Perspectives on Israeli Anthropology

Raphael Patai Series in Jewish Folklore and Anthropology

A complete listing of the books in this series can be found online at wsupress.wayne.edu

Perspectives on Israeli Anthropology

Edited by

ESTHER HERTZOG
ORIT ABUHAV
HARVEY E. GOLDBERG
and
EMANUEL MARX

Wayne State University Press
Detroit

14 13 12 11 10 5 4 3 2 1

Library of Congress Cataloging-in-Publication Data

Perspectives on Israeli anthropology / edited by Esther Hertzog . . . [et al.].
p. cm. — (Raphael Patai series in Jewish folklore and anthropology)
Includes bibliographical references and index.
ISBN 978-0-8143-3050-0 (pbk. : alk. paper)
1. Ethnology—Israel. 2. Israel—Social life and customs. I. Hertzog, Esther.
GN635.I78P47 2009
306.095694—dc22

2009004208

Typeset by E.T. Lowe Publishing
Composed in Palatino

Contents

Part V: Israeli Jewishness

A Note from the Editors

Israeli anthropology is special in two ways. First, most Israeli anthropologists are chiefly interested in the study of their own society, a trend reinforced by a growing contingent of colleagues from abroad. In most countries anthropological research emerged as the study of the Other and the exotic. Anthropologists explored other cultures by extracting themselves from the familiar territory of their own society, seeking to conceptualize the nature and ways of humankind on the broadest human foundations. The encounter with the estrangement of other cultures was fundamental to anthropological thought, both heuristically and theoretically. The application of anthropological theories and methods to researchers' own cultures has been a relatively recent development in anthropology. In contrast, this has been the starting point of Israeli anthropology, which has been motivated by empathy and shared identity. Anthropologists in Israel study groups and individuals with whom they identify politically and emotionally. The nuances and negotiations between these two contrasting attitudes are at the core of Israeli anthropology. As a discipline it explores the broadest foundation not only of humanity as anthropology has done globally but specifically of Jewishness. Its discoveries have expanded the varieties of Jewish identity.

Although Israel is a small country, it is populated by a multifaceted and changing society. The scope of research is unlimited, and in recent decades many more themes have become legitimate subjects for study. Political parties, army units, synagogues, old-age homes, prisons, ritual baths, expressions of collective memory, and the tribulations of new immigrants have all been studied, and each study has yielded new insights.

Second, though these scholars adhere to various theoretical and ethnographic traditions, they all treat Israel as a complex, modern, and open society. To the anthropologist, Israel is not so much the country and the state as the people and their far-flung networks and activities. The researcher studies each segment of society in its widest context, giving full recognition to the impact of the state and of the changing political and economic environment. This often requires the anthropologist to look beyond the state's geographical boundaries and to assess the impact of numerous factors on the social aggregate under study. Experience shows that seemingly distant and external forces, such as the American economy, the political dependence on America, the tense relations with neighboring countries, and the support of world Jewry, directly affect the lives of not only the Jews of Israel but also Muslim and Christian citizens, and even such seemingly isolated groups as the ultra-orthodox Jews of Jerusalem or the Bedouin of the Negev. Israelis living abroad, either as emigrants or as tourists, are also a part of Jewish society, and studies of such groups may reveal unsuspected novel aspects of Israel.

The social and cultural realities we study, and the diverse theoretical approaches we bring to bear upon them, drawn from the different countries in which we trained—Israel, England, the United States, and France—make us a diverse scholarly community. We in fact work in a postmodern environment that for us is not a scholarly trend but a reality to navigate and negotiate. The size of our country and the density of its population subject its people to constant interactions along multiple networks and cultural levels.

At the same time this collection of essays represents a truly provincial anthropology. We Israeli anthropologists are provincial in the fullest sense of the word. The positive side is that we deal with the people of a defined region and that we doggedly pursue our own lines of research, fully aware of the changing trends in the anthropological world. We also suffer from the drawbacks of provincials: we defer more to the writings of colleagues whom we consider to represent the mainstream than to the work of our countrymen, and we often feel that our achievements have not been fully recognized by colleagues in Europe and America.

Our aim has been to offer a selection of essays illustrating the range and depth of the anthropology of Israel, but not to present an integrated account of Israeli society. Almost all the essays in the collection have been written in the last decade, and only a few older, especially salient articles have been included. Almost all the articles were originally written and published in English. We have not been able to include all the authors whose work deserves to be in such a collection, and undoubtedly some subjects have not been given the emphasis due them. Our hope is that this book will stimulate future work in both established and unexplored directions.

Acknowledgments

We are grateful to all of our contributors and colleagues who cooperated in making possible this ethnographic "reading" of Israeli society. The volume is an ongoing project that grew out of our earlier work in Hebrew: *Yisrael: Antropologia Meqomit* (edited by Orit Abuhav, Esther Hertzog, Harvey Goldberg, and Emanuel Marx [Tel Aviv: Tcherikover, 1998]). Dan Ben-Amos played a key role in encouraging and guiding this parallel English volume, composed mostly of contributions not found in the Hebrew collection. Publication of the present work was partially aided by funds from Beit Berl College, the Hebrew University of Jerusalem, and Tel Aviv University. We appreciate the assistance of Sarah Willen, Ram Chopra, and Yoni Ventura in preparing the bibliography. Judy Goldberg helped with the typing and editing, and Emanuel Marx wishes to thank Dalia Marx for investing time and thought in the book. All of us are indebted to the expert and patient editing of Jenn Backer.

Introduction

Israeli Social Anthropology

Origins, Characteristics, and Contributions

ESTHER HERTZOG, ORIT ABUHAV,
HARVEY E. GOLDBERG, and EMANUEL MARX

Beginnings

Anthropological research in Israel had its beginnings in the mid-1920s during the British Mandate of Palestine in ethnographic field studies on the Arab population. These were soon followed by sociological and ethnographic studies of the Jews of Palestine. The early anthropologists were profoundly influenced by the rich travel literature on Palestine (see D. Rabinowitz 1998 for a full account) and in turn left their mark on future generations. The Palestinian researcher Tawfik Canaan (1882–1964) and the Finnish scholar Hilma Granqvist (1891–1972) are considered the founders of the anthropological study of Palestinian society. Canaan was a physician who devoted most of his time to studying Palestinian folklore and material culture. His principal works deal with sanctuaries dedicated to Muslim holy men in Palestine and with the Palestinian village home (Canaan 1927a, 1927b, 1933). Granqvist, a student of the eminent Finnish anthropologist Edward Westermarck, embarked on her research from the angle that the life patterns of the Palestinian villagers could serve as a source for understanding everyday life in biblical times (Weir 1975). Her work spans the life cycle of the villagers from cradle to grave, and is arguably the most comprehensive and empathic ethnography of an Arab society. Granqvist spent three years in the village of Artas near Bethlehem. In her first book she faithfully described the married life of the villagers (Granqvist 1931–35). She went on to write studies of childhood, adolescence, and death in the village. Many of the hundreds of photographs she took were published posthumously (Seger 1981).

A few years later two Jewish researchers, Erich Brauer (1895–1942) and Raphael Patai (1910–96), became the pioneers of ethnographic research of the

Jewish groups in Palestine (Abuhav 2002). Other scholars who might be viewed as harbingers of Israeli anthropology were Arthur Ruppin (1876–1943), Aharon Ze'ev Eshkoli (1901–48), and Yitzhak Ben-Zvi (1884–1963), who became the second president of the State of Israel. They were armchair ethnographers whose main interest was Jews from the Middle East.

The members of both groups, Jewish and Arab Palestinian alike, sought to document cultures that in their view had preserved traditional life patterns for centuries and that stood on the threshold of great changes. This concept influenced both the choice of research subjects and the selection of published material. Like many anthropologists of their generation, they viewed their principal role as saving (salvaging) traditional ways of life and did not address bigger theoretical issues or examine the influence of the surrounding world. The new reality that was being formed in Palestine—the constant flow of immigrants, the rapid economic development, the repeated revolts of the Arab population, and the sometimes violent encounters with the British Mandate authorities—at first appeared to the researchers as destructive influences that made their salvage efforts crucial. It was only in 1947 that Patai published a monograph focusing on culture change (1947a).

Erich Brauer emigrated to Palestine in 1925, the year in which his doctoral thesis on the Herero was published. He came from Germany, where he had been involved in Zionist activities with people like Gershom Scholem and Martin Buber. He wrote monographs on the Jews of Yemen (1934) and the Jews of Kurdistan (1947, 1993), and engaged in a scholarly dialogue with Shlomo Goitein (1983), who had studied the language and literature of the Jews of Yemen. A comparison of their works attests to the mutual enrichment between ethnographic research and research based on written texts.

Raphael Patai was a polymath who engaged in wide and varied research, published numerous books and articles, and worked in the fields of folklore, ethnography, Judaism, and the history of Zionism. He received his early education in Hungary in Jewish studies, which then was part of Orientalist scholarship, and was also an ordained rabbi (Patai 1988). Much of his published work was based on ethnological material from literature, but he encouraged other scholars to do field studies. In 1947 he founded the Palestine Institute of Folklore and Ethnology, which published the journal *Edot* and a series of books. These included, inter alia, the first Hebrew introduction to anthropology (Patai 1947b) and a book on the tombs of Jewish holy men in Eretz Yisrael (Ish-Shalom 1948) that was a kind of response to Canaan's book. After Brauer's death in 1942, Patai translated and edited his study on the Jews of Kurdistan (Brauer 1947). Both men devoted most of their efforts to preserving the traditions of Jewish ethnic communities, especially those from the Muslim world. Although Jewish researchers recognized the works of Palestinian scholars, there was already an almost total separation between the two groups, a separation that has continued to this day.

The promising beginnings of Palestinian and Jewish anthropology were not recognized by the academic establishment that was developing in Mandate Palestine at the time. Patai's ambition to introduce anthropology into the Hebrew University remained unfulfilled. The first difficulty in achieving the academic consolidation and continuity of the field was the fluid and controversial definitions of "anthropology." The discipline was accorded different definitions in different periods and countries, and even the terms "anthropology," "ethnology," and "ethnography" had a variety of meanings. Brauer, steeped in European academic tradition, viewed anthropology as a discipline that dealt not only with physical research but also with social and folkloristic study. In contrast, "social anthropologists" of the British school were engaged solely in social research. In the United States "anthropology" was viewed as an overarching discipline that included, in addition to social and cultural studies, physical anthropology, archaeology, and linguistics.

A second difficulty, linked to the first, was an ideological-ethical one that derived from the partial link of anthropology to race theories. The debates over whether the Jews are a single race or a number of races and whether the evidence to support such assumptions exists were part and parcel of a research tradition that dealt with the question of Jewish identity (Efron 1994; Hart 2000). These issues interested many Jewish scholars in Europe, and were discussed critically by Ruppin and Eshkoli. Brauer photographed the people he studied and intended to measure them. But Nazism and World War II made physical anthropology that "measured" Jews a questionable enterprise (Goldberg and Abuhav 2000).

A further obstacle to the development of anthropology was the priorities of the academic development at the small Hebrew University. At the time these scholars were active, it was the only institution of higher education in the country that offered study in the social sciences and humanities. The university discussed the possible introduction of anthropology, but it always remained at the periphery of its concerns. Ultimately, Brauer's untimely death and critical views toward Patai's anthropology shut the window of opportunity on the establishment of anthropology in Jerusalem. Patai emigrated to the United States in 1949.

Once Brauer and Patai had left the stage, Israeli anthropology became dormant. During the 1950s and the early 1960s anthropological activity was limited to a few individuals from abroad such as Melford Spiro (1920–), Stanley Diamond (1922–91), and Dorothy Willner (1927–), who came to do research or to explore possibilities for work but did not settle, and to a handful who developed their professional careers in Israel, such as Henry Rosenfeld, Alex Weingrod, and Phyllis Palgi. The Arab-Jewish fighting in 1948 (Israel's War of Independence), the expulsion and flight of the majority of the Arabs from the new state, the mass immigration of Jews from east and west, the economic hardship that was part of Israel's first years, and, above all, the mind-set of the country's leadership that the immigrants must be "absorbed" and assimilated as quickly as possible into Israeli culture all contributed to shaping the academic agenda of the social scientists working in Israel at the time.

The Revival of Anthropology

Ethnographic work was revived in the mid-1960s. A new generation of anthropologists picked up where earlier traditions had left off but also developed an anthropology with different characteristics. Continuity was manifested in the researchers' going back to work with Jewish immigrants, and many new ethnic groups were added to the repertoire. Over the years, they produced studies of Jews from Ethiopia (Abbink 1984a; Salamon 1999), Georgia (Elam 1980), India (Strizower 1966; Kushner 1973; Weil 1977), the island of Jerba in Tunisia (Deshen 1974), Kurdistan (Feitelson 1959; C. Cohen 1975), Morocco (Shokeid 1971b), Tripolitania (Goldberg 1972), the United States (Avruch 1981), and Yemen (Katzir, this volume; H. Lewis 1989). At the same time some anthropologists studied the Arab citizens of Israel: Arab villagers, the Druze communities, rural and urban Bedouin, and Arab residents of towns (see, e.g., H. Rosenfeld 1958; A. Cohen 1965; Marx 1967; Oppenheimer 1985; Kressel 1984; J. Ginat 1987). Anthropology, as a discipline, followed the manifold general trends that developed in Great Britain and the United States. But its emphases and pace also reflected local realities, including the fact that anthropology was always viewed as close to or, perhaps more precisely, placed in the shadow of sociology.

The local academic trends must be understood against the background of Israel's wider social and political history. Within three and a half years of Israel's establishment in May 1948, its Jewish population more than doubled as a result of immigration. About half of the approximately 650,000 immigrants came from post-Holocaust Europe and the other half from Muslim countries in the Middle East and North Africa. This made what Israelis called "the absorption of immigrants" a major societal goal, and therefore a central issue facing social research.

The sociologists in the country—then concentrated at the Hebrew University, which also supervised the sociologists at the recently founded colleges in Beersheva, Haifa, Ramat Gan, and Tel Aviv—formulated the conceptual framework within which immigration was studied. They stressed the importance of an analytic approach relevant to all immigrants (Ben-David 1953; Eisenstadt 1954). This stance implied criticism of a cultural anthropological outlook that paid more attention to the backgrounds and perspectives of the immigrants than did sociological investigations. In reality, more research was done on newcomers from the Middle East than on those of European background both by sociologists and by the few anthropologists who came to the country at the time. The overall bias toward making Middle Easterners the main object of study was criticized by the next generation of researchers, who saw the earlier social research as serving the emerging class structure in which the veteran Europeans established their superiority and control over resources and leadership. While this clearly was an emerging pattern, Jews from Middle Eastern countries also were gaining power and prominence in Israeli society and politics.

While the Hebrew University resisted the formal introduction of anthropology into its curriculum, in 1963 the new Tel Aviv University established a faculty of social sciences and recruited young scholars. The Tel Aviv faculty was the first group of scholars appointed without consulting the Jerusalem establishment. It recruited staff from European and American universities. Emanuel Marx, who had just graduated from Manchester University, was asked to set up a department of social anthropology. Because there were not enough suitable staff, Marx "temporarily" joined forces with sociologists and thus set a pattern that was to become the standard. The joint Department of Anthropology and Sociology at Tel Aviv University was emulated by Haifa University, Ben-Gurion University in Beersheba (which set up a Department of Behavioral Science that also included psychology), and Bar-Ilan University, all of which developed programs that combined both disciplines. In 1972 the Department of Sociology at the Hebrew University of Jerusalem changed its name to include anthropology. Both the recent and the older departments opened up to new and varied theories and developed new research subjects. Some new immigrants joined the new faculties, and Israelis who had been trained in other countries returned to work in their home settings. The 1960s thus became crucial with regard to the institutional setting of anthropology.

At the same time a new anthropological research program was launched in Israel, the aim of which was to study the integration of new immigrants. The program was funded by English donors, Lord Bernstein and his family, and was directed by Max Gluckman of Manchester University and Emanuel Marx. In the framework of this program, studies were conducted on the forms of settlement exclusive to Israel, such as communal farms, or kibbutzim (Evens 1995; Shepher 1983), cooperative farms, or moshavim (Abarbanel 1974; Baldwin 1972; Mars 1980b; Shokeid 1971a), and new towns (Aronoff 1974; Deshen 1970a, 1970b; Marx 1976). There was also a workshop for the rehabilitation of the elderly (Handelman 1977a). A second series of studies (Marx 1980a) added other research subjects, such as the Ashdod port (Mars 1980a) and the powerful Labor Party (Aronoff 1980). By then students of the Manchester group were contributing new field studies, such as the symbiotic relationship between the inhabitants of a Tel Aviv slum and the authorities (Ogien 1980), and the politics of an old-age home (Hazan 1980, 1992).

This research project produced a dozen books and monographs and an extensive series of articles. The results were published mainly in English, but some of the books and articles were translated into Hebrew and made their way into textbooks of various fields of study. All these studies emphasized the social forces with which people had to contend. Each person, whether in an official position or as an ordinary member of the public, was seen as having networks of social relations that transcended the formal boundaries of family, community, state, and so forth. These links conveyed all the forces affecting people and all the resources available to them. The total of the interactions flowing through these links at a particular moment was "society." This open system approach went beyond the functionalist paradigm and called for a rethinking of fieldwork methods (Marx 1980a). The fact that the project was funded and directed from abroad ensured its independence from governmental interference and also assisted some of the researchers in fully settling in Israel. The coincidence of an expanding and open academic system and the availability of funding for long-term field research encouraged the rapid growth of the new discipline.

The Bernstein Israel Research Project was thus instrumental in establishing anthropology in Israeli universities, and those involved in it felt that it was academically innovative. Max Gluckman felt that the project was another high point in his academic career. Working in "a group joined in exciting discourse about shared problems . . . has revived the excitement I enjoyed when I was a member of the group of not so much younger researchers based on the Rhodes-Livingstone Institute of Social Studies in Central Africa" (Gluckman 1970, xxviii). There was, however, a fundamental difference between the two projects: while the Rhodes-Livingstone scholars became the pillars of the "Manchester School" of social anthropology and made a profound impact on the discipline in England and America (Schumaker 2004), the Bernstein Israel Research Project had a more limited outcome. It successfully established anthropology as an academic discipline in Israeli universities, but it had little visible effect on the anthropological world. This was due neither to the conservatism and parochialism of British (or other) anthropologists of our generation, as Kuper (1983, 189) would have us believe, nor to the fact that most of the graduates of the Bernstein project remained in peripheral Israel or returned to Britain and did not transplant to the American center. It has much more to do with the fact that the discipline has expanded and that there is no longer a mainstream anthropology or a widely acknowledged leadership. Anthropology has broken up into numerous specializations and cliques, and within the confines of these groups the work of the Israeli anthropologists is known and recognized.

Continuities and Reorientations

What new trends did Israeli anthropologists introduce? First, they thought that the sociological studies of immigration in the first decades of Israel's existence were inadequate. Some scholars (e.g., Bernstein 1980) have argued that the sociology of that era fit the perspective of dominant elites. Immigrants were "absorbed" through bureaucratic structures, which enhanced dependence, exploited the newcomers, and limited their mobility (Swirski 1989). The early research had recognized the critical role of bureaucracies in Israeli life (Katz and Eisenstadt 1960) but considered them a "natural" or unavoidable aspect of dealing with mass migration. Furthermore, the authorities, as well as the sociologists, emphasized the cultural absorption of immigrants. Thus they thought that the first thing a new immigrant should do was learn the Hebrew language. This belief was based on the assumption that there was a monolithic Israeli language and culture, and that by adopting it the newcomer would integrate into the body social. Instead, the anthropologists employed a sociological notion of adaptation, based on the commonsense understanding that work, accommodation, and schooling for the immigrant's children were the most important first things. The immigrant's adaptation could be gauged by the growth of his or her social networks: the larger and more diversified they became, the better the adjustment to the new environment. Language was less important, for a new immigrant who worked and lived among more veteran immigrants from the same country of origin could establish these complex networks without relinquishing his native tongue and yet become fully absorbed in the new society. In due course, he would inevitably pick up some Hebrew.

Second, the topic of bureaucracy was not new to anthropological study. Both the earlier anthropological work (Weingrod 1966; Willner 1969) and that of the Manchester researchers placed a heavy emphasis on the organizational context of the "absorption" of immigrants. Immigrant cooperative settlements (moshavim) were a major focus of field research in the late 1950s and during the 1960s. The work on moshavim led naturally to studies of a second type of immigrant settlement, which emerged in the mid-1950s: the small new towns called "development towns." These towns were also planned and administrated from the center. But the policies decided at a national level were implemented and modified by bureaucrats in contact with local people, and were likely to be changed beyond recognition. Therefore, much anthropological research in these and other communities concentrated on the interaction between officials and immigrants along with other residents in the context of local political and economic developments (e.g., A. Cohen 1965; Aronoff 1974; Marx 1976; Goldberg 1984; Greenberg 1989; H. Lewis 1989). Although the population of the new towns was largely (but by no means exclusively) made up of Jews from Middle Eastern backgrounds (large-scale immigration from North Africa began in 1955–56), they came from a variety of countries and social environments, and could by no means be seen as continuing a single cultural tradition. One study explored the transformation of cultural traditions in a new town (Deshen 1970a, 1970b). It was only later that other anthropologists took up this last theme and examined the new towns as sites in which the traditions of Jews from North Africa were being reworked to become meaningful within the emerging Israeli setting (Weingrod 1990; Ben-Ari and Bilu 1997).

Another early focus of anthropological research was Arab villages and Bedouin communities. As indicated, this was a topic to which attention had been given in the 1920s. It took on entirely new aspects in the context of the new Israeli state. More than 600,000 (the number is still contested) Arabs fled or were expelled from the area that became the State of Israel after the 1948 war.

The Arab communities remaining in the new state became a minority within a short period of time. These Arabs were citizens of Israel, residing primarily in small towns and villages. For almost a decade they were supervised by a repressive military administration and were not the object of governmental development plans like those that aided Jewish immigrants. Also, the scholarly community paid much less attention to the study of these groups than to the study of Israeli Jews. The outcome was that anthropologists rather than sociologists did most of the early work.

This research, too, while focused on defined groups of villagers and Bedouin tribesmen, was keenly attuned to the wider and changing social context. Henry Rosenfeld (1964a) conducted fieldwork in rural communities in the north and, aided by the detailed ethnographic data of Granqvist (1931–35) and other sources, traced long-term social change. The turning of Arab villagers into a proletariat as a result of the loss of land and the growing industrial economy was a major theme. Another study, by Abner Cohen (1965), analyzed the changing nature of descent groups within Arab villages in terms of their relationship to Jewish society in the pre-state and post-state periods, in response to the powerful realities of the new Israeli state and politics. While Cohen's study was later criticized (Asad 1975) as representing a Zionist de-historicization of the object of its study, his book did highlight changes during the Mandate period and the first decade and a half of Israeli statehood, and analyzed the dynamics of internal village life in response to the wider social and political forces impinging upon it. Emanuel Marx's study of the Bedouin of the Negev (1967) took as a starting point the harsh rule of a military administration, which expelled the majority of the Bedouin and moved the remaining Bedouin population to a reservation in the arid eastern Negev. It took away most of their farmland and pastures, but did not allow them to work outside the reservation. Thus the Bedouin were forced to subsist on nomadic pastoralism and dry farming. Marx showed how these acts created a class system: those who still owned some land considered themselves "true Bedouin." They exploited a class of landless clients whom they called "peasants." While culturally almost indistinguishable, each class developed different patterns of marriage and nomadic movements, and even different ritual performances. Forty years later, in a totally transformed Bedouin society and economy, the classes are still in place (Ben-David 2004, 96).

Third, anthropological work also focused on communal settlements (kibbutzim). They emerged in the first decades of the twentieth century and were prominent in the growing Jewish society (Yishuv), in Mandated Palestine, and in the Zionist ethos striving to establish a Jewish state. Kibbutzim were studied intensively by American anthropologists such as Melford Spiro (1956, 1958) and Stanley Diamond (1957), and by sociologists at the Hebrew University, in particular Yonina Talmon and her students (1972). Both Spiro and Talmon were interested in questions surrounding the family in these ideologically conceived communities that were organized around socialist principles of economic equality and communal ownership of property, and entailed collective arrangements of daily meals and childrearing. Spiro's work focused on a single kibbutz community, which he utilized to analyze general anthropological questions about the existence of universal family structures and roles. Talmon's research was based on a sample of kibbutzim with a variety of backgrounds and different historical trajectories over a few decades. Even though only 3 percent of the Jewish population of the pre-state Yishuv and of Israel lived in kibbutzim, their thorough organization had made them politically salient. Thus they became a sector of Israeli society that was widely known abroad. After statehood, the contribution of kibbutz settlements to Israel's economy and defense waned in importance, but anthropologists never entirely lost interest in them (Tiger and Shepher 1975; Shepher 1983; Shapira 1987; Bowes 1989; Evens 1995).

Israeli Anthropology and Global Anthropology

After looking briefly at these foci of anthropological research in relation to the emerging Yishuv and new state (the absorption of immigrants, Palestinian Arab communities, and collective settlements), one might ask how Israeli anthropology fits into the developments of world anthropology that came to the fore after the 1960s. At that time there emerged a critique of anthropology as practiced during eras of imperialism and colonialism that presented the discipline as one based on creating a distance between itself and its practitioners on the one hand, and the "objects" of research on the other. Most typically linked to the study of faraway "exotic" societies, or non-Western groups that had been conquered, anthropology was characterized as creating its object as "the other." In addition, during the 1960s and the 1970s new theoretical orientations were being developed in the social sciences generally, both in the United States and in Europe. These developments reflected the conflicts and consciousness of the 1960s, such as the protest against the war in Vietnam and ethnic struggle in the United States, and the student rebellions in France and elsewhere. They stressed that conflict was endemic to social life, and that the source of much societal tension was the unequal nature of the "world system" in which smaller and poorer nations were dominated by larger and more powerful ones. They also argued that earlier social theory was an expression of this inequality rather than an independent stance that analyzed it critically. Social scientists trained in these perspectives came to teach and do research in the new and expanding university departments in Israel, but there is no simple answer to the question of how much these paradigms have influenced anthropology in Israel. For here, as in most provincial academic communities, fashions catch on very slowly, but once adopted may remain in place for a long time.

One of the hallmarks of Israeli anthropology has been the social involvement of its researchers. If in the first decades of the State of Israel researchers were committed to an ideology of national effort in the spheres of immigrant absorption, settlement, and security, they were also deeply concerned with the iniquities of centralized bureaucratic rule, the inequalities among the newcomers and veterans, and the discrimination against Arab citizens. They were also concerned with issues of social equity, such as individual and community rights, and multicultural identity. Sociologists and anthropologists sought ways of bringing the issues connected with depressed and disadvantaged groups to the center stage of academic discourse. All this was part of a worldwide trend focusing on the politics of identities and the processes of constructing power relationships in society. Anthropologists in Israel participated in these trends, but the evolution of the discipline there also reflected its own local dynamics.

Most of the early anthropologists in Israel were of middle-class European or American backgrounds, but this in itself did not turn them into representatives of an internal colonialism vis-à-vis the citizens of Middle Eastern origins. While participating in the Zionist project, some anthropologists were critical of policies toward the Jewish immigrants from Middle Eastern countries in the new towns and cooperative farming communities, and of the repression of the Arab population. Even though the first generation of Israeli anthropologists shared basic assumptions with practitioners of the discipline elsewhere, it was never exclusively concerned with the "exotic" and the implicitly "less developed" sectors of the population. This is shown by the numerous studies of the kibbutz, an elite population of mostly European origin, fairly well educated and deeply enmeshed in the state's power structure.

The fact that Israeli anthropology, from the beginning, pointed to the role of bureaucracies, staffed by European-derived old-timers (but also, fairly quickly, by people recruited from among recent arrivals), in the process of immigrant settlement meant that the study of "them" was also the study of "us." It is also worth noting that in the early years of the state, all the anthropologists working in Israel were Jewish. Many of them felt a deep and enduring commitment to the Jewish groups they studied, even when it was obvious that there were important differences in the particular Jewish histories that shaped the background of the researchers in contrast to those of the people being researched. Not only is this a retrospective evaluation of the situation from today's standpoint, but several anthropologists have reflected on this aspect of the nature of the relationship between the investigator and his "subjects" (Shokeid 1974; Goldberg 1985).

Trends of the Recent Decades

The new approaches gained strength from the 1970s onward, while Israeli anthropology began to diversify in line with trends in the discipline elsewhere. Consciousness of the role of the state and other formal institutions led to the continued study of bureaucracies, such as the welfare system (Handelman, this volume; Hertzog 1996). Much of the fieldwork from this period onward was carried out in urban settings, but the appearance of the new trends did not erase earlier approaches. The arrival of Ethiopian immigrants in the 1980s and 1990s brought in its wake studies that analyzed the issue of the adaptation of these immigrants in terms of culture shock and culture gaps (see, e.g., the 1985 special issue of *Israel Social Science Research*). These studies implied that there were cultural and social dichotomies separating the immigrants from Ethiopia and the "absorbing" Israeli society. Anthropologists suggested another approach, emphasizing the bureaucratic power relationships and dependency that shaped the experience of these new immigrants and set the terms within which they were perceived and treated (Ashkenazi and Weingrod 1984; Hertzog 1998, 1999). Less ethnographic work was done on the large-scale immigration from the former Soviet Union that began in 1989, but it did receive some attention, including work from anthropologists within that community (Siegel 1998, and this volume; Zilberg 2001). Because of their large numbers, nearly one million in a decade, these immigrants did not easily submit to the bureaucracies. They were provided with financial aid but were largely left to their own devices, and therefore adapted rapidly to the new environment.

The role of social power in defining identities and relationships is well documented in the gender studies that developed in the 1980s. These studies emerged against the background of feminist awareness and writings both in Israel and the world at large. In the social sciences the followers of this approach stressed the feminist struggle for equality. They gave prominence to gendered power relations in the family, the community, the labor market, the army, and so forth (see, e.g., Swirski and Safir 1991; Azmon and Izraeli 1993).

Anthropological research on gender relations incorporated the ethnographic perspective into this growing field. It highlighted the ways women deal with their inferior place in society and in the family, mobilizing alternative power resources and manipulating them in a society that structures their social and economic weakness and marginality. Women's voices are expressed in numerous works, including Yael Katzir's study on the economic power of women from a Yemenite immigrant moshav (this volume); the research by Rahel Wasserfall (1990) on women's use of the ritual pollution attached to their menstrual period as a resource in the definition of their identity and in their power relationships with men; and the work on the status of women and men in Bedouin society (Marx 1987; Abu-Rabia 1994). All of these studies shed new light on female endeavors to maneuver in settings in which they seem to lack formal power. Studies based on this viewpoint intensified in the 1990s (e.g., El-Or 1994; Hertzog 1999, and this volume), and attention to gender also encouraged the study of subjects like masculinity and war (Lomsky-Feder and Ben-Ari 2000), as well as the family and the welfare state (Handelman, this volume).

At the same time anthropologists turned their attention to the middle class. Research in the 1980s and 1990s posed questions regarding the cultural discourse and social patterns created and consumed by the members of this category, which was composed mainly of secular, urban Jews but also some Arabs. There are studies of secular urban neighborhoods (Birenbaum-Carmeli 2000), violence among schoolchildren (Furman 1994), wedding gifts (Abuhav, this volume), birthday celebrations (Shamgar-Handelman and Handelman 1991), remembrance days and sites like those related to Prime Minister Yitzhak Rabin (Vinitsky-Seroussi 1998; Hazan 2001, ch. 5), hikes organized by the Society for the Protection of Nature (Brawer Ben-David 1997), backpacking abroad as a preliminary stage of settling down to a bourgeois life (Selwyn 1995), memorializing trips to Morocco (Levy 1997), the sale of souvenirs to tourists (Shenhav-Keller 1993), the sales tactics of Arab shopkeepers in Jerusalem's Old City (Bowman 1996), Arab women forging new roles through shopping patterns (Forte 2002), and Israelis in New York manifesting a nostalgia for home (Shokeid, this volume).

Interest in the middle class did not mean that anthropologists were no longer attracted to diversity. It was becoming apparent that social diversity was intensifying. Traditions that had their origins abroad were reworked in the Israeli setting at the same time that former immigrant groups were experiencing social mobility and sharing political power. It became harder and harder to identify a single societal "center." At the same time, global influences that were both economic and cultural made Israel a site of striking social variety and self-awareness.

The new research paradigms and methodologies developed in the anthropological studies of the 1960s and 1970s, such as the social world approach (Hazan 1990) or an emphasis on life stories and life history (Lomsky-Feder, this volume; Bilu 2000), were now utilized to deal with urban life, its populations, and its settings. The overlap between anthropology and other disciplines also became more apparent, such as in many sociological studies based on ethnography, social historical studies (Deshen 1989; Goldberg 1990; Greenberg 1999; Zenner 2000), an analytic concern with diasporas and transnational relations (Levy and Weingrod 2005), works that bridged anthropology and folklore (Salamon 1999, and this volume), and analyses of rabbinic tradition that utilized anthropology (S. Cooper 1987; Seeman 1996).

Reflection, Assessment, and Commitment

As already suggested, Israeli anthropologists, in tune with the discipline in general, became more reflexive and conscious of the position from which their work was carried out. This took place on several levels. One was an attempt to examine Israeli identity from a new viewpoint, such as through a study of Israeli youth (Hazan 2001). This effort was enriched by the input of foreign researchers who examined, for example, the various definitions of "Israeli-ness," the relationship between "Israeli-ness" and "Jewishness," the state's construction and treatment of ethnic groups (Jakubowska 1992), the various definitions of "tradition" (Dominguez 1989; Paine 1992), and the probing of the cultural messages of Israeli archaeology (Abu El-Haj 2001). This trend has been paralleled by local reassessments, including an essay rethinking the way immigration and ethnicity have been studied (Goldberg 1987) and an edited collection that examines central values, images, and cultural constructions regarding "place and space" in Israel (Ben-Ari and Bilu 1997). Another area that addresses Israeli identity is the interest in constructing history and collective memory (Swedenburg 1995; Gefen 1997; Slyomovics 1998, and this volume; Schely-Newman 2002). There have also been critical studies on the cultural rhetoric of museums (Golden 1996; Katriel 1997; Ben-Ze'ev and Ben-Ari 1996), on the link between archaeology and nationalism (Weingrod 1995), on state ceremonies of remembrance (Handelman and Shamgar-Handelman 1997), on the place of the Holocaust in educational programs (J. Feldman 2001; Hazan 2001, ch. 2), and on the myths of Jewish heroism (Y. Zerubavel 1995).

Self-reflection has also led to more systematic introspection in anthropological writings. Researchers now, more commonly than in the past, include some personal exposure in the understanding of their subjects. Through the endeavor to deal with their place, role, and feelings in the course of a study, the anthropologist's understanding of her or his research subject becomes keener and clearer. Intentional reflexivity is prominent in the essays of Shokeid (1974) and Ben-Ari (this volume), while in other work it is implicit, still standing in the shadow of the research topic (El-Or 1994; Hertzog 1999; Lomsky-Feder, this volume). In all these studies we learn how an interest that stems from personal biography, or from a sphere of occupation, becomes a field of scientific research, or how the urge to study a subject may derive from prior social commitments.

The concern with reflexivity also touches on the presumed dilemma of the desirable degree of a researcher's personal involvement in a field of inquiry. Today hardly anyone would doubt the value of an anthropologist's involvement in the social milieu he or she studies. The more intimately she is involved, the more detailed the material she obtains and the more profound her understanding and empathy. Some researchers go further, unintentionally blurring the borderline between involvement and intervention. Others state explicitly that intervention in the everyday life of the "subjects" of a study is valid and might even contribute additional insights through the exposure of deeper layers of social experience. Beyond this, some anthropologists are systematically involved in political and social advocacy, such as defending the land rights of the Negev Bedouin (Marx 1990, 2000; Kressel 2003), protesting against the demolition of the homes of Palestinians (Halper 1993), or ending the segregation of Ethiopian immigrants (Shabtai 1999, 2001). Other studies deal with questions of social policy in medical and psychiatric anthropology (Palgi 1963; Basker, Beran, and Kleinhauz 1982; Minuchin-Izigsohn et al. 1984; Nudelman 1997; Brawer Ben-David 2005), urban renewal (Hazan 1990), education (A. Lewis 1979b; Abu-Rabia 2001), women in prison (Greenberg 1982), and geriatric care (Hazan 1992; Golander 1995; Gamliel 2005).

In comparison to the negligible and unrecognized discipline of the 1930s and 1940s, Israeli anthropology has, since the 1960s, become a fertile research field that attracts local and foreign researchers. In addition, the attributes of the ethnographic method have gained recognition by other social sciences as well as by the general public. Despite its representation by a small scholarly community, Israeli anthropology has gained a respected place in Israeli social science and the wider world of learning.

Finally, we are waiting for the day when more and more Palestinians will participate in anthropological research. Of course, the overall setting of the relationship of Jewish Israelis and of the state to local Arabs shifted dramatically in 1967 when Israel occupied the West Bank, Gaza, and Sinai, and came into direct contact with Palestinians living there. The few studies by Jewish Israeli anthropologists in the occupied regions were all motivated by resistance to the repression of the local population and to colonization by Jewish settlers (Ben-Porath and Marx 1971; Marx 1977; Lavie 1990; Stewart 1988–90). The ultimate test of the emergence of an anthropology of Palestinian society is whether erstwhile "Others" eventually become full partners in the study of their own societies. There are indications that this is indeed happening. We now possess detailed studies by Palestinian anthropologists in Palestine and Israel (Abu-Rabia 1994, and this volume; Hammami 1997; Khawalde 1994; Qleibo 1992), supplemented by the work of American and Israeli scholars (Bornstein 2002; Drori 2000, and this volume; D. Rabinowitz 1997, and this volume; M. Rosenfeld 2004; Slyomovics 1998, and this volume; Swedenburg 1995; Wesley 2005). Because of its inherently critical and sometimes "subversive" character, anthropology can only develop in an open and affluent society that does not need to struggle for survival, a society that can devote resources to the establishment and maintenance of autonomous academic institutions. We hope the day will come soon when Palestinian anthropology will blaze new paths.

Organization of This Collection

The essays in this book are organized into five parts that reflect issues that are important in understanding Israeli society and to which anthropologists, through their ethnographic work, have made important contributions. One basic theme stems from the fact that Israel has been a *country of immigration*. It was built up by immigrants during the pre-state period and witnessed mass immigration from both Europe and the Middle East during the first three years of existence. In the recent generation, there has been continued immigration, with the largest numbers of people coming from the countries of the former Soviet Union. This theme continues to be a central feature of Israeli life.

Immigrants to Israel, with varied backgrounds, joined those already present in the country within the contexts of a modernizing technological and economic framework and bureaucratic structures that impinged on all local citizens. As discussed, anthropologists in Israel recognized the complex and *pervasive influence of bureaucracies* in social life, as affecting both newcomers and old-timers and molding the patterns of social development.

The co-residence of various groups within the same settings and their participation in the same state institutions did not lead to the dissolution of social differences. Some differences did become less salient while others were maintained or even heightened. Israel is thus a site in which *social order is continually negotiated* among diverse and competing groups. Among Israeli Jews there are differences and conflicts between religious orientations (see part 5), between the political left and the political right, and even between middle-of-the-road Israelis with their contemporary sensibilities vis-à-vis the ideological rhetoric that previously dominated the country. Most prominent today are the tensions and accommodations between *Jewish Israelis and Palestinian Arabs,* most of whom live in the lands occupied by Israel after 1967, but others of whom are Israeli residents and citizens (see Ginat and Perkins 2001).

A number of these themes feed into an overarching question: what identities are common in Israel and how do they formulate notions of *Israeliness and Jewishness?* Within the contexts of a growing economy and society and a dynamic culture open to global influences, Israelis have found many ways of expressing specific identities and of contesting identities with which they disagree. The cultural backgrounds of immigrants have not been erased but have sometimes been reworked in new ways, and both Jews and Israelis residing abroad relate to and participate in the ongoing cultural debates, which constitute the ever-moving currents that enter into self-definition. Anthropological work has not only "studied" these developments but has become integrated in them.

In conclusion, our survey of past developments, and the collection of essays that follows, seeks to show the diverse and dynamic features of anthropology in its Israeli setting. In selecting essays for this book we have tried to draw on both early work and recent research, highlight different theoretical perspectives, and touch on a range of topics.

I

A Country of Immigrants

Continuing waves of Jewish immigrants have been a conspicuous characteristic of Israel, before and after its foundation. While the state sought to "absorb" the immigrants into an imagined national culture, each group of arriving immigrants and the indigenous Arab population have played a significant role in molding the culture of the country. Each group seeks to integrate in the political economy, while holding on to its customary culture, even as all traditions are exposed to worldwide influences. This cultural diversity has become more pronounced over the years and has yielded a rich harvest in every field of human endeavor.

Shlomo Deshen elaborates on the new meanings, in the context of Israeli society, that immigrants from Tunisia attach to rabbinic writings of former generations. Harvey E. Goldberg, relating to realms of popular culture, focuses on the mechanisms that allowed young newcomers from rural Libya to integrate contemporary Western dance into their way of life. Yael Katzir describes the empowerment of Jewish women immigrants from Yemen in a cooperative village (moshav). As the men were the state-approved breadwinners, they were tied to the formal marketing channels. Only their women dared sell their produce in open markets. Arnold Lewis stresses how the behavior of immigrants must be viewed in terms of the wider institutions in which they are enmeshed. He challenges the ethnic interpretation of the reality of an immigrant town and suggests instead class stratification as an explanation for the dilemmas in the realm of education. Dina Siegel analyzes the integration of the one million immigrants who arrived in Israel from the former Soviet Union in the 1990s. The immigrants set up their "own" economic and cultural organizations, culminating in a political party, in order to adapt more effectively to the new country.

1

Ritualization of Literacy

The Works of Tunisian Scholars in Israel

SHLOMO DESHEN

Introduction

Jewish immigrants from Tunisia have been part of the Israeli social scene for the past twenty years. They immigrated primarily in the mid-1950s, but there has been a steady trickle ever since. Of the 70,000 Tunisians in Israel, 15,000 to 20,000 originate from the southern part of Tunisia.

Tunisians face many cultural and social problems in the process of migrating to and settling in Israel. They face a heterogeneous society radically different from the traditional Tunisia they left behind. This essay examines these problems by focusing on their book publishing endeavors: a characteristic and remarkably intensive activity.

Background

Tunisian Jews regard themselves as different from the Jews of other North African countries because of their Judeo-Arabic dialect, lifestyle, and customs. Djerban Jews are especially proud of their origins and never tire of recalling their unusual beginnings. It was in Djerba that the *kohanim*[1] (members of the ancient priestly caste) lived, secluded in a separate village community nears the Ghriba, the hallowed ancient synagogue to which Tunisians flocked on pilgrimages. Djerba and its community were held in esteem by other Jews[2] and, in fact, most religious functionaries in Tunisia came from that area. While traditional Jewish education and scholarship had begun to deteriorate in many parts of the Maghreb, Djerba was less influenced by Western trends, and in the 1950s a Djerban rabbi was chosen as the chief rabbi of Tunisia. Accordingly, the religious status and self-esteem of Djerban Jews has risen considerably.

In Tunisian Jewish communities the viability of traditional learning was influenced by the extent to which modern educational institutions were accepted. For example, the Alliance Israelite Universelle[3] introduced the secular French school system with its first school in Tunis in 1878 and was able to expand and undermine the traditional educational system of the large Jewish communities of north and central Tunisia. In southern Tunisia, however, the Alliance met with much less success. The rabbis of Djerba firmly rejected the repeated efforts of the Alliance emissaries, and the form and content of schooling in Djerba and the surrounding communities remained free from French influence. Jewish culture remained paramount: the Bible and Talmud, taught at various levels at all ages, remained the major subjects of study. The first secular school was not opened until the 1950s, when most of the Jewish population had already emigrated and the community was in the process of dispersion.

One of the traditional didactic practices of Djerba is of particular interest here. Teachers encouraged students to write down interpretations of the texts they studied. As the student progressed, these notes became more original, and in time, the advanced student tackled scholarly problems on his own. Although the results were often nothing more than exercise books, the practice sometimes resulted in mature scholarship. If the work reflected traditional standards of outstanding scholarship, it was considered *hidushei Tora, novellae* of holy teaching.[4] The publication of *hidushei Tora* was highly valued, and a volume of *novellae* to one's credit raised the author's social standing.

Another significant factor that influenced and motivated the book publishing endeavors of Djerban Jews is that Djerban Judaism, in common with many other trends of traditional Judaism, is permeated with the spirit of the Lurianic Kabbala, and it is in this context (see Scholem 1946, 244–86; Scholem 1971a, 176–202) that the compilation and publication of one's religious writings have great mystical import. It is remarkable that Djerban Jews developed in practice the specific implications of the Lurianic Kabbala relative to book publications.[5] The following introduction in one book demonstrates a sentiment deeply rooted in Jewish mysticism and piety.

> And I have published this book not to gain honour, to display myself, or to make gains through it. But only so that with God's help I may through the sales of this book complete the publication of my other manuscripts. May the Almighty help me to find a publisher for them. I would let him have all my gain from the sales; only let him give me 50 copies for me to distribute to my friends. For the publication of my writings is mandatory upon me, as our Sages of blessed memory said: He who does not publish his *hidushim* will, Heaven forbid, be punished for doing ill to his soul (*'osheiq nishmato*), for the *hidushim* constitute part of his soul. (Shalli 1963, 7)[6]

If a man did not publish in his lifetime, for whatever reason, his sons considered it a major act of filial piety to have his works printed after his death. Financing the publication of writings of the deceased was seen in terms of deeds of ultimate altruistic charity, akin to the terms used in connection with the funeral and burial of the dead. Thus, in a eulogy for a deceased rabbi, after the orator had recounted all the scholarly works the deceased had produced in his lifetime, he concluded, "But to our sorrow the rabbi did not have the merit to complete and bring his *hidushim* on the *Ketubot* tractate to light and they are in my possession with other manuscripts of his. May the Lord cause merciful people (*anshei hesed*) to arise and bring them to light" (Hakohen 1972).

Sometimes people were prompted to publish their writings after having experienced an unusual and important event that they interpreted in terms of miraculous intervention in their favor.

> Blessed be He who does Good to the Unworthy. . . . On Thursday 28th Elul 5732 at a quarter to five I was walking on the road to Beit Hagadi and a vehicle flung me to the edge of the road . . . and there was only a hair's breadth between death and me. And I asked myself what shall I do in return. . . . And I said to myself I will do as our fathers and teachers did . . . and with the help of God in a few days I will start to print my small book *Yeshua Venissim* ("Salvation and Miracles"), a commentary on the Passover *Hagada*. (Haddad 1972)

In Israel Tunisian Jews adhere much less to the practices of orthodox Judaism than they did abroad; some of the minutiae of orthodox practice have completely fallen into desuetude, while others are only adhered to by a few people This is particularly obvious on the intergenerational level: the ritual practiced by the generation that has grown up in Israel is much more limited than that of the parental generation. Public synagogue worship in the recent Tunisian past was a daily practice that people attended for many hours. In Israel, public weekday worship is common only among the very old. The great majority participate only once a week, and an increasing minority participate only on major seasonal festivals.

Religious changes have also occurred at the deepest existential levels in the lives of people as individuals (for elaboration, see Deshen and Shokeid 1974). Faced with the drastic differences in religious atmosphere, the immigrants and the younger generation that immigrated as children experience a profound sense of loss and decadence. There is a deep feeling of religious failing and unworthiness. Despite the fact that these people have moved away from traditional ways, tradition remains legitimate to them, and there is no alternative system of values or beliefs that is acceptable to them.

Respect for the old rabbis is generally profound. In fact, the memories of ancient deceased rabbinical figures are being increasingly venerated in the form of renewed pilgrimages to synagogues named after them and to the tombs of Tunisian rabbis who died in Israel (see Deshen and Shokeid 1974).

In education, the position has radically changed. Tunisians[7] are particularly proud of their past high standard of traditional Jewish learning that was common in Tunisia to which they applied the idiom *ha'iyun hatunisi* ("Tunisian profundity"). The Hebrew meaning of *'iyun* is "study" or "learning," but in the usage of Tunisian Jews it connotes profundity, wisdom, and scholarly depth. A student who has reached a defined standard of scholarship is called a *me'ayein,* he who practices *'iyun. Ha'iyun hatunisi* recurs frequently in the Tunisian rabbinical writings of the past two hundred years.

In Israel, the education of Tunisian youth depends on educators to whom traditional Tunisian educational techniques are foreign. Most Israeli teachers are trained in secular schools, but even teachers who are sympathetic to tradition as such are generally ignorant of the peculiarities of traditional schooling in Tunisia (see Schachter 1972; Braham 1966). This secular education together with the fact that the practice of studying traditional texts by adults has been largely discontinued account for the near total decay of traditional learning as the immigrants knew it abroad.

The publication activities must be seen against this dual background: a rich religio-cultural heritage in which writing and publication figured prominently and a present that is conceived of as religiously impoverished and decaying.

Survey of Recent Tunisian Publications in Israel

During the years 1958–71 sixty-one books written by Tunisian rabbis and scholars were published in Israel by immigrants from southern Tunisia, specifically from the island of Djerba. The first four books appeared in 1958. In the next eight years the number of books published varied from one to five per year. In 1967 six books appeared; in 1971 there were thirteen. From the information I have on forty-two books, their print runs were as follows: twenty-three books, 700 copies; nine books, 500 copies; five books, 1,500 copies; two books, 2,000 copies; two books, 1,000 copies; one book, 300 copies. Since these figures include only the publications that came to my attention, my information is probably incomplete. Also, these figures do not include leaflets or periodicals. Since many belles-lettres works published in Israel are issued in small quantities (sometimes only 500 copies), the southern Tunisian print runs should be considered very large.

The publishing ventures were generally very successful; many of the books were soon out of print because of brisk sales. Since the appeal of these works did not carry far beyond the immediate southern Tunisian population in Israel, it is remarkable that the publishers found a large enough outlet for so many books.

None of the sixty-one books under discussion were issued by commercial publishers: eighteen were published by the authors themselves; eleven by close kinsmen of the writers; nine by local associations or committees of disciples and relatives of the authors, or by their followers individually. The main publisher, however, was the Organization of Immigrants from Djerba and Southern

Tunisia, a national association that published twenty-one books. (Two books were issued by a rival body that operated only for a short period.)

The Organization of Immigrants from Djerba and Southern Tunisia became prominent in the publishing field only after individuals and local committees had been active for some years. The publication committee that issued the first books in the late 1950s was organized in the village of Berekhya near the town of Ashkelon to perpetuate the memory of the deceased village rabbi. (For background details on this village, see Deshen 1966.) The rabbi had left behind many manuscripts of scholarly writings that the villagers undertook to publish; for some years they carried out the onerous and scholarly labor of editing, copying, and proofreading them. Later the villagers relegated most of the work to a disciple of their rabbi, who was himself a rabbi in another town. (To date, most of the rabbi's writings have appeared, making up ten sizable volumes.)

In the early 1960s Shmuel Eidan became the driving force of the committee. He was another disciple of the late rabbi, and he was able to solicit funds from southern Tunisians scattered all over Israel to mobilize the publication effort. The village committee readily entrusted Eidan and the new editor with its affairs and, subsequently, the committee grew into a national body (the Organization of Immigrants from Djerba and Southern Tunisia) devoted to the same goals as the local committee.

The emergence of an organization as a leading publisher is novel and significant. In the past, publication was the exclusive responsibility of individuals; today the formal institutional body assumes much of the responsibility for publication. The laymen and rabbis who constitute the active core of the Organization of Immigrants from Djerba and Southern Tunisia are imbued with a sense of responsibility for the perpetuation of Djerban tradition and culture. They consider themselves disciples of southern Tunisian scholars and therefore obligated to encourage the publication of their works. During the 1960s the organization assisted many authors and publishers and, in some cases (such as the renowned Berekhya rabbi), initiated the publication venture.

The organization does not operate as a publisher in the usual sense of the word, because it does not undertake financial liability for the venture. Its role is usually limited to matters of publicity and organization. It offers the publication venture its prestige, its extensive ties with southern Tunisian communities, and the practical experience of its officers. When the organization does initiate publication, it is dependent on individuals and local groups to collect funds for the venture. They usually have a particular interest in the publication as a result of their kinship with the author or their community ties, or because they are disciples of the writer.

The traditional financial operation is similar to newspaper advertising. The subscribers are allotted space in the book, and the amount of space per subscriber depends on the sum paid. Generous supporters can buy a whole page to commemorate dead relatives, while more modest supporters can buy one or two lines to request heavenly blessings for themselves and their families.

Two Publication Ventures

The obligation to publish the writings of deceased ancestors is felt most strongly by sons of authors and other immediate descendants. The publishing ventures of the Eidan family and the Farjon family are described below to help illustrate the mechanics of publication.[8]

The Eidan text was written in the 1860s by Rabbi Moshe Eidan, a prominent and revered rabbi in Djerba who died in 1894. His sons published the work in 1903. In 1966 his grandson Shmuel Eidan was moved by a vision to reissue the book. Eidan sent the following circular to fifty-eight relatives.

With the Help of the Lord 5th Tevet 5727, 18.12.1966.

Concerning the printing of the Passover *Hagada* of the Grandfather the mystical Godly genius, Rabbi Moshe Eidan, may the mention of the righteous and holy man be a blessing to us.

I hereby inform you with joy that last week I dreamt, and one of the rabbis came to me and requested that I issue a second printing of the commentary on the *Hagada* of the Grandfather, may the mention of the righteous and holy man be a blessing to us. I then asked the rabbi how to pay for this, for I don't have enough money. He replied "You can turn to all our families and every family will participate by giving a large or a small sum. Though most of our families have barely enough for their living, still go to them, and for this merit the Lord will have mercy on them."

Next morning I immediately went and handed the *Hagada* to the printer, and with the help of the L-rd in one-and-a-half months the *Hagada* will be printed on good quality paper and in a good binding. The total cost will amount to about IL.2,000.- and every copy will cost IL.2.-. I carry out the request of the rabbi and request you to try and send me immediately however much money you can. And through the merits of the rabbi, the author, the Lord will guard and have mercy on us and on you. Amen.

With blessing and much respect,
David Eidan

Within a few months 1,000 copies of Rabbi Moshe Eidan *Hagada* were circulated anew. The edition was a photo-offset reproduction of the 1903 printing, and it was financed exclusively by the descendants of the author. In most cases, publishers are unable to obtain financing exclusively through family sources, but because of the esteem and resourcefulness of Shmuel Bukhriss, his large family mobilized itself behind the publishing effort. On the obverse of the title page in small print appeared the name and address of the publisher and the following inscription:

Second Edition

Published with the aid of the family. May they be blessed from on High and the merit of the Pious man protect them and all they possess. Amen.

Shortly thereafter Shmuel Bukhriss won a large sum of money in the football pools, and his family saw this as divine compensation for his pious deed.

The Farjon publishing venture illustrates the efforts of ordinary people who seek to publish the writings of an unknown person. Ya'akov Farjon, an unskilled laborer, received a traditional education, studied traditional books and texts, and had accumulated reams of writings since his youth. He had assumed that his writings would one day be published and had begun editing them. His efforts were cut short by a fatal traffic accident in 1962. His widow and sons decided to compile the writings into a book, and they engaged an Israeli Djerban scholar to complete the editing, since they were not educated enough to do so themselves. The Farjon family wanted to finance the publication and donate the books to synagogue libraries as an act of piety in memory of the author. However, after four years of effort, they were unable to raise the money. In 1966 the family approached the public by circulating the following leaflet in southern Tunisian synagogues throughout the country.

Honored Congregation,

In the past years in the diaspora and particularly in Tunisia, when one published the work of a deceased scholar, one advertised in synagogues and public places and even in other towns in order to inform the generous public to give as much as possible. It was also the custom to publish the names of donors and to enable them to print memorials for deceased relatives.

We now inform you that we possess manuscripts of our deceased husband and father, Ya'akov Farjon, may the memory of the pious one be a blessing, that were written by the pious one in his life. He toiled in spirituality as any God fearing Jew, and we desire to honour him in death and to publish. . . . But now we have a great monetary problem of thousands of pounds needed to complete the holy work soon. Therefore we turn to you . . . the name of the giver will be published . . . and he will receive a copy of the book. May the merit of the deceased guard you and all Israel our brothers and may the merit of this *mitzva* ("pious deed") which is *hesed shel emet* ("genuine charity"),[9] cause God to cease our suffering and send Elijah to announce the Redemption, may it come about speedily and soon. Amen.

Contributions can be sent to the following address . . . and please write your name and address.

With friendly blessings and many thanks,
Fortuna Farjon and her sons.

The appeal was successful, and 1,000 copies of the book were finally printed in late 1966. The book listed about one hundred individuals, from seventeen different localities, who had made contributions. Another hundred donations were received while the manuscript was in press and thus the names of the donors could not be printed. The Farjon family also received contributions from the organization and from the Ministry of Religious Affairs. Two hundred copies of the book were distributed to the individual contributors, and 300 were given to the organization. These 300 copies could be ordered through a periodical for religious *novellae* that was published by a Djerban family with the assistance of the organization.[10]

Besides the writings of Ya'akov Farjon, the volume included a collection of southern Tunisian Jewish folktales the editor had included in order to appeal to people with little formal education. In the past such tales had often been printed in Hebrew characters, in the Judeo-Arabic vernacular; here they appeared in a modern Hebrew translation.

Compared with the Eidan publication venture, the Farjon venture was more difficult and required much more effort on the part of the immediate family. The oldest of the Farjon sons, a policeman who considered himself responsible for the publication, deliberately postponed his marriage until he saw the book through press. He felt that he did not have the means to marry, set up a household, and publish his father's book at the same time. It took three years for the book to be edited, copied, and published; considering the complications, this was not a very long period of time.

Conclusion

In the process of migration from the traditional communities of Tunisia to the modern and heterogeneous Israeli setting, the tenacious adherence to the many minutiae of traditional beliefs and practices has decreased and is continuing to decrease. People believe that they are losing hold of the means that lead to self-justification and salvation. This arouses feelings of unworthiness and malaise, for no clearly articulated secular or humanist ideology has been able to replace the traditional beliefs of the southern Tunisian immigrants. However, people can alleviate some of these feelings by participating in the publishing of holy books, for the publication of holy works is an act of great merit. Books are concrete, visible, and aesthetically satisfying, and their publication can engender ethnic self-respect. The publication of books is not an onerous task for the individual, although it is a great and complex burden for the publisher. The hundreds of people who assist in the financing, by merely undertaking to buy a single copy, gain religious merit at a negligible price and with no effort. Normally they will be esteemed by having their name included in the list of contributors. And most important of all, in buying such a book a person brings into his home a *seifer berakha* ("book of blessing") and a *shemira* (lit., "security," a talisman).

The most striking aspect of the publishing ventures of Tunisian Jews in Israel is that neither the people who publish and distribute the books nor those who buy them are likely to read them. The standard of southern Tunisian education, which is already low, is declining. There are very few people who are educated enough to study the books. In the past, in Tunisia, there was much more interest in the content of traditional texts; people met in study circles to discuss the books. In Israel today, the activity of publishing these books has great popular appeal,[11] but the people involved attribute decreasing importance to the actual scholarly content of the activity.

I suggest that the phenomenon be viewed as primarily symbolic and cultural. I have noted the religious importance that an author attaches to his scholarly writings, namely that his soul will benefit if his work is published. The author's descendants believe, in addition, that by publishing the writings of the dead their own souls will also have a better fate in paradise. In this sense, the scholarly content of the book is irrelevant to the publication venture. What is important is the inherent ritual value of the book as a vehicle for expressing filial devotion.[12] Following Goody (1968) and Meggitt (1968), I would conceptualize this as a kind of ritualization of literacy.

This interpretation is supported in three ways. First, many of the works published in Israel today are by Tunisian scholars of general Jewish renown, some of whom lived many generations ago, whereas the works commonly published in Djerba in the past were written by the immediate ancestors of the publishers. Very few works by ancient, virtually classical authors were published in Djerba. The traditional theological rationale for publication, filial piety, is therefore more tenuous in the case of many of the Israeli Tunisian productions than it was for the Djerban publications. Second, most of the southern Tunisian books published in Israel cannot be enjoyed by the reader as literature. In the past the content of the works was much more readily understandable to the reader because the authors were the immediate ancestors of the publishers, with whom they presumably shared a familiar cultural and social environment. Furthermore, the standard of religious learning was higher in Djerba than it is in Israel. This plus the fact that the Israeli Tunisians publish books of scholars who are not their immediate ancestors means that the writings seem esoteric to the reader. Third, in Djerba the books often included folktales in the Judeo-Arabic vernacular. Each page was divided in half: the Hebrew text was at the top, and the folktales were printed consecutively on the lower halves of the pages. Thus in addition to their interest as scholarly works, the books had wide appeal as folk literature. In Israel, however, there is some ambivalence about the traditional vernacular, and very few folktales have been published in that language. In other words, the books published by southern Tunisians in Israel do not contain material that can be appreciated by laypeople. They have ritual rather than literary value.

Books also have ritual value as talismans. In several of the posters and fly sheets advertising new publication ventures that are circulated among synagogue congregations the following appeals were made to the public:

> Take this book of blessing (*seifer berakha*) into your houses and enjoy its precious and sweet *hidushim*. May the merit of the Rabbi, the author, Avraham Hakohen Yitzhaqi and his teacher Rabbi Yeshua Bessis (may the memory of the righteous and holy men be a blessing) guard you and all the members of your households.
>
> And we call upon the public that they have the merit and acquire this holy book, and with the help of the Lord the merit of the holy Rabbi will guard them and the book will be a talisman and security (*qame'a ushemira*) in the house.

In other words, the books are promoted in terms of their prophylactic-magical value. The presence of these books in the house ensures the home against misfortune. (In the folk religion of many Jewish communities, as well as that of southern Tunisia, talismanic value is often attributed to ritual artifacts of the most diverse theological nature, such as pictures of rabbis, encased *mezuzot* inscriptions nailed on doorposts, and many others.)

I conclude by suggesting that the decrease in the attribution of weight to the literary content of books has been complemented by an increase in their diffuse prophylactic value. It is a case of extreme ritualization of letters. Southern Tunisians have substituted acts such as book publishing and pilgrimages,[13] which are now considered generally efficacious, for the many specific acts of piety that were formerly performed.

Notes

A version of this essay was read at the Israel Sociological Association meeting at Bar-Ilan University in January 1973. I am thankful for the comments of E. Marx, N. Rubin, M. Schwartz, M. Shokeid, and other participants at the discussion. This essay was first published in 1975 and the statements herein reflect that time period.

1. Although membership in the ancient Jewish castes has always had very little social or ritual significance, the castes still exist. Knowledge of who belongs to which caste has been kept alive because it is a sine qua non of Messianic hopes. Among Djerban Jews, perhaps more than any other Jewish community, being a *kohen* carried with it some actual social weight.
2. For the purposes of this essay there is no need to distinguish between southern Tunisian and Djerban Jewries. All Jews from the region look up to the leadership of Djerba and tend to identify themselves as Djerbans. The terms "Southern Tunisia" and "Djerba" are interchangeable in the present context. Elsewhere (Deshen and Jaeger 1971) I have discussed some of the fine differences that exist within southern Tunisian Jewry.
3. The Alliance Israelite Universelle, an international Jewish organization, was founded in 1860 and was based in Paris. It was organized primarily to defend Jewish civil and religious liberties and to prepare Jews everywhere for emancipation; it established an educational network that was strongly French in sentiment and cultural orientation. The network existed in many countries, especially in the Balkans, in North Africa, and in West Asia. However, some communities viewed the propagation of French culture in Jewish schools as a danger to traditional Jewish education.
4. The singular is *hidush,* and the contractive form is *hidushei* (from the plural) plus the word with which it contracts, i.e., *hidushei Tora.*

5. The medieval Ashkenazi pietistic book *Seifer Hassidim* was known to Tunisian scholars who have told me its ruling on publications: "And anyone to whom the Almighty has revealed anything, and he is able to write but does not so do, he does rob Him who revealed" (*Seifer Hassidim*, item 530).
6. My colleague Emanuel Marx has pointed out that this text implies that many people actually publish for gain. However, the Israeli Tunisian publication situation is such that it is inconceivable that an author could make any real profit; it would be much more likely to cost him money. The author's remarks should be evaluated in terms of his background. The man, who was over eighty, had been a prominent person in Djerba. In Israel he lived in Shelomi, an isolated and remote town, and he was largely out of touch with current developments. His writing reflects the experiences of his mature years abroad, where perhaps it was possible to make a profit from publication. But even that is doubtful; his words may be a mere figure of speech.
7. The terms "Tunisians" and "Djerbans" that I use are, of course, shorthand for "Jewish immigrants from Tunisia" or from Djerba. I use them for the sake of convenience.
8. The personal names in the following paragraphs have been changed so as not to invade the privacy of the people concerned.
9. This particular pious deed is termed "genuine charity" because the dead who are its object cannot repay.
10. I have no information on the financial details, but I believe that the proceeds of the sales revert to the Organization in return for its contribution in publishing the book.
11. In the past, fewer books were published yearly, the books were less voluminous, and the editions were smaller.
12. Chinese ancestor worship offers an interesting parallel. However, there are differences in the kinds of ancestors worshiped (distant or recent) and in the social import of the two kinds of worship (Freedman 1958).
13. Elsewhere (Deshen and Shokeid 1974) I have discussed the phenomenon of the increasingly popular *hillulot*, memorial pilgrimages, of Tunisian immigrants in Israel. Publication activities and *hillulot* can be interpreted in similar terms.

2

Cultural Change in an Israeli Immigrant Village

The Twist Dance in Moshav Porat

HARVEY E. GOLDBERG

Introduction

A common criticism of field studies of culture change is that they depend on a great deal of reconstruction after the fact. Even in instances where one community has been studied at two different points in time, these studies often do not reveal the intervening processes of change. Van Velsen (1967) has suggested the method of "extended case analysis" for studying these processes. This essay will utilize this approach in analyzing a case of trait adoption in an immigrant village in Israel.[1]

The community under discussion is a group of Tripolitanian Jews who migrated from North Africa to Israel in 1949–50. Originally they lived in two villages of the Gharian Mountain district of Tripolitania, Libya. There they worked primarily as merchants, peddlers, and artisans who serviced the needs of the majority Muslim-peasant population. This Jewish community was at least four centuries old (Slouschz 1927), and its social structure and traditions were not greatly affected by the Italian occupation and colonization in the twentieth century. The move to Israel abruptly took the members of the community from a traditional Middle Eastern milieu to the predominantly European-influenced setting of modern Israel (Goldberg 1972).

In 1951, after spending some time in immigration camps, the Gharian Jews settled a moshav (small-holders' cooperative) named Porat. During the next fourteen years the villagers learned the skills of modern farming, which is the main source of income in the village today. Most members of the community enjoy a comfortable standard of living based on the marketing of citrus fruit, vegetables, and poultry.

Socially, too, the community has fit well into Israeli society. The workers of the Land Settlement Department consider the moshav to be economically successful and socially stable. The villagers elect a moshav committee about once every eighteen months and the moshav is managed by a secretary, selected from among the villagers, who works constructively in conjunction with the employees of the department.

The economic development of Porat, and its integration into the wider society, thus has been relatively rapid. This does not mean, however, that Gharian Jews' former beliefs, attitudes, and customs have disappeared. On the contrary, any outsider familiar with Porat knows that it is one of the most "traditional" villages in the region, and one can observe there many old customs that have not survived elsewhere. It could be argued, in fact, that the quickness with which the villagers learned new techno-economic skills enabled them to preserve their traditional ways in areas that are not directly concerned with economics.

The tenacity of these traditions, and the complex ways in which they change, are the subject of this essay. My case study concerns a single culture trait, the "twist" dance. Since dancing, in Porat, takes place primarily in the context of marriage celebrations, I will begin my account by giving a sketch of the traditional wedding celebration of the Gharian Jews, phrased in terms of the "ethnographic present."

The Traditional Wedding

The legal consummation of a marriage takes place on Wednesday night, according to Mishnaic tradition (Tractate *Ketubbot* 1:1), but it is preceded by several days of ceremonies and celebrations. On the preceding Friday the cosmetic preparation of the bride begins when her hair is colored with henna by older female relatives and neighbors. The Saturday that follows is called *shabbat libnat*, the Sabbath of the maidens, when the first of parallel "bachelors" and "maidens" parties take place. On Friday night, after prayer, the young men gather at the house of the groom and the girls go to the house of the bride. After the Sabbath morning prayers the boys go to the bride's house, throw peanuts at the girls, and food is served.

On Sunday evening the groom sends a gift of clothes to the bride. These are brought by an old widow who specializes in this task, carrying them in a basket on her head. The old woman is dressed in white and leads a procession in which women sing Arabic songs and young men race on donkeys. After reaching the house of the bride the old woman takes charge of dressing the bride, combing her hair, and coloring it further. The bride is brought outside and sits on a low stool, her hair exposed and flowing, where she is surrounded by women and a plate is placed on her head. The young men, including the groom, then begin to take turns moving through the circle of women and placing coins in the plate. The women sing verses in praise of the bride, ululate in a high-pitched voice (*zgharit*), and call out the sum "contributed." The money is kept by the old widow as a form of charity (*tzedaqa*).

A somewhat similar ceremony takes place on Monday night. After undergoing further cosmetic treatment the bride sits outside, but this time her head and body are covered. Only her feet are exposed and these have been colored with henna. The young men, as during the previous evening, contribute coins, but this time they touch them on the toes of the bride before placing them in the basket. After this the bachelors retire to the house of the groom for a meal and the girls are served at the house of the bride.

Early Tuesday morning the bride is taken to the home of a friend or relative who has volunteered for the occasion and undergoes further preparation. Many women gather there and one older woman carefully removes the pubic and body hair of the bride with a special jelly that she prepares. (After marriage the girl will cleanse herself in the same manner as at the end of each menstrual period.) In the evening the men gather outside the house where they sing appropriate hymns (*piyyutim*) and drink. After dark there is a torchlight procession, led by the men singing hymns, in which a cloak is spread over the bride as she returns to her own home accompanied by the women. At her home the henna and coin rituals are carried out as they were on Monday night. After the rituals a meal is served.

On Wednesday, at noon, the notables of the community are invited by the *rebbi* (the main religious specialist—usually a prayer leader and synagogue teacher) to the writing of the *ketubba*, or marriage contract. The bride's father brings the dowry, consisting of clothing, silver jewelry, kitchen utensils, and bedding. Each item is publicly displayed, assessed lavishly by the notables present, and written into the *ketubba*, which (in the event of divorce or widowhood) will be about one-third higher than the sum of the enumerated dowry. The *ketubba* is later signed by the groom.

Toward the evening the bride is taken to the ritual bath (*miqve*) where, after immersion, she dons the clothes sent to her on Sunday. Later, the groom visits the *miqve* where he too dresses in new clothes and is given a new prayer shawl. He is then led, accompanied by song, from the *miqve* (near the synagogue) to his future home, usually a room in his father's house. Afterward another procession brings the bride from her home to his. The *ketubba* is read and given to the father of the girl, and the marriage is solemnly consecrated by the *rebbi*. A festive meal follows, after which the couple retires to their new home. The bride's female relatives linger nearby till evidence of the blood of virginity is shown. (For comparative descriptive material and analysis, see Goldberg 1990, 52–67.)

The round of celebrations and ceremonies does not end with the nuptial night but continues till the following Sunday. For the present, however, I wish to focus the reader's attention on the three celebrations before the nuptial night, which I will call the *henna celebrations*. (In fact, only Monday night is called "the night of henna.") Seven of the nine marriages that took place during my visit to

Porat involved village girls and men outside the village. In these cases there were truncated celebrations involving only one or two henna nights. It was these henna celebrations, at which unmarried boys and girls came into "contact," that provided the main setting for the introduction of the twist dance into Porat.

Throughout the week the celebrants are usually, though not rigidly, grouped as follows: young men (including younger married men), older men, unmarried girls, and married women. The groom spends his time with his age-mates and maintains an avoidance relationship toward his parents, particularly toward his father. The week of celebrations provides opportunities for marriage proposals to be made, from the boys to the girls, in the form of hints and rumors. The group of married women constitutes an important "relay station" in the transmission of these messages. The proposals are sufficiently veiled so that they can be ignored or rejected without causing anyone embarrassment, and without a face-to-face meeting of the boy and girl.

One more historical note is in order. The following account is taken from a book, written by Mordecai Ha-Cohen (Ha-Cohen 1978, 48; Goldberg 1993), and concerns a wedding that took place in the city of Tripoli.

> In former days no woman wore pantaloons, for it was a great shame to them. Instead they draped a sheet half-way down the thigh. The notable Shlomo Khalfon was the first to break with tradition. In the year 5492 (1732), he presented pantaloons in the dowry of his daughter, Miss Aziza, and it was an innovation and example. Then this custom began to spread for women can wear pantaloons if they wish. However, when they launder them, they do not dry them publicly in the sun, but in the innermost room.

This brief account indicates that, in the past, wedding celebrations were sometimes used as the *stage for the debut of culture traits.*

The Twist in Porat

My story of the twist begins in November 1963, before I selected Porat as a village of study and was surveying several Tripolitanian moshavim to locate a traditional community. In one moshav that interested me, the first villager I met was most cordial and, after engaging in brief conversation, invited me to attend a wedding that same evening. Being pleased at my initial reception in the village, I doubly welcomed the chance to observe a rite of passage so early in my fieldwork. During the course of the ceremony, however, I observed nothing "exotic" and was overwhelmed by ethnographic horror when, at the conclusion of the ceremony, the public address system began to play rock-and-roll music and boys and girls, in front of their parents, joined in dancing the twist. I knew I had to find another village.

I eventually located the community of Porat, which I selected as the site of my intensive study. I quickly learned that there the relations between the sexes were quite traditional. Adolescent boys and girls never met in public. "If you speak to a girl in public," the male youths said, "the village will have you married off to her." When groups of girls walked by groups of adolescent boys, there was not even an exchange of glances, to say nothing of an exchange of comments.

This set of arrangements, however, was quite unsatisfactory to the male adolescents. They were not too concerned with the lack of contact with the girls in their village, as they had known them since childhood (every girl, so to speak, was "the girl next door"). It did bother them, however, that their village was so "backward" and that their community retained social mores that were rapidly disappearing elsewhere. This perceived backwardness frustrated their strivings to develop a self-image of being "modern" (see Zenner 1963, 220). While the aspiration to "modernity" was shared by many of the boys, only a few of them had taken steps to realize these aspirations. With regard to heterosexual social contacts, several of them had learned some modern social dancing, but most of them remained socially gauche. The few boys who learned Euro-American dances, such as the twist, outside Porat would then teach them in the village to their more local-oriented male peers.

There were few organized youth activities in the village, though a number of attempts in this direction had been made by outside agencies such as the school and the political party. Another such agency was the army, which had a program of sending youth leaders to "outlying villages" to organize cultural-recreational activities. Several months before my arrival two female soldiers began to visit Porat weekly in order to hold dance classes. The soldiers intended to teach Zionist folk dances, but the boys knew that this was "old stuff" and insisted on being taught the twist. The soldiers agreed to teach modern dances if the boys would agree to learn the folk dances as well.

At first, adolescent girls also attended these sessions. After a few weeks, however, the rabbi of the village (who came from the island of Jerba in Tunisia; see Slouschz 1927, 43, 262, on Jerban links to Tripoli) began to speak against social dancing during his talks in the synagogue. He claimed that it was "shameful" (cf. Goldberg 1969, 62–63) and that dancing "could lead to other things." He exhorted the fathers to prohibit their daughters from attending the classes. The fathers followed the rabbi's teaching and the girls stopped going. (Some boys claimed that the rabbi forbade dancing because he had an adolescent daughter but would not have done so if he had a teenage son.)

Why was the twist readily accepted in the first village I visited and, initially at least, successfully opposed in Porat? One reason concerns the nature of the links between immigrant moshavim and the Israeli political structure. Each moshav belongs to a federation, which in turn is linked to one of the main political parties. In the first village described, there was no political commitment with respect to religion even though many of the people observed traditional practices such as the dietary laws and daily prayer. There was no resident rabbi in that village, though there was a ritual slaughterer and circumciser. Moreover, even if there were a rabbi, his moral exhortations would remain just that, and would have no organizational backing.

The village of Porat, on the other hand, is linked to the Po'el Mizrahi. As a religious party, it uses political means to preserve traditional religion in Israel (Fein 1967, 93–94, 174–76). The rabbi of Porat, for example, might have persuaded the moshav committee to fine fathers who allowed their daughters to attend dance classes. (Once the committee had fined young men who traveled, outside of the village, on the Sabbath.) In the context of Porat, this would have been entirely legitimate and legal.

The separation of the sexes in Porat, then, is not simply the maintenance of a traditional pattern (see the case of dancing reported from southern Algeria in Briggs and Guède 1964, 49). To some extent it should be seen as culture change in the direction of the "religious" sector of Israeli society instead of acculturation in a more secular direction. These varying acculturative trends are channeled by the national political structure.

Though the rabbi succeeded temporarily in keeping social dancing out of Porat, he did not revise the boys' goal of modernizing their own "youth-culture." In this they were assisted by two of the more "brazen" girls who were willing to challenge the prevailing customs regarding heterosexual contacts.

One of these girls, the daughter of a respected villager, apparently decided that she would marry a boy from outside the village (about 90 percent of the marriages were village-endogamous). She became engaged to an Iraqi whom she met while working in a nearby citrus-packing house. This boy was quite "modern," both from her viewpoint and in the eyes of the male youth of the village.

A few days before the wedding a henna celebration took place in Porat. The male adolescents were sure that they would have a successful party. They believed that the Iraqi boy would insist that modern music be played and that there be modern dancing. One of their peers was a brother of the engaged girl, and he promised everyone a "good time."

Most of the evening proceeded as usual. Late in the celebration, however, after many people had left, someone put a rock-and-roll song on the record player. One girl who, like the bride, was firmly committed to modern dating patterns, got up and danced the twist. She was followed by two or three *boys who danced primarily with one another*. One usually negative villager said to me, "Look at the whoring that goes on these days," but others displayed no reaction. After ten to fifteen minutes the dancing ended and the celebration reverted to its normal pattern.

During the evening there also had been sporadic attempts at organizing other forms of "modern" dancing. Schoolchildren grouped in a circle and began dancing kindergarten dances (in which a boy chooses a girl who chooses a boy and so forth). Some adolescent boys and younger adolescent girls participated in this dance, but most just watched. At other recent celebrations these circle dances had been organized and perhaps represented an incipient stage in bringing heterosexual dancing to the wedding celebrations. (Singing modern Hebrew songs, learned in school, was already part of the female side of the celebrations.) At an earlier henna night, when such a circle dance was organized, the boys expressed the hope that the twist would be danced, but their hope had not been realized.

Another henna celebration took place about two months later. In this instance, too, several boys danced the twist with one another late at night after many of the guests had dispersed.

The next wedding took place six months later when the sister of one of the more "modern" youths married one of the village boys. The brother promised his friends that there would be a "good time" on the night of henna. At this time there resided in Porat a youth of European background (associated with the Po'el Mizrahi), who worked as a part-time youth leader. During the evening of the henna celebration the circle dance was organized, but no one initiated the twist. The boys pressed the brother of the bride, but he was adept at finding excuses as to why the modern dancing had not yet started. As was common among the village adults, the boys were reluctant to assume leadership (Goldberg 1969), and asked the youth leader to organize dancing. The European youth had once told me that he thought it was permissible for immigrant youth to dance, as an educational device. He thus wished to comply and encouraged the boys to congregate in the room where the girls were gathered.

The boys hesitated at first until the brother of the bride received a message that the girls wanted to see Zakki (age eighteen) and Dido (age seventeen) dance. These two boys were quite popular among their age-mates. The male youths then entered the room where the girls were sitting, gathered in one corner, and twist music was put on the record player. Zakki was willing to dance, but Dido hesitated. At that point Dido's thirteen-year-old brother entered the room, indicating that he might dance the twist. This boy was mute and deaf, but could respond to the rhythm of the music. He, at times, assumed buffoon-like roles that were tolerated by the adults while the same behavior would be less well tolerated from other boys his age. Everyone encouraged him to dance with Zakki and he balked. Zakki tried to threaten him by saying that he should dance or get out of the room. (The "conversation" was, of course conducted in sign language.)[2] This approach did not work and I, letting participation get the better of observation, told the younger brother that if he were to dance I would take his picture the next day. He agreed and began to dance with Zakki and then Dido joined in. The boys clapped enthusiastically while the girls just looked on. After one record the dancers sat down and retreated to the male end of the room. The girls, after the one dance, got up and left. The boys seemed to relax, as things returned to "normal," but they were quite pleased that at their parties "people dance the twist."

That same evening another factor to the twist-complex was introduced. While the boys were still in the stage of talking about dancing someone received a message that Urida wanted the boys to dance. Urida was the sixty-one-year-old widow who specialized in organizing the female side of weddings (see above). Also, she had been a midwife in Tripolitania, which included preparing male children for their circumcision. (She continues to play the latter role in Israel.) No one seemed to pay very much attention to the rumor that Urida wanted the boys to dance, but, at the next wedding, it became clear that this rumor was firmly based.

At a henna celebration that took place about two weeks before I left Porat, twist dancing was initiated *immediately after the main ceremony* in which coins are placed in a basket on the head of the bride. This dancing, in which the boys

Table 1
Case History of the Twist Dance in Moshav Porat

Date	Circle Dancing	Twist Dancing	Occasion
November 1963	yes	no	celebration at the consecration of a synagogue built with funds given by a British Jew
December 10, 1963	yes	no	wedding of a village girl in a nearby Yemenite moshav
March 2, 1964	no	yes	wedding outside the village; two boys (one of them Zakki) danced the twist
May 18, 1964	yes	no	henna night
June 3, 1964	not seen	no	engagement; some boys said they hoped there would be twist dancing
June 7, 1964	yes	yes	henna night; late in the evening one girl danced the twist and several boys danced with each other
August 11, 1964	yes	yes	engagement; boys danced late in evening
February 7, 1964	not seen	yes	henna night; late in evening Zakki and Dido danced
March 29, 1965	not seen	yes	henna night; boys danced at a *central* point in the celebration, accompanied by the ululations of women

danced with boys, took place with seemingly little tension and apparent acceptance on the part of the community. This acceptance was signaled by Urida who (perhaps in an attempt to maintain her special prestige), while watching the dancing from a room in which the women were gathered, accompanied the music with the high-pitched ululations. Her female companions joined in the shrill singing, indicating that the twist had been integrated into the wedding complex of Porat. Table 1 summarizes the events that constitute the case history of the introduction of that trait.

In conclusion, the adoption of the twist in Porat grew out of a series of multidimensional events. The history of this adoption must take into account the Israeli political structure, traditional norms of heterosexual contacts, the acculturative aspirations of the youth, leadership patterns within the village, the presence of some mildly deviant individuals (and an anthropology student), and the traditional aesthetics of community celebrations. Some may prefer to see the community of Porat as being swamped by forces of globalization that carry Western "mass culture." My own inclination is to give equal emphasis to the local social viability revealed by particular case analysis.

Notes

1. The fieldwork reported herein was supported by a grant from the U.S. National Institute of Mental Health. Shlomo Deshen and Donna Shai provided helpful criticism of the original version of this essay. In this version, I provide the real name of the village, while the names of individuals remain fictitious. There also have been minor revisions in this version, mainly to incorporate material from endnotes into the text, and to provide a more accessible set of references.
2. There were about a dozen deaf-mute people in the community. They seem to have been accepted quite casually in everyday life, and there was a local "sign language" used by them and the rest of the community when interacting with them. A parallel situation is mentioned in regard to a Jewish community in southern Algeria (Briggs and Guède 1964, 12, 90).

3

Yemenite Jewish Women in Israeli Rural Development

Female Power versus Male Authority

YAEL KATZIR

The effects of development programs on rural women have been issues of considerable interest to social scientists. Most studies emphasize the adverse impact of government-planned development on rural women's status.[1] My discussion will show, however, that under certain conditions of rural development women may gain great informal socioeconomic power although male formal power (i.e., authority) is perpetuated.

This study explores the changing status and roles of women in a Middle Eastern peasant group relocated in a cooperative village in a new country under a centralized national resettlement and development program. Specifically, I will present sex-role adaptations of a rural Jewish group of weavers uprooted from their village of origin in Yemen and transplanted to a moshav, a smallholders' cooperative agricultural settlement in Israel.[2]

The vast anthropological literature on women, accumulated mainly since the mid-1960s,[3] has brought to light several major dimensions for the study of Middle Eastern (including Middle Eastern Jewish) sex roles.[4]

1. *Sex-role segregation.* Middle Eastern cultures are characterized by little overlap or exchange of male and female roles (i.e., there is a high degree of sex-role segregation).
2. *Domestic/private and public domains of action.* The physical and social spheres culturally defined as domestic and public are differentially accessible to men and women. Men are universally the family representatives in public political and religious roles and have full access to the public domain. Middle Eastern women's participation in the public domain is limited and ranges from confinement to the domestic domain and veiling in

the public domain to rural women's petty trading on markets and working in the fields.[5]

3. *Power versus authority.* This conceptual distinction derived from Weber differentiates between "power," the actual resource of control and decision-making, and "authority," the formal, recognized, and legitimate power. Most human societies entrust the men with authority in the public and domestic domains. Middle Eastern patrilineal cultures provide men with a high degree of authority over their wives and children; men have the formal domestic power of ownership and control over property, income and labor, and decision-making.[6]

   While women are universally recognized as subordinated to male dominance, their real power in the social process is often greater than expected. The "appearance and reality" of women's power in traditional societies had been an issue of major interest to anthropological research. Even in Middle Eastern societies with a high degree of sex-role segregation and great oppression of women, women may acquire considerable informal power and play a crucial role in the social, political, religious, and economic processes. Women use diverse manipulative strategies, such as gossip, as a means of social control. Women may serve as political mediators between their affinal and natal groups and transmit selective information. Often they are marriage brokers for their sons and daughters.[7]

   The analytical differentiation between appearance and reality has also been instrumental in providing a new perspective on women's personality. Middle Eastern women, like women of many other male-dominated societies with a high degree of sex-role segregation, are coy, meek, and submissive in the presence of men and authority, but are self-assertive, sometimes aggressive, and opinionated behind the scenes.[8]

4. *Friendship networks.* The informal networks of women in highly segregated societies, based on individual friendship ties, are a crucial element and a powerful social resource. Middle Eastern women who are excluded from the formal cultural institutions have developed elaborate female networks based on kin, affinal, and neighborhood ties. Such networks are used for the exchange of political, cultural, and kinship information. They often function in economic exchange and for emotional support among the women. They are imperative in the arrangement of marriage, and they can channel cultural diffusion leading to cultural change.[9] Middle Eastern female networks have well-established and ritualized mutual visiting patterns.[10]

This chapter deals with the appearance and reality of rural Yemenite Jewish women's power and authority in the public and domestic domains and the functions of their female networks in adjusting to the drastic change of moshav life and integration into Israeli society.

Studies of Middle Eastern women in development have conformed to the general conclusion of development studies that rural peasant women are negatively affected by development.[11] Studies of the sex-role adaptations of Middle Eastern Jewish immigrants to the Israeli moshav are rare,[12] and none has focused on Yemenite Jews.[13] Shokeid studied continuity and change processes in the division of labor by sex in a moshav of Moroccan Jews. Under economic pressures, women in this moshav, encouraged by their husbands, turned to wage labor in agriculture, which was a marked change from their economic position as housewives in Morocco. However, male dominance patterns persisted and women's total income was handed over to their husbands.[14]

My study shows that the people who were resettled in the moshav developed a dual economic system: a male-dominated formal economic system of the moshav as a cooperative, and a parallel female-dominated free enterprise private marketing of produce, which was illegal by moshav rules. The Yemenite men, who had created socioeconomic networks through trade in Yemen and who were literate in Hebrew prior to migration, remained socially and physically isolated from Israeli society and confined to the moshav and its environs, and to their kin and ethnic groups. On the other hand, the women who in Yemen had been isolated within the domestic domain, illiterate, and spoke only Arabic upon resettlement, developed extensive socioeconomic networks outside the moshav and outside their kin and ethnic groups. They quickly picked up modern Hebrew and achieved social mobility and integration within the larger society. This resulted in increased economic power within their families. Yet it did not increase their motivation to seize more authority in the family or to assume public roles outside the family. Despite the improved economic status of women in Ramat Oranim, the formal sex-role structure and authority within the family have not been altered by resettlement.

The moshav under study, Ramat Oranim (a fictitious name), was established in 1950 by a group of families from al-Gades, a village of Jewish weavers in Yemen.[15] By 1972 Ramat Oranim included 64 farming households of the original settlers and 11 non-farming households of younger or very old members and a total population of 750. The great majority of the families were nuclear. An average farming household had eight members and a non-farming household had four. The study focused on the 64 farming households' heads and their wives, a group of 123: 59 married couples, four widows, and one widower.

The members of the group selected for study, consisting of the original settlers and first-generation immigrants, were married before or shortly after resettlement in Israel. They were socialized into adulthood in Yemen and married between the ages of twelve and fifteen, the customary age range of first marriage among the Jews of Yemen. This culturally homogenous group, which emigrated from one village in Yemen, has been extremely stable throughout the years in the moshav, with relatively little turnover of moshav members. It was thus possible to acquire good ethnohistorical data on changes in the same population over time. Moreover, data on this very same population, its village of origin, and initial stages of resettlement are available through the ethnohistorical study of S. D. Goitein in Ramat Oranim in the early 1950s.[16] This is the only Yemenite Jewish group in Israel that has been followed systematically from resettlement to the present.

Jewish Sex Roles in Yemen

At the time of the mass exodus of Jews from Yemen in 1948, that mountainous, fundamentalist Moslem country located in the southwest corner of the Arabian Peninsula had been isolated for centuries from the rest of the world. Yemen had limited technology, road systems, and modern transportation, and an extremely high death rate. The Jews, the only non-Moslem religious group in Yemen, formed a castelike minority, distinguished by endogamy, religion, culture, and occupations. Jews were dispersed throughout Yemen, living in their own quarters mostly in villages. By Moslem law, Jews were dhimmi—second-class citizens, landless, and doomed to poverty and discrimination.[17] Yet there was constant interaction between Jews and their Arab neighbors. Yemenite Jewish folk culture was deeply embedded in local traditions, and there was a physical resemblance between Yemenite Arabs and Jews, indicating to a certain degree of genetic flow between the populations.

Within the highly stratified Yemenite society, Jewish males were artisans who came to occupy several economic niches through the monopolization of such crafts as silversmithing, weaving, tailoring, shoemaking, and so forth (vocations Moslems considered polluting). They thus played a key role in the Yemenite economy. Jewish men were respected by the Moslems for their vocational skills as well as for their great orthodoxy, literacy in Hebrew, and thorough knowledge of the Old Testament. Jews regarded farming as a very low-status occupation. By and large the Jews lived in great poverty.

Al-Gades was a Jewish village of patrilineal, extended-family households, located in the southern Yemen Highlands. Social life was marked by a high degree of sex-role segregation in which only men had access to the public domain and to the formal religious tradition. Men represented their families in all public political, religious, and economic roles, and in this way controlled the formal social and cultural system. Women were confined to the domestic domain and had no access to the synagogue or the market. Jewish al-Gadesi women lived in *purdah,* although they were not veiled like the local Arab women, who were allowed to sell agricultural produce on the markets.

The subsistence base of al-Gades households was a cottage weaving industry. All of the men worked in weaving and were independent, free enterprise, small-scale traders. They sold their products "door-to-door" or in the al-Gades market and in surrounding markets. They moved around the villages, forming socio-economic networks outside al-Gades. Men purchased all household supplies and goods in these markets, including clothes and accessories for the women.

Yemenite Jewish women were greatly subordinated to the men. Men controlled all household resources, including income, property, and the labor of their wives and children, and had absolute authority over their women and children. In the ideal patrilineal extended three-generational family, the married sons handed all cash income over to their father. In contrast to the women, married dependent sons eventually headed their own households.

Yemenite Jewry transmitted property solely to the male members of the patrilineage, and, unlike Arab women, Yemenite Jewish women neither inherited any property from their fathers or husbands nor received any dowry. Upon marriage, a woman was exchanged for bridewealth, which was kept by her patrilineal kin. A woman had no independent income and could not work for a living. Thus, an al-Gades Jewish woman had no property or income of her own and was completely dependent on her male kin by birth or marriage.

First marriages were always arranged, and a woman did not know her husband before the wedding. Girls were married between the ages of nine and twelve and boys between thirteen and eighteen. Bridewealth payment for first marriage was much higher than for second and third marriages.

Through bridewealth payment, the husband's patrilineage acquired rights to a woman's labor, sexuality, and offspring. If her husband died, a woman's children were to be supported by their father's lineal kin. Orphans often wandered among kin and were homeless. A new widow or divorcee remarried as soon as possible. Her late husband's brother (in accordance with the biblical law of the Levirate) could claim her for a wife; however, actual Levirate was not common. Life history data show low household stability in the Yemenite Jewish population. The death rate of women, men, and children was extremely high. The high death rate of infants added to a woman's precarious position in the household, because her status depended on how many children she had. Under Moslem influence, Yemenite Jewish men could relatively easily obtain a divorce from their wives. A woman could provoke her husband to initiate divorce by repeatedly escaping to her natal kin. Consequently, two or three marriages for men and women were not uncommon. For a woman, remarriage usually meant moving into a new household, sometimes in a new village, while the remarried man remained at home. A woman was thus likely to move several times in her life from one family and one village to another, and each time she was forced to adjust anew. In second and third marriages, women actively manipulated their environment or courted the potential husband to achieve a better relationship and socioeconomic status. Polygyny was legitimate among Yemenite Jews, but of low frequency.

If a woman's marriage lasted and her children survived, she acquired increasing power within the household through the number of children and her influence over them. Strong affective ties persisted within the uterine, mother-centered group of children with their mother and among siblings.

Women had individual friendship networks that were expressed in informal mutual visiting, institutionalized and known as the "women's visiting." While her husband was occupied by religious, political, or economic affairs, the woman would pack a bundle of *ja'ala,* dried nuts and fruits, which she would bring as a gift to the woman to whom she paid a private visit. Women also maintained close ties with their natal kin group through periodic visits to their village of origin. At the village springs, Jewish and Arab women struck long-lasting friendships and exchanged cultural information. As a consequence, women were often informal agents of change. These social networks with other Jewish and Arab women served as a crucial means of exchanging information and mediating between families. Thus, while men had the authority, women could manipulate the power system indirectly in the areas of political, economic, and marriage decisions.[18]

All Yemenite Jewish men could read Hebrew and had an excellent knowledge of the Old Testament. In this patrilineal society, the training of boys in the literary tradition of Judaism, particularly knowledge of the Old Testament, and in the craftsmanship and trade of weaving was the responsibility of the patrilineage—the father, the father's father, or an uncle. A father passed his vocational and intellectual skills on to his sons and hence was both their master and teacher, with total authority over them. The Yemenite Jewish man was typically an artisan-reciter who chanted the Old Testament while he labored and, at the same time, supervised his son, who was both apprentice and student. By the age of fifteen a young man was expected to have achieved adulthood through cultural and vocational maturity and thus be eligible for marriage. By that age he was expected to have become a "walking book," not only fluent in reading the Old Testament in Hebrew but also capable of chanting it by heart with perfect memorization, pronunciation, and intonation. He was also to have become a fully skilled weaver and trader. In contrast to the boys, Yemenite Jewish girls received no formal education, and were informally trained in domestic tasks by their mothers or mothers-in-law.

Migration and Resettlement in the Moshav

Upon the establishment of the State of Israel in 1948, the Jews of Yemen were declared personae non gratae by the Yemenite government and were forced to leave, abandoning all their property. That very same year they walked en masse from all over Yemen toward the British-dominated southern port of Aden. The 70,000 who reached Aden were flown on light aircraft by the Israeli government's Operation Eagles' Wings and arrived in Israel as destitute refugees.

During the early 1950s the *moshav olim* (immigrants' moshav) in Israel's development and border areas was one of the major resettlement techniques employed at a time when the newly established Jewish nation-state labored under heavy security, economic, and immigration pressures. The influx of about 750,000 Jewish refugees between 1949 and 1954, primarily from the Arab Middle East, more than doubled the Israeli population. The moshav form of settlement was selected to achieve national development and demographic goals: (1)

the provision of the agricultural produce supplied by the Arab sector prior to the 1948 War of Independence; (2) the settlement of border areas and population dispersal; (3) the prevention of the emergence of city slums; and (4) the rapid sociocultural and technological integration of the immigrants through planned change and development programs within the easily supervised small moshav organization.

Concomitant with these practical considerations were the interests of the European political elite to socialize the new immigrants into their particular pioneer, Zionist, socialist values and ideology, and through economic dependence to gain their votes for the ruling political parties. Thousands of former peasant and urban Middle Eastern Jewish artisans and traders were to become cooperative socialist farmers.[19]

As Sadan and Weintraub describe,

> A *moshav* (plural *moshavim*) is primarily a multipurpose cooperative society with limited ability, established to promote farming as the major occupation and source of living for its members. The nuclear family is the basic social and economic unit, but the various households—of which there are on the average 70 in a village—are bound together by mutual solidarity and aid as well as by common agricultural, financial, supply, marketing and other services. The village economy differs from place to place according to general economic considerations and local conditions; in each *moshav,* however, an equitable division of the means of production (chiefly in respect of public capital, size and quality of plots, and water resources) is maintained.
>
> Besides being an agricultural cooperative and upholding a specific way of life, the *moshav* constitutes a unit of local government with municipal duties. The authority over this and over the cooperative function is vested in the general assembly of the adult members, which decides upon matters of principle and lays down the general policy. The implementation of this policy is entrusted to the village council, assisted by various elected committees and a salaried administrative and professional staff. The council is chosen by the assembly in free, secret and universal elections. The two constitute, in fact, the executive and the legislative body, respectively; and their separation, together with the principle of democratic representation and responsibility, is an integral part of the *moshav* movement's value system and constitution.[20]

The moshav structure promotes farming with minimal socioeconomic differentiation and its economy—based on central planning, a subsidy, and a quota system for marketing produce—leaves little room for free enterprise. The moshav recognizes only the nuclear (not extended) family as the basic unit of production, consumption, and socialization. All households have equal status within the cooperative. The moshav recognizes each household as a single unit represented within the moshav by one of its members. By moshav rule, either a man or a woman can be the recognized household head, the legal owner of the homestead and farm, and the person entitled to control all of the unit's property and profit. The household head is also the "moshav member," representing the family in the public domain, for example, in the village council and at public events.

In the initial phase of resettlement, the "immigrants' moshav" was subject to the supervision of the government and moshav authorities and to planned change, development, and modernizing programs. Extension workers, mainly volunteer young members of veteran moshavim of European Jews, lived with the Middle Eastern newcomers for several years and guided them into the new modern socialist moshav way of life. They concentrated on retraining the men to be farmers and teaching the women new concepts and practices of hygiene, childrearing, and literacy skills, as well as new ideas about the status of women and their rights and duties in relation to men.

Male Authority and Isolation

Ramat Oranim was established in 1950 on top of an isolated hill near the Jordanian-Israeli border, on the dry and rocky Jerusalem hills. Though located only about fifteen kilometers from Jerusalem, Ramat Oranim was physically isolated from its surroundings. The few neighboring settlements, of European Jewish origin, made no effort at social integration. Until recently, the only contact with the outside world has been by bus directly to town.

The initial phase of resettlement was marked by a collapse of the old order and a great loss of status for the men. The moshav values were foreign to the inhabitants of al-Gades. Within this new agricultural environment, the al-Gades weaving tradition became obsolete and the former male artisans turned into unskilled laborers to be retrained as farmers. The once independent competitive retail traders now became members of an egalitarian cooperative, economically dependent on outside authority.

Initially the men became unskilled day laborers employed by the resettlement authorities to build their community; later they became farmers on their farms. They were thus isolated within the moshav by their new occupation.

As a cooperative of equal-status households, each working in its small half-acre holding, the moshav land was divided into equal plots and allocated to nuclear families by lottery. At first the heads of former extended-family households demanded and received the labor and income of their married sons, who by then were living in their own households. But within two years the sons stopped contributing their labor and income to the extended family.

Male status further declined through the devaluation of their biblical scholarship. Fathers could no longer be the sole masters and teachers of their sons at home. The state school system took over their teaching role, while their craft tradition was no longer a useful skill to be passed on to their sons.

The men were further isolated by the fact that they were not called to regular army service, an important male initiation rite and integrating force in Israel. Instead they were drafted locally to defend Ramat Oranim because of its vulnerable border location. Thus, instead of having the opportunity to develop friendship networks in an army peer group, as did others in the country, their isolation from mainstream Israeli society was deepened, and the contacts they had beyond the moshav were with their own kin in other communities.

Nevertheless, formal male authority within the family was perpetuated by the moshav structure. As in all Middle Eastern moshavim, the al-Gades families delegated the power of farm owner and moshav member to the man, and thus male authority within the nuclear family was maintained. As moshav members who have access to public, economic, and political roles, men dominate the formal structure. A widow or a divorcee can become a farm owner and a moshav member only if her son will eventually inherit the farm.

The formal status of women within their families was enhanced by national and moshav law, which raised the marriage age, forbade bridewealth and polygyny, and provided women with inheritance rights upon death and divorce. Husbands could no longer easily divorce their wives because by moshav law a divorced woman receives the house and farm from her husband as alimony. Consequently, the divorce rate dropped sharply. Moreover, the sharp decrease in the death rate and the continuing high birthrate increased the number of live children per family and hence the power of the woman within the family unit. Enhanced family stability resulted. Women were also exposed to development and modernization roles through their contacts with the volunteer female members of veteran moshavim and female soldier-teachers.

Following initial resettlement, the primary economic activity of Ramat Oranim became fruit production. The orchard plots, which were equally divided among households, were cultivated by the men. The men were full farmers until the Six-Day War in 1967, when the orchards were abandoned in the face of tough competition from the low-priced fruit imported from the Arab West Bank. As a result, egg production became Ramat Oranim's main economic activity. Chicken farming was and continues to be carried on mainly by women and children, with the proceeds going to the male household heads. The moshav members receive additional profits from collectively owned property of Ramat Oranim cultivated by outsiders. The net cash income of a moshav member is generally small because all dues, taxes, and debts are centrally calculated for each household by the moshav office. Ramat Oranim's men have turned increasingly to unskilled or semiskilled labor either within the moshav or in the surrounding area. However, 30 percent of the moshav's male household heads, especially the older ones, have chosen not to seek such outside employment and have remained idle.

Female Power and Integration

A private, free enterprise marketing system (illegal according to moshav law) has developed concurrently with the cooperative produce marketing system in

Ramat Oranim. This new system is controlled by women. Starting in the early 1950s, Ramat Oranim women made weekly excursions by bus to Jerusalem to purchase food and household supplies that were unavailable in the village store or in their own gardens. As a result of postwar rationing, agricultural produce was in great demand and the women perceived an opportunity for high profit. Encouraged by their husbands, they started to cultivate cash crops in their gardens, marketing them for excellent prices in Jerusalem. For thirty years now, Ramat Oranim's women have kept up this private marketing, taking first their fruit and later their egg trays by bus to the city several times a week. In 1973 each woman carried as many as eight to ten trays of thirty eggs each three to four times a week to Jerusalem, adding a total of roughly three million eggs to the free market.[21]

Ramat Oranim's cooperative egg production surpassed the allocated production quota and illegal marketing thus became a crucial channel for surplus eggs. For example, the annual production quota for Ramat Oranim in 1972–73 was ten million eggs; in fact, Ramat Oranim surpassed the quota and marketed some fifteen million eggs during that year. Each egg within the quota limit was subsidized by (Israeli Lira) IL0.01, while the penalty for each surplus egg was IL0.09, charged to the village's general account. In 1971 the heavy fine for surplus produce was finally canceled after a long bargaining process by Ramat Oranim officials, who demanded the quota be raised. This quota, once granted, was soon surpassed again.

The amount of produce carried from the moshav for private trade is limited by the trader's physical strength and the amount one is permitted to carry on the bus. Of course, there are seasonal fluctuations in how much produce is grown and in the supply of eggs (which depends on the hens' egg production cycle). Before the Jewish holidays in the spring and autumn, the women carry greater quantities of eggs to town and relatively lesser quantities are marketed through the cooperative. Because the women take care of the chicken coops, the number of eggs channeled into private marketing is determined by how much cash each woman needs. The women are also responsible for the egg-sorting process, so they can manipulate the quantities marketed centrally rather than through their private trading. A woman may select a larger number of "too large," "too small," or "broken" eggs (by definition not accepted for marketing through the cooperative system) if she needs more cash at any particular time. This demand for greater cash often coincides with the holidays and the markets' resultant demand for larger quantities. In this way, she can ultimately control the amount of cash that goes into her pocket rather than into the cash income her husband earns through cooperative marketing.

This new role gives women considerable economic power within their household. Because the men have earned little cash through the moshav system, the women have come to be the main providers of cash. Thus, contrary to family sex-role relations in Yemen, the women of Ramat Oranim control the household's daily budget and serve as the household's representatives on the market. When the men worked as farmers, they (and the households) depended on the women for cash, but even when the men eventually became wage earners and received their own cash incomes they could not stop the women's trade because of the surplus produce problem. Formally, the women are expected to hand all surplus cash income to their husbands, but they rarely do so, claiming that nothing is left. In fact, they earn a great deal more than they admit and use the extra cash for clothes, pocket money for their growing sons and daughters, and secret support of married daughters in town. Because money is not easily obtainable from the fathers, the mothers' status in the family is not only enhanced but openly acknowledged by the children, who have become increasingly dependent on their mothers. Most important, the extra cash income is used to raise the families' standard of living. With great persistence, the women of Ramat Oranim try to apply new ideas learned in town to their homes. They purchase new household goods with their own income and are thus instrumental in raising the standard of living. They also pressure their husbands to invest periodically in home improvements and sometimes stimulate their husbands' contributions by partial investment from their own savings in the purchase of an appliance or a piece of furniture.

Through trade the women have developed important socioeconomic networks in Jerusalem. Because their marketing is carried out primarily in one location within the Central Market, each woman has acquired, in addition to transient customers, a core of steady clients maintained over the thirty-year period. Moreover, each woman has developed close personal and economic ties with several merchants and traders and sells produce door-to-door to clients in surrounding residential neighborhoods. Over the years, Ramat Oranim women have cultivated and cherished the social ties developed with these patrons, whom they now term "friends," although they basically maintain a patron-client relationship. Informal visiting occurs when Ramat Oranim women make brief calls on their "friends" for trading and subsequently invite these "friends" to Ramat Oranim for family celebrations. In this way a feeling of closeness develops between the Yemenite women and their patrons, which is also partly a result of their sense of ethnic identity, since the "friends" tend to be of Middle Eastern and North African origin.

Through these contacts, the cultural perspective of the women has changed drastically. Their contact with city life has been the most important factor in their modernization; they have acquired new values and ideas about child-rearing, social mobility, and living standards, using their women "friends" as a reference group. Through these female "friendship" networks they promote social mobility for the entire family. They consult the "friends" on technical and personal problems, get information about the acquisition of goods and about schools and jobs for their children, and arrange marriages for their daughters. Because the networks are based primarily on lower-middle-class female clients and male merchants, they fulfill a crucial role for the Ramat Oranim families in the process of achieving upward mobility through marriage. The women actively accumulate information about eligible bachelors to whom they can introduce their daughters, thus promoting the marriage of daughters into a slightly higher socioeconomic class outside their own kin and ethnic groups. Toward this end, daughters are pressured to continue in high school, to acquire vocations and intellectual skills appropriate to city life, and to work for their living in an urban environment after graduating from high school.

This contact with urban life and lower-middle-class women in town has affected the self-image of Ramat Oranim women. Though in the very first stages their petty trade in town and independent income gave them a sense of partial liberation from their husbands, paradoxically, they have gradually come to see their trading activities as a low-class occupation. For Ramat Oranim women, then, the socioeconomic power and freedom provided by their independent incomes is now perceived as conflicting with their desire to move into the middle-class female status of housewives, and they have become ambivalent about their economic role. Some wives, particularly those of the moshav movement officials, have gradually decreased their private marketing and, at considerable financial sacrifice, have come to depend more and more on their husbands. Educated daughters with high school or vocational diplomas, married to urban men, rarely work after marriage.

Conclusion

The new equilibrium for Ramat Oranim's families has been achieved by a division of labor in which men and women prefer to maintain male authority within the domestic and public domains rather than change the formal sex roles within the family.

The moshav structure provided men with the opportunity to maintain their formal position of authority in the face of an otherwise sharp status loss, but the moshav also created constraints on the men, as moshav members representing the cooperative ideology and bound to the outside moshav authorities. By moshav law and by their own will, the men have remained in formal control of the moshav structure and household resources. The women have not attempted to interfere with their authority in the public or domestic domains. Under moshav law four widows with sons became household heads and owners of farms and acquired moshav member status, but they have never participated in the moshav assembly meetings. Nor have women tried to penetrate the other exclusive male club, the synagogue. Women have not raised their voices to interfere publicly with male political decisions. No woman, whatever her economic power within the family, has tried to question openly the male right to receive all the income from the cooperative egg production in which she actively participates.

Opportunities and constraints were provided by the moshav and Israeli society, not only for the perpetuation of male authority but also for informal female power. Within the new environment women have chosen to bypass the formal moshav system. By engaging in a free enterprise retail trade, Ramat Oranim women were able to create an economic niche unavailable to men. The retail trade conducted by the women provides the families with needed cash as well as a channel for surplus produce. The men were the moshav members and thus responsible for maintaining the cooperative system in which free enterprise is illegal. Because the women did not become co-custodians of the formal structure, they felt free to operate outside these moshav constraints. Even though they had acquired economic power, women preferred to keep a low public profile and not upset the formally male-dominated moshav and the household system.

The small-scale trade provided women with the opportunity to cultivate individual socioeconomic networks in Jerusalem. Such interactions based on friendship and informal situations promoted their objectives of economic security, independence, and sociocultural mobility and integration within the larger society.

Women were restricted to small-scale trade that fits in with their primary responsibilities of childcare and domestic services. The entire Jerusalem marketing operation takes only two hours in the early morning; it is therefore quite consistent with traditional sex roles. Other constraints on the acquisition of economic power by women included the ultimate authority of the men to stop this trade should its profits not be reinvested in the household. The evolving self-image of Ramat Oranim women from low-class to urban middle-class housewives was also a limiting factor in their economic activity.

State and moshav laws concerning marriage, divorce, inheritance, and so forth, as well as the sharp drop in the mortality rate, effected a drastic change in Yemenite Jewish family role relations: family stability increased and the divorce rate dropped compared to the previous rate in Yemen. The actual power of men over women and children decreased sharply, and their status within the larger society was shaken. Al-Gades families, resettled in Ramat Oranim, have reestablished their equilibrium by maintaining—as far as possible—male formal dominance within the household and delegating to the women the role of informal mediators with outside society and sociocultural change agents. The structural constraints imposed on Ramat Oranim men lowered their self-confidence, and they chose to avoid direct, personal interaction with Israeli institutions and society. The men retreated into isolation within the moshav.

Beyond these opportunities and constraints provided by the moshav and Israeli society, sex differences in adjustment to the new environment are also a consequence of behavioral strategies imported from Yemen. The social networks established by the women's small-scale retail trade were congruent with the general pattern of informal social relations among women imported from Yemen. Because Yemenite Jewish women were able to operate beyond the formal moshav system, they could establish individual social networks outside their homes and communities based on face-to-face interaction, which they used to manipulate the male-dominated public social process, to achieve social mobility, and to introduce cultural change. Women may also have been socialized in Yemen to be more flexible than men in adjusting to new environments. The Yemenite Jewish patrilocal family tradition and family instability frequently caused women to move from one household to another and readapt each time.

Thus, the evolution of the sociocultural role of Yemenite Jewish women and men in resettlement and development at Ramat Oranim was a product not only of opportunities and constraints provided by the environment but also of the behavioral strategies imported from Yemen. Ramat Oranim families overcame the crisis of cultural transition in part by maintaining male authority within the community and the family, yet delegating to the women economic power within the household and the roles of sociocultural change agents and informal mediators with outside society.

Notes

This study is based on fifteen months of fieldwork conducted in 1972–73 and follow-up visits to the community between 1976 and 1980. Data were collected by participant-observation and life histories methods. This essay was originally published in the early 1980s. The writings published since then on related topics such as Middle Eastern patrilineal cultures, Yemen, sex roles, development, and so forth have elaborated and refined many concepts used in this work. It is encouraging that later works on female networks in Yemen, Oman, Egypt, Morocco, and elsewhere support and validate the findings of this study.

1. For comprehensive reviews of the literature on women in development, see Boserup 1970; Bossen 1975; Mazumdar 1977; Olin 1980; Tinker 1976.
2. For a general description of the moshav organization, see Weintraub, Lissak, and Azmon 1969.
3. For general reviews and volumes on sex roles, see Ardener 1975; Friedl 1975, 1978; Hammond and Jablow 1976; Matthiasson 1974; Quinn 1977; Raphael 1975; Rapp 1979; Reiter 1975; Rogers 1978; Rosaldo and Lamphere 1974; Sanady 1973; Tiffany 1979, 1980.
4. For general reviews and volumes on Middle Eastern women, see Al-Qazzaz 1977 (an annotated bibliography); Beck and Keddie 1978; Fernea and Bezirgan 1977; Gulick and Gulick 1974; Meghdessian 1980.
5. Rosaldo 1974; Sanady 1974; Fernea 1975; Papanek 1973; Sharma 1978.
6. Michaelson and Goldschmidt 1971; Rogers 1975; Schlegel 1975, 1977). For Middle Eastern examples, see Fernea 1969; Maher 1974; H. Rosenfeld 1960.
7. For "appearance and reality" studies, see Chinas 1973; Denich 1974; Hunt 1973; Friedl 1967; Nelson 1974; Sweet 1967; Altorki 1977; Fernea 1969; Makhlouf 1979; Mernissi 1975.
8. M. Wolf 1972; Dwyer 1978b.
9. J. Barnes 1972; Boissevain 1974; E. Smith 1976; Stack 1974; Mernisse 1977.
10. Hamalian 1974; H. Rosenfeld 1975; Sweet 1974.
11. Olin 1980; Mernissi 1976.
12. For general studies, including family role relations, see Feitelson 1959; Shokeid 1963, 1967, 1971a.
13. One relevant psychological study is available: Sharni 1974.
14. Shokeid 1971b.
15. For a fuller description of moshav Ramat Oranim, see Katzir 1976.
16. Goitein 1955.
17. Katzir 1983.

18. Goitein 1955; Kafih 1962.
19. Shokeid and Deshen 1974; Weingrod 1962; Weintraub 1971.
20. Sadan and Weintraub 1980.
21. The figures of the illicit trade and its larger implication were calculated on the basis of field observation of market transactions. Because of the informal, illegal nature of the transactions, it is impossible to provide figures and tables for past activity.

4

Phantom Ethnicity

"Oriental Jews" in Israeli Society

ARNOLD LEWIS

As various collectivities have harnessed ethnic symbolism to political ends, the ethnic unit, long a primary concern of anthropologists, has blossomed into a phenomenon of general interest. In Israel, where the coming together of culturally diverse immigrants at Independence in 1948 was a salient social occurrence (Eisenstadt 1954; Patai 1970; Shuval 1963), the ethnic factor has been prominent in folk and sociological models of society. According to this perspective, the Jewish population of Israel divides into two major ethnic categories—"Ashkenazim" of European and American descent and "Eastern" or "Oriental Jews" of North African and Near Eastern origins.[1] The Ashkenazim, including among their numbers the pre-state Zionist "pioneers,"[2] make up most of the middle class and dominate elite positions in society. In contrast, the Oriental Jews generally hold working-class jobs, have relatively poor educational credentials, and have low per capita incomes (Eisenstadt 1967; Lissak 1969; Matras and Weintraub 1977; Smooha 1978). While accounting for more than half the Jewish population of contemporary Israel, they control relatively few economic, political, or social resources. Whereas high-status Israeli communities are populated predominantly by Ashkenazim, residents of development towns[3] and urban slums are mostly Oriental Jews. To pundits, the "social gap" between these populations is a central problem in present-day Israeli society. It is assumed that at the root of the "social gap" are fundamental differences between culturally disadvantaged Jews of the East and their more advanced compatriots of Western origins (Curtis and Chertoff 1973; Eisenstadt, Bar-Yosef, and Adler 1970).

In 1975, hoping to learn why Oriental Jews underperform at school (Lewy and Chen 1974), I set out for Israel. Working from assumptions in the literature (Minkovich 1969; Smilansky and Smilansky 1967), I hypothesized that cultural differences implicit in the ethnic structure of Israeli society inhibit the educational efforts of Oriental Jewish youth. Following the anthropological instinct, I looked for an appropriate community in which to develop holistic insight into the problem at hand. Helpful informants, knowledgeable about Oriental Jews, who they are, and where they live, were quick to suggest appropriate field settings. A typical candidate was Sharonia, a town of 3,500 working-class Israelis of North African and Near Eastern origins.[4] From afar, Sharonia clearly fit the classic profile of a low-status Oriental Jewish community. Large families, poor incomes, and low-status educational credentials were the rule. To government officials and community workers, Sharonia consisted of residents "in need of fostering."[5] To middle-class residents of Seaview, a nearby urban center, Sharonia was a poor satellite town. It was a good source of workmen and domestics. Its inhabitants were seen as culturally disadvantaged Oriental Jews (A. Lewis 1979a).

With the onset of fieldwork, my preconceived assumptions were quickly confounded by the "reality" of everyday life. Although the people of Sharonia were of North African and Near Eastern ancestry, I was hard-pressed to distinguish local cultural traits from those of their compatriots of European heritage. Among younger residents raised in the town, language, religious practice, national identity, styles of entertainment, aspirations for the future, and social expectations were similar to those of their higher-status countrymen. Discernible cultural differences between Sharonians and middle-class Israelis appeared to be more a function of socioeconomic possibilities than of primordial cultural characteristics. Although cognizant of their Kurdistani, Tripolitanian, or Tunisian origins, residents consistently characterized themselves as "Israeli in all matters" (A. Lewis 1979a). To these citizens, the ethnic category of Oriental Jews had little relevance.

These social facts contradict images of townspeople held by outsiders and implied in the literature. Thus the important question that must be asked is, "Who are the Oriental Jews?" or, more accurately, "What is the sociological meaning of the ethnic category of Oriental Jews?"

Fieldwork, the foundation of the anthropological enterprise, implies cultural confrontation between anthropologist and native. Yet the "thick description" (Geertz 1973a) we covet must be more than the product of idiosyncratic encounter. Separating anthropologist from erudite traveler is a toolkit of methods and models by which field material is collected and organized. What can the anthropologist draw from his professional knapsack in order to sort out contradictory information on ethnicity in Sharonia?

To begin with, what do anthropologists generally mean when employing the concept of ethnicity? Human beings create social meaning by assimilating disparate sensory stimuli into cognitive categories of things similar and different. To account for human differences, myriad principles by which to contrast and compare have been mobilized. Popular principles in the ethnographic literature include differentiation by sex, kinship ties, age, sets, and relationships to the means of production and ethnicity. The concept of ethnicity suggests the division of a given population into socially meaningful categories according to actor or observer evaluation of cultural differences.

Anthropological studies of ethnic phenomena tend to stress what has been characterized as cultural ethnicity or political ethnicity (Bennett 1975; Deshen 1974). The primary focus of study in cultural ethnicity is the culture bearing unit, a collectivity of people who share a unique set of cultural traits that exhibit underlying consistency over time (Naroll 1964). This is the ethnicity of the folklore specialist. It suggests that we view social behavior against the backdrop of a typology of cultural traits, which the anthropologist can distinguish from one another. Studies of acculturation and ethnic relations in complex societies that view the social behavior of a given population in reference to a primordial set of cultural traits adopt this perspective (Gans 1979; Sandberg 1974).

In contrast, political ethnicity switches the focus of study from the ethnic unit as a vessel in which cultural content is preserved to a social group that manipulates cultural symbols in a collective struggle for scarce resources in complex societies (Barth 1969; A. Cohen 1969; Despres 1975). As Fredrik Barth has postulated, this view emphasizes the social boundaries that define group competition, not the cultural stuff that boundaries enclose (Barth 1969). Thus, an ethnic unit becomes any social group that manipulates cultural symbols for political and social ends (D. Aronson 1976).

In what way can the concepts of cultural and political ethnicity assist in organizing ethnographic facts relating to Sharonia? Unfortunately, analysis proceeding directly from either perspective tends to obscure rather than illuminate. In social situations where ecological and socioeconomic boundaries clearly delineate one cultural group from another, the cultural ethnicity perspective has proved of high utility (Driver 1973). Researchers examining social processes in complex societies, however, have found this approach increasingly inadequate (Barth 1969; A. Cohen 1969; Yancey, Erickson, and Juliani 1976). Indeed, the political ethnicity formulation has developed in reaction to the explicit failure of the cultural approach to sufficiently account for the persistence and reassertion of ethnic expression in societies in which acculturation among social groups of divergent cultural traditions is well advanced (Glazer and Moynihan 1963; Van den Berghe 1973).

An attempt to view the contemporary lifestyle of Sharonians from a cultural ethnicity perspective generates inconclusive results. During thirty years of social life in Israel, townspeople have undergone rapid cultural change, assimilating a lifestyle markedly similar to that of urban Israelis of European origin (A. Lewis 1979a). Studies of other Israelis of North African and Near Eastern origins generally support this finding.[6] When cultural continuity with a pre-Israeli way of life has been identified, it has generally been associated with religious activity (Deshen 1976), a relatively marginal factor among the secularized residents of Sharonia. Although Sharonians continue to flavor their lives with ethnic foods and folk music, these artifacts of a cultural past are tangential to the dominant cultural thrust in everyday life. Pre-Israeli cultural characteristics explain little about life in present-day Sharonia.

The major contribution of the cultural ethnicity approach in exploring data from Sharonia is that it tells us where not to look for answers. Information organized from this perspective strongly suggests that the ethnic category "Oriental Jews" has little objective association with the pre-Israeli cultural characteristics of townspeople. Why, then, do middle-class Israelis insist that Sharonians, who are seen as Oriental Jews, are culturally different from other Israelis in ways that resemble their formative cultural heritage?

In exploring this question, the anthropologist might logically be expected to turn to the second model in the knapsack, political ethnicity. At first glance, this perspective appears to be a most promising one. After all, hasn't political ethnicity been conceptualized to deal with problems of ethnic categorization in complex, culturally fluid situations? Before this approach can bear fruit, however, another ethnographic fact must be confronted. The political ethnicity formulation suggests that analysis should be based on a group of persons who identify and manipulate salient ethnic symbols in pursuit of political, economic, and social ends. Hence, the anthropologist is encouraged to seek out persons who view themselves as Oriental Jews in certain situations and to examine the social import of consequent behavior. But it is rare that Sharonians identify themselves as Oriental Jews in political contexts. In some social situations, ethnic categories such as Kurdistani, Tunisian, and Tripolitanian help Sharonians differentiate themselves from others, but the category "Oriental Jews" is rarely used by local residents. When articulated, it refers to low-status Israelis, usually excluding the speaker, in much the same way that this image is projected by non-residents when referring to Sharonians.

The negative attitude of townspeople toward the ethnic category "Oriental Jews" is best illustrated by their response to the Israeli Black Panthers. The panthers, a group of young Israelis from Jerusalem, attempted to mobilize collective political action in the early 1970s by manipulating symbols associated with the ethnic category "Oriental Jews" (Smooha 1972). The activities of this group, while causing much alarm in the Ashkenazi-dominated national polity, gained little support in Sharonia and other low-status communities (E. Cohen 1972; Etzioni-Halevy 1975). Sharonians, with few exceptions, speak of the Panthers with great disdain. Townspeople symbolically distance themselves from this movement of persons they define as "good-for-nothings."

Who, then, are the Oriental Jews? To this end, it has been argued that a suitable answer will not be found in Sharonia. From the inside looking out, Sharonians are not Oriental Jews in either cultural or political terms. Yet, outsiders looking in on Sharonians are convinced that they are viewing Oriental Jews. Where should one look for a solution to this paradox? Might a sociological explanation of the ethnic category "Oriental Jews" be found through an analysis of the ideology of those who use the term? This possibility will be explored throughout the remainder of the chapter.

Analysis will proceed in three stages. First, the Zionist idea, the ideological underpinning of Israeli society, will be described. Second, the genesis of ethnic symbolism since statehood and situational use of ethnic stereotypes in everyday life will be examined. Third, the sociological meaning of ethnic symbolism in contemporary Israel will be discussed.

The impact of collective beliefs on social behavior has long been a central theoretical concern of anthropologists (Benedict 1934; Geertz 1964; Leach 1954; Redfield 1953). This suggests that a discernible compendium of beliefs in the public domain structures the meaning that people give to behaviors and events in everyday life. Often expressed in myth and folklore, these root paradigms, to borrow a phrase from Victor Turner, "affect the form, timing and style of the behavior of those who bear them" (1974, 67). In other words, root paradigms are collective cultural recipes for the construction of social meaning.

What root paradigm structures the meaning of ethnicity in Israeli society? To explore this question, one must turn to an analysis of Zionism, the national ideology by which most Israeli Jews evaluate their place in history, relationships to one another, and associations with salient others (Levy and Gutman 1976; Arian 1970). Explanations or pertinent social facts and the collective social consciousness of Israeli society are constructed in Zionist imagery.

In a classic discussion, H. G. Barnett (1953) has identified cultural innovation, the fusion of two or more elements into a qualitatively distinct whole, as a central mechanism in the process of social change. Zionism, as conceived in collective sociopolitical action in Europe and Palestine, is an innovative Jewish ideology. Synthesizing the Messianic image of Zion in traditional Judaism with nineteenth-century European nationalism, Zionism posited the concept of a Jewish national homeland in Palestine, the biblical abode of the Jewish people.[7] To numerous European Jews caught in deadly social crosscurrents of assimilation and anti-Semitism, the Zionist innovation offered existential safety on a distant shore. To the tens of thousands who journeyed to Palestine after 1880, the Zionist idea was a tangible call to action. These "pioneers" constituted the human vessels in which the Zionist idea was transported from Europe to Palestine. They became the nucleus of a new society, which gained nationhood in 1948.[8] In this, the immediate goal of Zionism came to fruition.

Yet, the Zionist idea suggested more than the concept of a Jewish state. It also offered adherents a model of the society they were leaving as well as a vision of the commonwealth that lay ahead. The meaning of ethnicity in Israeli society is anchored in these images.

Zionism was invented to explain social facts relating to the Jewish condition in modern Europe. Its prescription for social action is based on European nationalistic principles, but its existential thrust is deeply rooted in the ethnohistory of the Jewish people. In this, it adopts a conception of time implicit in the Bible, a view that suggests that the meaning of the Jewish people is intimately bound up with the working out of Jewish history.

The centrality of time in Zionist imagery is vividly expressed in the Museum of the Jewish Diaspora.[9] Ostensibly, the purpose of this impressive multimedia display is to commemorate Jewish existence before the reemergence of national independence. To half a million annual visitors, the museum is a profound statement of salient aspects of the Zionist vision.

The permanent exhibit, consisting of slide shows, mini-cinemas, music, pictures, sculptures, visual projections, artifacts, and the written word, creates images of Jewish existence in the many places where communal life was sustained over the past two millennia. In sections of family and community, and martyrdom and faith, symbolic continuity in divergent experience is suggested. Through diverse stimuli, the visitor learns how a people divided in social space preserved psychic unity through symbolic commitment to a common temporal vision, past and future. This is established as a dominant message in entrance and exit exhibits as well as in the context of various displays throughout the museum. Indeed, two millennia of Jewish life are portrayed as a single epoch bounded by contrasting social processes, exile and return.

In various contexts, the fundamental importance of heritage, collective purpose, remembering the past, and longing for future communal fulfillment are stressed. One is told that these values were nurtured through communal life, both spiritual and secular. Hence, "A tree may be alone in a field, a man alone in the world, but no Jew is alone on his holy days."

The visitor is able to reflect on these themes through a synergism of stimuli. For example, one display projects mezuzot,[10] candlesticks, a Hannukkah lamp, and a prayer book, core spiritual artifacts, against a backdrop of changing interior settings. In all, ten interiors from different Jewish communities are portrayed, each emphasizing the fashion prominent in the non-Jewish environment in which they are immersed. Herein, symbolic constancy is contrasted with transient lifestyles adopted from non-Jewish neighbors. In another section, twenty-one exquisite model synagogues are displayed. Although each reflects the architectural style of host peoples, the symbolic content remains fixed in time.

The visit ends with the return. Here, one is exposed to three related themes: Jewish yearning throughout the ages for a paradise lost, Zionist pioneers reestablishing the Jewish commonwealth, and the ingathering of the exiles. The final image expresses a moral imperative "To remember the past, To live the present, To trust the future."

Whereas the subject matter of the Museum of the Jewish Diaspora focuses on the quality of Jewish existence from exile to return, Zionist thought is equally concerned with social and spiritual contours of the future. During its formative years, the Zionist revolution bifurcated into religious and secular, socialist and non-socialist camps (Fisch 1978; Heller 1973; Sachar 1976). It was further divided by "political" and "cultural" schools of thought (Buber 1952). In polemic among adherents of each camp, the structure of the Zionist innovation was constructed. Through an examination of the dialogue among Zionist spokesmen, common underlying assumptions can be discerned.[11]

The Zionist vision of Jewish history postulates four historical periods in the development sequence—pristine paradise, diaspora, statehood, and utopia, mediated by three social processes: exile, return, and redemption.

Vigorous debate among Zionist adherents on the social content of each historical epoch and the transforming quality of mediating social processes is predicated on the fundamental acceptance of the underlying model. Concerned with European Jewry, Zionist thought focused particular attention on the maladies of diaspora, a historical period in which Jews were scattered among other peoples. From a Zionist viewpoint, diaspora is an unnatural condition, a negation of utopia, pristine and future. Thus, Max Nordau, an important political Zionist, bemoaned "twenty centuries of unutterable sufferings of millions of highly gifted human beings, artificially kept down in a low state of development" (1916). Rabbi Kook, a spiritual founder of religious Zionism, lamented the "destruction of the nation's life in its severance from its own place" (1975), and Achad Ha'am, the creator of cultural Zionism, postulated a need to "wipe out the spiritual taint of galuth (exile)" (1916).

Living in unnatural conditions, Jews of the diaspora were viewed as suffering a multitude of cultural and spiritual ills. To Zionist thinkers, the primary cause of cultural degeneration is the detachment of individual Jews from proper (Zionist) historical perspective and collective purpose, that is, the loss of temporal vision. This is succinctly expressed by Bertram Benas, a Jewish nationalist writing at the turn of the century: "Ghetto idealism derived its inspiration from a living present based on the future, but unhistoric assimilation, which has detached itself from the past and looks but to an amorphous future, deprives itself of the force necessary for a current vitality" (1969).

This theme is widely and consistently expressed in Zionist literature. Hence, Rabbi Kook argued that "Jewry in the Diaspora has no real foundation and lives only by the power of vision and by the memory of our glory, i.e., the past and the future" (Zionist Library 1972). Leon Simon, a disciple of Achad Ha'am, described the absence of "the normal relation of a people to its past and its future" (1916), and Louis Brandeis, the eminent American Zionist, worried over "a new generation left without necessary moral and spiritual support" (1916).

The Zionist solution to problems posed by diaspora was to instigate, through sociopolitical action, a return to Palestine and the establishment of the Third Commonwealth. It was reasoned that national independence would offer the Jewish people shelter from persecution, a hallmark of diaspora existence. Yet statehood was not viewed as a final goal but as a means to foster a historic end, the creation of a Jewish utopia. Thus, the moral legacy of the Zionist revolution was to be a society in which every Jew would be able to sustain a full spiritual and material life. This is expressed in the insistence of David Ben-Gurion, the first prime minister, that Israel must become "a model people and a model state" (Ben-Gurion 1963). How could utopia be achieved? Rabbi Bar-Ilan, a religious Zionist leader, pointed to the Zionist answer, suggesting that "our immediate preoccupation is with national redemption, with physical and spiritual deliverance" (1975). Similar sentiments are expressed in the Israeli Declaration of Independence: "We call upon Jewish people throughout the Diaspora to join forces with us in immigration and construction, and to be at our right hand in the great endeavor to fulfill the age-old longing for the redemption of Israel" (Ben-Gurion 1971).

The centrality of the quest for cultural regeneration is symbolized in the life and spirit of Aaron Gordon. Referred to as the "high priest of the 'religion of Labor'" (Levenberg 1945), Gordon was the prototype "pioneer." Leaving Russia in 1903 at the age of forty-eight, he came to Palestine to build a new life and renew the Jewish people. Although frail and often ill, Gordon relished in hard field labor, exemplifying in deed the social Zionist vision of redemption. The emphasis in Zionist thought on cultural revival as both an individual and collective quest is vividly expressed in Gordon's erudite words: "You will build the house of Israel; you will find the road on which we set our hearts, on which all the Jews have set their hearts from time immemorial, along which they will desire to go in the days to come. You will live the life of all Jews, and this life will be like an ever-deepening and overflowing spring. And your life will be renewed. This new life, like a tidal river, will go on, will renew itself, and flow onward, onward, onward" (Levenberg 1945).

Indeed, from a Zionist view, redemption is a moral imperative. Although divergent utopian visions have been promulgated, central to each is the assumption that a just society must be preceded by the creation of righteous men. Social perfection is thought to be a natural product of cultural revival. This is explicit in the temporal structure of the Zionist paradigm, which postulates the relationship between redemption and utopia as one of cause and effect.

To this juncture, three central themes in Zionist ideology have been described: negative images of diaspora Jewry, the moral imperative to create a Jewish utopia, and the saliency of redemption, cultural and spiritual, as a means to accomplish cherished ends. Embedded in Jewish history, these principles are posited in casual relationships to one another. Subsequently, I shall argue that the ethnic category "Oriental Jews" organizes central social facts in reference to these key assumptions.

In contemporary Israel, a society born of the Zionist revolution, Zionist ideology remains a moral measuring stick, a road map to collective salvation. Through ritual and public debate, Israelis evaluate social progress relative to national vision, past and future. To explain social facts bearing on collective identity and moral vitality, the Zionist paradigm is mobilized as a guide. From this perspective, a worrisome social problem is the issue of the geographic origin of immigrants and descendants in the socioeconomic stratification of society. Whereas persons of European and American descent dominate high-status positions, compatriots of low status are invariably of North African or Near Eastern origin (Lissak 1969; Smooha and Peres 1975).

Characterized in public discussion as the "social gap," this obtrusive social fact contradicts the moral imperative that the Jewish commonwealth must maximize the spiritual and material well-being of each Jewish citizen. Yet, if the contours of social issues are conceptualized in root cultural paradigms, so are their explanations. An examination of the literature suggests a collection of folk concepts[12] that have been generated toward this end.

The first Zionist "pioneers" entered a Palestine inhabited in part by an indigenous non-European Jewish population. These communities were composed of Jews from North Africa and the Near East, and operated from cultural premises alien to the European bearers of the Zionist idea. In European eyes, the language, attitudes, and actions of this population resembled those of the Arabs among whom they lived. As a result of social contact between settlers and indigenous Jews, the ethnic term "Oriental Jews" was used by ethnocentric Europeans and filled with negative cultural images (Eisenstadt 1954). Although eligible as Jews to join the Zionist experiment, its population was seen as requiring radical cultural transformation. However, the problems associated with Oriental Jews remained tangential to the central thrust of the Zionist revolution until independence.

With independence, the role of North African and Near Eastern Jewry in the Zionist revolution changed dramatically. In the period between 1948 and 1953, the Jewish population of Israel more than doubled from 650,000 to 1,450,000 (Patai 1970, 74–75). Of the new arrivals, half were of North African and Near Eastern descent. To the veteran Zionists, mass immigration suggested both promise and problem. In each newcomer, the historic process of return was enacted, the prospect of individual and collective redemption enhanced. Yet, the new immigrants were tarnished by diaspora experience.

From the viewpoint of the European elite, cultural imperfection was especially pronounced among immigrants from North Africa and the Near East. Like the native Jewish population they resembled, these immigrants were seen as lacking in basic social and psychological skills (Frankenstein 1953b; Ortar 1953). Examining ethnic imagery in leading Israeli newspapers in the early 1950s, Raphael Patai has catalogued a host of negative stereotypes associated with the ethnic category "Oriental Jews." These include instability, emotionalism, impulsiveness, unreliability, incompetence, habitual lying, cheating, laziness, boastfulness, inclination to violence, uncontrolled temper, superstitiousness, childishness, and lack of cleanliness (1970, 314). This array of negative characteristics are summarized in the folk concepts of "primitivity," implying cultural inferiority and "lacking culture" (314), suggesting an absence of social characteristics positively associated with being civilized.[13]

It would, however, be analytically incorrect to conclude that prejudicial stereotypes of immigrants from North Africa and the Near East are a product of a Zionist worldview. Spawned by veteran settlers and European immigrants, prejudicial ethnic imagery is a function of European ethnocentrism, not Zionist ideology. In light of the Zionist idea, the social meaning of culturally different newcomers was translated into a moral imperative for cultural change and social integration. Thus, the Zionist paradigm fostered ambivalence toward new immigrants who were otherwise seen as utterly repulsive. This is well expressed in the folk concept "Generation of the Desert," an allusion to culturally tainted Jews led by Moses at God's behest to wander about the wilderness until a new generation of culturally purified offspring were ready to inherit the Land of Israel (Friendly 1981, 5–6; Marx 1979, x).

Through this and similar analogies, social facts relating to culturally different and abhorrent immigrants were recast in terms of the Zionist paradigm. If the adult generation of Oriental Jews was beyond redemption, this was a lamentable, but anticipated, consequence of diaspora life and yet, as diaspora is a transitory phase in Jewish history, so are the negative cultural traits of diaspora Jewry, no matter how uncouth. In the act of return, immigrants had proceeded to a more advanced stage of Jewish existence. This was to be followed by redemption, the socialization of progeny into new Israeli men and women. The veteran Zionist population was to guide this collective cultural quest. Every effort was to be made to re-create these children in the image of their benefactors, not in that of their parents.[14] From the Zionist perspective, social progress required successful fulfillment of this mission. Pitfalls inherent in failure were vividly expressed in the folk concept of "Levantinization" (Patai 1970, 320–23; Zenner 1965, 323–24), the fear that cultural deficiencies of North African and Near Eastern Jews, if not eradicated, would stymie the utopian future postulated in the Zionist paradigm.

In contemporary Sharonia, the meaning of the ethnic category "Oriental Jews" is derived from folk concepts that originated in the 1950s. These have been updated to explain subsequent facts. Sharonia is a community of relatively poor residents of North African or Near Eastern origin. Its undereducated inhabitants have relatively large families, relatively little living space, and they finance their lifestyles on half the per capita resources of the average urban dweller (A. Lewis 1979b, 21–22). Nearly thirty years after their arrival in Israel, Sharonians remain on the socioeconomic edge of middle-class Israeli society. Thus, Sharonia and its residents, in light of the Zionist paradigm, is an ideological sore spot, a social occurrence in need of explanation and amelioration.

Toward this end, outsiders often conceptualize Sharonia as a community of the "Second Israel." First hinted at in the early 1950s (Shumsky 1955, 6), the image of a Second Israel has become a prominent means of expressing consequences of persistent ethnic stratification in Israeli society (Heller 1973; Selzer 1967, 51–86; Toledano 1973). In the public eye, the Second Israel is a stigma, an undesirable place to live that is inhabited by culturally deficient Oriental Jews. But it is also an indictment of the elite of the wider society for not fulfilling Zionist destiny.

How has the ideologically embarrassing Second Israel come about? In light of the Zionist paradigm, two logically consistent answers can be postulated. These are the culturally disadvantaged and institutional discrimination perspectives. The culturally disadvantaged argument suggests that socioeconomic inequality in Israeli society is primarily a result of persistent cultural differences between Jews of European and North African and Near Eastern heritages. This view, strongly supported by prevailing folk images, implies that national institutions generally operate in accordance with an egalitarian creed, but that Oriental Jews, as a category of persons, remain culturally distinct in ways that violate norms valued in the wider society. Thus, Oriental Jews are in need of resocialization, which must be accomplished before they can assume their rightful place as full citizens, contributors, and benefactors of the developing Jewish commonwealth. From this viewpoint, responsibility for negative social progress is seen to rest in the lifeways of relatively poor citizens of North African and Near Eastern descent.

The alternative institutional discrimination model also builds on the Zionist paradigm but interprets social facts differently. It assumes that immigrants and progeny of North African and Near Eastern origins have undergone prescribed cultural transformations and are presently similar to Israelis of European background. Thus, persistent social inequality is an end product of discriminatory practices on the part of public institutions. This line of reasoning faults the wealthy and powerful in Israeli society for ideologically unacceptable social inequality.

The culturally disadvantaged model is the predominant explanation by which relevant social facts are organized in Sharonia. Frequently used by the national elite and in the media, it draws on folk images, which give a history to the rationalizations inherent in the argument. In contrast, the institutional discrimination model is rarely applied to Sharonia. Efforts by townspeople and others (such as the anthropologist) to advance this argument are looked at askance by government officials, civil servants, educators, and middle-class observers of local social life. Indeed, such interpretations are invariably refuted by the reorganization of relevant social facts in reference to the culturally disadvantaged argument. The only consistent use of the institutional discrimination argument on the part of the Sharonians are the complaints of individuals claiming prejudice when turned away unsatisfied by authorities. Yet, to the present, such incidents have not been translated into a collective expression of institutional discrimination by the townspeople.

The potency of the culturally disadvantaged perspective in organizing social facts in contemporary Sharonia is evident in its frequent use by civil servants, educators, and townspeople in various social contexts. When budgeting resources for Sharonia, social planners and bureaucrats of various government ministries operate from the assumption that residents remain insufficiently socialized to the lifeways of the wider society. For example, a trailer camp was established in town to give temporary shelter to large numbers of new immigrants expected to arrive from the Soviet Union. Making little contribution to the community, the Immigrant Absorption Center was seen by townspeople as an unwarranted intrusion into their affairs. When asked by residents or the anthropologist to justify this project, officials invariably talked of the need to bring "new blood" to the town.

Folk concepts such as "primitives" and "lacking culture" are often used by civil servants to rationalize personal failings as well as to deflect social pressures emanating from townspeople and outsiders. The relationship between the local rabbi and congregants illustrates this point. The rabbi, a young man of European background, was assigned to Sharonia by the Ministry of Religion immediately after finishing his studies. Uncompromising in religious matters, he was poorly suited to serve the spiritual needs of "traditional,"[15] but not strictly religious, Sharonians. Many townspeople, finding the young rabbi too demanding, took a negative view of events organized under his auspices. To explain the behavior of uncooperative congregants, the rabbi pointed to what he characterized as the "primitive" religious traditions of Oriental Jews. In contrast to his European Jewish heritage, the rabbi felt that the cultural background of Sharonians was deficient. Thus, they had become morally degenerate. Ironically, nonreligious civil servants, when complaining that Sharonians remain relatively "primitive," often refer to what they see as a religious orientation in the townspeople.

Situational use of the culturally disadvantaged argument is perhaps best exemplified in the symbolic actions of educators. In light of the Zionist paradigm, education assumes a pivotal role in enhancing social justice. Through successful participation in extensive educational programs, youth of the "Generation of the Desert" were to be recast into new Jewish Israeli men and women. Thus, one of the first actions of the fledgling government after independence was to enact a compulsory education law. Today, youth are required to attend a minimum of one year of kindergarten and ten years of formal schooling. Sharonians accept this concept of cultural renewal and want their children to complete their education. Truancy is rare.

In dealing with youth from Sharonia and other low-status communities, the Ministry of Education has invented the concept of "those in need of fostering." Officially, this designation, based on socioeconomic characteristics, has been promulgated to enable the educational bureaucracy to target additional funds and special curricula to schools serving low-status Oriental Jewish communities. As used by teachers, this notion has become a euphemism for more provocative folk concepts such as "primitive" and "lacking culture" (Halper 1978, 270–78; A. Lewis 1979b, 88–89). Pedagogues entrusted with the task of educating Sharonian youth constantly refer to their charges as "those in need of fostering." Decisions on pedagogic methods, curricular content, grading policies, and other important educational matters are made in accordance with this perception (A. Lewis 1979b, 91–114).

Given the ideological importance of education in Israeli society, educators are constantly pressured to explain the poor achievements of low-status youth of North African or Near Eastern origin. Toward this end, teachers in Sharonia respond by arranging relevant facts in reference to the culturally disadvantaged perspective. Specifically, they argue that learning or behavior difficulties at school are a function of negative home and community environments. This explanation is strengthened in gossip sessions in which teachers exchange anecdotes on the "primitive" ways of pupils and parents (A. Lewis 1979b, 104–5, 117–37). Teachers view the official designation of Sharonia as an area populated by "those in need of fostering" as validation of the culturally disadvantaged contention (A. Lewis 1979a, 104–5).

Townspeople also use the culturally disadvantaged argument to advance and defend personal interest in certain social situations. In maneuvering to gain additional resources from national institutions, local politicians and community spokesmen often argue that greater efforts are needed to compensate for culturally backward elements in the local population. This stance is particularly useful in efforts by residents to gain further educational and welfare services. Individuals seeking aid from the local welfare office employ a similar symbolic strategy. In these circumstances, the symbolic perspectives of civil servants and clientele complement one another.

In another context, townspeople advance the culturally disadvantaged perspective to distinguish themselves from lower-status neighbors. In this, they emulate the posture that middle-class compatriots have adopted toward them. For example, in the early 1970s, the government constructed a new housing project for destitute persons. Over the years, families from various parts of Sharonia and adjacent communities have been settled in this complex. To distance themselves from the social implications of the project, townspeople have named it the "Refugee Camp," implying temporary housing for those who have yet to gain full entry into Israeli society. Residents portray persons living in this section of town as "primitive" Oriental Jews.

In the frequent use of the culturally disadvantaged argument to organize social facts in Sharonia, Oriental Jews as a category of people are constantly denigrated. In daily competition for economic and social rewards, a host of ethnically related folk concepts become symbolic weapons that individuals and groups can use to advance and defend their interests. The cumulative impact of these symbolic exchanges places Israelis of North African and Near Eastern origins at a disadvantage when interacting with others in everyday life.

Who, then, are the Oriental Jews? Implicit in the presentation of the data is a model suggesting that social meaning is synthesized through dialectical interaction between a root cultural paradigm and subsequent social facts. Specifically, it is argued that the meaning of ethnicity in contemporary Israeli society emerges from a confrontation between the Zionist idea and two salient social developments: large numbers of North African and Near Eastern Jewish immigrants who were deprecated by ethnocentric veteran and new immigrant European Jews, and division of society into social classes on the basis of primordial sociogeographic origins. In the diachronic analysis of this process, a sociological explanation of the ethnic category "Oriental Jews" is generated.

The meaning of ethnicity in Israeli society is structured by basic Zionist tenets. Spiritual unity of the Jewish people is recognized as the highest principle. Unity is expressed in two ways: shared vision of social time, past and future, and mutual commitment to sociocultural oneness through redemption and cultural renewal. Yet sociocultural differences among Jews in an imperfect present are also recognized and viewed as a legacy of diaspora existence. In this, an interesting paradox emerges. Although ethnicity is denied as a legitimate category by which to distinguish Jew from Jew in a utopian future, ethnic differences among Jews in the present are highlighted. Ethnicity is rejected as an ultimate principle, but acknowledged as a contemporary social fact.

With the arrival of massive numbers of Jewish refugees from Muslim areas of North Africa and the Near East, ethnic differentiation became a central issue in Israeli society. Articulated in the folk concepts "primitive" and "lacking culture," the ethnic category "Oriental Jews" was created and filled with negative cultural connotations. Nevertheless, the belief in the spiritual unity of the Jewish people bridged the social distance between the European elite and low-status newcomers from North Africa and the Near East. Through cultural fusion, the progeny of social strangers were to create the desired Jewish commonwealth.

In contemporary Israel, partial congruence between socioeconomic inequality and primordial sociogeographic origins contradicts idealistic egalitarian expectations. Nevertheless, these divisions have become a prominent feature of everyday life. How can this morally unjustifiable development be rationalized? Israelis have thought their way out of the dilemma through the use of the concept of the Oriental Jew. In this imagery, the division of society by social class is recast into social division by cultural characteristics. Thus, socioeconomic inequality, a stable sociological feature of Israeli society (Hartman and Eilon 1975; Lissak 1969; Smooha and Peres 1975), is transformed into a transient quality, a negative development, which can be set right by further cultural change among low-status citizens of North African or Near Eastern origins.

But the ethnic category "Oriental Jews" is not rooted in the cultural tradition and lifeways of concrete, living people. It has no tangible ethnohistory, rarely delineates an existentially meaningful identity, and lacks vigorous defenders. The anthropologist can identify and study cultural continuity and change among Moroccan and Tunisian immigrants (Deshen and Shokeid 1974), Jews of Tripolitanian descent (Goldberg 1972), Syrian Jews (Zenner 1965), Yemenite women (Katzir 1976), and working-class Israelis (Weingrod 1979). As I learned in Sharonia, however, Oriental Jews are difficult, if not impossible, to find, even if most Israelis are confident that they can point the way to them. Indeed, analysis has revealed that the ethnic category "Oriental Jews" is a phantom, a figment of collective Israeli imagination, a symbolic vehicle by which cultural differences capable of masking socioeconomic inequality are explained.

The elastic cultural content of phantom ethnicity is well illustrated in the folk etiology of lice. From time to time, elementary schoolchildren in Sharonia have been known to come to school with lice-infested hair. How are such occurrences explained? To teachers, lice are viewed as concrete manifestations of the primitive lifeways of townspeople. Educators often argue that lice and academic underachievement in Sharonia are tangible effects of a single underlying cause, the "in need of fostering" social milieu of low-status Oriental Jews.

Recently, an exposé on a popular television news program reported a surprising discovery: an epidemic of lice in fashionable, upper-middle-class neighborhoods of Tel Aviv and Haifa. On camera, one educator wondered aloud how youth from good families could possibly have lice. In the course of the program, an answer to this query was suggested: lice in high-status communities are a biological, not a cultural, phenomenon. In this, the social meaning of lice has been situationally defined. The appearance of lice in Sharonia and other low-status communities is viewed as evidence of the culturally disadvantaged background of Oriental Jews, while the explanation for similar manifestations in high-status neighborhoods eschews assumptions concerning the cultural characteristics of the infected.

The situational etiology of lice is a vivid example of the spurious cultural content of the ethnic category "Oriental Jews." Likewise, an endless assortment of undesirable events can be and are explained by invoking phantom ethnic imagery. In these symbolic actions Oriental Jews, as a category pf people, are continuously characterized as culturally tainted. In light of the Zionist paradigm, they remain in need of cultural renewal, an ideological prerequisite for social justice, a hope for the future. Yet, in the elastic cultural content of phantom ethnicity, perception of cultural change is perpetually blunted, and the realization of cultural renewal is consistently postponed. Hence, the vision of existential unity is sustained in the face of socioeconomic differentiation. The contradiction between the moral imperative of ultimate social justice and mundane political and economic interests in everyday life is dissolved.

Notes

1. "Oriental Jews" is the accepted English equivalent of the Hebrew term "Edot Hamizrach" (see Deshen 1970a, 10). The term "Sephardim," although occasionally used to label Jews of North African and Near Eastern origins, refers specifically to Jews of Spanish and North Mediterranean descent.
2. The term "pioneer" (*chalutz*), recognized in the formative years of the Zionist revolution, refers to persons who came to Palestine in order to actualize the Zionist idea. Pioneers and their progeny dominate elite positions in contemporary Israeli society. On the composition of Israeli elites, see Weingrod and Gurevitch 1977. On the pioneers and their descendants, see Elon 1971.
3. Development towns are immigrant communities planned from inception by the national government. They are constructed and maintained with public funds. See E. Cohen 1970, 1972; Aronoff 1973.

4. Sharonia is a pseudonym for a town in which I conducted fieldwork from September 1975 to January 1977.
5. The term "in need of fostering" (*teounay tipouach*), invented by the Ministry of Education to designate low-status clientele of North African and Near Eastern descent, is used by educators and others as a euphemism for persons viewed as culturally deficient. See Adler 1970, 301; Halper 1978, 270–78.
6. Myriad studies have examined cultural change among Israelis of North African and Near Eastern descent. Prominent examples of this work include: Deshen 1970a; Deshen and Shokeid 1974; Goldberg 1972, 1973; Matras 1965; Shokeid 1971a; Weingrod 1965; Weintraub 1971; and Zenner 1965. Although there has been some debate in the literature regarding the pace and process of cultural change (compare Ben-David 1953 to Deshen and Shokeid 1974), I am unaware of any work that would contradict the assertion that rapid cultural change has been the dominant trend among immigrants and their offspring.
7. For a general discussion of Zionism, the idea and the social movement, see Laqueur 1972; Vital 1975.
8. On the sociopolitical structure of the Jewish community in British Mandatory Palestine, see Eisenstadt 1967; Horowitz and Lissak 1978; Y. Shapiro 1976.
9. Located on the campus of Tel Aviv University, the Museum of the Jewish Diaspora is a multimillion-dollar exhibit of Jewish life over the past two thousand years. The project was conceived and is sponsored by the World Jewish Congress.
10. A mezuza is a religious artifact customarily placed on the doorpost of a Jewish abode.
11. My discussion of formative Zionist polemic is based primarily on the following anthologies and interpretive essays: Buber 1952; Fisch 1978; Goodman and and Lewis 1916; Hertzberg 1959; J. Heller 1949; Levenberg 1945; Tirosh 1975.
12. As used in this essay, folk concepts refer to informant-generated (emic), as distinct from observer-generated (etic), summaries of relevant cognitive stimuli. On the epistemological distinction between emic and etic constructions of social reality, see Harris 1968.
13. On ethnic stereotyping in Israeli society, see Peres 1971a; Shumsky 1955, 5–7; Tamarin 1971; Zenner 1965, 297–306.
14. On government attempts to actualize this ideological imperative, see Deshen 1970a; Shokeid 1971a; and Weingrod 1965; Willner 1969. On the role of educational services in efforts at cultural transformation, see Frankenstein 1953a; Kleinberger 1969; Kashti 1979; and A. Lewis 1979b.
15. Most Sharonians characterize themselves as traditional but not strictly religious in spiritual matters. In expressing this contention, they distinguish between religious sentiment and religious practice in everyday life.

5

The Political Integration of Russian Jews in Israel, 1988–1999

DINA SIEGEL

Introduction

In Israel ethnic parties have usually been considered an impediment to the union of the "Israeli people." It has been generally accepted that people may disagree on specific political issues, but not on what has been thought of as the essence of Israel—the gathering of exiles and building a new type of Jew, totally different from the stereotype of a diaspora Jew. Nevertheless, ethnic parties have often appeared in the Israeli political arena. Some of them, such as the German Jews' Progressive Party in the 1950s, Tami, an ethnic party of politicians of North African origin in the early 1980s, and the Sephardi religious Shas party, which won five parliamentary seats in 1984, booked a great success in Israeli politics. Russian Jews, however, had never succeeded in forming their own political organizations prior to the 1980s.

In the period of Great Immigration (1987–96) more than 750,000 new immigrants joined 200,000 old-timers (*vatikim*) from the former Soviet Union. The major wave of Jewish immigration from the former Soviet Union began in 1987, reached its peak in the years 1990–92, and continues at a steady flow to this day. Today they are the largest ethnic category after the Israeli Arabs. This immigration is also considered to have been the largest wave of immigration in the history of Israel. While the size alone of this influx of immigrants was amazing, its professional and educational characteristics made it even more remarkable: 40 percent had academic, scientific, or similar occupations.[1]

The huge number of Russian Jews requires a reconsideration of the relevance of the term "absorption" (*klita*) in general, since almost a million people cannot be "absorbed." They joined the society, while introducing their own culture and lifestyle and creating a new identity, that of Russian Jewish Israelis. Though maintaining their own new way of life, they combine their own cultural values and norms (which are gradually accepted by other Israelis) with what they learn and adopt in interaction with other Israelis. This ability to live their own cultural and social life, to set up their own political organization and public institutions, and to influence and introduce reforms in Israel indicates their full integration into Israeli society.

Since the beginning of the Great Immigration three periods of political activity of Russian Jews may be distinguished: 1992–95; June 1995 to the May election in 1996; and 1996 to the present. The first period was characterized by relative passivity, restricted to discussing and defining the problematic situation of new immigrants in Israel. It included debates and propaganda for and against the foundation of a Russian ethnic party and contests for leadership either between new immigrants and old-timers, or among the newcomers themselves. The second period was more active: the discussion of the definition of the problem was translated into action and the creation of symbols, which became the "vehicle for a conception." This phase culminated in the actual setting up of new political movements and integration into Israeli political life. "Israel in Aliya" became not only the first Russian party to pass the Israeli Parliament's (Knesset) threshold but also the first immigrant party ever to gain seven of the 120 seats, becoming in 1996 the fifth largest party. The third period may be viewed as a period of establishment, socialization, and ideological disagreement, as well as struggles for power between several Russian parties and individual politicians.

This chapter is mainly based on my fieldwork conducted between 1993 and 1995 among the Russian Jews in Israel. As only a few statistical and demographic studies on Russian Jews were available at the time, the main task of my research was to provide wide ethnographic data on different immigrant (and old-timer) groups in various settings. I found that the half-million Russian Jews cannot be dealt with as a single unit. Consequently I approached the study of the community as a series of small social aggregates. This approach allowed me to collect a wide range of information in different situations, examine their mutual influence and connection, and draw a sketch of the life of Russian Jews in Israeli society. One of these immigrant groups included the founders and members of a political movement that later became the Russian Jewish political party.

The material is based on both participant observation and detailed interviews with respondents. The observations were made during various public events, demonstrations, conferences, meetings, and debates, but also during "unofficial" and private gatherings. They included visits to a number of respondents at their homes and offices. During fieldwork I was in intensive contact with thirty-three respondents and their families. I conducted open interviews with many others, both Russian Jewish political activists and Israeli government officials and politicians.

In addition I applied content analysis of the Russian-language press and Russian-speaking radio and TV programs, and used this to discuss various publications and reports with my respondents. I also discussed the same issues with Israeli politicians in an attempt to understand the discrepancy between the official perceptions, as appeared in the Israeli press, and attitudes toward and views of the Russian Jews.

It is my intention here to analyze the dynamics of the development of Russian Jews' political organization as they used the power of their ethnic identity, their "Russianness," in Israeli society. I follow Edelman, who treats political developments as "creations of the public concerned with them" (1988, 2). In analyzing the process of shaping ethnic political identity I apply Barth's definition of ethnic groups as "categories of ascription and identification by the actors themselves" (1969, 10). These groups use their growing ethnic identity for various needs, for example, the accumulation of political power. Thus, I treat ethnic behavior as a political phenomenon, the result of power relations between different ethnic groups. This viewpoint allows me to analyze the struggle for power within and between the different groups involved.

Upon arrival in Israel the immigrants from Russia first underwent the usual short period of orientation and political quiescence. But they soon realized that their interests could be served by claiming their "ethnic rights." In the social context of an ethnically and religiously unequal Israeli society, Russian Jews faced stigmatization and economic difficulties. In this situation the symbolic significance of their Russian Jewish identity on the one hand, and their status as new immigrants on the other, became dominant. Their ethnic-political identification in Israel became organizationally and symbolically relevant.

The increase in numbers was the crucial factor in the growing movement for self-help. The Russian Jews realized that the Israeli government could not cope with the traditional "absorption" method with such a massive influx of mostly highly educated and trained new immigrants, and that it even obstructed their professional integration. The immigrants found that they could establish their own networks inside Russian circles without giving up their professional qualifications and cultural values. They concluded that it was up to them to achieve a satisfactory integration and that they had to organize for this purpose. The wide diversity among the immigrants, differences in social situation and educational level, lingering stereotypes of "elite" and "provincial Jews," and other obstacles prevented them from immediately forming a political organization, which would unite all Russian Jewish immigrants of the 1990s. They had to find a stable basis for uniting. Old-timers also joined the effort, because they realized the real opportunity of setting up an independent ethnic party, which the Israeli political establishment probably would not encourage but could not suppress.

The power of the "Russian vote" became evident when Russian Jewish immigrants were considered responsible for bringing two extra seats to the Labor Party in the 1992 election. The official explanation of their choice was that the new immigrants were ready to support any political party that would guarantee them proper housing, jobs, and education for their children. In their preelection campaign Labor promised them that instead of building new settlements in the occupied territories they would redirect money to the needs of immigrants; this promise was more important for Russian Jews than the ideological slogans of the Likud Party.

While Israeli politicians emphasized the importance of immigration, they did not consider the newcomers ready to participate actively in decision-making. Not a single immigrant was included in the major parties' lists of candidates. This triggered the formation of parties aimed at the immigrant vote: Tali, Am Ehad (One Nation) and Yad be-Yad (Hand in Hand)—a coalition of new immigrants and Israeli pensioners. The most significant was called Democratia ve-Aliya (Democracy and Immigration), DA for short, which also means "yes" in Russian. None of these parties crossed the threshold of 1.5 percent of total votes needed to enter the Knesset.

The Preparatory Period, 1992–95

After the 1992 elections many of the Russian Jews who voted for Labor were disappointed with the government's failure to keep its promises and claimed that in the future they would vote for other parties. Various Russian Jewish organizations recognized in these expressions of disappointment a sign that "Russians" were ready for self-organization. More and more often the phrase of the Russian popular writers Ilf and Petrov was heard in conversations among Russians: "To rescue a drowning man is the deed of a drowning man himself," by which they meant that it was up to them to help themselves.

The Russian immigrants' first real victory was achieved during the 1993 municipal elections in Jerusalem, Ashdod, Haifa, and a few other cities. The Russian-speaking press presented this achievement as the first step in the political development of Russian Jews and as a big step toward their integration in Israeli society. More and more Russian Jewish activists became involved in the debate about a Russian ethnic party. Representatives of almost all immigrants' organizations, from the Association of Single Mother Immigrants to Second World War Veterans, had regularly gathered under the umbrella of the Coordinating Council for Political and Public Movements of the Russian community to discuss a party platform and election campaign. They claimed that they needed to create their own party because they were treated like second-class citizens, insulted by top officials, faced the indifference of the general Israeli population, and were given no respect for their professional and cultural abilities. They emphasized the commitment to Russian Jews who remained in the former Soviet Union and set up innovative programs to help new immigrants. According to them, the sponsors of the new party should be Jewish businessmen from Russia who would be ready to invest capital as a way of safeguarding it if forced to leave Russia (in case of growing anti-Semitism, for example). This idea found great resonance in the Israeli media. Sensational stories of Russian mafia involvement in Israeli politics caught the headlines of the Israeli media. The assumption was that the Russian mafia subsidized the immigrant leaders in order to bring its own people to the Knesset. The Russian

Jewish activists were stereotyped not only as mafia and blackmailers but also as separatists and even hooligans who agitated for disorder and riots against the Israeli establishment.

In response, the Russian-speaking press opened a public discussion for and against a "Russian" party, which was not limited to "Russian circles" but also printed the opinions of politicians from the fight and the left, public officials and intellectuals. According to a survey in one of the leading Russian-speaking newspaper, 97.7 percent of participants were in favor of a "Russian" party.[2] Especially active in this debate were so-called olimologists, social scientists who focused on studying new immigrants (*olim*). Their studies were regularly published in the Russian-speaking press and presented at conferences and seminars attended by immigrant scientists. They dealt with demographic data, the potential electoral consequences of the Great Immigration, and the realization of this potential on the Israeli market. They also clearly defined the anti-immigrant tendencies in Israel and hostility toward immigrants in general, Russian Jews in particular. Their main emphasis was on "professionalism" and in-depth research, which would follow the setting up of the new "olim" party. This emphasis on "professionalism" of the founders of the new party may be viewed as a protest of the Russian Jewish intelligentsia against its inferior position in Israel. The personal status among (new and still unemployed?) immigrants is usually determined by the professional position that he or she held before the emigration, or the reputation of the university in which he or she studied.[3] In Israel, however, this distinction was ignored. Thus, for example, all Russian Jewish scientists were categorized as immigrant scientists (*mad'anim olim*), without distinguishing among them in terms of their level of education, experience, and achievements. For Israeli officials "Russians" remained one monolithic category of socially weak immigrants.

Russian Jews had a choice between forming a new party, based on this "intellectual elite" of the Russian Jewish immigrant community, or joining another Israeli party, which would combine the votes of Russian Jews and those of regular voters for that party. The calculation to join another, preferably small party was that even if the Russian ethnic party would not succeed, it would enhance the chance of representatives of Russian Jews in other parties to enter the Knesset.

During the debates it became very clear that the problem was that there was no one united Russian Jewish community in Israel: Russian Jews are spread all over the country and there is no real obvious basis for their unification. They did not have common geographical origins, and the new socioeconomic problems they faced in Israel did not provide a basis for establishing a common organization. Inside the Russian Jewish circles there were conflicts between religious and secular, Jewish and non-Jewish Russian immigrants, between those who came from big cities in Russia and those from small provincial towns from other former Soviet republics, between Ashkenazi (European) Russian Jews and those from Bukhara, the Caucasus, or the Central Asian republics. They emphasized differences in lifestyle, education, and cultural preferences. The main conflict was, however, between the new immigrants and the old-timers, Russian Jews who had arrived in Israel in the previous waves of immigration (in the 1960s and 1970s). The newcomers viewed the old-timers as stepchildren of the Israeli establishment who tried to "zionise" new immigrants, that is, to force them to accept the official Israeli ideology. According to the new immigrants the old-timers wanted to benefit at the expense of the socially weaker newcomers. The old-timers viewed the immigrants as anti-Israeli, anti-Zionist, and even anti-Jewish.

In spite of these mutual stereotypes, the groups made efforts to unite to set up a political organization and present a united front of Russian Jews in Israel. The disagreements between old-timers and new immigrants now focused on the strategy to be adopted in the political arena and on the structure and leadership of a new party. These arguments were one of the reasons why many Israeli politicians did not take the "Russians" seriously, believing that because of the inner conflicts they would never be able to unite.

The Russian politicians, however, realized the dangers of these internecine wars and made every possible effort to present themselves as representatives of one strong and united Russian Jewish community, at least for the wider public of their potential voters and other Israelis. This community allegedly had one common "enemy"—the Israeli establishment, which did not appreciate the Great Immigration, did not respect Russian Jews, and did not recognize their political rights. The message was very simple: if the establishment is convinced that the Russians are unable to unite and fight for their rights, let us show "them" that they are wrong. Setting up an ethnic union enhanced their own worth. The reinforcement of their perception of others (Israeli politicians) also defined their own self-identification (Russian Jewish Israelis). Attracting an audience to ethnic idioms also had implications for political mobilization; ethnicity became a combination of identity and rational calculation. It originates in a shared illusion on the part of the participants, and becomes a symbolic device that can be strategically used to mobilize power. It also lends itself to manipulation to promote specific interests. In this specific social context it becomes a useful political weapon of interest groups.

The Active Period, June 1995–May 1996

If during the first period Russian Jewish activists explored various strategies to address various problematic situations and the possibility of setting up a political party, the second period saw the actual foundation of Russian ethnic political parties and movements and pre-election campaigns.

The most important development in this period was the foundation of the Israel in Immigration (Yisrael be Ahya) movement on 7 June 1995. The organizers of the movement announced that their main tasks were to return to the Zionist idea of the mingling of exiles and to bring several more millions of immigrants from Eastern Europe, and provide them with all the necessary conditions for successful adaptation in Israel. Other political aims, such as security, economic growth, and the peace process, were presented as less urgent.

Although the program of the new movement had not yet been written and many questions still had not been answered, more than 14,000 immigrants joined the movement in the first days of its existence. Many others promised to join it the moment a definite program appeared. People wondered, however, why this was a political movement and not a political party. This question even led to a conflict within Russian circles. The opposition, which accompanied the setting up of the movement, argued that the fact that leaders were not ready to register the party meant that they did not really intend to run for the Knesset with an independent Russian Jewish party, and at the last moment might join one of the big political parties. The organizers, however, explained that compared with a political party, a movement might include people who did not agree on all the ideas but were united by one perception of immigration (aliya) and adaptation (*klita*). This argument was not convincing enough for many Russian Jews, because when the movement was registered as a political party, the same problem of ideological differences remained. There was also the practical aspect of organizing a movement and not a party, since political parties are not allowed to accept donations (they are financed either by membership fees or by state subsidies once they win the election). A movement, on the other hand, is based on donations.

The establishment of a new movement of Russian Jewish new immigrants caused concern among Israeli politicians and officials. Some of them warned the leaders of the party not to take anti-Zionist steps of ethnic separation. Others approached the leadership of the movement with proposals of cooperation. It became clear that in contrast to the political Russian Jewish movements in the previous election, Israel in Aliya was accepted in Israeli politics. What, then, was the symbolic meaning of this acceptance in Israel?

In the first years of the Great Immigration the "Russian" stereotypes still prevailed: Russians are not familiar with the capitalist economy, they have no experience with liberal and democratic practices, and they know nothing better than a one-party system in a totalitarian regime. What Israeli officials and politicians did not realize was that the new immigrants in the 1990s came from a totally different Russia than had the Russian Jews from the previous waves of immigration from the former Soviet Union. Their desire to leave the former Soviet Union was based on economic and social insecurity, a result of the changing policy of reforms. They would have preferred to immigrate to Europe or the United States had this been possible, but most of them landed in Israel. The size of this immigration proved that the old-fashioned Israeli method of dealing with such large numbers of new immigrants was no longer suitable. Russian Jews created new institutions, a social hierarchy, classes, a bureaucracy, and their own leadership. Israelis, however, did not attribute much significance to these developments. While the contribution of Russian Jews in Israel was obvious in all spheres of life, most Israeli politicians and officials preferred not to see these radical changes. Establishing an ethnic political movement and its victory in the political arena have been the most important responses of Russian Jews to this attitude. Israeli politicians had no choice but to become aware of the social and political power of the immigrants.

One of the most frequent arguments against the establishment of the Russian Jewish movement was that other ethnic parties had leaders (Tami, for example, had Aharon Abuhatzeira, who was a minister of religious affairs; Shas had the religious leader Rabbi Ovadia Joseph) but Russian Jews did not. And although Russian Jewish ex-refuseniks and Prisoners of Zion always occupied a special place in Israeli perceptions, they were considered "symbols of the past," historical figures, but no more than that. Though they became active in different political, especially right-wing, parties after their arrival in Israel, none of them entered the Knesset. According to some of them, they felt Israelis would like them to remain "passive symbols" and not to poke their noses into Israeli politics.

It is remarkable that most of the Prisoners of Zion became activists in ultra-right parties, identifying with nationalistic and religious ideas and expressing open hostility toward the Palestinians. Though not denying and even encouraging the possibility of setting up an ethnic Russian Jewish party, according to them such a party had to be nationalistic (and anti-Arab). The nostalgic link between the Land of Israel and the Jewish diaspora plays an important role in their attitude toward state problems. Having once been defined as "fighters for Jewish rights," ex-refuseniks, who experienced long years in Soviet jails and labor camps, use this image in Israel, fighting either the Israeli establishment or the Palestinians and left-oriented Israelis. This is their strategy to find their place in the Israeli political arena.

The most popular Prisoner of Zion, Nathan Scharansky, was accepted by the majority of new immigrants as a leader, especially through his image in the Israeli media as a human rights activist and an ex-refusenik, and through his activity as president of the Zionist Forum. Organized in 1988 by group of ex-refuseniks and friends, the Zionist Forum claimed in 1995 to be the official representative of Russian Jews in Israel, coordinating the activities of more than seventy immigrant organizations. The unique opportunity to set up a special institution concentrating on immigrant issues, which was the result of the Great Immigration in the 1990s, was used to create a wide network of relationships with other offices and to gain political power. Until the moment Scharansky entered the political arena, he appeared as a leader and non-political Russian public figure, but most of all as a symbol of Russian Jewry in the eyes of the Israelis. This symbol attracted not only Russian Jews but also many Israeli politicians who would readily use it for their own political purposes. The readiness of Israeli politicians from the left and the right to cooperate with leaders of the Zionist Forum was widely used for propaganda in the Russian-speaking press and allowed Scharansky to gain even more power. In 1995 all the activities and efforts of the Zionist Forum were focused on emphasizing the necessity of its existence and the importance of its coordinating role between Russian Jewish immigrants and the Israeli establishment. The symbolic strategies of the leaders, who shaped their own self-image as "patrons" and representatives of the Russian Jewry in Israel, served their interest in gaining political power.

Another symbol of the movement is its name. It contributes to the positive image of immigration in Israel. Instead of the neutral and sometimes negatively interpreted "Aliya in Israel," they have chosen to call it "Israel in Aliya," which has a twofold message: first, that Israeli society has made progress in most spheres of life because of immigrants; and second, that a new situation has developed in Israel in which immigrants are entitled to equal rights and equal positions in all areas. In this way, without emphasizing the ethnic character of the movement and without contradicting the tenets of Zionist ideology, the identity of the "immigrant" was presented as a basis for their organization and ideology. The claim to be a movement of immigrants in Israel had a "better" connotation than to be an ethnic movement of Russian Jews.

Although the Israeli media usually presented "Scharansky's movement" as the exclusive representative of Russian Jews in Israel, Israel in Aliya was not the only group with ambitions to enter the Israeli Knesset. The main criticism of the opponents from among Russian Jews was that the leadership of Israel in Aliya was too closely linked to the Likud Party. In politicized Israel not all new immigrants were prepared automatically to join the right-wing camp simply because it identified with immigration and adaptation. According to the opposition, Israel in Aliya tried to convince the uncommitted voters that the movement was a roof for both rightists and leftists, since in their view no single party can embrace such a wide range of political opinions.

In 1995–96 it became clear that Israel in Aliya had more than one rival; its biggest opponent in the Russian Jewish community was a party called Aliya, established on 14 June 1995. The leaders announced their party as liberal centrist, though the programs of Aliya party and Israel in Aliya movement were very similar, emphasizing primarily the necessity of socioeconomic reforms in Israeli society. The Aliya party used every opportunity to criticize Israel in Aliya, though no criticism was made against Nathan Scharansky, hoping that he would take advantage of the fact that Aliya was already a registered party with its own electorate and that he would become its leader. The activists from Israel in Aliya, however, considered Aliya party a "party of the offended": those who were not supported by the Zionist Forum and were now taking revenge. During the winter of 1995–96, some futile attempts were made to negotiate between Aliya and Israel in Aliya. However, no agreement on their position and place in the political arena was achieved.

New immigrants as well as Russian Jewish old-timers discovered that there was a unique historical opportunity in which they could promote their own interests using their Russian identity. The "Russianness" in this case was sometimes very tentative. Ephraim Gur, an old-timer from Georgia who immigrated in 1955 and did not speak proper Russian, organized his own movement called "Union for Aliya," emphasizing his links with the Russian Jewish community in Israel, as well as his own professionalism and experience as an Israeli politician. Non-Russian politicians also realized that something was changing: the number of Russian newcomers, that is, potential voters, was growing and the leaders were gaining power, using their ethnic identity. Both the Likud Party and the Labor Party started preliminary campaigns against the Russian Jewish movement. They organized various activities for new immigrants, including cultural evenings and ideological excursions to the Golan Heights or Samaria, explaining their own political ideas. The Russian lobbies in the Labor and Likud parties recruited "Russian" staff and employed Russian consultants to address immigration and adaptation problems. Israel in Aliya activists responded by emphasizing and interpreting any imprudent remark by high-level politicians on immigration or the ethnic identity of Russian Jews as a "slap in the face" to Russian Jews.[4] The popularity of Israel in Aliya grew during 1995–96. In February 1996, when it became clear that an early election would be held in May, the Israel in Aliya movement became an official political parry and started its pre-election campaign.

The campaign focused on two major issues. The first was a rethinking of the term "Zionism." Although emphasizing the importance of the "ingathering of the exiles," the main principle of Zionism, the party members considered themselves "New Zionists" because in their perception the old Zionism meant that Jews had to forget their diaspora traditions and culture and to accept the paternalism of the state. Their new slogan was "Immigration [is necessary] not only when Jews suffer in the Diaspora, but also because it is better for them to live in Israel," culturally, socially, and economically. The second issue was to create a positive image of the Russian Jewish immigrant. Party members did not talk about poor and miserable immigrants whose problems must be solved but about their power and success, the result of their *Yidische kop* (Jewish brain), and their ability to influence and change the whole situation in the state. Having no experienced members in the Knesset, the party emphasized other strengths. Thus, seven of the ten first candidates had Ph.D. degrees, two had been municipal councillors, and two were famous Prisoners of Zion.

All these aspects appealed to Russian Jews, in whose perception education and culture are the most respected values. And indeed, they are remarkably well educated and deeply committed (especially old people) to the Russian language, history, and way of life. Some of them consider themselves Russian émigrés, attending literary "nostalgia" evenings and lectures. In Israel, where Russian culture is flourishing, they can live a full "Russian" life. There are more Russian-speaking periodicals than Hebrew ones, as well as Russian theaters, cultural centers, bookshops, and groceries with "Russian" products. Many Russian Jewish immigrants found that they did not have to sacrifice their cultural traditions and professional skills in the process of adaptation to the new environment. A continuing rich cultural life remains the distinguishing feature of an educated and cultured person for the new immigrants, providing a set of unique cultural Russian-Israeli values as the basis for their new identity. During the pre-election campaign Russian Jewish politicians also used special "Russian" ways to appeal to potential voters. They spoke Russian on Israeli television. They also appeared on Russian television programs, knowing that most of the immigrants in Israel prefer it to Israeli television.

Establishing a political party of Russian Jews was a reaction to power relations both within the Russian Jewish community and in the Israeli society around it. It was a result of social developments, which triggered political discourse and activities denying the legitimacy of existing political parties. Its success was spectacular, and unexpected by most Israelis: Russian politicians gained seven seats in the Knesset. A few weeks after the election on 29 May 1996 the party joined the government with Nathan Scharansky as minister of industry and trade, and Yuli Edelstein as minister of absorption.

After the 1996 Election: The Ideological Split

The election results influenced the self-image of multitudes of Russian Jews, vindicated their sense of dignity, and inspired hopes for better economic conditions and improved social standing in Israeli society. Very soon, however, the Russian Jewish representatives in the Knesset found themselves under fire from critics from among immigrants dissatisfied with "unfulfilled promises." The new and unique Russian Jewish ethnic party could not escape the traditional Israeli political categorization of left and right. This categorization is based on three main issues: attitudes toward withdrawal from the Golan Heights, toward an independent Palestinian state, and toward the division of Jerusalem between the Palestinians and Israelis. The Russian Jewish politicians could avoid discussing these matters before the election, but not when they joined the coalition. The party appeared to be divided ideologically.

The first real split in Israel in Aliya occurred in December 1997 when two members, Yuri Stern and Michael Nudelman, left the party and started their own party. They explained that Scharansky considered Israel in Aliya a political party with a social agenda that can primarily serve the immigrants, while Stern viewed the party as an ethnic party, much along the lines of the ultra-Orthodox Sephardic Shas party. And although Stern emphasized mainly structural differences inside Israel in Aliya, he did not deny that the main reason for the split was "ideological conflict."[5] This manifestation of ideological differences is further proof of the full integration of Russian Jews in Israeli society. They no longer consider immigration and adaptation their main problems. The more urgent issues for them are security, peace negotiations with Arab countries, and development in the Israeli economy. They share these problems with other Israelis, and their status of immigrants becomes less and less important for their self-estimation in the new society.

The leaders of Israel in Aliya party realized that the rank and file no longer viewed the Israeli establishment as the "enemy." Indeed, many of them viewed Russian politicians as a part of it. To survive as an ethnic party, they began a search for a new rival. The advice of some politicians inside the party was to start an ethnic campaign against orthodoxy in general and Shas in particular. Since for many Russian Jewish immigrants Judaism as religion has no particular importance, and many of them do not approve of the standards of determining Jewishness by the Ministry of Interior, Israel in Aliya chose to fight for this ministry. The growth of the power and ambitions of Russian Jewish politicians was manifested during the pre-election campaign in 1999, when Scharansky announced that his party would vie for the lucrative Ministry of Interior. The Russian slogan *MVD pod nash control* (the Interior Ministry under our control), which became one of the highlights of the election campaign and a kind of "election folklore," led to open hostility between Moroccan and Russian Jewish politicians (the incumbent Minister of Interior was a member of Shas). Though presented in their pre-election campaign as insistence for Jews and non-Jews to be treated with similar respect, the campaign soon escalated into ethnic hatred and physical violence among members of both groups.

Israel in Aliya has strong opposition. The closest aide of Prime Minister Netanyahu, Avigdor Liberman, left the Likud Party and formed his own party, "Our Home Israel," to run in the next election. Stern and Nudelman immediately joined him. Israel in Aliya was presented as the "party of deceived hopes," and Russian Jewish immigrants had to make a choice between the minister and former Prisoner of Zion Scharansky and the "strong man" Liberman. According to one of the leading Russian-language newspapers, the support for Scharansky was stronger among more recent newcomers. They did not yet fully understand or identify with Israeli problems, and the slogan "MVD in our hands" received a very warm response among them. Another group of loyal "Scharansky people" were those who supported "our [people]" on any condition.[6] Thus, again the ethnic perception of the group of "us" against "them" (this time Moroccan Jews) played a very important role. The main argument was that "they," the members of Shas party, made it difficult for "our" minister to function properly in the interests of Russian Jewish immigrants. There is no "bad" minister but there were "bad" laws.[7] Perhaps this clear emphasis on ethnicity and its manipulation in the pre-election campaign allowed the leaders of Israel in Aliya once again to avoid making clear statements on their ideological position.

In contrast to the opacity of Israel in Aliya, Our Home Israel Party announced that it would be oriented to the right and would struggle against the establishment (or against bureaucracy, as it appeared in its program). It encouraged its supporters to vote for Netanyahu for prime minister. For many Russian Jews this was a good opportunity to combine their political ideas with their ethnic identity.

The power of the Russian Jewish political organization was reinforced in the 1999 election: Israel in Aliya and Our Home Israel parties won six and four seats, respectively, to the Knesset. The Ministry of Interior fell into "Russian hands" as well, with Scharansky as the minister. Socially and politically integrated Russian Jews changed the political arena of Israel, an outcome of strengthening their positive Russian Jewish identity and introducing reforms in Israeli sociocultural and economic life.

Notes

I would like to thank Emanuel Marx for his comments on this essay.

1. According to the Zionist Forum officials, in 1993 there were 50,000 engineers, 22,000 teachers, 12,000 physicians, 9,000 scientists, and so forth (Siegel 1998).
2. *Novosti Nedeli,* 27 January 1995, p. 18.
3. On some specific center-periphery and educational conflicts inside the Russian Jewish community in Israel, see D. Siegel, "Political Absorption: The Case of New Immigrants from the CIS in Israel," *Ethnologia Europaea* 25 (1995): 45–54.
4. This included the remark by the minister for Labor and Social Affairs that the majority of Russian immigrants were geriatric cases.
5. Yuri Stern, interview in *24 Chasa* [24 Hours], 18 July 1997, p. 4.
6. *Vremya,* Thursday, 6 May 1999.
7. Ibid.

II

Pervasive Bureaucracy

The state expanded rapidly during the first decades of Israel's existence. Its numerous bureaucracies competed for control of citizens' lives. The power of the state slowly declined from the 1980s onward, but bureaucratic control over basic public resources is still pervasive. The dependence of groups and individuals on state authorities still obstructs the growth of grassroots associations that could restrain and control it. Israel is thus made up of many competing bureaucracies, each with its own agenda and interests, each striving to increase its resources. However, local-level officials may develop their own agendas, often undermining policies of their superiors.

Ofra Greenberg offers a composite analysis of power relations and the mutual dependency of wardens and prisoners in the bureaucratic context of Israel's only prison for women. Much of social life in Israel is made up of close-knit networks that bring together people from the most diverse circles. Even the seemingly closed system of the prison is shown to be wide open to the outside world. Leah Shamgar-Handelman and Don Handelman argue that birthday parties shape children's age and aging experiences as part of their socialization to the bureaucratic ethos of the state. Reuven Shapira focuses on the bureaucratic and hierarchic aspects of a kibbutz-owned industrial plant, in which kibbutz members function as managers, while the menial work is done by hired labor from nearby towns. The managers are no longer controlled by the kibbutz and are not accountable to it, and their untrammeled inefficiency ruins the industrial plants.

Haim Hazan challenges the notion of "community," as used by the managers of a state-sponsored urban renewal project in a poor neighborhood. He shows that the implementation of community aims essentially to draw boundaries around the inhabitants of the neighborhood and to increase bureaucratic control over them. Esther Hertzog shows how functionaries in a state-sponsored "Absorption Center" turn female immigrants from Ethiopia into "Israeli women" in terms of gender roles in the family and in the labor market. She suggests that the prevailing gender stratification in Israeli society, rather than the immigrants' cultural past, affects gender power relations among them.

6

Prisoners and Guards

One Community

OFRA GREENBERG

My research in the "Teshuva" women's prison was carried out between April 1972 and April 1973, mainly through participant observation and backed up by interviews and other research. This essay is based on one chapter of the final report (which was published in book form in 1982).

To clarify the topic under discussion, I begin with a concise presentation of general data pertaining to the prison and its population, valid for the research period. The names of the women mentioned have been changed, and certain details have been altered so as not to expose their identity.

The prison, which occupied an area of 1.5 dunams (less than half an acre), was made up of several central structures: a residential wing, offices, a classification wing adjacent to workshops and classrooms, storerooms, and an isolation wing. The population was made up of prisoners and warders. Each of these categories was further differentiated according to both formal and informal criteria.

The senior, high-ranking warders worked daytime hours in the offices. Most had a high school education and had worked in the prison for several years. The junior staff primarily worked as guards in the residential wing, the workshops, and at the gate. They worked in three twenty-four-hour shifts. Most were young, with elementary education and were fairly new on the job.

The three categories of prisoner at Teshuva were recognized as such by the inmates themselves. I use the accepted terminology of the prison, since it alludes to the distinguishing characteristics of each category.

"Clever ones": women over twenty-five years old, with secondary education, who committed white-collar crimes, check forgery, or fraud. Some were married and had children, and maintained strong ties to their families.

"Small fry": young women aged up to twenty-one or twenty-two, with minimal education, convicted of vagrancy, theft, or prostitution. They were cut off from their families after leaving home, or since their parents wanted nothing more to do with them. Some had previously spent time in closed juvenile institutions.

"Securities": mostly Arab women, both Israelis and residents of the occupied territories, who were sentenced to long terms of imprisonment for crimes that threatened state security.

This division into "clever ones," "small fry," and "securities" was sharply reflected in day-to-day life, although it did not encompass the entire prison population. Some inmates fell between categories: uneducated Arab women convicted of murder, older women whose other characteristics were identical to those of the "small fry," non-Arab "securities," and other exceptions. This categorization is, however, significant in the formation of social relationships within the prison.

Life in the prison was ordered by an all-encompassing set of regulations and instructions. A strict daily schedule laid down detailed rules pertaining to the times of reveille, meals, work, leisure, and lights out. Prisoners were obliged to work, receiving minimal payment that varied according to type of work and length of stay in the prison. The branches of employment available to them included cleaning, agriculture, kitchen work, handicrafts, hairdressing, and sewing. Radio and television broadcasts were limited to certain hours stipulated in the regulations. Special permission was required by prisoners to keep personal possessions. Visits were limited in frequency (two per month), duration (half an hour), and in the number of visitors. The number of letters a prisoner could send was also restricted to two per month, and incoming letters were subject to censorship. Further restrictions applied to the nature and quantity of items that could be brought by visitors. For example, prisoners were permitted to receive a maximum of twelve packs of non-filtered cigarettes per visit.

The standard sanctions imposed on unacceptable behavior were to lock the prisoner in her room or in an isolation cell (in the case of violent behavior). Vacation was rarely granted, and was dependent on good behavior. This plethora of regulations provided ample grounds for bargaining, benefits, and differential treatment on the part of the staff. While the senior staff could exercise discretion in applying regulations, the junior staff could turn a blind eye to transgressions of the regulations (thereby taking the risk that their leniency might be reported to the senior staff).

On an average day some thirty warders shared this inflexible and restrictive regime with around thirty-six prisoners. During the year of my research a total of sixty warders worked in the prison (thirty of whom were recent recruits), and altogether eighty-two prisoners lived or passed through Teshuva. Prisoners and warders were in close day-to-day contact, got to know one another well, and were often dependent on one another.

Introduction

Blau (1974) has pointed out the discrepancy between formal rules of behavior and their actual application within functioning organizations: "Actually, the social interaction and activities in organizations never correspond perfectly with official prescriptions, if only because not all prescriptions are compatible, and these departures from the formal blueprint raise problems for empirical study."[1]

The questions investigated here are the following: in which situations do we come across informal reciprocal relationships in the prison, and what gives rise to this type of relationship?

Within the confined area of 1.5 dunams the entire prison population develops various types of contact that cross the boundaries of social categories. The varied relationships between staff and inmates constitute a microcosm of all the possible relationships between people: long and short term, broadly or narrowly defined, specific or diffuse. Owing to the ecological framework, the expression of these relationships acquires a special significance, specific to the location. But the truly significant point is that these relationships exist and develop in spite of everything: in spite of the structure, the law, and the formal regulations, which demand social distance between staff and inmates, as noted by Goffman (1961, 18–19). Several researchers have extensively discussed the formal arrangements governing contact between staff and inmates (Goffman 1961, 90–105, 124; Glaser 1969), but little attention has been paid to this topic and the possibility of informal relationships across these categories.

There are certain needs and possibilities that transcend the formal structure and that determine the quality of relationships between the people who inhabit this common space. There are times when the very need to operate according to the formal system requires informal contact in order to maintain the regular routine. I shall attempt to categorize the prison population in a different manner, taking into consideration informal relationships, both within and between the formal categories. This is done by presenting and analyzing two types of relationships that are generally ignored in discussions of total institutions, namely power relationships and friendships. I also examine the establishment of coalitions made up of both categories (prisoners and warders) and trace the links between these varied expressions of social relationship.

Power

Researchers dealing with the analysis of the characteristics of total institutions, such as Goffman (1971) and S. Wallace (1971), have noted that the staff has exclusive control over the lives of the inmates. In other words, staff members have a monopoly of power in the total institution, and the inmates are unable to exert any influence over events in the life of the institution. Goffman, it is true, does comment that inmates can exert some control over the staff through negative sanctions, such as reducing productivity or rejecting a certain item of food, but he fails to explain fully how the inmates acquire this ability to exert control.

A few more precise studies, such as those of Sykes (1958) and Strauss et al. (1963), reveal that the situation is not that clear-cut. Sykes found that warders required the prisoners' cooperation in order to do their job properly, since their power was not based on authority. The prisoners do not internalize the prevailing values of the prison, and thus are not motivated to behave according to them. If, on top of this, the staff has only limited discretion regarding rewards and punishments, the only means at their disposal to get their way is to resort to the use of force. However, since the frequent use of force is counterproductive and reduces its efficacy, the staff often chooses not to impose its will by force. As evidence of the staff's weak position, Sykes cites transgressions of prison regulations (e.g., theft among the inmates, refusal to work, and so forth), which constitute a source of constant conflict between the two social categories of warders and prisoners.

Strauss shows that the doctor does not impose his will on patients, who have a right to express their opinion. The form of treatment eventually given is the result of a compromise between the two parties. One may make the reservation that events in a hospital cannot enlighten us as to what goes on in prisons, which are the most extreme form of total institution. I would, however, go so far as to claim that even in prisons the inmates are not entirely powerless. Furthermore, in certain circumstances of contention between staff and inmates it is the latter who prevail.

For example, a struggle between the warder responsible for security in Teshuva and a prisoner named Hedda developed during the end-of-year theatrical performance held on the prison lawn in the presence of invited guests. Three performances were scheduled, and the argument between Hedda and the warder came to a head between the second and third performances. It revolved around the presence of two lighting technicians from the neighboring men's prison. The arrival of the two men during rehearsals gave rise to tension and excitement among certain prisoners. This disturbance worried the warder responsible for security, who decided to request that they be replaced. Hedda's sole concern was for the success of the performance, in which she had a starring role. She was adamant that the two experienced technicians should participate in the final performance. Both Hedda and the warder presented their case to the prison warden, who, after much deliberation and several interim conclusions, eventually decided in favor of keeping the experienced lighting men.

The warder was also angered by Hedda's blatant shirking of her work responsibilities and attempted to rectify this. Hedda justified her days off work by saying that she needed to rehearse, and that she was tired and in poor health. The upshot was that Hedda was granted time off work that was considered far too generous by the warder. Prior to the warden's decision, the warder tried to exert her authority over Hedda in various ways (e.g., by limiting the time allowed for rehearsals and giving her unpleasant work), but her victories were transient and incomplete.

Upon analyzing these events, it becomes apparent that Hedda's main source of power was the backing she received from the warden. This support stemmed from the warden's strong interest in the success of the performance, which rested on Hedda's shoulders. Hedda was the heart and soul of the performance: apart from playing the leading role, she had a say in the costumes, direction, and makeup, and she motivated her associates among the other participants. Consequently, the warden agreed to any request of hers that had a bearing on the success of the performance. This state of affairs may be better understood by considering their background. The warden was, to a certain extent, grateful to Hedda. The performance by the prisoners before a wide forum of guests was the first of its kind in the history of the prison (and presaged a series of such performances attended by outside dignitaries). The first two performances were enthusiastically received, and the warden considered Hedda largely responsible for their success.

Hedda, savoring her victory for a while, was well aware of her power and its limitations, and of the power of the warder responsible for security. At this stage she did not yet feel sufficiently confident to openly oppose a senior staff member. She had only recently won the warden's allegiance, and was unsure as to how far she could count on it. More precisely, she knew that this support was forthcoming only within the context of the performance and its success, rather than an expression of the warden's general disposition toward her. Hedda's status improved after the performance. Her power increased and extended to other spheres. Her confidence grew over time, and when the next test of strength came about, she gained the upper hand without being seriously challenged. The event related here also demonstrates that power is not a static characteristic. With regard to Hedda, we can trace a prolonged process moving in a clear direction, namely, the growing concentration of power in her relationships with members of staff.

The event described below took place in the kitchen, which was one of the central and most lively locations within the prison. It is a fairly large room (5 x 5 meters) and has an adjoining storage room, known as the "peeling room." This is where most of the kitchen workers spend their mornings peeling seasonal vegetables, such as eggplants, carrots, and potatoes, before cooking them for lunch. The kitchen staff is made up of seven women who work in two shifts. I shall focus here on the morning shift, which begins at 5:30. This shift prepares breakfast for all the prisoners, and then washes up and cleans the kitchen. Once the workers on this shift have eaten breakfast, they begin work on peeling and sometimes also sift rice. Upon completion of the peeling, between 11:00 and 12:00, they take a break and return to work at 13:15 to set the tables for lunch.

Their final tasks for the day are washing up after lunch and washing the floor. The kitchen workers in general, and the morning shift in particular, work according to assignments. This means that the sooner they complete their allotted assignment, the sooner they begin their lunch break.

On the face of it, this work schedule appears to be rather static, but this is not so in reality. It is interesting to trace the way in which a prisoner can modify the kitchen work schedule. Upon commencing work in the kitchen Hedda organized things in such a way that one and sometimes two women began peeling at 6:00 (instead of 8:30), thereby neglecting the preparation of breakfast. The kitchen team began to work more energetically, and the cleaning was neglected and performed superficially such that they completed their work around 10:00 (instead of 12:30). A short while thereafter a peeling machine and a machine for chopping vegetables were introduced to the kitchen, which reduced the peeling work to a quarter of the time previously required. The kitchen workers were then able to knock off at 8:00, and were free until 3:00.

When the other prisoners began complaining about the breakfast served, and the shift sergeant reported on the state of the kitchen, the matter was raised at the staff meeting. Several discussions were devoted to the problem in an attempt to find a solution. The issue came to a head when one of the kitchen workers complained that she had been left on her own to prepare breakfast while the two others had gone off to do the peeling. At this point it was decided to restore the previous schedule and begin peeling at 8:00. One of the sergeants was in favor of starting the peeling earlier, claiming that this did not cause any disruption. Eventually a compromise was reached, whereby the peeling would commence upon completion of the general breakfast, that is, at 7:00. Some days later a kitchen worker complained to a senior staff member that she had been left after breakfast to do all the peeling while the others had gone off. This complaint was found to be justified, and the matter was raised at yet another meeting. Complaints were aired about the slacking off in the kitchen, such as: "In the past everyone knew that between 7:00 and 8:00 the kitchen had to be cleaned; now they do nothing." It was decided that the peeling would begin at 8:00.

This decision angered Hedda. She let it be known that under these conditions she would leave the kitchen, adding, "Everything used to be fine, we used to help one another, like in a kibbutz. Now it's awful. We are forced to work late, and that makes us tired and irritable." She spoke of the solution that she had worked out: the morning shift workers smuggled the vegetables into the small peeling room, where they peeled them surreptitiously. After several days had elapsed peeling was once more done out in the open in the kitchen before breakfast (in contradiction of the decision made in the staff meeting). Hedda explained amid laughter, "All is well now, we start peeling early, as usual . . . last Saturday was Tsipora's shift. You know that on Saturdays we start work at 8:00. We asked her whether we could start peeling straightaway, so that we wouldn't have to stay late in the kitchen. She hesitated and asked us to wait until she finished her morning round. When she finished, at 8:20, we began peeling" (and this was before breakfast, which begins at 9:00 on Saturdays). "On Sunday it was Pnina's shift. We asked to start peeling earlier, and told her that on Saturday we had started earlier. She replied, 'I haven't seen anything.' We naturally started peeling earlier. On Monday, on Esther's shift, I began peeling in the main kitchen. When I saw that Esther did not react, I continued in the peeling room. . . . On Tuesday when Tsipora came, she had already allowed us before . . . we have now arranged that all the morning shift workers prepare breakfast together and then start the peeling. Now nobody will complain that she has been left to work alone."

Hedda is aware that the staff wants peace and quiet and does not really care when the peeling is done as long as there are no complaints about how the kitchen is run. She therefore yields on one point, making sure that all the workers (including herself) do the peeling together and thereby prevent complaints from other kitchen workers while still reaping the benefit of a free morning.

To summarize, instead of the prior arrangement, whereby the vegetables were peeled from 8:30 onward (generally until 11:00–12:00), work now begins at 6:30, so that by 9:00–9:30 the kitchen workers complete their task. The new arrangement leads to lower-quality breakfasts and a lower standard of general cleanliness. An additional element is the motivation of the workers, who now work energetically and efficiently thanks to Hedda's reorganization of the work schedule and the reward of a free morning. This contrasts with the staff's concern that the other kitchen tasks, including preparation of the breakfast and cleaning, should be methodically carried out.

An additional dimension to this issue is provided by the sergeant Esther, who originally raised the matter at the morning staff meeting. She approached Hedda's friend Jasmine, a fellow kitchen worker, asking whether Hedda was angry at her, and expressed her regret over the new regulation postponing the start of the peeling. The sergeant's behavior indicates the importance she attaches to the prisoners' attitude toward her, as well as her desire to maintain a cordial relationship with them.

This example demonstrates the way in which prisoners succeed in determining the procedures and actual conduct regarding one of the most important spheres in their lives, namely, the area of work. Their success was due, among other factors, to the senior staff's failure to monitor implementation of its decisions. Instead, it took action only after the prisoners themselves lodged a complaint. Its policy was to avoid resorting to coercion and to solve conflicts without reaching confrontation. The prisoners, who were aware of this approach, took advantage of it.

An analysis of Hedda's sources of power highlights the component of the warden's backing. Without this support her effectiveness would have been severely limited. It is expressed in two main ways. First, she is free to enter the warden's room (and that of the secretary) virtually whenever she likes and to remain there for a long time. Second, she has access to much confidential information. This information is beneficial to her in several respects: it can be used for one's own purposes; it helps one to get to know other people inside the prison, and thereby to control them; and it helps one to make sense of what is happening and to avoid feeling cut off from reality or helpless in the face of events.

Another important resource at Hedda's disposal is her connections with the outside world. She receives money from her relatives, and when she is given permission to purchase clothes or cosmetics she buys the most expensive brands. Her possessions attract the interest of warders as well as prisoners. On one occasion a long-serving warder asked her for a certain item (which was kept in a suitcase in the storeroom). In return, the warder supplied Hedda with important information: in one instance she gave her advance warning of visits by outside guests so that she could arrange her room and make it presentable. Moreover, because she receives money and goods from outside, she does not depend on the staff for satisfaction of her physical needs and can allow herself many days off work since she is not dependent on her salary. The only constraint she has to contend with is the need for permission to bring in banned items.

Hedda is very knowledgeable about fashion and cosmetics. On several occasions staff members sought her advice as to what to wear, how to match clothes, how to wind a scarf around their head, how to create a certain shade of makeup, and so forth. Another special skill she developed during her stay in prison was writing poetry and setting it to music. These songs were rendered by her and her friends on every special occasion in the prison and became a source of pride for both performers and the warden. Hedda's willingness to provide the staff with information no doubt contributed to their trust in her. She does not go running to inform on someone just to get extra cigarettes, as do the "small fry." Ostensibly, she reports to the staff with no expectation of being rewarded. She brings things to their attention because "it hurts me to see this going on," or "this is bad, it's harming them and I worry about them" (in the case of a lesbian relationship between two of the "clever ones"), or "things like this are not good for the prison" (with regard to a warder's "questionable" moral behavior). Hedda's communications are accepted by the staff at face value. They carry no negative connotations, and she is not considered an "informer," as are other prisoners in similar circumstances. The staff is, albeit unconsciously, won over by her subtle behavior, and she receives special treatment from them.

Among the prisoners Hedda denied that she reported anything to the staff. To preempt any accusations, she declared, "I know that some here think that I'm an informer, but the warden doesn't need my stories to know what goes on here." This tactic worked, and Hedda was only occasionally accused of informing by other prisoners, and was generally considered to be loyal to them.

Upon examining the resources of other prisoners, I found that some of them attained positions of strength even without the warden's backing. Since the prison's bureaucratic structure is hierarchical and centralized,[2] prisoners can ignore junior staff and direct complaints or requests for protection to a high-ranking member of staff, whose decision is final. The junior warders thus sometimes fail to exert their power, since they are loath to be openly embarrassed by their senior colleagues, who are likely to ignore their decisions.

While examination of each prisoner's power sources reveals her individual characteristics,[3] certain elements are common to them all. First and foremost is the staff's dependence on the prisoners, particularly the "clever ones."[4] The staff needs their services in various spheres, from maintaining routine day-to-day order to producing festive events. In order to maintain the smooth running of the kitchen and the sewing room, to ensure that the day passes without undue disturbance, and to lock up the cells in the evening without tension or outbursts the staff must accommodate the prisoners, accede to their requests, and on occasion yield to their will. The ability of some of the "clever ones" to organize other inmates at will, thereby presenting the staff with a united front that is prepared to act with or against it, also invests the leadership of this category with power. It is wise to treat them with consideration, since they control the reactions of other inmates.

Yet another source of prisoner power can be found in certain policies within the prison, with which the prisoners can either cooperate or hinder. The staff of Teshuva is eager to maintain peace and quiet, and this provides the "small fry" with considerable power. The trend toward opening up the prison to the public and encouraging contact with the outside world[5] gives rise to secondary requirements, such as the maintenance of a high standard of cleanliness, exhibition of attractive handicrafts, and production of theatrical evenings. All these require the prisoners' whole-hearted cooperation. They are thus given the ability to manipulate the staff into granting them benefits that would not otherwise have been forthcoming. For example, two inmates who were to participate in the end-of-year theatrical revue violated a regulation the day before the performance. They were put in solitary confinement, only to be freed immediately, since "we need them for the performance" and because of the possibility that they may refuse to appear altogether. We may assume that they had no hesitation in committing the transgression, knowing that they would not be punished. This incident reveals the staff as highly dependent on the prisoners, as its bargaining power and option to use coercion are severely curtailed.

All the events presented thus far portray the prisoners as wielding considerable power and being able to gain the upper hand in confrontations with certain staff members. This gives them a variety of opportunities to engage in activity that clashes with or runs parallel to the formal regulations. The prisoners' power lies in their control of resources required by the staff. This conclusion, however, is not all-encompassing; it is valid only in the context of the interaction between a certain prisoner and a certain warder. We must therefore carefully examine the traits and the connections of each party to the interaction.

One of the side effects of the considerable power enjoyed by certain prisoners is a sense of impotence among some of the staff, particularly among the junior warders. "She's friendly with the warden, so she does what she likes" and "She thinks a lot of herself" are common expressions. This feeling was tersely expressed by a sergeant who said to Hedda, "Here it's better to be a prisoner." When a remark was made at the morning staff meeting to the effect that Hedda was running the kitchen, the social worker added jokingly, "It's just as well that someone takes control of Jasmine when we can't control her."

Failure in the competition for influence produces feelings of jealousy. The external expressions of this jealousy are directed not only toward Hedda but also toward other prisoners who exert influence and enjoy special privileges. Attitudes toward Hedda are particularly vehement, since she has influence and privileges in abundance. The staff is often jealous and feels insulted. The junior warders are particularly sensitive to the behavior of "important" prisoners toward them. They feel offended by these prisoners, who often ignore and even ridicule them. A long-serving warder complained that Rivka had ignored her "good morning" greeting. Another warder took offense when Jasmine raised her voice in answer to a question. On a different occasion, another veteran warder remarked in a hurt tone that (Hedda's) "gang" ignored the warders, kept them at a distance, "and in general don't take any notice of us, as if we didn't exist."

Offense is generated only if the opinion of the person who gives offense carries some weight. If all the prisoners were treated in the same way, the warders would certainly not feel shamed and offended by their opinions of them. As one of the prisoners put it: "Here we don't treat one another as warders and prisoners, but as women." It would seem that merely getting attention from and being noticed by the administrative hierarchy (in which the undisputed authority, both formal and informal, is vested) has intrinsic value.

The events recounted here show that relationships are not restricted to two individuals, with every action affecting additional people. The implications of an action are taken into consideration by all the participants in the interaction. While this is true of society in general, the phenomenon is more marked in prison. The degree of dependence on one another, the constant contact at different levels in the life of the prison, and the intensity of relationships make it impossible to maintain an isolated relationship between two individuals. They have to carefully consider the implications of their actions for their relationships with others.

Proximity/Friendship

A different framework of relationships—whose very existence in the prison is surprising—is friendship between staff members and prisoners. Friendship is defined here as an exchange framework in which services, goods, and emotions are passed between individuals. (Although power is also a relationship that is structurally expressed in terms of exchange, it is generally imposed on one of the parties. In contrast, within the framework of friendship both parties voluntarily maintain a reciprocal relationship.) The friendships that grow between warders and prisoners are unusual in nature and are shaped by the location in which they develop and take place. The quality of these relationships is not uniform among all staff members and prisoners. Friendship is expressed in different ways and with varying intensity. Apart from being affected by personality traits, friendship is formed by structural variables (belonging to categories such as senior and junior staff), the existence of authority and regulations, and circumstances. All these factors come into play amid a complex system of various types of contact.

Without making a distinction between affection and friendship, I begin by presenting examples of close relationships between staff members and prisoners to provide the background for an extended case study of a particular friendship. These relationships cannot be understood without taking into consideration that in general the social distance in Teshuva prison is minimal.

One indication of the warders' involvement in the prisoners' lives is their active participation in the inmates' celebrations. Thus, for example, two warders on duty joined in the singing and dancing at a birthday party held for a young prisoner. On a separate occasion, a warder sat with a number of prisoners one Saturday night, telling them jokes and doing impersonations of various individuals. Eventually they all began dancing, with the warder partnering a prisoner. Such blurring of boundaries occurs at other times as well. A prisoner named Hava related how a warder had helped her clean the offices "and was nice to me, because we both like the same music, and we look at my fashion magazines together" (Hava receives foreign journals from outside sources).

These close ties generally develop between women with similar sociological attributes. "Small fry" make friends with junior staff members, and "clever ones" with the senior staff. For example, Sylvia (a "small fry") and Shula (a middle-rank warder) sat on either side of a locked gate, chatting at length about personal matters. On another occasion, Shula walked arm in arm with a prisoner in the yard. Dita (a "clever one") was very close to sergeant Esther, who tells her (in their shared foreign tongue) all about her problems at work.

Some of the staff are quite open about their friendships. One of the teachers confessed to me (and others) that "lately Hedda and I have become friends, and I'm very proud of it. There is virtually non-verbal communication between us." A senior warder spoke of a non-Israeli "clever" prisoner who had by then been released: "I grew very friendly with her. I did things that I did not allow myself to do with anyone else. When she got leave I took her to a nightclub and to a restaurant." She also had a special relationship with Hedda and with Jasmine, who spent hours in her room discussing their problems and hopes. She would try to help them and give them advice, and sometimes intervened in their private affairs. (For example, when Hedda and Jasmine drifted apart she repeatedly tried to get them to reconcile by speaking to them separately.)

The senior staff does not look favorably on close ties between junior and middle-rank warders and prisoners. A sergeant complained that a particular junior warder was too friendly with the prisoners: "She helps them put on makeup." Naomi, a middle-rank staff member, received many critical remarks about her ties with Jasmine. Strong pressure was put on Zipora (although a sergeant, she was marginal in many respects) to sever her friendly relationship with a "security" prisoner. It would seem as though the senior staff regards friendship with prisoners as one of its exclusive privileges, prohibiting its expression among the lower ranks. This conception was explicitly expressed on the occasion of a birthday party given for the daughter of a prisoner serving a long sentence. It was decided to celebrate the birthday in the prison and to put on a show attended by prisoners and outside guests. To keep the daughter company, the warden brought along her granddaughter and the adjutant came with her daughter. No junior warder was asked to bring her children. On another occasion when the daughter visited her mother she spent a long time playing with the adjutant's daughter.

In this case another special dimension came into play, namely, the gender of the prisoners and the staff. The fact that they were women—and thus also mothers in some cases—did much to bring these categories closer together. "We are also mothers" and "I know what it's like to be a mother" were expressions commonly used by warders. This common attribute fostered a certain sense of solidarity among them and to some extent counteracted all the other differences. When the social worker became pregnant, the prisoners freely gave her advice and recommendations. Warders regularly asked after prisoners' children, and vice versa. When one mother stood by another, many of their other distinguishing characteristics lost their significance.

The expressions of affection and friendship were mutual. Prisoners were also allowed to express their feelings, and not only verbally. Nira, the prisoner responsible for the upkeep of the warders' dormitory and dining room, for example, regularly served her favorite warders special dishes that were in short supply. Mati, a warder who sometimes helped out in the kitchen during her free time, explained that she liked to help the prisoner responsible for the kitchen. Ethel, a prisoner who was most affectionate toward Hedva, the warder in charge of the garden, volunteered to water the yard in the afternoons to make sure that Hedva's flowers did not wilt. Hedda's conduct is of particular interest. She advised the social worker to be less talkative after the latter had, on two occasions, complained about the warden in the presence of prisoners. Hedda found this behavior unseemly and warned the social worker that certain prisoners were likely to inform on her. Hedda acted as a friend, advising the social worker as to her behavior within the prison, thus treating her as her equal. She was in fact telling a member of staff how best to carry out her duties for her own good. The social worker accepted this conduct without query.

One of the most widespread expressions of closeness was the presents given to prisoners by staff members on various occasions, such as birthdays and holidays, and as goodwill gestures. Prisoners also gave presents to staff, but only to a limited extent, both because of their limited resources and owing to the strict prohibition on staff members' accepting gifts from inmates. Prisoners thus generally gave their gifts upon their release from prison, or on the occasion of a staff member's retirement. Although formal policy prohibited giving gifts to prisoners, the senior staff did so "on the condition that it is done openly," in the words of a senior staff member. "Openly" referred only to other staff, since they tried to keep all knowledge of such gifts from the other prisoners so as to avoid jealousy. In most cases, however, the junior staff was also not informed. The presents took various forms, including underwear, cosmetics, blouses, and other highly sought-after feminine items. The junior staff also brought gifts, but this was done clandestinely. All they were allowed to do openly was to offer prisoners food and sweets that they brought for their own consumption.

Ties with the outside world also tended to blur the distance between prisoners and warders. For example, the prisoner Leah and the warder Hadassah lived in the same neighborhood. When Leah returned from leave, she told Hadassah of a humorous event involving the local shopkeeper, whose store Hadassah also frequented. Hadassah sometimes brought regards from Leah's husband, whom she saw in the neighborhood (the two husbands worked in the same trade, and ran into each other on occasion). On rare occasions Hadassah conveyed messages from Leah to her husband.

The flow of information from the outside, coupled with the free exchange of information that accompanied close relationships within, meant that prisoners knew a lot about the warders' private lives, and vice versa. This tended to worry the staff. As one of the sergeants complained: "In other shifts they gossip all the time . . . here the prisoners know all about Shula, Hadassah, and Gila . . . with whom they sleep."

An additional dimension of the outside world that brings staff and prisoners closer together is the political sphere. Acts of terrorism (such as the Lod massacre and the Munich murders) unite all the Jewish women, prisoners and warders alike, whose immediate hostility is directed toward the "security" prisoners.

While close relationships and involvement in each other's lives remain problematic, there is another side to the coin. The staff genuinely cares about the inmates and perceives them as people. When decisions are made, treating the prisoner as an individual demands complex considerations that may have wide-ranging implications. If we add to this the personal sentiments involved in certain cases, the outcome is differential behavior on the part of the staff toward the prisoners. Theft committed by Ethel does not draw the same reaction as theft committed by Anna, since the staff considers the prisoner as a complete individual, together with her attributes, the expectations of her, the sentiments toward her, and her network of ties within the prison.

The following portrays in detail a relationship of friendship between a staff member and a prisoner.

Jasmine, a prisoner, recalled her friendship with Naomi, a warder.

> When I first arrived at the prison Naomi was very hostile toward me. When Nira attacked me in the hostel—we both worked there—she allowed her to continue, and even closed the door so that no one would intervene. Because of that I went on hunger strike for several days. Dr. Simhati [the prison service psychiatrist] came to talk to me, and persuaded me to end the strike. From then on Naomi became friendly toward me. Dr. Simhati must have spoken to her as well. In the beginning I didn't believe her, but after a while I saw that she really wanted to make friends with me. She visited my family, and her mother also visited them. When my mother fell ill, Naomi helped my family a great deal. She herself didn't tell me about it, but my family told me. Naomi's parents attended my mother's funeral. All the security wing is angry with me because of this, but they don't actually realize how close we are.

Jasmine declared that she felt this was a genuine friendship.

Naomi also declared her friendship for Jasmine in various contexts. The expression of their friendship took the form of many hours spent together, long discussions, and the exchange of opinions and information. Naomi gave Jasmine cooking instruction, and in return she taught Naomi to knit and embroider. All this took place within the prison. Only Naomi could be active on the outside. She paid regular visits to Jasmine's family, brought presents to the girls of the family, and took an interest in the problems of the other family members. (Naomi's activities were common knowledge, and she was reprimanded for them. But she was not explicitly prohibited from making these visits, even though she was transgressing the regulations, because of Jasmine's special status in the prison.)

Naomi came to Jasmine's defense on several occasions, including the event recounted below. Before describing what happened in detail, I shall provide some background to it. Naomi, as we have seen, was friendly with Jasmine. Zipora, a warder, was very fond of Ethel, a prisoner known for her quick temper. Hedda and Jasmine are friends, and both work in the kitchen. The event took place on the solemn holiday of Yom Kippur, the day of atonement. The food that had been prepared for the end of the holiday went bad after the refrigerator ceased to operate, and fresh food needed to be cooked. These facts are accepted by all the participants in the event. From this point onward the accounts of what happened diverge. Sergeant Zipora's version (she was the warder in charge of the shift on that day) was presented at the following day's morning staff meeting.

> When we found out that the food had gone bad, Naomi [Zipora's deputy on the shift] sent Ethel to the kitchen to ask for the book of menus. As soon as she reached the kitchen we heard shouts and screaming; Jasmine refused to give her the book. I arrived on the scene of the argument. Naomi was there already, trying to intervene. I said to her, "You stop interfering here." . . . I put her in her place in front of everyone. She was wrong to send Ethel; it was obvious

what would happen. Before I could stop her, Ethel was already in the kitchen. Afterward Jasmine yelled at me, "You're to blame!" Naturally I was angry and wanted to get her out of the kitchen, but Jasmine refused, and said that she had to prepare food for the girls. I shouted at her, "You are still a prisoner, and you can't talk to me like that!" During the ensuing discussion Zipora remarked angrily: "Naomi and Jasmine are just too much. . . . [*Shouting*] She knows everything!"

The following is Ethel's version of the event.

Zipora wanted to know whether there was any coffee, and so she sent me to bring the book of menus. Jasmine refused to give me the book, and said that the menu had been changed completely. I shouted at her, "You don't take care of us!" Hedda came to help Jasmine and I shouted at her as well. Naomi came and told Jasmine to leave the kitchen so as not to argue with me. Later on I told Naomi that it wasn't her job to defend Jasmine, and she answered, "Yes, I get paid for defending her."

Hedda's and Naomi's accounts differed slightly from each other and from the previous two versions. All of the accounts represent different perceptions of reality on the part of individuals who participated in the same event.[6] There is of course also the element of distorting reality for practical reasons. In recounting her version, Ethel changes the facts in order to portray herself as an innocent girl: she was "only" carrying out a warder's orders, and when she encountered a short-tempered prisoner (Jasmine), she responded likewise. The sergeant, on her part, emphasized that it was Naomi who sent Ethel, implying that she had sent her to Jasmine. In this way she was trying to express her displeasure at the special relationship between Jasmine and Naomi. Naomi, however, made it clear that she had sent Ethel to Sarah, the warder in charge of the kitchen. She was thus conveying that she had acted in a proper manner, approaching the person in authority; that she had not left the decision to Jasmine; and that she had had no contact whatsoever with Jasmine. Hedda, who at the time had serious complaints about Ethel with regard to other matters, embellished Ethel's negative role in the incident. She reiterated her threat that she would complain to the warden (and did in fact do so). In a fifth version of the event, the junior warder placed most of the blame on Naomi, who offended her.

The important point here is that Naomi supports Jasmine even though this leads to a quarrel with her superior, the sergeant. The predominant theme of the sergeant's version, on the other hand, is her anger at Jasmine's "disrespectful" behavior and Naomi's support for her. And indeed, Jasmine, with her good connections with the senior staff and with Naomi, felt herself to be the warder's equal. She was not prepared to accept a reprimand without answering back when she felt that she was in the right. Furthermore, she felt that she was entitled—as was the warder—to complain openly to the warder herself.

This case study reveals an additional interesting phenomenon. In the argument that developed in the dining hall two coalitions formed: on the one hand were Zipora (a warder) and Ethel (a prisoner), and on the other Naomi (a warder), Jasmine and Hedda (prisoners). We have noted that Jasmine and Naomi were firm friends, as were Zipora and Ethel. Furthermore, Zipora is generally hostile toward Jasmine. Zipora and Naomi thus give their support to Ethel and Jasmine, respectively, not because they are in the right but because of their connections in other areas. Even though Zipora and Naomi are friends, they feel no solidarity with one another as a result of their common role. Each of the staff members involved in the event related here chose to support a prisoner rather than standing by her colleague.

This is one of many examples of occasions in which a prisoner and a guard join forces against another guard. Such "mixed" coalitions are forged as a result of sentiments and interests that breach the formal boundaries of categorical ascription to either staff or prisoners.

A different type of close relationship that develops in the prison is that of supportiveness. This term refers to relationships between guards and prisoners that are often one-sided. Some guards adopt prisoners whom they take under their wing, bestowing favors upon them. These may take the form of merely expressing interest[7] in the prisoner but may go as far as intensive lobbying in support of the prisoner's cause. Examples of this type of relationship, which is widespread and takes a variety of forms and content, are presented below. The first example is provided by Leah, and describes her bond with the social worker.

Leah is thirty-five years old, is married with three children, and has a high school education. She was convicted of fraud and extortion, and was sentenced to a year and a half in prison. Leah had a host of problems. She was sickly and weak, had regular hemorrhages sometimes accompanied by pain, was undergoing lengthy medical treatment, and had been hospitalized. Finding a suitable solution for her children, as well as her husband's tenuous position at work, also caused her concern. She was always on the lookout for people willing to listen to her woes and to help her. While most of the staff disliked her intensely, both because they regarded her as a nuisance and because she had been labeled a "liar," the social worker took an interest in her, perhaps because she felt that she could actually help her.

Leah frequently approached the social worker with various requests to phone her parents or husband, to authorize a special visit, or to receive permission for a visitor to bring in some article. Each request entailed several visits by Leah to the social worker to check how the matter was progressing. In due course Leah began to visit the social worker just for a chat, with no particular objective in mind. Eventually she spent most of her free time with the social worker whenever she was available. Leah would sit and discuss her problems. The social worker would also talk about herself, and the conversation often resembled one between close friends. Leah, who devoted much of her time to knitting, mainly for her children but also for some of the other prisoners, began knitting for the social worker as well, who supplied her with wool. When the social worker had a lot of work and was under pressure to finish it, Leah would help her with filing. On several occasions Leah declared her love for the social worker, adding that without her she would have gone mad in the prison.

The social worker's patronage of Leah was expressed in the frequency of their contacts and in her readiness to go out of her way to further Leah's interests. In addition to taking care of Leah's various needs, the social worker had to wage a campaign to improve her ward's image in the eyes of the rest of the staff in an effort to gain her better conditions or to prevent sanctions from being imposed on her.

The relationship between Leah and the social worker was asymmetrical. There was no mutual give and take, since it was primarily the social worker who provided services (in this case as part of her job, albeit far and above what was expected of her) and Leah who urged her to provide them. Both women were well aware that this was an instrumental relationship, albeit one maintained through sentiments of fondness and sympathy. Leah's affection for the social worker is understandable. She was well aware of the campaigns waged on her behalf. No wonder, then, that she attempted to "repay" the social worker with various services, such as knitting and helping in the office.

Patronage relationships do not generally lead to conflict. On some occasions staff members who had such a relationship with a prisoner were actually asked to exert their influence on the prisoner to whom they were attached. The sergeant Esther, for example, was known to be able to influence Rina, a "small fry" defined as being "disturbed." Whenever a crisis erupted, the sergeant was summoned to speak to her and calm her down, and almost always succeeded in doing so. Similarly, the secretary exercised her influence on Judith (an older, uneducated prisoner, defined as "primitive") in order to calm her down during an attack (which took the form of tearing her clothes and smearing the walls of her room with excrement). Whenever Judith worked well or washed her clothes (she generally maintained a high standard of cleanliness), she proudly reported this to the secretary, who praised her and urged her to continue in this vein.

All these relationships may be viewed as a set of ties between a patron and her client. The prisoners are keen to maintain contact with the staff in general, and the senior staff in particular, since this may provide them with benefits and win concessions in various services.[8] The prisoner also has at her disposal a resource that takes the form of a public demonstration of this return (such as good behavior, informing, flattery, and service). The public nature of this reciprocity is meaningful, since the surrounding actors have sociological significance. But the most important point about this type of relationship is that it is founded on sentiment, and it is this that prompts staff members to support certain prisoners. Sometimes these sentiments develop during the course of the help-giving process. In any event, a guard will not go out of her way to help a prisoner for whom she feels no special attachment.

Fondness and patronage on the part of staff toward prisoners, which are repaid by gratitude, emphasize one's categorical association. Blurring of the boundaries within intercategorical relationships occurs because this pattern of relationship is not unidirectional; the quest for patronage is not unilateral. Some guards seek a form of "patronage" from certain prisoners (Hedda and Jasmine, for example). The content of such patronage is naturally different in this case, and takes the form of seeking attention, attempting to participate in the prisoners' lives, or seeking guidance from a prisoner on various matters. There is even latent competition among guards for the friendship of prisoners, and they are proud of being popular with inmates. For some of the guards this route leads to the top of the prison hierarchy, since the patronage of certain prisoners provides access to the warden.

Friendly relationships between staff and inmates also vary in content from one case to the next. For Leah, they serve mainly to satisfy her needs through the auspices of the social worker. In the case of Ethel, leniency and small gifts are given by members of staff in return for her services. The secretary provides advice, emotional support, and a willingness to listen to her favorites. In other words, the needs and attributes of both parties in the dyad determine the content of their friendly relationship.

However, a common attribute is evident in the behavior of all the guards, namely, protection of their wards. This may take the form of making a recommendation to another guard or of extricating the prisoner from precarious situations arising from incidents involving other staff members or other prisoners. This is a phenomenon rooted in the structure of the prison: the staff can enforce regulations, and this is one of its sources of power. The way in which the staff manipulates enforcement of regulations generates a high degree of prisoner dependence on the guards, since a prisoner can never be certain as to how the staff will react to a misdemeanor on her part. The discretion allowed senior staff regarding differential enforcement of regulations and the junior staff's ability to influence differential enforcement enable guards to play the role of protector in their relationships with prisoners.

Certain staff members tended to develop friendly and informal relationships with prisoners. The social worker, Naomi, the sergeant Zipora, Hedva, the guard in charge of agriculture, and to some extent the adjutant developed strong ties with prisoners, and on occasion this led to confrontation with other guards. The explanation lies in their position within the prison's social and formal structure. The social worker felt distanced from the staff, both because of the nature of her job and her superior education. She enjoyed a large measure of autonomy in her work and could thus easily develop informal relationships and form independent opinions, which she felt free to express. Zipora and Hedva, who had few connections among their senior colleagues, sought support from prisoners both by emotional investment in them and by furthering their interests, even in the face of opposition from other staff members. The adjutant, who was insecure in her position, gave support to a number of prisoners, but mainly to those in the "small fry" category.

In summarizing the elements common to close relationships among prisoners and similar relationships between prisoners and guards, we find that friendship within the prison is characterized by components of kinship, that is, an extensive and varied range of commitment. This may be in part a result of the lack of kin among inmates. The specific needs of those who engage in a dyad relationship determine the content of the commitment. In all the cases, however, we find an expectation that each partner in the relationship will come to the other's help in every situation and at all times. The intensity of the ties is primarily a result of the lack of other types of enduring relationships within the prison, such as kinship, neighborly, or work-based relationships.

The frequent mobility that disrupts and severs relationships among prisoners also affects relationships between prisoners and staff. The constant changes (following discharge from prison, moving rooms, or changing one's place of work) adversely impact associations, which then fail to fulfill the partners' expectations. On the other hand, the constant turnover in the prison and general instability in the prison environment generate a search for security and permanence. The partners in the dyad invest much emotional energy and go to great lengths to maintain and strengthen their close relationship, which may be the only permanent tie they have.[9] In a closed environment with few alternatives for establishing ties, the competition for friendship grows more intense, since this is the primary way to fulfill one's needs. The friendship lasts as long as it benefits both parties. As soon as the balance is disturbed, whether by design or as a result of a change in circumstances, the ties are severed. In some cases, owing to the nature of prison life, the intimate relationship becomes too demanding for one of the partners, who then initiates a separation. But in the prison one cannot ignore nor avoid a friend from the past, and severing relations thus often generates tension and hostility.

In concluding the discussion of informal relationships between prisoners and staff, which tend to blur the distinction between these categories, I shall summarize the factors relevant to the development of such relationships. These factors are invoked in order to explain one phenomenon: the existence of friendly relationships between women belonging to these two categories, relationships characterized by equality, and even by expressions of weakness on the part of the staff in its dealings with the inmates. The main explanatory factors are the following:

1. The ecological aspect, which has two dimensions. The *physical layout* of the prison is constricted, with only a few buildings. The offices are situated alongside the living quarters, leading to frequent contact between guards and prisoners. Relative freedom of movement in the yard and the see-through barbed-wire partition allow the prisoners frequent opportunities to

watch the staff and give them easy access to staff members. In terms of *policies and organization,* the detailed and controlled daily schedule, which applies to all the women (e.g., reveille, distribution of medication, and regular room inspections) generates frequent meetings with members of staff. The ample free time enjoyed by both prisoners and staff (particularly during the afternoon hours) enables both categories of women to sit together and talk. This leads to discussion of personal matters or to common social activities (singing and dancing). A treatment ideology stressing prisoner rehabilitation (although little is achieved in this area) combined with a liberal approach, both of which are applied in a centralized framework, contribute toward concessions and forgiveness in matters of discipline and to the narrowing of social distance. An additional by-product is the selective and inconsistent application of regulations, which enables prisoners to negotiate with staff and often allows personal sentiments to determine decisions.

2. Demographic attributes

   The demographic attributes of prisoners and staff play an important part in shaping their predisposition toward one another and in determining the nature of the relationships that develop over time. A "small fry" finds it easy to establish a close relationship with a junior guard, while an "intelligent" inmate is drawn toward the senior staff, owing to their common demographic characteristics.

3. Networks

   Connections with the outside world tend to blur the distinction between prisoner and guard. A prisoner may have connections with important people on the outside; a guard and a prisoner may belong to the same social circle on the outside. Since contact is maintained with the outside world, it affects life within the prison. These ties (and sometimes events that occur on the outside) have implications for prisoner-staff relationships within the prison. An individual's ties within the prison also influence the reciprocal relationships between guard and prisoner: the prisoner's selection of friends inside the prison and the guard's status in the prison affect the nature of the contact between them as well as their mutual expectations and may foster closeness between them.[10]

4. Seniority

   Guards who are new on the job are relatively strict with prisoners. In contrast, the long-serving staff (which is generally also the senior staff) is more lenient and forgiving. These contrasting approaches sometimes generate confrontation between staff members. As a result, the prisoners try to circumvent the new guards.

5. Mutual dependence

   The prisoners depend on the staff to ensure a reasonable existence (sufficient and varied food, permission to wear their own clothes, approval of an extra visit when needed, etc.). The staff, on the other hand, needs the prisoners' acquiescence to maintain an orderly routine. As far as actual activities are concerned, the staff depends on the inmates only for cleaning the buildings and cooking. No harm would be done by not performing other activities, such as agriculture, handicrafts, and so forth. But as we have seen, the staff is mainly dependent on the prisoners for maintaining "peace and quiet" in the prison. Both parties thus have much to gain by cooperating with each other.

Mutual dependence both affects the factors discussed above and is influenced by them. The physical structure and the policy determine the nature of dependence (in Teshuva prison they intensify dependence). On the other hand, external and internal ties (networks) serve to modify and weaken dependence. Seniority (both among prisoners and guards) makes for mutual relationships and leads to the establishment of mutual expectations and services. Dependence, for its part, dictates willingness to develop or maintain certain ties, or to form a coalition with women belonging to different categories. Transient external situations (such as a national disaster) as well as internal changes (moving rooms or place of work) generate realignments among prison inmates.

Van-Velzen (1973, 246) argues that environmental instability leads to rapid political change, since people try to evaluate and predict the future distribution of power and make their choices accordingly. The people involved, however, do not always have the ability to change partners in order to fulfill promises. One cannot oblige another to support him amid changing circumstances. The situation in prison changes frequently. Friendship serves, in part, to deal with this constantly changing environment by creating permanence amid mobility. Eventually, however, friendship itself becomes a casualty of this frequent change.

All these components, which are allied to personality traits, generate an entanglement of relationships involving both guards and prisoners. These are women who are thrown together in the same place, and to some extent share the same fate.

Notes

The essay appears here in its original version, slightly abridged, and without bibliographical updates.

1. Blau 1974, 29.
2. Centralization is an important attribute. Had the guards in charge of the kitchen or storeroom, for example, been able to make completely independent decisions, in the knowledge that the deputy, the adjutant, or the warden would not override decisions pertaining to their realm of responsibility, they would have been firmer toward the prisoners and could have had their way more easily.
3. According to Dahl's definition (1957, 203), an individual's power bases are made up of various types of sources—opportunities, actions, objects, etc. He can utilize all these to influence another's behavior.

4. Emerson (1962, 32) regards power as emanating from dependence on others.
5. The policy aims at bringing the audience and presenting the prison and staff to it, and does not seek to bring the inmates closer to the outside world. The prisoners, on their part, oppose this approach, which encourages frequent official visits. They see themselves as objects exhibited to provide for the visitors' curiosity. Expressions such as "it's as though we're in a zoo" or "they came to look at us as though we were animals in a cage" are frequently used.
6. Berger and Luckman (1966, 153) explain how reality is perceived in a subjective manner. According to them, external reality runs parallel to one's internal reality. Thus, objective reality can easily be translated to subjective reality, and vice versa.
7. Attention is an extremely important commodity in the prison, sought after by all the prisoners.
8. E. Wolf (1966, 7) argues that patron-client relationships are particularly functional in situations in which the society's organizational structure is weak and is thus incapable of providing a steady supply of commodities and services. In such places, clients seek insurance by attaching themselves to a patron. While one cannot characterize the prison's organization as weak, it does—by the very nature of its structure and definition—prevent the supply of many commodities and services. This leads to a search for patrons who are able to some extent to ease the shortage.
9. There is a parallel here to the situation described by E. Wolf (1966, 14–15). He found that in large-scale bureaucracies such as industry or the army, the instrumental function of friendship is to render an unforeseen situation more certain and to provide mutual support in the face of surprises from within and without.
10. It is important to stress that friendships also occur between prisoners and the senior staff. The sociological literature that discusses this area envisages only friendship between an inmate and a junior guard (McCorkle 1970, 420; Sykes 1958, ch. 3).

7

Celebrations of Bureaucracy

Birthday Parties in Kindergartens

LEA SHAMGAR-HANDELMAN and DON HANDELMAN

In the world of the Israeli Jewish child, the kindergarten is the dominant molder of experiences beyond the intimacy of the family. The kindergarten initiates the lengthy process by which a child is turned into a citizen, in large measure through the state system of education. Between the ages of two and six, the great majority of Israeli Jewish children attend kindergarten on a weekday basis throughout the school year (Shamgar-Handelman 1990). Within the kindergarten, the child participates frequently in two sorts of events that practice aspects of an ethos of statism and citizenship. One that we addressed elsewhere (Shamgar-Handelman and Handelman 1986) is the celebration of annual national and traditional holidays. The other is the birthday party, a celebration of age.

In that earlier essay we argued that the implicit designs and practices of these holiday occasions operate to shift the allegiance of the child from a social order within which the only hierarchy is that of the family to one dominated by the civil collectivity, within which the family is allocated a subordinate place. This shift in the child's perception of hierarchy (however it is accomplished in different social orders) is crucial to the reproduction, from generation to generation, of the hegemony of the modern state.

In this essay we discuss the pervasive motif of the birthday party, that of exact age. Ostensibly the party celebrates age for the sake of the maturity of the child. The child's passage from one numerical age to another is constructed to mark his growth and ongoing socialization into the norms of the collectivity (Weil 1986).[1] Although less obvious, we argue that the birthday party designs experiences of age and aging that prepare the child for his participation in the bureaucratic ethos of the state.

We will discuss three prominent, implicit messages of age and aging in the birthday party. One is the individuation of the birthday child in terms of a cultural taxonomy of time, that of age, which momentarily fragments the self according to temporal categories. Another is the child's reclassification from one age category to another, in accordance with this taxonomy of time. The third emphasizes the experiencing of time as continuity, for categories of age are shown also to be one's personal past, present, and future. The birthday party inculcates the youngster into a taxonomy of time.

This perspective stems from three premises. First, all social order depends for its coherence on systems of social classification. Second, in the modern state, ideas of exact age are "good to think," in Lévi-Strauss's terms, for they are integral to frameworks of classification used to create social order (Musgrove and Middleton 1981, 53). Third, modern bureaucracies invent social taxonomies and apply them to the citizenry of statist orders. The individual often is keyed by numerical age to these systems of classification.

The first section of this essay addresses the relevance of age to systems of classification in modern Western social orders. The second discusses the taxonomy of time communicated to youngsters through the birthday party. In conclusion we address the issue of how the taxonomy of time communicated to the child in the birthday party is of direct relevance, in the longer run, to relationships between the individual and bureaucratic ethos in statist orders.

Taxonomy and Age in the Modern Social Order

No cultural order exists without systems of classification—of ways of gathering, organizing, and making sense of knowledge (Lincoln 1989, 136; Lévi-Strauss 1966; Douglas 1966; Durkheim and Mauss 1963). Taxonomy always implicates practice.

Taxonomies are not solely intellectual—they should be good to use (cf. Bourdieu 1977, 97). One of the most important features of such structures of classification is that their constitutive grounds acquire a commonsensical, taken-for-granted character (164). In this regard, the role of age, often one's exact numerical age, is of special importance in modern Western social orders. Exact age is at once a classifier of oneself in relation to one's sense of self, and so too in relation to others. Moreover, numerical age both individuates the person and is used as a dominant criterion by numerous bureaucracies to place the individual in anonymous social categories.

Ostor comments that age and time "are categories and values in social relations. As categories they refer to culturally shaped indigenous concepts" (1984, 302). In the modern West, and elsewhere, age is an index of time. The age of the individual is his personal, autobiographical time, standardized biographically in terms of the regulation of cultural duration and other features. The following characteristics of temporal regularity are of relevance here. Western cultural time is usually conceived of as a rigid, sequential structure, lineal, and virtually irreversible. Time is divided mathematically into uniform durations that recur with fixed periodicity, through conventionalized rhythms (see E. Zerubavel

1986, 2–11). These characteristics enable the organization and experiencing of time as quantitative, and of its durations as exactly divisible, measurable, countable, and therefore comparable. Thus a length of time is composed of a number of durations of equal length added together (E. Zerubavel 1985, 59–60).

Age can be constituted from periods of equal length that are added together as a statement of being, and as a process of continuous duration. Yet, if Piaget was correct, this sense of temporal continuity—which synchronizes the durations that can join and separate people—is not inherent in children. This sense of continuous time, as a condition of being, must be acquired. Piaget (1969, 202–29) noted that the young child has a sense of age that is virtually discontinuous. Thus age is independent of the order of birth, while the arithmetical differences in age that separate persons exactly are thought to be impermanent and mutable with the passage of time (202). Therefore, the child must learn a temporal biography of self that will enter him into the continuous flow of cultural time. In the modern West this will also make him responsive to the taxonomic break between age categories based on the unit of the year. Each of these age categories is exclusive. Therefore, during a particular year, the child will learn that he is a member only of that category of age to the exclusion of all other age categories based on the year.

This taxonomic break is the abrupt movement from one unit of time to another. A child learns that each of these ages indexes different moral and normative practices. When he can turn these temporal rudiments of biography into autobiography, an important stage of personal maturity is evinced. In the recent past, the precision of personal age was not especially significant; birthdate might be remembered in relation to the closest historical event or calendrical holiday (cf. Myerhoff 1984, 159). Today, knowing one's own numerical age—one's exact location in fully synchronized time—is considered a basic index of individual competence.

The precision of personal age combines the idea of exact duration with the date of birth of the individual, his birthday. In reckoning age, the year begins and ends for every person according to their birthdate. In the life of the individual, the birthday not only imparts rhythms of periodicity and the momentum of lineality, but also that of personal climax. Thus the birthdate enables the individual to construct his private year, from one birthday to the next. These years are the cumulative, chronological durations of his autobiography, and often the temporal divisions of the self, of self-knowledge as a historical being (Kunz and Summers 1979–80). Moreover, the birthdate articulates the private year with the calendrical year, since they are both of equal duration and therefore comparable.

Chronological age is also used to separate and fragment persons from one another in Western social orders. This is imminent in Foner's (1975, 147) discussion of "age stratification": age grades and ranks all people and social roles, forming age strata that cut across the whole of society in relatively enduring ways. So, too, as the individual ages, he moves from one set of age-related roles to another, each associated with greater or lesser rewards, and so with upward or downward mobility (Foner 1975, 157–58; see also Johnstone 1970). Given the articulation through birthdate of private and public years, each individual can be isolated and counted separately, just as all individuals of a particular age category (or, for that matter, birthdate) can be aggregated and counted together as a cohort. The classification of cohorts expresses a numerical or statistical conception of the individual, one that is efficient for the operation of bureaucratic taxonomies, and thus for the controls practiced by the modern state.

Numerical age often abruptly crystallizes and synchronizes expectations about the biological, emotional, social, and intellectual qualities of persons. In Israel, for example, children aged six are expected to have an attention span of forty-five minutes, and this justifies placing them in the first grade of elementary school. Thus they are enrolled because they turn six, not because their attention span was proven. Similarly, at age eighteen, Israelis are expected to understand their political system and so they are enfranchised. They are not given the right to vote because they demonstrate any comprehension of the political system.

The taxonomic criteria of numerous obligations and rights are determined by age. Israelis are recruited for military service only after age seventeen. From that age one must carry an identity card that also entitles the holder to open a bank account in one's own name. A woman may marry without her parents' consent only on reaching age eighteen, not when she becomes physically and emotionally prepared for this undertaking. Of course, classification begins at an early age. For example, if a child turns six before November 30 of the calendar year, his parents should register him to begin the first grade in the next school year. But if he turns six after February 28, he can only be registered for the school year following the next one. All such age-dependent classifications are always subject to legislative or bureaucratic change, since they depend on the idea of exact, numerical age as a universal classifier of the individual, constructed, naturalized, and embedded in cultural order.

The early years of the child are thought to be a critical nexus for personal development and for inculcating the child in moral perspectives and normative practices considered necessary to function as a person and citizen. In this regard, knowledge and experience of the temporal order, its divisions, durations, and flow, and its synchronization of individual rhythms to those of social order are crucial. This may be the basis for Western (and Israeli) preoccupation with the chronological age of young children, and the concern that their characters and talents "conform as nearly as possible to our detailed expectations of their age groups" (Hughes 1989, 38). So, too, the near obsession with the age segregation of children. Many children spend an increasing proportion of their lives contained in educational institutions whose structures depend on age grading (Foner 1975, 151) where the higher the grade, the greater the prestige, status, and rewards (Burnett 1969, 7–8). As well, interaction among grades may be discouraged (Riley and Waring 1976, 407). "The school," comments Suransky, "separates the child not only from the adult but from fellow human children of different chronological ages" (1982, 20).

Educational institutions are central to reproducing ideological tenets of the modern state (Carnoy and Levin 1985, 20; David 1980, 50; Epstein 1978, 109; Lancy 1975, 379; Lewis 1979a; Parsons 1959; Willis 1981). Henry argued that "school metamorphoses the child, giving it the kind of Self the school can manage, and then proceeds to minister to the Self it has made" (1965, 292). In part this is the metamorphosis to citizenship and to loyalty to national hegemonies (Shamgar-Handelman and Handelman 1986; Gracey 1972, 271–72; Lawson 1963; Harrington 1973, 150). But this also is the inculcation of elementary categories of experience, like age, that are essential to the taxonomic practices of statist bureaucracies.

The modern state assumes extended jurisdiction over socialization (Tyack 1966), and so an increasing control over childhood education (Boli-Bennett and Meyer 1978, 802, 810). In this regard the early years of schooling undoubtedly are formative (Henry 1957). Moreover, given Piaget's contentions regarding the development of a temporal self, the kindergarten years may be the most powerful in organizing experiences for the child about the taxonomic structuring of age categories. These roles of kindergarten, and of its rituals, have hardly been examined, even though many anthropologists understand categories of social order to be constituted in part through ritual and ritual-like activities (cf. Ostor 1984, 297). When such studies are reported, they are unequivocal in pointing to the place of kindergarten in impressing the ethos of wider social orders on the young child (cf. Hendry 1986; Ben-Ari 1987; Norman 1991, 104–42).

The first Hebrew-speaking Zionist kindergarten in pre-state Israel opened in 1911. Kindergartens were linked closely to the practice of protonational ideology (Doleve-Gandelman 1987). Indeed, the founders of these kindergartens were directly influenced by the civil nationalism of the kindergarten movement in nineteenth-century Germany, which emphasized patriotism, citizenship, and political responsibility (Allen 1986, 437). Kindergartens in Israel are neither nurseries, crèches, nor babysitting arrangements. They are educational institutions run by graduates of teacher seminaries. Compulsory, free-of-charge education includes only one obligatory year of kindergarten, beginning at age five. Yet kindergarten is extremely popular: in 1988–89, over 74 percent of two-year-olds, over 95 percent of three-year-olds, and almost all the four-year-olds in the Jewish sector were enrolled in kindergartens.

The celebration of holidays in the kindergarten was and is perceived by educators as a powerful medium of enculturation (Fayence-Glick 1957, 141; E. Rabinowitz 1958). Kindergarten teachers treat birthday parties as festival celebrations, but ones centered on the child as "hero of the day."[2] It is customary to celebrate all children's birthdates that fall during the school year. Ways often are found to incorporate birthdates that fall outside this period. There is much variation among kindergartens in the scheduling of birthday parties. At the extreme, the birthday is celebrated close to the child's birthdate. At the other, a party is held once a month for all children whose birthdates fall during that period. Perhaps most common is the setting aside of a weekly time slot within which to celebrate the birthdates of the past week. In larger classes it is not uncommon for birthday parties to take place almost weekly; children who spend two to four years in kindergarten will participate in dozens of these celebrations.

Birthday Parties in Israeli Kindergartens

The organization and performance of birthday parties varies greatly among kindergartens. Nonetheless there are elements—architectonic and performative—that are widespread and even customary. The architectonic elements consist of a special chair for the birthday child, a garland of freshly cut flowers, candles, an album of drawings made by the children of the class and other gifts, and a cake baked by the birthday child's mother. Customary activities include garlanding the birthday child, birthday songs, lighting candles, biographical narratives about the birthday child, blessings for the birthday child, lifting the child in the special chair, gift giving, and eating.

Our interest is in the elements and activities that adumbrate the cluster of messages—individuation, reclassification and the fragmentation of temporal experience, and temporal continuity—which we mentioned in the introductory section. These messages are not tied to any particular sequence of activities in the celebration. Therefore our discussion is organized in terms of these messages, rather than any overall sequence of party activities.[3]

Nonetheless, the reader should get a sense of how a birthday party is enacted, even though there is no typical occasion of this kind, in order to appreciate that the performance of birthday celebrations is saturated with premises of taxonomic practice. Therefore, this section begins with an abbreviation of one party. This description is segmented, using Roman numerals to indicate different customary activities. We then discuss these activities in terms of the messages referred to above, with supplemental examples from other birthday celebrations in different kindergartens.[4]

The class consisted of thirty youngsters, aged four and five. The party was in honor of Amir (his name means the crown of a tree), who was turning five. From his arrival on that warm spring morning, dressed with care, his hair neatly brushed, he was singled out for special attention by the staff. For example, in the first period of free play he had the choice of playthings.

I. Architectonics: When Amir's mother and grandmother arrived in midmorning, they and the children were escorted inside by the teacher and her two aides. Along the back wall of the room were the children's small tables, temporarily out of the way, but each with a vase of fresh flowers on its white, plastic tablecloth. The children sat in their small chairs, parallel to three walls of the room. Next to the fourth wall stood an ornate, bright red chair. Its back was decorated with green sprigs and golden ribbons. The chair, used for all birthdays in this kindergarten, stood on a low podium of large toy building blocks covered with a small carpet.

Amir took his place on the red chair, his height raised above those of the other seated children. To his left sat the teacher, in an adult-sized chair; to his right sat his mother and grandmother in children's chairs.

A round table stood in the middle of the room, covered with a white, embroidered tablecloth. On it were a vase of fresh flowers, a plate on which stood six unlit candles, a garland of freshly cut flowers, an album of children's drawings, a coloring book, and a small box of markers. On the album cover the teacher had drawn a child holding five balloons. Each balloon contained an inscription, forming the following text: "Amir is five years old!"; "Congratulations!"; "An abundance of blessings!"; "Until one hundred and twenty!";[5] "Best wishes from the kindergarten children!"; and "Heartfelt blessings!" Each inscription was signed by the teacher and her aides.

II. Opening songs: The teacher opened the party by leading the children in two songs. The first was of a type used to focus attention and coordinate movement under the teacher's control. Following the opening words ("It's Amir's birthday, and a happy occasion for all the children"), the youngsters had to coordinate words with bodily movement: "With the hands, hakh, hakh, hakh (i.e., clap your hands); with the legs, trakh, trakh, trakh (i.e., stamp your feet); with the tongue, tak, tak, tak (i.e., click your tongue)," and so forth.[6] The words of the second song were as follows: "Birthday, lovely party, how pleasant and how lovely that every boy and every girl weren't born in a single day, but only Amir by himself [was born on this day]."

III. The garland: The teacher to the children: "Why is Amir sitting on a decorated chair, all dressed up so beautifully? What's he missing?" Children called out, excitedly: "The garland, the garland!" The teacher asked Amir whom he wanted to garland him. The four boys he called out paraded the garland around the room while the others sang: "Today is Amiri's [his nickname] birthday. He has a happy birthday and a garland of flowers." As the song finished, the boys placed the garland on Amir's head.

IV. Biography: The teacher asked the children: "What do you think, was Amir born so big? Amir's mother, perhaps you'll tell us how he was born?"

> Mother: "He was born in the north, in Rambam Hospital. We traveled through the night, and he was born there in the morning. He had very big eyes, and he looked at me. Father was very happy, and ran to tell grandfather and grandmother and all the uncles. And he said he'll be called Amir."
>
> Teacher: And how did you accept this, grandmother?
>
> Grandmother: With great happiness.

Teacher, to mother: Tell us how he grew up.
Mother: He ate and slept.
Teacher: What did he eat? Fish? Chicken?
Mother: No, he drank milk.
A kindergarten girl: Also porridge and tea and water.
Mother: And when he grew up a little bit, he began to eat more solid food. And when he grew up a little more, he started to crawl.
Teacher [to Amir]: Maybe you'll show us how a baby crawls. [She gave the mother a musical triangle.] When Mother strikes the triangle, you'll crawl. And when I beat the drum you'll walk like a big boy.

This sequence of activity was repeated twice.

The teacher told ten children to make five arches by facing each other in couples and raising their arms toward one another. Amir proudly marched through the row of "arches" as the children sang: "What's happened? What's occurred? Our Amir is five years old."

Teacher: "Amir, invite your mother and we'll teach her to dance." The teacher formed the children in pairs, and they, Amir and his mother, all danced and sang under the direction of the teacher.

V. Blessings: The teacher sang: "Amir has his birthday. Stop sitting down. Let's bless him on his birthday." Those who wanted to bless Amir raised their hands, and the teacher called them forward, one by one, to shake Amir's hand and utter their blessing. The following is a partial but representative listing of the children's "blessings."

Boy: Don't touch the electricity.
Teacher: It's very important to be careful.
Girl: May he help mother and father.
Teacher: What a wonderful blessing. It's so important to help mother and father.
Girl: May he travel by plane.
Girl: May he be healthy.
Teacher: This is a wonderful blessing.
Girl: May he not irritate his mother.
Boy: May he be a diligent student in school.
Boy: Both at home and kindergarten, may he be diligent.
Teacher: Lovely! Mother, how are you blessing him?
Mother: May he be a good boy.

VI. Candle lighting: All sang: "In our kindergarten again there is a birthday.... Candles are lit on the cake. And around them, games. And it's written in chocolate, 'Congratulations and all the best!'"

Teacher: How many candles are you going to light, Amiri?
Amir: Six.

The teacher turned to Amir: "Invite Grandmother to light the first candle."
Grandmother did so, and kissed Amir.

Teacher: Amir, don't forget to give Grandmother a kiss.
Amir: Now, Mother. Mother lit the second candle and kissed him.

Amir lit the remaining candles, even though a boy called out: Invite a friend.

Teacher: Amiri has chosen to light the candles by himself.

VII. Games: The teacher turned to Mother: "Now let's see if you know your child." She covered Mother's eyes with a kerchief and placed a girl before her. Mother touched her and said, "This is a girl. This isn't Amiri." She touched another child: "This is a boy, but he's not Amir." Then Amir stood before her, and she called out as she touched his face: "I think it's Amir. Sure, it's Amir." The games continued. Amir acted out an imaginary gift, and the children guessed what it was (a watch). Other charades followed in which children acted out imagined gifts while Amir guessed what they were.

VIII. Lifting the child: The teacher took Amir by the hand and moved him and the birthday chair into the center of the room. Together, teacher, Mother, and a number of children lifted the chair five times, and then one more for next year, calling out the number and lifting Amir higher each time.

IX. Gifts: The teacher announced the first of the true gifts, the album of drawings by children of the class, with empty pages at the end for Amir to add his own drawings. The teacher chose the children who would present him the album. Amir burst into tears. His mother tried to calm him and discovered (she said) that he wanted to choose the children himself, which he did. As children sang, "Here everybody, everybody comes; a large group is marching to the birthday party," Amir received the album, together with coloring book and markers, the gift of the kindergarten. In turn, Amir's mother (on his behalf) presented a gift (a large toy) to the kindergarten. The teacher then asked Amir to blow out the candles, which he did after strenuous effort.

X. Snacks: The aides rearranged the tables. At each child's place they set a slice of the birthday cake (baked by Amir's mother), half an orange, a piece of candy, and a small bag (called the "surprise bag") of sweets containing a small toy, the customary gift of the birthday child to each of the other children. The birthday chair was put at Amir's usual place; places were set for the adults at the round table. Amir reentered the room first, sat in the birthday chair, and cried, mumbling that he wanted to sit next to his mother. The teacher moved the birthday chair to the round table. When the children finished eating, they went outside to play; Amir's mother and grandmother said good-bye to Amir and left.

Together, these activities create a festive atmosphere, the basic premise of which is that it is a good thing to grow older and to grow up. Given the way the party is organized, this premise is not open to negotiation by any of the participants.

In what follows we discuss the birthday activities through the messages they carry in the following order: individuation of the person, reclassification according to exact age, and temporal continuity. Within a given activity, one message may lead to another so that different activities communicate combinations of the same messages. Therefore, the same sets of messages are entwined throughout birthday celebrations. This adumbration enhances the reception of messages with minimum distortion. In this regard the birthday party is more the performance of a context for experiencing sentiment. The party is not a rite of passage when this is understood as ritual that is intended to remake the person (see Handelman 1990, 22–62, for the logic of this argument).

(1) *The message of individuation.* The individuation of the birthday child is prominent in the architectonics of the room, in songs, in his garlanding, and in gift exchange. With regard to the architectonics (I), the chairs are placed in the format of an assembly, within which the birthday child is the focus of everyone's gaze. Facing youngsters of whom he is one on all other days, Amir is surrounded by adults, in whose direction he is moved on this special day. In his throne-like chair, he is separated from and elevated above the other youngsters.

The birthday child is individuated. He is treated as more of an autonomous being—a unique constellation of individual attributes according to Western perceptions.[7] As such, he is categorized and recast in terms of numerical age. Here exact (and exacting) age is the only category that separates him from the other children. On this day he is constituted by virtue of categories of time as a temporal being. The exact age that is only his is represented everywhere: in the number of rising balloons on the album cover, in the number of candles, in the act of lifting the child, and in the words of songs.

The process of individuation is one also of fragmentation, readying Amir to be recast as a new member of the category of age five. Thus Amir is made to stand by himself, in the words of the second song (II)—"how lovely that every boy and every girl weren't born in a single day, but only Amir by himself." This is made emphatic in the garlanding of Amir (III), in which the message of individuation also intimates reclassification. The garland motif entered the secular kindergarten likely as part of the celebration of Shavu'ot, a first fruits festival. Then children's heads were wreathed with flowers to signify them also as first fruits of Zionist practices to mold the land in the image of ideology. Comparably, the garland singles out the birthday child as the first fruit of his last round of maturation, the period of one year he has spent in the social category of age four.

In other kindergartens, the garland may be associated even more acutely with birthdate and reclassification by age. The following description is from a party for a girl turning five. Five children danced with hoops decorated with flowers, singing, "Today is a birthday . . . today is Orit's birthday." They placed the hoops over their heads and then down around their shoulders. As they sang, "And she has a garland of flowers," a sixth child garlanded the birthday child. Here hoops decorated like garlands are used as openings through which children pass head first, on a birthday. These hoops reflect the form of the birthday garland, that here signifies both the individuation of the birthday child and her reclassification by age, her movement through the threshold of an age category.

The gift exchanges in Amir's party are common to birthday celebrations in numerous kindergartens. Gift exchange (IX, X) joins individuation to classification, dramatizing the relationship between the individual and membership in a social category. While the birthday child is singled out temporarily from the category of kindergarten children, they remain generic members of this category.

They are an aggregate: during the party they are treated as similar and as interchangeable with one another. The individual and the category are the two parties that engage in gift giving here.

The gifts are unique and generic. Amir is given two gifts: a coloring book and markers, and the album of drawings. The book and markers are a generic gift from the kindergarten, as an institution. The album contains drawings, each the gift of an individual child. Each gift is the same (a drawing) but also unique (the particular composition of a named individual). The drawings are bound together in the album as an aggregate of individual compositions. Each is like and unlike every other, as are the children of the category, perceived as distinct individuals who are classified together. This gift demonstrates the viability of the generic category of children and of variation within it. Indeed, it constitutes the generic category out of an aggregation of unique individuals. So too the birthday child is expected to draw on the album's empty pages, thereby adding himself again to the aggregate of the category. Yet there he, too, is allowed space for self-expression, to inscribe his own individual mark. In turn, Amir gives one gift to the kindergarten. Later on, each child receives from him a surprise bag (X). The contents of each are the same, apart from the little toys that vary from bag to bag. The gift of the surprise bag internally differentiates the category of children, granting to each child a measure of uniqueness (the little toy). But this individuation is standardized, since the match between child and toy is one of chance.

The birthday child gives one gift (the large toy) to the kindergarten as an institution, and the same gift to each child (the surprise bag). Similarly, he receives one gift from the kindergarten (the coloring book and markers), and the same gift (a drawing) from each child. However, the drawings differ from one another, as do the surprise bags. Thus, although they are shown to vary within the category of children, the same rules of classification are shown to be embedded in each child. These experiences are made available to the birthday child from two perspectives: one from within the category of children that he is separated from, and the other from the outside, reflexively interacting with that category as a generic form. Gift exchange constitutes the birthday child as both unique and generic in relation to other members of the category of young children within the kindergarten. On this combination of the generic and the unique rests the reclassification of the individual.[8]

(2) *Reclassification by age.* In many kindergartens, reclassification is used to immediately relate individuation to obligations and rights that accompany the change in numerical age. The impact of reclassification by age is most weighty in what are called blessings (*brakha;* pl. *brakhot*) (V). In ordinary language usage, religious and secular alike, a blessing refers to a benediction, request, or hope for general or specific well-being and good fortune. But in the birthday party, the blessing often becomes a statement of social expectation directed toward the new member of the age category. Some of the blessings directed at Amir are more akin to benedictions (i.e., "May he be healthy"). Others are virtual imperatives, loaded with warning (i.e., "Don't touch the electricity") or with normative injunctions (i.e., "May he help mother and father"). Many blessings in these parties are not age related. For example, "May you be big and strong" and "May he be a hero" are adequate for every age. Yet in many instances these expectations are well adjusted to the numerical age of the child. A common blessing for five- and six-year-olds is, "May you be a good pupil in school" or variants thereof. But this blessing is rarely applied to children turning three. Then one may hear blessings like, "May you eat all the food you bring from home."

The repetition by children of blessings heard at previous parties especially constitutes the normative adumbration directed at the child. The children themselves bluntly tell their peers of the connection between reclassification by numerical age and acquiring new obligations. These blessings are highly reflexive, in that children take turns being the subjects and objects of participation. At parties of two- and three-year-olds, a child hears over and again the injunction, "May you not wet your pants." And then on his third birthday, it is his turn, the expectation directed solely at him because it is he, now, who has suddenly and abruptly reached the age of three. And the teacher may immediately add her comments, evaluating particular blessings (i.e., "What a wonderful blessing").

Messages of individuation sometimes lead directly to those of reclassification. After Gil was garlanded on his fourth birthday in another kindergarten, the teacher commented, "Now, Gil, you're happy . . . but" (she turned to the other children) "I'm terribly mixed up today. Perhaps Gil is only a year old . . . or perhaps two years old . . . or perhaps three . . . let's hear how old Gil is." Gil called out: "I'm four years old and one day." The teacher responded, "Yes, Gil? So you're already big and not small." Gil's mother added, "It's true. Yesterday was his exact birthday." Gil then recited the verse he had rehearsed, closing with the phrasing, "Today I'm four years old; I'm not little anymore." The teacher kissed him warmly, exclaiming, "You really recited it as if you were six!"

The garlanding of this child leads immediately to a recounting of his age as an additive sequence of years. This culminates in Gil's self-recognition of membership in his new age category, and indeed of his exact age as a sequence that inexorably progresses, as he exclaims, "I'm four years and one day." This leads to other byplays that broach more comprehensive issues of the child's continuity through time. Gil has become "big" in contrast to being "small" in his own past ages. He is no longer "little" because he is now four. And in doing the recitation "as if you were six," he is orientated toward his own future, constituted for him as a series of additional age categories that are part of the same taxonomy of numbers.

The highlighting of numerical age-classification practices abrupt discontinuity, perhaps even fragmentation, in a birthday child's sense of being. The child is taught to perceive himself as a person of parts—here these parts are blocks of time, measured by the year. The transition from one exact age category to another requires disjunction and recombination. Yet the child learns that age constitutes continuity of being. The transition between age categories also leaves those blocks of time that indexed his previous ages as integral to the child's personal history. Gil is not only four years of age—he is also one and two and three and . . . four years of age.

In these celebrations, adults stipulate the self of the child to be constituted continuously through numerical age. Children are made to become individuals who learn to count themselves into being through the exact addition of years. They learn to refer to, and to be referred by, these blocks of age. This is a segmentary, arithmetic continuity through time. These celebrations adumbrate age categories as numerical classifiers that signify time. Counting these numbers signifies increases in time that are unidirectional; one only grows older, becoming bigger, as in the following example.

After Oranit's garlanding, the teacher asked, "How old is Oranit? One year [she held up one finger]? Two years [she added a second finger]? No and no. Oranit is three years old [she held up three fingers]. And in Oranit's garland there are three flowers . . . one, two, and three, and one for next year." The teacher sang, "Yes, may you have a fourth birthday next year," and the children joined in, "Oranit is three years old. She was so, so small, and now she is so big. . . . Another year and another year and another year and we'll be big!"

Age categories as temporal classifiers are evident in the candle lighting (VI) and chair lifting (VIII) at Amir's party. The birthday child is identified with the number of candles—that is, with his reclassification. The order of candle lighting enunciates the co-presence of three age categories within the same family, activated in order of descending age. Grandmother, the most historical, lights the first candle, Mother the second, and Amir the third. This order is also that of three generations, related to one another both as kin and as members of different temporal categories within a taxonomy of generations. In this taxonomy, age not only separates but also relates persons to one another through their temporal differences.

The chair lifting also recapitulates the child's life through the enumeration of age categories. Each lift is higher, the number of the year called out in louder voice. Each elevation signifies the joyful growth of the child, year added to year, through the present and toward the future, in a taxonomy of being composed of blocks of time.[9]

(3) *Messages of temporal continuity.* The inculcation of the continuous flow of time is the necessary complement to taxonomic fragmentation by age. The continuity of the time-self, and of self in relation to other, is essential to self-recognition and autobiography. In the previous subsection we noted the kind of temporal continuity that emerges directly from the recounting of a sequence of categories of numerical age. This continuity is arithmetic. Adding together blocks of age, it gains coherence through chronological symmetry.

But birthday celebrations also practice a temporal continuity whose message is the unbroken synthesis of time. Here time is made to flow, without the abrupt disjunctions in shifting from one age category to another. This kind of continuity was encountered in the celebrations of Oranit ("She was so, so small, and now she is so big") and Gil ("So you're already big and not small"). Here size is a metaphor for age. The references to changes in size—then small, now big—are more ambiguous than the abrupt lurch from one age category to the next. Small turns into big through the continuous weaving and blending of strands of experience.

This seamless synthesis of the child's life course is holistic, rather than arithmetic. Its experiential significance suffuses the integrity of its entirety.

This kind of temporal continuity is most pronounced through brief biographical narratives, usually told by parents about the birthday child. These narratives provide the child with a past that grows and flows into the present and beyond but that does not depend on the absolute discontinuities of age classification. Time becomes profoundly integrative as the significant context within which the entirety of the child—past, present, future—takes shape. These narratives give the child a biography that tells how he has grown into his own present and provide an accounting of this from an adult perspective. At Amir's party (IV), his mother begins even before the birth, which is described as a joyous occasion for the entire family. The mother-child bond is iterated immediately ("He had very big eyes, and he looked at me"), as it is also in the first game (VII) following the candle lighting. The narrative moves on to growing up—to sleeping, eating, the shift to more solid food, and then the mobility of crawling.

The teacher makes of this a performance that immediately recapitulates the sequence of development narrated by the mother. At his mother's behest, Amir demonstrates how a baby crawls (and so how he crawled, in his own past), and then at his teacher's, how a big boy walks. He then is freed to march independently through the living arches of children as they sing, "What's happened? . . . Our Amir is five years old." Indeed what has happened is the passing of an age threshold, leading to even more complex behavior. So this sequence ends with Amir and the teacher teaching Mother how to dance. Dance, compared to crawling and walking, is the most complex of these motor activities; while the teaching of this to Mother reverses the outset of the mother's narrative—when Amir was a helpless tot, utterly dependent on mother. The entire sequence, combining narrative and drama, is fraught with developmental implications. Being a baby, a person of little competence, is linked here to mother, home, and the past self of the child. Greater accomplishments are articulated to contexts independent of the home—to teacher, kindergarten, and the present self of the child, thrusting toward the future.[10]

Later in the party, in the first game (VII), the teacher further dramatizes the issue of Amir's development. Blindfolded, his mother must recognize Amir by her touch. This raises the question of whether Amir has changed so much that even his own mother will not recognize him. Yet here she shows that her personal knowledge of her son is justified. The biography she has given him is indeed his past. This reiteration of her intimacy with him likely brings his biography home to him with added force.

Many teachers encourage other children to participate spontaneously in biographical narratives, as was evident at a party for Orli, who turned five. The teacher asked Orli why she had received such a wonderful garland, and Orli replied that it was her birthday. The following interchanges ensued. Teacher: "What is a birthday?" Child (1): "It's the day on which she was born." Teacher: "How old is Orli today?" Child (1): "She's five years old." Teacher: "She's really big already. Was she born so big?" Child (1): "What do you mean, she's very small!" Child (2): "She was very, very small, and every year she grew a little more." Orli's mother described how small Orli had been, "like a little package," how she cried all the time, and how one could not know whether she was cold, hungry, or thirsty because she could not talk. Child (3): "Babies even can't walk." Orli's mother continued, describing Orli when she began to crawl; Orli's father added that Orli had crawled into every corner, pulling things down and breaking them. Child (3): "Babies are allowed to break things." Child (2): "But they should be taught it's forbidden." Grandmother: "But now she's already a big girl. She's good and understands everything." Teacher: "Orli is now really a big, and clever and good girl, and I'm sure she'll keep on growing and learning more new things."

Orli is described as a small, uncommunicative, and chaotic being who then crawls, but breaks things indiscriminately. Yet now she has become both a big girl and an organized, moral being who will continue to develop. These and other rudimentary stories emphasize the flow of the child's growth through time, as one kind of behavior changes gradually into another, almost without mention of exact age.

Far from being the mere foils of adults, the children who participate here affect the story line, opening and closing issues of development and morality. Thus when one insists that Orli is very small, another puts this in the past tense, adding that Orli is growing away from smallness. Further on, a child interjects that babies cannot walk, and then Orli's mother switches topics to speak of Orli's development of mobility. And when a child states that norms are relaxed for babies, for they "are allowed to break things," another responds that they must be taught that "it's forbidden." The ease and fluency of unrehearsed participation in biographical narratives indicates that such story lines about development through time have become integral to the pasts of children. They not only listen to biography but make it integral to their own sense of self. These children are both object and subject of their own discourse. They have become autobiographical beings who share biographical features with others because each and every one of them encompass the continuity of time within themselves (Miller et al. 1990).

The messages of temporal continuity through biographical narrative are quite different from those of a chronological continuum of age categories. The narratives transform qualities of the child through time, weaving these differences into an unbroken but ever-changing sequence of development. Amir is described as looking, that becomes eating, and then movement of different degrees of complexity (crawling, walking, dancing). These are accompanied by developments in social capabilities (from being taught by his mother to teaching her; from being dependent on his parents to becoming the first among equals in his class on this day). In these biographical narratives the qualities mentioned do not depend on exact age but on self-transformation. The self is made through time, yet it does not depend for its existence on any blocks of time. Instead, these narratives emphasize the holism and continuity of the time-self.

By contrast, the counting of numerical age (in candle lighting and chair lifting) establishes a continuum composed of equal but distinct intervals. This produces a segmentary synthesis of time. This continuum of the enumeration of age imposes an external taxonomic scheme on the child. This, too, is biography that produces autobiography. But this kind of synthesis enables the fragmentation of the individual along lines of absolute fracture—those of numerical age. In this version of the individual, he can be taken apart by himself and by others, arithmetically, statistically. In this kind of synthesis, qualities of the child are understood to derive from categories of age, not from one's inner development. Here age is crucial to comprehending capability. Thus qualities are an index of age; a child of a particular age is assumed to have the qualities that adults think correspond to that age.

Though these parties are joyous occasions for kindergarten children and families alike, they are full of tensions for the birthday child. Toward the close of his celebration, Amir burst into tears (IX, X). Crying by the birthday child is fairly common at these parties. The usual explanations are those of overexcitement and overtiredness. Still one should not overlook the abrupt move from one absolute age category to the next, nor the impact on the child of contradictions between kinds of temporal continuity. All discontinuities are wrapped by the teacher, parents, and peers in a mood of consensus on the positive value of exchanging ages. The birthday child is continuously congratulated on this, as if it were his own personal achievement. Yet the child may feel that he is trapped by this consensus into the new obligations expected of him. In the life of a child the demonstrative addition of a whole year's block of time may well feel weighty and intimidating. A tearful child commonly will declare, "I don't want a birthday party anymore" and look for refuge in his mother, teacher, or an empty room. Nonetheless, he is returned to the celebration, accompanied by admonitions that he is no longer a baby and should behave in accordance with his new age.[11]

More than a few students of childhood socialization argue that children discover worlds of meaning through collective, public processes (Corsaro 1988, 2). For most children in Israel, age is the very first attribute of the individual to be turned into a taxonomic classifier. Only later will they come to know other of their attributes (i.e., gender, education) as classifiers. In Israel, the meanings of age in the kindergarten birthday party are far more complex and polyphonic than common sense dictates. Furthermore, the party is a locus of messages that are crucial to the development of the child, as both adult and citizen imbued with values of the bureaucratic state. Yet these messages already seed the child with an elementary contradiction—between the self segmented and continuous—that is deeply embedded in the modern condition.

Age and Bureaucratic Ethos in the Statist Social Order

The introduction to this essay discussed the prominence of numerical age as a classifier of the individual in the modern Western social order. Age classification constitutes a taxonomy of time that articulates the individual's temporal order to that of social order. We then analyzed messages of temporality in birthday parties, arguing that young Israeli children participate frequently in organized experiences of individuation, reclassification, and an arithmetic temporal continuity. Conversely, they also experience a more synthetic temporal continuity that does not depend on numerical age, and that emphasizes the holistic integrity of selfhood. In conclusion, we argue that these experiences of a taxonomy of time are paradigmatic of socialization into the bureaucratic ethos that pervades modern states and their classification of the person. For the person in the statist order, bureaucratic classification constitutes ongoing experiences of individuation, reclassification, and the segmented continuity of self. In Israel the practice of these experiences begins in kindergarten and in birthday parties there.

Bureaucratic ethos is intently entwined with the conception and practice of exact classification. The power of statist orders depends in part on their control over the means of classification. The idea of taxonomy is integral to that of bureaucracy. The florescence of systematic taxonomic thinking in the West may be traced to Renaissance developments in science (Foucault 1973, 54). Pervasive ideas of taxonomy provided for the locating of all phenomena—including the political and the social—through the smallest of distinctions, in accordance with invented logics of classification (Foucault 1979, 195). So too, new political visions of the perfectly governed society depended on invented schemes of classification (Eliav-Feldon 1982, 45; Foucault 1979, 205). Social classification was most elaborated at the social peripheries, where persons were most vulnerable to surveillance and control (S. Cohen 1985, 191). Yet no less pervasive were the applications of social taxonomies invented by statist bureaucracies to the everyday lives of ordinary persons.[12]

Bureaucratic ethos refers here to values of the conscious, systematic, categorical classification of information. The ethos is epitomized when the same principles of classification operate throughout the taxonomy; when the criteria of classification are categorically exclusive and exhaustive; and when the boundaries of categories are those of absolute distinction rather than those of polythetic clustering. The bureaucratic vision of time is taxonomic: of exact divisions and equal intervals, amenable to numerical manipulation. Much bureaucratic work deals with the principled invention and application of taxonomies of all kinds, in order to organize numerous domains of living in statist social orders. Bureaucracies practice their taxonomies incessantly and systematically, molding phenomenal realities in part by altering the criteria of classifiers (Shamgar-Handelman 1981). Weber noted that real power is practiced through everyday administration in the modern state.

Numerous "means of production" are concentrated in bureaucracy and its political masters (Mayer 1944, 60–61; Rizzi 1985). Perhaps we should begin to speak of a bureaucratic mode of production: the ownership or management of the means to consciously produce and apply taxonomic schemes of social classification.

In statist social orders the kind of person who is most amenable to bureaucratic classification becomes a critical issue. The axioms of Western, statist bureaucracy enable it to fragment any social whole into its smallest units for purposes of social classification. This minimal unit is the individuated person, the individual. The individual is most compatible with bureaucratic ethos and vulnerable to classification. Bureaucratic classification recasts individuals as members of aggregates or cohorts who share only the taxonomic criteria that categorized them together. In this bureaucratic mode of production, no organic relationships need to be taken into account, a priori. Neither kin ties nor friendship links, social networks nor community, have any principled, cultural mandate to reject the arbitrary (in the sense that consciously it could be otherwise) selections of bureaucratic classification (see Handelman 1981, 6–12; Handelman 1990, 76–81). The irrelevance of these relationships for bureaucratic premises is thought a criterion of their universalistic objectivity.

Bureaucratic ethos individuates persons and aggregates them in categorical terms as individuals. Statist bureaucracies work most efficiently and cost-effectively with an individuated cosmos in which individuals are sorted into different social categories whose criteria are open to conscious change. From the perspective of bureaucracy, the individual is the sum of all the classificatory indices applied to him. In this statistical notion of the person, the more information available on each individual, the more adequate is his categorization. Information-processing technologies are the only real limitations on the complexity of this bureaucratized individual.

We argued earlier that numerical age individuates the person and is used as a prime classifier of the individual. This effectiveness of numerical age is attested by its widespread prominence in bureaucratic classification. This idea of exact age depends on a segmentary conception of time. This conception of time is common to bureaucratic ethos and to the modern individual. In addition, this conception of time harmonizes the individual to the bureaucratic order and, through the idea of numerical age, opens him to the taxonomic manipulations of bureaucracy.

Persons generally relate to the bureaucracies that classify and segment them as natural, commonsensical means of making order, albeit carried to excess on occasion. For all that the system is criticized, the alternatives usually entertained are patently utopian. Since persons feel the significance of numerical age through a taxonomy of time, bureaucratic ethos classifies them in ways felt also to be natural. In other words, we learn to be the kind of people who resonate with bureaucratic ethos.

Such learning begins early. Still, there is little information on contexts that communicate such messages and feelings to the young child. One study of American kindergartens concludes that their experiences prepare children to work in bureaucracies (Gracey 1972, 279). Another argues that the American nursery school provides bureaucratic-like experiences for young children (Kanter 1972, 203). Still another emphasizes that American nursery schools create "time-objectifying" structures, mirroring the temporal constraints of "planned time" in wider social orders (Suransky 1982, 185).

In Israel, the ubiquitous kindergarten birthday party practices experiences of taxonomic time and numerical age that are essential to individuation and to the bureaucratic classification of the individual. Simultaneously, the child also experiences himself through a temporal synthesis of the unbroken coherence of the time-self. The birthday party provides no immediate, experiential solution to this contradiction between temporal selves at once segmented and synthesized. Nonetheless, the Israeli kindergarten birthday party is explicitly a celebration of the individual and implicitly a celebration of bureaucratic ethos. This conjunction of individuation and bureaucratic ethos may be significant for other social orders organized through premises of bureaucracy. There we would expect statist efforts to inculcate children in the sorts of experiences discussed here. Bureaucratic order may well depend in part on individuals comprehending themselves as certain kinds of temporal beings.

Notes

We would like to thank Eyal Ben-Ari for his comments on an earlier version of this essay.

1. For the sake of convenience we use the masculine gender to refer to the child in general terms. For the theory of bureaucratic logic that informs this essay, see Handelman 2004.
2. Over the years there has been much continuity in these and other themes of kindergarten birthday celebrations (Katerbursky 1962). In a description from the 1930s (Haskina 1941), the birthday child—wearing a crown and holding the Zionist flag—leads the children into the kindergarten to open the party, thus conjoining the celebration of individualism and nationalism.
3. Certain activities (i.e., garlanding) tend to appear near the beginning of parties, and others (i.e., lifting the child, gift giving) toward their close. These activities do frame some sense of sequencing, but one less definite than has otherwise been noted (Weil 1986).
4. Ethnographies of kindergartens were collected during the course of a seminar on this subject conducted by Lea Shamgar-Handelman at the Hebrew University. The ethnographers were supervisors of Jewish secular kindergartens, employed by the Ministry of Education, who observed kindergartens that they themselves supervised and with which they were conversant. Dialogues with the ethnographers and comments of teachers convinced us that the distinction between explicit and implicit designs of ceremonials was valid. These educators consistently understood birthday parties as the celebration of individual age, and nothing more. They did not acknowledge that the messages of these enactments implicitly saturated the education of children with bureaucratic, statist perspectives. There is very little material on birthday parties in instruction books and education journals. This deals in the main with how, rather than why, to celebrate.
5. In legend this is the age to which Moses lived; it is also a traditional benediction.
6. Ten songs, all joyful, were sung during the party. During birthday parties songs are used to shift children in unison from one kind of activity to the next. All the birthday songs mentioned in this essay rhyme in Hebrew. Kalkin-Fishman (1981) argues that the internalization of musical rhythm is used to inculcate control in Israeli kindergartens. To musical rhythm should be added those of rhymed song texts.
7. Our usage generally follows Dumont (1977, 1986) in distinguishing the individual from the social person. In this regard, the person is a negotiated social being composed of personae and roles, and therefore one whose holism is constituted and reconstituted through give-and-take with others, in a Meadian sense. By contrast, the individual is constituted as an autonomous, irreducible being, a holistic unit in and of itself. This conception of the individual is one basis for a statistical, bureaucratic notion of personhood in the modern West.
8. From a functionalist perspective, such symmetrical exchange ultimately engenders solidarity ties. However, in this instance we maintain that the route to this sort of conclusion—through the interplay of the generic and the unique—is of greater significance.
9. Through these activities the child practices the time continuum from opposite perspectives. The order of candle lighting proceeds from oldest (grandmother) to youngest (grandson), while the chair lifting begins with the age of one and ends in the child's future. For that matter, these two perspectives are conjoined in the candle lighting. The six candles signify the child's temporal continuum. However, lit in the order of generations, the child's temporal continuum recapitulates the history of his family.
10. Such short developmental sequences also implicate the transfer of control and primary loyalty of the child from family to state (Shamgar-Handelman and Handelman 1986).

11. Following Plessner (1970), crying during the celebration may signify the capitulation of the child to the social forces that are manipulating and redefining his relationships to others and to himself. Crying is the acquiescence of his body to this co-optation, and simultaneously the control of body over self. Crying thereby performs the surrender of the self to power beyond its control.
12. Max Weber's (1964, 329–40) ideal type of rational-legal bureaucracy is a form of organization designed to taxonomize information—to name and categorize phenomena—and to act on what it classifies. This perspective is discussed in Handelman (1981, 6–12). Our argument is phrased deliberately, if crudely, in terms of Western bureaucratic ethos, in recognition that groups no less than individuals may be used as minimal units of bureaucratic classification, and that there is evidence of this from other statist orders.

8

The Vanishing of High-Moral, Servant Leaders and the Decay of Democratic, High-Trust Cultures in the Kibbutz Field

REUVEN SHAPIRA

Introduction

What is the connection between leaders' morality and the performance of organizations? Can their morality explain, through trust, the dynamics of organizational cultures? Blalock Jr. (1989, 123) says that "the notion of 'trust' is a bit slippery," and while Bradach and Eccles (1989) perceive trust as one of three types of social control, which together with market and hierarchy creates plural forms, others see trust as an alternative to market and hierarchy: capitalist firms are based on market and hierarchy and tend to be low trust and coercive, while the kibbutz is based on high trust, democracy, and minimal coercion (Fox 1974; Riker 1974; Shapira 1987; Rosner 1993). However, even within capitalist settings many high-trust organizational cultures engender effectiveness, innovation, and prosperity (Guest 1962; Dore 1973; Rohlen 1974; Ring and Van de Ven 1992; Semler 1993; Fukuyama 1995), though the exact causality is not very clear. Hosmer concluded his review of organizational trust thusly: "If researchers can show empirically that there is a connection—through trust—between the moral duty of officers and the output performance of organizations, there would be an obvious impact upon philosophical ethics and—I would like to think—upon organizational theory as well" (1995, 400). For Hosmer, trust is based on one's expectation of ethically justifiable behavior on the part of the other person(s); ethically justifiable behavior consists of morally correct decisions and actions in which the "interests of society take the degree of precedence that is right, just and fair over the interests of individuals" (399). Thus defined, it is clearly relevant to Michels's (1959 [1915]) "Iron Law of Oligarchy": the head of a large organization in his decay phase (Hambrick and Fukutomi 1991) betrays participants' trust by self-serving conservatism aimed at continuity, enlarging personal and staff privileges, promoting and rewarding only personal loyalists, shifting organizational goals to serve his own aims, and thus castrating democracy by various means. Opposite examples of high-moral deeds conducive to trust were George Washington's and Thomas Jefferson's refusals of a third term in office (in 1797 and 1809, respectively), limiting Iron Law's deleterious effects on U.S. democracy by an eight-year norm for presidents. Other organizations used a norm of periodic officers' replacement (hereafter Rotation). Latin America's presidents are Rotated by constitutions that bar second terms (Mainwaring 1990), officers of ancient Athens were Rotated yearly (Fuks 1976), and China's district magistrates had three-year terms (Chow 1966), as did officers of U.S. and Israeli armies (Gabriel and Savage 1981; Vald 1987), Israeli universities, and kibbutzim (Leviatan 1992).

However, did Rotation really prevent the Iron Law and distrust caused by self-serving continuous leaders? This essay examines this question by using the framework of kibbutzim, whose innovative and adaptive cultures have recently declined. Both their decline and previous long success will be explained by a new, revolutionary paradigm (Kuhn 1962) that perceives them and their hundreds of federative organizations (hereafter FOs) as a field (Bourdieu and Wacquant 1992), contrary to customary kibbutz research (CKR), which ignored FOs even though thousands of kibbutz members administered them and their heads dominated the field by Iron Law continuity, enhanced rather than prevented by Rotation of lower-level officers. However, the new paradigm's task is not simple, since it has to explain many decades of kibbutz innovation while the field was dominated by FO heads' conservatism. Moreover, this task is complicated since crucial behaviors of FO heads and executives as members of their respective kibbutzim were rarely studied because of CKR ignorance of FOs.

The Kibbutz Field's Sudden Decline from Adaptive Creativity

The kibbutz communal movement, with 270 kibbutzim and 125,000 inhabitants, was a leading force in the creation of a Jewish homeland and establishment of the state of Israel (Kanari 1989; Near 1992, 1997). It has been described as "a highly successful enterprise by virtue of its longevity . . . as well as any other criterion by which the success of social systems is judged," as well as "adaptive and highly creative" (Krausz 1983, 4). Moreover, it remained adaptive and creative long after the idealism of the first generation's pioneers had vanished, when primarily second-generation pragmatists made main decisions, introducing industrialization, higher education, and regional cooperation into agricultural cultures (Gamson 1977; Don 1988; Niv and Bar-On 1992).

However, during the recent past the kibbutzim have been troubled by a huge debt crisis, with few signs of the creative innovation that once distinguished them, preferring instead conservatism, bureaucracy, and technocracy (Ben-Rafael 1988, 1996). Their industry, formerly innovative, remained in mature sectors, rather than turning to high-tech areas (Leviatan 1997), and suffered from brain-drain (Sheaffer and Helman 1994). When executives of their main FO faced dilemmas, they avoided decisions (Avrahami 1993). Kibbutzim imitated the surrounding society, used its concepts, and reinterpreted their values accordingly (Kressel 1992b; S. Ravid 1992). They lack trusted leaders: officers did not view themselves as leaders, nor did most members see them as such, and often with good reason (Kressel 1991; Leviatan 1992). Officers often turned to outside consultants whose solution packages rarely help ailing kibbutzim and instead engender distrust and paralysis of organized change in many cases (Shapira 1993; Pavin 1994; Bien 1995).

How, then, can one explain the relatively sudden reversal, whereby creativity vanished and was replaced by conservative imitation of capitalist society? Why has the democracy practiced by kibbutzim with relative success for three quarters of a century failed to produce leaders able and willing to cope with their crisis by creative innovation, as had been the case in the past? Has Rotation really prevented the Iron Law, or has the Law somehow reigned, even though CKR did not expose this and its deleterious effects? But if this is the case, how have most kibbutzim remained "adaptive and highly creative" for so many decades, and why have they lost creativity recently?

Kibbutzim and FOs: Creativity versus Imitation of Capitalist Firms

Kibbutzim are democratic, self-managed organizations, owned and managed by their members/workers. Managerial creativity is vital to their unique cultures, and its loss threatens their long-term viability (Stryjan 1989). Initially successful, such organizations eventually failed, as success led to growth, which led to imitation of capitalist firms (i.e., hired labor, hierarchy, bureaucracy, and stratification), declining democracy, and conservatism (i.e., the minimizing of change). Stryjan explained the success of kibbutzim in their use of a federative structure, optimally combining the advantages of small units, which have remained creative (i.e., devised original solutions to problems) and shared creative solutions among themselves, and their use of federative organizations (FOs) that performed functions for which each kibbutz is too small.

FOs are ubiquitous: Hamashbir Hamerkazi supply FO was founded in 1916, Tnuva marketing FO in 1925, and kibbutz national federations (hereafter NFOs) in 1927–29 (Near 1992). At their peak, the mid-1980s, NFOs and their subsidiaries were administered by some 2,500 kibbutz members called *pe'ilim* (activists), who enjoyed the use of 900 company cars (Yadlin 1989; Lifshitz 1990) and employed many hired workers. Another FO type, Regional Enterprises, consisted of twelve commercial-industrial concerns with some 110 plants, 1,200 *pe'ilim,* almost each with a company car, and 7,000–8,000 hired workers (Atar 1982; Bar-On and Shelhav 1984). These FOs and a hundred others imitated capitalist firms' multilayer hierarchies; hence car models and ages were finely graded in accordance with *pe'ilim* ranks in FO hierarchies (Tzur 1980; Shapira 1987).

Stryjan ignored the possible negative impact of large, hierarchic, stratified FOs on kibbutz democracy and creativity. He followed CKR, which perceived FOs as external, not part of the kibbutz field. Hence, studies of FOs have been rare (cf. Krausz 1983), and much of my FO data is from non-research sources although a kibbutz is defined as a "community affiliated to a NFO and is misunderstood outside this context" (Rosolio 1993, 10). Kibbutzim have carried out national missions, and FOs have been the vehicles through which Israeli society rewarded them (Ya'ar, Ben-Rafael, and Soker 1994). FOs were also dominant because they controlled vital kibbutz interests and their heads and deputies generally held the same office for decades, compared with a few years for kibbutz Rotational officers (Lifshitz 1983; Arieli 1986; Ringel-Hofman 1988). Main NFO heads, Tabenkin, Ya'ari, and Hazan, held their positions for forty, fifty, and fifty-seven years, respectively, and they and twelve of their deputies became Knesset (parliament) members for twenty to thirty years (Shavit 1985; *Kibbutz*, 20 May 1987; Near 1997; Tzachor 1997). Some deputies were cabinet ministers, one was deputy prime minister, and another held the position of deputy prime minister informally.

In accordance with Iron Law, continuity turned high-moral, hard-working, austere, radical leaders of the 1920s–1940s into self-serving, privileged conservatives. In the early 1950s, midway through their half a century of dominance, Ya'ari and Hazan of the Artzi NFO rejected all new ideas raised by kibbutz officers to help with the huge national task of absorbing a million immigrants (Kynan 1989) and sidetracked innovative leaders of the new generation (Beilin 1984; Dagan and Yakir 1996). Tabenkin, who headed the Meuchad NFO (Kafkafi 1992), acted similarly. The Regional Enterprises were conservative both in their technological and social choices: employees had no say in management, nor was there any gain-sharing, while *pe'ilim* were a privileged group that received generous benefits (Atar 1982; Shapira 1987, 1995b). NFO heads enjoyed minister-style large American cars with chauffeurs (Tzachor 1997, 180) and promoted loyalists who eventually succeeded them, but they lacked critical thinking (Hirschman 1970) and continued anachronistic policies: in 1982 heads of the Takam NFO (an amalgamation of the Meuchad and Ichud NFOs) promoted "national missions" as if it were the 1930s–1940s (Rosolio 1999, 61).

Kibbutz versus FO Cultures: The Moral Dimension

While kibbutz internal Rotational officers have a heavy workload and responsibility without formal rewards, continuous *pe'ilim* usually have a lighter workload, similar responsibility, and ample rewards (Shapira 1987). Regional Enterprises *pe'ilim* legitimized privileges by self-aggrandizement: plants were allegedly enlarged owing to economies of scale and other advantages for kibbutzim, which were refuted upon close scrutiny (Shapira 1978–79). Kibbutz officers were coerced into supporting this growth, as their subsequent careers were largely dependent on senior *pe'ilim* (Shapira 1995a). NFOs supported capitalist industrialization of kibbutzim, by few members managing hundreds of hired workers (Kressel 1974), and opposed kibbutz egalitarianism: in the 1960s, as the number of *pe'ilim* cars soared, some kibbutzim initiated sharing them on weekends. FOs' resistance slowed down the proliferation of the norm to other kibbutzim and caused widespread violation (Ginat 1981; Atar 1982; Shapira 1993).

FOs' behavior raises the question as to which moral commitments (Etzioni 1988) had influenced *pe'ilim*. Russell (1991) found FOs of Israel's urban cooperatives aimed mainly at controlling their member cooperatives rather than promoting their cause. The above-mentioned low-moral deeds by *pe'ilim* indicate that kibbutz FOs were no different, and this is explained by the low morality of FO heads. However, did these heads behave the same as influential kibbutz members in their respective kibbutzim, or were some of them high-moral servant leaders (Graham 1991) who preferred public interests over their own (Hirschman 1982) in the other context, that of the kibbutz? Did they back democratic rule while opposing many decisions initiated by kibbutz officers? A leader's actions have more impact than his assertions (Geneen 1984). Did such high morality explain the successful high-trust cultures in some kibbutzim where free flow of knowledge enhanced problem-solving (Zand 1972) and innovation risks by creative officers (Ring and Van de Ven 1992; Shapira 1995b)? Could imitation of these creative kibbutzim by most others explain the creativity and adaptability of the kibbutz movement for seven decades?

Moreover, as a result, Rotation kibbutz chief officers were relatively young (mostly thirty to forty years old) and had been junior figures in the field controlled by FO heads. Nevertheless, some of these juniors defied seniors and initiated egalitarian norms such as sharing FO company cars. Can the high morality of three powerful, and quite conservative, FO heads, who dominated a particular kibbutz, explain the fact that the juniors' innovation succeeded although it negated the views of these heads and taxed *pe'ilim* privileges? Could the low morality of power elites at a liberal kibbutz, which, according to Peters and Austin (1986), would have been expected to be innovative, explain its anarchic conservatism (Shapira 1993)? And, more generally, did kibbutz decline result from the vanishing of high-moral leaders and the rise of lower-moral, self-serving powerholders who caused descending trust spirals that stopped original solutions and ruined uniqueness?

Methodology, Kibbutzim, and the Case of Rama

The extended case method (Burawoy et al. 1991) is employed in order to investigate the above questions. Though the reader would benefit from a fuller profile of the four kibbutzim studied, due to space limitations and ample previous publications on the kibbutzim, only crucial differences among the four cases will be provided. As historical context and environmental forces were much the same with the two pioneers established in the 1920s, their detailed comparison will make up the main proof that powerholders' behavior was the dominant factor in creating and changing cultures. The two younger kibbutzim will be dealt with briefly, only as proof that their cases do not negate the main thesis. A fuller ethnography proving this in detail is in preparation.

I will commence with a medium-size kibbutz (650 inhabitants), which I shall call Rama (some details have been changed to preserve anonymity). This case will expose a causal link among low-moral, self-serving powerholders, distrust, lack of creativity, decline of democracy and egalitarianism, and FOs' oligarchization. Then Rama will be compared to successful Kochav (almost 1,000 inhabitants), which is distinguished by creativity and egalitarianism. It was studied earlier during fieldwork that took fifteen months to complete. In addition to observations and a study of its records, information was gathered from 123 people, mostly officers and *pe'ilim* of all ranks and generations, as well as ex-members who became nationally prominent. They were mostly formally interviewed; interviews lasted between thirty minutes and several hours, and some interviewees were accorded several sessions. In the two younger (established in 1949 and 1954) and smaller kibbutzim (450 and 300 inhabitants, respectively, in 1990–91), which were studied previously (Fadida 1972; Topel 1979), fieldwork lasted three months in each and involved a study of records, observations, and interviews with 35 and 29 people, respectively, much like what had been done in Kochav. In Rama similar fieldwork took six months, but in this case no ex-members were among the 51 interviewees, who included most of its chief officers during 1986–92, sector managers, committee heads, outside workers, and others. None of the members of Rama who read the research report expressed reservations, further strengthening the validity of the findings.

Rama has approximately 400 members and 250 children. During 1990–92, its membership decreased by 30, and the total number of its inhabitants by 50. While less committed youngsters left, families stayed, twelve new families were absorbed, and others applied for membership. Such relative stability, despite a deteriorating economic situation and standard of living, resembled other kibbutzim (Maron 1997) and can be explained, inter alia, by Israel's unemployment and housing problems at the time (R. Cohen 1991). Rama is encumbered by a fairly average debt. As a result of late and conservative industrialization, it depended until recently mainly on agriculture, which had become less profitable. Its plastics plant, the main business, employs 60 workers, most of whom were hired, and sells mature products in shrinking markets, both domestic and for export. More profitable are a small chemical plant with 15 employees, most of whom are kibbutz members, several workshops (3 or 4 workers each), and a new food plant with 25 employees, established after outside consultants forecast a further decline in the plastics plant. The latter is based on imported expertise and hired labor.

Another change was that various service branches sought outside business: a small museum was enlarged and became a tourist attraction, and a kibbutz old-age home, dental clinic, nurseries, elementary school, high school, and workshops began serving outside clients. Parallel to this outside work by members increased and was legitimized by setting a minimal condition: that members be paid at least the national average wage. However, because of employer taxes, having a member work outside and hiring an outsider to take his place at the kibbutz is worthwhile only if the outsider is paid much less than the member. Usually this has not been the case. Alas, outflow of labor from the kibbutz has risen. "The kibbutz's ability to assign members to jobs is negligible," confessed its chief work officer; thus hired labor supplanted outside workers.

The outflow of labor was also related to Rama's plants' use of hired labor, as it encouraged labor-intensive, tedious techniques (Zamir 1979), deterred women from taking industrial jobs, and caused conservatism and brain-drain (Shapira 1979, 1980). Both the manager and chief engineer of the plastics plant moved to top jobs in neighboring kibbutzim. Their know-how and expertise commanded high salaries, company cars, and expense accounts that elevated their status. Yet the kibbutz loses: without the engineer, the plant has lost its remaining technological edge, while the manager's exit helped thwart a major change of which he had been the main driving force, and which would have generated revenues many times greater than the outside salary he brought in. Much the same happened in the garage with the chief mechanic. An experienced cook turned to baking cakes at an urban wedding hall for a very modest wage even though she was much needed at the kitchen. This is common in today's kibbutzim (Leviatan 1995); their values lost meaning and personal motives guided behavior (March and Olsen 1989, 131).

Outside work has magnified problems of equity, the solutions to which were often unfair and caused widespread distrust. Many outside workers held company cars, so the kibbutz decided it would provide a car for anyone with a salary of over $3,000 a month (6,000 new Israeli shekels). This was not fair for male members earning $1,801–3,000: if they received a car costing $300–400 a month, they would still be bringing in more than the required national average of $1,400. However, the cook mentioned above was allowed outside work, even though her employer deducted $250 from her $1,000 salary (the minimum required for women) for her company car. This was a clear circumvention of the norm without a convincing explanation. Another woman, a qualified and highly paid professional, did not receive a car for several part-time outside jobs, preventing her from continuing her outside work.

Such decisions have limited outside employment and eased some kibbutz worker shortage, but its values were undermined, as in many other cases of unfair norms or unfair implementation by officers, who sometimes do not even abide by their own rules. The new uses of outside markets were presented as a necessity in a bad situation that required any kind of solution, but they were selective and opportunistically used by officers. Trust was ruined as "the interests of society" did not "take the degree of precedence that is right, just and fair over the interests of individuals" (Hosmer 1995, 399).

Violations of Egalitarian Norms by the Talented Power Elite

However, market forces were used opportunistically also by outside workers who followed the low morality of veteran elites, including *pe'ilim*. For example, after work and on the weekends kibbutz cars have to be at the disposal of all members, according to a car-sharing norm adopted long ago. However, this norm was not enforced in the case of three high-status professionals who worked outside, for whom Rama had purchased cars some years earlier, despite members' complaints and bitter criticism by present and past kibbutz secretaries.

> They [the three violators] attained powerful positions and determined norms their fellow members no longer have the strength to cope with. All those who violate norms have tall trees to lean on. For instance, G. [a professional with his own office in town] does whatever he wants, as if it was his own car, he buys a new one every other year and has not put it at the disposal of other members, despite its being formally owned by the kibbutz.

The speaker did not mention some *pe'ilim* who had done the same ever since the car-sharing norm was adopted. Moreover, from time immemorial some *pe'ilim* violated egalitarianism by acquiring luxury goods with money saved from expense allowances received from FOs or which they had obtained as gifts from high officials with whom they became acquainted as *pe'ilim*. Authors, editors, professors, and professionals with successful outside careers acted similarly. Let us call the latter the Talented Elite, to be distinguished from the competing Economic Elite of *pe'ilim* and ex-*pe'ilim*. The Talented Elite subdued Rama's Rotational officers and violated egalitarian decisions owing to their prestige, independent resources, and considerable influence, rendering them immune to negative sanctions against norm violators. In one case efforts to impose a norm on a rebellious editor caused him to relinquish formal membership while remaining a resident because of his wife's membership. He stopped giving Rama his salary and paid only a small fraction of the real cost of the services his family received from the kibbutz; later, six others followed suit.

So, who would accept authority jobs that had little power and no formal rewards? Past treasurers and economic managers who became *pe'ilim* and accumulated power, prestige, and privileges by circulating in managerial jobs help provide an answer.

The Kibbutz Career Ladder, FOs, and the Economic Power Elite

CKR ignored FOs and the power and various kinds of capital (Bourdieu 1996) *pe'ilim* accumulated there, though Rosenfeld (1951) found that some of them held supreme status in a kibbutz. However, neither she nor others saw FO jobs as the main career ladder of kibbutz officers, which helps explain the acceptance of powerless and negatively remunerated internal kibbutz offices. Internal offices were short term, while lucrative FO jobs could last for the rest of one's working life when taking into account job circulation (see below), and provided ample prospects for promotion. But CKR did not study officer careers, although the higher probability of kibbutz economic managers and treasurers becoming *pe'ilim* compared to secretaries (Helman 1987) can explain better than the reasons provided by Am'ad and Palgi (1986) why it was harder to fill secretary jobs. A related reason was the dominance of economic discourse in the kibbutz field (R. Cohen 1978).

Such dominance was revealed in 1987 when Rama's norm of boarding children in nurseries with their peers was changed to boarding with parents. However, at that time, funds for enlarging flats were scarce. Most of the families put their children up in the modest living room of their tiny, fifty-square-meter, one-and-a-half room flats, with no solution in the foreseeable future. Soon afterward the norm of collective construction collapsed. The father of the first family to build an addition to his house at his own expense was the non-member editor mentioned above. He was encouraged by many members who saw no prospective solution to their plight. Soon other non-members followed, and then others, until private construction was formally authorized.

However, private construction was not restricted to those who needed it for boarding children; among the first to enlarge their flats after authorization were middle-aged (forty-five to sixty years old) members of the Economic Elite, present or past *pe'ilim* without small children, who had extra money from fringe benefits derived from FO or other outside jobs. On the other hand, as Rama's economic committee members, they found little kibbutz money to enlarge other people's flats, though they did find a relatively large sum, $120,000, for new offices for the food factory, an expenditure the factory manager had deemed inessential. Thus they ignored the plight of half of the kibbutz, preferring a lower-moral alternative, a marginal interest of their sector.

Self-serving tactics were also used against potential new leaders, innovative young sector officers whose success could threaten elites' standing (Stryjan 1989, 90). Following other kibbutzim, a young consumption manager proposed to budget electricity, which had previously been provided free of charge and had caused much waste. In other kibbutzim, budgeting had led to savings of 20 to 25 percent, in addition to infrastructure savings. His suggestion was thwarted, despite five years of planning and information gathering on consumption habits that made it quite simple to budget without causing injustice to anyone. Two female officers of preschool education initiated a policy of accepting outside toddlers for a fee, and persuaded the nursery teams to make the necessary extra effort through their own example of hard work. However, the economic committee refused to allocate any of the profits accrued to a renewal of the old buildings and a modest purchase of toys. The two officers resigned, ostensibly as part of ordinary Rotation, but interviews showed frustration. Pretending it was a usual Rotation, they prevented any appearance of criticism that might have damaged future managerial careers (Shapira 1995a). A similar instance also occurred in one of the kibbutz's farm branches.

Pe'ilim *Circulation, "Parachuting," and Patronage Regimes*

Fears by the Economic Elite of the rise of junior officers are better understood when one considers the overall threat to its power and standing. Its control of main kibbutz decisions was limited by some juniors who had already been promoted to chief offices and by the power of the Talented Elite. Other factors were the need of most of its members to find new managerial jobs every three to five years, their problematic circumstances in these jobs as "parachuted" officers (see below), and the dependency of job continuity and promotion in FOs on loyalty to conservative patrons, mostly FO heads.

FOs enabled *pe'ilim* to preserve and enhance their status, power, and privileges by circulating among their thousands of administrative jobs. Without preserving their status by circulation, very few would have left lucrative FO jobs at the end of a short term (Shapira 1995a). However, even if a job opening was found, obtaining it and succeeding in it were difficult tasks. As in similar circumstances in the United States (Maccoby 1976), the honesty and sincerity of FO officers were poor (Shapira 1987). Rotation accentuated short-term perspectives, which were especially prone to distrust and lack of cooperation, causing failures (Chow 1966; Jay 1972; Axelrod 1984). FO jobs were also hazardous because "parachuting" (as it is called in Israel) to an unfamiliar unit renders one a complete outsider, lacking knowledge of people, technology, domains of authority, and industry problems, much as a paratrooper on enemy land. His superior could arrange to have him sent back to his kibbutz, ostensibly by the kibbutz's own request (Shapira 1995a). Success was largely dependent on hired foremen and technicians, some of whom competed for the job the "parachuted" officer gained, and who for a variety of other reasons were unreliable (Shapira 1987). Creating mutual trust with them required risky self-exposure (Zand 1972). Prone to failure as a result of a dearth of local and tacit knowledge (Geertz 1973a; Dodgson 1993), with all the implications of failure for career prospects, "parachuted" officers mostly preferred coercion (Kipnis 1976), were ineffective, shifted efforts to private aims (Hirschman 1982), and were caught in a vicious circle of distrust and tricks to defend status (Shapira 1995b).

Moreover, even if effective, an officer's continuity was dependent on a conservative, less- or non-Rotated FO head to whom he must prove his loyalty (Hirschman 1970). Heads of Regional Enterprise FOs concerns nominated loyalists as deputies and plant managers, thus strengthening cliques aimed at dominating decision-making and helping each other's promotion (Dalton 1959; Shapira 1987). Patronage regimes were also crucial in the three other kibbutzim studied here. Each was dominated by three patrons who accumulated preeminent power by being among the first kibbutz chief officers, advancing to the status of *pe'ilim,* and sometimes returning to manage the kibbutz for a while or settling into powerful behind-the-scenes posts such as comptroller, as happened at Rama, or other pivotal offices (Leshem 1969). Patrons nurtured loyal clients who had been promoted with patrons' help to chief kibbutz offices and then to FO jobs (Fadida 1972; Topel 1979; Dangoor 1994). Thus officer careers were dependent on patrons who rarely promoted radical creative junior officers, in accord with Hirschman (1970). Moreover, FO jobs were filled through old-boy networks of patrons; thus a patron controlled promotion not only to FO jobs under his jurisdiction but also to many others through his FOs' network of relationships.

The Rotation norm exacerbated Hirschman's (1970) negative selection of radical creative officers in promotion by guaranteeing their early removal from successful jobs into career paths that sidetracked them. The most talented and ambitious usually left to succeed on the outside, or turned to outside careers like Rama's "tall trees," while others "left inside" found a relatively autonomous interesting job, declining any managerial office (Shapira 1990; Am'ad and Palgi 1986). Thus the conservatism of Rama's low-moral Economic Elite was also a result of selective promotion of officers, which favored uncritical loyalists over radicals.

Low-Moral Conflicting Power Elites, Ailing Democracy, and Failed Remedies

Rama's conservatism can also be explained by the rivalry, both open and latent, between power elites. The Economic Elite and its followers controlled the money and the economy, most promotions to FOs, and most general assembly decisions, but failed to enforce decisions on Talented Elite members whose success provided an alternative career path to FO career ladders. Moreover, the Economic Elite's dubious morality caused much distrust, while some Talented, former kibbutz chief officers who did not advance to FOs because of their radicalism and turned to professional careers were highly trusted by many members. This trust also helps explain some of the latter's violation of decisions initiated by the Economic Elite that did not result in a public outcry.

Low-moral power elites thwarted efforts by Rotational officers to solve problems democratically, and anarchy caused Rama to be considered "liberal" by both members and outsiders. Liberalism is usually associated with innovation (Peters and Austin 1986), but the opposite was true here. Similar to other conservative kibbutzim, management staffing was problematic (Am'ad and Palgi 1986). Many talented members preferred outside careers (Gelbard 1993), creating a self-enhancing process: innovation fell prey to managerial incompetence, and creative junior officers, perceived as threatening by weak seniors, were sidetracked. Furthermore, rivalry between power elites made innovation especially risky, as it was anyone's guess as to who would violate a decision and who would follow suit; nor was it clear whether officers' authority would be upheld at all.

The lack of communal solutions to escalating problems eroded involvement in Rama's public life (Hirschman 1982), undermining the authority of democratic organs. The general assembly "dried up" (Kressel 1983, 154): only a handful of members continued to attend regularly, while most did so only when interested in the topics on the agenda. In accordance with Parkinson's (1957) Law, crucial topics were often dealt with in brief discussions involving few members. Often, interested parties would appeal a decision and reverse it by mobilizing support. General assembly decisions lost the legitimacy of representing public judgment (Yankelovich 1991). Two former secretaries tried a remedy: a ballot box vote, whereby not only those in general assembly attendance could vote. This practice, however, was limited to the acceptance of new members. Thus, the main problem, public democratic authority on other crucial matters, was not solved.

Other secretaries failed likewise. In general they were inexperienced, came from the ranks, and were expected to return there (A. Helman 1987). Weakness drove them to various subterfuges. For instance, a decision to construct sixteen flats of a special type was handled by one secretary without consulting the planning committee, whose chairman was known to oppose it. Other committees were eliminated and information monopolized by officers, as in other crisis-ridden kibbutzim (Zamir 1996). Resistance to change grew with members' distrust of officers' integrity, perceiving them as impostors without much credibility (Kets de Vries 1993; Kouzes and Posner 1993).

Without trusted leaders, the economic crisis also became a social one: youngsters left while communal activities declined and were later abandoned, as is usual in cooperatives during periods of downturn (Hirschman 1984). Interviews indicated feelings of helplessness, distrust, and suspicion concerning others' morality, as happened in a backward, low-trust Italian village with selfish officers (Banfield 1958). The kibbutz social worker stated, "The kibbutz is stuck . . . the system is not working . . . committees that are still functioning have a great deal of responsibility but hardly any authority. All authority has been transferred to the economic committee and everything depends on them to the point of paralysis. All the others prefer not to take responsibility."

One of the main reasons for paralysis and backwardness was the separation of formal authority from power, a result of Rotation and "parachuting," much like Chow's (1966) findings in China. Informal powerholders evaded responsibility for public interest, and weak formal officers were unwilling or unable to risk grappling with challenges. A lack of creativity ruined self-management (Stryjan 1989), but unlike in Stryjan's analysis, FOs were crucial agents of the change. Prospects of promotion and circulation in FO jobs gave officers a good reason to play safe and refrain from radicalism, and *pe'ilim* circulation enhanced FO heads' Iron Law continuity, power, and conservatism, thus securing the suppressing of radical creatives before they gained much public trust required to overcome entrenched powers (Shapira 1995a).

A Comparative Perspective on the Loss of Creativity

Kochav is a veteran kibbutz that was initially similar to Rama. It coped with much the same hardships and used the same austerity measures. However, its democratic, egalitarian culture enhanced creativity and growth to some 1,000 people, one of the few kibbutzim of such size. However, Kochav is not among the richest kibbutzim and was only slightly better-off economically until the crisis, in which it suffered heavily. For instance, in 1985 alone its losses amounted to $3,500,000. However, by 2000 its economic and social situation was much better than that of Rama. For instance, almost all of Kochav's family flats had been enlarged within a few years after deciding to board children with parents. In contrast to Rama, Kochav's economic officers gave this project high priority, seeing it as their own responsibility.

One reason for success was early industrialization, which happened two decades before it did in Rama. At first, Kochav's factory used hired labor. In the early 1960s, new, young managers made hired labor redundant through automation, new products and technologies, a new shiftwork system in which kibbutz members who were non-factory workers participated, and later a new kind of partnership with another kibbutz. It wasn't until the late 1960s that Rama bought an old plant, which remained a technological latecomer and used hired labor at a time when kibbutz industry was innovative and almost all new plants used self-labor (Rosner 1992). Likewise, they differed in most farm branches, as well as in consumption. In 1962, Kochav pioneered the sharing of *pe'ilim* cars by all members after work hours and on weekends. Rama adopted the norm much later but never enforced it, as was noted. Kochav also pioneered self-service in the dining hall, which supplanted forcing members to take turns in unwanted waiters' jobs.

Kochav's innovation was largely due to the many talented people involved in its management; Rama's talented people sought outside careers (e.g., Gelbard 1993). Kochav's officers enjoyed strong authority, since they were trusted and considered among the most talented (the two groups were quite identical in education, age, and sex composition). Their managerial socialization began in minor kibbutz offices, where grassroots democracy taught how devotion to goals agreed upon by a team would be rewarded by dedicated work, which brought about their sector's success, rewarded by promotion to chief kibbutz offices. Many of Rama's chief officers lacked such socialization, as talented, successful branch managers were repressed by power elites, while less competent ones were promoted to chief offices.

Patrons' Morality, Role Modeling, and Creativity

Socialization, however, does not explain how and to what extent Kochav had avoided much of the negative effects of conservative FOs on managerial creativity for half a century, as promotion to FOs had been the main career ladder of its chief officers as well. Different powerholder morality helps explain this.

As explained above concerning patronage regimes, three patrons who were among the founding leaders of Kochav chose loyalists as successors when they turned to the founding of FOs or were promoted to existing ones. As FO heads or executives they later helped loyal clients' promotion to FOs. The vertical cliques thus created (Dalton 1959) provided mutual aid in promotion and dominated decision-making. Beginning in the 1950s patrons and cliques were conservative, used defensive tactics against radical officers, and foiled many of their initiatives and later promotion to FOs. Iron Law continuity in FO offices assured patrons' power (Shapira 1990), and Rotation exacerbated Hirschman's (1970) negative selection of radicals in promotion, guaranteeing their removal from jobs before or soon after original solutions succeeded, preventing them from capitalizing on their success and sidetracking their careers.

However, Hirschman's process came relatively late, as Rotation was not used in the kibbutz's first decades in some cases of successful officers who continued innovating before they had been promoted to be *pe'ilim* with the help of Kochav's would-be patrons, who were also innovative in those early days. Some of these *pe'ilim* also returned to minor offices or even to the ranks at the end of their term. In Rama, and more so in younger kibbutzim (see below), *pe'ilim* rarely returned to minor offices or to the ranks, while radicals were never promoted to FO jobs with patrons' help. Thus Kochav's patrons' early radical, visionary leadership (Bennis and Nannus 1986) created a truly democratic tradition in which radical creatives, including intellectuals and artists, thrived. Before FOs turned oligarchic, Kochav's patrons modeled asceticism that inspired high-moral dedication to egalitarianism. Moreover, even when they later became conservative FO oligarchs, they never emasculated democratic decisions after approval, and almost none of the 123 Kochav interviewees suspected them of objecting to inventions for personal reasons. This is in sharp contrast to Rama, where such accusations were common. Even some of their few critics grasped their conservatism as caring for the public good.

This high-moral tradition enabled Kochav's officers to persuade members to override patrons' opposition to radical changes such as industrialization. Later another wave of radical officers introduced shiftwork sharing, discontinued hired labor, and introduced creative solutions to inequality caused by growth and success, such as car sharing. Later self-service in the dining hall was introduced and was soon imitated by all kibbutzim and became the norm. However, Ran, the young kibbutz secretary who initiated and led car sharing and self-service introduction in the early 1960s, returned to a minor job, was promoted to an FO job once for a short term, and was not selected for another term in a kibbutz chief office, as was the case with many loyalists of patrons.

However, even many loyalists as kibbutz chief officers worked for the public good and rarely used offices for private gain; thus their credibility (Kouzes and Posner 1993) remained intact. They followed patrons' overarching commitment: decades after establishing and heading large FOs, patrons devoted a large part of their meager free time to Kochav's committees and general assembly. Their involvement enhanced high participation rates in democratic organs, hence disobedience was negligible. Their conservatism frustrated radical officers, but when crowded assemblies approved the latter's inventions, patrons backed implementation. This was true even when their views were rejected and privileges curbed, as high involvement made them sensitive to public opinion. On the other hand they could afford to do so, given their secure status as FO heads, which made them immune to losing standing to successful inventors, as R. Dore (1973, ch. 9) explained with regard to innovation in Japanese firms.

Though opposing industrialization, Kochav's patrons helped overcome a serious crisis caused by it when, in the early 1960s, new kibbutz officers initiated Rotation and self-labor at the plant, contrary to its old-guard policy of hired labor and continuity. The latter resigned, refusing to impart their information and know-how to their successors, causing serious disruption. Only patrons' help rescued the plant and the kibbutz from the strife that created two nearly warring camps. Patrons also helped prevent the problematic status of nonmembers, husbands of women members, such as those mentioned in Rama. Such problems were solved creatively through a standing appeals committee that was invented in Kochav's early days and always included one of the patrons. Its meetings were confidential and the general assembly could only either approve its proposals or reject them, in which case the problem was referred back to the committee for a new solution. This process helped enforce problematic decisions and enhanced trust in kibbutz leadership. Only minor damage was caused to patrons' authority when two of them, national figures, violated the car-sharing norm on the grounds that they needed their cars constantly. No one emulated them and the norm remained in force.

Without such a high-status, no-standing appeals committee and no such high involvement in kibbutz problem solving, Rama's high-moral informal leaders, mostly ex-secretaries, failed to cope with violation of egalitarianism by fellow *pe'ilim*. Their influence was further diminished with growing Talented Elite who followed such *pe'ilim*, and with failures in enforcing egalitarian solutions such as car sharing and shiftwork sharing, which tried to follow Kochav's example. Both succeeded in Kochav as a result of elite members' serving as high-moral role models, a service Rama's power elites mostly abstained from.

Kochav's Creativity Decline and the Vanishing of High-Trust Culture

As late as 1987, no member of Kochav's elite violated car sharing, and many *pe'ilim*, the kibbutz secretary, and other elite members put in a weekly evening or night shift at the plant, to mention just two of the many instances of altruistic behavior. However, Hirschman's (1970) process combined with Rotation eliminated creativity much earlier. As in Ran's case, creative radicals were rarely promoted to FOs; they were Rotated from successful jobs, their careers were sidetracked, and most of them left. Although their creativity brought success to Kochav, and later to most kibbutzim that imitated it, loyalists of conservative patrons were promoted to FOs, later circulating back and forth between

FOs and chief kibbutz offices; one loyalist of the main patron served as Kochav's secretary seven times; between secretary terms he was a *pa'il* until he became a Knesset member. Rotation, which was applied at the end of a two- to three-year term, was strictly enforced ever since the 1960s crisis, so that the short time horizon of officers also hampered cooperation (Axelrod 1984) and creativity (Jacques 1990). It exposed officers early on to FO conservatism and privileges, while "meteoric" promotion (Luthans 1988) of few loyalists further curbed effectiveness.

Kochav's creativity gradually lessened with the ascendance of a conservative, circulative elite of loyalists who lacked the high-moral and critical thinking (Hirschman 1970) of the old guard. Their promotion—a result of self-serving loyalty to patrons—modeled low morality and inspired conservatism, while the sidetracked careers of the previous generation's radicals such as Ran deterred youngsters. Ran's creativity failed and he was sidetracked again in the 1970s: as a successful but new minor department foreman in the factory, brought in for its renewal, he proposed a major innovation that succeeded a decade later but was rejected at the time because of a lack of formal backing by a young Rotational factory manager who liked Ran's idea very much but yielded to pressure by veterans of the main department who would have lost a main product and prestige by its implementation.

Kochav's success, with its concomitant growth in size and complexity, also carried the seeds of its own undoing. It was double the size of a "tribe," where leaders can be acquainted with everyone personally (Jay 1972, 106), and with an aggregate sales volume of $17,000,000, lack of creativity caused cultural decline and growing imitation of capitalist society. For example, in the recent past fewer members from outside the plant have volunteered for shiftwork, and as the kibbutz with which Kochav had been in partnership established its own plant, a manpower shortage has resulted in a partial return to hired labor. In addition, many other recent changes imitated those of the surrounding society.

Distrust and Conservatism in Patron-Controlled Younger Kibbutzim

Finally, let us consider the two younger kibbutzim mentioned above (they were established in 1949 and 1954, respectively, and numbered some 450 and 300 people, respectively, in 1990–91). Their early years were fraught with much hardship, though these groups of novices were better helped by FOs, the Jewish Agency, and the government than were Kochav and Rama a quarter of a century earlier. The main drawback, however, was not dependency on FOs that enhanced complacency, as Rosolio (1999) has argued, but patronage by conservative FO heads of loyal chief officers who in the 1950s tried emulating the kibbutz of the 1920s. As Rotation was adopted from inception, these chief officer loyalists became *pe'ilim* in their mid-twenties, nominated loyal clients to succeed them in kibbutz chief offices, and the heavy price of their early ascendancy was "fortified power structures" (Topel 1979, 119) of cliques with ultraconservative patronage that did not hesitate to detract from democratic decisions.

In 1959, a referendum was held in the kibbutz established in 1949 on allowing children to sleep in their parents' flats instead of in nurseries. Fully 62 percent of the voters favored the proposed change, but since only half of the membership participated in the vote as a result of patrons' unified antagonism (which accorded NFO heads' position), the patrons could "bury" the issue in committees. The will of the majority was realized only eighteen years later after many veteran kibbutzim had made the change.

Industrialization was also thwarted. In 1952 an ex-officer who was a qualified engineer was sent to work in an outside plant, as it was informally agreed between him and the would-be main patron that he would acquire expertise and later found and manage a plant on the kibbutz. Four different proposals offered by him during the next decade were rejected by his former backer, who in the meantime became the main patron. He allegedly did it since he favored agriculture, but in reality he defended supremacy: had the engineer succeeded with the plant, he might have become a new patron, as had happened with several other kibbutz plant managers (e.g., Kressel 1974). Even after the kibbutz assembly rebelled and decided to set up a plant in 1963, the main patron's opposition blocked this move until 1976, long after the engineer had left and had become manager of the plant at which he had been working (which had 1,500 employees). The kibbutz plant suffered a shortage of skilled managers and specialists as a result of a previous brain-drain and the negativism of two patrons toward its management by the third patron. The clients of the two, who managed the kibbutz, sent too few members to work at the plant, which then had to hire most of its staff from the outside. After six years, the third patron gave up and left the kibbutz, along with the chief engineer. The two patrons tried to manage the plant, but they never succeeded in turning a profit.

The early use of Rotation brought, in this case, early promotion of conservatives to FO jobs, as well as early nomination of loyal clients to chief kibbutz offices and soon after to FO jobs, which created "fortified power structures" never found in Kochav and Rama. When a patron finished a term in an FO job and could not find another one, a client helped him return to a chief kibbutz office by vacating it, while the patron and his clique helped this client find another managerial job. In the kibbutz established in 1954, patronage developed more gradually as it was at first an independent kibbutz and joined an NFO only a decade after its founding (Fadida 1972). However, the failure of its industrialization is also largely explained by conservative patronage. Its partnership in the very successful factory of a nearby veteran kibbutz elevated the principal patron to an executive position there, giving him little incentive to erect a subsidiary in his own kibbutz with the veteran kibbutz's help, as was initially planned and as Kochav had done in helping its younger partner's industrialization.

For three decades both of these younger kibbutzim were controlled by veteran patrons. The outcome was brain-drain of talented, critically minded officers, followed by a massive exit of supporters and others who learned that egalitarianism and democracy were a bluff, consisting of patrons' control through clients. Exits resulted in the relevant NFO sending fresh groups of youngsters to fill the ranks, from among which patrons promoted new loyalists. The latter enhanced patrons' power and suppression of their fellow radicals, causing their exit. Recurring cycles of suppression and subsequent brain-drains conserved patrons' rule, as did the dependency of these kibbutzim on the NFO for reinforcements where patrons were well networked in top echelons. Both kibbutzim failed to emulate the egalitarian solutions of Kochav and other creative kibbutzim, and in both elites' behavior ruined trust (Fadida 1972; Topel 1979). Both suffered heavily; approximately 80 percent of their members left. The 1954 kibbutz rented dozens of empty flats to outsiders and underwent a wholesale reversion to traditional modes of privacy and personal property that left little of communal life intact. In the 1949 kibbutz, young members urged the adoption of this model, but veterans' opposition caused a stalemate, a massive brain-drain, and growing dependency on outsiders whose aim was the same non-communal model.

The chances of both kibbutzim renewing communal cultures based on trust and democracy appear slimmer than those of Rama, owing to a much more severe brain-drain over the years. Only Kochav seems to have some chance of reviving its creativity and communal culture viability, should a high-moral servant, transformative leadership (Burns 1978; Graham 1991) appear, accumulate enough confidence to institute major changes, and replace Rotation by a real solution to the Iron Law so creative radicals will be rewarded by continuity in office and promotion, as long as they remain high-moral servant leaders.

Conclusions: High-Moral Leaders, Trust, and Creativity

Anthropological studies of four kibbutzim, helped by earlier findings of FOs that were ignored by CKR, substantiated "empirical . . . connection—through trust—between the moral duty of officers and the output performance of organizations" (Hosmer 1995, 400). The success of high-trust cultures for some seven decades was dependent on high-moral, servant radical leaders, who inspired creative innovation by "decisions and actions in which the interests of society take the degree of precedence that is right, just and fair over the interests of individuals" (399). By high intellectual ability, they created and explicated a new vision, as well as an asceticism that raised them to the highest level of morality in the Jewish tradition (Looz 1982), engendering ascending trust spirals (Fox 1974). While later on Iron Law continuity, patronage regimes, and self-enhancing accumulation of power, prestige, and privileges (Lenski 1966) caused oligarchic conservatism, grassroots democracy raised, to kibbutz sector management and eventually to kibbutz chief offices, many who followed their high commitment to the radical ethos. Where and when high-trust cultures reigned, radical officers coped with problems creatively and with democratic support overcame patrons' conservatism. However, creativity succeeded only when high-moral patrons stuck to democracy, even when their views were rejected and their own privileges restricted. Aside from dedication to the kibbutz cause, this is explained by patrons' sensitivity to public opinion as a result of their high level of involvement in kibbutz deliberations and secure top positions, which made them immune to early loss of standing to successful juniors (e.g., Dore 1973, ch. 9).

Radicals used kibbutz autonomy in a federative system to nurture creativity. But while creativity enhanced the success of their kibbutzim, and later of many others that imitated them, it also increased the power of FOs, the self-serving conservatism of rarely or non-Rotating FO heads, and Hirschman's (1970) negative selection of radicals in promotion, which was exacerbated by Rotation. Early removal from office prevented radical creatives from capitalizing on trust created by success for more inventions, and caused their sidetracking and/or leaving. Even high-moral patrons mostly preferred loyalists for FO jobs. Radicals were filtered out of the field's managerial strata, with continuity and promotion becoming more dependent on patrons' and cliques' help than on job effectiveness, creative coping with problems, and members' trust.

While innovation by radicals prolonged communal viability, major original solutions, democratically approved and implemented and conducive to communal ethos, ceased with the departure of the high-moral old guard. Their loyalist successors lacked critical thinking (Hirschman 1970), having mostly been managerially socialized by low-trust FO cultures, which associated authority with private gain rather than public service, and as personal interests became dominant (Hirschman 1982), descending trust spirals (Fox 1974) depressed creativity, causing a brain-drain, a decline of democracy, anarchy, and conservatism. Both CKR and Stryjan (1989) failed to detect this and the dominant role of low-moral, oligarchic FO heads in this decline of communal cultures.

The failure to see this is all the more critical. With FO growth, Rotation was no longer an egalitarian, high-moral practice, as it turned into circulation. Kibbutz chief officers rarely returned to lower echelons and in general became *pe'ilim* and circulated in lucrative FO jobs and/or between them and kibbutz chief offices until they found a continuous top FO job. It created multilayer stratification, finely graded status symbols and privileges to which CKR was blind (Shapira 2008), and engendered vicious circles, especially in younger kibbutzim, whose patronage regimes were especially conservative, as patrons became early clients of FO heads already in their oligarchic phase. The distrust of patrons' non-democratic control and the disenchantment with FO heads who supported them caused diminishing cooperation (Hirschman 1984), recurring cycles of brain-drain, massive exit, "leaving inside" (abstention of the talented from public office), inefficiency, and ineffectiveness. The growing dependency of these kibbutzim on NFOs enhanced patrons' power and furthered distrust, conservatism, and backwardness (Banfield 1958).

Although I have no representative sample of kibbutzim, it is clear from the vast literature, which space considerations prevent from adducing here, that since the 1940s, with NFOs' oligarchization, fewer and fewer kibbutzim were "adaptive and highly creative," and for shorter periods, while conservatives and imitators increased in number. Until the 1980s, creative kibbutzim were imitated; subsequently, capitalist firms came to supplant them, as formerly creative kibbutzim ceased to be both successful and creative. As kibbutz second-generation power elites adapted their morality to that of oligarchic FO heads, creativity in the service of public interest was suppressed, and even though some powerholders were troubled by the gap between their morality and kibbutz ethos, little action was taken. That gap paved the way for change, triggered by the debt crisis. Its direction however, was determined by the previous half a century's domination of the kibbutz field by oligarchic FO heads (cf. Bourdieu 1996).

While Rotation seemed to further creativity by constantly vacating offices, permitting the promotion of trusted, creative young officers, in reality this promotion was short-lived, after which even most successful radicals were rarely promoted or received another job of equivalent rank, their careers were sidetracked, and most left. Rotation made the success of their inventions dependent on patrons' adhering to democracy, since without it patrons' opposition blocked implementation. Rotation enhanced the power of FO heads: as gatekeepers of the circulative privileged strata, old-boy networks helped them select loyal conservatives, and if a radical was mistakenly chosen, he was weeded out after a single term. Failure prevention became the prime aim of most members of the privileged stratum, since one failure might be enough to ruin a career (Shapira 1987, 1995b).

Periodic Rotation is no real solution to the Iron Law; its unavoidable price is weak, ineffective officers who lack crucial intangible resources, and fearing exposure of this deficiency cannot remedy it (Shapira 1995b). Many other deficiencies have been detailed above, the worst being negative selection of talent, caused by a mismatch between power and responsibility, and conservative anarchy from conflicts between powerholders and officers. Aristophanes, Athens' famous playwright, depicted the Rotation regime as "the rule of embezzlement and evil . . . leadership is the interest of the completely ignorant and the lowest of degenerates" (Fuks 1976, 56). Dr. Vald, a former colonel in the Israeli army, has written, "Rotation turned into a sacred ritual kept zealously because it serves promotion needs . . . of unprofessional, inexpert and inexperienced officers" (1987, 158). Other works substantiated that fixed, short periods in office are a Procrustean bed for creative leaders, preventing their success, while conservative continuous powerholders pull the ropes (Chow 1966; Gabriel and Savage 1981; Mainwaring 1990; Shapira 1990, 1995a).

Implications for Further Study of Kibbutzim

Before dealing with the sociological implications of my findings, let us look at some open questions on kibbutzim. Why had their FOs never practiced self-management as had the Mondragon cooperatives' FOs (Whyte and Whyte

1988)? An obvious reason was Rotation of *pe'ilim*, which rendered it impractical. However, did institutionalization of Rotation precede FOs oligarchization or was it a part of leader efforts to accumulate power? A related question concerns *pe'ilim* privileges: were they enlarged to attract kibbutz talents that found weak, Rotational FO jobs unattractive? Did FOs' competition for these talents inhibit cooperation in devising solutions to kibbutz needs? Power struggles between FOs and FOs versus kibbutzim point in this direction (Shapira 1978–79; Ginat 1979), but further research is required for definitive results.

Another question is how much the leftist political turn by main NFOs in the 1940s to a reverence of Stalin's dictatorial regime (Tzachor 1997, 188), contrary to kibbutz democratic ethos, was aimed at serving power needs of oligarchic leaders. Historians explained this turn by the political situation, but as it legitimized power concentration by leaders, it is better explained as a part of NFOs' oligarchization, though further study is required.

Opaque Systems: Implication for Sociology of Organizations

Trust is crucial for understanding organizations, especially innovation, and their heads play the main role in engendering ascending or descending trust spirals (Fox 1974; Shapira 1987; Fukuyama 1995). The efforts to prevent the Iron Law, a major cause for distrust and conservatism, commenced in Athens 2,500 years ago, and since then periodic succession norms have lacked clear long-term success. The price paid by organizations for the Iron Law is enormous and the phase of leaders' ineffectiveness (Hambrick and Fukutomi 1991) may continue well over half a century if ruling periods of loyal conservative successors are taken into account (Hirschman 1970). In such long periods of organizational decline successive generations of young, talented radicals learn the problems and invest vast efforts in inventing solutions called off by oligarchs. They may exit after investing their best years in an opaque system, taking with them ample knowledge that successors had to pointlessly relearn. The Iron Law negative effects are profound and lasting, but organizational sociologists neglected to search for solutions.

There is one explanation—aside from kibbutzim being a clear success—why CKR ignored Iron Law in FOs. Without going into the details of other explanations for its ignorance (Shapira 2008), one main reason for its failure is quite clear: as a result of a mistaken perspective (Martin 1992), it did not study FOs and thus served the interest of top kibbutz leaders in continuity. The price was a gross misunderstanding of the kibbutz field's various cultures, belief in the positive effects of Rotation, and no help toward solving the Iron Law. Worse still, hailing Rotation as a success supported other organizations' use of it, for instance, the Israeli army. The failure of CKR proves that organizational sociologists must be aware of leaders' actions aimed at private interests, disguised as serving organizational ones (Dalton 1959). The kibbutz case proves that such disguises can mislead an army of educated social scientists and hundreds of studies for many decades, if cross-sectional, longitudinal, historical, and anthropological data are not properly integrated. Only such an integration, as done here, coped with the complex dynamics of a field whose elites created hybrid organizations as shields against surrounding society pressures, the latter becoming Trojan horses that helped ruin the very cultures they were to uphold.

Organizational sociologists must be reflexive toward their epistemology, and they must aim at buttressing its robustness (Bourdieu and Wacquant 1992) to prevent grave mistakes like that of CKR. They must problematize the boundaries of the field they are studying to prevent powerholders from externalizing some parts of it that do not help the image they seek to maintain. Officer careers must be studied in wider contexts, not only of the field's variety of organizations but also of societal and even international contexts where careers can be promoted in literally thousands of organizations.

Present Solutions and a Proposed Growing Trust-Dependent Succession

Ya'acov Hazan, the Kibbutz Artzi NFO head, was right when he stated, "Leadership is not forged by Rotation"; a new solution is required. Large American firms use "golden parachutes," generous retirement benefits to encourage leaders' succession (Vancil 1987). This expensive instrument, however, is based on egoism; thus, it may not promote servant leaders, or radical ones. Servant leadership that is transformative whenever required (Burns 1978; Graham 1991) is based on power accumulated by consecutive successes of coping with essential tasks of growing scale and importance that create ascending trust spirals, resulting in the sincere, optimal pooling of intangible resources at the leader's disposal (Zand 1972; Shapira 1995b). Thus, a manager's continuity in office must be dependent on members' trust (Semler 1993); this, in turn, must be based on high-quality judgment (Yankelovich 1991), which is feasible where information and knowledge flow freely and sincerely, that is, in a high-trust culture (Dore 1973; Fox 1974).

The challenge is thus to devise a succession system conducive to high trust by making continuation in office conditional on growing trust in a leader. It may be done by periodic tests, analogous to the second-term vote for U.S. presidents. However, as Washington and Jefferson well knew, motivating their refusal of a third term, reelection as a result of power accumulated over eight years of incumbency is quite probable, even if considerable distrust prevails. However, as an officer's effectiveness may begin to decline only after eleven years (Hambrick and Fukutomi 1991), it is desirable to require special criteria for allowing a very effective officer to remain beyond two four-year terms, and perhaps even stricter criteria to permit him to retain his position for a fourth term if he continues to excel. Thus, a new built-in mechanism against oligarchic continuity is required, which would counteract the automatic advantage of an incumbent of eight years or more over competitors. Such a mechanism would make third and fourth terms conditional on passing a higher trust test, rather than on a simple majority. Hence, only a small number of very effective, much trusted officers would be reelected to a third term, and fewer yet to a fourth. However, since prestige tends toward exponential growth (Goode 1978), a test of exponentially growing trust for these terms seems desirable. If, under this principle, a third term would require, let us say, a two-thirds majority, an exponential fourth would require 89 percent, and it would create a built-in mechanism against the Iron Law, as a 119 percent majority is impossible. However, only with experience can the precise degree of exponentiality be properly defined.

The other major question is, whose trust must a leader gain in order to continue in office? In small communes where officers and their achievements and failures are known to everyone, all members can vote. More complex and crucial is this question in large, industrialized communes and FOs. In *Union Democracy,* Lipset, Trow, and Coleman (1956) suggested that in large, multi-unit organizations, only bipartisan politics prevents the Iron Law. The idea raised above may do that without bipartisanship, which seems inappropriate as it does not prevent oligarchy within parties and the rise of "warlords" instead of creative, high-moral servant leaders. Both kibbutzim and Mondragon (Whyte and Whyte 1988), the two most successful federative cooperatives, have no partisan politics. Representatives of constituent units, with some FO staff members, create a quasi-parliament. This may be the right constituency for FO leadership succession decisions if, and only if, almost all of its members are the freely, periodically elected representatives of constituent units, and are also subject to the growing trust clause to prevent their own oligarchization, a known problem of presidential regimes (Mainwaring 1990).

The above ideas are preliminary and comport with FOs of self-managed organizations. However, the case of Semco, a private Brazilian firm that became a unique federative, original industrial democracy (Semler 1993), points to the possibility of much wider applicability. It calls for research that would further reveal the dynamics of oligarchization and leadership succession in various communities and organizations and the possibilities of Iron Law prevention by norms that engender democratic, high-trust cultures.

Notes

The author acknowledges the helpful comments on earlier drafts of this essay by Gideon Kressel, Moshe Schwartz, Israel Shepher, Emanuel Marx, Ze'ev Shavit, Pinchas Shtern, Gila Adar, Yuval Milo, Mira Baron, Dani Zamir, Amir Helman, Dafna Izraeli, Yehuda Bien, Dani Rosolio, Leora Ya'acobi, Dvora Kalekin-Fishman, Zachary Sheaffer, Michael Harrison, Haim Shferberger, Daniel De Mal'ach, Martin Kett, and Avi Kirschenbaum.

9

The Disguised Egg

Four Narratives of Acculturation

HAIM HAZAN

Introduction

Anthropological deliberation over the concept of "acculturation"—itself largely the product of anthropological thought—varies considerably in form, structure, meaning, and importance (see Keesing 1974; Carrithers 1992). Engaged in the construction of a scientific façade for and about "acculturation," namely the relinquishing of one "culture" in favor of another, many anthropological works seldom evaluate their own premises with regard to it. Anthropologists have traditionally viewed processes of cultural change through the development or modernization perspective. This perspective, although involving "images of the telic evolution so despised by persons trained in the Boasian tradition" (H. Schneider 1988, 61), has become prominent among "practical anthropologists" who "roamed the (Third) world of development, working as consultants or employees for institutions such as the World Bank or The U.S. Agency for International Development (U.S. AID)" (Escobar 1991, 659). The development perspective has also been common since the 1960s among many Israeli anthropologists employed by the Jewish Agency (Ha-sochnut) to research immigrant settlements and immigrants' "acculturation." As a research tradition, it entailed the use of a functional mode of representation as a framework for understanding cultural change. This mode of representation is arguably still prominent among many Israeli anthropologists. I will return to this argument in the conclusion after developing my own account of three stories of "acculturation" as told in an urban renewal setting not very different from the "immigrant settlements" of the 1960s. Indeed, like many other "deprived" localities in Israel, the one studied here was also the outgrowth of a residence inhabited by Ma'abara (the transition camps for new immigrants in the early 1950s) evacuees.

What follows, then, is not intended to be a systematic discussion of the sources, derivations, and ramifications of the concept of "development" in anthropology. Since the 1990s there has been a steady accumulation of critical literature discussing anthropology and the colonial encounter or the politics of ethnography in "developing" societies (see Escobar 1991; Apfell-Marglin and Marglin 1990; Asad 1973; Bennet and Bowen 1988; Clifford and Marcus 1986). Instead of "development," which has come to signify linear evolution as associated with the Western doctrine of progress, I use here the term "acculturation" as a more neutral umbrella concept. True enough, "acculturation" has its own historical record, which is not entirely innocent (see Hoben 1982 for a historical review). However, it is arguably more neutral than "development," at least grammatically speaking. In this essay, therefore, "acculturation" signifies a plethora of alternative routes to cultural change, one of which is the "modernization" model of the development perspective, the others completely different narratives. The aim of this essay is to undo, and to some extent classify, narratives of acculturation from the social text, rather than construct an understanding of the social, which builds on a prior concept of "culture." "Culture" is therefore in quotes here in order to focus on its emergent, contextual, and ideological enactments rather than its pre-established, singular, and static abstraction. My premise is that every definition or formulation of "acculturation" is a narrative—a story about something or other—which, when studied analytically, is likely to reveal a weltanschauung with regard to man's place in his environment, his ability to act within it, the importance of his desires, and the ways in which he constructs his identity within it.

Acculturation as a narrative is addressed in various ways in the literature. Astington (1991) describes the formation of the cultural narrative in the socialization process undergone by the child. This psychological position is adopted by Carrithers (1992), who views culture, and hence "acculturation," as a kind of sociocognitive narrative about the human condition. Regarding "culture" as a narrative rather than an objective entity "out there" has opened up a whole array of critical self-examination in the social sciences. Anthropology itself has come of late to be regarded as a kind of narrative, such as "the writing of culture" (Clifford and Marcus 1986; Tyler 1987; Clifford 1983), a kind of rhetoric (R. Rosaldo 1987), or secondhand representation (Myerhoff and Ruby 1982; Pels and Nancel 1991). Some have even ventured to claim the precedence of folk models of culture over scientific models (Holton 1992). I intend to address this crucial issue by examining the way in which the concept of "acculturation" has been traditionally applied by anthropologists to the Israeli context, and—by way of comparison—let the "natives" speak their own mind about this concept. This speaking has produced a much more refined and elaborated view of "culture" as a multifaceted panorama of realities and hyperrealities. In contrast, Israeli anthropologists working (or employed) in similar contexts have often reduced and interpreted "culture" within a parsimonious functional framework, reproducing the perspectival order of "nation building" as indoctrinated by the

Israeli political establishment, of which they were part (Kimmerling 1992; Ram 1989). In doing this, Israeli anthropologists were operating in a similar manner to "development anthropologists" who recycled and reinforced the dominating (First World) views of modernization, social change, and the Third World.

The ethnographic scene I now turn to invoke is an Israeli "renewal neighborhood." This concept became part of Israeli social life after the initiation of "The Program for Rehabilitation and Renewal of Neighborhoods in Israel" in 1977 by the government of Menachem Begin (see Carmon and Hill 1984; International Committee on Project Renewal Evaluation 1981). The following section is an invocation of one such renewal neighborhood, beginning with the "hard facts" that determined the day-to-day conditions of existence of the residents, and then proceeds to the world of images and metaphors that residents "live by" (Lakoff and Johnson 1980; Wagner 1986).

The Field

The neighborhood in which the research was conducted—which I shall call Arod—is part of a city situated in the center of the country, and has a population of about 6,000 (for more details see Hazan 1990). It is located on the outskirts of the town and is separated from most of its other residential areas by open land. The neighborhood's residents were characterized by extremely heterogeneous ethnic origin, stemming from some thirty-two countries, mostly from Asia and Africa (some 63 percent of all residents; the "Sephardic"). Approximately 14 percent were Israeli-born and 22 percent (the "Ashkenazis") were born in Europe (mainly eastern Europe) and America. In 1982 the rate of those with partial or complete elementary education among the 15–44 age group in the neighborhood was 30 percent, and the unemployment rate was above the national average: 48.7 percent among men and 72 percent among women (the respective rates in the general population are 32.9 percent and 55.8 percent). The level of family income was also relatively low, standing at 34 percent below the national average.

The range of employment and housing opportunities available to most of the residents was limited, and they were well aware of this. Moreover, an improvement in living conditions could have been gained by a move to less expensive areas, such as a development town or a community settlement on the West Bank, or to a different part of the neighborhood itself. For most residents, any thought of moving to the central area of the large city that lay in enticing proximity was but an unrealistic dream. Nevertheless, many of the residents reported a feeling of belonging to the place in the sense of its being a human environment rather than an area of residence. A taxi driver expressed this sentiment: "I'll do my best to leave this neighborhood, but my heart will remain here forever." The main expectations of Project Renewal were that an improved quality of life and a more agreeable physical environment would be expressed in a commensurate rise in the prices of apartments, the sale of which would enable a move to a different area. Identification with the neighborhood, such as it was, took the form of dependence on a local social network, the importance of which is evident among a population that struggles to fulfill its material, employment, and educational expectations on its own. This mutual support was not attributed to the neighborhood's existence as a socio-territorial entity. On the contrary, residents felt that "in spite of this screwed-up neighborhood, the people here are nice."

A paradoxical need thus arose to abolish the neighborhood while maintaining it for the ways in which it provided social security. Residents spoke with revulsion about various aspects common in the neighborhood, such as drug abuse and crime, and went as far as to condemn the place as a neighborhood without a future. Many of these same residents, however, referred with affection to what they termed "the neighborhood spirit." The dilemma confronting residents was whether and how to rid themselves of the neighborhood while conserving its "spirit." As we shall see, the various images prevalent in the neighborhood, which constituted the verbal expression of this "spirit," will serve as building blocks for the acculturation narratives recounted below. It is important to note that the terminology employed to label the social images is not the result of academic abstraction and generalization but, as in the case of professional argot, part of the rhetoric found in a certain speech community. It was, of course, not a language in general use, but, like all languages, its use was limited to the people and situations it was likely to serve.

An additional point that should be made here has to do with the decisive role played by Project Renewal in imparting, justifying, and disseminating this language. Residents learned that in order to communicate usefully with project officials they would be advised to adapt their speech to the argot of the organization that concentrated such vast resources. The ability to negotiate a share in the distribution of resources, such as housing allowances, establishment of various clubs in the vicinity of their homes, positions on the project's staff, and so forth, was largely determined by the residents' contacts with local centers of power. These centers—local committees, officeholders who owed their livelihood to the project, and various community services—were all part of the project's organizational structure and thus partook in the ongoing organizational discourse. This discourse took place in many meetings at which interests were presented, debates held, and decisions made, as well as in the course of daily chats and contacts among providers of services, and between them and residents. This discourse, which originated in a bureaucratic argot foreign to the local residents and typical of Project Renewal in general, facilitated communication in four spheres: among project officials; with residents; with the authorities and institutions to which the local project was linked and which served as its basis; and with the "adopting" community in the United States.[1] The communicative power of the project's language thus acquired a local dominance that relied on ideological hegemony, according to which the project's objective was to enable the local community to merge with (or become acculturated to) "mainstream" Israeli society while abolishing the neighborhood's (and residents') original identity/stigma. I will outline the rough contours of this discourse by describing five of its "root metaphors" (Turner 1976).

"Residents"

These were perceived as a generalized entity, not necessarily identified with place of residence. The "residents" are not equivalent to the neighborhood, and may thus be separated from it. This is a dynamic entity that possesses a dual transformative potential. It may join up with the "unhealthy" elements found in the neighborhood, or sever its connections with the neighborhood and reach the level of "ordinary Israeli citizens, as in Ra'anana, Kiron or Tel-Aviv," in the words of one of the project activists. The "positive" potential was to be encouraged by adopting certain lifestyles, with particular emphasis on complementary education, that characterize well-established localities. Thus, computer courses, various educational clubs, and sports activities flourished in the neighborhood. All these were supposed to make up a cultural mechanism whereby the symbolic entity called "residents" was to elevate itself from the stigma of its neighborhood. Alongside this mechanism functioned a political mechanism termed "resident participation," which was designed to allocate a role to neighborhood residents in the decision-making process with regard to priorities and distribution of resources concerning the planning of their lives in their place of residence. This "resident participation," which supposedly occurred on several decision-making levels, from steering committees to implementation of the programs in the field, was the object of severe criticism, open ridicule, and expressions of skepticism as to its sincerity. As one of the residents put it, "In Herzlia there is no 'resident participation' because there the residents participate anyway. Only here is this fig leaf necessary, so that they can do what they like, supposedly with our consent." "They" are the establishment's representatives, who include the project's salaried officials—both locals and those from the outside—and other officeholders involved in decision-making at the local level. But "they" is also Israeli society, since serious questions about their sense of belonging to it constituted one of Arod's residents' central dilemmas.

"Israeli Society"

This is an ambivalent image signifying belonging and identification on the one hand, and a sense of rejection and detachment on the other. The tension between these two poles was generally apparent when "Israeli society" was mentioned; while national symbols such as the army and even "good old Israeli songs" engendered enthusiastic identification among residents, much frustration was caused by the labeling of their neighborhood as a deprived area. The neighborhood's very inclusion in Project Renewal, in itself considered an achievement to which many deprived areas aspire, exacerbated the sense of detachment and alienation from Israeli society. When the local project was praised for its achievements, one of the residents reacted by quoting a Hebrew proverb:

"We were head of the foxes, not even a tail to the lions." Both the residents in general and those active in the project were well aware that full integration into what they conceived as "Israeli society" could take place only at the expense of denouncing the neighborhood's identity. The attitude toward the country's political regime reflected this ambivalence. The prime minister at the time, Menachem Begin, who had been among the initiators of the national project, enjoyed widespread admiration, expressed in terms such as "Begin is our father, we owe him everything." Several ministers in Begin's government, however, who were involved in Project Renewal, were at times roundly criticized, as were their minions—directors of ministries and their officials. The residents' attitude toward the army was stamped with the same duality. Admiration of military symbols was shared by most residents. This was apparent in the adoption by the local youth movement of a military style uniform, and in the manner that visiting army officers were feted. But the fact that some of the local youngsters were not drafted into the army on grounds of social incompatibility was a sore point about which people were embarrassed and complained. Rehabilitation programs operated by the army, in which several of the neighborhood's youngsters were included, served only to exacerbate the feeling of rejection within the general sense of identification with the national collectivity. A television documentary portraying the arduous and tortuous process of the acceptance to an army unit of one of Arod's youngsters was conceived by residents as a mark of Cain on the neighborhood's forehead. One of them put it this way: "Now the entire country knows who we are, and all who see us shall know us" (an explicit allusion to the biblical mark of Cain). Whereas the project set itself up as a leverage to ease the process of integration into "Israeli society," its very existence paradoxically loaded even weightier stigmas than before onto the neighborhood's image. Any activity regarded as evidence of the project's success also emphasized the neighborhood's degradation and marginality, which had necessitated the activity in the first place.

Community

According to the neighborhood's residents, this concept was not in daily usage before the project entered their lives. The term became one of the national project's main semantic apparatuses, since it was extremely useful in creating a smooth rhetoric in all spheres of the project, thereby helping blur the conflicts inherent in them. Its qualities of symbolic opaqueness and social cleanliness rendered the term acceptable and innocuous.[2] In this respect "community" is an undefined social unit that is neither a "neighborhood," a "development area," a "special attention area," nor a "deprived neighborhood." It signifies rather a framework that transforms all these into a desirable way of life without any negative connotations, suited to the modern, Western world to which it aspires. This Western world was represented in the project not only as an ideal model incorporating quality of life, technological sophistication, comfortable housing, and attractive surroundings, but also as a concrete entity manifested by the adopting twinned communities from the diaspora. These were regarded not only as a bountiful source of funds that would help the neighborhood develop into a "community" but also as a model to be emulated, and to which the neighborhood was now linked by a strong, continuous bond, expressed in reciprocal visits, hospitality, and joint planning of services and facilities, which had replaced the "haphazard and casual connection of the past." The concept was freely bandied about at every opportunity. It was easier to talk of "communities" rather than of "neighborhoods," since the expression did not require territorial definition or accuracy, was free of unpleasant connotations, and enabled the establishment of a rhetorical relationship of equality between adopter and adopted, purveyors of services and their clients, establishment figures and residents. It replaced existing images with new ones, and belonged to the language of "renewal" and "well-being," rather than the language of "development" and "welfare." However, the most important characteristic was probably the nucleus common to every settlement or group of people seeking a future with a quality of life independent of any previous economic, social, or cultural background. The proliferation of "community settlements" during this period, and the attendant media campaign encouraging the young, energetic, and ambitious to join them, added a taste of belonging to a different Israeli society, one that was able to shed the impediments of past divisions. The aspiration to become a "community" was presented by the project workers in Arod as a vision of a different social future, which the neighborhood's residents would be able to realize only if they were to change beyond recognition. The binding quality of the concept of "community" facilitated rhetorical patching up of differences and rivalries that were presented as the outcome of local disputes, most of which involved different ethnic groups. Ethnicity was indeed an additional characteristic of "neighborhood" life that had to be blunted in order to join up with "mainstream Israel," or "First Israel," as it was labeled in contrast to the "second Israel" of the margins.

Ethnicity

Because of the great variety of ethnic origin among the neighborhood's residents, no single political dominance was expressed in ethnic terms. Apart from the Yemenites, who constituted the nucleus of the neighborhood's first inhabitants, no areas were identified according to the origin of their residents, owing to the desire to preserve the delicate balance between various areas of the neighborhood characterized by ethnic homogeneity. People were particularly careful not to connect political disputes with ethnic variance, and any attempt to do so was rejected. Nevertheless, the predominance of those of oriental, and particularly Moroccan, origin left its mark on the structuring of residents' cultural identity. The status of rehabilitation neighborhood, in which economic differences between residents were relatively small, taken together with its ethnic variety, provided evidence, in the words of one of the residents, that "we're all in the same boat and there is no one to envy." Accusations of relative deprivation and discrimination according to the oriental/Western (Sephardic/Ashkenazi) divide lost most of their sting, since it was the eastern European immigrants, most of whom were old and received welfare support, who occupied the bottom rung of the economic ladder in the neighborhood. In addition to this, several of the local positions of power had for many years been in the hands of the Yemenite veterans, and if there was any sign of a political struggle couched in ethnic terms, it was between the old-time members of the neighborhood council in pre-project days and a young generation, most of whom were involved in the project and of second-generation Moroccan origin. Ethnicity was of value in presenting the neighborhood as a pluralistic cultural territory characterized by mutual respect, each part of which proudly preserved its traditional cuisine and dress for special occasions, such as the Mimouna celebrations at which, as in many other places, interethnic brotherhood was advocated by way of publicly displaying a variety of presumably authentic ethnic folklore.

The City

The neighborhood was separated from its city center by a few kilometers of a mainly non-built-up area. A public transportation service connected the neighborhood to the city; regular and frequent buses and taxis provided easy access to its shopping and entertainment centers. In addition, the neighborhood bordered on another residential area that was considered to be more affluent and was thus not included in Project Renewal. Nevertheless, the feeling of isolation among residents was widespread. They did not see themselves as residents of the city but as residents of the neighborhood, and since convenient transportation was also available to the nearby metropolis of Tel Aviv, many of them preferred to do their shopping and to seek their entertainment in its anonymity rather than being exposed in the city. The feeling of isolation was fueled in no small measure by the belief fostered by the local leadership that the neighborhood was greatly deprived with regard to the municipal distribution of resources. At the same time, many of the residents sought to improve their standard of living by moving to the city, and were extremely proud of the fact that another rehabilitation neighborhood in the same town was regarded as a failure, and that in comparison Arod was a symbol of success, both at the national and municipal levels. As was the case in all the previous images discussed, the attitude toward the city was ambivalent, incorporating contradictory attraction and rejection.

These five local idioms provided the raw material for the three narratives of acculturation to which I now turn.

Three Narratives of Acculturation

The following section describes three accounts of how the neighborhood was cleansed of its residents in order to emerge as a "community." That is, these accounts tell and enact the story of cultural effacement and change. The first two accounts maintain representational relationships with those residents—albeit by means of a reflexive wink in the second case—whereas the third dispenses with representational relationships and creates a simulation as an alternative to both the neighborhood and the residents.

The Disguised Egg

The neighborhood's elderly residents were a secondary target of the project. A large and active day center had been opened for them, but their status within the "community" was problematic. They were seen as representatives of the former, pre-project ethnic neighborhood identities, and many of them received welfare support. The welfare services were perceived as a threat to the creation of the community within the project, since their existence perpetuated the stigma of poverty. It had thus been decided to physically separate the community center from the welfare office, which had been moved to another street. Nevertheless, a series of activities for the elderly were initiated, aimed at integrating them into the community. The first and most important of these was a literacy program. The idea of integration into the community was presented under the auspices of developing intergenerational relationships between grandparents and their grandchildren by enabling the grandparents to assist their grandchildren with their homework and in reading stories. Only elderly women participated, however, since the neighborhood's old men were literate in Hebrew and spent most of their time in the local synagogues, which served as social centers for them. The participants did not attach much importance to the stated objective of learning to read and write. Some even ridiculed the idea, claiming that the grandchildren did not need their assistance in doing homework, adding that the relationship with them was based, as one of them put it, on "what's in the heart and what's in the pot." As is customary in literacy classes for new immigrants, the course material was very simple, consisting mainly of children's stories. At the end of the course the participants were asked by their instructor to write an essay that would demonstrate their command of the language by describing the particular study material that had made the strongest impression on them. The essays were collected and published in booklet form for local distribution. Without exception the women chose one story—"The Disguised Egg"—by Dan Pagis, a well-known Israeli poet and writer. This story recounts the adventures of an egg that became fed up with its eggy identity and decided to seek its fortune in other roundish forms in which it hoped to find true happiness. This journey of self-revelation passes through a balloon, an apple, a ball, and other oval-shaped objects, but brings only disappointment. The egg eventually reaches the conclusion that it cannot change into something else, returns with relief to its egg shape, and hatches a chick. The women, each in her own words, offered almost identical explanations as to why the story had struck a chord with them. They saw the text of the story as an allegory of their own fate. They had immigrated to Israel from the countries of their birth, whose culture they had internalized. In Israel they had passed through various phases, at each of which an attempt had been made to transform their basic identity into something else. In the immigrants' camp they had been expected to become Israelis, and later on in the neighborhood others had tried to impart a culture foreign to them. They claimed, however, that their true selves were to be found only in their origins, in their undisguised ethnic affiliations. Some went still further in developing this theme, remarking in their essays that only once it had accepted itself for what it was could the egg become fertile. In their case, too, only once they had resigned themselves to what they were, not through necessity but by choice, would they be of any use to their grandchildren. The main lesson to be learned from the parable of the disguised egg is therefore that one's disguise must be removed before one can know one's true self and view oneself as a complete person. Removing these disguises, however, means the abrogation of Israeli reality in general and that of the neighborhood in particular. Thus, the story is employed as metanarrative capable of renarrating experience.

The Natural Selection

To mark the project's first anniversary, the project board met to discuss ways of celebrating the event. In contrast to the gravity and heated discussions that characterized other meetings, this one was conducted in a humorous vein and was devoid of tension. The participants, most of whom were residents of the neighborhood, made various lighthearted proposals as to "how to entertain our residents." Someone suggested a boxing contest, since "if they don't see blood they won't be satisfied." Another suggested a "Moroccan feast," because "that's what suits them and what they'll enjoy most." There was a general consensus that this type of entertainment would please the residents, attract an audience, and meet their expectations. The initial proposals, however, which had obviously been made in jest, and betrayed more about attitudes toward the residents and the neighborhood than any intention of implementing them, were rejected. The reasons put forward for their rejection were of the kind that "the project can't be identified with events such as these" and, in particular: "Who can tell how the residents will behave? Perhaps they will go wild and run riot, and then what will we look like to the invited guests?" The consideration of the community's appearance to outsiders was sufficiently weighty to induce more serious suggestions. Thus, for example, the idea was put forward to invite the "Pale Tracker" (Hagashash Hachiver) entertainment group, well-known for its ethnic humor, "so that the residents can laugh at themselves a bit," but this was rejected because of the high cost involved. Agreement was eventually reached on holding an exhibition of armaments to be set up by the army unit adopted by the residents and on inviting a performance by "The Natural Selection" group, to be held at the center of town rather than in the neighborhood. The Natural Selection is a musical ensemble that strives to lend an authentic-classical air to oriental music, thereby staking its claim to status and legitimacy in the field of serious music. The ensemble had won critical acclaim and recognition and was considered "civilized" entertainment as opposed to "cassette music" with which popular oriental music is often identified in Israel. The choice of the city as the venue for the performance was not fortuitous. The excuse that no suitable place was available was unconvincing, since well-attended events had taken place in the neighborhood, where a suitable hall had been built. The territorial detachment was part of the cultural isolation. Bringing Arod's residents to the city symbolized the neighborhood's abolition for both its residents and the project team. The event was widely publicized, but demand for tickets was small and much of the audience at the performance was made up of non-residents. The complete disappearance of the neighborhood and its residents will be demonstrated in the next narrative.

An Invitation to the Community

The inauguration ceremony for Arod's community center was held before a large gathering. Careful examination of the invitation sent to guests reveals some of the main characteristics of the concept of community and the ways of implementing it. Invitations were sent out to neighborhood notables, activists in Project Renewal, Jewish Agency officials, representatives of government ministries, senior municipal officials, and many other guests from all parts of the country, including contributors from the twin community in the United States. The invitation's design indicates its purpose and significance. It was printed on top-quality paper in Hebrew and in English. Apart from its value as a communication bridge between the two communities, the use of English establishes the community's standing within a wider, modern, Western, and universal culture, one of whose ingredients is the English language. Thus, the neighborhood not only breaks out of the narrow confines of "the second Israel" but also extends beyond mainstream Israel and Israel altogether. With a mere wave of an invitation, the neighborhood becomes part of the sought after, rational, scientific, free, and "cultured" world. At the top of the invitation were the emblems of the various bodies involved in establishing the center—first, the coat of arms of the city in which the center was located, followed by the insignia of the Jewish Agency, of the twin city abroad, and finally of the neighborhood itself. The name attached to the illustration betrays the problematic nature of the center's essential function. In Hebrew it is called a "palace of culture and sport," whereas in English it is a "community center." The Hebrew language imparts a combination of a "modern" meaning to the center (culture) and a religious one (palace). This combination has become part of everyday speech, indicating a site for ongoing activity, irrespective of any specific time and place. The concept of "community," on the other hand, is identified with a given time and place, and as we have seen, the people of the neighborhood seek to break out of the problematic confines of their place and time, in other words, of the neighborhood. This internal contradiction between the necessity to be part of an existing reality and the desire to repudiate it and to regard it as part of an alternative and sought-after life cycle is evident from the other parts of the document in question.

As in other invitations to family events, such as weddings, circumcisions, or bar mitzvahs, the "parents/in-laws" also appear on Arod's invitation. In this case, these are the Jewish Agency, the municipality and the neighborhood committee, and the twin Jewish community. These three "take pleasure in inviting you to the inauguration ceremony of the Palace of Culture and Sport."

As in other family events, the inauguration ceremony was a rite of passage, that is, a festive-symbolic designation of the important and marked change that has taken place in the identity of the participants. During the ceremony outlined in the invitation, a neighborhood "becomes" a community. Yet this narrative of "becoming," rooted in the very essence of the project of "renewal," was actually a simulation, a staged production bearing little or no connection to the lived experience of residents.

During the inauguration ceremony, the heads of Project Renewal and its patrons made speeches before a selected audience that had gained admittance to the grounds of the center by invitation only. An appropriate and evenly balanced audience was thus ensured, one that could be relied on not to disrupt the ceremony and to bring credit to the organizers. The mezuzot (parchment scrolls) were fixed in place amid much song and dance led by a well-known rabbi from another part of the country. This is an interesting fact when one considers the large number of synagogues and rabbis in the neighborhood. The invitation of a rabbi from the outside not only avoided local factionalism but also imbued the neighborhood with an aura of belonging to the entire religious establishment. Following a tour of the building's components, the library in particular, as befits a "palace of culture," groups of neighborhood women appeared before the guests dressed in original ethnic attire. The picture was one of cultural diversity whose roots were not in the present time and place and which, moreover, presented the "authentic" people of the neighborhood as apiece of folklore. The gulf between the "exotic" apparel and ornaments and the modern, European dress of the visiting members of the American "twin" community placed the former in the category of a museum exhibit, in contrast to the modern power and vitality of the latter, who, moreover, were economically in a position to enforce their way of life on the local residents. The image of this cultural subjugation was artistically formed during the ceremony.

The program was presented to an invited local audience that filled the lavish hall to capacity at the beginning of the evening, but which steadily dwindled, with only a few people remaining to the end. This did not prevent the program from running its full course. It included an appearance by the municipal orchestra, which set the seal of approval on the acceptance of the out-of-the-way neighborhood into the fold of the city to which it belonged. The inclusion of the neighborhood in the city was affirmed immediately afterward during a series of greetings and speeches made by the mayor, a senior government minister who read a telegram of greeting from the prime minister, representatives of the neighborhood and of the project, and a representative of the twin community. In the cultural events that followed, the center's dancers performed jazz numbers, devoid of any folkloric elements, while a local school choir sang songs from musicals, many of them from *Fiddler on the Roof.* The high point of the evening was a performance by a well-known singer who combined "good old Israeli" songs, with which the new community could now identify, with a visual "then and now" slide show. Pictures of the neighborhood's degenerate and neglected past were shown side by side with those portraying the present achievements of an exemplary, well-tended, clean, and orderly place. The contrast was so blatant that there seemed to be no connection between the two periods, and the audience was no doubt torn between its degrading past as residents of an isolated neighborhood and the present, with its promise of a bright future as citizens of the nation, the country, and the world. In fact, only a few of them remained in their seats to the end of the event. Most exited during the early stages of the evening, leaving behind them the youth movement youngsters and the local hacks.

This vision of the future, almost eschatological community created by the project spells the abolition of the neighborhood and its residents as a significant entity worthy of mirroring or even winking at, as was the case in the ceremony described. It is also an abrogation of every system of symbols that connected the neighborhood and its residents to the concept of the community. The community has, in fact, become a self-display with no "self," a signifier with no signified, or, in the words of Baudrillard (1983, 1988), a "simulation."

Conclusion: The Wink of Self-Awareness

This essay has portrayed three contexts for the enactment of acculturation: a literacy class, the Project Renewal anniversary, and the "community" anniversary. All three contexts involved a group of people telling and enacting their story of "acculturation," of the possibility of change, of renewal. All three contexts present a rather negative and futile perspective of acculturation. The elderly women of the literacy class tell the story of the disguised egg, the story of the impossibility (and futility) of changing one's original cultural identity. The gap between the ideological façade of "successful acculturation"—as enacted in the project's anniversary and the community anniversary—and its practical failure in terms of participation and identification tell a similar story. These three contexts signify not acculturation but the opposite: the collapse of the ideology of acculturation, the bankruptcy of the idea that a new culture can be freely imposed on some passive recipients. The story of modernization, so often told by anthropologists and Project Renewal officers alike, is completely missing from the first context, and appears in the second and third as an ideological façade, remote from the everyday experience of "the residents" subjected to it. It appears to be one of the disguises worn by the egg from the first story.

Moreover, the three contexts present three different frames of relationships between the narrator of acculturation and his or her audience. The elderly students of the literacy class, reading their own story and the story of acculturation in general into the text of "the disguised egg," were their own audience. They narrated their story in the context of the class, signifying their own experience, each sharing the other's life experience, enacting together as a Greek chorus. The project's board members, in contrast, were the narrators of an acculturation story to be presented before another audience: the residents of the neighborhood and the city. This audience played a role (minor, partial, but existing) in the formation of the social text presented to it. Finally, in the case of the "community anniversary," only the narrative of presentation remained, while the audience (literally) disappeared. This third narrative in fact existed in a world of its own, a world devoid of audience participation, a world of pure simulation, of bricolage. It signified no reality, only ideological façades.

Having recounted these three narratives of acculturation, it is time to consider the fourth. In spite of the variety and richness to be found in Israeli society, anthropologists who have researched it have made little use of the three narratives presented here. Generally speaking, anthropologists have largely refrained from elaborating the views of residents regarding their "culture" and have almost never attempted to describe acculturation as a playful, winking performance or, even worse, an empty simulation. In contrast, anthropologists (in Israel and elsewhere) have largely imposed their own serious view, their own functional narrative of acculturation-as-development. In this they were no doubt reproducing the ideological worldview of the state institute employing them, as well as the ideological discourse of their own profession and its claims for objective, scientific knowledge.

One would have perhaps expected that in just such an immigrant society like Israel, grappling with questions of cultural identity and image, anthropological attention would be directed to the possibility that people may wish to repudiate the reality of their lives through cultural means, thereby either transforming it or abolishing it completely.[3] Not only has the question of the representation of cultural repudiation been all but ignored in Israeli anthropological literature, but a persistent and apparently ideologically inspired attempt may be discerned in many of its researches to substantiate the view that, despite the differences and the variety in what is termed Israeli society, it nevertheless possesses a depth of meaning that unites and bonds its members, even once they have cut the umbilical cord joining them to society. This view served as justification for decades of harsh immigration "absorption policies." Employed by many Israeli anthropologists, it serves as evidence of their ideological bias toward the central value system of Zionist nationalism (see a recent discussion of this debate in Shokeid 1992; for a critique of the failure of reflexivity in most Israeli anthropology, see Kunda 1992a and Gurevitz and Aran 1991). Many "applied anthropologists" working in the 1960s for the Jewish Agency in immigration settlements were committed to the view of "preservation of authentic cultural identity" while simultaneously submitting to the worldview and prescription of the state's development perspective. This paradox became the leitmotif in the narrative of Israeli anthropology, whose story is of course too complicated to be summarized here.[4]

Were the anthropologists who hold such unstated positions to examine their findings through the three viewpoints presented here, they might well arrive at a different kind of explanation. I am arguing here in particular for the need to problematize the existing dominance of mimetic representation. Israeli anthropologists, even when freed of the burden of development perspective, have kept their serious preconceptions about "culture" as an ontological essence to be found "out there" in the field. Rather than being a narrative, "culture" or "acculturation" was supposed to be "objectively" deduced from the rituals and ceremonies of the field. Rather then being a staged performance addressing, winking at, or denouncing a certain audience, the respondents' and anthropologists' accounts of "acculturation" were perceived as functional representations of a lived reality. A one-to-one link was thus established between the narrative and its contextual reality, and the multiple existence of alternative links was dismissed. Let me illustrate this argument with several examples. For example, the wink of self-awareness can be revealed in ceremonial revelry and saintly cults, so often discussed in Israeli anthropology as functional symbols of "authentic," (counter-)cultural identity. An analysis of this sort is already concealed between the pages of the research by Bilu and Ben-Ari (1992) into the creation of "cults of the righteous" by the Abu-Hatsera family. Or, the alternative interpretation proposed here can be used to show how birthday celebrations in kindergartens are not only "functional national ceremonies of socialization" but mainly a game (see Weil 1986; Shamgar-Handelman and Handelman 1991). Likewise, the element of simulation present in community singing among Israeli émigrés in New York, seen by Shokeid (1990) as a functional resort from cultural alienation, can be thrown into relief. A similar Baudrillardian simulation is associated with the practical Bible lessons attended by ultra-orthodox women, seriously interpreted by El-Or (1990) as a functional gender socialization mechanism. Such an alternative view can elucidate the well-developed self-awareness, among these women, of the paradoxes that create their status. Only moderate theoretical flexibility is required to demonstrate that the revelations of Moroccan dreamers (Bilu and Abramovitch 1985), the religious lessons in Jerusalem (Heilman 1983), or the structuring of the past by residents of an old-age home (Hazan 1992) do not conform to traditional representational relationships with the surrounding reality, and that an association of simulation would afford just as good an understanding of them as does the usual symbolic relation. In a society whose literature has already discovered rootlessness, rejection of reality, and the attempt to abolish it, one may have expected that anthropology, too, would find the appropriate theoretical tools for describing and discussing these phenomena.

Such alternative interpretations may well be put to the anthropologist by the people he investigates. This is the view currently addressed by various proponents of "dialogical" anthropology. This view emphasizes the sharing of ethnographic authority with the voices of informants (see Clifford 1983, 1986; Sanjek 1990; Kirschner 1987; and the special 1990 issue of the *Journal of Contemporary Ethnography,* dedicated to ethnographic research writing). This call is becoming ever more urgent as "the former subjects of objects of study are not only becoming an audience, and a critical one at that, but they are becoming anthropologists themselves" (Caplan 1988, 17). Part of the socio-anthropological literature dealing with postmodernism is currently searching for conceptual ways of formulating a possible theory of representation, despite the premise of infinite possibilities. The popularity of social philosophers such as Baudrillard, whose influence permeates this essay, is also evidence not of straying from the path but of breaking new ground. Will a different anthropological approach emerge from all this, one that in Baudrillard's words is a simulacrum of its predecessors and will thus abrogate both itself and that which it no longer represents? Will the discipline, rather than reinventing its own tradition, rid itself of some of its sacrosanct assets, such as authenticity, meaning, and claims of representation? The anthropological future, if there is one, holds the answer.

Notes

1. The principle of "adoption" by a "twin" community from the diaspora was one of Project Renewal's innovations. This enabled direct transfer of funds to the adopted community and active participation on the part of the adopting community in the physical and social planning and in the distribution of resources in the locality.
2. The popular employment of the concept of "community" in Arod was similar to its appropriation within the more "scientific discourse" of sociology. "Community," although regarded as a sociological unit of analysis and comparison, is in fact a mixture of commonly accepted denotation and lack of definiteness, of international meaning (Warren 1973; Schneider 1979) as well as unique locality (E. G. Cohen 1982). The rhetorical nature of "community" may well render it analytically questionable, turning "community studies" into a myth, as Stacey (1969) suggested. One wonders what the results would be of employing a similar, critical analysis toward the recent rhetorical upsurge about "communitarianism" in America.
3. Deshen's (1970a) argument concerning the destruction of symbols fits this line of thought but fails to address the theoretical implications of the phenomenon and ignores its significance for the intellectual destiny of social anthropology.
4. It is interesting to point out, in this context, that "applied anthropology" is still invoked as a neutral concept, as well as a guiding motto, by current Israeli anthropologists. Consider the following opening lines from a well-known Israeli anthropologist: "In recent decades, anthropology has proved to be of value in many fields of social practice. The achievements of applied anthropology are particularly salient in medical training and practice, in agricultural and community development, and in education. But in many other fields the application of anthropology has hardly begun" (Deshen 1993, 58). Such an enthusiastically unreflective view of applied anthropology is perhaps not surprising in the Israeli scene, although mildly shocking in the larger historical context of anthropology.

10

Gender and Power Relations in a Bureaucratic Context

Female Immigrants from Ethiopia in an Absorption Center in Israel

ESTHER HERTZOG

Introduction

Some thirty thousand immigrants from Ethiopia were brought to Israel between 1982 to 1993 and were sent to absorption centers[1] owned by the Jewish Agency.[2] Once there, they were treated as a homogeneous social collective of "new immigrants in special need of help," which implied the immigrants' weakness and otherness.

As a part of this "special" care, female welfare aides were introduced as instructors of the immigrant women. They were added to the various other workers employed in the centers.

In this essay I discuss the bureaucratic control of women immigrants from Ethiopia that developed in the context of absorption centers in Israel. I argue that the bureaucratic treatment influenced the emergence of gendered power relations and gendered role division among the immigrants. The officials encouraged the development of an "Israeli female" identity in the women immigrants. This process developed in direct relation with the existing gendered power structure in Israeli society and out of the bureaucratic setup. However, the officials explained the gender gaps and their gender-based treatment of the immigrants with cultural rhetoric.

The immigrants were treated by officials as belonging to distinct categories, mainly as family members, men, women, or children. I suggest that by transferring resources to "family units" and by allocating them through the men, the officials enhanced the bureaucratic "family" unit and the gendered power division within it. Housing was delivered to the family through the men; sustenance allowances were passed to "family heads," most of whom were men;

health insurance for the family was issued in the man's name; and vocational training was granted mainly to men. Moreover, the welfare aides, who related mainly to the women, asserted social control over them and transmitted through them the prevailing gendered social order. I suggest, therefore, that the family unit, the gendered disparity within it, and women's dependence on men emerged from the bureaucratic practices employed in the absorption centers and from the gendered power structure in Israel.

This essay is based on eighteen months of fieldwork conducted by the author during 1984–85 while living among the immigrants in a caravan in an absorption center (Hertzog 1999).

Theoretical Background

Following scholars like Freedman (1970), Yanagisaco (1979), and Buijs (1993), and Israeli scholars like Swirski (1984) and Marx (1987b), I suggest that gender relations and the "family" should be analyzed as a part of the surrounding economic and political forces. According to this approach, the family system is not an independent entity and neither the family nor the power relations in it are "natural" or self-evident. The "family" is rather a social construct, defined, shaped, and changed by the economic and social forces in society. I suggest that state bureaucracy is one of the major forces involved in constructing the "family" and in shaping the gendered power and role division within it. I shall use the case of female immigrants from Ethiopia in an absorption center in Israel to illustrate how and why state agencies influence the emergence of the "family unit" and the gendered power within it through their bureaucratic practices and agents. I contend that gender role division and family structure of immigrants from Ethiopia, in absorption centers, reflect the gendered stratification in Israel and are endorsed by the bureaucratic treatment.

Analyzing women immigrants' integration in bureaucratic terms is consistent with Marxist and feminist studies of scholars like Mcintosh (1978), Ferguson (1984), and Rein (1985). These studies point to the connection between bureaucracy and capitalist oppression. They criticize in particular the state welfare bureaucracy. Rein emphasizes the role of the "social welfare industry" in producing a growing separation between male and female occupations in the segregation of the last and in the feminization of poverty. Feminist studies indicate the indirect oppression of women by men, through women who act as social supervisors within bureaucracy, especially welfare bureaucracy, over other women. The welfare state structures a distance between groups of women and recruits some of them to key positions in the patriarchal systems and allocates them a major part in reproducing the patriarchal patterns.

Most of the vast research on absorption of immigrants published in Israel since the 1950s emphasized "cultural" differentials of the immigrants to explain integration processes (e.g., Ben-David 1953; Frankenstein 1953b; Eisenstadt

1954; Bar-Yosef and Padan 1964; Shokeid and Deshen 1977). In these studies, which focused on immigrants from Islamic countries in particular, the immigrants' collective inferiority and backwardness were implied. The "cultural theories" suggested that the family structure of the immigrants and the gender power division within it derived from a patriarchal culture brought by the immigrants from their homelands. Most of the studies about immigrants from Ethiopia continue to focus on cultural explanations (e.g., Y. Kahana 1977; Messing 1982; Rapoport 1983; Ben-Ezer 1985; C. Rosen 1985).

However, a few scholars, the most prominent of whom are Weingrod (1966), Willner (1969), Marx (1976), Bernstein (1981), and S. Swirski (1989), have revealed the patronizing policy of "absorbing" immigrants in Israel and criticized the ethnocentric "cultural" theories that have given academic credibility to the absorbing systems. They have indicated the central role played by the intensive bureaucratic intervention in integration processes of immigrants in Israel, and described how state authorities turn the immigrants into a needy category that is forced to be dependent on state officials. I follow this approach in describing and analyzing the bureaucratic control of female immigrants from Ethiopia and the use of cultural explanations by the bureaucratic establishment to justify its control over them.

Bureaucratic Patronage and the Emergence of Gender Power Relations

In the bureaucratic context of absorption centers women and men were treated as family members: the women were considered "housewives" and "mothers" and the men were "family heads" or "providers." I suggest that in their interactions with the immigrants the officials tried to restrict the woman to the home and to the absorption center, thus enhancing her dependence on the man as provider and on themselves as "helping" patrons.

Treating the immigrants as "families" included the delivery of resources through one of the family members, mostly the man, who represented the others in negotiations over these resources. I contend that gendered role division and power relations in the absorption center emerged from the categorized treatment of the officials and the bureaucratic mechanisms used in the distribution of resources. Ethiopian female immigrants were largely ignored in relation to employment opportunities and were excluded from vocational training. The differentiating attitude grew out of bureaucratic needs just as much as from bureaucrats' gendered and ethnic stereotypes stemming from the immigrants' cultural characteristics. Moreover, the officials transferred their treatment of the Ethiopian immigrant women as "housewives" and "mothers" from the gendered power structure in the larger society to the immigrants' lives.

I shall demonstrate these arguments by referring to officials' monologues, officials' written and verbal discourse, and daily encounters between female immigrants and workers in the center, female instructors in particular.

The following monologue from the center's director illustrates this patronizing bureaucratic attitude, which was rationalized by the immigrants' social and ethnocultural needs and background.

> It's about women. Here we have a dilemma. On the one hand we want to advance the women, give them some tools so that we can advance them to the level of women in Israel. We tell them that it is impossible to make a living with only one salary. We have to help them to a stage where they can begin to work. On the other hand if they go to work, the children will be neglected. They do not have the same responsibility that men and women of the twentieth century have. They do not know that if they go out to work the house has to be in order and the children looked after. They do their day's work and they come home and lie on the bed. The children wander about outside all day. I have experience in this area. It is a disaster to push these women into work. A disaster. My social worker in my previous workplace said that the children were neglected, ran about in the streets, and were filthy dirty. They had no proper food. The immigrants began to fight with each other. This destroyed the family. She got them to return home and started to invest in improving their self-image as housewives. It was not only the kids who were destroyed but also the wife and the home. It caused fights. The woman runs off and he murders her.
>
> Then we say O.K., we will not push her out to work—the opposite. We will try to stop her working. But we have to give her some kind of enrichment—after all it is they who educate their children. They should be in a position where they are able to sit with the child and see what he is doing. I don't say they have to guide them—they are not able to reach that stage. But at least let them not be afraid of their child's exercise book or of singing a Feast of Light songs with the child. We have to give them some enrichment so that they can guide their child. It will take another year or two.
>
> I say to them that they must first check themselves and ask how much you can take upon yourself. You must first be sure of yourself as a woman, sure of yourself in the role of woman. Only if you feel that you have other potential can you develop it and cope with home and work together. We will let you. We will help you. But let us not push everyone into work only for the money, because in the end we will pay for it. They might earn a few pounds as industrial workers but it will cost us more than they earn. It is better to put this money into the home and train them as housewives. In most cases they love this.
>
> They go out to work only for money. If you honor her position as a housewife and see her as equal to the male within the system and her job just as important as that of the male, perhaps even more—to educate the children, etc. When they want to leave the home we won't say no. But we should not encourage this idea. When they understand what it is to be responsible towards the family and the children, only then can we say O.K. Fine. They will explode if they try to do everything together.

> The immigrants are going through such a severe crisis and harsh dissolution of all frameworks and values. That's why we must preserve one fraction linked with reality. Someone has to pay the price of the tough cultural crisis they are going through. The women have to be empowered as mothers and wives. They don't know what is cleanliness, cooking, and childcare. All they know is extended family.

The director's words illustrate a deep patronizing and ethnocentric attitude toward the immigrant women. In such discourses, immigrant women appear to exist only as mothers to their children and wives to their husbands. They are perceived as primitive and irresponsible people whose primary raison d'être is to enable their children's integration into the host country. They are expected to weather the impact of the "cultural crisis" of immigration and to prevent the "destruction of the family." When resources are allocated to them for activities and training, this is for empowerment for the sake of their children.

The ethnocentric rationale was not only verbally expressed but was also an integral part of bureaucratic practices. One of the Absorption Ministry supervisors said once,

> I have stopped women's vocational training. We had the experience in Pardes Chana, where the women had started to work and then they have ignored any responsibility. They were leaving the children alone all day at home or thrown outside. Then I said that it is impossible to do this and we must think how much damage it will cause the Israeli society in the future. The changes are so drastic anyway because the men did almost nothing in Ethiopia. There they used to work three months a year in agriculture doing nothing afterwards. All the work was on the women, the water, graining the coffee, and the men were near the fire and did not even always nurture it. Now we want them to cooperate and help at home, as the woman goes out to work.

These monologues, apart from exposing paternalizing practices and stereotypes, demonstrate how officials presented their work as "professional" caring, protecting, and supervising of the immigrants. The officials needed the women in the absorption centers for the sake of their employment. Moreover, the women, kept within the center, enabled the control over the Ethiopian families, which entailed control over resources meant for the immigrant families.

The workers in the center used different means to limit the women's prospects in the labor market and their motivation to work outside the center. First, only men were sent to vocational training, which was offered to them to help them attain better employment opportunities. The man was considered responsible for providing a living for the other members in the family. Second, the officials reproached mothers who went out to work for "neglecting" their children. In fact, the officials' actions and perceptions derived from the gendered economic and social reality in Israel, where "home-sphere" activities are most commonly dominated by women, and the public sphere is primarily dominated by men. The labor market is characterized by a limited range of poorly paid "female occupations" and a large range of better paid occupations, held mainly by males. Organizing vocational training for male immigrants as family heads, rather than for women, stems from Israeli ideas of "normal" roles for women and men. However, discrimination against Ethiopian women with regard to vocational training was rationalized by the Absorption Ministry in terms of the immigrants' traditional background, rather than with reference to the preexisting gender division of labor within Israel. For example, a bureaucratic working paper stated that

> different types of action have to be taken in relation to women and men. This is based on the assumption that . . . in the traditional pattern of this immigration, the man is responsible for providing for his family and its welfare. From this, his status as the head of the family is derived, and he will continue to function as such for quite a long time.
>
> His role in the traditional society, the extent of responsibility which goes with his roles, and the education he has internalized since his childhood toward fulfilling this role make him unable to be flexible or easily influenced. Therefore, the general orientation for him is to adjust roles intended for him in the process of absorption to those that are inherent in him—vocational training and vocational advancement—which will increase his income and his economic self-confidence, and enlarge his options in broad social directions. (Gdor, Astman, and Salmon 1985, 104)

It was also explained that "the problem of the women in the Ethiopian ethnic group is the gap between their potential role in the absorption process and their ability to integrate in practice. Being busy with taking care of young children, their limited range of experience (including elementary education), and limitations derived from cultural norms concerning their role within the group delay the pace of their progress, in acquiring the language, a profession, and integrating in work and taking part in educational programs)" (4). Another bureaucratic working paper stated that

> The integration process of the Ethiopian women is slow and complicated in comparison to the men's because they not only have to overcome the cultural gap, they also have to adapt themselves to a sex role that will result in readiness to go out to work. In addition, the women must, like women in the modern world, fill a variety of roles, as woman, wife, working woman, and achieve some balance between them. Considering this process as a slow one, which will not take months or years, but rather generations, will help to see the changes in a realistic perspective and with realistic expectations for change. (Eran 1989, 221)

The officials, so it seems, blamed the women's ethnic origin for their discrimination. The cultural arguments were offered to explain, justify, and make self-evident the actions and decisions that derived from a social system that expects the women to be responsible for raising children and running the home. Men are considered, in this context, responsible for providing for their families. Even more important is the connection made by the officials between the "slow change" to be expected from the immigrant women and the dimension of time, which calls for their long-term involvement in the process of integration.

However, the officials' antagonistic attitude toward women's work outside their homes and beyond the center's borders could change when the conditions and their interests have changed. The officials could even become interested in sending the women to work outside the center. For example, when the manager of a factory for medical gloves asked the center's director to send women to work in the factory as soon as possible, the director instructed the staff with these words: "There is the problem with children. It is needed to be arranged for the working hours of the mothers. It should not be difficult to lengthen the opening hours of our kindergarten, if it won't work by the women's self-organized babysitting in the caravans. But this must be done quickly, because otherwise the factory managers will turn to other centers."

When the director became interested in sending the women to work outside the center he changed the rules. For the sake of organizational networking and for presenting himself as efficient in supplying workers, the director used the immigrant women as a resource in his interactions with outside factors. In that case the "cultural" considerations were put aside.

The absorbing agencies could find an encouraging support for their policies on academic grounds. Many scholars attribute the immigrant women's marginalization to their cultural background, perceived as opposed to the prevailing gender relations in Israeli society. I will use some examples to illustrate this point.

Ben-Ezer describes an immigrant's family as "a big patriarchal, traditional family with a clear role division based on gender. In the Ethiopian family the husband-father is responsible for economic, employment, educational and religious spheres. He usually represents the nuclear family in relation to the extended family or the community. Much respect was given to the woman-mother, who is responsible for taking care after the children, their education at home and different home tasks. Clearly, the children's rights and obligations are determined by their sex" (1983, 21). Schoenberger states that "there is a great gap between the woman's position in the Ethiopian family and that in the Israeli . . . the position of men and women in the Falasha[3] society is such that man's position is superior and woman's position is inferior. A woman is expected to perform only service jobs and she can not voice her opinion . . . all she is expected to do is to fulfill her obligations to her father or husband . . . women are just a property, like donkeys" (1975, 267).

Apart from their common stereotyped and ethnocentric attitude, these two descriptions seem to contradict each other, as one (Ben-Ezer) suggests that "much respect was given to the woman-mother," while the other claims that the women were considered "like donkeys." Moreover, various studies suggest that in Ethiopia, women have participated in "outside home" work, including agricultural work and trading their craft works (Faitlowitz 1959 [1908]; Y. Kahana 1977; Weil 1985; Banai 1988).

A study conducted between 1992 and 1993 (Benita, Noam, and Levy 1993) indicates, contrary to the "cultural orientation" studies, that dichotomized gendered division of labor cannot be inferred from the immigrants' interviews about their past. Rather, they indicate that 26 percent of the women worked outside their homes in Ethiopia and that no gender differences were found in terms of agricultural work, even though women were occupied in hand crafts more than men were.

Furthermore, the survey findings (Benita and Noam 1995) lend support to the claim that the absorption policy plays a significant role in affecting women's prospects in the labor market. It appears that the discrimination against women in vocational training led to their discrimination in the labor market later on. The absorption policy has channeled the women into "female" occupations: at home and outside, taking care of children and other dependents. The bureaucratic control and policies could not prevent the Ethiopian women from working outside the home and center. Economic needs, no less than personal aspirations, induced women to work out of the home. A single income, especially that of low-paid workers, and immigrants' special need for greater resources in order to get settled made an additional income essential. Therefore, women who managed to find a substitute to look after their children went out to work. They went to work in faraway places in seasonal, poorly paid, and physically demanding jobs.

Comparing unemployment rates of immigrants from Ethiopia to those of immigrants from Russia suggests that the participation of both in the labor force is significantly affected by gender. Female immigrants from both regions have higher unemployment rates than male immigrants. Some 30 percent of the immigrant men from Russia were unemployed in 1992, whereas 55 percent of the immigrant women were unemployed (Handels and Bar-Zuri 1994, 164).

The differences in unemployment rates for male and female immigrants seem to be in accord with the differences in unemployment rates of veteran Israeli men and women. Between 1991 and 1993 about 50 percent more women than men were unemployed (National Insurance Institute of Israel 1996, 76).

I conclude, therefore, that the gendered structure of the labor market and governmental policies are the main factors affecting women's employment. This is true for all women, whether veteran women or immigrant women from Russia or Ethiopia.

The *Somchot:* Controlling Women by Women

The bureaucratic control over female immigrants from Ethiopia in the absorption center was enhanced by women's support, namely by *somchot* (singular, *somechet*). Somchot are female welfare aides, "grassroots" workers with a limited education, supervised by social workers. Somchot were introduced into the welfare services in Israel twenty-five years ago with the aim of instructing women in housework and childcare (Etgar 1977). Somchot are usually instructed to intervene in "families with disabilities in social functioning." The welfare department in the Jewish Agency has adopted the role of somechet as "a guide for implementing trained skills . . . a tutor, an educator and an orientator for the Ethiopian family . . . for implementing learned skills needed for integration in the Israeli society" (Jewish Agency 1984, 9).

I suggest that through her "work relations" with the women, this welfare agent influenced the woman's position in the family. The role of the somechet was based on the similarities between her role at work and at her own home. Therefore, the unique role of the somechet was her personal embodiment as a living role model for women as "mothers" and "housewives" according to so-called Israeli standards. The social structure outside the center was thus transmitted by the somchot through their interactions with the women. A Jewish Agency document (1984) describes the qualifications expected to be found in a somechet as follows: "basic knowledge in running family life and the home in Israel. At least 10 years of schooling. A neat appearance, expressive skills and having a family." It appears that by introducing the somchot into the welfare "absorbing" services, the "absorbers" tried to resocialize the immigrants by transmitting the values and standards of the "absorbing" society to the immigrants. The center's secretary explained to me how she chose somchot, illustrating the aspect of embodiment of the female identity in the role of the somechet: "I didn't know a thing about what a somechet is and what is expected from her, so I asked each of them if she had children."

There were six somchot in the absorption center. Each was attached to ten families—or, rather, ten women—in practice. The immigrant women were encouraged by the somchot to fulfill the conventional "normal" Israeli woman's role, namely to accept responsibility for child and home care.

The following interaction between a somechet and a female immigrant, in the presence of the center's cultural coordinator and me, shows the extent to which the "woman's role" is self-evident for all, immigrants and somchot alike.

One day I was chatting in the office with a somechet and another worker, and an immigrant woman came in. The somechet turned to her and told her aggressively, "Enough with the coffee. You sit for two hours with one woman, then she sits for two hours at your place." Then she turned to us and added, "Instead of drinking coffee all day long, she should wash her child's head. What do I do? Every day I comb my daughter's head and check it. The child herself says, 'Ma, look and see if I have lice.'"

I asked the somechet what was wrong with drinking coffee with your friends, commenting that I do the same. She said, "We too have this problem in our neighborhood, but I'm not like that. With me the house has to be clean before I do anything else." Then she turned to the woman, saying, "Enough coffee," and pushed her toward the door.

The somechet acted like a role model, basing her reproach on her own experience. She referred to her duties as a housewife and a mother. Her excellence in performing these tasks, proudly presented by her, justified, in her eyes, her authoritative, patronizing attitude toward the woman. My resentment over the woman's humiliation did not include a denial of the assumption that it is women who have to take care of the cleaning and who are responsible for their children's well-being. In fact, I admitted my responsibility for the cleanliness of my home. The three of us took for granted the woman's responsibility for the household.

This example also illustrates the immigrant women's vulnerability to officials' denigration in this context. Pushing the woman was the physical expression of the unequal relations that developed between the two groups of women. The situation in which somchot would enter the immigrants' caravans without knocking on the door, criticizing the women about dirt, cooking, childcare, and so forth, was an everyday occurrence. Criticizing a woman with regard to her personal affairs and her socializing with other women was a way to exert social control over the female immigrants. The expression "to drink coffee" was used by the somechet to denote "a problematic" and an unacceptable behavior that allegedly causes the woman to set aside "important" duties such as cleaning the home and her child's head.

This situation emphasizes how daily prying into women's lives through an inspection for tidiness was legitimized. Blaming the women for failing to clean their homes entailed both tying them to the home and care of children and a profound stigmatization. By criticizing the women's cleanliness the somchot created a social distance and their authoritative position was asserted. Thus the interference weakened the woman's position.

"Taming" the female immigrants also included positive gestures, encouragement, and compliments, not only criticism. The following case illuminates this point.

One day the center's director asked the workers present in the office whether anyone was interested in joining him on a visit to a cooking workshop. The secretary and I accepted his invitation. In the room where the workshop was taking place some twenty women were sitting around the table. The cultural coordinator was there, tasting the baked cookies. He complimented the women for their work. The somechet was standing at the head of the table kneading cookie dough and cutting slices for baking. She talked very loudly to the women and was almost yelling at them. The director tasted the cookies and commented that he wished the women would learn to cook so well that they would be able to invite him to taste cakes at their homes. Then he patted the somechet in a fatherly way on her back.

Approval and compliments were, so it seems, used to promote women's compliance with their responsibility for house and family duties. The director's visit was a gesture of respect toward the "students" and an act of appreciation for the excellent job of the somchot. Praising the women's activity and diligence is associated with cooking for the family. The exclusivity of women's participation in the workshop elucidates that the home jobs were intended, by those in charge, exclusively for women. The teaching was also performed by women, who derived their experience and knowledge from their kitchens at home and not from any professional background. The officials perceived housework, such as baking and cooking, as self-evidently female tasks.

An exchange with a young couple illustrates this. The wife told me that she was participating in the cooking workshop. I asked whether any men were participating. The husband replied, "No, it is not for the men." I asked him whether the men want to participate, and he answered: "The officials say it is for women." It seems, therefore, that engendering the treatment of immigrants in the absorption center served to push the women into the female niche. The bureaucratic patronage minimized the chances that men would take part in "female" activities meant for women alone. The instruction aspect in the encounters with the women was rather marginal. In fact, the main activity of the somchot can be seen as "placing" women in their "right" place.

Discussing the matron's demand that I evacuate my caravan for four days (to accommodate two women soldiers) with my Ethiopian friend illustrates this point. Trying to sympathize with me, she told me how women were treated by the somchot: "My somechet is not good. All the time she says, 'Why don't you clean up?' I tell her that I am pregnant, my back hurts and I can't stand, but nothing changes her attitude." She continued, telling me about the other somchot. "They come to women who have had many guests and say, 'Why is it dirty? Why don't you clean up?' The woman answers, 'I am tired now. I shall clean in the evening.' "

It seems that the somechet took it for granted that the women were responsible for the home caravan cleanliness. My friend complained about the unkind and inconsiderate attitude of her somechet regarding special circumstances, such as being pregnant or having guests. She did not, however, reject the interference in her private life. Neither did she complain about how she was treated as solely responsible for cleanliness while her husband's share in the responsibility was ignored. This example illustrates once more the legitimate daily prying of the somchot into the women's lives. As the somechet was authorized to supervise the immigrant women, they became subordinated and were expected to conform.

The hierarchical structure of the absorption center introduced inequality into the relationships between the somchot and the immigrant women. The formal position of the somechet prevented, a priori, equal relationships from developing between the somechet and her "trainee," the immigrant woman. These bureaucratically constructed encounters forced the women to comply with prying into their lives and with constant criticism of their behavior as housewives and mothers. This structured power imbalance allowed the somchot to invade the privacy of the women but not the other way round. It follows that the bureaucratic indirect control, through the somchot's inspection, caused the women to comply with their perceived female roles.

The following example reveals how far the somechet could go in terms of interfering in "her" woman's life. A short time after a one-year-old baby had died, the somechet of the baby's mother told me, "I am going to take out her diaphragm. I have fixed her an appointment with the doctor for tomorrow." The somechet meant well. She thought that taking the diaphragm out would be for the woman's own good as it would help her to become pregnant and overcome her agony. The somechet never thought to turn to the husband. Needless to say, she did not think it was a matter that was too intimate for her to interfere in.

The issue of pregnancy suggests itself in this context. The Ethiopian women had been firmly encouraged by the matron and the somchot to use a diaphragm, not the "pill," to prevent pregnancy because the immigrants were considered too forgetful and irresponsible to stick to the daily routine of taking it. Thus, the bureaucratic construction of gender identity in Ethiopian women involved both pushing them to adapt to "modern Israeli" concepts of "birth control" techniques and an ethnocentric attitude toward the "primitive" Ethiopian women. In practicing their power over the immigrant women in female affairs, such as the use of devices for birth control, the somchot presented themselves as experts on female issues. Thus, women's sexuality played a significant role in daily power relations between somchot and immigrant women.

The case of the breastfeeding further illustrates the intense interference of the somchot in "women's issues." During my fieldwork a young immigrant woman had difficulty breastfeeding her premature baby. When her somechet wanted to provide Materna powder for her, the matron told her that she must try to convince "her" woman to breastfeed the baby.

The somechet said she had tried it already and the mother did not want to hear about it. The matron said, "You have to tell her she must breastfeed the baby. She is so lazy. She is so apathetic. She must try. You give her Materna only if there is no choice. Tell her that if she does not breastfeed the baby, he will die."

In their encounters with the immigrant women, the somchot exerted social control over them. The relationship between the woman and the somechet defined and symbolized, for those involved in the interactions, both directly and peripherally, the woman's duties and responsibilities. Through the somchot and other officials as well, the social environment influenced the women to comply with "their" niche as "women."

The bureaucratic control in the absorption center enabled organized interference in the immigrants' lives, women's lives in particular. Being tied down to their homes in the center made it easier for the officials, somchot, and others to approach the women. Thus the female immigrants became captive residents in the hands of the officials who needed them to establish their positions. Withholding the Materna from the needy mother was a means of ensuring her continuous dependency on the somechet and her superiors. The matron expressed a total disrespect for the mother. She treated her as being so stupid and primitive that she would believe her somechet if she told the mother that her baby would die if she did not breastfeed it. The belittling of the women as rational human beings as well as reasonable mothers was inherent in the encounters between immigrant women and the somchot. The following case emphasizes the power-dependence relations between the women and the somchot in the center. One day I was invited by one of the somchot to accompany her on a visit to one of "her" women. I followed her into the woman's caravan, which she entered without knocking on the door.

A woman was washing the floor inside the caravan. It was flooded with water. The radio was on and very loud. With no hesitation the somechet stepped straight ahead to the bedroom and came back with a baby in her arms. She was excited and full of pride and said, "I am crazy about this baby." I asked her cautiously if the baby had been asleep. She answered, "This is not what I care about." She came closer to me and showed me how sweet the baby was, boasting of how much money she could get from the American visitors for taking pictures of this baby. She said, "This is the prettiest baby in the center."

During all of this the mother continued to wash the floor. The radio continued playing and the somechet seemed very triumphant over every smile of the baby, who was trying to close his eyes. Then the somechet turned to the woman, reproaching her loudly, "All you need is that the maintenance worker will see you washing the floor like that." When I asked her what was wrong with the way she was washing the floor, the somechet explained, "This is a PVC floor and flooding it with water spoils it. It must be washed only with a rag." Later on I asked her if she was instructing the woman. She replied, "What for? She does not need to be taught any more. She knows everything. I come only to see how things are . . . if everything is O.K."

Feeling free to enter without knocking on the door; to step inside the caravan when it is being washed; to take the baby without asking for his mother's permission, disregarding the fact that he is asleep; reproaching the woman like a little girl in front of me—all of this reflects the structured control of the somchot over the immigrant women in "women's affairs." The immigrant woman seemed passive and helpless, as though she had no choice. It seems that she did not perceive it possible to reject the intrusion into her private life or to object to the domination of the somechet over her baby. All she seemed to be able to do was to ignore the offense and keep doing what she was busy with and make herself unfelt. It should be stressed that the dependency was not one-sided. The somchot depended on the women for their jobs. This explains the obsessive intrusion of the somchot, pretending to be vitally necessary on the premises. Instructing the women in housework was marginal or even nonexistent and the somchot had to convince their superiors constantly of their exclusive and unquestioned "expertise" in women's affairs. Finally, the officials in the center needed the "family," especially the women, to justify the need for their work. It has been argued that through the somchot the bureaucratic social environment influenced the women's compliance with their gendered affiliation and roles. The supervision and control exercised by the officials, especially by the somchot, over the Ethiopian women increased the latter's dependence and passivity.

Conclusion

I have discussed the bureaucratic treatment of women from Ethiopia in terms of power relations, focusing on how and why they were patronized and socialized into "Israeli female" identity by the officials. The case of Ethiopian female immigrants in an absorption center has been used to illustrate the role of state agencies in constructing gender stratification and the "family unit."

I conclude that intensive bureaucratic care of women is a powerful way to influence the gendered role division and power relations within the bureaucratically constructed "family." By treating the immigrants from Ethiopia in the absorption centers as "family members," the officials channeled them into the gendered power structure that prevails in the larger society. The officials in the various absorption agencies related to the family as a unit with a self-evident existence, irrelevant to their own actions. They treated the family as a closed and distinct system, and its members as belonging to different subcategories. While distributing resources on a family and gendered basis, the officials influenced the immigrants' gender roles and power relations.

The role of one specific worker, the somechet, has been emphasized and discussed as a powerful social mechanism in socializing women and channeling them into the female niche in society. Introducing somchot to instruct the women from Ethiopia but not other immigrant women reveals the latent bureaucrats' stereotyped attitude toward them.

Considering the implications of the bureaucratic "absorption" of Ethiopian female immigrants in Israel brings into the discussion the question of alternative courses for the absorbing policy. It is suggested that "direct"[4] rather than "indirect" absorption would have helped accelerate the integration process as well as avoid the humiliating interference in the immigrants' lives. Turning the immigrants, the women in particular, into captive citizens in the absorption center while being supervised by officials, especially the somchot, prolonged their dependence. I suggest that a "passive," almost invisible female behavior emerged as an indirect result of the intensive intervention in the women's lives.

The ethnocentric attitude, which has been implied mostly toward the women, was largely rationalized by the immigrants' cultural background. I suggest that while the bureaucratic establishment had a major role in the emergence of gender gaps and differences, it used cultural explanations to justify its policy. In fact, the cultural explanations were often used to mask gender-based discrimination.

Notes

1. Absorption centers form an Israeli social framework. They concentrate Jewish immigrants and offer them various services that are intended to facilitate their adaptation to their new context. Absorption centers were established in the 1960s to accommodate immigrants from Eastern Europe and Anglo-Saxon countries. In the 1980s and 1990s they were used mainly for immigrants from Ethiopia and for some immigrants from Russia. The immigrants were taken di-

rectly from the airport to the absorption centers. Forty-five centers were made available to accommodate the Ethiopian immigrants who arrived during Operation Moses in 1983–84. Another thirteen centers were filled by March 1985, and about eleven hotels were rented and used as temporary accommodation for the immigrants. As this arrangement was very costly, the immigrants were transferred to absorption centers after about a year. Only immediate families were sent to the same place by the Jewish Agency officials. Extended families were sent to different sites, depending on the space available. Young immigrants were sent to special absorption centers. Children under seventeen who arrived without their parents were referred to youth boarding schools. Soon after arrival at the centers the immigrants underwent medical examinations and treatment. A few days later they started their language studies in the "Ulpan," Hebrew classes for adult immigrants. The Ethiopian immigrants were offered ten months of Ulpan studies. Immigrants were meant to stay in the absorption center for one year, but the majority of them stayed for two or more years.

2. The Jewish Agency is a worldwide Jewish organization, founded in 1929, that encourages Jews to settle in Israel and assists them in doing so. The absorption centers founded by the agency are one of its main means of assisting immigrants during their first years in the country.
3. Falasha is the name given to a Jew in Ethiopia by the Christian Amhara. It means strange, or foreigner, someone who does not have the right to own land in Ethiopia.
4. Direct, as opposed to indirect, absorption refers to the immediate integration of Jewish newcomers to Israel without staying in absorption frameworks beforehand. This term (and policy) has been introduced into the absorption discourse since the beginning the 1990s, when the mass immigration from Russia started. Over the 1990s around a million people arrived in the country and received generous financial aid from the state. This absorption is considered as having been very successful.

III

Negotiating Society

Israeli society is still in a state of flux and does not yet hide the chaotic reality under a cloak of order and polite manners. It thus offers many opportunities for the study of negotiated order. The following chapters discuss the range of negotiated arrangements in various sectors of Israeli society and in diverse realms: work, politics, interpersonal relationships, socialization, and inculcation of the society's central messages. They illustrate the strategies used in these encounters, the topics and sites of the disputes, and the emerging social constructions of the ongoing negotiations.

Gideon M. Kressel discusses ideological negotiations over the notion of work. He shows how the spirit of cooperation among the members of cooperative villages (moshavim) was eroded when unskilled Arab labor entered the scene. This is one example of a general movement away from socialist ideologies to individualistic and capitalistic ideas. Tamar Katriel analyzes the practice of youth movements seeking to communicate their core messages through fire inscription ceremonies. The destructive forces of fire are harnessed in the form of blazing letters, conveying Zionist slogans that the impressible youths are supposed to take to heart. Orit Abuhav discusses the practice and norms of giving wedding presents, and how the dynamics of social exchange are disguised as acts of generosity. Hagar Salamon illustrates how bumper stickers are mobilized in the emotional battlefield of politics, engaging "left" and "right" in written repartee on Israel's streets and roads. Edna Lomsky-Feder shows that Israeli soldiers elide their involvement in warfare from their life histories, although soldiering is intimately interwoven in their daily lives. Tamar El-Or and Gideon Aran demonstrate how metaphors of motherhood and birth are used in the political discourse of the Jewish colonists in occupied Palestinian territories as they carry forth a political program that is hotly debated within the larger society.

11

"He Who Stays in Agriculture Is Not a *Freier*"

The Spirit of Competition among Members of the Moshav Is Eroded When Unskilled Arab Labor Enters the Scene

GIDEON M. KRESSEL

Dilemma at Work

One works for a living, but the function of work in higher forms that concerns us here can be derived from two basic aspects under which we meet it: as a contest for something or a representation of something. These aspects can be linked in such a way that the work represents a contest or else becomes a contest for the best representation of something. Representation means display, and this may simply exist in the exhibition of something naturally or culturally given before an audience.

The purpose of competition at work in Zionist-Socialist Israel was to establish a strong and just society of people living by their own labor (i.e., turning the Jewish occupational pyramid upside down[1] or the implementation of Hebrew labor) to consolidate the new nation building. Jewish immigrants to Eretz Israel were competing at work in pioneering, deliberateness, dedication, perseverance, risking of their own resources, and putting their life in danger. They competed at work with body strength, determination, dexterity, proficiency, knowledge, and sacrifice.

Usually a contest is not devoid of purpose; that is, the action does not begin and end in itself: it contributes to the necessary life process of the group. Moral values then stress physical and intellectual fitness as part of the work ethic. The more this ethic raises the intensity of life in the individual or the group, the more readily it will become part of civilization. The object for which we compete is first and foremost victory, and victory is associated with the ways in which it can be enjoyed. The fruits of victory may be honor and prestige, or they may be material or symbolic values that affect the life of the worker and the welfare of the whole group.

Competition over outstanding achievement in Israel in the 1990s did not affect the workplace as it had in the past for two reasons: the spirit of capitalism in its local expression removed the stress from the way a fortune was made and placed it on the amount of money amassed, and the process was accompanied by the increase of Arab labor at the workplace alongside Jews. The Arabs' entrance, at first to infrastructure jobs, diminished the willingness of members to compete at work even in situations in which they could perform better than Arabs. The view of the workplace as a racetrack suggests an addition to current sociological explanations of the choice of future occupation and of vocational behavior.

Cooperation is requested for the maintenance of public institutions and in extending a helping hand to members in need.[2] Competition has been confined to implementing skillful, diligent, and productive agriculture. A change of values in Israeli society and, recently, in government policy pertaining to the rural sector has disrupted these two tracks. Infusion of individualism and capitalism into the arteries of the moshav has brought about the dismantling of cooperative institutions and the liquidation of mutual guarantee agreements. Mechanization through the 1960s increased work efficiency, and the saturation of markets, quotas on production imposed by the Ministry of Agriculture, and the law of inheritance (which prevents fragmentation of the small holding) spurred competition in which the better fit were supposed to survive. However, in moshav Noon Yud (pseudonym), an unexpected change of circumstances has encouraged the tendency of the most able entrepreneurs to quit farming. Employment of Gazan workers in moshav farms beginning in the summer of 1968 has disrupted the conventional code of fairness in competitive behavior based on self-labor.

While the innovation of modern agricultural technology distinguished the most capable farmer and enhanced the attractiveness of farming, the farmers' reliance on unskilled labor harmed their professional reputation. Now, ambitious members who strive to demonstrate excellence must seek to achieve this outside the moshav.

Since striving for excellence is strongly inculcated, many people in their search for arenas of performance leave farming because they do not find it challenging enough. *Homo competitivus* will endeavor to accumulate capital, scrupulously implement socialism, or strictly obey religious commandments, finding it difficult to live without criteria for achievement. Anomie is explained as confusion over the rules of the game and a lapse of controls ensuring fair play whereby cheating prevails (Huizinga 1950).

By 1970, 400 moshavim, 250 kibbutzim, and a variety of private farms were supplying the local market with large quantities of farm products, and since opportunities for export remained limited, the number of people that could be profitably employed in agriculture was proportionately restricted (Gvati 1981). To maintain sufficient income, there was increased effort in mechanization to save on manpower and to increase work efficiency. Family members whose work was no longer required looked for employment elsewhere; they joined the armed forces or the civil service. The laws of inheritance, which prevented the splitting up of the small holdings, also encouraged the tendency to leave as a way of providing a variety of sources of family income. State institutions provided loans on easy terms to improve homes and public buildings, thus offering some compensation for the widening gap between rural and urban incomes. The road system was also improved to shorten the time it took to travel to and from the towns.

Then, the income from external work outgrew that from the small family farm. The improved quality of village life thus became suited to the raising of families; young couples began to acquire houses from farmers whose own children had grown up and had preferred the comforts of the city. The average age of the population of the moshavim decreased, and initially, along the coastal plain, the proportion of residents (those owning no farmland or with no on-the-spot income) gradually overtook that of the farmers who remained (Applebaum 1974, 1979, 1983; Shoresh 1988). A few efficient farmers took over the cultivation of plots belonging to those employed outside the moshav, exploiting technological advances and hiring farm workers (Zussman 1988). In this way, the principles of equal distribution of productive capacity were broken; the community, which had measured diligence and manual dexterity in terms of material success when everybody occupied farms of similar size, lost its yardstick for comparison. As the balance tilted toward the non-farmers, there was also a change of values; Arab labor became more acceptable.

Noon Yud: From Moshav to *Kfar* to Suburb

The first decade of statehood was marked by a great flow of immigration, by massive investment in establishing new moshavim, and by the encouragement of movement from town to the country in order to increase agricultural production and to overcome the austere conditions and need for rationing. But by the end of the 1950s, agricultural production had grown to such a degree that the Ministry of Agriculture had to apply strict production quotas to small holdings;[3] it also favored the moshavim on the periphery over those in the center of the country. In Noon Yud, a moshav of the Ha-Ihud Ha-Hakla'i, in the center of the country founded in 1954 on an area of 2,400 dunams (400 acres), the family farms were dismantled one by one.

At the beginning of the 1970s, three dairy farms were still operating, and by the end of the decade, all had shut down. Of sixty-five poultry houses in the 1950s, only five were still used in 1991. Of forty-five families that earned their living from farming, three were left. Of two hundred families in the village (inadvertently, the term *kfar* [village] was used to replace "moshav"), thirty-six still gained some income from the cooperative orchard (560 dunams) and from family orchards. Overall, the number of full-time farmers totaled ten; these included vegetable growers (whose fields covered the entire arable area of the village, plus additional plots belonging to other settlements, on which watermelons were grown), poultry farmers, a young man specializing in greenhouses, and a young man who grew mushrooms.

Noon Yud's founders, immigrants from Argentina, understood the importance of economic diversification and set aside an area for crafts and workshops, allocating small plots to members who did not intend to devote themselves entirely to agriculture (maximum area of six dunams, compared to complete small holdings of twenty-eight dunams). When most of the original members abandoned agriculture, whoever did not take the opportunity of developing a small craft or industry turned to trade or employment outside the farm. Houses changed hands as well. In these circumstances, the standard of living of those working outside rapidly improved in comparison to those who kept farming. This trend continued; sometimes prime plots lay fallow or farm buildings and installations that were built at great expense were neglected. Keeping open the option of directing unsuccessful farmers to more suitable branches of agriculture is not easy to accomplish; professional training and capital are needed to develop alternative branches in highly advanced agriculture, while fluctuations in the cost of credit (as in 1984 and 1985) can overwhelm the borrowers and threaten their chances of success.

Most of the investment in developing the industrial area, therefore, came from outsiders, some of whom even settled in the village. In this way, local residents could find alternative employment close to home. The settlement of people of means added to the village's coffers, improved its status, and attracted more new settlers of means. The demand for houses, even those that had remained unimproved since originally being handed over to the settlers as Jewish Agency houses in the early 1950s, increased in value. Whoever had previously wanted to leave but had not had the means of doing so, including those in debt whose farms and homes had been mortgaged, were able to find buyers and thus set themselves up in a town.

The recession in the Israeli economy from 1965 to 1967 and the resulting unemployment strengthened the members' desire to hold onto their homes and even caused some to return to their fallow fields, but not for long.

The Six-Day War extricated the economy from the recession, improved the employment situation, and at the same time transferred emphasis in agricultural development to new settlements beyond the Green Line. In the veteran moshavim, agriculture as a percentage of all types of employment was reduced (Applebaum 1986), which prompted further suburbanization of moshavim. Those in the central area close to arterial roads and the cities were in particular demand, although not all to the same extent.

According to Applebaum (1986), with members, the demand for housing was particularly great when (1) the cooperative was strong enough to prevent members from becoming embroiled in debt (because property under mortgage does not attract buyers until the owners' debts are met); (2) the cooperatives were not too strong to the point of enforcing mutual guarantees among the members for payment of each other's debts, something that keeps people of financial means at arm's length; (3) questions about equality among members of independent work or of Hebrew labor were suppressed and did not overly concern the moshav institutions; (4) the community did not place a premium on its agricultural character and actually limited the spread of livestock farms because townspeople tended to be put off by the smell; (5) a well-defined community character was maintained, and the moshav chose not to absorb more than a few families at a time, did not permit private buildings to encroach on public areas or fields, prevented multistoried buildings, and so on; (6) the community was zealous in maintaining living standards and keeping up public institutions and surrounding greenery and controlled the cleanliness of public areas; and (7) out of responsibility to the local authority, the growth of competitive power centers was discouraged and the development of special interest groups and struggles between *hamulot* (groupings of related extended families) was prevented.

In Noon Yud, all the aforementioned elements were generally present; it was highly in favor of housing and was the most prosperous of the villages in the area. Its outstanding characteristics were the following:

1. It exhibited a stance independent of party politics or movement ideology. Despite its linkage to the Ihud Hakla'i (a national organization of middle-class settlements founded in 1944), it was not obligated to the organization, which in any case was weak and made fewer demands of its settlements than, for instance, the Moshav Movement. Even though most of its members were formerly in pioneer youth movements in their countries of origin and included former kibbutzniks who did not conceal their inclination toward the values of the Labor Movement, their demands of the moshav institutions were limited to the subject of public services. The moshav secretary, not a resident, was hired by public tender, and an interview to assess his or her qualifications for the job according to his or her education and managerial skills was conducted.
2. It supplied green lungs and cheap seasonal fruits to the residents in the extensive orchard areas (mostly citrus [Grossman 1987]). The limited number of livestock farms (that nevertheless supplied neighbors with low-cost produce) and the industrial factories set up according to a master plan at some distance from the residential area offered additional income and products at bargain prices to the residents.
3. It was secular but liberal; that is, it was supportive of members who followed religious traditions and ceremonies but noncoercive. The village had a synagogue and an occasional *minyan* (a minimum of ten adult men, a quorum necessary for community prayer), mainly on religious festivals

and, in particular, on the high holy days. It was also widely used for family ceremonies such as bar mitzvahs and memorials.

4. It was Ashkenazi in character; though dozens of members were from families that came from Arab countries, or themselves emigrated from an Arab country, they mostly displayed outstanding economic success and a Western approach to planning and family and to their children's education. In comparison to the moshavim of the oriental aliyah (wave of immigration), the members of Noon Yud resisted the tempting offers of grants and subsidies by the settlement authorities and thus did not allow them to run their businesses. They had to achieve their goals by their own efforts. They also kept strict control over the cleanliness of public areas, prevented the development of internal feuds to the point of undermining the authority of the cooperative, did not allow members to be late in paying debts, and sometimes even forced those who did to sell their farms and leave the village.

Alternation in the Approach to Agriculture

The founders of the village remember years of toil and trial and initial hardship. They saw it as one of the obligations of the individual to bring about the needed statistical change in the national character (an indirect relationship to Borochov's model of inverting the pyramid).[4] This was required by the reality of the situation if one wanted national independence. They saw it as a way of fighting against the negative stereotype of Jews in the diaspora and therefore as a means of changing the image of the Jew held by the non-Jew. It was a *mitzva* (a good deed) essential for the renewal of the people's connection with its soil, to prove its right to its land, and so on.

For the sons of the founders (i.e., the generation that grew up or entered the circle of employment in Noon Yud in the 1970s), manual labor was viewed as nonessential. Of fourteen high school graduates who were asked in 1972 about their plans for the future after their army service, only two indicated that they looked to agriculture or an academic profession connected to it. The others felt that agriculture was only suitable for the young, while they are preparing themselves for a serious, real profession. In one's twenties, one must learn a profession to replace agriculture. A person who respects himself, they said, cannot remain in agriculture beyond the age of thirty. When one is established one ought to be far, far away from it.

Dani, a son of the moshav, a student in the Haifa Technion, described what passed through his mind until he settled on this point of view based on events that influenced him when he was positioned to do farm work on a kibbutz in the Jezreel Valley along with his military service.

> One winter's afternoon, I was shepherding the kibbutz herd of sheep on the hills to the south, and heavy rain began to fall. At first I thought that it was

> stopping; I sat behind the stone terrace wrapped up in my poncho, till I noticed that everything was soaking, from my poncho to my clothes, to my boots, till I was like a sopping rag, and it went on and on and on. When you're on guard duty in uniform and with a weapon, and that happens to you, at least you know you are on duty, standing under fire and rain. But I was dressed in blue work clothes and it made me think of my father tending his bit of orchard in Noon Yud. I felt as if he was, at that moment, in this flood, soaked to his bones and wretchedly dragging himself home. I pitied him so much, and myself put in his position when I'd already be old, with children, a respected individual and looking like that. That's when I decided that farming was not for me.

The devaluation of the status of manual labor and of farming, which then provided employment and a source of income for many of the members, came as a surprising disappointment, which was received with deep sorrow. With the pain came the realization that the farmers must analyze and understand what was happening to answer the question, Why are the young not following in our footsteps? Their answers are varied and can be divided into two categories: farmers who blamed themselves and farmers who blamed outside factors in general and the leaders of the country in particular. In the quote below, one of the founding members reflects on the situation and tries to explain why the second generation is uninterested in the farm. Ya'acov, a fifty-five-year-old production engineer, explains (recorded in the autumn of 1978 while orange picking in his orchard).

> Keeping a full orchard farm [twenty-eight dunams] today, with technical equipment and with growing and organizing arrangements [using contractors who employ wage laborers], is less of an effort than it used to be when we started . . . production costs are less than they were. All the same, if you want to save money and you've got the energy, you can always go out and do it right yourself. . . . That way the harvest is complete [the workers always leave fruit on the trees], the pruning is more responsible [one doesn't break branches like the laborers], irrigation is more economical [if you see a leak, you fix it at once], and the things you do with responsibility and love are felt at once. It also pays in the long run, perhaps not much. That is why [to make up for the low income relative to the effort] the traditional subsidy was granted [that the Labor Alignment Governments paid to the farmers]. So now, when they are reducing that subsidy, how can they complain about the youngsters? The present government is harming the profitability of farming, and the understandable reaction is pullout. Where great effort is optional, show me anybody who chooses the hard way. Look at myself, for example!
>
> When I finish work at the factory I'm happy to change my clothes and come out here till sundown . . . for me it's like sport and recreation, looking after my orchard although it brings in no income. I'm even ready to spend the

> money I earn at Tadiran on this hobby, on the understanding that it goes in cycles and that next year we'll succeed, and what we earn will pay for what we lost this year . . . but if we have to keep absorbing losses year after year, my wife, Esther, won't agree.

According to Ya'acov, doing things without getting a reasonable profit from them hurts the pride of youngsters who can't overcome the values of Israeli society in general and can't allow themselves to be presented as a *freier* (sucker, an idiot; a term of considerable contempt in modern Israel).[5] For himself, again, fruit growing is not viewed as employment in the sense of work to earn a living but an occupation, a way of preserving his health and sanity. Michael (sixty-five years old) also belongs to the original group of settlers, a former kibbutznik who works for the Histadrut (the General Federation of Labor) controller. Like Ya'acov, this afternoon farmer places the blame on the country's leaders. However, he puts particular emphasis on how American values have pervaded Israeli society as being responsible for the results, not only the poor income from farming. He says that while it is true that he is not dependent on the few pennies his orchard brings in, he does not hoe it as a *Beschüftigung für Kalikes* (work for cripples, a Yiddish expression stressing its unimportance; a way for the pitiable to pass the time). Michael explains (recorded as he was moving aluminum irrigation pipes in his orchard in the summer of 1977).

> It's man's nature everywhere to try to become bourgeois, while socialism was and remains a vision and ideal based on overcoming egoism, that's to say, *virtu* (in French), that's to say, giving up some personal benefits to allow society to progress. To maintain the orchard by the work of the members alone [with some hesitation] O.K. . . . perhaps you don't have to do every last thing yourself, but as much as possible, that, for us is a necessity of existence . . . because if we don't make the younger generation face, on the one hand, its weaknesses, and on the other, the need for every person to be aware of, and ready to contribute to, improving society, there is little chance of changing things for the better. We can only do that together.
>
> People who don't have the means of facing themselves can't make a society. The trouble is that in the media and in the schools of today [most of the moshav children study in comprehensive vocational schools in the neighboring towns], they teach you to rate people by their clothes, so who am I to tell my children that a blue collar is beautiful? Status symbols are taking root in society and setting the tone. It's a broadcast on a different wavelength, in a different code. And today it's not just clothes. Once they used to say *Kleiden machen Leute* [clothes make the man, viz, his value], but nowadays, to be exact one ought to say *Die auto machen Leute* [the automobile makes the man, viz, his status]. Not to look ridiculous, you need to buy everything and eliminate the impractical.

The retreat by the youth of Noon Yud from agriculture was influenced, according to this explanation, by its becoming an embarrassing visiting card for them. Even though in and of itself the work is enjoyable and good, and engaging in it adds to the internal beauty of the community, it spoils their image in the eyes of their friends from outside. Does this mean that it is the status of a tiller of the soil that has been injured and no longer bestows respect on the young people of the maturing generation in the new Israel? (See Ortiz 1979 on the devaluation of agricultural labor.)

We can obtain a partial answer to this question from the point of view expressed by sons of a moshav close to Noon Yud who left a life of plenty with their parents to set up a unique farm under difficult environmental conditions in the Negev desert in southern Israel. They partly expressed their stance during a conversation I had with them in January 1988.

Mediator: This is your fourth year here . . . , and if you haven't yet achieved economic stability, at least you've proved that one can make a living on an arid hillside like this. [*A look of astonishment, a shrug of the shoulders from lack of desire to relate to this.*] It makes one respect you because it requires a constancy of purpose and no small measure of self-sacrifice.

Alon: What's that?!

Mediator: There must have been other short-term volunteers, let's say for a month, who came to the area or were ready to work, even by your side, for a certain period, but determination is measured over time, and for four years now you've kept going. It's not been easy for you, but you haven't given up, and now you can begin to see results. You are leaving footprints in the sand. Stamina is also a measure, isn't it?

Nurith: It's not as hard for us here as you think; it's just nice here. [*They notice my embarrassment at having entangled myself by my taking a high tone and come to my aid.*] The moment it stops being a pleasure, we'll just stop and go somewhere else.

Mediator: What things in particular make life here on the hillside so pleasant?

Alon: First of all, life is quiet here. From morning to night, there's nobody to order you about; and another thing, only someone who loves the nature of the region can understand.

Mediator: Alright, but all the same, you're surrounded by desolation, so there are those who would call your putting down a stake in this hill a pioneering act. Don't you feel like pioneers? How is that you're seen as pioneers and you don't care?

Alon: If we had found the quiet and the nature we have here in the center of the country, we wouldn't have come here. Just go near Tel Aviv and see what it's like [*having second thoughts*].

Nurith: We don't say it's bad in Gush Dan [the name given to the highly populated central coastal region], we just say it's hard to find there a mince spot like this.

Mediator: And what's bad, say, in the hills of Kashmir, the Appalachians, or the Andes? Does the farm have to be situated in Israel?

Alon: We think in Hebrew, and here [in Israel] it's comfortable, although we can get by in English and Spanish. We've no reason not to move somewhere else if it's worth it, why not? We've already toured many countries and laid our eyes on quite a few spots. We've no special obligation to this country . . . if they were to offer us a place abroad with conditions like here? Sure we'd consider it on its merits. [*After further thought.*] But the offer would have to contain no less than we have now.

Mediator: Why are you so against the notion of being called pioneers?

Alon: [*After thinking for a minute and throwing a stone at a dog sniffing around the cattle trough.*] First, if you say pioneer, it means that later on others have to follow, right? And we don't want to be flooded. We want to stay here in peace. Second, people place their hopes on a pioneer; he's expected to do certain things, yes? And we don't want to have to do anybody a good turn, or even indirectly glorify or humiliate somebody by means of the life we've chosen. We want to live private lives, obligated only to ourselves, and that's all.

Mediator: So O.K., you live your lives without giving yourselves fancy names. But how can you prevent the interest you are creating? People look at you from outside and see you as accomplishers. There is some vision to which you are connected . . . does that bother you? Do you want to prevent it?

Alon: Sure! [*With some qualification after further thought.*] It's not that we want to or can interfere with the thoughts of others . . . journalists come and publish articles about us that bring curious people out here in their wake.

Nurith: Afterward there are those who offer to lend a hand, or are sympathetic and offer us sums of money, which we usually politely decline. . . . The trouble is that we, ourselves, begin to see us as part of a venture; then we begin to complain about government offices we actually don't give two hoots for and want nothing from, and that gives life a bitter taste.

Mediator: Do you follow the anarchist doctrine, that we can do without the state and national institutions? For instance, when, against your wishes, you're bouncing around government offices among the dumb bureaucrats, what complaints do you make to them?

Alon: To give you an example: the road from Eilat to Tsnifim is excellent. The road from Makhtesh Ramon to Beer Sheva is good. But the section of road from Ma'ale Ha-Meishar to Nahal Faran and Tsnifim, only a forty-kilometer section, is old, full of potholes, and dangerous. A few million are needed for repairs and they'd be able to attract . . . if just 5 percent of the internal tourism that flows down to Eilat via the Arava road were to return by the hill road and stop off at the Ramat Hanegev tourist sites—the restaurants, the gas station, the guest houses—they'd spend some money and provide employment for hundreds of local families. Such a simple idea to get things moving. . . .

Mediator: It sounds as if you suddenly got turned on by something Zionist, don't you agree?

Nurith: [*Self-justifying and wiping an unwanted grin off his face.*] It's not that we're against Zionism; we simply want to say that what brought us here was not Zionism. . . . Let us tell you, we're nobody's *freiers!*

The young people talking like that are Ashkenazim, in their thirties, and wiry laborers who were educated to lend a hand in the creation of Israel, to make the deserts flourish. They have also learned a chapter in the book of veering winds of ideology, one that sends people out on self-sacrificing missions and then washes its hands of them. The deteriorating status of agriculture is not foreign to them, and they are aware of the growing tendency to measure things in terms of material profit. They solve the conflict between Zionism without quotation marks and Zionism with quotation marks paradoxically by performing Zionist deeds, camouflaging their motives with statements suited to the spirit of tough individualism and achieving their vision of personal fulfillment. Their words are similar to those of their own generation in the West, translated into Israeli Hebrew of the 1980s.

Far Away from the Fields

We left Noon Yud, whose sons have extricated themselves from the short-lived tradition that their parents established,[6] understanding that climatic influences holding sway in the surrounding Israeli society have been responsible for the consequences. An analysis of Nurith and Alon's words shows that one cannot talk of a general turning away from farming. One cannot dismiss it as work unsuited to the Jewish nature, as some who were sickened by the conditions of farming work in moshavim in the center of the country in contrast with that in the periphery tried to explain to us. The connection between the external and internal circles are illustrated by the results of a survey of the graduation classes of youngsters from Noon Yud from the years 1978, 1982, and 1986. Tables 1, 2, and 3 list their study programs and their employment or choice of preferred employment for those still studying. Eleven completed their schooling in 1978, seventeen in 1982, and twenty-nine in 1986.

As shown, the tendency is toward the academic and service professions and away from production. What explains the youths' change of mind? What follows are some comments, beginning with those of Haim (among the last of the farmers in the village growing vegetables in the open). Haim (forty-five years old) explains the retreat from agriculture as a drastic, rapid development that had already begun in 1968 with the employment in the village of workers from the territories (Arab laborers from the West Bank and Gaza who became widely employed in Israel after the Six-Day War). Haim opens by making a rebuke.

Table 1
Trends of Study, Career Tracks, and Present Employment for Noon Yud Graduates, 1978

Study program/ number	Level of training	Employment
theoretical (5)	academic (4)	social worker (1)
vocational (3)	seminar, etc. (3)	engineer (1)
agricultural (2)	other (4)	vet (1)
incomplete (1)		lawyer (1)
		teacher (2)
		paramedic (1)
		housewife (1)
		farmer (1)
		workshop owner (1)
		transport worker (in U.S.) (1)

Table 2
Trends of Study, Career Tracks, and Present Employment for Noon Yud Graduates, 1982

Study program/ number	Level of training	Employment
theoretical (10)	academic (4)	economics (1)
vocational (4)	other (12)	education (1)
agricultural (3)		biology (1)
		engineer (1)
		computers (1)
		teacher (3)
		farmer (3)
		service worker (2)
		mechanic (1)
		insurance agent (1)
		housewife (1)

Table 3
Trends of Study, Career Tracks, and Present Employment for Noon Yud Graduates, 1986

Study program/ number	Level of training	Employment
theoretical (16)	students at academic institutions (12)	studying (12)
vocational (7)	other (17)	management/sales (3)
agricultural (5)		teacher (3)
incomplete (1)		full-time army (3)
		nurse (2)
		hotel service (2)
		building worker (1)
		goldsmith (1)
		on a trip abroad (2)

How are they [our sons] to blame? If I were their age and took a blow like that, I doubt I would choose the occupation I have today. As soon as the workers from the territories came, all the work could be carried out here at low cost by a third party . . . , so why work hard? It occurred so fast that even I didn't grasp what was happening to us . . . and then the Yom Kippur War came and caught us in the middle of the autumn harvest without the workers from Gaza. [During the emergency situation from October 6 to the end of the war, Arab workers generally stayed away from work inside the Green Line.] Nobody had realized how fast we had become accustomed to that ease and comfort. We had to rely once more on our own workforce, so it didn't seem unreasonable to do what had to be done, simply and obviously to bother our kids to come and help. . . . In any case, there were no classes and they had nothing to do except to be glued to the radio. . . . So we notified them to assemble at 6:00 A.M.; we expected between thirty and forty and only nine turned up. Another three girls and a boy arrived at the field at 8:30 A.M. . . . Then we talked about money, eight lirot for six hours of work [to midday], and seventeen came. The second day of work was also so-so, and you could still understand it. It takes time for the body to get used to bending over. . . . In six hours they managed what a regular worker does in one; they cracked jokes, ate and drank, went to the side to piss . . . , still, finally you must get used to it, don't you? But with them it got worse from day to day till it became intolerable. When they couldn't handle it anymore, you could sense it by the damage they left, pelting each other with zucchini! They played tag, they ran around and

> rioted among the rows, uprooted seedlings. . . . In the end we had to kick them the hell out.

Dalya and Ronith, both seventeen years old and in the eleventh grade, were there, and they tell another version of the same story.

> The work was fun until some workers from Gaza had returned, to whom he [Haim] paid by the end of each day. We got used to the physical toil with no problems, and the team, including some grown-ups, was effective and pleasant; but he who was all-out thankful to us at the beginning began yelling at us, showing the manners he had acquired talking to his Arab workers and calling us spoiled brats. And when we talked back to him, to keep us quiet, he began to play on the money string. So far we were all engaged doing voluntary work and no one mentioned money. But if on a payment basis, the little he offered and the trouble he caused us bossing around . . . was no fun any longer.

Harvesting the Washington orange begins in November, and in 1973 the number of Gaza workers at the worksites of Israel was small. The local youth were summoned to the harvest; a few arrived, and for a fortnight the team work continued while the man in charge of the grove complained about the meager output, accusing the kids of being lazy and careless. Mariana (twenty-seven years old), a housewife and formerly a volunteer from Holland who had joined the team, explains her view of what happened: "As long as the local team was all by itself, it was pleased; the work was done considerably well, with jokes flying around. Being together with cheerful young people, then who cares about mud on the shoes or socks soaked with dew and rain? But then came the Arabs back to work together with a team of men, faces of dummy expression, greedy eyes, hanging jaw, and brown teeth; who wouldn't mind mud on the shoes?"

Whom Can We Keep Up With?

When the unemployed workforce from the administered territories began to return to the moshav fields, the departure of the youngsters from the fields and orchards increased. The large number of available workers reduced the cost of simple labor and lowered the status of blue-collar workers, in particular among Jews of oriental extraction and Israeli Arabs (Kressel 1992b; Semionov and Lewin-Epstein 1987). Moshavim that were based on arable farming, especially those of the eastern aliyah (wave of immigration in the early and mid-1950s) and other moshavim that had not established bounds of permitted and forbidden with regard to the principles governing work ethics to help fend off the flood of workers from Gaza, altered beyond recognition. The norm changed imperceptibly, and false justifications were given for it, as Michael explains:

"It's preferable and right, taking the social dimension of the problem into account [since we are presently responsible for the welfare in Gaza], not to take away from them [the Arab workers] the simple jobs both they and we can do, and for us to do the work that only we can."

In the beginning, operating tractors was included in the work members carried out, but later on that too was given over to skilled Arab hands. In parallel, it became necessary not to be seen toiling over dumb physical work more than was essential; as one of the veteran members, a graduate of a youth movement in Argentina and a former kibbutznik, contemptuously said of the moshav youngsters: As for them, they mustn't make a mistake and exert themselves [working] during the day whenever it's possible to save a little energy for the evening.

As they describe it, overseeing the work done by the Arab laborers is necessary, but one must take care to do so sitting in the driver's seat of your car. In the fifth year of the existence of the Green Line, not only the operation of mechanical equipment but also the overseeing of the Arab laborers from the driver's seat has been largely handed over to Arab subcontractors; since they have been seen driving around the moshav on tractors, accepted conventions have changed. Thus, the members' own habit of using tractors around the village to run their daily errands has faded; it's too much like the Arabs. From this point on, use of the Ferguson has been left to the subcontractor, while the members, even for the shortest of local journeys, use the car. The question then arises: What is the force caused by the presence of the Arabs that so repels their Jewish colleagues? One Saturday evening, a group of members discussed the subject (recorded in the winter of 1980); Akhino'am, a thirty-eight-year-old resident of Noon Yud and a nurse in the local hospital, expressed her opinion and explained an important point.

Akhino'am: In the hospital, side by side with us, there are dozens of Arab doctors and nurses who come from the local towns and also from villages in the north, and so far there has been no special problem accepting them as colleagues. It's a plain fact that the Jewish teams don't switch their work because of them.

Mediator: Perhaps what counts in the hospital is their relatively small number [compared to the number of Jewish workers]; as long as there are few of them, it doesn't matter, because their participation doesn't worry the others.

Akhino'am: It's true there are hardly any Arab nurses, but with the sanitary workers, who are mostly Arab women, we also have a large total number of Arabs.

Mediator: Then perhaps it's because the respect accorded to doctors and nurses is guaranteed; perhaps the good salary makes the difference. If you don't mind, let's take an opposite case; suppose the demand for unskilled workers was so great that they offered, say, to fruit pickers, the wages they give a doctor. Would that be enough to increase the willingness of the village youngsters to work in their company, to see them as colleagues?

Akhino'am: If, for instance, the heads of the hospital departments were clever and talented Arabs? A good question. If they were the modern, cultured people and the Jews were the trainees, then perhaps they'd be like the Jews and we'd be like the Arabs. [*General laughter.*] Then we'd surely be the ones seeking their company, and maybe they would avoid us.

Mediator: If that's so, perhaps it's easier to accept the Israeli Arabs as colleagues, especially those who have made progress, while the Arabs from the territories who are relatively more primitive are harder to accept.

The question is answered by Yavin, a forty-five-year-old village member and manager of the large regional citrus-packing plant.

Yavin: You'll be surprised to hear that quite a few of the fruit pickers and building workers are high school graduates and even have technical college diplomas from Egypt and goodness knows where else.

Mediator: Then it's likely that the problem of their presence is not actually in the bad name it brings to the job, as it were, of work for the unfortunate but in the climate, work relations, and the sometimes unpleasant friction.

Yavin: If there's a retreat from farming, that's not yet a sign of friction. It may be the opposite, that work relations are based on a clearly defined ladder of authority that doesn't allow any clashes. What may be and is probably at the heart of the matter is the rotten feeling those in authority have working with them, chiefly the Gazans. Just thinking about this Gaza, a bottomless pit of problems, makes you want to run a mile.

This last explanation for the retreat from farming in the village highlights what the presence of the Gazans (in particular) on the farms has done to the connection between the member and himself. That is, it is not simply a question of the depreciation they have brought to the job but the touch of guilt that penetrates the members' hearts when they put them to work and see themselves as wrongdoers (Semionov and Lewin-Epstein 1987). This perhaps explains how the subcontracting of farming on the moshav passed so quickly into the hands of Arabs.

Since the company of the workers from the territories is not unpleasant for all the members (there is the motivation to work with them), we tested another explanation offered by the forum: the infiltration of their (the Arabs') traditional system of values, which conceals a contempt for manual labor, into the local circle of members that worked with them. Haim explains,

For me, working was in my blood. During the first period [of employing Gazans] I worked with them at everything, but right away you see it doesn't improve your standing in their eyes. It's not like with us [the industrious are

> better than the lazy]. They uneasily hint that it's not necessary . . . when I used to load the crates, my *rais* [foreman] would take them from my arms saying, *Mush lazem! Mush lazem!* [not necessary that you tire yourself out] . . . It's not that they just want to curry favor, they simply want to see you as the boss, and a boss who sweats harms his status, and when you go down in their eyes, you endanger your authority.

The value system of the Arabs from the territories is a matter for specific research. If, however, their representatives working at the various Noon Yud sites cast their cultural shadow over the Hebrew work ethic, it is worthwhile to test the question, How did it happen so easily?

Here is a description of talk recorded at one of the moshavim in the Negev that forcefully raises some points not mentioned in the above discussion at Noon Yud. Eli, a fifty-year-old Tunisian from a moshav with members from a variety of family origins and owner of a fruit-tree farm and a herd of sheep, explains how the entrance of Gazan workers began and what their influence was (recorded in 1988).

> Workers from the [Gaza] Strip first came for the citrus picking in the cooperative orchard, directed to us by the labor exchanges, in the winter of 1969. Our contact man with them was Moshe Mizra'i from the second generation [in Israel] of immigrants from Syria who was fluent in Arabic. After the citrus harvest, he kept a few of them on to pick apricots in his own plot, and actually, from then on they stayed with him and not just for seasonal work. . . . At the start, there was some criticism, mainly because at the end of the day he'd let them sleep in sheds in the courtyard, but all in all, it wasn't a bad arrangement. Moshe was able to supply workers to whoever had urgent need of another pair of hands and became a big man. When the matter was raised at the general meeting [winter of 1971], there were already a number of farms with subtenants like that. At first they still looked pretty shabby and weren't very noticeable. There were those at the meeting who called for their expulsion, while a few took pity on them.
>
> The Arabs slowly learned more and more from Moshe, and those who picked up some Hebrew no longer needed a translator. The presence of this reserve of assistants quickly spread, and the members who resisted employing them began to feel they were being left behind. In some bitterness, they asked for the intervention of the Movement, transferred the matter to what we call the Institutions, and under their wing tried to take up the fight again at home. But it was already too late to change the situation. They remained a minority, not just in our moshav. Whoever carried on doing the work themselves became exhausted. Perhaps the moshavim of the Arava [the rift valley running from the Dead Sea down to Eilat], like Ein Yahav, which don't have the administered territories next to them, can play at principles, but here they [Arabs looking for work] are swarming everywhere.

In 1989, two of the village youth, waiting to be called up for their army service, took on the job of cutting lawns. Another two together raised a field of fodder that they sold after its harvest to horse breeders in the neighboring village and made a nice profit. Another four worked as shop assistants in local towns, three were counselors in children's summer camps, and the rest (the majority) waited for the call-up and did nothing. These few representatives of the large graduation class, who could be seen every day in their work clothes, focused on their work and, pleased with themselves, were approvingly received by their parents and their friends' parents. They were produced as evidence to support the statement, Look, it's possible, the chain has not been broken.

Others were less impressed and preferred to mourn the spirit of the past. Pessimism over the chances of the village surviving as a village, which I had already recorded in 1978, reflects this mood. Dov, an eighty-year-old father of five and grandfather of twelve from Bielorussia who was raised in Argentina and immigrated in 1951, concludes,

> They're not the reason [the Gazans]; it's our politicians, from the Jewish streets. They [the politicians] go up and down between Jerusalem and Gush Dan (Tel Aviv area) all the time, passing by us just a couple of meters away, but they never stop. Maximum, they stop off at the Ramle market where the agricultural produce is good and cheap. . . . What would happen to them if they were to spend a little time in an orchard picking fruit? So people should see they know well enough how to bring along a photographer and a journalist to preserve them for posterity, putting on a pair of boots for a little fruit picking! That would influence the youngsters' scale of values more than a hundred Arabs. Everybody should look, the Arabs too, at the prime minister or one of the members of the cabinet putting in a little time in work clothes. What would be wrong with that? Then a negative label for such beautiful work wouldn't be possible. All we've got is a Knesset [parliament] of white collars and ties, lawyers from Tel Aviv with lily-white hands like fine gentlemen. . . . Look, I'll tell you about my kids, something that happened a month back; they were quarreling about who was going to roll up his sleeves and, actually, who wouldn't lend a hand to finish putting in the drip irrigation in the orchard. I had bought the materials [plastic tubing and drippers] and left it beside the trees, ready for them to come. Earlier, we'd talked about a special effort; all three of them would come, with their children, for a weekend of hard work, once again together with their dad, like when they were growing up. Well, they arrived and they hadn't even gotten out of the car before they were fighting about who should do more and who should do less.[7]
>
> Finally they got out of the cars, drank some coffee, and ate some cake, and the time came to roll up their sleeves. They did that and got a little done, a very little. Most of the special effort they left to the granddad, to somehow get it done with the Arab workers. After all, they were educated to the work, were always energetic, ready for any effort. At first, after they went away and set-

tled into work in the city, they used to come back on weekends to help on the farm, they used to say they missed working outside in the open air . . . and now, psshh . . . an attitude like that, where does it come from? Perhaps they're embarrassed in front of their wives and children, or their new city friends. In the city, a game of tennis is the acceptable way of stretching your bones, and for village air you go on a picnic; and a Jew who still works the fields is a sad sack, someone who hasn't found a way to get out of it [farming] in time, someone who, at best, is a nature preserve [staying on because of idealism].

The feeling that the authorities are responsible for national morale and the spirit of the next generation is shared by most of the members. The criticism of the unchecked flow (or, as they called it, nonstop policy) of workers from the territories to the moshavim was also linked to the activities (or failures) of the government. On the basis of the understanding I gained from Noon Yud, I formulated this question: In what way, in your opinion, is the government failing, in view of the resulting attitude of the moshavim to work? This question was put to moshav members in the western Negev by student researchers with whom I worked from 1986 to 1989.

The answer given by David (a forty-six-year-old born in Romania, a graduate of Youth Aliyah, and a member of a Negev moshav from the 1960s) was recorded in the winter of 1988, and in essence it agrees with what Dov said. He also believes that the behavior of the younger generation, avoiding responsibility for the village fields, is influenced by a public climate of evading responsibility for public (national) property evident, he says, throughout the country. This is influenced, he believes, by a lack of personal example from the country's leaders. However, his point of view is different in his identification of the guilty leaders and in his demands that they correct the situation.

David: It's all a matter of education, and just as you can compete over how much output you can accomplish at work, you can also compete over your achievements in not working. It all depends on the agreed rules of the game, and I had the opportunity to learn that immediately on my arrival in this country. I was fourteen years old. I had no family and I was sent to the Ahava orphanage near Haifa. . . . There, the education emphasized love of work according to Gordon's gospel [a famous pre-state socialist of distinction] to the extent, for example, that the undisciplined kids were punished by taking away their right to work.

Once, they caught one of our group pinching some stuff from the economia [storage cupboard]. His punishment was particularly charming in its phrasing: removal of the privilege of working [on the institution's farm] for a whole week. We received it with sad laughter, as something serious and at the same time entertaining. It took us some time to learn how to react to the attitudes of the teachers with an independent mind of our own. . . . In a spirit of *dafka*[8] as a game, we set up a rule book for energy savers. We imposed bans and boycotts on ourselves for the crime of unjustified wasting of energy. And we instituted half-mocking punishments for anyone caught breaking the norm and making too much of an effort. Like, for instance, going to the dining hall was a must, you had no option, but to make the effort to turn the door knob or push the door open, we decided, was excessive. So we'd stand near the door to the hall, pretending to read the notice board, till somebody would go in and then we'd quickly squeeze in behind them. They had a kind of springy swing doors there that would swing in and out till they settled down.

Another method was to accompany some girl [the group excluded girls from the secret roll call], who would innocently push the door open for herself and us. It was a kind of sport: the main thing was not to touch the knob, to enter without taking one's hands out of one's pockets. Once we caught a boy called Hilik not restraining himself, opening the door, and running to eat. His penalty was to schlep Isaac on his back, like a sack of flour, all the way back to the dormitory. You might say we expended vast energy for the saving of negligible energy. But those were the rules of our game. We were lucky, of course, that we were not required to slave in order to live. They gave us all our meals in the dining hall without considering if, how, or how much, we worked . . . when you're supplied from the horn of plenty, it's easier to develop games of taboo.

Mediator: Are you saying that the comfort in which the children are living spoils them to the extent that they escape to a land of games, a land of dreams?

David: From newspapers and books you can learn that even on the poverty line, clochard cultures develop of conscious, born beggars who sleep in the refuse but will do everything not to be ashamed and to seem to be working. It's a matter of outlook, but . . .

Mediator: You are really saying that perception is what actually determines experience and not the other way around, as Karl Marx put it?

David: Everyone's perception here can determine his own experience, even to the point of death. And what brings people to suicide if not a state of perception? No, but what I'm saying is that education will determine how we live here and how . . . the education I got at the orphanage won in the end, and I bring up the matter in connection with our kids. It was the orphanage that taught me to handle tools, got me used to the personal discipline of getting up and going to work, of a full day's work, and I know today that not everyone who's inured to manual labor has a hankering for physical work. . . . But there are those who get genuine satisfaction from doing something well with their hands, like a moshavnik who is still skillful in harvesting with a scythe, or a carpenter whose profession is right there in his hands. A carpenter like that will feel he's withering away if he can't feel his tools in his hands. He'll thank you for letting him go to his workbench but not at the price of the contempt of his environment. The woman is the barometer. If she forbids her husband to carry on, he'll give in for the sake of peace at home. Healthy youngsters are ready to climb mountains, to tour the world with a backpack . . . my eldest has a horse that he looks after with much effort and goes riding with his friends in his spare time, while my second goes yachting till he's exhausted. In all, they're not lazy, but if they're going to work up a sweat, they won't do it to for work.

Mediator: If that's so, what do you want of the politicians? Were they the ones who changed the rules of the game, like your energy savers rule book? I'm sure some of them toil away hard enough at their job.

David: They've got to understand that studying for agriculture, or for vocational training, must be part of the general education of every youngster in Israel. Just as it's important to impart knowledge of Judaism, and how to handle a weapon, it's important to impart the perception that we cannot survive here except by our own labors; that every high school graduate and every doctor can tend his own garden with his own hands, fix up furniture in his house, repair an electrical switch, solve a plumbing problem. . . . After we took the leap from a diaspora mentality, a people of *Luftgeschäften*, to a mentality of nation building, we've got to secure what we have achieved. . . . When, in the educational system, vocational training is left to those who fail academic studies, when they brainwash us with American movies full of beautiful people with time to spare and hardly anything about life in the country or what goes on in factories . . . that way one can forget everything we renewed in this country, the mentality of our old lifestyles . . . that's the way we're letting the diaspora saturate our country again.

Here the criticism of the leadership focuses on pedagogy. Its essence is the lack of care in education for values essential for the national morale. Reinforcement of this criticism comes from Shaul, a forty-nine-year-old Tripolitanian from a religious moshav in the western Negev who blames the authorities for not controlling television programming.

It [turning your back on farming] comes from outside, not from inside. Western ideas have taken over the country. In Western Europe and the U.S.A. nobody cares for work anymore. They have the blacks do the work for them. They bring in blacks for any unpleasant job. Just pay and sit back in comfort. Bow down to money! Our kids imbibe that from the media. It drips into the mind from what Israeli television broadcasts. It's all entertainment . . . that's what decides for our youngsters what they want to be when they grow up. Look, for instance, my grandson, aged four and a half, loves helping me feed the chickens in the afternoon. I used to take him with me until my son-in-law [twenty-seven years old], also from the moshav, came up to me and demanded that I leave the boy alone to watch children's television programs.

> I answered in my own way, all honor to the television, but that it was also important to help him love looking after animals. To that, he answered, What do you want, that we should raise the children the way you raised us? And he made what he meant quite clear: to work all day like an ass and be a cheapskate all your life!

This version concludes that the laws of osmosis, which also apply to life in society, do not permit the existence of small isolated cells such as a moshav community. The cell walls are permeated by the surrounding Israeli environmental influences, and parents want their children to move up to more prestigious and better-paying professions than their own.

During 1991, as a result of the intifada and the scarcity of Arab farm workers and, at one and the same time, the major influx of immigrants and the unwillingness of both immigrants and locals to take on the status of wage earners in agriculture, the Ministries of Labor and Finance announced their readiness to compensate workers directed into agricultural labor, with a sum of 15 shekels per day over and above the wages paid by the farmer. The effect of this step on the placement of workers in Noon Yud's fields and orchards remains limited. During the previous year, members of the cooperative won their battle to rezone agricultural land to build houses for the younger generation and thus signaled their intention to slowly divorcing themselves from farming.

Conclusion

Sending immigrants to the moshav and encouraging a movement from town to country were both short-term arrangements in opposition to the modern worldwide trend of drastic reduction in the number of farmers. Development of the means of production and investment in modern technology continued apace even though a plentiful supply of agricultural produce to the local markets had been achieved (at the end of the 1950s) while attempts to widen Israeli export markets were meeting with difficulties. From then on, the numbers who could live comfortably from farming dwindled, and competition among them increased. The most highly mechanized and efficient farms survived. To meet the need to settle the country and to distribute the population widely, it was the government's policy to direct farm subsidies to the moshavim on the periphery and to deny them to those in the central area. The result was the exit of many farmers from the circle of production.

The Moshav Law, which prevents the splitting up of the family farm and according to which only one of the children can inherit, acted to direct the other children from infancy either to establish their own farms or to find alternative employment outside agriculture. The numbers of those who left the moshav to go to work increased with the development of various industries and services in the country and with the proliferation of the bureaucracies. External employees who continued to live in the village and other settlers from outside contributed to its change in character and transformation into a suburb. Most of the farming plots that remained were rapidly handed over for cultivation to Arab workers or a few Arab subcontractors. A desire for increased efficiency led farmers to move from labor-intensive crops (such as vegetables) to orchards, which were compatible with outsider labor but only at harvest time.

From 1968 onward, the cost of manual labor was significantly reduced by the availability of Arab workers from the territories, and this lowered the status of blue-collar workers on the moshav. At the same time, the desire to avoid the negative label attached to employers of Arabs became a feature that characterized, in particular, moshavim of the western (Ashkenazi) aliyah.

The alternative solutions to the challenge in the various production areas were in essence these: (1) to avoid crops needing much back-breaking labor[9] in favor of other high-tech crops; (2) to avoid agriculture and work on the moshav altogether; (3) and to ignore critics and avoid self-criticism, to bend with the wind, and thus to profit from the labor of workers from the territories. The choice was not easy for three reasons. First, to develop alternate, high-tech crops requires considerable capital investment, while the volatile cost of credit (typified by the situation at the end of 1985) can intensify the difficulties of the borrowers. Second, branches that are more or less impermeable to the entrance of Arab workers are the civil and national services, in particular the defense forces and the police, and also defense and high-tech industries. However, one must have professional training and talent to be employed by them. Third, employment of Arabs impairs the motivation to work and erodes the justification of the moshav ethic and personal pride.

It has been years since agriculture ceased to be the source of income for most of the families in the village. It is apparent that the philosophical links that were the initial basis of attitudes toward it have also vanished. This is heartbreaking for the veterans, all the more so since the younger generation's attitude of turning one's back on any form of physical labor has deepened. However, the placement of the children in alternative employment has been as much influenced by families' desire to guarantee their future than by the surrounding Israeli cultural climate that has begun to reject the dream of national renewal in the homeland.

The use of Gazan workers in Noon Yud farms hampered the attractiveness of agriculture for the young and ambitious moshav members. There are three reasons for this. First, since the time most of the rough work was deposited in the hands of Gazans, farming has been losing its sportive value. Demonstration of individual ability, as in competitive games, must follow clear rules that should obligate all participants equally. The quantity and quality of production by the end of a day of work or an agricultural season resembles the results of a sprint at the finishing line. The entrance of Gazans into the farms of the less sportive farmers could not leave their decently competing colleagues indifferent (see Eli's words). Eventually, all who continued to farm had to thus employ

Gazans or quit. As in long-distance running, we find an analogous image of a retired farmer in the eyes of his maturing son (Dani's confession) who consequently shuns farming. Second, socialist consciousness (paying a great deal for maintenance of cooperative institutions, thus paying homage to egalitarianism), which had given a collective significance to individual work, compensating for hardships, and lack of comfort in the life of a moshav was of no avail once Gazans were let in to fulfill the dirty jobs (see Michael's words and Yavin's words). Third, striking the Zionist chord (the words of Nurith and Alon) did not lead to an understanding that people were getting their living the hard way for the sake of a collective goal (i.e., nation building).

Attempts to instill competition among teenagers with work quotas (see Dalya and Ronith's reports) began when big (Zionist) words lost their effect. The offer of extra payments as a means to spur competition or just increase the output in orange picking by taunting the feebleness of workers as their shoes get soaked in mud had an adverse effect (Mariana's report) because as long as the Gazans were present, money could not make a difference. Why did moshav members rule themselves out of competition with the Gazans?

Homo competitivus searches for tracks where ability can be shown, be it through achievement or through resolute laziness and the saving of bodily energy (David's story). Speeding up work is motivated by the income greater output yields, as well as by the fashion according to which the income can be spent. Spending and saving also serve as tracks for competing, and, interestingly, these two alternatives are interrelated. We find that the choice of vocation is made not only on the basis of the income it will provide, but also in the conventions of its work effort, creativity, quotas of production, and in the standard of living such a salary may afford. The image of one's future colleagues and their standard of living or the fashion by which they spend the salary are also important. To this way of thinking, cheating as a means of winning a game robs the action of its play character and spoils it altogether because for the actors, the essence of play is that the rules be kept so that it is fair play (Huizinga 1950). This aspect should be added to the various factors appearing in the literature pertaining to choice of vocation (Lissak 1969; Holland 1973; Ortiz 1979; Wallman 1979a, 1979b; Super 1980; Krue 1983; Nevo 1987).

In accordance with this analysis, the Gazans and their preferences for spending the work revenues earned in Israel affect the way their occupations are viewed. The apparel of the Gazans at the workplace and at their homes now color the jobs in a way that moshav members do not want to be painted.

Notes

1. The phrase appeared with the effort to make the Jews return to primary occupations, such as the labor on the land, with early Zionism.
2. On the interplay of winning through cooperation, see Orlick 1978.
3. See Schwartz and Giladi 1993.

4. Dov Baer Borochov (1891–1919), the first theorist of Socialist Zionism, advocated the normalization of the Jewish vocational structure by turning manpower from secondary occupations (craftmanship, trade) to primary ones (farming, mining).
5. For the use and the implications of the term *freier* in Israel, see Roniger and Feige 1992.
6. For parents having children and then helping their absorption outside the moshav in the western Negev, see Shokeid 1990.
7. I asked about the details of the argument, and here is the explanation: The dispute was over who would excavate the channel with the digger to lay down a section of two-inch pipe across the exit road between the plots. There the ground was harder and relatively difficult to break up, and the second son (thirty-nine years old) said it would take half an hour or so. However, on principle he was waiting for his older brother (forty-one years old) to go first for once and dig the hard section because the last time they had both come for fruit picking, the older brother had taken it upon himself to stay behind and load the crates in the van (having come late) but then remembered he had to hurry back to town; so his brother (with his brother-in-law, thirty-seven years old) had to stay and do that job, too.
8. This is an untranslatable word with many shades of meaning depending on the context. Here it means something like "just because!"
9. We now record expressions such as angle crops (literal translation) for the culturing and harvesting in vegetable gardens that rise to a level of bitterness in nicknames like Boazim (Boaz, the owner of the fields in which Ruth the Moabite gleaned), which are given by the younger generation to the moshav farmers employing Arab workers.

12

Rhetoric in Flames

Fire Inscriptions in Israeli Youth Movement Ceremonials

TAMAR KATRIEL

Introduction

Fire has become a central element in the ceremonial idiom of contemporary Israel and is found in a variety of "civic rituals" (Bocock 1974; Liebman and Don-Yehiya 1983). For example, fire symbolism is used on such calendrical occasions as the festive lighting of "commemoration candles" in front of the Western Wall on Memorial Day, and in the lighting of twelve torches by carefully selected members of the populace on Independence Day on Mt. Herzl in Jerusalem. The Hanukkah festival of lights is occasion for repeated reenactments of traditional Jewish symbolism of fire and light in a variety of private and public settings—from the lighting of the candelabra in private homes to the symbolic torch run that connects Israel to Jewish communities abroad in a gesture of flames to the bonfires that today serve as a focus for youngsters' celebrations of the traditional annual holiday of Lag Baomer all over the country. These calendrical occasions are regularly televised by the National Television Network and large segments of the population participate in them vicariously. Even such home-centered, fire-related traditional practices as the lighting of Hanukkah or Sabbath candles are modeled on TV on a regular basis so that their symbolic communal import is underscored.

A special use of fire symbolism found in a variety of Israeli public ceremonies involves the practice of lighting "fire inscriptions" (natively known as *ktovot esh*) as a highly impressive celebratory move at the closing of public occasions. This particular practice, which involves the lighting of large-lettered slogans on festive occasions, was the subject of considerable elaboration in the Israeli youth movements in the nation-building era. Youth movement documents abound with references to the fire theme in general and to the art of pyrotechnics in particular, and publications specifically concerned with fire have been compiled (Naor 1949; Tal 1963; Zilka 1970). The effectiveness of fire inscriptions as enacted cultural forms is attested to by the fact that they have been in continuous use for more than half a century and have become an official element of other traditional Israeli ceremonials, notably military ceremonials and kibbutz celebrations, as well as high-profile public occasions such as Independence Day celebrations. They are also used more sporadically on such occasions as, for example, the closing ceremony of the Soviet Jewry Month celebrated in the spring of 1985, when Anatole Sharansky was honored by being invited to light a fire inscription in a highly visible, televised ceremonial gesture.

In attempting to account for the particular rhetorical effectiveness of these words-in-flames, fire inscriptions are considered here as a form of ephemeral art, a category of aesthetic objects found cross-culturally in a variety of ritual contexts. In Marilyn Ravicz's explication of this notion, "'ephemeral' includes visual phenomena created or assembled with conscious knowledge that they will be destroyed, dismantled, or permitted to decompose within hours, days, or, at the most, several months. 'Art' designates visual phenomena created so that they incorporate structural, decorative, or other stimulatory characteristics perceived as aesthetically rewarding to the members of the culture concerned" (1980, 115).

The frequent and integral part played by repetitively used ephemeral forms in ritual communication can be accounted for in terms of their role in bridging the two fundamental, formal aspects of the ritual experience, an experience described as encompassing "carefully orchestrated packages of (1) highly stereotypic activities, including familiar roles and ideas; and (2) what Turner has called mandatory improvisations, or the liminal aspects, replete with change, ambiguities and surprise" (Ravicz 1980, 124). In Roy Rappaport's formulation (1979b), these two aspects of ritual involve the transmission of two orders of information: (1) canonical information, which involves messages not encoded by participants but part of the "liturgy." These messages tend to be invariant, durable, and are mainly conveyed through the symbolic dimension of the signs participating in ritual communication; and (2) indexical information, which concerns (or points to) participants' own current physical, psychic, or social states, especially as they relate to the manner and degree of their engagement in the ritual action. Ephemeral art forms are designed in such a way as to combine these two types of messages: whereas the aesthetic forms in which they are cast and the symbolic vehicles used are part of a canonical, often sanctified, symbolic idiom, they are clearly designed to affect participants' current states and dispositions through their arousal potential. Ephemeral art forms, as used in ritual communication, thus serve as a medium of a particular kind of ritual learning, in which the kinetic, cognitive, and sensory systems of participants are engaged through specialized techniques and thereby "prepare the human organism to act by structuring attention and learning, and by mobilizing motivations and resources" (Ravicz 1980, 124).

This approach to ritual communication has its theoretical foundation in C. S. Peirce's semiotics (1955), specifically in his well-known trichotomy of signs, made up of a symbolic, an indexical, and an iconic dimension. A number of anthropologists have explicitly drawn on Peirce's approach to the study of signs in exploring cultural communication processes (Silverstein 1976; D. Murray 1977; Rappaport 1979b; Daniel 1984). A major contribution of these studies has been to bring out the centrality of the indexical dimension of signs, as well as its role in the attainment of ritual efficacy. Clearly, fire is only one of the many materials used cross-culturally in the construction of ephemeral art forms. Other such forms include body-enhancing decorations of various sorts (e.g., headdresses, body paintings, masks, costumes, and so forth), paintings on walls, structured objects, kites, and sky writing. The analysis of fire inscriptions must, therefore, address the issue of the particular effectiveness of this specific visual metaphor in the context of the culture studied, as well as explore its shaping in verbal and emblematic signs.

Symbolic Antecedents

Given the essentially pedagogical nature of ritual and ceremonial events, it is not surprising that youth movement ceremonials, with their explicit and implicit socializing agendas, should have proven such fertile ground for the intense shaping of ritual symbolism during the Israeli nation-building era. The centrality of the youth movement ethos in the development of modern Israeli culture is widely recognized, as is summarily acknowledged in a retrospective account by a well-known literary critic, who went as far as to say, "Anybody who wanted to belong to the new Israeli culture had to accept the rules of the game formulated within the youth movement culture" (Shaked 1983, 21).

The search for a language of word and symbolic gesture that would encapsulate the experience of a newly emerging culture in a publicly shared expressive idiom has been a persistent concern in Israel from the days of the early pioneers up to the present (Y. Zerubavel 1995; Even-Zohar 1981; Oring 1981; Liebman and Don-Yehiya 1983; Katriel 1986; Doleve-Gandelman 1986; Weil 1986). The youthful quest for new cultural symbols finds its vivid expression in both the documents and the literary writings of the early part of the century. Moreover, the forging of such symbols was a task explicitly entrusted to the young by members of the older generation of pioneers. For example, Berl Katzenelson, the influential leader of the Socialist-Zionist movement in pre-state Palestine, lamented his movement's overemphasis on matters of ideological content and its neglect of form and style. In a speech delivered in the 1927 convention of Hanoar Haoved youth movement, he called upon the young to take the lead in generating a distinctive ceremonial idiom, noting that "people are educated not only by the contents but also by the forms of life" (1946, 189).

Notably, despite the pioneers' conscious effort to reject both European and Jewish cultural ways, the task of symbolic reconstruction did not begin "from scratch," as the revolutionary stance would have it: traditional Jewish as well as European cultural contents and forms were selectively—though not always consciously—drawn upon in this culture-creation enterprise. The use of fire inscriptions as a ritual symbol in youth movement ceremonials provides an intriguing example of such a newly elaborated symbolic form, whose meanings and shaping can be traced to general European traditions, specifically to the influential youth movement culture of the turn of the century, on the one hand, and to Jewish lore, on the other.

Fire has, of course, been used as a multivocal symbol in many cultures.[1] Psychoanalytically oriented scholars have adduced both mythological and clinical materials in exploring the symbolic role of fire in human experience, stressing its psychosexual underpinnings. Both Sigmund Freud (1964) and Carl Jung (1956) regard fire as a symbol of a life force (libido or energy), and Gaston Bachelard (1964) offers a phenomenological account of the human experience with fire along these lines. Elias Canetti (1966) is similarly oriented toward the universal aspects of fire symbolism but transports the discussion from the realm of individual to social psychology, offering an intriguing interpretation of fire as a symbol of the crowd.

Citing scores of fire-related practices associated with the fire festivals of Europe (and other lands), James Frazer is similarly oriented to that which cuts across cultural differences, identifying similarities in the underlying functions of fire symbols: "Whether applied in the form of bonfires blazing at fixed points, or of torches carried about from place to place, or of embers and ashes taken from the smoldering heap of fuel, the fire is believed to promote the growth of the crops and the welfare of man and beast, either positively by stimulating them, or negatively by averting the dangers and calamities which threaten them from such causes as thunder and lightning, conflagration, blight, mildew, vermin, sterility, disease, and not least of all witchcraft" (1935, 329).

The effect of fire was ascribed either to its function as a stimulant, ensuring a needful supply of sunshine (hence, the use of disc- or wheel-shaped fire contraptions), or as a purifying element, a disinfectant designed to burn up and destroy all harmful influences. The fascination with fire and what were originally divinatory practices (e.g., jumping over a bonfire) became part of the ceremonial idiom of European youth movements at the turn of the twentieth century, most notably in Germany (Laqueur 1962; Schatzker 1969; Stachura 1981). These practices were appropriated in one form or another by subsequent generations of youth groups, including the Jewish youth movements, whose ethos was so influential in the development of modern Israeli culture. The bonfire, and the circle of light and warmth it defines, has been a central symbol of youth movement solidarity since its very inception. The German poet Stefan George

(1868–1933), who was an influential figure in the German youth revolution, articulated the force of the fire symbol, saying, "Who once has circled the flame / Always shall follow the flame" (1943, 211).

The conceptions of fire as a stimulant and as a purifying element have both found their way into the Israeli youth movement ethos, although, of course, in a different ideational context: the cosmological beliefs of earlier times have been replaced by a highly compelling psychic metaphor. An entry in a collective diary compiled by a group of young pioneers and first published in 1922 under the title of *Kehyliyatenu* (our community) accordingly reads, "I believe in fire, in its enormous power, in its symbolic power. . . . Fire awakens the sleepy, it brings people closer" (Tsur 1988 [1922], 43).

The centrality of fire symbolism in modern Israeli ceremonial idiom can only be partly attributed to the European youth movement heritage, however. Images of fire and light also echo deeper historical roots associated with the central role of fire in Jewish religious symbolism—from fire-related myths such as the story of Moses and the burning bush that was never consummated, which clearly brings out the role of fire as a mediator between God and human beings, to central Jewish practices, such as the lighting of candles on various religious occasions, to collective memories of destruction by fire, notably the burning down of the Jerusalem Temple in 70 A.D. Furthermore, a tradition of using fire to relay messages and connect through a fire-borne act of communication, mainly in the form of a bonfire kindled on the top of a hill, has a long history in ancient Israel. Despite the strong sense of a cultural revolution that permeated the Jewish youth movement, as it did the European youth culture in a more generalized way, a sense of continuity was nevertheless maintained through the use of symbolic media.

Fire inscriptions manifest a culturally distinctive shaping of the general theme of sacred fire: unlike the ritual symbol of the bonfire, which is widespread in European and American youth movements, words-in-flames seem to be a uniquely inspired form of ephemeral art in the Israeli context (and have been "exported" to some Jewish youth movements in the United States). They echo an age-old tradition that associated fire with writing and divine speech and in which the letters of the alphabet are the mystical instruments God placed in the hands of humans, making them partners to the act of creation through the gift of language and speech (R. Kahana 1985). In the letter-centered Judaic tradition, the letters of the alphabet are a source of enlightenment both literally and metaphorically. Indeed, the Hebrew word for letter, *ot*, can also mean sign or symbol. The link between letters, fire, and light has found its expression in many legends associated with the bestowal of the Torah upon the children of Israel. According to some legends the Torah was written as black letters of fire inscribed in white flames; other legends link the letters of the alphabet to the act of creation and the light of creation is said to inhere in them; and legends about the destruction of the Jerusalem Temple describe the indestructible letters of the Hebrew alphabet flying out of the burning Torah scrolls.[2]

In contemporary Israel, fire, then, can be considered a "key symbol" (Ortner 1973). As such, it serves to mediate between the disparate, originally mutually exclusive cultural orientations that ground modern Israeli culture, traditional Judaism on the one hand and the secular civil religions of Socialist Zionism and statism on the other (Liebman and Don-Yehiya 1983). Initially, the appropriation of European youth culture symbolism by Zionist youth groups was an act of rebellion, part of the larger Zionist revolt against traditional Judaism. Even then, however, the focal place given to fire was seen in association with the place of fire in Jewish tradition. A German youth movement source explicitly articulates this symbolic conquest of fire by fire, saying, "In the radiance of the voluntarily embraced fire of Goethe, Fichte and George, we are putting out the candles of the candelabra lighted by our fathers who demanded obedience and assent to barely comprehensible religious formulas" (cited in Schatzker 1969, 151). Thus, the fire inscriptions kindled in present-day youth movement (and other) ceremonials draw some of their force from the fire images of times past, and at the same time they give renewed meaning and a new direction to the past by adding a link to this ancient fire chain, a link shaped by the spirit of youth.

Fire Ceremonials in Contemporary Youth Movements

The use of fire inscriptions is the most salient aspect of the youth movement ceremonials in which they figure, and these events are often generically labeled as fire events in both formal and informal discourse (formerly they were referred to as *mifkad esh* [fire parade], and today the most common term of reference is *tekes esh* [fire ritual/ceremonial]). These ceremonials tend to be punctuated by a festive tone that stands in contrast to the gaiety associated with, for example, Fourth of July fireworks displays in the United States, the smaller-scale firework displays in Israeli Independence Day celebrations, or the intimacy and playfulness of youth movement bonfires.

The description given in this and the next section is based on material collected between the years 1982 and 1986 through participant observation (seven youth movement fire ceremonials were directly observed) and ethnographic interviewing of participants in such events (Spradley 1979, 1980). Additional information was drawn from discussions with Israelis of various ages and personal backgrounds, relating to both present and past occasions of this kind, as well as a consultation of relevant youth movement documents (e.g., Tal 1963; Zilka 1970). The account offered here differs in its orientation from available sociological discussions of the Israeli youth movement, which tend to focus on ideological and social structural issues (Adler 1963; Eisenstadt 1967; Eaton and Chen 1970; Shapira and Peleg 1984). The focus here is on an interpretive account of enacted symbolic forms, along the lines of the "comparative symbology" approach developed by Victor Turner for the study of ritual symbolism.

Of the three dimensions of meaning for the interpretation of dominant ritual symbols distinguished by Turner (1977)—the exegetical, the operational, and the positional dimensions—the first two dimensions—the exegetical and operational—will be specifically addressed in this section. The positional dimension, which refers to the "intertextual" relations of the symbol with other dominant symbols in the culture, was addressed in the discussion of the symbolic antecedents of fire inscriptions and will be taken up again in the concluding remarks.

The exegetical dimension consists of explanations the actors themselves give the investigator. Discussions of fire inscriptions with participants in such ceremonials tended to lead in two directions: comments of a historical flavor invoking the symbolic antecedents described in the previous section; and stories and descriptions relating to the art of pyrotechnics, interspersed with aesthetic evaluations of the events that were often expressed in animated, hyperbolic terms.

Elements of such exegetical discussion, which gave the original impetus to the whole inquiry, are incorporated in the following account, but my main focus in this section will be the operational dimension of fire inscriptions as enacted symbols. In studying this dimension of symbolic meaning, "the investigator equates a symbol's meaning with its use—he observes what actors do with it and how they relate to one another in this process" (Turner 1977, 190). This particular focus requires a detailed consideration of the contextual features and organization of the activities involved in the fire events. Their significance will be assessed by considering them as situated enactments whose meanings derive from the complex interplay of the words conveyed, the medium of fire in which this is done, the organization of the activities (sequential ordering, participation roles), and aspects of the physical setting. In this section I address relevant features of the situational context in which youth movement fire ceremonials typically take place, and in the section that follows I focus more specifically on the act of reading fire inscriptions.

Fire inscriptions are typically used as part of several celebratory events during the year. The most spectacular one is usually associated with the celebration of the youth movement itself—for example, *yom hashevet* (Troop Day) in the Scouts or *hag hama'alot* (Holiday of Ascendance), which marks the beginning of the activity year in Hanoar Haoved Socialist youth movement. Other occasions, such as national holidays celebrated by the youth group, or summer camp celebrations, may also be concluded with a fire display of greater or lesser elaborateness whose function is to elevate the tone of the occasion, endowing it with a festive mood. These ceremonials are literally framed by fire: they start out with intimations of fire in the form of candle-like contraptions placed in sand-filled paper sacks that form a path leading to the darkened area participants are to occupy, and the actual lighting of fire inscriptions is the climactic closing of the event. All the other ceremonial acts, such as speech making, music, and poetry reciting, are used as a means of leading up to the fire spectacle in a movement of ascending suspense.

The ideal location for such a ceremony is a relatively remote spot of natural elevation, preferably on the top or slope of a hill. When such a location is chosen, an ornamental effect is added through the scenery, as the hill slope becomes the page on which the words and images of fire are momentarily inscribed before they turn into smoke and disappear into nature again.[3] The important point here is that fire inscriptions involve a magnifying effect as compared to regular writing, thus invoking a sense of the gigantic. As Susan Stewart (1994) points out in her discussion of the gigantic and the miniature, these spatial manipulations have come to be associated with the public domain and with an enclosed personal domain, respectively. Thus, the size of the fire inscriptions bespeaks publicness in a way that, for example, the lighting of many candles does not do (a ceremonial practice I observed in a Fourth of July celebration in a university stadium in the United States in 1979).[4]

Some of the events observed in the course of this study came close to this ideal, while others used different types of locations, such as a hilltop with a monument of historical value, which the children reached after a daylong hike, or the open-air village stadium, where most important communal events take place. In all cases, an open space bespeaking non-restrictiveness and a closeness to nature was chosen, and a basically ground-level orientation was maintained so that the event could embrace, or attempt to resurrect, the small-scale community in a way that the use of fireworks, an essentially mass phenomenon, could not do.

Ceremonials of the type discussed here usually involve two orders of participants: members of the youth group whose celebration it is and guests (parents, siblings, and sometimes other community members). The two groups arrive independently and stand separately. The youngsters come first and stand closer to the ceremonial center, which punctuates their role as focal participants and "hosts" of the occasion. Parental presence and community involvement is a relatively new development: today parents emphatically note that they do not remember such involvement in the equivalent occasions of their youthful days. Contemporary youth movements have renounced the symbolic stance of youthful separateness of times past that was, paradoxically, accompanied by a wholehearted embracing of adult-sponsored ideologies. Today parental participation in such high-profile ceremonials is both expected and solicited through written invitations (whose program may explicitly mention the prospect of fire inscriptions). At times the guests' presence is explicitly acknowledged in a fire inscription that reads *bruhim haba'im* (welcome).

Contemporary fire ceremonials are partly a breathtaking show and partly a ritual-like shared experience, encompassing both parents-as-a-group and youngsters-as-a-group. The parents participate primarily in an audience capacity, and their representative may greet the assembled in their name. The youngsters alternate between the role of audience and performers. Some perform in readings or music pieces (as representatives again; in none of the occasions I have observed was the identity of the performers made much of). More significant, however, they all perform as a group in call-and-response chants that occur at various points in the ceremony and that are always initiated by adult counselors (e.g., as a completion marker, crowning the end of a speech, or as a controlling device used to command the youngsters' attention when it seems to wane). This differentiation in the participation roles is utterly obliterated when the climactic lighting of fire inscriptions is reached and all join in a moment of shared, silent appreciation, their eyes fixed on the images that take their shape in flames.

The preparation of fire contraptions is the youngsters' province and it is in this collective task that the real test of performance lies. The inscriptions are made up of big letters of wire padded with jute cloth that are soaked in oil just prior to being kindled. As the detailed instruction manuals dealing with the art of pyrotechnics indicate, the construction of these inscriptions is considered a most serious matter requiring specialized skill and much care. In some youth troops, particular individuals are considered local "masters of fire," to borrow Mircea Eliade's term (1956). A successfully constructed fire inscription is one that burns itself out without falling apart. Even today, when many of the fire tricks mentioned in instructors' manuals are not usually practiced, this one performance test remains. Youngsters say it is a matter of pride to construct successful inscriptions, and the gift of skill is well-received by parents and community members whose representatives sound an appreciative note in praise of "the wonderful youth of this town."

A similarly appreciative note can be found in some of the lore surrounding the fire events. Year after year, I heard tales of devotion as parents praised the commitment of the youngsters who worked hard to prepare the inscriptions, and then, fearful that they might be stolen or destroyed, stayed all night in the field to keep an eye on them.

The youngsters' own fire lore sounds a different note, indicating their concern with a high level of performance in the pyrotechnic arts. An example

Figure 1.
Youth movement fire ceremonial, October 1985. Photograph by Guy Katriel and Shimon Kogan.

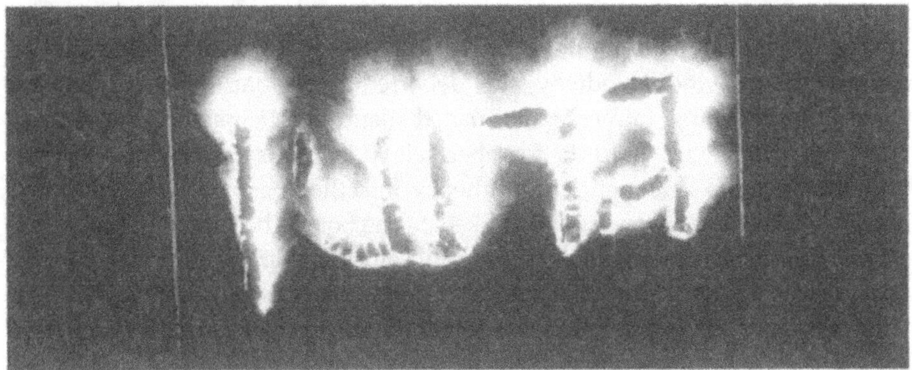

would be the story about the "stupid Scouts" who fastened the jute cloth with a plastic band so that it melted the moment it was touched, causing the whole inscription to fall apart. One parent's comment in response to a similarly unfortunate occasion indicates that parents are attuned to the youngsters' interpretation of the fire event as primarily a test of performance with mildly sacrificial overtones. Commenting on a recent fire event, she said, "My heart broke when these inscriptions suddenly began to fall apart."

Even though the fire inscriptions are put together by the youngsters, their contents are drawn from a rather small repertoire of conventionalized expressions, whose pathos and elevated style mark them as particularly far removed from the youngsters' own expressive idiom. Indeed, my young informants, who were willing to go into the details of pyrotechnics practice with considerable zest, became singularly vague when asked about the choice of messages to be inscribed. These would generally be "one of those things we always use," or whatever the troop counselor found fit. The slogans used give expression to essentially adult-sponsored ideologies and values, and are rather obviously pedagogical in intent.

Notably, there is no slot at any point in the whole ceremonial in which youngsters' spontaneous self-expression is invited or their verbal cleverness exercised, as is the case, for example, in the Boy Scout Campfire Programs described by Jay Mechling (1980). Rather, the youngsters recite, sing in unison, provide set responses to set calls, which allow for no individual variation, or call out formulaic yells of the "troop x is the greatest" variety, which, are, again, a form of collective self-assertion. Moreover, throughout the ceremony the youngsters are addressed as a group, never as individuals: the change in status celebrated in some of these ceremonials relates to the ascendance of the whole group from one stage in the youth movement ladder to another. Even in more spontaneous address, as in disciplinary comments made by counselors in attempting to control unruly conduct, it is common to hear the whole group addressed by its group label, which signals their age-related position within the youth movement hierarchy, and is replaced with each change in the group's status.[5]

This quiescent and participatory attitude reaches its peak as all participants join in the ritualized act of discerning and admiring the fire inscriptions kindled at the close of the ceremony. The particular form of bonding thus achieved is most telling. Standing side by side, debarred by the dark from making eye contact, not touching, immersed in hushed silence, participants' attention and gaze are galvanized toward the fire spectacle. It is in this shared orientation to a focal source of excitement and authority that they become joined without, however, becoming interpersonally linked. Susan Sontag has pointed out the less savory aspects of the impersonal grouping of people around an all-powerful force, arguing that it is an aspect of what she calls "fascist aesthetics," which "flow from (and justify) a preoccupation with situations of control, submissive behavior, extravagant action and the endurance of pain" (1972, 91). The more sinister implications of fire displays, however, were rarely mentioned by my informants.[6]

Somewhat paradoxically, this highly collectivist experience is primarily constructed by mobilizing the sense of sight, the most individuating of senses (Ong 1982). The specifics of the uniquely structured visual experience involved are discussed in the next section.

On the Phenomenology of Reading Fire Inscriptions

A youth movement instructor manual specifically devoted to the preparation of fire ceremonials recommends the use of fire inscriptions since "the fixed or moving fire has a strong experiential impact on the onlookers" (Tal 1963, 2). Whether they take a verbal or an emblematic form, the signs used in contemporary youth movement ceremonials fall into two broad categories, which serve to anchor the ritual occasion in terms of its indexical meanings, as they relate to the social situation in which the ceremonial action takes place, and in terms of its symbolic meanings, as they relate to the broader cultural context in which it is embedded.

The social occasion is indexed by signs that provide a definition of the situation in terms of the identity of the group celebrated (the youth movement and local troop names and emblems) and the particular occasion thus marked in the youth movement calendar. Some of the messages inscribed have a similar indexical function: *heye nahon* (be prepared) was observed in a Scouts' ceremonial; *gar'in* (youth settlement group) was observed in the Holiday of Ascendance, which celebrates members' ascendance up the Noar Haoved youth movement ladder, until they reach the ultimate official goal of settling the land; and *nizkor tamid* (we shall always remember) was observed in commemoration ceremonies in both youth movement and other contexts.

The cultural meanings more broadly shared in the community at large are invoked by signs that are good for all seasons. These may depict both traditional and newly adapted emblems such as the Star of David, the menorah (candelabra) that symbolizes the State of Israel, the image of the pillar of fire that led the Children of Israel to the Promised Land (and served as the title of a popular historical TV series aired in the early 1980s), or the image of the map of the State of Israel. Alongside these emblems are formulaic expressions selected out of a more or less set repertoire of slogans and clichés, including shalom (peace) and *hazak* (strong, a formulaic phrase traditionally used in completing the round of weekly readings of the Torah, which has come to have a general celebratory role in modern contexts). Although analytically distinguishable, these two levels of context (the situational and the cultural) often blend into each other. Notably, ideologically colored slogans such as the rather outmoded *la'avoda vele'amal* (to work and labor), which was observed in a Socialist youth movement celebration, are often more of an index of affiliation to a particular social group than a statement of wider ideological commitment.

Fire inscriptions frequently take the form of injunctions or vows—they draw their substance and force from the past as a source of shared communal values and patterns of sentiment, and yet are explicitly oriented to future action, conjuring a moment of renewed awareness and commitment.

My own and my informants' observations and memories, as well as the documentary material consulted, indicate interesting changes that have occurred within one generation with respect to the content, style, and number of fire inscriptions used in youth movement ceremonial occasions. Thus, an inscription photographed in 1943 in a youth movement ceremonial that read *batelem batelem neleh ad hasof* (we shall always take the appropriate path) would be unthinkable today; not only is the message of total conformity and obedience no longer palatable to contemporary youth but the language of this inscription is overly dramatic to patho-filled. Similarly, the photograph of a fire inscription that reads *nitka yated ledorot* (we shall fasten our hold—literally, "stick a peg in the ground for generations to come") that was used in a ceremonial inaugurating a swimming pool in a young southern kibbutz in 1954 has made many of my informants smile. At the same time, photographs of a whole stadium sprinkled with over a dozen fire inscriptions, which are common fare today, were very surprising to older informants who have been out of touch with youth movement ceremonials since their own youth.

It appears, then, that contemporary youth movement fire ceremonials rely more heavily on the dramatization provided by the visual impact of fire than on the ritual invocation of shared values and ideological commitments. The frequent use made of group labels in a sheer assertion of existence seems to suggest that—given the present de-emphasis of ideology—group membership remains the most clearly shared common base beyond which no exhortation or vow can be meaningfully inscribed. Regardless of what the inscriptions signify, contemporary fire ceremonials are essentially about the act of signifying, drawing attention to itself through what Barbara Babcock has called a "surplus of signifiers" expressed primarily as a sensory overload, a surfeit of signification which, by disrupting the complementarity of signifier and signified, calls the meaning of everything into question and playfully "creates a realm of pure possibility" (1978, 294). Babcock's comments on the semiotics of fire in firework displays seem to come in some respects close to describing the effect of the more flamboyant fire displays of contemporary youth movement ceremonials: "As pure pattern and pure possibility fireworks are the epitome of a superabundance of signifiers. They are everything and nothing or, to be more precise, a lot of sound and light (*son et lumière*) signifying nothing. And, like fireworks, a surplus of signifiers is potentially dangerous as well as entertaining and enlightening. A symbol of revolution, it is itself a revolution in a suspension of serious and normal modes of signification" (296).

The underlying visual metaphor of the spectacle, however, is not the free play of fire but rather its domestication—the channeling of the ravenous tongues of flame, incessantly struggling to find their own willful shape, into the form of letters, the paradigmatic embodiment of human culture. The constant movement of the flames is an ever-present reminder of the potential danger of fire getting out of hand, and the ritual action is one of constraining it. The tension thus induced is keenly felt and often commented on by participants. The natural, open setting in which the events take place serves to further accentuate the play of contrasts: nature versus culture, the chaotic versus the orderly, the random and whimsical versus the expected. This play of opposites, and with opposites, is carried into the structuring of the visual experience involved in the very act of reading fire inscriptions. A closer look at this act reveals some of the ways in which (as distinct from the grounds on which) fire inscriptions construct their rhetorical appeal.

The most immediately obvious contrast is, of course, the play of *light and dark*. The ceremonial center, the circle of light in which speeches are made and greetings extended, initially stands in sharp contrast to the surrounding darkness. As a result of the gradual manner in which the inscriptions are kindled, participants are faced with a crescendo of fire that then again becomes diminished in a gradual movement. The darkness/light binary contrast becomes transformed into an analogical dimension. The particular effect thus achieved is that of time stretched out, as in the experience of watching the sun rise or set.

Another effect has to do with the intricate play of *movement and fixity:* in reading fire inscriptions there is a reversal of the usual relationship holding between "the arrested image and the moving eye," to use a phrase coined by the art critic Ernst H. Gombrich (1982). Rather than the eye moving along the fixed letters, the letters are moved along by the spreading fire. Once they have come into existence, the flaming letters keep waving in the wind, thus blurring their contours and further diminishing the sense of fixity they carry. At the same time, observers make an effort to fix their gaze so as to be able to identify the imperfectly shaping and jumping letters in front of them: this is truly a case of reversal with the image moving and the eye arrested. As a consequence, participants become highly involved in the visual construction of the image. Moreover, a high level of outwardly directed attentiveness is maintained, which prevents them from falling into a reverie—that contemplative, inwardly directed look that is so often induced by gazing at a fire (Bachelard 1964). The hypnotic effect of the fire is balanced out by the alertness required by the deciphering effort.

At another non-material level, however, the sense of movement is counteracted by the demarcation and fixity of the ideological message as a form of "authoritative discourse" in Mikhail Bakhtin's sense, a discourse that "remains sharply demarcated, compact and inert: it demands, so to speak, not only quotation marks but a demarcation even more magisterial, a special script, for instance . . . its semantic structure is static and dead, for it is fully complete, it has but a single meaning, the letter is fully sufficient to the sense and calcifies it" (1981, 343).

The ever-shifting movement of the fire stands in sharp contrast to this underlying message of ideological fixity. The momentary, highly evocative clash of directional orientations further underscores its perceptual evocative force; the initial emphasis on the *vertical* dimension, associated with the positioning of the signs, the use of a hill slope as a preferred site, and the upward movement of the smoke is punctuated by the *horizontal* movement of flames as they run their course in giving shape to the letters.

Fire has a transformative effect when used in fire inscriptions both in terms of their material substance and in terms of their linguistic status. Indeed, as both Gaston Bachelard (1964) and Elias Canetti (1966) have pointed out, one of the outstanding qualities of fire as a medium is that it produces quick changes in the form and substance of everything it touches and typically joins the things affected by it as they become welded together. In dramatizing the vitality of movement and change, fire inscriptions serve as a visual metaphor for a directed, rhetorically oriented, spiritual force that can bring people together in joint action as well as mediate disparate realms of experience, the realms of *inner feeling* and of *public action.*

As forms of ephemeral art, fire inscriptions involve an extraordinary joining of *the fleeting* and *the timeless:* in what may be referred to as a dislocation of medium and message, the inscriptions give expression to what are taken to be (or strategically presented as) eternal communal values or truths, while the ritual action itself consists of their being literally consummated within minutes in a burst of flames. The contrast between the act of inscribing and the use of fire as a medium for so doing is punctuated by the gross, thing-like character of the inscriptions compared with their short, spiritualized, speech-like ephemeral life. Paradoxically, in their most grossly material state the inscriptions stand as a mere language potential, as a skeletal language form waiting to be turned into utterance. It is only by going up in self-consuming flames that this language potential is actualized in an act of speech.

Thus, it seems that, ultimately, fire inscriptions provide a reflexive statement on the process of signification itself. Various aspects of this process are deconstructed and recombined in unusual ways: the surplus of signifiers disturbs the complementarity of signifier and signified; the fleetingness of the spoken word is combined with the materiality and fixedness of the inscribed letter; the conceptions of language as form, as event, and as product are juxtaposed and contrasted in the course of the ceremonial action; the nature of the act of reading as a play of eye and image, and as a variously textured activity of recognition and decipherment, is probed. It is by providing an unusual, complexly structured visual experience, one that self-reflexively dramatizes the possibility of signification, that fire inscriptions exert their "strong experiential impact on the onlookers."

Conclusion

The widespread use of fire symbolism, in the form of fire inscriptions or otherwise, as a persistent element in the rhetoric of identification that characterizes present-day Israeli communal conversation points to a consolidation of a public idiom of symbolic expression. In recent years, fire inscriptions have been observed (either by me or by my informants) in a variety of contexts in which their use was rather unexpected and indicated the extent to which this symbolism had become diffused: in a school-based ceremonial occasion, in a demonstration by orthodox Jews in Jerusalem, in bar mitzvah parties and wedding celebrations held in private suburban gardens, and—in Arabic letters—in ceremonials held by agricultural clubs whose membership consists of youngsters who are Palestinian citizens of Israel. On all these occasions, the use of fire inscriptions is clearly metaphorical and builds on the cultural definitions generally given to fire ceremonials. Paradigmatic fire ceremonials are occasions that are public rather than private or familial; they involve voluntary commitment rather than required participation; they involve messages that are consensually oriented and self-addressed rather than provocative and addressed to outsiders; and they are broadly associated with the Zionist ethos. The use of fire inscriptions on other occasions is designed to sanctify the messages conveyed, endowing them with the legitimization of an authoritative communal voice.[7]

There has, however, been a gradual movement of de-semanticization of fire inscriptions. The fire inscriptions of yesteryear would carry little validity in contemporary youth movement ceremonials, which tend to replace even worn-down slogans by explicitly indexical signs. Whereas the lure and effectiveness of the fire displays is widely recognized, the problematic standing of the kind of authoritative discourse they embody is not. As Alain Goldschlager (1985) argues, such discourse is marked by a particularly shaky relationship to reality. This is brought out by the little attention generally paid by the participants in these ceremonials to what the inscriptions say, as well as by the humorous attitude often disclosed toward the inscriptions they manage to recall. Participation in such events seems to involve a specialized interpretative norm that allows participants to discount the contents of the inscriptions. In the usual course of events, this norm allows participants to be duly impressed by the fire display without being disturbed by the remoteness of the quasi-canonical messages conveyed.

At times, however, this gap becomes disturbingly conspicuous, as, for example, in the use of the slogan "It is good to die for our country," which was reportedly uttered by the early defender Joseph Trumpeldor on his deathbed (1920) and has since become part of Israeli official heroic lore. Although by now it has become the butt of many jokes (Zerubavel 1995), it appeared as a fire inscription during a youth movement ceremonial held in commemoration of Trumpeldor in the middle of the Lebanon War (1983), when the whole country was torn by disputes over both its justifiability and its cost in human lives. The insensitive use of such an inscription at this particular moment in history points to the degree of its semantic vacuity (unless we assume that it was deliberately chosen to invoke a heroic spirit, which contradicts both ethnographic observations of how the inscriptions are selected, as well as the overall political orientation of that particular youth group).

Another example, from a different angle, demonstrates the voiding impact the fire inscriptions themselves can have. Following a decree by the Ministry of Education stipulating that during the 1985/86 school year the educational system should make the concept of "Democracy" its focal educational theme, "democracy" appeared in one of the slogans inscribed in fire in a Socialist youth movement ceremonial in late 1985. The word replaced the third member of the tripartite formula "Zionism, Socialism and the Brotherhood of Nations." This substitution of "democracy" for "the brotherhood of nations" passed largely unnoticed by the participants in this ceremonial, who were highly appreciative of the impressive fire display. To the critical observer, however, there was something eerie about the use of "democracy" in this context. The image of "democracy" exorcised into a verbal flame has little in common with the idea of democracy as grounded in a laborious, uncertain quest for reasoned discourse and considered assent. Fire inscriptions, indeed, invite participants to succumb to the all-too-human desire "to short-circuit the process of rational apprenticeship" (Goldschlager 1985, 175), letting the hidden flames in their hearts light up with an uplifting promise of unity and bonding. Having once gone up in flames, "democracy" can now be safely deposited into the communal bag of truths, to be periodically resurrected in an image of wire and yute cloth by some teenage "master of fire" for whom "democracy" will have become another one of what the youngsters call "those fire inscription words."

In contemporary contexts, in Bakhtin's words, fire inscriptions constitute an authoritative discourse largely deprived of its living authority, a hard-edged discourse marked by inertia, by semantic finiteness and calcification, a discourse that becomes "an object, a relic, a thing." It is a discourse that is not surrounded by "an agitated and cacophonous dialogic life" (1981, 344) but is playfully, deceptively turned into a grandiose celebratory gesture. Thus, fire inscriptions are not only shaped by the ideational contexts in which they are used; in turn, they become a shaping force in them as they both embody and dramatize the gap between youth movement ideological discourse and the ideational and social worlds in which it is currently deployed. In a way, perhaps, they help bridge it by framing this discourse as a playful curiosity or by eroding its ideational content.[8]

In tracing the "semiotic career" of fire inscriptions as a cultural form in Israeli youth movement ceremonials, I have emphasized their essential context-embeddedness in both cultural-historical and situational terms. Because I have regarded the use of fire inscriptions as a rhetorical act, which is part of a particular idiom of public expression, the kinds of issues I have addressed are, naturally, very different from those raised in the psychoanalytically or ethnologically oriented discussions of fire symbolism mentioned in the introduction. Whether we regard fire as a universal symbol of transformative energy or as a universal symbol of the crowd, the fact still remains that in different cultural contexts, it is symbolically shaped in different ways and is used in various forms and degrees on different occasions. Even the use of fire inscriptions in other cultural contexts would require a detailed analysis of their deployment as situated cultural forms to be fully appreciated and meaningfully compared with the discussion presented here.

A cultural-semiotic reading of the use of fire as an ephemeral art form thus requires that we go beyond noting the fact of its use and pay attention to the shape it is given and the manner in which it is deployed on given occasions. Such inquiry would address both the indexical and the symbolic dimensions of the flaming signs involved. The changes that have been noted in the enactment of fire ceremonials in Israeli youth movement contexts, with respect to the type and number of inscriptions used, the nature and structure of participation, the shift in the function of fire from a primarily sanctifying force to one that has a semantically voiding impact, all further reinforce the need for a context-sensitive approach in the study of symbols, whether they appear to be culture specific or traceable to universal aspects of human experience. It is my hope that this extended case study has demonstrated the fruitfulness of such an approach for understanding rhetorical forms in their cultural contexts and for assessing their critical implications.

Notes

1. The role of fire symbolism in various cultures is discussed in many scholarly and more popular sources. The main ones consulted in the course of this study are Cirlot 1962; de Vries 1974; Gaskell 1981; J. Cooper 1978; Cavendish 1970; Farbridge 1970; Eliade 1956; *Encyclopedia Britannica,* vol. 9 (Chicago: William Benton, 1972); *Encyclopedia Americana,* vol. 11 (Danbury, CT: Glorier Ive, 1981); *Encyclopedia Hebraica,* vol. 7 (Jerusalem: Encyclopedia Publishing Company [in Hebrew], 1958); Hastings 1951; Plimpton 1984.
2. According to Carl Jung, "It is probably no accident that the two most important discoveries which distinguish man from all other living beings, namely speech and use of fire, should have a common psychic background. Both are products of psychic energy, of libido or mana" (1956, 165). He goes on to cite a Sanskrit term, *tejas,* whose meanings include fire, energy or vital force, passion, sharpness or cutting edge, and spiritual power. Thus, it is probably no etymological accident that the Hebrew word for flame (*lehava*), for enthusiasm (*hitlahavut*), and for the cutting edge of a knife (*lahav*) come from the same root-stem. Whether the link Jung points out is universal or not, it certainly has been amply elaborated and amplified in Judaism. As Jung points out (1956, 162), the language of the Old Testament repeatedly associates the mouth, fire, and (divine) speech: for example, Psalm 29:7 says, "The voice of the Lord scattereth flames of fire," and Jeremiah 23:29 asks, "Is not my word like a fire?" The link between fire and passion appears in youth movement parlance in the expression *lihyot saruf al hatnu'a* (literally, to be "burned on the movement," to be utterly committed to it).
3. According to Sutton (1977), in sixteenth-century Italy a tradition of pyrotechnic theatrics evolved that did not involve the presence of actors onstage. When this tradition moved north, Teutonic productions came to reflect "the architectural preferences of northern Europe and were often skillfully deployed against dramatic backdrops, thus utilizing the entire landscape as a stage set for pyrotechnics" (25). A somewhat similar spatial predilection can be seen in Israeli pyrotechnic art, which, again, traces it to its roots in the German youth culture.
4. The size of the letters varies with the number of participants and the layout of the inscriptions, which generally determine the distance from which they are to be viewed.

5. The call-response pattern does not always involve fixed pair-parts. For example, a highly flexible call-response pattern is reported for African American communication in Daniel and Smitherman (1976), and a partly improvisational call-response pattern was found in the Boy Scout Campfire Program described by Jay Mechling (1980). The ideological and collectivist orientation of Israeli youth movement fire ceremonials stands out even more sharply when juxtaposed to Mechling's account. That this account is relevant to the larger American scene is brought out by a reading of official Boy Scouts of America literature published in Irving, Texas. See Boy Scouts of America 1985b, 1980, 1984. In addition to these differences in ceremonial idiom, it should be noted that in American Boy Scout lore fire symbolism stresses the dangerous aspects of fire as a destructive force (cf. Boy Scouts of America 1985a), whereas in the Israeli context it is generally presented more in its benign aspects as the Helper of Mankind (cf. Naor 1949).
6. Cf. Speer 1976; Friedlander 1985. These authors discuss the fascination with and manipulation of fire as part of the official aesthetics of the Third Reich. It is interesting to note in this connection that the Olympic torch was first introduced into the symbolism of the Olympic Games in modern times in the 1936 games held in Nazi Berlin (Durantez 1985).
7. As the example of fire inscriptions used in the context of a demonstration indicates, they can be used in protest as well, in which case they retain their full semantic load. An example of this, also associated with the First Lebanon War, was the use of the archaic phrase *Halanetsah tohal herev*? (Shall the sword forever devour?) in a kibbutz Independence Day ceremonial where public sentiment, which amounted to a rejection of official policies, was expressed in a fire inscription. Whereas this inscription was surely a direct statement about the war, I do not think the same could be convincingly said about the Trumpeldor phrase.
8. According to one of my youth movement sources, a further step toward the semantic devoiding of fire inscriptions and the carnivalization of fire displays was taken in the late 1980s in the name of efficiency: he reported that the fire inscriptions for the 1989 Holiday of Ascendance were being prefabricated in a regional youth movement center and sent to all the different troops. All they had to do was wrap the inscriptions with jute cloth, which turned many days of work into just a few hours of play. My young informant promised me that there would be lots of inscriptions and seemed to consider my questions about what they would say quite secondary.

13

Wedding Gifts

The Wrapping and the Content

ORIT ABUHAV

The subject of this essay is wedding gifts in Israel of the 1990s. The discussion of gifts is almost as old as anthropology itself but has not yet been exhausted despite the theoretical transformations the discipline has undergone. Since it is vital for understanding social relationships in general, and reciprocal and exchange relationships in particular, I will begin with a discussion of wedding gift giving and indicate the methodology of gathering data and documentation. I will relate gift giving to the various aspects and sociological and anthropological distinctions that derive from the ethnography, and through them attempt to depict the wedding gift given in Israel; I will also address the question of whether these wedding attendants—the gifts—are monetary or tangible.

Wedding Gifts in Israel: Presenting the Dilemma

"Gifts are the main exchange mechanism in numerous 'primitive' societies, in which a multifaceted system of obligation between family or community members mandate a continuous two-way exchange of various kinds of goods and services . . . with social differentiation and decrease in the potency of personal contacts, this regulation is weakened. Traditional gift-exchange relationships are gradually becoming business relationships."[1] The "gifts" cited above contain the seeds of the main sociological questions that will be discussed in this essay.

The first issue that needs to be addressed deals with the problem of social distinction that stems from an examination of the "wedding gift." Mechanical solidarity, according to Durkheim, is the social glue that characterizes "primitive societies," originating in the sense of similarity that society's members feel for one another. This feeling unites and joins them and enables them to live together, through the recognition that social order is based on the sense of "we"—we, who are alike.

However, the concept of exchange itself embraces differences and distinctions. In their various transactions, parties to the exchange transfer goods from one to another. Since similar people possess similar goods, exchange can exist only between those who are dissimilar. Exchange in a ("primitive"?) society, based on mechanical solidarity, indicates in fact the dissimilarity between the various units, whether the matter at hand is gifts or the exchange of other items. A gift is, therefore, a sign of distinction. In her article on wedding gifts and their role in Ethiopian group relationships, Salamon (1994) underscores the communicational aspect of gifts when examining the kind of gifts exchanged. In Ethiopia it was customary among Jews and their Christian neighbors to attend one another's weddings and bring gifts unique to each group, thus emphasizing the differences and distinctions between them. Jews would give their Christian neighbors knives used for farm work or animal sacrifice, while the Christians would, in addition to the knives, give money.

The essence and symbolic value of the exchanged objects take on different forms in different societies, and may be business oriented to a greater or lesser degree. Moreover, following Appadurai (1986a), there is room to challenge the polar dichotomy between "solidarity" and "modern" societies, based on the attitude of their members to goods and gifts. I will examine the characteristics of the distinction existing in the exchange of gifts in Israeli society, and focus both on the diversity of gifts (what people give) and that of those participating in giving (the givers).

Another interesting issue relates to knowledge. To what extent do the gift givers deliberate, to what extent are their options clear to them, to what extent are they au fait with what is accepted, and exactly what is considered "good taste." I will argue that in a diversified society like Israeli society, we will find a considerably large category of fence-sitters for whom the norms are unclear. They simply "do not know" what or how much to give. In the Jewish ultra-orthodox or Bedouin societies, all the members know what a proper gift consists of, inter alia, because information on the exchange of gifts is open and public. Arab and Bedouin societies have extremely structured characteristics and present themselves as such (e.g., in the museums of Arab and Bedouin culture in Israel). The praxis is well-known, clear, and undisputable to all; a guest knows what to bring and how to give a gift at any given social event. But in mutlicultural societies that are in a constant state of change, creating a unified and consensual archetype is a protracted process and its necessity demands agreement.

One suggestion for interpreting the bewilderment that exists when choosing a gift and the lack of knowledge regarding what is proper is presenting gift giving as a cultural byproduct of what is stereotypically called "*Sabra* [native-born Israeli] culture," which has been coalescing over recent generations and is characterized by contempt and disregard for manners and a scant expression of feeling. The *sabra* regards courtesy as hypocrisy, while the anthropologist sees it as the lubricant of social relationships. When drawing his portrait of the *sabra*, Oz Almog attributes these characteristics to the fact that the *sabra* grew up during the early years when Israel was a "small and rural frontier society . . . characterized by initial and non-institutionalized relationships" (1997, 332), as well as to an ideology that supported the rejection of manners, which were considered characteristic of bourgeois decadence, and regarded courtesy as an expression of hypocritical and false relationships, which were part and parcel of bourgeois life. Appadurai also mentions the bourgeois existence that characterizes the French bourgeois class, one of the hallmarks of which is the knowledge of what constitutes "good taste."

Gift giving at weddings serves as an ethnographic observation point—a unique, albeit narrow, perspective of Israeli society. I do not intend to delve deeply into the theoretical-conceptual discussion of the entity called "Israeli society"; I will only say that in my opinion the concept comprises a wide variety of social groups and categories. This kind of perspective of Israeli culture has resulted in a series of studies that have examined the characteristics of Israeli society by shedding light on a social phenomenon from a limited ethnographic standpoint that relates to a small segment of social behavior. These include Katriel's (1982) article on Friday night "complaining" get-togethers, which examined the social-value characteristics of the period in which these gatherings took place, as well as her well-known study (1986) of the term *dugri* (Arabic: blunt, direct speech and behavior); Roniger and Feige's (1992, 1995) study that examined the term *freier* (sucker, patsy) as an expression of a value-ideological change in Israeli society; Goldberg's (1971)[2] study of the introduction of the twist dance to Moshav Even-Yosef as a sign of cultural change, as well as his study (1998) of the Jewish and universal aspects of the custom of breaking a glass at the wedding ceremony; and Tittmuss's (1970) study of blood donation as an analogy to overall exchange-relationships in society.

The Israeli social custom of giving wedding gifts will become clearer when considered in the wider context of gift giving. A brief review of events in which gifts are given shows that this custom is prevalent in the following circumstances: (1) life-cycle events: Brith Milah (circumcision), as well as the Brita (a party held in honor of the birth of a girl), birthdays, bar mitzvahs, bat mitzvahs, weddings, and silver and golden wedding anniversaries (no gifts are given at the termination of life); (2) spatial change: a housewarming party, hospitalization and discharge, first visit to a home; (3) holidays: Jewish—Rosh Hashanah, Hanukkah (Hanukkah coins given to children), Passover, Purim (sending of gifts); civil—Mother's Day; and (4) personal events: commencement of studies, graduation, induction to the military, discharge from the army, rise in military rank, work promotion, retirement, a trip abroad, return from a trip abroad (the traveler brings gifts), for special personal service, as compensation for injury, or as a gesture of peacemaking.

Whatever the gifts, their main and salient characteristic is diversity. To the surprise of many (myself included) who have addressed this topic, the heterogeneity of wedding gifts and its place in the social discussion—among the hosts, guests and relatives, and those specifically requested to state what they bring as wedding gifts—is extensive and not self-evident. This heterogeneity makes the examination of the phenomenon extremely challenging. The majority of interviewees, who expressed their opinions openly, were amazed by the fact that not all participants in the discussion held similar views and in most cases were not even familiar with the different strategies that others adopt in similar situations.

Hence the question that must be asked is, how does the variety of wedding gifts reflect the diversity of present-day Israeli society? Explanations for the diversity of gifts may derive from two sources. The first is the diversity of social spaces the gift givers come from and who are gathered under one roof. The second is that despite the fact that we expect that people who belong to specific "social spaces" will behave similarly to their neighbors in this space, the degree of similarity is not so great that we can expect uniformity. I presume that in traditional societies the variety of options open to the gift giver was narrower, and the list of customary gifts was more limited, as in rural Arab society. In contrast, culture currently provides a variety of choices and wedding guests are expected to select one of them. This variety enables the expression of nuances of social relationships, but also challenges the person to choose, a dilemma similar to that confronting the consumer at a modern supermarket. Hence this is characterized by confusion and lack of knowledge about what to give.

Research Method

A methodology of building a wedding gift ethnography can be accomplished in two ways. The first way is a diachronic view that systematically follows the sequence of the exchange of wedding gifts along a period of time, while focusing on the social fabric in which reciprocity takes place. This is possible when discussion is anchored in a number of figures within the fabric, among whom friendship or kinship relationships exist, and we examine who brought whom what and when, or when we follow a cycle of gifts that one person gave and received (see Brumann 1996). The second way is a synchronic one, which I chose for this ethnography. A personal, unmethodical, and inconsistent interest in the topic opened a window of opportunity for me to a socially wide-ranging methodical and consistent research. While closely following the gifts brought to a wedding of a relative of mine, I asked various people, "What do you bring to a wedding?" I posed this question to a wide variety of people of different ages, social status, and place during the years 1994–96. I interviewed approximately 150 students from two teachers' seminaries, and approximately 50 relatives and acquaintances.

It is worthy of note that I was initially inclined to roughly divide the entire society into basic divisions, according to accepted variables of ethnicity, social status, or age, but I did not find diversity of gift giving based on ethnic group or age. (In this regard it is worth noting that in her discussion of the Israeli family's characteristics, Lea Shamgar-Handelman [1995] found that the classic divisions of society, accepted in statistical analysis, did not enhance her understanding.) On the contrary, as time passed the complexity of the phenomenon, which I will now discuss, was revealed.

It appears that this seemingly innocent question, "What do you bring as a wedding gift?" aroused disconcerted, emotional, and excited responses on the one hand, and marked bewilderment on the other. Indications of these responses were evident as early as the discussion on the variety of gifts, and should not be surprising. Although exposing the strategies adopted by the interviewees often demanded their candidness, their wish to share their strategies with the interviewer and other listeners was also apparent. Blunt exposure of their considerations for choosing a gift embarrassed the speakers and was ten times more difficult when attended by listeners' criticism.

After the question was posed to the group of interviewees, the subject was discussed and various ways of meeting the social obligation of gift giving were presented. When I conducted individual interviews with each of the interviewees, a more complex picture was revealed, which also included the various deliberations that attended the decision of choosing the gift, accompanied by daily examples that illustrate the principles.

Variations on a Wedding Gift: A Story of Gifts at One Wedding

I conducted a telephone conversation with a young couple on the morning after their wedding. The conversation opened with their complaint that they did not "cover the wedding," that is, the cost of the wedding was greater than the sum of money they received in gifts: the sum they were committed to pay the hall owner, the band, the florist, and other expenses incurred in the wedding's production was greater than what they had received. The large box brought by one of the family members, lying desolate in the gift cradle at the entrance to the hall, had aroused my curiosity, and I inquired about it. It turned out to be a "nice practical dinner service" in the eyes of the gift bearer, but was "the lesser of two evils" in the eyes of the recipients, who were happy that they had received only one tangible gift.

Friends of the bridegroom's parents who lived abroad sent the young couple (via the parents) a silver platter and picture frame. The gift was received several days prior to the wedding and was met by anger and resentment, mainly on the part of the bride. She claimed that she would have preferred money, and (rhetorically?) asked whether they could send the gift back or sell it. The groom's response was more moderate, evidently because he was familiar with the custom prevalent among his parents' generation abroad of giving ornamental silver items as a wedding gift.

At the entrance to the hall the groom's parents, the bride's parents, and siblings stood in the receiving line. Next to them were the video photographer and his assistant, who filmed all those who crossed the threshold, including the exchange of good wishes and kissing of the guests, and, of course, the retrieval of gift envelopes from pockets and bags and their transfer to the celebrants. It is worthy of note at this stage that this footage would later serve as a documented list of the wedding guests and would assist in confirming the list of gifts, checks, and givers. In cases when there was doubt regarding the presence of certain guests, the video documentation was decisive.

During the event the couple circulated among their guests in order to chat with them, to have their photographs taken together and thank them for coming, to see whether they were satisfied with the hosting and meal, and, albeit less noticeably, to assess the number of guests and ascertain who was absent. The celebrants were well aware of the fact that any uneaten meal, any empty seat or plate, meant an expense that would not be covered by any income. As mentioned earlier, the couple received money from their guests and in general were disappointed by the overall sum, the individual sums received from their relatives and friends, and the fact that many of those invited were absent. The blunt and explicit way in which they expressed their disappointment, without attempting to disguise it, revealed to me a world of calculations of which I was unaware, and which later became a window through which I chose to study the phenomenon of wedding gifts. The data and classifications in this essay are a result of accumulated information gathered at numerous weddings and about numerous gifts and attitudes of people who come from different social spaces.

Considerations Related to Gift Giving

Analysis of the question, "What do you bring as a wedding gift?" shows that choosing a gift-giving strategy is determined by a number of principles: the wedding's venue, the number of guests, timing, the type and degree of relationship, the guest's and host's status, and "how much it is customary to give." These principles and their interrelations are what will be, in the end, decisive in choosing between a tangible or a monetary gift, the type of tangible gift, or the sum of money in the envelope that will be transferred to the hall safe or directly into the bride and bridegroom's pocket.

The Venue of the Wedding and Number of Guests: Cost per Person/Cost of Gift

In recent years the trend of hosting weddings at event centers in a garden setting has grown. These are wedding reception gardens situated in "natural" venues that have been transformed into reception grounds. Many couples prefer to marry in a free and informal atmosphere that is perceived as "natural" and "outdoors," in contrast to indoor halls. In addition to the outdoor venues, it is customary to conduct family celebrations in specifically designated halls, some of which are situated in industrial zones and others in the city center.

More costly weddings take place in fashionable hotels in the big cities and at "exclusive" gardens and outdoor reception grounds.

The cost of holding a wedding is in the range of $25–50 per head. This includes food, serving, and at times hall decoration and flower arrangements. A band, disc jockey, or a dance troupe is an additional cost that does not depend on the number of guests (therefore it is worthwhile for the host to invite more guests who will bring more gifts and thus cover the cost of the wedding, which includes, in addition to the price per person, additional costs). Guests are conversant with the price per person as a result of their knowledge of the market or because they were directly or indirectly informed of the cost by their hosts. Information pertaining to cost is cast like a fisherman's net through the social network with the hope—usually realized—that it will reach its target audience. The intensive social interaction between colleagues, or between family members, leads to the dissemination of information regarding the cost per person among guests so that they have a basis for calculating the appropriate cost of the gift. Calculations are conducted in the following manner: cost per person, based on venue and menu, is the index for determining the cost of the gift, with the addition of the Value Added Tax, of course.

The cost of the gift is weighted according to the number of guests who give a collective gift. A couple will bring a sum of money that is equal to twice the cost per person, plus some. This principle is somewhat more complex when a family with two children is involved. On the other hand, a single person who comes to a wedding will bring a gift equal to the cost per person plus 50 percent. It is worth noting that when the interviewees voiced their deliberations as to the pros of giving a tangible gift (compared with a gift of money), the number of guests "included" under the same gift was not very important. The number of participants was more important when the gift in question was money.

The Timing of the Event: "This Summer You Will Be Dressed in White" (from an Israeli Song)

Unlike many other life-cycle rituals—from the Brith Milah through the bar mitzvah and funerals—the timing of a wedding varies. For numerous reasons the summer months are preferable for wedding ceremonies. Outdoor reception gardens can only be used during the summer because of the weather; the wedding season also falls during the summer break at institutions for vocational training and academic studies, where the majority of couples are young people who are at a turning point in their professional lives—either studying or in a transition period between studies and work. The spring is more limited because of the Jewish law prohibiting marriage in the seven weeks between Passover and Shavuoth (Pentecost), and "there are a lot of religious festivals" in the fall that would overshadow a wedding. Despite the higher cost of weddings during the summer months—price per person, band, and so forth—marriages usually take place during this season.

Despite the advantages of the summer, the frequency of events and religious festivals that mandate gift giving will make it more difficult for givers to bear the financial burden and will compel them to reduce the amount they are able to give for each gift. Therefore, hosts will consider holding the wedding within the following framework of constraints: not too close to the High Holy Days, when the cost of hosting and gifts is great in any event; not at the end of the month, when salaries have been used to the full; and, if it is possible, not during the summer months. Young women in particular explicitly voiced these considerations related to timing, which take into account the financial burden on the giver. Among older and more financially well-established interviewees, this was not one of the crucial considerations. This distinction raises the question: does the gift constitute such a heavy economic burden for the lower-middle class and the poor? Do harsh conditions prevail over the social obligation to reciprocate gifts? However, failing to relate to these considerations, as manifested by more affluent people, does not necessarily reflect the fact that they do not relate to the financial burden involved in gift giving. They may be camouflaging the economic dimension of the gift and underscoring its social facet more successfully.

Who Is Getting Married?

One of the immediate and spontaneous responses to my question, "What do you bring as a wedding gift?" was "It depends on who is getting married." The degree of kinship of the bride or groom, or both, to the gift giver, even if it is not the primary consideration in determining the type and scope of gift, may be a decisive factor in choosing a gift and determining its worth. I noted four degrees of kinship, which I put into four categories.

1. The first category comprised close relatives, such as siblings, nieces and nephews, and cousins, who received gifts of the greatest value. Monetary gifts are usually in the region of 1,000 shekels (about $240) and in special cases are even higher (here I did not include parents' gifts to their children).
2. The second category comprised more distant relatives and close friends, as well as children of close friends. These people give tangible or monetary gifts of lesser value than those given by members of the first category, but relatively higher than those of the third.
3. The third category, which most married couple–gift giver relationships fall into, comprised various kinds of relationships and ties with the married couple, but nevertheless gifts were uniform or nearly uniform. The analysis conducted was not based on a social relationship hierarchy, which is determined in accordance with the closeness of the social ties between giver and recipient. Uniformity in this category is perhaps the result of criteria that were not dependent on the degree of closeness, such as

the venue of the wedding, and stems perhaps from their feeling no necessity or desire to invest thought and resources in determining the nuances of the differences between different kinds of social ties, and from the convenience of generalization. In general, the interviewees answered the question, "What do you bring to the wedding of those to whom you are not particularly close?" with "Whatever is customary." This kind of answer was a subject for a separate discussion, since "customary" is a main subject of social research (see, e.g., Bourdieu 1972).

4. The fourth category comprised couples and guests who were socially distant from one another. This type of guest includes relatives whom couples meet only once every few years—at family events such as weddings—or children of colleagues, who were invited anonymously to the wedding and their invitation was noncommittal in the extreme. In such cases guests will deliberate as to whether they are obliged to participate in the wedding, and when they decide in the affirmative, their gift will be the minimum that can be given without causing embarrassment or shame. One way of indicating distance is a telephone (not a written) invitation, made by the couple and their families close to the event. In such cases, if the guest comes to the wedding, he or she will give a modest gift and leave immediately. A half-hearted invitation means a half-hearted gift.

Sometimes groups join forces in order to give a communal gift. This kind of group gift presents complex dilemmas and even more complex solutions. For example, a group of colleagues, which comprises both the managing director and the sanitation staff, get together and buy a microwave oven (extremely popular in recent years), or a group of friends, in which the relationship of its members to the couple is differential, organizes to buy a communal gift. A communal gift annuls the variance between the givers themselves toward the recipient. Annulment of variance is preferable for those lower in the hierarchy (those who are distant or poor), but it also means that those of higher rank (closer, more affluent) cannot demonstrate generosity and financial ability. Therefore, this kind of gift is a compromise that is manifested in social pressure to join the group of givers and, despite its numerous disadvantages, is extremely popular.

Among the considerations involved in choosing the gift and its characteristics, the giver's place in relation to the host is of great import. This place, like any other social position, is characterized by its flexibility and is the object of social maneuvering. In comparison with the cost per person and the place and timing of the wedding, over which the giver has no control, definition of the degree of relationship to the couple is a tool for realizing interests, establishing or weakening ties, becoming closer or more distant, and expressing hostility or sharing. For this reason, giving that takes into account the quality of the relationship is an opportunity for a redefinition of relationships, whether it strengthens or weakens them. It is also the channel for transmitting messages related to the relationship's quality: for example, giving an ambivalent gift to someone who is defined as genealogically close or emotionally distant, or to someone who is defined as an longtime friend but the relationship is no longer close.

The Status of the Recipient and the Giver: Each According to His or Her Ability? Each According to His or Her Needs?

Regarding gift giving as a demonstration of status is a natural interpretation arising from observing wedding gifts from the perspective of exchange. Emanuel Marx (1980b), for example, points out the economic status role of gifts in the Bedouin society in the Negev desert. He claims that because of the life circumstances of the desert people, they cannot demonstrate their economic wealth in consumer goods or real estate. Therefore people give valuable gifts, which are public items of exchange whose value is clear-cut, and through them they can demonstrate their wealth more directly, openly, and clearly. In comparison with Israeli society, where the value of a gift is an encoded social fact that is usually not discussed, in Bedouin society the public declaration of the value of the gift is an inherent part of its essence and objective.

The pairs of relationships between givers and recipients can fall into three general categories: the recipient and the giver are of equal status; the recipient is of a higher status than the giver; and the recipient is of a lower status than the giver. In each of these categories a number of *modi operandi* are open to the giver. I will now analyze the social significance of these different *modi operandi*. It is clear that by their very nature the categories are inclusive in such a way that they blur nuances of differentiation. Therefore, relating to the bride, bridegroom, and their parents as one category diminishes sensitivity to possible status differences between the bride and bridegroom, and between their families. However in an extremely schematic way it can be presented as follows: if the giver and the recipient are of equal status, and the value of the given gift is the same as that of the received gift, the relationship is seemingly symmetrical. Despite the fact that the reciprocity principle of exchange pulls in the direction of equality, the received gift will never be entirely identical to the given gift. For example, those giving money must weight their gift in accordance with the rise in prices from the time they received the gift. But beyond considerations related to weighting, givers will usually try to increase the value of the gift even symbolically so that they "will not be shamed." Bourdieu, who relates to a situation in which the recipient is eager to give a countergift of similar value, or equal to the given gift as soon as possible after receiving it, is of the opinion that this kind of behavior may be interpreted as a rejection on the part of the recipient of the giver's gift, and, moreover, a gift identical to the received gift should not be given in the case of a tangible gift, nor an equal sum to that of a gift of money. Bourdieu notes that we can observe in all cultures that in order to avoid insult, the countergift must be different. Immediate and equal exchange invites rejection (Bourdieu 1972). But in order to maintain the principle of symmetry, an equal, but different, gift can be given. I shall illustrate using the following example. On her marriage, A. received a monetary gift of 2,500 shekels (just over $600) from her cousin, who got married three days later; A. gave her cousin and bridegroom a countergift of airline tickets of about the same value. (A.'s father used to refer to the wedding invitations he received in the mail as "traffic tickets" he had to pay under protest.)

In the second category, when gift givers are of higher status than the recipient, they will act in one of three ways: they will give a costly gift; give a gift compatible with the recipient's status; or give a particularly modest gift. If he gives valuable gifts, and in this case both sides are aware of the fact that when the time comes the recipient will have difficulty in giving an equivalent gift, the recipient will be grateful. Inequality between the giver's and recipient's gifts will emphasize and highlight their difference in status; what the giver "wasted" from the point of view of general resources he or she gained in social resources. This is a classic example of converting economic resources to social ones and is highly compatible with the theory that deals with conversion of resources.

Among mountain-dwelling Jews in the Caucasus, the bride used to dress in rags in the company of her relatives during one of the days of the wedding feast, and they would give her gifts. The bride, deliberately wearing rags, diminished her status in order to get support from her relatives and enable them to demonstrate their financial superiority. She underdressed demonstratively as a kind of social etiquette so as not to constitute a burden for her relatives who would, in such a situation, feel obliged to overdress and to show her true generosity. If she minimized herself, her guests would not feel obliged to climb too high in order to be considered generous.

The giver may also choose to give a gift equal or parallel to that given by the recipient or which he or she might have given. Thus the giver relinquishes flaunting his own superior status, saves on resources, and does not bind the recipient to him in any way whatsoever. The giver thus artificially lowers himself in relation to the recipient and creates an artificial symmetry. The recipient will undoubtedly criticize the giver on his miserliness and will bear contempt because "he could have afforded much more," but it is possible, however, that he will be pleased that he released the giver from the shackles of gratitude and saved him the price of social arrogance.

Finally, the giver might give a modest gift, which will diminish the giver and place him "beneath" the recipient. This is uncommon but not unreasonable. This type of behavior is plausible in cases in which the giver chooses to demonstrate extreme modesty with an educational and patronizing nuance, as if to say, "True, I am rich and can afford it, but giving a wedding gift is not an occasion for ostentatiousness." This way the giver broadcasts asceticism and demonstrates modesty and defiance of the practices of other affluent people or the nouveaux riches, who flaunt their wealth. Perhaps he does not want to demonstrate his wealth and financial ability and chooses to convey a message of minimalism. This kind of message can, of course, be interpreted by the recipient as an expression of animosity, obligatory giving that is insincere, or in the vein of "only a rich person could allow himself to buy so cheaply." It may well be that the social price rich-modest givers pay by giving an insignificant gift is bearable, and may even be desirable in the event that they want to sever ties with the recipient. Another way of interpreting a categorically modest gift given by the wealthy is that wealthy people do not feel compelled to prove their wealth. As a student from Tirah (an Arab town) said, "Rich people do not have to prove their wealth and can permit themselves to give a modest gift—even a miserly one. I, who am not rich, always give generously because I do not want to appear poor."

Should the givers of the gift be of lower status than the recipient, they will be likely to choose one of three stratagems. If they choose to give the equivalent of "what is accepted" they will put themselves in the "middle ground" where no great financial effort is required, and at the same time they will not demean themselves by displaying their limited means. This alternative seems to be the most common, albeit it is the least interesting. The second choice is to give the wealthy person an expensive gift. In this situation, the giver tries to somewhat diminish the recipient's superiority and the economic price he or she pays is very high. It is quite possible that considerations of the "price per person" are relevant to the giver, since according to them his gift is supposed to at least cover the cost of "his plate," although it is clear that holding an extravaganza is designed to show off the recipient's economic power and thus maintain his high social status. He cannot allow himself to be modest because then he will lose social status and narrow the gap between his own ability to be profligate and the ability of those beneath him on the social scale. The potlatch, on which Ruth Benedict reported in her book on patterns of culture (1934), is reincarnated at a wedding. The wealthy man throws his money around, just like the Native American chief who smashes his pots and throws out the rugs woven by his people over a whole year just to show the power of his wealth and his ability to be extravagant, apart from display purposes. Therefore there is perhaps no point in trying to hoist the wastrel by his own petard, that of uncontrolled waste. Only a chief of the same ability and control of resources can face him and conduct a duel of equals. The third way is, of course, that the giver of limited means gives the wealthy person a gift of modest value, thus contributing to maintaining the wealthy person's superiority, while his own money, which in any case is limited, stays in his pocket.

Giving "What Is Customary"

Another answer to the question, "What do you give for a wedding?" was, as mentioned above, "What is customary." This is a statement deriving from the conception according to which there is "something that is accepted." When one is exposed to many wedding celebrations, mainly when the giver or his friends are of marriageable age, or when their children or their friends' children are of marriageable age, the meaning of "what is accepted" is clearer and unequivocal because the discourse on it is more open and frequent. On the other hand, a dissociation of a number of years from "the wedding market" that occurs during the interim between one's own wedding and those of one's children causes obscurity and blurring of what is meant by "what is accepted." I was told by E. (a sixty-year-old woman who married off her son about a year prior to our conversation), "When I'm invited to a wedding and don't know how much to give, I consult other people with the same relationship to the celebrants who have been invited, and this way I'm updated on what is accepted. It's always better to give 50 shekels (about $12) more than what I think is accepted, if the sum is not clear, and this way I don't humiliate myself." E.'s awareness and sensitivity toward what is accepted to give heightened, so she says, after her son's marriage. Since then she has "paid far more attention to how much to give." In E.'s social circle, the accepted sum ranged between 200 and 300 shekels ($48–72). There are those who give a sum that is a multiple of 18 (Hebrew numerology = "life"), that is, 180 or 360 shekels (about $43 or $86). Some give a round sum in hundreds and add the 18 ("life") shekels. However, E. stated categorically that she sometimes goes as high as 600 shekels (about $145) for a gift if the bride or bridegroom is the daughter or son of very close friends or a close relative.

Knowing what to give is based on circumstantial factors, such as familiarity with the wedding market or the giver's location in the center of numerous social events. But knowledge of "habitus," as defined by Bourdieu, plays a decisive role in the formulation of gift knowledge. Because of the lack of an objective model, only a "social juggler" well versed in the cultural capital defined by Bourdieu as "the art of life" can maneuver in the various aspects of gifts. There are those who are equipped with this cultural capital—in France, mainly members of the upper-middle class—and those who do not have this capacity. "Good taste" in exchange is expressed by knowing what to give and when to reciprocate with a countergift. The timing component in giving—when to give—and its content component—what to give—are the cornerstones on which the praxis of gift giving is built.

A special but common way of interpreting "what is customary" is comparing it with what the giver received from either the bride or groom in an exchange of gifts. Knowing how much each of the guests gave is basic social information, whether it was stated openly and demonstratively or accumulated in secret lists that accompany the conclusion of the marriage ceremony with the opening of the envelopes containing money and the wrapped packages. At the weddings of Georgian Jews, it is customary for one of the groom's relatives, a brother or uncle, to publicly announce the value of the gift as the guest makes his or her entrance, and at the same time record and document the sum: "In the course of the banquet, an announcer rose and described each gift the bride had received from her own family and that of the groom, with the giver's name, as well as the list of gifts received from the groom's side. . . . The bride's mother told me that the presentation of the gifts is a clear means of creating new social connections and reinforcing them, while the announcement from the stage creates communication between the people at the tables" (Moldavski 1983, 85). The list of gifts, mainly dollars, serves as a basis for understanding how much should be given when the celebrants have to reciprocate when they are invited to a future celebration by their guest. Announcing the value of wedding gifts is also accepted practice among other groups, such as the Jews of Tripoli.

As I noted above, the list of gifts is compiled when they are opened by the couple, either in the presence of their parents or in private. Accurate documentation of the gifts is essential so that the recipients can know whether their debt has been repaid or, alternatively, what their own debt will be in the future. Moldavski notes that at the weddings of Georgian Jews at which colleagues who are not from the Georgian community took part, the "Israelis" gave wrapped gifts with a greeting card, or envelopes containing checks, and these were not recorded by the gift collectors but were handed over to the parents of the young couple.

In an Arab village in Israel (in the Wadi 'Ara region) it was customary during the wedding celebration to pin a covering of banknotes to the groom's suit. One by one, the guests would pin the notes to his suit. Recording of the gifts was not done through an announcement but through a groomsman, an older friend and representative of the groom's father, who stood behind the groom and who knew everyone, saw everything, remembered everything, and recorded everything. The givers of gifts of money thus discharge their obligations to the father of the groom or his elder brother and thus the father is the one responsible for the deals and ensuring that the debt is repaid. Today, however, it is customary to give money in an envelope because it is "more elegant." "We have taken this from Jewish culture," says A. The custom has undergone several transformations, from pinning notes to the groom's jacket (according to A. this stopped because of damage to the jacket), through collection of the money by the groomsman who would pass among the guests carrying a large case, to giving a check in an envelope directly to the groom.

In conclusion, gifts of money were the most common at Israeli weddings in the mid-1990s. Yet the custom of giving tangible gifts has not completely disappeared and their exclusivity is worthy of a separate discussion.

A Tangible Gift and a Gift of Money

In the preface to his book on the social life of things (articles), Appadurai (1986a) presents the social qualities of commodities (articles, products, goods). He opposes the concept of many theorists, including Bourdieu, who differentiate between societies with a capitalistic economic infrastructure that place emphasis on the "accounting" aspect of the gift, and those often described as having an infrastructure of solidarity in which the gift has great emotional and societal value. In Appadurai's opinion, this dual approach causes numerous researchers to view a commodity as a "type" of "thing," thus limiting their discussion to the question of what "type" it is. For a better understanding of the uniqueness of commodity exchange, it is not enough to distinguish it from barter or the exchange gifts. One must identify how the "accounting" aspect appears in each of these forms of exchange. Appadurai suggests that we view the commodity as "a thing" in a certain state, at any time and at any place in its social life. In other words, he suggests looking at the commodity's potential to be anything instead of making a purposeless distinction between commodities and other things.

There are two types of tangible gifts: a nondescript and non-exclusive tangible gift that is not intended to transmit anything related to the giver's or recipient's taste, and an "arrow gift" that is supposed to hit the target of the recipient's taste and needs. In contrast to a gift of money, the giving of an arrow gift has the value of taste: that of the giver who has chosen the gift, the way in which the giver perceives the recipient's taste, the way in which the giver maneuvers and shapes his own image in the eyes of the recipient, and the flavor of social investment. Schwartz (1970), a social psychologist who dealt with these aspects of gifts, argues that through the gift the giver conveys his thoughts regarding the recipient's desires and needs. In this way, parents who give their children gifts shape their identity and the image of others which defines itself once it becomes public. Accordingly, accepting a gift is accepting the identity of the other, while rejecting it is rejecting the other.

The gift of an article in general, and a more binding arrow gift in particular, is perceived as a very personal way of giving a gift and expressing heartfelt feelings. A gift of this kind contains an investment of thought—"what to give"—which is a conscious addressing of the accepted norms in the locale under discussion: an investment of thought on "what is suitable" for the specific couple to whose wedding one has been invited, an investment in looking for the suitable item, and a financial investment in its purchase. And above all, there is an investment in risking one's reputation in the event of that the recipient's and the giver's expectations are not met. Together with the possibility of a successful choice of gift, the giver of an arrow gift takes a great risk when the arrow misses its mark. The miss, which damages the giver's reputation, derives from his inappropriate image of the recipient's taste, which may be inferior to the latter's self-image. Arrow gifts are therefore rare, even among the congeries of article gifts, and even rarer are those that are the fruit of the giver's own creation: a picture he has painted, a jug he has made, a statue he has sculpted, or a book he has written.

The tangible gift, given as it were out of generosity, which is a product of a mixture search and personal matching, also involves an aspect of control. The giver of a tangible gift who, in fact, decides what to do with his money, dictates to the recipient his scale of priorities and taste, and thus there is an aspect that might be viewed as educating or even patronizing. A recently married young female student said that had she received a bookstore gift certificate she would have been insulted as it would have shown the giver's intention to educate her

(her education, as it were, being lacking), and she remarked derisively, "That's an educational gift."

A tangible gift is sometimes viewed as a prudent way of giving a gift whose monetary value is low but which, on the face of it, appears respectable. Numerous interviewees noted that one can buy an article gift cheaper than what is considered respectable and appropriate to put into an envelope in the form of a check or cash.

In conclusion, gifts of money are mutually exchanged products—coins and notes—whose immediate value can be measured against clear criteria and whose current value can be assessed in comparison with a gift of money given in the distant past. As the saying goes, "Money has no smell," nor does it have a history. Every note is identical to its fellow and is thus an ahistorical representative of its value. Therefore, money transactions are anonymous and the social identities of the giver of the note and its recipient are not embodied in the note itself. Money is all-embracing and is measured by its cumulative value, and only this aspect is taken into account when assessing money as a gift. Money is not attributed to its owner's unique personality, but indicates overall and covert financial ability. Despite the presentation of money and tangible gifts as being mutually exclusive, the possibility exists of a kind of mediated gift between these two types of gifts. In Turkey, for example, it is customary to bring a gold coin (whose current value is about $100) to the circumcision ceremony, and it is quite possible that this custom also pertains to wedding gifts. It is also possible for gift certificates (envelopes containing a note of a fixed value) to be given, which are used for purchases at a specific store in a well-known chain that sells a specific product or at a large department store.

Graeber (1996) compares money gifts to the exchange of beads in Madagascar and claims that money gifts are gifts without a history in contrast to necklaces, jewelry, or other articles, which have a historical value and bear the social identities of their previous owners. However, in contrast to this type of gift, tangible wedding gifts open a historical chapter or write an additional section in it. Their power is in the degree of their topicality, and the more contemporary they are, the greater their value. Articles given as gifts are the *dernier cri* in fashion (dishes and silverware, bed linen, or home furnishings). Objects of Judaica are given only infrequently in the secular Jewish sector and have an overall historical value as representing tradition, even though the item may have only recently come off an industrial production line. It can be argued, with some reservations, that many people who give gifts view the giving of money as a "negation" of the sentimental and social value of gifts in general, and of wedding gifts in particular.

An extreme expression of the relegation of the personal and sentimental value of the tangible gift, which turns it into something more like a money gift, is the initiative of the Visa credit card company, which made the following offer to its members:

> Holders of this Visa [card] can purchase gifts for the wedding gift list without leaving home. . . . The wedding gift list, the solution to the eternal problem: what to buy. According to their taste, the young couple compile a list of gifts they would like from the huge selection offered by all departments of the Hamashbir Letzarchan [department store]. . . . Call the toll-free number. . . . We will help you choose your gift by phone and send you a lovely greeting card for the young couple that tells them something about the gift you have bought for them. The gift will await the couple at the Hamashbir Letzarchan branch.

This is an attempt to manage an exchange that is supposed to be personal from an anonymous control center by remote control, as if it is "untouched by human hand." It is presented by the advertiser as a time-saving investment and is compatible with the increasing tendency to turn the gift into something less personal and more instrumental.

Thus far I have described the ethnography of the wedding gift in Israel and its various aspects. Emphasis has been placed on the degree of behavioral variety, despite its being perceived by the majority of the participants in the social act as being standard, and the different variations of deciding considerations in the choice of the type and value of the gift were presented. I will now attempt to indicate the overt and covert characteristics of giving a gift.

Visible and Hidden in a Wedding Gift

The Wrapping

Gifts given at a wedding are brought wrapped in elegant colored paper and tied with shiny, colored ribbon crafted into ornate bows. Generally, the wrapped gift comes in a plastic bag given to the purchaser with the store's logo. Wrapping style varies according to current fashion. Today it is widely accepted at prestigious gift stores, and particularly of gifts in the "natural" style, to wrap the gift in brown recycled paper or "simple" and "natural" brown wrapping paper, and to wrap a bundle of wheat stalks or raffia around it. The investment in the gift packaging, whatever its style, is considerable: one has to wait until the wrapping operation, with all its style and details, has been completed, and it appears that the cost of the gift also includes the salesperson's investment of time and packing materials.

After observing the wrapping and packaging, one might ask: why wrap, hide, and cover the gift given to the couple at their wedding? There can be no doubting the fact that the wrapping hides the article that passes from the giver to the recipient. One interpretation of this is that recipients seek to conceal their gift so that they will be able to pretend it is extremely valuable, since with the exception of the couple and perhaps their parents, no one else will know what it actually is. The strategy adopted by the giver of hiding the gift enables him to maneuver in a way in which he will be perceived as generous, even if his gift is not sufficiently respectable. Some say that the wrapping of a gift is designed to avoid shaming the recipient, so that he is not humiliated by the fact that he is compelled to accept something from his fellow. This approach was presented by H., who was very close to the ultra-orthodox circles in Jerusalem. He claimed that there is a similarity between gift wrappings and the covering of Purim festival gifts. These gifts are covered in order not to embarrass the recipient. Deeper inquiry shows that at Purim, there is a double commandment: the giving of gifts, which is an exchange between equals, and giving to the needy, which is a one-way transfer of goods from the wealthy to the poor. The innocent bystander in the street will be unable to distinguish between Purim gifts and alms for the needy and this is the purpose of covering the gift.[3]

Gifts of money—checks or notes—are usually placed in a white envelope with the name of the celebrant—the bride or the groom—inscribed upon it. At the entrance to some wedding halls one can find a writing desk with envelopes on it. At weddings of Jews of Ethiopian origin, a family member stands at the entrance giving out white envelopes upon request. The more anonymous and impersonal the gift, such as gifts of money, the greater the anonymity and formality of the wrapper. The wrapping of money has no added value in terms of an emotional-social or financial investment.

Wrapping gifts can also create a barrier between the giver and the recipient, and between an impersonal object which, when standing on a store shelf, is just another consumer "product" and the gift when it is wrapped (elegantly or simply). In the course of an object's social life, Appadurai discerns the stage at which the object is defined as "a commodity." This stage is the time at which the article is still on the shelf. But from the moment the article—a product or a commodity—is perceived by the buyer as a gift, it shifts and becomes a gift and its wrapping turns it into a tribute. Appadurai indicates the commodity's potential of being anything, including a gift. Not every article has the potential of being a gift; despite the numerous existing possibilities, there are some things that will not be given as a wedding gift, such as a commodity whose monetary value is very low—a broom, for example—or one whose cultural connotations are linked to bodily secretions, such as toilet paper. A further characteristic of a commodity is its context. A thing whose place is in a commercial context will become a commodity. In contrast, a gift store is a social arena in which things are gifts by definition and there we can find things that can be defined as wedding gifts a priori. The very fact of their location in a store of this type turns them into possible gifts.

The wrapping is a barrier that also creates a distinction between the neutrality of transferring an article from hand to hand and the symbolic and emotional intention inherent in gift giving. An analogy may be drawn from the world of the tangible gift with that of art: just as a picture frame has meaning as an aesthetic barrier (known as "aesthetic distance") between the wall on which it hangs and the work of art itself, between sacred and profane, thus the wrapper separates the mundane from the exclusivity of the symbolic social event. In addition to its creating a degree of distancing the vitality of the work of art, aesthetic distance also serves as a liminal area separating the ordinary object from the tangible gift. Furthermore, the purpose of wrapping the gift is also aimed to surprise the recipient. Sometimes—if the gift is opened in public—the time elapsed between the announcement of the solving of the enigma and exposing the core of the gift is designed to accord the gift a greater symbolic value and extend the liminality in which the gift is no longer an ordinary article and still not an item in the economic and emotional exchange process.

The gift is an irreversible riddle which, like any other, is an enigma calling for a solution. Solving the riddle is a process constructed through hints and codes that are gradually revealed by the solvers, sometimes alone and sometimes through interaction with others. The riddle as a genre in Jewish culture has been discussed at length by Galit Hasan-Rokem in her book on the Book of Lamentations (*Tissue of Life*, 1996) and also by Dan Pagis (1986) in a description of the Hebrew riddle in Italy and Holland. Both propose a distinction between the "riddle" (text) and "a riddling situation," the essential characteristic of the riddle, which separates it from other types, in particular from two standpoints: its designation as a challenge, either public or private (a situation of riddling), and its verbal form, that is, the text's ability to serve as a challenge (and this is the attribute of riddling). The riddle can also be a gift in itself. Pagis describes riddles—rhymed one-language or multilanguage texts composed for a wedding in the seventeenth to the nineteenth centuries. The riddle was sometimes combined with other works—poems, cantatas, and plays—submitted by writers in the framework of a competition between them at wedding celebrations. The riddles were usually presented at the weddings of intellectuals and the author would "precede the riddle with words of greeting, affection or flattery that reflected his status and relationship with the celebrants" (Pagis 1986, 72). Sometimes the author would distribute the riddle among the wedding guests a few days before the celebration to enable the awarding of prizes on behalf of the couple. Following the riddle set by Samson at his wedding feast (Judges 14), the riddlers viewed the relationship between the wedding and the riddle as self-evident.

The riddle, the enigma, and the mystery that are solved at the wedding are given expression in an extraordinary manner. Quite a large number of wedding ceremonies in contemporary Israel involve a couple that have been living together for a long time, and even if they do not share a house, in most cases they do share a bed. The "one-timeness" of the new intimacy created on their wedding night—a significant concept of an extremely important event in the life of the young couple—between bride and groom, has lost its old meaning. We usually say that in contrast with the past, when the young couple ran off to fulfill the commandment of intimacy immediately after the ceremony, today they hurry to their hotel room to open the gifts and count the checks. Breaking the hymen has been replaced by ripping the wrapping from the gifts. The bridal gown, too, is like a gift wrapping: it is dramatic, "festive," elegant, and theatrical, tied around the waist with a beribboned belt; it is a one-time wrapper and a great deal of time is spent in its preparation and wearing. "Undressing" the gift from its wrapping is like removing the bridal gown from the bride's body. (There is a formal similarity among the gift, the bridal gown, and the decorated limousine that brings the bride and groom to their wedding ceremony. All three are tied in the middle with a ribbon and decorated with bows and tassels.) Moldavski, in her study on gifts among Georgian Jews, quoted a woman who, when asked why it is important to be invited to the wedding, replied, "Seeing a bride is worth paying for a gift" (1983, 82).

The Invisible Gift

Although the guest participating in the wedding celebration is part of a group of gift givers just like him, he does not discuss the subject of gifts with them. The binding string that ties the wedding guests together is the fact that they are linked to the celebrants in one way or another but they are not necessarily connected to one another socially. Despite the congregational character of the celebration, the subject of the gift is concealed and is not a topic for conversation among the guests. Even close relatives or friends do not publicly discuss what has been brought as a gift, and it would not be an exaggeration to describe the absence of this subject as a paradox of a taboo that everyone knows about, to which they have all devoted time, thought, and money, but no one talks about. This open social "secret" is an expression of the attitude toward the gift as it is perceived: an obligation, a façade of generosity but also discretion, and a zealous guarding against non-transmission of information.

The guests sitting at their tables, ten at each round table, or those mingling with the other guests as they taste the delicacies at the buffet will inevitably engage in small talk on any subject under the sun, with the exception of the gift. As the guest arrives at the affair, he gets rid of the white envelope, which his wife is carrying in her purse or he in his jacket pocket, with a discreet, even disguised movement by handing it to one of the bride's or groom's close relatives (his or her father or sibling). It is customary for the guest to slip it into a safe near the receiving line, which will be guarded throughout the evening under the eagle eyes of the couple or someone they have appointed for this task, lest the safe be stolen. Even a cradle for the gifts, if there is one, will be given the same treatment. At some halls or gardens there is an inner room in which the gifts are collected (the couple's traditional private room after the ceremony?) after being handed to a close relative who later takes them to the room.

Discussion of the gifts still takes place, but only in a close family circle that may have some ceremonial aspects. Talk about the couple's sexuality is customarily limited to jokes about "the morning after" in which the couple awaken to their new status after a night in which their conjugal intimacy is realized. These sayings express a type of humor, such as "Everyone knows why a bride stands under the wedding canopy but no one talks about it," when there is agreement among all the speakers that it has sexual overtones. However, the speakers immediately delineate the meaning given to the wedding night and relate to it as "the night of opening the gifts." Again, the pattern arises of relating to the gift as a necessary evil in the public context, but as an aspired-toward good in the intimate context, which includes close relatives.

The day after her brother's wedding celebration, T. "innocently" called at her parents' home, where the young couple had spent the night. At the family breakfast in which she participated, the couple intended to open the envelopes in the presence of the groom's parents and sister, but then the bride asked that the envelopes addressed to her family (those bearing the letter "A" not "N") be opened in the presence of her parents who lived a long distance away, and whom she intended to see shortly. The bride viewed this as safeguarding her family's territory from which no one could expel her and gave deep meaning to the "breaking of the hymen" of the envelope in the presence of her parents, who were the primary addressees for the money/checks.

Open Camera and Candid Camera

One of the points of view that illustrates the attitude of Israeli society toward wedding gifts, that same ambivalent attitude of generosity and necessity, was given humorous expression in two television programs screened some time apart and on different channels, and which employed a similar principle. One, using a hidden camera, documented the facial and verbal expressions of guests who were asked what they had brought as a wedding gift by the waiters serving light refreshments. After hearing their reply, the waiter said, "That's not enough, you're not getting any canapes," and went on his way. The waiter did this systematically to a number of guests, whose response was generally one of silent embarrassment and astonishment. In the second program, the director studied the reaction of the mothers of both the bride and groom as they opened the gift envelopes and discovered, to their great surprise, that their generous guests had given them sums of money or checks to the value of only a few shekels. The open and blunt "truth" is not spoken aloud, and the categorical exposure in "candid camera" shows, which elicits an embarrassed reaction, is a means of entertainment. The embarrassment stems from exposing the façade of generosity to the lens of the hidden camera. Things that are never said openly are given brusque expression that is surprising in its directness.

At the same time we are currently witnessing the spread of the custom of videotaping the wedding, which expressly follows the ceremony from the moment the guests enter until the last one leaves. From this place and time begins a full and detailed documentation of the guests, the speakers, the kissers and handshakers, and, of course, the check and gift givers. This detailed documentation enables the hosts to systematically and exhaustively record all their guests: who came, how many came, and especially who was absent. The videocassette will serve the couple in the future as an alternative to memory, that same social memory whose value cannot be underestimated when it comes to exchange and reciprocity. The video is a means of preserving information and documentation, as well as the list of gifts. In contrast to the "candid camera" that documents the embarrassment once the disguise is revealed, the overt video film provides documentation of the social memory as well as the legitimate aspects of heartfelt giving: kisses, greetings, congratulations, and gifts.

Perhaps social obligation mandates that we make a show of heartfelt giving and that wrapping the bitter pill of the gift (bitter, to the giver's pocket) in a saccharine-sweet wrapper of a sincere desire to give and give generously is stronger, more compelling, and more binding among the wealthy than the lower-middle class. The person of lower status can afford to be blunter and more extrovert in a public display of his calculations, because "noblesse [does not] oblige." What the wealthy person loses on the status front is not lost by those who have no status. Expressions of overt and covert principles of exchange of wedding gifts are an important axis in analyzing the phenomenon in Israeli society in which many people are frequently invited as wedding guests. The exchange of wedding gifts is a routine matter for the guests and a one-time event for the bride and groom. However, the camouflage of generosity and closeness, which everyone takes care to cover themselves with, is on numerous occasions frequently torn away or removed. An event such as this is perceived as a malfunction, an obstruction in the constant and well-oiled flow of exchange and gifts that are given along its route. Moreover, according to Ben-Menahem (1999), camouflaged messages are sometimes more efficient than direct ones, and a wrapped interest is sometimes preferable to a naked one.

In characterizing wedding gifts in Israeli society of the 1990s, I have followed Marcel Mauss (1954), whose name is mentioned in the same breath as "gift." Mauss laid the foundations for the discussion of the gift and determined the three main obligations related to it: the obligation of giving, the obligation of receiving, and the obligation of reciprocating. From this stem reciprocity and obligation, which are the mirror-image of social order, in which are reflected rules, customs, expectations, symbols, rewards, and norms. The gift is a total social fact that embodies different aspects of social life. Lévi-Strauss, who to a certain extent is Mauss's disciple, developed the idea of reciprocity and exchange and indicated that discrete social units exchange women, symbols, and objects (1987). Two exchange products intersect at the wedding: gifts and women (albeit the exchange of women in marriage is rare in Israeli society). The symbolic aspect expressed at the ceremony itself intensifies the act of exchanging gifts of money and tangible gifts. Bourdieu's words on gifts and their exchange (1990a) add a further dimension to this exchange, which is the power of decision in the individual's hands and his ability to maneuver within borders demarcated by these rules.

Bourdieu also indicated that in the giving of a gift, although it is a voluntary act, there is an appearance of generosity and of prima facie heartfelt giving. Generosity and obligation are contradictory even though all those participating in the social act deny this contradiction and try to camouflage it. The contribution of Mauss and Lévi-Strauss was in the shaping of the theoretical and structural aspects of exchange, while Bourdieu, Appadurai, Smart, and Graeber contributed a touch of understanding of the act, from their observations of the acts of human beings. Natalie Zemon Davis, who conducted a research on gifts in sixteenth-century France (2000), reveals the ways that gift exchange is crucial to understanding alliance and conflict in daily family life, as well as in the domains of religion, economic activity, and politics. As a social historian she draws a complex picture of the role of the gift in different contexts of people's lives, and in this sense I follow her view. In contrast, I chose to focus on one context: wedding gift.

The ethnography of giving gifts at the Israeli wedding shows their diversity on the one hand and the removal of the veil of generosity and heartfelt giving on the other. A gift is a sign of social distinction by means of which one social unit can express its uniqueness to the other. Knowing what to give is the kind of social capital with which some are blessed, and there are those who nurture it as part of their status. The gift has both visible and invisible facets and its enigma is expressed in its wrapping. The considerations taken into account when choosing the gift are the status of recipient and giver, the bride's or groom's relationship to the giver, the timing of the wedding, its location and cost, and even an attempt to hit the mark of the recipient's expectations and taste, while considering what he either gave in the past or will give in the future.

Notes

I wish to acknowledge my debt to Miriam Talisman and Anthony Berris for their sensitive translation of this article from the Hebrew, and to Irit Milo for her enlightening artistic comments.

1. E. Cohen 1967.
2. See Goldberg, this volume.
3. Moreover, Harvey Goldberg told me that Jews from Moshav Porat, whose origins are in Tripoli, used to send Purim gifts to their Muslim-Libyan neighbors on the pretext that the gifts were "alms for the poor" so that the "real" charity, given to Jews of their community, would not be discovered.

14

Political Bumper Stickers in Contemporary Israel

Folklore as an Emotional Battleground

HAGAR SALAMON

My daily journey to campus on Mt. Scopus in Jerusalem is more than an everyday act of commuting. I usually follow a route that crosses the borderline, officially obliterated but socially still very much in existence, between West Jerusalem (which was under Israeli sovereignty prior to the 1967 war) and East Jerusalem (under Jordanian sovereignty until the war). Sometimes this route is blocked because of political tension, demonstrations, or visits by foreign dignitaries. If this is the case, I take an alternative route, crossing a second dividing line within Jerusalem between the neighborhoods inhabited by secular or moderately religious Jews and those inhabited by ultra-orthodox and often anti-Zionist Jews. In this case, I must avoid being delayed by an ultra-orthodox demonstration, wedding celebration, or funeral of one of the ultra-orthodox rabbis.

Even if my journey passes without incident, however, it offers an opportunity to consider the complex and multifaceted nature of Israeli political reality as embodied by these dividing lines. The cars on the road are themselves emblems of the profound emotions of owners and audience alike. The cars that pass me are plastered with political stickers, creating a rich mosaic of terse slogans engaged in a dynamic and profound discourse. Thus metallic vehicles of transportation are transformed into the vehicles of political sentiments, through which a complex process of political communication takes place. This cultural phenomenon of folk politics expressed in the dynamic and public genre of bumper stickers is not unique to Jerusalem and has become widespread throughout Israel over the past decade.[1] The personal experience that led me to write this essay is one shared widely in Israel, where members of the public are involved as willing or unwilling participants in this popular discourse of the roads.

In the postmodern world, of which Israel and Jerusalem form an idiosyncratic but integral part, bumper stickers are an increasingly common expressive medium.[2] The Israeli variant of this iconic phenomenon shows specific characteristics, including the rapid growth of the medium since the early 1990s (reaching new peaks of folk innovation and creativity in the context of the peace process, and above all following the assassination of Prime Minister Yitzhak Rabin in November 1995) and its predominantly political nature.[3] This lively and animated folkloristic political discourse offers an alternative perspective on major political developments, which occur at a dizzying pace in Israel, and on the hegemonic political discourse that takes place in this country.[4]

An analysis of the "discourse of stickers" may cast light on social and political processes in Israel; the forces active in these processes; the level of involvement of specific groups in this discourse; and the relationships between these groups. These aspects, while not the focus of this essay, are the background for the present study of bumper stickers as a folkloric phenomenon. This essay attempts to unravel and interpret the popular political discourse embodied in this postmodern genre, and to discuss the interrelationship between this form of popular expression and the discursive nuances it embraces. Such discussion may further our understanding of such aspects as the definition of folklore in the modern world; the fluid boundaries between folklore, popular culture, and media; and the place of folklore in multicultural societies that are the arenas of complex covert and overt struggles between various groups representing competing political and even cosmological perspectives.[5]

The sticker—a visual expressive medium that must be read by its audience—seeks to convey social and political complexities in short messages of a few words that can be absorbed at a glance. As with other forms of expressive folklore, stickers are phrased with terse poetics that address a world of shared images. In attempting to interpret the message, the audience further expands the exegetical game through attention to aural aspects (such as rhythm and rhyme), multiple meanings, and other exegetical acts. This essay seeks to document the complexity and sophistication of this unique form of discourse, focusing on the experience of exegesis it inspires. The documentation process included open-ended and semi-structured interviews. The enthusiasm with which interviewees tackled the task of interpreting the messages revealed an argumentative and sermonizing rhetoric in which dexterous textual analysis is rife with powerful emotions. Popular discussion of these short and transient messages also reveals a surprising measure of emotion that emerges in all the participating voices.

The present analysis positions folklore as a cultural arena in which the distinctions between addresser (deliverer) and addressee (audience) are constructed and deconstructed through an emotive process. The presence of affective affinities emerges as the central feature of folkloric discourse. Due attention to these affective affinities in theoretical discussion of the nature of folklore and the experience it embodies may help define this field and conceptualize its characteristic dynamics.

Shalom Akhshav and *Shalom, Chaver*

The first documented political bumper sticker in Israel is usually considered to be ***Shalom Akhshav*** (Peace Now),[6] designed by David Tartakover in 1977.[7] This sticker is still in circulation today, many years after it was first introduced. This essay is based on material documented in Israel between November 1995 and May 1999, some twenty years after the production of the first bumper sticker. The material thus testifies to the generative qualities of the first sticker as expressed in the formation of the entire genre in Israel, and specifically the cluster of stickers on which this chapter focuses.

At the beginning of November 1995, in the midst of a controversial peace process, Israeli prime minister Yitzhak Rabin was assassinated in the main public square in Tel Aviv after stepping down from the podium where he had addressed a large gathering of supporters. The public reaction was one of extreme shock, which intensified after it emerged that his assassin was a young religious Jew who had acted on the belief that he was obliged by religious law to stop the peace process.[8] This brutal challenge to the foundations, boundaries, and adherents of Zionist nationalism would become a central theme in the public discourse that was to emerge on Israel's roads. Rabin's funeral was attended by numerous leaders from around the world who came to express their sorrow and show support for the path of peace he adopted. U.S. president Bill Clinton, a key partner in this peace process and arguably the most influential leader in the world, was among the mourners who gave eulogies. He ended his speech dramatically, repeating the Hebrew phrase from his response to the assassination just days earlier in Washington. Moving the crowd, in a sincere display of grief, he called out toward Rabin's coffin, "Shalom, Chaver!" ("Shalom, Friend!").[9]

Almost immediately after President Clinton's speech, this phrase became a written text with the appearance of a bumper sticker bearing the words ***Shalom, Chaver***. More than one million copies of it were produced and distributed.[10] The ***Shalom, Chaver*** stickers, in which the word "Shalom" uses the same biblical-style font as in the ***Shalom Akhshav*** sticker, were placed on the rear windshields of a high proportion of cars in Israel.[11] The sticker became a personal expression of mourning and separation on the part of the car owners, as well as a unifying ritual in the face of the divisions highlighted by the assassination.[12] At the same time, stickers expressing opposition to Rabin's government and policies were quickly and quietly removed from many cars.[13] In a popular game of ping-pong embodied in the discourse of stickers, however, it was not long before stickers began to appear challenging the perceived messages of ***Shalom, Chaver***. From this point onward, a cluster of stickers deriving from ***Shalom, Chaver*** began to emerge alongside other existing generative clusters that continued to develop to varying extents.

The research process began with casual observation that grew into a more intensive, long-term visual documentation of the cluster of stickers, which continued to expand and change throughout the research period. Though covert and overt connections existed between the different clusters of discourse, the descendents of the sticker ***Shalom, Chaver*** clearly belonged to a distinct and closely related family. As will become clear, the analysis of this phenomenon revealed a diverse range of tactics "employed" by the stickers in order to maintain this "familial" affiliation. In addition, we interviewed drivers who were asked to comment on the stickers that appeared on their vehicles. The repertoire of stickers was also presented to some one hundred interviewees—drivers and others—who were asked to discuss each sticker, as well as the phenomenon of the discourse of stickers in general. After a brief explanation, the interviewer pointed to each slogan, without reading it aloud,[14] and the interviewees were asked to comment on the slogan as they saw fit. Interviews concentrated on readings of the stickers associated with ***Shalom, Chaver*** and with the unique popular experience expressed and indeed created by this folkloric discourse, in an effort to develop a phenomenological theoretical perspective based in this folkloristic experience. In keeping with this approach, we were not concerned with ascertaining the creator of each sticker. Our approach was consonant with the anonymity of the stickers for the audience, with the exception of the generative sticker in the cluster, "authored" by the president of the United States, and with the exception of stories we heard during the interview process concerning popular copywriters whose personal ideas for stickers had become widely disseminated, usually without their involvement.[15]

As will become evident from the quotes throughout this chapter, the interviews expressed the wealth of interpretations and the divergent and sometimes contradictory directions taken by the interviewees. This diversity not only reflects the fact that the interviewees represented a variety of political and religious positions within Israeli society, but also bears witness to emotional variance and tremendous creative capabilities on the individual level. During the research for this essay, over thirty different stickers were documented on the roads, all of which were part of the popular political discourse that ***Shalom, Chaver*** generated, and continued to generate at the time of writing. During the interviews, these stickers were presented to the interviewees in a manner that created an internal research chronology which, while attempting to reflect the actual chronology on the roads, inevitably differs from the chronology of each individual's encounter with the stickers in the ethnographic field.[16] Accordingly, the interviewees were asked to recall the interpretative experience they underwent in the original encounter, as distinct from the research context.

From the outset, it was evident that the generative capacity of the apparently simple phrase ***Shalom, Chaver*** is due not only to the powerful emotional con-

Figure 1.
A group of four related bumper stickers.

text in which it entered public discourse but also to the inherent ambiguity of the two words from which it is composed.[17] Above all, the complexities of the Hebrew word *Shalom* must be appreciated. *Shalom* may carry the meanings of the English words "peace," "hello," "good-bye," and "farewell"; it is also a male first name, as well as a family name. As for the word *Chaver,* this is the masculine form of the word "friend." The word may be used to refer to a specific personal friend, but it is also widely used in colloquial Hebrew as a generic and amicable term of approach to an unknown (male) stranger in the street, and as such may address the reader of the sticker. *Chaver* may also mean boyfriend, and in a specifically Israeli context it may also refer to a member of various social and political institutions, particularly the kibbutzim, the General Health Fund, and the "Histadrut" Trade Union, all bodies closely identified with the Labor Party and the left wing of the Israeli political spectrum. In the specific and original context of the sticker ***Shalom, Chaver,*** "Chaver" naturally refers to Prime Minister Yitzhak Rabin, by implicit reference to Clinton's address. The ambiguity and multiple meanings of this short text are central to the generative function of this sticker; changes in punctuation within the text and those it generates may also offer additional interpretations.

The following list of thirty-two versions included in the cluster of stickers generated by ***Shalom, Chaver*** and presented to the interviewees illustrates the vitality and diversity of this phenomenon. The English translation adopts the most probable interpretation intended by those producing the sticker. Ambiguities and alternative interpretations are discussed later in the chapter.

Hebrew	**Translation**
Shalom, Chaver	Shalom, Friend
Shalom, Chaverim	Shalom, Friends
Shalom Balahot	A Nightmarish Peace
Ze Lo Shalom, Chaver	This Isn't Shalom, Friend
Ze Lo Shalom, Moshe	This Isn't Shalom, Moshe
Shalom, Leah	Shalom, Leah
Chaver, Ani Zokher	Friend, I Remember
Chaver, Ata Zokher?	Friend, Do You Remember?
Chaver, Lo Nishkach Velo Nislach	Friend, We Won't Forget and We Won't Forgive
Chaver, Ata Chaser	Friend, We Miss You
Shalom, Ata Chaser	Shalom, We Miss You
Shalom, Ata	Hey, You
Chaver, Ata Chaser Yoter Veyoter	Friend, We Miss You More and More
Hazman Over Ve'ata Chaser, Chaver	Time Passes and We Miss You, Friend
Chevron, Ata Chaser	Hebron, We Miss You
Chaver Mevi Chaver, Ve'el Ha'emuna Nitchaber	One Friend Brings Another and We Join the Faith
Chaver, Ani Gomer	Friend, I'm Finishing
Chaver, Ani Mokher	Friend, I'm Selling
Bye-Bye, Chaver	Bye-Bye, Friend
Bibi, Tagid Shalom	Bibi, Say "Shalom"
Shalom, Shalom	Shalom, Shalom
Kimat Veshakhachti Shalom	I Almost Forgot Shalom
Shabbat Shalom, Chaver	Good Sabbath, Friend
Shabbat Shalom, Tel Aviv	Good Sabbath, Tel Aviv
Shanah Tovah, Chaver	Happy New Year, Friend
Chaver, Ani Zokher Et Hashabbat	Friend, I Remember the Sabbath
Chaver, Ani Zokher!! Et Hashabbat!!	Friend, I Remember!! The Sabbath!!
Shalom, Beineinu	Shalom—Among Us
Shalom Beineinu Levein Hakaba	Shalom between Us and God
Shalom, Yedid	Shalom, Buddy
Hayita Chaver, Shalom	You Were a Friend, Shalom
Sticker, Ata Chaser	Sticker, We Miss You

Having presented the cluster of stickers discussed in this study, I shall now examine the unique characteristics of this genre in general, and the ***Shalom, Chaver*** cluster in particular. The discussion will combine theoretical aspects with descriptions and insights offered by the interviewees relating to this folkloric encounter.

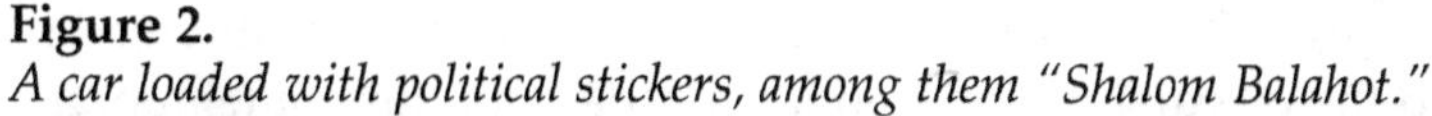

Figure 2.
A car loaded with political stickers, among them "Shalom Balahot."

The clarity with which the cluster of stickers generated by ***Shalom, Chaver*** reveals itself as a cohesive group is reflected both in the fact that all these stickers include at least one of the two words in the original slogan,[18] and in the fact that all the stickers, without exception, use the same typography for the word *Shalom*—a typography which, as noted above, dates back to ***Shalom Akhshav*** and is reminiscent of the style used by scribes in preparing parchment copies of the sacred Jewish texts. In most cases, the text appears in varying shades of blue on a white background; these are the colors of the Israeli flag, and hence associated with Zionism, nationalism, and patriotism. In addition to the graphic design of the sticker—an important factor in unraveling the message—the discourse of stickers makes its interconnected nature evident in the use of grammatical forms and syntactical rhythms common to most of the slogans. Thus the slogans announce their belonging to a single family, however fraught the internal relationships may be. This fact will be of central importance in interpreting content and in the process of popular exegesis.

After discussing various aspects of the sticker medium as a folkloristic genre, I shall progress to a concrete illustration of the interpretative discourse relating to the cluster of stickers examined in this chapter. The reader will best appreciate the interrelationships between the stickers by reviewing the entire cluster presented below.[19] This illustration will in turn lead to a concluding discussion relating to the discursive and emotional aspects of this contemporary folkloric discourse, and the manner in which these are embodied in the connection between medium and message in new genres.

Characteristics of the Genre

The Car and the Road

In Israel, stickers appear most frequently on cars.[20] Since Israeli cars are often encountered traveling bumper-to-bumper, the "bumper sticker" is in most cases raised to the rear windshield. The selection of the car as the forum for popular intertextual and interpolitical negotiation requires specific attention. The road experience, which includes both rapid travel and much time spent in traffic jams staring at the car in front, represents life in the modern technological world. In terms of the specific discourse on the subject of the peace process, the road and car—as path and vehicle leading from one place to another—mirror the "process," while the concept of movement, with its associations of political movement, adds to the explicitly political organizing spectrum of meaning.[21] The experience of the rapid encounter between messenger and audience—sometimes for a fleeting moment, sometimes during a prolonged period of staring—also constitutes a significant component in the intertextual encounter engendered by the discourse of stickers.

One of the respondents relates,

> I sometimes play a kind of game with myself, a sort of quiz. While I am still quite a long way behind the car, and can't yet see exactly what stickers they have, I try to guess their political orientation. For example, I go by the type of car, how many people are sitting in it, or whether there are a lot of children. Sometimes—and I can really get mad at myself about this—I even go according to how they are driving: if they're driving badly, I tell myself that they must have a particular political leaning. I know all these generalizations are really dangerous, but unfortunately in most cases it turns out to be true. . . . All this happens at once. Sometimes I get a chance to see the face of the driver and the stickers, and check whether I was right—I mean, whether the face matches the stereotypes.[22]

Similar comments, though with numerous variations, were made throughout the interviews. On one level, such comments reflect a need to identify and categorize, reflected in an exegetical structure centered on the political dialectics of left-right and secular-religious. On another level, however, the combination of the diachronic axis of time and distance, and the competitive nature of driving in Israel—almost to the point of a struggle for survival[23]—with the synchronic axis that seeks to cope simultaneously with information from differing and opposing directions constitute a constantly changing popular arena for the

Figure 3.

"Shalom Akhshav" and "Shalom Chaver" stickers, among others.

political debate that takes place in this society. This framework exemplifies a popular political struggle articulated through myriad voices and a particularly vital process of generativity. Yet the very arena for this struggle also includes a unifying potential, since it demonstrates the common foundation underlying all these voices—a foundation symbolized by the single, shared road along which all travelers pass, as well as the fact that, as noted above, within this discordant and divergent cluster of stickers, not one "dared" deviate from the identical graphic design of the word *Shalom*.

Mixed Messages

In the interviews we conducted, the respondents described the dynamic and complex experience of the discourse of stickers, repeatedly claiming that they interpreted the message in the context of several factors: the car, the driver, all the stickers on the car, and the way the different stickers were positioned. This last element became particularly important in the case of numerous documented cases of stickers that were cut and re-pasted or organized in order to create different and sometimes unique meanings. The following are two typical examples.

> If you're asking about specific stickers, then there are some cases where it is obvious to me what they mean, while in other cases I have to see all the other stickers on the car in order to work out the meaning. In 99 percent of cases, all the stickers on a car are in the same [political] direction. It's interesting, though: I've noticed that sometimes people put apparently contradictory stickers next to each other, such as ***Chevron Me'az Ul'olam*** [Hebron: Now and Forever][24] next to ***Shalom, Chaver*** or, worse, ***Shalom Akhshav*** [Peace Now].

> Maybe the idea is to "confuse the enemy," or maybe it's as if they are saying, "Don't put me in a box—look, I've put both these messages on my car!"

Another interviewee comments: "I feel uncomfortable about all these stickers we see all the time. I drive along and in front of me there is a car full of stickers. From a distance, it's sometimes hard to see if they are right-wing or left-wing stickers. The colors look the same, and sometimes you can only tell when you get very close. You must have seen those recent stickers that turn the original message on its head, but look just like the original from a distance."[25]

A Removable Medium

The physical characteristics of the folkloric discourse of stickers have an additional significance unique to this medium. The sticker—a piece of paper approximately 25 x 5 centimeters—bears a short slogan on one side; the other is adhesive. The sticker is a popular artifact in its own right, readily available to all. The phenomenon as a whole engages participants in a quasi-ritual process of adhesion, removal, and addition. The voice that participates in the discourse is a printed message, placed on a private car and representing its owner. Yet when necessary, it may also be removed. Removal may occur as the car changes drivers or owners, or as changes occur in the collection of stickers. The relative ease with which stickers may be removed enables a dynamic approach; thus the temporary nature of this medium contrasts with the totality of the political message, which is often perceived as an emblem of affiliation in Israel.

When asked about the stickers seen on their cars, some respondents gave replies such as "it was like that when we bought it" or "someone stuck it on," thus denying their own responsibility—despite the evident ease with which the stickers might be removed. This dynamic also operated in the reverse direction: in many cases the audience, as an active player in the drama, engaged in the removal of stickers that they opposed, in an act identifying the discourse of stickers as the arena for a literal public struggle. This act itself becomes the focus of an additional duplication of meaning that may be seen as a semiotic moment subordinated to the total discourse, as people rationalize that they do not put stickers on the car because they are afraid that their cars will be damaged. For example, one interviewee confessed, "I'll tell you the truth. I'm not proud of this, but I'm afraid to put a sticker in favor of peace on my car, because I'm worried about my car. I even remember that I once put a ***Shalom Akhshav*** sticker on my car, and then just before I took the car into the garage, I removed it, because . . . well, you know."[26] Another comment was made by an interviewee who stated that he had right-wing sympathies: "Most of the stickers you see are right-wing. I think this is because left-wingers are afraid that their car will be damaged by right-wingers. I'm very sorry about that. This is a fear that doesn't exist the other way around."

The temporary nature of the sticker is reflected not only in conscious removal but also in gradual fading and disintegration. For example, many stickers were documented in which the slogan ***Shalom Akhshav*** had disintegrated, leaving only ***Shalom*** or ***Akhshav***.

A further avenue of reflexivity concerns the question of the popular nature of stickers; I shall return to this question below from a theoretical angle. The respondents' comments on this medium presented a class hierarchy between those who put stickers on their cars and those who do not. The assumption is that the widespread availability of stickers—distributed free of charge at intersections, in newspapers, and on the streets and squares—detracts from their worth, and potentially projects on the drivers as well. One respondent explained, "You don't see so many stickers on Volvos or Mercedes,[27] because putting stickers on a car makes it more 'popular' and less stylish." Another commented, "I've got a new car, so I won't put stickers on it, because I don't want it to get damaged." And a third emphasized: "I think that cars with lots of stickers are unaesthetic. They're usually old cars."

Rhetoric and Popular Exegesis

In this section I shall present interpretations of the cluster of stickers generated by ***Shalom, Chaver***, which are thereby indirectly related to ***Shalom Akhshav***. As noted, one may identify a number of clusters of political stickers in contemporary Israel that maintain an extensive system of communication through imagination and imagery. In order to convey this complex and multilayered reality in written form, I needed to sequence the material in a manner that created internal textual cohesion. Thus, although the diverse and even contradictory interpretations of the stickers clearly reflect a large number of possible structures perceived by the audience, the order in which the slogans appear in this essay is the product of the structure I formulated during research. This structure attempts to reproduce development along a diachronic axis. Naturally, such an approach contradicts the blurring of time and the simultaneous presence of messages as perceived in folkloric time.

Shalom, Chaver

"When Clinton said *Shalom, Chaver,* I was very moved by these words. Clinton became a member of our family with that slogan. I felt a kind of pride, tinged with sadness, that the president of the United States had become so close to us." Another interviewee noted, "Whenever I see the sticker, it immediately reminds me of Rabin's funeral. [He was a] *chaver*—because you could rely on him. All kinds of people put that on their car: Arabs, Jews, people from all sections of society. Everyone was behind it."

The narrowing of power discrepancies and the dismantling of the hierarchy between the president of the United States and the prime minister of Israel expressed in the words *Shalom, Chaver* became a focus of significance in dismantling social hierarchies. The words *Shalom, Chaver* are simple and mundane words of greeting, without any specific political intent. The popular and routine nature of this greeting seems to enable it to contain both a personal farewell on the part of many Israelis, as well as an expression of pain, protest, and personal shock at the assassination. Although the general phraseology of the slogan could allow different political interpretations—such as farewell in sorrow and farewell in joy—all those who were asked about the sticker were completely unequivocal that it related to the assassination of Rabin; the vast majority agreed that the sticker expressed sadness over his death. This sticker appeared mainly alongside stickers identified with the left wing, although cars were also observed on which it appeared alongside right-wing stickers. This fact, and the fact that in many cases this was the only sticker on a car, relates it to a sense of national unity and common fate. The unifying basis of this sticker lies in the shared understanding that this ostensibly mundane daily greeting actually relates to a shared and known friend who is being greeted not on arrival but on departure, after his assassination. However, many interviewees were aware that subsequent developments transformed the sticker from one belonging to the "whole people" to one identified in political terms mainly with the left wing.

Shalom, Chaverim (Shalom, Friends)

"You see this on cars of people who want peace between all the different groups. They want compromise among everyone, among friends." Another interviewee took a very different view: "It's a right-wing slogan. Very cynical. It's saying that there are others in the ranks who will find the same fate [as Rabin]. It's real incitement. Whenever I see that sticker I expect to see religious Jews in the car."

This sticker was one of the first to appear following the widespread circulation of ***Shalom, Chaver***.[28] The appearance of this sticker immediately after the generative one, and the daring act of changing the slogan from a single, known person to the plural form, channeled the respondents' interpretations of this slogan toward the world of the complex political divisions and discourse of Israeli society. The seemingly neutral character of the slogan in linguistic and syntactical terms led many respondents to hesitate as to its message, allowing the simultaneous existence of contradictory interpretations. Thus, while some claimed that it was a play on words with no political overtones, intended merely as an aesthetically pleasing variant of the generative slogan, others argued that it had a clearly political thrust, though, as noted, different and even contradictory views emerged as to what direction this might be. Another noted, "When you come to a group of acquaintances you say *Shalom, chaverim* ["Hey, guys!"]. It's Jewish solidarity, a way for one driver to greet another." Those who identified this slogan with the right wing claimed that it expressed a desire to extend the circle of "friends" on the left to whom they would like to say "shalom" (in the sense of good-bye). A similar explanation links "friends"—*chaverim*—with the traditional Israeli left: "This slogan identifies *Shalom, Chaver* with the kibbutzniks of the previous generation—the generation that founded the State of Israel, the members of the Labor Party[29] and the left, and says shalom to all of them." Similarly, another respondent said: "It makes me think of the members [*chaverim*] of a kibbutz; a meeting of kibbutz members." There were those who interpreted the sticker in the context of the 1996 Knesset elections, implying that all those from Rabin's party would not stay in power.

Some respondents, however, identified the sticker with the period of Palestinian terrorist attacks several months after the assassination of Rabin, explaining, "The sticker bids farewell to those murdered by terrorists during this period, and says that they were also friends and they were also murdered—not just Rabin." Another interpretation: "It means that we still don't have peace, friends."

Shalom Balahot (Nightmarish Peace)

This sticker first appeared after the Oslo Accords and before the assassination of Rabin, and all the respondents identified it with the right-wing opponents of the Oslo Accords. This sticker related to ***Shalom Akhshav*** in graphic and semantic terms before the appearance of the powerful and generative ***Shalom, Chaver***. The respondents who presented a chronology of events as the basis of their attempt to interpret the message dated the appearance of this sticker as the period of large-scale terrorist attacks that followed the Oslo Accords—some of which occurred before the assassination of Rabin and some after.

The word *Shalom* in this sticker, which first appeared before Rabin's assassination, uses the same typeface and color as the generative ***Shalom Akhshav*** sticker, while the word *Balahot* appears in red[30]—a color that would later appear repeatedly in slogans expressing opposition to the peace process. Many respondents claimed that the red signified danger and warning, and alluded to the bloody price that the peace process would exact. At the same time, red is identified, in Israel as elsewhere, as the color of the left wing.

The phrase *Shalom Balahot*[31] alludes to the compound Hebrew word for "nightmare" [*chalom balahot*], implying "something we must awake from as soon as possible, before it is too late"—the explanation offered by a respondent who had placed this sticker on his car. While all interviewees associated the explicit message with the fear that "the peace process will prove to cause more harm than good," some emphasized the internal rifts: "It represents people for whom I feel the absolute opposite of closeness and joint destiny. Those who are doing all they can to destroy peace." Another interviewee added, "I see this sticker as part of the incitement that led to Rabin's assassination. It went along with the sticker ***Rabin Boged*** [Rabin Is a Traitor] that was very common—and that, the day after the assassination, as if by magic, was suddenly removed from all the cars."[32] Indeed, many interviewees found that the most convenient way to explain the ***Shalom Balahot*** sticker was simply to note which other stickers they would expect to find together with it: "This sticker goes along with others: ***Chevron Me'az Ul'tamid*** [Hebron: Then and Always]. You know, those national-religious ones." Many saw this sticker as part of the wave of opposition and incitement that preceded the assassination of Rabin. The slogan ***Shalom Balahot***, which had often appeared with ***Rabin Boged*** before the assassination, was taken as a single, continuous sequence: ***Shalom Balahot***, then ***Rabin Boged***, and then condensed and reappropriated by the left as ***Shalom, Chaver***. In this act of replacement, the facetious *Shalom* as a rhyme for the *chalom* component of the compound word for nightmare (see note 31) was thus reconverted into a uncynical usage of *Shalom* as "peace" and "good-bye," while Rabin was transformed from *Boged* ("traitor") into *Chaver* ("friend").[33] The rhetoric employed by interviewees commenting on this sticker was particularly emotive, containing explicit expressions of fear, anger, frustration, and even hatred.

Ze Lo Shalom, Chaver (This Isn't Shalom, Friend)

"This is a sticker of the opponents of the peace process. The *Chaver* ['friend'] is whoever happens to be reading the slogan." The interviewee added, "The slogan refers to the hopes raised by the possibility of peace, but states that what has actually occurred is nothing like that. It's a good play on words, drawing on cultural forms. They took an existing form and turned it into something else, altering its meaning. *Shalom* here means a particular political reality, while *Chaver* is no longer Rabin, but rather whoever sees the sticker. I like these wordplays—they reflect a kind of human imagination that I can enjoy, even if it doesn't match my own political beliefs."

One interpretation sees the words *Ze Lo* ("this isn't") as implying that *Shalom* is to be understood here as meaning peace, rather than as good-bye in the original *Shalom, Chaver*. *Chaver* in this sticker may be interpreted in two ways—as the same specific "friend" who made the peace accords, and who is addressed here after his death, or as a generic and non-specific friend—an individual approach to each participant in this folkloric discourse. In this sticker, the first three words (including the word *Shalom*) appear in a font reminiscent of Hebrew handwriting, while *Chaver* appears in the same form as in the generative sticker (both in terms of typeface and in terms of its position in the slogan). Most of the respondents identified this sticker with the right-wing opponents of the peace accords and as referring to the bloody events that followed. Surprisingly, one respondent suggested a very different interpretation: "It's as if they are saying to Rabin, 'we're not saying good-bye to you or to the path you took.'" This interpretation requires borrowing from English idiomatic usage to translate the slogan, as in "This is not good-bye, friend."

Ze Lo Shalom, Moshe (This Isn't Shalom, Moshe)

"Moshe is meant to be anybody—a kind of generic name, since it is very common. Using Moshe to refer to a Jew is like using Muhammad to refer to an Arab." This sticker constitutes a satirical play on the previous one, using the same typeface and colors. Here, *Shalom* is interpreted as neither "peace" nor "good-bye" but rather as a male first name,[34] placed next to another common male first name—Moshe. This slogan blurs the possible interpretations yet still leaves open the political interpretation of *Ze Lo Shalom* as "this isn't Shalom." One respondent complained, "I don't know what this is meant to be. Who's Moshe?" In another interview: "Well, I really don't know what this is meant to be. It doesn't mean anything . . . Moshe is just a name. I guess postmodernists would put this one on their car—they don't have any God!"

Shalom, Leah (Shalom, Leah)

"This relates to Leah Rabin and the terrible suffering she has undergone." While none of the respondents doubted that the reference is indeed to Leah Rabin, the widow of the late Yitzhak Rabin, most disagreed with the charitable interpretation offered above: "This is a hateful sticker addressed against Leah Rabin, telling her to watch it." Similarly: "It's not a pleasant sticker. As if they want to kill her, too. A right-winger would post this sticker."

This sticker was not widely distributed, perhaps because of its explicit message, which led one interviewee to describe it as "a very cynical statement and a blow beneath the belt," and perhaps because of its personal and non-political character. This sticker was also explained in various ways. Some associated it with a period after the assassination when Leah Rabin frequently expressed her opinion on political issues; the sticker is interpreted as criticizing this behavior. One interviewee explained, "Leah Rabin's image does not win people over. Women are associated with warmth and the family, but she expressed political positions and took them to the extreme, so she was no longer seen as a woman to be pitied because she lost her husband."

Some respondents who placed great importance on the diachronic axis in their interpretations claimed that this sticker appeared in response to Leah Rabin's comment that she intended to pack her bags and leave Israel after Netanyahu's victory in the 1996 elections: "It made me think of all those jokes about Leah Rabin. . . . It may also be connected to the comments about leaving Israel. . . . It's a spiteful concoction, just like the jokes about Sara Netanyahu."

Chaver, Ani Zokher (Friend, I Remember)

"It says that people remember Rabin, and don't forget him even though time passes." Similarly: "It's a left-wing sticker. We won't forget that a prime minister was murdered here. We'll support your heritage, and make sure it doesn't happen again. It's a sticker as part of the war against Alzheimer's."

All the respondents interpreted this sticker as referring to Rabin, as in the generative sticker. "I remember" was interpreted as a personal statement on the part of the owner of the car relating to his memory of the association—a kind of "renewal of the covenant" with the late Rabin and the memory of this event. Once again, the chronological approach was evident: many respondents stated that this sticker appeared on the first anniversary of Rabin's assassination. All the respondents identified the sticker with the left wing, although some noted that it might also be used by right-wingers who wanted to emphasize that despite the stereotype of right-wingers as supporting the assassination, they also remember and condemn it. Although many respondents expressed this "renewal of the covenant" in positive terms as close in meaning to the original sticker, some described it less positively: "It kind of irritates me. They're stretching out a good gimmick beyond its natural lifespan. It's all starting to seem a bit pathetic." Right-wing respondents stated that this "renewal of the covenant" is immediately associated with the political accusations leveled against the right by left-wingers: "This sticker really annoys me. They bear a grudge against a particular group, against the national-religious sector. It's as if they're saying 'I remember what you did, and I won't forget.'" Thus many respondents, both left- and right-wing, associated this sticker with the related slogan ***Chaver, Lo Nishkach Velo Nislach*** [Friend, We Won't Forget and We Won't Forgive], although the second part is implicit in this case. In this interpretation, the message becomes overtly political, directed at those identified with the assassination in political terms.

Chaver, Ata Zokher? (Friend, Do You Remember?)

"It's as if one driver turns to another and implies that they have forgotten him [Rabin]. It feels pretty gross." Another respondent: "They're trying to be smart; I don't know what it really means. It's kind of neutral." Another comment, implying indignation at the apparent reproofs of righteous left-wingers, was: "What's the idea here? They're turning to *me* and reminding me not to forget?"

All the respondents noted that *Chaver* in this slogan no longer relates to Rabin but to a living, though generic, "friend," that is, the person driving the car alongside them. Many respondents claimed that the message was unclear but noted that it made them feel vaguely uneasy, as if the assassination were being belittled. The demand for an answer contained in the slogan may have created this sense of unease. Another possibility was also raised: "This is an internal sticker among left-wingers—do you remember that we were on the path to peace? *Chaver* here means their own friends—fellow left-wingers." Or: "It's exactly the same as ***Chaver, Ani Zokher*** [Friend, I Remember], just phrased from a different standpoint. The first one declares that he is among those who cherish the memory of Rabin, while the second demands that others remember the assassination." This comment reflects an organizational axis arranging stickers from inclusive to exclusive.

Chaver, Lo Nishkach Velo Nislach (Friend, We Won't Forget and We Won't Forgive)

"This is addressing him [Rabin], promising him that they won't forget or forgive the perpetrator—just as it states." Although the word *Chaver* here could be interpreted either as referring to the original *Chaver* (Rabin) or to the "friend" reading the slogan, all the respondents adopted the former interpretation, seeing the slogan as a declaration of loyalty to the memory of the assassination. As in the case of ***Chaver, Ani Zokher*** [Friend, I Remember], many respondents stated that the phrase "we won't forget and we won't forgive" implies that an entire section of the population is being blamed for Rabin's assassination. One example: "These are real die-hard Rabin supporters. It's a kind of thirst for revenge. A desire to take it out on the other side." Several respondents associated the turn of phrase "won't forget and won't forgive" with the Holocaust. For example: "It's a reference to the Holocaust, to a profound trauma. . . . Seeing this sticker makes me again blame the person who murdered [him] and those who provided support. It rekindles feelings of anger against these people." From another angle: "I strongly identify with the sticker. I identify with the meaning, and with the sense of vengeance against those who portrayed Rabin in SS uniform and pushed him around at Wingate.[35] It tires me out just to remember all that."

Chaver, Ata Chaser (Friend, We Miss You)

"This sticker expresses mourning at the assassination of Rabin, and longing for him. I see this as a legitimate sticker." Similarly: "This sticker says that Israel misses Rabin a lot, as a leader and as a general."

All the respondents explained that this sticker refers to Rabin, expressing personal and national longing for the leader and the path he led—and thus implying direct political criticism against the present leadership.[36] The slogan addresses Rabin directly, as if he were hearing the comment. One respondent stated: "All those who loved Rabin, from all sectors. Even from the Likud.[37] Everyone loved Rabin—maybe they didn't agree with his way, but they loved him." Another interviewee explained: "This is the sticker I most identify with, all the time. It expresses a very great sense of loss. Personally, I was always very much in favor of Rabin, even when it wasn't fashionable. . . . I really miss him, on a personal level."

Given the clarity of this message, the following subversive association is particularly fascinating. In one of the interviews, a respondent, asked to relate to this sticker, said that he would tell a joke instead: "You can change the meaning of one of the stickers just by adding a word. Which one?" When the interviewer replied that she did not know, he continued: "But I have to tell you that I'm only kidding. It isn't as if I really mean it. We have enough tension in this country; you've got to have a laugh sometimes. Well anyway—what is the word you have to add?: *Erekh*! So that it reads: *Chaver, Ata Chasar Erekh* [Friend, You're Worthless]!"[38]

Shalom, Ata Chaser (Shalom, We Miss You)

"It implies a kind of despair at the state of the peace process in the Middle East. It's dead. It's all over. Nothing will come of it. This sticker appears on the cars of people who think that Bibi killed the peace process." Another interviewee claimed, "It refers to the way the present government is fudging the peace issue." Although the message is ostensibly "neutral" in political terms, reflecting a general longing for peace that has always been part of the official Israeli ethos, the immediate association with ***Shalom, Chaver*** [Shalom, Friend] and ***Chaver, Ata Chaser*** [Friend, We Miss You] led most respondents to identify this sticker as criticizing the Likud-led government for its equivocal attitude toward the peace process. Some respondents interpreted this message on the basis of the replacement of the word *Chaver* with *Shalom,* implying that what is missed is not the individual, but peace.

Interestingly, this sticker was sometimes also found alongside clearly right-wing stickers. Thus, although the responses to direct questions showed that it was identified with the left, it reflected a sentiment that the longing for peace is not the monopoly of one side of the political divide in Israel. Thus, right-wing use of this sticker implies rejection of the alleged expropriation of the desire for peace by the other side. As one respondent explained, "I put this sticker alongside ***Chevron Me'az Ul'olam*** [Hebron: Then and Always],[39] because I was sure that it was a right-wing sticker. Then my wife told me that she thought it was a leftist sticker. But I left it on my car because we also long for peace. It's just that giving up Hebron and other parts of the Land of Israel won't bring peace for the Jewish people."

Shalom, Ata (Hey, You)

"I think it's really nice. Warm and welcoming. 'Hey, how're you doing?' Kind of easygoing, smiling, and simple. I don't know who you are, but hey there."

This sticker was observed several times, though it was never distributed in this form. Some claimed that it reflected a desire for peace: "You, he, and I will make peace. Vote for the party of peace. You are the person who will make peace." Others, however, claimed that the change in the slogan removed its overtly political content. The subversive nature of the slogan was perceived as coming from the use of an existing sticker, cutting out the word *Chaser;* for some, the cutting of the slogan was interpreted as a sophisticated reference to the interruption of the peace process. This response relates directly to the fact that this sticker was created by cutting the sticker ***Shalom, Ata Chaser,*** leaving out the word *Chaser* and thus blurring the original interpretation of *Shalom* as peace. The result is a slogan that is overtly vague, in which *Shalom* seems to be more readily interpreted as the regular daily greeting ("hi" or "hey"). One respondent commented, "This is another of those alienated postmodernist jokes. I'm not sure what it's making fun of. I don't think it means anything apart from just cutting off the end of the slogan." Similarly, another interviewee explained, "The whole point is that people won't understand it. Maybe the idea is that I should put my brain to work trying to think what's happening to peace. I don't really know." Another respondent offered a particularly creative interpretation: "It's a play on words—*Shalom, Ata* in the sense of 'peace, now.'[40] This is a sticker for the settlers: they're trying to say that there is no way to peace. It's a cynical comment on ***Shalom Akhshav*** [Peace Now]. 'Peace, you' implies that the peace is not for us, only for you."

***Chaver, Ata Chaser Yoter Veyoter* (Friend, We Miss You More and More) *and Hazman Over Ve'ata Chaser, Chaver* (Time Passes and We Miss You, Friend)**

"These are very emotional stickers, in my opinion. They convey a sense of desperation—longing and intense desperation." Another respondent added, "These always seem exaggerated to me. Even when Rabin was around they weren't satisfied. But it's true that as time passes the situation gets more screwed up and the past starts to look better, even if it wasn't really so wonderful." Another more overtly political interpretation: "Left-wing. It tries to inspire longing and sympathy in us." Yet another respondent explained, "You find this on the cars of Rabin admirers who are frustrated with the deteriorating peace process, and with the fact that Israeli society is becoming less concerned with Rabin's assassination. It's a statement of a political position." Another respondent was more forthright: "Crybabies! Right, maybe we should all pack our bags and fly away from here? Crybabies, for heaven's sake!"

All the respondents interpreted both of these stickers as relating explicitly to the original *Chaver,* Yitzhak Rabin. Both stickers were interpreted as critical of the Likud-led government that came to power after the assassination, expressing personal and national longing for the slain leader. These stickers were never found alongside overtly right-wing slogans.

***Chevron, Ata Chaser* (Hebron, We Miss You)**

"Those people who think that we mustn't give back Hebron. It's a right-wing sticker." This sticker is a rare, individual cut-and-paste creation, though it has been documented more than once. The majority of respondents interpreted this sticker as an expression of right-wing regrets over Israel's withdrawal from much of the city of Hebron.[41] Some respondents, however, interpreted *Chevron* (Hebron) as a diminutive and possibly derogative form of the word *Chaver* (Friend). One respondent pointed out that this sticker includes a grammatical error: since cities are grammatically feminine in Hebrew, the slogan is incorrect.[42] She explained that she associates such an evident grammatical mistake with right-wing extremists of American origin who are unfamiliar with the details of Hebrew grammar; this interpretative comment thus addresses content and intent, as well as grammar.

The sticker is also associated with the sticker ***Chevron Me'az Ul'tamid*** [Hebron: Then and Always]. Thus it forms part of a separate cluster of stickers. The two slogans also reflect the emotive interpretation of changing political circumstances, with the self-confident and stable message of "Me'az Ul'tamid" ("then and always," or "since forever and for eternity") giving way to the somber and uncertain "Ata Chaser" ("we miss you" or "you are absent").

***Chaver Mevi Chaver, Ve'el Ha'emuna Nitchaber* (One Friend Brings Another, and We Join the Faith)**

"Shas[43] and the like. The rhyme is weak. It's about bringing people 'back to the faith'—each religious person will bring someone else along, and then we'll all be 'born again.'" Most respondents stated that the sticker is clearly identified with a religious political party that aims to bring the message of religion to as wide a public as possible. "Religious" stickers are becoming increasingly widespread, including many that relate to ***Shalom, Chaver***. On the semantic level, this slogan relates both to ***Shalom, Chaver*** and to the humorous use of a commercial slogan, *Chaver Mevi Chaver* [One Friend Brings Another].[44] These cultural contexts are thus used as vehicles for the central message of this political party. One respondent noted, "This is a religious one. People should 'return to the faith.' If you bring someone else into the fold, you get a discount from God—you are forgiven for a few of your sins." Another commented, "Religious preachers are using the *Chaver* from the advertisement of the health fund. As if there's a 'special offer'—bring a friend into the faith, and you'll get special privileges. Even God will give you some bonus points if you bring a friend along to the next 'revivalist' meeting."

Chaver, Ani Gomer (Friend, I'm Finishing)

"It makes fun of all the stickers—all those people who get an orgasm out of messing around with all these slogans. It's saying that for these people, the sticker has become the main thing."

This sticker has an overtly subversive message, based on the rhyme between *Chaver* [friend] and *Gomer* [finishing]. Some respondents reported that this slogan was based on a joke about Clinton that was popular around the time he made his speech. The impact of the slogan is based on the various possible meanings of the Hebrew word *Gomer*. In standard Hebrew, *Gomer* simply means "finishing" or "ending"; some respondents followed this line, suggesting that the sticker refers to the end of Rabin's life, as some interviewees suggested. Most respondents, however, discussed the more common use of this word in modern Hebrew slang as meaning "to come," that is, to reach orgasm.[45] Moreover, both the people referred to in the slogan—the *Chaver* and the "I" who is "coming"—are masculine; apart from anything else, this is required in order to maintain the rhyme. Accordingly, the slogan raises associations of homosexual relations. One respondent commented, "It's just a joke. If someone is 'coming,' that's his own business. It's a gay thing really, isn't it? Otherwise the sticker would have to be *Chavera, Ani Gomer* or *Chaver, Ani Gomeret*."[46]

One woman's comments clarify the subversive nature of this sticker.

> You know what sticker I'd put on my car if I could find it, only I can't? This is the only sticker I'd put on my car: the one that says ***Chaver, Ani Gomer***. You get the meaning? . . . Because all they've done until now is screw our minds with Bibi-Shmibi, "*Chaver Ata Chaser*," "*Chaver Ani Zokher*"—do remember or don't remember, one lot say day and the others say night. So now all we can say is *Chaver, Ani Gomer*—I mean, they're screwing with us so much that we're coming. That's the message of it. We're sick of being screwed about by this lot

and that lot [i.e., by the left wing and right wing]. When someone screws you, you come. . . . Of course it's a political sticker. It's saying that they're all the same—all they do is screw us.

Chaver, Ani Mokher (Friend, I'm Selling)

"It's cute. This is a nice sticker, kind of personal." Another respondent noted, "This sticker leaves all the lofty issues and comes down to daily life, to selling and buying cars."

This slogan is a prototypical personal creation inspired by the political stickers. Here, too, it is interesting to note that the sticker strictly follows the typeface and structure of the general cluster. The sticker met with a mixed response among the interviewees: "I like the sticker. It's awesome." Many shared this perspective, though others remained within the general political direction of the cluster: "It relates to the claim that Rabin was 'selling off' the Land of Israel. I imagine it's someone from the right wing, but it depends which stickers appear next to it." One respondent was inspired to make a broader comment on the cluster as whole: "The things they've done with that '*Chaver*' business. . . . I'm telling you, Clinton's provided employment for the whole country."

Bye-Bye, Chaver (Bye-Bye, Friend)

"It's just like ***Shalom, Chaver***, but it expresses contempt. It's as if they're saying farewell, but actually they are happy about it, in a kind of light mood." Another added, "This is a terrible sticker. Simply vindictive."

In this sticker, the Hebrew word *Shalom* is replaced by the universal, English *Bye-Bye* (written in Hebrew letters; this greeting is well-known and widely used in Israel).[47] The fact that the sticker uses the English *Bye-Bye* raises another association, interpreted as a message to Clinton. In other words, just as he used a Hebrew word in addressing Rabin, now an English word is being used to address him—with the implicit hope that he will go home. For example: "The sticker was distributed immediately after the Monica Lewinsky affair erupted into the headlines." Yet another explanation relies on the similarity between *Bye-Bye* and Bibi, raising the possibility that Netanyahu is the friend who is being wished *Bye-Bye*.[48] This line of interpretation was also followed by some respondents in addressing the next sticker in the cluster.

Bibi, Tagid Shalom (Bibi, Say "Shalom")

"This is a sarcastic one. A contemptuous comment to the prime minister." This sticker is one of the most sophisticated examples in the whole cluster, containing numerous covert meanings. One interpretation is that the slogan addresses Netanyahu, in place of the original *Chaver*, and orders him to say *Shalom*, in the sense of "bye-bye." The clever play on words between "Bibi" and "Bye-Bye" was certainly appreciated by the audience. However, the slogan was also interpreted as telling Netanyahu to say *Shalom* in the sense of "hello" or in the sense of "peace." Moreover, the overall structure of the slogan in Hebrew is reminiscent of a common form of address to very small children who are learning the basic rules of behavior: "Little boy, say 'Shalom.'" Some respondents combined this apolitical social context with a specific political argument relating to Benjamin Netanyahu's refusal (during a certain period) to shake hands with Yasser Arafat, the implication being that he could not bring himself to follow a basic rule of courtesy learned in childhood.

Shalom, Shalom (Shalom, Shalom)

"It reminds me of "Peace, peace—but there is no peace" (Jer. 6:14, 8:11). Another respondent commented, "There won't be peace this way. The first *Shalom* is saying 'good-bye,' the second means 'peace.' This sticker appears on the cars of left-wingers who are worried that peace isn't coming." Similarly, an interviewee stated, "This is a short and concise expression of the feeling that the longed-for peace is slipping away."

All these interpretations see the sticker as protesting the lack of progress in the peace process, saying that Israelis could say *Shalom* ("good-bye") to *Shalom* ("peace"). Another, more optimistic explanation was offered: "It's nice—I like this one. Let there be peace. I'd be glad to see this everywhere. It's fun. Someone who puts this on his car wants peace between everyone, not just between Jews and Arabs. It's a really nice slogan that makes me feel good."

In addition to these two opposing interpretations, many others were also offered. For example, one respondent explained, "There's something a bit old-fashioned about it. I imagine that today a left-wing religious person might put it on his car, because of the association with Isaiah: 'Peace, peace, to those far and near, said the Lord' [Isa. 57:19]. It's a sticker for Meimad or Netivot Shalom.[49] It belongs to my father's generation—they used to say `Shalom, shalom' as a greeting, using the word twice."

Kimat Veshakhachti Shalom (I Almost Forgot Shalom)

"It's saying that peace has been forgotten, removed from the national agenda and become a matter of history."

The word *Shalom* appears in the same typeface as in all the others that relate to the generative sticker. However, this is one of the few cases that does not rely on a rhyming allusion to the generative ***Shalom, Chaver***. This fact seems in keeping with the verbal message of the sticker, which relates to something cardinal that has been marginalized and forgotten. The interviewees saw this sticker as a counterpoint to ***Chaver, Ani Zokher*** [Friend, I Remember]: "Peace has been forgotten. . . . Sometimes they remember it and say the word just to pay lip service, right before leaving."

One printed version of this sticker makes a direct reference to a children's television program watched by an entire generation of Israelis, in which a puppet character always ended the show by saying "Kimat Veshakhachti Shalom" in the sense of "I almost forgot to say good-bye."[50] This sticker uses a somewhat childish font, with two figures on either side: to one side the puppet from the old television series, and to the other side, Benjamin Netanyahu.

Shabbat Shalom, Chaver (Good Sabbath, Friend)

"Religious people. When I see it, I think how nice it is that religion has this desire to welcome people without any personal interest." Another respondent noted, "This is a friendly sticker, because it is saying *Shabbat Shalom* to everyone, whatever their political opinions. It's trying to bring everyone closer. It isn't necessarily a religious sticker—it could reach out to anyone. You can't interpret it negatively, only in a good way."

This sticker was observed with increasing frequency toward the end of the research process. The force of this sticker comes from the fact that by adding just one word to the generative sticker, a tremendous change in meaning is achieved. This sticker represents a different kind of subversion, associated with the religious group of stickers. The sticker is based on the traditional greeting *Shabbat Shalom*![51] The greeting maintains the meaning of *Shalom* as "peace," but the peace alluded to is no longer a political one, between Israel and her neighbors, but rather peace in the personal, family, and national Jewish sense. Despite the ostensibly mundane nature of the greeting *Shabbat Shalom,* its attachment to the word *Chaver* constitutes a subversive statement that seeks to shift the balance of gravity to a new point, focused on the Jewish faith—in which the Sabbath is a cardinal element.[52] In the context of this sticker, it is worth noting a traditional Jewish legend that is often quoted in debates on Sabbath observance in Israel. The legend states that if all the Jews would keep the Sabbath just once (in the sense of observing the religious commandments related with the Sabbath), full redemption would come to the People of Israel; naturally, such redemption would also include peace.

Shabbat Shalom, Tel Aviv (Good Sabbath, Tel Aviv)

"This is addressing residents of Tel Aviv, who are mostly secular. It's a call from religious people who are tolerant of the secular." Another respondent offered a similar view: "[It's] someone religious who wants to gently remind the residents of Tel Aviv that Shabbat exists, and it would be nice if they observed it a little." A third perspective returns to the political tensions between religious and secular: "Maybe it's religious, or [maybe it refers to] traditional people who want to emphasize that they observe the Sabbath even in secular and depraved Tel Aviv. But you could also see it on a restaurant that opens on the Sabbath."

This sticker relates to ***Shabbat Shalom, Chaver,*** but here the reference is specifically to Tel Aviv—Israel's most "secular" city, promoted under the slogan "The Non-Stop City." Interestingly, this slogan not only appeared on car stickers but was also hung weekly on Friday afternoons just before the approach of the Sabbath. The enlarged version, posted on giant billboards at the entrance to Tel Aviv, apparently by a religious group, was an appropriate medium for a slogan that addresses an entire city.

Shanah Tovah, Chaver (Happy New Year, Friend)

"This is a really cynical sticker. I can't stand it. I bet they produced it on the first anniversary of his murder.[53] It's a right-wing slogan, telling the 'friend' that they had a good year since he died." Another respondent offered several possible interpretations: "It's turning to Rabin up there. Greeting him in a very uncynical way. Or it could be addressing any individual in the street. But it might also be an ironic comment about how bad this year has been—that is, that since the assassination it's been a bad year."

This slogan appeared on the front page of one of Israel's leading daily newspapers in the issue published immediately before the Jewish New Year. In our fieldwork, we documented cases where it was cut out of the newspaper and stuck on the windshield of cars. Since the greeting *Shanah Tovah* relates specifically to the Jewish New Year, all the respondents focused on this point as symbolizing the end or the beginning of periods. One respondent noted, "This is another cynical sticker, but it depends on timing. If it appeared immediately after the assassination, then it's bitter and angry, because clearly this was a bad year. . . . But if it appeared a long time after the assassination, it's saying that we still remember you."

Chaver, Ani Zokher Et Hashabbat (Friend, I Remember the Sabbath), and a close variant, *Chaver, Ani Zokher!! Et Hashabbat!!* (Friend, I Remember!! The Sabbath!!)

"This is a disgusting sticker. First of all, it's saying that the memory of Rabin and his assassination is completely unimportant. All that matters is the Sabbath. Now since we also know that the person who murdered Rabin was a religious Jew, who certainly kept the Sabbath, and, even more important, that the assassination was encouraged by a group of rabbis who justified it in terms of religious law, then it really annoys me and repulses me and God knows what. All this preaching is just unbearable as far as I'm concerned." Another interviewee offers a quite different view: "It's saying that we should remember the Sabbath. Jews should remember and keep the Sabbath. It's a kind of playful comment on ***Chaver, Ani Zokher*** [Friend, I Remember]—'Friend, I remember the Sabbath.' I like it."

Shalom, Beineinu (Shalom—Among Us)

"Before we make peace with our neighbors, we must make peace at home—among the Jews." Or, similarly, "The stickers all talk about yes to peace or no to peace, and everyone argues with each other. So before we make peace with our enemies, we must first make peace among ourselves."

In the context of the central discourse discussed here, this sticker relates to the previous one but without the specifically religious and cosmological orientation. Thus the slogan becomes a call for internal peace. When asked to discuss the meaning of this sticker, there was universal agreement: This sticker seems to relate directly to ***Shalom, Chaver*** from a particularistic perspective cloaked in a garb of unity and inclusiveness. One respondent approved of this approach: "It's an excellent sticker! In order to stand up to someone from outside the family, the family must be united." Another reacted quite differently: "This is the sticker that most annoys me. Phony harmony. It's an anesthetic in the war[54] that's going on here."

***Shalom Beineinu Levein Hakaba* (Shalom between Us and God)**

"It's a message from the religious, who say that there must be peace between the Jewish people and God because so many people here do not believe." This sticker is another "religious" member of the generative family. This time, the message is conveyed explicitly through the image of peace between Jews and God: "This is one from the 'God squad'[55] who think they know best what people should do, and try to claim that all our problems from A to Z would be solved if we all became religious like them."

***Shalom, Yedid* (Shalom, Buddy)**

"It could be anyone. Who could be a 'buddy' instead of the 'friend?' Maybe Bibi?" Another respondent suggested: "I think it's when they said farewell to Hussein. It's saying that Israelis mourned his death."

This slogan appeared as the headline of a report on the funeral of King Hussein of Jordan in the winter of 1999 featured in a leading Israeli daily newspaper. It reflects the close relationship between folklore and the media.[56] The word *Chaver* used to address Rabin is replaced by the word *Yedid*—another Hebrew word for "friend" but one that is less intimate.[57] Among its uses, *Yedid* is also associated with the adjective used in the media for countries that are "friendly" to Israel. The slogan also conveys the strong sense of loss and mourning in Israel over the death of Hussein, who was profoundly admired and even loved by Israelis.

The remarkable creativity of the interpretative process was also evident in the case of this sticker. One respondent, for example, drew an analogy between the textual and contextual character of this sticker and the generative ***Shalom, Chaver***: "When Hussein died, it was important to recall that he made peace alongside Rabin, so they bid him farewell in a similar manner. But I think they should have produced a sticker in Arabic. It's a pity no one thought of that."

***Hayita Chaver, Shalom* (You Were a Friend, Shalom)**

"It's a fine address to Hussein, who passed away. They want to tell him that just as all Israelis mourned for Rabin, so they mourn for him. He was very widely loved in Israel." Another respondent recalled, "Hussein came to Israel to visit the bereaved families of young girls murdered by a Jordanian soldier. Although he was a king, he came and knelt down before them and asked for forgiveness. The Israelis appreciate this and remember that he acted like a true friend."

This slogan also appeared in the press after the death of King Hussein, who was widely respected and even admired by many Israelis. It was understood as a direct address to the late monarch,[58] based on the inversion of ***Shalom, Chaver*** [Shalom, Friend] to *Chaver, Shalom* [Friend, Shalom], as well as the addition *Hayita* [You Were], emphasizing the past activities of the king and the nature of the address as an oration for the late king. One interpretation maintains the reference to King Hussein but perceives the sticker as expressing fears about the future of peace as a result of the change of rule in Jordan: "It's saying that peace was our friend, and now we're worried what will happen under the new ruler in Jordan."

Sticker, Ata Chaser (Sticker, We Miss You)

"This summarizes a comment about all the stickers. After all these variations and slogans, the end result is that what's missed now is not the *Chaver* 'friend' but rather the sticker itself."[59] Another respondent was angered by the sticker: "Contempt! After all, a sticker is just a sticker. It's not important. Here they talk about it as if we miss a sticker like we miss a person, and I think that's a contemptuous comparison. I'd never put a sticker like that on my car. It's really annoying." A third respondent explained, "They're making fun—as if what matters to everyone here is just to find some slogan to follow."

This sticker is evidently satirical, overturning the intense political weight attached to the stickers. It first appeared in a satirical column in a leading newspaper. However, we also saw it on cars, enlarged and taped on the rear windshield. Within the overall discourse discussed here, the respondents related to this sticker in various ways. One explained, "The message is that we need to find a sticker that will unite us all—religious and secular, left-wing and right-wing. We really need a sticker like that."

Discussion

The future of folklore studies depends on its ability to respond to the challenges posed by expressive genres that are not conveyed through interpersonal interaction.[60] This understanding, according to Kirshenblatt-Gimblett, together with the deconstructivist tendencies currently evident among folklore researchers in various places,[61] is currently at the center of the field's debates. It is in this context that Briggs and Schuman[62] note the need to dismantle the dichotomy between traditional and modern and replace it with a discussion of traditionalizing as a central cultural dynamic. The rich interpretations that make up the Israeli road discourse, with their deep historical and cultural roots, reveal a folkloric, multivocal dialogue conducted through a contemporary medium. This dialogue offers a unique empirical contribution to understanding the dynamics of traditionalizing.

In recent years Israel has seen a cultural phenomenon of lively and public folk politics, embodied in the iconic genre of bumper stickers. In addition to providing insight into issues relating to contemporary Israeli society and culture, documentation and analysis of this genre creates theoretical potentialities, extending our understanding of the nature and limits of folklore in the pluralistic postmodern era, and confronting traditional definitions of this field with new cultural phenomena. In focusing on a dominant cluster of stickers in the Israeli ethnographic field, we sought to learn about the popular experience and unique interpretation that is expressed, and indeed created, in this folkloric discourse. The scope of creativity and interpretation revealed to us during the course of the study reflects the local characteristics of the genre which, as part of the process of the globalization of culture, has moved overseas from one ethnographic field to another and has assumed unequivocal folkloric form.

As is evident from an analysis of the reactions and intracultural interpretations relating to the discourse of stickers, this phenomenon shows a particularly high level of folk political debate and embodies an exegetical and persuasive aesthetics. This folk politics is organized in argumentative spirals, creating a broad structure of discourse and meaning, the different parts of which replicate and are subservient to each other. The argumentation is embodied in the diversity of versions in the cluster; in the fact that all the versions relate to a single sacred text, albeit in differing manners and degrees; and in the intricate and sometimes abstruse nature of popular interpretation, which is reminiscent of traditional Jewish exegesis. An analysis of the range of interpretations offered reveals a number of organizing axes around which interpretative rhetoric is structured. In some cases a single axis may be followed, while in others the interpretation vacillates between different axes and combines them in the act of exegesis.

a. A diachronic axis, according to which the interpretation is based on a chronological sequence of political events. This axis is expressed in rhetoric such as "This sticker bids farewell to the victims of terror during that period"; "the sticker was produced on the first anniversary of Rabin's assassination"; "It's connected with the Oslo Accords"; "It depends on the timing—if it came out immediately after the assassination, then I think it's very cynical. . . . If it was a long time after, then it means 'We still remember you.'"
b. A synchronic axis relating to the simultaneous presence of a range of stickers and to the encounter between these stickers. This axis draws its interpretative legitimacy from the broad context underlying the different stickers. For example: "This one goes along with 'Hebron: Then and Always'"; "[My interpretation] depends on which stickers appear together with it—whether they are right-wing or left-wing."
c. A sectarian axis that establishes meaning through factional categorizations. This approach is characterized by rhetoric such as "This is a sticker of the settlers"; "a left-wing sticker"; "religious Americans, you know what I mean?" and so on. This axis emphasizes the dialectics of inclusivity/exclusivity, reflected both in the slogan on the sticker and in the varied associations of solidarity and alienation: "It's saying that we

all want peace"; "they're blaming a whole section of the people for Rabin's assassination."

d. An axis bridging copywriter or creator and audience, and offering explanations relating to the creation and "invention" of the sticker. This approach focuses on an imaginary copywriter, often entails value judgments as to his or her level of sophistication and aesthetic creativity, and often blurs the dialectics between copywriter and audience. For example: "They came with a reference to the Holocaust. It's clear that they're trying to link the assassination to an enormous trauma"; "plays on the association of Rabin and peace"; "a nice invention—a very cute idea." The attempts by many respondents to offer their own slogans for stickers may be included in this axis.
e. A private axis, transferring discussion of the various stickers to the personal level of aesthetics and emotion. Typical comments reflecting the private axis include "I didn't like that one"; "it doesn't really move me either way." These comments are always accompanied by others relating to different axes and employ a characteristically capricious rhetoric; arguments are drawn mainly from the emotive sphere and the level of cognitive processing is minimal.

These axes emerged repeatedly in the respondents' interpretative comments, blending public, private, emotional, and reflexive levels. In some cases this resulted in exegetical corroboration, in which the different axes contributed to an interpretive totality, while in other cases, incompatibility along the axes made for incoherent dissonance that may result in an unnerving lack of exegetical clarity.

An increasingly important characteristic in illustrating the nature and borders of folklore seems to lie in the distinction between folklore and popular culture.[63] Hasan-Rokem defines the difference[64] as relating to the level of mutual activity between the subject that makes the creation and the subject that consumes it, and to the ability to distinguish between the two.[65] In contrast to popular culture, folklore is created through a mutual action involving the talents and cognizances of singers and audience alike, of storytellers and listeners—in a manner that blurs the distinction between them. These mutual relations raise the folkloric experience to the level of *jouissance*—a feature that would seem to be absent from popular culture. Popular folkloric creativity, therefore, is characterized by the simultaneous presence of artist and audience, by the constant dismantling of the partition between the two, and by the principled dialogics they embody, at the levels of both conscience and emotion. For Hasan-Rokem, the attempt to reveal all these while continuing to acknowledge the creativity of the individual is the act of acrobatics practiced by researchers of folklore.

The discussion in this essay on the dialogue of stickers generated by *Shalom, Chaver* enabled a close examination of the nuances involved in folkloric creation, as well as the operational mechanisms unique to this genre. Our research showed that on the folkloric level, the creation was expropriated from the "creative individual," commuting the acrobatic act of research from the individual to the collective domain. This process was surely realized by the creative individuals themselves; for their part, they appear to have cooperated with the processes by which the identities of copywriter and audience were blurred. The public in Israel was involved as both copywriter and audience in the discourse of stickers derived from *Shalom, Chaver* on various levels, from the level of diverse and creative interpretation, through criticism and the creation of imaginary slogans, through the rituals of placing and removing stickers, and by overcoming technological barriers in order to create "homemade" stickers. Thus discussion of the discourse of stickers as folklore focuses attention on the mutual affinities connecting and differentiating popular culture and folklore, and the mechanisms involved in their creation. As we have seen in this essay, the discourse of stickers of such impressive popular force generated by ***Shalom, Chaver*** associates itself with the mythological ***Shalom Akhshav***. Yet this latter sticker, for all its many years of existence, has not developed into a full-fledged folkloric entity. While this may be due in part to the explicitly sectarian political identity of ***Shalom Akhshav***, the main reason probably lies in the other slogan, that is, ***Shalom, Chaver***, which generated an emotionally charged folkloric discourse, dismantling barriers between copywriter and audience. The founding moment of this discourse, and the traumatic juncture at which the words *Shalom, Chaver* were spoken, in an American accent by the president of the United States, was one of emotional force and the transcendence of hierarchies. Thus, this slogan possessed a founding potential to create a folkloric discourse that also invited blurring, such as that of the distinctions between copywriter and audience; both are fed by and flood emotions.[66] This discourse blends aesthetics and humor along with profound emotions of fear, frustration, anger, sadness, identification, joy, and the pleasures of gloating.

The discourse on the cluster of stickers discussed here draws its interpretative authority from processes that create diverse, even contradictory, readings, reflecting the emotional dimensions of the political folkloric arena. In our case, these dimensions are characterized by an argumentative aesthetics that hints, through form, content, associations, and connections between them, at various levels of explicitness, to the common and the divisive underpinnings of this entire discourse. On the basis of this understanding, one might propose that "text" and "context," as two distinct concepts, may be transferred in theoretical and methodological terms into the "moment of semiosis" at which several discourses meet and intertextual relations occur in the spaces between the discourses.[67] Forms of transmission, the relations between form and content, messenger and audience, tradition and innovation, original and dissemination, and, above all, the relations between folklore, emotions, and power continually generate new forms of folkloric discourse. The bumper sticker discourse, as a focal point for these dialectics, challenges and widens traditional limits of the folkloric scope.

Figure 4.
A "homemade" bumper sticker.

Figure 5.
A new sticker to the cluster, "Hakol Biglalcha, Chaver" (Everything because of you, Chaver).

Postscript

The cluster of stickers branching out from ***Shalom, Chaver*** continues to grow. While completing this essay, around the time of the 1999 general elections in Israel, the stickers ***4.11.95, Bocher, Ata Zokher?*** [November 4, 1995, Voter, Do You Remember?][68] and (with a more explicit message as to the political ramifications of memory) ***Chaver Ani Zokher, Barak Ani Bocher*** [Friend, I Remember, Barak I Vote][69] appeared before the election, while the stickers ***Chaver, Hashalom Chozer*** [Friend, Peace Is Returning] and even ***Chaver, Ani Chozer (Bitshuva)*** [Friend, I Return (in Repentance)][70] were seen shortly after the elections. ***Salaam, Chaver***, substituting the Arabic *Salaam* for *Shalom*, is the most recent variation. The continuing evolution of these stickers is further evidence of the vitality of folkloric discourse and its ability to contain and produce new voices, and to react creatively to a dynamic and changing reality.

Notes

I would like to thank Sarina Chen and Hannah Zik, who helped document the material for this study. I am grateful to Professors Galit Hasan-Rokem, Victor Azaria, and Steve Kaplan, as well as Dr. Meskerem Brhane for their important comments, and to Shaul Vardi for sharing the struggles of the English translation. Last, but most important, my thanks go to the many interviewees who were kind enough to share their experiences, thoughts, and creativity with us.

1. For a discussion of the phenomenon as a "plague," see Levinson and Ze'evi 1995, 15 Kislev 5756.
2. In the United States, bumper stickers are a widespread phenomenon and are usually considered part of a related group of genres including other car signs, buttons, and T-shirts (H. Smith 1988; Case 1992). Articles on this subject have addressed the medium either from the historical and historical-parricide perspective (H. Smith 1988, 141–43) or from the functional standpoint (Case 1992, 107).
3. The pioneering literature on this genre has hitherto concentrated on the ethnographic field of the United States. Theoretical works have assumed without question that stickers are a genre of popular culture in which political themes play only a secondary role. Research in this field has concentrated on classifying the phenomenon according to predetermined criteria, and on using the external exegesis of researchers to order the messages according to clearly delineated categories (see, e.g., H. Smith 1988; Aguirre 1990; Case 1992; Endersby and Towle 1996).
4. The popular engagement in this form of creativity emerged clearly both in the existing material I collected and in the slogans people spontaneously offered when I mentioned the subject of my research.
5. On the connections between folklore, politics, and nationalism, see Dow 1991.
6. The use of a text box to offset the sticker slogans is intended to allude to the respondents' experience in the field, acknowledging the limitations of a written academic text as a vehicle for examining a dynamic real-time visual experience.

   Shalom, Chaver was documented both with a comma between the two words and without punctuation; for the sake of convenience, the comma has been used universally in this essay.
7. On the Peace Now movement, see M. Bar-On 1985. On the connection between this movement and the sticker, see Levinson and Ze'evi 1995.
8. For a discussion of the conflict that the assassination brought to the fore, in which new political forces challenged some of the most deeply ingrained paradoxes of the vision of the modern Israeli nation-state, see Hazan 1998.

9. See below for discussion of the various meanings of this expression. Since the ambiguities, nuances, and sounds of the Hebrew slogans discussed in this chapter must be understood in order to appreciate the generative process presented here, all slogans will be given in transliterated Hebrew, with a basic translation in parentheses.

   It should be noted that although President Clinton first used the phrase *Shalom, Chaver* shortly after learning of Rabin's assassination, most respondents in this study associated the expression with his funeral oration in Jerusalem.
10. The sticker was produced and distributed on a voluntary basis by the employees in an advertising firm and by a printing house. A further 500,000 copies of the same sticker were printed and distributed by a leading Israeli daily newspaper. The main competitor to this newspaper also produced its own sticker expressing the sense of shock at the assassination, and bearing the words ***Dai La'alimut*** (Enough Violence); this slogan belongs to a parallel cluster of stickers in Israel.
11. Though the level of dispersion is not central to this essay, a random examination we made of several parking lots during this period showed that three out of every ten cars bore political stickers; in some parking lots, four out of every ten cars in a row bore stickers.
12. For discussion of other manifestations of "mourning rituals" after the assassination of Rabin, see Hazan 1998.
13. They were removed, most likely, by the car owners, perhaps as a result of their recognition of the potential destructive impact of anti-Rabin rhetoric or perhaps to avoid being identified with the accused camp. In some cases, vengeful mourners removed stickers without the consent of the owners.
14. Standard modern Hebrew orthography, based on an essentially consonantal alphabet, creates numerous ambiguities and multiple readings, as will be noted in the discussion of the specific stickers. Accordingly, it was important for the interviewer not to direct interviewees to any particular reading of the written text.
15. In this context, for example, H. Smith notes that this genre is a form of folk poetry with iconic characteristics, adding that "their analysis requires the reader-viewer to reread and review formal content in several explicit and implicit contexts in order to decode them" (1988, 141).
16. Naturally, alternative categorizations of the stickers could have been followed. One approach that seems logical at first glance is to order the stickers according to political orientation (in the Israeli context, this would require attention both to the left-right axis and to the religious-secular axis). This was inappropriate for this study, however, since our central goal was to examine the respondents' categorizations and interpretations. Moreover, and as is clear from the detailed discussion below, we were surprised to see that respondents offered diametrically opposed interpretations even of stickers that seemed to us to present an unequivocal political perspective.
17. This explains the complexity encountered in attempting to translate the stickers from Hebrew to English. As mentioned in note 14, the solution I adopted is to introduce each sticker in its Hebrew form, in transliteration. The Hebrew transliteration is intended to be functional, not academic, and to enable non-Hebrew speakers to gain some appreciation of the aural aspects of this phenomenon. In standard Israeli speech, the combinations *ch* and *kh* both represent guttural "h" sounds.
18. The one exception, which maintains the pattern "X, We Miss You," replaces the word "friend" with the word "sticker."
19. Some readers may prefer to simply review the two-column list of stickers and proceed directly to the summarizing discussion, using the detailed discussion only for reference.
20. In addition to stickers displayed on cars, the research also identified cases where stickers were displayed in homes—particularly, and I believe significantly, on entrance doors. Other locations included bags, T-shirts, and diaries; the common denominator is that all these locations are particularly exposed to audiences likely to read the stickers; they also constitute border markers of personal identity.

21. In this context, see Aguirre (1990, 92), who reflects on the manner in which people communicate on highways and the function of stickers in this discourse. He claims that the road is a significant element, insofar as it relates to the concrete and symbolic question as to where one is "coming from" and where one is "going to."
22. This comment, and others in this essay, must be understood in the unique Israeli context, where the orientation of an individual as left- or right-wing, and their often related identification as secular or religious, may in many cases be inferred from aspects of physical appearance. A beard and/or skullcap (for a man), or a head kerchief and long sleeves (for a woman), will be interpreted as implying a level of orthodoxy in religion and a right-wing political orientation; a man with an uncovered head who is shaven and wearing a certain type of round eyeglasses will be seen as a left-wing secular intellectual. While these are naturally stereotypes, such external characteristics are probably more accurate indicators of religiosity and political leanings than they are in most Western countries.
23. Israeli driving is notoriously aggressive and is exacerbated by poor infrastructure and an exponential increase in the rate of car ownership.
24. This is a sticker opposing any Israeli withdrawal from Hebron—a position that would not usually be expected to go along with the message of the other stickers quoted by the respondent.
25. For example, ***Ken Lashalom, Lo La'alimut*** (Yes to Peace, No to Violence) was turned into ***Ken Lashalom, Lo L'Oslo*** (Yes to Peace, No to Oslo), and in a personal version into ***Ken Lamashiah*** (Yes to the Messiah). "Oslo" in Israeli political discourse means the peace process with the Palestinians, started through clandestine discussions in the Norwegian capital. The second syllable of the name Oslo is the same as the Hebrew word "no," a coincidence that has been exploited by slogan makers. The very personally prepared version ***Ken Lamashiah*** transferred the whole debate to the religious sphere.
26. The interviewee is reflecting on the situation in Israel, in which blue-collar workers are identified with a hawkish political position.
27. Two brand names which, in Israel, serve as a code for prestigious cars.
28. This sticker intensifies the Israeli-American connection underlying the entire cluster. "Shalom, chaverim" are the opening words of a song that was popular in the United States in the 1950s. This song is still sung by many in the American Jewish community, forming part of a limited repertoire of Hebrew songs sung in the original. Although the song is completely unknown in Israel, for a small number of respondents with American ties these words aroused associations with American Jewish culture.
29. Rabin's party.
30. The allusion is emphasized by the use of a "dripping" effect on this word.
31. The word *balahot* appears in modern Hebrew only in combination with the word *chalom* (dream): *chalom balahot* = nightmare. Thus the slogan draws on the rhyme between *chalom* (dream) and *shalom* (peace). *Shalom balahot* might be translated "Peacemare."
32. See note 13.
33. Other stickers similarly capitalize on reversal and contrast, such as *Chevron Me'az Ul'tamid* (Hebron: Then and Always), which is a politically opposing variant on *Shalom Akhshav* (Peace Now).
34. In modern Hebrew, this entails a shift in the stress of the word: while *Shalom* is usually pronounced with the stress on the second syllable, when used as a first name the stress colloquially shifts to the first syllable.
35. The interviewee notes two of the incidents during the period immediately before the assassination. In the first, montage photographs of Rabin in SS garb were disseminated at a right-wing demonstration. In the second, Rabin was accosted in public by citizens who opposed his policies.
36. This refers to the Netanyahu government, which came to power six months after the assassination and was in power during the research and writing of this paper (prior to the May 1999 elections).

37. The Likud is the mainstream right-wing party that was opposed to Rabin's policies (and which, under Netanyahu's leadership, subsequently won the 1996 elections).
38. The joke is based on taking the word *chaser* (missing or lacking) and transforming the affective word meaning "missing," in the sense of longing, to the word that signifies straightforward absence of something, then adding the word *erekh* (value or worth). Strict Hebrew grammar requires a slight change in pronunciation (from *chaser* to *chasar*), but this would not always be evident in colloquial speech, and in any case there is no change in the unvocalized written form of the word.
39. A clearly right-wing message expressing opposition to the transfer of Hebron to Palestinian control as part of the Oslo Accords.
40. In addition to the word *Akhshav* (Now) as in the classic *Shalom Akhshav* (Peace Now) sticker, there is another, more literary word for "now": *'Ata,* which most Israelis pronounce the same as *Ata* (You), though the spelling is different.
41. Hebron has a special status for Jews as a historio-religious place, and the withdrawal thus created particularly strong emotions.
42. The words *Ata* and *Chaser* are both marked as masculine in Hebrew; a grammatically correct version of the sticker would read *Chevron, At Chasera.*
43. This is a religious party that has gained strength in Israel over the past decade, building its political base largely on its image as a religious antithesis to secular Zionism.
44. The slogan was used by a health insurance company, where existing members received various benefits if they persuaded new members to join.
45. This use of the verb has become so ubiquitous that many Israelis now avoid using the form *Gomer* to mean finish or end, using a different verb instead (a process akin to the narrowing of meaning of the English word "intercourse").
46. The respondent offers two other versions of this phrase; both also translate into English as "Friend, I'm Coming," but the first presupposes a male speaker talking to a female friend, while the second presupposes a female speaker talking to a male friend.
47. The disparaging aspect comes from the semantic field of "bye-bye" in Hebrew—and perhaps in English as well. Wishing "bye-bye" to Yitzhak Rabin might be compared to a sticker in Britain saying "Ciao, Diana."
48. Indeed, stickers bearing the legend *Bye-Bye Bibi* were seen around the time of the 1999 elections in Israel.
49. The respondent mentions two organizations representing the minority of orthodox Jews in Israel who support dovish and left-leaning policies in terms of the peace process.
50. Some respondents interviewed after the decision to hold early elections in 1999 developed this line of association, claiming that the slogan was implying that Netanyahu had almost reached the end of his "program" and it was time for him to say good-bye.
51. Literally "A Sabbath of Peace," though the usual equivalent greeting among English-speaking Jews is "Good Sabbath!"
52. This combination of innocence and subversion is also evident in another successful sticker of indirect relevance to this cluster: ***Shabbat Shalom Akhshav*** (Shabbat Shalom Now), which performs precisely the same operation on the original sticker (*Shalom Akhshav*) as the present sticker does on the generative (*Shalom, Chaver*).
53. The respondent means the murder of Rabin and assumes there is no need to state this explicitly.
54. In context, the "war" to which the respondent alludes is clearly that between religious and secular Jews in Israel.
55. The respondent uses the modern Hebrew slang "dos" to relate to the religious; depending on context, "dos" can vary in tone from the humorous to the contemptuous.
56. See, e.g., Degh 1994.

57. "Buddy" is only an approximate translation, used to indicate that the Hebrew word is not *Chaver*, as in the other stickers. *Yedid* is, perhaps, halfway between "friend" and "acquaintance."
58. The fact that the interviews took place shortly after Hussein's death meant that most interviewees immediately associated these stickers with this event.
59. Interestingly, this interpretative perspective relates to Haim Hazan's discussion of the absence of commitment to identity inherent in practices of commemoration (1998, 743).
60. Kirshenblatt-Gimblett 1992, 1998. Examples of these genres include e-mail folklore and the folklore of the office photocopier. On urban office folklore, see in particular Dundes and Pagter 1978, 1987, 1991; in this context, see also Abrahams 1993; Dorst 1983, 1990.
61. For various developments of this discussion, see, e.g., Georges 1991; Kirshenblatt-Gimblett 1988, 1996, 1998; Ben-Amos 1998; Bendix 1998.
62. Briggs and Shuman 1993.
63. The concepts of popular culture and folklore are often used interchangeably. For a discussion of the similarities and differences between these two concepts, see R. Bauman 1992; Levine 1992; Hanson 1993.
64. Hasan-Rokem 1997, 12, in the preface to the special volume of *Theory and Criticism*, which she edited.
65. In the context of this distinction, Richard Bauman notes that the definitions of these two phenomena sometimes overlap and are sometimes counterpoised (1992, xvii).
66. For a discussion of the connection between emotions and discourses, see Gumperz 1982 and particularly Abu-Lughod and Lutz in the introduction to their book on the language and politics of emotions (1990, 1–23).
67. Earlier in the essay I used the notion of "semiotic moment." For a discussion of the term "moment of semiosis," see Mechling (1993), who also advocates for research into new folkloristic contexts in which creator and audience are distinct yet simultaneously connected. A central concept in this new understanding is that of intertextuality as coined by Kristeva. On the development of this concept, see Ben-Porat 1985; Boyarin 1990. Such concepts as structure, form, function, or even meaning are no longer immanent components of the discourse, but rather the products of an ongoing process of production and reception of discourse. Important for our purpose, this process is located not in the moment of delivery, or even the moment of creation itself, but precisely at the junction or point of encounter of a number of directions of discourse.
68. This draws on yet another rhyme between *bocher* (voter) and *zokher* (remember). The date is immediately recognized by most Israelis as the day of Rabin's assassination.
69. This sticker uses the same underlying rhyme as the previous slogan, though *Bocher* is here a verb rather than a noun.
70. This syntax, awkward in English, is a literal translation of the Hebrew phrase "to return in repentance," used to describe a process of drawing close to God through taking on the commandments. The presence of parentheses around "in Repentance" allows for interpretations that employ a non-idiomatic usage of the verb "to return."

15

The Meaning of War through Veterans' Eyes

A Phenomenological Analysis of Life Stories

EDNA LOMSKY-FEDER

Introduction

Haggai, tanks brigade: "When I think about war, half of my life has passed since then. I was nineteen then and now I'm thirty-four. It is almost insignificant. It seems to me truly anachronistic. Almost. . . . The war didn't change me at all. I always wanted to travel and I always loved to travel. I never took things too seriously. That's all."

Zohar, tanks brigade: "It is so much more dramatic than life, so crazy, dramatic, and intense. I have no doubt that . . . that my life is divided into before the war and after the war."

These two quotes illustrate two different outlooks on the meaning of war as a factor in the personal biography of the speaker. They were culled from life stories of two Israeli men who participated in the 1973 Yom Kippur War as part of their regular military service. Both were combat soldiers from a similar sociocultural background. The two men look retrospectively on their war experience of fifteen years ago, trying to evaluate its place in and importance to their life stories.

Which of these quite different perceptions characterizes the personal meaning the Israeli man lends the war experience in his life story? What is the nature of the difference, and how can it be explained?

The research literature that focuses on the influence of war on veterans states that the view of war as a crisis or transition (as expressed by Zohar, the second subject) typifies the place of war in the veteran's course of life (see, e.g., Card 1983; Figley and Leventman 1980; Laufer 1988a, 1988b; Lifton 1973; Milgram 1986; Modell and Haggerty 1991). This approach uses psychological models to explain the difference between the two speakers. The first veteran, Haggai, who asserted that his life was not affected by the war, would be said to lack self-consciousness or to be compelled to repress or deny his awareness of the influence of war on his life.

Is the underlying assumption that war is a traumatic experience a necessary one? Is the psychological explanation of Haggai's statement the only way to explain his remarks? And is there a sociocultural context in which the non-crisis outlook can characterize the meaning the individual gives to war in his life story? Can the differences between the speakers be explained through cultural rather than psychological models?

The decisive answers found in the existing literature express assumptions about the predominantly traumatic effect of war on the individual. This approach views war as foreign to the course of normal life. War is perceived as a difficult and stressful experience with far-ranging and traumatic repercussions (Danish, Smyer, and Nowak 1980; Reese and McCluskey 1984).

Because of these assumptions, the prevailing research does not ask whether and how far war experience is integrated into the world of the individual, or whether the experience necessarily distorts and disturbs his life. The researchers' certainty about the severe impact of war and their neglect of the social context have largely overshadowed veterans' responses to the question of whether or not they interpret the war in traumatic terms. The phenomenology of war is perceived as unimportant, and the authors are hardly, if at all, attentive to the meaning the war receives in the eyes of those who fought it.[1]

This is especially problematic when we wish to examine the meaning of war among veterans in societies such as Israeli society, where the wars are frequent and are given social and cultural centrality.

Given this background, the aim of this study is twofold. First, I will deal with the phenomenology of the war experience, that is, to discover the personal interpretation of war as revealed in the Israeli veterans' life stories, and to understand the interpretive mechanisms through which the war experience is integrated into the course of their lives. Second, I will explain the war's personal meaning within the cultural context in which the veterans live and construct the reality of their lives.

The central thesis here is that the phenomenology of war must be understood in context. More specifically, my claim is that because war is not a shocking and transformative factor in Israeli society at the macrosocial level, it is not so at the individual level. It seems as if war is institutionalized and normalized into the Israeli social order, and thus the individual also integrates and co-opts it into his personal biography.

Life Stories and the Phenomenology of War

The meaning of war was examined through life stories of war veterans.

A "life story" is the individual's description of the course of his life. This story is a collection of events and experiences that the narrator chooses (consciously or unconsciously) to present as his or her personal story along a time axis. According to this perception, a life story does not represent a random collection of events but is "narrative rather than a chronicle; in it resides the evaluation of one's own existence" (Frank and Vanderburgh 1986, 186).

In researching the life story, it is necessary to examine not only the contents of the narrator's biography but also the formal or "literary" aspects through which he or she shapes the story. The researcher must therefore also relate to the rhetoric of the biography and the manner in which life is articulated as a narrative (Bertaux and Kohli 1984; Bruner 1987; E. G. Cohen 1982; Corradi 1991; Crapanzano 1984; Denzin 1989; Sarbin 1986). The goal of the researcher studying the life story is not to reconstruct actual reality as such but to extract the story of a particular narrator concerning this reality and to expose his or her perceptions of it.

In general, the phenomenological approach to life stories focuses on the individual's interpretation of his or her world, rather than on his or her behavior or personality (Berger and Luckmann 1966; Schutz 1970; Schutz and Luckmann 1974). The life story as interpretation takes a personal story and embeds it in a larger sociohistorical context. The sociohistorical context provides narrative content for the life story; at the same time, the life story is a significant sociocultural document, as the individual constructs a personal version of the common social-historical context. Life stories are a mediating mechanism between society and the individual; between the cultural meaning attached to events and experiences and their personal meaning; and between collective memory and personal memory. For this reason our interest in the life story stems from the phenomenological constructions of the narrator (Ryff 1984).

The life story or, according to Schutz and Luckmann (1974), the "biographical articulation" of the individual, is one of the means used by the individual to construct his or her world. In particular, it is a tool by means of which the individual cruises through different levels of time and links them to his or her world. According to Schutz and Luckmann, biographical articulation is conditional upon society: "The categories of biographical articulation are not really categories of inner duration as such, but rather are categories which are formed intersubjectively and established within relative-natural world view. They are basically imposed upon the individual and become interiorized by him" (1974, 57). The social categories of biographical articulation are part of a worldview assumed to be self-evident. Moreover, the individual experiences these categories as part of his or her world, as part of the reality of his life, and they define the operational limits for him (94). Schutz and Luckmann are aware of the unique nature of the individual and maintain that it is important to examine how personal experience is reconstructed in the life story. They posit that the unique nature of the individual is expressed in the way he organizes and arranges his life experiences on the continuum of time, and in the relative weight he lends these experiences (58).

Although Schutz and Luckmann emphasize the way the subject perceives his world, their analysis focuses on the intersubjective construction. Therefore, they argue that the individual's perception of his life is largely determined by the sociocultural context. The individual can do no more than choose one from among a number of available "typical biographies" (94–95). The degree of openness and variety with regard to the selection of typical biographies depends on sociohistorical and class contexts; it also varies according to gender.

Watson (1976) attempts to forge a systematic link between the phenomenological approach and the "life story" approach. He claims that the situation in which a subject recounts his life story to the researcher is a special situation of biographical articulation. According to Myerhoff (1980), by complying with the request to tell about himself, the subject is compelled to contemplate his life, thereby formulating conscious thoughts into a more coherent articulation. In this situation, the narrator departs from the spontaneity of his existence in the world, becomes more aware of his "natural points of view" concerning his life that he has taken for granted, and adopts a more phenomenological position regarding the world (Natanson 1962). In other words, he examines and investigates his natural assumptions about the world and makes his own experiences the object of examination. This situation emphasizes the significance and meaning of events and experiences in the narrator's life—such as the war experience.

The experience of war is of special significance in the life story. In his seminal article "The Homecomer" (1944b), Schutz argues that war is a unique experience in the context of the phenomenology of man. This is because war has the potential to shatter "taken for granted social knowledge." The emphasis in Schutz's article is on the detachment from home and the return home with a different perspective. The subjects are soldiers who spent long periods at war, that is, a situation in which the dimension of time is of central significance in the construction of the soldier's memory of home and family. The act of coming back home confronts these constructs of memory with the reality of the encounter. To a large extent, the return is also a transition from one reality of life—war—to another reality—home. This transition locates the soldier in a position of "phenomenological strangeness"—a position that is largely unexpected, since this strangeness occurs within what used to be familiar. This position inevitably shatters what used to be taken for granted. Returning home disrupts the natural and spontaneous continuum according to which the soldier used to perceive his home reality. Largely against his will, he is pushed from natural observation to phenomenological observation of the reality of home life. The emphasis in Schutz's analysis is therefore not on the essence of the war experience as one which undermines that which has been taken for granted, but on the quality of the return from this experience. In this respect, each return home has the potential to disturb that which has been taken for granted. Even returning home from a vacation, in Schutz's opinion, unsettles to a certain extent what used to be seen as something that did not even require consideration. From this perspective, the longer the absence from home, the more significant the experience of return; the more different the "other reality" is from the "home reality" to which one returns, the more dramatic the new encounter.

It thus follows that return from war carries the potential for crisis, since it cancels the rules of the game to which the soldier has become accustomed in the war reality and forces him to confront the radically different rules of the home reality.

I would argue that this mechanism of challenging that which has been taken for granted is potentially present in the moment the soldier is "thrown" into the war reality. Thus, not only is the return from war significant in terms of the perception of everyday life but the actual encounter with war as a unique phenomenon is as well. This particular point is not emphasized by Schutz, who deals with the nature of the experience in the context of the process of homecoming. Given its powerful emotional and moral impact, the experience of war carries the potential to challenge the social presumptions that structure the home reality. The war experience forces the individual to confront extreme and abnormal situations in which the fighter is pushed toward a phenomenological position regarding his life world. War is vastly different from what was previously familiar, known, and expected in the home reality; experiences in war also usually differ from the soldier's expectations of war itself. These gaps—between the soldier's social knowledge of the reality of his life and of the reality of war on the one hand and his actual experiences in war on the other—may potentially lead to the breakdown of the individual's natural assumptions about his life.

War, then, is an event that carries the potential to break down the models according to which one interprets the everyday world. Is this potential always realized? Does the social context in which this experience takes shape influence the realization of this potential?

The goal of this study is to examine the meaning of the war experience in the life story within its cultural context and by means of a phenomenological framework. More specifically, through the life story I seek to clarify whether war is presented as part of the "typical biography." I examine the connection between war and other events perceived as part of the typical biography; the "natural" assumptions concerning war and the "phenomenological" points of view; whether war is taken for granted in social terms or is seen as an experience that challenges natural suppositions concerning the world, leading to a phenomenological perception of life.

My analysis of the stories stemmed from the term "interpretive relevance" as developed by Schutz and Luckmann in their book *The Structure of the Life-World* (1974). According to them, when a subject or event receives conscious attention and is the object of focused discussion (i.e., when it is of thematic relevance), the narrator does not usually confine himself to presenting the matter, but also interprets it and determines its significance and meaning on the basis of the interpretive schemes available to him. "Interpretive relevance," then, is the encounter between the individual's experience and his social knowledge by means of an appropriate interpretive scheme (Schutz and Luckmann 1974, 207). As long as events, incidents, and experiences are familiar and do not create "noise," they are interpreted in a routine and almost automatic manner. The interpretation will be in accordance with familiar and approved categories of meaning, which can be seen as the norms in the construct of reality. When an experience shatters and violates the ongoing and routine continuum of how the individual "reads" the environment, to the extent of undermining norms, it receives more attention.

I use the conceptual framework set by Schutz and Luckmann to examine how the speaker conceives and interprets war in the context of his prewar knowledge that was taken for granted. Is this an experience that has led to a "disturbance" in routine interpretation, to the point of destabilizing knowledge that has been taken for granted, requiring a purposeful, conscious, and reflexive grappling with its meaning? Against this background, what meaning does the experience receive in the context of the veteran's perception of the continuum of his life?

The objective is to understand the way in which war relates to the world of "the taken for granted" and to unravel the interpretive solutions, proposed by the storytellers, to confront the experience. These outlooks expose an important aspect of the repertoire of cognitive strategies, which the subjects use to incorporate the experience into their lives. The assumption is that the more the war experience is presented as an event that did not break down "taken-for-granted" social knowledge, the more normalized it has become in the course of life.

Methodology

My research is based on sixty-three life stories, gleaned from in-depth, open-ended interviews. Israeli society is engaged in a constant struggle and offers an especially interesting case for studying the meaning of the war experience among war veterans. There are several reasons for this: (1) war occupies a special place in Israeli culture and ideology, since the idea of being a "besieged" nation is a central component in the country's self-image; (2) war is one of the primary factors in building social institutions, developing the economy, and maintaining social solidarity; (3) within a relatively short period of time, Israeli society has been involved in many wars, each of which had its own character and own set of social implications; and (4) military service in Israel is compulsory, universal, and long (both regular service and reserve duty). As an experience shared by almost all Jewish men and by many women, it transcends differences of social class and ethnicity. Because Israel has been involved in a number of wars, most Israeli men have fought in at least one war and have been forced to deal with this experience (Horowitz and Lissak 1989; Kimmerling 1985, 1993; Mintz 1984).

Given these factors, it is clear that military service and the war experience are deeply rooted in the reality of life in Israel and are central to defining the identity of the Jewish Israeli and the constructs of his or her day-to-day existence. The interviewees were men born between 1952 and 1954 who fought in the 1973 Yom Kippur War as part of their regular military service. Half held combat positions and half were support staff.

For our purposes, the 1973 Yom Kippur War is especially pertinent to the phenomenology of war in Israel. This war is universally regarded as the most traumatic of Israel's wars. Absolute faith in the power of the Israel Defense Forces (IDF) was shattered and feelings of impermanence and insecurity that were put to rest in the 1967 (Six-Day) War, and supposedly banished from individual and collective consciousness, were reawakened. This crisis of faith in the power of the IDF forced Israelis to reexamine the meaning of war on the individual and the societal level.

The interviews took place between 1987 and 1989, about fifteen years after the Yom Kippur War. The men told their life stories and talked about this from a retrospective viewpoint. This cohort is interesting because the men entered adolescence when Israel was basking in the euphoria of the 1967 war; they were brought up with the values, images, and symbols that had become entrenched as a result of the 1967 war. There is a special significance to the fact that this generation came fully of age around the time it had to fight in the Yom Kippur War—a war that, from a military and morale point of view, was the antithesis of the 1967 war. Later, when the members of this cohort were about thirty years old, they served as reservists in the Lebanon War (1982–84) and have since taken part in the IDF response to the Palestinian Intifada (uprising), which broke out in 1987. Both the Lebanon War and the Palestinian Intifada have further divided national opinion and shattered collective faith in the role of the IDF. These additional experiences with war doubtless influence the way in which war is perceived—specifically the Yom Kippur War—and lend an additional dimension to the veterans' retrospective interpretation of the meaning of this experience.

The stories were chosen from a clearly defined social group: middle-class, educated, secular men—the group from which most of the Israeli "elite" comes. This point is extremely important because, to a great extent, the interpretations presented here express a hegemonic ideology, that is, the cultural models of the dominant groups in Israeli society. Even the "other voice," critical of the IDF, is phrased in conceptions that are meaningful for dominant Israeli groups and are not the interpretations typical of a person from the social periphery of the society, such as criticisms developed among marginal groups like women, lower-status second-generation immigrant groups, and Israeli Palestinians.

Findings

Before presenting the different meanings of the war experience in the life stories, it is important to stress that this study is concerned with the interpretive level of the individual, not with behavior or personality. In other words, the focus is on the way in which the subjects interpreted and explained the effect war had on them. It does not claim to answer questions such as "Does war have an impact on life?" or "What sort of an impact does war have?"

An analysis of the life stories reveals a number of interpretations of the war experience. In what follows, the different interpretations and the relationships between them are discussed. These various interpretations are not necessarily mutually exclusive; generally, the interviewee presents a number of interpretations in the course of a single story. The relationships between the different interpretations are an additional factor in the analysis of the material and in understanding the interpretive mechanisms through which the individual integrates the war into his life story.

The "Dominant Voice" Interpretation of Continuity

The interpretation of continuity integrates war into the course of life by means of previous social knowledge. This interpretation is the dominant voice, expressed in some 75 percent of the life stories. Whether they served in combat or noncombat positions, most of the veterans perceive the war as a significant experience, but one that did not undermine their taken-for-granted knowledge of the world. Life is perceived as a linear continuum; war has a localized place on this line but did not alter it. Even if the interpreter wonders about social or personal truths, the experience of war did not substantively change his understanding and feeling of control in the external and internal environments. This interpretation of continuity receives many meanings, and several variations can be identified within the dominant voice of continuity. As mentioned earlier, these meanings do not necessarily preclude one another, and some tellers simultaneously present a number of interpretations to establish the interpretation of continuity.

The most routine interpretation of war is heard in the stories in which war is perceived as an event integrated into a period of conscious lethargy, which the tellers claim is characteristic of youth, and specifically of regular military service. An example of this is the following comment by Amnon, a paratrooper:[2] "We didn't have the faintest idea what was happening to us, we were jerks. Regular soldiers aren't . . . their lives don't belong to them. I think it's partly a matter of age, and partly the context of being a regular soldier, that makes you not think in terms of profits and losses."

These stories portray the army as a totalitarian institution, which fosters mechanical, automatic, and herd-like behavior. According to these veterans, military service silenced their emotions and vulnerability, and dulled their ability to think independently and critically. They claim that "being in the army" took control of how they dealt with war experience. Expressions such as "brainwashing" and "deadening" are used to describe this outlook.

Another expression of the interpretation of continuity originates in acceptance of and fundamental identification with the hegemonic Israeli ideology of war. Koby, a pilot, expressed it this way: "I was into the whole business of Zionism and heroism—the same things that now seem a bit stupid to me. But I remember that because I was too young, they didn't let me fly for the first two days. I went on a hunger strike. I refused to shave and I went around barefoot, until they let me fly. I was injured slightly once, and some of my friends died and some were taken prisoner, and it was . . . but it wasn't even traumatic, because it all happened completely under the banner of Israeli heroism . . . that's it."

While Koby's comments have a dimension of self-irony, this is combined with his nostalgia for the enthusiastic, believing, and committed young man he used to be. The war experience was shaped by the cultural models that led him to enlist and according to which he acted during his service. The war did not challenge his interpretative patterns; indeed, he claims that it even reinforced them. A further example is Chaim, a personnel officer in the armored corps.

> All those people who say that it destroyed things for them . . . that it destroyed myths for them . . . what did it destroy? . . . On the contrary, this was the just war . . . we didn't start it, we didn't want it, we didn't have any goal. These evil guys came and surprised us on Yom Kippur. At that time, the mere fact that they came on Yom Kippur[3] was considered a serious sin. So I'm not convinced that myths were really destroyed, I think that in some ways it strengthened the myth. . . . Certainly the war strengthened the connection with all these things. Look, this is our war. Each generation has its own war, and this was our war.

These subjects speak about identification, rather than a sense of "deadening" or the absence of criticism. Most proponents of this interpretation view the war as just. The tellers accept the cultural assumption that as long as a war is justified, it should be seen as a political means based on rational and utilitarian considerations. The Yom Kippur War did not destroy this basic conception, and these individuals justify the war in defining it as an experience of continuity. Avi, a flight supervisor, was asked how the war influenced his life: "I'm not sure how to isolate the war. Because there is no doubt that we were attacked in the Yom Kippur War, and we had to defend ourselves, which is what we did. . . . We were educated to fight in an unavoidable war, an ethical war, a war that couldn't be prevented. . . . But the war took place and had to take place. What can we do? This is part of life. Death is part of life."

According to Avi, a justifiable war should be seen as part of life. The Yom Kippur War fulfilled this criterion, but the war in Lebanon—which undermined Avi's conception of war in Israeli society—did not. Many of the stories that present the Yom Kippur War as an experience of continuity through identification compare this war to the war in Lebanon. In this they differ from the subjects who viewed the war as an experience of discontinuity and who often speak about the 1967 war as a heroic war in collective memory.

Stories in which the identity-based interpretation is particularly strong are ones where the narrator presents himself as a young man who was, before military service, rather alienated from the ethos of the army. In these stories, the war is portrayed as an event that reinforced his links and identification with such an ethos. This type of interpretation is particularly evident in the life stories of interviewees who spent long periods of their youth outside Israel and felt somewhat marginal in Israeli culture, especially given its militaristic element. Army service was a particularly significant experience for these young men in the process of their induction and integration in Israeli culture.

Another voice in the interpretation of continuity through identification is expressed in the stories presenting war as a rite of passage to the fighter role. Yuval, an officer in the infantry, expressed this view: "This was the first time I tested myself in truly difficult situations. All the time you ask yourself how you will react under fire, if you will be able to assist others in difficult circumstances. On the one hand, this is a difficult situation, and all that, but on the other hand, I . . . it's not nice to say, but I felt a certain personal satisfaction because I was pleased with myself."

This outlook sees war as an experience that binds the individual with the cultural models addressing the nature of the good soldier. According to this interpretation, war accentuates the connection between "common knowledge" and action on the battlefield. This interpretation of continuity is latent in most of the stories but is especially prominent when the teller feels a certain dissatisfaction with his military service or the war. The emphasis on functioning successfully on a personal level compensates for feelings like "my role wasn't sufficiently combat oriented" or "I wasn't able to integrate into the army" or "I didn't fight in the war with my buddies."

Until this point, the tellers have presented themselves as passive interpreters who adopt cultural models without criticizing them. Some interviewees present themselves as more active interpreters who take part in more conscious negotiations with their interpretive schemes. In this case they are critical—but the criticism existed before the war and was reinforced by it. War is an experience that confirms and promotes the process of undermining the social norms that previously existed.

An example of this is given by Rafi, a soldier from the intelligence corps. Later in his life, Rafi became one of the leaders of the Peace Now movement.[4] In his story, the Yom Kippur War is perceived as an experience that strengthened the way he challenged things that were taken for granted, an experience that reinforced a separation and detachment from hegemonic cultural models.

> At a very young age, my opinions were very unmilitaristic. . . . In these matters, I was very different, even before we went to the army. I mean, I always expressed very clear views on this matter. My big brother, let's say, was in a combat unit, but I wasn't. I already had objections to this even at this stage. . . . I never identified, I mean when I was very young I didn't identify really with what they were doing. Even when the Labor Party was in power, I was very much in opposition. I mean, that they weren't doing enough, and that they were putting us in danger, etcetera, etcetera. Yom Kippur was the proof of this.

Rafi's comments convey his basic interpretation of the war as an event that confirmed his opposing stance. The war was additional evidence for an already consolidated viewpoint.

While in some cases the war brings confirmation of a critical standpoint that had taken shape before military service, in other stories it is the nature of the encounter with the IDF during military service that leads to a significant challenging of social norms. The war experience becomes integrated in a process that had begun earlier.

The last variation of the interpretation of continuity appears in stories that define war an experience that raised awareness and put an end to youthful naiveté. Here, the war is integrated into the natural process of maturation. The subjects do not perceive war as an event that caused a dramatic change, a shock, reform; war is presented as a catalyst—a meaningful experience that propelled a process that would have taken place in any case. War did not cause a conscious revolution but raised questions and thoughts that characterize the maturation process.

In stories characterized by highly routine interpretations, the sobering up that comes with maturity is presented as occurring after the period of service. Here, however, the war serves as a catalyst, accelerating processes that are characteristic of the natural process of maturation.

To sum up, for the time being, the stories illustrate that interpretation of continuity is dominant in the life stories. According to these veterans, the war did not undermine the models that interpret the world and did not interrupt the flow of life.

The "Other Voice" Interpretation of Discontinuity

Despite the dominance of the continuous voice, we must also consider the less common voice, which presents the war as an experience that disturbed the ongoing interpretation, destroyed understood assumptions about the world, and interrupted the continuum of life. This is termed the "interpretation of discontinuity."

This interpretation was heard in about 25 percent of the life stories, is far less common, and can be seen as the "other voice" in the stories. At the same time, it is presented with emotional and dramatic power. It is voiced more often but not exclusively by combat soldiers.

Haggai, an operations sergeant in the air force, relates: "Suddenly I couldn't identify with anything happening here. Everything looked awful. Awful, shocking. In one fell swoop, the Garden of Eden became Hell." And Ze'ev, a pilot:

> What did you do in the war?
>
> I was a pilot in the air force. The Yom Kippur War was a trauma. It was a turning point in my life, in all respects, in all respects. And within a few hours of the war beginning, I really felt that I was a totally different person.

In response to an innocent and conventional question in the Israeli context, Ze'ev presents the war as an immediate, direct, and spontaneous turning point in his life. His first association with his military service is the war and its being a transforming event. The revolution was immediate and absolute—he was "a totally different person."

Stories that present war as an experience that interrupted the course of life have a common narrative core: a youth who is obligated and believes in hegemonic cultural models goes to war. During the war he undergoes difficult experiences but meets the demands of the Israeli fighter ethos and functions as dictated on the personal level. His encounter with war is a source of great disappointment to him and he acknowledges the gap between reality and image. Because of this insight, he seriously questions these images and takes a critical stance, sometimes even adopting alternative models. The shock lies in the interpretive schemes that construct the relationship of the teller with his society. The disturbance in the flow of life is translated into sociopolitical terms more often than into psychological-existential ones. This approach undermines the interpretive schemes dealing with the relationship with the society, and purifies the schemes dealing with the "self."

In the interpretation of purification, war is defined as an event that shocked the taken-for-granted accepted dogma; later, one tries to recover what is truly important and significant. For example, Ofir, an infantry soldier:

> At that point, the whole world of values crumbled. All that was left were the simple questions that I don't see now I'm quoting to you from my life then. At that point, there was no Schopenhauer or Hegel or Nietzsche, no "relative good" or Socrates. There was just one desire, and in the end one feeling: fear. Then you ask yourself "why am I afraid" and the answer is real simple and not at all sophisticated: "Because I want to live." So then you ask the question that led to all the philosophies in history: "Why do you want to live?" And the answer is real simple: You want to live because, and I remember the answer, because you want to see Tali [his future wife] and the family, and I want a red-roofed house in a green field in Australia. Now, after you return, part of the answer becomes your ten commandments, because these are the things that were the very kernel of your life then, in these sacred and honest moments. Later, you can argue with this, and ask whether these minutes really represent something in life, or whether they are actually removed from life. But when I came back from the war, my feeling was that these feelings bind me.

This interpretation neither undermines nor combats accepted norms but consciously deals with the same knowledge as a way of separating the wheat from the chaff. According to this interpretation, war enables the veteran to construct a "cleaner," "truer," and "purer" interpretive scheme for the meaning of existence.

The undermining of the interpretive scheme focuses on the model that deals with the social meaning of war. The interviewees assert that the process begins with a difficult encounter with the IDF during the war, engendering feelings of helplessness and despondency. The gap between expectations and reality was so enormous that some refused to acknowledge the reality and interpreted the situation as a tactic, an exercise in camouflage.

Their stories express the shock, despair, and pain in the meeting with war. The war was so different from what they had been promised, so different from what they believed it would be, so out of line with what they were trained to do.

They were deeply disappointed by the IDF's performance and arrogance. According to these veterans, the IDF was neither "strong" nor "good." The stories present a different picture of the IDF, one far removed from the traditional image and the Israeli fighter ethos. Yigal, in the tanks brigade, expresses this view: "Myths like, you don't leave the wounded, you don't leave them behind on the battlefield. The commanders are like that . . . all that disappeared . . . when you see how they leave the wounded, how they leave bodies, how . . . hysterical commanders do not command, don't have control, when you see how the soldiers don't believe in their commanders, how the soldiers avoid their responsibilities, so as not to be wounded. So . . . maybe myths aren't broken, they simply fade out."

Belief in the IDF (and the idea that it is a strong, advanced, and ethical army) was shattered. The interviewees present the IDF as a physically and morally battered army.

It is no accident that the 1967 Six-Day War is always present. The comparison with this war is interwoven (at both explicit and implicit levels) in all the stories that present this interpretation. The interviewees undergo profound soul searching when confronted with militaristic worldviews and with the feeling of collective arrogance that became deeply rooted after 1967.

The undermining interpretation also incorporates the alternative interpretation that was more strongly voiced in the Lebanon War (S. Helman 1993; Lieblich 1989) and continues to be heard during the Intifada. Although the undermining interpretation is not the dominant voice in the life stories of the Yom Kippur fighters, the manifestations of this interpretation are powerful in the overall context of the "war voices" heard in the social group that we investigated. The obvious questions are: Who is doing the undermining? Can these subjects be characterized in terms of their patterns of involvement in the war?

Three characteristics are typical of this group which, as stated, comprises about one-fourth of all the interviewees: First, most of them are combat soldiers who do not express any doubts about the extent to which they were combative participants in the war. Second, most were involved (through combat experience or otherwise) in the battles and events that have come to symbolize the Yom Kippur War and constitute its collective memory. Third, most finished their army service shortly after the end of the war and did not spend a prolonged period serving in the military.[5]

The "Accompanying Voice" Interpretation of Isolation

Although the interpretations of continuity and discontinuity lend different meanings to war, they both acknowledge the direct tie between war and life, and both view war as part of the course of life. In addition, there is a third interpretation as well: the "interpretation of isolation." Here, war is seen as a separate, unrelated experience, not part of the social models that construct the reality of daily life. War is presented outside the continuum of life.

If the interpretation of continuity is the "dominant voice" and the interpretation of discontinuity is the "other voice,"' the interpretation of isolation is the "accompanying voice." To differing degrees, this voice appears in most of the stories. This interpretation appears beside and always accompanies the interpretation of continuity or discontinuity. The interpretation of isolation does not stand alone.

This interpretation has two central meanings. In the first, war is defined as a "different world" and therefore irrelevant to daily reality; the models that interpret the reality of war are neither valid nor relevant to constructing the course of life. Arnon, a soldier in the infantry, describes this well: "Life and war are parallel, and do not intersect." Ilan, an infantryman, concurs: "A different planet.... You can't apply it at all to any other area of life."

The second interpretation of isolation defines war in psychological terms as a repressed experience, hence one that is not present in daily life. The veteran does not consciously deal with the experience and therefore it is not part of the daily interpretive "game." This psychological meaning is clearly expressed by Moshe, a member of the armored corps: "It passed for a simple reason—my repression mechanisms are very strong, very sophisticated. I didn't even have one nightmare at the time I saw all the horrors of war, all the horrors!" Moshe uses psychological jargon of "repression mechanisms," as do many other interviewees.

The two meanings of the isolation of the experience from life are fundamentally different. There are two types of narrators present here: the "phenomenological" narrator who defines the war as "other reality" and the "psychological" narrator who defines the war as "suppressed reality." The "phenomenologist" focuses on the war, emphasizing the nature of the experience as a social entity; the "psychologist" concentrates on the fighter who has been through the war and is busy coping with memories of the experience. The phenomenologist examines the relevance of this experience to the everyday social environment of the actor; the psychologist relates to the presence of war in the inner environment of the actor. The phenomenologist defines the war as a totally different experience from normal life; the psychologist defines it as a particularly difficult experience. According to the phenomenologist's interpretation, the experience was outside life, since these are two social entities that do not meet; the psychologist assumes that there is an encounter between war and life but that this is on the unconscious level, since war is so difficult to cope with. The isolation of war from the life course is mainly evident when veterans seek traces of the experience in their private lives. In this regard, the notion of isolation—especially in the psychological definition—offers an easily accessible cultural model for veterans, who explain why it is difficult for them to place, identify, and articulate the influence of war on their lives.

The "Voices of War" Dual Interpretation

On the face of it, the interpretation that isolates war from life runs counter to the other interpretations—of continuity and discontinuity—which tie it to life. How can war simultaneously be defined as part of life and outside it? It appears that lack of consistency is one of the means of dealing phenomenologically with complex situations, including the war experience. I would argue that the internal contradiction in presenting the war in the life stories is what enables the veteran to live with and "normalize" war in his daily life.

The different interpretations should be seen as a complex of "voices of war" that construct a dual perception of experience—simultaneously part of life and outside life. The dual perception is an additional interpretive mechanism used to integrate war into the course of life.

The dual interpretation coalesces war into the course of normal life, but at the same time it remains a "lacuna." War is a meaningful event in an autobiography but one that generally leaves no obvious traces in the life story. This experience constructs the veterans' reality of life but is at the same time defined by them as a different reality, neither relevant nor present. The dual interpretation of war is a paradoxical concept—the normal in the abnormal. War is integrated in life by removing it from life; war is normalized by delimiting and isolating it.

I claim that the tension and the lack of consistency between the interpretations allow the individual interpretive flexibility and degrees of freedom in coping with the experience. This dual interpretation does not present a continuum from isolation to connection. These are two important facets of the same outlook—sometimes one is referenced and sometimes the other is. The question is: in what context does the teller employ the interpretation that connects war to life and in what context does he use the interpretation that isolates war from life?

Analysis of the life stories demonstrates that interpretation depends on context: the connection of war to life (in a continuous or a discontinuous way) comes to the fore when the teller is concerned with the public sphere of the experience and his role as a citizen. The isolating aspect is more common when the veteran deals with the experience as a person and speculates about the meaning of war in his private life—career, family, friends, and so on. The interpretation of continuity appears when the veteran faces the fact that every few years he is exposed to a war situation and sometimes is sent to the front. In this context, he cannot ignore the presence of war and its relevance to his public life. War must be seen as part of life, whether by accepting or rejecting it. In contrast, removing war from private life is an extremely effective interpretive model for explaining why war did not affect the personal biography and why it is difficult to distinguish its marks on the course of daily life.

The more difficulty the veteran had in identifying the vestiges of war in his private life, the greater his need for the interpretation of isolation. What is striking and interesting is that in the stories which presented the interpretation of continuity, the teller had greater difficulty pinpointing the impact of war on the private life story and he expressed the interpretation of isolation in a more powerful fashion. And so, paradoxically, the more a person integrates the war into his life, the more he removes it from his life. When he strongly expresses the dominant voice—the interpretation of continuity—the dual interpretation plays a greater role in his life story.

Discussion: The Personal Meaning of War within the Cultural Context

An analysis of the "interpretative relevance" of war in the life stories of Israeli soldiers shows that war is not perceived by the interviewees as a traumatic experience but as one that is integrated in the flow of their lives. War is thus a "normalized experience" in their lives, contrary to the findings reported in the general literature relating to the impact of war on demobilized fighters (see also Syna-Desivilya 1991). The life stories reveal two interpretative mechanisms used by interviewees in integrating and normalizing the war experience in their lives. The first is the continuous interpretation of war, that is, integrating the war into the flow of life by means of interpretative schemes that existed prior to the war. The second mechanism is the dual interpretation of war, that is, representing it as an experience that was simultaneously part of life and removed from it.

It is precisely this perception of war, as a "normal" experience integrated in the flow of expected life without any "noise," that expresses the centrality of war in Israeli life. This perception reflects the definition of war as an integral part of life in Israeli society, as well as an additional "voice" in the construction of this meaning. Subjects' interpretation of war is an expression of what Kimmerling (1993) calls civil militarism or cognitive militarism, which characterizes Israeli society, that is, a state in which the members of a society take the centrality of war in life for granted. The expectation that war will break out sooner or later is part of the collective, as well as personal, identity and conscience.

The interpretive mechanisms seen in the life stories—the interpretation of continuity and the dual interpretation—are symbolic expressions on the individual level for the routinization of war into the life world. These cognitive "strategies" can be seen as mediation mechanisms that translate the collective meaning of the war experience as a "normal experience" into personal meaning. These interpretations enable the individual to satisfy the social demand that war be smoothly integrated into his life. Put differently, when war does not cause social change, it will probably not affect the personal biography. In the

Israeli context, coping with war means living as if the war had not taken place—on both the societal as well as the individual levels.

I would contend that the personal meaning of war, as voiced by these interpretations, allows veterans to cope with the frequent demand to participate in war as well as to live their lives as though the war had not taken place. This outlook on the experience not only serves the society; it also allows the individual to live with war, without shocks or extreme changes, in the demanding context of Israeli society. It therefore recruits the commitment and conscription of members of society and controls the disruptive effects of crucial changes for the individual that arise in a war situation.

It is hard not to be impressed by the way subjects integrate the war into their lives and by their commitment to the social meaning attached to war. It appears that this is linked to a large extent (or even dependent on) to the institutionalization of relations between society and the army (Horowitz and Lissak 1989) or to the characteristic nature of Israel's wars (in close proximity and short term), which enable a rapid return to routine on the general societal level as well as the personal level (Kimmerling 1985, 1993). However, there are also macrosocial arrangements that construct the normalization of this experience on the individual level and serve as mechanisms for social control. Several such arrangements can be suggested.

The first arrangement is the entire range of socialization processes in Israeli society during childhood and adulthood, which prepare the youngster for the role of soldier and for a state of war. The recognition of war and of the army as part of reality is consolidated in light of the repeated picture of a father going off to the army and accompanies the life cycle until the stage when the youngster himself becomes a father accompanying his own sons as they go off to army service (Katriel 1991b; Lieblich 1989). The war and all that goes with it are among the most central themes reflected in formal and informal curricula, overtly and latently (Bar-Tal and Zoltak 1989; Bet-El and Ben-Amos 1995). In addition, the army and security are daily and central features in the media (Herzog and Shamir 1994; Katz et al. 1992). The Jewish Israeli prepares for war and faces war throughout his life: the internalization of the war as part of life is the result of socialization processes.

An additional social arrangement structuring the normalization of war on the individual level is military service. The army is apparently a central social institution that functions as an agent for socialization for fighting situations through regular service and reserve duty. However, in terms of its significance in the construction and preservation of the war experience, as part of life and beyond life, military service is much more than just another socialization agent. Regular service is a central element in the social and cultural construction of the stage of youth in Israeli society (Azarya 1989; Lieblich 1989; Rapoport and Lomsky-Feder 1994). The frequency of wars and the need to recruit youngsters for the sake of the collective have obliged the Israeli state since its establishment to shape what Mosse (1990) terms the "myth of participation in war."

In other words, society has systematically and deliberately reinforced the noble facets of military service and war. The heroism of war is culturally structured through the myth of the warrior hero, which is a key element in the ethos of the sabra (native-born Israeli) and has served as a model of identification for generations of young Jewish Israelis (Gal 1986). Israeli society has succeeded in channeling the aspirations of its youngsters into military service and in structuring the characteristics of youth through the role of the soldier.

The institution of reserve duty is also central in terms of the social structuralization of the significance and normalization of war within life. This is one of the key mechanisms focusing male discourse around the army and war (Ben-Ari 1992; S. Helman 1993). Reserve duty is an "island" of the army within everyday life, exposing participants to fighting situations in an interrupted continuum over decades of their life.

A third social arrangement that fosters the normalization of war on the individual level is the continual and intensive preoccupation with the war experience in the different "cultural fields." Israeli society is preoccupied with war—particularly with its painful and critical aspects—in the various channels of its culture. Social time is dotted with wars—from the Memorial Day ceremonies immediately before Independence Day through the anniversaries of the various wars (Handelman and Katz 1991). Relative to other societies, the culture of commemoration in Israeli society is exceptional with regard to the number of memorial sites and the extent of memorial literature (Levinger 1993; Sivan 1991). War is a central theme in Israeli literature, drama, and poetry (Katz et al. 1992; Meron 1992; Shaked 1988). It occupies artists (Ofrat 1991; Tzalmona 1993) and appears as a central theme in popular culture, on the radio, in the movies, and in rock music (Katz et al. 1992).

This intensive and public preoccupation removes the subjects from the private domain and implies an acceptance and institutionalization of the "naturalness" of war in the Jewish Israeli's life. Addressing the cost of war, from a position of empathy for pain or from a critical standpoint, through so many channels and on an almost daily basis, leads to the expropriation in the collective arena of the personal experience of coping with these subjects. This may also allow the pain, tension, anger, and criticism to be channeled into the public arena, enabling the individual to continue life as usual. These "cultural fields" can be seen as arenas for a form of catharsis that is at once collective and individual.

Notes

1. Exceptions to this is, e.g., the study by Schütze (1992), which discusses the way in which the collective guilt of the German people affects the individual memory of German soldiers and civilians who lived through World War II.
2. The following analysis of the material includes excerpts from life stories. The excerpts are transcribed with minimal editing to ensure optimal proximity of the reader to the manner in which the narrator expressed himself. Where the narrator's comments included breaks in

speech ellipses are used. Although the excerpts were not edited, the very choice of excerpts includes a significant dimension of editing.

3. The narrator refers to the Jewish mourning customs that are also part of rituals for Yom Kippur (Day of Atonement), a highly significant day for observant Jews. The war began on this religious holiday. This description is interesting and unique, because the narrator is not religious; this is an instance of the absorption of religious symbols into a secular context.
4. Peace Now is a social protest movement established in the 1970s to push forward the peace process between Israel and the Palestinians.
5. A detailed discussion of the connection between the personal, crisis meaning carried by war among this group and patterns of participation in war appears in Lomsky-Feder 1994.

16

Giving Birth to a Settlement

Maternal Thinking and Political Action of Jewish Women on the West Bank

TAMAR EL-OR and GIDEON ARAN

On October 27, 1991, a Jewish woman named Rachel Drouk, a settler in the West Bank, was killed by Palestinian Intifada fighters. Twenty-five women spontaneously gathered at the site of the murder and held a vigil—a vigil that eventually developed into a protest settlement. The women, all of whom were married mothers, presented their initiative in maternal narratives: grounds, motives, and justifications for the act, targets, and anticipations were all related to the practice of care. This essay conducts an artificial dialogue between the women's discourse and Ruddick's theory of maternal thinking (1989), enabling deconstruction of the former and a critique of the theory of care.

On October 27, 1991, busloads of Jewish settlers from the West Bank, members of the right-wing political movement Gush Emunim,[1] made their way to a mass demonstration in Tel Aviv to protest the beginning of peace negotiations in Madrid. Their banner read "You don't sell out your mother," reflecting their fear that the meetings would lead to the withdrawal of Israel from the West Bank. A Palestinian attack on one of the buses left two dead: the driver, a Jew from West Jerusalem, and Rachel Drouk, a settler from Shilo and a mother of seven. After Rachel's funeral, twenty-five women from settlements all over the West Bank made their way to the site of the killing—a barren, rocky hillside in Samaria—set up tents, and stayed the night. Their stay stretched into a week (the traditional mourning period), then a month, and finally culminated in the founding of a new settlement. The women called it Rachelim[2] in memory of Rachel Drouk, Rachel Weiss, who burned to death with her three children in a Palestinian attack on a bus near Jericho on October 30, 1988, and Rachel, one of the four matriarchs of the Jewish people.

The act of founding Rachelim was highly exceptional. Right-wing women—most of them orthodox, all married, all mothers—established a protest settlement in the West Bank. Most of the women, who were college educated and aged thirty-five to forty-five, worked, and some held political positions in their community. Orthodox women are accustomed to operating separately from men because of the traditional seclusion of the sexes. This separation created a vital society of women capable of carrying out spontaneous acts on a community level, as well as organizing in large leagues. Emuna is the largest such league of religious women (Sasson-Levy 1993).

Religious-Jewish fundamentalism as metanarrative contains numerous and varied references to women's roles, status, motherhood, and femininity. Since it constitutes a holistic religious worldview based on mainstream orthodoxy, while tending toward a radical interpretation, these references are in dispute with Western feminist ideologies (Davidman 1991; Heschel 1983; Kaufman 1991; Koltun 1976; Weidman-Schneider 1984).

The expansion of traditional women's performances beyond founding day crèches and girls' schools and beyond performing acts of charity is indicative of essential changes in the status of these women. These changes stem from the open cultural market and the democratic state within which the women live, causing them to reinterpret the feminist messages embedded in Jewish culture. The Rachelim event is a prime example of the extension of orthodox women's performance. It was an attempt to operate as women and mothers within the political arena—not as supporters of the men and not as claimants for a fair share, but as initiators of a novel strategy based on novel arguments.

It is tempting to analyze the event according to feminist theories of motherhood, peace, and political action. Evaluating fundamentalist women's actions in terms of Western feminist theory, however, produces unsound results. In Western feminist theory, religious women, especially those who are not part of the West, are seen as a homogeneously powerless group, as victims of their culture (Mohanty 1988). We suggest that it is more appropriate to listen to the narrative presented by the women involved in the Rachelim event. We attribute significance to their experience of motherhood and its political potential in the local cultural context, and we reread the narrative through the theory of maternal thinking (Ruddick 1989). The insights gained from the local event also serve as a critique of Ruddick's essentialist and universalistic theory. Examining the feminist value of the act of founding Rachelim reveals the significance of the event for the women and their society, at the same time unveiling basic social structures underlying the gender category (Strathern 1988).

The Chain of Events

Immediately following the funeral in the settlement of Shilo, twenty-five women made their way to the site of the murder. Inside the tent erected at Rachelim, Naomi Sapir recounted the following.[3]

> It could have been me, just the opposite of the sentence we use so often in Israel, "It can't happen to me." I, like each woman there, felt that it could easily have happened to me. Orphaned children were sitting now in some house, and that was what was so acutely distressing. Rachel was the first woman from the settlements who was killed, and for us that was the shock. We understood the price we might have to pay, we grasped the enormity of the risk, the responsibility we have toward our children who travel the roads every day, and mainly the helplessness. We made the decision—we were staying. It was a form of protest, a kind of cry to the world. We are still here, going on with life, still founding settlements. In a place of death, lights will begin to twinkle at night. There will be life. We decided to name the spot Rachelim in honor of Rachel Drouk, Rachel Weiss, who was burned to death with her three babies in a bus attack near Jericho, and, of course, after our biblical matriarch, Rachel.

The husbands of the women were not partners in their decision or the act. Their role was limited to the technical matters of preparing the equipment needed for staying the night at the bare, hostile location. Both the Israeli military and civil administrations in the area opposed the women's move and raised logistic and legal obstacles in an attempt to persuade them to go home. Finally, both authorities agreed to allow the women to hold a vigil at the site until the end of the traditional week of mourning. Through parliamentary and extra-parliamentary actions and negotiations with the military, the seven-day period was extended to one month, then two months, with the women still in place.

The army erected a large tent for the women and a smaller tent opposite it to house soldiers guarding them. The original twenty-five Rachelim women took turns sitting in the tent, accompanied by another two hundred women who came in shifts from all settlements in the territories. Girls of all ages from all over the country made pilgrimages to the site, and organized groups of girls arrived from diverse public and religious schools to study in the tent. Rabbis and male and female teachers gave lessons in Judaism. The Rachelim women related their story to visitors—the chronology of events leading up to the founding of the settlement—over and over again. During the first week, the women remained day and night; later, they began going home in the evening, leaving their husbands, sons, and brothers to stand guard.

Three weeks later, the women of Rachelim issued a call to other women in the territories and Israel. It was published in *Nekuda*, the settlers' monthly periodical, distributed in leaflets, and hung on a large poster in the tent. It read:

> We the women of Judea, Samaria and Gaza have established a memorial vigil. We demand we be allowed to found the settlement of Rachelim at this spot, on this hill, where the murderers lay in ambush. There are sufficient government lands for the establishment of a permanent settlement. We remain at this site demanding to found a settlement, for this is the only Zionist response to this criminal murder. We hold vigil at this place, and we will persevere in the

> hope that the Government of Israel will decide to found a civilian settlement at the spot from which the shots were fired. This will be the way to prove to those who would uproot us that they will never achieve their goal. Not only will we not be uprooted, our roots will only grow deeper. We call upon every woman and mother in the settlements and every woman and mother in Israel to stand up and be counted with us at this memorial vigil. And, of course, men too, husbands and sons, are invited. Let us find comfort in the building of the land. (Haim 1991, 13)

The women called it "The Feminist Manifesto." The gender used throughout the document was feminine plural—a powerful statement in Hebrew, which is a gender-sensitive language and in which the generic plural is masculine. The ending explicitly includes men and brings the feminine formalization to a climax.

The choice to unite spontaneously and act on a separatist basis is formalized here. The call is addressed to Jewish residents of the territories and Israel, as well as the government, and is completely by and for women. It concludes with the call to all women and mothers in Israel to express their support for the vigil. The call to men begins with "And, of course," but the opposite is implied: men are addressed only as an afterthought. There may or may not have been a brief ideological debate on this point, but the upshot was that the ladies of the manor had decided to invite the lords as well.

One could say that the tent guards had been invited to step in. Once the seven-day mourning period was over, the women no longer stayed at the tent during the night. Their men, while not part of the protest settlement, stayed to guard at night—perhaps out of concern or worry. Some came to visit during the day, bringing the children to see their mothers, but they were always visitors. The invitation "to step in" seems more like a plea for consent and support rather than for joining in.

"The Feminist Manifesto" and extensive media coverage brought a massive response throughout the West Bank. Following vigorous public lobbying by the women, the government approved Rachelim as a permanent settlement and study center for women. Within three months of the Rachelim incident, two more Jews from the territories were murdered, and other settlers adopted the women's model and established memorial settlements at the sites. The women of Rachelim had revived an act from Zionist history in which a settlement was founded at a site where Jews were killed and the site was named after them. Unlike Rachelim, the two subsequent memorial settlements did not last. Following the change of government in June 1992 from Right to Labor, all projects in the West Bank, including the development of Rachelim, were frozen.

Doing It Their Way: The Appropriation of the Political Act

The women passed the time at Rachelim debating their case with the military and the civil administration, attempting to regulate and contain the storm they had created. They prayed, kept the dietary laws with respect to food delivered to the tent, and studied. Traditionally a male endeavor in Judaism, religious study has for some time been undergoing female appropriation (El-Or 1993, 1994; Weissman 1976).[4] Local rabbis arrived to teach the women at Rachelim; it was reminiscent of how women used to go to mostly men's settlements to cook and launder for them.

In the November 1991 issue of *Nekuda*, journalist Emuna Elon wrote about the reaction of non-orthodox Jews to the phenomenon: "Anyone passing by would probably have been surprised to see a group of tired, eccentric women dressed in long, full skirts and head scarves, sitting around a rabbi and listening to a lesson. The soldiers who came to guard there had never seen such a sight. These poor men had to stand there in the biting cold. But the women went up to them and offered them homemade cakes sent by their families. They invited them to warm themselves by the small heater" (44).

The Rachelim women told guests from outside their political group about soldiers guarding the site who wrote words of admiration in the guest book. Some of these were kibbutz-born men who were identified with the left-most sectors of Israeli society. The women told of officials and senior army officers who expressed admiration for their courage and resolve. The women took every opportunity to thank these people; they referred to them by first names so as not to disclose their identity and to show their familiarity with them and their gratitude for the personal connections. While visiting the tent, we watched the women receiving reporters and visitors in traditionally feminine ways: they smiled, played the role of gracious hostess, and offered food and drink and warmth by the stove. Numerous children ran underfoot, and the women's arms were full of the babies they had not left at home.

Conversations in the tent were "women's room" ones; the tone and content were set by the women. Visitors, including us, were obliged to acknowledge that the primary actors were mothers and women and that the topics of discussion were children and motherly concerns. One way or another, it led to talking about their men and to listening to criticism and a rereading of masculine politics. The women also wished to speak about their appearance. With a reflexivity typical of women and minorities, they repeatedly and somewhat sarcastically alluded to how the press was not accustomed to their "garb," their long full skirts and dresses, in the bitter cold, barren landscape. Their head coverings were wrapped in the manner of religious women. They objected to the description of them in the media as "sloppy orthodoxesses" and to the detailed account by a Tel Aviv female reporter of the mud around their tent and the filth in their makeshift toilet.[5] As Geula Tzroia said, "It's important to us to look pretty and feminine. We have no need to come across as Amazons on the mount. Our strength is quiet, beautiful, and positive."

At a political rally at the Jerusalem Theater (described below), the women of Rachelim were elaborately dressed, wearing fashionable hats and earrings, and among the one thousand women present that evening, the women of Rachelim stood out for the elegance of their clothing.

The act of Rachelim was neither perceived nor depicted by the women in violent heroic terms. No alienation was created between those disobeying the law and those upholding it. The women were tired, the soldiers were cold.[6] The women were not afraid to couch their political action in terms of the interaction between the players. These terms were not abstract; rather, they referred to the people behind the action. They chose to diminish the political struggle and to emphasize instead the possible dialogue between the rival Jewish sides. Thus, the traditional rivalry between those who believe in the Greater Land of Israel and those willing to give it all back for peace became mere appearance and the shared human values were underscored—the hunger and cold, and the presence of both parties in the occupied territories—soldiers, government officials, and citizen-residents.

The Sensibility of Women's Irrationality

Women are often described as acting instinctively and emotionally. Rationality and sensible thought are reserved for masculine action (Harding 1986; Ortner 1974). The women of Rachelim employed this convention for the express purpose of deconstructing it. They were proud to describe their action as motivated by a bundle of feminine (motherly) emotions, free of the institutionalized and abstract thought of the dominant male group. They described their action, however, as spontaneous, as the only possible path of rational action, and therefore blurred the accepted distinction between the rational (masculine) and the irrational (feminine).

In the November 1991 issue of *Nekuda*, Emuna Elon's article stressed the spontaneity of the act of founding Rachelim by referring to a tale from the Midrash (a major corpus of biblical explication) known to every orthodox girl and boy. The tale attributes the Hebrew people's delivery from bondage in Egypt to the initiative of the Hebrew women, who were pious and righteous. Pharaoh, king of Egypt, sentenced all the newborn Hebrew males to death—a decree, the Midrash intimates, that caused celibacy among the men. The Hebrew women, nevertheless, went out to the fields, seduced the men working there, and became pregnant. They hid from the Egyptians, bore their infants alone like the beasts of the field, and hid their babies. God helped the women's initiative with miracles that provided them with the food and shelter necessary to raise their children. These "madwomen" were the progenitors of the next generation, which was responsible for Israel's salvation and exodus from Egypt. These "madwomen" combined their powers of seduction and drive for pregnancy and childbearing with the feminine optimism that sees raising children as feasible under any circumstances. The men, on the other hand, were fearful, obeyed authority, and tried to act rationally.

Elon compared the settlers' wives to these Hebrew women in Egypt. Today's men, she claimed, were once radicals under the Labor government in the mid-1970s but became part of the establishment when the Likud Party, which favors annexation of the territories to Israel, came to power in 1977. Today the men fill official positions and work to further their objectives through accepted conventional channels, while the women do not feel constrained by the establishment and are free to act as "madwomen." This is no time for "rational" conduct, said Elon. "It is an emergency—a time for 'mad' action" (1991, 44) to continue the previous policy of Jewish settlement of the West Bank despite the political changes and the Intifada. The women realize this and will be the ones to jar the system, carrying both men and women in their wake. A seemingly irrational act, according to Elon, has become a necessary and logical strategy: women can accomplish what the dominant but immobilized men cannot permit themselves to do. The article described the motherly practice itself as madness: "One hand stirs the soup, the other bandages a scraped knee, the third holds the telephone and the fourth turns up the volume on the radio to catch the news" (45). According to Elon, women with four hands can do anything.

In the past, these women were in no hurry to free themselves from the group's policy. They progressed in step with the men, following their vision and distinguishing themselves at the tasks the men vacated for them (Aran 1991). This active involvement did not prevent Elon from saying, "We've been wasting our time. Giving birth and making homes isn't enough. The feminine voice (in Hebrew, *Hakol Hanashi*) should have been heard in the political system too" (44). The women's voice had not been silenced previously, but its tones had been in harmony with those of the men. For several years, a woman named Daniella Weiss held the position of secretary general of Gush Emunim, and women established Eli—Mothers for Israel—an organization that mobilized support based on concern for the well-being of the children in the West Bank. Now, however, as women reflected on the past, they were intensely critical of their previous efforts: "We attended parlor meetings after the children were fed and put to bed, after we had hung the laundry and washed the dishes. We held a large assembly at a Jerusalem hall, everyone applauded the beautiful speeches and drove home. But we stayed on the dangerous roads, went on having more babies, carefully monitoring high-risk pregnancies and tending husbands with flu" (Elon 1991, 44).

Politics custom-tailored for men and the masculine fantasy of transcendence were not suited to the women's lives. In the act of founding Rachelim, their point of departure was the practical reality—acts, not words, the concrete concern for their children, which men customarily translate into ideology. They were not afraid of the kitsch or sentimentality that is attributed to motherhood. They accomplished a political appropriation with unique features that derive first and foremost from their experience, from the basic commonality that unites orthodox Jewish women—motherhood. Together with the practical concerns, they drew the suitable images of women from the Midrash about the women in Egypt. This configuration, when given historical-cultural legitimization, allowed them to come close to Western feminist experience.

The appropriation of political action by the women of Rachelim is made up of two central moves: adoption and feminization.

Adoption

The women chose to lay claim to a symbolic tract of land. It is accepted strategy in Zionist history to settle sites identified as ancient Jewish settlements and disputed lands that represent a risk to the reemerging Jewish entity. In this sense, Gush Emunim sees itself as following the pioneering Zionist line formerly dominated by the local labor movement. By the mid-1970s, Gush Emunim was appropriating Zionist politics, in both ideological and practical terms (Aran 1991). While Gush Emunim represents itself as the authentic interpreter and implementer of pioneering Zionism, the women now wished to single themselves out as bearers of a flag the men had tired of carrying. The women of Gush Emunim were doing to their men exactly what the movement as a whole had done to the Zionist pioneers before them.

Feminization

Feminist action or research may be defined as having the following characteristics: an organization based only on women; the determination of a feminine-maternal motive as the motive for acting; the description of the aim of action as treating a problem with special ramifications for children and mothers; the aspiration to create widespread identification with women and children outside the acting group; criticism of male politics; and construction of fields of feminine creativity and response (Duffy 1985; Reinharz 1992). The Rachelim event demonstrates such features. It also includes references to Israeli women outside the territories, a certain reflexivity relating to Palestinian women and left-wing Jewish women, a reinterpretation of the history of Gush Emunim, an on-site designing of feminine discourse about women and mothers, feminine media coverage, attempts to change the image of the female settler, and amplification of the feminine (Jewish and orthodox) voice in the local and national political discourse.

We Are Here Because We Have Children: The Maternal Motive

Inside the army tent on a cold rainy day, a group of women sat around a makeshift table as a small gas stove struggled to warm the area. Miri Mass, a woman of about thirty-six years, a textile artist and handicraft teacher, told us the following:

> First of all I have an obligation to my children, as all of us mothers do. I'm a mother of seven children, God be blessed, and I'm responsible for their safety. The children travel to school every day by bus, and to after-school activities

> every afternoon. They come home and ask, "Why is nothing done? Why aren't they shot? Why doesn't someone finish off those Arabs?" These are natural questions for a child to ask when he is attacked. His bus is escorted by the Israeli army and what does he see? He sees that when stones are thrown at him the soldiers either flee or do nothing. We, of course, raise him to revere the soldiers and our sons enlist in the elite army units, so what can I tell him? How should I raise him? I should also raise him not to hate Arabs, shouldn't I? And not to want to kill them, I should convey that to him too. What can I tell him? So this is my answer! I'm building a settlement. This is how to live in peace. Not by killing and war. By creating.

"Yes, but this settlement is dangerous," one of us offered. "It just increases the risks." Miri replied,

> Childbirth is also dangerous, isn't it? Have you considered that? When a woman becomes pregnant she is taking a risk. So? Do women stop having children? There are still places in the world with a 40 percent risk of infant death during labor. Do women stop having babies there? Giving birth is a huge beginning, with some amount of risk. We are the ones who know how to do that. And I'll have you know that our settlement here has given the children a lot of strength and a lot of meaning. Someone is doing something, not just sitting and waiting for the Arabs to throw stones. I can tell you stories that would set your teeth on edge about what we have gone through here in five years of Intifada. How my husband and myself with nine children (two of them friends' children) happened into a village by mistake and how the women closed in on us. Yes, yes, the women blocked the way and I could already glimpse my approaching death. I radioed the army and got no answer. Finally, there was no choice. My husband got out of the car and fired a few shots in the air. The women moved aside, the army arrived, and we were saved. And the children have come home many times through a hail of stones and I've never heard them say, "Mother, I don't want to go, I'm scared." I must think of my children and that's that.

Naomi, also one of the founders of Rachelim, was standing on the side and interrupted Miri at this point: "And have you ever thought of the Arab children? Of a child who is awakened in the middle of the night, in the cold, so they can search his house? Have you thought of him?" Miri replied, "I think of him at the humane level, of course I do. But his parents are the ones who aren't thinking of him. They should have made sure there would be no reason to search their house. Just like they take him to demonstrations and then they're surprised when he's wounded." Naomi went on to express what we, the researchers, refrained from saying: "They have no tanks or rifles to bring to demonstrations, so they bring women and children. I really respect the

Palestinian woman. Her perseverance. She knows that the one who is stronger will be the one who will stay here. I have a lot of respect and admiration for her—she acts." "And 'Women in Black'?"[7] one of us asked. Geula answered.

> Those women? They're barren. They do nothing but stand and talk. I respect their persistence but not the practical application or the attitude. They know very well how to count the Palestinian children killed in the territories but not the Jews who are killed. Why didn't they express their sorrow about the murder here? When they went to kiss Hanan Ashrawi [spokeswoman for the Palestinian delegation to the peace talks] before she left for Madrid, they could have stopped at Mrs. Rofeh's [the wife of the Jerusalemite driver killed in the incident] and offered condolences, without going out of their way. But no, that didn't occur to them.

Naomi said, "I have no problem with the Palestinian women. As a mother, I totally understand them. The problem is that their leaders and our leaders aren't doing what has to be done. So they're on the roads and we're here." Miri responded, "That's really the point. It's not the problem of feelings that I don't have for those children and those women, it's the political dispute I have with them over who should be landlord here."

This emotional identification appears to be fed by the steadfastness attributed to women, especially mothers. The Palestinian women are perceived by the women of Rachelim as their counterparts: bearers of life, caregivers, and victims of male politics. The practice of motherhood that they share includes three basic tasks: works of preservative love, nurturing for personal growth, and training for social acceptability (Ruddick 1989). These are expressed overtly by the women of Rachelim.

Works of Preservative Love

As Ruddick has written, "Preserving the lives of children is the central constitutive invariant aim of maternal practice; the commitment to achieving that aim is the constitutive maternal act" (1989, 19). The primary importance of the physical safety of children was stressed by the women of Rachelim, the Jewish women who came to visit and offer support, and newspaper articles written by women. In a lucid voice, uncamouflaged and unafraid of being accused of melodramatics, they pointed out the direct danger to the children as well as the indirect danger to them should one of their parents be injured or killed. The women described in detail incident after incident in which their own lives and those of their children were nearly lost. After five years of Intifada, there was no lack of such incidents: stones thrown at the windows of the yellow school buses carrying the settlers' children, roadblocks, and, recently, attacks with firearms.

As Hanna Dotan asked during our conversation in the tent, "What good is the lovely house I built with my own hands if I can't go outside? True, the children aren't scared, but I am very worried. Things can't go on like this." None of them raised the elementary question, "Why are we here in the first place?" Their presence in the territories required no explanation, especially in view of Israel's possible full or partial withdrawal from these territories. Holding fast to the demand for a Greater Israel, the women refrained from ideological discussions and focused on the practical matter of the children's safety. By working the maternal issue, they shelved the unbridgeable political debate between themselves and other schools of thought in Israeli society. They felt that on that issue they could garner a broad base of support. Speaking about the safety of children, they urged listeners to accept a fait accompli in which the children were there (with the government's support, of course), and their safety somehow had to be ensured.

When forced to address the ideological issue, the women of Rachelim tried to bring it in line with the questions hurled at the settlers by their opponents, and the doubts and dissent sometimes voiced among the settlers. Their answers were part of their firm belief that Israelis are duty bound to occupy and hold all parts of the historical land of Israel, that living in the territories was a risk to be taken today in the interest of securing complete safety in the future.

At this point, it is tempting to analyze the women's structured discourse with their surroundings as a play between maternal *practice* and maternal *rhetoric.* Direct concern for the children's safety requires immediate departure from the area, while the rhetoric exploits the danger surrounding the children's lives. Did the event emerge as a maternal reaction to the reality? Or was it a counterfeit maternal discourse plucked from an altogether different discourse, one of nationalism and the legitimate ownership of lands, of a messianic dream of the Greater Land of Israel—in short, the macronarrative of Gush Emunim? To discern which interpretation is appropriate to the event, the maternal narrative must be heard before it can be critiqued.

A novel element in the act of founding Rachelim was the women's lack of shame in verbalizing their fears for the safety of their children and the settlers in general. Their action, they claim, had originated in a mortal fear for the lives of their children. They introduced fear into the discourse of the settlers' community, a subject absent from the male ideological discourse and thus denied. The women's admission of fear was a source of empathy and identification. True, they did not seek the legitimization of this fear, as did the "Women in Black." They intended to eradicate it by harnessing its reverberations to the drive for increasing security.

Developing a Feminist Standpoint(?)

The fact that the women of Rachelim were not alienated from the value system in which family and maternity are central accounts for their ability to draw strength from the maternal practice. Using their maternal power, they strove to better their position in the social arena, or even control it for a while. In doing so, they somewhat paradoxically reformed (or redefined) maternal practice. The same traditional maternal motif that mobilized them was in partial contradiction to the task they had undertaken. In this sense, they may have been giving precedence to their responsibility to the new baby—the settlement. They had left their homes and had gone off and left their children, husbands, jobs, kitchens, and households. It was not a total absence. The distances are short and they could and did travel home from Rachelim in no more than one hour; yet the act of founding Rachelim, at least in its initial spontaneous stages, separated the women from their homes and routine roles.

Through these transitions between home and the camp, the women were rediscovering their practical status, by no means novel, but partially obscured by their traditional roles. They were discovering the motherhood that lies outside the glorifying discourse of family in Gush Emunim (Aran 1987; Burgansky 1977). They were experiencing the beginnings of acknowledgment of their status as fighting women capable of overcoming the guilt feelings cast at them from every direction. They enjoyed putting aside their sense of duty to husbands and children and carrying on with the task they had set themselves. As Avigail Haim of *Nekuda* reported from one of the women, "The kids are okay, the women next door are helping out, there isn't much in the fridge, but so what; it's no catastrophe" (1991, 12).

The women's settlement increasingly resembled a consciousness-raising workshop for women. With their husbands back home, at work, at the house, or at their studies and teaching, the women of Rachelim remained in the tent and came to reflect on their femininity. Through dialogue—among themselves; between themselves and the rest of the Jewish population of the territories; with the authorities, the army, the government, the media—negotiations on the subjects of their femininity, religiosity, and radical womanhood developed. Reckoning a whole rereading of the history of Gush Emunim was taking place, singling out and underlining the women's role in the success of the settling of the territories, even to the point of reducing the entire saga of the Greater Land of Israel to the women's unswerving, radical belief and devotion. In the interviews granted to journalists during the first few days, women avoided the term "feminism."[8] They replaced it, when offered, with terms including "motherhood" or "daughters of Israel." In time, however, new formulations began to appear. After hours of discussion and thought, and encouraged by the relative success they were gradually able to claim by staying put and becoming a role model for other groups, they dared to change their terminology. The following are selected quotations from Shelomo Dror's article titled "Women Settlers on the Frontier Line," which appeared in the newspaper *Hadashot* on February 2, 1992.

> [Naomi Sapir:] We didn't come here out of boredom or to rebel against conventions. We were the ones who created them in the first place. It was we who built this society.

The men need to undergo a process to make them understand that we are equal partners. Fifty percent of the settlers are women. How can anyone come and tell me to stay at home. That's absurd. The women can go out and make their own livings and ensure their own security. We came out of the kitchen long ago.

[Miri Mass:] They ask us how our action is viewed by the religious society around us, which wishes to see woman as "a helpmate" (Gen. 2:18). I answer that for me coming to Rachelim didn't mean going beyond the pale. It wasn't the act of a woman who wanted to show the men that she too can do things like this. That much is clear by now. The distance between me and my grandmother is as vast as the Middle Ages. Once, women used to walk behind the men and even hide themselves. Today it's different.

[Naomi to Miri:] I'm not crazy about all the violent action that's been taken by men recently. It lets a genie out of the bottle, and who's to guarantee that extremist elements won't jump on the bandwagon and hurl it downhill? We women don't believe in the use of force but rather in quiet protest and persuasion.

Naomi summed up the feminine thesis that motivated the act of founding Rachelim and served as a kind of ideology.

> By remaining here we express the idea that life for us in Judea and Samaria[9] is not a political demonstration, but a simple and day-to-day wish to live. We state that life goes on and that our answer to death is—life! We organized on a feminine basis because the women provide the emotional and organic justification for the entire idea of settling. As to the political authorities, some of us are of the opinion that we should make do with exerting influence on the decision-makers, while others think that we should actually be in there [in parliament]. Either way, we've wasted a lot of time and there's a lot to do.

In February 1992 the women of Rachelim, with a large number of supporters (one thousand of whom were present at the Founding Conference), founded a women's lobby. They called it the Zionist Women's Lobby, since a nonpartisan women's lobby already existed. They claimed the existing lobby worked exclusively for the advancement of women's personal status and avoided confronting social and political issues. Their lobby did not deal with women's personal status, since they maintained they were satisfied with the status assigned to them within traditional Judaism. The new organization was founded to rejuvenate the nationalist-Zionist ethos as they understood it on a foundation of women's solidarity.

At this point, the initially spontaneous activity began to take on organized aspects. The original act of the women was being formulated and distributed in pamphlets. The former government had promised the establishment of a permanent settlement at Rachelim, but the women continued their vigil in the tent for two years. Major political changes in the region prevented the site from becoming a settlement; today fewer and fewer groups of female students go there to study.

Ruddick has defined a standpoint as an "engaged vision of the world opposed and superior to dominant ways of thinking" (1989, 128). The women of Rachelim were attempting to form precisely such a vision. Again, Ruddick's definition of a feminist standpoint is "to generalize the potentiality made available to the activity of women, i.e., caring labour—to society as a whole" (132). This was what the women of Rachelim were speaking about. Still missing is an examination of how these actions and experiences, and the feminist consciousness they created, relate to political conclusions and the pursuit of peace. It remains to be seen just why all the women of Rachelim agree that there is no rightful place for Palestinian children and their mothers on the political level.

Giving Birth to a Settlement: From a Case Study to a Test Case

The Rachelim event can serve as a test case for two major theoretical concerns in feminist research.

1. The discourse about the practice of care. The essentialistic attributions rendered to this practice such as the pursuit of peace and the impact of an expressed maternal discourse on alternative ones (e.g., Chodorow 1974; Gilligan 1982; Kruse and Sowerwine 1986; Rosaldo and Lamphere 1974; Ruddick 1989).
2. The discourse about feminism and fundamentalism. There appears to be something attractive about the connection between fundamentalist radicalism and women's activism. Much has been written on this topic, especially on Middle Eastern Muslim women (e.g., El-Guindi 1981; Kandioti 1991; Macleod 1992; Moghadam 1993a, 1993b; Williams 1979).

The Practice of Care

Gush Emunim, of which the women of Rachelim form an essential part, is doing its utmost to sound a voice that has been growing progressively weaker in Israeli discourse. This voice conceives of the relations between Israel and its neighbors as a state of either war or surrender. Within this voice, the women of Rachelim were attempting to improvise a feminine chord. They sat in the tent and studied the Bible while their husbands were uprooting olive trees in Palestinian olive groves, obstructing highways, and demonstrating outside the homes of Intifada leaders with firearms in hand. The women preferred to describe their political action in a terminology of creating, giving birth, continuity, and education, which supplanted the usual vocabulary of seizing, struggling, constructing, and resisting. They claimed to have chosen a nonviolent way of remaining in the territories. The fact that they wished to depict their activities in these terms while dissociating themselves from the male choices should not be underestimated. These choices were important, even if the women were not actually changing the objectives toward which the men were striving.

There is no doubt that their variation on the theme bears a close affinity to the model of "maternal thinking" and contains many of the elements identified by Ruddick. From their point of view, the women were responding to the violent acts of the Palestinians. Had they discussed Ruddick's theory, they might have wished to employ her sentence that at times it was necessary to "refuse to judge from a distance the violent response of others to violent assault on them" (1989, 138). The women of Rachelim were contending that until now they had stood behind and beside the men. Now, in this hour of urgency, they could no longer settle for this: the time had come to stand in the place of the men, or in front of them. Disappointment in the men's spirit led them to propose a feminine alternative. Although graceful and pleasant in tone, this alternative was actually a form of feminine radicalism.

The women of Rachelim accepted as given the nationalist religious Zionist interpretation formulated in radical Jewish groups since the early 1970s. The roots of this interpretation, which is shared not only by radicals, originate far from maternal practice in totally different layers of Israeli social reality. The essence of motherhood as expressed by the women of Rachelim—of responsibility for their children's well-being, of concern for their nurturing and social training—can only be understood within the context of that interpretation. The practice and experience of care indeed form a unique discipline bearing both emotional and mental power. This is a power immanent to the practice itself, a practice that at the moment is carried out mainly by women. The hermeneutics of this practice do not take place within a domestic void. It exists within a rich and complicated cultural structure.

The full realization of the experience of motherhood would mean evacuation of the territories, or at least an acknowledgment of the contradiction between the wish to ensure the safety of one's children and the national conflict. Other women in Israel face a similar problem. A mother in Tel Aviv can also be said to be undertaking unnecessary risks in the interest of realizing a given social goal—life in an independent Jewish state. If this mother does not believe in a totally national narrative, she may experience the contradiction between her two tasks and acknowledge the fact that her life in Israel poses a continuous threat to herself and her children, as well as a threat to the Palestinians. This is a difficult and demanding but real possibility. The women of Rachelim cannot live this incessant tension, which would endanger the messianic dream of Gush Emunim. Instead of combating the danger, they cultivate a metaphor in which the risk becomes an opportunity; thus, they desired the impossible: to realize the totality of a messianic, religious, radical dream through feminist practice. Since the feminine practice triggering the event in question bears only an artificial tie to peacemaking, the very nature of this maternal practice is undermined. The sentimental peace of the women of Rachelim—which they represented as a kind of metaphor, a dream that will come true only with the coming of the Messiah—in turn presents motherhood under the same metaphor. By so doing, they are able to dodge their human/maternal responsibility for the safety of their children, or the safety of Palestinian mothers and children, and supplant it with the rival strugglers' duty to endure and win. They described Palestinian mothers and children as respected rivals with motives identical to theirs and their children's. The entire conflict between Jews and Arabs was recast by the women of Rachelim as a struggle between the mothers and children on either side. The grounds for identification become the grounds for the struggle.

The reports they stimulated in Israel's critical press took a skeptical, cynical view of their femininity, their motherhood, and their feminism. The practice itself, which drew all its strength from an authentic feminine and maternal experience, could not be expressed because it was held captive by a fundamentalist religious worldview in which peace is part of a utopian messianic discourse.

Feminism and Fundamentalism

The combination of feminism and fundamentalism carries major dilemmas. At the beginning of this essay, we noted the gap between the metanarrative of Western feminism and the Middle Eastern context. After several years of political-cultural efforts to detach the Jewish Israelis from the Orient, it is time to draw more on local experiences and decode them within their own context. Rather than going into cross-cultural comparisons, we suggest another dialogue: one between the local feminism/fundamentalism experience and the self-awareness of the group being examined. One would study a practice carried out and experienced by women in terms of whether there is a growth of reflexivity of self-awareness, of observing other groups and thinking and talking about them (and sometimes criticizing them). A growing self-awareness, a consciousness, can indicate empowerment. This parameter of self-awareness can serve as a tool for cross-cultural comparisons.

Epilogue

Feminist research drawing on the ideas of "maternal thinking" must examine the local context of each group of women. It must examine the cultural richness and diversity, the perceptions of history, and the overt and hidden social levels on which the maternal experience takes place. It is only within this context that the unique local meaning of the universal experience of care may be understood. There is no doubt that in making an effort to design a feminine solution of their own to a problem shared by the entire public, the women of Rachelim were involved in innovation and in improving their status as women; however, from the standpoint of peacemaking, there is no automatic or even evolutionary connection. This kind of connection will be possible only when women and men together create a society within which the pacifying attributes of the practice of care are freed from their particularistic, nationalistic, and glorifying meanings.

Notes

We wish to thank Judith Lorber, Daphna Israeli, Nitza Yanai, and Sarit Hellman for their helpful comments on this essay. A previous version of this essay was presented at the annual meeting of the Israeli Anthropological Association in February 1993.

1. Gush Emunim is a radical offshoot of religious Zionism associated with the teachings of Rabbi Abraham Isaac Kook the senior (d. 1935) as interpreted and taught by his son, Rabbi Yehuda Tzvi Kook (d. 1982) (Don-Yehiya 1987). This religious-political movement embodies ultra-rightist hawkish politics that focus on the "Greater Land of Israel" view that resists all efforts to dismember present-day Israel. Behind this ultra-Zionist ideology lies an original, mystical messianic theology. The combination of mystical religion and political activism puts Gush Emunim under the canopy of fundamentalism (Aran 1991).
2. Rachelim is a Hebrew plural of Rachel. Interestingly, it is a masculine form of the plural. *Rachelot* would be the feminine form.
3. We obtained this quotation and others in the essay through interviews conducted between November 1991 and June 1992. El-Or interviewed the women and Aran interviewed some of their husbands.
4. Even today, most orthodox women do not study Talmud, the major Jewish corpus that informs and determines the substance of religious life. They do, however, study the Bible, biblical exegesis, Mishnah, and works of Jewish philosophy and moral philosophy.
5. Women's appearance has become a major issue when they become visible as political actors. The women of Greenham Common, for example, received fairly extensive coverage in the British press. But Ruth Walesgrove (1984, 21) points out that all the papers focused on the women's looks. They mocked their vulgar, sloppy, and dirty appearance, described the mud around their tents and caravans, and doubted their feminine sexuality. Gabriel's (1992) work on "Women in Black" addresses the same issue (see note 7).
6. Both men and women in Gush Emunim show a warm, hospitable attitude toward the soldiers because of their positive attitude toward the army, which they see as "the army of God." It carries a different meaning when done by women in the traditional context of domesticity.
7. "Women in Black" are Israeli women who maintain a peace vigil every Friday afternoon at several major intersections throughout Israel. Initiated as a result of the Intifada in 1988 by former activists in other peace movements, they wear black and carry placards reading "Stop the Occupation." Some women base their motivation for peace on their maternity. Passersby mock and curse them and tell them to go home and prepare the Sabbath and take care of their kids. One time one of them answered, "I am here taking care of my child" (Gabriel 1992, 320). Gabriel points out that these women stand quietly, passively, while the counterdemonstrations and onlookers are noisy. The women of Rachelim hold this against them and claim, "They do nothing, they are barren."
8. Israeli-born women hesitate to refer to themselves as feminists. Because of the Socialist-Zionist ideology that offered equality and because of their reluctance to associate themselves with the Anglo-Saxon aura attached to the feminist movement, they tend (or perhaps tended) to overlook the discrimination against women and deny its political aspects (Izraeli 1991; Swirski and Safir 1991).
9. The settlers insist on calling the West Bank "Judea and Samaria" to stress its Jewish past and present. Other Israelis use designations like "the bank" (*hagada*) or "the territories" (*hastachim*). People on the political left refer to it as the "occupied territories."

IV

Accommodating Palestinians

The longstanding tragic conflict between Jewish and Palestinian nationalisms is reflected in every facet of their daily life. Both contesting parties are aware that they are bound to live in the same country and to constitute one economy, and this both exacerbates the conflict and results in many forms of cooperation. It is not surprising, then, that the Jewish-Palestinian conflict has been studied from many different angles. The chapters in this part discuss various aspects of the confrontation between the two peoples, such as personal and collective patterns of adaptation and state mechanisms of oppression.

The political conflict concerning the occupation of Palestinian territories by the Israeli army is expressed in the behavior of the individual soldiers. Eyal Ben-Ari describes strategies of personal transformation used by Jewish men who reject the Israeli occupation when they have to face Palestinian civilians as soldiers. Whatever their political opinions as citizens, during their military service they adopt different norms. Dan Rabinowitz discusses daily situations that entail both risk and trust in a mixed city of Arabs and Jews. It seems that ethnic distinctions are overcome by trust where professional and personal interactions are concerned. Shulamit Carmi and Henry Rosenfeld analyze the role of the state economy in widening the gaps between Arabs and Jews. Susan Slyomovics discusses the narratives of Palestinians and Jews in the village of Ein Houd, now settled by Jewish artists. The former Palestinian inhabitants were expelled from their homes and "temporarily" reside in a nearby village that has only very recently been recognized by the state. While the artists indulge in humanistic ideologies of peaceful coexistence with Arabs, they conveniently forget the past and ignore their neighbors. The chapter illustrates a common phenomenon: Israeli Jews tend to deny the circumstances of Israel's establishment and its impact on the Arab population. Aref Abu-Rabia shows that childbirth customs reflect the Negev Bedouin's social world, including the expropriation of their land and their concern with pastoralism. Israel Drori studies a garment workshop that employs local women in an Arab village in

Israel. He discusses the contradictions in the role of the female Arab departmental supervisors who mediate between local cultural traditions and the economic considerations motivating the male Jewish managers. The chapter demonstrates how globalization threatens the wages of the local female workers, who are in constant fear of losing their workplace. Soon after the events described in the chapter, the firm was moved to Jordan and the workers were dismissed. Emanuel Marx describes the often unexpected results of the protracted negotiations over land between Negev Bedouin and the Israeli authorities. The State of Israel owns 93 percent of the land, much of it expropriated from Arab owners. The expropriation continues in the Negev, where Bedouin owned or used large areas of land.

17

Masks and Soldiering

The Israeli Army and the Palestinian Uprising

EYAL BEN-ARI

Personal Circumstances, General Questions

I write like a soldier
alienated from any political awareness,
and the feelings alternating during this guard shift
are wary of looking at each other.
—Z. Sternfeld, "Intifada Diary," 1988

From mid-April to mid-May of last year (1988) I served a month-long stint with my reserve unit in the Hebron area of the West Bank. During this period my battalion performed all of the "usual" activities Israel Defense Forces (IDF) units are entrusted with in the occupied territories: for example, setting up roadblocks, maintaining patrols, and carrying out arrests. A few weeks after this period of duty I helped organize a party for the unit's officers and senior NCOs (noncommissioned officers) in a Jerusalem night club. Such parties—which take place in civilian establishments—are held not infrequently by many of the army's reserve units. This gathering—which was attended by wives and girlfriends—was not held in order to conclude the period in Hebron but as a farewell party to two officers who were leaving the battalion. Having come back deeply troubled by what I saw and felt in Hebron I think that I expected the party to provide an opportunity for us to discuss, to raise questions, or at the very least to hint at what this particular period of duty (our first during the Intifada, the uprising) had "done" or meant to us as soldiers, as human beings. In short, I expected the party—set apart from the period of active duty in terms of space, time, and rules of behavior—to provide an occasion for reflection. The hints, the questions, let alone the full-blown discussions that I had half-hoped would be heard, were not raised at all.

The curious combination of troubled citizen and anthropologist that has guided me in the last four years when looking at my society questioned why this was so. Part of the answer lies, I soon realized, in the character of such periodic parties as opportunities for celebrating the solidarity and essential unity of a combat unit. This was not a suitable occasion, I further understood, for raising potentially divisive issues, or for openly acknowledging the personal difficulties many of us had endured during the period of time spent in the territories occupied by Israel.

Beyond such answers, however, I kept on wondering. I continued to be troubled, to be disturbed by wider issues that I would like to discuss here: how do army reservists interrelate and reconcile their experiences of serving in the territories during the Intifada (the Palestinian uprising) with those of living their "normal" everyday Israeli lives? To be sure, Israeli forces have carried out similar "missions" associated with the occupation of the territories (the West Bank and Gaza) long before the uprising (see, e.g., Lieblich 1987, 322; Zucker et al. 1983). But as it sometimes happens when one is thrust into an extreme situation, one can begin to examine and illuminate many features that are ordinarily rendered invisible by the "normality" of this same situation. So it is with the Intifada. The uprising raises the following question: how do people perform—within the context of their army service, and for its duration—acts that are totally different from and in direct contradiction to the way in which they behave while they are civilians?

On one level this question is a psychological or social psychological one.[1] Here one may well ask what are the mechanisms or techniques by which people who see themselves as members of a "normal" democratic society use to cope with their participation in policing activities within another society that is governed by different rules and expectations: the ways, to put this by way of example, in which reservists contend with their participation in such activities as daytime and nighttime arrests, dispersal of demonstrations, or forcing "local inhabitants" (always Palestinian Arabs) to clear away roadblocks.

Yet this question is not limited to the realm of psychology or social psychology. It also involves issues that have to do with army service as the enactment of meanings. What I am proposing, in other words, is the need to view service in Israel's army reserves from what is perhaps a novel perspective: that is, as an activity through which different meaning systems are produced and reproduced. More specifically, I will attempt in this analysis to situate some of the more individual-centered mechanisms and small-group dynamics by which reservists cope with their tours of duty during the uprising within three wider processes: the construction of (male) identities through military service, the transition between civilian and army lives, and the workings of the interpretive schemes that underlie military activities.

Before moving on to the analysis I should, perhaps, outline the limits of the present argument. What follows is based on the impressions and observations of a deeply troubled participant. While I am by profession an anthropologist I did not carry out a piece of systematic fieldwork while in Hebron, nor did I envisage a systematic analysis of the situation while there. Along these lines, my discussion is based primarily on my own experience during the early stage of the uprising, on a small number of interviews I conducted with some of the battalion's officers, and on a review of many articles from popular journals and newspapers that have been devoted to the subject.

The Battalion

Let me begin with a short description of the army unit to which I have belonged during the last five or so years. The battalion is part of one of the army's elite infantry brigades: it is distinguished, to put this by way of that combination of abstraction and preciseness characterizes military parlance, by a high level of readiness and combat effectiveness. Yet it is an organization that is made up exclusively of reservists, of *miluim-nicks* (literally, people who fill in the gap). These soldiers and officers volunteered for one of the "crack" infantry forces[2] during their compulsory term of service and upon completion of that term (usually three years) were assigned to our unit. By law every man who has completed compulsory service can be mobilized (until the age of fifty-five) for a yearly stint of up to forty-two days.[3] In reality units like our battalion are usually called up at least twice a year and for longer periods. As in other parts of the army (Gal 1986, 40), the burden shouldered by officers and senior NCOs is considerably greater than that of lower-ranking soldiers. The former are continuously involved in such matters as briefings, staff meetings, additional training, or tactical tours.

Like many reserve units in the army, the general atmosphere in the battalion tends toward the informal and the familiar. A close relationship and understanding holds officers and other ranks together. Rank is not emphasized and everyone (including the unit's commander) is called by his first name (or equivalent nickname). All of us serve under similar conditions: the same beds and barracks, the same food and canteen services, similar clothes and equipment, and approximately the same kind of furloughs. The battalion is, to borrow a term often used in the IDF, an "organic unit" (*yechida organit*). Organizationally this implies a framework characterized by a permanent membership and structure of roles, and that upon mobilization the whole battalion (as one complete organizational unit) is recruited. "Socially" this term implies a military force characterized by camaraderie, a high level of cohesion, well-developed primary groups, and, no less important, a sense of a shared past. Let me give a few examples.

Like the "buddy system" found in the American and Canadian armies (Kellett 1982, 99; Moskos 1975) or the "comradeship" found in the British forces (Richardson 1978, ch. 2), so too the battalion is made up of a number of close groupings that often developed over the course of a number of years. This is clearly evident in the happy renewal of friendships that goes on at the beginning of each tour of duty. Yet it is also apparent in the attachment of nicknames used only during *miluim*, the emergence of "characters" within the battalion's subunits (e.g., the company clown or the platoon's "expressive" leader), or the knowledge many men have of each other's personal lives and interests. Many of the quieter periods during reserve duty are devoted to the recollection and creation of shared experiences: the war of 1973 for a few of the remaining older soldiers, the war in Lebanon, skirmishes with terrorists, or the hardships of training endured during previous stints of duty. On other occasions parties and picnics are held either on the last day of duty or upon a return to civilian life (with people's families). It is during these occasions that the solidarity of the force is celebrated and what the British term "regimental spirit" is displayed and subtly honored.

Every year on the morning of Remembrance Day many soldiers and officers join the unit's veterans to gather at the battalion's memorial site. This site—which is situated in one of the hills surrounding Jerusalem—was built to honor the battalion's dead from the 1973 Yom Kippur War. During the short ceremony prayers and songs are sung, flowers are placed next to the small memorial tablets, very brief speeches are given, and again people meet, renew acquaintanceships, and share memories. Some of us would later proceed to other military cemeteries across the country to join smaller family services for men who had been killed in the previous few years.

And myself? During reserve duty I become an army bureaucrat. I am the battalion's adjutant (*shalish*)—a staff officer—and hold the rank of captain. With the exception of a brief period during my compulsory term of service, I have been in such a noncombatant support role in frontline units for almost all of my military career. My responsibilities are varied and include such matters as helping the battalion's commander issue orders, mobilizing and demobilizing the whole unit, and dealing with personnel issues (soldiers who have gone AWOL, promotions, and so forth). I have been with the battalion since returning from four years of study abroad and volunteering—upon my return—for service in a frontline unit.

Preparing for Hebron

Nails and nails,
rust and rust at their edges
and a long wooden handle
intended to pierce
the flesh of our faces,
to pluck.
Our women,
pluck their eyebrows.

—Z. Sternfeld, "Intifada Diary," 1988

While being inducted a day or two before moving to the Hebron area, the special role we were to carry out in relation to the Intifada became clear: we were ordered to become policemen. This was evident first of all in the nonstandard gear that was issued: rifles for shooting canisters of tear gas, special helmets, visors, and shields (for protection against rocks), clubs (which were, by order of the battalion's commander, later left unused in the barracks), and implements mounted on standard rifles for shooting rubber bullets (one of those unique technological innovations that military industries continually take pride in). Next the terms used during the preparatory briefings belonged to the world of policemen (see, e.g., A. Reiss 1971, xiii): search and seizure, stop and frisk, squelching disturbances, maintaining order and quiet. Finally, overlaying all of this was a heavy emphasis on the legal aspects of our activity. We were reminded that the "objects" of our activity were civilians, that all of the activities undertaken by the battalion's soldiers had to be properly (i.e., lawfully) "covered" by regulations, that the right forms (for evidence and complaints) had to be filled out at local police stations, and that all of this be done under the supervision of suitably authorized officers.

Yet this was not a smooth process. During these first few days the usual gripes about army life (or more specifically about the transition to army life) were compounded by new complaints centering precisely on our new role: army soldiers, most of the arguments went, were being taken to do police work. We were being turned from soldiers into policemen. The army, as the more sophisticated soldiers put it, is an organization entrusted with training and preparing for an attack by the forces of an external enemy. Here we were being ordered to become a policing force charged with enforcing law and order. The complaints, while not questioning the deeper issues of Israel's presence in the occupied territories, nevertheless well underscored the basic unease that many soldiers felt at having to be deployed in one of the major urban centers of the West Bank.

This unease must be understood against the backdrop of how the uprising was perceived by many, if not most, of the unit's soldiers and officers. The picture we had received of the uprising through the mass media had been one of mass demonstrations, concentrated rock throwing and tire burning, and the constant use of Molotov cocktails. This situation led, of course, to the emergence of anxieties and apprehensions at being mobilized in order to deal with these expressions of Palestinian anger and frustration. In one of the interviews I held with the unit's officers, a young commander recalled, "It looked as though the uprising was very, very violent, very, very difficult. That's what was shown on television. And I expected it to be very hard, that we were going to war. It was not a matter of routine. And I came with a lot of apprehensions about how one deals with these circumstances."

Compounding such anxieties were the interpretations many men gave to the Intifada in terms of their experience of the war in Lebanon.[4] A number of men thus related to me how the uprising in the West Bank had raised recollections, triggered associations of the lawlessness and utter chaos they had encountered in Lebanon. Having been away doing a Ph.D. in England and fieldwork in

Japan during Israel's Lebanese debacle, I was spared these kinds of associations. For me, however, the thought of serving in Hebron during the Intifada raised memories and fears I had thought forgotten. I found myself transported back to the Yom Kippur War of 1973, when as a nineteen-year-old infantry soldier I was wounded by an Egyptian sniper and taken out of action for a number of weeks. The uprising had thus "succeeded" in jarring me: jarring me to the extent of experiencing anew at least some of the fears I had felt during that war.

Two soldiers refused to go to Hebron on moral grounds. Some effort was made—and this is no doubt a reflection of the fact that the battalion was an "organic unit"—to persuade them to come with us. They were given assurances, for example, that they would not be put in situations where contact with the "local population" was inevitable, or that their duties would be limited to guarding strictly military installations. When they stood by their decision both were sent to be court-martialed by the commander of the brigade. Both soldiers received a sentence of one month in jail. The treatment they received after being sentenced also reflects the atmosphere of our unit. As their trial was held late in the evening, and as they could be sent to the military prison only on the following day, both men were sent back to their companies. They spent that night, in other words, with their "buddies" and friends. The general attitude toward these soldiers was not one of censure or banishment. Rather, it was a mix of respect for their ability to stand by their beliefs and a feeling that they were somehow misguided. Indeed, later when we were in Hebron, a number of their friends telephoned their families to find out how they were doing in prison. Others approached me for news about them (being formally in charge of discipline in the battalion I had asked for information about the two men from the brigade's adjutant, who had visited them). In mid-April, four months after the beginning of the uprising, we moved into Hebron.

Masks and Disguises

Though the boys throw stones at frogs in sport,
yet the frogs do not die in sport but in earnest.
—Plutarch, quoted in Fine 1988, 43

Soft people
prefer to stay at the observation post
Uri with the diamond earring.
He is the first casualty of the uprising;
I hit him with the communications gadget
(bleeding in his right eyebrow).
Does not react—
One shouldn't give pleasure to the locals.
Uri has a soft voice

and an English accent.
He tells with a smile
how he was Charles Bronson;
Kicked the doors of night.
—Z. Sternfeld, "Intifada Diary," 1988

In attempting to understand my battalion's experience during our stint in Hebron, let me suggest a somewhat unconventional viewpoint in regard to reserve duty in general, and then relate it to the case of the uprising. Essentially the argument is the rather obvious one that going into *miluim* involves entering a special behavioral frame (Bateson 1972b; Handelman 1977a) that is governed by rules different from (and even contradicting) those of civilian life.[5] What is less apparent, however, are the peculiar patternings of and assumptions that lie behind these rules. Let me try and make this clear by way of a metaphor some of my army friends use to characterize their induction into *miluim*. Many soldiers refer to the wearing of uniforms on the first day of reserve duty as the donning of disguises, as the bearing of masks. What I would suggest is that this metaphor illuminates how the transition to soldier involves more than a "mere" transition to a new social role and its attendant norms and expectations. This is because the use of masks or disguises involves a special potential for behavior that is at one and the same time normatively different from civilian life and in a special sense also non-normative.

As Honigmann (1977, 275) has shown, masquerades are often special means that facilitate a temporary separation between the personal identity of the "users" and the behavior that is being enacted. For the duration of their performances, the disguised are in a position to express hostility with impunity because they are "not themselves" (Honigmann 1977, 272; Walter 1969, 83). Along these lines, I would suggest that for the limited period of *miluim* the reservists cease to be the normally identified, circumscribed, constrained members of Israeli society who must be concerned with how they are regarded by themselves and by others. On one level these circumstances work toward allowing many reservists to display "irregular" public behavior like cursing and swearing, belching and farting, urinating and spitting, or talking dirty. This situation also allows many men to freely exhibit the "macho" dimensions of their army character. This point is readily evident in regard both to nonverbal behavior—posturing, hunching of shoulders, excessive preoccupation with guns and equipment—and verbal behavior—free use of the imperative, barking words in a forceful manner, the abandonment of politeness forms.

On another level, however, the disguises donned during reserve duty have had a number of implications for the way in which relations with local Palestinians have taken shape during the uprising. One prime example, noted by many people in my battalion, is how the special circumstances in Hebron allowed them to play with relatively few restraints. Some talked of chasing rock throwers as games of "hide-and-seek" or of "catch-as-catch-can." Others characterized these games as battles of wit in which each side attempts to outfox the other. One man's observations evoke Czikszentmihalyi's (1975) characterization of the "flow" element in play: "Many times it's like a game. A game of learning how to deal with it. There is a certain problem and you have to give a solution. You—I think—cut yourself off from all sorts of thought about what you're doing, and how and what's happening here. It's a game like a crossword puzzle, of technique, of how you deal with a problem." Another example was provided by the commanders of one company in developing what in their words was a game of "bingo." At the roadblocks they manned, they looked for license plates of "hot" cars: not stolen vehicles but those owned by suspects wanted by the General Security Service.

On yet another level, the use of disguises and masks has, to state the obvious, very serious and direct implications. A company commander's words: "From what I saw many of the locals there also thought of us as partners in a sort of game until something happened, someone got hit or something like that." Here the argument is that use of masks and disguises provides at least some reservists with a legitimate license to behave in ways that they would not normally—that is, within the bounds of their everyday civilian life—associate with themselves.[6] One example (about which I sensed quite a bit of unease among a number of officers and soldiers) were nighttime arrests. These forays into Hebron's urban neighborhoods or the city's adjoining villages often consisted of a similar pattern of actions: knocking on the door in the middle of the night, seizing the suspects against a background of crying women and children, handcuffing them with plastic handcuffs, blindfolding them, and then moving them out to detention centers for questioning by the General Security Service. Other, perhaps less extreme but no less serious, instances of the special kinds of behavior that I witnessed were purposely making people wait for hours in the hot sun until given permission to proceed beyond army roadblocks or, when riding army vehicles, contravening local traffic rules (going up one-way streets, or expecting a line of cars standing at a traffic light to let one through).[7]

When conceived in these terms the dynamics of military service within the context of the uprising may be better understood. Thus, reservists during their stint of duty are temporarily not themselves but people placed in special circumstances that in themselves may allow (or, more forcefully, demand) a certain type of behavior.[8] Indeed, this kind of explanation is one that is often found at the end of the account many reservists give in regard to their stints of duty in the territories: highly delimited—spatially as well as temporally—episodes during which they become an-other person (a certain "other" to themselves).[9]

A Benign Occupation?

In the beginning there was fear,
the heart beat hard.
Then came black anger,

like a cloud of black smoke rising—
and their hate clung to us.
I raised my hand to strike,
I saw nothing—
until my club of anger grew heavy.
I stood in disbelief
staring through my tears
at the empty hand now strange,
at the hand that beat, until hate was quenched—
and at the blood that clung to my hand.
—A. Arzi, "A Cloud of Smoke," 1988

This kind of explanation—of becoming an-other person in the army—may well illuminate the type of behavior found in a large number of specific situations in which soldiers find themselves. At the same time, however, it tends to deproblematicize the actual act of disguise as well as the continuing need at least some soldiers feel to somehow relate their "masked" behavior (and the behavior of their comrades) to their identity as ordinary Israeli citizens. Two examples related to the Intifada and through that to one of Israel's most durable oxymorons—the attempt to manage a "benign occupation" in the territories—may bring this point out.

The first example is a personal one. One day I was asked to take a Palestinian arrested that morning to brigade headquarters some four kilometers away. Before asking the man to get on the vehicle I was driving, I allowed the soldier accompanying him to take off his blindfold and the plastic handcuff on his hands, and to let him urinate. The Palestinian managed a short, tear-choked thank you in Hebrew. The second instance was related to me by one of the battalion's clerks (a soldier I am directly responsible for). He was ordered to accompany a busload of detainees to the nearby military prison. According to his story, as the detained men were let off the bus one of the prison guards asked him, "How many pieces (*chatichot*) have you brought today?" When he replied that they were human beings and not things, the guard was struck temporarily dumb, only to retort some minutes later with, "Are you some kind of leftist or something?" Both instances—and they can be multiplied many times over—exemplify two interrelated processes that form part of masked behavior. On the one hand they represent a process Lifton (1973, 206–7) terms resensitization: that is, a situation in which despite encounters with an enemy in stereotypic terms (or as an object), they are nevertheless turned into individual people. On the other hand the two examples illustrate one of the prime paradoxes of behavior in disguise: despite the disjointedness of identity engendered by the use of masquerades, one always remains (albeit to a limited extent) a human being. Hence the need I felt—and according to their testimony many other soldiers feel as well—to account for our actions in terms of somehow humanizing the occupation, of somehow presenting a more humane face to the occupying force.

There are yet other mechanisms, techniques of neutralization (Sykes and Matza 1957), that individual reservists employ to deal with the situation in the territories: repressing memories associated with *miluim,* playing down the seriousness of their behavior, or isolating their experience (stating that army and civilian "lives" are essentially unrelated). Another coping strategy has been characterized by Stanley Cohen (1988, 61) as a sort of ritual incantation: people believe and account for their actions in terms of their forming part of the military effort to "restore law and order until a political settlement is reached."

For all this, however, while these kinds of explanations well illuminate the problematic nature of disguised behavior, and highlight the type of accounts people (myself included) mobilize to deal with the contradiction built into service in the territories, they still do not suffice. This is because, as I will presently show, they still fall short of explicating the way these mechanisms that operate on the individual or small-group levels are enveloped within wider processes of the production and reproduction of meaning in the army. This may be understood through referring again to my battalion's experience in Hebron.

Clean Work

As I described before, our movement into the city and its environs also signaled a movement into the role of policemen (and all that this role entails in terms of tasks, equipment, and legal terminology). What happened, however, was that in the space of a few short days everyone—officers and soldiers—reverted to the typical mode of military thinking and perception that Hasdai (1982) has called the "doer" (*bitsuist*) orientation.[10]

This development was reflected, in the first place, in the kinds of terms people used. Terms like *nikui shetach* ("clean up" or "mop up") were in constant use: clean up this village or mop up that street or avenue. This expression, which is usually used in times of war or skirmishes to refer to the elimination of pockets of enemy resistance in a given area, was now used with regard to clearing away "civilian" (i.e., Palestinian) roadblocks, stones, tires, PLO flags, and demonstrators. Other military terms that crept into use included not only the usual array of army acronyms or the expressions officially designated by the signals corps, but also such words as deployment (*prisa*), breakthrough (*pritza*) into houses, raids (*peshita*), and parallel uses of forces (*avoda bemakbil*).

What is perhaps of greater significance from the point of view of the present argument, however, was not only that the usual terms and perceptions used within the context of the army were infused into the policing activities of Hebron and its environs. What is of greater importance was that after a few days in the *shetach* (which is the way army men refer to the field), the criteria by which officers, single patrols, companies, or the whole battalion itself were appraised were the type of standards that are used with regard to regular army tasks (whether in times of war or along the country's borders during those misnamed periods of peacetime). Thus, for example, one set of criteria that was utilized time and again in evaluating how a certain unit carried out its mission was whether it had done "clean work" (*avodah nekiya*): that is, operated with minimal damage to "our" forces, efficiency, smooth execution, and no delays in the designated timetable.

Two excerpts from the interviews I conducted may well illuminate this point. One young officer who had joined our unit two or three years prior to this time put it in the following terms: "When you're there and you've got a goal—that everything will run smoothly (*yidfok*) like the army wants it to run—then it really becomes a personal matter. There has to be a solution to a problem and I have to find it immediately."

Another officer—one of the company commanders—told me how they had entered a village and given chase to hundreds of people who had subjected them to a barrage of rocks: "It worked really well, and from this aspect I was satisfied, from my point of view as company commander and how the people functioned (*tifkedu*) in situations where they were put under pressure."[11]

A related set of criteria revolved around the success of the commanders of a unit in exploiting the stint in Hebron in order to "solidify" or "crystallize" the unit (*gibush yechidati*) (see Katriel 1986, 30–31). This refers to the success of officers in fostering a sense of solidarity among their soldiers and their channeling of this solidarity to the practicalities of coordination between soldiers, smooth intra-unit communication of orders, or mutual help between its members. To reiterate, these are the type of standards that are usually applied to army units that carry out "regular" military missions: border patrols, incursions into enemy territory, and combat missions.[12]

The use of these criteria is summarized in the words of a company commander from the paratroopers (a unit very similar to ours) who was asked in a newspaper interview about his experience in the territories (*Kol Ha'ir,* February 10, 1989): "We came out better soldiers than when we went in because we saw it as a military mission. Individual soldiering, the movement of the whole company, and our familiarity with combat in built-up areas all rose to a higher level."

Military Culture

What does all of this imply? Here again I would suggest looking at the army experience from a rather unconventional viewpoint: that is, viewing army life as organizational culture, as the enactment of certain meanings. When viewed from such a perspective, I would argue, the developments I have described are evidence of a process of "naturalization" (Dolgin, Kemnitzer, and Schneider 1977, 39) that the battalion underwent during the first week or two in Hebron. In a word, given the organizational structure and rules through which the battalion operated, and given the criteria and terms through which the environment and the unit's activities within it were appraised, it is only "natural" that the uprising began to be perceived through an essentially military (as opposed to police) orientation.

The unit's reality constructors (Morgan 1986, 132), such as the officers and NCOs, because of their conceptions of "what we are" and "what we are trying to do," established points of reference that "properly" belong to the domain of the military. The argument, then, is that the interpretive schemes suited to "ordinary" army contexts formed the framework for understanding (and acting on) the new circumstances of the Intifada: that is, to a situation in which the army is in heightened contact with civilian populations and has to react to types of resistance it is not trained to deal with such as stone throwing, flag raising, demonstrating, burning tires, and using Molotov cocktails.

Yet this is not just a simple shift from an emphasis on policing to one that has to do with the tactics of military warfare. The shift is much more subtle and has to do with the nature of the IDF as a certain kind of army. The Israeli army, like many other modern military forces, is guided by a very strong managerial ideology.[13] As Feld (1977, 52–53; see also Lang 1972, ch. 2) notes, the commanders of modern armies are often guided by a desire to gain the maximum utility from the machines and manpower at their disposal and inclined to employ these items according to the prevalent managerial standards rather than force them into the mold of military code and traditions.

Along these lines, it may be better understood how my battalion's commanders—and I would argue that this holds for many other reserve units as well—came to define and react to various problems posed by the uprising not only in military terms but in the special terms of military technology and organization. To borrow from Lifton's (1973, 65) remarks about another situation, the problems posed by Palestinian resistance came to be seen as problems to be solved by the application of the right technique, the proper know-how.[14] In this way the recourse to military interpretive schemes allowed for a redefinition of some of the personal (or ethical) problems involved in serving in the territories into questions of an essentially professional military nature. In a word, moral misgivings were, in effect, displaced onto an organizational plane. An analysis of the types of self-reflection that are encouraged in these circumstances may make this point clearer.

Continuities in Identity

Let us begin by way of the kind of reflection that is promoted within the context of the army itself. Here what is evident is that the process of "militarization" of the Intifada operates to channel away any basic questioning of the situation. By allowing, indeed even actively encouraging, field commanders to reflect on and consider such tactical issues as deployment, the efficient use of manpower, and other resources, or "creative" reactions to local action, there is a diffusion of reflexivity on a deeper level: the level of basics such as Israeli presence in the territories or the impact of this presence on Israeli society. In other words, the promotion of reflection about "role performance"—a reflection that is consistent with other facets of Israeli male identities—tends to reduce consideration of the basic legitimacy of this role.

The diffusion of a more penetrating self-analysis is reinforced by two further points. The first has to do with the fact that despite the events of the last decade—especially the war in Lebanon—for most Israeli men participation in the army is still considered to be a reward in itself. As Horowitz and Kimmerling note, such "participation defines the extent to which an individual is in the 'social-evaluative' system of Israel" (1974, 265). Any acute self-reflection engendered by service during the uprising then by definition touches on the right of reservists to be part of this system of evaluation. It may disrupt, given the tendency of military identity to be a central component of Israeli male identity (Lieblich 1987, 11), their conception of themselves as Israelis.

At the same time this situation is intensified in the case of "organic units." In units like my battalion the close primary-group ties and the "spirit" of the unit also work to channel away a self-reflection that may touch on the deeper problems of the Intifada. In other words, because soldiers and officers evaluate themselves and are evaluated within the context of tight groups of important others, self-analysis may come "dangerously" close to questioning the feelings of belonging and solidarity, the sentiments of pride and unity of purpose, and the common experiences and ideals represented by the unit.[15]

Against the background I have just traced out it may now be clearer how some reservists may return to their ordinary, everyday existence and account for their period of duty in terms of another—perhaps slightly more difficult but nevertheless just another—stint of *miluim*. What are thus experienced upon a return to noncombatant life—and it is just this meaning of civilian that takes precedence in this context—are certain sentiments of empathy with the "locals" and astonishment at one's actions, but also very deeply felt emotions of pride at army missions well done, of solidarity with one's comrades, and of sharing with them another military experience. The observations of a company commander from the paratroopers that I quoted before bring this out (*Kol Ha'ir*, February 2, 1989): "I have no doubt that against force you have to react with force, and that the missions defined for the army are legitimate. At the same time you see that the local population are suffering . . . and I did these things. As a soldier I am at peace with myself regarding my actions. As a human being I am not at peace with myself."

At the Edge of My Society

Stones and pebbles cannot be tamed,
until the end they look at us with very quiet,
very clear eyes.
—based on Z. Herbert, *Poems*, 1984

When a colleague and friend read an earlier version of this essay he observed that permeating my whole analysis is a deep sense of guilt (he is an ex-therapist). Yet guilt can be a "positive" motivating force. Telling this tale—or, more precisely, relating my personal story to the more distanced analysis—has provided me with a means for confronting the experience of Hebron as well as for facing some of the deeper implications of my actions and those of my friends and comrades. This, of course, has been far from easy. I state this in no way in order to minimize the sufferings of the Palestinians or to overstress the "psychology" of the rulers at the expense of the oppressed (Bishara 1989). Rather, I believe that in order to understand the complexity of the situation one must take into account both the patterns of thought of the Israelis who are charged with managing the occupation of the territories and the process through which someone such as I begins to tell you such a tale.

Although I was rarely in direct contact with Palestinians while in Hebron, I found myself in a state of turmoil for weeks after my return: I did not sleep well, could not concentrate on my teaching and research, and was short with my children. Above all, however, I was very defensive about any criticism of the army and of the actions of soldiers in the territories. As I then only vaguely sensed and now more explicitly realize I took these criticisms and questions personally: that is, as attacks touching on my identity as an army officer and through that as an Israeli, and as assaults on my commitment to the army and by way of that to my own society.

These circumstances were made more difficult by the unfulfilled expectations many people had (myself very much included) that stints in the occupied territories during the Intifada would effect an immediate political backlash leading to mass movements for change. If anything—as my analysis tries to explain—what I witnessed at that time (a few months after the uprising's beginning) was the basic resiliency of the situation: in other words, how the application of "double standards" to behaviors within and across the Green Line could continue. It was against this backdrop that sometime in June I was asked to make a short presentation at a roundtable discussion organized at my department about the Intifada. This discussion grew out of the feeling some of us held that we should and could react to the uprising as anthropologists and sociologists (ours is a joint department). At the beginning I toyed with the idea of presenting some kind of general and of course very distanced analysis about the microeconomics of the Intifada or about its implications for territorial behavior. I sensed very quickly, however, that this just would not do and that I needed to present something that grew out of my own turmoil and as yet only vaguely defined questions. Yet this was problematic to say the least. I was one of those Israeli academics Stanley Cohen (1988, 95) talks about: most of my academic colleagues have no sense of being on the edge of their society, of seeing it from the outside. As a result, they are reluctant to take a stand that might be interpreted as "disloyal" or "unpatriotic" or (worst of all) "anti-Zionist." So, even today, they defend an idealized version of Israeli history and culture as though it were reality.

The presentation I eventually gave—a short, ten-minute talk based on some very rough notes—was trying. It was my first public attempt to divulge a deeply personal story and to analyze some of its implications, to own up to my experience and yet to subject it to the anthropological scrutiny that I apply as a matter of course to my normal subjects of research.

During the summer I spent over two months doing fieldwork in Japan. It was only at the end of this period, however, that I finally felt that I could commit my experience to writing. I had to literally travel away from my society in order to travel to its edge, to be able to look at it from an external vantage point. Yet I am still very much part of my society. These days I return home dreading to look at the mailbox: will a new mobilization order be there?

Notes

I would like to thank U. Almagor, Y. Bilu, E. Cohen, R. Gal, D. Handelman, S. Heilman, R. Kahane, B. Kimmerling, A. Levi, A. Lieblich, B. Lomsky-Feder, A. Seligman, and especially G. Aran for comments on an earlier version of this work. The Harry S. Truman Institute and the Koret Foundation granted me financial aid toward completing the manuscript. Translations of the poems from the Hebrew are my own.

1. Indeed, a number of Israeli psychologists (see, e.g., Bar-On 1988) have raised this question.
2. A description of one such force, the paratroopers, can be found in Aran 1974, 149.
3. A fuller exposition of the army reserve system can be found in Gal 1986, 38.
4. Lieblich's (1987) sensitive account of the experience of soldiers who went through the war in Lebanon brings these points out. Some of the soldiers she describes are the kind of men who, upon completion of their compulsory term of service, joined our unit.
5. See Feige (n.d.) for an analysis along these lines.
6. Sutton-Smith and Kelly-Byrne (1984, 187) point out that behavior termed "play" or "playful" may often be used as masks for other forms of behavior such as cruelty or violence.
7. Indeed under certain circumstances one may well hypothesize that the wearing of uniforms induces a certain process of deindividuation: entering a state of lessened self-awareness, reduced concern over social evaluation and weakened restraint against prohibited forms of behavior (E. Aronson 1988, 216).
8. Although very little is known about their activities I would suggest that the secret Intifada committees (the invisible Palestinian government in the territories) may be analyzed along the lines I am suggesting in regard to the Israeli army. These committees—which function, it seems, not unlike the secret societies of West Africa (Walter 1969, ch. 5)—also use masks to dissociate themselves from as well as cover their public identities as individuals. Their effectiveness, however, in contrast to the army depends on mystery, dramatic intervention, and the sudden return to invisibility.
9. This situation is not unique to the situation that I am describing. First take the following account of the Poro secret society studied by Harley: "Gbana . . . was a grand old man with pure white hair when I last saw him. He always had a kindly smile. At the height of his influence he was judge for a total of nine towns. . . . It is hard to reconcile the gory history of [his] blood stained mask with the benign clear-eyed patriarch" (Walter 1969, 85).

   Next take the example of a Vietnam veteran related by Lifton: "I came to be fascinated by my threatened life and to enjoy the immediacy of it, and yes, to hate it too and to hate myself for enjoying it. . . . I was two of myself, one human and the other inhuman. . . . At a time like that you find out what man is like" (1973, 104–5).
10. On the psychological background of this kind of mentality, see Lieblich 1983; Lieblich and Perlow 1988, 44.
11. Later on in the talk we had this same man noted how important it was to fulfill the officer's role despite any misgivings he had: "I tried to disconnect myself from the whole idea of

whether we should be there [in the territories] or not because after all as the company commander I always had to tell the soldiers that we have to do it, and we have to do it well, and with a lot of motivation."

12. A somewhat less pronounced set of criteria for appraising activity can be seen as a direct outgrowth of the fire and movement emphasis that is part of Israeli tactical doctrine (Kellett 1982, 250). These criteria had to do with the degree to which actions were created and initiated by various commanders (*pe-ulot yezumot*) rather than being reactions to the initiative of the "locals."
13. Historically, of course, many modern managerial codes were developed during the modernization of the Prussian army (Morgan 1986, 23–24).
14. Sadly, later developments bear this point out. The Israeli army has, over the course of the Intifada, attempted to deal with the situation through introducing a series of different "technical solutions": using clubs, administrative arrests, house explosions, rubber bullets, plastic bullets, special cannon for shooting glass marbles, and so on.
15. This kind of analysis brings out, I would further argue, how many soldiers, despite misgivings and doubts they may have, are "gently" swept into a situation that is "beyond their control." It is beyond their control not in the sense of their inability to direct the practical consequences of their actions, but on the deeper level of not controlling the assumptions that lie at the basis of these activities. Along these lines one implication of my discussion involves realizing how facile may the army's future moves be into "new" and, for many Israelis, unthinkable activities. If the IDF has so readily adapted to police work against Arabs, will we be witness to a relatively easy adaptation to "work" (*avoda*) against Israeli citizens—Arabs and Jews—first beyond the green line and then (within appropriate contexts) within it as well?

18

Risk, Rationality, and Trust

Israeli Responses to Palestinian Arabs in Authority Positions

DAN RABINOWITZ

Illiberal Squad

Natzerat Illit has one competitive basketball team, Hapoel Natzerat Illit (HNI). Formed in the 1970s, when it joined the bottom (fifth) division of Israel's National League, the team took a few years to be promoted to the fourth division (Liga Bet), where it competed from 1984 to 1990.[1] Affiliated with the nationwide network Hapoel, the sports arm of the Histadrut trade union federation, HNI was and still is operated and financed by the local workers' council (Moetzet Hapo'alim), the standard name for local branches of the Histadrut.[2]

The 1988–89 squad offered a fairly representative cross-section of the Israeli population of the town. The eldest player was a twenty-eight-year-old driving instructor. The youngest players were three seventeen-year-old schoolboys. There were two conscripts, a policeman, a shopkeeper, a technician, and a bank clerk. Five players were of North African origin, and seven were East European, three of whom were natives of the Soviet Union who arrived in Natzerat Illit as toddlers in the early 1970s. There were no Palestinian players on the team.

Having played for clubs in higher divisions of Israel's national league, I joined HNI soon after moving to the town. At thirty-four, I was past the zenith of whatever basketball career I may have had, and was looking mainly for a way to stay in shape. Being more or less on a par with the team in terms of ability, I was able to be an active player on the squad. Players as well as management were vaguely aware that I was engaged in a social study of the town as part of some university degree. Like me, however, they saw no link initially between my presence on the team and my investigative persona. None, in fact, seemed particularly preoccupied with the details of my research. This was unlike my experience in other arenas in Natzerat Illit, where my identity as an investigator was always paramount. More on this shortly.

Natzerat Illit is often portrayed as an island of bigotry and racism. However, I found the Israelis in Natzerat Illit to be, on the whole, as liberally minded as their compatriots elsewhere. Their unique circumstances expose the failure of liberal ideology to prescribe behavior to match ideals and principles it ostensibly stands for.

The case of HNI players, most of whom displayed stark illiberal worldviews, presents a further twist. Whereas many Israelis in Natzerat Illit are critical and apprehensive about the Palestinian presence in their town, most HNI players were also loud and clear regarding "Arabs" generally. One of the conscripts, a military policeman, was stationed as a warden at a nearby military prison, guarding Palestinian prisoners apprehended during riots in the Intifada. On one occasion, when the team was at a restaurant for lunch, he gave the rest of us a chilling and totally non-reflexive account of a riot that had taken place in the prison a few days earlier and of the measures taken to suppress it. His gleeful, gruesomely detailed anecdote included clubs and hosepipes, black eyes and blue faces, streaks of blood, broken toes, twisted fingers, and heavily breathing Palestinian prisoners. The undivided attention he was getting at the table may have pushed him to overplay the brutality of the affair. But even allowing for some exaggeration, his account was truly sickening.

Most of his audience was as sympathetic as he was proud. When one of the younger players queried whether "you guys ever show mercy," the answer was a recitation in unison by two or three of the older players to the effect that "these sons of bitches, who throw stones at our soldiers and hurl abuse at the state and the army—they deserve no mercy." Toward the end of his account two players inquired eagerly whether they could possibly visit the prison with him. They said they wanted "to take part in the action, you know. Have some fun, club some Arabs, do our bit." Astonished, I heard the interlocutor promise to check the possibility with his commanding officer.

Another player, a police sergeant, was occasionally summoned with his unit for tours of duty in Jerusalem to police the Friday prayers at the al-Aqsa mosque on Temple Mount (Haram al-Sharif). On one occasion he announced that he was going to miss an approaching training session. "We are going to Jerusalem," he explained, "to beat and blow those Arabs to bits. Show them the cost of messing with the police."

One player complained on several occasions that his family's transport business was systematically ruined by unfair competition from local Palestinians. One time he told me of his plan to move to adjacent Migdal Haemek[3] since, as he put it, "Natzerat Illit is gradually becoming an Arab town. They are allowed to come in here, rent, buy, take us over. In Migdal Haemek everybody knows: no one moves into the town without approval of the mayor. And he has said on various occasions that he is not allowing a single one of them to move in."

In December 1988 a Pan American airliner was blown up above west Scotland killing hundreds—an event known as the Lockerbie disaster. The event coincided with an initiative on the part of the United States for rapprochement with the PLO. A player on HNI, an avowed supporter of Meir Kahana's ultra-right Kach movement, had this to tell me about the affair shortly after it happened: "That's good. It will teach the Americans who Yasser Arafat really is, and that they should not deal with him. That is what the Arabs want to do to everyone. This is how they are, and this is why I don't want them here or anywhere else."[4]

These statements were admittedly made in public, in the context of a relatively young, all-male, exclusively Israeli sports team, where discursive survival hinged on lucidity. Debates, many of which took place in a minibus on the way to or from away games, tended to consist of short, bold statements, often breeding verbal extremism. In private conversations some players came across somewhat more restrained. The overall picture, however, was clear enough. HNI players, more than many others in Natzerat Illit, had definite ideas regarding Palestinians who, as far as they were concerned, were as dangerous to the state as they were detrimental to the town. At the end of the day they are out to get all Jews and Israelis, who must in turn get tough.

The Palestinian Coach

As the 1988–89 season approached,[5] HNI management began looking for a new coach who could harness the talent and ambition they believed was present in the squad and help promote the team to the third division. Financial limitations and a shortage of qualified candidates in the region narrowed the choice considerably until the team administrator, a devoted volunteer on behalf of the local workers' council, came up with a surprising choice. In August 1988, following extended negotiations, he hired Ra'id Riziq, a thirty-year-old Palestinian from a veteran Christian family in Nazareth, as team coach. Riziq, who teaches physical education in a government school in Nazareth and who had been coaching basketball for nine years, came with an impressive record. Six previous seasons had seen him coach three clubs, all of which were promoted under him by at least one division. One of the three, the YMCA club of Nazareth, was promoted from fifth to fourth to third division in two straight seasons, missing further promotion the following season by a whisker. This was corrected in 1987–88, Riziq's fourth year as coach, when history was made: the club was promoted again, becoming the first Palestinian club to make Israel's National Basketball League Division Two—a fully professional, big league.

Typical of many peripheral clubs in Israel, once it had been promoted to the senior division the club chose to drop their local coach and hire a better-known one—in this case a veteran Israeli coach from Haifa, experienced in the major leagues. Ra'id Riziq was thus fired after his most successful season. Frustrating as this may have been for him, it enabled him to respond positively to HNI's offer and to become the first Palestinian to coach an all-Israeli team in Israeli team sports.[6]

10 August 1988. 19:55, at the gym. HNI players are casually warming up for the first official practice of the new season. Club officials watch them intently from the sideline. Standing next to them in a fashionable track suit is a well-built young man, with a whistle on a cord around his neck. The new coach, Ra'id Riziq, has come for his first practice session.

20:00: Riziq stands up and nods to the team manager, who calls the players to the bench. Basketballs stop bouncing instantly, their thuds replaced with squeaks of rubber soles on the wooden floor. Then an attentive silence settles in as the players seat themselves on the low bench along the wall.

The new coach walks slowly to face the row of players. Muscular, tall, his posture is impressive as he waits there motionless, hands behind his back. He glances at his watch, obviously ready to begin. The team administrator appeals for a few more moments while he goes out to look for one other official. The coach nods his consent. The administrator goes out shortly, then returns alone. Riziq does not wait for an introduction and begins.

"First of all, if any of you consider being late even by one second for a practice, or for any drill I set, he'd better not come at all. Likewise, if anybody has a pain in his hand, in his leg, in his stomach or whatever, he'd better stay away. I don't like these stories. This must be understood now. My Hebrew is good enough. You will understand whatever I have to say.

You probably know me, or have heard of me. So far, every team I coached was promoted. And I intend to go on that way. You will all have to work hard. I may not be here next year, but you will. You remain here. This is your team. I shall insist that you give everything [to the team], which you will.

"I did not come here to make new friends. I do not want you to be my friends, I don't need it. My wife back home, she loves me, and that is enough for me. We are here to work, and work hard. I shall not let you off or exempt you from anything. What I want is to practice as much as possible. We have a month and five days until the first match. I would like us to practice five or six times a week, including a concentrated day of training on Saturdays, from morning to evening, or at least from morning to noon. If anyone has a problem with this, let him speak out now."

The players are silent, somewhat overwhelmed. The tone and content of the speech already represents a quantum leap for this essentially amateur club. A brief but inconclusive discussion of dates and times for approaching sessions ensues, and the practice gets under way.

The team walks on court. The coach explains the first drill. It is a standard one: players running to the basket in single file. A teammate, waiting stationary at the corner, passes the ball to each running player, who takes it to the basket. A simple move, but Riziq introduces a snag. He insists that each running man should call out for the ball. This act, so natural in real game situations, looks contrived during a practice, when all moves are prescribed, repetitive.

Two minutes into the drill Riziq whistles and the action stops. He assembles the players in the circle at the center of the court. "I do not hear you calling," he says. "All together now, call out. I want to hear you calling together as if you are asking for the ball." His demand—halfway between an educational exercise for a particularly slow group and a punishment for unruly youngsters—verges on authoritarianism. After all, the players are adults. Incredibly, we all respond, shouting in somewhat embarrassed unison: "Op. Op. Op." The coach is still not satisfied, and wants it louder. The cries go stronger: "Op. Op. Op."

Practice commences again. Riziq proves concise and eloquent, meticulous in his demands and very tough. Players are penalized with extra runs for imperfect execution of exercises, including failure to complete drills within the time allocated. The practice is not only relentless but exceptionally long. The coach does not smile, makes no jokes, and reprimands players who attempt to exchange hushed words with one another. Two short intervals for drinking water are all we get in the way of repose. The intervals are timed—three minutes each. Players are not allowed to sit on the floor during these intervals or, for that matter, at any other point.

22:00: Two strenuous hours after he began the session, Riziq finally blows the whistle to signify that it is over. He utters a rapid "Good night" and is out of the gym. Exhausted players, distorted with pain and effort, collapse on the floor. One of them exclaims, "This is not a training session. It is the Intifada." Another adds that "this guy has had specific orders from the PLO: he is here to kill us." Nobody laughs, and there are no more remarks. People pensively collect their gear and leave.

Riziq's opening speech, outlining a contract with the players that would determine the atmosphere for the weeks and months to come, shattered a number of implicit assumptions that Natzerat Illit Israelis, like Israelis generally, have regarding interpersonal relations with Palestinians.

First, the very role of a Palestinian publicly addressing Israelis broke the mold of Palestinians as obedient, silent listeners. The speech, moreover, had a dominant, confident, often threatening tone in which a Palestinian resolutely issued commands to Israelis. He did this in immaculate, authoritative, and confident Hebrew, including the prediction (or was it an order?) "you will understand everything I have to say."

The coach's disposition, more like an army officer talking to subordinates than a Palestinian addressing Israelis,[7] portrayed Riziq as an ambitious, successful professional, by no means an underdog. His hidden message was that in the present company it is Israelis, not Palestinians, who are prone to underachievement ("I may not be here next year. You stay here"). It had a proud Palestinian rejecting the potential closeness of his Israeli counterparts ("I do not need you as my friends"). The introduction of an invisible but loving woman, unattainable for Israelis by virtue of being both Palestinian and married ("my wife back home loves me. That is quite enough for me"), further accentuated his autonomy.

I had heard about Riziq. Some Palestinian friends in Nazareth, aware of my interest in basketball and in the recently promoted all-Palestinian YMCA club, had told me about the club, its players, and the unusually talented and tough coach who was in charge there. I even wrote a newspaper feature article about the club's promotion in mid-1988, although I did not speak to Riziq while preparing it.

When later that summer I heard that Riziq was about to become coach of the all-Israeli team I had just joined, I realized that this sporting aspect of my routine was about to take a surprising turn. The practice session and the speech preceding it convinced me that I faced a unique conjuncture, an opportunity anthropologists seldom manage to create but are sometimes fortunate enough to stumble into.

My original intentions notwithstanding, HNI gradually became a central arena for me as an ethnographer. I was immediately forced to make a number of decisions regarding my relationship with my teammates, the visibility of my investigative persona, and how to manage and present my own positionality. As often happens during ethnographic fieldwork, the need to differentiate between myself as anthropologist and as a person took me by surprise. Rightly or wrongly, I judged the situation in which I found myself in HNI—a legitimate participant and only marginally an observer—as beneficial.

Not wishing to compromise this unexpected vantage point, I decided to carry on just as I had done before the team became so promising a scene for my research: refrain from positive acts of inquiry and limit myself to silent observation. I hardly posed questions to those around me, and when I did it was in passing, mostly leading to one-off exchanges rather than fully developed discussions. I never had a notebook, writing utensil, or recorder with me at practices, matches, or team meetings, and certainly did not conduct anything remotely like an interview with any of my teammates. The only exception was Riziq, with whom I became friendly in 1989 after the end of his period as HNI coach. I visited his home on many occasions, had him and his wife visit our home, and held prolonged discussions with him about basketball, his time as HNI coach, and politics. I let him read a draft of a journal article (Rabinowitz 1992) based on his story, where he appears under the pseudonym Shafik Daher. In April 1995 I read him the final draft of this chapter and received his consent to use his real name.

Most of the material I present on HNI here, however, pertains to the time before Riziq and I grew closer. While my special relationship with him may well have colored my emphasis and interpretation, the ethnographic detail I present here is based exclusively on observations written at night, immediately upon returning from practices, matches, and meetings. Fortunately, the gym was only minutes away from home by car.

Boundary Concealment: Who Are "We" Anyway?

Riziq's capacity to depart from stereotypical modes of behavior that Israelis expect to find among Palestinians was demonstrated on various occasions. He was, for example, astutely inquisitive and matter-of-fact when the military service of conscripts and reservists clashed with practices and matches.

> 22 August 1988. Following a practice session, a player approaches Riziq with a problem: he had been called up for a stint on active military duty that was to last fourteen days, beginning the following Sunday. The stint obviously coincides with the all-important build-up for the season, and the player will miss a number of practices and preseason matches. The following dialogue ensues.
>
> Riziq: Any chance of you getting a sick note[8] and giving this call-up a miss? I once knew a player who used to do this regularly and quite effectively.
> Player: Well, technically it is possible. But I would really feel uneasy about it. The unit I am with is very easy-going, and people are really considerate. If you have a real problem, others will help you out, including the commanding officer and officers. There is trust. So if I do this, not show up at all, I will really be letting them down.
> Riziq (nodding in understanding): I see. What about matches, though? Could you have an evening or two off for matches?
> Player: Yes. That will definitely be all right.

Riziq was quite prepared to draw his own discourse and metaphors from the domains of military valor. Esprit de corps, fighting spirit in battle, mutual dependence under fire, and control of territory popped up more than once.

> 26 August 1988. Approaching the end of a practice session. Riziq requests a particularly demanding drill. He is adamant on perfect performance and counts down aloud the final twenty seconds. The players are pushed to the limit. As his count goes under ten, some players cheat, relaxing and letting the clock run out. One gives up altogether and stops running five seconds before time. Riziq assembles everyone at the corner of the gym, and turns to him.
>
> Riziq: You stopped five seconds from time. Why? (Tense silence.) Don't you know it is the final seconds which are the most important in basketball? Why did you give up? Would you stop running in the last and crucial moment in a battle, too? Would you leave your mates without cover in war and just stop

running? Do you know how many bullets you would get? (points at his own belly repeatedly, as if being hit successively by bullets).

This discourse deviates sharply from the image Israelis have of Palestinian citizens of Israel as people who shy away from anything remotely linked to military matters. The place of values such as military valor, camaraderie, and soldier-like responsibility in the definitions of Israeliness in general and of Israeli manhood in particular has been alluded to by several writers.[9] Israelis find great difficulty in extending these values and applying them to non-Israelis, least of all to Palestinian citizens of Israel. Riziq's resilience and choice of metaphors thus effectively appropriated these values from their normal Israeli exclusivity.

Riziq often used the terms "us" and "our mentality" in referring to the team, thus temporarily obliterating the all-pervasive abyss between Palestinians and Israelis, two groups normally assumed to be dramatically different and distinct.

26 August 1988. At the end of practice, a birthday party. One of the players, twenty-six today, rushes to the changing room, returning shortly with a plastic bag. Out come a rich birthday cake, complete with cream and icing, disposable cups, bottles of soft drinks. Using a chair as a makeshift surface to work on, he hurriedly cuts the cake, pours the fizzy drinks, then dishes them out to the players, who are seated on a bench along the wall. He remains standing near his chair.

Riziq is on his feet as well, but slightly to the side. Someone makes an improvised speech. There is laughter: Then Riziq asks, "What about songs? Don't you people sing on birthdays?" His suggestion and question are met with silence. First, birthday sing-along is somewhat out of place in the context of an Israeli men's basketball team. Second, his use of "you people" is ambiguous. Does he mean "you Israelis"? "People in this town"? "This particular basketball club"?

Someone cracks an unrelated joke. Grateful, we all return to nibble at the bits of cakes we hold in paper napkins.

Throughout his period as HNI coach Riziq strictly avoided direct reference to his national identity. He took great care, for example, not to use Arabic words in his speech.

28 August 1988. A practice session in the gym. Riziq explains a new drill, clear and concise as ever. On route, however, a mishap: he bridges two sentences with the Arabic word *ya'ani*. The term, which in this context means "in other words," makes perfect sense to the players: *ya'ani* is one of an assortment of Arabic words fully incorporated into spoken Hebrew. This notwithstanding, Riziq is acutely embarrassed. He fumbles, as though he had just committed a

terrible faux pas, then stops dead, shaking his head disapprovingly. Finally he takes a deep breath and starts over, replacing the unfortunate word with its proper Hebrew equivalent.

> 14 August 1988. At the end of a practice session. Riziq announces that he and the team administrator are planning to attend an approaching basketball tournament near Tiberias, where top professional clubs from Tel-Aviv are scheduled to play. They think it would be nice if some of us came along. "The tournament will take place in S'amakh," Riziq tells us, then quickly realizes this appellation is inappropriate. S'amakh is the Arabic name of an old Palestinian village that stood at the southern tip of the Sea of Galilee (Lake Kineret in Hebrew, Bahrat T'abariya in Arabic) before it was destroyed by the Israeli army during the war of 1948. The site, which Israelis have since named Tsemah, now has local government buildings and other facilities, including the large conference and sports center where the approaching tournament will be held. Having realized he just used the old Palestinian name of the place, Riziq quickly regains control and corrects himself. "No, that is Arabic. I mean . . . Tsemah."

The few acknowledgments of his identity as Palestinian Riziq did allow were of a folkloristic nature.

> 19 August 1988. At the end of a practice session, near the gym's door. Riziq turns to some of the players and says, "Among us [the Hebrew word he used was *etslenu*] there is a saying that if you eat Zaa'tar you become leaner, have much energy and speed, and, most important of all, your head is 'opened,' you think more clearly. So before you come to the next session make sure you have some Zaa'tar."

Zaa'tar, the Arabic word for thyme, is also the name of a popular spice, made in many rural Palestinian households by grinding thyme with other herbs. In recent years, however, it has become immensely popular among Israelis, who can buy it ready-made and packaged in most supermarkets. While the name "Zaa'tar" has been incorporated into Hebrew with no alteration, every Israeli knows its Arabic origin. Its use by Riziq, complete with his reference to the popular Palestinian belief in its potency, all prefixed by "etslenu" was a clear and conscious reference to Riziq's own identity and culture.

> 14 August 1988. At the end of a practice session in the gym. The team attempts to fix an extra practice session for the following week. Players' schedules and priorities are not easy to coordinate, but Sunday finally emerges as the best option. It is almost finalized when Riziq, who is normally the one pushing for extra practices and training sessions in spite of his rather laid-back players, is forced to decline. He tells the team, "This time it is I who cannot make it. My cousin got married this week, and having spent all evenings this week in

> practices,[10] I have not yet been able to visit and greet him. Sunday, unfortunately, remains my only available evening."

Riziq's explanation meets instant sympathy and understanding. The practice is rescheduled. While extended formal wedding celebrations are known in some communities of Mizrahi Jews in Israel, its practice among Palestinians is almost taken for granted by Israelis. Riziq's reference to a family wedding, or for that matter to the beliefs regarding the use of Zaa'tar, thus clearly signified his cultural and national identity. These references, however, were essentially "soft." They colored his Palestinism in folkloristic, depoliticized shades while at the same time breaking the silence that shrouded his otherness. This enabled a relatively relaxed treatment of a loaded issue. The alternative—an unbroken, ambiguous silence regarding the coach's national identity—might have been construed by players as more menacing.

I subsequently discovered that Riziq's political inclinations reflect a consensus among young Palestinians in Nazareth and elsewhere in Israel vis-à-vis the state that can be summarized as accepting it as a necessary evil. It is a stance many Israelis in Natzerat Illit regard as tantamount to treason. A choice on his part to delve into issues of identity and politics would have strained his relationship with players and management to the limit.

Authority Questioned

The weeks just prior to the start of the formal season and immediately thereafter exposed a growing rift between Riziq and his players. The players, most of whom had never played professionally, found it exceedingly difficult to adjust their demanding basketball schedule to their professional, familial, and social commitments. The main problem was attendance at practices and matches. Many sessions took place with less than ten men—the all-important quorum needed for exercising game plans. Ra'id Riziq grew bitter and frustrated with these lapses in attitude and commitment and made no secret of his misgivings.

> 19 September 1988. The team is about to leave Natzerat Illit on its way to a friendly match in adjacent Migdal Haemek. Some have already gone in one minibus. I find myself with Riziq on the pavement outside the gym, waiting for the other hired vehicle. Riziq laments the poor discipline of the players as well as of the management. He is clearly preoccupied with the issues of order and authority. The conversation turns to earlier experiences in his career as coach, and he offers his interpretation of the events that led to his departure from Nazareth YMCA the previous year, immediately following the most successful season he and the club have ever had.
>
> "I was becoming weaker," he said, "less authoritative, yielding. You have to understand, the way I was in YMCA throughout my time with them was

> not at all the way you see me here. There I had always been hard on the players and on the management. I was genuinely tough. I had my ideas and I pushed them and never gave way.[11] Then, last season, I softened. I started giving way. I was letting people off the hook, was not single-minded enough. This was the beginning of the end. One thing then led to another, and at the end of the season, with all this historic success, I was out.
>
> Unfortunately, now I am coaching here, I have had this mentality rubbed off me further. One guy is late. Another has a pain in his hand. A third, something is wrong with his sister, a fourth has troubles with his grandmother. And I . . . somehow I go along with these things. I tell you, I am becoming soft, like you Jews. It is really bad."

The first matches in September brought less than satisfactory results. Defeat in the first two matches made the season look unpromising. The players' attendance did not improve, and an early crisis was clearly in the making. We also learned that Riziq had not been getting as much support as he had expected from management, particularly from his official employers at the local workers' council. Most of them, I later discovered, had been uneasy all along about hiring a Palestinian coach.

In mid-October, an emergency meeting was convened by one of the veteran players and the team manager. Attendance was for once complete: all the players, the coach, and the team manager were there. During the meeting another fact emerged: Riziq, who had begun coaching more than two months earlier, was still awaiting his first paycheck. The meeting ended with the players pledging to attend all practices and management promising to recruit more players to the squad and to facilitate the smooth running of the team for the rest of the season.

Conversations between players even before that meeting reflected their preoccupation with Riziq's motivation to coach a fourth division club so soon after promoting his former club to the second division. The new situation deepened people's bewilderment: why was their coach willing to continue for so long without pay? One day, as the team was in the minibus returning from an away game without Riziq, who drove his private car, a highly regarded veteran player volunteered an explanation: Riziq, he said, elected to coach HNI simply to demonstrate that he can manage an all-Israeli team. "He needs to prove it," said the player. "It is the key to his future career as coach." This interpretation, which seemed plausible to most players, was adopted as the standard solution to the riddle and was repeated by other players on subsequent occasions.

In the aftermath of the mid-October meeting, however, Riziq came to the correct conclusion that the promises given to him by management were not going to be fulfilled and that neither wages nor new blood was forthcoming. He decided to suspend himself for two weeks. His idea, he later told me, was to see whether management was going to make drastic changes and thus decide whether there was any point in carrying on with HNI.

This move had immediate implications, though hardly those Riziq anticipated. The team administrator, who had recruited him in the first place and who remained the mediator between him and the local workers' council, immediately resigned. Three volunteers from outside the inner ring of Labor activists quickly stepped into the void, becoming the new management committee.[12] The new committee soon embarked on an energetic and successful fundraising effort. Unrestricted by any moral obligations to the self-suspended Riziq, they appointed a new provisional coach—a player whose long experience with HNI, considerable natural leadership, and immediate availability made him the obvious choice. The new player-coach ended up coaching the team for the rest of the season, doing reasonably well.

By the time the team seemed to be functioning smoothly under the new management and coach in early November, the local workers' council had lost even the limited interest they may have had before in Riziq as an employee, effectively disowning him. His demands to be paid for the time he had worked were denied, as the council claimed he had left the team unilaterally, thus breaching his contract. His court claim against his ex-employers dragged on until late 1992, at which point he was granted compensation in court.

The players, too, were quick to lose sight of their former coach. Riziq's considerable professional impact on the team was soon eroded by the ideas and emphases of his successor. His name was hardly mentioned anymore.

> 3 December 1988. During practice at the gym. The [new] coach explains a drill. One of the players finds it similar to a drill he already knows. He turns to his mate and says, "This is like the drill we used to have with . . . this guy. . . . He used to do this with us. What was his name? The Arab!"

Doctors and Patients

Like most new towns in Israel, Natzerat Illit suffers from a chronic shortage of physicians. None of the doctors serving the community is a long-term resident of the town. Many, particularly specialists, live elsewhere, attending local clinics once or twice a week. There is no hospital in Natzerat Illit. Kupat Holim Klalit (KHK)—Israel's largest health insurance company, run by the Histadrut trade union federation—operates medium-sized clinics in the town but requires patients to travel to Afula or even Haifa for most non-routine visits and treatments. Macabbi, the second-largest health insurance company, has a single clinic in Natzerat Illit.

Neighboring Nazareth, on the other hand, has a thriving medical community. It has three hospitals (all run by Christian organizations) and a large number of resident specialists—Palestinians who are either hospital staff themselves or have ready access to hospital facilities. A decade-long crisis in public health in Israel that left KHK impoverished discouraged specialists in Nazareth from making themselves available to patients exclusively through KHK. One result is that private health care thrives, with most physicians operating private clinics.

Dr. Nawaf Sa'adawi, a resident of Nazareth, is a pediatrician. Originally from a village in western Galilee, he is one of a handful of Palestinian citizens who graduated from the prestigious medical school at the Hebrew University in the 1960s. After his graduation, he worked for KHK for a while, then moved to Nazareth, set up a clinic, and quickly gained a reputation that spread to neighboring Natzerat Illit. Veteran Israeli residents often described Sa'adawi as "the doctor who raised our children." Upon arrival at Natzerat Illit for my fieldwork, my spouse and I inquired about medical care for our daughter. An Israeli resident, herself a mother of four, said with exaggeration, "There is only one pediatrician around here. His name is Dr. Sa'adawi."

A keen, experienced diagnostician, Sa'adawi commanded an impressive knowledge of therapeutic methods and a close acquaintance with specialists. Operating mainly from his private clinic in Nazareth, he was also available three afternoons a week in Natzerat Illit, where he attended patients in a clinic run by one of the health insurance companies.

It took a while to discover that many of the Israeli patients who worshiped Sa'adawi's excellence came across on other occasions as vehemently anti-Palestinian. One example is Brakha Benisho, an Israeli resident of Natzerat Illit of Moroccan origin. Aged twenty-five at the time of fieldwork, she had recently given birth to her second child. Returning from the maternity ward of the regional medical center in Afula, she had the following to say of her experience.

> It was OK generally. But the Arab women really brought me down. They really are like cattle, giving birth year in year out, no fail. They are so primitive—you should have heard them scream in the labor room. It made me so angry. And they take so much space. Imagine—Arab women all over the place, with millions of noisy relatives around them, all chattering in Arabic. It is disgraceful, the way the hospital authorities put them with us Jewish women. The least they could do, if they insist on helping the damned Arabs multiply, is put them separately.

On another occasion Brakha complained about KHK, of which she is a member. She talked of queues, of rude service, and of incompetent doctors, and she related the following incident.

> My older daughter was once ill with a rare infection which no one in KHK tracked down. It went on and on. The child was suffering. We had no sleep for weeks. Eventually it was too much to endure, and I went to Sa'adawi. Imagine—going to his clinic in the *shuk* [Hebrew for market] in downtown

> Nazareth. All those Arabs, and the dirt. So foul. But then Sa'adawi, I swear, had one quick look at the poor child and knew exactly what was wrong. He told me, then and there: it was an infection. A rare one. He wrote the prescription. I got the medicine. The child was well within a day. Not that it did not cost. It did, and how: those Arabs know too well how to take money. Especially from the United States.[13]

Dina Hirsh, an Israeli resident of European origin, aged twenty-seven at the time of fieldwork, was a mother of a one-year-old. She was once present when a neighbor, who had recently given birth in the medical center in Afula, told of a Palestinian woman who had given birth to a stillborn baby. "She was so stupid and primitive, that Arab woman," the raconteur said, "that she completely lost control, and the baby ended up suffocating." Dina's reaction was instant and spontaneous: "Oh, good. One less Arab."

This notwithstanding, Sa'adawi was Dina's ultimate authority on childcare—from nutrition to hygiene to treatment of real and imagined illnesses. There were times when she attended his clinic three or four times a week. She refused to consult any other doctor, insisting that the efficacy of his treatment was unsurpassed.

Brakha Benisho and Dina Hirsh obviously hold extreme views about Palestinians and their relations with Israel and Israelis. For Benisho, everything about her experience with Sa'adawi that is objectively "Arab" (the location of the clinic in Nazareth, the *shuk,* the people on the way) is negative and threatening. All aspects of the experience that are objectively negative (the cost, the distance, the dirt in the *shuk* at the end of a business day) she subjectively links to "Arabness."

Hirsh, on the other hand, resolves the problem of Sa'adawi's identity by other means. Being a member of the health insurance company with which he is affiliated, she is not normally forced to attend his private clinic and is thus spared the "Nazareth experience" Benisho so resented. In the context of the Natzerat Illit clinic where he sees Hirsh and her infant, Sa'adawi's national identity is virtually forgotten. His (real) family name is not stereotypically Palestinian and is neutralized further by the prefix "Dr." His forename, a more typical name with obvious Muslim connotations, is omitted from spoken and written communication. His immaculate Hebrew, often sprinkled with English and Latin, radiates authority.

Brakha Benisho's single episode with Sa'adawi, while obviously trying, had one aspect that stood out for her in glorious isolation. She attributes her daughter's recovery to a magic moment in which health was restored through a succession of almost simultaneous acts: Sa'adawi observed, identified, pronounced a diagnosis, and cured by prescription. That was the instance in which, for her, Sa'adawi momentarily ceased being "Arab."

In the case of Dina Hirsh, who sees Sa'adawi much more frequently, the moment is extended to a routine and is buttressed by her insistence that this particular doctor's efficacy is unrivaled. As far as she is concerned, it is a professional, trustworthy doctor who looks after her son, not an "Arab."

Trusting the Suspect

Dina Hirsh, Brakha Benisho, and the basketball players of HNI, while subscribing to crude essentialist generalizations regarding "Arabs," are nevertheless willing, in certain circumstances, to trust and even subordinate themselves to Palestinian individuals.

In *The Rebirth of Anthropological Theory*, Stanley Barrett defines the notion of "contradictions in personal attributes" (1984, 150–58). People's stereotypes and preconceptions of personal attributes, he argues, tend to be arranged "in binary opposition" that "push[es] toward polar extremes" (157). Thus the "dumb blond" syndrome reflects an ostensible contradiction between being intelligent and being beautiful; Falstaff and Cassius reinforce the stereotypical opposition in Shakespeare's mind between being fat and being gloomy; and so on.

Barrett concentrates on the classic contradiction represented by the black professional in North America. White people, he asserts, have certain assumptions about blacks: they are supposed to be poor, or slaves, or field hands, or migrant laborers, or factory workers, or some combination of these. When one comes across a black physician, which of his (or her) statuses dominates, race or profession (1984, 157–58)?

This problem had been addressed by sociologists decades earlier. Hughes (1945, 355) observed that non-white, female, non-Protestant physicians of "lower social stock" are accepted by white Americans only in the most acute emergencies or as exotic healers for the desperate. This assertion, while probably more true of the United States in the 1940s than of the reality in certain states today,[14] is nevertheless relevant for this discussion. More recent research indicates that the chief negative characteristics white Americans tend to attribute to blacks are lack of ambition, lack of competence and intelligence, underachievement, laziness, and inconsistency (see, e.g., E. G. Cohen 1982, 1984). Schuman (1982, 346–49) asserts that the psychogenetic beliefs regarding the sources of black underachievement held by American whites in the early twentieth century were replaced in the second part of the century by a kind of environmental determinism. The key characteristics, however, seem to remain at the level of blacks' performance (see also Campbell and Schuman 1968).

When white Americans face black professionals their difficulty is in reconciling professional performance with the stereotype of blacks as poor achievers—an incoherence revolving around blacks' *capabilities* or, more precisely, the assumed absence thereof. The case of Israelis in Natzerat Illit is different. Exposed to a relatively affluent, urbane, and educated Palestinian community, they have long internalized the notion that many Palestinians have impressive careers. The contradiction in personal attributes triggered by a Palestinian professional or a Palestinian in a position of authority is thus considerably weaker.

The negative views of Palestinians held by Israelis have been monitored periodically by means of attitude and stereotype surveys.[15] One striking feature of most survey results is that the qualities Israelis attribute to Palestinians, including citizens of Israel, are primarily related to intent. When asked to comment on "the Arabs," Israelis tend to focus on ascribed intentions and conspiratorial designs. Peres, who asserts that "Attitudes of Jews towards Arabs are obviously dominated by the struggle against the Arab world," indicates that 76 percent of Israelis of European origin and 83 percent of those of oriental extraction believe that "every Arab hates all Jews" (1971a, 1029). Peres and Levy (1969) likewise suggest that Israelis view Arabs as potentially violent.

In her much-quoted survey of 1980, Mina Zemach asked Israeli respondents to specify the first five words that spring to mind upon hearing the term "Israeli Arab" or upon thinking of it. The words respondents came up with were arranged by meaning into fourteen subgroups. The subgroup that had the highest frequency (35.2 percent of the expressions used) was characterized by Zemach as "reflecting (the attribution to Arabs of) negative emotions—hatred, fear, suspicion" (1980, 82). An additional 13 percent were citations associated with the Israeli-Arab conflict ("PLO," "terror," "murder," "hatred of Jews," "the enemy") or with the Holocaust ("concentration camps," "anti-Semitism," "Germany"). A total of 48.2 percent of the labels were directly linked to ill intentions which, Israelis believe, Palestinians have toward them. Only 16.5 percent of the expressions cited referred to perceived inherent qualities of Palestinians, including "family oriented," "dirty," "lazy," "savage," "diligent," "ignorant," "poor," and "miserable."

Trope likewise indicates that Israelis' stereotypes of Arabs primarily reflect perceptions of Arabs' intentions (1989, 135).[16] In his treatise on Israeli ethnocentrism, Sami Smooha attributes the way Israelis feel regarding Palestinians to the persistence of the Israeli-Arab conflict and to the dissent of Palestinians within Israel (1988, 1989–92, 150). The stereotypes of Palestinians Israelis hold may thus be characterized as self-referential, indicating primarily what Israelis think Palestinians want to do them. It could be further argued that such stereotypes entail the attribution of irrationality, with Palestinians essentially seen as hot-blooded murderers primarily motivated by hatred. Revengeful rather than self-seeking, they are perceived as potentially given to uncontrollable malice, often at the expense of careful choices and designs that could have better served their own best interests.

The notion that any Palestinian can turn his skin at any time, deny his own interests and allow some dark, demonic alternate self to possess his actions, features regularly in the discourse of right-wing politicians in Israel. Often reflected in printed headlines describing Palestinian assaults against Israelis,[17] it is present in a more sophisticated guise in the less-likely quarters of Israeli liberalism. Amos Oz's description of demonic Palestinian twins in *My Michael* (1984) is one example. Adir Cohen's study of the image of the Arab in Israeli literature (1987) cites an array of similar depictions.

The problem facing Natzerat Illit Israelis once confronted by a Palestinian in position of authority is not his faculty. In their view being Palestinian does not exclude excellence. Their difficulty lies in reconciling being Palestinian with the benevolent *intentions* required for responsible authority and proper professional performance. The issue of trust, not aptitude, is at the core.

Professional Trust

Trust has a special place in the relationship between professionals and clients. Willensky's discussion of the service ideal and of the place of trust therein argues that professionals as well as clients must believe that the client's interests are paramount—a belief that cements the client's trust in the professional. This trust in turn secures free flow of information without which the professional is unable to perform (1964).

Goode has argued that wider society grants guilds professional autonomy only when it is deemed essential for adequate performance of the service. In exchange the profession exercises effective internal control over practitioners' ethics and performance. The more the clients are exposed to potential damage, the more important it becomes to exercise the checks and penalties that would protect them (1969, 292–93). Goode goes on to identify the "person professions"—those dealing with the individual's body, personality, or reputation—as ones in which the public is particularly aware of the professional's capacity to harm the client, intentionally or inadvertently. Clients are reassured by the belief that person professionals like physicians, psychiatrists, accountants, and divorce attorneys are restricted by particularly elaborate and stringent codes of conduct, ethics, and ideology. Paradoxically, it is in the person professions that clients often feel they are best protected from the potentially hazardous side effects of being handled by professionals.[18]

Brakha Benisho and Dina Hirsh could thus be seen as taking a double risk with Dr. Sa'adawi. One is the conventional risk that the physician might harm their children or families by misuse of the powerful tools of his trade—his expertise, his prescriptive authority, intimate details about the family he may have gathered. The other is the specific danger that in being Palestinian he would attempt to cause indiscriminate damage to his Israeli patients. It is, after all, the same sort of damage which, according to their worldview, every Palestinian always hopes to cause to every Israeli, and which they themselves sometimes openly wish for Palestinians, including children.

One conclusion then is that where personal well-being is at stake, distrust of Palestinians' intentions is subordinated to the basic faith in the professional integrity of physicians, whatever their national affiliation. Also, in the well-ordered context of their encounter with Sa'adawi, Brakha Benisho and Dina Hirsh were clearly confident of their ability to distinguish good faith from malice—a certainty that underscores their willingness to trust the Palestinian doctor.

Coaching basketball, at least in Israel, does not constitute a profession in the normal sociological sense. For one thing, neither coaches nor players explicitly subscribe to the service ideal. The interaction between coach and players is better described as one where interests are fused—not as one in which the interests of players (or the club) override those of the coach. Ra'id Riziq poses less of a potential threat to his players and to management than a physician would to patients. This is not to say, however, that the perceived danger is completely gone. What if the coach discriminates against a particular player because of the player's political leanings? What if he is out to harm the club representing the Israeli town that so obtrusively asserts itself in the coach's Palestinian heartland? What if the coach sees his unusual position, in charge of young Israeli males, as an opportunity for sweet revenge for the humiliation and suffering inflicted by Israel and Israelis on his people for decades? What if he does, after all, get orders from the PLO, as the remark made at the end of the first session jokingly suggested?

As it happened, HNI players ended up displaying a remarkable ability to disregard their attitudes vis-à-vis Palestinians and Arabs generally, to trust Riziq, and to accept his authority. This is but one of many cases whereby Israelis invest trust in Palestinians in a variety of non-professional contexts, including commerce, industry, and government (see Horowitz and Lissak 1989, 78–79). This clearly calls for an alternative explanation, one that would apply beyond the context of professional interaction.

Exorcising the Fear of Irrational Malice

Trust features in sociological literature in two major perspectives (Zucker 1986). One, the origins of which are traced back to Parsons, "asserts trust resides in actors" and assumes that participants to an exchange put self-interest aside in favor of "other orientation" or "collectivity-orientation" (57; after Parsons 1939, 1969). The other, which Zucker traces back to Garfinkel, "rests on some degree of collective orientation at the beginning of interaction, but self-interest is often expected and legitimate at subsequent stages of the exchange" (1986, 57).

Much of the sociological literature on trust[19] highlights the function of trust as "a deep assumption underwriting social order" (Lewis and Weigart 1985). Likewise, studies of trust as a social reality (Lewis and Wiegart 1985), of trust as a commodity (S. Shapiro 1987), and of the concerted efforts aimed at creating trust (Zucker 1986; Roniger 1990) depict trust as a "climate" regulated by society and for it. My perspective here departs from these attempts: it looks at trust primarily in interpersonal relations. More specifically it focuses on the relationship among danger, rationality, risk-taking, and trust.

Trust occupies what Spencer-Brown (1971) calls the unmarked space between the familiar and the unfamiliar. Luhmann (1979, 1988) sees this space as the transition zone between cosmology, where the world is assigned with distinct, fixed dangers, and technology, where the sensation of precariousness gives way to a new belief in technical solutions. It is in this essentially modernist middle ground that we meet the rational construction of risk and trust—a complimentary opposition that has become a feature of virtually every venture and decision in modern life. Trust, where it exists, is a tentative bridge, consciously constructed and culturally mediated between the impossible and the feasible. This approach informs, to an extent, Hart's depiction of the Frafras of Acra (1988), Gambetta's analysis of the nineteenth-century mafioso in southern Italy (1988), and Lorenz's treatment of the relationships between industrialists and subcontractors in France (1988).

For many Israelis, trusting Palestinians hinges on departure from a state of primordial fears of Palestinians' bad intentions and on arrival in a universe whereby Palestinians are seen as having rational interests like everybody else. Given the extent to which the orientalist perspective has penetrated Israeli life and consciousness, complete with emphasis on the ostensible irrationality of Arabs (above), this task is by no means trivial.

Ra'id Riziq displayed a persona with which HNI players were quite familiar—that of the determined and successful competitor. His sportsman's image was buttressed by consistent concealment on his part of aspects of his person not directly linked to being an ambitious coach. He repudiated personal encounters to the extent of remaining unaware of his players' surnames or, for that matter, of their ignorance regarding his.[20] A resident of Natzerat Illit's al-Kurum neighborhood since the early 1980s, he was oblivious to the fact that many of his players erroneously believed him to be a resident of Nazareth. Likewise, he carefully circumvented uncontrolled references to his national affiliation, making sure this emotive issue cropped up only in innocuously folkloristic and depoliticized contexts, willfully reducing the range of attributes in terms of which the players could relate to him. This restriction was so effective that it arrested most players' personal loyalty to him, a fact that became painfully clear when the coach found himself isolated from club management and felt compelled to quit.

In 1995, as I read this analysis to Riziq, he had this to say:

> I think you have a point here. In fact this is something which has perplexed me for a while now, as it came up in almost every place I coached. Take the YMCA, for example. The squad of 1987–88 had historic success under me, when we repeatedly broke all previous records of promotion and got as far up as Division Two. When we were finally promoted to Division Two, there was that terrible row with management and I was forced to leave. I sat at home and waited for the players to make a move on my behalf, to raise their voice, but nothing happened.
>
> Or take Shaf-'amr. When I took the team, we started the season with nine wins in a row, and looked pretty good for promotion. But my salary was not

> paid, and I quit. I thought the players might make a stand, say they do not want another coach, whatever. Nothing. Another coach was hired to replace me, the streak of victories was broken, and they failed promotion.
>
> So obviously there is a valid point here, and it probably has to do with my way of dealing with my players, the discipline, the distance which I keep. But let me tell you this: I love the way I work, I think it is professional, and I have total faith in it. I will continue like this, although it is clear to me that there is and will always be a price to pay.

The preoccupation of HNI players with their coach's intentions, followed by their conclusion that he saw his stint with HNI as an important stepping-stone for his career, were congruent with their view of him as someone primarily seeking personal success. This discovery exempted them from the endemic search for cryptic explanations for his choice to work with Israelis. Their distrust of Palestinians' intentions, while not eradicated altogether, was easily suspended.

Both Riziq and Sa'adawi were identified by their Israeli counterparts as highly rational and calculating. This represented a significant departure from the stereotype of irrational malice that Israelis so often attribute to Palestinians. The ambitious coach is interpreted as being there because he seeks a brilliant career. The doctor wants to remain a doctor, and—at least as far as Brakha Benisho is concerned—is out to get the client's money. Likewise, Palestinian keepers of shops in Nazareth, which Israelis regularly patronize, Nazareth garage owners, and Palestinian partners in joint ventures have long-term interests in cooperating with Israelis that the latter quickly discern and readily endorse. This gives the Palestinians a solid cover of predictability and hence trustworthiness. The omnipresent Israeli anxiety of Palestinian irrational malice is offered a sensible, context-related exit.

Self-Interest in the Adversarial Context

This discussion raises the problem of rational self-interest and its place in the adversarial context. As indicated, once Israelis interpret Palestinians as acting out of rational self-interest, the old "all Arabs hate us all and are out to get us" approach is eclipsed by the essentially pragmatic position that "Arabs, like all other people, are out first and foremost to help themselves." This in turn allows Israelis to develop ad hoc trust, or minimal trust—at least within specific limits such as commerce, industry, or the person professions. Analytical attention thus shifts from the relatively well-documented rationality of actors who *invest* trust to the less obvious notion of the rationality actors *attribute* to others as a prerequisite to trusting them.

The fact that Israelis sometimes perceive an actor as rationally inclined toward cooperation in spite of being Palestinian has a further implication. A Palestinian perceived by Israelis as someone who has somehow overcome his irrational destructive drives and is now willing to cooperate with Israelis so as to serve his own interests is inevitably accredited with a high degree of rationality and calculation. This in turn enables Israelis to invest more trust in him than they would have done in a potential Israeli partner, whose motives for cooperation might always be unclear. If rationality and predictability are indeed so highly valued in business and professional encounters, there follows the paradoxical, counterintuitive notion that interpersonal trust can in fact sometimes be found in the adversarial context.

An interesting problem is the extent to which actors tend to generalize from specific interactions involving ad hoc trust to wider and more clearly politicized arenas—in this case from the positive experience with a doctor or a coach to Israeli-Palestinian relations generally. My observations from Natzerat Illit indicate no such transference. Neither HNI players nor Sa'adawi's patients allowed their extended encounters with the two impressive men to modify their attitudes regarding Palestinians or Arabs generally. This seems consistent with my impressions of economic cooperation. Israeli partners, customers, employers, and employees tend to associate their Palestinian counterparts primarily with the legitimate and predictable *homo economicus.* The initial tendency to see all Palestinians as irrational bloodthirsty creatures may be mitigated by the discovery of familiar calculations. But however effective within specific, recognized contexts, these realizations do not appear to spill over to other spheres.

The involvement of Palestinians in Natzerat Illit's real estate market provides another vivid illustration. Negotiating real estate deals with prospective Palestinian buyers, many Israelis become aware of the sensible self-seeking aspect of individual Palestinians and their conduct. As mediation unfolds Israeli sellers often learn about specific circumstances and considerations surrounding the Palestinian buyer's desire to move to Natzerat Illit. Most negotiations proceed and are concluded in good faith, with both sides treating circumstances and self-interest as not only legitimate but self-explanatory and hence acceptable.

Things are not as placid, however, when Israeli residents, including ones who have successfully completed sales to Palestinians, think of real estate in terms of the more general panorama of "Palestinians moving into Natzerat Illit." The same Palestinian who was depicted earlier as party to a rational and mutually rewarding deal is now construed as part of a sinister and threatening Palestinian conspiracy to take over the town, outnumber its Israeli residents, and dominate them.

The lack of transference demonstrated here suggests that positive interaction between individuals, even when it happens over extended periods and with numerous participants, does not guarantee coexistence between groups. Only a conviction that the other side *as a collective* guides itself rationally, predictably, and in accordance with mutually acceptable rules of play can facilitate such a sweeping shift of attitude. This, I argue, is what happened in the summer and autumn of 1993 when Yasser Arafat's personal predicament, the institutional and economic crisis of the PLO and the political decisions taken by the Palestinian leadership, convinced most Israelis that the Palestinians' willingness to deal with Israel was driven by rational calculations. The rationality now attributed to the Palestinians created a swing in the views of many Israelis regarding negotiation with the PLO and the eventual relinquishing of territories occupied in 1967—two issues that had been taboo in mainstream Israel for decades.

The tension between treatment of individuals and a generalized attitude toward an outgroup is not unique to Israeli-Palestinian relations. A Christian Palestinian with whom I shared some of the notions presented here had this to say about his strained relationship with Muslim Palestinians and Islam.

> Although I lived most of my life with Muslims here in Nazareth, I still find myself referring to them as something different and inferior. I sometimes think of them as Znuj (black Africans) or Hnud (Indians). With time we Christians were educated to believe that we are one step above them. Perhaps by seeing them like this we try to put ourselves in the position of the Jewish guy who looks at us from above.
>
> When I meet a Muslim professor, will he change my view of Muslims? I think not. Meeting someone who is extremely educated will not change my attitude to Muslims as a whole. And I know I do not have any faith in their intentions. Perhaps it all goes back to childhood memories. When I was little, we had a Muslim family as neighbors. And when my mother would throw away the washing water through the window, the Muslim woman living underneath would shout, "First we'll finish off the Jews, then it will be you lot." This is one reason why although I want a Palestinian state, I am not at all sure I could ever live in it.

Do Palestinian citizens of Israel attribute rationality to their Israeli partners? Arguably they do. True, the relentless preoccupation of Israelis with the formidable problems associated with infrastructure and economic development, housing, agriculture, industry, and more has all too often been directly at the expense of Palestinians. It involved seizure and expropriation of Palestinian land and is continuing to fuel discrimination in budget allocations, inequality of opportunities for Palestinian individuals, limited access to resources, and more. No one is more aware of the ubiquity and gravity of these inequalities than the Palestinian citizens of Israel themselves. And yet, I argue, most Palestinians in Israel do not attribute to Israelis an irrational obsession to cause them harm at all costs. This is reflected, among other things, in the pattern of mobilization adopted by the Palestinians within Israel. The level and intensity of involvement on the part of Palestinians in parliamentary and local-level politics as a medium for public action implies a certain faith in a negotiated improvement. This sentiment could hardly be sustained if Palestinians assigned Israelis with irrational malice against all Palestinians always.

A major distinction thus emerges between the Palestinian citizens of Israel and Palestinians and Arabs elsewhere—including those in the territories occupied by Israel in 1967. The overriding interpretation of Israel in the Arab world remains an essentialist, and self-referential one, portraying Israel as an evil entity, irrationally and inexplicably obsessed with dominating Arabs and harming them. The rhetoric of war and politics across the Arab world is rife with references to Israel as driven by satanic forces rather than by reasonable pursuits of realistic goals and interests. Not so among most Palestinian citizens of Israel.

Finally, I have indicated that HNI players are not representative of average liberal-minded Israeli. And yet their bigoted, unshakable dispositions vis-à-vis Palestinians did not stop them from displaying a remarkable level of trust of, cooperation with, and even subordination to Ra'id Riziq. Significantly, this took place with no signs whatsoever of what one might call consciousness-raising. The assumption, grounded in the liberal emphasis on enlightenment that progress comes with moves from theory to knowledge to ideology to norms to attitude and finally to action emerges as highly problematic. Likewise the continuum, implicitly assumed in liberal thought, from racist to indifferent to liberal to trusting and cooperating, is constructively ruptured. Paradoxically, not only does this rupture fail to arrest desired progress toward cooperation, in certain contexts it could even enhance it.

Epilogue

April 1995, in Ra'id Riziq's living room. Having just read the final version of this chapter to Ra'id—my free translation of English text into Hebrew mixed with Arabic—I sit and wait for his response. He is pensive, intent, as if weighing his options. Finally he turns to me and says,

> You know, I coached a Jewish squad again not long ago. The youth team of Kibbutz.
>
> Gevat. It went quite well. We finished second in their division, and they wanted me to continue. I was considering their offer, and suddenly understood this weakness that I have. When I work with Arabs, I am as strong as God, and I succeed. I put everybody, even rebels, back in line. No one gets smart with me, not even management.
>
> When I work with Israelis, I go back to that wretched point where it is not only they who look down at me, but I as well. This sort of attitude enters into me as well! Perhaps it is because you see for yourself and you realize that everything on the Jewish side is better. The roads, education, culture, the way people are treated, life in general. The Jewish child gets more social security, better conditions, better support.
>
> I know that I can be as good as any of them, but I also see that they have better lives. Like when I was at the physical education academy at the time. I knew how well I competed with all my Jewish classmates—in physics,

chemistry, gymnastics, basketball, volleyball, swimming, English. There were so many fields in which I knew I was better. And yet I felt inferior. And they all made sure I felt that. Not my mate. The system. It works that way.

No matter how much you develop and progress, you still know that you have the lower hand. I feel I am near, but then a silly thing like the way a stupid secretary treats you puts you back in that inferior place.

This is the feeling that takes over when you come to coach a Jewish squad. It is even there when you coach an Arab side with a Jewish star: not only a Jewish guy, but the star of the club. So you think to yourself: I'll be soft on this guy, considerate, democratic. Gain his trust and eventually get confirmation that I am all right. This was the way I felt with many Jewish guys I coached. And I know it is all wrong. It is only recently, with a Jewish guy I had in the last club I coached, that I started to feel that I have the hang of it. Actually I am waiting now for the next Jewish guy whom I will coach. I tell you, he is not going to have an easy time. I have had enough. And I also think I am more ready than ever to coach a Jewish team again. I just heard from Hapoel Natzerat Illit again. They say they want to talk to me about next season.

Notes

This essay is based on fieldwork conducted in Natzerat Illit in 1988–89.

1. Following the 1990 season Hapoel Natzerat Illit was promoted to the third division. In 1991 it competed for promotion to the second, eventually losing by a narrow margin. Playing in the third division until 1995, when it was demoted to the fourth, HNI remains Natzerat Illit's only competitive basketball team, and is one of the town's chief sporting representatives.
2. Competitive sport in Israel is controlled by politically oriented sports federations. Hapoel is the biggest federation. Others are Maccabbi (historically affiliated with the liberal party, now part of the right-wing Likud coalition); Betar, affiliated with the right-wing party Herut; and Elitziir, associated with the national religious party Mafdal.
3. Migdal Haemek is an Israeli new town established approximately six kilometers southwest of Natzerat Illit, on the site of the large Palestinian village Mjaidal, which was destroyed in 1948 and reduced to rubble shortly afterward.
4. Investigations in Britain and abroad have since established unequivocally that the PLO was not involved in either planning or executing the operation.
5. Most sports in Israel are played in seasons that correspond to the academic calendar, beginning in September or October and ending in May or June. Summer months are used for resting, regrouping, and preparing for the coming season.
6. Palestinian coaches have not ascended to significant heights in any of Israel's main sporting establishments. Two outstanding examples are the rather marginal sports of weightlifting and boxing, which are considerably more popular among Palestinians than they are among Israelis, and where Palestinian coaches and managers have made their mark. The head coach of the Israeli national boxing team in 1991, for example, was a Palestinian.
7. Riziq's proficiency in such parlance was probably acquired during his academic training at Israel's main sports academy, the Wingate Institute (named after the British colonel Charles Lord Wingate). The institute trains students to use curt, military-like speech when issuing exercise demands to trainees and students.
8. Although this conversation, like all others Riziq had with players of HNI, was conducted in Hebrew, the term "sick note" was said in English. Significantly, Israeli army jargon still retains

a few British Army phrases (e.g., pass, after-duty). Sick note, however, is not one of them. The player seemed to take a while to realize the meaning.

9. See Horowitz and Kimmerling 1974; Katriel 1986, 30–31; Ben-Ari 1989; S. Helman 1993; Kimmerling 1993.
10. Riziq coached another team—a youth team in Nazareth—on alternate nights.
11. In April 1998, when I read the final draft of this chapter to Ra'id, he was even more emphatic. He said, "When I began coaching at the YMCA, it was a different world, in terms of my demand and my insistence that I get my way. One time, when I discovered that management had failed to provide the players with pen and paper to take down my brief, I made a fuss and got what I had asked for. I tell you, I was as harsh with management as I was with the players."
12. A nationwide crisis in the Hapoel sports federation in the late 1980s brought about a similar solution in many branches. Locally organized voluntary associations were often invited to take over the responsibility for senior competitive teams, sometimes even of youth activities. Relinquishing some control over potential foci of public interest, local workers' councils thus nevertheless freed themselves from crippling debt and a considerable workload for their officials.
13. Since Sa'adawi is presently not affiliated with KHK, through which Brakha and her family are insured, her visit to him had to be paid for privately. Because there are not many Israeli specialists in Natzerat Illit to choose among, she would have had to have gone to Haifa or Afula to find one.
14. E. C. Hughes goes on to indicate that the common solution in the United States seems to be voluntary segregation by which, for example, women lawyers represent women clients and black personnel managers "act only in reference to negro employees" (1945, 3).
15. See Peres and Levy 1969; Peres 1971a; Robin 1972; Levy and Guttmann 1976; Zemach 1980; Bizman and Amir 1982; Smooha 1988, 1989–92.
16. These findings, with their emphasis on intention rather than attributes, suggest certain modification of Said's assertion that the Zionist view of Palestinians, which he sees as an amplification of the Western view of the orient, portrays the Palestinians as vicious and stupid (1980, 26).
17. A headline in *Yediot Aharonot* of July 16, 1991, which deals with an assault committed by a Palestinian, reads, "He ran with the axe, waved it about and assaulted as if possessed by a craze." Such characterizations are commonplace in cases in which Palestinians have attacked Israelis but are hardly featured when Israelis use violence against Palestinians.
18. There are, of course, cultural and historical variations. An impressionistic view of mainstream Israel, for example, would suggest that physicians, judges, professional soldiers, and civil engineers enjoy a fair amount of popularity. Advocates, clergymen, academics, and media people, on the other hand, are not as fortunate.
19. Theoretical discussions of the main issues related to trust can be found in Blau 1964, 1968; Deutch 1962; Garfinkel 1963, 1967; Henslin 1972; Luhmann 1979, 1988; Barber 1983; Lewis and Weigart 1985; L. Zucker 1986; S. Shapiro 1987; Roniger 1990.
20. For non-Arabic speakers such as HNI players, Ra'id Riziq's real name is somewhat awkward to grasp: both parts could denote either a family name or a given name. In fact most players were unclear as to which was what. Some addressed him and referred to him only by his surname, Riziq, thinking this was his given name.

19

Israel's Political Economy and the Widening Class Gap between Its Two National Groups

SHULAMIT CARMI and HENRY ROSENFELD

Unlike the situation in many longer-established states, in Israel the state's ruling power, not class power, set in motion the process of class formation and continues to hold the primary role in the process. In this work we view the widening class gap between the dominant Jewish national majority and the Arab (Israeli Palestinian) national minority from the perspective of over four decades of Israel's political economy.

The striking feature of the Israeli political economy is the salient role of the state, not only in class formation but also in its direction of an aggressive militaristic policy and in its capacity to attract unprecedented foreign financial aid, both of which are of fundamental importance in class formation.[1] Through its successful Middle East military policy, the state has adopted privileged national prerogatives in regard to the Palestinians, both those who are its citizens and those in the occupied territories, and through its financial attainments and military takeovers it has supported a developed, expanding, affluent, welfare, and warfare economy. The political economy, with the state ruling power taking the lead, has thrived and, in certain respects, the living standards of the Arab minority population have improved. However, militarism and national privilege have been structured by the state ruling power into class inequality, closing off avenues of advancement for Arabs.

The Nation-State and the (Remnant) Other Nation: Militaristic Nationalism from the Outset

As an outcome of the 1948 war, by the end of 1949 Arabs had become a small minority in Israel: 160,000 compared to 1,013,900 Jews. Loss of family and kin, 650,000–700,000 persons who became refugees, the virtual destruction and disappearance of hundreds of villages, and entire towns empty of Arabs resulted in a population of just one hundred villages (in the Galilee area, in a small concentration in the Little Triangle, and encampments in the Negev, with some 20 percent living in the towns of Nazareth, Shafar'Am, and the mixed Jewish Arab cities). This was a poor, desolate, remnant population that had lost its urban centers of business, learning, and employment, as well as its social and regional links inside the country, not to mention the termination of political, cultural, and other ties outside the country. The entire Palestinian Arab agrarian and commercial political economy with its upper-class echelons of landowners, rentiers, merchants, officeholders, and professionals, along with a religious hierarchy, was destroyed and/or dispersed, and the proletarianization of Arab peasants[2] that had begun in Palestine prior to 1948 was halted.

Throughout the first decade of Israeli statehood Arabs in Israel were faced with the problem of sheer survival, since, among other things, state policy assigned them the role of the enemy. The military government imposed by the state placed Arabs under the watchful eye of the multiple provisions of the British Mandatory government's 1945 Emergency Regulations. Indeed, the military government was the local manifestation of a regional and general Israeli policy determined to preserve by force the 1948 war gains, essentially the non-return of the refugees and state takeover by decree of their land and property. The policy of non-return highly augmented state power by making the state the owner of 93 percent of the country's land, as well as of entire urban areas, public buildings, tens of thousands of dunams of orchards, and so forth, turning the state bureaucracy into the primary authority over land and property management and distribution.

The politics of national dispossession did not flow from the essence of Zionism (as in Rodinson or Asad),[3] nor was it drafted beforehand or dictated by the logic of the war victory (as in Fapan and in Morris).[4] It was a matter of choice and the result of a decision made by the dominant political party, Mapai, and within that party by the prime minister/minister of defense, Ben-Gurion, and his followers. Expropriation of land and property from one nation and its transfer to the other was presented as the necessary condition for mass absorption and settlement of tens of thousands of Jewish immigrants, for agricultural and industrial development, and as indispensable to Israel's national security and survival. Militaristic policy was immediately highly profitable and convenient for the regime, no doubt a victory for the right wing (Mapai) of Labor and the Zionist right, and would be a crippling blow for the Zionist socialist movement.[5] The non-return policy of Israel was denounced in the United Nations and it was not fully approved by the United States.[6] Since the United States occupied a special place in the economic salvation of the Israeli state as early as 1948, it could have curbed Israeli militarism, but it did not do so. Success in mobilizing external financial aid without the obligation to adhere to UN Resolution 194 of December 11, 1948, recognizing the right of return of, and/or compensation for, the Palestinian refugees, was perhaps the outstanding achievement of Israeli policy. U.S. economic aid, which began as a $100 million loan, became a permanent component of the Israeli political economy.[7] Since American aid was not made contingent on Israel's retreating from some of the gains of its military victory, the United States lent sanction to them and, by so doing, gave Israel a free hand in its relations with the remnant Palestinian Arab population, as well as in terms of their land and property.[8]

External economic and political aid, alongside the war spoils, were fundamental factors in further enhancing the centrality of the state. Almost all the aid was structured in such a fashion that it went straight from government to government. That is to say, the determination, planning, budgeting, and execution of its programs for growth and development essentially were in the state's hands. Militarism as policy (the use of force and military superiority as the solution to the national problem), statist centrality, and external aid formed a coherent structure, implemented by the state bureaucracy into facts on the ground.

A mass immigration of Jews, survivors and refugees of Nazism, many of whom were barred from entrance into Palestine by Mandatory government policy and by the Arab Palestinian leadership, and those who fled Middle Eastern countries in the wake of war and Israeli statehood—750,000 during the first three to four years, 1948–51—replaced, as it were, the number of Arab refugees. The Arabs, the population of the other (Palestinian) nation—who were few in number and were living in small and scattered pockets in the country—now existed at the edges of Israeli society. Former Arab towns and mixed Jewish Arab cities were populated by the new immigrants. Arab refugee houses and property were expropriated by the government, and the tiny Arab populations in these towns and cities were forced into depressed areas. During this period of mass immigration, approximately five hundred Jewish settlements, townships, and camps were established.[9]

There is nothing more pertinent to the meaning of class privilege and order in Israel than the centrality of the state, and there are only two factors—military power and the external aid it receives—more important than land takeover in understanding how its central powers were augmented. The land confiscations and expropriations from the remaining Arab villages and owners took place against the background of the grand takeover by Israel of land and property of the refugees whose rights, while recognized by international law, were ignored by the state. It is estimated that 4–5 million dunams of refugee land ("abandoned land") were taken over by Israel.[10] With regard to the Palestinian Arab citizens of Israel, 50–70 percent of their land was confiscated by the state mainly during 1948–53. Takeover has not ceased, and Arabs in Israel now own 400,000–450,000 dunams (not including land in the Negev) out of approximately 1.5 million dunams of land originally theirs prior to 1948.[11]

While the long-term impact of the military government on Arab life, labor, and property is still not fully known, there is no doubt that the extent of its control was even more restrictive and pervasive than its eighteen years (1948–66) of formal operation alone indicate. The military government directly intervened in matters regarding the return of refugee family members, in local politics, in village leadership, in court matters, in civil concerns, in clan and intercommunal conflicts, and so forth, and not only in the areas of Arab livelihood and economic conditions.

The first years of statehood carry with them all the indicators of radical change, especially those of (Jewish) national, state growth on the one hand and of (Palestinian Arab) national marginalization on the other. From what was to be approximately 40 percent of the population in the area allotted to Israel in the 1947 UN Partition Plan, Arabs became 10–12 percent of the new state's population; the Israeli government turned a binational reality into an almost but not quite pure nation-state. One-fifth to one-quarter of the Arab population were turned into "internal refugees," uprooted from, and not allowed to return to, their former homes and lands and forcibly appended on or into other Arab village communities. Migrant laborers and others were confined to their home villages. Housing conditions and food shortages for the small Arab populations in the mixed cities were the worst of all. Nonetheless, refugees, suffering from hunger and poverty, often waited on the borders opposite their villages to return to their homes and land.

The Exclusion of the Arab Village from the Agricultural Revolution

From the 1949 armistice agreements and the start of the mass Jewish immigration to 1960, Israeli agriculture underwent a revolutionary development and in many respects became similar to what it is today. That is, agriculture became highly intensified, mechanized, and diversified. The amount of land under cultivation increased from 1.65 million dunams to over 4 million dunams (in 1985 it was 4.35 million); the amount of land under irrigation increased even more sharply from 300,000 dunams to 1.3 million dunams. By 1960 it was completely different agriculture from that of 1948–49: the plantations area had doubled; egg production (formerly an import item) increased from 3 to 8 million units per year; the number of milk cows almost quadrupled; and dairy farming reached a productive capacity not far below that of today while the population has since more than doubled. Water input for agriculture, a good indicator of the revolutionary change, quadrupled from 257,000,000 to 1,060,000,000 cubic meters; this was achieved mainly through the introduction of regional water carriers in the north and east, and the countrywide carrier from the north to the arid areas in the south. (By the beginning of the 1980s it had risen only to 1,212,000,000 cubic meters.) The number of tractors increased from 1,300 in 1949–50 to 7,400 in 1960.[12]

The number of Jewish settlements increased from 333 in 1949 to 721 in 1953. Many of the settlers were newcomers to farming. During the first decade the absorptive capacity of agriculture increased as did innovation. In 1955 approximately 17 percent (102,000 persons) of the total employed (585,700 persons) in Israel were in agriculture (including forestation, land reclamation, and so forth). While we cannot here discuss the social structure of agriculture, because communal and cooperative movements with their accumulated knowledge and local experience were among its main components, their countrywide federations provided an organizational base allowing even newly established settlements to take part in the transformation.

The annual rate of economic growth in Israel during 1950–65 was 10–11 percent, "more than for any other state for which data is available"; for 1950–55 it was 12–13 percent, and for 1955–65, 9–10 percent annually.[13] The rate of growth in agriculture was fairly similar: 13 percent until the mid-1950s when it began to decline, mainly as a result of overproduction, falling prices, storage problems, and limited export outlets.[14]

The central role of the state was even more important in agriculture than it was in other economic branches; thus, the exclusion of the remaining 100–120 Arab villages from effective areas of the agricultural revolution must be regarded as a matter of policy. When opportunities for jobs opened up in Palestine's World War II economy of the late 1930s and the 1940s, approximately half of the Arab rural male workforce, in an Arab population that was predominantly village-dwelling, were wage workers or peasant wage workers. The dry, extensive grain farming in Arab villages did not provide a livelihood for the majority of their inhabitants. Thus road building, transportation and hauling, maintenance work in British army camps, and other jobs in the ports, refineries, police force, and so forth attracted thousands of peasants up until the 1948 war. All this halted after 1948, and at the same time the Israeli government did not include the remnant Arab villages in its development program—Arab agriculture did not receive means for diversification or water for irrigation, did not undergo mechanization,[15] and, on the whole, continued cultivating traditional crops (wheat, barley, sesame, melons, olives, and so forth).

Therefore, when we read that 49 percent (21,800 out of an Arab labor force of 43,400) were employed in agriculture up to 1955, and 45 percent in 1959,[16] we might think that Arabs existed in a separate subsistence economy and not within the Israeli economy. The reverse was in fact true. The military government insisted that all Arabs who worked outside their home villages prior to the 1948 war had to return to them. In addition, the military government kept them, and most others, inside their villages for years afterward. Taking into account the fact that up to 1953 the state expropriated approximately half the land of the Arabs, and with their existing means and techniques the Arab villages could not possibly "employ" 45–49 percent of their labor force in agriculture, the percentages are better grasped euphemistically to indicate that Arabs were contained within their villages against their will and were denied employment; many eked out their living as best as they could from the land.

Agricultural growth and development in Israel were essentially dependent on investments and outlays from the state (and with regard to the hundreds of new Jewish settlements, entirely so). Centralized planning coordinated the settlement of groups, as well as their farm buildings, animals, inventory, machinery, water installations, housing, and so on. During 1949–61, of $4.6 billion in capital import, $1.6 billion was invested by the government in development projects, roads, electricity, and land reclamation; agricultural settlement and water resources received 30 percent of this amount.[17]

From the beginning, the state mobilized two main elements for growth and development from outside the system and tenaciously safeguarded their continuous inclusion within the system. The capital for the machines, installations, seeds, and so on came mainly from American Jews, the U.S. government, and, from 1953 onward, German reparations. Since most land was provided via military takeover from the Arabs, the state was not under pressure either to buy land in the market as was done during British rule or to include those from whom it took the land (both the Palestinians outside and those in Israel) in its development schemes.

Under this policy of expropriation and exclusion, not one Jewish settlement lacked piped water, while during the first decade the overwhelming majority of Arab communities were without running water. It is not our purpose to detail comparisons, only to provide some insight into the state at work. Over 40 percent of "Jewish" cultivated land (3,202,000 million dunams) was under irrigation in 1959–60; under 4 percent (728,000 dunams) of Arab cultivated lands were irrigated. (In 1990, 65 percent of "Jewish" cultivated land and 8 percent of Arab cultivated land were irrigated.)[18]

To no small extent this tremendous undertaking in agriculture and settlement relied on militaristic prerogatives. That is, without the military government the ruling party could not have had a free hand to convert land takeover into an elaborate system of national privilege. In the summer of 1948, the military government undermined Arab citizens' property and communal rights by leaving them open to arbitrary ruling power interpretations. (Even a rare instance of intervention by the Israeli High Court was overruled by military force.)[19] "Reasons of security" provided rationalizations for the military government's actions ("the Arabs are enemies of the state," "they haven't accepted that this is a Jewish state," "our policy is necessary for the absorption of the new immigrants"), and "reasons of culture, national character, and tradition" for why Arabs were not amenable to agricultural development and modernity (e.g., "the backwardness of the Arab peasant," "their sectarian habits and factionalism," "their land division practices").

Nation-state privilege defined class relations between Jews and Arabs, that is, who has the means of production, a developed infrastructure, electricity, and so forth—the haves and the have-nots. How, then, does a democratic, pluralistic society with advanced socialist and liberal movements and parties accommodate itself to a policy of privilege and expropriation? As we have discussed elsewhere, the pluralistic character of the Israeli political structure should not deceive us because at the same time it was—and long remained—a highly centralized power system.[20] The answer, then, comes down to the centrality of the state and the ruling party. All the political and economic institutions of the Histadrut (trade unions), including the Union of Agricultural Workers, all the retail, wholesale, and marketing cooperatives, Tnuva, the financial institutions, the Agricultural Bank, the water companies, the specific associations of agricultural growers and professions, and so on were under the authority of the party, Mapai, that ran the government, and controlled the Zionist Congress, funding, and settlement institutions. The non-return and land takeover policy turned nearly every Jew into a complicit partner and defender of its terms. Moreover, the strong lasting pressure of army service, numerous armed skirmishes alongside outright wars, the direct participation in events of a relatively small population, and so forth were conducive to the acceptance of the dominant role of the prime minister/defense minister. Nonetheless, the policy of separation and imposition of a military government on Arab citizens had, as is well-known, opponents from the left, the liberals, and the right. The latter opposed the political and electoral monopoly that the military government provided the ruling party. The Zionist left, not only the Communist Party, had Arab members and were firm critics of national inequality and military government. However, the opposition failed over many years to change the situation by parliamentary and political means.

The Resumption of Arab Labor Migrancy under Harsh Economic Conditions and Political-Military Restrictions

In order to gain a livelihood, simply to survive, Arab villagers sought work in their immediate neighborhoods. However, they were faced with military government tribunals, fines, and jail sentences. Villages were closed off, limited movement areas demarcated, and severe restrictions imposed, allowing for only a minor trickle of favored individuals to join the job market. Christians (20 percent of the Arab population and mainly urban) had a somewhat easier time than did the Muslims (70 percent of the Arab population and mainly rural). And while the rural Druzes (10 percent of the Arab population), unlike the Muslims and Christians, were looked upon favorably by the authorities because of their military service, it had a minor effect on their chances of securing jobs.

Since government labor exchanges served local residents only, the migrant Arab laborer could not turn to them. In addition, the cities were crowded with Jews looking for jobs and with the unemployed in general, and the labor exchanges primarily allocated relief work in road repair, forestation, and a twelve-day month in public works at a minimum wage. In all areas and in all the cities there was a surplus of workers: Jews from new immigrant camps, villages, and new towns looking for work. Histadrut officials adopted the same exclusionary policy toward the Arab as worker as did state and municipal officials to the Arab as local inhabitant and military government officials to the Arab as citizen.

It is important to point out that the number of Arabs within both the population and the labor force was also very small. In 1949, the 160,000 Arabs were 13 percent of the population; in 1954 there were 192,000 Arabs (11.3 percent of a population of 1,718,000). In 1954, 38,300 Arabs were employed out of an Arab labor force of 43,000. Officially they were 6–7 percent of the employed in the country and most were recorded as being "employed" in agriculture. In 1961 there were 53,500 Arabs employed (7.5 percent of the total employed), and in 1964, 66,200 Arabs were employed (7.7 percent of the Israeli labor force and 11.3 percent of the population).[21]

Unorganized Arab labor had to accept low wages and was often illegal. Arabs worked at temporary employment as laborers on infrastructure projects (such road construction, sewage, land reclamation, and forestation). They worked the longest hours and received the lowest pay, and were away from home, often without kin and without union or any juvenile or worker's protection. They were also at the mercy of the military government and/or ready informers.

During most of the 1950s Arab labor migration remained more or less a trickle as a result of the sealing off of the Arab villages by the military government and the loss of former sources of urban employment and housing. But the most important factor was the ongoing general unemployment and partial employment in the Israeli economy. In 1956, 250,000 Jewish immigrants were still in camps. The daily lineups at the labor exchanges continued and thousands were on relief work. Only when this situation changed did Arab labor migrancy gain some momentum and then, with full employment in the 1960s, become Arabs' main way of earning a living.

Some improvement in economic conditions was noticeable during the mid-1950s after mass immigration slowed, but it was more obvious after the finalization of the German reparations agreement in 1953–54. Increased imports of machinery and raw materials for agricultural infrastructure and industry expanded the job market. Rationing was abolished as a result of agricultural successes and, because the financing of food imports, ceased to be problematic. Reparations payments encouraged rising housing standards, and the building industry regained its position as a leading employer. These years are known for rapid economic growth, 10 percent or more,[22] but unemployment remained a major problem, and in some areas of the country, particularly in the north, where most Arabs lived, it was even more acute. Only in the aftermath of the 1956 Suez War, with the accumulated effect of extended foreign aid, did workers begin to enjoy full employment.

The Centralist State Combined High Military Performance, High Foreign Aid, and Growing Domestic Affluence

It is difficult to say that the economic gains of the first (1948) war were matched by those of the second (1956) war despite the fact that Israel distinguished itself militarily and two colonial powers, England and France, stood by its side. There were no permanent territory or property acquisitions, and most of the 1956 national budget had to cover the cost of the war. Nevertheless, for almost a decade following the Suez War the economy experienced extensive development. Local activity was spurred by the growth in capital transfer from the same sources: West German reparations, grants and loans from Jews worldwide, and U.S. aid. Transfer was generally from government to government. The state became more practiced in its capacity to attract foreign aid that responded favorably to war victory.

The effect of foreign aid was seen in a number of ways, particularly in the steep increases in the goods and services imported each year. For example, in 1959 imports to Israel totaled nearly $600 million, while in 1964 it was twice that amount. Israel's exports in 1959 totaled $267 million; by 1964 they more than doubled. However, the gap of almost 50 percent between imports and exports remained. While the import-export gap in 1959 was $319 million, unilateral transfer covered $250 million of the deficit, with an additional $90 million coming from long-term loans. In 1964 the gap was $564 million, since the country imported twice as much as it exported; unilateral transfers covered $330 million of this with the remainder covered by long-term loans, again leaving a reserve.[23]

This is another way to look at the central place of the state in the economy, a place far superior to what was exhibited by its sectoral employment or welfare services. Economic aid enabled Israel to operate a planned economy and more: the state was a major employer, the main owner of land, and the main investor in all branches of the economy. Unlike other planned and developing economies, the state did not have to depend on internal accumulation to finance its high rate of economic growth; it could and did rely on heavy imports not matched by exports without falling into the debt trap. Generous aid, which was not essentially military (at this time) and not only "foreign" in the strict sense (Jewish, German, U.S.), allowed Israel great economic flexibility in terms of investment in production and consumption, warfare and welfare.

Defense outlays did not fall below 8–10 percent of the GNP between the 1956 and 1967 wars, but the defense burden was more than ameliorated by improved conditions of aid.[24] Thus, economic growth was not curbed by government defense outlays, and most Israelis managed to improve their standard of living during this period.

Building and public and other services were the growing areas of the economy as far as employment was concerned. In 1961 agriculture accounted for less than 12 percent of Jewish employment (down from 18 percent in 1950), and less than one-fourth of Israelis (23.2 percent) were employed in industry.[25] Even with the great land takeover from the Arabs, and mass immigration of Jews who were supposed to be the peasant replacement (mainly Oriental Jews), Israel retained its main (Jewish) pre-state Mandatory characteristics of an urban service economy.

Local industry was not overly pressed to develop import substitutes or to meet the demands of the rising standard of living enjoyed by the overwhelming majority of the public. For most of the 1960s, full employment and reparations enabled a growing sector of the public to purchase modern household equipment, radios, washing machines, and even cars, when 90 percent of these goods were imported. Israeli industry remained small to medium sized and was concentrated in the traditional branches of citrus growing, food, textile, and pharmaceutical and chemical production, phosphate mining, and diamond polishing. Such was the picture, more or less, until slightly after the third war in 1967.

Class Dimensions: Processes in the Formation of the Jewish "Upper Half" and the Ethnic and National Composition of the "Lower Half"

Class formation took place mainly via government assistance and financing in various contract opportunities in combined public-private ventures in finance, importing and exporting, real estate, commerce, entrepreneurship, management, and legal and professional establishments, as well as in the great expansion of and openings provided in upper-level government administration. The upper half of earners consisted primarily of veteran Ashkenazi Jews. The new strata included those with education, professions, skills, some means, or a business, property, or real estate, whose standard of living improved most in terms of property ownership, profit, and income.[26]

All social groups benefited from the expansion of the economy in the second decade; the standard of living rose as people enjoyed increased income and consumption. However, the neediest made the fewest gains. Among Jews, most of the latter were Oriental immigrants, heads of big families, less educated or less skilled, or less connected. Many were settled in the peripheral, rural areas or development towns, or in immigrant camps where social, welfare, municipal, and other services were underdeveloped and where the job market had little to offer. Textile or food-processing plants set up to ease local employment pressures were primarily projects that had high installation costs and yielded low wages, forcing the townships and the surrounding areas into all the instabilities and insecurities of dependence on labor-intensive, mono-industry. The differences in pace and scope of economic development during the first two decades had far-reaching effects on class formation and the preservation of ethnic conflict and antagonisms. What the lower half gained from economic growth was relative full employment in building and manual services and, over time, in the second generation, the advances created from improved local education and welfare and health services.

In the 1960s Arabs remained a small fragment (7 percent) of the labor force, and almost all were at the bottom of the lower half. Employment in government bureaucracy and the status of "state employee" was, with very few exceptions, a Jewish monopoly; the same can be said about the more secure jobs in Histadrut workplaces. Even after the gradual removal of restrictions leading up to the formal abolishment of the military government in 1966, Arabs remained migrant laborers who sought jobs wherever they could be found. They did not move their families to the urban or rural areas where they were employed.

During the full employment of the 1960s, 80–90 percent of employed Arabs became wage workers, most outside their home villages and in jobs that were the least desirable, paid by the day or the hour, and physically the most demanding. Arabs in these jobs rarely accumulated the social benefits that had been the cornerstones of Jewish workers' rights (sick days, annual vacation, severance pay, promotion, and so forth). By dint of their persistence and perseverance under these conditions, Arabs remained in the labor market. The pattern of Arab proletarianization, labor migrancy, hard physical labor away from home, but high to full employment held up to the recession of 1965 that ended with the 1967 war.[27]

During the first fifteen to twenty years of Israeli statehood there were obvious similarities in class terms between Arabs and (mainly) Oriental Jews, most of whom were in the four lowest deciles and endured long stretches of unemployment and temporary low-paying jobs. Nor was labor migrancy strictly an Arab phenomenon. High population turnover characterized Jewish localities and townships; Jews often moved to the urban centers in search of jobs and a higher standard of living. This kind of residential change was not possible for Arab laborers.

With the upsurge after the 1967 war employment rose sharply, and toward the end of the decade there was a shortage of workers. Full employment was the single most important factor for Arabs, who were the least secure among the wage workers. What did and did not change for them? The differences between Arab and Jewish workers narrowed with regard to the rate of unemployment (since Arabs were prepared to continue under conditions of migrancy), and the gap closed somewhat in terms of family income since, among other things, the number of earners per Arab family was relatively greater. The wage gap narrowed significantly, primarily because Arabs were to be found in the, at the time, better-paying contract work branches such as construction and infrastructure projects. Hostels were not built for Arab migrant workers, nor did they receive travel allowances. But the availability of work, and good wages, and the demand for skilled workers in building, as well as the purchase of pickup trucks and cars by Arab subcontractors, helped raise the Arab wage-earning family's standard of living and had a visible impact on village life. Better and regular wage income helped many Arab households and locales pay for the installation of piped water and electricity. The fact that many Arabs worked as plumbers, painters, masons, electricians, carpenters, or skilled workers was perhaps more important in this respect since the government invested nothing in Arab housing and little (with the exception, at the time, of primary schooling) in the basic installations of electricity, water, and roads in Arab communities. With these skills and their savings, Arabs built their own homes with indoor toilets, kitchens, showers, balconies, and so forth, and gradually acquired modern home appliances in line with Israeli standards.

Greater Militarism: Conquest, Military Aid, and Industrial Changes

With the 1967 war and the occupation by Israel of the West Bank and the Gaza Strip, the government's role in the economy reached new heights. In particular, the state succeeded in attracting even greater levels of external aid. The major sources remained Jewish (national) funds and German reparations, but, unlike 1956, these were quickly overshadowed by military and economic aid, mainly from the U.S. government, which apparently began to regard the arming of Israel as a project. Even prior to the 1967 war, when Israel's alliance with France was still strong, there was a sharp rise in U.S. military aid to Israel. In 1971 U.S. unilateral aid alone reached $800 million; over the decade it jumped to more than $2 billion and in 1980 reached $3 billion annually. (The foreign debt nevertheless increased but remained essentially long-term government-to-government debt.)

External aid generously nurtured all facets of local economic activity. Exports jumped from $1.1 billion in 1968 to $1.8 billion in 1971 and reached $10 billion in 1980. Imports rose even more sharply from $1.8 billion in 1968 to $3 billion in 1971 and to $14 billion in 1980. Israeli defense outlays rose from (the very high) 10.4 percent of the GNP before the war in 1966 to approximately 30 percent throughout 1970–80.[28] The main items on the military budget were armaments, upkeep of the army, local purchases, and investment in local military production.

The rates for employment, consumption, imports, and exports all grew, but most outstanding were military purchases and orders from all branches of the economy for goods, food, clothing, building, services, and so on in order to maintain a larger, more active, and better-equipped army. The 1967 war and occupation resulted in new Palestinian refugees (250,000), more Israeli land takeover, new Jewish settlement, roads and neighborhoods, and, for the deployment of the Israeli armed forces, new camps and fortifications. It is clear that this economic and territorial expansion, compared to that which followed the Suez War, relied heavily on U.S. government money and extensive U.S. military aid, by means of which local armaments and arms-related industries received a new impetus. (There was also a complete transition from French to U.S. armaments.)

It is within this joint (U.S.-Israel) strategic-military understanding that structural change within the Israeli economy took place. The rapid growth of military and high-tech industries was the outstanding feature of this change. The ministry of defense became an important producer, while previously it had been essentially a large-scale purchaser and importer. Up until the 1967 war the ministry had mainly affected local production as a major buyer of local goods such as shoes, clothing, and building materials. The radical leap to heavier military production began with government investment in assembly and repair plants, local production of replacement items, and import substitutes that pushed production for export. The development of a more sophisticated local armaments industry was connected to a combination of extensive imports fueled by tremendous external capital aid. Armaments and arms-components companies (Bedek, Military Industries, Raphael, Air Force Industries, Soltam, and so forth) grew rapidly. The state was not necessarily the owner of all military enterprises, but it did own most, was the main investor and initiator, and in one form or another was also connected with Histadrut and private companies (e.g., Tadiran) that participated in military production for the Israeli army and for export.

These capital-intensive, mostly high-tech companies employed highly skilled professional labor. They included plants with large (often the largest) workforces such as those that developed the Lavie fighter plane and the Merkavah tank as well as smaller companies that produced sophisticated components, electronics, optics, radar systems, and so forth. Such enterprises required long-term research, planning and investment, international marketing connections, and civilian and military management. The expanding armaments industries attracted highly trained scientific and engineering personnel, along with skilled workers, and offered favorable conditions for their future training and advancement.

By the middle of the 1970s the military industries had become serious exporters of armaments: by the 1980s, they contributed one-fourth of Israel's industrial exports.[29] Nonetheless, at their height, the yearly export sales of armaments fell still below the annual military grant of approximately $1.8 billion from the United States. With the success of the local military industry, smaller arms defense-connected plants were also established through government promotion and investment in many of the peripheral Jewish townships in the north (e.g., Qiryat Shemona, Ma'alot) and south (e.g., Ofaqim, Bet Shemesh) and in the occupied territories (e.g., Ophra, Hebron), areas and places that had been dependent for the most part on labor-intensive plants.

Even though Israel has engaged in five wars and has maintained a conquest state for decades, it is obvious that we are not dealing with a war economy but with a political economy that has a high, continuous stake in militarism. We have explained elsewhere that it was not the occupation of the West Bank and Gaza Strip in 1967 that served as the major factor in the developments that restructured Israeli militarism into a militaristic political economy. Rather, it was the overwhelming, massive U.S. military and other aid, and the place Israel held within U.S.-Middle East policy. With the occupation, the aid and the strategic linkage reached more sophisticated levels.[30] Occupation and conquest certainly provided further ideological raisons d'être for ongoing militarism, firmed it, as it were, but a constant show of military force, successive wars, and confrontations also served the same ends.

Heavy armament imports extending over many years, along with the increase in local production and export, gave rise to a burgeoning group of Israeli arms dealers who, alongside importers, bankers, industrialists, big contractors, corporation lawyers, and so on, amassed great wealth. Not only were Arabs outside this proliferation, but they were disqualified from seeking employment in the majority of enterprises in the developing branches. Security disqualification encompassed not only government military establishments but also private and Histadrut high-tech plants. The rising branches further altered the wage structure, mobility patterns, and the differentials between occupations in the economy, confining Arabs to the lower half of the wage-earning population.

Class-National Differences in the Expanding Branches of Employment (Government and Office Jobs, Business Services, High-Tech and Arms-Related Industries)

In 1983 one-fifth of Arabs employed in Israel (22,700) worked in construction, while the number of Jewish employees declined to 4.1 percent (52,900). Indeed, building was a growing "Arab branch."[31] Another 30–50 percent of the employed workers (officially 43,000 in 1983) were Arabs from the occupied territories.

Industry became an equally important branch of employment for Arabs. According to the 1983 census, 20.2 percent (24,000) of Arabs and 21.7 percent (282,000) of Jews were employed in industry. But, the proportional similarity went no further; branch composition was very different. Arabs were absent from all the high-tech, electronics, and military-affiliated industries, which were also the higher-paying ones that required more qualifications. Arabs remained primarily in the food, textile, and plastics industries, as well as assembly line production, where wages were low and conditions far inferior. The industrial branches from which Arabs were absent were also those with close ties to higher academic institutions that provided training, grants for advanced studies, job recommendations, and so forth. There is a direct link between professional and management posts and partnership in the advanced industries—where the rising upper echelons also managed to combine high salaries and high profits.

The proliferation of military-related, high-tech industries and occupations following the 1967 war (and, even more so, the 1973 war) provides a partial, but important, explanation for the widening gap between Jews and Arabs in terms of standard of living and economic status. The rise of new and advanced opportunities remained beyond the reach of Arab young people, qualified students, professionals, and so forth, who also continued to suffer under previously mentioned depressive factors such as the need for labor migrancy, which was itself the outcome of underdeveloped villages devoid of employment opportunities. Unlike Jewish townships, Arab locales were not included on the government's development list. Exclusion sharpened further the fact that most Arab workers were employed by Jews, in itself a sufficient reason why work relations are strongly marked by a class-national dimension.

The new industrial, technological, and professional opportunities added strong state military systemic connections, a factor that helps explain their exclusionist nature and their contribution to the widening class gap.

We discussed the industrial branches that expanded greatly in personnel and production during the 1970s and 1980s. However, industry in general provided fewer new jobs than did other branches of the economy and even declined in relative terms. Financial, business, and public services provided most jobs for those joining the labor force and/or for those who left industry, primarily Jews.[32]

The fact that Arabs were mainly rural and that their educational level was relatively lower than that of Jews, and that ministries and central banks were Jewish and not Arab, explains to a certain extent the continuing low representation of Arabs in state public and business services. Offices chose their personnel and workers and they did not choose Arabs; and, if pressed to account for the almost total absence of Arabs in the state ministries, vast bureaucracies, or local offices, "security" was given as the reason.

During the first decade of statehood, Jews and Arabs found jobs primarily in agriculture, public works, and construction. In the second decade agriculture declined, but construction remained an important branch that compensated for the skills and efforts of Jews and Arabs. In the third and fourth decades, those following the 1967 war and the occupation, Jewish workers began to leave jobs in construction and no new Jewish workers replaced them. During the fourth decade (1989), the two previous mass employment branches, construction and agriculture, together employed fewer (9.6 percent) Jews and local Arabs than did either finance (10 percent) or business services (10 percent).[33]

The rapid decrease of Jewish construction workers has generally been attributed to the influx of low-paid Palestinian labor from the occupied territories. This explanation is incomplete. Work in agriculture and construction is hard physical labor, and workers have always sought opportunities for more secure, less seasonal employment. Such possibilities for veteran workers and for those who had recently joined the labor market were made available through the state's expanding services and the expansion of business services (banks, financial institutions, the stock exchange, brokerage firms, and so forth). Finance and business jobs grew from 5.2 percent of the total employed in 1970 to 8.2 percent in 1980 and 10 percent (146,000) in 1989. Public and community services jobs for the same years grew from 24 percent (1970) to 29.6 percent (1980), where it remained up to 1989 (431,000).[34] That is, the expansion of state and business domains (far more than high-tech and armaments production) gave Jews the opportunity to leave agriculture and construction. The great expansion of these services followed the increase in military and other grants, loans, and government debit financing. From this standpoint, after the 1967 war and occupation, the vast import of capital and the possibility to further enlarge it turned Israel into more of a service economy than ever before.

Thus, the radical factor that contributed to the widening socioeconomic gap between Jewish and Arab working-class families was the growth of services that supplied employment not only for Jewish men but mainly for Jewish women. The government provided more, and a wider range of, welfare, health, and educational services (e.g., free education up to age eighteen, training centers, welfare services for the elderly), and of local, municipal services in the townships and locals. In addition, private services such as banks and tourism expanded. The number of jobs in financing, trade, and tourism grew by more than 50 percent during 1970–82, and women became the majority of employees in these areas. However, the main employers of women were and have remained the government and municipalities and other state and public administrations (from 44 percent in 1970 to 56 percent in 1982). These branches were the major contributors to the growth of Jewish female employment from 25 percent in the 1960s to 40 percent of the wage earners in the 1980s. In 1975, for example, there were 1,006,700 Jewish employed; in 1987 the number rose to 1,245,800. Of the additional 239,100 Jewish employed, two-thirds were women; 353,300 Jewish women were employed in 1975 and 519,700 (39 percent of all Jewish employees) in 1987.[35]

In social terms the change meant that from the mid-1970s onward, two-earner families ceased to be mainly Ashkenazi and spread to the majority of young Jewish Israeli families, including more and more of those of Oriental origins. In standard of living terms it meant that car ownership, a three-room apartment, travel outside the country, and more became matters of popular and no longer conspicuous middle-class consumption. Often of the two earners at least one enjoyed job permanency as a government or municipal employee. Job security carried with it possibilities for holding a mortgage, obtaining low-rate loans, and so forth. Although Israeli-born Jews of Oriental origin are not proportionally represented in the universities, in high-income professions, or in business ownership and contracting, they have greatly improved their conditions as earners.

The increase in two-earner families is enough to explain the widening income gap between the Arab and Jewish working populations. Male Arab workers did not advance into the new highly favored, better-paying employment branches mentioned, and the vast majority of Arab women remained outside the labor market. In 1980 the number of Arabs employed (including East Jerusalem) was 127,500, of whom 15 percent (20,000) were women (in 1989, the figure was 16 percent [28,000]).[36]

Even though Arabs had a very minor share in the employment possibilities as a result of the development in health, welfare, and education services, the rising level of social welfare did not bypass them. Similar to other families with limited financial means, Arabs enjoyed the reforms that provided free secondary school education. At the time (the 1970s and early 1980s), university student fees were also highly subsidized. The small increase of Arabs in public services correlated primarily with the rise in numbers of Arab teachers and school personnel, which in itself was connected to the high rate of growth of the numbers of Arab school-age children. Over time the establishment of local councils in approximately half (55) of the Arab villages and townships (with another 35 connected to regional councils) also provided some local employment.[37]

Meanwhile, Israeli occupation of the West Bank and the Gaza Strip in itself wrote large the implications of the military aspect of the economy together with its differential impact on Jews and Arabs. Although this is at the (militaristic) heart of the matter—the occupation of the territory of another nation and the control of this nation by armed force—we cannot here deal with its political, economic, ethical, or social facets. We touch on only two points: some of the advantages accruing to Jewish groups from the occupation, and the exploitation of Palestinians in the labor market. The government's action concerning land expropriation, settlement, building, infrastructure investment, and large military outlays in the occupied territories attracted numerous Jewish groups: contractors and subcontractors in every imaginable field, along with their political supporters and legal advisors, were some of the known beneficiaries. The control of Palestinian markets ensured the monopolistic position of Israeli goods and services. The government's Civil Administration provided better-paying jobs and contracts for Jewish employees who lived inside the green line. The huge upsurge in government settlement policy following the victory of the right in the 1977 election obliged it to invest in infrastructure housing and finance the upkeep of public and communal services.

As far as labor is concerned, up to the end of 1987, 80,000–120,000 Palestinians from the occupied territories worked daily in Israel (these numbers were often severely reduced by curfews, closures, and other security restrictions).[38] Most Palestinians were low-paid laborers in construction and manual services (restaurants, quick-food stands, municipal and public sanitation and maintenance), in markets and shopping malls, in small industry, in the citrus industry, in agricultural work, and so forth at wages often 50 percent below the going rate for Jews and, in general, under unprotected conditions. Contract and piecework along with the employment of children and women for long hours and at low wages were common among Palestinians. Most of the wages paid to workers from the occupied territories returned to Israel through the daily purchase of goods and services by the Palestinian population, as well as in the form of taxes and fines levied by the state.[39]

Since the employment of numerous Palestinians from the occupied territories was arranged through work contractors, the job market has tended to become employer- and/or contractor-controlled. Trade unions in the occupied territories were not recognized by the Israeli Histadrut or by the state. These two were the largest employers in the Israeli economy. In spite of their highly unionized tradition, Israeli labor institutions got along with split, nationally differentiated wages paid in the same market. In class terms it was not a win-win situation. Thus in the beginning of the 1980s, when the first signs of a recession in Israel were becoming evident, the unemployment of local Israeli workers did not affect the employment of the Palestinians from the occupied territories (similar to the situation in Europe in the 1970s and early 1980s, where high unemployment went hand-in-hand with large-scale employment of migrant workers).[40]

The Political Economy Receives Much and Needs More: High Aid and Armaments Outlay Alongside Shortcomings in the Service Belt

The rise in unemployment in Israel during the 1980s (from 5 percent at the beginning, 8–9 percent midway, and 10–11 percent at the end of the decade) followed nearly twenty years of relative full employment. During the 1950s–1960s, recession was evident primarily in layoffs in construction. Although in the 1980s the construction branch was also affected as a result of reduced government input, cuts were also made in the defense budget with reduced purchases of locally produced defense items. The strongest establishments were most affected—the armaments and high-tech, military-related industries which, as mentioned, were the most subsidized as well as the most rapidly growing component in Israel's export production.

The cuts by the ministry of defense in orders from local industries after the Israeli invasion of Lebanon in 1982 were paralleled by an increasingly problematic general market for military hardware and arms, a market that has become more competitive and was experiencing shrinking demand. Since this production requires heavy financial outlays, U.S. collaboration has always been critical. Major local Israeli projects (e.g., the Lavie airplane, the Merkavah tank) were canceled, and others, such as participation in the SDI project of the United States, are in doubt. Though these cutbacks in production were not accompanied by a reduction in U.S. aid, they could have survived only by means of increased U.S. funding, which was not forthcoming.

The crisis in a modern, capital-intensive, dynamic industrial sector, one employing highly qualified personnel, furthers our understanding of the pitfalls, and even contradictions, stemming from the "most favored" cash and military position reserved for Israel by the United States. Israel's favored status remained as strong as ever. (For Israel, the major beneficiary of U.S. aid, the package officially stood at $3 billion annually: $1.8 billion in military aid, $1.2 billion in economic aid.) At the same time that many Third World countries, new states, are imprisoned by their debts to the big banks, the conditions under which Israel received its cash were better in its fourth decade than ever before; all its yearly aid was provided as a grant.[41]

Much as it was difficult for Israel to compete in the automobile or electrical household appliance markets (refrigerators, washing machine production after armaments, still the heaviest import items) since well-established, stronger industrial producers made entrance into them difficult for newcomers, so it proved to be, in many respects, with military hardware and the high-tech sector as well. The point is that the availability of foreign capital did not solve this basic problem of industrial development. The success of the Israeli armaments industries, 20–25 percent of all industrial export during the 1980s, followed the agreement by the United States to include Israeli local production of arms as a limited aid item.[42] Export was further bolstered by special arrangements with foreign governments, facilitated through the good offices of the United States in addition to their battle-tested proficiency, and the military training that often accompanied sales. The shutdown of a number of large and advanced production plants and the retraction in employment were nevertheless great since much was invested in them and they were regarded as model enterprises, and relatively strong economic groups were affected. In Israel such plants are neither multinationals nor privately owned but are mainly public, state enterprises whose employees are highly organized as academics, professionals, or highly qualified technical personnel.

The limitations in advanced Israeli industry are more obvious in the area of its job-generating capacity than they are in that of investment and production. Prior to the recession, the new, most modern plants did not employ more than 15 percent of the 300,000 employed in industry, and the long-term decline in employment in agriculture and building was not compensated for by growth of employment in industry. Employment expanded in the "production" of services, not in the production of goods, with every third Jew a state employee (not including those in the army). Services absorbed most of the demand for jobs in the labor market, especially that of women, and we can surmise that they helped keep the rate of unemployment down to 5–6 percent during 1980–86. Indeed, services are the government's social remedy to the ejection of workers from the labor-saving, technologically advanced branches, as well as a shelter against other market hazards. Nor did the expansion of services take place at the expense of the government's direct and ongoing investment in and subsidization of industry.[43]

Israel's political economy was and is cushioned by an affluence of means that made possible resilient (if not entirely multiple) lines of development. Thus, the years of government high investment in industry, in civil administration, and in services were also the years that its investment in defense was between one-fourth and one-third of its annual GNP.[44] During the 1980s the government's over-involvement and over-investment in all economic areas brought it to finance its budget by means of heavy local borrowing. Approximately two-thirds of its annual budget was spent on interest payments and defense, and in 1988 local debt rose to 1.5 times its GNP. The assumption that government spending fueled inflation brought the authorities in 1985 to introduce another round of devaluation and budgetary restraints, as well as cuts on defense and public services such as education and health, on subsidies to industry, and on food subsidies. As a reaction to budgetary cuts unemployment rose to 8 percent in 1988, 9 percent in 1989, and approximately 10 percent in 1990.[45]

Shifts Caused by Recession: The Rich Become Richer and . . .

Periods of recession underline the class terms and contradictions within the political economy. We look at the employment-occupational structure during this period and explain why and how specific class and national groups fared differently. Alongside the high rate of unemployment new workers entered the workforce, and during 1985–89 the number of employed grew by 110,000 persons. (Excluding the Palestinians from the occupied territories, the total number of employed in 1989 was 1,460,000; 172,000 of these were Arabs, including those from East Jerusalem. The total number of unemployed was 150,000.) An examination of economic branches shows that agriculture, industry, and construction continued to eject workers during these years: in 1985 agriculture employed 72,000, in 1989, 67,000; industry remained at its low level of 300,000; construction declined from 70,000 employed in 1985 to 60,000 in 1989.[46]

The branches that absorbed new workers were commerce, restaurants, and hotels, which saw an increase in the number employees from 167,000 to 211,000 (most were sales personnel in shopping malls, retail shops, and wholesale and import trade); the number of public and community service employees grew from 400,000 to 430,000; the number of employees in personal and other services grew by 20,000 (household services, garages); and some 15,000–16,000 found new employment in financing and business services.[47] These employment openings were characterized by a high level of part-time employment, hourly work, mainly unskilled labor, and urban maintenance jobs. Employment in these branches represented the lowest level of wages, occupational status, and job security, and their expansion illustrated the growing numbers of urban working poor.

This pattern of absorption in urban services is linked to the fact that the recession did not affect the public equally. The upper half further indulged itself in consumerism, thereby generating demand for more goods and services (e.g., shopping malls, urban housing, home electronics, air conditioners, cars, delayed installment payments, and so forth). Since many of the consumption items they sought are imported, the impact on local employment was mainly in terms of services. Family net income fell below the average family expenditure during the 1980s; such an income-consumption gap thrives on consumerism (e.g., credit cards, installment payments, etc.).[48]

A few words should be added on car ownership, since its consistent and extraordinary rise during the extended recession writes large the striking feature of consumerism and unemployment occurring at the same time for different strata. (The state's involvement in support of both the rich and the poor, differentially of course, makes it appear as though there is no contradiction in the simultaneity of the phenomena.) During the 1980s the number of private cars almost doubled (409,000 to 778,000), and the growth spread almost equally over the period (statistically, nearly one car for every 1.5 of the 1,200,000 families in Israel). The increase was most prominent for 1989 and 1990: 60,000 new cars were annually purchased at an estimated cost of $1–1.2 billion each year. A (modest) new car costs approximately $20,000, government taxes constituting some 115 percent. Yearly upkeep is estimated at $8,000, or the yearly wage of an industrial worker in many of the industrial plants and not only of workers in agriculture or construction.[49]

Perhaps most noticeable in this decade of recession, a period that included the war in Lebanon during the first half and mounting unemployment in the second half, was not only the popular consumerism of the two-earner family but even more the conspicuous affluence of the upper decile. The monthly salaries of top management in public and private establishments exceeded, so to speak, a car per month (that is, over $20,000 a month).[50] Even if such salaries were trimmed by taxes, their earners were well protected by a highly satisfying legacy of fringe benefits, pensions and insurances, stocks, loans, company cars, and so forth. The top stratum includes representatives of various economic branches, including banks and insurance companies, import and export businesses, industry, holding companies, professional service firms (lawyers, accountants), building corporations, and real estate firms. Captains of industry were joined by former high-ranking army officers. Many in this stratum were commonly linked to government businesses in both Israel and the United States. An outstanding contribution of the Israeli government toward their upkeep was its financial rescue of these top groups from the morass of the 1983 banking crash.[51] The large middle class did not lag far behind the upper class, generating an unceasing demand for housing, travel, and their rising standards. In 1988 only 7.5 percent of the apartments built had fewer than four rooms, and the other 92.5 percent had at least four rooms; the figures for 1989 are fairly similar.[52]

The recession in general, therefore, and not only the high rate of unemployment, further widened the gap between the upper and lower halves in Israel. In statistical measures the upper decile's share of total income rose from 29 percent in 1988 to 30.8 percent in 1989. Gini's coefficient, the measure for inequality in income distribution, rose from .457 in 1988 to .472 in 1989, a rise of 3.7 percent in that one year.[53] Although the Israeli political economy differs from other capitalist economies because of the large amount of external aid it receives, and in certain respects because of the distinctive role of the state in the economy, the systems' accommodations to unemployment are similar. This can be seen in the provision of several months' unemployment insurance, and in the government's and media's contention that 10 percent unemployment rates are tolerable.

In 1989 the incomes of 33 percent of families (304,000) in which the family head was either a wage earner or nonemployed were below the poverty line. National insurance benefits along with child allowances and old-age and survivors pensions raised two-thirds of these families to just above the line.[54] The unemployed were only a small group, some 10–20 percent, among recipients of national insurance, since only 35 percent of the 150,000 unemployed in 1989, for example, were eligible for unemployment insurance; eligibility is dependent on prior employment, accurate registration is a factor, and insurance is provided for limited time periods only. The occupational characteristics of the jobless in 1989 present a reverse picture to that found in the demand structure for workers during 1985–89. Those who gained employment did so mainly in services and in metropolitan centers, while the unemployed included large groups of industrial and building workers from Jewish development towns and Arab towns/townships/villages (officially, 10 percent and 12 percent, respectively, of the labor force of each but undoubtedly much higher).[55]

From the beginning of the recession unemployment in development towns was higher than the national average even though 30–40 percent of the workers in these towns were employed in industry compared to 23 percent countrywide, and industry had been regarded as workers' safe haven in troubled times.[56]

While the state succeeded in its policy of industrializing the development towns, it did not sufficiently diversify their local economies and, therefore, the recession that hit certain industries put the townships at the top of the unemployment list. In addition, development towns led the list only in regard to Jews. Arabs held the unemployment record in Israel, despite the fact that Arab towns and villages are the least industrialized in the country (this, of course, is an understatement). Indeed, three of the half dozen industrial plants owned by Arabs are located in a neighboring Jewish township so that they can be eligible for government subsidies provided by the Law for the Encouragement of Capital Investment.[57]

Differential Vulnerability to Recession: Jewish Development Towns and Arab Villages/Townships

Labor migrancy in the beginning of the 1990s was a central political and economic feature for Arabs in Israel, even though much has changed since it became so prevalent four to five decades ago.[58] According to government data, 50 percent of Arabs are employed outside their area of residence;[59] field studies for specific villages/townships have found that the percentages were 75–90 percent.[60] (Using the lower figures, approximately 90,000 Arabs in Israel and, prior to the Intifada, 120,000 Palestinians from the occupied territories working in Israel, together 20 percent of the wage earners, were migrant Arab Palestinian workers.)

During the years of economic expansion and full employment, Arabs in Israel did not accumulate the political and economic influence required to deflect in their favor some element, if even fragmentary, of the state's productive means similar to what was gained by their Jewish neighbors in the development towns. It is to this fundamental differential that we now turn. A parallel development would have meant that the majority of Arabs would not have had to earn a living outside their home communities or locales. And another "Arab trait," no less significant than those of their rates of unemployment and labor migrancy, that of the economic-occupational status of Arab women, would also have changed completely. For example, in 1989 among Jews there were more unemployed women than men (65,100 women, 57,700 men); meanwhile, only 8 percent of the registered Arab unemployed (18,000 men, 1,600 women) were women.[61] That is to say that for Arab women, employment, and therefore unemployment insurance (from which we take the above percentage), are still not recognized civil rights. If two-thirds (approximately) of Arab men are in the labor force, only one-sixth (approximately) of Arab women are. Arab women do not have the right to wage work, and Arab men do not have the right to employment inside their home villages, townships, and cities, though men and male youths have adapted (and had to adapt) themselves to labor migrancy and the demands of the countrywide economy and labor market.

Arab workers from villages in the north and the "triangle," the two main concentrations of Arabs in Israel, work in the urban centers of the coastal plain, but when they are laid off from their jobs in Haifa and Tel Aviv, these cities do not take care of them and they join the ranks of the unemployed in their home area (Nazareth, Taybe, etc.). Under conditions of redundancy in so many work branches where jobs have already become temporary and part-time, many men, and especially youths, find it difficult to put together the four to five months of consecutive employment necessary to draw unemployment insurance. (The ratio of unemployed to those receiving insurance is estimated at 3:1.)[62] The recession offered employers grounds to fire workers quickly and arbitrarily. Although this applies to Jews as well, it holds doubly so for Arabs and occurs in a multiplicity of work branches and workplaces including Histadrut factories, kibbutzim, and moshavim, where Arab workers have been employed for years.

In order to give the reader a sense of the atmosphere of recession in a climate fairly saturated with nationalistic overtones, we quote from an open letter that appeared on a half page of a noted liberal Israeli newspaper. The letter was written by someone who had been awarded the title of Distinguished Industrialist 1991, and he addresses his employees in the following way: "My thanks to the devoted workers of our plant, who are all of the Jewish faith" (in Hebrew, *asher kulam bnei dat Moshe*).[63] True enough, following the racist rabble-rousing of a Kahane gang in Jerusalem and their plea that employers post notices such as "[We employ only] Jewish labor" and "We've fired all the Arabs,"[64] we found a statement by the city's Manufacturers Association that in Jerusalem 30 percent of the factory workers are Arabs[65] (presumably from East Jerusalem). However, it is doubtful whether the competitive wage rates and skills of the Arab workers will be sufficient for them to keep their jobs if the recession continues, the incitement mounts, and the Histadrut has not become a champion of workers' solidarity.

Even in the building trades where their position is strongest, Arab workers are the least institutionally protected in terms of the labor market. During the 1960s and 1970s, when Arab workers gained mastery of entire segments of the building trade, contracting, engineering, financial services, and management remained almost completely Jewish. Wages are determined, practically speaking, by building contractors including large government and Histadrut building and construction corporations. The Building Workers Union within the Histadrut, once a strong union, saw its membership drop to 10–15 percent of the workers (20,000 out of 150,000) by the 1990s, most of whom were probably former Jewish construction workers who gained supervisory and maintenance jobs. Most Arab building workers labor under the contract system; this holds for each trade with its special skills. Each Arab contractor often puts together a family, kin, or local work group, takes care of its transportation, and sometimes provides its own heavy equipment. Wages are at day rates, even the most skilled workers lack job security, amortization is rapid, the physical risk is high, and the work is unsuitable for middle-aged and older employees. There was a time when the Histadrut dealt with the harsh conditions in the building trades and endeavored to control competition through a highly organized labor market and, within its own building concern, Solel Boneh, offered tenure and sought suitable jobs for its veteran and disabled workers. In the 1980s these facts belonged to a bygone past.

But while Jews experienced many new and more advanced employment openings, Arabs remained trapped. Upward mobility remained a very narrow path. Since the government distributes education much more equally than it does jobs, there are now many thousands of young Arab people with secondary school and higher education and professional qualifications.[66] We have already noted the barriers that prevent Arabs from entering high-tech industries. This is particularly disastrous, since these are considered to be the industries of the technological future, and when the state closes off these jobs to Arabs, it sentences its national minority to service the public at the hardest, lowest-paying, manual labor or to seek their future outside the country.

The pitfall of the migrant worker is that he does not have a proper base from which to negotiate working conditions. We see this especially in times of recession in the form of competition from low-paid Palestinian workers brought from the occupied territories and in some employment from subsidized workers such as Russian Jewish immigrants, whose low wages are supplemented by the government. When the Higher Surveillance Committee for the Affairs of the Arab Population called the public out for a countrywide Equality Day strike (June 24, 1987), Arab workers demonstrated in their villages/townships for equality between Arabs and Jews—not at their insecure and shifting workplaces, but at home where there is no employment but where they feel secure in asserting their rights.

When Arab workers, especially migrant laborers, are discriminated against and finally fired, they land in their villages/townships where job possibilities are practically nonexistent. The labor of two to three generations in the late 1980s to early 1990s provided for the maintenance of families, perhaps larger, healthier, and better-educated ones, and for often spacious and modern homes. But just as Arab migrant workers did not accumulate realistic social benefits, job security, or economic advancement, neither did Arab communities succeed in accumulating economic means and employment opportunities for the present and future generations.

This political economic situation is comprehended for what it is by the Arabs who live by its terms, and their awareness is sharpened by what they see in the Jewish townships across the road. Most of the Jewish development towns began, and essentially remained, townships of wage earners and more specifically of manual workers (the "lower half" of Israel, with only a small middle-class component). However, unlike Arabs, most of the Jewish workers are employed in their townships in the local factories, offices, and schools. The great change that brought about this situation occurred after 1967 with the economic expansion that followed the war. Prior to this time, the men in most development towns in the north were in buses at dawn on their way to work in manufacturing plants, oil refineries, or electrical and water installations in the Haifa bay area, or they were queuing up at the local labor exchange. Jewish townships were usually located on their Arab neighbors' or refugee land, where the government had set up housing projects and other facilities for new inhabitants. However, neither nationalized land and subsidized housing nor the preferred treatment given the new townspeople by the government was sufficient to bring about the transition from labor migrancy, a low percentage of gainfully employed and among them few women, to that of growing local employment (up to the recession of the 1980s).

Government remained for many years (and through many losses and economic fiascos) the planner of local industrial enterprise, as well as its faithful provider of grants, loans, and tax relief. Direct industrial ventures were offered free land, as well as extensive and continuous input on the part of the government in roads, sewage, electric installations, and other infrastructure, including schools, clinics, and housing. Government financing and subsidies encouraged firms and industrialists in the areas of textiles, food, pharmaceuticals, building materials, and car manufacturing to set up new industries or branches of existing ones in development towns. In other areas the government, as well as the Histadrut, set up their own plants.[67]

In the 1970s, the government's Military Industries and Airforce Industries established and expanded defense-related industries, among which were high-tech and electronic plants. These possibilities for industrial development were an outgrowth of the U.S.-Israeli political-military build-up, with the government the financier and manager of the high-tech plants and the Israeli army the first main client for its products. (The atomic plant in the tiny township of Dimona was in many respects a precursor to a military agreement with the French government.) These workplaces have a high percentage of scientific and administrative personnel, while less than half are production workers. Together with the most modern technology and high productivity, wages are relatively high with supplementary bonuses and advanced training. The metropolitan area benefited most from advanced industrialization, but the peripheral, development townships also received a share and it is to some of the social consequences that we now turn.

The two types of industries in the development towns employ 30–40 percent of the local labor force. Government initiative and continuing high subsidization have remained the prime movers since even now the towns do not attract private capital.[68] Even when the textile and chocolate plants in Upper Nazareth and Hazor had a surplus of goods piled up in their warehouses, and when the Soltam plant in Yoqne'am lost its Iranian market for artillery shells and laid off almost all the township's factory workers, and when the protective battle clothing and gas-mask plants did the same in Qiryat Gat, these retreats and hazards fell on a more diversified, more educated, more qualified, and richer social community.

Industrialization and the development projects that accompanied it helped halt the population turnover that characterized the 1950s and 1960s. Women found permanent jobs in industry and, more important (often part-time), in government and municipal-related services (education, health, and welfare). The importance of these services cannot be overstated, since trade and business (jobs in sales and office work) remained fairly insignificant as sources of local employment. Thus, in the development towns as well, albeit late and partial, the new Israeli Jewish two-earner family way of life became a real possibility and, over time, the rule for young couples. Jewish workers in the development towns now have a base from which to defend their rights by means of strikes against government cuts in wages, jobs, or managerial arbitrariness that is enhanced during times of recession. The consequences of industrialization and municipalization in the broader contexts we have mentioned help explain why struggles for social justice have lost, to the largest extent, ethnic expressions that characterized them in the 1950s and 1960s in the same locales.

In the early 1980s industrial growth came to a halt in the development towns and the layoffs began. Unemployment rose still further in 1985 when the government enacted a policy of reduced industrial subsidization and cutbacks in social spending. The names of many townships in the north and the south became associated with some of the most bitter and lasting workers' strikes. In the Histadrut-owned tire factory at Tirat Carmel workers were forcibly evicted by a hired security company, and in the Yoqne'am munitions factory attack dogs were used to disperse strikers. Workers fought bitter and long strikes in Upper Nazareth, Qiryat Gat, Dimona, Beit Shemesh, Qiryat Atta, and elsewhere. The National Organization of Workers in Israel Defense Industry, usually a very restrained group, published in the press their intention to go on strike with the claim that "the Defense Ministry prefers to import armaments rather than to buy them from us . . . because it has more dollars through U.S. aid than [Israeli] shekels." They added that this policy "which will increase unemployment and plant closures . . . will be the death blow of the development towns."[69]

Workers in the Jewish development towns are used to expressing themselves in nationalistic language and chauvinistic concepts. They stress the state's obligation to them, in terms of their position as frontline buffer settlements vis-à-vis the Arabs, the demographic and territorial importance of their locals, their army service reserve duty, and the secret nature of their workplace. Thus, when the moment came to incite against striking workers in townships, management called them *ashafistim* and "terrorists." Clearly, nationalistic political viewpoints and attitudes are part and parcel of the social milieu and accepted expressions in Jewish municipal and workers' councils, local offices of government, the army, the police, and so on. Superiority and privilege are anchored in land laws and land transfer in such policies as the "Judaization" of the Galilee and the establishment of outposts (*mitzpim*) on the land of Arab neighbors (as late as the 1970s). Arabs rarely have direct conflict with their Jewish neighbors, and development towns are rarely in open disagreement with Arabs. Perhaps it is absolutely clear to both, and visually marked in the political-economic geography of national distinctions, that the local privileged status and condition of their Jewish neighbors is a matter of state policy implemented by force and by law.

On the Other Side of the Road

The politics of exclusion of Arabs from the agricultural revolution in the 1950s was repeated in terms of the industrial developments that took place from the late 1960s onward. Meanwhile, the Arab population in Israel doubled from 1970 to 1990 (as of 1990 some 700,000, not including East Jerusalem). By 1990 there were four Arab cities and three dozen large villages/townships with over 5,000 inhabitants. Within these neither the Histadrut nor the government has established one industrial plant, not even for the publicity it might gain. With regard to general municipal development, as late as the mid-1980s the government budgets provided for this purpose to Jewish and Arab municipalities of the same size favored the Jewish population by a ratio of 3:1 (and stood previously at 5:1 and 9:1).[70]

There are certainly differences among the Arab cities and villages/townships themselves; they are, after all, historical communities. Arab Nazareth, for instance, is not only distinct from Upper Nazareth, the Jewish city affixed alongside it, but also from most other Arab townships. It has a large and mixed intelligentsia of writers, journalists, academics, poets, and professionals, has publishing houses and local newspapers, and is the active center for numerous political organizations and religious establishments, world-renowned churches and orders, monasteries, schools, and hospitals. However, what is common to all Arab cities and villages is that the state's policy toward them determines their place in the political economy. Government policy did not endeavor to expand the employment capacity of Arab townships and cities so as to provide the growing population of young people with a better future. These areas have no proper industry or local services, and, with the exception of education, employ very few people. In addition, it is extremely difficult both economically and socially for Arab families and individuals to move to more favorable job areas.

In Arab villages and townships there are, practically speaking, no local employers, and, with the exception of teachers, a handful of municipal workers, and a couple of bank clerks, few earn their wages locally. In the large Arab locales there are many shops and workshops. Most of these are small family businesses owned and run by fathers and sons (and/or brothers) who have learned and gained their trades and skills through work outside the village and have set up shop on family premises. These businesses include carpentry, foundries, plumbing, electricity, cement and brick production, and auto repair shops. Each business employs up to five workers and, as family members, they draw "wages" by agreement. The list of occupations and professions indicate that home building, from planning to TV installation, can be done locally; the same is true for most phases of car and truck repair, as well as medical care provided by local doctors and national health clinics.

Two interrelated points with regard to local economic life need to be mentioned here. Even in communities where there are fifty or more shops and workshops, the number of people employed in them is minor relative to the local labor force. Moreover, such workplaces do not tend to expand in size but multiply as some of the partners or employers establish their own place. The second point further illuminates what we have analyzed with regard to the Jewish development towns, namely that small workshops do not develop into big plants. Industrialization and employment openings and infrastructure development did not evolve from local craftsmanship or manufacture, that is, they did not grow from within.

The infusion of state means and planning stopped short of the threshold of Arab communities. Underdeveloped locales not on the government development-investment list do not attract Jewish capitalists seeking cheap labor or Arab entrepreneurs versed in local conditions.

Small trade, like the small workshop, includes several types of shops (grocery stores, cafés, clothing stores, hair salons), often positioned one opposite the other, and functions under the familiar conditions of available premises, family labor, and the clientele of close kin. Workshop owners and tradespeople do not enjoy the benefits of business with the government or its protection, but when the government does appear in Arab communities, it is usually through the income tax and the value-added tax, as well as inspectors and collectors. It seems that holes in the tax collection net are designed primarily to catch the small fish. During the first half of 1991, for example, the rate for those (heavily) fined for tax evasion was three times higher among Arabs (18.8 percent) than among Jews (6.6 percent).[71] (The hardest hit of all are the weakest: the Palestinians from the occupied territories where workers and others are required to pay income tax at rates often double those prevailing in Israel.)[72]

Is the callousness of the government and the punitive face of the law toward the Arab self-employed to be understood as measures designed to restrict tradespeople and artisans from conducting business within their villages and townships, and thereby limit retail and wholesale competition with Jews and restrict the growth of an Arab middle class? In terms of the existing data, it is obvious that Arab economic activities, whether in trade, crafts, or local production, do not represent any sort of threat or form of competition to Jewish interest groups in the Israeli economy.

While Arab communities provide little employment opportunities for male wage earners, women are able to find work mainly in locales where agriculture for the market is developed and where textile plants operate local workshops. In textile workshops wages are based on piecework, and since pay in the textile branch throughout the country is at the lowest scale, the Arab village seamstress likely earns little. Women are also employed in large textile plants outside their home communities (e.g., in the Jewish cities of Upper Nazareth and Hazor), usually under arrangements made through local Arab male contractors who organize their transportation if necessary, are responsible for their replacement, and are paid a percentage of their wages.

A substantial number of women work as agricultural laborers (picking, weeding, vegetable gardening, and flower cutting, as well as seasonal labor in citrus and other fruit tree groves). Women are employed in groups, mainly in Jewish locales but also in Arab townships or large villages that became large producers of agricultural produce for local markets or exports. Contract labor is separate from household agriculture that increasingly is the responsibility of women whose families still retain agricultural land and/or home vegetable plots. Female agricultural work groups are mainly composed of unmarried young women and those with little schooling. Wages are by hour, day, or piece. Throughout the country agricultural labor pays the lowest wages, is physically demanding, and is seasonal. Work organized under a contractor is probably still more exploitive since there are no worker's rights, insurance, compensation, sick pay, or vacation, and, with regard to Arab women, the contractor or subcontractor takes travel costs out of their pay, often makes patriarchal arrangements with wages going straight to fathers, is not connected to a labor exchange, and so forth.

Trade in female labor by contractors is commonly regarded as a strictly Arab phenomenon stemming from a demand for the preservation of family honor (women will be under constant supervision, the contractor is a relative and/or takes on responsibility, and so forth). No matter the extent to which "traditionalism" is invigorated by the system, we understand the phenomenon, in its local guise, as a Jewish Arab or Israeli one. The government, the Histadrut, other state agencies that deal with labor and labor organization, and, in the past, the military government, which controlled travel, movement, and work permits, are partners with labor subcontracting (the institution of the *rais*) by turning a blind eye to the practice and by shoring up the institution and enjoying its benefits.

Labor subcontracting is not limited to Arabs in Israel. The military and civil administrations in the occupied territories hand out labor subcontracting concessions to Arabs on both sides of the green line. Nor is the phenomenon limited to Arab women. It extends to both genders, and subcontractors bring thousands of laborers under their supervisory arrangements to work in Israel. Thus we can see that this so-called Arab entrepreneurship owes much of its success to state political and economic backing. The low-paid, highly experienced, agricultural labor of Arab women and men is beneficial to Israel's agricultural export as well as for keeping down the cost-of-living index. Trade in labor power has meanwhile transcended Arab-Palestinian boundaries and risen in stature with dozens of "manpower" agencies in Israel dealing with Portuguese, Philippine, Romanian, Polish, and other workers: their passports are confiscated by the "manpower" agency, the agency's profits are a private matter, the condition of the worker is unknown, and the Histadrut asks no questions.

The wage-contract labor of Arab women usually takes place during a transitional period before they are married and have children and does not lead to an individual employment status, nor does it lead to a two-earner family. On the contrary, contract labor is antithetical to an independent wage-earner status, emphasizing the inferiority of the woman's position and her dependence on male supervision, a throwback to a patriarchal household economy after it has long been superseded by wage labor in the market. The two-earner family was not the precondition for industry and local services on the other side of the road and in fact the opposite is true: the two-earner family became possible via these industries and services, which led to the reduction of family size and changes in family lifestyle.

The very large family has barely declined in size among Muslim Arabs, except with regard to the two-earner family.[73] The latter refers mainly to Arab families in which the wife is a teacher (half of the gainfully employed women in these situations are teachers). Indeed, despite the fact that Arab schools are understaffed, teaching is the only real wage employment available to Arab women. The number of Arab women teachers in 1986–87 was approximately 4,000, or 40 percent of the 10,000 Arab teachers in primary, intermediary, and secondary schools. Even in primary schools more than half of the teachers are men, and in secondary schools only 20 percent are women. Meanwhile, 75 percent of the 74,150 Jewish teachers are women.[74] Teaching is one of the few professions available to Arabs that has job security, paid vacations, pensions, and so forth. But being accepted for teacher training programs and being able to keep a teaching job have so far also carried with them security checks and conformity tests. Tight political control probably explains the acquiescence of Arab teachers with regard to professional schooling demands and their low profile as an intelligentsia acting on behalf of the Arab public. (Jewish teachers do not face political scrutiny, and their unions are separate by a long historical tradition and by language.)

Even when Arab teachers and professionals (many of them two-earner families) do have the personal incomes necessary to enjoy better living standards, the amenities and services (streetlights, sidewalks, nurseries, recreation and cultural centers, parks, and playgrounds) are mostly absent in their home locales. A quote from a recent newspaper advertisement paid for by the ministries of housing and labor and welfare, and by the local council of the Jewish development town of Ma'alot, demonstrates the differences between what is offered in Jewish versus Arab towns. The advertisement was designed to attract new inhabitants to the township's population of six thousand, despite the fact that it was at the height of the recession and there were no local jobs to offer. The ad runs, in part, as follows: "Ma'alot offers: quality housing at an attractive price, ministry loans toward purchase, superior educational and health services, ministry adjustment grants, partial tax exemptions, great reductions in public services, subsidized kindergarten, extended school-day, special subject lessons, subsidized summer camps," and more.[75] Among Ma'alot's closest neighbors are Arab villages and townships similar in size; however, not one small or large Arab village or township could publish a list like that describing Ma'alot. Thus, rising advantaged groups (teachers, professionals) within Arab locales find themselves in communities deprived of services. Some Arab two-earner families who are searching for services unavailable in their home villages/townships move to the main Arab city, Nazareth, or to predominantly Jewish cities, like Haifa, Upper Nazareth, or Carmiel; in some, like the latter two, they often confront open nationalist rejection.[76]

Ma'alot exemplifies some of the more modest possibilities available. Moreover, even though it is a small remote township, it is nurtured by the center; two ministries are listed in the ad, and a third (interior) is represented by the local council. There are dozens of other Ma'alots and, within the overall system, those within the pre-1967 Israeli boundaries have to compete with dozens of the most advantaged Jewish townships established in the occupied territories. The latter are only "a half-hour from Petach Tikvah" or from other metropolitan areas. Nevertheless, settlements in the occupied territories received extra-high levels of state financing.[77]

The government did not and does not plow back even some of the surplus labor value extracted by the system from its underpaid Arab migrant laborers and experienced agricultural workers (not to mention other extracted capital such as land and property). The good housing conditions and the high level of consumption of cheap agricultural produce are characteristic of the Jewish Israeli standard of living. Many Arabs also live in better homes[78] and have a diet rich in vegetables and fruit, but they lack village sewer systems, building permits, proper school facilities, local industry and employment, and so on, which are allocated according to nationality. Although 80 percent of Arabs in the labor force are wage earners (similar to the Jews), only 17 percent are employed in public, municipal, or Histadrut offices (or 7–8 percent of all those in administrative and professional jobs are Arabs). The class gap between the nations is built into the system and develops with the system.

We have provided examples from Jewish agro-technical, industrial, and other developments to explain that solving the problem of the gap does not lie with the local people. Political-economic centralization is such that Arabs will never be able to do it on their own. Communities composed almost entirely of workers and other wage earners cannot become their own entrepreneurs and/or take the place of the state, especially in a wealthy entrepreneurial state like Israel. That is to say, it is up to the government to reverse the magnitude of its investment and subsidization in the appropriate areas to 5:1 or 3:1 for five years to the benefit of Arabs. Whatever the case, the state continues to move in an opposite political-economic direction. The former ruling rightist and coalition governments played the national game (e.g., "it's a Jewish state," "the Arabs are really enemies") with class cards, that is, the national minority was expropriated, excluded, and exploited. Under this policy the Likud government differed only in degree, if at all, from the previous Labor-etatist governments.[79]

Indeed, the militaristic system of rule by force that became the letter of the law and the practice of the state bureaucracies forty-five years ago, which allowed the Jews to enjoy the class privileges of conquerors, is alive and well: land confiscation, the demolition of unlicensed building, the outlawing of forty small rural communities by refusing to recognize them and depriving them of water and electricity, barring Arabs from holding or renting of what is called national land, treating Arabs as separate religious sects (Muslims, Christians, Druze) and thereby denying them national minority rights, basing army service on nationality, and so forth. The state preserves the military relationship between the two nations with Arabs as either enemy or potential enemy; when it wishes it invokes the necessary rules and laws, including the 1945 Emergency Regulations, in arbitrary determinations of its, the ruling nation's, needs.

Conclusion

Through a detailed examination of the Israeli political economy we have attempted to explain why the class gap between the two nations has widened. The state's policy and the means it has used to put its policy into practice are the main reasons for the widening of the gap. In this conclusion, and from only a slightly shifted, but updated, perspective, we restate our point of view.

Alongside more elaborate forms of class control that have developed over time, when so disposed the state has no compunctions about employing might. Thus, the policy in operation in regard to the 1990–91 Russian immigration to Israel used directives held in abeyance for more than a decade, and once again the state expropriated land from Arab villages and townships. It is clear that a system that links the right of free entrance of Jews into Israel ("the law of return") to that of land confiscation from Israeli Arabs relies on its capacity to use force if necessary.

Applying extra powers specifically toward Arab citizens, mainly in the form of expropriation, demolishing homes, and, until recently, administrative arrests, is kept alive, to a large extent, by the ongoing occupation of the West Bank and the Gaza Strip where they are carried out to a massive degree. The militaristic regime tends to equalize the status of the Palestinians on both sides of the "border," that is, from time to time to downgrade the status of the Arab citizens of Israel to that of subjects.

The politics of land confiscation and of dismissing Arabs from jobs and replacing them with, and/or hiring only, new immigrants whose wages are subsidized by the state hurt Arabs, inflamed nationalistic emotions, and served the interests of the Likud-led right-wing government, while its actual contribution to immigration was less than negligible. To face the real problems of mass immigration, creating jobs, and large-scale housing, the Israeli government requested an additional aid package amounting to $10 billion from the United States. This has been the historical "open-sesame" of Israeli militaristic nationalism.

All Israeli governments have acted in this fashion and, to different degrees, all have been successful. Successful financing after a successful war, over a period of five to six wars, has created a fairly comprehensive Jewish consensus that inequality based on dominant force is irreversible, that the Jews will not have to forego their privileges, and that their government defends them against those who insist otherwise. In this respect policy is bipartisan, tried out by the (Mapai) Labor-Alignment that led successive Israeli governments until 1977, and pushed further by that of the Likud that followed it. The Likud government moved further right, carrying with it even more nationalistic groups that turned racism into a springboard for electoral gain. (Since June 1992 a Labor-dominated coalition has ruled.)

Israeli militarism has always been tied to the key condition of mustering massive external aid. Over forty-five years this condition has completely undercut a serious political struggle in support of non-militaristic options, or what was once up to the 1970s a cherished aim of economic independence. Proposals to mobilize the means to provide employment, to accelerate growth in the economy, to enhance health, education, and welfare services through changes in allocation of resources, to terminate all building and settlement in occupied territories, to cut defense spending, and to negotiate for joint (Middle East) regional economic development in industry and in the main branch dependent on peace in the region, tourism, have been put forward, at one time or another, not only by political parties on the left (Jewish and Arab) but also by liberal groups. Indeed, parliamentary political opposition and public criticism expressing support for a Palestinian state, for negotiations with the PLO, for ending "emergency" regulations within Israel proper, and for full equality, including that of equal employment opportunities for all citizens, have always been present in Israel. However, it has never succeeded in halting the consistent drift to the right. It is in this perspective, and under such conditions, that the widening class gap between Jews and Arabs is to be understood.

Notes

We wish to dedicate this study to the memory of Simha Flapan and Yosef Washitz, forerunners, and to present it to Eric Wolf, in friendship, now also in memory. Henry Rosenfeld wishes to thank the Joint Committee on the Near and Middle East of the American Council of Learned Societies and the Social Science Research Council for a grant with funds provided by the National Endowment for the Humanities and the Ford Foundation.

1. We have discussed elsewhere the Israeli political economy, one guided by militaristic nationalism, in terms of a threefold construct or model that included the central power of the state and state bureaucracy, militarism as policy, and external economic and military aid. See Carmi and Rosenfeld 1989, 1991.
2. Openings for livelihood on a large scale began to crystallize around British Mandatory regional development through Jewish immigration building and service requirements and especially through the demands generated in the World War II economy in the Middle East. For different economic and social reasons, a major process of urbanization of peasants did not follow in the wake of this partial proletarianization. Carmi and Rosenfeld 1974.
3. Rodinson 1973; Asad 1975.
4. Flapan 1987; Morris 1989.

5. See Carmi and Rosenfeld 1989.
6. See McDonald 1951, 181; Weitz 1965, 4:42.
7. See Israeli 1961, 98–99.
8. Nor was traditional U.S. Jewish financial aid independent of U.S. pressure. In a totally different fashion, German reparations to Israel, which began in 1953, were mediated by the U.S. government. See Balabkins 1971, 82–94.
9. Bein 1952.
10. Estimates differ somewhat on the amount of Arab land transferred by Israel to its ownership following the war. The first minister of agriculture (Zisling 1988, 8) wrote that 5 million dunams of cultivated and non-cultivated land, not including 1.8 million dunams in the northern Negev owned by Bedouin (and not including the land of the Arab citizens of Israel), were involved. The Conciliation Commission for Palestine estimated that "Of the roughly 6,400,000 cultivated dunams held by Jews in Israel with the signing of the armistice agreements of 1948–49, 4,608,000 (72 percent) were Arab owned before statehood" (Rudey 1971, 135). Meanwhile the Israeli government claimed that it had taken over as "abandoned land" only 4,183,669 dunams of which 2.5 million dunams were cultivated. See Peretz 1958, 165n16; Abu Kishk 1981; Oded 1964.
11. H. Rosenfeld 1978, 390–91.
12. Central Bureau of Statistics, *Statistical Abstract of Israel* (hereafter *SAI*), 1987, no. 38, 354–59.
13. Gaaton 1969, 48.
14. See Bank of Israel 1960b, 32.
15. H. Rosenfeld 1968.
16. Zarhi and Achiezra 1966, 6; Khalidi 1988, 88–90; Haidar 1995.
17. Bank of Israel 1964.
18. Haidar 1995, 19–20.
19. Ikrit and Biram were bombed by the Israeli Defence Forces the day after the High Court decision. See Chacour 1984.
20. Carmi and Rosenfeld 1989, 14–28.
21. The compilations are our own from different sources including the summary tables in *SAI* 1987, no. 38, and *SAI* 1990, no. 41.
22. Bank of Israel 1969, 48–50; Bank of Israel 1960a, 13.
23. Halevi 1983.
24. Halperin 1987, 1007; Carmi and Rosenfeld 1989, 38.
25. *SAI* 1987, no. 38, p. 7.
26. Rosenfeld and Carmi 1976.
27. H. Rosenfeld 1978, 392–99.
28. Berglas 1983, 52–53.
29. Halperin 1987, 1002–3, 1008–9; Rotem 1988.
30. Carmi and Rosenfeld 1989, 37–39.
31. *SAI* 1987, no. 38, pp. 306, 728; Haidar 1995, 81.
32. The figures for "employed persons by economic branch, population group and sex" are in *SAI* 1990, no. 41, pp. 336–37; see also p. 352 for "non-Jewish employed persons."
33. *SAI* 1990, no. 41, p. 336.
34. Ibid., 336–37.
35. Ibid.
36. Ibid.
37. Al-Haj and Rosenfeld 1990; N. Reiss 1991; Swirski 1990.
38. The head of the Israeli Civilian Administration in the Occupied Territories (Goren) put the number of workers at 120,000 (see *Yediot Ahronot,* January 11, 1991); another estimate (*Ha'aretz,* November 22, 1990) is 100,000 (Hebrew newspapers).
39. See Arnon 1988. In 1986 Israel's import from the occupied territories of goods and services, mainly in the payment for labor, was $1.1 billion. Meanwhile, its exports to the occupied ter-

ritories were $1.2 billion (ibid., 265); for taxes, see *Yediot Ahronot,* January 8 and 11, 1991; for work conditions, see *Yediot Ahronot,* January 11, 1991. For "court matters" concerning public order (excluding matters in military courts) in the occupied territories, which almost quintupled between the years 1968 to 1986 (from 20,000 to 106,000), see *SAI* 1987, no. 38, p. 747.

40. For example, during the same period (June 1991) that 110,000 work permits to work in Israel were issued to Palestinian workers from the occupied territories, "there are now 125,000 unemployed in the [Israeli] economy" (see *Ha'aretz,* June 17, 1991). Meanwhile, wages for a Palestinian building worker from the occupied territories were 1,000–1,400 shekels a month. (There are no additional labor costs, e.g., social benefits.) An Israeli building worker (who is usually an Arab) received 1,800–2,500 shekels; a new Jewish immigrant in training for work received 1,600 shekels (see *Ha'aretz,* February 26–27, 1991). In 1986 (prior to the Intifada) the average daily wage for a Palestinian worker working in Israel was 18 shekels; the average daily wage for a worker in Israel was 29.6 shekels. The average labor expense for a worker per day was 39.7 shekels. See in *SAI* 1987, no. 38, pp. 442, 728. Under the title "Income Tax, Additional Revenue from the Occupied Territories," the economist G. Eshed writes that "According to calculations the income tax on earnings of $800 per month for a Palestinian family with two children in the occupied territories is $140, while in Israel no income tax is payable on such earnings. The answer of the Civilian Administration to our question of 'How come?' was 'Thus.'" Eshed, *Yediot Ahronot,* May 7, 1991. (We have changed shekels into dollars at the rate of two shekels to one dollar.)
41. Both the high level of local consumption and the state's turn to capital-intensive industries are connected to the relative ease with which the government continues to mobilize the high investment required. The "relative ease" here is, of course related to the support of American Jewry and its influence on the U.S. government and, as said, Israel's strategic importance for the United States in terms of Middle East stability. As a result of this aid and loans, Israel continues to import 25 percent more than it exports or produces; that is, the gap, which is sometimes termed "the chronic deficit," "the structural imbalance," or "dependency" remains a major built-in feature of the economy.
42. See Evron 1980, 439–41, 447–48.
43. See ibid.; Bruno 1989.
44. Carmi and Rosenfeld 1989.
45. Yaniv 1990, 128; *SAI* 1990, no. 41, p. 358.
46. We worked out the figures following the listings for "employed persons, by economic branch, population group and sex" in *SAI* 1990, no. 41, pp. 334–37.
47. We follow the calculations in *SAI* 1990, no. 41, pp. 334–37, 352–53, 358–59.
48. *SAI* 1990, no. 41, pp. 296–97.
49. See table 18/18 in *SAI* 1990, no. 41. For auto sales, see also *Yediot Ahronot,* November 21, 1990, where we learn that 61,000 new cars were purchased in 1989 and 60,000 in 1990. For car upkeep, *Yediot Ahronot,* April 29, 1991, provides figures.
50. The salaries of high officeholders such as judges, ministers, and government bank officials are far below those in top businesses. We have treated the subject elsewhere mainly in regard to movement out of the one and into the other (Rosenfeld and Carmi 1976). Here we mention that although there is a clear contradiction in salary levels, there are also points of compensatory linkage, e.g., similarities in fringe benefits, the holding down of multiple directorships, honorary presidencies, chairmanships, and so forth.
51. The economist Arnon (1988, 262) writes that "the monetary situation is the Achilles' heel of the government's policy. We are threatened this year with the government's refund of four billion shekels [$2 billion] for the bank shares that it undertook to repay in the banks' stead. . . . Finally, the government will apparently pay out seven billion shekels" ($3.5 billion).
52. *SAI* 1990, no. 41 p. 473.
53. Achdut 1990, 43–91. See also Lever and Huhne 1985, 101.
54. Ibid., 78.

55. Yaniv 1990, 127.
56. Borochov 1989.
57. Khamaisi 1990; R. Khalidi 1988, 161–63.
58. H. Rosenfeld 1964a, 1978.
59. *SAI* 1990, no. 41, p. 352.
60. Haidar 1990; H. Rosenfeld, "Discrimination Creates the 'Sector'" (unpublished ms.).
61. *SAI* 1990, no. 41, pp. 352, 358.
62. Yaniv 1990, 127.
63. *Ha'aretz,* March 29, 1991.
64. *Yediot Ahronot,* November 22, 1990.
65. *Ha'aretz,* February 27, 1991.
66. Swirski 1990; Al-Haj and Rosenfeld 1989, 210; Yogev and Ayalon 1987.
67. Up until 1985, when it altered its policy, the government contributed 60–75 percent of the financing of development town industry. See Borochov 1989, 268–70. A Bank of Israel survey shows that the government grant provided to 200 large companies in Israel equaled their profits during the same years (1968–70). That is to say, the subsidization in the development towns was not out of the ordinary. See "Profit and Profitability in Industrial Firms in Israel, 1965–70," *Survey,* no. 40 (October 1972).
68. Borochov 1989, 268.
69. *Yediot Ahronot,* March 5, 1991.
70. Al-Haj and Rosenfeld 1990, 153.
71. *Ha'aretz,* June 6, 1991.
72. *Yediot Ahronot,* May 7, 1991.
73. The percentage of Muslim women with six or more children declined between 1955 (37.8 percent) and 1985 (23 percent). They were high, however, compared to those for Jewish women for 1955 (13 percent) and 1985 (5.1 percent). See *SAI* 1987, no. 38, p. 121; see also Khamaisi 1990, 40.
74. *SAI* 1987, no. 38, p. 580.
75. *Hadashot,* June 21, 1991.
76. See H. Rosenfeld 1988.
77. Concerning the new Jewish city, Beitar, located outside Jerusalem in the occupied territories, we read in *Ha'aretz* (June 18, 1991) that "it received 10,000 dunams [2,500 acres] of expropriated land, that the entire housing project is at the initiative of the ministry of housing," that the "new inhabitants enjoy far higher grants and better mortgages than for which they are eligible according to the law," and that "they were allotted larger areas for public community institutions than is usual." We also read in the same issue of the newspaper that the plants in the industrial area set up in Barkan, located in the occupied territories but near the center of Israel, receive the highest benefits that the government allows according to the Law for Encouragement of Capital Investment.
78. H. Rosenfeld 1978, 392–99.
79. Carmi and Rosenfeld 1989.

20

Post-1948

The New Ein Houd

SUSAN SLYOMOVICS

The Palestinian Arab village of Ein Houd is located in the Carmel mountain range near Haifa. Volume 1 of the Bir Zeit University series Destroyed Palestinian Villages (*al-Qura al-Filastiniyah al mudammarah*) is dedicated to the Palestinian Arab village of Ein Houd. This series focuses on the more than 418 Palestinian Arab villages that were either depopulated during the 1948 Arab-Israeli war or destroyed in the five subsequent years.[1] The authors, Sharif Kanaana and Bassam al-Ka'bi, point out in their introduction that the village chosen for the first volume is an anomaly: Ein Houd remains a rare example—not only in the Palestinian ethnographic series but also in Arab-Israeli history—of an Arab village that was not physically destroyed during the five years after 1948. The village was transformed into Ein Hod, a Jewish artists' colony (*kfar ha-omanim*). Its inhabitants, all belonging to the same *hamulah* (clan) of Abu al-Hayja, were dispersed, were exiled, or went into hiding in the nearby hills.[2] This chapter sketches the post-1948 history of the Abu al-Hayja in Israel. While Jewish Israeli Ein Hod wrote its history linearly in time as it developed from a weekend retreat for a small core of artists to a place with a renowned artists' exhibition center, a national museum, art schools, and training workshops, Palestinian Arab Ein Houd al-Jadidah was slowly and painstakingly rebuilding itself; of the two villages, Ein Houd al-Jadidah is currently the more populous.

Expulsions (1948)

The history of the clan of the Abu al-Hayja and their expulsion from Ein Houd in 1948 is a chronicle of successive waves of escape, first to the nearby caves and forests, then to an interim, temporary refuge further afield in the Druze village of Daliyat al-Karmil, and finally into exile. The majority of the Abu al-Hayja dispersed throughout the Arab world, though a small group was able to remain close to their village. In general, for Palestinian Arabs in the Haifa subdistrict, the end began with the fall of, and the exodus from, Arab Haifa; starting April 22, 1948, Haifa's Arab population left.[3] The Jewish forces (Haganah) then moved south of Haifa, attacking the villages of the southern Carmel range: first, the village of Balad al-Shaykh, and then, on April 25, al-Tirah was assaulted with mortar and machine guns. Women and children were evacuated from al-Tirah, Ein Houd, and al-Mazar but the men remained and defended their villages until July.[4]

Each memorial book in the Destroyed Palestinian Villages series devotes a section to the 1948 expulsions specific to the described village's history of depopulation. These sections are based on tape-recorded accounts of villagers who experienced the traumatic, unforgettable events.[5] Although the taped accounts were collected forty years after 1948, many researchers affirm their accuracy. One narrative about Ein Houd's defense in 1948 was recounted by Muhammad Mahmud Muhammad 'Abd Al-Salam, known as Abu Faruq, in tape-recorded interviews conducted by Sharif Kanaana and Bassam Ka'bi, coauthors of the memorial book to Ein Houd. Abu Faruq, sixty-five years old at the time of the 1985 interview, was twenty-eight in 1948 when he was expelled to Jenin refugee camp where he died in 1991. He never returned to his Ein Houd house that became Marcel Janco's or to his vineyard where the Janco-Dada Museum now stands. Abu Faruq recalled that each village was left to defend itself; no outside leaders aided them and no leader arose within Ein Houd. Within the village, old men acted the most bellicose, he noted, tripping whenever they brandished their ancient, unwieldy swords. During and immediately after World War II, while employed in the nearby British army camp at al-'Aziziyah or in the British-run prison at Atlit, as many as thirty Ein Houd male villagers had received basic instruction in the rudiments of military drill and small firearms training. The Abu al-Hayja's skills as builders began their association with the British; first hired to erect the prison camp fenceposts, they subsequently formed a construction crew for the army barracks, moving, as they say in the oral interviews, from the outside to the inside. Additionally, villagers recounted that during World War II, several men served in the British police force.[6]

The Jewish forces approached Ein Houd twice, each time from the south and east. Twice they were repulsed, Abu Faruq narrated, and on one occasion the villagers captured a tank immobilized in the ditches they dug to defend the perimeter.[7] Khalidi's description of the last days of Ein Houd, based on contemporary newspaper reports, confirms memories of the Abu al-Hayja.

> A force of 150 Jews struck at 'Ayn Hawd and the neighboring village of 'Ayn Ghazal in an attack on the evening of 11 April 1948, according to the Palestinian newspaper *Filastin.* The attack was repulsed, as was a more serious one the following month. The villagers of 'Ayn Hawd remained in their village after the fall of Haifa in late April. 'Ayn Hawd was stormed in late May 1948 after Arab snipers had allegedly halted traffic on the Tel Aviv–Haifa road. An

unnamed informant told a reporter from the Associated Press that 'Ayn Hawd and 'Ayn Ghazal had been broken into on 20 May. The residents of 'Ayn Hawd apparently stayed put after that attack.[8]

Partly sustained by radio broadcasts from Transjordan's King Abdullah, the villagers heeded the king's transmitted messages and quoted his words decades later: "Be steadfast. Whoever leaves his village will be punished."[9] The villagers waited in vain for the Arab forces to come to their rescue. Two historians, Walid Khalidi and Benny Morris, maintain that only joint Israeli naval and ground operations succeeded in expelling the villagers of Ein Houd along with those from the nearby Little Triangle, the name for the adjacent villages of Ijzim, Jaba, and 'Ayn Ghazal.[10] Khalidi summarizes the last days of Ein Houd.

> 'Ayn Hawd was probably one of a number of villages south of Haifa (including al-Tira, Kafr Lam, and al-Sarafand) that were occupied in a limited operation launched during the "Ten Days" (the period between the two truces.) If so, it fell to Israeli forces around 15 July 1948 in an operation that was distinguished by the participation of Israeli naval forces. These assisted the land-based attackers by providing covering fire and by bombarding the villages.[11]

According to Abu Faruq, Ein Houd held out until July 1948.

> The first to fall was al-Tirah, whose inhabitants numbered fifteen thousand. They passed through our village, heads bowed carrying guns. . . . Kennedy guns from the British army, they gave them [the Jews] the newest weapons, Sten and Bren guns, don't ask about the weapons. The Jews bang three times and you face east to Mecca. The whole group left and we remained and Ijzim and Jaba. Jaba, by God, fought. They had young, good fighters and they used *batiriyat* against the tanks which passed through the village. . . . We stayed, us, Ijzim, Jaba, the three. The last thing: we took the children and put them in the huts and they ate and drank and made bread. The last thing: they brought on the Atlit coast, launches and boats to the village and four or five airplanes above us like fire and they hit us and bombed us and what was there for us to do? I want to ask you, what could we do? We took ourselves and we left most things and went to the Druze, those who put goats and furnishings with friends of course they guarded them. . . . They left in stages. The last stages, we were in it, me, my four brothers; with us, two cousins, and we came to the Druze. My father was alive, and the women and daughters were with him. We told him: "Stay here, O old man, if something happens we return; if nothing happens, may God make it easy." He gave each one of us thirty dinars, his guns, blankets. If we return we will find him, if not, may God make it easy. We left in the last caravan from Ein Houd to the Jenin area by 'Ara which was the camp for the "courageous" [said with sarcasm] Iraqi army.[12]

Abu Faruq lived in the village of Yam'un for seven years, where a distant branch of Abu al-Hayja relatives had settled, moving only in 1956 to nearby Jenin Camp (under Jordanian rule during 1948–67) to join the rest of the Abu al-Hayja from Ein Houd. In 1985, replying to the Bir Zeit researchers' question about when the villagers thought to leave, Abu Faruq insisted that the villagers' only concern was "*sharaf al-bint* (the honor of the girls); the first thing we left our village was *'ird* (honor), only *'ird,* not money, not children, just *sharaf,* because we heard about Deir Yasin and al-Tanturah next to our village where they did things to the girls."[13] Abu Faruq was referring to the most famous atrocity of the 1948 war carried out on April 9 in Deir Yasin near Jerusalem. Approximately two hundred and fifty Palestinian villagers were massacred by Jewish forces. Closer to Ein Houd, villagers from al-Tanturah on the coast south of Haifa were expelled on May 22.[14]

At the end of April—between the first and second attacks—three of the Abu al-Hayja's well-known village house builders, Muhammad, Mahmud, and Miflih, joined their families, who had been temporarily evacuated outside Ein Houd in the higher mountains to the east. They headed to the nearby Druze village of Daliyat al-Karmil, where a lucky few were crowded into houses while the majority of villagers remained outdoors sleeping and eating under the trees. Refugees expelled by the Israelis from surrounding villages continued to swell the population of Daliyat al-Karmil by the thousands. Afif Abdul Rahman, son of Muhammad the builder, was ten at the time of expulsion. He recounted a vivid memory of a visit by an Israeli military leader whose purpose was to threaten the Palestinians, all of whom were waiting in Daliyat al-Karmil for the opportunity to return to their homes. The officer informed them that they must leave Daliyat al-Karmil by the following Friday.[15] The villagers did not flee at the behest of any Arab orders; they were ordered to do so by Israeli army officers.[16] One Friday at eight in the evening, late in April 1948, columns of Palestinian peasants departed the Carmel region. They trekked southeast down the mountain range to the plain of Marj Ibn 'Amir (Esdraelon Valley), a forced march without food or water, reaching Wadi 'Ara the next day at ten in the evening. A village thirty-nine kilometers southeast of Haifa, Wadi 'Ara is strategically located at the gateway to the plain of Marj Ibn 'Amir, near the intersection of the Haifa-Jenin road.[17] Many peasants from villages in the Haifa region followed this route to exile, one that led them to the town of Jenin where Jenin Camp was built to house the refugees.[18]

Other places of emigration opened when an Iraqi delegation arriving at 'Ara as part of the Iraqi army deployed around Jenin announced their country's willingness to accommodate several thousand refugees.[19] Despite the three Abu al-Hayja brothers' desire to keep their families together, one brother, Mahmud, elected to leave for Baghdad with his family.[20] Another brother, Miflih, was held prisoner by the Israelis for several months until he was deported to the West Bank. Muhammad, the master builder, reached the Jenin-Yam'un area with his family. Thereafter, in various refugee camps throughout the West Bank, Muhammad continued to build as part of the construction crew for schools run by the United Nations Relief and Works Agency for Palestinian refugees (UNRWA) in Nablus, 'Askar, and Fara'ah camps. He is credited with building the vocational training center in Qalandiyah Camp.[21] Although he constructed houses throughout the Haifa-Carmel mountain region, he did not enjoy the promise of the traditional Palestinian blessing—*insallah bi-tithanna fiha* (May God grant you to live happily in the same house)[22]—recited whenever a house is completed. In 1964 at the age of forty-eight, Muhammad 'Abd al-Qadir 'Abd al-Rahman 'Abd al-Rahim Abu al-Hayja died of a heart attack, a refugee in Fara'ah Camp near Nablus, then under Jordanian rule.

Post-1948: Ein Houd al-Jadidah (New Ein Houd)

Satuhi satuhi
kullu qarana min jadid.

[They will be resurrected, they will be resurrected
All our villages anew.][23]

The best view of Palestinian Arab Ein Houd, now Jewish Israeli Ein Hod, is from the east. Standing at the crest of the higher hills that make up the Carmel mountain range, at a place called Jabal al-Wustani (Central Hill) by Palestinians, sits the post-1948 new Arab Ein Houd al-Jadidah. From Jabal al-Wustani, the Abu al-Hayja can look down at their former homes. On a small segment of nineteen dunams that was once part of the lands belonging to the Abu al-Hayja from their pre-1948 ownership of over 12,500 dunams, they began their resettlement and relocation immediately after the forcible depopulation of Ein Houd was completed by the Israeli army during the summer of 1948 (fig. 1).

Figure 1.
View of Ein Houd al-Jadidah, August 5, 1995. (Photo by the author.)

Figure 2.
'Asim Abu al-Hayja' ca. 1986. Courtesy of 'Asim Abu al-Hayja'.

Figure 3.
Muhammad Mubarak Abu al-Hayja'. Courtesy of Muhammad Mubarak Abu al-Hayja'.

To rewrite, reconstruct, and document this earlier history, as well as to chronicle the present struggle for recognition, is a project that complements and parallels the Abu al-Hayja's stated political goal of recognition. The intertwined endeavors of writing and engaging in national politics are consciously pursued by the Abu al-Hayja, and multiple forms of evidence are willingly disseminated. There are the many books and newspaper articles, mainly in Hebrew and Arabic, some in English, written by and about the Abu al-Hayja as well as a village archive supported by 'Asim Abu al-Hayja (fig. 2), in his home, who provides copies of material as requested. More important, the Abu al-Hayja, as part of an organization to promote the rights of Palestinian Arab villagers in Israel, have published since 1989 the monthly newspaper *Sawt al-qura* (The voice of the villages). They have prepared photographic exhibits and several videotapes that are widely distributed. They moved easily into the Internet era with informative and activist websites; they support both their own writings and the research of outsiders as effective tools to publicize the plight of Palestinian villages in Israel.

One leader, Muhammad Mubarak Abu al-Hayja (fig. 3), mentioned his seventy-page (incomplete) memoir written in Hebrew, and begun when he was seventeen as a chronicle of his village's early history. Muhammad Mubarak defined his task as the redactor of Arab oral traditions and village histories that have validity only if in printed form.[24] Orally transmitted history, he noted, carries neither legal value nor political clout. Once published, he believed such documents are crucial for establishing the rights of the Abu al-Hayja to their former villages, a right they insist upon in order, paradoxically, to give it up: " 'We have to be realistic,' says Mubarak. 'We are not going to get our original village back and we have nothing against the Jews who live there today. All we want is official recognition for the new village we have built, and the services to which we are entitled.' "[25] The Abu al-Hayja endorse an approach best articulated by the Palestinian Israeli Azmi Bishara, a professor of philosophy: "There could not begin to be an equality until stones mark the graves of what were once villages nor an historic compromise until Palestinians obtain their tombstones; the victim must be recognized in order for him to forgive."[26]

Information about Ein Houd al-Jadidah's early days was also obtained, at several removes, from Ein Hod's Jewish artists who tell how the Abu al-Hayja once supported a traditional clan historian, an oral poet who declaimed and improvised odes and epics in the Palestinian Arab dialect. Unfortunately no poems were transcribed, nor did the poet leave a successor trained in his repertory, though some Abu al-Hayja are still familiar with parts of his poems and tales. The poet Carmi vividly recalled visits in the 1950s to the Abu al-Hayja village in the company of Moshe Barak, an Arabic-speaker; Carmi listened to a poetry performance while Barak translated two poems from Arabic. The poems, obviously addressed to the two Jewish visitors from Ein Hod, were odes expressing the difficulties of the Abu al-Hayja's life under military rule. One recurring metaphor was that of flies destroying the olive trees; the flies, according to Carmi, were symbols for the police. The theme of a second poem was one of longing for beloved ones in distant lands and for dear friends that could not be visited.[27]

The history of the Abu al-Hayja encompasses not only the 1948 dispossession shared by all Palestinians but includes a newer, post-1948 experience of potential expulsion from their current homes, the predicament of many Palestinian Arab citizens within the Israeli state. Two laws passed by the Israeli Parliament in 1950 define the circumstances for expulsion. The Law of Return grants every Jew throughout the world the right to immigrate to Israel while excluding Palestinian Arabs. More threatening to the Abu al-Hayja is the Absentee Property Law, which classifies them as "absentees," encompassing in that classification their lands and homes as "absentee property."[28] Although they are citizens of Israel, because they left villages even for a brief time in the midst of war, their rights to homes and lands were deemed abandoned, and when they built new villages nearby, recognition in the form of municipal services—electricity, water, and sewage—has been denied. The provisions of the Absentee Property Law were reproduced for a photographic exhibition and accompanying pamphlet that Dror Yekutiel produced in 1990 with the Abu al-Hayja, an exhibition and booklet whose name was derived from the current

Abu al-Hayja status: citizens of Israel oxymoronically designated as "present absent" (in Hebrew, *nokheah nifkad,* in Arabic *al-hadir al-ghaib*).[29]

It is noteworthy that the community of Palestinian Arabs remaining in Israel, despite threats of expulsion and depopulation, are called "absentees" by Palestinians forced to flee to the surrounding states. "Absentee" in this context shifts meaning according to cultural and geopolitical perceptions yet with the contrast between those "inside" Israel versus those "outside" firmly in place: for Jewish Israelis, the Palestinian Arabs within Israel have always been "present absentees" even though the Arab inhabitants of Israel for a period of nineteen years (1948–67) were denied access to Arabic books, newspapers, and movies produced outside Israel. Because no telephone or mail service connected Israel to the Arab world during these nineteen years, the divided Palestinian nation relied on radio broadcasts to communicate messages from various refugee communities to Palestinians inside Israel by *rasail al-ghaibin* (messages to the absentees).[30] Relationships among the Abu al-Hayja living inside the Green Line, the name given to Israel's pre-1967 armistice line, with their *hamulah* (clan) outside were only reestablished after 1967 when the "present absentees" of Israel encountered the exiles in the Occupied Territories. The Israelis consider the Abu al-Hayja to be "present absentees" whether they are in Israel or Palestine. The Arabs consider the Abu al-Hayja to be absentees if they are not in Palestine.

Collective Political Action: The *Hamulah*

One introductory approach to what has been accomplished by the Abu al-Hayja in building Ein Houd al-Jadidah is to begin with a review of the Abu al-Hayja clan system and genealogical history. The *hamulah* (clan) is defined by Palestinian sociologist Majid al-Haj as "a patrilineal descent group composed of all members related biologically to a common great-grandfather, or members who have related themselves to a certain *hamulah* by fictive relatedness in order to obtain *hamulah* protection and rights, along with *hamulah* responsibility and commitments."[31] During the late Ottoman period, Palestine was largely agrarian and the village lands of Ein Houd were held in common but periodically redivided among the different members of the *hamulah*.[32]

Descent claims by individual clans have played a role in determining prestige and status. The primary claim, as in many Arab and Islamic countries, is direct descent from the Prophet Muhammad or his family, from the Prophet's tribe of the Quraysh, from other religious figures of that era such as the Ansar, or from the Prophet's companions, unrelated but staunch supporters. A second prestigious lineage in Palestine is descent from any military figure who arrived in Palestine with the Muslim conquest or one who, later, fought against the Crusaders. Both claims presuppose long residence in Palestine.[33] The Abu al-Hayja trace their lineage to one of Saladin's famous generals, thereby accruing prestige as defenders of a Muslim-Arab Palestine against the invasions of the European Crusaders. Their tenure on their lands is also linked to these wars.

Pre-1948 Arab Ein Houd consisted of the Abu al-Hayja *hamulah,* a single clan divided into five large lineages or subclans. Each *dar* (subclan) traces its descent from an early generation of four brothers and a sister, all five of whom claimed Husam al-Din Abu al-Hayja as their eponymous ancestor. Husam al-Din was one of Saladin's generals granted the territory of Ein Houd as a reward for his martial prowess at the Battle of Hittin against the Crusaders. The historical and genealogical connection to a medieval past and the awards from their heroic leader, Saladin, illustrate the ways in which the contemporary Palestinian narrative is not separable from the Palestinian people's existence in Palestine and their subsequent displacement from their homeland. The Palestinian national narrative cannot be reduced to a response to Zionism; in the case of the history of the Abu al-Hayja clan in Ein Houd, the story stems from Saladin's twelfth-century conquests.

The five original Abu al-Hayja subclans are the following: Dar Ibrahim, Dar 'Ali, Dar al-Hajj Sulayman, Dar Ahmad, and Dar 'Abd al-Rahim. Dar 'Abd al-Rahim is the subclan responsible for populating Ein Houd al-Jadidah above Ein Hod on the Carmel mountain region. Narratives about the Arab *hamulah* are an essential and controversial aspect of the discourse of social science about Palestinians. In 1977, for example, Khalil Nakhleh undertook a comprehensive critique of Israeli social science studies about the Arab population in pre-1967 Israel.[34] In particular, he targets the ideological nature of Israeli social science, whose research findings often conclude with the notion of an immutable Arab social structure epitomized by the *hamulah:* "the [Israeli] focus on the immutable and 'self-juvenating' hamula is no accident, due mainly to the peculiarities of anthropology."[35] What Nakhleh terms the "peculiarities" of Israeli anthropology are a tight bundle of theories based either on recourse to an Ottoman and Mandatory past or, more frequently, on explanations linked to Arab traditional kinship organizations brought forth to account for the retrograde condition of Israel's Arab sector. Subsequent research by Elia Zureik and Aziz Haidar demonstrates that studies based on *hamulah* organizational structures have as their underlying premise a denial concerning the current socioeconomic oppression of Arabs under Israeli rule.[36] Both scholars demonstrate that issues of land expropriation, the proletarianization of the Arab peasantry, the Israeli authorities' intention to maintain the *hamulah* structure for political expediency—in sum, the totality of external political pressures—are rarely or imperfectly correlated with whatever changes are predicated for internal kinship structure. Instead, theories of change or lack of change in the *hamulah* claims are allowed to stand independent of a sociopolitical context as if what is said about the *hamulah* represents metonymically the reified Arab village.[37]

Accounts of the *hamulah,* thus, stress its changeless qualities, emphasizing an ideal and idealized structure that is patrilocal, patrilineal, and endogamous. Israeli anthropologist Abner Cohen, for example, believes that despite modernization processes linked to the establishment of the State of Israel, the extended kin group in the form of the *hamulah,* rather than the nuclear family, is the continuous vital component in village politics.[38] His ethnography of the village of Kafr Qasim charts the centrality of the *hamulah* organization as the determining principle of local political control at the same time as he points to a contingent, historical periodicization—the *hamulah* lost its economic base under the British but has been undergoing a revival under the Israelis. The emphasis on an abstract category such as the *hamulah* is a departure point for anthropologist Talal Asad's critique of Cohen's research and, by implication, the ideological basis on which much Israeli ethnographic research on Palestinians rested. The *hamulah,* Asad writes, "constituted a mode of control and an imputed identity for the only political existence allowed to Arab villagers in Israel."[39] Because the *hamulah* social structure is interpreted as a microcosm of Palestinian Arab culture, it is held accountable for Palestinian Arabs' failure to establish cooperatives or to initiate modernization. Thus, the *hamulah* is either an obstacle to or a victim of social progress.[40] Indeed, in many analyses, it is precisely the importance of the *hamulah* that is thought to ensure the absence of collective political action.[41]

Both Majid al-Haj and Henry Rosenfeld have studied the preeminence of the *hamulah* on the local political scene, showing the ways in which the clan system has adapted and been integrated into the political life of Arabs in Israel. They maintain that the *hamulah* no longer functions through traditional hierarchical relationships; it is has become a framework through which its individual members effectively promote social and political changes.[42] Al-Haj and Rosenfeld rethink the borders of kinship; the Abu al-Hayja who attribute their successes and limitations to the power of the Palestinian Arab clan confirm such a viewpoint. The extreme case of the Abu al-Hayja as "present absentees" in an isolated rural enclave presents a history of the ways in which their *hamulah* has provided the essential link and motivating principle for political organization. While the eponymous *hamulah* founder-figure of Arab Ein Houd was Husam al-Din Abu al-Hayja, medieval warrior and general of Saladin, on whom the Carmel mountain lands were bestowed for himself and his progeny, the post-1948 Ein Houd al-Jadidah owes its origins to several twentieth-century charismatic leaders who have emerged from the Abu al-Hayja clan and whose biographies are reconstructed according to written and oral sources.

In the case of the Abu al-Hayja of Ein Houd al-Jadidah, displaced within their country by processes of internal colonization, how could disenfranchised Palestinian Arabs build their new village—what is now Ein Houd al-Jadidah—two kilometers above their former homes? Their struggles are then related to the history of Kawkab Abu al-Hayja, a village in the Galilee where a *maqam,* an ancestral Abu al-Hayja shrine dating from the medieval era, persists as an important site of pilgrimage. Finally, the organizational structure of twenty-seven Abu al-Hayja families who resettled in Jenin Camp, Jordanian territory from 1948 until 1967, is considered. What is the nature of relationships among the Abu al-Hayja who inhabit at least these three disparate geographical locations in the light of a historically lived experience and as a study of texts and representations? At issue here is the relationship between the experiences of displacement and the cultural, as well as the literal, construction of house, home, and community.

Biography: The Life of Abu Hilmi

As the last *mukhtar* of the pre-1948 Arab Ein Houd, Ahmad Mahmud 'Abd al-Ghani became the village's chosen successor to Zaydan, who was deposed by the British in 1939. In 1948, Ahmad Mahmud was expelled from Ein Houd to the refugee camp in Jenin where he died in 1954. He never returned to his village nor was he able to meet again with his brother, Muhammad Mahmud 'Abd al-Ghani, who remained to build and become the founder of Ein Houd al-Jadidah. The new Ein Houd was born from the families of two cousins, Muhammad Mahmud 'Abd al-Ghani 'Abd al-Rahim and Mahmud 'Abd al-Hadi Husayn 'Abd al-Rahim, both of the subclan Dar 'Abd al-Rahim.

Both Jews and Arabs agree that at the beginning of Ein Houd al-Jadidah there was a forceful, charismatic leader named Shaykh Muhammad Mahmud 'Abd al-Ghani, known throughout the region, according to the custom of taking one's name from one's eldest son, as Abu Hilmi (father of Hilmi): " 'We cannot talk about the village without talking about Abu Hilmi,' his grandson 'Asim says, 'The history of the new village is linked to him.' "[43] With a few families, Abu Hilmi sought refuge in the early 1950s higher up in the hills where they had pastured their flocks of sheep. At first, helped by Druze neighbors in nearby Daliyat al-Karmil, who fed, housed, and then schooled the Abu al-Hayja children, a small nucleus under Abu Hilmi's leadership were able to avoid forced emigration from the Druze village that scattered the rest of the Abu al-Hayja among other villages in Israel as internal refugees or further afield in Jordan and Iraq.

Interviews with the inhabitants of Ein Houd al-Jadidah conducted by Dror Yekutiel in the 1980s record the Abu al-Hayja clan's recollection of the expulsion: "Echoing shots rent the hills. Soldiers were climbing from the Wadi towards Ein-Haud. In that instant the villagers became present-absentees. The sheik gathered his sons; silently, they walked to the huts on the opposite hill, where the herds were gathered to protect them from beasts of prey. They dare not look back upon the stone houses they abandoned."[44] The early settlement that brought Jewish Israeli artists to their former Ein Houd homes is remembered by the Abu al-Hayja with pain: "The first attempt to resettle the stone houses of Ein Haud in the 50s is clouded in mystery. They say that the mountain vomited the new settlers out from within it. . . . They remember how, in the dark, thousands of eyes watched from the mountain ridges all around. Stones rained down on the village and funeral processions sang dirges underground, from inside the mountain. They fled from the place in fear, leaving the stone houses deserted behind them."[45]

"My father refused to leave," Abu 'Asim explains. "There was shooting, panic, and confusion. We fled here to what had been for our flocks of sheep two miles away."[46] Ein Houd al-Jadidah's founder, Abu Hilmi, had settled on a spot of pasture land, the *izbah* (hamlet) where prior to 1948 the clan resided each summer though always returning to their homes below. In the 1950s during the first years of resettlement, the Abu al-Hayja lived in mud-brick huts covered with roofs of mud mixed with branches. According to Ruqayyah, one of Abu Hilmi's daughters, life was difficult, and shacks and tents sheltered humans and animals alike. Houses were huddled together and the winter rains frequently washed away houses and walls.[47] As the clan pooled their resources to convert to cheap cement-block houses—because traditional stone construction was four times more expensive—Abu Hilmi conceived a new village layout inspired by the mountainous terrain, not by traditional Palestinian social structures for housing placement (fig. 4). Most Palestinian Arab villages have densely built centers, houses with shared walls, and narrow alleyways; Abu Hilmi's village has houses widely spaced and defensively circled as if to ward off attack. Taking the highest point of one of the central Carmel hills, Abu Hilmi chose the four cardinal points as his frame of reference. Forming a large circle and serving as a perimeter of security, houses were spaced far apart. Buildings on the north, south, and west sides precariously hug the inaccessible mountain slopes. Each cardinal point was allocated to the one of the four main male household heads: 'Abd al-Rauf guarded the west, 'Abd al-Ghani the north, and 'Abd al-Halim the south. To the east is the sole access to the village, a single dirt track watched over by Abu Hilmi's son, Hilmi. By 1964, sixteen houses, mainly one-room, cement-block structures, were completed. To this day there are no state-maintained paved roads; building material and all supplies were brought up the mountain on donkeys and more recently by truck.

A grandson and village leader, Muhammad Mubarak 'Abd al-Rauf, says that Abu Hilmi always assumed he would return to his land and house, which became the property of the artist Isaiah Hillel, his wife, Sarah, who named Ein Hod, and their only daughter, Sophia, who now lives there alone.[48] Hillel tried to pay Abu Hilmi for the house, according to the architect Giora Ben-Dov, who lives in what was once the home of Muhammad 'Abd al-Hadi and his wife, Ruqayyah, who now reside in Ein Houd al-Jadidah. Ben-Dov's gesture is the only known documented one: when Hillel received the title of ownership to the house he walked up the mountain to visit Abu Hilmi to offer financial recompense.[49] Hillel, fluent in Arabic, was graciously received and thanked, but with these much-quoted words Abu Hilmi refused: "Because it is a house and you cannot sell a house."

Abu Hilmi's children say he believed that just as the Turks and the English had come and gone, so too would the Jewish newcomers. Between 1952 and 1959 Abu Hilmi fought the Absentee Property Law ruling that had dispossessed him of original Ein Houd and also threatened the newer settlement. Although he lost the court case, the authorities never executed the court order,

Figure 4.
Strategic map of Ein Houd al-Jadidah drawn by Muhammad Mubarak, August 23, 1991.

and negotiations continued until 1962 when he was offered three options: to purchase the land he lived on, to rent the land he lived on, or to cede all claims to Ein Hod in return for the land he lived on. He is said to have replied: "How can I buy or rent my own land?" When the offer was repeated in 1964, Abu Hilmi decided to buy his land but when he tried to do so, he was informed that the State of Israel does not sell land.[50] Within a few weeks of his attempted buy-back, the Israel Land Administration constructed the first of many fences that would enclose the nineteen-dunam area of Ein Houd al-Jadidah. The religious kibbutz of Nir Etzion, athwart on the mountain to Ein Houd al-Jadidah, bars access to the road on the Jewish Sabbath. A resident of Ein Houd al-Jadidah describes the village's boundaries.

> I've defined the location of the village thus: We are in an open prison. Surrounding the village is the first fence. . . . Above the village and beyond the fence is the park. That's the second wall. The third wall around the village and part of the park is the military firing zone. And the last gate: The Sabbath gate of Nir Etzion. . . . For this gate the Nir Etzion gate, anyone from the village—anyone—can get a key—no problem—just take a key. I don't take one. . . . I make a detour of thirty kilometers in order not to pass that gate and be in need of a key. I'm prepared to walk but not to use a key. On principle. That's the third prison. That in a way is the fourth wall. The Sabbath Wall.[51]

Muhammad Mubarak jokes that because of the closed road he is the only Muslim to keep the Jewish Sabbath. When he passes the chicken coops of Nir Etzion on his long detour homeward he notes that the chickens have electricity whereas he, his family, and fellow villagers in Ein Houd al-Jadidah do not.[52] When the fence was built, villagers lost direct access even by a dirt road to their village and olive orchards could not be harvested outside the boundary fence. Their recollections described life before the fence even as the government squeezes them into constricting enclaves and replaces their olive trees with cypresses.

> The tantalizing smell of warm pita from the oven, dipped in olive oil and wiped in dark green zater [thyme], with hot minted tea afterwards. Young olive trees in the village enclosure, their fruit full and succulent. The olive orchard used to extend along the slopes from the village down to the valley. Their blanched remains are withering beneath the cyprus [*sic*] trees planted by relief workers. In 1964 the village was fenced in by a two-wired fence; the park surrounds it within the military firing zone from Nir Etzion to Kerem Hamaharal; the double Sabbath gate leading in and out of Nir Etzion opens onto a rocky path which climbs to the ridge and skirts the wadi on its way to the village. A reserve within a reserve within a reserve. A place which doesn't exist. The address written on the village inhabitants' identity cards is Nir Etzion.[53]

The Abu al-Hayja did not willingly leave Ein Houd and their homes. Like many other Palestinian peasants during the early years of the establishment of the State of Israel, they made numerous attempts to regain lost homes and farmlands. Tuvia Iuster, gifted both as a sculptor and a strongman, recalls an event in 1960 that precipitated his invitation from Marcel Janco to join Ein Hod. Asked to guard the Jewish village's northern perimeter, Iuster was allocated the three-room stone house that had belonged to Rashad Rashid, who died in 1992 in Jenin Camp; the house was later transformed architecturally by artist Arik Brauer. Iuster took up his duties of artist and guard.

> One day I got a cable from Janco in French: "Viens maintenant, viens urgent," [come now, come urgently] . . . so I come, and what was the matter was, on this side of the village of Ein Hod, it wasn't yet part of the village but was optioned, there was this ruin and where Brauer lives there were three rooms. Arabs made what you called here a *plisha.* Squatters. Their rooms were empty, so they come in, and according to the law of asylum, comes from the time of the British or the Turks, if you live three days in a house which was empty, you get the rights to the house. . . . Anyway they were supposed to be people who lived in the village, and because the house was empty and because at this time were elections, so one of the parties promised them they will help them get their house back if they vote for their party.[54]

Iuster, who calls himself a giant two meters high and two meters broad, thereupon took up the position of *atran* (village watchman) at the urgings of Janco and Itche Mamboush, another resident artist. One morning he was called on by Mamboush to defend a house.

> So when I hear that the Arabs have made a *plisha,* I took my tools, which was a little axe, and I go to liberate the country . . . and I find *effendi,* some Arab who was sitting in one of the rooms that was supposed to be mine . . . from the family of Abu Hilmi. So I explained to him in Rumanian, Yiddish, and a few words in Hebrew that it was my house, that the Sokhnut [Jewish Agency] gave it to me and they made an invasion in my house. To which [they replied] they didn't understand my language, they didn't want to get out.[55]

Iuster describes his confrontation with the Abu al-Hayja as a melee of women wielding brooms and children throwing stones. The confrontation ended in favor of the Jewish artists when Israeli police were called in as reinforcements; the Abu al-Hayja clan were re-expelled, and the post-1948 order restored. Another indication of the Abu al-Hayja's attempts to return home is found in a 1954 newspaper article in which it is noted that artist Moshe Barak, doubling as the village watchman, "has already apprehended one infiltrator";[56] the label "infiltrator" applied to a homesick peasant returning to his own possessions.

Throughout the 1950s and 1960s, until he was halted by age and infirmity, Abu Hilmi regularly descended to Jewish Ein Hod. Arik Brauer remembered how he first met Abu Hilmi. After watching Brauer add to what was formerly the house of Rashad Rashid, Abu Hilmi thanked Brauer and said, "I see you are building me a second story."[57] Ovadiah Alkara, from nearby Daliyat al-Karmil and the only Druze artist living in Ein Hod, claimed that these words were actually uttered by a Jewish artist whose Ein Hod home was visited by its former Arab owner. The new owner conducted a tour for the previous owner, pointing out, "Here is the new kitchen I added for you, here is another bedroom I built for you."[58]

According to his daughter, Ruqayyah, Abu Hilmi's daily walks about Ein Hod were part of a deliberate strategy to maintain the Abu al-Hayja presence.[59] 'Asim called his grandfather's gesture *tahaddi* (a challenge and a provocation).[60] After 1948, the 156,000 Palestinian Arabs remaining in Israel seemingly vanished. The majority of those who stayed were villagers governed by a system of military laws confining them to the immediate perimeters of their legal residences and further restricted by the near unobtainability of travel permits.[61] Other considerations are said to have prompted Abu Hilmi's survey of what he insisted belonged to the Abu al-Hayja: he needed to touch the land and see his house. In person, he countered the phenomenon of the vanishing Arab by being the ubiquitous Palestinian. Abu Hilmi's grandson Muhammad Mubarak recalled that much of the women's time and labor was spent washing and pressing his sweeping cloak, white robes, and head cloth—at a time when the Abu al-Hayja were still living in huts with no water or electricity—so that Abu Hilmi might walk his lands daily and make the Abu al-Hayja presence known.[62] Unlike other post-1948 destroyed Palestinian villages, there is no lack of knowledge among Arabs or Jews concerning ownership histories of the houses and the land of Ein Houd/Ein Hod: "It is said when there is a dispute about property boundaries, they [the artists of Ein Hod] call on the Arabs of Ein Houd to be the judges"[63] is a frequently voiced statement.

While I lived in Ein Hod during the summer of 1991, Muhammad Mubarak acknowledged that by an unspoken, but mutual, agreement between the two communities, there were no longer any Abu al-Hayja working in the Jewish Israeli Ein Hod. This agreement ended a longstanding arrangement in which former Arab owners had been brought in to renovate their houses and garden their lands. Muhammad Mubarak described what it meant to work on your own house: "Only in 1976, when I was twenty-two, did I come to work here for the first time. Renovations. I renovated old houses. You know what 'old' means. Even when I went in, I didn't feel any emotion. To this day I don't feel anything about what was here. Why don't I? I can't tell you."[64] In the 1990s, Arab labor imported from the Occupied Territories of Gaza and the West Bank worked in Ein Hod's restaurant and gardens.

Abu Hilmi was not only the *mukhtar;* he was also *abu al-balad* (the father of the village) in every sense: founder, visionary, dispenser of group hospitality in the guesthouse, and progenitor.[65] Mufagah, Abu Hilmi's daughter-in-law, confirmed that the high birthrate of Ein Houd al-Jadidah was his deliberate policy to populate the village after the catastrophe of 1948. Abu Hilmi fathered fifteen children: eight children with his first wife, 'Afifah Husayn, a cousin from the lineage of Dar Ibrahim, who died in 1975; seven children with his second wife, 'Ayshah, whom he married in 1967.[66] A 1976 photograph of Abu Hilmi taken in Jenin shows a striking, tall figure with blue eyes and a long, flowing beard that grew longer each year as a testament to his famous vow that it would not be cut until he returned to his former village. In 1982, one year before he died, Abu Hilmi was permitted by the Israeli authorities to make the pilgrimage to Mecca. Along the way he visited his kinsmen in Irbid, Jordan, the site of the guesthouse of Ein Houd reconstituted by refugees and exiles. The Jordan-based Abu al-Hayja understood the significance of his midriff-long, white beard as a sign of deep mourning: "You are near our village living on a small part of its lands where you can see it daily; yet you are still in pain. Then should we, here in Jordan, all die? You are still living on the soil of our village, breathing its air, what should we do here in Irbid?"[67] Abu Hilmi died believing the village of Ein Houd al-Jadidah he helped found was nothing more than a prison for his descendants.

Political Organization and Intellectual Upheaval (1978)

The power relationship between Arab and Jew in Israel is masked by an apparently universal right to citizenship.[68] When the Abu al-Hayja titled a 1994 video recording "Not on Any Map: The Unrecognized Arab Villages in Israel," they spoke both symbolically and literally: the numerous attempts to efface Ein Houd al-Jadidah, their post-1948 village, so that it is but a blank space on Israeli maps are not imagined but real.[69] This spatial context illustrates that both metaphor and reality constitute the very ground of the Abu al-Hayja existence. Another exhibition of documentary photographs, titled "The Forgotten Ones," was inaugurated in Haifa in 1993 to describe the everyday experiences of Arab residents in "unrecognized villages." Muhammad Mubarak introduced the exhibit, saying, "No matter what the photos can express, the reality of life is more miserable."[70]

Ein Houd al-Jadidah is an example of how Palestinian Arab space in Israel is the site of a social, political, and economic struggle.[71] Azmi Bishara points out that even legal Arab villages in Israel are not reference points on government maps; they are marked by signposts only at the village and thus are not defined as known and named Israeli space: "Big green signs in the north point the traveler's place as being between Shlomi and Acre. Arab villages do not exist in the public spaces called 'green signs.' They get a small white sign only next to the entrance of the village. The village is signified only if it is immediate."[72] Many Palestinians have developed the capacity to see palimpsests: Jewish Israeli Achziv functions as a sign for Palestinian Arab al-Zib, Tirat Haifa for al-Tirah, and so on. Legal, recognized Arab villages in Israel have white signposts; handwritten signs to Ein Houd al-Jadidah posted on trees off an unmarked, unpaved road were repeatedly torn down during my 1991 stay.

The politics of marginalized, unrecognized Palestinian villagers, a minority within the Arab minority of Israel, was to change the stories told about space on Mount Carmel and to contest the vocabulary created about Arabs by Jews. Ein Houd al-Jadidah has been castigated by Israelis as an ecological disaster for the Carmel Park lands as well as a demographic time bomb: "now the Arabs are two hundred, soon they'll be four thousand."[73] Historically, the Abu al-Hayja have been relegated to the Israeli vocabulary as "hostile Arabs," "fanatics," and the "enemy" (*oynim*)—phrases successfully carried over time from their armed resistance before 1948 to their current successful organizational strategies. The Arab as Other and the Arab as an ecological disaster are intimately related: once Jewish Israelis characterize all that is Arab, Muslim, Bedouin, or Turk as the malevolent Other, with the years of the Ottoman Empire (1517–1918) as the dark ages of the Holy Land, the malevolent Arab is conjoined to his people's historically disastrous agricultural practices. The opposite characterization—the good Israeli occupied in the beneficial, modern agricultural practices of Jewish settlements—is advanced as the solution to the putative deterioration of the soil and the primitivism of its native Palestinian Arabs.[74] To such characterizations, the Abu al-Hayja respond with a counternarrative of films, photography, newspapers, books, and websites. Because their villages do not exist in terms of government cartography, the Abu al-Hayja's most important activity has been to put their and other unrecognized Arab villages in Israel on the map. To do so, a master plan for all the unrecognized settlements was commissioned and paid for with the help of the Association of Forty, an organization founded by the Abu al-Hayja.

Before the Abu al-Hayja created the Association of Forty, they transformed their internal village practices and organization. Abu Hilmi pursued the only available, political course, one that placed his village in a traditional patron-client relationship under the protection of a particular patron, Avraham Melamed, an Israeli politician residing in the adjacent religious kibbutz, Nir Etzion. Melamed's wife, Yael Taub, was an artist with a house in Ein Hod. During Abu Hilmi's later years, Melamed was a powerful figure in Israeli politics and thanks to his patronage, the villagers were permitted to tap into Nir Etzion waterlines and became members of the kibbutz medical clinic.[75] Beginning in 1948, Abu Hilmi (as the *mukhtar*) was forced into the role of mediator between his people and the new state. According to Brenda Danet's study of the phenomenon of "pull" or "pulling strings"—called *protekzia* in Israeli society—four-fifths of the Arab population in Israel act on the assumption that a Jewish Israeli official cannot be approached directly while 100 percent believe that payment must be given to receive a service: "Thirty percent thought the payment could be symbolic; fifty-five percent thought it would have to be a substantial payment, either a sum of money or an expensive gift."[76] As "payment,"

Abu Hilmi regularly delivered the Abu al-Hayja as a bloc vote in favor of Melamed's party during elections. The village headman reprised an aspect of his pre-1948 Mandatory assignment, in which he was appointed or allowed to remain in place depending on his degree of compliancy with the authorities. Historically, the Abu al-Hayja had already undergone the removal of one *mukhtar* in 1939: for his support of the Arab Revolt, the British government had deposed Zaydan. In Ein Houd al-Jadidah, other seemingly traditional village institutions and structures were re-created. Abu Hilmi maintained a rebuilt village *madafah* (guesthouse), which functioned as a meeting place, a center for hospitality, and a mosque for the Abu al-Hayja clan just as he done for his 'Abd al-Rahim subclan lineage in his pre-1948 Ein Houd home.

Abu Hilmi, affectionately and reverently referred to as the shaykh who ruled on all matters, declared in 1978 that he could no longer lead the village. He resigned, saying to his clan this much-quoted statement, "I am tired, oppressed, I've no place to go, only God can help, complain to Him" (*tishki 'amrak li-llah*). He assigned himself the role of advisor. Following his successful plan to educate his descendants at Israeli universities, he resolved to let the younger generation, born or raised in Ein Houd al-Jadidah, the opportunity to take over. Abu Hilmi had completed the fourth grade in nearby al-Tirah, a village that had supported two elementary schools under Ottoman rule.[77] He read and wrote Arabic. One of Abu Hilmi's grandsons, Muhammad Mubarak, is a civil engineer and a graduate of Haifa's prestigious Technion Institute. He became an acknowledged village leader.[78]

The Abu al-Hayja characterize 1978 as a year of *inqilab fikri* (intellectual upheaval).[79] The transitional framework was a group of four men—Abu Hilmi's grandson Muhammad Mubarak, along with 'Asim, 'Abd al-Ghani, and 'Ali—chosen to form the first committee to govern the village. Though Muhammad Mubarak was the youngest, he was acceptable to all as the new leader. Eventually, men and women—voting rights were granted to women in 1990—over the age of sixteen were eligible to vote or become candidates in future village elections. According to Israeli law, a legal committee consists of at least seven members. In 1983, the Abu al-Hayja added three members to constitute *al-lajnah al-'ammah* (general committee). The committee held weekly meetings, expanding membership to nine to allow for women's attendance, which the Abu al-Hayja acknowledged was often determined by the family situation: young mothers were the most likely to be absent for legitimate reasons. Following Israeli committee rules, five consecutive absences by any elected member resulted in dismissal. Subcommittees were created to address budget, culture (including education and managing the school), sewage, street maintenance, and religious matters (mosque and graveyard).

Finances are shared and disbursed from a single fund (*sanduq*).[80] Each resident who is able pays a family tax. Based on the combined earnings of all Abu al-Hayja families in Ein Houd al-Jadidah, Muhammad Mubarak reported in 1991 a monthly income of US $500 for the entire village, a figure below the poverty line.

In comparison, he calculated Jewish Ein Hod's annual income for municipal services at approximately US $200,000. In Ein Houd al-Jadidah, to maintain the 1991 low level of municipal services for water and sewage costs and to upgrade the road and provide electricity would have required an expenditure of US $30,000 per year. The Abu al-Hayja cannot apply legal pressure through the Israeli court system to enforce delinquent tax payments from clan members, nor would they. The Abu al-Hayja rely on social cohesiveness and pressures exerted by clan members; they say they must get along with each other to form a unified front. In every way, they contrast their new administrative structure with their previous system: the Abu al-Hayja instituted democracy to replace *ihtikar,* rule of the village headman.

The 1978 upheaval that changed the internal governing structures of the Abu al-Hayja was not an isolated political act by one clan reacting to the pressures of an untenable legal and existential situation. Changes in Arab local self-government parallel a concurrent awakening of the Arab minority in Israel, a process called "Palestinization" by Israeli sociologist Sammy Smooha.[81] The tactics and strategies of the Abu al-Hayja were influenced by many factors; the watershed event the Abu al-Hayja say was the first Land Day—March 30, 1976—when Palestinians in Israel organized to protest repeated Israeli land expropriations "Judaizing" the Galilee, a process described by Azmi Bishara as "the bluntest expression of the state's treatment of its non-Jewish citizens as aliens and outsiders. Israeli authorities reacted to this aspect of national organization and civil rebellion in an unequivocal fashion as if to make clear that the state is not your state and we will not tolerate any act of rebellion!"[82] During the protest marches and demonstrations, six Palestinians were killed and some seventy injured. These deaths are commemorated annually with cultural and political events produced by the Arab minority in Israel in order to link their struggle for civil rights with their national conflict. The celebration of Land Day, instigated by Israeli expropriation of Arab land, has encouraged organization and institution building among the Palestinian Arabs who are citizens of Israel.[83]

To begin the process of organizing Ein Houd al-Jadidah, one of the first acts of the Abu al-Hayja general committee was to take back their village's name. Until 1978, though their village was not on any map as a place or a mailing address, it was locally known by the name of Kfar Abu al-Hayja, a combination of the Hebrew word *kfar* (village) and the clan name. To promote geographical and historical continuity, and to perpetuate memory—'Asim explicitly used the word *dhikra* (memory)—the Abu al-Hayja emphasized their original, pre-1948 name of Ein Houd. They believed this return to the name Ein Houd would be understood by Israeli society, in general, and the artists of Ein Hod, in particular, as a radical, incendiary gesture because there is an Ein Houd but it is Jewish Ein Hod. Nonetheless, Hebrew-language newspaper articles and the Ein Hod artists stubbornly continued to use the Israeli-approved appellation Kfar Abu al-Hayja for many years. Just as "Palestine" and "Palestinians" as terms referring to a place and a people were long taboo words in Jewish Israeli discourse, so too was the legal recognition of the Abu al-Hayja's existence, which they now tied to their original, recuperated, pre-1948 village name.

In 1978, the general committee of Ein Houd al-Jadidah also decided to breach the hated fence erected in 1964 to impede village growth; slowly the leaders convinced the clan to expand beyond the perimeter set by Israeli government authorities. Relying on many capable builders from his clan, Muhammad Mubarak, a civil engineer, functioned as head builder and general contractor for the new houses that were slowly heading down the steep and verdant hills wholly out of view of kibbutz Nir Etzion or Jewish Ein Hod. Dwellings often take more than three years to construct because materials must be brought up the mountain either by truck, by donkey, or by hand. Muhammad Mubarak intends to make Ein Houd al-Jadidah a paradise—an Arab village in Israel with its own sewage system. The Abu al-Hayja insist they will never leave; paradise is to be created in the small northeast corner of pre-1948 Ein Houd that is left to them. Being denied expansion, the Abu al-Hayja say they can and will build underground.

Israeli government authorities have waged an unceasing battle to dislodge the Abu al-Hayja and disperse them for resettlement elsewhere in Israel. Although the Abu al-Hayja have successfully fought several expulsion attempts from Ein Houd al-Jadidah, their struggle to remain intensified as a result of the Markowitz Commission Report, the popular title of a 1986 survey of illegally constructed housing, mainly Arab, undertaken by the Ministry of the Interior. For the Arab sector, the Commission on Illegal Construction documented over 6,000 instances of illegal houses under demolition orders or pending demolition decrees. The commission reports, for example, that as of July 1986, the Druze village of Daliyat al-Karmil had 174 demolition decrees with an additional 153 pending.[84] Though three Abu al-Hayja houses were involved in court cases, the survey records no demolition decrees against Ein Houd al-Jadidah. With the release of the Markovitch Report, fresh suits were filed and new litigation was initiated against the Abu al-Hayja's houses.

Paragraph 3.8 of the Markovitch Report describes the situation of "Abul Haija"—the Israeli authorities use the clan name for place and recognize neither the village nor its name change to Ein Houd: "Abul Haija (block 11956) is located southeast of Nir Etzion, within the Carmel Park, where twenty-four houses have been built. The commission recommends freezing all new construction at the site and proposes that the Israel Land Authority negotiate with the local residents in order to settle them in one of the recognized settlements. The commission recommends taking administrative and legal procedures to prevent any additional construction at that site."[85] The report's proposal for Ein Houd al-Jadidah was negotiation followed by relocation. The Markovitch Report created three categories of housing: "white" meant legal; "black," illegal; and "gray" houses (*batim aforim*) were neither black nor white but an amalgam of the two. "Gray" structures were not to be demolished immediately but allowed to be inhabited with requisite services of electricity, water, and telephones. "Gray" houses are under government surveillance: aerial photography and regular visits during which village housing is photographed to ensure that minimal, basic repairs to the exterior or any attempt to enlarge are not effected—in the language of the report, repairs are "frozen." Houses are deliberately permitted if not encouraged to deteriorate, an affront to the architecturally minded Abu al-Hayja, who have painstakingly rebuilt domiciles over the years. Should a house become uninhabitable, which occurs sooner or later when repair is forbidden, authorities declare it unsafe and then destroy it. In every instance, the permit for "gray" is for a limited time; once the permit expires, the house becomes "black" and is subject to demolition. The Markovitch Report painted the entire village housing of the Abu al-Hayja "gray," condemning housing to deterioration that in turn ensured subsequent demolition. Before the Markovitch Report, twenty-four dwellings illegally constructed by the Abu al-Hayja had escaped notice with no demolition decrees filed against the houses.

Consequences for Ein Houd al-Jadidah were enumerated by 'Asim. The freeze on new building construction or renovation since the 1986 Markovitch Report meant the Abu al-Hayja are mousetrapped again by conflicting Israeli government directives. Education, for example, is compulsory and the State of Israel pays the salary of the village schoolteacher. However, unrecognized villages are denied municipal services; such villages must pay any other expenses required to comply with the law of compulsory education: a schoolhouse, usually constructed by the state as a municipal service, must be provided for the state-supported teacher—in other words, a building that can only be built illegally. Whatever action the Abu al-Hayja take, they are in defiance of a law: in this instance, the Abu al-Hayja proceeded to construct an illegal building to house their elementary school up to the fourth grade (fig. 5). 'Asim provided another example, one concerning individual residences. When a house is designated "gray," the exterior does not belong to its owners, and minimal repairs, such as changing windows, are forbidden. More worrisome is the issue of family cohesion; as the population increases, sons and daughters forming newly married couples are forced to leave the village in search of housing elsewhere.[86] Demolishing Arab houses or appropriating them, generalized attacks on Arab landholdings, are seen by Anton Shammas as methods of space deprivation: "The Arab house has not only lost its original inner space, which was based on the harmonious tension of the arch stones, it has also lost its outer space. 'Building without a permit' has become synonymous with Arab building."[87]

In 1989, Israeli lawyer Michal Fox joined Anat Fisher and Adam Fish for the legal defense of the three (seven were originally cited) Abu al-Hayja houses illegally constructed in 1986 and therefore subject to new demolition orders mandated by the Markovitch Report. According to Fox's description, the government case rested on convicting the Abu al-Hayja for building activities, but

Figure 5.

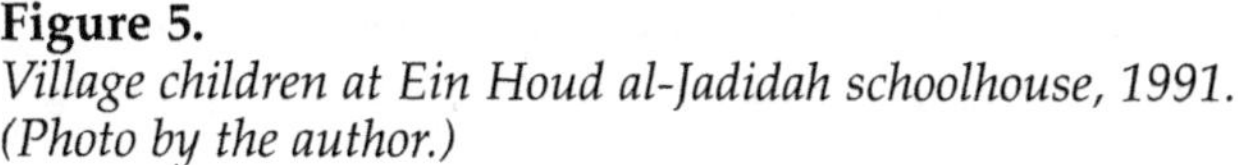

Village children at Ein Houd al-Jadidah schoolhouse, 1991.
(Photo by the author.)

they were not prosecuted for inhabiting illegally constructed houses. The Abu al-Hayja's defense was argued according to Israeli concepts of homeownership that assume an owner is not the builder. Lawyers, in asserting that builders of illegal housing were not necessarily owners, disregarded the true situation of the Abu al-Hayja as renowned and skillful Palestinian Arab builders. Because illegal construction of housing is, by its very nature, accomplished without the required paperwork documenting ownership, the court had no record of ownership and no evidence with which to prosecute owners. Written proof of construction is required to demolish a building. To build illegally is to be without papers. The Abu al-Hayja chose to plead not guilty to owning the houses they inhabited in order to avoid another common, legal Israeli government tactic: being sued repeatedly. Throughout the trial, the Abu al-Hayja steadfastly refused to acknowledge ownership or construction. Adam Fish represented the Abu al-Hayja in the three original cases: *State of Israel vs. Basmat Abid Abu al-Hayja* (3753/87); *State of Israel vs. Muhammad Yusif Abu al-Hayja* (3754/87); and *State of Israel vs. Abid Rauf Abu al-Hayja* (3756/87). On March 20, 1990, after three years of uncertainty and tension for Ein Houd al-Jadidah, the Haifa Court resolved the cases in favor of the Abu al-Hayja. According to Fox, the government lawyer resorted to name-calling during the trial, invoking appellations that date from resistance during the 1948 war: once again, the village and its inhabitants were "hostile" and "enemies" (*oynim, shodedim*).[88]

Founding the Association of Forty (1988)

Palestinians in Israel are designated by both Arabs and Jews as "absentees," politically, culturally, and existentially. Even more so were more than 60,000 Palestinians in Israel living in unrecognized villages. A Ministry of the Interior survey from 1992 in the Northern District identified 96 unrecognized Arab villages. An Association of Forty survey described 179 unrecognized settlements, typically consisting of 140 persons, though some have populations of 500, and divided them into three categories: unrecognized villages adjacent to recognized ones; those within a defined area; and isolated villages such as Ein Houd al-Jadidah.[89] To organize the unrecognized villages, in 1988 Muhammad Mubarak Abu al-Hayja founded the Association of Forty ("forty" commemorating the fortieth anniversary of the United Nations 1948 Universal Declaration of Human Rights). The first meeting of the Association of Forty was held in Ein Houd al-Jadidah. The organization's aims appeared in its promotional pamphlet: "public activities to achieve governmental recognition for the villages, preparing both a national zoning plan and local plans to obtain building permits, providing legal counseling in the face of demolition orders, fines and sentences for constructing without permits, and improving the living conditions by obtaining basic necessities for them."[90]

The Abu al-Hayja clan has become experienced in resisting and organizing to protect Ein Houd al-Jadidah against the most terrifying threat—a house demolition order mandated by any state agency. "The Road," a video made in 1987, chronicles one government attempt; on July 17, 1986, court orders were posted to demolish three Abu al-Hayja houses.

> "We don't want to be turned out of our homes in the area where our families have lived for generations and become refugees a second time around," said Muhammad Abulejah, who heads the committee pressing for official recognition of Ein Hud.
>
> The residents fear that demolition of the three partially constructed homes is just the first step toward razing the entire village.
>
> "If the settlement has no official status that means all the houses were built illegally. If the authorities can order the demolition of three homes, there is nothing to stop them from pulling down the rest," said Abulejah.[91]

Mounting an effective publicity and lobbying campaign, the Abu al-Hayja vowed to stop bulldozers brought to demolish homes by employing nonviolent tactics. Refusing to be displaced a second time, the entire village, including women and children, waited at the village entrance, prepared to lie in the path of the machines. Amir Mahoul, then chair of the Arab Students Union of Haifa

University, described groups of both Jews and Arabs staffing the night vigils to help villagers outnumbered by the police.

> Now the custom with the Ministry of Interior is that they don't come and demolish in the middle of the day—during the hours when all the villagers are there—they try to find more convenient hours. Either at night when everyone is asleep, coming to them one by one to get the people out of the houses and demolish them; or coming during the morning when the men have gone to work outside the village. During that time the villagers of Ein Hud didn't go to work because guarding their houses was important to them, so what was left, from the point of view of when the Ministry of Interior—the "Green Patrol"—would come were the nights. . . . So the only option we had was to come at night in groups and sit in all sorts of points in the village such that if someone tried to approach the village from any direction, someone would alert all the others.[92]

Fortunately, the Abu al-Hayja's lawyers found a technical irregularity in the government paperwork such that the presiding judge upheld the *hamulah*'s appeal, and the three houses were spared.[93]

Muhammad Mubarak describes the link between the origins of the Association of Forty and the plight of Ein Houd al-Jadidah, his village and the first village to employ unrecognized status as a strategy to unite one sector of dispossessed Palestinians in Israel by the tenets of nonviolent resistance.

> Suddenly they served us with demolition orders. We were desperate. We began to look into it and found out that there were many unrecognized communities. We decided to found the Association of the Forty in 1988 and the first meeting was here in Ein Houd. . . . The moment we reach violence—we "open fire"—the cannons of the state can wipe out the whole Arab population and in my opinion they are waiting for us to change our nonviolent approach. It may be that they don't see this as a nonviolent approach; they think it is most violent when we open our mouths and explain what we lack and demand these things.[94]

Unrecognition, Recognition, Unrecognition, and Partial Recognition: 1992 Onward

In June 1992, a special commission put together by Aryeh Deri, then Israel's minister of the interior, officially recommended recognition of five unrecognized villages: Ein Houd al-Jadidah, El-Aryan, El-Khawaled, Domeida, and Kammaneh.[95] Specifically, Ein Houd al-Jadidah was to be included in the Regional Council of Hof Ha-Carmel as is Jewish Ein Hod, a recommendation the Regional Committee in charge of planning and construction only endorsed four years later on January 6, 1996. Between June 1992 and December 14, 1994, when official recognition of Ein Houd al-Jadidah occurred, the Association of Forty, under the leadership of Muhammad Abu al-Hayja, continued to exert legal, moral, and political pressure. Consequently, on January 3, 1995, the government of Israel recognized four villages: El-Aryan, El-Khawaled, Domeida, and, for the second time, Ein Houd al-Jadidah.[96] Almost a year later, on December 21, 1995, official approval was given to construct the road to and infrastructure for Ein Houd al-Jadidah. Five days later, on December 26, 1995, four additional Arab villages were granted recognition: Husseiniya, Humeira, Kammaneh, and Ras El-Ein. By early 1996, it seemed that the Association of Forty had prevailed. A series of government and court decisions were passed, though not enacted, on behalf of the unrecognized villages: on February 1, 1966, the Council for National Gardens decided to give 170 dunams from Carmel Park lands to Ein Houd al-Jadidah (these dunams were lands confiscated in 1948 from the original patrimony of the Abu al-Hayja); on March 10, 1996, Yossi Sarid, then minister of the environment, endorsed the placement of the road, the paving of which was finally agreed upon by various government agencies; on March 19, 1996, the Regional Council of Hof Ha-Carmel agreed to the disposition of 170 dunams of park land to Ein Houd al-Jadidah; and on May 19, 1996, the government allocated 50 million Israel pounds ($15 million US) for the villages recently recognized plus 5 million Israeli pounds specifically targeted for Ein Houd al-Jadidah's electricity and road, while the Israeli government's Finance Committee endorsed the decision to allocate immediately 5 million pounds to Ein Houd al-Jadidah. A timetable was announced by the Ministry of the Interior for completing the work to bring municipal services to the recently recognized villages.[97] Progress was halted on May 29, 1996, when the Likud Party under Benjamin Netanyahu's leadership won the Israeli national elections. The new minister of the environment, Rafael Eitan, refused to abide by and to implement decisions of the previous government concerning recognition of Arab villages.[98]

During the years before 1996 when recognition was government policy, Muhammad Mubarak registered Ein Houd al-Jadidah organizationally as a cooperative (*kfar kehilati,* in Hebrew; *ta'awaniyah,* in Arabic) to be a part of the general movement of smallholders' cooperatives, the well-known Jewish Israeli institution of the moshav. He claimed Ein Houd al-Jadidah was the first Arab village to be designated a moshav by government bureaucracy.[99] Plans for the village as an agricultural enterprise called for an equitable redistribution of the former Abu al-Hayja lands currently in the hands of the surrounding Jewish Israeli settlements. Another possibility he envisioned was returning approximately one thousand dunams under the authority of the Carmel National Park lands to clan control. For the right to farm an additional one thousand dunams, the Abu al-Hayja clan was willing to forego the notion of land ownership. Farmland would have enabled Ein Houd al-Jadidah to expand and build for the future by granting each household approximately four dunams for family vegetable gardens. Muhammad Mubarak foresaw that the Abu al-Hayja would engage productively in mountain agriculture using the latest greenhouse techniques. He cited markets abroad for flowers and herbs, especially for thyme and honey. Plans to establish an agricultural enterprise in Ein Houd al-Jadidah drew explicitly on the pre-1948 Mandate period of Ein Houd as a recognized exporter of carob, olive oil, and honey to Haifa.[100] Income was to be allocated for offices, playgrounds, a village clinic, and a larger school. In addition to sustaining the clan economically, village agriculture means many Abu al-Hayja may choose to work within the village as opposed to current employment opportunities that are limited to commuting throughout Israel as low-paid laborers.

Michael Turner, the architect hired by Jewish Ein Hod to work on future planning, building, housing, and tourism needs, was also paid by the Ministry of the Interior for Ein Houd al-Jadidah to plan and, according to Turner, to facilitate and mediate among various ministries the complex negotiations involving sewage, electricity, water, and a road.[101] Since 1974, when Ein Houd al-Jadidah's lands were declared a national park and nature preserve, laws have been passed to protect the environment: no above-ground electrical wires may traverse a national park and provisions must be made for installation underground. Zoning laws must change Ein Houd al-Jadidah's post-1974 legal status from national park land to land zoned for residential, agricultural, and commercial use. The nineteen-dunam area of Ein Houd al-Jadidah must be enlarged, if only to conform to health codes that forbid human habitation within two hundred meters of a cemetery. Enlarging Ein Houd al-Jadidah's boundaries by allocating five dunams per family, in contrast with each family's current allotment of six hundred square meters, would accommodate three times the current population, an act, Turner maintained, that would ensure continuity of the traditional family structure of an Arab village. Many of Turner's infrastructure and planning requests on behalf of the Abu al-Hayja clan were, in fact, what Jewish Israeli settlers on the Palestinian Arab West Bank routinely receive under principles set in motion by General Ariel Sharon, minister of agriculture and settlements in the first 1977 Likud coalition government. Turner was asking for similar central government planning on behalf of twenty-seven Abu al-Hayja village houses.

A master plan prepared by an architect and presented to the Ministry of the Interior was one step in the process of becoming formal, legal, and recognized. To Turner's plans, Muhammad Mubarak added a guesthouse for the village. Calling it in Hebrew *bayt margo'a* (a house for relaxation) and in Arabic *masayif* (summer resorts and rest centers), he envisaged a modest complex of fifty to one hundred rooms with a swimming pool. In this way, he hoped tourists attracted to the village to enjoy Arab hospitality, Palestinian mountain agriculture, and rural life would also enjoy the amenities of a modern resort.

At the dawn of the twentieth-first century, Ein Houd al-Jadidah has finally achieved official recognition, a process that began in 2004 by saddling them with yet another inadequate, restrictive, state-imposed master plan. To challenge the village's newest geographical and architectural limits, and in partnership with the Foundation for Achieving Seamless Territory (FAST), a

Dutch-based non-governmental organization led by Israeli architect Malkit Shoshan, Ein Houd al-Jadidah actively solicited alternatives by holding an international architecture and planning competition.[102] In the meantime, Muhammad Mubarak's tourist development plans produced Ein Houd al-Jadidah's sole restaurant and major village employer called *Habayit* in Hebrew and *al-Bayt* in Arabic (home). Listed as an alluring tourist stop on numerous travel websites, it is noteworthy as a building purposefully constructed in the village to be a commercial restaurant: "Habayit itself is located in a rare spot. Large glass windows look out on green hills and the sea. Safia and Muhammed Abu-el-Hija have opened their home to guests. Safia cooks and the children help. She uses a variety of herbs such as wild arum, mallow, chicory, and cyclamen leaves. The menu changes with the seasons, and some 20 courses are served, including chicken with rice, stuffed peppers, grilled eggplant, and a wide variety of salads."[103]

Nonetheless, despite local changes, international attention and a measure of renown as a tourist destination, as of July 2007, only Muhammad Mubarak's house was connected to Israel's national electrical grid, while the rest of the Abu al-Hayja awaiting building permits that few expect will soon be granted, must take their electricity from him.[104]

Kawkab Abu al-Hayja: Tourist Village

The mix of tourism and agriculture that holds for Muhammad Mubarak the possibility of economic independence for his family and clan has been initiated elsewhere, notably in the clan village of Kawkab Abu al-Hayja, approximately a half-hour car trip from Nazareth north to the Galilee. Both Ein Houd al-Jadidah and Kawkab Abu al-Hayja are Muslim villages but with different post-1948 histories. In July 1948, according to historian Benny Morris, the Israeli army captured several Arab villages in this region during the northern sweep called Operation Dekel. Among the villages were al-Ruways, one of the settlements founded by Husam al-Din Abu al-Hayja and belonging to the Abu al-Hayja clan, and Kawkab Abu al-Hayja, the site of the shrine where the founder of the clan is buried.[105] According to observers' accounts, the Israeli army distinguished the Muslim population from Christians and Druzes, characteristically "'cleansing the area of Muslims and [taking] an easier attitude towards Christians . . . [and] Druse.'"[106]

Palestinian Arab inhabitants of Kawkab Abu al-Hayja claim a history of resistance not only to Jewish settlement but also to British Mandatory rule. From the Jewish Israeli viewpoint, the reasons why some Palestinian Arab villages were allowed to remain after 1948 depended on various factors: the degree of resistance by the villagers, their religion, and, finally, independent, field decisions made by local Israeli army commanders.[107] As an Arab writer Emil Habibi's responded to the perennial question of why he elected to stay in Nazareth under Israeli rule.

> Why should I go into exile? I've never dreamt of it. I would die if I went into exile, like a fish on the shore. I never thought of this. Why should I go? These theories were inserted into our minds by Zionism, that one can choose his homeland. They not only choose their homeland, they change their names as well. There is a movement of changing European names into Israeli/Jewish . . . Hebrew names. What is this? I told you about this niece of mine, a student here in the U.S. She sent me a questionnaire: "Why did you stay?" Why did I stay? It is a very natural thing to stay in one's homeland.[108]

For the inhabitants of Ein Houd and Kawkab Abu al-Hayja, it was natural to remain in their villages. Both villages were largely depopulated by the Israelis in 1948, and both reestablished themselves. What both villages share, however, are the efforts of a charismatic leader who kept a core population in place and on the land: Abu Hilmi took on this role for the Abu al-Hayja of Ein Houd and the villagers of Kawkab Abu al-Hayja recount the story of their revered leader, the tenacious Shaykh Hamid 'Abd al-Halim.[109] Oral interviews conducted in the 1990s have elicited a founder and founding moment structurally analogous for Kawkab Abu al-Hayja to the 1948 events surrounding Ein Houd's destruction and rebirth as Ein Houd al-Jadidah. Shaykh Hamid was a scholar, a graduate of Cairo's famed Al-Azhar University. Although blind, during the attacks on Kawkab, he hid on the roof rather than flee, claiming blindness and other physical infirmities prevented his departure. A small group of villagers, some 150 people, stayed behind to be with him. Villagers recall that a British soldier helped the shaykh down from the burning roof of his house where he had sought refuge, carrying the shaykh on his back. The shaykh is reported to have declared, "They burned our village yet we will ride on them." Encouraged by these words, villagers say they began their post-1948 life by building simple mud houses. Unlike Ein Houd, little remains of the traditional stone buildings of Kawkab. Indeed, Kawkab's houses were first burned down by the British in the 1940s, a scorched earth policy to eradicate resistance before Jewish Israeli attacks. In Kawkab, there are no houses from the pre-1940s but the shrines in the village endure, most of which are tombs for soldiers, notably the tomb of Shaykh Sa'id, who had accompanied Husam al-Din Abu al-Hayja and Saladin in the campaign to rid Palestine of the Crusaders in the eleventh century.

The charismatic Shaykh Hamid 'Abd al-Halim died in the nearby village of Kafr Manda in 1990, at an age reckoned by the villagers to be more than one hundred. Then, the population of Kawkab numbered 2,220, some 600 of whom claim Abu al-Hayja lineage. The two main divisions in the village are called the Fellahin (farmers) and the Fuqara (six subclan lineages of Hajj, Hajuj, Mansur, 'Ali, Salih, and 'Odeh), both of whom controlled the land and agricultural production. The third clan grouping, the Abu al-Hayja of Kawkab, never owned land and were notable for their religious devotion and their role as dervishes.

At the time of my first visit to the *maqam* (shrine) in Kawkab on August 3, 1991, Nayif 'Abd al-'Aziz Abu al-Hayja was seventy-nine years old (fig. 6). He

Figure 6.
Nayif 'Abd al-'Aziz Abu al-Hayja', keeper of the Kawkab Abu al-Hayja' shrine, August 3, 1991. (Photo by the author.)

is the keeper of the tombs that include, outside the shrine, an eastern tomb housing the body of Husam Abu al-Hayja who is called, according to the inscription on his grave, Abu al-Hayja son of Hamdan.[110] On his tomb are inscribed these words: "You are Abu al-Hayja son of Hamdan, you are his son, the son resembles the generous father." A western tomb, also outside the shrine, is for 'Ali Badawi Abu al-Hayja, who died 1183 (fig. 7).[111] The founder of Arab Ein Houd, Husam al-Din Abu al-Hayja, the warrior-general granted several villages by Saladin, is buried in Kawkab Abu al-Hayja and his grave is often visited both by the clan and by Christian, Jewish, and Muslim pilgrims to pray and to seek cures.[112] The shrine is always open with blue ribbons tied to the entrance gate, a signal that anyone may enter at any time. Visitors pull threads from these ribbons to wrap around throats or wrists. Threads are said to remind wearers to pray and perhaps cure illness. Nayif's son, Fuad, a schoolteacher in nearby Sakhnin, gives tours of the shrine. Most visitors arrive in the summer because the village's high altitude harbors cold and snowy winters. Among the pilgrims visiting are the Abu al-Hayja from Israel and Jenin Camp.

Figure 7.
Exterior of Kawkab Abu al-Hayja' shrine.
(Photo by the author.)

The Abu al-Hayja of Jenin Camp

In 1948, Rashad Rashid 'Abd al-Salam of Dar Ahmad subclan, a *mukhtar* of Arab Ein Houd, was forced to leave his village. Accompanying him was a group of Abu al-Hayja families, and many eventually regrouped in Jenin Camp by 1959. During my 1995 visit, there were twenty-seven families numbering 216 people. The head of Jenin Camp, 'Abd al-Raziq Mar'i Hasan, was from the Abu al-Hayja clan; his former house in Ein Houd is a library. When Rashad Rashid died in 1992, a refugee under occupation, the Abu al-Hayja of Jenin Camp, asked to appoint another headman by the Israeli military authorities, say they refused. Just as their kinsmen in Ein Houd al-Jadidah replaced the *mukhtar* with a democratically elected, nine-person committee in 1978, the younger generation raised, if not born, in refugee camps declared allegiance not to the Abu al-Hayja but to the larger family defined as the Palestinian people. Because clans and families promoted *infisal* (divisiveness and separatism), the younger generation chose to be active in various political parties, mainly the Palestine Liberation Organization (known by its initials PLO in English and by Fatah in

Arabic). 'Abd al-Raziq not only headed Jenin Camp but also, as a Fatah representative, held an important post in charge of *lajnat al-islah* (a seventeen-person committee to settle disputes) with jurisdiction over the town of Jenin, its refugee camps, and sixty-five villages in Jenin district. His role was to solve every family's problems not just those of the Abu al-Hayja. Inspired by his family genealogy, the generals and leaders of Saladin's armies who liberated and conquered Palestine from the Crusaders, he noted parallels to their contemporary political and national struggle under Israeli military occupation: "We are not less than they."[113] Both Murad Rashad Rashid, the son of the *mukhtar,* and 'Abd al-Raziq said they have not returned to see their houses, though they regularly visited Ein Houd al-Jadidah and Kawkab Abu al-Hayja, the latter as a pilgrimage to their ancestors' shrine and an outing to the calm beauty of the Galilee countryside (fig. 8). Not able to bear the emotions experienced when facing a lost childhood home, they cited instances of dangerous and humiliating encounters with Jewish Israeli residents of Ein Hod who call on the police to eject visiting Abu al-Hayja.[114] Zahiyah Muhammad 'Ali Nimr, wife of the *mukhtar* and mother of Murad, was uninterested in any discussion concerning payment or reparations for her house: the building in which Arik Brauer lives belongs to her and she wants it back.[115] Though 'Abd al-Raziq ran as an independent candidate from Jenin during the 1996 elections to form the parliament of the Palestinian National Authority, along with many Abu al-Hayja, he, too, shares the hope of a return to their village of Ein Houd because without it, he says, they are like bodies without souls never able to achieve their humanity.

Conclusion

When first interviewed in 1991, Muhammad Mubarak insisted that even if a Palestinian state formed by a union of the Occupied Territories of the West Bank and Gaza should arise, such a state would neither influence nor guarantee the rights he sought as a Palestinian Arab who is a citizen of Israel. The 1993 Oslo Accords initiated what seemed unlikely in 1991: the possibility of a Palestinian state. In contrast, most Jewish Israeli analysts assumed that achieving a settlement between Israel and a Palestinian nation was the only factor determining Israeli attitudes and laws related to the Arab citizens of Israel.[116] Muhammad Mubarak believes in pressing for Israeli acknowledgment of Palestinian Arab rights as a minority in Israel regardless of the outcome in the West Bank and Gaza. Muhammad Mubarak may never establish a sovereign state nor shape a nation, but he can define a community.

At the same time, the Abu al-Hayja and the Association of Forty define what they mean by equality. One example is equal protection of sites sacred to Muslims, specifically the preservation and care of mosques and cemeteries; this is an issue that unites Palestinian Arab civil rights activists and the Muslim religious leadership in Israel. Desecrated mosques, such as the one in former Salamah, currently Tel Aviv's Kfar Shalem neighborhood, are documented in

Figure 8.
Murad Rashad Rashid and 'Abd al-Raziq Mar'i Hasan of Jenin Camp and 'Asim Abu al-Hayja' of Ein Houd al-Jadidah in Jenin Camp, August 11, 1995. (Photo by the author.)

the Palestinian memorial books;[117] in Salamah, a Muslim cemetery threatened with destruction is located where Halamish, an Israeli construction company, plans to build.[118] Another site of contention is the cemetery of pre-1948 Arab Ein Houd, where the main visitors' parking area and the garbage dumpsters were located in 1991;[119] Michal Fox, a lawyer for the Abu al-Hayja, noted that in this case both Arabs and Jews agreed on the location of the cemetery. The two parties turned to the Ministry of Religion to question why funds for a fence around the dumpster were not available, only to be told that the priorities of the Ministry of Religion are cemeteries in use, not former Muslim ones.[120] For Jewish Ein Hod and Arab Ein Houd al-Jadidah, this dispute about boundaries and yet another fence—one to protect the sacred Muslim burial ground from the adjacent Jewish-built garbage dump and parking lot—foregrounds Jewish Israeli erasure of non-Jewish religious spaces.[121] Related issues are the opposition to further transformations of mosques into museums, a spatial repurposing that deprives Muslims of legitimate places of prayer. In 1992, discussions were held on two cases: the plan of the mayor of Tiberias to turn the Dahir al-Umar Mosque, part of a restaurant since 1948, into a museum despite pledges from Muslim leaders to renovate it, and actions of the municipality of Beersheva then in the process of converting a mosque to a museum.[122]

When feasible, the Abu al-Hayja tie the fate of unrecognized villages explicitly to the State of Israel's attempts to eradicate individual dwellings, communal structures, and religious property, acts perceived as attacks on the civil rights of the Arab minority as well as their history.

> In addition . . . is the problem of 132 unrecognized Arab villages, which lack services as basic as drinking water. Consider, too, the problems of the Negev Bedouin, many of whom are being transferred from their homes and lands. In mixed Arab-Jewish towns, Arabs are being pressured to leave in order to obliterate the many meanings that the collective Palestinian memory holds for these towns. We are facing an effort to kill our memory. Our waqf properties are not being respected. Mosques are turned into nightclubs, cemeteries into shopping centers and residential complexes.[123]

Accordingly, the Israeli polity is viewed as "includ[ing] citizens who enjoy full rights and undertake full obligations, while others are deprived of political and civil rights."[124] Place is obviously not devoid of politics. The Abu al-Hayja once defined Ein Houd al-Jadidah as a reserve within a reserve within a reserve. Ein Houd al-Jadidah is a site that does not exist on any map; identity cards listed the address of the adjacent religious kibbutz, Nir Etzion. Recognition means not only construction permits and municipal services but that the village of Ein Houd al-Jadidah will appear on the map and in their identity cards.[125] The Abu al-Hayja have created communities of resistance based on the possibilities of real and imagined geographies. The geography of the Carmel Mountain is full of gaps and contradictions into which the marginalized, "absent present"

Palestinian Arabs have been able to inscribe for themselves new mappings and sites. They keep alive the story of this specific, contested space, and in so doing they continue to affect radically the ways Jewish Israelis codify the past; at the same time, they dare to envision a different future for Palestinian Arabs who have come to invest in the spaces of Israel. In the moments when they are heard in their fight for recognition, especially when winning recognized-village status for nine villages in the north of Israel—their own village of Ein Houd al-Jadidah plus El-Aryan, El-Khawaled, Domeida, Arab El-Naim, Husseiniyya, Humeira, Ras El-Ein, and Kammaneh—the Abu al-Hayja clan challenges the Jewish Israeli understanding of collective memory to include the Palestinian Arabs of Israel.

Notes

1. On the Bir Zeit series, see Slyomovics 2007.
2. Kanaana and al-Ka'bi 1987, 3–6. The clan name appears in English transliteration according to various spellings, among them: Abu El-Hijja, Abulhaija, Abulheja, etc. I use "Abu-al-Hayja" to follow Library of Congress protocols (minus diacritical marks and in contrast to my original chapter in the book, *Object of Memory*). Similarly, the village name, Ein Houd, also appears as 'Ayn Hawd, Ein Hud, Ayn Khud, and so forth.
3. Useful works on the fall of Haifa are Palumbo 1987; W. Khalidi 1959b; and Morris 1989, 73–99. A review of the scholarly historiography on the events of 1948 is Shlaim 1995. See also "Special Issue: Israeli Historiography Revisited," *History and Memory* 7:1 (1995).
4. Morris 1989, 93–94. See also Nazzal 1974.
5. Michael Palumbo, for example, claims accuracy for Palestinian memoirs when juxtaposed with Western, non-Arab sources (American, United Nation, British, and Israeli) (1987, 17). In contrast, Israeli historian Benny Morris "very, very, rarely" used interviews to establish facts: "While contemporary documents might misinform, distort, omit or lie, they do so in my experience, far more rarely than interviewees recalling highly controversial events some forty years ago. My limited experience with such interviews revealed enormous gaps of memory, the ravages of aging and time, and terrible distortions or selectivity, the ravages of accepted information, prejudice and political beliefs and interests" (1989, 2). For an excellent critique of Morris's refusal to conduct research that included oral interviews, see Teveth 1990, 214–49.
6. Sharif Kanaana and Bassam Ka'bi, taped interview with the Abu al-Hayja, Jenin Camp, February 14, 1985, cassette 2 (Ka'bi, Arabic transcription, p. 19). The events surrounding 1948 in the Ein Houd memorial book are based on their interviews and summarized, see Kanaana and Ka'bi 1987, 47–58.
7. Muhammad Mahmud Muhammad 'Abd al-Salam (Abu Faruq), taped interview with Kanaana and Ka'bi, Jenin Camp, February 14, 1985, cassette 3 (Ka'bi, Arabic transcription, pp. 33–34).
8. Khalidi et al. 1992, 150.
9. Khalidi (1959a) demonstrates that Arab leaders opposed a Palestinian exodus and their radio broadcasts to the population were to encourage villagers to stay. Claims and counterclaims regarding the role of Arab leaders and their radio messages are summarized in Kanaana 1992.
10. Khalidi et al. 1992, 178. Morris's preliminary map lists Ein Houd as no. 170, dating its fall and final evacuation around July 15, 1948 (1989, xvi), though his book does not give the specific history of what happened to Ein Houd. However, he states that with the exception of isolated villages such as al-Tirah, 'Ayn Ghazal, Jaba, and Ijzim (which surrounded Ein Houd), the Arabs of this area had evacuated their homes and villages (118).

11. Khalidi et al. 1992, 150.
12. Abu Faruq interview, cassette 3 (Ka'bi, Arabic transcription, p. 36; translation by Susan Slyomovics).
13. Ibid., cassette 3 (Ka'bi, Arabic transcription, p. 35). These concerns are attested to in interviews conducted by Warnock 1990; Sayigh 1979, 87.
14. There is a vast literature on the Deir Yasin massacre; see Morris 1989, 113–15; Khalidi et al. 1992, 290–91. The fate of al-Tanturah is discussed in Khalidi et al. 1992, 194–95.
15. Afif Abdul Rahman, interview, Irbid, June 24, 1994. Unless otherwise indicated, all interviews are by the author.
16. See Norman G. Finkelstein's analysis of Benny Morris's book (1995, 51–87). Finkelstein notes this scenario occurred in other villages citing Beit Naqquba (56). See also Morris (1989, 227) for the situation in the village of Ar Rama.
17. Khalidi et al. 1992, 201.
18. Oral histories collected in Lynd, Bahour, and Lynd 1994 confirm narratives similar to the Abu al-Hayja; see their interview with Bashar from Jenin Camp:

    I was born in 1932 in a little village next to Haifa. . . . In 1948 . . . there was a war. We left when there was bombing from planes and bombardment from the sea. We went inland because we thought that was the only place where we could be safe. We came here to Jenin, walking from Haifa, wearing our pants and our shoes and carrying our clothes. That's all we had with us. The strongest of the village left first. Those who had less strength left next. Those who were not able to make it were taken in vehicles and dropped in Jenin. I came with my mother and brothers. We left at 6:00 at night. We got here at ten o'clock the following morning, walking. (31)

19. UN census figures for 1949 put the Palestinian population in Iraq at 4,000; see *United Nations: Report of the Economic Survey Mission of the Middle East* (New York, 1949), cited in Brand 1988, 9. See also Eppel 1994.
20. Kanaana and Ka'bi, taped interviews with the Abu al-Hayja, Jenin Camp, cassette 1 (Ka'bi, Arabic transcription, p. 11). Reasons given for a group heading to Iraq were that in 1948 Iraqi army leaders, hearing the name Abu al-Hayja, called out among the refugee groups, announced that they too were part of the Abu al-Hayja (though also called al-Rayahiyya in Iraq) and offered sanctuary to their kinsmen.
21. For maps of these camps, see Plascov 1981, appendix 11, which consists of United Nations Relief and Works Agency for Palestine Refugees (UNRWA) foldout maps in the back pocket, especially two maps of 'Askar Camp, and a third map locating schools built in West Bank camps.
22. Canaan 1933, 18.
23. Jabra 1959, 68–69. These are the last two lines of his poem to the massacre of Deir Yasin (translation by Susan Slyomovics).
24. A similar need to document in print was demonstrated for newly literate Bedouin writers in Jordan by Shryock (1996).
25. Quoted in Gavron 1986.
26. Bishara 1995.
27. T. Carmi, interview, Ein Hod, August 14, 1991. Carmi mentions that one poem, "She-artsenu yafa" (1956, 103–6), written in 1955, is about the landscape of Ein Hod and Arab children.
28. The Absentee Property Law was passed March 14, 1950, and appears in *Sefer ha-khukkim* (Book of Laws), no. 37 (2nd Nisan, 5710; March 20, 1950), 86.
29. Yekutiel 1990, n.p. Text in Arabic, Hebrew, and English; quotes from the English.
30. Kanaana 1975, 4.
31. Al-Haj 1993, 49.

32. On the complex history of the land system in Palestine, see Hadawi 1988, especially the section titled "Palestine System of Land Tenure" on pp. 35–46.
33. Sabella 1971, 26–27.
34. Nakhleh 1977.
35. Ibid., 65.
36. Zureik 1979; Haidar 1987.
37. Eyal 1993. Eyal contrasts the current discursive objectification of the Arab village (that produced harsh military rule policies) by Jewish Israelis with the pre-1948 state period that romanticized the Arab village as a locus for an authentic Jewish identity rooted in biblical ways.
38. See A. Cohen 1965, and his "Hamula," *Encyclopaedia of Islam* (1979), 3:149–50.
39. Asad 1975, 274.
40. This is also the view of Nakhleh, who described himself as "an indigenous Palestinian anthropologist and member of the group being studied" (1977, 55).
41. A summary of these positions are in al-Haj 1993, 49–50.
42. H. Rosenfeld 1980; al-Haj 1987; al-Haj and Rosenfeld 1990.
43. Abdel Fattah 1987, 13; Natur 1980; Livav 1980.
44. Yekutiel 1990, n.p.
45. Ibid.
46. Abu 'Asim speaks in Hebrew to the camera operator (the film has English subtitles) in a thirty-minute video titled "The Road," written and directed by Yitzhak Rubin (Haifa: Teknews Ltd. Production, 1987). Oral histories collected by Rosemary Sayigh (1979) among Palestinian refugees in Lebanon attest to Palestinians' frequent attempts to return to home villages; see her section on uprooting.
47. Ruqayyah Abu al-Hayja, interview, Ein Houd al-Jadidah, August 13, 1991.
48. For the story of naming Jewish Ein Hod, see Slyomovics 1998, 66–67.
49. I have found only one documented instance in which Jewish homeowners offered to renounce or pay rent to former Arab owners; see Ofer 1993. Dalia Landau's parents, Bulgarian immigrants to Israel in 1948, were given the Al-Khayri house in Ramle, which had been deemed abandoned Arab property: "When her parents died Dalia inherited the house, and she and her husband Yehezkel (formerly director of the religious peace movement Oz ve Shalom) decided to dedicate it to some form of Jewish-Arab reconciliation. They first thought of selling the house and giving the money to the Al-Khayri family, but the offer was refused. Bashir Al-Khayri, who had left the house at the age of six, suggested turning it into a kindergarten for the Arab children of Ramle 'so they will enjoy the childhood I couldn't have.'"
50. "Kharij al-qanun" [Outside the Law], *al-Mursal* (June 26, 1964), n.p.
51. Yekutiel 1990.
52. "The Road."
53. Yekutiel 1990.
54. Tuvia Iuster, taped interview, Ein Hod, August 19, 1991. An abbreviated version of these events is recounted by Iuster in "The Road."
55. Iuster interview.
56. Bat Haim 1954.
57. Arik Brauer, interview, Ein Hod, August 16, 1991.
58. Ovadiah Alkara, taped interview, Ein Hod, July 30, 1991.
59. Ruqayyah Abu al-Hayja, interview, Ein Hod al-Jadidah, August 13, 1991.
60. 'Asim Abu al-Hayja, interview, Jenin Camp, August 11, 1995.
61. Eighty percent were villagers and only 6 percent of 200,000 Arab city dwellers remained in urban areas after the war. See al-Haj and Rosenfeld 1990, 24; Lustick 1980.
62. Muhammad Mubarak, interview, Ein Houd al-Jadidah, August 5, 1995.
63. "The Road," voiceover narration.
64. Quoted in Grossman 1993, 95–96.

65. Sharif Kanaana has defined the *mukhtar* (literally, "the chosen one") as "the headman chosen and appointed by the government while a sheikh is a traditional informal headman of a village or tribe" (1975, 4). Abu Hilmi was the shaykh; he was both chosen by his clan and recognized by the Israeli authorities as the *mukhtar.*
66. The general Palestinian community of Israel shows a quadrupling of the Arab population since 1948 as a result of high fertility and low mortality rates, according to the section titled "The Population, by Religion," in Central Bureau of Statistics 1995, 43–45.
67. Afif Abdul Rahman Abu al-Hayja, interview, Irbid, June 18, 1994.
68. Relations between Arabs and Jews are formal, asymmetrical, and filled with tension (Smooha 1989–92).
69. "Not on Any Map: The Unrecognized Arab Villages in Israel" (1994), thirty-minute videotape, sponsored by the Association of Forty.
70. "Photo Exhibition in Haifa: 'The Forgotten,'" *Arabs in Israel* 3:2 (1993): 8. See also the Association of Forty 1993, with photographs by Walid Yassin, Peter Fryer, and Dror Yekutiel. For a review of the exhibit, see "Photo Exhibition in Haifa" 1933.
71. Theories concerning the production of space are from Lefebvre 1991 and Soja 1989.
72. Bishara 1992.
73. Tuvia Iuster, interview in "The Road." From a comparative perspective, their situation is similar to that of Native Americans in the United States as well as the Maasai of Kenya and Tanganyika: "one of the first steps in establishing a national park is to rid the region of its initial caretakers" (Deihl 1985).
74. "Conservation of the landscape, and intimate contact with it, thus appears as the surest way of protecting the nation as a whole, both from internal schisms and external influences and threats. . . . To a significant degree, defending nature is inseparable from defending the State: a case of defending a metaphor with an army" (Selwyn 1995, 131).
75. On the role of local political considerations as determinants in voting patterns of Palestinian villages in Israel, see al-Haj 1981, 1979.
76. Danet 1989, 249–50.
77. Khalidi et al. 1992, 196.
78. The ways in which Arabs have attempted to change their marginal status in Israel through educational attainments is the subject of al-Haj 1991. Between 1970 and 1975, Arabs in Israel with higher education increased by 150 percent according to Rekhess (1981, 114).
79. This roughly corresponds to "the (ac)quiescent first period, 1950–75," characteristic of Palestinian Arab political activity in Israel, described by Lehman-Wilzig (1993, 131). However, the existence and establishment of the Abu al-Hayja settlement during the so-called quiescent period constitutes a radical protest and a nonquiescent act. Another contributing factor is that in 1977, the right-wing Herut Party–led coalition came to power after twenty-nine years of Labor (Alignment/Mapai parties). This, too, called a political upheaval (*mahapakh,* in Hebrew), was a factor that contributed to the Abu al-Hayja's radical change in voting patterns. See Ben-Dor 1980; cf. Rouhana 1986.
80. Contrary to Jacob Landau's assertion regarding the decline of the Palestinian *hamulah,* which he sees as possibly the result of the extreme circumstances of the Abu al-Hayja *hamulah* of Ein Houd al-Jadidah, the economic significance of the clan has increased (1993, 49). Sociologist Majid al-Haj notes that for the Arab town of Shefar'am, the economic role of the *hamulah* is negligible; only 9 percent of informants receive financial support from their kinship group (1987, 79).
81. Smooha 1984, 5, 162–63.
82. Bishara 1993, 90L.
83. Joel Beinin (1988) demonstrates continuities between the 1976 Land Day demonstrations and the successful strike in 1987 by Arabs in Israel on another occasion, Equality Day. The beginnings of Land Day organization and interviews with its leaders are in Majalli 1990.

84. Ministry of the Interior, State of Israel [Markovitch Commission Report] (Jerusalem: Ministry of the Interior, 1989), 50, paragraph 3.5. The Markovitch Report is translated into English by M. Ben Joseph with typescript copies available from the Association of Forty.
85. Ibid., 51.
86. An early study points to the phenomenon of "cumulative in-situ urbanisation": "the bulk of the labor force works away from the village but continues to live in it. . . . In the course of this process (stemming from the political and social state of the Arabs in Israel, and from local geographical circumstances), the villages assume a peculiar character, no longer truly rural while still not urban" (Meyer-Brodnitz 1967, viii).
87. Shammas 1983, 42.
88. Michal Fox, interview, Haifa, August 15, 1991.
89. "Statement by the Association of Forty: Association Calls for Solving the Problem of All the Unrecognized Villages," *Sawt al-Qura* [The Villages' Voice] 12:9 (1994): 24; also cited in *Arabs in Israel* 2:12 (1993): 6.
90. Association of Forty pamphlet, n.d., n.p., Arabic and English, states that "it will accept with gratitude support and donation from public organizations and from individuals who perceive our activity as humanitarian, which struggles for coexistence in peace between Arabs and Jews."
91. "The Road"; Rudge 1986; Minns and Hijab 1990, 50–57; Goodman 1986.
92. Amir Mahoul, interview, in Nunn 1993, 31.
93. "The Road."
94. Mohammed Abu al-Hija (sic) interview, in Nunn 1993, 30. See Abdel Fattah 1995 for a six-year review (1988–95) of the accomplishments of the Association of Forty.
95. "Official Recognition for Arab Village 'Ayn Haud," *Arabs in Israel* 2:4 (1992). Arabic transliterations for village names are according to the Association of Forty.
96. "After Long Years of Struggle and Suffering," *Sawt al-qura* 30:6 (January 1995): 28.
97. "Development of the Recognition Process of Eight Unrecognized Villages in the North" (Haifa: Association of Forty, 1996), unpaged press release; Association of Forty 1996.
98. Association of Forty, "Israel's Measures against Its Arab Citizens," letter to the U.S. House of Representatives, August 1996.
99. Muhammad Mubarak Abu al-Hayja, interview, Haifa, July 26, 1995. "'Ayn Hawd qaryah ta'awaniyah jamahiriyah" [Ein Houd Cooperative Village], *Sawt al-qura* 30:6 (1995): 5. Bar-Gal (1190) dates the first Arab cooperative to 1924 by tobacco growers of Acre, and describes various obstacles to a cooperative movement in the Arab sector by the British in pre-1948 and the Israelis in post-1948.
100. Kanaana and Ka'bi, taped interview with the Abu al-Hayja, cassette 1 (Ka'bi, Arabic transcription, 4).
101. Michael Turner, interview, Jerusalem, July 24, 1994.
102. Master plans submitted from an astonishing range of architects were posted on FAST's Web site, http://www.one-land.org/.
103. "In and around Ein Hod," http://www.ynetnews.com/articles/0,7340,L-3245558,00.html.
104. Fadi Eyadat, "After Sixty Years of Statehood, Electricity Begins Flowing to Ein Hud for the First Time," *Haaretz*, July 31, 2007, http://www.haaretz.com/hasen/spages/888225.
105. Morris confirms that in certain cases where "the IDF encountered no, or no serious, resistance, at least a core of inhabitants stayed put usually by clan" (1989, 200–201).
106. Morris quotes Yitzhak Avira, "an old-time Haganah Intelligence Service hand and something of an Arabist," who was critical of this procedure because Avira believed the Christians and Druzes were equally dangerous (1989, 201).
107. Much has been written on the subject of which Arab villages remained and why. A selection of readings would include works already cited by Benny Morris, Norman Finkelstein, and Walid Khalidi.

108. "Literature and Politics: A Conversation with Imil Habibi (Interview Conducted by Allen Douglas and Fedwa Malti-Douglas)," *Mundus Arabicus* 5 (1992): 27.
109. Versions were recounted by my host, 'Ali Khajuj, who learned his history through oral transmission from his family. In addition, the local council of Kawkab commissioned Palestinian geographer Shukri 'Arraf to produce a volume describing the history and geography of their village.
110. The gravestone of 'Izz al-Din Abu al-Hayja, the son of Husam al-Din Abu al-Hayja is currently in the Islamic Museum, Jerusalem. See Burgoyne and Abul-Hajj 1979.
111. According to Ottoman Land Law, the shrine and its lands are deemed *waqf* (land assured to pious foundation).
112. Taufik Canaan notes, "Many peasants and Bedouin come to the tombs of their dead to swear fidelity to the clan, innocence when falsely accused and to tell their difficulties and ask for help" (1927b, 76).
113. 'Abd al-Raziq Mar'i Hasan, interview, Jenin Camp, August 11, 1995.
114. According to 'Asim, two Ein Hod residents, Itche Mamboush and Givon, have resorted to the police. Mu'in Zaydan recounted that his visit to his former house, currently inhabited by artist Zeva Kainer, was cut short by the police; Tuvia Iuster, another Ein Hod artist, recounted an episode when he called the police (cf. Slyomovics 1998, chapter 3).
115. Zahiyah Muhammad 'Ali Nimr, interview, Jenin Camp, August 11, 1995.
116. Kretzmer 1990, 1–6.
117. Kanaana and al-Hadi 1986.
118. Halamish cites "a decree issued twenty years ago by a Muslim religious figure divesting the site of its holiness and permitting construction on the premises" (Levin 1992).
119. Moshe Barak, an early settler in Jewish Ein Hod, is remembered more vividly in Ein Houd al-Jadidah for the offense of burying his favorite dog among the Muslim Abu al-Hayja family tombs.
120. Michal Fox, interview, Haifa, August 13, 1991.
121. See the summary of the dispute by Drori-Wilf 1991; "Arab Cemetery Desecrated," *Sawt al-qura* 28 (October 1993): 9; and "'Ein Hod' Society Demands Preservation of Local Cemetery," *Sawt al-qura* 32:6 (March 1995): 24.
122. "A Demand to Stop Turning Mosques into Museums," *Arabs in Israel* 2:10 (1992): 10. Approximately 850 mosques were destroyed between 1948 and 1949, with some 100 mosques remaining intact, according to Sarsour 1993.
123. Zaydan 1993.
124. Kimmerling 1992, 443.
125. Cook 1995.

21

Childbirth in a Traditional Bedouin Society

AREF ABU-RABIA

Bedouin women are assisted in childbirth by a midwife (*daya*), a righteous woman considered to be graced with healing powers and possessing blessing (*baraka*),[1] the power to cause material and spiritual well-being, and one or two other women. This privilege is reserved first for the mother-in-law, and the eldest daughter may be called on to help if necessary. No one else is allowed to be present.

Immediately after the baby is born, the mother, who is attended by one of the women, holds the newborn in her arms while the cord (*sirr*) is tied (*tasrir*) and cut. The midwife holds the end of the umbilical cord and says, "In the name of the Merciful Lord." If the baby is male, she stretches the cord up toward his shoulder to symbolize that he will grow up to be fearless, to carry a gun or sword on his shoulders, and to bear the responsibility of his family and tribe. If the newborn is female, the cord is stretched in the direction of her thighs to symbolize that she will grow up to be a good housewife and mother, will skillfully operate the spindle (*maghzal*) (which is worked manually by spinning thread against the thigh) to weave tent flies, tapestries, and carpets for her new home, and will raise her children responsibly and faithfully.

The midwife then takes a strip of clean white flannel, one-half to one centimeter wide, and winds it round the umbilical cord at a distance of two fingers (three centimeters) from the navel. She winds a piece of white sewing thread twice around this material and ties it with a strong knot to hold the cord rigid. Four fingers (six centimeters) from the first knot, she loosely knots another thread round the cord, cuts the cord[2] above this knot, and smears the cut end with kohl (*kuhl*)[3] to stop the bleeding and close the cut. She severs the cord with a sharp razor blade that has been sterilized in a flame. Within a week the section of the umbilical cord between the two knots dries up and falls off.

Bedouin women believe that the newborn baby, like the embryo, breathes through the umbilical cord. Thus, great care is taken to prevent the first knot from becoming loose or untied for fear the baby's breath will escape through the cord and he will die. (Henceforth both male and female babies will be referred to as "he" unless otherwise stated.)

It is customary for the midwife to hide the umbilical cord under the supporting pole of the tent (*wasit al-bayt*)[4] or in the tent lining (*btanit al-bayt*) to symbolize the baby's continuing loyalty to his family. One old woman—Um Mahmud—told me she hung her son's cord on the neck of a she-camel (*naqa*) to symbolize his connection to camels; indeed, when he grew up he loved tending camels and was even nicknamed "father of the camels" (*abu al-niaq*).[5]

Following the tying and cutting of the umbilical cord, the Bedouin midwife washes and removes the birth stains from the baby with a clean white cloth or sponge soaked in lukewarm water and soap. Some midwives smear olive oil (Olea europaea L. [*zeit zaytun*]) and a little salt over the baby's body[6] to strengthen his bones and muscles and to prevent diaper rash (*nasaf*) and frostbite (*qarsih, saqi'*). The midwife then swaddles the baby (*tamqitt*) in strips of cloth prepared in advance by the pregnant mother. She binds each leg separately and then together, and wraps his entire body in a cloth (*sumsar*), which is secured by winding a piece of white flannel folded to the width of the palm of the hand (eight centimeters) around his waist.

During the following weeks the mother prepares a special head cover or bonnet (*augayyih*), on which she hangs light-blue beads (*kushshash*) and amulets (*ihjabat*) to ward off bad spirits and the evil eye (*nafs, 'ayn*). Bedouin women believe that certain characteristics of the midwife are transferred to the baby, particularly personality traits associated with temperament, greed, and generosity. After swaddling the baby, the midwife or one of her helpers places a little kohl in the baby's eyes (*takhyl*) to strengthen eyesight, prevent infections like trachoma (*ramad*), and ward off the evil eye. Bedouin women also cure babies' eye infections with drops of mother's milk, the best of which is a black woman's (*'abdih*).[7]

The Bedouin midwife then ties a scarf (*'asba*) around the mother's forehead, knotting it at the back to fortify her. Her mother-in-law or one of the other women prepares her a drink of lukewarm sugar water.[8] She consumes a half to a whole liter of the drink, sitting upright and taking little sips so as not to vomit. This drink assuages her thirst and promotes the flow of milk to her breasts. The midwife and one or both helpers then prepare the baby's first nourishment (*luqun*). Composed of several ingredients, most of them medicinal plants, the mixture is prepared in a small cup by mixing one tablespoon of sugar or honey (*'asal*), preferably honey, with one tablespoon of processed butter (*samin*) and a quarter teaspoon of myrrh (Commiphora myrrha [*murr batarikh*]). The sugar/honey symbolizes the baby's good and sweet life, and the butter signifies that the baby will be blessed with many children, great riches, generosity, and Bedouin hospitality. The myrrh, which has a bitter taste, symbolizes that the child will grow up to be brave and unafraid to confront problems, and will not be fastidious in matters of food. The mother or the midwife dips her finger into the soft creamy mixture and puts it in the baby's mouth. The baby usually eats between a quarter and a half a teaspoonful.[9] An inventive Bedouin midwife may add certain ingredients.[10]

This mixture is fed to the baby several times during the first day and serves as a substitute or supplement for the mother's milk during the first three days until she is able to breastfeed and the baby adjusts to her milk. The mixture is also used to prevent disease and infection. Feeding the baby by this mixture (*luqun*) is called *talqiin.*

While the baby's food is being prepared, one of the women takes a few coals from the fire and places them a meter from the mother. She puts incense (*bakhur*) on the coals and reads the following verses from the Quran (the Daybreak Sura): "In the name of Allah, the Beneficent, the Merciful. Say: I seek refuge in the Lord of Daybreak. From the evil of the darkness when it is intense. And from the evil of malignant witchcraft" (Quran 113, 1–5); (the Mankind Sura): "In the name of Allah, the Beneficent, the Merciful. Say: I seek refuge in the Lord of Mankind. The King of Mankind. The God of Mankind. From the evil of the sneaking whisperer. Who whispereth in the hearts of mankind. Of the jinn and of mankind" (Quran 114, 1–6).[11]

The incense serves a number of purposes: it keeps the evil eye and other bad spirits away from the mother and her baby, it fills the tent with a pleasant smell, and it cures a mother possessed by a female demon (*qarina*) who can cause madness or various postpartum depression in a new mother or instant death to her newborn baby. The burning of incense is called *tabkhiir.*[12]

During the first week the mother exposes her baby to many scents. She does this to prevent him from developing allergies, nausea, vomiting, vertigo, and dizziness from scents he will encounter as he grows up. The Bedouin believe a person can die from strong smells that he has not been exposed to as a baby, and therefore during these first days of life he is introduced to a resin from Assafoetida (Ferula assafoetida or Ferula narthex [*jiddih, anjudan, haltit*]) with very pungent scents.[13]

The baby sleeps next to his mother during the night. After forty days he is placed in a special cradle (*zuqaha*) during the day made from a blanket stretched between two ropes inside the tent. This cradle can be easily rocked and keeps the baby out of the reach of children and animals. When the mother puts the baby down anywhere she says, "In the name of the Merciful Lord, may He preserve you from dangerous men and evil spirits." Bedouin women believe that invisible spirits residing above and below the ground fear God and will not touch anything over which this sentence has been pronounced. One old woman—Um Usif—told me the following story.

> One day a woman placed her newborn baby in the cradle and said "In the name of the Merciful Lord," and went out to the field to gather firewood. As she was lifting a piece of wood she was captured by jinns, bound, and brought to their leader. The jinns, who dislike righteous, honest, God-fearing

people, wanted to put her on trial and their leader ordered them to kidnap her baby. The jinns went to capture the baby, but returned after an hour empty-handed. When the leader asked what happened, they said that they could not capture the baby because the mother had said "the heavy sentence" (the way jinns refer to the mother's utterance) when she placed the baby in the cradle. The jinns were overcome by the fear of God, and their leader ordered them to release the baby's mother. The mother hurried back to the tent, where she found her baby healthy and content.[14]

The mother changes her baby's swaddling clothes several times a day and washes him once a day if there is enough water. She is assisted in these tasks by her mother, mother-in-law, daughters, sisters-in-law, and, of course, her own sisters, who usually visit during the first week after the child's birth.

The women bring gifts of money (*nuqutt*), the equivalent of fifteen to twenty-five dollars, or food such as rice, sugar, and live fowl (chickens and pigeons) for slaughtering. Bedouin women attach great importance to feeding the mother well, since the child depends on her for nourishment and because her strength must be built up. The visitors put the money in the mother's hands or in the baby's swaddling clothes (*magayitt*), taking the opportunity to look at the baby's face. A gift to the mother is called "midday meal" (*ghada*), and the bearers are called "givers of the midday meal" (*mghadyat*).

A gift of money is the exclusive property of the mother and she may use it as she sees fit. She usually buys something for herself or clothes for the new baby, or she may keep the money in her purse. She may lend the money to other women or even to her husband on the condition it is returned within a reasonable period of time. A woman who receives a gift of money must return it or its value to the giver on a similar occasion, such as a birth. When a woman is sick or unable to visit, she can send the gift with her mother, married sisters, mother-in-law, or sisters-in-law.

The birth of a boy is a joyous occasion.[15] Women bless the mother, saying, "Congratulations on the birth of a son, groom, shepherd of livestock" (*mabruk al-walad, al-'aris, ra'y al-ghanam*). The baby's mother or paternal grandmother ties a white headkerchief (*mandil/shash abyadh*) or piece of white material (*rayih baydha*) to a rope in the women's section of the tent as a good omen (*fal*) and a sign of gratitude to God.

The husband's male friends and relatives congratulate him on the birth of a son, and during the first week he holds a ceremony (*muruq, isbu'*) to celebrate the birth of a new male and his acceptance into the family. This ceremony symbolizes the rite of birth. Both male and female relatives of the husband and wife are invited to this ceremony, which consists of a large banquet at which animals are sacrificed. The ceremony, which is usually the evening meal, is served separately to the men and women, and sweets (*fraha, hilu*) signifying joy and happiness are distributed to the women and children. Before the bowls of meat are removed at the end of the meal, the guests bless the father, saying, "Congratulations on the birth of a new son," to which the father replies, "God bless you." This ceremony symbolizes the acceptance of the newborn into the tribal society.

By the time the ceremony takes place the father has announced his son's name, which he has chosen after consulting with the baby's paternal grandfather, and in some cases with the grandmother. Sometimes the baby's name is chosen before birth. Um Sliman—an old woman—told me the following story: "When my son's wife became pregnant for the fourth time after having given birth to three daughters, I told her that if she had a male baby he must be called Mhammad [Muhammad]. As I said this I pointed my forefinger at her womb. She gave birth to a boy and I told my son the baby must be called Mhammad. My son agreed and that is the name of my grandson." Another old woman—Um Ahmad—told me, "When my son's wife became pregnant after giving birth to two daughters, I told her that if she had a son he would be called Isma'il, and so it was."

A baby boy is named after his grandfather or his uncle on his father's side or after one of the prophets (Mhammad, Ahmad, Musy [Musa], or Ibrahim), or he is given a name attributed to God to ward off the evil eye, like Abd Alla or Abd al-Karim. Some names are intended to mislead the evil eye and prevent bad spirits from harming the child, such as Shihdih, which means beggary, and Bnayyih, which means daughter.

When a daughter is born the father does not hold a ceremony and usually is not congratulated by his male relatives and friends. The women comfort the mother with the following blessing: "Congratulations on the birth of a daughter, bride, gatherer of firewood and shepherdess of livestock" (*mabruka al-bint, al-'arus, al-hattabih, ra'yt al-ghanam*).

The daughter's name is usually chosen by the mother together with her husband and mother-in-law. Sometimes it is chosen by the mother and mother-in-law and only told to the husband for his formal approval. When a mother of daughters gives birth to another girl, she and her mother-in-law choose a name that symbolically expresses hope, like Kfayih, which means "enough daughters."

The birth of sons is much more valued than the birth of daughters. Only males are permitted to succeed the father, and they represent pride and prestige. And, it is the males who defend the honor of the family. Thus, a man with no sons is in an inferior position among his family members, who say, "Poor man! He has no sons to succeed him and no one to defend the family honor."[16]

The mother may not leave the tent for forty days except to tend to her daily needs. During this time she is released from all social obligations and most of her household duties are taken over by her daughters, mother-in-law, sisters-in-law, neighbors, and her own mother and sisters. This includes taking care of younger children, carrying water, preparing food, taking care of the domestic animals, and doing laundry.

The baby is not permitted to leave the tent during this period and, as far as possible, other people are prevented from seeing him. The newborn baby is regarded as vulnerable (*najmih khifif, hassas*) to a strange glance, which may bring sickness or the evil eye. According to Bedouin women, a covetous look toward the baby that stems from the jealousy of supernatural powers has the potential to jeopardize his well-being. It is also felt that undesirable traits may be transferred to the baby through a touch or a kiss.

The mother is in a state of impurity (*nafasah*) for forty days,[17] during which she is forbidden to prepare food for her children and husband, to sleep next to her husband, and to have conjugal relations with him. He is obliged to sleep on a separate mattress at the far end of the tent, or even outside, and to eat in the male section with his brothers, who are responsible for providing his midday and evening meals.[18]

After forty days the mother washes (*ghassalat*) her body with water in which she has put an "impurity bead" (*kharazat kbass*) and a gold coin (*dhahab*) to symbolize the end of her impurity. She is then considered pure (*rab'anat*) and allowed to have conjugal relations with her husband, as well as to carry out her household duties. She takes her baby together with some candy to the tent of his paternal grandmother for blessing. This first departure from the home tent is called *awwal tulu'*. The paternal grandmother gives him a gift (*'attiyih*) of a female sheep or goat to symbolize his connection to livestock, and the offspring of this animal are the baby's property and not to be shared with any of his brothers.

Bedouin take extensive measures to protect the health of both mother and child. The mother is careful to eat nourishing food, particularly during the first forty days after giving birth, and the baby is fed on demand. A popular dish considered to have nourishing and healing properties, eaten at least once a day by new mothers, consists of compressed dates (*'ajwih*), raisins (*zibiib*), pure olive oil, black cumin,[19] fenugreek (*hilbih*), and saffron (*za'faran*). These ingredients are simmered over a low flame for four to six hours; they can be prepared during the ninth month of pregnancy or the first week following the baby's birth and preserved in a jar. This dish nourishes and fortifies the mother, increases her milk supply, and enhances her immunity to disease. The husband is charged with buying the ingredients, which are considered to have nourishing and medicinal properties, both preventive and curative.

During the second or third month of a baby boy's life he is brought by his brother or mother to an elder of the family, someone regarded as righteous and respected for his generosity and courage. This man, usually the baby's paternal grandfather or uncle, possesses blessing power to cause material and spiritual well-being. He takes the baby in his arms, saying, "May Allah protect you," spits into his mouth, and wishes him a long and happy life. He returns the baby to his brother, saying that with the help of Allah the child will grow up to be brave and loyal to his family. The baby's brother thanks the righteous man and takes him back to his mother. This act (*tariiq*) is based on the belief that the characteristics of the righteous man will be transferred to the baby through his saliva (*riq*). He is not paid for this service; his reward is being deemed worthy of the task. The baby's mother is, however, expected to provide a festive meal.[20]

Bedouin believe that two-thirds of the child's character is inherited from his mother's brother, and one-third from his father (*thilthiin al-walad il-khalah*). Thus, in this respect, the mother makes no contribution to the baby's character. Since descent among the Bedouin is patrilineal, the act of spitting is probably intended to enhance the traits inherited from the father's family and diminish those inherited from the mother's side.

When the baby sucks his thumb, the Bedouin believe that Allah has given him the instinct to suck "fresh nourishment with the taste of honey from the Garden of Eden."[21] They also believe babies are innocent of all sin and go directly to heaven if they die young.

When the mother decides it is time to feed her sleeping son, she rouses him by touching him lightly on the nose and repeating the words "In the name of Allah, the Beneficent, the Merciful." Sometimes she wakes him by holding *jiddih,* which she has wrapped in a small piece of cloth and heated on coals. A daughter is allowed to sleep until she awakens on her own. When it is time for her feeding, her mother encourages her to nurse by singing

ya hamdih dufy, dufy
ya khashim ma'tufy
naymih taht ghtaky
zay al-qutun al-mandufy

[O sweet Hamdih, come to me
You have an aquiline nose
Asleep under your blanket
Soft like combed cotton]

When she cries for no apparent reason, her mother sings,

ya bnayyih la tightadhy
siaqky 'ashr niaqy
wa khaylih wa makhladyih
wa buky mahu radhy

[O sweet daughter, don't be angry
Your bride's price is ten she-camels
And a khaylih and makhladyih[22]
But your father isn't contented]

The Bedouin mother never feeds her baby, male or female, lying down. She sits and holds the baby in her arms at an angle, holding his head up toward her nipples. She believes this position allows the milk to flow directly into his mouth and stomach and prevents choking, and is pleasant for him as well as a sign of respect. The mother will say, "I never feed my baby lying down, only while sitting or standing, like a noble Arabian mare preparing for a race." Likewise, the mother does not feed her baby while walking.

The mother's mood is believed to strongly affect the baby's feeding, especially that of a boy, and she will not feed him when she is angry, irritable, or sad because such moods will prevent his benefiting from her milk. She calls this "milk of anger" (*halib al-ghaydh*) and believes it can cause vomiting or diarrhea. A girl, on the other hand, can drink milk of anger without harm because a daughter, unlike a son, can tolerate moodiness; females can adjust to any moods, as well as the ups and downs of life.[23]

The mother feeds her baby whenever she interprets its crying as a sign of hunger. Some mothers pay more attention to their sons than to their daughters, which explains why boys are fed more often than girls. Moreover, boys are breastfed for one to two years while girls are breastfed for only six months to a year. A woman who has no sons might breastfeed a daughter even less than six months because it is believed she cannot conceive while breastfeeding, and she is anxious to raise her status in the eyes of her husband and his family, especially his mother, by having a son. The constant threat of divorce or of her husband taking a second wife forces her to shorten time span during which she breastfeeds a daughter.

During the first year of life the mother immunizes her baby against scorpion stings. Uttering the word "rabbit" (*arnab*) to trick the scorpion and avoid frightening her baby, she catches a yellow scorpion (*'aqrab safra*) and roasts it over the fire. She strains the ashes through a thin scarf and lets the baby suck them off her breasts. This act of immunization is called *irdha'it al-'aqrab*. The Bedouin also use Heliotropium for treatment of scorpion stings because this plant's blossoms resemble the scorpion's tail.[24]

The *Hawi/Hawy* (snake charmer) is also responsible for rendering babies immune to scorpion stings and snakebites. The *Hawi* is renowned for his ability to capture snakes, and he usually carries around a few in a sack. The *Hawi* immunizes by placing a teaspoon of sugar in his mouth, moistening it with saliva, and giving it to the baby to swallow. The *Hawi* is paid for this service with money or with an object of value.[25]

Bedouin women use a number of animals as both cures and preventives. Um Salim—an old woman—told me that when her son was about six months old, her husband hunted a crow (*ghrab*), cut it open with a sharp knife, removed the liver, and gave it to her to roast and feed to the baby. Bedouin believe that crow's liver makes the baby sharp and attentive like the crow; when the baby grows up it will be as difficult for his enemies to trap him through fraud or deception as it is to capture the crow. With the exception of the heart and liver, which are eaten for medicinal purposes, Bedouin do not eat crow meat as it is considered tainted. Um 'Ali told me how her husband caught a crow, removed its heart, and gave it to her to roast and feed to their one-year-old son. It is believed that a baby who eats the heart of a crow will grow up to be brave and unafraid to walk alone on dark nights. And, indeed, this woman's son is known in the family as a brave young man.[26]

Bedouin women have great fear of the *qarina*, especially during pregnancy and immediately after childbirth. The *qarina* can take possession of a woman and cause the death of her baby in childbirth or infancy. The *qarina* can be exorcised by surreptitiously feeding the possessed woman cooked donkey meat. Afterward, when she is told what she has eaten, the *qarina* will hear the words and immediately leave the body, not wanting to inhabit a woman who has consumed donkey meat.[27]

Another animal assigned curative powers is the Palestine mole rat (*khlund*). The following story illustrates. One night a pregnant woman, who had lost all her children in childbirth, dreamed that the *qarina* came and stood some distance from the tent and said, "Were it not for that which is on the pitchfork (*minsas*), acting as a barrier between you and me, I would enter into and kill the fruit of your womb." In the morning the woman related the dream to her husband, and the husband told her that the day before he had killed a mole rat and its blood had splashed on the pitchfork. The woman went into the field to retrieve the mole rat, cut it open, removed the insides, salted the body, and hung it on the supporting pole of the tent to dry. When it dried she cut it into pieces and put them in her and her husband's pillows. She eventually gave birth to a healthy son and, subsequently, to four more healthy children. This event strengthened the community's faith in the mole rat as a powerful curative and preventive agent against possession by the *qarina*.

The *qarina* can also be thwarted by an amulet prepared by an amulet writer during the eighth or beginning of the ninth month of pregnancy; it is hung on the baby's head immediately after birth. It usually contains verses from the Quran and other phrases and numbers known and understood only by their creator. Some sample verses taken from the Quran are: "Allah, There is no God save him, the Eternal. Neither slumber nor sleep overtaketh him. Unto him belongeth whatsoever is in the heavens and whatsoever is in the earth. Who is that intercedeth with Him save His leave? He knoweth that which is in front of them and that which is behind them, while they encompass nothing of his knowledge save what He wills. His throne includeth the heavens and the earth and He is never weary of preserving them. He is the Sublime, the tremendous" (Quran 2, 255). It should be noted that the Bedouin attribute sudden infant death syndrome (crib death) to the *qarina*.

A woman who is pregnant for the first time or has given birth only to girls may swear an oath to Allah in return for his granting her a son: "Lord! I beg and beseech you to allow me to give birth to a son to succeed my husband. I pledge you a goat or a sheep." She may swear this oath over a tomb of a holy person, and, if she bears a son, he may not leave the tent until he has been taken to visit the tomb of the holy person where the oath was sworn.

All members of the family take part in this pilgrimage (*zwara*) to the holy tomb, where the father reads the Opening Sura from the Quran, and then moves some distance away to let his wife and children express their thanks. In a special place adjacent to the tomb the mother burns incense (*bakhur*), reads verses from the Quran, thanks Allah for granting her a son, and asks Him to watch over her son and grant him good health and long life. She also asks personal favors, which she reveals to no one.

The husband then cuts the ear of the promised sheep or goat next to the tomb of a holy person so the blood splashes on the tomb as a sign of the pilgrimage. The animal is taken back to the tent, where it is slaughtered to signify fulfillment of the oath, and the husband and his wife invite their relatives to a celebration. This pilgrimage signifies the baby's leaving the home for the first time; this is a rite of passage and the fulfillment of the oath. Before the meat bowls are removed at the end of the feast, which is usually the evening meal, the husband asks the guests to read the Opening Sura (*al-Fatiha*): "In the name of Allah, the Beneficent, the Merciful. Praise be to Allah, Lord of the World. The Beneficent, the Merciful, Owner of the Day of Judgment. Thee alone we worship. Thee alone we ask for help. Show us the straight path, the path of those whom Thou hast favoured. Not the path of those who earn Thy anger nor of those who go astray" (Quran 1, 1–7). The guests say, "By the help of Allah, your oath has been accepted by Him" (*zwaritku maqbula*). The husband replies Amen, and he is then permitted to remove his guests' bowls.

Bedouin believe that young boys are more vulnerable than girls to the evil eye and therefore go to great lengths to protect their sons, including hanging blue beads or amulets on them, dressing them in girls' clothing, and giving them a girl's name. The custom of not cutting a boy's hair until three to five years of age is designed to hide his sex and fool the evil eye into thinking he is a girl.

A special ceremony is held to mark the boy's first haircut (*hlaqa*). His mother, together with his father and brothers and sisters, make a pilgrimage to the tomb of Abraham in Hebron (*Ibrahim al-khalil*), where they pray and ask Allah to grant them health, happiness, and wealth. The boy's mother holds her son in one arm, touches the tomb with the other hand, and says, "Oh *Ibrahim al-khalil* our Father, I am giving my child to the care and patronage of Allah and to you. May you preserve him from sickness, from bad people and from devils. Oh *Ibrahim al-khalil* our Father, today my son's hair is to be cut for the first time, his face will be as light as the sun, please preserve this light and do not let it go out. Oh *Ibrahim al-khalil*, you who are our Father, as the devoted Father never forgets his offspring and cares for them day and night, please do not forget us." The father then takes the boy to the barber where a razor touches his head for the first time and his hair is cut. From this day on, the boy may have his hair cut.[28] On the way home the family celebrates with sweets bought in Hebron. Animals are sacrificed at the tribal encampment and the relatives of the husband and wife are invited to a festive meal. At the end of the meal the Opening Sura is read aloud. This haircut ceremony symbolizes the boy's rite of passage from an indeterminate state to male status.[29]

Notes

My fieldwork was conducted in the Negev and Sinai deserts during the last fifteen years.

1. *Baraka/barakah* blessings are sent to man by God. The word can be translated as "Beneficent force, of divine, which causes super abundance in the physical sphere and prosperity and happiness in the psychic order." *Encyclopaedia of Islam* (Leiden: Brill, 1960), 1:1032.
2. In Egypt, the midwife cut the cord, took some blood from the cutting of the umbilical cord, and used it to "clear her—the female baby's—throat and the roof of her mouth." This practice is followed to "help the child eat well" or "to prevent rash inside the baby's mouth" (Morsy 1982).
3. Bedouin women prepare kohl (*kuhl*) by pouring olive oil into a small bottle and inserting a wick of clean white cloth secured against the neck of the bottle with a piece of dough. The wick is lit and held under a pan or sheet of clean metal. The soot that sticks to the bottom of the pan is collected with pigeon feathers. Out of that, antimony is usually made.
4. For more details about this term, see Havakook 1986.
5. There are similar beliefs among other peoples in the world. See, e.g., Frazer 1935, 247–67; Blom 1992, 37; Hernandez 1992, 152–53.
6. Compare this ritual to that found in Egypt (Morsy 1982, 165) and among the Slayb tribes in Syria. Jabbur 1995, 429–30.
7. The milk of a black woman is considered to be exceptionally effective in safeguarding the child's well-being because Allah had blessed her (*baraka*) with medicinal powers. The logic behind this strategy was not "racial" but based on a belief in the therapeutic powers of opposites (medication works through its opposite—*dawa' al-shay' bi-didihi*)—the black woman and the white milk (Abu-Rabia 2005b). For more details about the evil eye, see Abu-Rabia 2005a. For more details about eye diseases and treatments, see Abu-Rabia 2005b. This custom is well-known in Kerala, India: "fresh breast milk [is used] as a disinfectant for eye diseases, perhaps the RNase enzyme in it neutralizes the viruses" (Pisharoty 1993).
8. See Morsy 1982, 162–70, for a similar ritual in Egypt.
9. Compare to the rituals of Mexican women when they give birth in Hernandez 1992, 153, and Gomara 1992, 165; for Samarkand's women, see Frazer 1935).
10. Some of these ingredients are common ash (Fraxinus excelsior [*lesan al-'asfur*]), cinnamon (Cinnamomum zeylanicum [*dar siny, qerfeh*]), sulphur (*kabrit*), black cumin (Nigella sativa L. [*habbet al-baraka*]), garden cress (Lepidium sativum L. [*habb al-rashad*]), safflower (Carthamus tinctorius L. [*'usfur, qurtum*]), white lead (*isbidajeh*), and ginger (Zingibar officinalis [*zanjabil*]).
11. Literally, "from the evil of blowers" (feminine), referring to a common form of witchcraft in Arabia in which women tie knots in a cord and blow on them while uttering a curse. The Daybreak Sura is a prayer for protection from fears proceeding from unknown. According to Prophet Medicine, *Ruqa* (sing. *Ruqya*) is the recitation of some divine verses as a treatment for a disease (*Ar-Ruqa* with the last two Suras of the Quran, nos. 113, 114). See also Khan 1974, 423–24.
12. Compare with Bilu 1993, 86–87.
13. In Egypt, if the infant is very still after delivery, the midwife asks for an onion and puts it on the infant's nose, whereupon she sneezes (Morsy 1982, 169). In Yemen, after childbirth, the resin of Assafoetida is burnt and the smoke placed between the mother's legs to contract the vagina (Ghazanfar 1994, 208).
14. For more details about kidnaping by jinns, see Bilu 1993, 32–33, 57–59, 86–87.
15. Compare to Egypt (Morsy 1982, 162–70) and Palestine (Abu-Rabia 2001); see also Granqvist 1947.
16. See more details in Eickelman 1993; Morsy 1978; Patai 1971, 84–113; Patai 1983, 25–40.
17. For further details, see Morsy 1982, 171–73; Inhorn 1994.
18. For the Nubian of Egypt, see Kennedy 1970, and compare to Pilsbury 1982.

19. In the *Prophet Medicine: Narrated Abu Huraira:* "I herd Allah's Apostle saying, 'There is healing in black cumin for all diseases except death' " (Khan 1974, 400).
20. Use of saliva/spittle (*riq*) is mentioned in the *Prophet Medicine* (Khan 1974, 429). For similar traditions in Morocco, see Westermarck 1968 [1926], 1:93; among the Bedouin of Sinai, see Shuqayr 1916, 369; among the Bedouin of Egypt, see G. Murray 1935, 197; in Arabia, see Doughty 1923, 1:527, 2:164. In ancient Jewish beliefs, spittle possesses much curative power. Sometimes the spittle of persons in key positions is used to give blessings (Douglas 1979, 120). See also the rites of *Tahnik* in Morgenstern 1966, 34–35.
21. Abu-Rabia 2007.
22. There are numerous strains of Arabian horses: Koheilah or Qhayleh, 'Obeyah, Dahamah, Shuwaimah, Makhladyih, and Saqlawiah (Abbink 1984b; Hamdan 1974; Westermarck 1968 [1926], 1:99; Musil 1928, 383.
23. Compare to Creyghton 1992.
24. See Abu-Rabia 1999, 47, 75, 77.
25. For more details, see Abu-Rabia 1999, 54, 77; Lane 1981, 170, 370–81.
26. Compare to the Bechuana (Frazer 1935).
27. Compare with Abu-Rabia 1999, 43; Bilu 1993, 86–87; Morgenstern 1966, 7–21.
28. Compare with Morgenstern 1966, 36–47.
29. Relevant sources about traditional childrearing among the Arabs include Ammar 1954; Canaan 1927a; Dickson 1949, 172–80; Diqs 1967; Granqvist 1947; Musil 1928, 243–66.

22

The Supervisors

Go-Betweens

ISRAEL DRORI

The process of industrialization in the periphery, particularly in industries employing women, has created open tension between women's traditional role in their family and society on one hand and the need to adapt to industrial working life on the other. This tension generates a series of issues relating to adaptation to work life, the social relations of production, management systems, family intervention, and the impact of work and wage earning on the individual's status, role, and autonomy. The textile industry is the prototype setting for studying the impact of industrial work on women in traditional societies. The Israeli case is particularly interesting as it combines both typical and non-typical "ingredients"—Arab workers and Jewish managers, women and men, traditional and modern, minority and majority.

The analysis of the dynamic interaction between managers and workers is important for addressing several themes. How do these two seemingly opposing interests merge for the sake of a common purpose? How does the work culture in the textile plants satisfy the needs of both workers and managers? How do their conflicting values, norms, and worldviews affect the production process? What implications does ethnic diversity in the workplace have on the production process and the evolution of a work culture? What is the outcome of the interaction of the traditional values and norms of Arab workers and the management style and methods of Jewish managers?

In this essay I unveil an intricate culture-building processes of conflicts and negotiations, social relations replicating the family at work, reciprocity, fairness, and mutual aid in day-to-day interactions on the shop floor. It is a dynamic process that ultimately helps alleviate the alienation generated by the industrial setting. The plant has multiple roles as a participator in a competitive industrial market and an interactive member of its social environment, accountable for the seamstresses it employs and sensitive to their personal needs.

To meet their business goals, the managers must cooperate with the tradition-bound community that provides them with their workforce—adopting its norms and appropriating its worldview. The managers harness and manipulate traditional family values to foster personal commitment, furthering production goals through normative control. The consequence of this personal commitment is a workforce that relates to the organization as family, identifies with its goals, and internalizes feelings of loyalty and belonging to a distinct social group.

For the seamstresses, work at the plant is their first and often last exposure to the wage-earning world outside the family. In their new context, they undergo a transformation that both serves the ends of the organization and strengthens their status within the traditional society they safeguard. They emerge as active cultivators of the organizational culture that ultimately furthers the manager's production goals. The managers, in turn, find themselves subjugated to their workers' traditional perception of work.

This chapter deals with the supervisors, women who are promoted from among the seamstresses. While they supervise departments, they act essentially as mediators between managers and workers and the sewing plant and the local community. The supervisors are the guardians of the social organization of production and the bearers of the shared meaning of work values and practices.

The Supervisors: Go-Betweens

> But when I lie in my bed at night, I have only one thought: "Almighty God," I think to myself, "help me to give absolute satisfaction to my superiors!" [I think of nothing else.] Whether they choose to reward me or not, of course, that's their affair. [If I can see a clean, well-cared for town, the convicts properly looked after, not too many drunks in the streets—there's the satisfaction of a job well done. What more could I want?] I'm not after honours and decorations. . . ! Of course, that sort of thing has its attractions, but as the poet says, compared to the joys of a job well done, everything else is dust and ashes!
>
> —N. V. Gogol, *The Government Inspector,* Act I, Scene III, p. 57

The position of departmental supervisors is held by women only. All the supervisors are promoted from the rank and file of the plant. Most supervisors are in their twenties and thirties; a few are in their forties. Most of the supervisors are unmarried and live with their families, who depend on their economic contribution to the home. They do not have a common educational background. Some have completed only elementary school, others are high school graduates, and yet others have acquired professional training in accounting, secretarial work, or sewing. Most of the supervisors are from the village in which the plant is located. In Nazareth and Kfar Tavor, they come from different communities. In sewing plants located in Druse villages, such as Beit Jan and Julis, they are mainly Druse;

in mixed communities, such as Maghar, there are Muslim, Druse, and Christian supervisors; in Nazareth there are Christians and Muslims; and in Kfar Tavor there are only Muslim supervisors. The religious affiliation of the supervisors reflects the demographic composition of the plants.

The supervisors manage departments of thirty to seventy seamstresses. The departments are responsible for either specific operations or products. The management is integrative and extended; the supervisors manage both the production and the seamstresses. The supervisors are also the representatives of the managers and the plant in the community, and their role extends beyond the sphere of work into the personal lives of the workers at home. This chapter aims to characterize the intricate and complex role of the supervisors. It reveals the double meanings and ambivalence in the supervisors' life and work and their contribution to the process of creating shared meaning in the plant. It shows how the supervisors construct their role and their self in the plant, taking into account the demands and rules of work as well as the values, practices, and worldview of the community. Furthermore, this chapter elaborates on the role of the supervisor as mediator.

The Essence of the Role

The job of the supervisors includes dealing with the multiple aspects of running a sewing department in its day-to-day management and requires both good human relation skills and professionalism. It also includes grasping the needs of the company: its goals, priorities, operational principles, values, and norms. The supervisors view themselves as managers working under pressure, required to provide quick answers to pressing problems, while meeting clearly defined overall goals.

The supervisors serve as mediators in the plant. First, the supervisors are the instructors in the plant and are the ones who teach the seamstresses the basic techniques of sewing. They convey the rules, procedures, hierarchy, authority, and appropriate behavior of the plant in all aspects of production to the workers. Second, the supervisors are the translators and interpreters of the two different sets of meanings, values, assumptions, and practices of the seamstresses and the managers, creating a common language and an open channel of communication. The need for interpreting managerial policies for the workers leads supervisors to develop a system of informal accommodations that flexibly reconcile with shop floor constraints (Thurley and Wirdenius 1973). Third, the supervisors are mediators between the seamstresses and their families regarding incidents and behavior at work. Fourth, the supervisors mediate between the plant and the community, mainly advocating for the plant following controversial events. They convey the mood, attitude, and feelings of the community to the managers of the plants.

The supervisor's job is rooted, first and foremost, in her great sense of commitment and responsibility to her work. The sewing plant is her arena for self-realization, achievement, and the development of her career, especially because a number of the supervisors do not see themselves as potential wives and mothers.

Nehaye, a supervisor, told me the following:

> The work is very hard because you have to work with the women and, at the same time, make sure that there is a high level of production. Sometimes there are lots of problems with the machines or with the raw materials and everything falls on the supervisor's shoulders. Not to mention that problems of discipline with the women also take up a lot of time. Sometimes one of the seamstresses is your cousin or maybe even your sister and you have to yell at her. You can't show favoritism. At home is one thing—work is something else. Very often you have to stand up for your department and fight with everyone else, even with the managers and the machinists to ensure that the department comes out as well as possible. But what can I tell you? The work gives me a lot of satisfaction. I'm not ashamed to tell you that my job is my life. What else do I have? I don't have a husband, I don't have children. At work I get a lot of respect and I can really show what I'm worth here. And at home I'm the main provider, helping my sister buy clothes, my brother, who is studying to be a dentist in Romania, and my other brother pay off his mortgage.

The unmarried supervisors, who have no obligations of raising a family, shift the balance of their self-realization from the private sphere to the public sphere of work. Their role at work becomes a simulation of patriarchal relations at home, whereby the supervisors embrace a version of the father, mother, and older sister. As "fathers" they are managers, as "mothers" they care and mediate with the managers, and as "older sisters" they are the friends of the workers. It is the work that provides them with self-esteem and prestige, since they become one of the main breadwinners in their families. Their strength in the family increases, especially in decision-making matters regarding household issues. The interface between these roles is sometimes a problematic endeavor that creates tension between the supervisors and either the seamstresses or the managers, who require them to continuously reconstruct their role and self.

The supervisors must first of all be excellent seamstresses, familiar with both sewing techniques and production details. Aida describes the supervisor's characteristics.

> A good supervisor is first of all a good seamstress, that's why she was promoted. She knows all the sewing operations and gets everything ready in time—thread, fabric, elastic. She knows what someone needs without waiting to be told. She knows that a woman who is finishing one job has to have more work waiting, even before she finishes. She knows how to fix the machine, how to let women work by themselves. A good supervisor knows how to in-

> troduce new merchandise and new lines into the department. She has to be independent and she has to have her own methods.

The emphasis on professionalism is an important aspect of the supervisors' role. Supervisors consider themselves facilitators in addition to being managers. Their main goal is to help and serve the seamstresses and to ensure the flow of work, which is the key to ensuring high production. In this sense, the supervisor is a field manager, who apart from managing and supervising has substantial physical work to do. She must constantly provide work to the seamstresses and simultaneously continuously control and monitor the production level. In addition, she must solve production problems as they arise. The flow of work has multiple facets—constantly coaching the workers, ensuring a smooth production process, and meeting the department production and quality requirements. This means that the supervisors must maintain tight control of their departments, in terms of both production and human relations.[1]

The supervisor must expend extensive professional and managerial efforts to attain a stable department. The supervisors train their seamstresses and build up their departments over a long period of time, encouraging the workers to raise their output, maintain high quality, and show sewing flexibility in a variety of items. A well-functioning department has a balanced workforce that enables the supervisor to manage production and quality with maximum results.

Fatma describes her system of management.

> The supervisor is both mother and sister to the seamstresses in the sewing plant. She is the link between them and the manager. She is responsible for production, quality, and raw materials. She is required to break in new women and make sure that production never lags. First of all, a good supervisor never loses her temper. She listens to what the women have to say, tries to understand whether their problems are related to work or to their private lives. She is, in fact, more like a friend than a boss.[2] The supervisor has to have an overview of the situation. It doesn't make any difference if the woman is working at a machine and the supervisor is doing some other kind of work. They are both here to work. The supervisor has to have a very good grasp of exactly what is going on in every part of her department. She has to listen carefully to what the manager has to say. She has to check out the merchandise in accordance with the proper forms and production schedules. A good supervisor has to be very conscientious about quality when there are problems with merchandise that is sent back from central quality control.

The primary managerial aspect in the plant is meeting departmental production goals, and this serves as the criteria by which supervisors are evaluated. It determines their bonuses and premiums, which is an addition to the regular salary and dependent on performance. Their ability to succeed depends on an ongoing track record of high quality and production levels. Achieving this track record ensures them high esteem at work and in the community.

Relations between the Supervisor and the Seamstresses

The relationship between the supervisors and the seamstresses is multidimensional. The double meaning of their role constitutes an integral part of their interpersonal relationships with the seamstresses. On one hand they are the managers, who exercise authority over the workers, command them, and scold them if necessary. On the other hand, they are often members of their workers' families or are personal friends. The boundary of this ambivalence tends to be manifested at work.

Noal, a supervisor, comments,

> The supervisor has to know how to be a friend to the women. She has to be like the manager, whose word is law but who at the same time has a sympathetic ear for their problems. But she has to attempt to keep work problems separate from their problems at home. She has, first and foremost, to understand the women and try to help them in every way possible, like their friends. The women will do everything for a supervisor they like. It is very important to train them properly from the beginning, to educate them, to explain everything to them very clearly and in detail. In this respect the supervisor is like a mother to them. The women come to me with all their problems, professional and personal. I have thirty-eight women in my department, Bedouins and *fallahim* [farmers] from a number of villages. There are not too many differences among the women. They are all more or less alike. You have to treat them all the same way, regardless of their religion or the kind of village they come from.

The relationship between the supervisors and the seamstresses is seen in familial and emotive terms. The supervisors "take care of the women," and the women "love" the supervisor. Demonstrations of affection are as common as cross voices and angry looks. There is an expectation of mutual consideration alongside the acceptance of authority.

> Raja: We yell at the women if we have to. People get angry at times but if the supervisor makes a mistake it's up to her to apologize to the women. A few months ago, I was in a terrible state because of personal problems. I had tears in my eyes all the time. I spoke to the women and told them that I was having some trouble and needed their help. I asked them to try and work quietly and stop bothering me with all kinds of nonsense. It really helped.
>
> Drori: How did the women take it?
>
> Raja: Most of them knew my story and helped me. I have really good relations with my workers. They tell me all about their problems with their

> families and with their boyfriends. I feel like their mother or sister. I don't want to feel like their boss. I want them to know and to feel that I'm just like them, working in the department—no different.

The managerial styles of the supervisors vary. It can be authoritative toward the seamstresses, though most of them prefer a more warm and "feminine" style. The seamstresses obey because of their personal loyalty, commitment, and intense emotions toward the supervisors. This "feminine" management is accompanied, however, by authoritative measures. The seamstresses' main loyalty is to the supervisors, not to the work per se.[3]

The relationship between the supervisors and the seamstresses is reciprocal but also complex. The supervisors tend to present these relationships as dyadic, obliging both sides equally. In practice, however, this perceived mutuality is not always congruent. The relationship between the supervisors and the seamstresses can be described as one of mentoring, whereby the supervisors serve both functional and psychological roles. Their functional role includes coaching and protecting their workers. The psychological role includes personal support, friendship, acceptance, counseling, and role modeling.

The issue of fairness is also a part of the supervisors' managerial style. Although a supervisor may come from the family or *hamula* (clan) of some of her workers, she cannot allow herself to show them the slightest partiality. She has great power to help or harm the workers individually, with regard both to work and to relations with the senior management. As long as she remains aware of the extent of her power, she is also aware that the only way she can preserve feelings of fellowship and unity among the women is by scrupulous impartiality. It is usually women from the supervisor's own family or *hamula* who sometimes complain that they are treated unfairly.

Hoda, one of the supervisors, states,

> It is important for me to demonstrate the same attitude toward all the women. They can feel if they are being discriminated against. Once I saw one of the women sitting and crying all the time. I went over to her and asked her very tactfully what was wrong and offered her some advice. The other women declared that I was showing favoritism and I had to make it clear to them that they were all equal in my eyes, all one family. But regardless of what I do, there are always those who claim that I am partial to the women from my own family and my own village. It's important to give them the feeling that their supervisor is a good person who is ready to help them, regardless of what village they come from.

Embracing both the authoritative and hierarchical aspects of work while complementing them with friendship and togetherness enable the supervisors to use a wide range of tactics and pressure on the workers. These can be either formal or informal, thus embodying both the managerial and familial value systems.

Munira tells me the following:

> You treat the women well without yelling at them and then everything goes smoothly. You have to have good work relations, to be a friend to all of them. Work is work and if everything is going well, the supervisor is like a sister or friend. But if there is trouble with quality or quantity or with discipline, I have to deal with it. For example, there was a seamstress who promised to work on Friday and didn't show up. Then she was asked to work overtime and she refused. I took the problem to the manager, who threatened the woman. The next day the seamstress took sick leave because she didn't feel like working. So I asked the manager to let me handle the case. I didn't let her come to work until she agreed to sign a form, agreeing to work on Fridays and overtime and quit taking unnecessary sick leave. Since then, I've had no problems with that seamstress.

One integral aspect of the supervisor's job is outside the physical boundaries of the plant—in the homes of the seamstresses. She regularly visits the women at home and knows their families. The families recognize the supervisor's authority as representative of the plant and see her as the guarantor of their daughter's interests—health and honor. They are prepared to discuss with her various issues pertaining to their daughter's work. She also serves as a channel of information for family members on a variety of subjects concerning work, such as possible overtime, management plans, and activities of the plant for the benefit of the village, spiced, perhaps, with a little gossip.

The supervisors are attentive to the complex issues associated with the seamstresses' entry into wage labor, especially in terms of the relationship with the worker's father. They were in the same position once, they come from the same community and set of assumptions, and their relative experience in these matters enables them to address new issues in the workers' lives. The supervisors sometimes serve as mediators and advocates for seamstresses on internal familial matters.

Jihan tells me the following story.

> One of the women bought herself a new blouse and a pair of pants. When her friend saw her, she went out and bought the exact same outfit—to show that they were good friends. Then the second woman's father began to beat her up. Why? Because he said that she had to give her money to the family and save up to buy things for her wedding. The woman was angry at her father and angry at the whole family. That's bad. So she asked me to go and talk to her father. I told her I was ready on condition that her father also agreed. At first he refused. But then my brother, who knows him, spoke with him and told him that this way he was ruining his daughter, that his sister, who was her supervisor, would solve the problem. So he said that because he respects my brother he would agree to talk to me. I came to their house and we sat around drink-

> ing coffee and talking and in the end the woman agreed that she wouldn't buy things just for the fun of it and would give her paycheck to the family. Her father agreed to give her 100 NIS (New Israeli Shekel) a month for pocket money. I told him that if the woman never saw any of the money she earned, she would stop working hard and wouldn't have any reason to earn premiums.

The supervisors also mediate between the needs of the plant and the needs of the families of the seamstresses. This mediation is necessary because of the frequent tensions between the family and work regarding overtime and low pay. The family sees the supervisor in multiple roles—as a member of their social group, as women, and as managers in the plant—in that order. This means that she is expected to give precedence to the community and the family over the workplace. The supervisors realize that they are walking on a tightrope. In their interactions with the families of the seamstresses, however, the interests of the work are primary.

Supervisors and Managers

In the plant's hierarchical structure there are precise status differences between supervisors and managers with regard to function, responsibility, and authority. Nevertheless, the position of the supervisors in the overall structure is closer to that of the managers than that of the seamstresses. The supervisors are expected to present managerial competency in spite of the fact that in practice they do not have a formal management education.

The supervisors enjoy relative autonomy in managing their departments even though they do report to managers. According to Su'ad, a supervisor,

> The managers usually rely on the supervisor. They give her the right to manage the department the way she sees fit, providing she delivers the goods. But it's not as if the managers and the supervisors function separately. We work together and our goals are achieved together. If, for instance, the managers don't pay enough attention to quality, neither will the supervisors. If the supervisors and the managers don't meet together regularly to decide how to work together, there will be problems. The supervisors don't always understand exactly what the managers want from them. Every manager has his own system and even though we may be experienced supervisors, we still have to get used to every new manager and his methods. There is nothing that can be done about this. We stay in the same job for years, doing the same thing over and over again. Managers come and go. We even teach them a thing or two when they're just getting started and once they learn they start telling us what do and how to do it and begin changing things that we've been doing for years. That's why they are managers. But the supervisor is always the manager's right hand and has to help him in everything, especially with the women. A good supervisor takes a big load off the manager's mind.

The supervisors are the most stable group in the plant. They are the ones who retain the shared meaning of work values, norms, and practices, both those of the managers and those of the seamstresses. Managers come and go, and it is the supervisors who maintain the guidelines for behavior under the various circumstances and events at the plant. They constantly attempt to incorporate the managerial system into the seamstresses' behavior. The supervisors embody both sets of rules, procedures, norms, and behavior, and translate them into practical behavior as a mechanism for absorbing conflict and delineating moral codes at the plants.

The supervisors accept the manager as the highest professional authority, aware that he is working under constraints dictated to him by his superiors. They also accept that he has a broad grasp of the overall operation of the plant whereas they focus largely on running their own departments. Thus, in the daily reality of the sewing plant, only the manager can really judge whether one department needs to relinquish some of its workers or machines for the benefit of the plant as a whole, a situation that may cause tension between the supervisor and the manager. This kind of conflict can be expected from time to time. The manager has to weigh his general priorities and those of the plant against the priorities and schedules of the supervisors and their individual departments. This may adversely affect the achievements of a particular department. Zohara, a supervisor, comments on this issue: "If I have to send some of my seamstresses to another department, it will be to my disadvantage, since I will certainly not be able to fulfill my work schedule."

In situations of this sort, the supervisor may feel that the manager's decision is directed against her personally and arbitrarily. Loyalty to the manager is one of the central values in the job of the supervisor as well as one of the central facets of managerial strategy. Loyalty is understood on a personal level with reciprocity as an integral component. A manager who undermines the authority of a supervisor in the running of her department is perceived as breaking the rules of decency and loyalty, which are the cornerstones of the managerial system in the sewing plants.

The loyalty of each supervisor to her department and to her workers is a matter of great sensitivity in itself and has little relation to the needs of other departments in the plant. The dual loyalty to the department and the workers, on the one hand, and the loyalty to the managers, who sometimes harm the department for the sake of the general interest of the plant, on the other hand, raises inner tensions. For example, the level and quality of production determine the supervisor's personal evaluation and salary. If, however, the manager withdraws one of the supervisor's seamstresses from the production line because of an urgent need elsewhere, the performance of her department is immediately affected. Thus the supervisor is torn between her loyalties to the department and to the performance of the plant as a whole. This tension is part and parcel of her work that cannot be avoided and demonstrates the inner contradiction in performing the job of supervisor.

One source of tension between the supervisors and the managers is the disruption of the solidarity and togetherness that develops between the supervisors and their workers. The supervisors build a sense of unity and accountability within the department through department participation in seamstresses' personal events such as birthdays and engagement parties, and by giving departmental presents at these events. Achieving departmental unity and solidarity takes a long time and entails both an emotional investment and physical energy. Any disruption of the departmental flow of work, particularly by a manager's intervention in the supervisor's department, is perceived as a blow to the supervisor, a threat to the stability of her department, and blatant disregard of her efforts. Disruptions hurt their ability to meet their production goals and maintain their sense of excellence, and thus infringe on the equality between the supervisors. The following story illustrates the local patriotism of the supervisors to their department.

Salweh tells the following story.

> My department is set up to produce 1,500 pairs of boxer shorts with Lycra elastic bands. I have two women who know how to sew the Lycra but only one machine for it. So I asked for another machine. Eran, the production manager, told me there was another machine in Rudeina's department and I should transfer the woman there. I thought that the woman should be working for me on the boxers but they told me that she would be working for Rudeina, and I didn't agree. I'm not ready to train a woman in order for her to work for another department. Then I'll be stuck. The other day they brought me Cacharel shirts for finishing. They shouldn't have done that. Rudeina's department was doing that and they brought her another product. Whoever sewed the shirts from the beginning should do the finishing as well. But the production manager didn't want to make it hard for the women in her department so instead he made it hard for me and my department. They're out to get us and I don't know why. I just don't have any luck. My department is my first priority. If I give a woman to Rudeina's department I'll be hurting my own department; the merchandise will suffer and our output will fall.

In conflicts whereby the manager undermines the supervisor's authority, she converges into her department and expresses loyalty to her workers. The department, for her, is the source of loyalty, unity, solidarity, and mutual assistance. This leads to managerial ambiguities, whereby the supervisor takes a stand in favor of her department and the manager takes a stand in favor of the plant. In the background are not only department cohesiveness and the message she wants to send to the workers of protecting them at all costs, but also concern for professional performance. If her department is hurt, she will not make her production goals and will be accountable to the manager. The dispute about managing and organizing the work between managers and supervisors becomes a social drama, whereby the supervisor gains emotional support and high esteem for her persistence from her workers but suffers inconveniences, as she ultimately must comply with the manager's requests.

The managers of the sewing plants are interested in crystallizing a hard core of experienced department supervisors who are capable of independent action insofar as it is possible. There are supervisors who are extremely professional in their work and highly motivated, so much so that the managers have little need to interfere with the management of their department. Moreover, the supervisors would view such interference as a personal affront. In this respect, the hierarchical divisions of authority between managers and supervisors become somewhat indistinct, and the latter are able to acquire significant power. This power expresses itself in having a free hand to do in the department what she pleases, as long she as meets her production and quality goals.

The autonomous management of a department by a supervisor is conditioned by a high level of personal loyalty to the manager; the two are mutually interdependent. The loyalty involves full agreement on the part of the supervisor to the methods, goals and needs of the manager. Thus the supervisor must conform to the manager's view, styles, and priorities in order to gain autonomy in running her department. A supervisor does not necessarily see this type of relationship with the manager as an advantage, as it creates more friction within her department. Taking an a priori pro-managerial stance implies that the supervisor has relinquished her function as a spokesperson and advocate for her workers. Only a few supervisors agree to uncritically identify with the manager, as eventually it lessens their independence, autonomy vis-à-vis the manager, and bargaining power with the workers.

The supervisors expect managers to recognize their professionalism and exhibit reciprocity in their relationships. Ignoring the supervisors' experience and their role as facilitators of the production process is viewed as breaching the implicit contract between them and the managers. The entire value system developed in the sewing plants is a reflection of this bond between the two. The supervisor is the extension of the manager, the mediator and translator of the manager's outlook and worldview, and the one who implements the manager's work plan. The relationship must be harmonious and reflect deep understanding and trust.

Managers have varied attitudes toward supervisors. They grant considerable autonomy to those who are professional, have proven themselves at work, and obey the manager unquestioningly. These supervisors give up resources of their departments without fearing a loss of status. They are pillars of the plant and enjoy high status with the manager at work. The manager consults with them and respects their advice. They are the legacy of the plant, those who for years participate in reshaping and renegotiating all aspects of work and life on the shop floor.

New supervisors have a more fragile relationship with managers. They have to deal with their lack of professional management skills and the difficulties of performing all of their professional-organizational duties. Furthermore, their dyadic relations with the managers have not yet crystallized.[4] At times they are hesitant about approaching the managers to clarify some issue, simply because in their former position in the plant they had no direct access to him. Establishing a close working relationship with the managers is part of the supervisor's job. It ensures that the manager will actively support her and back her in all of her department matters. This support is a prerequisite for success.

The Supervisors and the Company

For most of the supervisors, the company has no direct impact on their work. Their frame of reference is their department. This perception stems from their minimal tangible connection with the company, except for the occasional visits of one of the directors and the rare extension course they take at the division center in Carmiel.[5]

The supervisors' connection to the company is expressed mainly through team meetings with functionaries from the division, who pass on information about the obligations to fulfill orders, raise quality levels, or meet production schedules. The company managers consider the supervisors as those who have direct influence on the quality of the merchandise, which gives the company its competitive edge in the international market. The supervisors accompany customer representatives who come to check the quality of the merchandise. Such visits instill in them a sense of pride that they belong to a large company with an outstanding international reputation. This feeling is reinforced when they make visits, from time to time, to "sister" plants or participate in yearly events arranged by the company for all of its employees.

Smooth operation of the sewing plants depends on good planning and logistics, cutting, delivery, and inventory management. If this support is not provided on time or with the needed quality, the plant cannot meet its production goals. This puts a lot of pressure on the supervisors because it is beyond their ability to influence. Although it is perceived as the prerogative of the managers, the supervisors are the ones who face the consequences of logistical problems. In instances, for example, when the materials do not arrive or are damaged, the managers must confront the supervisors' justified claims regarding their inability to meet their goals. On many occasions this raises tensions and confrontations as the supervisors are frustrated by the managers' blind support of the company.

Flora, a supervisor, is extremely frustrated. She goes to the manager and tells him that she has failed in her role and is quitting. Dror, the manager, tries to persuade her that she is a good supervisor and shows her graphs and data proving that her output, quality, and absenteeism is the best in the plant. Flora is not convinced: "There is too much pressure. I can't take it anymore. Especially the new product of Marks and Spencer. It is made of thin material that curls up. All the women are depressed—they can't reach their norm and there are quality problems. Then their salaries will be low and they'll come to me with complaints. I don't have energy anymore. I want to leave. This problem with the raw material is hurting my department."

Dror backs Flora up and says that he has talked to the cutting manager and the division manager but they don't understand. To placate her, he suggests she write a letter to the division manager. She likes the idea and says, "I'll write. But it's the last chance. If it doesn't work then I'm leaving and *hallas* [the end]."

Flora wrote the following letter:

A Letter to the Division Manager about Raw Materials

I would like to notify you in this letter about the condition of the raw materials in the last period which is getting gradually worse. There are problems that repeat themselves—cutting, asymmetry, unequal parts, the material curls up, the color tones are not uniform. Imagine to yourself the pressure on me and my department. Every morning we come to work with enthusiasm. We begin to work and suddenly encounter a catastrophic problem that messes us up for the whole day. The department and I get into a lot of pressure and the seamstresses take advantage of this. On one hand we have quantity and quality obligations. On the other hand, problems with the raw materials hurt us from all sides. The seamstresses have to cut and sort and waste productive time. I understand that the raw material can't be perfect. But you'll agree with me that there's a limit. I want you to understand the pressure on me. All the seamstresses are on my case. The plant is meant to produce underwear, not problems. The customer should be satisfied with our products. I occasionally get material that is garbage—forgive the expression—and we all know that from garbage you can only make garbage. Even though we try our hardest, it's hard to overcome the problems if they repeat themselves.

Hoping that you will help us,
Flora M.
Maghar Sewing Plant

The manager never passed the letter to the company. He had only wanted Flora to stay at work and used the letter to appease her. Eventually this line of product ended and a new line, one that did not curl up, was given to Flora's department.

In the course of time, the company has acquired a good reputation among the Arab and Druse villagers because of the way it ensures the women's safety and good name. It has become known as a firm that accepts the special cultural and behavioral norms of the seamstresses as part of its organizational culture. Many of the supervisors told me that they went to work at these plants because "they were the only places where their parents would let them work." Many said that they would recommend "only this company" to their sisters or relatives who wanted to work in industry "because it shows respect for all the communities and their customs."

Conflicts over Backing

The supervisors expect the backing of the managers in issues related to decision-making in the department. One day around noon, Amneh sees that she does not have enough fabric to finish making one of the products. She decides to send four of the women home. The production manager is not at the plant that morning and when he returns toward the end of the day, Amneh tells him what she had done. He becomes incensed and tells her that she should have checked with the manager as to whether they might be of some use in another department. Amneh is offended.

> Not only did he shout at me, he didn't help me. Perhaps I made a mistake but it's his job to explain things to me and not to shout at me. I'm fed up with that sort of behavior. If that's the way he acts then he doesn't care a straw for me. If he doesn't agree with the way I do things, I can stay home. I've got everything I need at home. Let him give me official notice and I'll say, "Bye, see you." He thinks he's the only one who knows anything. Nobody else understands anything. Maybe I did make a mistake, but that's no way to behave. I can't get used to that. At home my brothers all have the highest respect for me. My mother waits at home for me till five o'clock and doesn't eat a thing until I'm back from work. He yelled at me for letting the women go home instead of making sure that there was enough fabric. What does he think? Let him shout at his wife, Mr. Manager.

Offending the supervisors breaches their perception of reciprocity.[6] When a supervisor's interpretation of events is not accepted or a manager scolds her, she has a choice. If she categorizes the insult as a severe breach of reciprocity, she can resort to a solution of "exit"—leaving work. If she complies, she can use her "voice" to defend her position and point of view, thus reiterating the norms and values of the work. The following story illustrates the latter option.

Najah has worked as a supervisor for fifteen years. Her story illustrates how professional and personal backing plays a role in managerial methods. Any departure from these norms is immediately grasped as a lack of respect and leads to a breakdown in relations.

> The whole mess started when the division quality controller stopped the work of Fahimeh, the other quality controller. She [the division quality controller] said that Fahimeh approves defected merchandise. I went over to her and she showed me an example. I thought it looked fine. I told her that I thought we could continue anyway but we had better go and talk to Rami. We

came to the office, you know, in a friendly way, I showed him the merchandise and I said to him, "Take the underwear and see if there's a problem and tell me if we can continue to work." I was really sure that he would agree with me because we had had the same problem a month before and then Rami had agreed that we could continue. So Rami looked at the underwear and Fahimeh asked him to give her permission to continue. He said it was no good. I explained to him that we had a problem sewing the legs.

Fuad, the production manager, saw that there was going to be an explosion and walked out of the office. Believe me, if he had stayed on nothing would have happened. But he didn't want to take sides in the argument and so he pretended that he had something urgent to do and left. I told Rami that I couldn't go on like this and he answered me in an angry tone that I shouldn't think I was doing him a favor. That's what he said after I'd been working under pressure for months, working overtime without end and working Fridays until 2:00 in the afternoon. He was the one that was holding up the smooth flow of work. I told him thanks a lot, if that's the way you thank me for all the work I've invested. You're trampling on everything and I don't like it.

She looked at me and then she lowered her large brown eyes and spoke softly.

"I took off my smock."

I looked at her with surprise and she smiled. "You know that I took off my smock, so why are you looking at me like that?"

Taking off your smock at the sewing plant is equivalent to saying, "I quit." It is a symbolic act of resistance usually performed in the presence of the worker and the manager and is considered a burning insult to the management. A woman who takes off her smock in front of everyone is, in effect, declaring that she has lost faith in the management. The managers, too, see this act as a particularly vehement form of protest.

Rami tells me,

It makes my blood boil to see a worker take off her smock so boldly. It's like a rebellion. If a woman or particularly a supervisor, who is an example to everybody, does that, I'll kick her out of the plant. I never want to see her again. At that point I don't care what happened or who was right. A woman who takes off her smock in front of everybody is disgracing the plant. It's like putting a stigma on the plant and its managers. It's a vote of no confidence in the managerial abilities of the supervisors and me, in our ability to solve the problems of the seamstresses. That's perhaps the most important point of all—personal management. All the time I am trying to get it home to them that the manager solves all their problems—at work and outside of work. The manager is a fair person, doesn't play favorites and doesn't hand out demerits. When one of them takes off her smock, it means she isn't giving the manager a chance, that she doesn't believe in him.

The manager must be sensitive to the style and content of using his authority toward the supervisors. The content of the hierarchy is not pure control; it is "mellowed" and includes compassion, consideration, and friendship. If the manager ignores these new contents and resorts only to authoritative justifications and displays of power, then he openly changes the rules of the game and the supervisor has no avenue but to quit. Nonetheless, the conflict is open to negotiation.

"What happened after you took off you smock?" I ask Najah.

> Fuad grabbed me on the stairs and asked me to stay. I was burning up inside. Nobody appreciates what you do. Rami had to show that he's a man, so he wanted me on my knees, and that's just not my style. I stayed at home for three days. Rami called me up at home and asked me to come back. I told him I wasn't coming. If you want, I said, you can come over here, we'll have a cup of coffee. He said, you come for a cup of coffee and after that I'll come to you for a cup of coffee. I didn't want to insult him so I came for a cup of coffee.
>
> After three days, my friends from the department told me that they missed me and I shouldn't leave them. I still don't respect Rami, but I decided to return to work for my workers.

Najah's story reveals the drama behind the intricate relationship between the managers and the supervisors. The game has distinct rules. The manager is entitled to dispute the supervisor's decisions within a prescribed framework as long as he maintains respect. For the supervisor, it is important that the form of the manager's expressions still preserves her status as part of management. Only then can the supervisor affiliate with the manager despite their differences of opinion, thus strengthening her "organizational self."[7] Confronting her with a decision that contradicted her professional judgment, Najah took a symbolic act in front of the whole plant by taking off her red smock. This bold gesture was aimed directly at the manager and challenged his legitimacy, power, and proficiency. Although the manager has the power to fire the supervisor, he lost the battle in the moral field.

The managers try to avoid prolonged conflict because they have little leverage in risking the cooperation of the supervisors. In such conflicts the supervisors implicitly remind the manager that he must resort to a course of action and behavior in which both sides save face. These cases illustrate the limit of the managers' power, whereby their misuse of it can adversely affect them.

The managers' tendency to see the plant as one integrated system and to base their decisions on the interest of the entire plant often collides with the supervisors' territoriality and desire to preserve the integrity of their departments. Flexibility is an issue that often raises friction, particularly during times of changing products and styles from one season to another. For the managers, the change in the seasons is a time for reorganizing the assembly lines and mobilizing seamstresses within and between departments. The basic criterion for mobility relates to the seamstress's qualifications, abilities, polyvalence, and proficiency. Although reorganization is accepted by the supervisors, friction and complaints are part of the ritual. The supervisor must tackle a practical problem—how to explain the transfer of seamstresses to other departments. These transfers are characterized by mini-crises whereby seamstresses cry, yell, and threaten to leave work, and supervisors quarrel with managers.

Iman's department is strong and cohesive. The relationships between the seamstresses are friendly, they spend time together outside of work, and they attend each other's celebrations. With the coming of the summer season, the managers decide to reorganize the department. Iman complains bitterly and objects, crying and claiming that it is not fair: "I've been working many years to train my workers and now they are taking them from me." As a protest, she decides to take a special vacation, claiming that she has to help her sister who had just given birth. The manager apparently is quite satisfied with her decision and uses the opportunity to personally reorganize the department. When Iman returns to work three days later, she finds an already established new reality. She bursts into the manager's office and lays down her protests.

The manager lets her blow off her steam and then says, "I have learned an old Arab proverb, 'He who is in the market is the one who buys and sells.' You were not here, so I changed your department." Iman is speechless and leaves the office.

When I ask her why she let the manager reorganize her department, she comments, "I did it on purpose. I wanted him to be the bad guy. Now the whole plant knows that he took advantage of my absence to make these changes. Nobody blames me for cooperating with him. I retained my reputation of taking care of my workers first and foremost."

The option of exit can be seen as a resistance strategy to the manager's policies, particularly its apparently arbitrary decision-making process. For Iman, it is an active option that sends a message of noncompliance to both the manager and her workers. Although she does not have the power to curb the manager's decision, she does not accept its rationality either. She takes a definitive stand and prefers the integrity of her department.

Wages and Remuneration

The supervisors see the issue of salary as problematic, and it is always on their agenda in deliberations with the managers, as wages are not commensurate with their responsibilities. This is particularly evident when compared with the seamstresses' wages. An experienced supervisor, with years of seniority, makes only a few hundred NIS more than a good seamstress. The supervisor cannot advance in the management hierarchy but there is a wide range of jobs she can fulfill at the supervisory level. She can be in charge of a large department that sews elaborate products; she can be responsible for packaging; and she can serve as chief quality controller for the plant or as chief instructor. While all of these jobs require a good deal of professional expertise, the responsibilities they entail are not reflected in the basic wage.

The managers determine bonuses and premiums for the supervisors above their low basic wage, and this "extra" becomes an important component of their take-home pay. Before the passing of the minimum wage law in 1996, the average basic wage of a supervisor came to about 1,600 NIS a month. A quality controller earned a premium of 40–50 hours' pay while more demanding jobs earned the supervisor another 60–80 hours' pay. A quality controller thus earned 1,900–2,100 NIS a month while a supervisor earned 2,300–2,500 NIS a month. This salary is in accordance with the collective agreement, with differentiation dependent on seniority. Since the passing of the minimum wage law, supervisors receive the same basic salary as the seamstresses and depend on management bonuses to supplement and raise their income above the average seamstress's salary. The company prefers to use managerial bonuses instead of raising their basic salary—this way the social benefits remain the same as before the passing of the law. Customarily, there is an annual increase according to seniority, but the difference in pay between one level and the next is almost negligible. These increases, therefore, are not viewed as either a form of remuneration or a professional promotion.

The management is well aware of the problem and seeks various means to raise wages. Bonuses may be given for special effort. Additionally, if one of the supervisors has a car, she may earn additional money by driving the women to and from work.

The supervisors always know that their contribution is higher than their pay and accuse the company of lacking gratitude. The managers attempt to justify the supervisors' relatively low wages by pointing to the low profitability of the textile industry in general and the ever-present threat of international competition from countries in which wages are much lower. They repeatedly cite the example that a supervisor in the company's plant in Egypt earns $120 a month, whereas in Israel she earns about $800.

With all the complaining, dissatisfaction about salaries never translates into group action or group demands for a raise. The supervisors discuss their bonuses individually with the managers. It is assumed, for the most part, that the company is tight-fisted and that the managers have little leeway to be generous with compensation. As far as the supervisors are concerned, it is a situation they have to live with.

The managers themselves try to maintain a balanced policy with regard to the remuneration of the supervisors. The more experienced and the more capable among them receive a higher wage than those just starting in the job, both because of seniority and larger bonuses and premiums. The supervisors acknowledge the existence of an informal wage scale, whose standards are strictly adhered to. In theory, the salaries of the supervisors are their own private business but, in practice, each of them knows what the others are earning. If one of them gets "too far ahead" with bonuses and premiums, there will be a long line of supervisors at the manager's door petitioning for their "rights." Money is the surest sign of a supervisor's worth, beyond the attention or kind words given her by the management.

Ivtesam shares with me her feelings on the subject.

> The managers get ahead but the supervisors stay in the same place. You think that if you have a lot of seniority you're really making progress. But it's not so. A supervisor with seniority doesn't have any advantage. I'd like to know why we don't get ahead, why we're practically in the same place we started from. What is 2,300 NIS for a supervisor who has worked for more than ten years. The supervisor does all the work and in the end she goes home empty-handed. The supervisor has all the trouble but she only gets *grushim*.[8] They don't see us as managers, like them. We are not more than the seamstresses to them, Arab village women.

The issue of remuneration emphasizes the inequalities inherent in the entire textile industry in the Arab villages. Even though the supervisors' contribution is recognized, they are still not considered full-fledged managers in the company. The fact that they are supervisors does not fundamentally change their income, only their responsibility. In this sense the exploitation of the supervisors is strongly apparent. The managers draw them into the realm of management, but with regard to remuneration they are confined to the realm of the seamstresses.

Relations among the Supervisors

The value of teamwork is considered the key to success at the plant.[9] At the plants, team-related values are harmony, reciprocity, and recognition of achievement. When teams do not operate in accordance with these values, the climate of the plant is hostile. Hostility is felt among the seamstresses, between the seamstresses and the supervisors, and among the supervisors. Furthermore, the discord spills over into relations outside the plant and affects personal friendships.

The repertoire of relations among the supervisors is large and runs along a continuum from deep friendships, to solidarity and mutual esteem at work, to dislike, to hatred. Most of the conflicts among the supervisors simmer for some time under the surface. Those involved are usually not interested in bringing them into the open and thus generate an open crisis at the plant. But if a conflict does erupt—and it is not important how trivial its source—it does not take long before it engulfs everyone in its wake, both in the plant and at home in the village. Such a conflict requires the interference of a moderator, and it is usually the manager who tries to resolve the conflict through arbitration and compromise. He must intervene boldly if he is to get the plant back on track.

The following story illustrates a case of an "all-out war" that took place in the wake of a conflict between two supervisors, Suha and Johara. The two had worked together at the plant in the same capacity for a long time. One might say that there was a certain symmetry between them. They were both highly esteemed by the manager of the plant and both ran large departments that produced similar kinds of merchandise. There seemed to be an unwritten agreement between them. They presented a united front to the manager, to the other supervisors, and to the seamstresses, and appeared to be good friends. The manager, for his part, was careful to preserve their status as senior supervisors and never showed favoritism to one over the other, either in his personal relations with each or at team meetings. The united front burst wide open the day that Suha decided that the time was ripe for her to take professional precedence over her erstwhile colleague.

Suha had to sew examples of a product on a machine that belonged to Johara's department and asked permission from the manager to take the machine. She did not bother to mention the fact that the machine belonged to the department of another supervisor.

This is the way Suha saw it.

> We had a fight over a certain problem. Once I had a single-needle job to do. I went to Jacob, the manager, and asked for a single-needle machine. He said, okay, there's no problem. The machine was in the blouse section of Johara's department and I saw that nobody was using it. Jacob was in the dining room so I decided that I would take the machine, put a woman to work, and when he finished eating I would tell him about it. Johara saw that one of my seamstresses was working at the machine and lost her temper. She threw a spool of cotton at the woman and nearly hit her in the eye. I saw the whole thing and I told Johara she should be ashamed of herself. [Suha also added an epithet but refused to tell me exactly which one.] Johara began to scream insults at me and I answered her back. She has a sister, Feize, who worked in her department as a quality controller. Feize saw us quarreling and came over and began to hit me with her shoe from behind. Some of the women from my department also came over and told her that she should be ashamed of herself, doing something like that. In a few minutes all the women from the two departments were shouting at each other. There were even women with sisters and cousins in the other department who were shouting at each other and it was a big mess until the manager turned up.
>
> I left the department and went home. My quality controllers told Jacob that they didn't agree that I should stay home while Johara continued working. They said that if he didn't send her home they would all walk out. He told Naif, the driver, to take Johara home. I told my parents and my brother what happened. My brother went to the plant and told Jacob that if Johara and her sister come back to work they would be dead for what they did.

Jacob had a dilemma. On the one hand he wanted to end the fracas, arrange a *sulha* (reconciliation), and get the plant back into working order, with both supervisors working. On the other hand, he could not ignore the fact that Suha was from one of the most respected families in the village, whereas Johara came from another village. Suha's father and brother spoke with the village elders and consequently a delegation arrived at the plant and bluntly presented to the manager an ultimatum: either fire Johara and her sister or all the women from the village will leave the plant.

Jacob had no choice. He insisted, however, on handling the matter in his own way. First he suspended both supervisors and Feize from work for two weeks. After this cooling-off period, Jacob decided that Suha would come back to work and Johara and Feize would be transferred to another plant.

Suha said, "When I came back to the plant I told Jacob that he hadn't behaved properly. She should have been kicked out of the company altogether. She was always opening her mouth at me because she was jealous and no matter how much I felt sorry for her, she always crossed me. She thought that she was better than me. That she deserved the same as me. I was a supervisor in the plant when she still worked for me as a seamstress. I'm stronger and smarter than she is. If you put her and a snake in the same pit, the snake will run away."

In the aftermath of this conflict[10] the plant underwent many changes. The structure of the departments changed as a result of changes in product lines, which caused large departments to be broken up into smaller ones. With time, Johara's and Suha's seamstresses were dispersed among the new, smaller departments. Many got married and left. From those in the plant who were part of the conflict, only a few dozen remained. The story continues to circulate, however, in the plant. Seamstresses and supervisors still identify themselves with either Suha's or Johara's party, even new seamstresses who did not work at the plant at the time of the quarrel. Apparently Suha and Johara represent diverging work philosophies. Suha's approach represents a more considerate and consensual management style that gives priority to the plant as a whole. Her party consists mainly of village women. Johara's approach, still proudly represented by a few supervisors, entails uncompromised departmental coherence. They are territorial about their departments and guard their boundaries carefully.[11]

The conflicts between supervisors are multilayered. Regardless of where conflicts begin, they tend to accumulate additional issues, related to style of work, personal matters, and familial or community matters. These conflicts create camps in the plant. Sometimes when friends or relatives belong to different camps tensions arise, and efforts at a *sulha* are made. The workers realize that conflict is never simple but multidimensional.

Conclusion

Supervisors are in a unique position in the sewing plants. They rise from the rank and file of the shop floor to being in charge of a department. Their primary responsibility is organizing their department's production and managing the seamstresses. They play the role of mediator between the managers and the workers, particularly in crisis situations. They serve both sides as cultural interpreter. They are advocates for the workers to management and, in turn, translate the management's point of view into a language workers understand.

The affinity of the supervisors to the cultural traditions of the workers and their ability to adapt them to the demands of work in the plant enable them to translate the meanings of the social relations of production. The supervisors see themselves as gate-keepers and mediators, capable of preserving and interpreting managerial and local sets of cultural values and bridging them. In their mediating role, supervisors find themselves in a self-contradictory position. Although they are expected to be loyal to management, they still feel a sense of responsibility toward the seamstresses they manage. They have to solve this inherent dissonance by recognizing this conflict and sometimes bearing its consequences.

The work enlarges the supervisors' personal and professional horizons and contributes to their sense of independence. They feel that they have greater control over their own lives. Being a manager at work develops their sense of self-importance and expresses itself in their relative independence from their families and increased power within it.

Notes

This chapter is based on long-term field research conducted between 1994 and 2002. The field research was based mainly on participant observation as well as on structured and unstructured interviews.

1. Blauner (1964) and Edwards (1979) recognize the overseeing nature of the social relations of production on the shop floor, particularly between supervisors and workers. They emphasize strict control as a key to smooth operation.
2. On the double role of the supervisor as both boss and friend, and the blurring of these roles, see Kung 1981.
3. The notion of loyalty in the sewing plant has multiple meanings and expresses both interpersonal and work relations. As such, loyalty is a principal value in the sewing plant work culture. Many have claimed that loyalty to the workplace in the traditional sense (a covenant in which companies offer job security, flexibility, and rewards in exchange for adequate performance and occasional short-term sacrifices) is dead in the era of modern competitive capitalism (see, e.g., Thurow 1997). Loyalty in a competitive capitalist environment may best be defined as a desire to remain an employee of the organization, or continuous commitment as opposed to active involvement and identification with the organization. Clearly in the sewing plants the more traditional (and more profitable) sense of loyalty to the organization prevails (see Reichheld 1996).
4. The characteristics of dyadic vertical relationships, such as the relationship between managers and supervisors, have been analyzed in the context of role theory and social exchange theory. According to role theory (Katz and Kahn 1978), the process of defining one's role occurs through interactions with the other member of the dyad as well as with other people in the organization who convey important role information. Social exchange theory (Emerson 1962) discusses the relevance of alternative exchange partners from whom members can gain valuable resources for the balance of power and influence within the dyad.

5. In recognition of the importance of the professional contribution of the supervisors to the sewing plant and their key role in motivating seamstresses, the division sporadically initiates professional training. These trainings concentrate on issues such as human relationships, sewing technology, production procedures, and updating on company structure and strategy. These trainings are offered to all of the supervisors from the sewing plants and serve as a stage for exchanging ideas and making interpersonal contacts. The supervisors see these trainings as bonuses because they take place in Carmiel and entail tours of other plants and festive meals, as well as a break from work.
6. Research has demonstrated (see, e.g., Dawes 1992) that high levels of group solidarity and cohesion facilitate reciprocity. This kind of reciprocity, involving many actors and described as indirect, can be characterized as a social exchange system (see Ekeh 1974). In such a system, members help each other without expecting immediate reciprocity, but it is expected at some point in the future by anyone in the organization. It is in the manager's interest to facilitate this kind of social reciprocal relationship by exhibiting solidarity and cohesion with the supervisors. See also Gouldner 1960.
7. According to Kunda (1992a), the "organizational self" is the subjective experience resulting from the balancing of the acceptance of the ideology of the work organization (in the case of the sewing plants, that which is embodied by the managers and its rejection). On the various aspects of self-definition within work settings, see, e.g., Van Maanen 1976.
8. *Grushim* is the Hebrew equivalent of pennies.
9. Extensive literature deals with the importance and benefits of teamwork in various organizational settings. See, e.g., Kasl, Marsick, and Dechant 1997; LeClair 1996.
10. The incident took place in May 1994.
11. Intragroup conflict within the same organization is studied by Pinkley (1990), who found that people differentiate between two types of conflict. The first are task-based conflicts, based on disagreements about the performance of the job. The second are relationship conflicts, arising from interpersonal disagreements not related to the work itself. Jehn (1995) demonstrates negative implications of relationship conflict, including tension and animosity between the groups, lowered satisfaction, frustration, and a desire to withdraw.

23

Land of the Negev Bedouin

EMANUEL MARX

Introduction

The states of the Middle East have always tended to treat the Bedouin as second-rate citizens. Even today many government spokesmen and experts argue that the Bedouin contribute little to the region's national economies, that they live apart from the settled population, and that they raise animals only for their own subsistence (League of Arab Nations 1965, Abou Zeid 1996).[1] Their nomadic way of life was viewed as little more than an attempt to opt out of civil obligations, such as military service and payment of taxes. By settling the Bedouin, governments hoped to make them more productive and more governable. As they were thought to practice a subsistence economy (see, e.g., Cole 1975, 145), the loss of land and production caused by settlement was often ignored. On the contrary, the officials believed that as settled peasants the Bedouin would at last enter the market economy. This policy was often informed by the fact that Bedouin own large tracts of land, parts of which the state requires for various purposes from time to time. As the Bedouin move with their herds for part of the year, they are generally widely dispersed and incapable of concentrating large forces. Therefore they are incapable of effectively controlling their lands and are easily subdued by the greater power of the state. It is precisely because state authorities view Bedouin as candidates for land expropriation that they deny the very real contribution of their herds to the national economy (Gardner and Marx 2000, 21–22).

The preconceptions of the government officials as to the nature of nomadism affected their settlement policies: they tended to concentrate on housing the pastoralists in permanent villages and on converting them to an agricultural way of life. From the mid-nineteenth century onward, governments made numerous attempts to force or persuade them to settle. In the Negev these projects began in the 1870s, slightly later than in other regions of the Ottoman Empire. They were partly inspired by the completion of the Suez Canal in 1869, and partly by the growing importance of the barley grown in the Negev for

European beer brewers. The grains were exported from the port of Gaza. In the two last decades of the nineteenth century the Ottoman authorities set up a series of villages for the Bedouin in the vicinity of Gaza (Gazit 2000, 185–86). The villages took root because they fit into the Bedouin's mixed economy: now they marketed both grain and animals. However, they put more labor and capital into animal husbandry, which still provided the greater part of their income (Abu-Rabia 1994, 107–27). In 1896 the Ottoman authorities founded the town of Beersheva, which rapidly became the administrative and commercial center of the Negev. It attracted numerous Bedouin settlers, among them tribal chiefs (Ben-Arieh and Sapir 1979, 56). Even more incisive was the impact of World War II. It brought about the economic and occupational diversification of the Negev Bedouin, affecting more than those who moved into towns.

In complex modern economies the population gravitates to urban centers. As the regions around the cities become more densely settled, land becomes a scarce commodity. This is the case in Israel's Negev. As the Bedouin use large areas of land near the cities for extensive herding and dry farming, they own a commodity of enormous value. Therefore the Israel Lands Authority (ILA), the government agency that controls 93 percent of Israel's land, is constantly being pressured (or tempted) to allocate the land to more powerful groups, such as the army, Jewish settlers, and commercial interests. The state then expropriates large tracts of land in the name of security considerations, progress, and economic development, but does not necessarily use the land more intensively or profitably than the Bedouin. Some 80 percent of the land in the Negev has been allotted to the army and is mostly reserved for bombing ranges, training terrains, and camps. In some outlying regions land was awarded to the Nature Reserves Authority, another state agency. Thus the ILA unceremoniously expropriated the 'Abde ('Ovdat) canyon from the Kishkhar Bedouin for a nature reservation for ibex and gazelles. In recent years it leased large parcels of former Bedouin land to Jewish settlers to prevent what the officials describe as the "encroachment of Bedouin on state land."

In reality, the state and its agencies have generally met with little resistance as they have gradually appropriated Bedouin land. Yet the struggle between these unequal forces continues unabated. It has gone through three major stages. First, in 1950 Israel registered all the Negev as state land. As the new owner of the land, the ILA progressively seized all Bedouin common pasture areas to which, incidentally, the Bedouin did not claim ownership. The ILA also gradually took over 80 percent of the individually owned cultivated land (1 million out of 1.2 million dunams). Second, the authorities' efforts to expropriate the land still remaining in Bedouin hands eventually led to the establishment of Bedouin towns, in which every Bedouin could acquire a subsidized building plot. Bedouin who had never owned land bought most of the building sites. Third, the struggle over land affected the Bedouin economy in a variety of ways. The Bedouin who decided to stay on their land did not improve their farms, had difficulty obtaining pastures, and received inferior government services. Those who moved into the Bedouin towns sought to increase the areas controlled by their group, and paid scant interest to the development of local employment opportunities. The agencies of the state were concerned with concentrating the Bedouin in the towns, but did little to develop local public services and even less to foster local trade and industry. As will be explained below, all this led to very high unemployment among the Bedouin.

Land Expropriation

In the 1940s the Negev was inhabited by some 75,000 partially settled Bedouin who had developed a differentiated economy in which nomadic pastoralism continued to play an important role. Most of the Bedouin were concentrated in the relatively fertile western Beersheva Plain, where they engaged in pastoralism and dry farming and worked in the numerous army camps in the region. Most of the farmland was owned by Bedouin tribesmen, who sold some of it to wealthy Gaza notables, to the Bedouin's "peasant" clients and sharecroppers, and to the Jewish National Fund, an arm of the Zionist Organization. The Bedouin's main crops were barley and wheat. Many cultivators built mud-brick storerooms for grain (*baika*). These also doubled as shelters in winter, such that the Bedouin could be viewed alternately as settled when they engaged in farming and as nomadic when they engaged in herding.

During the fighting that accompanied the establishment of Israel in 1948, most of the Bedouin were driven out or went into hiding. Some of them returned when the dust had settled, but most became refugees in the Gaza Strip, North Sinai, and the West Bank. The new state set up the Military Administration that moved the remaining Bedouin to two reservations in the Eastern Beersheva Plain and north of Beersheva. During the following years the army expelled more Bedouin such that the first Israeli national census in 1950 found only 11,000 Bedouin in the Negev. In 1950 the state declared all the Negev south of Beersheva as state land. This area of approximately 10 million dunams, nearly half the total area of Israel, included 1.2 million dunams (some 300,000 acres) owned and cultivated by individual Bedouin. Only Bedouin who had previously lived and owned land in the reservation maintained (tenuous) possession of their land, but even their rights were continually contested and challenged by the state. Bedouin households with no access to land, whether they had owned land in the past or not, were each leased 100–150 dunams (about 25–35 acres) of this newly acquired state land, enough to meet their subsistence requirements. This land was subject to annually renewable leases, and in the early years tenants were often moved around to prevent them from acquiring rights of tenure. The Military Administration strictly controlled the movements of Bedouin by a pass system; "movement permits" were issued only for short periods and specific purposes. The Bedouin thus had to rely on the resources available in the reservation, and inevitably became nomadic pastoralists and cultivators. Because they were not allowed to settle and to construct houses, they lived in black goat-hair tents. To an external observer, unaware of the heavy coercion involved, this could appear like an ideal Bedouin society.

This situation continued until the early 1960s, when the rapidly developing Israeli economy required ever-growing numbers of workers. The restrictions on the movement of Bedouin were gradually lifted and the Military Administration was finally abolished in 1966. The Bedouin gradually entered the wider economy not only because it offered higher incomes but also because the population in the reservation grew rapidly—it doubles about every fifteen years and now exceeds 130,000—while land became scarcer. The Bedouin entered many different occupations; they became factory and farm workers, builders, truck drivers and tractor operators, traders, artisans, and building contractors. They are now fully integrated—though on the lower rungs of the national economy. Yet many households continued to raise sheep, generally as one of several economic ventures, and some even owned large flocks of up to 500 heads. Occupationally the Bedouin had become urbanized, but only a few households moved to the towns. Instead, the members of each descent group settled on their own or on leased land to protect it against incursions from the authorities. Those who still owned land hoped that their physical presence, in addition to the regular cultivation of the land, would protect them against expropriation, whereas the landless Bedouin, the tenants of the state, were no longer being moved around and were gradually establishing a hold on the land. These Bedouin felt so secure that some of them manured their land and planted trees. Thus, some 150 hamlets sprang up that are spread evenly over the cultivated parts of the Bedouin reservation. The goat-hair tents in which the residents of these hamlets first lived gave way to the much cheaper wood or tin shacks. Gradually they built houses of cement blocks, but without foundations. The idea was to construct a fixed abode without antagonizing the authorities.

The authorities feared that if these hamlets became permanent they would prevent alternative land uses and, because they were widely scattered, would require expensive infrastructures and services. Therefore they decided to remove the whole Bedouin population from their land and settle them in towns. The Jewish towns in the Negev refused to even consider setting up Bedouin quarters, although Bedouin families trickled into Beersheva, Arad, and other towns. Therefore the authorities decided to set up a number of towns for Bedouin only. First they made a false start. In 1965, they built a series of concrete houses at Tel Sheva, near the mound of ancient Beersheva. The plots were minute and left the occupiers little room for extensions, storage space, or a garden. The land was to remain the property of the ILA, as was standard practice all over the country, and the Bedouin tenants were to receive renewable forty-nine-year leases. Furthermore, they were expected to sign away all claims to land owned in the past. The ILA hired a town planner (who "knew what was good for the Bedouin") who designed small, two-room houses, which emulated the customary division of the tent into a section for men and another for the family. But the Bedouin had enough experience with urban living not to want to live in such cramped conditions. The ILA did not consult with the Bedouin and took for granted that they would submit to its wishes. To facilitate this policy the authorities sought to curb the construction of permanent dwellings in the countryside. But the combined limitations were too much for the Bedouin to take. They did not trust the authorities, which in their experience had always sought to take away but not to yield up land. They did not buy the houses, even when the authorities offered valuable incentives, including one that was rather unusual, namely leases on farmland. The town became derelict and was not revived until the 1980s in the wake of the construction of other Bedouin towns.

Rahat

In the early 1970s the authorities came up with a new concept. They designated five sites for new Bedouin towns, in which they offered developed building plots of about one dunam (1,000 square meters) each. To make them attractive to the Bedouin, the authorities charged nominal prices, amounting at first to about 10 percent of the value of the land, gradually rising to 60 percent. Only Bedouin residents in the Negev were allowed to acquire these plots. Each plot owner had to commit to building a house within a year. Regulations as to size and style were kept to a minimum, but most Bedouin eventually constructed large homes. At this stage, the settlement scheme did not spill over into the land issue. Most Bedouin were still considered to have no title to any land. Therefore the new towns attracted buyers from among the landless Bedouin, who could thus improve their situation. Bedouin who still owned or had claims to land in the Negev held out hope of eventually regaining their land or at least obtaining fair compensation.

This plan was first applied in 1972 to an area sixteen kilometers north of Beersheva, which was densely settled by numerous Bedouin descent groups. Each group had built several clusters of semi-permanent dwellings on a hilltop overlooking its tract of land. For over a decade they had successfully resisted attempts by the ILA to move or dislodge them. On this issue the members of the descent group were firmly united. Now the authorities sought to regularize the situation and to prevent further expansion of the Bedouin by incorporating the various hamlets into the framework of a town. They offered Bedouin the incentive of building plots in freehold (*mulk*) for each household head and for each son over the age of twenty-one. This was a revolutionary step for the ILA, which had never voluntarily relinquished its hold over land. Under its regulations land could not even be leased to "non-Jews" (Lehn with Davis 1988, 186–91). For the first time since the establishment of Israel it allowed large tracts of state land to revert to freehold and, in this case, to non-Jews. This time the Bedouin were not asked to forgo their claims on land and property confiscated by the state in the past. The Bedouin now demanded that each descent group reside in a separate neighborhood so that strangers, including members of other Bedouin groups, could not see or molest their women. In this manner the members of a descent group sought to maintain effective control not only over a contiguous area with a large number of building sites but also over a reserve of land that would supply building plots for their children and grandchildren. The government's experts on "Bedouin mentality" considered these demands quite reasonable. They sought to overcome the Bedouin's "natural" resistance to settling by complying with their wishes.

The town planners appointed by the authorities took the situation on the ground as a starting point. They left all the existing hamlets in place but made provision for groups residing outside the boundaries to set up new quarters in the town. As a result, they designed a town quite unlike any other in Israel. Its main features were a circular inner road from which feeder roads led like the spokes of a wheel to each neighborhood. The neighborhoods were separated by stretches of wasteland and were not connected to one another by roads. At the hub of the wheel, public buildings and commercial premises were to be located (Kaplan and Amit 1979). The neighborhoods were parceled into building sites of about 1,000 square meters each. The plots were leveled so as to be ready for construction, and asphalt roads, electricity, water, and telephone lines were brought up to each plot. The authorities named the town Rahat (Hebrew for "trough"; they did not know that there was an Arabic word *raht* [leather loincloth]), which could be interpreted as an allusion to the pastoral antecedents of the inhabitants. The elected Municipal Council that has run the town since 1994 has not changed the Hebrew name. It depends too heavily on the ILA and the ministry of the interior to take a step that could be construed as insubordination or an outright expression of Palestinian national sentiments.[2]

The town grew rapidly, as far as residential development was concerned. The settlers built spacious, comfortable houses; even the smaller ones had a floor space of at least 150 square meters. The Bedouin viewed the houses as a good investment, perhaps due to the absence of alternative investment opportunities. Most houses stand on tall concrete pillars, which provide the owner with covered storage space and allow him, at any time, to construct a ground floor at minimal expense. Most houses are faced in stone and are surrounded by well-tended gardens with fruit trees and flowerbeds. Some Bedouin set up tents in the gardens that serve as cookhouses and are frequented in summer by old men and women who feel more comfortable in the open air. The main entrance of the house opens onto the largest room, the men's assembly room (*diwan*). It is furnished with a variety of armchairs and coffee tables, as well as mattresses. A side door gives access to the other rooms. Most of them, especially the bedrooms, contain wardrobes, plaited straw mats, and mattresses that are piled up during the day. Only young couples tend to sleep on beds (Jakubowska 1988, 143). Most kitchens are equipped with gas ovens, refrigerators and washing machines.

Each house is inhabited by one household, which often includes unmarried grown-up children of the head of the family, as well as elderly relatives. Extended families do not easily develop in a situation in which every male adult can acquire a valuable building site at a low price and must start construction almost immediately. But kinship and agnatic ties remain strong, for social control is facilitated by living in a neighborhood of agnates. Some descent groups have demonstrated their solidarity and their adherence to the spirit of Islam—and, through it, to the Arab world—by building their own neighborhood mosque. Each member subscribes according to his financial ability. The elders of the descent group tend to live near the entrance of the quarter, where they can watch and monitor the movements of members and visitors. While they have the leisure to take care of the interests of the neighborhood vis-à-vis the local authority, the pressure of local politics, often requiring sustained negotiations with a variety of authorities, is such that mostly younger men versed in Hebrew are elected to the Town Council.

The town provides little employment for its inhabitants. Only a handful of stores and workshops have been set up in private homes in some neighborhoods. In the first years, when a Jewish official assisted by an appointed Town Council ran the town, these entrepreneurs were prosecuted for infringing on the planning regulations. A modest shopping center was constructed near the town hall and the police station, right in the middle of town, but even now, thirty years later, little business is conducted there. The distance between the outlying neighborhoods and the center is so great, the variety of goods on sale so limited, and the prices so high that most inhabitants find it more convenient to do their shopping in Beersheva. Many men work regularly in and near the city, and make it their business to buy the provisions. They buy staples such as sugar, rice, and oil in bulk and truck them home, thus undermining the possibility of setting up well-stocked local food stores. Schools, nurseries, and dispensaries had to be constructed all over the town in order to provide services for children, the sick, and the elderly.

The physical layout turns the town into a dormitory suburb. The discriminatory practices of various state agencies—such as the small grants-in-aid by the ministry of the interior, the lack of funding for improvements in schools, and the long delays in the provision of roads, water, electricity, and public transportation—further reduce the opportunities for local employment. A handful of professionals, mainly doctors and teachers, as well as civil servants, are employed in the local branches of ministries and in the municipality. Most men are compelled to commute to workplaces in and around Beersheva. A survey commissioned by Rahat Municipality in 1997 found that 66 percent of men over eighteen and only 13 percent of women work outside the home. A full 64 percent of these men find work outside Rahat (Rahat Municipality 1997, 16–18) in construction, trucking, industry, agriculture, and services (Jakubowska 1992, 103). Such a clear-cut sexual division of labor is found wherever a high proportion of the working population engages in migrant labor: the women generally stay behind to take care of the children and the home while the men go out to work. Because of economic uncertainty people put their trust in children and produce large families. With a natural increase in the population of around

5 percent (Meir 1997, 109), many women of childbearing age are either pregnant or nursing for long periods of time. This situation results in an absolute rate of unemployment of 29 percent for men and 85 percent for women (Rahat Municipality 1997, 18). In my estimate, this is the highest rate of unemployment in the country.[3]

This condition has persisted since the founding of Rahat and is replicated in the other Bedouin towns. It is conducive to the growth of seemingly primordial beliefs about the nature of the genders, in which men are thought to be rational, hard, and strong, and women emotional, nurturing, and dependent (Abu-Rabia 2000, 85–86). Indeed, most women in Rahat, women whose contribution to the pastoral economy had been considerable, became housewives who relied on the income of their menfolk. This is not to imply that women are powerless. As most men work outside the town, women maintain and manipulate the family's network of social relations and control a great deal of vital information. As mothers, especially, they mediate between the diverging interests of husband and sons. The chief limitation of their power is the constant threat that the husband may find local employment, return home, and take over the reins.

More Bedouin Towns

Rahat has a population of 34,000 and is by far the largest Bedouin town in Israel. The number of inhabitants is expected to rise to 90,000 by 2020–25. Two additional towns were set up in the early 1980s in entirely different circumstances. Under the terms of the 1979 peace treaty with Egypt, Israel was to evacuate Sinai. The Israeli air bases in Sinai were to be relocated in the Negev, and one of them was to be constructed in the Eastern Beersheva Plain in an area inhabited by Bedouin. Most of the land still remaining in the Bedouin's possession was to be expropriated, and the 5,000 people living in the area were to be resettled in new Bedouin towns. But when Bedouin in another part of the Negev fought police and officials of the ILA who were trying to build a road on land that had been earmarked for a new Bedouin town, the authorities realized that the Bedouin would resist their removal. In order to avoid a violent confrontation with Arabs, so soon after the conclusion of a peace treaty, the government decided to settle the matter by negotiating with the Bedouin. It appointed a committee that negotiated an agreement with elected representatives of the Bedouin community. The agreement was approved by the government and ratified in a special law, commonly called the Peace Law of 1980 (Marx 1990).

The agreement marked a new departure in the state's relations with the Bedouin and, by implication, with the Palestinian Arabs. For the first time the state recognized the rights of the Bedouin to receive equitable compensation for expropriated land. As the legal issue of land ownership was still being debated in the courts, the state now treated the Bedouin "as if" they had such rights. The Bedouin entered the agreement on the assumption that it would set a new standard that would be applied retroactively to Bedouin whose land had been expropriated in the past and who had never been indemnified. One outcome of the agreement was that it immediately halved the area to be expropriated from 65,000 to 35,000 dunams (from 16,000 to 8,500 acres). No less important was the principle that all the transactions would be handled at market values. Thus, on one hand, the Bedouin would receive the full market value of their land and chattels and, on the other, would pay the full price of the building plots or irrigated land that the authorities would put at their disposal. This principle put an end to the coercive aspect of the resettlement project. Hitherto the government had paid only nominal sums for expropriated land, but also charged a nominal price for building plots in the new Bedouin towns. That arrangement had left the Bedouin no alternative but to move into the towns. Now they had the option to invest the compensation money in any manner they chose, even if in practice they knew that because the state owned 93 percent of the land, the value of privately owned land would rise faster than that of all other commodities. Every Bedouin to a man decided to put all his money into land.

The negotiated accord of 1980 between the state and the Bedouin offered a fair and workable solution to the seemingly intractable problem of Bedouin lands. It is likely to serve as a paradigm for negotiations with Negev Bedouin who have never been compensated for land sequestered by the state in the early years. It may even serve as a point of departure for a settlement with the Palestinian refugees in the framework of a comprehensive peace treaty between Palestine and Israel.

Two new towns were to be set up for the evacuees, 'Ar'ara and Ksefa. While the planners sought to apply the lessons learned in Rahat and to construct a more compact town with a commercial center and an industrial park, the Bedouin wished to retain as much land as possible. Therefore the new towns became almost identical to Rahat: they consisted of a series of widely dispersed neighborhoods, each inhabited by members of one descent group. Here, too, each family, and every man over the age of twenty-one, was entitled to acquire at least one developed building site. At first the negotiations proceeded to the satisfaction of the Bedouin. About 150 households received compensation, and the towns developed by leaps and bounds. But once the Bedouin had vacated the land the authorities lost interest and the negotiations slowed down. Some Bedouin are still negotiating with the authorities, while others have given up hope or are waiting for better times and terms. While the population of Rahat is constantly rising, and even Tel-Sheva is growing, 'Ar'ara and Ksefa are developing only slowly. During the 1980s three more concentrations of Bedouin settlement were officially recognized as towns: Shqeib (Segev Shalom), Hura, and Laqiya. Today over 80,000 Bedouin, more than half the population, reside in seven new towns (see table 1).

In spite of the setbacks, both the Bedouin and the authorities consider the new towns a success story. Both parties believe that they have achieved major objectives. The ILA and some other agencies of the state claim that they vacated

Table 1
Bedouin Towns in the Negev, 2002

Name	Founded	Inhabitants
Rahat	1972	34,100
Tel-Sheva	1965	11,200
'Ar'ara	1981	10,500
Ksefa	1982	7,900
Shqieb (Segev Shalom)	1984	5,300
Hura	1989	7,600
Laqiya	1990	6,100
Total		82,700

Source: *Statistical Yearbook of the Negev Bedouin* 2004, table II/1.

large areas in the Negev for alternative uses and concentrated the majority of the Bedouin in towns where they can pursue their own way of life. The authorities do not raise awkward questions, such as whether the Bedouin are receiving a fair share of state services or whether the structure of the towns prevents the Bedouin from contributing adequately to the national economy and to political life. The same attitude has prevailed with regard to the towns set up in the 1950s for new Jewish immigrants. Therefore, we must attribute the neglect of the Bedouin not simply to discrimination on ethnic grounds but rather to the fact that they still own some land that the state wants. Indeed, the state's efforts to establish its ownership over the rest of the remaining Bedouin areas continue unabated. The Bedouin Development Administration, affiliated with the ILA, was set up in 1980 and has attempted to move the 50,000 Bedouin living in 150 or so hamlets scattered in the Eastern Beersheva Plain to the existing towns. In order to put pressure on them, the Bedouin Development Administration holds back the provision of government services and infrastructure, like roads, water, electricity, public transportation, and telephones. The ministries of education and health do not fully go along with this policy, and run schools and health services for the Bedouin. The Bedouin have also been able to make up for some of the missing services; for example, the advent of cellular phones has eliminated the need for phone lines. Many Bedouin have acquired water tanks and mobile generators. They have organized an efficient and economically viable system of transportation for schoolchildren and workers. In 1999 the Bedouin Development Administration came up with an alternative plan that would allow the inhabitants of the hamlets to retain some of their land. It would construct two or three new government service centers, which would attract the population of the hamlets like a magnet. Eventually these would become the nuclei of additional Bedouin towns. The project is underpinned by an ideology that views the Bedouin who live in the hamlets as a "diaspora" (*pezurah*) that awaits ingathering. Because the project has ignored the Bedouin's concern with land ownership, its success is not assured.

The agencies of the state have never accepted the Bedouin's concern with the perennial issue of landownership, nor understood the "tribal organization" that defends their interests. Just as the descent groups allowed the Bedouin in the 1960s to maintain some control of their land under the repressive Military Administration, they now help them obtain more land in the new towns. The issue of land has remained dominant among the Bedouin and has caused them to put the interests of future generations above short-term economic advantages. This attitude has pervaded Bedouin thinking from the days of Tel-Sheva. Only the Bedouin's bargaining position has improved over the years. They believe that the towns have provided them with a secure base on the ground, one that is capable of growth and expansion and will yield building sites for their descendants. As the task of protecting land is unending, the continued survival of the descent group is assured. Therefore, the descent group as neighborhood organization also affects municipal politics. Whenever elections take place, the descent groups rise to the surface and submerge party political affiliations (Parizot 1999). Furthermore, the open plan of the town's neighborhoods with the intervening empty spaces gives every Bedouin the option of resuming pastoralism at any time. There are 218 households in the towns that maintain flocks (*Statistical Yearbook of the Negev Bedouin* 2004, table IV/11). Sheep pens are set up on the outskirts and the flocks are taken out to nearby pastures.

At present there appears to be no way to overcome the combined resistance of the Bedouin and the neighboring Jewish local authorities, with the connivance of the Bedouin Development Administration, to town development. The experience of the Rahat town planning team (in which I participated) is characteristic. The project to prepare a new town plan was initiated by Rahat Municipality and the planning division of the ministry of the interior in 1995 because of the rapid growth of the town population. There was no more land available for new inhabitants, because each of them was expected to acquire a one-dunam building plot. While the Bedouin Development Administration had raised the price of a plot to 60,000 NIS (New Israeli Shekel) (approximately $14,000), this was still only half the real cost of developing the land. As every Bedouin wished to benefit from the bargain, the demand for plots was insatiable. The municipality was therefore under pressure to use the town plan as a lever for obtaining additional land. The planning team, however, also had to consider the disastrous employment situation. It therefore suggested that an entirely new town be built to the south of the present town, with a business center, commercial and industrial areas, and densely built-up residential areas. The older part of the town (8,560 dunams) would then become a residential suburb of the new part of town. The ILA allocated another 10,940 dunams to the project, thus increasing the town area to 19,500 dunams, a 130 percent increase (M. Ravid 1999, 5). Yet the Rahat municipal councillors opposed the project, arguing that they would never be able to attract industry to the town and that the inhabitants had no desire to live in densely populated residential areas. They openly admitted that if they set up more residential quarters they would run out of building plots within ten years and demand more land. They received support from an unexpected quarter. On June 27, 1999, the mayor of Rahat and the head of the Bnei Shimon Regional Council signed an agreement to put the industrial park under the joint management of the Rahat Municipality, the Regional Council, and the new Jewish town of Lehavim. The Regional Council appointed a planning team for the industrial park, without waiting for the approval of its partners. A month later, while the planning team was putting the final touches on the Rahat town plan, the ministry of the interior's planning division informed it that the area designated for an industrial park had been taken out of the planning area and handed over to the neighboring Bnei Shimon Regional Council. As the implementation of the town plan is in the hands of the Rahat Municipality, it is very likely that the new areas allocated to the town will be distributed to descent groups for low-density residential housing. They will have won another battle over land, and lost another on employment. And the ILA will have given away still more land in pursuit of its major objective of taking over Bedouin land.

Notes

An earlier version of this chapter was published in 2002 (Marx 2000). I thank Moshe Ravid, head of the Rahat town planning team, for four years of fruitful collaboration. I am grateful for the very useful comments of Dawn Chatty, Ann Gardner, Avinoam Meir, and Moshe Ravid.

1. There are a few exceptions, such as the Oman government's attempt to revive pastoralism (Chatty 1996).
2. The other six Bedouin towns retained their Arabic names. Only one of them, Shqeib, also received a Hebrew name, Segev Shalom.
3. Only the Ethiopian Jewish immigrants have such high rates of unemployment. A 1999 survey by the Brookdale Institute found that 68 percent of men and 90 percent of women were unemployed (quoted in Isaacs-Elazari 1999, 58). The severity of the situation is not reflected in the official statistics, which count only the number of persons registered at the Labor Exchange.

V

Israeli Jewishness

The diversity emphasized in parts 1–4 leads to an overarching question: what Jewish identities have emerged in the context of an Israeli national state? The numerous cultural responses to this question were initially shaped by two main factors. One was the deep divide between secular and religiously observant ways of life that characterized Jews in Mandate Palestine and was formalized in orthodox governmental institutions after Israel was established. The second was the mass immigration of Jews from Middle Eastern countries whose styles of Jewish belief and practice differed both among themselves and from European versions of Judaism known to most of the old-timers. Israeli society is now marked by the dominance of various forms of orthodoxy in league with the state. Each possesses thriving systems of education and social welfare that are safeguarded by political parties. The different styles of orthodoxy reflect specific historical experiences that shaped Jewish life in Europe and the Middle East, which have been adapted to the exigencies of Israeli life. The Conservative and Reform streams of Judaism that are important in American Jewry are represented by small groups that receive almost no support from the state and struggle for legitimization. Whatever the background of Israeli Jews, it is abundantly clear that religious commitments did not dissolve in a "modern" secular state and that Jews of all backgrounds found ways of asserting their identities and contesting those with which they disagree. Thus many different specific expressions of Jewish life and identity have been forged. The chapters in this part reveal how Israeli and Jewish identities are constructed by the tension between the religious establishment and the man on the street, by innovative religious practices—often presented as a return to the sources—of both a personal and more public nature, and by meetings of Israelis abroad with Jews and non-Jews.

Henry Abramovitch provides an example from "daily life" about the highly charged tension between religious and secular definitions of Jewishness. He shows how a funeral becomes a "misleading" encounter between secular and religious Jews. Yoram Bilu and Yehuda Goodman provide an example of processes internal to the ultra-orthodox (*haredi*) world, showing how haredim manage cultural influences that penetrate their way of life from the outside world. Their chapter describes performances that use autistic children in an ultra-orthodox community to transmit otherworldly messages. Two contributions illustrate implications for Jewish life abroad that have emerged with the creation of an Israeli state and culture. André Levy, an Israeli anthropologist, explores the consequences of the existence of Israel for a depleted diaspora. The remaining Jewish community of Casablanca, Morocco, one of the few in the Muslim world that is available for a study, bears the scars of mass immigration to Israel and forges a new Jewish identity that carries echoes of the Israel-Palestinian conflict. Within a New York setting, Moshe Shokeid shows how new forms of Jewish identity are generated among Israelis abroad that draw on their Sephardi past and help them accommodate to a new and perplexing life situation.

Within Israel itself, Alex Weingrod discusses parallels between Jews from Morocco and European-derived Hasidim in the way they have expressed their socioreligious formations and concretized them in space. He compares the architecture of two buildings in Israel, erected with the aim of marking two distinguished religious dynasties: the tomb of the Baba Sali revered by North African Jews and the exact copy of the Lubavitcher Rebbe's home in Crown Heights, New York. Jews in Israel are able to influence and shape the public sphere to a degree that was usually not possible in their diaspora communities.

While historically, men have been the main public actors in Jewish life, ethnographic research has depicted both continuity and change in the religious activities of women in Israel. Rahel Wasserfall points to continuities and developments that have taken place among Israelis from Morocco in rituals of family life. She shows how the ritual bath (*mikveh*) taken by Jewish women after their menstrual period reconfirms both the Jewish and the female identity of members of this group. In the public sphere, new religious initiatives by women have become a source of struggle among various approaches to Judaism, as illustrated by Susan Starr Sered's chapter on women worshiping at the Western Wall of the temple site in Jerusalem. The contestation there weaves together new understandings of gender in relation to Judaism and the will of orthodoxy to maintain dominance in the religious life of the state.

24

The Jerusalem Funeral as a Microcosm of the "Mismeeting" between Religious and Secular Israelis

HENRY ABRAMOVITCH

Funeral: Text and Performance

The study of death rituals provides a key to understanding the core values of a society (Palgi and Abramovitch 1984). Confronting death forces each community to deal symbolically with the question: "What is the meaning of life, for us as a community, when faced with such loss?" In Madagascar, when I had conducted my previous fieldwork, the ancestors were in the center of social life. The most important life cycle event for each Malagasy occurs years after his biological death, at the second funeral during which their bones are removed from the earth and placed in coffins above ground. In a moving and joyous ceremony, the chief mourner asks that the soul of the deceased be received in the realm of the "Great Ancestors." The successful completion of this final rite of passage places an enormous economic burden on the living descendants. The ancestors, however, are conceptualized as the actual leaders of the corporate kin group and their impact may be felt in a wide variety of ways, through dreams, illness, prophesy, sacrifices, and spirit possession. As Roger Bastide has noted, the African community is a dialogue of the dead with the living.

In Israel, the customs and relationships connected with death are undergoing rapid and controversial changes. Burial, the sole form of disposal of the body, remained until recently a religious monopoly of orthodox Judaism establishment, under bureaucratic control of the ministry of religion and its affiliated religious councils or burial society (Hevra Kadisha). In the past, the Hevra Kadisha was an exclusive, voluntary society affording high social status. Their status has declined both in the religious community and even more so in the secular one. The dead themselves who as in Madagascar occupied an important role in social life are now increasingly left out and marginalized. In order to better understand the changing Israeli attitudes toward death and the internal dynamic between these ritual experts and their increasingly secular clients, I conducted field work as a participant-observer of a Jerusalem Hevra Kadisha. Before discussing the results of the fieldwork, I want to mention some dilemmas I encountered during the fieldwork, especially regarding the sense of entry into a stigmatized work identity.

Entering the Field

At the beginning my fieldwork with the Hevra Kadisha, when I asked for permission to participate in their activities, I was overtaken by sudden anxiety: "Would they accept me, a stranger, in their holy work?" To my surprise, I was accepted willingly and "with a blessing." The officers of the Hevra Kadisha were aware of the decline in their social image in Israeli society and were very interested in seeking ways to improve that image. They saw my work as a way of doing so and, as it were, of getting their side of the story across. I quickly learned how the members of this "holy brotherhood" suffered from stigmatized work identity, which clashed with how they wished to perceive themselves as doing the "highest form of loving-kindness," since the dead could never repay their kindness. In the past, I was told, one could join the Hevra Kadisha by invitation only, making it an exclusive club as well as a cornerstone of Jewish life. With the rise of secularization, there was a growing antagonism between religious and secular Jews, heightened by the sharp decline in the belief in an afterlife. What had been sacred and honorable had become a stigmatized and debased job. Secular critiques accused the Hevra Kadisha of making money from the dead. Some regular workers remained proud of their work and its traditions, but others would avoid admitting the exact nature of their work out of fear of social exclusion. I recall one man who actually worked only in the office and had no direct contact with corpses at all. When asked where he worked, he would reply mysteriously, "The last stop."

As a participant-observer in the Hevra Kadisha, I was present at many funerals. At first I was an observer, looking on from the side. Gradually I became one of the workers. I carried the body on the stretcher, I traveled in the van with the body, I carried the body to grave, and I helped with the burial itself. I then rushed back for the next funeral. Eventually, I even observed the purification rituals themselves. I went through a process of becoming one of them. In doing so, I violated a number of social taboos, doing things that others never do, things they prefer to leave to others and afterward despise those who do the "dirty work" for them. During funerals I often felt that I was violating my own sense of privacy and perhaps the privacy of the mourners, even though a funeral is in its essence a "public event." It was as though "acute grief" was not a subject that should be investigated. In time, as I was increasingly accepted by the Hevra Kadisha, these sentiments disappeared and I had a work routine. Acceptance by my fellow workers also allowed me to see "behind the scenes." For example, while riding in the van with the corpse, the fellows would recite Psalms, especially Psalm 91. Suddenly, the walkie-talkie came on in full volume calling: "hesed 3, hesed 3" ("hesed" is the term for "loving-kindness"). It was an absurd moment that combined piety and electronic technology. Following this interruption, the prayers often stopped and conversations, usually in Yiddish, turned to daily concerns. In this way, I could sense how the routinization of funerals for these ritual experts often detracted from the uniqueness of the event. For the family of mourners, the funeral is a one-time event; for the Hevra Kadisha, it was just another funeral.

In this chapter, I consider two distinct aspects of the Jewish funeral in Jerusalem. First, I present an anthropological/ethnographic description of the unique aspects of Jerusalem mortuary against the background of more general Jewish custom. In addition, symbolic aspects of the ritual are discussed in an attempt to reveal social and psychological functions of funeral ritual as part of the mourning process.

Second, I discuss the Jerusalem funeral as it is performed in practice. Specifically, I focus on the situation in which secular mourners (Israeli Jews from a nonreligious background) participate in the burial ceremony as part of the religious monopoly of rites of passage, such as weddings and funerals. As a result, nonreligious, non-observant secular Israeli Jews are forced to participate in an orthodox religious ceremony. Such an orthodox ceremony reflects basic values dissonant with those of secular Jews. Instead of reinforcing basic shared values and group cohesivenesss (Durkheim 1969; Huntington and Metcalf 1979), the funeral promotes dissension and dis-harmony. Indeed, the confrontation of values in the Jerusalem funeral may be seen as a microcosm of the "mismeeting" between the secular and orthodox Jewish communities in Israel as a whole.

I examine the funeral, in its ideal form, as a text for a central social-religious drama. Later, specific performances of the social drama are analyzed against the backdrop of the secular-religious conflict. Material for both sections was collected as part of a participant-observer study of the major Jerusalem burial society, which handles over half of all funerals in the Israeli capital and by far the majority of funerals for secular Jews. By presenting both sides of the religious-secular divide as faithfully as possible, I hope to clarify the position of each and show the basic points of their mismeeting.

The Religious-Secular Continuum

The terms "religious" (*dati*) and "secular" (*hiloni*) require some clarification. In practice, these polarized social categories reflect the contemporary folk classification of Israeli society. As in many other cases of conflict, be they religious, political, interethnic, or economic, there is a pervasive tendency to dichotomize social categories into in-group/out-group, with-us/against-us polarities. Such a split serves to reinforce rigid group boundaries and exclusive identity, feeding the cause of extremists on each side. The social reality is much more complex, resembling a continuum more than a dichotomy. There are ultra-orthodox individuals who hardly come into contact with nonreligious individuals and institutions. Likewise, there are atheist Israelites who have no contact with religiously minded Jews of any group, do not celebrate Jewish holidays, know little or nothing of Judaism, and even overtly refuse to participate in a religious burial ceremony. Both extremes, however, constitute tiny minorities. Most Israelis lie on a continuum of more religiously minded or more secularly minded. Many members of the Hevra Kadisha studied do reserve army service, albeit often in the burial unit. At least one has an advanced secular degree, though a majority studied primarily in religious educational settings. Most so-called secular Jews celebrate at least some religious holidays, in addition to the holidays of the Israeli civil religion. Many secular Jews have or had religious parents or grandparents who directly or indirectly influence their perceptions. A common occasion of mismeeting is the situation in which an observant parent is buried with full ritual to the dismay of the nonreligious children. Many secular Jews sit shivah (observe the seven-day mourning period) and observe the thirty-day commemoration (*shloshim*). Most observant Jews, the so-called knitted skullcap (*kipa sruga*) Jews, participate fully in mainstream secular Israeli society, with its mix of civil religion and Judaism. These individuals, while clearly in the religious camp, often have attitudes, opinions, and even behaviors similar to those of their nonreligious fellow citizens.

There are always individuals who defy the simple continuum, for example, an ordained orthodox rabbi who works for the secular Citizen's Rights Party, or secular Israelis who keep no rituals but following a death begin religious observance or, in extreme cases, become "born again" Jews (*hozrim betsuva*). Thus the dichotomy religious-secular, while reflecting a basic cleavage of Israeli society, hides at least as much as it reveals.

In terms of funeral behavior, individuals on the religious side of the continuum are more likely to understand and share the worldview of the burial society. As mourners, they are more likely to "know their parts" and to participate in the religious drama as it unfolds, without prompting. Individuals toward the nonreligious side are much less likely to comprehend or accept the orthodox worldview. They are more likely to be confused by the sequence of events and react angrily to the imposition of specific customs that offend their sense of a funeral aesthetic. Secular Jews are therefore less likely to agree with the ritual script that the burial society proposes. The struggle in extreme cases is often acute, precisely because funerals are occasions in which the basic group values of a community need to be reinforced. The polarized extremes have few if any values in common, and the funeral ceremony becomes the battleground over which a set of values will be reinforced, elaborated, and even celebrated. Death is a time when people need to feel they have an answer to the meaning of life, to feel there is a reason to continue living. The tragic mismeeting occurs when the values and answers of the burial society seem irrelevant to or antagonize their secular clients.

The Task of Funerals

Funerals, like other rites of passage, perform a number of simultaneous tasks in the social and psychological life of a community. In this section, I discuss the interrelationships between three of these tasks. For convenience, I shall refer to these three tasks as initiating mourning, providing social support, and ushering the soul of the dead into the afterlife. Each task refers primarily to one of the three main actors in the funeral drama, respectively, the chief mourners, the rest of the community, and the body and soul of the deceased.

Although ritual initiation of grief often begins long before the ritual disposal of the body, it is with the funeral that the initiating of grief is most pronounced. The survivors are confronted with the reality of the death and their loss. Their social status is typically altered or reduced. They are obliged to display signs of their grief, such as changes in diet, habits, clothing, ritual pollution, and so on. These changes help the mourners in contouring the grief process and ultimately allow them to successfully resolve the loss.

Funerals are also occasions that bring people together. The community gathers in support of the mourners and helps them in their ritual tasks. Like other ceremonies, these rites provide a renewed sense of togetherness and social solidarity at the very moment when the continuity and permanence of the social group is threatened by the loss of one of its members. Providing social support takes many forms. It might include comforting the mourners, feeding them, or just sitting together in silence. The comforting presence helps the mourners overcome the sense of aloneness that death almost inevitably brings and helps them complete the tasks of mourning.

The primary formal task of funerals, however, involves the dead, not the living. It is connected with the parallel obligation of appropriate disposal of the corpse while ushering the soul of the dead into the culturally conceived afterlife. This transition is often fraught with dangers and is in part dependent upon the behavior of the mourners. The successful navigation of this transition, however, reenacts a symbolic victory over the reality of death through reference to a sacred order that transcends everyday experience, which Geertz (1973a) has called a "religious perspective." Although the funeral usually only begins the process of ushering the soul into another realm, it does provide a collective sense that, even in death, there is a potential for continuity and even the regeneration of life.

These three tasks in the funeral process usually go hand in hand and indeed are interdependent. The mourners are supported by the entire community, who as a whole take solace in ushering the soul of the dead into the afterlife and the symbolic victory over death this provides. The fortunes of the mourners are in some complex manner linked to the successful transition of their relative who might return as a wandering ghost or an agent of misfortune if the transition fails. The dead man's soul is often in turn dependent upon the performance of specific rituals by his relatives and, occasionally, the community to complete this passage to the other world.

In describing the funeral process in these terms, I have emphasized their functional aspect. Circumstances might occur in which the tasks might clash in a dialectical process, in which the demands of one are temporarily set aside in favor of the needs of the other. In this study, I want to describe a somewhat anomalous case, in which I will argue that the demands of providing social support to the mourners are set aside, indeed negated, at a crucial moment in ushering the soul in his passage to the afterlife. Specifically, I shall discuss an aspect of the Jewish funeral in the holy city of Jerusalem.

Prior to the start of a father's funeral, all lineal descendants, literally "all those who have issues from his loins" (children and grandchildren), are forbidden to follow the funeral procession. In former times, when the body lay in state at home, these children were left behind and did not attend the funeral at all.

More recently, following the letter of the injunction not to follow their deceased father, children are sometimes permitted to walk in front of the procession, ahead of their father's body, and arrive at the graveside in advance of the rest of the funeral party. In either case, this injunction, known as *herem Yehoshua bin Nun* (Hebrew, "the ban of Joshua son of Nun"), serves to set off a man's children and grandchildren not only from his body but also from the rest of the community at the very time when these lineal mourners are presumably most in need of psychological and social support.

The Jerusalem Funeral and the Jewish Mourning Cycle

Before analyzing this custom of ritual exclusion, it is necessary to place it within the context of the Jerusalem funeral practice and the Jewish mourning cycle. In the course of this discussion, I shall restrict myself to orthodox Jewish custom, which follows the *Shulhan Aruch* and other standard codes of Jewish law. The contours of orthodox Jewish mortuary ritual are shared by most Jewish communities, although there is considerable heterogeneity in the details of burial and mourning. In Jerusalem, for example, during the British Mandate period in the 1930s, there were at least thirty-two different burial societies, and each Hevra Kadisha jealously guarded the specific traditions of its own religious practice.

In the 1950s their number was reduced, and today there are about twelve active burial societies. Most of these are geared toward an ethnically homogeneous immigrant group, for example, Persian Jews, North African Jews, or specific religious sects such as Hasidic Jews. The burial society in which I was a participant-observer is the sole nonsectarian organization and is used by Jerusalemites of diverse ethnic backgrounds, religious and secular Jews alike.

In practice, they are responsible for over half the funerals performed in Jerusalem.

Most Jewish communities oblige descendants, especially children, to escort their father to the grave. Indeed, the Hebrew word for funeral, *Levaya,* derives from the root *laveh,* "to accompany." All Jews are required by religious law (halakha) to follow the funeral cortege, at least a number of symbolic steps, even if they are simply passersby. This restriction on children in Jerusalem burial custom stands out all the more in contrast.

Orthodox Jewish funerals are simple, standard, and rapid affairs. Virtually the same service is performed for all. No great expense is necessary. In Israel, standard burial plots and burial garments are covered by social security, though one can buy a specific plot if one wishes, and the erection of a tombstone can be a considerable expense. In addition, some Jews specify in their will that they be buried in Jerusalem, and the transportation from overseas plus the obligatory purchase of a plot and tombstone can run as high as ten thousand dollars. However, most people are buried free of charge.

Ideally, a dead person should be buried as quickly as possible, preferable before nightfall of the same day. In many communities it is, however, acceptable to postpone the funeral to the following day or until the heirs and chief mourners arrive. In Jerusalem, the importance of immediate burial is greatly stressed because of the sanctity of the holy city. As a result, individuals are often buried within hours of their demise, even at night. Because burial is not permitted on Saturday, the Jewish Sabbath, funerals on Saturday night, after the Sabbath is over, are common.

The Jewish mourning cycle divides up mourning into four distinct and time-limited phases. From the moment a person learns of the death of an immediate relative (father, mother, brother, sister, child, or spouse) until burial, he is considered an *onen.* An *onen,* "one whose dead lies before him," is absolved of the fulfillment of all positive commandments. He is not required to pray or even answer greetings. His entire attention is absorbed by the obligation to make arrangements for the burial. After the funeral, the mourner becomes an *avel* (mourner) and begins the prescribed initial seven-day period of mourning, *shiva* (Hebrew, "seven"). During the first seven days, a mourner is forbidden to work, to wash, to have sexual intercourse, to study, to offer greetings, to wear freshly washed clothes, to cut his hair or beard, and to participate in any festivities. Usually he sits on the floor or on a low stool. He is not permitted to prepare his own food nor should he leave his house. It is customary for members of the community to visit and sit with the mourners during the shivah. The shivah period is typically ended by a visit to the grave of the deceased.

Some of the prohibitions of the shivah continue until the thirty-day *shloshim* (Hebrew "thirty"), for example, wearing new clothes or cutting hair or beard. The *shloshim* is usually celebrated by a visit to the grave and a large meal, called the feast of the thirtieth day (*seudat shloshim*). Except for parents, formal mourning is completed on the thirtieth day. Mourning for parents continues for twelve months. The anniversary of the death is likewise observed by a visit to the grave, recitation of prayers, and often a meal. The anniversary is observed in a like manner every year.

These four phases, or statuses, *onen, shiva, shloshim,* and, in the case of parents, the remaining eleven months of the year, make up the four divisions of the Jewish mourning cycle. For each of these divisions, there is culturally appropriate social support that relatives and friends are expected to offer. In addition, each phase is said to mark stages in the transition of the soul of the deceased in the other world; the fate of the soul and the cycle of mourning depend on the actions of the mourners, who pray, study, and give charity in honor and aid of the deceased. The cycle is completed when the soul reaches its place in Paradise and may act as a cultural resource and intercessory on the behalf of his relatives, especially his children.

Initiating Mourning

Rather than present a chronological sequence of Jewish Jerusalem funerary ritual, an account will be given in terms of three tasks of the funeral discussed previously. Unless noted, customs apply to Jewish funerals generally.

Upon learning of the death of an immediate relative, one is obliged to "rend one's garments." Although this obligation should be performed at the moment of learning of the death, standing, saying the phrase, "Blessed is the True Judge," in Jerusalem, and elsewhere, it is also formally incorporated into the funeral ritual. Thus, just prior to the beginning of the formal ritual prayers, the leader of the Hevra Kadisha cuts a garment, such as a shirt or scarf, with a razor, which the mourner continues to tear. The mourner is then instructed in the appropriate phrase. The tear is the first behavioral indication of loss and seems to symbolize the tearing of the psychosocial fabric of society. The tear is never meant to be fully repaired, evoking the sense that once a close relative dies, something in the inner world of the person is irrevocably torn and can never be fully mended.

It is also customary in Jerusalem to spill all standing water. The reasons for this are complicated, even contradictory: to avoid effects of ritual pollution, lest blood somehow enter the water supply, or to avert the Angel of Death. In any case, spilled water in a Jerusalem courtyard was a sign that a death had occurred. With the advent of indoor plumbing, this custom is infrequently observed.

Concerning the status of *onen,* Lamm has written, "Practically, then, the *onen* must make immediate and significant decisions based on the reality of death. Psychologically, however, he has not yet assimilated it or accepted it" (1969, 21). This initial phase corresponds to the stage of shock and disbelief, with a subtle psychological identification between the *onen* and his dead relative in that both are cut off from the demands and requirements of social and religious life. It is significant that at the funeral, which ends the status of *onen,* the mourner's main task is to say the Kaddish prayer and reaffirm his belief in God.

Traditionally, family members participate in a vigil over the corpse because a dead body ought not to be left alone. In Jerusalem, in most cases in which the funeral is delayed overnight, the body is refrigerated, and in many cases no vigil is conducted.

At the end of the ritual purification in Jerusalem, it is customary for the members of the burial society to invite the eldest son to place earth over the eyes of his parent. My informants told me that this is done because the eye is the organ of desire and envy, and needs, as it were, to be specially treated in order for it to accept its demise. The symbolism of "earth to earth, dust to dust" was also cited in this connection. For the son who places the earth over the eyes, this last direct encounter with the body dramatically brings home the reality of death. Although most communities outside Israel use some sort of coffin, traditional Jewish practice, which is still followed in Israel, rejects absolutely the use of closed coffins, and the deceased is dressed in seven burial garments enclosed by a winding sheet. These shrouds are often prepared by the deceased while still living, and in such cases, it is a family member who makes them available to the burial society. Moreover, the body wrapped in a plain white sheet, lying on a simple bier, is itself another poignant reminder of the fragility of human life.

In Jerusalem, the funeral begins when the leader breaks a bit of porcelain over the doorway and recites the Hebrew phrase from Psalm 124:7: "the snare is broken and we have escaped." My informants were not clear about the meaning of the phrase, whether it referred to the soul of the deceased (in which case it concerns the ushering of the soul into the afterlife), or whether it concerned the break between the world of the living and the realm of the dead. In any case, like the rending of garments, the metaphor of something broken is clear.

In the funeral service, the chief mourner's main task is to recite the Kaddish. Although the Kaddish is often referred to as the prayer for the dead, it literally means "sanctification," and its use is not limited to mortuary ritual but is a regular element in daily prayer. It contains no personal reference to the dead person. Rather, it is a public declaration of faith and an affirmation of divine sovereignty now and in the time to come. The text of the prayer, however, is mostly in Aramaic, a language incomprehensible to Israeli Hebrew speakers, and so it has some of the mystic flavor of an incantation.

From a dramatic point of view, the recitation of the Kaddish by the eldest son or other male relative is the high point in the funeral service. It is at this moment that great emotion is displayed by both the man reciting and the assembled crowd. Often the chief mourner has difficulty completing the prayer when he is overwhelmed by feeling. It is at this point that he must show publicly that he accepts the divine decree.

The structure of the prayer is a sort of ritual dialogue between the individual mourner, who recites the main text, and the assembled quorum, who respond "Amen" or "May His Name be blessed" in the appropriate places. The Kaddish highlights the interdependence of mourners, the community, and the dead. In

Jerusalem, the Kaddish is recited three times, once before the funeral, again when the body is placed in the funeral van, and again in a more elaborate version at the graveside after burial.

Social Support

Social support for the family of the deceased is provided by the Hevra Kadisha and by the community of relatives, friends, and neighbors. The Hevra Kadisha, literally a sacred society or holy fellowship, takes upon itself the work of preparing the dead for burial. Originally, it was a voluntary organization of high status and prestige in the community and only members of highest standing were invited to join in this highest form of loving-kindness (*gemilut hesed shel emet*). However, with the bureaucratization of mortuary care and the increase in the number of daily funerals, the status of the individuals who work full-time in the Hevra Kadisha has declined, especially in the eyes of secular Israelis. This clash of values in the Jerusalem funeral between secular Israelis and religious Israelis is exacerbated because burial is a monopoly of the ministry of religion, which at the time of my fieldwork did not allow, except in kibbutzim, any secular funeral. Moreover, the black garb of most of the workers of the burial society and the routinization of this sacred activity have contributed to their stigmatized work identity.

From a religious point of view, however, the Hevra Kadisha performs a vital function. When a death occurs in a town, according to orthodox law, there must be an organized burial society to see to the needs of the deceased, then work and normal social life for those not immediately involved can continue. In addition, some authorities argue that once the Hevra Kadisha assumes responsibility for the care of the dead, the mourners are released from the constraints of the *aninut,* that is, the status of *onen*. The Hevra Kadisha brings the body home from the hospital, undertakes the ritual purification of the body, dresses the body in shrouds that they provide (except as stated above), and makes all the formal funeral arrangements. At the funeral, the leader performs *kri'a,* the rending of garments, breaks the shards, recites various prayers, and assists the chief mourner in reciting Kaddish, if necessary, while the rest of the members of the society make up a prayer quorum, if there are less than ten adult men. They also help carry the body and accompany it to the cemetery while reciting Psalms. At the grave, one of the members lays the body in the ground and assists in covering it with earth while the leader performs further prayers. As in many communities, in Jerusalem the mourners are given a pamphlet that explains most of the mourning customs and memorial prayers. In addition, a rabbi associated with the burial society visits the family during the shivah period.

As we shall see below, most of the activities of the burial society are for the purpose of honoring the dead (*kvod hamet*), but many of their actions provide practical help for the mourners, who would otherwise be obliged to carry out many of these duties themselves. Despite their loss in status and their stigma, the Hevra Kadisha act as ritual experts guiding the mourners through the funeral drama, coaching them in their roles, and reminding them of the religious commandments. It is the leader of the Hevra Kadisha who informs the children of the ban of Joshua son of Nun.

Members of the community provide a display of support at each step of the funeral. Their very presence reassures the mourners that they are not entirely alone. In cases where there are no mourners, the Hevra Kadisha performs the funeral.

During the formal prayers, community members surround the mourners and say the responses in Kaddish. Often they will carry the deceased, first to the funeral van and later from the van to the grave. At the grave, they follow the example of the leader of the Hevra Kadisha, shoveling earth into the grave, taking care not to pass the spade directly from hand to hand. Later, they will also place a stone over the covered grave, a custom common in Jerusalem and a number of other communities.

The nonmourners assume their ritual roles as comforters in the recessional from the grave. At the end of the graveside service, they form two lines, through which the mourners pass. As the mourners walk by, those present recite the formal words of comfort: "May the Lord comfort you among the other mourners of Zion and Jerusalem." Concerning this custom, Lamm has written, "The purpose of the recessional is to redirect our sympathies and concerns from the deceased to the mourners. It marks the transition from *aninut* to *avelut,* the new state of mourning which now commences. The theme changes from honoring of the dead to comforting the survivors" (1969, 66–67). Comforting the survivors is continued through visits to the shivah, bringing food, which serves to nurture the mourners, and participating in a special prayer quorum at the house of mourning.

Ushering the Soul of the Dead to the Afterlife

Hertz (1960) first discussed the parallels "between the state of the corpse, the fate of the soul and the ritual condition of the mourners." As we have observed, everything up to the funeral is done to honor the dead, and thereafter in support of the mourners. The fate of the soul, however, is bound up with the actions of the mourners but also with the decomposition of the body. Only at the end of the mourning cycle, when the body has decomposed to the bone, may the soul achieve its ultimate destination and be bound up in the "bundle of life" (*tsror hahayim*). Death merely initiates the ultimate process of separation of body and soul to their respective fates. This attitude is aptly summed up by the motto, written in large Hebrew letters above the funeral chapel of the Hevra Kadisha in which I did my study, that read, "The body returns to the earth whence it came, while the soul returns to Him who gave it."

Jewish custom forbids touching a dying man unnecessarily lest this hasten the departure of the soul. Ideally a prayer quorum of ten adult males should be present to attend him, to hear his confession, and to help him with his final prayers. If he is reluctant to make his confession (*vidui*), he is reminded, "Many have confessed and not died; many have died and not confessed." In one Jerusalem hospital, it was the custom for one God-fearing man to say the confession publicly with all the patients answering "Amen." If a person cannot speak aloud, he is permitted to say it in his heart.

After death, candles are lit, windows are opened, and the body is undressed. Covered by a top sheet, the body is later lowered to the floor so that the back is in contact with the floor. Thus begins the symbolic journey of the body toward the earth. Special care is taken so that the face is covered because one is forbidden to look into the eyes of the deceased. Usually mirrors and pictures are likewise covered.

The body should be watched at all times and Psalms recited during this vigil. Eating, drinking, blessings, or study are forbidden in the immediate presence of the corpse. These prohibitions are based on the notion that one must not "mock the poor," as the dead are called, in their impoverished ability to perform any religious commandments. It further seems to serve as a guard against the envy that the dead would thus feel toward the living.

The handling of the corpse is guided by three concepts of Jewish culture: the honor due to the dead (*kvod hamet*); the uncleanness of the dead, or ritual pollution of the corpse (*tum'at hamet*); and ritual purification of the dead (*taharat hamet*). The honor due to the dead, as discussed above, requires that the dead body be treated with appropriate respect. Common American mortuary practices, such as embalming, autopsy, wake, viewing the remains, and cremation are all forbidden because they are not in keeping with the notion of *kvod hamet*.

Rabbinic literature often compares the dead body with an invalid ritual object, such as a defective Torah scroll. Such a scroll is proscribed for ritual use, yet it must be handled with the care and respect of a valid one, in accordance with the holiness it once possessed. Likewise, a dead human body must be treated with respect. Like the dead body, any ritually defective material bearing the Divine Name must be buried or stored in a *geniza* (repository), and the Hevra Kadisha has set aside a plot of land in which such material is buried. Under certain circumstances, a Torah scroll will be given funeral honors.

Honor due to the dead requires that the corpse undergo ritual purification and, in Jerusalem, that it be buried according to the burial custom of the holy city. Alternative forms of disposal are unacceptable to orthodox Jewish law. Even the ashes of one burned to death must be buried. Likewise, a corpse ought not to be left overnight because it is not keeping with the honor due to the dead, the sanctity of Jerusalem, or the danger that an unclean spirit might enter the dead body. At the close of the graveside service, the leader, in the name of the Hevra Kadisha and all those assembled, addresses the spirit of the dead person. He says that if any fault was unintentionally committed, it was performed "in his honor according to the custom of Jerusalem." He goes on to ask forgiveness from the dead person and absolves him of membership in any association of which he might have been a part. Stripped of his social roles and any grudge toward the living, the soul is free to make his journey toward the world to come.

Jewish beliefs concerning purity and pollution are exceedingly complex and intricate. For the purposes of this essay, it is important to note that human corpses are a major source—and, in some senses, are considered the archetypal source—of pollution (*avi avot hatumah,* literally, "the father of fathers of uncleanness"), that is, the primal category of pollution. Corpse pollution transmits uncleanness not only to anything that comes in direct contact with it but even through the shadow of a building in which the corpse lies. Moreover, any person or object polluted in these ways becomes a carrier of the ritual pollution. For example, a man might become ritually unclean if he touches a vessel that has lain in the shadow of a house in which someone has died. The earth is the only object that does not receive nor transmit corpse pollution, and once the corpse is buried it is no longer subject to the laws of uncleanness.

Prior to burial the corpse must undergo ritual purification (*taharat hamet*). The purification process is divided into two parts: the physical cleansing of the body and the actual ritual of purification. It is a fixed rule that men wash men and women wash women, in keeping with the "honor due to the dead." My informants did mention one unusual case in which no woman was available in the Hevra Kadisha to perform the cleansing and purification. In this case, a man was blindfolded and participated in the ritual cleansing. It is important that the members of the Hevra Kadisha themselves undergo daily ritual immersion to remove the source of corpse uncleanness and restore themselves to a state of purity and hence be in a ritually pure state during the act of purification of the dead body.

Before beginning the purification procedure, the senior member of the company leads a prayer for mercy and forgiveness on behalf of the deceased. The physical cleansing of the body commences following right-left, sacred-profane dichotomies first noted by Hertz (1960). The head, neck, and right side of the body are washed to the accompaniment of special prayers for each body part. The left side is treated without any benediction. The body is then turned over and once again the right side is washed, with prayers, the left silently. Finally the body is placed on its left side and the anal cavity is cleansed by enemas until the water comes out clean without any smell. The anus is then sealed with a wad of cloth. This "internal purification" (*tahara pnimit*) is peculiar to the burial custom of Jerusalem, but it is not performed in the case of infectious diseases, or upon doctor's orders, or in the presence of blood, such as after an operation. If at any time the presence of blood is detected, the internal purification procedure is stopped. Indeed, any individual "whose blood is upon him" such as in violent death receives no purification, external or internal. Such individuals are often buried in their bloodied garments because blood in equated with life (compare Gen. 9:5).

In many communities, care is taken to trim fingernails. In Jerusalem, however, all the dirt under fingernails and toenails is removed so that no direct barrier can be said to come between the body and the waters of purification.

After the physical cleansing is complete, the body is immersed in a ritual bath (*mikveh*), if available. If no *mikveh* is available, or when it is used only for the highest-status individuals, the corpse is raised to an upright position and about twenty liters (the so-called 9 *kavim*) are poured over it. The corpse is then declared pure by the threefold repetition of the Hebrew word *tahor* (pure). At this point, the corpse is in an inner state of purity, while continuing to radiate corpse pollution.

The shrouds are made of plain white material, flax or cotton, and should be hand sewn. In many communities, a man's *kittel*, a long white garment used for his wedding, for the Day of Atonement, and for Passover festivities, is used. There are seven standard burial garments. They are put on in the following order: a square head covering, a loincloth, pants without openings for the feet, a tunic, (or *kittel*), a long thin triangular eye cover, a hood, and the winding sheet. During the dressing, the eldest son is invited in to place earth over the eyes. Three external knots are tied to keep the arms and legs together during transit to the grave and are only untied when the body is placed in the grave, so that the person leaves the world as he entered, "without ties."

A large prayer shawl is placed over a male body; a *parochet* or Torah curtain is used for females, once again highlighting the equivalence of Torah and human body. The body is then placed on a bier and carried across the hall from the purification chamber to a small chapel where candles are lit and the family may gather for a prayer vigil and a last, intimate farewell.

The ban of Joshua son of Nun is announced to the children just prior to the funeral proper. None of my informants could give an explanation for the ban or even whether this Joshua is the same man as the one described in the Bible. It is possible that the name is meant to give the relatively recent practice an aura of antiquity. Scholars (Tuchinski 1948; Scholem 1965b) assert that the ban is probably no more than 250 years old. All those who have issued from his loins are informed that according to the "custom of Jerusalem" (*minhag yerushalayim*) they are prohibited from following their father to the gravesite. The ban applies to both sons and daughters, grandsons and granddaughters, of deceased men, not of deceased women. Formerly, when the body was taken from the home of the deceased, the children would recite the traditional prayers at the doorstep of the house. They would remain behind while the funeral procession continued in stages to the cemetery.

Although the language of the injunction forbids actually following, it is permissible to walk in front of the father and arrive at the grave ahead of the rest of the funeral party. Many observant Jerusalemites elect to follow this practice, fulfilling the letter, if not the spirit, of the injunction. In contrast, secular Jews, unfamiliar with this practice, often react with anger and confusion. Many refuse to comply. I have heard reports in which the children were forcibly prevented from following in the procession, although I never witnessed such an altercation. On the contrary, the members of the burial society where I did the bulk of my observations stated that it is not their job to enforce the ban, which in any case was for the honor of the deceased father. As one man put it succinctly, "We are not policemen."

It must be emphasized that this ban on children is not only peculiar to Jerusalem, within Judaism, but apparently anomalous within the anthropological literature on mortuary ritual (Rosenblatt, Walsh, and Jackson 1976; Aries 1977; Huntington and Metcalf 1979; Humphreys and King 1981; Bloch and Parry 1982; Palgi and Abramovitch 1984).

Moreover, the custom seems to violate one of the cardinal functions of such rites of passage. Durkheim taught that one of the major functions of funerals is to bring together the survivors in an increased sense of social solidarity. "The foundation of mourning," he wrote, "is the impression of a loss which the group feels when it loses one of its closer relations with one another in associating all in the same emotional state and therefore in disengaging the sensation of comfort which compensates for the original loss." He concludes, "Since they weep together they hold to one another and the group is not weakened in spite of the blow which has fallen upon it" (Durkheim 1969, 401).

The ban of Joshua son of Nun sets off the children physically not only from their fathers but also from all other nonlineal relatives and the rest of the community, just at the very time when they are most in need of a reassuring sense of solidarity and emotional support.

The Flaw in Male Sexuality

In religious (halakhic) terms, burial marks the ritual transition from the deeply liminal status of "those whose dead lie before them" (*onen*), who are absolved of all positive religious commandments, to the social status of *avel* or mourner, who, sitting low on the ground, have a restricted but clearly defined social standing. For the children who do not follow their dead father, the passage from *onen* to *avel* is blurred. They do not actually witness the burial itself and therefore do not know precisely when the change of mourning status is effected.

How are we then to understand this ritual separation? One hint comes from the liturgy of the funeral itself. It begins with an extract from the *Ethics of the Fathers* (3:1).

> Akavia Ben Mehalalel used to say:
> Look upon three things and you shall not enter into sin: Whence have you come?
> Where are you destined to go?
> And before Whom you must stand in final judgment?

The answer to the initial ontological question, "Whence have you come?" is given in an undertone, sotto voce so that none of the assembled can actually hear what is being said. The whispered answer is "from a vile drop," that is, one's father's semen; and the text is not spoken aloud out of respect for the children of the dead man.

The great student of Jewish mysticism Gershon Scholem has discussed the background to this peculiar doctrine.

> To the Kabbalists, the union between man and woman, within its holy limits, was a venerable mystery, as one may judge from the fact that the most classical and widely circulated Kabbalistic definition of mystical meditation is to be found in a treatise about sexual union in marriage. Abuse of man's generative powers was held to be a destructive act, through which not the holy, but the "other side," obtains progeny. An extreme cult of purity led to the view that every act of impurity whether conscious or unconscious, engenders demons. (1965b, 155)

Spilling one's seed even in a nocturnal emission constituted a terrible flaw in the nature of masculine sexuality. Such wasteful ejaculation was considered worse than murder, creating irreparable damage to the "upper spheres" and, moreover, an act not amenable to repentance (Zohar 62a; Green 1981, 56; Benayahu 1983).

The flaw in masculine sexuality derives from the fact that a man's first sexual experience is a wet dream or nocturnal ejaculation. This dream experience was conceptualized by the Kabbalists as a sexual encounter with female demons, usually Lilith, Adam's first wife. Cohabitation with such demonic female spirits engenders the "semen demons" who are relegated to the spirit world but nevertheless seek to claim paternity from their erring father. It is noteworthy that Lilith, according to well-known Midrash, separated from Adam because she wished to engage in "forbidden" sexual intercourse. Since then Lilith, symbolizing the banished destructive feminine aspects, is conceived of as a threat to infants, newlyweds, and other liminal individuals because she is often in search of semen with which to construct bodies for her wandering spirit children.

Ejaculated semen engendered a sort of disembodied demon, ever seeking to incarnate. Unless prevented from doing so, these "spirits of harm that come from man" would appear at their father's funeral. Their appearance was not only out of keeping with the honor due to the dead, but worse, these "semen demons" might dispute or demand their share of the father's inheritance or harm the more legitimate heirs. To prevent this, a series of antidemonic rites were devised to guard against these illegitimate demon children.

One of these devices was a strange "dance of death" that is still performed by request in Jerusalem for men of high standing.

> Before the body was lowered into the grave, ten men danced round it in a circle, reciting a Psalm which in Jewish tradition has generally been regarded as a defense against demons (Ps. 91), or another prayer. Then a stone was laid on the bier and the following verse (Gen. 25:6) recited: "But onto the sons of the concubines, which Abraham had, Abraham gave gifts, and sent them away." This strange dance of death was repeated seven times. The rite, which in modern times has been unintelligible to most of the participants, has to do with kabbalistic conceptions about sexual life and the sanctity of the human seed. (Scholem 1965b, 154)

Many diverse cultures express the mysterious connection between sexuality and death in mortuary ritual (Bachofen 1967; Bloch and Parry 1982). In many cases, the victory over death or transformation into rebirth "is symbolically achieved by a victory over female sexuality and the world of women who are made to bear the ultimate responsibility for the negative aspects of death" (Bloch and Parry 1982, 22). The dangers of the female might be implicit in Jerusalem rite because formerly, in many cases, women did not accompany the corpse to the grave or even attend the funeral at all. What is unusual in the custom of Jerusalem is the focus on masculine sexuality as "dangerous and destructive" when separated from the sanctified fertilizing act of procreation. It is precisely this disembodied masculinity that endangers the funeral process.

The sixteenth-century Kabbalist Abraham Sabba, according to Scholem, was the first to formulate the funeral link between father and his spirit children. He poignantly describes the final meeting: "For all those spirits that have built their bodies from a drop of his seed regard him as their father. And so, especially on the day of his burial, he must suffer punishment; for while he is being carried to the grave, they swarm around him like bees, crying: "you are our father," and they complain and lament behind the bier, because they have lost their home and are now being tormented along with other demons which hover (bodiless) in the air" (1965b, 155).

To prevent such a tormenting a pathetic scene, various antidemonic tactics were contrived. The most potent was a sort of sympathetic magic. The presence of a man's biological offspring seemingly allows the "semen children" to attend the funeral as well. By banning one set of heirs, the absence of the other is assured.

This explanation is the one my informants gave me and continue to give bereaved children just prior to the funeral. As in other cultures (Bloch and Parry 1982), there is a folk explanation that parallels the official esoteric account. I heard this explanation mostly from women. They claimed that all children are prohibited from following a father's bier because a man is never sure whether his children are truly his own biological offspring. The ban acts to prevent the public disgrace of a bastard being included in the funeral procession, even if the father is not aware that a child is from another's seed. What is interesting is that the folk explanation and the official explanation deal with the same issue, namely, the exclusion if illegitimate offspring. Whereas the official version focuses on illegitimate beings in the spirit realm, the folk version is concerned with illegitimate children in the flesh. Both versions agree that there is no need for a similar ban in the case of mothers, who are in all cases sure about the maternity of their progeny in a way that no father can be confident about his paternity.

There is at least one matrilineal society, the Fante of West Africa, in which the children, who have no share in their father's inheritance, are set apart during the funeral procession. The children, who provide only the coffin and no other funeral expense, walk in front while the rest of the relatives follow (Chukwukere 1981). Unlike the Jerusalem case, Fante children are obliged to walk in front of the coffin and certainly to attend the funeral rite. Chukwukere convincingly argues that their position within the procession reflects their peculiar status within their father's family and the more general male-female dichotomy in which a man's children belong not to his own but to his wife's lineage. Similarly, Goody (1962, 1976a) has shown how peculiar customs might reflect changing conflicts concerning family and inheritance.

Separation of Body and Soul

Kabbalistic views of death emphasize the separation of the soul from the body. One tradition, for example, described how the soul leaves the body organ by organ and continues to wander from the grave to the home of the deceased in the initial period following death. Moreover, the separation of the body from the soul was said to parallel the original fusion at the moment of conception. My informants stated that the soul could hear everything said in the presence of the corpse at least until burial. Indeed, the graveside service is only complete when forgiveness is asked of the dead man, as well as absolving him from any lingering obligation. The soul in its wanderings from house to grave is said to be "mourning" over its body, and the link is only finally severed with the decomposition of the flesh, whose duration is said to equal the period in which the soul undergoes punishment for his sins. In the rocky soil of Jerusalem, certain plots are favored for their alleged capability to hasten decomposition. In this way, as in many cultures, the fate of the body to a large extent parallels the fate of the soul in the afterlife.

Death, however, places both body and soul in a vulnerable position. Some texts (Trachtenberg 1974) pictured the dying man surrounded by evil spirits waiting to pounce. Demon spirits were thought to try to gain possession of the corpse in the period between death and burial. This danger is expressed in the phrase, "The body is like a house and the soul its inhabitant; when the tenant leaves the house there is no one to look after it" (quoted in Trachtenberg 1974, 47). Numerous aspects of Jewish mortuary ritual were designed to guard against such demon attacks. The vigil, the sealing of orifices, rapid burial before nightfall—a time given over to unclean spirits—were all designed to protect the body against such evil influences. In Jerusalem, right-left dichotomies during ritual washing/purification and the recitation of antidemonic chants, for example, Psalm 91, were added for additional protection against the dangers of the liminal phase. Only with burial did the danger of demons cease because it was well-known that demons have no power under the earth (Tuchinski 1948; Benayahu 1983).

Funeral ritual everywhere enacts a symbolic victory over death. Often, achieving a collective sense of symbolic immortality (Lifton 1979) requires overcoming the biological material nature of man (Bloch 1982). In Jewish funerals, this physical aspect of man is usually represented by the "stinking corpse," the archetypal source of ritual pollution. The material aspect of the person, in this case the physical body, must be cast aside in order to release the crucial nonphysical essence, which then begins its journey to Paradise in the afterlife. In Jerusalem, this physicality takes on an additional presence, in the form of the felt presence of a man's ejaculations that come to haunt him and his children in the cultural entity of spirit or demon offspring.

The Kabbalists focused on spilt semen as the epitome of the antireproductive act, which threatened the triumph over the physical nature of man and hence the funeral process itself. In this process, the image of these semen demons became an "image of ultimate horror" (Lifton 1979), that is, a collective image of extinction.

This image crystallized the fear that a man will leave behind him not children and children's children but only a vile drop. This spilling of the seed is considered an expression of the anti-life forces, which work against the symbolic continuity of father and son. The danger represented by these symbols of disembodied masculinity threatens the very principle of biological continuity represented by lineal descendants, and indeed the very symbolic victory over death.

Funerals, we have argued, initiate mourning, provide social support, and usher the soul of the deceased into the world to come. In normal circumstances, these three functions go hand in hand, mutually reinforcing each other, as in the Jewish funeral outside Jerusalem. In Jerusalem, the special cult of purity and Kabbalistic concerns over the sacred nature of procreation led to a series of ritual innovations in which the demands of social support were momentarily set aside in favor of the special needs of helping the spirit of the deceased make the dangerous transition to the world to come. Because of the flaw in masculine sexuality, which conceived of a man as inevitably the father of semen demons, the presence of any children would threaten the funeral process, especially the symbolic victory over death, sin, and the biological, material nature of man. The needs of the descendants for social support could thus be sacrificed in favor of ensuring magical protection for the soul of the deceased.

This anomalous case highlights how different cultures selectively use diverse aspects of the funeral process to mediate and modulate various dilemmas on its own cultural agenda. Indeed in the Jerusalem case, the usual rhythm of initiating mourning, followed by ushering the soul to the world to come, and then providing social support is maintained. It is precisely at the transition point between ushering the soul and providing social support that the two clash. Once the man is buried, however, as in all Jewish practices, the nonmourners make condolence visits to the house of mourning.

The custom emphasizes the latent role of sexuality and fertility in funerals even when it is not overt in the ritual. As Maurice Bloch (1982) has argued, societies with traditional authority based on a timeless ancestral realm have difficulty with temporal, unpredictable events like birth and death, which seem to violate the realm of eternity. Such societies, he claims, tend to bifurcate their relation to the body and soul of the deceased, identifying the corpse with dirty pollution, something to be thrown away, as the spirit ascends to the ancestral realm, which is associated with the eternal values. Bloch gives examples from the Merina society of Madagascar, which has a second funeral in which the bones are removed from the earth and placed in communal ancestral tombs.

His argument, however, seems to apply to the Jerusalem material as well, which is likewise a religious system based on a purported timeless ancestral realm of values. The corpse is considered archetypically polluting and, in that sense, needs to be thrown away to allow the soul to rise to Paradise. Unlike the Merina, in which the rotting corpse is identified exclusively with women and female values, Jerusalem Jewish custom adds to that dichotomy the male division between fruitful and barren sexuality, that is, between sacred sexual procreation and intercourse with demons in the form of seminal ejaculations. Just as the spirit must be separated from the body, so too must the demons be kept away from their father.

We have examined an anomalous funeral custom of Jerusalem, *herem Yehosua bin nun,* in which lineal descendants are prohibited from escorting their father to his grave. This practice effectively isolates these sets of mourners, just at the very time when it is expected they would most be in need of social support. The emic explanation concerns the Kabbalistic conception about the flaw in male sexuality. A father's seminal ejaculations engender disembodied half souls, or demons who would seek to claim paternity at the funeral unless all children were banned.

For the Kabbalists, the funeral initiates a process in which the body and soul of the father begin a process that leads to ultimate separation, the body returning to the earth and the soul to its Creator. Just as body and soul need to be separated, so too a man's biological children need to be distinguished from his unwanted spirit offspring. Whereas the former are vital symbols of continuity, the latter are considered threatening and disruptive. In a symbolic sense, these two sets of creations should not meet at the time when the separation of the father's body and soul begins.

From a functionalist point of view, the prohibition remains problematic. Nevertheless, one can discern in the structural contrast of sacred fertility with barren masturbatory sexuality and the difficulties inherent in the task of the funeral, namely, the symbolic victory of the spiritual over the material.

Religious Ceremony/Secular Mourners

Until now, I have presented the funeral dynamics from the perspective of the burial society and the religious establishment it represents. I have also tried to make sense, in symbolic anthropological terms, of some of the peculiar customs of the Jerusalem burial tradition.

The performance of the funeral, the actual versus the ideal, varies tremendously. I have seen beautifully evocative ceremonies "which not only do the work of burial, but also much of the work of mourning, creating a momentary sense of unity among the mourners, but also uniting all those gathered" (Abramovitch 1986). In particular, one is impressed with the person who enters the open grave to receive the corpse as it is passed down. He lays the corpse in the grave and undoes the last slipknots in the shroud, symbolically undoing the final ties between the dead and the living. Likewise, asking for forgiveness from the deceased is often a beautiful moment, indicating the reality of dialogue between living souls and dead ones. In describing such a funeral ritual American scholar Jacob Neusner has written, "Jerusalem's Hevra Kadisha is deserving of its name, 'the holy society.' Those beautiful Jews showed me more of what it means to be a Jew, of what Torah stands for, than all the books I ever read. They tended the corpse gently and reverently, yet did not pretend it was other than a corpse" (1974, 158).

Not all funerals are so successful. I have also witnessed embarrassing, disruptive burials. The initial dilemma concerns the asymmetry between the bereaved and the Hevra Kadisha. As in other professions, the emergency of the former is the routine of the latter. Individuals who participate in funerals on a daily basis do not always display a sense of empathy and concern concomitant with the mourners' unique feeling of loss. Indeed, for the members of the Hevra Kadisha the emphasis is on finishing the ceremony as quickly as possible, often in order to set the stage for the next funeral. As a result, corpses may even be buried before most of the bereaved are assembled. Even more disturbing, it is not unheard of for the driver of the funeral van to honk noisily just after the conclusion of the graveyard service to call the pallbearers to reassemble.

The handling of the corpse in practice does not always attain the ideal of reverence. I have seen corpses get wet in the rain, splattered with mud, and banged as they are placed in the grave. But perhaps the most astonishing thing is the simple fact of the corpse wrapped in shrouds lying on a bier. Coming from a North American background, I found the stark confrontation with the shrouded corpse to be the most striking and disturbing aspect of the funeral, far more disturbing than the collection of alms at the graveside, which many secular informants found exceedingly distasteful.

At the end of the graveside service, it is traditional to place a stone on the grave and to do so on the occasion of each visit to the tomb thereafter. The number of stones thus becomes an indication of postmortem popularity as well as an unobtrusive indicator to regular visitors to the grave that others have been there as well. The origin of the custom is obscure but probably derives from the use of rock cairns instead of gravestones in former times. Stone, however, is an appropriate symbol of permanence, highlighting the separation of the decaying body from the eternal soul. In contrast, many secular mourners bring flowers to the grave. To the orthodox, flowers are inappropriate not only as non-Jewish symbols but also because of their impermanence. Flowers that wither cannot symbolize the cultural values of eternity, union with the Creator, or the passage to everlasting life. The clash between the Hevra Kadisha and its secular clients is a conflict of differing basic enduring cultural values to be reaffirmed as part of the ritual process.

Many nonreligious Jews in Jerusalem are passively compliant with the guidelines of the Hevra Kadisha. This is not surprising because many disoriented individuals are glad of the structure the ritual provides, even allowing a culturally sanctioned regression to acts and attitudes belonging to their own childhood. Others, however, are deeply disturbed, even enraged, although part of their anger might be displacement of the anger felt concerning their loss. Some of the secular reaction must be seen as part of the resentment at encroaching religious control of social life. Religious monopoly on burial is seen as a case in point. In addition, the physical appearance of the members of the Hevra Kadisha makes them the target of epithets like "crows" or "vultures." Professional mortuary care, formerly a voluntary activity, is considered by nonreligious as a stigmatized occupation, in contrast to the traditional Jewish view in which it is the highest form of charity (*gmilut hesed shel emet*).

Most of the rituals done in accordance with the custom of Jerusalem are incomprehensible and often offensive to secular Israelis. It is also my feeling that many secular individuals are upset by the lack of any artistic contouring to the funeral proceedings. The absence of a coffin, the ban on lineal descendants, the rapidity of burial, the collection of charity, the frequent lack of solemnity, and even the placing of burial implements on tombstones go against their Westernized sensibilities. Secular mourners do not know their roles in the funeral drama. They need to be coached when to say Kaddish, where to stand, and when to pass through the lines of consolers, as well as on the details of observance of the shivah period in the seven days following burial. On the other hand, I have occasionally seen secular Jews perform a funeral within a funeral: after passing through the lines of consolers, the traditional exit from the cemetery, the individuals return to the grave for further orations, devotions, or tears. It is at this secular funeral, resembling the kibbutz funeral in some ways, that secular mourners and their friends are able to express some of the positive basic values of their culture and special relationship with the deceased, unfettered by halakhic restraints.

The basic clash between religious and secular cultures is one of worldview. Within the context of funerals, the orthodox perspective is personal, mystical, otherworldly, and concerned with the unseen. Their task in the funeral is to aid in the transition of the soul from the body to the status of ancestor dwelling with the Eternal in Paradise, reunited with the Creator. The funeral is also the occasion for the demise of the social person, as well as the end of the status of *onen* for his or her ritual mourners and their transition to the status of *avel*. The entire ritual is based on a profound belief in an afterlife under a Just Judge; that death can be retribution for sin; and as we have seen, that there is a hidden connection between death and male sexuality.

In contrast, most secular Israelis are uncomfortable with such eschatological notions of reward and punishment, afterlife and paradise, eternity and damnation. The soul of the deceased is not usually understood to continue a nonmaterial existence, except perhaps in the memories of loved ones. The burial is thus a marker of the transition from life to "nonlife." Those who ordinarily engage in such ritual are implicitly stigmatized and tainted by their regular contact with the dead in a way quite different from halakhic concerns with ritual impurity. Moreover, the Jerusalem funeral does not include any spontaneous personal expression of one's emotional relation to the deceased beyond the standard tears and eulogies. Such a personal relationship is one of the basic life values in secular society, and the development of the funeral within the funeral is therefore one attempt to reaffirm this basic cultural value.

If funerals are social occasions for reasserting basic life values, which address questions of ultimate meaning in the face of ultimate loss, then Jerusalem burials are indeed a flash point in the ongoing tensions between orthodox and secular Jews. Each group or ideology struggles to maintain its worldview as paramount. In the funeral, this struggle centers on the question, implicit in alternative worldviews, "Where are the dead?"

For the orthodox, the answer is clear, if mystic. The dead, separated from the body, return to the Creator where they may find response in Paradise. The main function of the funeral is to help the soul attain its proper position in the hereafter, a transition that is full of dangers.

For secular Israelis, the dead do not function as cultural resources, mediating between man and God. Hence, there is no need for prayer, charity, and good works to ensure that the soul completes his spiritual journey. Secular Jews come to the funeral mostly, I believe, to say good-bye, to mark the parting from life. There is a general concern for the peace of the deceased, but it is not tied to any specific ritual tasks, as it must be for the orthodox. Once the dead are buried they might not be forgotten, but in a metaphorical sense they are, indeed dead.

The Mismeeting

Martin Buber created the word *vergegnung* (mismeeting) to designate the failure of a real meeting between men. In his *Autobiographical Fragments* he discusses how he learned from a playmate, a girl several years older than he, that his mother would never return. He writes,

> We both leaned on the railing. I cannot remember that I spoke of my mother to my older comrade. But I still hear how the big girl said to me "No, she will never come back." I know that I remained silent, but also that I cherished no doubt of the truth of the spoken words. It remained fixed in me; from year to year it cleaved ever more to my heart, but after more than ten years I had begun to perceive it as something that concerned not only me, but all men. Later I once made up the word "Vergegnung"—"mismeeting" or "misencounter"—to designate the failure of a real meeting between men. When after another twenty years I again saw my mother, who had come from a distance to visit me, my wife and my children, I could not gaze into her still astonishingly beautiful eyes without hearing from somewhere the word "Vergegnung" as a word spoken to me. I suspect that all I have learned about genuine meeting in the course of my life had its first origin in that hour on the balcony. (1971, 18)

Although Buber is discussing his parents' divorce, all experiences of loss and reunion are fraught with the danger of mismeeting. In this essay I use Buber's notion of "mismeeting" to discuss the failure of a real meeting in Jerusalem funerals, which in turn mirrors the broader social conflict between religious and secular Jews in Israel. The conflict becomes more acute when those in charge of running the funeral, members of the Hevra Kadisha, who are exclusively orthodox, if not ultra-orthodox, religious Jews, serve fully secular Jews who do not share the worldview of the religious community and indeed are actively hostile to it. The service relationship common in American funeral homes in which the mortician seeks to accommodate or ingratiate himself with the client mourners does not exist. The Hevra Kadisha is a charitable, honorary voluntary association, formerly of very high social status. Its allegiance to the precepts and values of its religious community involve religious concepts of the "honor due the dead" (*kvod hamet*), ritual purification of the deceased (*taharat hamet*), and the sanctified local burial custom, known as "the tradition of Jerusalem" (*minhag Yerushalayim*). Everything up to the actual burial is done to honor the dead; afterward it is the mourners who might take precedence. From a dramaturgical point of view, the religious members of the burial society perform the funeral to assist in the final separation of body from soul so that the latter might begin the dangerous and difficult transition to the next world (*olam haba,* literally, the world to come). Most of the complicated and strange prayers and rituals are designed to further this mystical transition. The secular families of the deceased, who usually reject any notion of an afterlife, misperceive these rituals as an attempt by religious ritual experts/authorities to impose their will on secular outsiders. Far from seeing these actions as part of the honor due the dead, they see in many of the rites indignity and humiliation, which block their own spontaneous expression of grief and secular life values.

If many secular Israelis reject the religious text of the Jerusalem funeral, they are hard-pressed to replace it with a ceremony of their own. Secular Jews do not dwell on issues of death, transitoriness of human life, and the reification of transcendent values. In this way, they are at a great disadvantage in relation to the religious communities who have a tradition and ideology that addresses such issues in theory and praxis. In the one instance of the secular funeral, in kibbutzim, no established form of ceremony for funeral and burial has taken hold, in contrast to their success in many aspects of communal ritual life. Indeed, the very first kibbutz funerals were held in silence or inevitably fell back on variations of traditional Jewish custom. For a secular community, constellated only in polarity to the religious communities' attempt at domination, it is not clear what basic group values should be celebrated.

Unlike those who fall in the mid-range of the secular-religious continuum, for those near its secular pole, the funeral does not serve as a holding environment, containing the intense conflicting feeling to which death and loss inevitably give rise. As a result, angry feelings might be inappropriately vented toward the Hevra Kadisha in a way that interferes with the natural mourning process. Most secular Israelis do perform the shivah, at least in part, staying at home to receive condolence visits but not reciting shivah-appropriate prayers or sitting on low seats. Often the bitterness of the mismeeting within the funeral remains, however, leaving a lasting sense of grievance and mistrust. Such a sentiment is poetically expressed in a contemporary Greek funeral lament, which seems to express sadly the potential for mismeeting.

> Songs are just words. Those who are bitter
>   sing them
> They sing them to get rid of their bitterness
>   but the bitterness doesn't go away. (Danforth 1982, 146)

Within the contexts of such mismeeting and misperception (witness Franz Rosenzweig's bitter motto: "It is worse to be misperceived than to be mistreated"), there is a further struggle over the priority of the tasks of the funeral. While the members of the Hevra Kadisha formally do the work of initiating mourning, they are unable to provide much social support, especially because their main task is focused on ushering the soul into the afterlife. Secular Israelis, bereft of an afterlife, find much of the funeral ritual absurd. Many seek to avoid the ritual act of rending one's garment, the formal sign of mourning. Their feeling is, "I refuse to place myself under your moral authority" or, more simply, "You cannot tell me what to do." This struggle over moral authority and the transcendent group values is at the heart of the mismeeting between religious and secular Israelis.

25

"What Does the Soul Say?"

Metaphysical Uses of Facilitated Communication in the Jewish Ultra-Orthodox Community

YORAM BILU and YEHUDA C. GOODMAN

Introduction

The empirical question underlying this essay concerns the peculiar ways in which a set of techniques, originally designed to improve the communication skills of children suffering from pervasive developmental disorders, is used in the Jewish ultra-orthodox community to defend its boundaries and reassert its values.[1] The functional analysis that unfolds is informed by the following theoretical approaches.

First, the case study raises questions that highlight mental disorders (and other forms of deviance) as culturally constituted and historically situated (e.g., Gaines 1992; Kleinman 1988; Kleinman and Good 1985; Littlewood 1990). Students of mental disorders may note that profound mental retardation and pervasive developmental disorders such as autism are culturally malleable to a fairly limited extent given, indeed, the pervasiveness of "primary" biological and psychological malfunction. Taking account of the distinction between disease and illness (Kleinman 1980), however, we nevertheless would like to illustrate how, even in the case of a disturbance as encompassing as autism, the particular systems of local knowledge in which the malfunction is embedded might substantially reconstitute it. Of special interest to us is the process whereby, in a given historical moment, specific mental disorders (or other forms of deviance) are selected and transformed into highly ritualized and stylized performances in a dramatic morality play encapsulating core dilemmas and contested values of the community. Thus, without underestimating the biological bases and psychological meanings of mental aberrations, the question at issue here is how individuals suffering from specific forms of personal distress are culturally deployed in such a way as to articulate and encounter collective concerns emerging in a particular historical context (cf. Foucault 1973).

Second, focusing on the politics of deviance, we rely on a well-established sociological tradition originating in the work of Durkheim (1933, 1938), which highlights the functions of deviance for creating integration, cohesion, and solidarity (Ben-Yehuda 1985, 1990; Erikson 1966; Farrell and Swigert 1982). Specifically, we are interested in the construction of deviance as a rhetorical device and in the dialogical possibilities that this construction opens for reaffirming or changing the boundaries of symbolic-moral universes (Ben-Yehuda 1990; Berger and Luckmann 1966). Our focus is thus on the transactional process between center and periphery through which deviance is confronted, appropriated, and remade by powers representing (or aspiring to represent) the society's core values.

In depicting mental disorder as a vehicle for attaining sociocultural goals, we wish to emphasize, following Littlewood, that culture is also constituted "by mystification and control of people through limitations on access to different types of knowledge. . . . Diagnoses and illness experiences are . . . also interpretations, reinterpretations, co-options, concealments, repressions, transvalorizations and commentaries on social conditions and cultural hegemonies" (1990, 321; cf. Scheper-Hughes and Lock 1986; Frankenberg 1989). In the case under discussion, the system of local knowledge that informs the cultural construction of deviance, and the moral-symbolic universe that is consequently reaffirmed, are not biomedical but mystico-religious. As a result, the "commentaries on social conditions and cultural hegemonies" are recounted in the language of the otherworldly.

A third perspective pertinent to our analysis is that of globalization (Appadurai 1990; Hannerz 1989). The case under study demonstrates how even bounded cultural enclaves become partially enmeshed in the interactive systems that constitutes the modern world. At the same time, however, it serves to highlight the *selective* permeability of group boundaries in the age of global cultural flow. In Appadurai's terms, the commodity trafficking across the borders of the community under discussion refers to *technoscape* rather than to *ideoscape*. The fast (though not uncontested) adoption of augmentative communication aids by Jewish ultra-orthodox individuals and groups seems to support Appadurai's contention that "technology . . . now moves in high speeds across various kinds of previously impervious boundaries" (1990, 8). But this trafficking was not accompanied by a similar incorporation of the ideology and rationale underlying the original use of the techniques. Rather, an extensive process of "indigenization" (Hannerz 1989) could be noted through which the aids and the mental problems for which they were elicited were reframed and realigned in keeping with the community's hegemonic ideology.

The emphasis on interactive systems and communication networks in the globalization model resonates with the multiple levels of communication generated by the introduction of the procedures to the ultra-orthodox community. Ostensibly, the techniques are designed to improve the communication abilities of their users. But beyond that, they provide the means for the intriguing dialogue mentioned previously between moral agents of the social order and deviants at the margins of society as well as for an intergroup dialogue, with the secular world outside the community, and a metaphysical dialogue, with the afterworld "above" it.

The Controversy over Facilitated Communication

The set of procedures known as "facilitated communication" (FC) was developed in the 1970s by Australian educator Rosemary Crossley to train individuals with severe communication impairments in the use of augmentative communication aids. "To get the words out" (Crossley 1992), the facilitator provides continuous physical assistance to the handicapped person, helping him or her in pointing to pictures or letters on a communication board or in typing out messages on a computer keyboard (Schubert 1991). Sitting next to the handicapped person, the facilitator usually starts by holding the person's hand, isolating a finger for pointing or typing. Theoretically the method involves prompt fading by gradually moving the point of physical contact from the hand to the wrist, forearm, elbow, upper arm, and shoulder. But in practice, fading may or may not occur (Eberlin, Ibel, and Jacobson 1994). A critical aspect of the technique is that the intention of the movement is supposed to originate in the message sender: "The message receiver is making physical contact with the sender only to overcome psychoemotional and/or neurophysiological problems affecting success" (Prior and Cummins 1992, 332).

Crossley's work in the center she founded in Melbourne, known as Dignity through Education and Language (DEAL), portrayed FC as a revolutionary breakthrough in the treatment of severe cognitive and communication impairments and developmental disabilities, including autism and mental retardation. Using FC, many individuals who had previously shown extremely limited communication skills putatively reached normative or even superior levels of communicative performance. This astounding observation has led Crossley to a reconceptualization of autism and mental retardation as volitional motor control disorders (1992).

Douglas Biklen, a professor of special education who had visited the DEAL center and published an enthusiastic report about FC in the *Harvard Educational Review* (1990), became the apostle of the technique in North America. He founded the Facilitated Communication Institute at Syracuse University and initiated a series of qualitative observational studies of FC (Biklen and Schubert 1991). Through this ethnographic-style research program, insightful, creative, and humorous messages, reflecting rich inner life and advanced literacy, were putatively elicited from individuals hitherto viewed as extremely deficient in cognitive and communicative skills. Since autism is characterized by pervasive impairments in these areas, it is not surprising that the spread of applications of FC to individuals displaying autistic features "seems to have reached the status of minor epidemic" (Prior and Cummins 1992, 332). This "epidemic" was sustained by many desperately hopeful and committed parents and professionals seeking to give voice to the "silent wisdom" traditionally believed to be hidden within autistic children (Dillon, Fenlason, and Vogel 1994). It was further bolstered by the establishment of training workshops throughout the country that promoted the uncensored use of FC and by the hyperbolic presentation of FC in the media as a "miraculous" breakthrough in the treatment of autism and other developmental disabilities (Eberlin, Ibel, and Jacobson 1994; Prior and Cummins 1992; Bebko, Perry, and Bryson 1996).

The mounting popularity of FC was counterbalanced by a subsequent wave of controlled experimental studies that failed to replicate the positive effects attributed to the technique in naturally occurring contexts. Reviews of these studies have usually echoed the unequivocal conclusion reached by Eberlin et al.: "At the present time there has not been one scientifically valid confirmatory finding supporting the claims that FC produces independent client-generated communication" (1993, 528). Using effective modes of experimental control, many of the studies have demonstrated that the communicative outputs attributed to the handicapped persons were in fact produced by the facilitators, probably without intent or awareness (e.g., Bomba et al. 1996; Dillon, Fenlason, and Vogel 1994; Eberlin, Ibel, and Jacobson 1994; Montee, Miltenberger, and Wittrock 1995; Moore, Donovan, and Hudson 1993). To the critical eye, this ample documentation of "facilitator influence" has reduced FC to "unwitting ventriloquism" (Routh 1994).

The uniformly disenchanting conclusions of experimental research studies have stirred a heated controversy. Proponents of FC have attributed the experimentalists' failure to replicate the naturalistic findings to the impersonal and discouraging ambiance and intrusive design of most experimental studies that cast doubt upon the aid user's competence and the facilitator's credibility (e.g., Duchan 1993). Under these inauspicious circumstances, so markedly at odds with the humanistic, respectful, and optimistic assumptions ostensibly guiding facilitators in naturally occurring situations (see Mundi and Adreon 1994), the salutary effects of FC could not be materialized. The debate grew bitter when moral and ethical issues involved in the use of FC came to the fore. One noted example has been the salvo of allegations of physical and sexual abuse made through facilitation (Bligh and Kupperman 1993; Moore et al. 1993). A special issue of *Child Abuse and Neglect* (Jones 1994) was devoted to this subject.

One consequence of the ongoing controversy over FC has been the mushrooming of professional publications on the subject. As mentioned earlier, even though the procedure is not specifically designed for people with autism, a brief review of journals such as the *Journal of Autism and Developmental Disorder* and the *Journal of Pediatric Psychology* clearly shows that autism is the clinical category most thoroughly researched with regard to FC. Autistic children also loom high in the particular context of FC application to which we now turn.

Facilitated Communication in the Jewish Ultra-Orthodox Community

Since the beginning of 1995, a succession of reports in Israeli newspapers depicted the growing use of and subsequent controversy over FC in Jewish ultra-orthodox (*haredi*) circles.[2] Before discussing the form and meaning of the employment of FC in this particular cultural context, a brief discussion of the ultra-orthodox community is necessary.

In terms of religious commitment, Israeli Jews are distributed along a wide spectrum, from complete atheists to devout observants (Sobel and Beit-Hallahmi 1991). The sector designated ultra-orthodox, about 500,000 strong (8 percent of the population), is located at the most religious pole of the continuum. The members of this sector, clearly distinguished by their peculiar appearance (beards, earlocks, skullcaps, and sect-appropriate, old-fashioned dark uniforms for men; wigs or headdresses and modest clothes for women), are noted for their uncompromising adherence to the strictest version of halakha (Jewish religious law). As a result, the sacred becomes a "phenomenological constant" for them (Csordas 1985), regulating every aspect of their daily life.

Although unified by religious fundamentalism (Heilman and Friedman 1991; Marty and Appleby 1993), augmented by deliberate attempts to retain sociocultural life patterns as crystallized in the traditional Jewish communities of former centuries, the ultra-orthodox are far from constituting a monolithic bloc. In fact they are sharply divided into many sects and factions, marked by bitter struggles over political power, material rewards, and religious hegemony (Shilav and Friedman 1985). The historical watershed that separated enthusiastic, mystically oriented Hasidim and their rationalist adversaries (Mitnagdim) has been blurred in the twentieth century; but the two camps, and many of the parties within each of them (particularly on the Hasidic side), have preserved distinct religious sensibilities. Another historical rift, between Ashkenazi and Mizrahi or Sephardic Jews (of European versus Middle Eastern and North African backgrounds, respectively), has been strongly maintained among strictly religious Israeli Jews, as evidenced by the persistence and growth of ultra-orthodox political parties and educational systems in keeping with this ethnocultural division.

The various ultra-orthodox groups also differ in their attitudes toward the Zionist state, ranging from reserved acceptance to total condemnation of Israel as a political entity. The groups are united, however, in their unequivocal opposition to the secular lifestyle of mainstream Israeli society. Striving at all costs to insulate themselves from the polluting effects of modernization, they tend to concentrate in well-delineated neighborhoods. Most of the ultra-orthodox live in Jerusalem (over 100,000) and in Bnai Brak, an all-religious town near Tel-Aviv;

but today, because of population pressures and shortage in accommodations in these centers, *haredi* neighborhoods can be found in many urban settlements throughout the country.

Life in ultra-orthodox neighborhoods unfolds according to sociocultural codes so much at odds with those of the rest of society as to fashion a sharply distinct subculture that institutes (and is being instituted by) a social reality (Berger and Luckmann 1966) and a behavioral environment (Hallowell 1955) of their own. For those immersed in this subculture, the twin spiritual ideals to be relentlessly pursued are the strict fulfillment of all religious precepts and the study of Jewish sacred texts, especially the Babylonian Talmud, in religious academies (*yeshivot;* see Heilman 1983; Helmreich 1982). Women are expected to contribute to the second goal, limited to men only, by taking care of the household with its numerous children (as procreation is a cardinal commandment to be strictly pursued) and, if necessary, by becoming the breadwinner.

The puritan character of the family is manifested in an elaborate decorum of modesty and a strict separation of the sexes. This separation launches boys and girls into entirely different socialization orbits. Three-year-old male children are already engulfed in religious study, which will remain their main vocation for years to come, while the learning path of girls is geared toward more mundane (and lucrative) jobs. Female work, together with the community's well-established support system and state-sponsored subsidies, have all made the pursuit of open-ended religious study realizable for many young adults. Consequently, the ultra-orthodox community is becoming "a society of learners" (Friedman 1991). Outside the world of learning the most important institution for the ultra-orthodox man is the synagogue, where he prays three times a day. Of immense importance also are spiritual leaders of the community, always ordained rabbis, whose moral authority and advice are sought and accepted without challenge.

Despite their separatist ideology, the ultra-orthodox have not been self-sufficient enough to entertain a complete disengagement from the secular society within which they are uncomfortably situated (El-Or 1992; Friedman 1991). On the contrary, their growing empowerment has resulted in a stronger involvement in Israel's central political, economic, and social issues, and an increasing dependence on state resources. The outcome of these dialectics is a complex negotiation process with the secular world through which the community seeks to maintain and even fortify its boundaries but is also being subtly transformed (Ravitzky 1993). The drift of various ultra-orthodox groups toward the right end of the political spectrum in Israel is one of the more noticeable changes that the community has been undergoing in recent years.

The constant influx of *hozrim betshuva,* secular Jews embracing the religious way of life, into the ultra-orthodox community in the last thirty years (Aviad 1983; Beit-Hallahmi 1992) is another manifestation of the shifting boundaries between religious and secular worlds in Israel. On the one hand, the fact that many thousands of secular Israelis from all walks of life "saw the light" and joined the ultra-orthodox community contributed to the latter's growing self-confidence and proud assertion of its heritage and calling. On the other hand, the "returnees" (*hozrim*) have endowed their new ambiance with knowledge, sensibilities, and coping modes derived from the modern secular world.

If the extreme conservatism of the ultra-orthodox and their endless efforts to insulate themselves from mainstream secular society are taken as their overriding characterization, then the fact that in Israel the spread of FC was primarily associated with strictly observant individuals and groups[3] may appear quite puzzling. We seek to alleviate the puzzlement by pondering this phenomenon in the light of the complex negotiation process conducted between the two worlds. The stereotypical image of a community averting its gaze from the swarming activities and innovations in the secular world "out there" is no longer (and perhaps has never been) accurate. Rather, another dialectical process seems at work now: cultural products from the secular world, while still generally deemed pernicious and "polluting," may be borrowed and reshaped to strengthen the boundaries between the ultra-orthodox community and the rest of society (cf. Appadurai 1990).

As a matter of fact, orthodox Judaism is not intrinsically hostile to the introduction and distribution of novel educational or medical procedures, provided they do not infringe upon religious precepts or proscriptions (Preuss 1978). But this general orientation has been historically translated into a cautious and suspicious attitude toward innovations. Against this background, the entrepreneurial role of strictly observant individuals in promoting a recently introduced, controversial procedure such as FC and their readiness to examine to that end a large quantity of scientific data published in specialized professional journals, from which the ultra-orthodox are usually estranged, cannot be taken for granted. The acquaintance with popular television programs on FC that this promotion involved is particularly remarkable, given the pernicious image of television in the ultra-orthodox community and the general proscription to watch it. All this unusual reaching out and barrier crossing may suggest that FC is believed to hold a special promise for religious believers, beyond the ambitious goal of improving the communication skills of severely incapacitated individuals. The essence of this significance became crystal clear with the first media reports on FC in ultra-orthodox settings. The communication was geared toward otherworldly planes; the impaired children were perceived as mediums susceptible to supernormal agencies and able to impart knowledge derived from them.

According to Israeli religious newspapers, this esoteric use of FC had been cultivated in ultra-orthodox circles in the United States and was then imported to Israel. In the new surrounding it has been promoted by a collection of committed individuals and voluntary associations situated in Jerusalem and Bnai Brak, the two urban strongholds of Israeli ultra-orthodoxy. The individual advocates of the system, rabbis coming from a variety of orthodox backgrounds, have been primarily engaged in FC sessions conducted in private family settings. The voluntary associations, less inhibited in their eagerness to publicize the elicited communications, specialize in public displays of FC sessions in front of big audiences. In both settings the overwhelming majority of the message senders were impaired children coming from observant families. Likewise, most of the facilitators were women from strictly religious backgrounds. The sessions were run by the religious promoters who presented the questions to the children. Mystically oriented rabbis and religious activists seeking to bring secular Jews back to religion were particularly instrumental in promoting FC. A wide plethora of tools has been employed to document and distribute the communications extracted in private and public performances, to expound their meaning, and to amplify their reverberations. These tools include posters, articles in newspapers and periodicals, brochures, lectures, and even audiocassettes and videocassettes for rent and sale.

This propagation of "metaphysical FC" in the ultra-orthodox community was not left unanswered. A series of critical articles in religious newspapers, bearing titles such as "autism and charlatanism" or "autism without mysticism," have cautioned against the esoteric use of FC by mobilizing against it venerated rabbinical figures, as well as observant physicians, psychologists, and educators. Many of the arguments of the religious professionals resonated with the methodological caveats in the aforementioned scientific reviews of the phenomenon, while the rabbinical figures reacted to FC from the classic hyperconservative stance, claiming that any system of ideas or set of procedures not grounded in Jewish tradition should be shunned.[4] These critical voices, however, have not been successful in discrediting the phenomenon and in stopping its spread. We are even tempted to suggest that the heated controversy that followed the introduction of the system into the ultra-orthodox community may have contributed to its growing salience there. FC continues to thrive in religious circles, as autistic and other incapacitated children disclose through it messages from otherworldly planes. Before discussing the contents of these messages, the religious rationale underlying their use should be clarified.

The Theosophical Basis of Facilitated Communication

Judging from their publications, the religious promoters are well versed in the scientific literature on FC. But they promulgate it in a very selective way, focusing on the reported dramatic improvements in communication skills while seeking to minimize the wealth and weight of disproving data. In dealing with the alleged achievements of FC, the promoters confound scientific and religious discourses. The brochures and cassettes they distribute always start with detailed depictions of the professional history of the procedure. This introduction appears rigorous and sober-minded as it focuses on the empirical evidence that supports FC and on the professional experience and academic background of its proponents (Crossley and Biklen star in several publications). It may come as a surprise that in order to increase the credibility of FC effects, the promoters bask in the glory of research methods and academic affiliations pertaining to a scientific meaning system from which they are ordinarily quite alienated. But the reliance on scientific status symbols appears as part of a rhetorical scheme hiding specious reasoning, since it always ends with a narrative twist. In the last analysis, all the religious reports assert that the scientific-positivist paradigm, despite its enumerated achievements, fails to account for the entire gamut of FC effects. As phrased by one of the publications, "we are facing a phenomenon scientists have no idea how to cope with."

The shift from scientific to religious idioms is marked by reframing allegedly inexplicable FC effects as "miracles." These "miracles" include anecdotal reports on advanced literacy without prior exposure to reading and writing, fluent communication in foreign languages, elicitation of coherent messages without staring at the keyboard, communication during states of deep coma, absorbing written material and conducting complex calculations with enormous speed, and knowledge of Divine Truth. All these "miracles," except the last one, are elaborations on arguments raised by facilitators (and popularized by the media) without manifest reference to otherworldly reality and metaphysical entities. The religious promulgations capitalize on these extraordinary anecdotal reports, presenting them as rigorous scientific findings, only to expose the limitations and shortsightedness of the empirical perspective.

Two well-known talmudic references constitute the starting point for the ultra-orthodox exegesis of FC effects. The first one asserts that "since the Temple was destroyed, prophecy has been taken from prophets and given to fools and children."[5] In the second reference it is contended that an embryo in its mother's womb "looks and sees from one end of the world to the other."[6] This amazing farsightedness is correlated with no less amazing insight or introspection, as the embryo is also believed to master the entire corpus of the Holy Scriptures. A metaphorical reading of another phrase in this reference—"a light [literally candle] burns above its [the embryo's] head"—serves as a mediating link in accounting for these prodigal embryonic capacities. The candle stands for the soul, viewed as the godly element in human existence,[7] which, in the embryonic state, still enjoys a free-floating, extracorporeal position. As a divine spark unconstrained by material limitations, nothing physical or spiritual is beyond the pale of the soul. This blissful state is short-lived, however. From the moment of birth onward, the soul, encased in a limiting bodily habitat, is bereft of the prenatal spectacular faculties. According to a talmudic legend, the loss of these faculties is triggered by an angel who strikes each newborn on its mouth at the moment of parturition. This act may be viewed as the Jewish version of birth trauma.

Following the erasure of the prenatal Platonic traces of erudition and unobstructed vision, learning becomes strenuous and slow. The laborious process of secondary acquisition is mediated by the brain which, being a material organ, is more limiting than enabling. Cherished by science as the site of high mental processes, the generator of human intellect and creativity, the brain is pondered here as a confining device, a screen that distances humans from their divine source, the pure omniscient soul. The knowledge it can grasp, perforce constrained by human inherent fallibility, is but a small fraction of the endless primordial wisdom lost upon parturition.

This line of reasoning renders the prophetic powers of "fools and infants" comprehensible. The maimed bodies and injured brains of severely impaired persons, viewed in mundane life as the source of unending misery, constitute an asset from a mystical viewpoint since they allow them privileged access to their god-given soul. Dialectically, the more incapacitated the individual, as reflected in both physical and mental dysfunction, the more permeable the bodily screen that effectively separates "normal" people from their divine, supernormal source. This dialectical process is responsible for the "miraculous" performances of children suffering from autism, cerebral palsy, and severe mental retardation in FC sessions. From a mystico-religious perspective, the procedure is an effective tool for bypassing the afflicted body and making direct contact with the pure soul. Through this contact, extraordinary information from otherworldly spheres may be obtained which, as one of the brochures puts it, "enables us to get rid of any doubt regarding the foundations of our faith."

"What Does the Soul Say" in FC Sessions?

Cloaked in this metaphysical garment, FC-cum-séance provides a meeting ground for the transcendental and the mundane that is otherwise uncommon in Judaism. Kabbalists throughout the centuries have sought to induce themselves into ecstatic and contemplative states in which they could experience the presence of the divine (Idel 1988). But these experiences were typically private events, limited to mystical virtuosi, and highly ineffable. FC sessions, in contrast, often take place in public settings in front of a large audience, and their messages are lucid and easily conveyable. These messages, "the secrets of the soul," are disclosed by the impaired child with the facilitator's assistance in response to questions addressed by the rabbi in charge of the session.

The most compelling theme dealt with is divine providence. The children report that they are strongly aware of God's existence and, based on the experiences of their souls in the afterworld, are cognizant of his omnipresence and guidance. Having faith in God, loving and worshiping him, and following his will in learning and piety are depicted as the most important things in life. These objectives are not external prescriptions, difficult to accommodate, but reflections of human intrinsic motivation. The incapacitated children, stripped of the distorting constraints of base bodily desires, are able to articulate through facilitation the genuine wishes of their souls, thus providing evidence as to the innate spirituality of human nature.

Once God's immanence (in the world as well as in humans) has been established, it is important to reconcile it with the miserable fate of the impaired children. Since the notion of divine providence, based on the moral principle of divine restitution as individually geared to each believer (Hebrew, *hashgaha pratit*), is a cardinal pillar of faith in Judaism, the agony and pain of the children and their families must be accounted for. This is particularly true in the case of pervasive developmental disorders like autism and mental retardation, in which early onset discredits any explanation focusing on the victim's sins. One of the publications responded to this moral challenge with the following generalization, based on repeated messages from the children: "All the brain-damaged without exception know that they had lived in this world before, know their former name and parents' names, and *know the sin for which they came to this world in such a miserable form.* They all know that they did not come to this world to do penance, since they know the ultimate truth and do not have [the option of free] choice. They came to the world simply and solely to endure this anguish, which for them is a rectification of the sin for which they came into being" (italics added).

As in other religious systems, the notion of reincarnation, designated *gilgul*, "the transmigration of souls," in mystical Judaism (Bilu 1985),[8] serves to account for apparent aberrations in the principle of divine retribution, embodied, in this case, in the mutilation of innocent children. The possibility of rectification makes the Jewish variant of reincarnation a demonstration of divine grace, given the opportunity imparted on the transmigrated soul to improve its transcendental status in the hereafter. In the sessions, the vicissitudes of the souls in their former incarnations and in afterlife were minutely portrayed with special emphasis on their sins. Among the transgressions responsible for the message senders' present wretchedness, moral breaches on the interpersonal level were particularly noticed. Of these, *lashon ha'ra*, "evil tongue," encompassing a variety of verbal misbehaviors from gossiping to vilifying and slandering, appeared as a cardinal sin. The salience of this category of misdeeds in the context of autism, mental retardation, and cerebral palsy reflects (and further reinforces) the principle of divine retribution: those who had sinned with their mouth were doomed to suffer from gross communication impairments in their new reincarnation. Other reported sins included adultery, embezzlement, and apostasy. The depictions of the souls' wanderings in the afterworld focused on the celestial jury and the penalties it imposed on the culprits.

The information on the children's former incarnations, vices, and punishments is elicited in the course of a staccato succession of questions and answers. The publications, claiming to bring an accurate documentation of the sessions, present these dialogues verbatim. Less typically, a coherent "autobiography" of an impaired person, presented as a confessional memoir, would be elicited in response to a request to relate a life (or rather former life) story. In both genres the message senders express total acceptance of the impairment, presented as an opportunity to ameliorate the transcendental status of their souls, and beseech others in their vicinity to subscribe to this point of view. In unfolding the suffering they endure because of their deformities and limitations, however, the impaired launch pointed criticism against the rejection and contempt they face in the wider society. Their plea for human tolerance and compassion (rather than heavenly mercy) resonates with similar complaints raised by autistic and other afflicted children in nonreligious FC sessions.

The privileged access of the impaired children to their souls endows them with special divinatory skills amply tested in FC sessions. Even though the publications admonish against engaging the children in petty matters, the personal sphere is represented in the communications in attempts to disclose the causes of individual life problems, from illness and economic misfortune to truancy, heavy smoking, and marred family relations, or the unfolding of future events, such as winning in lottery and success in the religious academy. The fact that the disclosed causes always pertain to the religious domain attenuates the relative insignificance ascribed to these mundane concerns. The wide spectrum of the questions in FC sessions, spanning the trivial and the sublime, is illustrated by the following passage taken from a dialogue with a seven-year-old autistic child.

Question: Is the presence of the divine clear to you?
Answer: It is as clear to me as the reality of sunlight is clear to you.
Q: Why did you come to the world in this form?
A: There is no suffering without sin, and I sinned in forsaking the study of the Torah.
Q: Why have so many troubles been occurring recently?
A: Because of [the prevalence] of "evil tongue" and sexual relations with menstruating women.
Q: Why are you crying?
A: Because I can see through you.
Q: Why have there been so many cases of divorce recently?
A: Because adultery breeds divorce.
Q: Is God with us now?
A: He is all over.
Q: What precept should be emphasized to draw the redemption nearer?
A: Showing love without expecting reward.
Q: When I reached Rabbi Elazar [a well-known charismatic rabbi] I went back and refused to receive his blessing. Why?
A: Your soul, contaminated by your body, drove you away.
Q: Is midnight prayer (*tikun hatsot*) conducive to drawing the redemption nearer?
A: It is conducive to both personal rectification and (collective) redemption.
Q: Is it recommended to work and study at the same time?
A: [Yes]. It is correct to do both. Laboring hard on both of them may cast vices into oblivion.
Q: What about séances?
A: [The messages are] valid. But it is forbidden to conjure the dead.
Q: How to choose between schools?
A: The pupil should decide, following his own heart.

Q: Is it permitted to engage in karate?
A: [No]. This is a vain entertainment of the gentiles.

Concerns related to the current political scene in Israel are addressed in many communications. In line with the growing nationalistic sentiments among religious circles in Israel, the children expose the futility of the peace process, condemn the former Labor government, sympathize with families of soldiers missing in action, lament the suicide bombings in Israeli buses (which in some cases they reportedly had foreseen), and warn against an imminent Arab assault on Israel. A question about the cogency of the controversial slogan of the right wing in the 1996 elections—"Netanyahu is good for the Jews"—was answered with a pseudo-biblical verse composed of words forming an acrostic with Netanyahu's full name.

Many of the sessions, particularly in public settings, are pervaded by strong apocalyptic and revivalistic tones. In fact, the disclosure of personal and political matters merely serves as a prelude to highly charged communications asserting that redemption is imminent and urging the people around to repent and thus facilitate its coming. Repentance, in the form of meticulous religious observance and moral awakening, is presented both as a prerequisite for the coming of the Messiah, without whom salvation will not unfold, and as a last-moment opportunity to be spared God's wrath. These messages clearly constitute the emotional climax of the encounters and, in the eyes of the organizers, are their raison d'être. Their significance is indicated by the disproportionate space assigned in the publications to gloomy depictions of the plights and predicaments dialectically preceding redemption, to spirited exhortations to go back to the fold and repent, to frightening admonitions portraying in vivid colors the terrible fate facing those who would not, and to shining promises about the eternal bliss awaiting those who would. A special periodical, designated *The Last Words for the Last Generation,* of which two issues have already appeared, is devoted almost exclusively to dispatching these messages. The quotations on the cover of the second issue, taken from recorded FC sessions, convey the sense of fervor and urgency imbued in these apocalyptic messages.

"We who look asleep come to wake up those dormant in deceitfulness."

"This is a frightening and sad situation which begs for redemption. The world in its present form is doomed to disappear in the near future and we must—a life or death matter—make Jews repent. This is the task of the present generation. This is the end."

"In a little while the world will cope with the final ordeal."

"God saves the souls just before the very end."

"Those opposing our mission will not be able to stop us nor to extinguish the truth."

"You live like drunks, not paying attention to the signs God is sending to you."

While the dramatis personae in the sessions—the organizers and most of the facilitators and the impaired children—had religious backgrounds, the catchment population of "metaphysical FC" has been secular no less than religious. The repeated messages to repent, in particular, which make the public sessions akin to Evangelical churches' revivalistic meetings, are primarily outer-oriented, even though the function of invigorating those within the ultra-orthodox and larger religious fold should not be disregarded. Given that in their communications the children posit the unity and solidarity of the Jewish people as a key to salvation, their messages to the nonreligious alternate between beseeching and admonition. Addressed rather than excluded in order to expedite the coming of the Messiah, they are also threatened with eternal damnation if they do not yield to the messages.

The controversy over FC within the ultra-orthodox camp also reverberates in the sessions. Some promoters, apparently ill at ease with the hostile approach of some renowned religious authorities, extract messages from the children that support the use of FC and praise its achievements.

Comparative Notes

As a peculiar mystical elaboration, "metaphysical FC" may be taken as a measure for the cultural distinctiveness of the ultra-orthodox community. At the same time, however, it also serves as a reminder that even a religiously fundamentalist enclave cannot altogether insulate itself from the wider secular society within which it is uncomfortably situated. After all, the procedure was imported from the outside,[9] and its astounding effects, to the extent that they were designed to move nonobservants, are outer-oriented. The dialectical reality of greater insulation incongruently interspersed by more points of contacts and permeability appears as an emerging characteristic of ultra-orthodox life in the present-day, postmodern world.

Starting with a comparison between clinical and metaphysical FC, we proceed by exploring synchronic and diachronic aspects of the multifaceted relations between the ultra-orthodox and the secular society, extrapolated from the case under study. First, we discuss the ultra-orthodox's changing attitude toward science. Second, we examine how disordered children are employed as mediums for obtaining transcendental knowledge from a historical perspective. Generalizing from this historical comparison, we conclude by suggesting a dichotomous model of mystical avenues in Judaism that seeks to relate modes of transcendental involvement to aspects of the social structure.

Between clinical and metaphysical FC. Ambitious as the objectives of clinical FC may appear, particularly in the context of dramatic displays of improved communicative skills and rich inner lives of severely incapacitated children, they seem pale in comparison to the paranormal claims of mystically induced FC. And yet, notwithstanding the gap between scientific (or pseudo-scientific) FC and its metaphysical counterpart, the similarities between the systems transcend common procedure and administration. In particular, the emergence of metaphysical FC may shed light on the "mystico-religious" aspects of clinical FC. In both settings FC is used to bypass gross physical deficits in order to give voice to hidden aspects of the psyche. This basic resemblance is clouded by epistemologically divergent rationales. According to the psychological model underlying clinical FC, the hidden psychic aspects to be retrieved are located in the brain/mind; whereas the mystical model separates between the disembodied divine soul and the brain/mind and assumes that the more damaged the brain the louder and clearer the voice of the omniscient soul. It might be suggested that the two systems use different idioms of transcendence, hidden and internal in the clinical case (cf. Shweder 1991), exteriorized and cosmological in the metaphysical case. Yet the boundary between the two may at times become blurred, as terms prevalent in the professional discourse indicating transcendence in the first sense (for example, "idiot savant" in the case of mental retardation and "silent wisdom" in the case of autism) may be imbued with "spiritual" overtones.

The near miraculous accomplishments claimed for FC in clinical settings, the strong emotions and moral concerns that the procedure has instigated, and the "*veritable religiose adherence* by its most extreme proponents" (Jones 1994, 492; italics added) all cloak clinical FC in a near mystical atmosphere. It might be argued that in the secularized version of transcendence reflected in clinical FC the mystique of the mute as self-creatively intelligent, poetically sensitive, yet trapped in a broken body and bereft of the means to articulate and express the richness of its inner life resonates with the divine spark that constitutes the soul in metaphysical FC. In the same vein, the image of clinical FC as an empowering technique put forth to liberate autistic children from the dark recesses of their mental prison by helping them communicate and realize their inner potential resonates with the soteriological messages that the children convey in metaphysical FC, related to their imminent salvation from the sins they had committed in previous incarnations, their happy compliance with God's harsh verdict, and their exalted status as prophetic messengers.

It is interesting to note that in both settings, the children's messages are marked by a strong sermonizing aspect. This moralizing draws the communications in the clinical setting closer to the religious exhortations of the children in the ultra-orthodox context. Moral complaints over the ill treatment of invalids and misfits are prevalent in both forms of FC. In clinical settings allegations of physical and sexual abuse have become particularly noted, further embittering the controversy over FC. Without going into the specific contents of these allegations, it might be argued that in the context of psychological (inner and hidden) transcendence, the retrieval of covert sexual traumas appears as the secularized equivalent of the unraveling of mystical secrets in metaphysical FC. In orthodox settings the allegations against abusers have been generalized to charges lamenting the growing moral deterioration and nonobservance and denouncing religious transgressions. Intriguingly, in an oft-quoted case study of sexual abuse allegations, made through facilitation, "a religious value system and mention of God was evidenced even though the child had received no religious education" (Bligh and Kupperman 1993, 554).[10] It might be concluded that in both settings, FC enables autistic and other disabled children to appear as resolute moral critics of their respective milieus.

The optimistic and humanitarian tenor of clinical FC has been retained and even enhanced in the religious setting. Secular and observant proponents alike emphasize, beyond the technical improvement in communication that facilitation brings forth, the favorable change in the children's status and their greater acceptance by their parents. But beyond that, metaphysical FC endows the children with a distinctive transcendental aura, highlighting their access to their omniscient souls and their exalted stance as intermediaries with the hereafter. In secular settings FC is viewed as conducive to disclosing human potentials which, at best, may put disabled children on a par with "normal" ones; but metaphysical FC further magnifies the position of the children, reframing their afflictions as an innate moral asset that even great rabbinical figures do not naturally possess. The religious publications amply depict the favorable attitudinal transformation that parents of disabled children have undergone once they became aware of their children's privileged mediational status and superhuman abilities. The humane, benevolent orientation toward autism, mental retardation, and other pervasive disorders that the supporters of metaphysical FC display stands at odds with the traditional attitude toward mental illness and physical stigma in the ultra-orthodox community characterized by shame, denial, and concealment. The change may be viewed as the tacit influence of modern life facilitated by the tremendous toll that physical and mental stigmas cast on the ultra-orthodox family. Traditionally, the exposure of such blemish could tarnish all family members and particularly harm the prospects of finding a worthy spouse through matchmaking (Goshen-Gottstein 1987).

Whether clinical or metaphysical, the redemptive presumptions of FC have met with fierce opposition in both settings. As mentioned earlier, the skepticism regarding the efficacy of FC, which the results of rigorous experimental studies raised, was reiterated in ultra-orthodox circles. And in both settings the moral preaching of FC proponents, emphasizing the humane aspects of the procedure and the hope it has been giving to the afflicted and their families, was countervailed by criticism accentuating the damage that unrealistic expectations regarding the children's abilities might cause their families. The public sessions of metaphysical FC have drawn most of the fire in the religious camp. They were denigrated as circus-like performances in which the children's precarious well-being was put at extra risk because of their harsh exposure to the limelight. The controversy in the ultra-orthodox community over the legitimacy of metaphysical FC may be viewed as one manifestation of the age-old tension between rationalists and proponents of mysticism in Judaism (Horodetsky 1947).

Between science and mysticism. Against the image of the ultra-orthodox community as an insulated enclave, the swift absorption of FC and the acquaintance with the scientific debate it stirred appear intriguing. Popular television programs no doubt familiarized wide circles of watchers with FC, but strictly observant Jews are hardly exposed to the electronic media. In any case, the intimate familiarity with the controversy over FC that some promoters and critics in the ultra-orthodox community demonstrated indicates that they went beyond popular media presentations and perused the professional journals for data. We believe that this involvement reflects a significant change in the general attitude of the ultra-orthodox community toward science as the spearhead of secular progress and enlightenment.

Based on skepticism and empirical investigation, the tenor of scientific endeavor appears inimical to religious faith. The historical process of modernization and secularization that has been corroding the Jewish traditional way of life since the nineteenth century has left many rabbinic authorities wary of the heretic potential of enlightenment and inculcated a strongly ambivalent approach toward scientific claims and discoveries. Particularly in areas where theories and findings challenged religious convictions (e.g., Darwin's theory of evolution), the orthodox response was one of denial, exclusion, censorship, and parochialism (Katz 1961). This ultra-conservative approach, indicating an inherent weakness and insecurity vis-à-vis the secular mainstream, appears to be changing. The historical process of contraction and attenuation which, in the aftermath of World War II and the Holocaust, had put into question the perseverance of organized forms of Jewish ultra-orthodoxy, has recently been blocked and even reversed (Friedman 1991). In terms of numbers, resources, political influence, and religious adherence, the ultra-orthodox communities in Israel enjoy a period of consolidation and expansion accompanied by a growing sense of self-confidence and assertiveness. The appropriation and adaptation of FC may be viewed as one example of this process of empowerment.

As against the traditional evasive approach to science, a new confrontational view can be discerned in the ultra-orthodox community that is characterized by appreciation, challenge, and contestation. Applied science and technology are held in high esteem, as illustrated by the case of FC, and their contributions to human welfare are not disputed unless they openly clash with religious dogma and practice. But the prestige accorded to science only serves to accentuate the shortsightedness of scientific *theories* that fail to explain a wide gamut of special phenomena, whether naturally occurring or the product of advanced technology (like FC). In recent years attempts have been made by ultra-orthodox advocates to peruse popular and professional publications on extraordinary and enigmatic phenomena that reside in the borderland of scientific inquiry to expose the ineptness of their rational-empirical explanations, and to reframe them within an all-embracing metaphysical account. Salient among these occurrences were those involving altered states of consciousness and parapsychology, such as near-death and out-of-body experiences, trance and possession, spirit mediumship, telepathy, telekinesis, precognition, miraculous healing, reports on former reincarnations, and hypnotically induced paranormal skills. In this context

FC holds a special fascination for religious advocates. As a computer-based device it is an appreciated status symbol of technological sophistication. But the data it produces include transcendental communications inexplicable by science, which endow the procedure with a mystical aura. The assertive pursuit of esoteric phenomena, of which metaphysical FC is but one conspicuous example, thus emerges as a feature of the novel ultra-orthodox approach that does not shy away from science but seeks to confront it and expose its inherent limitations.[11]

Between FC session and dybbuk possession. While the efficacy of metaphysical FC as a means for invigorating religious faith may explain its *maintenance* despite vocal rabbinical opposition, the reasons for its *introduction* still must be accounted for. Three attributes of FC, resonant with mantic traditions in Judaism, could have been conducive to embracing the procedure in the face of resistance to innovations. First, it is possible that the salience of the letters of the alphabet in the augmentative communication aids of the procedure might have had a special appeal in a scripture-based religious system that imbues these letters with a strong supernatural flavor. In fact, of the rich array of divinatory and therapeutic techniques in Jewish folk religion, "the magic of the letters" has been by far the most popular (Idel 1995). This is hardly surprising given the primacy of the text in Judaism and the deep-rooted mystical tradition that deems the letters of alphabet the primordial vessels from which the world was created.[12] Second, in various forms of Jewish divination, as in many other non-Jewish mantic systems, prepubescent children, deemed pure and innocent, have been viewed as expedient mediums (Bilu 1982, 1990).[13] Third, the attribution of prophetic powers to deranged people could also be traced to classic Jewish sources.[14]

Within the traditions of using children and deranged persons for divinatory purposes, metaphysical FC appears particularly akin to the exorcistic ritual of the *dybbuk,* the Jewish classical variant of spirit possession (Bilu 1985, 1997; Nigal 1983). *Dybbuk* possession had plagued many Jewish mystically oriented communities, first in the Mediterranean basin and the Middle East and later in the Hasidic concentrations of eastern Europe. Documented cases of *dybbukim* (pl.) span four hundred years, from the first half of the sixteenth century to the beginning of the twentieth century. As in many other instances of possession (e.g., Bourguignon 1976; Boddy 1994; Lambek 1989), females were overrepresented among the afflicted, while most of the intruding agents were males, viewed in the Jewish mystical context as spirits of notorious sinners who took possession of their victims in order to flee from the endless persecutions that were their share in the hereafter. The exorcistic ritual was usually public, conducted in the local synagogue by a kabbalist or a Hasidic master. It followed a predetermined sequence of steps in which the recalcitrant spirit was compelled to betray its identity, to confess its sins, to portray the punishments and suffering that were its lot in heaven, and to give its consent to depart harmlessly through a minor part of the victim's body. During exorcism the spirit would disclose many mystical secrets, either spontaneously or upon the rabbi's request.

The similarities between metaphysical FC and *dybbuk* exorcism are striking. In both settings deranged persons were maneuvered, through a complex elicitation technique and an interrogatory dialogue with a rabbinic authority, to retrieve transcendental secrets. The imparted knowledge, ordinarily blocked from "normal" people, could be reached because of the afflictions of the communicators that granted them privileged access to metaphysical entities, in the form of divine souls or spirits of the dead. The mystical secrets disclosed through the communications provided a convincing "eyewitness" testimony that validated fundamental religious convictions. Both autistic children and *dybbuk* possession victims openly and minutely discussed the vicissitudes of their previous lives and afterlives and justified their present misery as a celestial verdict, a restitution for their sins. The doctrine of the transmigration of souls (*gilgul*) thus confirmed added to the cardinal tenets of Jewish faith, such as God's immanence, divine providence, and divine retribution, vividly illustrated in the public arenas of FC sessions and *dybbuk* exorcism. In both cases, the communications were elicited in front of a large audience, in a dramatic spectacle in which bits of transcendental reality were brought down, as it were, and impinged upon mundane reality. It is not surprising that then as well as now the communications had a considerable impact on the community, invigorating religious faith and propelling nonbelievers back to the fold. Consequently, special efforts were made to publish cases of *dybbuk* possession and FC sessions under moving and colorful titles. As against appellations such as *What Does the Soul Say* and *The Last Words for the Last Generation,* typical of publications on FC, brochures dealing with *dybbuk* cases had titles such as *The Spirits Recount* or *A Terrible Deed of the Spirit.* While the material on *dybbukim,* confined to the written word, lacked the variety of electronic devices now available for the promoters of FC, this literature was quite popular at the time. The literary style in which the promulgated materials were written in both settings had a strong sermonizing accent depicting in vivid colors the moral fallibility of mortals and urging them to repent.

Thus, *dybbuk* exorcism and FC sessions reflect the triumph of the social order. In both cases deviance is confronted, highlighted, and "rectified" by religious authorities in order to enhance conformity and invigorate faith in the community. "Rectification" is double-edged in the two settings. On the manifest level *dybbuk* exorcism was a healing ritual, an impressively efficacious therapy in which the expulsion of the possessing spirit was an almost inevitable outcome of administrating the proper incantations and spells. From a psychodynamic-etic perspective, which would attribute the spirit's blatant aggressive and sexual verbalizations and behavioral manifestations to the victim's own (repressed or suppressed) wishes, the brutal assault on and domestication of the spirit meant the frustration and taming of the victim's true desire. Given the portrayal of the possessing spirits as the epitomes of vice and depravity, the dialectical process whereby deviance was transformed into a lever for inculcating conformity was particularly impressive.

No such notion of evil accompanies the forms of childhood disorders represented in FC, where deviance is even treated as meritorious because it paves the way to the divine; but the afflicted children do refer to their past vices to justify their misery. "Rectification" here is particularly complex, as the children are not healed. The contrast with the dramatic success of the exorcistic performance in *dybbuk* cases reflects the enormous gap in prognosis between reactive-episodic and chronic-pervasive disorders. At the same time, however, FC does empower the incapacitated children in a double sense, allegedly improving their communication skills and assigning them a high status as mediums. In terms borrowed from psychotherapy, *dybbuk* exorcism and FC sessions follow diverse models of healing. The former is based on symptom elimination while the latter espouses a "sacrificial" paradigm (see Eade 1991), according to which the ailment is cognitively restructured in mystical terms and thus made more acceptable.

The similarities shared by spirit exorcism and FC sessions should not overshadow the obvious differences between them. Most noted among the latter is the diverse nature of deviance employed in the two settings. The turn from spirit possession to autism and other developmental disorders provides a fascinating case of a historically situated folk employment of shifting psychiatric categories. While attempts are now being made to introduce spirit possession-cum-illness to psychiatric classifications,[15] common medical wisdom tended to associate it with the classical hysteria, and particularly with the dissociative form of hysterical neurosis (Bourguignon 1976; Krohn 1978), which in DSM III has become Dissociative Disorder (American Psychiatric Association 1980). Of the subtypes of this category, multiple personality disorder appears as the present-day kin of possession illness (e.g., Putnam 1989). It is interesting to note that *dybbuk* cases that flourished throughout the nineteenth century began to attenuate in the first decades of the twentieth century—a trajectory convergent with that of classical hysteria. Childhood Autism, the disorder most strongly associated with FC, is a fairly modern category first introduced to the psychiatric discourse as a distinctive diagnosis in the 1940s (Kanner 1943).[16]

The fact that autism is an established diagnosis within the psychiatric classification, while *dybbuk* possession was a folk category outside the medical realm, comprehensible only as a mystically based cultural meaning system in Judaism, may in itself serve as a measure for the ultra-orthodox move toward "modernization." A cultural enclave as this community may still be, it does not produce its own forms of psychopathology anymore.[17] This point increases in significance when the different clinical pictures of possession and autism are evaluated in terms of their different cultural input. The *dybbuk* manifested itself in a wide array of symptoms—the behavioral manifestations of the possessing spirit—informed by an elaborate cultural script. The possessed were able and willing to enact internalized variants of this script, to articulate their personal distress in terms of a dramatic ritualized performance based on the shared symbolic vocabulary of the spirits as collective representations. This enabled the peculiar collusion between healer and deviant realized in the smooth unfolding of the exorcistic dialogue and its conformity-enhancing effects (see Bilu 1985; Krohn 1978).[18] In many cases the cultural constitution of personal distress resonated with major collective concerns prevalent in the community. Therefore, the success of the exorcistic ritual, aside from being an effective individual intervention, also had an impact on the community as a whole. As a culture-specific syndrome, emerging from the myths and beliefs of the community but also alleviated through them, the proliferation of *dybbukim* was indeed a testimony to the viability of folk religion in traditional Jewish society and to the extent to which it could shape as well as help cope with personal distress and collective concerns.

In contrast with *dybbuk* possession, the cultural shaping of the *primary* symptomatology in autism appears modest at best. Designated "the empty fortress" by Bettelheim (1967) and characterized by gross *deficits* in many areas of functioning, it appears as the mirror image of the rich, culturally based performative surplus of the *dybbuk*. Needless to say, involving autistic children in metaphysical FC constitutes a massive cultural construction of the disorder. But here the cultural script is not built into the primary symptomatology, as was the case with the *dybbuk*, but rather imposed on it through thick layers of mediation. Metaphorically as well as metonymically, the physical molding of the communicator's fingers by the facilitator in FC appears to stand for the tight grip of the religious authority on the communicator. To be sure, the rabbis' compelling orchestration of the ritualized encounters with the deviants had their effects in both settings; but in the *dybbuk* case, a *direct* cultural dialogue with metaphysical entities could take place through "oversocialized," highly communicative deviants, while in FC it was precisely the manifest emptiness of autistic children and other "undersocialized" noncommunicative deviants that could be filled with proper cultural contents through heavy mediation. The communications in FC are based on literacy as befits the proliferation of learning in present-day ultra-orthodox communities.[19] As means of communication, writing (or pointing to letters on the board in the noncomputerized sessions) and reading are certainly more heavily mediated than the oral dialogues between the exorcist and the *dybbuk*. The Jewish traditional society of previous centuries was no less scripture-based, but literacy among females, the typical victims of possession, was significantly low. *Dybbuk* possession, resembling a theatrical performance, was based on oral transmission, role modeling, and embodied learning—"low" sediments in Jewish folk culture that were relatively text independent. Written charms, however, did play a decisive role in the exorcism of the *dybbuk*. Replete with esoteric appellations derived from mystical sources, they were burnt down and put before the victim's nostrils to scorch and suffocate the possessing spirit. But this blatantly magical use of the written word was a far cry from the "ordinary" informative input of the written messages elicited through FC. In the contemporary ultra-orthodox community, where the ideal of establishing the ultimate "society of learners" has never been so close to being achieved, even prophetic messages and transcendental communications ought to be encapsulated within a lettered rather than oral framework.

Concluding Note: Center and Margins in the Search for the Transcendent

Mystical phenomena constitute experiential links between the believer and the divine conducive to transforming the transcendent from a remote particle of faith into a deeply felt conviction (e.g., Csordas 1994; Spiro 1987; Stromberg 1993; Obeyesekere 1981, 1990). For religious experiences to be thus "oxygenated" and invigorated, religious systems must maintain institutionalized avenues to the sacred. Seeking to situate our historical comparison within a wider analytic framework, we would like to conclude by charting a dichotomous model of mystical pathways to the sacred, based on the differential location in the social order of the actors serving as mediums.

In Jewish mysticism many patterns of establishing contact with the divine have been noted throughout the ages in which the mediums were part and parcel of the rabbinic elite, from talmudic sages to noted kabbalists and Hasidic masters. These luminaries experienced an abundance of prophetic revelations related to diverse celestial powers, from the Holy Spirit (*Ru'ah Ka-Kodesh*), the Heavenly Voice (*Bat-Kol*), and the female counterpart of God (*Shekhina*) to Elijah the Prophet and various angelic messengers called *Maggidim* (Bilu 1997; Werblowsky 1977). The induction methods to summon the heavenly messengers ranged from the meditative to the ecstatic, and the experiential modes through which they found expression included a wide variety of altered states of consciousness such as dreaming, trance, reveries, and automatic writing. But in terms of the social order, most of this rich mystical activity occurred in *the center of society*, as the kabbalists and sages involved in it, though not necessarily the leaders of the community, were ordinarily deemed men of high standing and prestige.

In contrast with center-based mystical productions created by religious specialists and virtuosi, the mediums in the divinatory settings described in this work were recruited from the stigmatized margins of the community. The young protagonists of FC sessions, suffering from pervasive developmental disorders such as autism, mental retardation, and cerebral palsy, may be viewed as the modern, medicocentric addition to the quota of deviants and misfits employed for mantic purposes in the past. Following our comparative analysis, it might be argued that within Jewish ultra-orthodox communities the female victims of *dybbuk* possession were the eighteenth- and nineteenth-century counterparts of present-day FC mediums. Bearing in mind that the selection of the misfits was historically situated, it could be illuminating to compare the peculiar social and cultural circumstances under which a given category of deviance became an established avenue for divination. Such a study is certainly beyond the scope of this essay, but the following illustration may serve to whet the reader's appetite as to the creative possibilities entailed in this selection process.

A series of Hasidic stories in a pamphlet of praises dedicated to a nineteenth-century *tsaddiq*, Rabbi Mordechai of Nadvorna,[20] focus on the rabbi's involvement in the mystical business of rectifying the transmigrated souls of ex-sinners. What made these stories unique was the fact that here the objects of transmigration were not human beings but black bears. In a peculiar narrative fusion of the mundane and the transcendent, the recurring plot depicts the rabbi as stumbling upon a band of gypsies performing with a dancing bear. After a tough negotiations the gypsies agree to sell the bear to the *tsaddiq*, who brings it to his house. A miraculous dialogue between the rabbi and the animal ensues in which the bear divulges its Jewish origin and confesses the sins responsible for its base reincarnation. While these dialogues were short and condensed, always ending with the bear's sudden death, the theme of divine retribution, so salient in FC sessions and *dybbuk* exorcism, appeared in a nascent form in all of the stories. To illustrate: one of the bears rectified by the rabbi was in his first incarnation a pious Jew who fulfilled all the commandments except one: he did not pay respect to brides and bridegrooms and never danced in their wedding ceremonies. To make up for this sin, his soul was transmigrated into a bear condemned to dance with a band of gypsies. In the social microcosm of east European shtetls, "black" gypsies (this is how they were designated in the text) with their black bears were an emblem of peripherality and otherness.

Thus, in different historical periods different marginal categories—gypsies and their bears, victims of spirit possession, and mentally disturbed and organically incapacitated children, to mention but a few[21]—were employed in traditional Jewish society for mantic purposes. In terms of sex and age roles, females and children, the more inferior groups in the population, were overrepresented among the mediums. The center-periphery bifurcation portrayed here should not be viewed as representing mutually exclusive or antagonistic pathways to the transcendent. It would be all the more incorrect to portray the mantic communications from the margins as a manifestation of the power of the weak, seeking to subvert the existing social hierarchy and religious authority. Quite the opposite is true. In terms of power relations, the center-periphery division is deceiving as in both settings the mystical and divinatory activities were monitored by leading rabbinical figures. The ability of the religious elite to reach out for the deviant and the marginal and to cast their messages in the mold of the religious canon is a testimony to an all-embracing hegemony typical of close-knit fundamentalist societies. It is true, however, that the dramatic mobilization of the margins by the center may come in times of social unrest and cultural change in which the society, under a foreseeable risk, ought to be cemented and its underlying myths and beliefs to be galvanized and rejuvenated (see Bilu 1985). Outside the Jewish realm, the witch craze in post-medieval Europe may be similarly viewed (e.g., Trevor-Roper 1967).

Placing peripheral mantic activities under the hegemonic canopy of rabbinical authorities, however, should not blind us to the significant differences between the two types of mystical avenues discerned above. Center-based revelations of mystical rabbis have typically been conveyed through *willfully sought private experiences* that had to be *remembered* in order to be transmitted. The rabbis' role in promoting and mediating peripheral divination has been decisive too because the conveyers of the messages—whether black bears, possessed women, or autistic children—have been characterized by a *total lack of awareness,* either permanent or transient (as in the *dybbuk* case marked by dissociation and amnesia). Thus, the recalled private experience of the mystic has become in the marginal arena a *public performance* moldable by authority figures (e.g., an exorcist or a facilitator), of which the medium is liable to remain totally *unaware.*[22] It was this muteness (literal or metaphoric), powerlessness, and plasticity of the innocent mediums that afforded the massive crystallization of their communications into a conformity-enhancing output.

In the light of these differences, the coexistence of the two mystical avenues in Judaism (and in other religious systems) does not appear surprising. Peripheral divination has not been redundant and dispensable even in times when a rich mystical creation kept flowing from the center. The mystics ordinarily produced and reproduced esoteric knowledge, promulgated in cryptic texts and distributed among small circles of scholars. Ironically, it was the misfits and outcasts at the margins of society who served as the "oxygenation basins" of religious beliefs. They revitalized religious experiences in dramatic, theatrical spectacles in which their misery and agony were morally expounded and rationalized in a most convincing way. Deviance has thus been effectively employed to objectify and validate core religious principles.

Notes

1. The data were collected during 1995–96 in the context of a larger study dealing with communication patterns and boundary maintenance in the Jewish ultra-orthodox community in Israel. We are grateful to the Schein Foundation of the Social Science Faculty at the Hebrew University of Jerusalem for supporting this project.
2. See, e.g., Ha'aretz, 20 January 1995; Yediot Ha'hronot, 10 May 1996; Hamodi'a 28 June, 19 July, and 2 July 1996.
3. Unlike the core of the ultra-orthodox community, which is clearly defined, at the margins the boundaries between gradations of religious adherence are blurred. When we use terms such as "strictly observant" or even "orthodox" we wish to convey the idea that the religious use of FC, although primarily associated with the ultra-orthodox community, may sometimes exceed it.
4. The controversy is related to the ongoing tension in the ultra-orthodox communities between rationally and mystically oriented forms of religiosity (see Horodetsky 1947).
5. See Baba Bathra 12b (Babylonian Talmud 1976).

6. See Niddah 30b (Babylonian Talmud 1959).
7. A major doctrine of Jewish mysticism views mental life as a tripartite system divided into *nefesh* (psyche), the vital principle that is the lowest grade of the mental apparatus, *ru'ah* (spirit), the intellectual faculty in the middle, and *neshama* (soul), the highest element representing moral consciousness (Zohar 1956 II, 402–3).
8. The doctrine of the transmigration of souls, absent in the Bible and the Talmud, first appeared in mystical circles in the twelfth century, where it was presented as selectively implemented for specific transgressions only. In sixteenth-century Lurianic Kabbala it was extended into a universal law (Scholem 1971b).
9. It is significant that the procedure first penetrated ultra-orthodox circles in the United States. By and large American Jewish orthodoxy is less stringent than its Israeli counterpart (Soloveitchik 1994).
10. As in all other experimental studies, the allegations, made by a ten-year-old mentally retarded blind girl with autistic characteristics, were ascribed to "facilitator effect."
11. Admittedly, our depiction of the change in the ultra-orthodox attitude toward science is oversimplified. Historians have noted that some degree of openness toward scientific innovations, and an active confrontational approach toward secular and particularly Zionist historiography, were evident already in the nineteenth century (Bacon 1984; Bartal 1993). But there is a general agreement that these processes have intensified considerably in recent years (e.g., Soloveitchik 1994).
12. The idea that the universe was created from letters is elaborated in the mystical Book of Creation (*Sefer Yetsira* 1962).
13. Aside from the use of children as mediums in divination (see Bilu 1982), they also appear in Jewish texts as possessing profound mystical secrets (Tishby 1949) and prophetic insights (Eshkoli 1956).
14. See, e.g., In Praise of the Ba'al Shem Tov (1970, 4).
15. A category of Trance and Possession Disorders was recently introduced to ICD-10 (World Health Organization 1992). DSM-IV now includes a Dissociative Trance Disorder. Various possession disorders are included in appendix 1 of the manual devoted to culture-bound syndromes (Kirmayer 1992).
16. Childhood Autism should not be conflated with the term "autism," one of the "four A's" introduced by Bleuler as primary markers of schizophrenia (the others are affect, association, and ambivalence).
17. *Dybbuk* possession may be viewed as a Jewish culture-specific syndrome. See Bilu 1985; Csordas 1994, 298.
18. Krohn (1978) maintains that the common thread underlying the wide historical diversity of hysterical symptoms has been the tendency of hysterics to act out dominant cultural character, albeit in extreme and caricatured ways. For a discussion of the interface of sociodynamics and psychodynamics entailed in hysteria, see Bilu 1985.
19. For an insightful analysis of the new and controlling role that the written word now plays in contemporary Jewish religious life, see Soloveitchik 1994.
20. The pamphlet, designated the Centennial Letter (*Michtav Shnat Ha-Me'ah*), was published in 1995, one hundred years after the rabbi's death.
21. Other marginal mediums include impure animals such as mice, frogs, and ravens, and children and adults on their deathbed (e.g., In Praise of the Baal Shem Tov 1970).
22. The distinction between central and peripheral mystico-mantic activities partially corresponds to Bourguignon's (1979) division of ceremonial altered states of consciousness into nonpossession and possession trance and to De Heusch's (1981) distinction between shamanism and possession.

26

Playing for Control of Distance

Card Games between Jews and Muslims on a Casablancan Beach

ANDRÉ LEVY

"If we hadn't had our exclusive (Jewish) clubs . . . if we didn't have these Israeli enclaves, we couldn't survive here. We wouldn't stay even one day in Morocco!" declared Joe Almakeias[1] during a card game. This assertion appeared to be a common truth for everyone sitting within the sheltering walls of a Jewish club in Casablanca. As my thoughts about Jewish existence in contemporary Morocco became clearer, I realized how statements such as the one above reveal the centrality and importance of what I term "contraction"—that is, the simultaneous demographic decrease and practice of self-seclusion in enclaves while identifying with the exterior poles of identification (mainly France and Israel). These enclaves have become a basic strategy for the Jews in this community to cope with the fluctuating aspects of their continuous social and spatial contraction.

Societies are increasingly experiencing demographic fluxes. Although migration is a popular research topic, few scholars have studied the effects of steady out-migration on the groups remaining behind (Bottomley 1992). Researchers tend to "travel" with migrants who become a minority group, sojourners, or any other kind of long-term residents. These researchers are often intrigued by the interactions between migrants and their host societies, while ignoring the crystallization of sociocultural mechanisms that deal with the repercussions of migration on the society of origin. These are profoundly related to the crux of social stamina, especially when small minority groups are involved as in the case of Moroccan Jews.

Combined with other political and historical circumstances (presented below), the dwindling of the Jewish population in Morocco provokes in Jews feelings of fragility and vulnerability. The Jews' basic reaction to their decreasing numbers is to create and exploit to their advantage various social frames for managing their relations with members of the larger Muslim society. These social frames orient the behaviors of the actors (Berger and Luckmann 1966) and grant a sense of predictability and control vis-à-vis Muslims who are a priori perceived as menacing.

This essay proposes a close look at contemporary Jewish-Muslim relations in Casablanca by depicting the interactions of Jewish and Muslim card players on a private beach named Tahiti. As a frame of ritualistic behavior, card games provide a reliable shelter for Jews to interact with Muslims. As play, that is, as an activity that calls into question social order (Handelman 1977b), however, card games seem to contradict the desire for peaceful and controllable relations with Muslims. Thus, I wish to account for the reasons that motivate Jews to meet Muslims under such complex conditions.

This essay presents the Jews' perspective without getting into a politically biased and judgmental position regarding the *quality* of Jewish existence within Arab or Muslim societies. Researchers who have studied contemporary Jewish-Muslim relations have tended either to ignore the Jewish perspective (see, e.g., L. Rosen 1968, 1972, 1984) or to describe Jews as passive subjects in the face of great historical and political forces (see, e.g., Tessler 1978, 1981; Tessler and Hawkins 1980; Tessler, Hawkins, and Parsons 1979). Both perspectives disempower Jews and disregard their status as active social agents. Moreover, while the former view ignores the influence of migration on Jewish lives, the latter accepts the Jews' current retreat from their Muslim surroundings as a conclusion and not a theoretical issue to be studied. Here I wish to re-present the perspectives of the Moroccan Jews and the ways in which they *actively* construct and exploit to their advantage the social frames of the beach and the card games in the context of their demographic, social, and spatial contraction.

The fieldwork was conducted primarily in Casablanca between July 1990 and September 1991. My broad theoretical goal was to comprehend how Jews cope with their apparent future death as a community and to understand what kind of social mechanisms and discursive articulations they developed in order to face this seemingly doomed future (Levy 1996). My data indicate that the fundamental response of Casablancan Jews to their future dissolution is a rather complex mode of isolation: they strive to retreat from their immediate Muslim surroundings and create isolated places to establish zones that permit connections to the more remote poles of identification—primarily France and Israel. This basic attitude is epitomized in the opening statement made by Joe Almakeias.

As a tiny and diminishing community, however, Jews cannot be self-sufficient and must meet Muslims in various circumstances. In this essay I will confine myself to the intricate problem of the Jews wishing to be sheltered from Muslims and at the same time having to meet them. The basic solution to this conflicting situation is for the Jews to contain their relations in well-defined and bounded spaces and within clear social frames over which they aspire to hold some control.

This way of constructing a world that conflates community, culture, and space is not unique to Moroccan Jews. As a result of recent sociological, economic, and political processes, there are a growing number of transnational and postcolonial communities spread throughout the globe. Groups and individuals travel more than ever (Piore 1979), although they did not refrain from doing so in past historical moments (Clifford 1997). The various sorts of outsiders (such as expatriate groups and diasporic communities) reveal a deep need to reduce feelings of strangeness as a result of their encounters with the new surroundings since strangeness generates fear and anxieties. According to Erik Cohen, who relies on Schutz's (1944, #166) seminal work on "strangehood," "[t]he strangeness of a foreign environment is the key element in the expatriate's experience as well as the principal problem with which he and his community have to cope." Hence, he continues, "expatriate communities become structured through their efforts to resolve the problem of strangeness" (1977, 15). Establishing a cultural enclave is a relatively common solution for communities that will not or cannot confront strangeness. Within this cultural enclave people construct an infrastructure that supplies varying degrees of needs that substitute for those available in the host country. The degree of its boundaries' rigidity is also an outcome of the willingness (or capability) of the expatriate to be exposed to the strange surroundings.

Without dismissing the above, one wonders why such little attention has been given to groups that turn into a sociocultural enclave without even emigrating, that is, without the notion of "strangehood." It seems that several groups—that for long historical periods used to be an inherent segment of a society—find themselves alienated in their own countries. They develop structural characteristics parallel to those of expatriate communities without exiling from their own spaces. The causes of confinement into cultural enclaves may change: political change, internal migration, demographic diminution, and so forth. Unlike the expatriate experience, the emergence of enclaves has to do with internal, local circumstances. These circumstances affect the need to develop an alternative pole of reference, as the surrounding entity becomes (or always has been) a rejected society; a "hosting" country. In cases of dominating minority, it is most likely that the need for exterior reference will not emerge. Whites in South Africa, for instance, did not develop an imagined homeland outside their spaces. Unlike the too specific diaspora model introduced by Safran (1991, #160),[2] they evolved enclave traits without constructing an imagined homeland.[3] According to Crapanzano, although whites in South Africa situate themselves between Western Europe and the United States, that is, between the Old World and the New World, their "identity seems at times to be constituted by their defense against outside influence of whatever sort. They draw a tight boundary around themselves—a laager" (1985, 184). Moroccan Jews, however, do not enjoy the status of a dominating minority. Hence, they have a desperate need to invent an alternative, imagined homeland.

In what follows I will briefly introduce the historical and political context that prompts the diminishing community to adopt the solution of isolation from the Muslims surrounding them in favor of identification with remote poles of identification.

Sociospatial Contraction: Past and Present

Essentially, a tendency for Moroccan Jews to withdraw from contact with Muslims has always prevailed. The daily religious practices of both groups have dictated a certain extent of spatial separateness, a practice vividly demonstrated by the confinement of Jews behind the walls—real or symbolic—of the *mellah* (Jewish quarter/ghetto) (Hirschberg 1968). Some scholars have described this confinement not as an intrinsic process related to differences in daily religious practices but as a demonstration of the Jews' low legal and social status as *dhimmis* (see, e.g., Stillman 1979). Whatever their interpretation, however, most scholars agree that Jews were part and parcel of the Moroccan sociocultural reality in the past. Their widespread immersion into Moroccan spaces—although frequently in confined or well-bounded areas—is a fundamental manifestation of it (Goldberg 1983).

In the late nineteenth century, French colonialism prompted dramatic changes in the Moroccan landscape. One visible example was the acceleration of a flow of people from small villages in the hinterland primarily, but not exclusively, to the coastal cities. This movement was provoked by socioeconomic changes that were generated by the French presence and influenced Muslims and Jews enchanted by the allure of modernism. Casablanca demonstrates this spectacularly: the city's population grew by approximately 170 times in the course of a single century (Adam 1950) with Jews making up the most enthusiastic part of that human tide. Moroccan Jews wished to proximate those urban spaces that French colonialists inhabited as they aspired to benefit from the seemingly egalitarian promise embodied in the universalistic rhetoric of French colonialism (Bensimon-Donath 1968).

Nevertheless, after the establishment of the State of Israel (1948) and the end of French colonialism that was followed by Morocco's independence (1956), and the ensuing migration of Jews to Israel, France, and Canada, Morocco's Jewish population rapidly decreased. In the 1940s the entire Jewish community in Morocco numbered more than 250,000 people; by the end of the 1990s that number was 6,000 (see fig. 1).

The more the total number of Jews in Morocco diminished, the more their relative proportion in Casablanca increased (see fig. 2). For instance, in 1951, 20 percent of the entire Jewish population lived in Casablanca; by the early 1990s roughly 70 percent of the estimated Jewish population had come to reside in Casablanca (about 4,000 Jews).[4] Their demographic diminution continues to this day. From the 1970s to the 1990s, the community lost approximately 5 percent of its members annually, mostly due to migration.

Figure 1.
Decrease of Jewish community between 1948 and 1994 (in thousands).

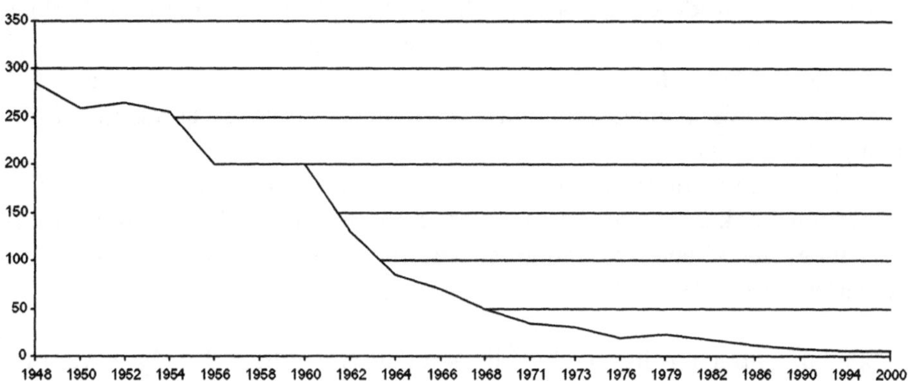

Sources: *American Jewish Yearbook* and American Joint Distribution Committee reports.

Figure 2.
Rate of Jewish population in Casablanca compared to total Jewish population, 1936–2000.

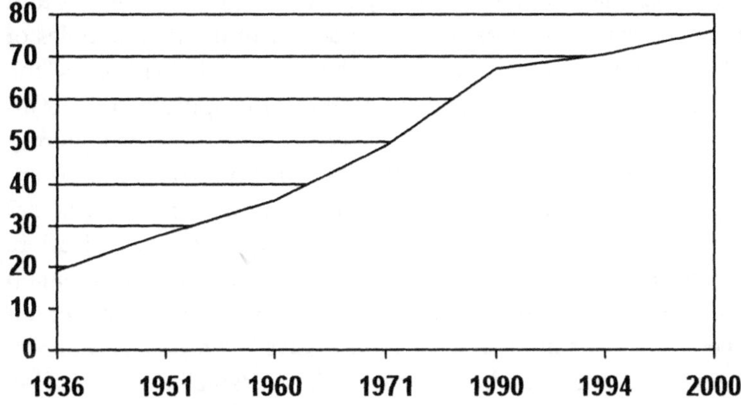

Sources: *American Jewish Yearbook* and American Joint Distribution Committee reports.

Several external forces mold and nourish the Jews' disengagement from Muslims. For the purposes of this essay it is sufficient to state that the definition of the Moroccan collectivity that leans on Islam (Bourqia 1987; Suleiman 1989; Tessler 1978)[5] and the roles that both France and Israel play in the Jews' lives affect this disengagement greatly. The aspirations of Jews to identify with French culture during the colonialist era—which they hoped would carry benefits such as the annulment of their inferior legal and social status as *dhimmis*—brought about a detachment from the Arab majority (see, e.g., Memmi 1975). Today, for instance, Jews do not speak *fusha* ("classic" Arabic) and few youth speak fluently *darija* (the colloquial Arabic). Also, the recurrent involvement of Israel in violence in the Middle East raises feelings of insecurity among Jews (Laskier 1990; L. Rosen 1968), particularly because the identification of Jews with Israel cannot be made public. All these factors give way to and nourish existential fears and anxieties among Jews, and accelerate the process of disengaging from their surroundings.

"[L]ooking for the frontier," writes Fatima Mernissi in her fictional autobiographic book *Dreams of Trespass*, "has become my life's occupation. Anxiety eats at me whenever I cannot situate the geometric line organizing my powerlessness." (1995, 3)

Spatial contraction in the Jews' lives today is manifested daily in various ways. As individuals Jews refrain from entering into the houses of their Muslim neighbors, thus deterring reciprocal visits. The community's institutions contribute to this process by supplying services that maintain seclusion. For example, La Comité de la Communauté (the Jewish Community Council; henceforth the JCC) has a special worker who deals with the issue of passports, thereby attenuating the need for contact with the Moroccan bureaucracy. Passports and visas are central emblems in the Jews' lives and preoccupy much of their conversations, especially in moments of political tension.[6] Passports and visas represent the capacity to maintain free contacts with the remote poles of identification. According to the JCC worker who deals with passports, the "passport is the Jew's modern walking stick." Without the approval of this institution, Jews find it hard, if not impossible, to receive passports. This prerogative grants the JCC enormous power to control its members. This power is enhanced by the process of disengagement from Muslims, a form of social contraction into which the JCC has invested much energy. This organization, which in fact represents Jewish elite interests, needs its constituents to remain in Morocco; it seduces its members and even competes for them: "We never felt the JCC's involvement in our lives as we do these days," complained a member in the management of the Ittihad (Arabic for Alliance Israélite Universelle). The Jewish educational system of the Ittihad used to (Laskier 1983)—and still does—try to preserve its independence from the JCC. Nevertheless, as expressed by this high-level officer, it is a difficult task.

This seclusionist stance was presented by one of the community's functionaries, Moise Ladany, when he proudly recounted his successful attempt to "kidnap a Jew."

> I heard from someone that there is a lone Jew living in Tadla. I was told that he is neglected, dirty, and that he is habitually searching for food in the garbage; he never bathed, he slept in the streets, outside. . . . I drove there with Madam Aflalo [one of the JCC's social workers] and my wife, Babette. However, when this Jew saw us while we were approaching him, he started

to yell that he doesn't want to see any Jew! He doesn't want to meet Jews. "So," I thought to myself, "tact is needed . . . I have to use my brain!" First, I treated him; I paid for his coffee and for a haircut, too. Meanwhile, I sent Madam Aflalo to get an authorization from the local police to take him by force. And then I spoke with him quietly, gently, sweet talk; the cops carefully approached him, and we all quickly seized him and put him into my car. Poor Babette—she was sitting in the back seat beside him—and she wanted us to wash him up first, but I said no. It was better to take him directly to Casablanca. And you should see him today—he has clean clothes, and he lives in our "Home.". . . You can visit him—he is at the psychiatric wing there.

This story suggests that it was too challenging for the community to have an "unleashed" Jew. By his independence this anonymous Jew escaped the community's social control and defied the prevailing stance of contraction. From the point of view of those managing the institutions, he was better-off behind the walls of the Jewish psychiatric institution and filled with drugs than being "on the loose."

This inward inclination enhances the vitality of the community's institutions. In a paradoxical way, the smaller the community the more vigorous its institutions. The Jewish community in Casablanca has lively private clubs and youth centers, educational systems (from daycare to high school), a medical center, and a social support system managed by the JCC. To these institutions, one must add the religious infrastructure of synagogues, a slaughterhouse, kosher supervision, and so on. Most of this structure is condensed into less than one square kilometer. These mechanisms of social and spatial contraction reinforce feelings of a self-imposed seclusion. Thus, many parts of Casablanca are "terrae incognitae" for Jews: most of its districts are unvisited and unknown. "There . . . Casablanca is a real Arab City!" stated Daniel after accidentally entering one of these ideational faraway places.

Exposure on the Beach

At a certain point during my fieldwork I noticed that the usual sites Jews habitually attend became less attractive, and Jews were going to the beach. Dede Aflalo told me, "You should go there. . . . We have fun, we play cards with Muslims there." I was surprised. Not only do Jews go to the same beach that Muslims frequent, but they are involved in a competitive activity with Muslims. In addition, I thought that the "frivolous" elements of the beach might be intimidating for Jews. Moreover, had I been asked to make a prediction, I would have said that Jews will tend to avoid a space that might cruelly highlight their diminishing numbers. Like pilgrimages and funerals, I thought, this ability to capture visually the progressive decrease in number might be unpleasant (Levy 1994).

"Like our club," lamented Momo, "so is the beach. It is a refuge place and not a pleasant site to enjoy. I go there because it is a place other Jews attend. In that way we create a ghetto. It is our own doing!" This is not the case for all Jews, and my assumption, like Momo's statement, reveals only a partial truth. Jews enjoy going to the beach, even if it is accompanied by a free-floating—most of the time latent—feeling of distress and anxiety. Their anxiety is attenuated by various sociocultural mechanisms that are exploited to establish a feeling of control over interactions with Muslims. Apparently, the elements of re-creation (i.e., those that disconnect people from everyday bonds [E. Cohen 1979])—undressing is perhaps the most representative of these—generate an enactment of rigid sociocultural restrictions and rules of conduct on the beach (Edgerton 1979). Loose instances, Turner emphasized (1967), are the most socially controlled. Or, to use Goffman's words when relating to the naked body, "When bodies are naked, glances are clothed" (1971a, 46). The societal "clothing" restrains the anarchic potential of the metaphoric nakedness.

The persistence of boundaries running along ethnic lines is a fundamental rule, and maintaining these boundaries is especially important to Casablancan Jews. The most acute threat made by the concrete and metaphoric exposure of the body is set against the stability of relations between Jews and their primary "Other": the Muslims. They seek to control these relations, or at least to manage them peacefully, and achieve this by recruiting various codes of behavior on the beach to their advantage.

Social Repercussions of Spatial Ordering

Casablancan Jews frequent the beach quite often, letting the harsh sun burn their skin for long hours during the summer. Men attend the beach for a couple of hours during their lunch breaks and for several hours after work. Wives frequently join their spouses to lunch together. The beach is more populated on Saturdays and Sundays than on weekdays, and people occasionally stay from morning to evening. Tahiti, the preferred beach for Jews, is located in the midst of many other private beaches. Like the others, it is a very small and condensed space.

Two of the beach's gatekeepers play to the Jews' advantage in their pursuit of control. By "gatekeepers" I mean the sociocultural and economic barriers that regulate the profile of those who enter the beach. First, only people who can afford the admission price can enter. Second, cultural restrictions contribute to the beach's exclusiveness: those who do not approve of body exposure will not come. Thus, orthodox Jews and Muslims will not go to the beach. These gatekeepers serve as equalizers that blur external differences between Jews and Muslims. People from both groups are part of the same socioeconomic stratum that, essentially, is associated with a local version of French culture. It is clearly manifested by the use of French (although Muslims tend to use more colloquial Arabic at the beach) and the manner of dress.

The pathway connecting the several corners of the beach witnesses a colorful parade of men, women, and children wearing the latest fashion in swimwear.

Figure 3.
Schema of the beach: (a) entrance; (b) bungalows; (c) coffeehouse; (d) water pool; (e) pool with water slides; (f) suntan chairs zone; (g) cabins; (h) wardrobes and restrooms; (i) kiosk.

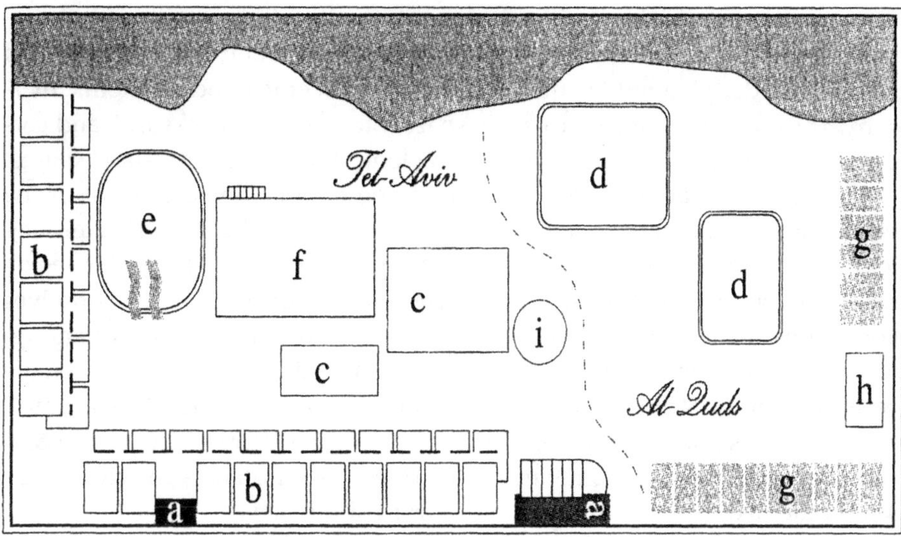

Bikinis and other swimsuits are changed often—every two hours or so—which turns the parade into a colorful and lively event in which people are both watching and being watched. Fashion, partial nakedness, and suntans blur distinctions that are already attenuated by the socioeconomic and cultural gatekeepers. Hence, no apparent division between groups appears when one first watches beachgoers. When looking more closely, however, one realizes that partitions do exist. These partitions are apparent in the way the beach space is physically organized into several distinct areas (see fig. 3).

Bungalows. There are two levels of bungalows. The lowest is populated almost entirely by Jews. Muslims usually inhabit the top floor, although there may also be many Jews on this level as well. The upper bungalows are not as prestigious as the lower ones because they are away from the activity below and are exposed from above to the direct gaze of bystanders who cannot afford to pay the fees. The concentration of Jews is achieved by a collective rental of the bungalows, organized by a JCC member. The bungalows are the women's domain, where they fulfill their traditional tasks as housewives. They prepare snacks and refreshments for family members, supervise their children, and chat with neighbors. They rarely interact with Muslim neighbors.

Cabins. Opposite and at a distance from the bungalows stand two short lines of tiny cabins used for storing clothes. A few Jews (usually the younger and less affluent ones) rent these cabins. The division between the storage places and the bungalows indicates and symbolizes an unmarked yet well-conceptualized boundary between the two spaces of the beach: Muslim and Jewish. This division is conceptualized in the nicknames that Jews and some Muslims ascribe to these spaces: "Tel-Aviv" and "Al-Quds" (Arabic: Jerusalem), respectively. This naming expresses the institutionalization of this division as well as the common recognition of it. The social division is a manifestation of contraction and carries an underlying hidden message, based on an ethnic socioeconomic hierarchy. The use of the cabins turns this space into a Jewish "backyard" and corresponds to the Jewish practice of avoiding long stays within "Muslim" spaces.

Playground. In accordance with that socioeconomic division, most of the recreational equipment (such as the only waterslide or the largest swimming pool) is within the boundaries of the Jewish space. Muslims who wish to enjoy these must go to the "Jewish" space. When Jewish children find themselves alone without a Jewish friend nearby, they usually play by themselves and ignore nearby Muslim children. Jewish mothers immediately intervene when the (rare) possibility of interaction occurs: children are considered "hazardous" and may release undesirable information to Muslims. Parents frequently told stories of embarrassing, sometimes even dangerous instances in which their child recounted a joke about Muslims in front of Muslims.

Sunbathing Chairs. Chairs can be rented on a daily basis and are used by those who cannot afford to rent bungalows. Because space is limited, few chairs are available. Hence, a notion of limited good prompts a fierce competition over space and chairs. An intricate dynamic evolves because ethnic parameters do not determine who rents the chairs, and there seems to be no apparent way to create Jewish enclaves. Nevertheless, Jews tend to arrive in small groups, take over spaces, and create small "islands" that constantly grow as the day passes.

Sometimes Jews find themselves "isolated"—alone among Muslims. In that case, they signal their desire to be secluded by clear codes such as wearing large hats that cover their face, by putting on dark glasses to avoid eye contact, by listening to music with earphones, or by scattering bags, towels, T-shirts, and other belongings to mark the border. Sometimes they simply fall asleep.

Limiting the analytic gaze to the ordering of the beach accentuates the success of Jews in maintaining the demarcation of ethnic division through spatial parameters, and it overemphasizes their ability to constitute hierarchical relationships with Muslims. The actual interactions, however, constantly challenge this image of social and symbolic control because Muslims evidently do not accept Jewish definitions and perceptions. This becomes clear when one watches the interactions of the card players sitting around the coffeehouse tables located within the "Jewish" space.

Card Players on the Beach

Card games are a popular recreational activity among Jews. Many men and women play cards on a daily basis within Jewish clubs and on the beach. Although I watched and participated in many of the activities at the clubs, I will concentrate on the card games because these games offer the steadiest, and almost the only, social frame for encounters between Jews and Muslims.

I was invited to play cards when the games did not involve large sums of money. As an outsider who did not agree to be involved financially at these games, I was trusted. I enjoyed some success and was awarded the title "professor." When games involved high-stakes bets, however, no one agreed to have a "non-involved" player. This allowed me to watch "serious" games from the side and to concentrate on the dynamics between players, and between the players and the kibitzers. It was impossible for me to follow much of what was happening around the games while playing; the activity is too sweeping, seducing, and addicting.

The dynamics of card games change from one setting to another. The most solid ones take place at the CU (Cercle de l'Union) club, a prestigious institution that established tough rules regulating the acceptance of new Jewish members. Most of this club's members belong to the relatively thick layer of well-to-do Jews. There, card games involve people of both sexes and are conducted in a peaceful manner. Many members play bridge as well as more popular French card games such as *belote.* This club stands in sharp contradiction to another, more inclusive, Jewish club—the CA (Cercle de l'Alliance). Card games there are noisier and exclude women. Quarrels often evolve, mainly when someone is suspected of cheating. Women are not supposed to witness—let alone participate in—such dubious incidents. "We are not like the CU, where women participate in card games," said Sam Buhtseira. "They have many problems there. Since married couples play together there, they find it hard to close the club at reasonable hours. Husbands do not have any restraints; they can stay for long hours since their wives are with them. And it's also not polite that women witness all the aggression and the scandalous cheating."

At the beach one can find players of both sexes, although women are not involved in "serious" card games that involve bets of large sums of money. "Simple" games are played for soft drinks, or even for "nothing." "Mixed" games—games in which Jewish and Muslim males are involved—usually entail bets of large sums of money.[7] Women play cards among themselves and sometimes with their male relatives or friends within the bungalow compound. They do not play with Muslims—males or females.

In colonial times, Maghrebi Jews and Muslims were involved in a variety interethnic games, including various sorts of football (Herr 1982) and violent versions of tag (Bilu and Levy 1996, 296–97; Pascon and Schroeter 1982). These games were usually seen and organized through the prism of ethnic cleavages. Hence, as political tensions grew stronger—for example, after the end of the Qaramanli regime in Libya—accusations and incidents occurred during the interethnic games. Ha-Cohen, for instance, testifies that because of these "incidents the games were curtailed by the Turkish authorities in 1845 . . . and were completely eliminated in 1850" (quoted in Goldberg 1990, 34).

Even today, interethnic games are seen by Jewish organizations as a (naive) indication of political rest (Laskier 1990). As a rule, today only few Jews play cards with Muslims outside Tahiti beach. I did not witness these instances as, the clubs that hosted them were off-limits to me as well as to most Jews. There was only one occasion during the Jewish calendar in which several Muslims were invited to play cards within the Jewish clubs: it was during the Jewish holiday of Purim. This carnival-like holiday has many scenes of inversion: people dress up in disguise, children are permitted to publicly smoke cigarettes, young students are allowed to mock and ridicule their rabbis, and so on. Important to our purpose, however, is the mitzvah (religious command) to rejoice and drink wine to a degree that one will not distinguish between Haman (the mythological archenemy in the story of Purim) and Mordechai (the Jewish rescuer). This mitzvah demands a momentary suspension of religious and ethnic boundaries. Within Purim's ephemeral time frame Muslims are allowed to enter into the Jewish enclaves.

The most popular game between Jews and Muslims at the beach is "Rami Couple." Basically, this is a very simple game with fixed and well-defined rules: players are supposed to organize their cards in series. A couple wins a turn when one partner finishes organizing his "hand." When this happens, the remaining cards in the hands of their rivals are counted as negative points. Therefore, players should dispose of part of their hands by exposing series of cards they have already ordered. Reaching a set number of negative points means losing the entire game. Card games are thus perceived as "rule-bound" activities in which the rules are not to be bargained. When Michael Kruyat, considered one of the finest ("fin") players, doubted a certain rule of a *belote* game, he encountered the opposition of Sam Buhtseira. The latter said that this contested rule appears in *The Book of Belote,* published by the *belote* organization in Paris. Kruyat first denied the existence of such a book, and then later disagreed with Buhtseira's version of that rule, claiming that "anybody can write a book. If they say this is the rule then you can tear apart this book." All the people around opposed Kruyat and looked shocked by his blasphemy. Apparently, rules of the game are not to be contested.

Although card games are "rule-bound," they are a social event that is related to and occurs within a specific context. They are not free-floating events disconnected from cultural settings but a "medium for rich, metaphorical discourse that plays out some of the most essential themes" of Jewish-Muslim relations. However, unlike Herzfeld's Glendiot case, in which the fixation of the rules of the games are "of relatively little interest in the serendipitous idiom of Glendiot life" (Herzfeld 1985, 152), within the Moroccan context the rules are of utmost importance. As I will show later, they regulate the most fundamental problem for Jews—the complex schism from Muslims.

Even if the basic rules are fairly simple and few, players establish a large number of subrules and tactics for the best way to win a game. Based on probability logic, these strategies are supposedly aimed at reducing the effect of chance and luck. These subrules and tactics are concerned with the ways in which players track their rivals' and partners' course of play. Mastery over them distinguishes a sophisticated and shrewd player from an unskilled one. The latter relies only on random distribution for composing series of cards. Good players know how to follow and analyze the situations and unseen cards of their partners. They know what their rivals' situation is and what cards they need, and then make appropriate efforts to keep those cards in their hands although they do not need them. Good players choose the correct moment for disposing part of their "hand" in order to escape negative points, or in order to assist their partners by presenting more possibilities to finish the game. Good players also know when to hold their hand in order to prevent their rivals from achieving the same possibility. In short, there are a multitude of aspects to take into consideration, all of which relate to the need to follow others and to be attentive to counterparts and rivals.

Players and kibitzers alike are supposed to keep quiet while playing. At the end of each turn, however, conversations suddenly erupt; people usually try to demonstrate their canny movements, their sophisticated ideas, and their knowledge and mastery of the game. Losers do it with greater enthusiasm since they must prove that it was only bad luck that prevented them from winning. Partners analyze their hands, taking pride in their mutual understanding when they win, and blaming each other when they lose.[8]

Like the need to follow one's partner and rivals during the game, this act of proclamation and interpretation demands a great deal of sensitivity to the "Other"—whether a Jew or a Muslim. What complicates the need to be attentive to the "Other" is an unvoiced rigid rule regarding the way Muslims and Jews play together: a Jewish couple never plays against a Muslim one. As if without noticing, Jews and Muslims form mixed couples. This is not accidental. Even if not spoken, it is an intentional and conscious construct. While driving back from the beach after one of my first days observing card games, Roger 'Adas indicated this principle: "Did you notice that Jews never play against Muslims? We do it on purpose. We don't want them to think that Jews cheat Muslims. To think that we are making a *combine.* Who needs that trouble?" The Jews wish to avoid allegations and accusations that run along ethnic lines. Another way to maintain peaceful relationships is to have more or less permanent players who know each other. This ensures a predictability within the game scene that is hazardous by definition. Occasionally Jewish players who are not satisfied from their Muslim partners will continue with the same partner rather than take on a new one. Even if it is explained (as Jews often do) as a reluctance to restart the process of mutual understanding and a desire not to change their luck, this preference also indicates a wish for steady and anticipated relations with Muslims.

At first glance, the mingling of couples, like the need to follow the "Other," appears to break the basic rule of separation. But, as it may be deduced from 'Adas's words, this is not the Jews' intention. Instead, it is part of their wish to hold untroubled relations with Muslims. Interestingly, the mingling of couples *in the game* is an indication of deep social division *outside it*.

The relevance of an ethnic dichotomy between card players is not limited to the conscious composition of mixed couples. Teasing relationships relating to the ethnic division occur often in the course of the games. For instance, when David Cohen bragged when he won a game, his Muslim rival, Sa'id, immediately responded, "You—*ya Shrif*—you don't 'play it' right!" By that Sa'id declared that Cohen was cheating. Interestingly enough, however, he nicknamed Cohen "Shrif," that is, a descendent of a holy Muslim family.[9] Like Muslims who are linked to the Prophet's family (Shrif), David is also a descendant of a priestly Jewish cast. Thus although Sa'id used an Islamic term in order to express the notion of holy genealogy, he also used this term in order to tease and even criticize the Jew: he accused David of playing an "unholy" game. Not only is David playing a "profane" game, but he is also cheating. The specific setting made it even worse as he played in a frivolous setting (the beach). Moreover, David was betting on Shabbat; according to halakhic laws Jews are not allowed to handle money on this holy day.[10]

Teasing relations that run along ethnic lines are mutual. Sami Gazizy, for instance, mocked his Muslim rival, Mahmid, who lost a game (and money): "Why are you crying so much about the money you lost? You can earn all your loses by selling in [a] few minutes ten grams of gold to some Jewish suckers!" Another Jew, who wished to encourage Mahmid to give up his place, continued: "Go to work! You should open your jewelry store! Many Jews are waiting in line for your gold!" Mahmid responded immediately: "What are you talking about? It's Shabbat; no Jew will provide for me today."

This short episode, like the previous one, both manifests a reduction of complex social actors into simplified symbolic types (Handelman 1991) and expresses various role reversals: a Shrif who is a Jew. A Muslim who is a jeweler (traditionally, Jews dominated this craft because it is religiously forbidden for Muslims to mold precious metals). We also see a Muslim who is accused by a Jew of being a miser. For my purpose here, however, the important point is that, like the mingling of couples, these reversals accentuate the ethnic division. It is an extremely relevant issue among card players.

Despite the fact that games are rule-bound (that is, they are supposed to construct ritualistic social relations), and although participants tend to avoid ethnic rivalries, ethnic-based disputes do occasionally erupt (although not as often as among Jews in the CA). The detailed specifications for the correct way to win a game cannot present an absolute solution. There is no limit to the interpretations of one's actions as a card player. The range of interpretations given to what is eventually considered a wrong move is vast: it can be seen as stupidity, a moment of distraction, cheating or conspiracy, and even an oversophistication that misleads the partner. This diversity of interpretations makes one wonder why quarrels are not more frequent.

Aimed at reducing tensions based on ethnic grounds, this mingling of couples prompts a boomerang effect: it deepens the division and creates another sort of tension. Couple games inherently contain a tension between the drive to act as an individual (a virtuoso) and the crucial need to cooperate with the partner. Cooperation might necessitate an acknowledgment that the partner's hand is better than yours. By implication this means a recognition that one is, momentarily, inferior to one's partner. This also means subsuming one's own whim in favor of that of one's partner, who is, in most cases, one's "Other."

Jews talk about the problematic need to yield among themselves, although they do not recognize that it as an immanent problem for couple games. Instead, they usually blame Muslims for not knowing how to yield. "A Muslim partner is usually very stubborn," said George Levy when he wished to praise his partner's excellent manner of play. According to George, his partner, 'Abdallah, had repeatedly agreed to expose series of his hand, giving George more room to get rid of his spare cards. That way they won many times, explained George.

Tensions between Jews and Muslims occur most often when one side accuses his counterpart of cheating. Public and open allegations are almost always a Muslim privilege. Jews usually do not publicly challenge Muslims. The Jewish silence is related to the fear and anxiety Jews have in the presence of Muslims.

Muslim kibitzers who follow the games are sometimes part of the cheating. They signal to their friend-players the situation of their adversaries. Occasionally they also give away kibitzers and players who cheat. Nevertheless, even when they clearly see someone cheating, Jews do not interfere—even if their friends lose. In addition to suspecting kibitzers, a player might accuse his partner of being a collaborator with his rivals. It is common to suspect that partners help their adversaries, and later on divide the lot. These allegations are also usually made publicly against Jews.

Moreover, accusations are often directed against players who do not pay their debts. Since payment was not always made on the spot, participants frequently owed money to others. Some Muslims were categorized by Jews as players who never pay their debts. Such accusations are made only in their absence. This issue was raised during a conversation among several Jewish card players who constantly mentioned 'Azuz's name. The discussants agreed that 'Azuz was a person one must avoid playing with. Gey Malcka stated, "He always teases us [Jews], and you can't retaliate." All nodded their heads in agreement.

The following story in which 'Azuz again stars, recounted by Albert Ohayon, testifies to the Jews' inhibition in confronting Muslims. A number of years ago Richard Balili came to the beach after mourning his father's death. "Richard was still very sensitive about it," explained Albert, "but 'Azuz, as usual, cursed Richard's father during a card game, when he realized that he was losing. 'Azuz did not know about Richard's father. But Richard almost beat him to death, and punched him on his face until 'Azuz just fell on the ground!" Moshe Cohen interrupted, affirming Albert's version, and added that on the next day 'Azuz was beaten once more because he purposely cursed Richard's father again. "But," Cohen finished, "the third day Richard had to run away from the beach. Many Arabs . . . on the beach were furious that a Jew kept on beating an Arab, one of their brothers. He couldn't go to the beach for several months. After that, when he came, Richard greeted 'Azuz nicely, and that ended the story.

Albert, who had carefully listened to the story, added his own conclusion: "Yes, one should know that it's better to behave correctly with Arabs! They speak nicely to Jews, but if they have to take a stand—they'll always support their brothers."

It was not coincidental that the fact that Richard was still mourning his father's death was interpolated into the story. In fact, it "justified" Richard's outburst against a Muslim and explained his atypical behavior.

Jews see tensions arising in the course of mixed card games as especially dangerous because they believe that Muslims will never see the tensions as conflicts between individuals but as conflicts between ethnic categories. In this story, Albert's conclusion thus reaffirms the Jews' inclination for self-restraint; it is pointless, even dangerous, to get into a situation in which one cannot control one's emotions in front of Muslims.[11]

"Even playing," Fatima Mernissi's fictional mother cautions her young daughter, "is a kind of war." (Mernissi 1995, 3–4)

Exciting Encounters within Well-Framed Settings

In contrast to previous times when Muslims were involved in intricate and patterned relations through Jewish rituals and games (see, e.g., Ben-Ami 1984; Benech 1940; Bilu 1980, 1988; Bilu and Levy 1996; Deshen 1989; Flamand 1960; Goldberg 1978, 1983; Shokeid 1971a, 1982), today Muslims are excluded from rituals (Levy 1994).[12] The only voluntary and formally patterned relationships between Jews and Muslims are those that take place during card games. This is particularly surprising since, while rituals act as a conjunctive social event, "Le jeu apparaît donc comme *disjonctif:* il aboutit à la creation d'un écart différentiel entre des joueurs individuels ou des camps, que rien ne désignait au depart comme inegaux" (Lévi-Strauss 1962, 46).[13]

Not only do games produce schisms where none previously existed, but in this case they deepen an a priori schism between Jews and Muslims that the former seek to control. The fragile situation of the Jews, therefore, enhances the puzzle. Keeping in mind that card games involve fierce contests, one should ask why Jews voluntarily meet Muslims on such shaky and risky ground. The frivolous nature of the beach setting complicates the riddle but also points to the possible answers.[14]

As for the beach, I suggest that its ordering is appropriated as a mechanism for Jews to attain some degree of control. Although their spaces are constantly shrinking, Jews somehow manage to mark boundaries of separation. It is within this sheltered space that card games take place. In a deeper sense, it appears that because card games are rule-bound activities they offer a security net. Within them, Jews can constitute safe and even controllable relations with Muslims. This goal is achieved by the preacceptance of a "meta-message" about the universalistic nature of rules of the game—that is, an acceptance that the rules are not culturally specific or negotiable. That image of uncontested rules enables dialogue between Jews and Muslims. There is also a "pre-contract" in Durkheim's terms (1933) that requires all parties to be obedient to its rules.

Another "meta-message" is the "non-serious" nature of the play. Bateson has emphasized this ideational aspect when referring to the meta-message "This is play." According to him, this framing guides the cognition of the participants and establishes a line demarcating the boundary between non-play and play (1956, 1972b). Players are frequently reminded of this boundary by statements such as, "It's only a game." Through such statements players step out of the game and seriously indicate that it is a non-serious event[15] and thus express their wish to defuse tensions. Parallel messages, although more culturally specific, played at yet another level. When wishing to loosen strained situations, players invoked the well-established cultural code of honor and shame: "It's only money," "I play for the fun, not for the money," and many other similar statements aimed at both defusing potential eruptions and saving face for the losers were used. They indicate a mutual acceptance of cultural idioms.

Likewise, attitudes about the presence of women and cheating indicate common cultural ground. Respectful women should not witness or be exposed to male canny and aggressive behavior. Also, the ability to handle dubious activities and to have an accepted definition of cheating testifies to the existence of a dialogue. "It is not *tricherie* [cheating]," explained Dede Ben-Baruch, "but rather *tricotage* [knitting]," when he wished to clarify the thin and elusive distinction between cheating and slightly bending the rules of the game. As the similar sound of the terms in French indicates, only a hair's breadth separates the two. Successfully "knitting" a situation in one's favor not only demands quick hands but also—perhaps most important—smooth talking and a high level of discursive articulation, all of which must be accepted by both Jews and Muslims.

What I have presented to this point explains how the frame grants a stable setting; I have not attempted to provide an explanation for the need to enter into the interactions in the first place. I believe Jews cannot permit themselves to ignore Muslims in such a condensed and small space. In addition, the frame offers an opportunity for the individual to convey messages. The statement "it's (only) a game" establishes a well-defined border between the world inside and the world outside; it demarcates a clear border between the world of the game and the world of the "ordinary." Within the "abnormal" sphere of the game, players can permit themselves, and should allow others, conduct that in the outside world would be considered threatening, improper, or insulting (like the teasing relationships that convey messages regarding the identities of both groups). Because they effortlessly try to deter reciprocal relations, however, they can only convey frugal and parsimonious messages, using simplified discourses regarding "symbolic types." Hence, Jews can enter into ritualized social exchanges with Muslims under this sheltering umbrella. Moreover, the arbitrary distribution of cards and the canny and astute character of the game offer grounds for successfully competing with Muslims at a relatively low level of risk. The game offers a fairly equal opportunity to defeat the adversary while protecting the winner by the message of non-seriousness. Jews seek to enter into thrilling interactions, to convey messages that are dangerous outside, and, in a more existential way, to look into the Muslim world while being protected by the frame of the game.

To conclude, it seems to me that in the same way that the Jews' own existential situation as individuals who undergo a process of contraction that involves a contradictory situation, that is, an intense social control (especially by their own active institutions) and a gradual diffusion of their community at the same time, so do the beach and card games inherently contain a tension between social diffusion and rigid rules of conduct. Within the compound space of the coffee tables at the beach, Jews encapsulate and enact their larger, more diffused contradictory life experience.

Notes

Many institutions financed the fieldwork on which this essay is based. I would like to thank the Shain Center for Research in Social Sciences, the Center for the Study of Zionism and Yishuv (Hertzl Fellowship), the Institute for Research on the Sephardi and Oriental Jewish Heritage (Misgav Yerushalayim), the Levi Eshkol Institute for Economic, Social and Political Research, the Morris M. Pulver Scholarship Fund of Israel, the Memorial Foundation for Jewish Culture, the Ben-Zvi Institute for the Study of the Jewish Communities in the East, the World Sephardi Federation and Israeli Sephardi Federation, and the Jerusalem Center for Anthropological Studies. The Fulbright Foundation and the International Sephardic Education Foundation (ISEF) generously financed my one-year postdoctoral stay in Cambridge, MA. Also, I would like to thank the members of the Center for Middle Eastern Studies (CMES) and the Anthropology Department at Harvard University for their hearty hospitality. Special thanks to Susan G. Miller for her insightful comments.

1. All names have been changed, although I tried to maintain their ring (whether Arabic, French, biblical, or Israeli). Almakeias's use of the term "Israeli" indicates the complex role Israel plays in the Jews' lives. However, an elaboration of this point is beyond the scope of this essay.
2. "[E]xpatriate communities' . . . members share several of the following characteristics: 1) they, or their ancestors, have been dispersed from a specific original 'center' to two or more 'peripheral', or foreign, regions; 2) they retain a collective memory, vision, or myth about their original homeland—its physical location, history, and achievements; 3) they believe that they are not—and perhaps cannot be—fully accepted by their host society and therefore feel partly

alienated and insulated from it; 4) they regard their ancestral homeland as their true, ideal home and as the place to which they or their descendants would (or should) eventually return—when conditions are appropriate; 5) they believe that they should, collectively, be committed to the maintenance or restoration of their original homeland and to its safety and prosperity; and 6) they continue to relate, personally or vicariously, to that homeland in one way or another, and their ethnocommunal consciousness and solidarity are importantly defined by the existence of such a relationship" (Safran 1991, 83–84).

3. Clifford introduces a trenchant criticism on this too particularistic model (1994, #52).
4. For a relatively reliable assessment of the size of the Jewish community in Morocco, see the *American Jewish Yearbook.*
5. For a general introduction on this issue, see Tibi's discussion about the perception of Islam as *din wa dawla* in various Muslim states (1990).
6. During the Gulf War, Jews talked endlessly about the virtues of foreign passports; Canadian, American, and French were considered the best ones.
7. In contrast to card games among Tiwi women (Goodale 1987) or among the Daulo (Sexton 1987), no meaningful economic repercussions are involved. Games are among more or less equal and affluent participants.
8. Jews and Muslims alike tend to use both Arabic and French interchangeably. As a rule, however, Jews are inclined to use more French than Muslims. When the conversations are intense, vivid, or even fierce, both Jews and Muslims tend to use Arabic. When conversations turn more sober, people from both groups speak in French. Interestingly, I never heard remarks made on the use of language during the games.
9. The popular notion of the term "Shrif" among urban Moroccans does not necessarily carry a holy meaning. They may use it when addressing an older or senior person, friends, and sometimes even a non-Muslim (S. Miller, personal communication). However, in this case Sa'id deliberately chose this term to indicate he was aware of David's "holy genealogy." He pronounced it in such manner that accentuated the "holy" meaning of the term.
10. Sa'id probably was ignorant of many aspects of halakhic laws. However, it is important to note that like women and children, gamblers are considered unreliable and thus incompetent witnesses in court. For communal and institutional sanctions against gamblers, see Goldberg 1993, 166–67.
11. This might explain the absence of women in mixed games. The rules with regard to games with Muslims also reflect a *shared* image of the dangers embedded in the emotionality and uncontrollability attributed to women (for the symbolic images of both Jewish and Muslim Moroccan women as dangerous and uncontrollable, see Bilu 1980 and Dwyer 1978b, respectively). As dangerous beings, women might endanger the fine and fragile ethnic borders separating players. Moreover, women are primarily perceived as sexual beings who, as unrestrained persons, might inflame tensions. Therefore, they should be symbolically kept within confined social spaces so that they are not exposed to the heated encounter of card games laden with sexuality (Herzfeld 1985, 157–59). For an in-depth presentation of the mechanisms of female concealment in the Maghrebi context, see Mernissi 1975.
12. For the complex representation of a Jew in a Muslim ritual in the Maghreb, see Hammoudi 1993.
13. "Games thus appear to have a *disjunctive* effect: they end in the establishment of a difference between individuals players or teams where originally there was no indication of inequality" (Lévi-Strauss 1966, 32). I would like to thank Professor Sally Falk Moore for pointing out this quotation to me.
14. Since I focus on the Jewish perspective, these questions ignore an important angle: Why are Muslims involved in these games? For primarily political reasons my fieldwork was restricted to the Jewish community; thus, I cannot provide a good explanation for this intriguing question.
15. For an insightful analysis of this paradox embodied in the boundary itself, see Handelman 1992.

27

Israeli Emigrants in New York

The Hasidic Option

MOSHE SHOKEID

This chapter is part of an ethnography that presents a population of Israeli emigrants (derogatively nicknamed *yordim*—those who "go down") who are residents of the Borough of Queens. I conducted fieldwork among the emigrants for two years during 1982–84 while staying with my family in Queens, and studied nearly two hundred Israeli men and women, families and singles, whom I met in various venues (home, work, social and cultural public events, an Israeli club, and so on). The ethnography portrays the relationships of *yordim* among themselves as well as their relationships with American Jews. A major finding of the study is the absence of Israeli organizations, when compared with American Jews' remarkable tendency to build communal and national institutions. It also highlights the inability of secular Israelis to affiliate with American Jewish organizations that are closely associated with synagogue participation. This chapter focuses on a specific sector of the population studied: Israelis of Sephardi background. In contrast with *yordim* of Ashkenazi origin, they were more receptive to outreach initiatives from a Hasidic movement actively engaged in the recruitment of newly arrived fellow Jews.

The Lubavitch Hasidic movement, also known as Chabad,[1] was established in the late eighteenth century in Russia under the leadership of Rabbi Shneur Zalman (1745–1812).[2] His eldest son, who succeeded him as "rebbe,"[3] settled in the town of Lubavitch—hence the name. The Lubavitch movement is unusual in its policy of proselytizing, which is directed to bringing unobservant Jews back into the orthodox fold.[4]

My first acquaintance with Chabad's activities among the Israelis in Queens occurred when I was invited by my garage mechanic and his wife to attend the weekly evening lectures on Judaism held at their home. Shlomo and Shula were both hard workers. The garage was open every day but Saturday, and their workday often ended after 8:00 P.M. Nevertheless, they considered it essential to spare some time for spiritual and cultural activities and to try to involve their friends in these activities. Shlomo and Shula, both born in Israel of Yemenite extraction, were in their late twenties, intelligent, jovial, and well liked by their loyal customers. Shlomo had come to the United States with a friend ten years earlier, soon after completing his army service. He had felt an urge to leave Israel and to try whatever awaited him in a new place. Shula arrived a few years later to pursue professional studies.

At the time I met them, both were worried about the prospect of raising a family in New York and were anxious to go back to Israel. At the same time they were frustrated by the financial difficulties involved in giving up their business (on which they still owed a considerable mortgage) and starting from scratch in Israel. Shlomo's father, who had arrived in Israel at a very young age, was not orthodox, and Shlomo, upon his arrival in America, was remote from religion. Shula's parents, who were raised in Yemen, continued to preserve an orthodox way of life in Israel. The couple's association with Chabad and Shlomo's gradual return to orthodoxy played an important role in easing their continuing hand-wringing over their return to Israel.

The participants at the gatherings in their home usually included about ten men and women in their late twenties and early thirties. About two-thirds were of Middle Eastern extraction and a third Ashkenazi. Most of the men in the group were car dealers, and the few women were mainly employed as shop assistants. Almost all the men had been living in the United States for more than five years; the women's stays were of a shorter duration.

The Chabad teacher—as in most other congregations, he was referred to in his absence as the "rav" (rabbi) and otherwise by his first name—was on close terms with Shlomo and Shula, who considered him a personal friend. He too was an Israeli who had been living in the United States for about seven years (where he also got married). He served on the Chabad Committee for Hebrew Speakers and worked among Israelis.

The teacher recommended that I attend two other similar groups in Queens. The second group was also hosted by an Israeli-born young couple in their late twenties who had come to the United States shortly after their marriage. Their parents, who immigrated to Israel in the early 1950s from Kurdistan, lived in Jerusalem. The young couple could not afford to buy an apartment in Jerusalem and had decided to try their luck in the United States. When I met them three years after their arrival in New York the host was driving a truck, of which he was part owner. They were managing nicely in a comfortable, rented two-bedroom apartment and seemed satisfied with their achievements in America. The other attendants, mostly in their twenties and early thirties, were friends of the hosts. Most were of Middle Eastern extraction and were employed in blue-collar occupations. The meetings were attended by five to ten male participants.

The third Chabad congregation, hosted by Reuben, had been meeting for the longest time. Reuben, in his late thirties, born in Israel to parents of Iranian extraction, had done extremely well in America. After seven years in the United States he owned a number of successful stores and an impressive ranch house, and he displayed other marks of affluence as well. Attendance at Reuben's home ranged from five to fifteen male and female participants. Many were recruited from among the hosts' business acquaintances, including owners, salesmen, managers, and employees in the garment industry. Most participants were of Middle Eastern extraction. Reuben's extensive economic connections and his determination to hold the meetings regularly enabled the uninterrupted life of this congregation for more than three years.

In all three cases the core of participants was based on the hosts' personal networks, of which business and friendship bonds were dominant. Other recruits were informed either by Chabad activists or by Israelis who had some experience with the movement.

For a few weeks I also attended meetings at the Piamenta family home in Crown Heights (the major neighborhood concentration of Chabad in Brooklyn, where the movement's central institutions are located). The Piamenta congregation was regularly advertised in the local Hebrew newspapers and on a local Hebrew radio show. These announcements invited Israelis in New York to combine lectures in Judaism with music led by the host, whose family had a longstanding reputation in Israel for musical talent and performing skill. The members of this congregation were not part of the hosts' personal network of friends. Many were students from the nearby Lubavitch Yeshiva, which included a group of Israelis. Here again the majority of participants were of Middle Eastern extraction. The crowd of men and women was considerably larger and more diverse in its occupations than at the less advertised congregations. No less than thirty participants were present at the meetings. The women, though seated separately, were not secluded from the men, who sat around the main table. At the other groups the women sat with the men around one table. Music performed by the host or visitors added a convivial atmosphere to these gatherings.

Meetings at the home congregations started at 9:30 P.M. and lasted for about two hours. The congregants usually had some time to socialize before the rabbi's arrival. Only a few participants attended the weekly meetings regularly. Most others attended once every few weeks or months. Some came regularly for a few weeks and then disappeared for a long time.

I also spent a day at the Chabad Yeshiva in the company of a group of Israelis undergoing training in Judaism and Chabad theology. The group included about twelve men in their twenties to late thirties, two-thirds of whom were of Sephardi extraction and the rest Ashkenazi. In the home congregations about 50 percent of the participants were married and the other half single or divorced; among the Yeshiva participants most were single or divorced. On the whole, many of the participants at Chabad activities had recently arrived in the United States, although there were also some who had been there for more than five years.

Chabad teachers never declined an invitation to address a group of Israelis, and they also lectured at the Israeli Club in Forest Hills[5] at two Wednesday meetings during Hanukkah 1982 and 1983. The teacher-rabbis at the home congregations were assigned to specific groups, with which they met every week for as long as the group survived or as long as the teacher remained in New York. The same teacher, for example, was associated with Reuben's group for more than three years. When a teacher could not attend a meeting, another teacher was immediately assigned to replace him. The temporary assistants were either from the Chabad Brooklyn community or newcomers from Israel who had come for a short visit to the headquarters. In most cases the permanent teachers were former residents of Israel who had been summoned by the rabbi for an unspecified period in order to work in New York. They all spoke the modern Hebrew used by most Israelis without an accent that could be associated with American English, Yiddish, or Arabic. Most of them, if not all, could speak Yiddish fluently. Attired in a somber outfit (dark suit and hat) and with a command of Yiddish, they looked like orthodox Ashkenazim, although a few of them were of Sephardi extraction. They rarely used Yiddish idioms at their lectures, but often switched to Yiddish with their colleagues.

None of the participants was orthodox prior to association with Chabad. One participant told me that although his parents were very religious, he himself had given up orthodoxy during his army service and since then paid an annual visit to the synagogue on Yom Kippur only. Although he had recently discovered the importance of Judaism, he still did not consider himself orthodox. He thought that many other participants also felt that they missed Judaism since coming to the United States. He argued, however, that some participants came to the meetings at Reuben's home in order to please the host, with whom they did business. He also claimed that the host himself used Chabad for his business interests: "In order to do well in business here you need to master Yiddish or wear a skullcap. The Jews control the textile business in New York and it's enough that they extend their credit to you for a longer period in order to succeed. Chabad is Reuben's alibi in business. If they see you from time to time at the rabbi's *hitvadeu't*,[6] or if you get the rabbi's recommendation, then you'll get special treatment." Reuben, who indeed may have profited from his relationship with Chabad, also reciprocated with generous financial contributions. In addition, he provided employment in his stores for Chabad's new recruits.

This instrumental reciprocity between the Hasidic movement and its new disciples was less noticeable at the other home congregations although the teachers offered help and support to whomever seemed to be in need. Chabad's worldwide organization, its local connections, and its abundant resources appeared to be able to provide easy solutions to most problems.

The participants showed great differences in their commitment to religious observances. Shlomo, for example, closed his garage on Saturdays and on all Jewish holidays (he stayed open on Sundays and other American secular holidays). The teacher at Shlomo's congregation must have had this increasingly observant attitude in mind when he commented: "You need patience; after all they come from an orthodox background." When I asked the teacher if Reuben was strictly observant, he answered, "No, but he is making good progress."

Chabad's efforts at proselytizing did not seem very successful among *yordim* of Ashkenazi extraction. Most puzzling was the particular appeal of Chabad's activities to Sephardi *yordim*, whose religious experience and cultural traditions were remote from those represented by Ashkenazi Hasidim. The Sephardi male participants, most of whom were born in Israel, had not been observant prior to their involvement with Chabad, although their parents were often observant. Most of them had been through junior high school in Israel[7] and were employed there in small business and in technical and blue-collar occupations. In New York they were mainly employed in business or had become independent craftsmen.

The association of the few Ashkenazi male participants with Chabad seemed to be more often related to a turbulent personal history of soul-searching and disappointing experiences. In most cases, this was their first encounter with the Jewish religion, which had not been practiced by their parents. The women, both of Ashkenazi and Sephardi extraction, were in most cases single and their participation also entailed the expectation of meeting a male companion.

The following discussion of the major themes raised by the teachers and a consideration of some other characteristics of Chabad may offer an explanation for the particular appeal of an Ashkenazi Hasidic movement among Sephardi *yordim.*

The Message: The Unity of the Jewish People

The lectures at the home congregations usually began with a reading from the two-page Hebrew weekly pamphlet. The pamphlet, based on the rabbi's Sabbath afternoon *drasha* (rabbinical lecture), was often related to the portion from the Torah (Pentateuch) read in the synagogue during the morning service (*parashat hashavua'*). Other texts often used were *Pirkei Avot* (Ethics of the Fathers) and, for the more advanced, the *Tanya,* the major book of Chabad scholarship and beliefs.

Although the texts or the context of the lecture and its subject matter might differ at the various types of Chabad meetings, in all settings the teachers consistently conveyed the same specific messages. I once recorded two lectures by different teachers on the same cassette. When I transcribed them, I could hardly differentiate between the two, since both teachers used a similar style and structure of presentation, as well as similar intonations. At all meetings and with all audiences the lectures clearly led to the same ideological and practical conclusions.

Most lectures touched on the revelation of the divine ingredients of the Jewish soul. This interpretation was new to me, as well as to most other participants. We were all well aware of the special position supposedly bestowed upon the Jews as the unique chosen people, *am segula,* but not as being "next to God" in their personal substance. The idea of the divine quality of each and every Jew thus shifted from the tradition of a collective attribute into the domain of personal attributes.

At a meeting during Hanukkah at Reuben's home, the teacher argued that every Jew has two souls: the natural, animalistic soul (composed of fire, wind, water, and soil) and the divine soul (the container of pure oil). The gentile lacks this divine substance, and even his animalistic soul is of an inferior quality. While a gentile can be taught to be good, a Jew is inherently good. The teacher used as evidence the Germans, who, although famous for their good manners and civility, as well as their celebration of philosophers and sociologists—the reference to sociologists was made by the speaker while looking pointedly at me—succumbed to the leadership of a madman. The teacher went on to claim that the Jewish soul is part of God. As it is written in the Torah, "Israel, you are my first-born child," and "you have blown life into me." God blows life from his own soul into every Jew, thereby adding the special quality to the Jewish soul.

At a lecture on Hasidic theory presented one Sunday morning at the Chabad Yeshiva, an Israeli in his mid-twenties of Ashkenazi extraction, who prior to his involvement with Chabad had been far removed from Jewish religious life, asked, "Why were the laws of the Torah given only to the people of Israel?" He got an immediate answer: "If you are an engineer, you don't ask, 'Why aren't I a janitor?' Don't ask why you aren't a slave and don't ask 'Why am I not as base as others?' We have a mechanism which ignites immediately. Every action you take transforms you into a divine creature. I may go hungry for two days and then come upon a nice piece of meat. But I will not eat it because it has not been ritually cleaned and prepared according to Jewish custom." He continued in a conciliatory manner to explain that we should differentiate among Jews, gentiles, and pious gentiles (a select category of gentiles whose noble character has been proved through their humane actions). The Jews receive directly from the source of holiness, the pious gentiles receive something from the same source, but the ordinary gentiles are completely removed from holiness. This special substance[8] was also used to explain why the Jews do better than others in so many spheres. Even a Jew who does not fulfill God's commandments is superior to the ordinary gentile. This conclusion, as evidenced more clearly in the following observations, ultimately leads to an eradication of the separation between religious and secular Jews.

A major theme in Chabad's teachings stressed that since all Jews are part of the same entity, they are mutually responsible and accountable. As expressed by one teacher, "From the point of view of the rabbi there are no secular Jews and orthodox Jews. All Jews perform *mitzvot* [precepts], some do more and some do less." As evidence, he quoted the rabbi's letters, which are always addressed to "All the sons and daughters of Israel" and not to particular Jews. This concept of the unity of the Jewish nation and the indispensability of every individual was symbolically expressed through the rabbi's project of inscribing every Jew on a list, since it is believed that every letter in the Holy Scripture stands for a living Jew. At all Chabad meetings the participants were encouraged to inscribe themselves and their relatives on this list, which, it was claimed, already included six million names.

The message conveyed by Chabad's teaching was flattering indeed. It endowed every participant, including those whose material or intellectual achievements and social or moral standing were less than satisfactory in their own eyes, with an undeniable innate value and status. The rabbi's representatives, who were themselves successful in many ways, were most sincere in their offer of this new sense of self-esteem. I never saw a Chabad teacher falter in his expression of respect toward anybody, even when provoked by obscene or offensive behavior, by conspicuous ignorance of Judaism, or by irritating demands. The lectures at Shlomo and Shula's home, for example, were often interrupted by jokes and obscene sexual references to the participants and their past experiences. At one meeting a young car dealer of Moroccan extraction seemed to be trying to test the teacher's patience. He continuously made bodily gestures toward a good-looking female participant, focusing attention on her breasts. Moreover, he made frequent jokes about the teacher's moral and sexual life. For a long hour the teacher made only feeble smiles of protest at this continuing offense, which gradually made it impossible for him to teach. At last he could no longer restrain himself and asked the troublemaker whether he had nothing on his mind except cars and girls. Seemingly offended, the young man retorted, "So it seems you think me no good and wish me to leave." The teacher immediately apologized—"No, you are a saint [*tzadik*]"—and brought as proof an ancient saying that claims all children of Israel are *tzadikim* even when they do not seem to be so. Moreover, if the young man promised to put on phylacteries,[9] he would present him with a one-dollar bill that he had carried in his inside pocket as an amulet ever since the rabbi had given it to him. The young man, though touched by the offer, refused politely. He promised to let the teacher know when he felt ready to put on phylacteries. At a later meeting the teacher told me that he had a lot of patience in dealing with his audience and added, "You need to get close to them; they come from a religious background [implying their parents' generation] and can be recruited back to orthodoxy."

The differences between Chabad's Ashkenazi Hasidic tradition and the Middle Eastern religious traditions, the background of many if not the majority of the Israeli participants, were never referred to. The teachers addressed the participants in the neutral Israeli Hebrew dialect and emphasized the intrinsic importance of every Jewish individual regardless of religious status and cultural background. They were never carried away into a discussion about the differences between Ashkenazim and Sephardim, even when provoked. Once during an intermission, for example, Reuben seized the opportunity to share an idea that had occurred to him during the previous Sabbath service in the synagogue that he thought "might explain the ethnic disparities [*pa'ar adati*] in Israel." "I go to an Ashkenazi synagogue," he began. "While the congregants gossip (since they know each other well and possibly speak to each other in Yiddish), I read. I was reading in Genesis how Canaan, the son of Cham, and his descendants were cursed by God to be slaves forever. It suddenly struck me that since Sephardi Jews have been dispersed for many generations in the lands of the children of Canaan, they must have been infected by their hosts' impurity and therefore arrived in Israel disadvantaged in comparison with Ashkenazim." As proof of his hypothesis Reuben quoted a verse from the Book of Genesis and went on with his argument: "If you look around [in Israel] you always see the Sephardim in manual jobs while the Ashkenazim do office jobs. It is a fact that the Sephardim arrived in Israel disadvantaged, but not because of a lower IQ." The teacher reacted to Reuben's insight briefly and in an unimpressed tone: "I have never thought about it—we always think about what unites the Israeli nation rather than about what divides it." The host retorted, "I agree with you, but if everything is written in the Torah, then this too is written there. This chapter shows the destiny of the Jews in the lands of Canaan." At that the lecturer resumed the theme he had been discussing before the interruption.

Our host, Reuben, had not been satisfied in Israel with his economic and social standing and, according to a close family member, was bitter about the ethnic prejudice he thought had adversely affected his achievements there. He now seemed greatly reconciled to his existential position. Economically successful and enthusiastically embraced by an Ashkenazi establishment, he looked back without bitterness at the Israeli ethnic reality, which in the past must have caused him considerable pain.

The only reference made by the teacher to the ethnic divisions in Israel was intended to demonstrate how alien any such divisions are to Chabad. Answering a question about the rabbi's opinion on Israeli politics, the teacher mentioned that while Prime Minister Golda Meir held office, she was reported to have expressed resentment about the rabbi's intervention in Israel's internal affairs. The rabbi reacted to her complaints by relating a parable: "Imagine, a simple Jew from Brooklyn." At this point the teacher interrupted his own narrative and said: "But let me add, 'and one who doesn't speak Yiddish,' since according to Golda those who can't speak Yiddish are not Jews!" He then continued with the parable: "This Jew from Brooklyn phoned her up and told her about a bomb due to explode in her Jerusalem office. Wouldn't she accept his call?" Thus the secular Israeli prime minister had apparently used Yiddish as a criterion for distinguishing between Jews. But although Chabad people used Yiddish for many purposes (including the rabbi's periodic appearances in front of his disciples, which were also broadcast on radio and television), it did not serve as a barrier between Jews, who were all considered equal.

The notion of embracement by Chabad once led Reuben to relate in an amused mood an early life experience. While still a teenager employed in Tel Aviv at a workshop owned by Ashkenazim, he overheard somebody saying he had a *goyishe kop* ("a gentile head," a Yiddish term for incompetence). Yiddish, although largely alien to most Sephardim, did not seem to deter them from joining a movement noticeably Ashkenazi in its symbolic expressions.

The Essence of Judaism and Its Transmission

At one session at Reuben's home, after reading from the weekly Torah portion (which dealt with Noah's Ark), the teacher argued that it is commonly assumed that a person who lives in Israel, speaks Hebrew, and serves in the army is Jewish. But if this is the case, then Israeli Druse citizens are also Jewish, since they, too, fulfill the same three criteria. And what about Russian Jews, who do not live in Israel, do not serve in the army, and cannot speak Hebrew? Would we not consider them Jews? The teacher went on to reassure his listeners that Jewish identity cannot be defined as evenings of folk singing or dancing, thus alluding to a major manifestation of secular Israeli culture. Jewish identity is what we call "Judaism," it is the "ark" that reappears every generation. Otherwise, he explained, there would be no reason to retell the story of Noah's Ark and the flood. Judaism is the "ark" that survives the continuing deluge of foreign cultures and senseless pursuits.

A similar theme was repeated by another teacher, whose lectures I attended at both the Chabad Yeshiva and at the Israeli Club and who used the image of *pach hashemen* (the container of oil), which kept the menorah lit at the temple in Jerusalem and which is symbolized every year by the Hanukkah candles. The oil represents the substance of Judaism. He said that the Torah holds everything, including the technical inventions and scientific theoretical revelations of which the modern world is so proud. He promised his audience that learning the Torah was not the study of the irrelevant past but a way of improving their general education in fields about which most of them were uninformed. He also reassured his listeners that the practice of Judaism would not interfere with their individual professional lives.

The teacher, who revealed that a few years ago he too had been "anti-Torah," related his recent experience in the army, where he witnessed highly educated men "go nuts" from boredom. They could not concentrate on books related to their professional work and absorbed themselves in pornography. They phoned their wives and complained as though they had been away from home for a few years. Yet, once home, they immediately rushed out to see friends and find entertainment. The speaker himself had had no problems whatsoever during his seven weeks of army service because, as he said, "The Torah is with you everywhere and it answers all problems. It is a way of life. Without the Torah people escape from themselves. They search for entertainment, which is no more than a method of escape. Judaism calls you to come and learn about yourself, which is a world in itself!"

The teacher thus invited his listeners to share his recent Israeli experiences. He was also associating Chabad with major issues of Israeli life, army reserve duty in particular, and at the same time raising doubts about the strength of

Israeli Ashkenazi secular culture, often associated with higher education and professional skills (of which most participants of Sephardi extraction were deprived). Pinpointing the weaknesses of secular education, the teacher presented Chabad's education as a modern system capable of solving problems inherent in contemporary life.

Israelis of secular background commonly perceive Judaism as a body of archaic and demanding precepts as well as a corpus of complicated texts that requires many years of learning. The Chabad messages, however, presented Judaism as a goal easily attainable by all Jews regardless of their religious status. To be Jewish by birth allowed one to be halfway toward the attainment of this goal, and the rest of the way was not burdensome. Participation in Chabad's relaxed meetings was an important step in this direction. The participants were not questioned about their practice of religious observances. It was assumed that they would gradually, at their own pace, commit themselves to increasing their load of daily observances.

One of the regular participants at Reuben's congregation told me that he had transferred his seven-year-old son from a Jewish school to a public school, an action he knew would greatly displease the Chabad teacher. He explained that he was not satisfied with the standard of teaching at the Jewish school. This action might also have been influenced by financial considerations (in 1982–83 the annual fees of Jewish schools in Queens, unless subsidized, ranged from $1,250 to $2,700). He also worked on the Sabbath, since he might otherwise have lost his job as store manager. He went on to point out that Reuben himself, who appeared to be a pillar of orthodoxy in Chabad circles, kept his stores open on the Sabbath. The teachers, however, did not criticize their recruits' behavior and treated the participants and the hosts in particular with much respect.

A Saint in the House

The Chabad teachings also stressed the importance of the association of its disciples with the leader of the movement, the venerated Lubavitch rabbi, Menachem Mendel Schneerson, who at the time was over eighty years old. The involvement of Reuben's family with Chabad was most noticeable upon entrance into their spacious home, which was like a shrine to the Lubavitch leader. The walls were decorated with photographs of the rabbi, one of which showed Reuben in his company.

A young Israeli of Middle Eastern extraction who lived in the Chabad Yeshiva compound and knew the rabbi's daily schedule took me to see the rabbi when he arrived at his office for the morning session. At 10:00 A.M. the rabbi's limousine stopped in front of Chabad headquarters. I remained in the small corridor leading to his office with an Israeli friend and a few women who were waiting for the opportunity to be blessed by the rabbi's presence. All other local attendants disappeared into the adjacent corridors and rooms. Suddenly a dead silence fell upon the busy place. The rabbi marched alone along the path leading to the building and into his office. I was impressed by his firm walk and authoritative expression. Our guide, who reappeared after the door closed behind the rabbi, told us he felt very small in the presence of the rabbi. An Israeli of Ashkenazi extraction who was visiting the Chabad center for a few weeks appeared on the scene and explained that the women waiting for the rabbi had already sent him a letter requesting his help. He also told us that a relative of his, a thirty-eight-year-old woman of many talents who could not find a suitable spouse, sent a letter to the rabbi and came to see him from Israel. "It is enough that the rabbi looks at you," he explained. She returned home after seeing the rabbi in this corridor and soon was happily married.

The reverence and adulation the Hasidic leader enjoys, as expressed in his presence as well as in the stories relating his mystical powers, resemble those of religious leaders of many groups of Middle Eastern Jews, particularly in North Africa. As I have described elsewhere (Shokeid 1979), these leaders were scholars whose authority was invested with charismatic traits demonstrated by the individual, as well as by the family patrimony, best expressed in *zekhut avot* (merit of the fathers). The leaders, who were not formally appointed and who did not receive a regular salary, were known for their extraordinary deeds and the power of their blessing. In Israel this type of leadership could not easily accommodate itself to the religious bureaucratic system (based on, among other things, formal appointments to various offices). Consequently, the authentic leadership of many Middle Eastern communities lost its position among its constituencies. The sense of loss and the yearning of Middle Eastern Jews for their traditional leaders manifest themselves in Israel particularly in the popularity of pilgrimages to the tombs of scholars and saints[10] and the *hilulot,* the commemorative celebrations dedicated to sages from earlier times.[11]

In Israel, the Ashkenazi Hasidic movements led by charismatic families (which remain unaffected by the religious bureaucratic establishment) are on the whole removed from the Sephardi community. In New York, however, the Sephardim are enthusiastically encouraged to join the flock of Chabad and share with its disciples the power and blessing of the illustrious Lubavitch leader.

Once, during a home congregation meeting, the participants were discussing the rabbi's good health and youthful appearance, as well as the enigma of his childless marriage. A participant of Moroccan extraction suggested that the rabbi would one day reveal himself as the Messiah for whom the Jews have waited so long.

Chabad and Israel

Although Chabad teachers were mainly involved in the revival of Judaism and the redemption of individual Jews, Israeli affairs were constantly brought up during the sessions, often by the teachers themselves. Moreover, they mentioned

Israel mainly in reference to controversial political issues, seemingly far removed from the goals of religious teaching. These references repeatedly attacked Israeli groups and individuals who expressed opposition toward the Likud government. The teachers manifested an unreserved nationalistic orientation. Thus, for example, when discussing the continuing dangers of the "flood" from which the Jews can find refuge in the "ark," the teacher added sarcastically: "But instead of searching for the Torah, people look for Peace Now or for a guru." Peace Now, an Israeli political movement associated with leftist parties, represents the strongest ideological opposition to the Likud and its political partners. In the same breath, the teacher was also alluding to the various Eastern religions that have reached Israel. A similar reference was made while reading from the weekly Chabad Hebrew flier related to Hanukkah: "the Hellenistic and liberal party which emerged among the Jewish people and wished to integrate Judea within the Greek world of cultural normality." The teacher added by way of explanation: "As is the case with Peace Now . . . while the Greek empire, its culture, and way of life are now the subject of historical research, the Jewish people and its Torah are eternal!"

On another occasion the teacher explained the rabbi's support of the occupation of the West Bank as based on the biblical promise to Abraham. He quoted the rabbi, who argued that had Israel shown to the nations God's written promise and particularly the contract detailed in Genesis of the sale of the Patriarchs' Cave in Hebron to Abraham (who first bought it as a graveyard for his wife, Sarah), international pressure would quickly have subsided. The rabbi was reported as supporting the Lebanon war, which, in his view, would have attained its goals had the Israeli government not been inhibited by various cabinet members and by the opposition parties.

The rabbi's political stand, enthusiastically presented by the teacher, suited the political attitudes of most if not all regular participants. The opposition parties in Israel and particularly the Labor alignment (which ruled the country until 1977) and its present-day leaders seemed to be resented for more complicated reasons than their political stand over the West Bank. An opportunity for airing these opinions was offered before the start of meetings, when the participants usually listened to the news on the Israeli radio program "Kan Israel" at 9:30 P.M. It often mentioned the latest debates in the Israeli parliament and quoted the arguments and mutual accusations made by the leaders of the coalition and the opposition parties. On hearing these announcements the participants added their own offensive ridicule and evaluations about the personal characteristics and the policies proposed by the opposition leaders. Support of the Likud government and its nationalistic policies was prevalent also in other segments of *yordim* population. But the unanimous consensus in support of the Likud and the vehement resentment toward the opposition parties was particularly overwhelming among Chabad's congregations.

On various occasions participants asked why the rabbi never visited Israel. On one such occasion the teacher reacted with emotion: "There isn't a more dedicated Zionist than the rabbi. In recent years no other movement or organization, the Jewish Agency included, has recruited more immigrants to Israel than Chabad. Go and see how many neighborhoods in Israel have been built by Chabad. Chabad started its settlements in Israel before Hashomer Hatzair [a kibbutz movement associated with a more extremist socialist ideology] and it is now planning a settlement on the West Bank." He went on: "If the rabbi stays in America it is because it is better for the Jewish people, most of whom are still in the diaspora and shouldn't be left alone. The rabbi can better support both Israel and the Jews from here. The time is not yet ripe for the rabbi to leave America. Furthermore, he cannot visit Israel because he wouldn't be allowed to leave again [as prescribed by the *Shulhan Aruch,* a guide to rules of conduct in daily life]." But although the rabbi had never been to Israel, the teacher insisted, he knows it as intimately as if he had walked throughout the land. Alluding to the imminence of the rabbi's arrival in Israel, he ended his defense by informing the group that a fully equipped apartment is ready and waiting for the rabbi in the Old City of Jerusalem.

When the teacher was challenged by a newcomer of Ashkenazi extraction that the survival of Zionism necessitates living in Israel, the teacher stingingly retorted, "Is Udi Adiv a Zionist? He lives in Israel!" Udi Adiv is a young kibbutz member who was convicted for espionage and whose trial and verdict shocked the Israeli public. He went on to explain: "Wherever they are, the people of Israel are attracted to Judaism. There are many important values in Judaism and one of them, though not the most important, is Zionism. The fact is that the young people brought up on the values of Zionism, including those raised in the kibbutz, have left Israel or even cooperated with the PLO. It is Judaism which is at our roots, it is Judaism which carries the true promise for the return to Israel, for the return to values, and for health."

Chabad's position was positively committed to Israel. It presented a clear nationalistic viewpoint associated with the Israeli right wing's wishes for a "greater Israel." It supported Israel's government and its policies at a time when these were less than popular with the American government and the American mass media. At the same time, however, Chabad's position toward immigration to Israel was ambiguous. While assuming it to be an important religious duty, residence in the United States was not stigmatized, since the battle for the survival of Judaism was more important. Chabad Hasidim were called upon by the rabbi to leave Israel for America or vice versa, according to the tasks he considered vital at a specific time. As one of the teachers exclaimed, "We have a task and it doesn't matter whether it is to be carried out in Israel or in New York." The trouble, he pointed out, is that "in Israel, too, the Jews are in exile—spiritual exile [*galut ruchanit*]." This attitude was often adopted by participants who interpreted their own stay in America in mystical terms.

When Shlomo confessed that living in the diaspora was a source of pain to him, the teacher insisted that although he was residing outside of Israel he was not in exile. He thus differentiated between territorial exile and spiritual exile (*gola* versus *galut*). Shlomo often argued that exile was most probably "forced upon us," implying the other participants as well. He attributed the responsibility for his departure from Israel and his prolonged stay in New York to an external force. He thus assumed circumstances similar to those of Chabad missionaries summoned to the United States by the rabbi's command. Although the teacher gave no support to this interpretation, Shlomo did not give it up. Reuben once aired a similar idea. When the teacher expressed the wish that Reuben might go back to Israel next year, Reuben responded in a wishful tone, "I hope he [God] who took me out of there will also take me back." The teacher made no comment at this transfer of responsibility to the Almighty. Another participant once commented, "We don't know why we are here, but I believe we are serving as delegates for some good reason. God must know why we are here."

Compatibility between Chabad and Its Sephardi Constituency

The data available on Chabad's achievements in its proselytizing activities among Jews seem to indicate that Chabad's missionaries are satisfied with much less than full "conversion" and with modest numbers of converts. As reported by Mitchell and Plotnicov (1975), in over forty-five years of work among Pittsburgh's Jews, the Lubavitchers have succeeded in attracting only six new recruits. However, within four years of missionary work at centers situated near colleges and universities of Los Angeles, Singer (1978) reported forty-five converts to Chabad.[12] Among the Israelis I observed, the impact of Chabad activities was varied. Without taking into account the Chabad Yeshiva students, whose social characteristics were possibly similar to those of the Los Angeles recruits, the hosts of the home congregations seemed closest to the status of converts. Most other participants developed a positive attitude toward Chabad teaching, but their lifestyle was otherwise very little affected. Although they did not become either synagogue congregants or observant, their participation produced a new awareness of their Jewish identity and provided them with an experience of social and cultural belonging in an alien environment. The teachers, for their part, seemed gratified by any act that involved their audience in Jewish activities. This tolerant approach was remarkably different from the image of Ashkenazi orthodoxy as most participants had experienced it in Israel.

Although the Chabad movement is rooted in a Hasidic Eastern European tradition, whose major features have been remarkably preserved in its voyage from the shtetl to New York, the majority of Chabad's new recruits from among the Israeli *yordim* were of Middle Eastern extraction. Three elements of compatibility seem to have given rise to Chabad's particular appeal among this segment of Israeli immigration: between the religious demands made by Chabad and its pattern of religious leadership with the religious tradition of Middle Eastern Jews; between Chabad's ethos and its strategy of relating to the existential experience of Sephardi Jews in Israeli society; and between Chabad's nationalism and the "rightist" tendencies among Sephardim in Israel.

In a study of contemporary trends in the religiosity of Middle Eastern Jews in Israel, I observed the development of a particular style of religious behavior that I called "*masoret* religiosity" (Shokeid 1984). This mode of religiosity involves a deep attachment to a diffused conception of *masoret beit abba* (tradition of the father's home), which is usually connected with synagogue life but more specifically entails an attachment to the religious details of family ceremonial life on the Sabbath and the festivals. This type of attachment is remarkably tolerant toward partial participation in synagogue life, as well as toward the selective preservation of religious observances in public and at home. The ethos distinguishing this pattern of behavior suggests a scale of religiosity that ranks and rewards each believer according to his particular existential circumstances. The believers perceive this scale as the natural order of religious life, which endows contemporary leaders, as well as scholars and saints of the past, with the spiritual power to supplement their own religious deficiencies. The leaders of past and present provide seasonal opportunities for religious elevation, as for example during the pilgrimages to the saints' tombs and other celebrations. This mode of religiosity is characterized by spiritual and emotional involvement and the notion of belonging, rather than by the strict practice of religious observances.

Chabad's particular ethnocentric religious theory, which attributes a special religious status to all Jews, regardless of their religious comportment, and which accommodates a relaxed attitude toward religious observance among the new recruits, is remote from the severe attitude toward partial observance held by Israeli orthodoxy. Thus Chabad's position was compatible with the religious experience and affective modalities that characterize Israeli Sephardim. Chabad's anchoring in the rabbi's charismatic leadership added a further element to the compatibility between the seemingly distinct Ashkenazi and Sephardi cultural traditions. Further evidence for religious attitudes among Sephardi versus Ashkenazi *yordim* may be found in Korazim (1983, 104), who reported that among his sample of Israeli families in New York the majority of Sephardim (60 percent) defined themselves as "traditional," whereas the majority of Ashkenazim (58 percent) defined themselves as "secular." This information supports our observation that the Sephardim were more receptive to Chabad's proselytizing activities.

Sephardi immigrants in New York include some, if not many, who harbor bitterness about their disadvantaged position in Israeli society, where the Ashkenazim still control important resources of power and prestige. Chabad, however, included Ashkenazim who seemed to be openhearted and anxious to absorb them as equals among their ranks. Chabad's theological message, as well as its missionaries' behavior, placed great emphasis on the indispensability of every individual to the welfare of the Jewish people. In contrast, both the secular and the orthodox establishments in Israel had looked down at their brethren arriving from the Middle East, who were expected to strip off their cultural and behavioral traditions as soon as possible. The saga of Middle Eastern Jews' journey to a new country was now being repeated, but this time for the better. The Ashkenazi Jews they met at the other end, as represented by Chabad, exhibited the hospitality, love, and understanding that had been missing at the earlier encounter.

Chabad's position on Israeli politics also seemed compatible with dominant attitudes among Israeli Sephardim. Chabad's support of the Likud was mainly related to its interest in annexing the West Bank. Chabad's political sympathies coincided with the popularity of the Likud among the Sephardi constituency (see, e.g., Arian 1981), which was influenced by additional motivational factors. Although the Likud had Ashkenazi leadership, it was nevertheless able to contain a Sephardi protest against the veteran Ashkenazi establishment. This veteran establishment, mainly associated with the Labor Party, had ruled the country since the attainment of statehood. The Labor governments were responsible for the absorption of all immigrants and were therefore accountable for the failures in the integration of the newcomers and the gaps that continue to divide the Sephardim and the Ashkenazim in Israel.[13] Finally, Chabad's nationalism, combined with a relaxed attitude toward residence outside Israel, helped relieve the dilemmas with which most *yordim* were besieged. Its message offered an alternative version of identity, which, while preserving Israeli loyalties, also incorporated a newly acquired American component. That part, however, was not associated with the dominant American Jewish self-presentation and institutions, which lay beyond the reach or aspiration of many Israelis.

This chapter analyzes the attraction that Chabad Hasidism has for Israelis of Sephardi backgrounds living as immigrants in the United States. Part of the analysis illuminates the general question of why and how a European-derived Hasidic group proved attractive to Israelis of Middle Eastern background, whether in Israel itself, in France where similar developments have taken place among North African Jews who migrated there, and in North America. Another aspect of the argument shows why affiliation with this orthodox movement is meaningful to Israeli emigrants still trying to make sense of their long-time stay on American soil. At about the time that this field study was concluded, the Shas Party made its debut on the Israeli political scene. Its electoral success since then also represented a novel merging of influences from the world of Ashkenazi orthodoxy with the social background and contemporary dilemmas of Middle Eastern Jews in Israel. This chapter thus gives a hint of developments that have since become more prominent, entailing both general global phenomena such as migration and the globalization of Jewish identities and religious issues that have echoes both in Israel and abroad.

Notes

This chapter is taken from M. Shokeid's *Children of Circumstances: Israeli Emigrants in New York* (Ithaca: Cornell University Press, 1988), 139–60. The introductory paragraph was added by the author for this volume. The concluding paragraph was supplied by the editors.

1. "Chabad" is the acronym formed from the Hebrew words for wisdom, understanding, and knowledge.
2. The Chabad movement sprang from the fragmentation of Hasidic Judaism, founded in the mid-eighteenth century by the Baal-Shem-Tov (1700–1760). Hasidism advocated the introduction of joy and emotional fervor into traditional Judaism, which was hitherto characterized by a life of strict observance guided by a learned elite.
3. The title "rebbe" refers specifically to the head of the movement. The Israelis and their teachers, however, pronounced his title somewhat differently, "rabee," without the Yiddish intonation. I shall therefore use the customary term "rabbi."
4. See Shaffir 1974; Mitchell and Plotnicov 1975; Singer 1978.
5. For more details about the Israeli Club in Forest Hills, see Shokeid 1988, 71–103.
6. *Hitvadeu't*—the rabbi's periodic appearance in front of his disciples. These appearances are usually associated with the major holidays.
7. Korazim's survey of Israelis in Queens and Brooklyn (1983) revealed that the educational level of families of Sephardi origin was significantly lower than that of Ashkenazi families (84–85)..
8. The substance of holiness embedded in each individual was often phrased in terms of vessels such as the container of oil associated with the miracle of Hanukkah (when the menorah at the Temple was kept lit for eight days by the oil provided from one small container) or Noah's Ark. These containers and their contents were at the same time associated with the essence of Judaism as a system of belief and a way of life. The divine soul, as well as the substance of holiness, were described as aspiring to infinity.
9. Phylacteries (tefillin)—two black leather boxes containing scriptural passages that are bound by black leather strips around the left hand and on the head and worn during the morning services on all days of the year except the Sabbath and scriptural holy days (see *Encyclopaedia Judaica*, 15:898–904).
10. See, e.g., Shokeid 1974; Ben-Ami 1984; Ben-Ari and Bilu 1987.
11. See Deshen 1974.
12. One should probably compare Chabad's achievements in Los Angeles with those of other proselytizing movements active among university students.
13. The support of the nationalistic policies of the Likud might also express a latent protest against old-style Zionism, which did not greatly involve the Sephardim.

28

Changing Israeli Landscapes

Buildings and the Uses of the Past

ALEX WEINGROD

A number of recent anthropological studies have sought to interpret the design of a building or an entire urban landscape within the context of a cultural system. Emphasizing such topics as shape and color or how space is conceived and organized, these studies explore relationships between the ways in which structures are crafted and their underlying cultural conceptions. To cite briefly several examples, Rabinow (1989) explains that the French redesign of Moroccan cities was conceived by an elite nurtured in nineteenth-century social theory and the spirit of colonial mission; Geertz (1989) shows how the new designs of dwellings in a Moroccan town became part of an intense political-cultural debate that resonated widely; and Kapferer (1988) suggests that Australian monumental structures can be seen as expressions of a pervasive national mythology. The relationships indicated in these studies between physical structures and their cultural meanings are intriguing: styles of architecture, or several particular buildings, are portrayed as evocations of basic cultural processes. Thus, as Blier indicates in her finely detailed analysis of Batammaliba buildings and their builders, architecture becomes "a kind of script that can be read" (1987, 10).

This chapter focuses on these themes—or, following Blier's phrasing, it examines two Israeli structures as if they were "scripts" and proceeds to "read them" within the unfolding contexts of Israeli society and culture. The two buildings that form the center of this analysis were built during the 1990s. The first consists of a shrine and associated buildings constructed on the outskirts of the small Israeli town of Netivoth, focusing around the grave of the great new Jewish *zaddik* (saint), Rabbi Israel Abouhatzeira, popularly known as the Baba Sali. Standing in or near what had once been open fields, these structures have been designed to express a distinctly Moroccan or Maghrebian set of motifs. The second is the exact, brick-by-brick replica of the red-colored, three-story Brooklyn building that serves as the headquarters for the Jewish Hassidic religious movement known as Lubavitch (sometimes called Chabad). It was built in what had once been an open field overlooking the main Tel Aviv–Jerusalem highway.

These are both extraordinary buildings. What makes them unique is that they transfer and implant faraway places—Morocco and Brooklyn—directly into the Israeli scene. This chapter addresses the issue of how to decipher their script—how to "read them" in order to understand what they are meant to signify—and, more generally, how to consider these particular representations in the wider theoretical context of physical structures and their meanings.

The Structures

Let us first examine the Moroccan building, the Baba Sali's shrine. Rabbi Israel Abouhatzeira, the Baba Sali, is undoubtedly the most famous of the new Israeli saints (Ben-Ami 1984; Ben-Ari and Bilu 1987; Weingrod 1990). A member of Moroccan Jewry's leading religious dynasty, he immigrated to Israel in 1964 and subsequently settled in the small southern town of Netivoth, where he established and became the head of a yeshiva, or religious academy. In Morocco, Rabbi Abouhatzeira had already gained the reputation of a learned sage and, more important, of a miracle-working holy man. He became famous for his ability to heal and cure—he was particularly known for blessing bottles of water that had recuperative powers—and consequently was besieged with requests not only to resolve thorny issues in religious law but also to assist persons who suffered from barrenness, illness, personal misfortune, and the like. When, in 1984, Rabbi Abouhatzeira died at the age of ninety-four, it was immediately apparent that he would become a *zaddik,* just as his grave would become a holy shrine. He was buried close to the local town cemetery in what was at first a solitary, simple grave. Soon thereafter, the grave was capped with a small, domed, whitewashed structure, becoming a marabout's grave in the distinctly North African style.[1] Standing by itself in the midst of a large space, baked and glaring in the desert sun, this plain, primitive, whitewashed shrine glistened in a dazzling, powerful fashion.

The story of the Netivoth buildings belongs not to the Baba Sali but to his son and successor, Rabbi Baruch Abouhatzeira, the Baba Baruch. Here the tale proceeds on more slippery ground. Baba Baruch, who quite literally seized his father's mantle from other competing claimants, has been the wayward son. With the reputation of a rogue rather than a saint, he has nonetheless developed the shrine with great energy. Each year, on the anniversary of the rabbi's death, a *hillula,* or pilgrimage and memorial celebration, is held at the grave site. Baba Baruch, who has true entrepreneurial skill, has been the catalyst in promoting the pilgrimage into a widely publicized event that attracts tens of thousands of participants.[2] He has also been occupied with reformulating, designing, and constructing the physical setting. The tomb and shrine, which at first had a plain maraboutic design, have been subsequently enlarged and redesigned. The tomb is now presented inside an outer wrapping of rows of rectangular white stones: separate entrances and spaces for women and men are marked off, and the saint's grave, covered by an elevated tombstone, is enclosed so that the crowds of supplicants cannot touch or place objects upon it. A synagogue has also been built adjoining the tomb, and its outer stone walls climb upward in a regular placing of walls, turrets, and towers. If anything, the shrine now appears less maraboutic and more like a miniature of the walls that encircle Jerusalem.

Of greater interest are the new buildings that have gone up about a kilometer away from the shrine itself, on the outer perimeter of the town of Netivoth. Baba Sali had lived there in a modest home, studying and praying in the synagogue and yeshiva built for him. Baba Baruch is presently transforming this site into a modern "spiritual complex," referred to in his public relations booklets as Kiryat Baba Sali, or the Baba Sali Complex. It is here in particular that Morocco is being built in Israel's Negev Desert region.

When observed from a distance, these new buildings have the appearance of common or "typical" Israeli structures. They consist of a white rectangular building covered by the kind of sloping, red-tiled roof that has become a mark of contemporary Israeli architecture.[3] From a distance, nothing appears out of context or exceptional; on the contrary, the building appears to be well within accepted conventions and perfectly "Israeli" in design. It is only when one turns the corner to stand at the entrance that the building's real character is revealed: the outer Israeli packaging or container is opened—voilà—to reveal the Maghreb within.

The bold design is striking (fig. 1). The architect—born in Marrakesh, trained in architecture at an Israeli university, and secular in outlook—conceived and then succeeded in implementing this unusual structure. A large plaza built of red and black tiles flows in front of the building designed in stark, strong colors of white and a kind of ocher, or deep-purple red. The outer walls of white are low-slung, but towering above them are wide ocher columns that culminate in a white maraboutic cap. The tops of the walls are regularly turreted, with notches climbing up and down, while the curving windows set within them act to soften what is otherwise a kind of desert fortress appearance. The entrance is placed beneath the purple columns. Gazing inside (the opening is meant to be peeked into), one sees that everything flows in curves and arabesques. The floors are made of alternate lines of white and darker tiled mosaic, and they connect with arched, flowing porticos that provide shade cover for the four sides of rectangular space. Each portico is itself held up by a series of alabaster-like white columns, and between them there is a rolling wave of arches. The large inner courtyard is open, uncovered, and darkened only by shadows as the sun moves across the sky. The centerpiece in this composition is a fountain placed in the middle of the courtyard: at certain moments the quiet sound of trickling water provides a backdrop to this imagining of the past. For it is certainly the Maghreb, Morocco, Marrakesh perhaps, that this extraordinary building is meant to represent.

Figure 1.
The Moroccan building at Netivoth.

The semiotic meaning is clear enough. The building functions in part as a study center for the yeshiva, and the upper story provides quarters for some of the students. But these functions hardly seem relevant: the real message is in the design, and the design is of Morocco. Indeed, as if to remove any uncertainty, a sign affixed to the building's outer facing announces that this is "Yechivat Babe Sale," the Hebrew transliterated and written in French.

The second structure is both similar and different. Chabad, or as it is often called, Lubavitch (named after the small Russian town that was its original center), is one of the many Jewish Hasidic religious sects that sprang up in Eastern Europe during the eighteenth and early nineteenth centuries. The word *chabad* is an acronym standing for the Hebrew *chochma* (wisdom), *bina* (understanding), and *da'at* (knowledge). The sect's members and followers travel a special path that often places them occupationally or professionally in the secular world, while they observe strict ritual prescriptions as well as the directions of their leader, the rebbe.[4] The present leader of the Chabad movement, Rabbi Menachem Mendel Schneerson, moved from France to the United States in 1940, where the previous rebbe, his father-in-law, had established his synagogue and "court" in the Crown Heights section of Brooklyn. In an erstwhile middle-class neighborhood with a spacious boulevard, grass, and trees, 770 Eastern Parkway became the movement's center. Over the years, the immediately adjoining buildings as well as other homes have been acquired and incorporated into the Chabad headquarters.

As viewed today, there is nothing exceptional about the structure itself: it is only one of a large number of similar red-brick row house–type buildings that were built in this section of Brooklyn in the early 1930s. But the address has a unique, wondrous aura for Lubavitch Hasidim. It is a special place because the rebbe is there (although he does not actually live there), and therefore, in keeping with Hasidic religious beliefs, the structure itself partakes of the rebbe's holiness and sacred powers. What is more, this building is known personally by Lubavitchers everywhere, as it seems that practically every Lubavitch Hasid anywhere in the world has visited the building, and they are familiar with many of its features.

During the 1950s, the Chabad movement established a small community in Israel. Kfar Chabad, as it is called, is a residential and educational complex located near Tel Aviv. Among other things, it serves as a showplace for their activities. In 1985, in the course of one of his periodic personal discussions with a group of visiting Hasidim, the rebbe alluded to the idea that he wished to have a building like the present Brooklyn structure built in Kfar Chabad. Because the rebbe, who was then in his eighties, had never visited Israel, this sudden request sparked great interest and speculation among his followers. Following discreet inquiries, it was determined that the rebbe did indeed want a new building to be built in Kfar Chabad. What is more, he wished that it be identical to the center in Brooklyn: it should, quite literally, be an exact replica of 770 Eastern Parkway. The Hasidim immediately became energized to carry out his wish. One does not, after all, question the rebbe, because he has profound wisdom and foresight. Thus in 1985, the Chabad Hasidim began making plans to build a duplicate of the Crown Heights building in Kfar Chabad.

The story of the building's construction is an important piece of its overall significance. The initial problem was finding the proper place. A large undeveloped area outside the Kfar Chabad complex was located. This field had the advantage of providing wide-open space; what is more, because it was slightly elevated, it could be seen from every angle, including the major highway several kilometers away. This particular parcel of land did not belong to Chabad, but they applied to the Israeli Land Authority for permission to build there, and their request was quickly granted. (Speed and success in conquering elements that could potentially have slowed the project—bureaucratic as well as technical—are important in the tale of how the building was built.) The main problem, however, was how to build an exact copy of a Brooklyn row house–type structure. There were no plans or exact measurements of the rebbe's building, and it was clear that a great deal of the work had to be specially designed and crafted. The committee in charge of the project selected several architects (who were themselves members of Chabad) and instructed them to begin working. A building contractor was chosen, the necessary funds were made available, and the building's inner scaffolding was quickly set in place. But then the difficulties became more acute: what were the exact measurements? Where would the red bricks come from? And what about the lintels and the doors? One of the architects flew to Brooklyn to measure, sketch, and photograph every inch of the building, and orders were placed with artisans to build or mold particular sections of the house.

And then the rebbe again spoke about the building: he chastised them because it was taking too long, and he went on to say that it should be completed by the 12th of the Hebrew month of Tamuz, the day on which Chabad celebrates Israel's redemption, only thirty-three work days away.[5] This was a stunning, seemingly impossible request. It was the rebbe's wish, however, and consequently from that moment on the contractor, his workers (nearly all of whom were Palestinian), the architects, and many Chabad volunteers worked literally around the clock. The tiles were flown in from Holland, craftsmen built the door frames and white lintels, the roof went up at the proper height and pitch, a tree was planted at exactly the same spot as in Brooklyn, and finally, at the end of the appointed period, the building was actually complete. Exhausted and exhilarated, all of those who had taken part agreed that it was a wonderful sight, and that completing it at that speed had certainly been a miracle.

The replica does seem perfect (fig. 2). It is a Brooklyn row house, and even though the red brick is a bit off-color, the effect is truly extraordinary. Of course, the building is totally out of context. It is a row house without the rows, as it were, not to mention everything else that is completely different—but this makes the effect even more stunning. The arrangement of inner space is not quite identical to the original in Brooklyn—a library and bookshop are located on the ground floor, a synagogue on the second floor—but the rebbe's office, where he receives individuals or small groups of Hasidim, is designed precisely as in Brooklyn. And most important, the building's number is 770. As if to answer any doubts, this address (just as the Moroccan building, its signature) is affixed to the doorway entrance of the building in Israel as if it were in Brooklyn.[6]

Reading the Script

These are, in capsule form, the two buildings. Each is bold, powerful, and unquestionably distinctive. What do they signify? Why have these two foreign, distant motifs and places been transplanted to Israel?

We can begin with features that they have in common. Both buildings share a certain significance when seen from the perspective of the participants or social actors—that is, from the points of view of the Hasidim and others who come to visit the Israeli copy of 770, and the North Africans, mainly Moroccans, who can be seen strolling about the new buildings at Netivoth. By their own testimony, visitors to both sites find that being there has the extraordinary effect of overcoming both space and time. To be in the rebbe's building in Kfar

Figure 2.
The Israeli replica of the Brooklyn building.

Chabad—to be in 770 on a hot Israeli morning—is also to be in Brooklyn and, most important, to be close to the rebbe. The Lubavitch Hasidim are quite explicit about this. Both in discussion and in their published statements, they attest to the power of the building to make them feel as if they were once again near to the rebbe, as if they were, quite literally, back in the hubbub of activities as well as holiness that characterizes his court. They recall situations and persons from when they visited there in the past and recount experiences that took place "in this very building"—but in Brooklyn. What is missing, they continue with a wistful smile, is the rebbe. The building—and, in fact, the entire experience—is not the same without his presence. But it is as close to it as they can come while in Israel, and they value the experience.

The same can be said for the site in Netivoth. Lighting candles and praying at the Baba Sali's grave revives memories of Morocco. The people, faces, smells and foods, singing and dance, and language bring them back to another time and place. The same rituals are performed, often with family members and old friends. Walking through the Baba Baruch's newly constructed yeshiva, or taking part in one of the "celebrations" that he organizes and presides over, can also conjure up a vision of the Moroccan past. These are memories revived for the older pilgrims and participants, while for the younger generation born and reared in Israel, the site evokes images of what Morocco is said to have been like. The younger participants are sometimes quite explicit about this. They relate that "this is what my parents told us about." Some can even be heard explaining to their children that "this is what Morocco was like."

None of this as yet explains why these buildings are there or what renders them significant. In order to answer these questions, it is necessary to leave personal experience and move to a broader historical and contemporary sweep. Here the central issues begin to take shape, and they focus on ideology, belief, and power.

Both of these buildings signify a deep break with the Israeli cultural past, and more particularly with the Zionist ideological system that has been the dominant discourse within the Jewish community, initially in Palestine and subsequently in Israel. This is not a small matter: it is, rather, the statement of a wholly different cultural age.

Zionism took as its goal not just the creation of a homeland for the Jewish people but also the formulation and development of a new Jewish culture.[7] At the core of its ideology was the belief that coming to Palestine-Israel meant leaving the past behind: the young Central and East European Jews who emigrated to Palestine in the first half of the twentieth century urged themselves to turn their backs on their previous materialist, bourgeois, sometimes orthodox religious way of living and start a secular life afresh in their new land. "Anu banu artza livnot u' lihibanot bah" ("we have come to the land to build and to become rebuilt by it") is a singsong refrain of those days that makes the point perfectly: coming to "the land" would bring about a new life, inspire the creative act of inventing the new. In a practical sense, this meant that the new arrivals struggled to master a new language (Hebrew), wore different clothing in different styles, sought to develop new themes in art and music that grew from "the land," began to write poetry and plays about different motifs, and talked and argued about their new lives, all in a conscious effort to remake and thereby "rebuild themselves." It was an odd mixture of materialism and idealism: these new conditions of their existence would generate different, and truer, forms of culture.

Moreover, the logic of this movement was to denigrate or almost despise their own cultural pasts. The *galut* or exile way of life prior to arriving at the shores of Palestine-Israel was depicted in dark, negative tones. This term, in fact, was always pejorative—*galut* expressed what one should not be, how one should not behave. There was a *galut* mentality, for example, a term that described how in the diaspora Jews were always uneasy and fearful of the *goyim,* and how they had become spiritually or culturally crippled by imitating the majority culture. As others have argued, this Zionist critique of the Jews' past at times seemed to accept anti-Semitic caricatures (Rubenstein 1984, 5). The various diaspora histories, whether in Poland or Iraq, were thus constructed in dark, negative terms. The cultural and political elites, the community's censors, stood on guard against expressions of the *galut* past, and they took part as well in the creation of the new.

To be sure, a small ultra-orthodox religious community rejected the Zionist ideology, and many of the post-state immigrants to Israel (including those from Morocco) also did not fully adopt this interpretation of their past and present. Nonetheless, this was the reigning ideology, and immigrants as well as the religious minority were forced to at least contend with it.

It is against this background that these two structures—the one a duplicate of Brooklyn, the other an imagining of Morocco—stand out in stark relief. What they surely represent, if not cry out, is that it is now possible and indeed legitimate for the *galut* to be literally transported to Israel and openly displayed there. The buildings are not tucked away in places where no one will see them; on the contrary, they are proudly displayed in locations where they are certain to be seen. The duplicate of 770 stands like a beacon overlooking a busy highway, and busloads of pilgrims regularly visit the Moroccan structures at Netivoth. It is difficult to imagine that these buildings could have been built a generation or two ago: the reigning cultural and political elites, the censors, would have criticized, derided, mocked, and hounded them in various ways. In all of these respects, these buildings thus represent a kind of "end of Zionism" or, to shift to a different metaphor, an ending of the Zionist hegemony.[8]

There is yet another feature that is shared by both buildings. Not only do they mark the end of one cultural age, they also are significant voices of the newer, ongoing cultural contest that seeks to define the present and the future. In this instance, the issue is not just that of fashioning the new but also and more importantly that of determining what its character should or will be. The problem, perennial perhaps, is who or what is an Israeli?

At some time in the past—say, during the 1940s, 1950s, or even 1960s—this issue appeared to be clear-cut, even obvious. The Israeli persona or character was then encapsulated in the image of the sabra.[9] Sabra, the native born and reared, the second and succeeding generations of diverse immigrant parents, was represented by the spiny desert cactus: prickly and tough on the outside, soft and cool on the inside. When all of the spines were correctly removed, one was left with the stereotype of a secular individual, European in appearance and bearing, cocky and outwardly confident, a pragmatic doer who also had a feel for community and perhaps also, uncertainly and vaguely, for morality. This was considered a unified and unifying symbol—it was what being or becoming Israeli was supposed to mean. But the term, and presumably also the vision, has literally disappeared from present-day Israeli discourse: it is rarely used by the media, and it seems absent from informal settings as well. Israel has in recent decades become too diverse and divided along religious, ethnic, political, ideological, communal or national, and other lines for a single unitary symbol to find wide popular acceptance. What is more, plagued by failure and uncertainty, the old political and cultural center, socialist in orientation, has itself retreated, if not dissolved (Avishai 1985; Eisenstadt 1985).

Nonetheless, an explicit and implicit debate regarding "Who is an Israeli?" continues. Some of the claims and assumptions that inform this controversy are represented in the two buildings. Their topics and messages are quite different, however, and it is therefore necessary to consider them separately.

We can begin with the building in Netivoth, the Moroccan structure, or better still, the "imagining of Morocco." What is unfolding there can best be understood as a response to the longstanding Zionist hegemony. In order to understand this properly, one needs to recognize this ideology in its various dimensions. For it has never been just or only "Zionist." From its inception, roughly at the turn of this century, it has also been a European or, to use the proper label, an "Ashkenazi" hegemony. The ideal was not just to build a new culture but to build a culture based on European or Euro-American styles and practices, while other cultural formats were attacked, denied, and often denigrated. This has been a continuing conflict: while Ashkenazic hegemony was established early, it has been challenged by various waves of non-European newcomers. This is the significance of the Moroccan structures: they are part of the process of counterattack, the statement of a new mythology, and a contemporary attempt to deal with the still-powerful hegemonic system.

The prevalence of Ashkenazic hegemony in Israeli society and culture has been documented in many studies, and there is no need to repeat it at length (see Ben-Rafael 1982; Smooha 1978; Weingrod 1965). Beginning in the late 1960s and 1970s, however, and continuing to the present, a new ideology of "cultural pluralism" that includes ethnic revivals of various kinds has succeeded in changing some of the previous cultural assumptions. Of special interest is the fact that Moroccans in Israel have taken the lead in this process. The best example is their phenomenal success in transforming the *mimouna* celebration, a relatively minor holiday celebrated at the end of Passover, into an Israeli national event that is, in effect, a celebration of Moroccanness.[10] Along similar lines, the emergence of a score or more of new Israeli *zaddikim,* best personified by the Baba Sali, is also closely connected with members of this ethnic group. Moroccan Jews have, in brief, taken the lead in challenging the Ashkenazi hegemony, thereby seeking to locate themselves more centrally within the mainstream of society.

These encounters are rarely if ever ended once and for all. Cultural contests that essentially are political continue over time because they are waged over vital issues. The Moroccan revival of the *mimouna* celebrations took place more than two decades ago, while the Moroccan buildings at Netivoth, Baba Sali, and certainly Baba Baruch are more phenomena of the 1980s and, probably, the 1990s. There is a certain continuity and consistency between these two sets of phenomena, but the issues and the idioms are considerably different.

No one accuses Rabbi Baruch Abouhatzeira, the Baba Baruch, of not being an "authentic Israeli." No one argues that he does not speak the language properly or that his Hebrew has the wrong (that is, Moroccan) accent. These are old issues, and they are no longer relevant to the contest. True, in public he commonly sports a traditional Moroccan *jellaba,* yet he appears to be Israeli to the core. And so are his buildings, the new "Kiryat Baba Sali" that he is building at Netivoth. The entire building project expresses themes that are in tune with contemporary Israel. Baba Baruch is building buildings, transforming the land, and setting men to work with bulldozers and precast concrete as they put up one structure after the next. In many respects this parallels other well-known Israeli political builders, such as Teddy Kollek, Jerusalem's mayor, whose efforts in transforming Jerusalem have been compared with those of the ancient King Herod, or the mayor of Tel Aviv, who has also been redoing his city at a furious pace. Moreover, just as with other "Israeli projects," Baba Baruch travels widely in Europe and Israel to raise funds for his building program, and potential donors receive slick publicity booklets that describe his activities in three languages (Hebrew, French, and English) alongside color photographs. What is more, an Israeli design or aesthetic has been stamped on the buildings themselves. This is an important point. The architect took care to represent Morocco within a recognizable Israeli container. It will be recalled that when observed from its entrance, "Yechivat Babe Sale" is Moroccan, but from all other angles it appears to be characteristically Israeli. In much the same way, the Baba Sali's grave, originally presented as a marabout's shrine, was refashioned to appear as a kind of Jerusalem miniature. This is, in short, an Israeli production: the building project represents Morocco, but it is wrapped in the cultural formats of contemporary Israel (Bilu and Ben-Ari 1990).

This does not mean that there is no controversy over Baba Baruch's projects. On the contrary, his message has been fiercely contested. The issues are anything but trivial, and the debate has been lively and spirited. Yoram Bilu and Eyal Ben-Ari report having collected more than one hundred Israeli newspaper and magazine articles that are, in effect, scornful attacks on Baba Baruch and his activities (Bilu and Ben-Ari 1990). There is no other contemporary Israeli figure, they write, who has been the target of such fierce sarcasm. This media attack is often comic and derisive. To cite a few examples, the main protagonists are renamed "Baba Business," "Dynasty Baba," or "Baby Sali," and events such as a son's marriage or the yearly pilgrimage to the saint's tomb are drawn as starkly negative cartoons. The articles (many of which are written in a pseudoethnographic style) are also caricatures and "cultural alarms" aimed at those who take part in these activities—the "Moroccan masses," in other words. They are described as "primitive people," followers after "idols and magical incantations," persons "whose traditions have been rubbed out, whose dreams are ended, and who are momentarily sustained by the promise of a blessing and a drop of magical water" (Bilu and Ben-Ari 1990, 57).

These are, to say the least, stinging attacks. The issues and what is at stake should be clear. The Moroccan structures at Netivoth are a statement of legitimate cultural and political power, and they consequently represent an attack on the Ashkenazic hegemony, while the media attack, led by the elite censors, aims at maintaining the older centers of power and privilege.

We turn now to the second structure, the exact copy of a Brooklyn building built at Kfar Chabad. What does this building stand for? Why was it so important to build a replica of 770 Eastern Parkway in Israel?

In order to understand the issues and the processes involved, it is necessary again to provide some background. Chabad is a Hasidic group that has, over the course of several centuries and a succession of seven rebbes, formulated its own distinctive doctrines, practices, and views of the world. In addition to being ritually orthodox, fully observant Jews, members of Chabad typically have at least one foot in the secular world. Not only did the present rebbe study at the Sorbonne in the 1930s, Kfar Chabad offers technological training as well as religious instruction to the movement's youngsters. As one expression of its modernism, the rebbe periodically addresses his Hasidim on a worldwide radio and television network via satellite. The movement is also uniquely open to and engaged with the secular world, Chabad encourages conversion to its ranks, and it has a lively feel for public relations that includes presenting declarations to various world leaders. Finally, in contrast to other orthodox and ultra-orthodox religious groups in Israel that are anti-Zionist and reject the Israeli state on the grounds that it is secular and was not brought into being by the coming of the Messiah, Chabad has adopted a more Zionist political position: some of its male members serve in the Israeli army, the Hasidim vote in Israeli elections, and they are involved and take an active part in everyday Israeli affairs.

The figure of the rebbe plays an absolutely central role in all of the Hasidic groups, and the Lubavitcher rebbe is crucial in understanding the copy of the Brooklyn building at Kfar Chabad. The duplicate of 770 was built there because of his explicit instructions; however, he never explained why it was necessary to build an exact replica. There is mystery here, just as there often is in understanding or interpreting the rebbe's wishes. Why build an exact replica of 770 Eastern Parkway in Israel?

There are at least two different solutions to this puzzle. The first suggests that his building—this structure that is connected with his holiness and mystical power—was built there in anticipation of the rebbe's imminent arrival in Israel. As we already know, he has never been to *eretz ha'kodesh,* the Holy Land, and those who anticipate that the rebbe may arrive there in the near future explain that this exact replica awaits him as his old-new home. But there is much more that is said—or, better still, implied—by this interpretation than the mere readying of a familiar abode for one's rebbe and leader. The Lubavitch Hasidim, as well as their rebbe, have for some time been speaking about the Messianic Age that is about to arrive.[11] In sometimes indirect, sometimes more direct ways, they have spoken among themselves and with others about the numerous signs of *geula,* the Period of Redemption that is fast approaching, or what still needs to be done in order to ensure that "the Messiah will come now." There is an obvious clue in the rebbe's instruction that his building be completed on *yom ha' geula,* the day that Chabad celebrates the People of Israel's redemption. The precise details are vague, but the dreams, hopes, and emotions are evident. And, should the Messianic Age be fast approaching, there is also the belief that the Lubavitcher rebbe is in some mysterious fashion connected with this process. Perhaps he actually *is* the Messiah; at the very least he is closely related to the events and processes through which the Age of the Messiah is shortly to arrive.

The beliefs and understandings are, in brief, eschatological: the end of days, the redemption, is fast approaching, and the rebbe is a part of the unfolding. This is why 770, this sacred space, has been built in the Holy Land. It is part of an extraordinary, fabulous process.

This is one explanation, and it is certainly bold, if not—as the critics say—outrageous and blasphemous. The second interpretation also sees the building in symbolic terms. It, too, focuses on the rebbe but seeks to unravel the mystery more in terms of the movement's practical problems of leadership and succession. Chabad is facing a difficult dilemma: the rebbe, Rabbi Menachem Mendel Schneerson, was in his eighties when the building was built, and he died in 1994. He had no children, nor were there any serious claimants to succession within his family. Hasidim without a rebbe would seem to be a contradiction in terms, since these sectarian groups require a charismatic leader. Indeed, in the past the absence of an authoritative rebbe has led to internal dissension and near disintegration. The building's construction, according to this interpretation, signifies that there is about to be a new period of autonomy in which each large community of Hasidim will have to find its own direction from within itself. There is now a 770 in Israel just as there is a 770 in Brooklyn. Each symbolizes Lubavitch and the rebbe, and both announce the profound lesson that it will be both necessary and possible for all of the Hasidim to discover ways to continue until, finally, the present rebbe's successor emerges. This is what the rebbe meant when he commanded that 770 be built in Israel.

Two final points need to be made. First, in contrast with the Moroccan buildings at Netivoth, no attempt was made to design or otherwise connect 770 with its immediate Israeli locale. The building stands starkly by itself—the Lubavitch architects and the committee that approved the design conceived of it as the rebbe's building and consequently felt no need to represent it in association with Israeli motifs. On the other hand—and this is the second point—the building is closely connected with Israeli realities. While Chabad earnestly goes about its task of bringing good to the world, it is also deeply involved in various controversies. The religious world in Israel is fiercely divided between Zionists and anti-Zionists; between those who are Hasidim and those who, like the *misnagdim* or Lithuanians, adhere to a more rationalist view of traditional practices; and between various Hasidic sects that compete vigorously with each other. In addition, Chabad's increasingly public pronouncements that the Lubavitcher rebbe is, or may be, the Messiah have been scornfully ridiculed by others within the orthodox community.[12] What is more, many of these religious groups are allied with competing Israeli political parties, or they constitute warring factions within the same party. This is, in short, a field of intense religious and political conflict and competition.

It is in this regard that the building transported from Brooklyn to Kfar Chabad takes on additional significance. Positioned starkly by itself, able to be viewed from afar, 770 symbolizes Chabad in its continuing campaign for influence and effectiveness. This, too, is a claim to hegemony, to the rising eminence of the rebbe and his followers: it is a statement about a political today and tomorrow.

Conclusion

What messages or meanings are being conveyed by these buildings? More generally and abstractly, what conclusions regarding structures and their interpretation can be drawn from these two cases?

The two new Israeli buildings can be seen to convey significantly different messages. Juxtaposing them so that they reflect on one another can help clarify their "scripts." The Moroccan structures, to begin, were built to represent Morocco and the Jews' past there. This is a complex message, and its various dimensions need to be clearly stated. First, the bold presentation of Moroccan buildings transfers Morocco, the *galut,* to Israel, and thereby renders it legitimate in the new land. By bringing Morocco to Israel, this diaspora is retrieved, raised up so that the historic experience of the past can henceforth be viewed positively, practically on a par with the ideology of Zionism and the Ingathering of the Exiles. In this regard, the buildings at Netivoth are also part of a developing new mythology regarding Morocco and its place in a Jewish past. Morocco was different, it is now claimed, and unlike other diasporas, Jews lived there in favored circumstances under Muslim rule.[13] Second, the fact that the buildings exhibit common, easily recognized Israeli designs is no less significant; as was emphasized, Baba Sali's shrine and the new yeshiva are presented within an Israeli container. The message is Morocco—but Morocco now set in Israel. This is a statement about the continuing Moroccan presence within the Israeli social fabric, or, to put it in terms of current Israeli ideologies, it is a claim of Moroccan "integration" into a more pluralistic Israeli society. Third, while the buildings are representations of the past, their meanings are situated within the present; they are closely intertwined with cultural-political power and hegemony in present-day Israel.

These features contrast in practically every detail with the replica built at Kfar Chabad. Building a copy of 770 Eastern Parkway in Israel has literally nothing to do with Brooklyn, New York City, or the United States. None of these places is represented by this 1930s-style building, nor are they imagined to have been transported to Israel. After all, what was built at Kfar Chabad is not an architect's rendering or conception; rather, it is the precise, brick-by-brick copy of an existing structure. It is also significant that a copy of a Brooklyn building was built, rather than a replica of the group's original center in the Russian town of Lubavitch. Whereas several other Hasidic groups have built replicas of their former East European–styled synagogues in orthodox neighborhoods in both Jerusalem and Bnai Brak, a mainly orthodox town that adjoins Tel Aviv, Chabad has sought a connection with the rebbe and the building made holy by his presence. As Green points out (1977), in Hasidic thought the rebbe's dwelling can become a kind of *axis mundi,* the sacred center of the earth. Chabad, therefore, turned to Brooklyn rather than to Eastern Europe. Clearly, there was no reason to enclose this building within an Israeli design. If the replica of 770 awaits the rebbe's arrival there as the Messiah or as part of the messianic process, adorning it with Israeli motifs would have been irrelevant or, more likely, improper and profane.

There is, moreover, the matter of *galut,* the diaspora. To be sure, for the Lubavitch Hasidim, Brooklyn (and every place else outside Israel) is thought of as *galut,* whereas Kfar Chabad and Jerusalem are perceived as *eretz ha'kodesh,* the Holy Land. But matters are not so simple. The rebbe also is holy, and the space where he resides, his building, partakes of holiness. This is especially evident in the mounting excitement brought about by belief in the rebbe's, or possibly the Messiah's, imminent arrival. What is being represented in the 770 at Kfar Chabad is the union or merger of sacredness: it is a building that will become holy when the rebbe-Messiah arrives in the Holy Land. The issue is not, as in the Moroccan structures, one of lending eminence and difference to a particular diaspora experience; rather, it is that of taking a step toward the End of Days, enabling the process by which *galut* itself will be ended and Israel redeemed.

In addition, there is an even more encompassing difference between the two structures: they can be seen to relate differently to time. The Moroccan buildings are "in time," whereas the Brooklyn structure has, in effect, been placed "outside of time." Suggesting that the Moroccan buildings are "in time" means that their conception and design are closely related to events in the present-day world. To be sure, they make use of images of the past, but this is done in order to score points on issues in the present. While the same can also be said of the Brooklyn building—that it symbolizes some present-day Israeli political contests—it is also associated in a very different way with time. The 770 building is connected with holy cosmic forces and the eternal, and consequently it is "outside of time." This conceptualization follows what Eliade calls "eschatological" time and what Robert Paine, in an essay on some related features of Israeli culture, has termed "totemic time" (Eliade 1954; Paine 1983). Being "outside of time" means that the building is not merely tied to the present but is also more profoundly connected to the timeless unfolding of religious redemption and eternity.

Finally, these conclusions regarding structures and the uses of the past have a wider relevance. Representations, including buildings as well as other constructed objects, are frequently shaped and adorned with images from the past, but just as frequently their message is closely interwoven with the present. Two examples, drawn from recent work in history and anthropology, illustrate this process. The point is made in Maurice Agulhon's analysis of the changing depiction of Marianne, the youthful female symbol of Republican France (1981). Agulhon describes how throughout the nineteenth century, the varied busts or statuettes of Marianne were shaped politically—"politics laid down the directives for art" (1981, 81)—so that in radical districts she appeared with Phrygian cap, the Roman symbol of freedom, and bared breast, while in politically rightist zones she was capless and modestly draped. The past in these cases was used in the service of the present. Similarly, Rabinow has shown how, in establishing the tone of the French Protectorate in Morocco, the planners tore down some structures that signaled European modernity (a tennis court, for example) in order to rebuild a ruined mosque and tower. The message, Rabinow concludes, is the necessity of a new "historical consciousness" in which the ruling French attest to the authentic power of the native culture (1989, 300). It is, once again, the past in the service of the present. This process is widespread, and many more examples might be cited. These intersections of politics and culture spark invention and creativity in many diverse realms of social life.[14]

Notes

I am indebted to a number of colleagues for their suggestions and critiques. My special thanks to Gary Gerstle, Amiran Gonen, Menachem Lorberbaum, Daniel Meijers, Stephen Sharot, Moshe Shokeid, Lucette Valensi, and Yael Zerubavel. Earlier versions of this essay were presented to several audiences: the 1990 meeting of the Israel Anthropological Association; a conference on power and prayer held at the Free University of Amsterdam; Department of Anthropology seminars at

Barnard College, the University of California–San Diego, the University of California–Los Angeles, and the University of Toronto; and the Social Science Seminar at the Institute for Advanced Study. This essay was written while I was a John D. and Catherine T. MacArthur Fellow at the Institute for Advanced Study. It is a pleasure to thank the Institute's faculty and staff for providing so pleasant and stimulating an environment. Ruthe Foster helped draft various early versions, and I thank her for her assistance.

1. The design of Moroccan maraboutic shrines is described in D. Eickelman 1976; see also Geertz 1968.
2. See Weingrod 1990 for a description of the pilgrimage to the Baba Sali's grave.
3. This format or style is what Harlap terms "Southern Mediterranean" or "French Mediterranean" (1982, 42). It has become prominent especially in local "build your own home" (*Bnai beitcha*) projects that are essentially clusters of single-family homes. For a review of the development of Israeli architecture, see Harlap 1982.
4. The classic analysis of Hasidism is Scholem 1961. Chabad's history, doctrine, and orientations are described in a number of texts. See Mindel 1973; Meijers 1986; and Sharot 1982.
5. How the building was planned and built and the festivities that took place when it was inaugurated are described in a special publication (in the form of a newspaper) that was issued by Chabad to commemorate the building's third anniversary.
6. Both of these sites have been expanded. At Netivoth, a new Moroccan-like façade was added to what had been Baba Sali's home, and a school was built nearby, the design of which is almost identical to the "Yechiwa." Plans were also announced to build a home for the Lubavitcher rebbe in a site next to the 770 building. However, these plans were laid aside following the rebbe's death in June 1994.
7. This emphasis on designing a new and different culture is described in a number of studies and memoirs. See, e.g., Eisenstadt 1954 and A. Elon 1971, especially chapter 6.
8. The various features that characterize the "crisis" or "end" of Zionism have been described in many publications. See, among others, Avishai 1985, especially chapter 7; Eisenstadt 1985, 403–42; Rubenstein 1984. Yael Zerubavel (1992) also has discussed this in the context of the changing interpretations of Israeli mythologies.
9. See A. Elon 1971 and Rubenstein 1984. For a symbolic analysis of the term within Zionist ideology, see Doleve-Gandelman 1987.
10. This process and some reasons for it are discussed in Weingrod 1979.
11. The Hasidic expressions, or interpretations, of Judaism have always placed a significant emphasis on the Messiah and the Messianic Age. See Sharot 1982.
12. Chabad's pronouncement that the Lubavitcher rebbe is the Messiah created an uproar in early 1992. In Israel, posters and billboards were prominently displayed calling on Jews to "prepare themselves for the Messiah's coming," and the newspapers were filled with reports of his Hasidim's activities designed to "bring the Messiah now." The *New York Times Magazine* carried a lead article on the rebbe, and the media worldwide publicized reports of preparations being made to greet the Messiah. These "promotional activities" continued for more than a decade following the rebbe's death.
13. There have been various expressions of this new ideology that "Morocco was different." The historical experience of Moroccan Jews is being recast as positive: Muslims and Jews lived there in peace and harmony, it is now said, and the king of Morocco and his regime favored and protected the Jews. Thus, for example, when an Israeli historian of Moroccan origin argued publicly that King Mohammed V had not always opposed the anti-Semitic Vichy regime, he was attacked by Moroccan spokespeople for his "lack of scholarship." To cite another example, an Israeli political figure, again of Moroccan origin, remarked that he had "never felt so much at home as during his visit to Morocco"; this is another strand in the "Morocco was not *galut*" approach. As a third illustration, in the midst of a traditional pilgrimage some

Moroccan Jews prominently displayed poster-sized photographs of Hasan, king of Morocco, in the Moroccan-style tent placed near the center of the celebration (C. Geertz, personal communication, 1991). Needless to say, one can hardly imagine any other Israeli ethnic group proudly displaying a photograph of a Muslim ruler.

14. These issues are related to what Hobsbawm and Ranger (1983) have termed "the invention of tradition"; that is, a past is invented, but the reasons why this process takes place can be explained by present conditions or situations.

29

Menstruation and Identity

The Meaning of Niddah *for Moroccan Women Immigrants*

RAHEL WASSERFALL

This chapter deals with the meanings of *niddah* (menstruation and associated laws of purity) among Jewish women who emigrated from Morocco and settled in a moshav in Israel in the 1950s. It is based on ethnographic fieldwork and interviews carried out in 1981.[1] The women studied ranged in age from thirty-five to seventy-five. I did not have a particular interest in the topic of niddah when I began my fieldwork. Rather, I began with an interest in understanding how women of Moroccan origin shape their identity and how they construe their sense of self. I sought to reveal how these women conceive of what it means to be a Moroccan Jewish woman. But I quickly realized that it was impossible to deal with this question without taking account of the meaning of niddah for these women. Indeed, I discovered that religious identity and gender are inextricably entangled in practices related to the female body, specifically to menstruation.

In classic Hebrew literature niddah means "separation" and "seclusion" and refers to a woman who is menstruating and who has been separated for a specified period after her menstrual flow has ended. In Jewish law, niddah refers to a whole complex of regulations concerning the behavior of the menstruating woman including, perhaps most importantly, the prohibition on sexual relations during this period.[2] But niddah has a very different set of meanings from the perspective of the women whom I interviewed, and who did not have a formal religious education. Their conceptions of niddah differ from the meanings encoded in classical religious sources. This analysis, then, allows women to speak for themselves about a fundamental set of Jewish regulations. It shows how the regulations of the female body are taken up by women themselves and become part and parcel of their own identities. In addition, niddah is associated with notions of healthy reproduction and has implications for women's social placement in the community and in relations within the family.

The importance of niddah came home to me at the very outset of my fieldwork when I was conversing with a young woman (age thirty-five) born in Fez but educated from childhood in a large town in Israel; with some reticence she told me about her problems with her mother-in-law, problems that influenced her decision to build a separate household and to leave the common roof of the extended family. She urged her husband, who was the firstborn in his family, to build a new house, near the common house. The point of contention in this dispute was the mother-in-law's insistence that her daughter-in-law obey the laws of niddah and go to the *miqve* (the ritual bath that ends the period of separation following menstruation).

There are a number of ways of interpreting this argument. Quite plausibly these two women were in conflict for influence in the house, love of the son or husband, the division of common labor, and so forth. Yet it is interesting to note that the dispute crystallized around the issue of niddah. The laws of purity, then, served as the institutionalized, and hence legitimate, means of channeling the tensions between mother-in-law and daughter-in-law.

This incident intrigued me, and I looked for an opportunity to ask the older women about niddah. Given my own background as a French-born, Ashkenazi Jew, I regarded these matters as personal and intimate, and hence difficult to bring up in conversation. I therefore tried to approach the subject circuitously, by framing my questions as ones regarding Jewish law and by asking them what *mitzvot* (commandments) they actually perform. To my surprise, they mentioned only the education of their children and charity. No one mentioned the laws of menstrual purity or kashrut (the dietary rules). It was as if niddah had nothing to do with Jewish law. After circling around the subject, I realized that without a direct question the subject would never be broached.

But as soon as I put the question directly, the women cried out, "You are not Jewish?" (F; don't you know that for us niddah is essential?) or "Are we Arabs?" (F; for not obeying the laws of niddah). From these reactions it was obvious to me that niddah occupies a central place within these women's thinking about themselves as Jewish women.[3] It also turned out that niddah was a subject about which these women felt entirely comfortable speaking. Among women, niddah was not intrinsically a shameful or private subject. It became shameful, as in the case of the mother- and daughter-in-law incident, when sexual relations were at issue. For example, I was told that "it is shameful" (F) and "it is not honorable" (F) for a mother to educate her own daughter on sexual relations that included the teaching of laws of niddah because the subject of niddah in itself is relatively public, and it is available as a symbol through which personal and communal identity can be expressed and behavior evaluated. Before exploring these various significations of niddah, I will present more background on the village and its residents.

The Moshav Setting

My fieldwork was carried out on a moshav that was founded by immigrants from Morocco.[4] In the early 1950s a nucleus of ninety-four families (ninety from Fez and Sefrou,[5] and four from Gilmama in the south) bought plots of land and houses from the Jewish Agency. The first settlers had enough money to change the standard architectural housing plans. A majority of the immigrants were merchants who were for the most part financially secure enough to invest a large sum of money, immigrating to Israel in 1955.

The nucleus of settlers from Fez, who were religiously traditional, had established criteria of religious observance as a precondition for candidacy to the group.[6] For example, families were not accepted if the head of the family shaved. The strict criteria of observance made it difficult to assemble the one hundred families required for the formation of the moshav (only a third were found). For this reason, the Jewish Agency envoys turned to the township closest to Fez, Sefrou. The two communities maintained constant family, economic, and religious relations.[7] Of the moshav population today, one-third originated in Fez, nearly two-thirds are from Sefrou, and four families are from Gilmama.

A number of families left the moshav at the start of the settlement, but members of established families bought out their shares and replaced them. The moshav was not without political rivalry between the two groups. Today, two synagogues stand side by side in the center of the village, relics of past problems. For a variety of reasons, including problems of ideology and farming, the settlers abandoned their first occupation in favor of trade. According to my informants, Jews from the towns of Morocco were not accustomed to the hard physical labor of agriculture, which was linked in their minds with devalued Arab labor.[8]

In 1981 the moshav had a population of six hundred, composed of 120 families. In the early 1980s, twenty families were engaged in full-time or part-time farming, fifteen families in the market gardening of vegetables, and five families in growing and exporting roses. Most of the settler population had established a variety of businesses in the small town about ten minutes from the moshav. Among the settlers we found occupations such as bank employees, bureaucrats, and career army officers. From an Israeli point of view, the architecture and interiors of the new houses could be considered very comfortable since they contained a great variety of household appliances.

For the purposes of analysis, I classified my informants into two age groups: fifty to seventy-five years of age; and thirty-five to forty-nine years of age. The average number of children per family for the moshav as a whole was 7.8. The average number of children according to the family's community of origin and the mother's age group is shown below.[9]

Age Group	Fez	Sefrou
50 to 75	6.5	9.4
35 to 49	5.4	6.4

The average number of children in a family is somewhat lower for the younger women, but it is clear that reproduction and family were still strongly valued in moshav life. It is possible that the moshav members were sufficiently well off not to be under economic pressure at the time of initial settlement and that this economic independence helped maintain or even strengthened the traditional role of the women I interviewed.[10]

The great majority of women had never worked for a salary. In the first group, not a single woman had worked outside her home, while among those originating from Fez, two women had been employed as secretaries before marriage. As for the second group, of those from Sefrou, one woman had been employed before her marriage as an embroiderer. Among those coming from Fez only one woman worked outside her house (as a nurse); another told me she had taught dressmaking before her marriage. A majority of women had received a formal education. In the first group, six out of the seven women from Fez had received a formal education while only four out of the ten from Sefrou had that advantage. All the women in the second group originating from Fez and Sefrou reported receiving formal education.[11]

Niddah and Jewish Identity

It is important to distinguish between "official" religious meanings attached to niddah and those attributed to it by my interlocutors on the moshav. In this community, the observance of niddah was not primarily considered a mitzvah (religious obligation) but helped articulate and was entangled in what it meant for the women to be both female and Jewish. These women described menstruation as "our way" (*haderech shelanu*) (H; i.e., the way of women). The use of the Hebrew idiom "our way" is significant. It indicates that they understood the observance of niddah not only as a distinguishing mark of being a woman but also as a sign of their being Jews. The use of the Hebrew idiom "our way" is apparently the same expression used by Jewish women in Algeria at the beginning of the twentieth century. According to Marcel Cohen (1912), Algerian Jews used this expression of Hebrew origin (see Gen. 18:11) as part of their Judeo-Arabic dialect. This linguistic feature illustrates the way in which niddah observance was construed as a specifically Jewish practice rooted in Jewish tradition and distinctive in the Muslim host cultures.[12] In fact, niddah observances perform a crucial role in the articulation of Jewish identity.

Niddah is a complex cultural symbol through which women interpret a specific bodily process, namely, menstruation. It is a symbolic process referring to (1) the flow of menstrual blood, "our way" in the words of these women; (2) the seven-day period of purity following the cessation of the menstrual flow, an interim period during which spouses should refrain from sexual relations; and (3) the miqve in which a woman should immerse at the end of the seven-day wait, an institution marking the resumption of sexual relations between the spouses. I now explore each of these three dimensions of niddah.

Menstrual Flow

Older women reported that during their period of menstrual flow, they had tended to neglect their physical appearance, did not wash, and had continued to fulfill their other obligations as housewives (cooking, educating the children, and so forth). The majority of prohibitions during this period are connected with abstinence from relations between spouses. The woman does not pass any object directly to her husband but instead places it on a table so that the latter does not come into physical contact with her, a contact that could arouse a husband's sexual desires. She must not speak "too much" with him, nor enter into either the bathroom when he is present there or their bedroom to arrange the beds, wipe his face, and so forth. During the first three days of their menstrual period, older women also tend to refrain from preparing and blessing the hallah (bread used for the ritual meals on the Sabbath). They recited the blessing only if there were no other women in the house. The correct preparation of the Sabbath loaf, lighting Friday-night candles, and the laws of niddah are the religious observances that apply especially to women, according to the Mishnah.[13] Elsewhere in North Africa there have developed various popular notions of the link between them (Schely-Newman 2002, 79, 81). In the moshav, popular ideas and practices related to niddah appear in other realms. Women do not generally participate in synagogue services, and after menopause very few even follow religious services on the Sabbath and high holidays. Some women mentioned that they refrained from going to the cemetery while menstruating.

Days of Purity

As soon as a woman's menstrual flow ends, she must daily verify that no blood-colored flow is seen.[14] According to Jewish law, if she discovers no blood, she must count seven days and then take her ritual bath. All the older women referred to the days of purity as the "safety period" (H), a period that ensured her purity when she took her ritual bath. In other words, this period ensures "that she had nothing left" (H), that the woman no longer had any flow of blood and therefore that sexual relations with the husband would take place at the legitimate time. Guarding the purity of sexual relations is believed to protect any fetus that might be conceived. The women in the younger group spoke of observing only three or four days as a period of safety. In practice, matters are even more complicated when one considers that women of both age groups do not automatically go to the ritual bath after having counted the specified period of time.

The woman's going to the bath also depends on the husband's involvement and reflects informal negotiations between the spouses. From the perspective of rabbinic law, the prohibtion against sexual relations during a woman's menstrual period is directed toward men. In the moshav, a man was expected "to send" his wife to the miqve when he deemed it appropriate. In other words, not all of the responsibility lies with the wife. If for various reasons the husband does not send her, the woman abstains from going to the miqve. She remains in a state of limbo, during which sexual relations are forbidden, but she can perform domestic functions.[15] Thus niddah as a symbolic system not only concerns the woman's persona but is linked to the *relationship between* her and her husband. This would seem to confirm the public authority of the husband in Judeo-Muslim culture. But further examination of niddah symbolism will demonstrate how niddah observances are actually negotiated.

Miqve (Ritual Bath)

A certain proportion of the water in the miqve must be rainwater. In Morocco, it was not heated because in the Judeo-Moroccan cultural system only cold water is considered to have purifying powers while hot water is reserved for hygiene (Bruno and Malka 1939, 338). In the moshav, as elsewhere in contemporary Jewish world, the miqve is heated with the hope that it will attract younger women. After counting the seventh day, the woman must wash herself in her home before nightfall and then go to the miqve. The miqve is open daily at nightfall and is maintained by an old woman (who a few years before the time of my fieldwork had tried unsuccessfully to persuade the young women of the importance of the miqve). The miqve is in a non-obtrusive location, its architecture the most banal possible. It is near a school that is empty in the evening when the women arrive. The women go to the miqve by indirect routes, hiding their towels so that their own children and neighbors will not guess from their behavior that sexual relations are to take place between the women and their husbands that night. Older women relate that if on leaving the ritual bath their eyes fall on an Arab or a donkey, they must purify themselves again. Deshen (1981) writes that during the nineteenth century this belief caused the closure of a Jewish store in a *mellah* (Jewish quarter in a Moroccan town). This store was located next to the miqve and the returning women would encounter Arab customers. The community exerted pressure on the storekeeper to close his stall. Malka (1946) recounts that a Jewish rabbi was in the habit of coming to recite psalms in front of the miqve so that the women's first glance would fall on him. Those attitudes are linked to the belief that the first glance after the bath affects the conception of the potential child.

Different Meanings of Niddah

The women in the moshav ascribed three distinctive kinds of meanings to niddah observances. Niddah (1) plays a role in the construction of religious/ethnic identity; (2) is embedded in ideas about the physical and spiritual well-being of the Jewish people; and (3) is strongly linked to matters of public honor. Like all mitzvot, the practices of niddah may or may not be observed. Religious commandments, by definition, are characterized by the possibility of nonperformance. If nonperformance were not possible, then the obligations could not be commandments, since there would be no choice or will involved on the part of the religious actor. However, when a commandment, such as niddah, becomes constitutive of identity, the actor ceases to recognize the possibility of refusing or failing to perform it. As an element of one's identity, the commandment must be performed for the actor to implement his or her identity, that is, to be who he or she is. As noted above, women in this community did not explicitly include niddah among the religious commandments they perform. Women mentioned only childrearing and charity as religious duties. The observance of niddah, therefore, was so deeply connected to their identities that its performance was simply taken for granted.

In their eyes, niddah practices distinguish Jewish from non-Jewish women. This is evident in the way in which the miqve serves as a sign of female Jewish identity. I am not suggesting that the miqve has completely lost its status as a mitzvah but that in the minds of these women its primary importance is its ability to differentiate them from their neighbors. Consider the following quotations from my informants that illustrate the way in which an ideology of identity is linked to the niddah observances: "What! We are Arabs" (F; for not going to the miqve). "You are not Jewish?" (F; for asking such a question and showing your lack of knowledge). "In Fez, in Sefrou, the rabbi does not have to ask for a proof that the bride has been to the miqve as is standard practice in Israel today; no woman would think of marrying without going to the miqve" (F).

It is only possible to understand this transformation, whereby the practices of niddah become not only a religious duty but in fact a marker of identity, if we consider the way in which the institution of miqve is symbolically linked to the physiological processes of women's bodies. Menstruation is considered essential to female identity; it is what makes a woman out of a girl. But the miqve not only signifies this developmental change. The miqve, as these women see it, *is also* what makes a Jewish woman out of a menstruating woman. To understand this point, I will explore the ways in which women describe and how they feel about their menstrual blood and the ritual of going to the miqve.

Blood, Miqve, and Feminine Identity

The appearance of blood is "their way," the feminine way of being: "she must have blood to become a woman, it is nature, so that she should give birth" (H). "Blood is natural for the woman. It was usual not to touch the husband. That is how it was" (H). Menstrual blood, then, is considered an expression and symbol of the feminine essence. It signifies the potential of conception, the construction of the Jewish household, and the continuity of the Jewish people, all of which are central values in Judeo-Moroccan culture. A woman who does not menstruate is considered an anomaly. In this community, which cares deeply about the fertility of couples, the absence of menstruation, like sterility, becomes a personal and family tragedy.

The blood that appears each month symbolizes the capacity to reproduce and thus transforms a young girl into a woman.[16] But in going to the miqve, these women understand their behavior to stem directly from their identity as

Jews. According to my informants, Muslims in Morocco did not institutionalize any observances with regard to menstruation.[17] As understood by my informants, then, menstruation involves two different, meaningful processes that are linked. It is simultaneously a personal and universal symbol of a girl's transformation into a woman. But this physiological event has become institutionalized in a set of practices that superimposes references to Jewish identity on these personal meanings. It is the ritual bath that enables the women to identify collectively as not just women but Jewish women. If blood turns a girl into a woman, the miqve turns the woman into a Jew. Niddah thus provides the link between personal identity (I am a woman) and collective identity (I am a Jew).

It is incumbent upon the mother-in-law and the sisters-in-law to convey to a young bride the normative behavior prescribed by niddah observances. The Jewish mother has no role in that education.[18] In traditional Judeo-Moroccan culture, the interaction between mother and daughter around matters pertaining to niddah is more than problematic. Mothers do not guide their daughters when they first menstruate and a number of firstborn daughters were inclined for several months to conceal from their mothers their new state of womanhood.[19] Mothers, like daughters, were too embarrassed to discuss this subject with each other. This reticence in fact signifies that the daughters have entered a new state of being in which their potential fertility could become a reality through sexual relations.[20] Mothers are reticent to intervene in anything concerning their daughters' sexual relations, and in this setting menstruation and sexuality are deeply entwined. Miqve, we recall, is itself a sign that sexual relations have resumed between husband and wife, and menstruation itself is a sign of a woman's reproductive potential. In a culture in which sex is basically regarded as a means toward procreation, the ability to menstruate is seen as making women desirable. Before menopause, women regard themselves as sexual beings because of their potential fertility. The stage in life when niddah rules must be observed thus represents women's active sexual period when they are desired by their husbands.

Personal Health and the Well-Being of the Jewish People

Proper observance of niddah practices is critical for the health of a woman and her loved ones. For the women, menstruation is a sign that she is cleansed. The flow of blood is regarded as very beneficial for the women, and some men said that because of this monthly cleaning, women live longer. Menstruation is regarded as a potential danger to a husband, who may become ill if he comes in contact with this blood. Miqve is the means of preventing menstruation from "soiling" the husband and making him ill. More important, the health of a potential child is also endangered unless a woman immerses in the ritual bath. Only with the protection of the miqve is the child born pure and healthy. And without the miqve, the child risks "sullying" (*tum'ah*) the whole Jewish people when it in turn matures and has its own children. Because husbands are perceived as being more interested in sex than their wives, it is therefore the responsibility of husbands to abstain from all relations with their wives during the period of menstrual flow.

Women referred to all of these different "perils" of niddah in the same interviews. It is important to note that it is only the anticipated Jewish community of the future that is in danger of being defiled by menstrual blood. The actual Jewish community in its present concrete form is apparently not endangered by menstruation. Thus women sit beside other men in the community while they keep a distance from their husbands. In the Moroccan community, niddah is institutionalized as a *matter of importance between spouses.* This, I believe, is because niddah refers to the sexual preoccupation between spouses and thus belongs in the domain of sexual modesty. It is not about protecting other men or the extant community from impurity. This contrasts with the behavior of men and women in Ashkenazi ultra-orthodox communities where every woman is potentially a niddah and thus must be avoided.[21]

Personal and Communal Health

Why is menstruation simultaneously conceptualized as the condition of being "sick" and as a process of cleansing and gaining potential longevity? I suggest that there is a connection between the restrictions on menstrual blood and the biblical prohibition against eating blood because "the blood is life" (e.g., Lev. 17:11). Ingesting blood thus constitutes a mixing of life and death, since the blood from a dead animal is being used as nourishment. It is this mixing of life and death that is prohibited and perceived as repugnant.[22] Analogously, the blood of menstruation signifies that an opportunity for conception has been missed and that the potential for new life has been lost. One must be on guard regarding this ambiguous blood, which while once potentially life giving now signifies loss of life.

This is why sexual intercourse is regarded as dangerous to the potential infant. It might mingle menstrual blood, which is linked to death, with the potential blood of the infant. In the writings of Aristotle (Barnes 1973), a fetus is created when blood is coagulated by the sperm. When conception does not take place, unfertilized blood runs off as menstrual blood. This understanding of conception is found in some rabbinic *midrashim* (D. Feldman 1974, 133) and seems to underlie statements by my female informants: "the blood of menstruation is the blood of a dead body" (F; le sang des regles c'est le sang d'un mort); "death is in your belly" (F; la mort est dans ton ventre).[23]

Although the women knew that from the perspective of modern medicine the chances of becoming pregnant at the time of the flow were infinitesimal, they continued to think that sexual relations were prohibited so as to prevent the blood of the potential child from becoming impure. The flow of menstrual blood signifies that the potential for this blood to be transformed into a fetus had passed and that this blood, previously available for life, had become a symbol of death. Menstruation, then, appears to both a woman and her husband as a blatant sign that conception has not taken place. Yet at the same time menstruation is an agent of the woman's health, for through this process her blood is cleaned. Here again we see the dual and oppositional life-death symbolism operating in the menstrual blood. For this reason, women would appear in this culture as ambiguous beings, bearing within them symbols of both death and life. Menstruation is the point of convergence for two sets of concerns: concerns about women's health and the larger concern with the Jewish people's well-being. In addition to these broad cultural-symbolic and personal meanings, niddah has implications for daily interaction in the community and the family.

Public Honor

Both older and younger women speak of honor in relation to the miqve. By fulfilling the laws of niddah, women are in fact preserving their honor vis-à-vis their husbands. Why is honor, a central element of culture in the Magrheb, linked to the practices of niddah generally and to the ritual of the miqve specifically? Fertility in this culture brings honor, and firstborns are often called "my honor" (*kavod*) by the women. By performing the ritual of the miqve, the women not only help their husbands and themselves reproduce the Jewish people but maintain the purity of the Jewish people by preventing the child from "turning out a mamzer."[24] On the night of women's return from the miqve, they or their mothers-in-law prepare a festive meal, a kind of symbolic wedding ceremony. As the menstrual blood renews the woman's body, the miqve renews the relationship between the couple. Going to the miqve symbolizes the end of sexual abstinence and revives desire in the couple. Sexual intercourse is incumbent on husbands the night the woman returns from the miqve. In this way, too, the couple renews their marriage contract that they understand as their potential to build a house in Israel, to "reproduce" the Jewish people.

Interaction between Marriage Partners

Thus far, I have interpreted the meanings of niddah mainly from the perspective of Jewish women. But as I will now suggest, niddah also is the symbolic site where the division of power between husband and wife is enacted. As mentioned earlier, it is incumbent upon the husband to send his wife to the miqve. Women say that in cases of conjugal fights, husbands might delay sending them. In such cases, sending one's wife to the miqve is the means of reconciliation between husband and wife. Women, I was told, sometimes insist that men "beg" them before they actually go to the miqve. Expressing interest in going to the miqve is in fact a way of indicating interest in sexual relations, and sex is an important area of domestic bargaining between husbands and wives. My informants agreed that if the men do not ask their wives to go to the miqve, a woman can remain in this situation for an indefinite period, which does not keep her from carrying out her other tasks and duties as a housewife. One woman described how her husband would prevent her from going to the miqve if on the night she was permitted to go he came home and found her still at home. That day, he would declare, did not count as one of her clean days, and thus he would establish himself as the expert.

Thus the husband exercises a great deal of control with regard to a woman's visit to the miqve. But at the same time going to the miqve is fraught with symbolic significance. A woman who goes to the miqve without the instruction of her husband is regarded as declaring her sexual desire. Women talked with pride of their spouses waiting impatiently for their return from the miqve, representing them as more sexually desirous than they themselves felt. It is interesting to note that the men with whom I talked described the situation differently; they said that the women were more sexually desirous. The visit to the miqve thus entails a kind of game of power in which the one who is labeled as more sexual desirous is perceived as the loser.

Strategies of Power and Miqve

A husband may manipulate niddah observances in one of three ways: (1) he can make his wife have sexual relations before going to the miqve; (2) he can insist that his wife cut short the days of safety and go to the miqve before the completion of the seven obligatory days; and (3) the husband can "forget" to send his wife. Of these three possibilities, the second is the most common. The others, though possible, are not very common for specific reasons. Were a man to have sexual intercourse without his wife going to the miqve, he would have to be willing to ignore the conception that niddah can make him ill. At least in theory, this possibility is recognized, as illustrated by a woman who said, "The husband was kind; he knew how to wait" (H). Her statement implies that if he were not kind, he could have taken her by force. But fear of personal illness and concerns over the well-being of the Jewish people act as important deterrents against this kind of behavior.[25] As one of the men expressed it, "If anything would happen to the child, I would feel guilty; I would think it was because of that" [the infraction of the laws of niddah] (H).

The third possibility—not sending his wife to the miqve—may occur in one of three situations: (1) sexual intercourse is seen by the man as a "service" he provides to his wife; (2) his virility is not in question because he already has a large number of children; or (3) he presents himself as a religious expert and is a stickler for the regulations. In this case, he may insist that his wife delay the miqve one or two additional days. What is interesting to note here is the symbolic manipulation of sexuality; both partners present the other as more desirous of sexual relations. As one of my male informants explained, "If one could do without it, everyone would feel better" (H). "It would take away honor and contribute nothing to it" (H), said another. Whoever wins in portraying the partner as having more interest in sex thus appears to be doing their spouse a service. The denial of sexual desire, therefore, conceals a move to gain symbolic and social power. To deny one's own desire is to accrue symbolic capital, to win the game of distributing power.

Women play this game as well. The women I interviewed consider the Jewish Moroccan woman as having no social power. "The Moroccan woman is a zero" (H), several women cried out. Thus women have a variety of strategies for gaining and exercising power in their relationships. Since a man's virility lies in the number of children he has fathered, by shortening the waiting time women provide men with the ability to demonstrate their virility. While it is ultimately the husband's decision as to when the wife should go to the miqve, women accrue symbolic capital by agreeing to go early.

The concept of impurity enters in a critical way into this ongoing negotiation over who is pleasing whom more. By going to the miqve before the end of the period of safety, the wife exposes herself to a risk; as one informant put it, "If any [blood, impurity] is left, it is my illness" (H). To go to the miqve early is to risk becoming ill. But in taking this risk, a woman accrues "points" in the game of power. Women are willing to take this risk because they gain what they could not acquire by other means. Thus the manipulation of wives by men, which at first glance exhibits their social power, proves in fact to be a feminine gain.[26] Women would capitalize on this gain in arguments with their husbands.

But there is a second strategy by which women seek to exercise power in their relationships. Women spoke of putting off their visits to the miqve and not paying heed to the constant demands of the husband to go to the ritual bath. Indeed, delaying the miqve ritual and thereby postponing sexual relations seemed to be the principal source of feminine power in the eyes of these women (Deshen 1981). The man waits with impatience and brings his wife presents on the evening of the miqve. Since masturbation is religiously prohibited and visiting prostitutes is frowned upon, men have no other licit outlets. By delaying the miqve, then, women make the desires of their husbands more obvious and thereby emerge victorious in the game of power relations.

Conclusion

Among Jewish women from Morocco niddah observances are both symbolic representations and cultural practices. As representations, they help articulate what it means to be a woman and a Jew. Niddah is one of the core symbols of women's identity. It serves as the link between their personal identities as a woman and their collective identity as Jews. Niddah is also what links a Jewish couple to Jewish tradition. As practices, they are the sites in which men and women seek to develop and exercise power in their marital relations. As this analysis has suggested, although social authority is represented as masculine, it is in fact moderated by informal female power. Women see themselves as dominated by their husbands, yet they are not completely subordinated. Niddah remains one of the important contexts in which women can finesse their husbands in the game of authority. Therein may perhaps lie one of the causes for the profound attachment to niddah by these women, who viewed it as one of the main symbols of womanhood.

Notes

This chapter has been translated and adapted for the present volume from *Mishpahot Be-Yisrael,* ed. R. Bar-Yosef and L. Shamgar-Handelman (Jerusaelm: Akademon, 1991). I would like to thank Harvey Goldberg and Madeleine Adelman for their comments on the original version. Another version of this material has been published in *People of the Body: Jews and Judaism from an Embodied Perspective,* ed. Howard Eilberg-Scwartz (Albany: State University of New York Press, 1992). The fieldwork on which this essay is based was funded by a scholarship from the Ben-Zvi Institute of Jerusalem.

1. The residents of the moshav came from the cities of Fez and Sefrou in the Middle Atlas region of Morocco. The interviews were conducted in French or Hebrew. The older women from Fez spoke French and Hebrew. One single woman born in Sefrou had trouble speaking Hebrew. For the younger ones the use of French was difficult and the interviews were generally conducted in Hebrew. In regard to the quotations below, those translated from Hebrew are followed by an "H"; those translated from French are followed by an "F."
2. Niddah is a Hebrew word meaning "a menstruating woman." The rules concerning niddah are compiled in a number of rabbinic legal codes including the tractates *Niddah* in the two Talmuds and in the *Shulkhan Arukh* (*Yoreh De'ah* 183–200). Jewish law prohibits sexual relations between husband and wife while the woman is menstruating and seven days after the end of the period. A woman must count five days for menstruation and add seven days of purity. After that period, the woman must immerse in the ritual bath, the miqve, before resuming conjugal relations. Similar purity rules, restricting access to the sanctuary, apply at childbirth according to the Bible (Lev. 12:1–8). For the birth of a boy, a woman is in a severe state of impurity for seven days and a lesser state of impurity for another thirty-three days. Both of these periods are doubled after the birth of a girl. A man who had sexual relations with a menstruating woman was subject to *karet* (being cut off from the community). These biblical restrictions, applied to the realm of sexual relations, remained in force even after the destruction of the second temple in 70 C.E. For a more detailed discussion, see "Niddah" in *Encylopaedia Judaica* (1972); Eilberg-Schwartz 1990, 177–94; and Wasserfall 1999.
3. Kashrut plays a similar role. That subject is beyond the focus of the present inquiry, but see note 22 below.
4. Studies of other moshavim of immigrants from North Africa are found in Weingrod 1966; Willner 1969; Shokeid 1971a; and Goldberg 1972.
5. Sefrou is one of the Moroccan towns that, after the large-scale emigration of Jews, was studied by several American anthropologists (Geertz, Geertz, and Rosen 1979). These scholars allude to the important economic situation occupied by the Jewish population. Many of the aspects of the traditional Jewish culture are documented in Stillman 1988.
6. The moshav is registered with the list of moshavim aligned with the Hapoel Hamizrahi movement of the National Religious Party.
7. The historical relationship of these communities has been documented by Bar-Asher (1977). The Department of Jewish Communities of the Israel Museum treats both towns as a single ethnographic complex although it is possible that at the level of gender ideology the similarity of the two groups also stems from their contiguity on the moshav.
8. Shokeid (1971a, 178), in his work on immigrants from southern Morocco, describes the belief regarding physical agricultural work as Arab labor. Such labor in the eyes of the villagers is a symbol of poor education and lack of humanity. Women did not want to be photographed in the fields and said, "Don't take our photographs when we are working like Arabs." The expression "like Arabs" is a common idiom used to condemn a person's manners.

9. The statistical data represent the replies of twenty-seven women, while thirty-one moshav members were interviewed in depth. For technical reasons, four people were not interviewed: two younger women from Fez and two older women from Sefrou.
10. This is different from the moshav studied by Shokeid (1971a), where economic problems were one reason women were forced to redefine their traditional role and relations with their husbands. Goldberg's analysis of a moshav of Jews from Libya (1972) claims that economic success was one factor that allowed the preservation of other aspects of the villagers' traditional life. Donath writes, "a study in depth of structures of the Jewish family and their evolution in contact with different host nations remains to be made" (1962, 113). For the concept of gender ideology in a general Moroccan setting, see Dwyer 1978b.
11. Women were not particularly precise about their years of schooling. One woman born in 1908 in Fez received a bachelor's degree.
12. There apparently were also several circumlocutions in local speech for referring to a woman during her menstural period, perhaps used more commonly when addressing a man (cf. Stillman 1988, 65–66, 84–85, 104–5).
13. Mishnah Shabbat 2:6.
14. The color of the flow is one of the problematic subjects discussed in the Mishnah. See Fonrobert 1999.
15. This is different from what was observed by Rhonda Berger-Sofer (personal communication) among Ashkenazi Jewish women in the ultra-orthodox Mea Shearim section of Jerusalem, where women went to the miqve at their own initiative when the seven "clean days" were over. There, a woman's own sense of purity seems to be a motivating factor. See Berger-Sofer 1979. See also notes 18 and 21.
16. B. B. Harrell (1981, 817) argues that during the pre-industrial period, menstruation was uncommon because women passed from one pregnancy to the next. She interprets menstruation as a borderline period that is also symbolic of feminine fertility and sexual attractiveness: "Menstrual flow would thus symbolize the height of female sexual capacity vis-à-vis the male as well as the female's liminal freedom from biological and culturally mandated intensive infant parasitism."
17. Islam does prohibit sexual intercourse during menstruation but does not have an elaborate set of rules parallel to the "miqve" complex of norms.
18. With reference to Algeria, Briggs and Guède write that the mother avoids connection with the procedure of the miqve when the bride goes to purify herself toward noon on the day of her wedding: "It would have been considered shameful for her mother to take part in such physically intimate proceedings" (1964, 50). In the research I conducted in 1983–84 in a Moroccan moshav in Israel, the mother indeed took part in the miqve procedure before the wedding (Wasserfall 1987). In ultra-orthodox Mea Shearim the role is incumbent upon the mother just before the marriage ceremony (Berger-Sofer 1979, 149).
19. Goldberg (2003, 116) notes that recorded Jewish practice provides few instances of formal reactions to the onset of menarche, but he does give a few ethnograpic examples from North Africa and elsewhere. See also Schely-Newman (2002, 31–33).
20. For an interpretation of the mother's role in the marriage ceremony that supports this argument, see page 65 of "The Rite of the Table" in Rosen (Wasserfall) 1981.
21. In the Mea Shearim community, for example, women do not go to public ceremonies such as circumcisions while they are observing niddah (personal communication from Miriam Janyanti, who conducted fieldwork there).
22. See S. Cooper 1987. An ethnographic analysis dealing with symbolic links between the realms of food and menstrual rules among Jews in Ethiopia is found in Salamon 1999.
23. There are conflicting opinions in rabbinic literature on the role of the woman in conception. The Talmud reflects a view different from that of Aristotle. It suggests that both the woman and the man contribute to the body of the child. In the Midrash, however, the Aristotelian idea is reflected. The occasion for this comment is the verse from Job 10:10–22, "Hast thou not

poured me out like milk and curdled me like cheese?" The Midrash comments: "A mother's womb is full of standing blood, which flows there from menstruation. But at God's will, a drop of whiteness enters and falls into its midst and behold a child is formed. This is likened unto a bowl of milk. When a drop of rennet falls into it, it congeals and stands, if not it continues as liquid" (Leviticus Rabbah 14:9; Yalkut to Job 10:10; cited in D. Feldman 1974). See the work by Nissan Rubin (1995), which surveys relevant literature.

24. The term *mamzer* formally refers to a the status of a child born of an illegitimate union as defined in biblical law, such as an adulterous union between a man and a married woman or an incestuous union. The women of the moshav also apply this term to a child conceived before the woman has been to the miqve.
25. In another moshav (Wasserfall 1987), I was told by a Tunisian woman that once she complained to her mother that her husband wanted her to shorten the days and send her to the miqve before she was due. Her mother said that her husband was behaving "nicely" and told her that her own father did even worse and had intercourse when she was menstruating. Gilad (1989) notes a specific ritual Yemenite women used when defiled by their husbands, as for example when their husbands forced them to have intercourse while still in a state of niddah.
26. This woman's choice to shorten the "security days" may be linked to the fact that in Jewish tradition the seven days of purity is not a biblical rule. The period of seven days was institutionalized later, in the time of the Mishnah.

30

Women and Religious Change in Israel

Rebellion or Revolution

SUSAN STARR SERED

Introduction

During the past half century, gender and religion have been negotiated by numerous groups in a variety of contexts (Callaway and Creevey 1994; Neitz 1987; Shiman 1986). Yet even within specific cultural frameworks, the outcomes of these negotiations often seem inconsistent. For example, despite monumental changes in the autonomy enjoyed by Catholic nuns and women pastors, the church continues to refuse to ordain women as priests (Iadarola 1985; R. Wallace 1993). Despite the enormous increase in Muslim women's access to religious learning, unveiled women have been stoned on the streets of Iran (Darrow 1985). And despite the increasing number of Protestant denominations that now ordain women ministers in the United States, Christian (not only Catholic) anti-abortion activists have firebombed abortion clinics. All of this raises questions about the factors that affect the outcomes of challenges to traditional religious gender roles. This chapter sets out to ask why, in some cases, traditional religious systems are able or willing to modify their notions of gender roles, while in other situations they violently oppose such changes. When analyzing gender conflict in religious systems it is crucial to understand that two ontologically different sets of issues are involved. The first set is "women"—that is, female people who have varying degrees of agency within specific social situations. The second set is "Woman"—a symbolic construct composed of allegory, metaphor, fantasy, and (at least in male-dominated religions) men's psychological projections. Although "Woman" may have little or no grounding in the real experiences of "women," when conflict arises over the role or status of "women," religious leadership often responds to "Woman" rather than "women." "Women" trying to get a bigger piece of the pie are often seen as "Woman" being deconstructed as a key theological symbol—as a move to throw away the entire pie and bake a new one. That kind of response does not easily lead to resolution of religious conflict for the simple reason that "Woman" as a symbol is often associated with some of the deepest and most compelling theological and mythological structures in the religious tradition.[1]

What I have said about "women" and "Woman" seems, in many ways, to also be true of nonreligious conflicts. In political and economic conflicts in the United States, for example, women are both agents (e.g. consumers and voters) and symbols (e.g., of fertility or sexuality). Women as agents have long won their major American political battle of universal suffrage; however, "Woman" as a symbol is still abused in, for example, exploitive advertising. Yet despite certain similarities, it can be argued that religious and secular conflicts do differ in important ways. In one of his classic studies of Ndembu religion, Victor Turner found that in the course of a conflict regarding who would take leadership roles in a circumcision ritual, the outcome of the conflict hinged upon whether it was understood as religious or political: "When the situation was defined politically, it seemed that E faction (the upstarts) might succeed in at least nominating the senior circumciser, since they were numerically superior and better organized and could appeal to those elements most sensitive to modern changes. But when the situation was defined ritually, and when several ritual situations followed one another immediately, traditional values became paramount and A1 played on the relative conservatism of Ndembu to maintain and even enhance a status that had political implications" (1966, 246).

What Turner seems to be saying is that religious conflicts include a dimension that is generally absent from other types of conflict. Religious conflicts tend to be, by definition, conflicts over symbols (symbols are, after all, the currency of religion). In religious conflict the issue of divine legitimation comes into play; religious symbols are eternal symbols—they are symbols of the very order of Heaven and Earth, and thus intrinsically harder to change. In cases of religious conflict, to use Gluckman's terminology, those who favor religious change generally see themselves as involved in a rebellion—in a situation in which subordinates turn against a leader without revolting against the authority of the office he occupies. Those who oppose religious change generally see the change as revolution—an attempt to alter the nature of religious institutions and of the structure in which they function; revolution sets out to change the fundamental rules of the game (1965, 28).

To summarize what I have argued thus far, when conflicts are understood as involving immutable symbols (revolution), resolution becomes much more difficult than when the conflict is understood as one of relative political power or access to economic resources. How the conflict is understood has to do with a number of factors. First, the symbolic value of the matter under dispute in part determines the outcome of conflict. An object, a ritual, a role, or an idea with high symbolic value is more likely to be understood as immutably religious. Second, the social locations of those involved in the conflict have a great deal to do with the outcome. Relevant aspects of social location include insider-outsider status, caste, class, and political power. During the process of the conflict both the symbolic value of the matter at hand and the social location of those involved in the conflict can be contested; that is, neither is an absolute given. Thus, a third factor that affects the outcome of conflict is rhetoric: how successful the two sides to the conflict are at "framing" or "packaging" the conflict in a way likely to lead to the outcome they desire.

It is within this context that I shall present three instances of religious conflict involving gender in contemporary Israel. In one of the instances ("Women of the Wall") the conflict centered on a highly valued Jewish symbol (the Western Wall), the women who tried to bring about change were perceived as outsiders and marginal, and the rhetoric involved in the case left no room for redefining the problem as nonreligious. Throughout the conflict, those who opposed the proposed change addressed the women in symbolic language as "Woman," and the conflict has not yet been resolved.[2] In the other two cases (women on religious councils and electoral bodies that choose chief rabbis) the matter under dispute involved a relatively new and symbolically shallow institution, the women who demanded the change were perceived as insiders in Israeli society, and the rhetoric offered by the women stressed that the issue is in essence a political one, not a religious one. Although the religious establishment initially resisted the change, they entered into negotiations with "women"—with people capable of agency—and the conflict has been resolved.

Background

Contemporary Israeli society represents a curious mixture of secular and religious institutions (Sobel and Beit-Hallahmi 1991). Although in most ways Israel resembles other Western democracies, orthodox Judaism in Israel is institutionalized through a system of state-run religious schools, state-funded synagogues and religious services, municipal religious councils, orthodox rabbinical control of weddings and divorces, and municipal and national chief rabbis whose public stature and Jewish legal rulings carry a great deal of cultural weight. Although they have never constituted more than a minority, orthodox political parties have representatives in the Knesset (Parliament) and have been part of almost all government coalitions since the founding of the state. Religious orthodoxy in Israel is composed of a multitude of subgroups. One stream of orthodoxy, associated with the National Religious Party, is highly nationalistic and seeks to combine modern life with traditional religion. The ultra-orthodox stream, which endeavors to isolate its adherents from the modern world, supports its own political parties.

Traditional orthodox Judaism dictates distinct, gender-determined roles and positions. Men and women are believed to be essentially different, with different natures, spiritual paths, and legal statuses. Women are seen primarily as domestic beings, whereas all public and official leadership roles (rabbis, cantors, judges, circumcisers, and ritual slaughterers) are the province of men (Heschel

1983). In Israel, until a few years ago, men continued to occupy all leadership positions that fell under the auspices of the orthodox Jewish establishment: municipal religious council members, chief rabbis, kashrut supervisors, judges in religious courts, and cabinet ministers from orthodox parties were all men.

During the late 1980s through the late 1990s a series of cases unfolded, each challenging, in different ways, the traditional orthodox Jewish religious gender roles that had been institutionalized by the modern Israeli state.[3] In this essay I look in some detail at three of these cases: the struggle over the right of women to serve on municipal religious councils; the battle by women to serve on the electoral bodies that elect chief rabbis; and the fight over the "Women of the Wall," who have demanded the right to pray at the Western Wall in Jerusalem while adorned with traditional male religious symbols. Although these are not the only clashes over gender and religion that have occurred over the past ten years or so, their particular importance is reflected in the fact that all three eventually reached the Supreme Court, all three received a great deal of media coverage, and all three were concerned with key symbols and structures of power.

I demonstrate that the "pro-change" sides consistently endeavored to sell their struggle as—what Gluckman (1965) called—rebellion, a subordinate group's effort to get a bigger piece of the pie. In two of the three cases, they were successful. After a process of negotiation, the "pros" and the "cons" agreed that the women's demands were *not* a challenge to fundamental religious tenets concerning gender or sacred power but a (perhaps unfortunate) side effect of belonging to a secular state. In these instances, the matter was fairly quickly resolved. Inasmuch as the conflict was interpreted in secular rather than religious terms, the system was able to absorb the rebellion and the outcome, as Gluckman would have predicted, was increased social cohesion.

In the third case, that of the Women of the Wall, the "pro" side tried to package its cause as rebellion, but the very symbols that they publicly and flamboyantly employed belied their claim. The "con" side perceived the women's demands as revolutionary, that is, efforts of a subordinate group to overthrow the system and change the essential rules of the game. The conflict was interpreted as a challenge to sacred power, and religious fundamentalists responded violently—as if to a revolution. Because the authority of the "cons" is curtailed by the secular Israeli state, however, no resolution has yet been reached. The Israeli Supreme Court, after four years of deliberation, recently ruled that the case involves sociopolitical rather than legal issues and turned the matter over to the legislative branch of the government.[4] Put differently, the Supreme Court seems to share the "con" perception of the case as revolutionary.

Women on the Religious Councils

In each Israeli township, a municipal religious council arranges and oversees a variety of public religious institutions. In 1986 Leah Shakdiel was elected to serve on the municipal religious council of the desert town of Yeruham. Her election, like all religious council elections, had to receive the approval of the minister of religion.[5] The minister refused to sign her appointment because, as it was later made clear, Shakdiel is a woman. The case went to the Knesset and finally to the Supreme Court. The Court ordered that Shakdiel be allowed to serve on the religious council. Since that time, similar cases have come up in other municipalities, and the result has always been the same: women now sit on religious councils in cities and towns throughout Israel.

The "Pro" Opinions

"Pro-change" forums mustered four main arguments: discrimination on the basis of sex is against Israeli secular law: halakha (Jewish religious law) does not forbid women to sit on religious councils; the councils deal with issues of particular importance to women (such as ritual baths); and Shakdiel is suited to the job because she is orthodox, knowledgeable about Judaism, and has generally good character traits. It should immediately be clear that none of these arguments is revolutionary: all claim to fit already existing laws (secular and religious). The fourth argument in particular serves to clarify that no one was questioning the fundamental rules of the game.

In Shakdiel's petition to the Supreme Court, her lawyers (from the Association for Civil Rights in Israel) stressed that men who sit on the religious councils are not required to be learned in halakha; thus it is discriminatory to demand it of women. This argument was accepted by the Court. In his ruling, Chief Justice Menahem Elon (an orthodox judge who sits on the Israeli [secular] Supreme Court) wrote, "The religious council . . . has no authority regarding *halacha,* it does not rule on matters of Jewish law, and according to its makeup the men are not able to make rulings of *halacha*. . . . All that is done on the religious council is to arrange religious facilities, to take care of erection and maintenance of ritual baths, to spread Torah learning and Judaica among the masses. And also to take care of organizing *kashrut* services." Elon quotes Shakdiel as saying that if this were a body that made halakhic (Jewish religiolegal) decisions, she would not ask to be on it. In sum, according to Elon's ruling, "Not accepting a candidate to the religious council because the candidate is a woman is against the basic principle of the Israeli legal system according to which discrimination on the basis of sex is forbidden."

To summarize, the "pro" forums presented a range of arguments, one of which was selected by the orthodox yet sympathetic chief justice. The particular argument he selected is significant: he was convinced by the claim that the issue at hand in fact has nothing to do with religion—that traditional religious mandates are not being challenged.

The modern orthodox camp was split regarding the case, with the more liberal elements of the National Religious Party supporting Shakdiel and the more conservative elements, together with the ultra-orthodox parties, opposing her. Once the case was ruled on by the Supreme Court, the National Religious Party began to nominate their own women for various municipal religious councils. Today, the National Religious Party claims that it finds both the Supreme Court ruling and the argument that the religious councils do not deal with halakha to be convincing. Ultra-orthodox parties, on the other hand, cooperate with the Court's decision—that is, their representatives serve on councils where women serve, yet they refrain from nominating women for religious councils.

The secular newspapers, and letters to the editors of secular newspapers, were highly supportive of the right of women to serve on religious councils. They presented it as an issue of the sphere of power of the rabbinate versus the sphere of power of the state. Gender remained tangential to their discourse, and more to the point, religion remained tangential to their discourse. As we shall see in the case of the "Women of the Wall," when the newspapers interpreted the issue as concerned with gender and religion, they were far less sympathetic to change.

The "Con" Opinions

What I loosely label the Religious Establishment (the ministry of religion, the chief rabbis, orthodox and ultra-orthodox political parties, and orthodox and ultra-orthodox newspapers) developed an extensive arsenal of "con" rhetoric (Y. Cohen 1991). Their main arguments were the following: (1) modesty prohibits men and women from sitting together; (2) it is not the custom for women to serve on religious councils; (3) women are not represented fully on secular bodies either; (4) women are debased in secular society (e.g., pornography, high divorce rates); (5) according to Jewish law women are not allowed to govern; (6) rabbis will not participate if women sit on the council; and (7) Shakdiel was not genuinely interested in serving the religious public—she was a publicity-seeking complainer. The bulk of their rhetoric concentrated on the dual issues of modesty and the refusal of important rabbis and scholars to sit with women. For example, according to Ashkenazi chief rabbi Shapira, if women serve on the religious council, "[male] religious scholars [*talmidei hachamim*] will not be able to sit and so it will turn into a council of wimps [*nmushot*]" (*HaAretz,* June 1, 1988).

In the previous section I showed that the "pro" side's most successful argument was that since the religious council is not a religious (halakhic) body, there is no prohibition against including women. The "con" side at first disagreed. When asked why it is permissible to have women in the Knesset but not on the religious council, an ultra-orthodox Knesset member replied, "Also in the Knesset women's participation is not to our taste. But that is still as far away from the religious council as east is from west. In the Knesset they talk about economics, society, welfare, politics—and not about things that have to do with the religion of Israel" (*HaTsofeh,* September 26, 1990).

"Even if a person knows Torah and halacha, and even if he is a big religious scholar, how can he interpret halacha? Halachic interpretations can be given only by halachic leaders, and definitely not by the [secular] Court. When the

Chief Rabbis say no [to Shakdiel], when the Rabbi of Yeruham says no, when the custom is that way and the law is that way—it is impossible to change things just because one lady wants to [has a whim] to sit with men" (Rabbi Shapira, quoted in *Maariv,* May 31, 1988). The essence of Shapira's stance is that traditional frameworks of authority should not be tampered with; knowledge alone does not give an individual the authority to rule in matters of Jewish law.

The theme of who has authority was reiterated on a number of occasions. For example, the Chief Rabbinical Council condemned the Supreme Court's decision as improper interference in religious affairs. When Sephardi chief rabbi Eliahu was asked by a reporter why women cannot sit on religious councils, given that the municipal rabbi and not the religious council rules on halakhic matters, Eliahu said, "A woman will do what she wants, and not listen to the opinion of the municipal Rabbi" (*Hadashot,* May 31, 1988). Eliahu's comment clarifies the position of the Religious Establishment: women's participation on the religious councils is a challenge to male, rabbinical hegemony in religious matters.

Rabbi Eliahu Bakshi Doron, the former chief rabbi of Haifa who is now the chief Sephardi rabbi of Israel, announced that "there is nothing prohibiting a woman from joining the religious council . . . but one must take into consideration that this has not been done in the past. And now, the matter has become one of *davka* [being contrary for the sake of being contrary]. . . . If all of the fight [concerning Shakdiel] on this matter was in order to break the framework [of traditional Judaism], if they want to put on a woman in order to change how things are always done, it seems that this is an issue that must be opposed" (*Kol Haifa,* May 17, 1988).

To summarize what we have seen until now, the "pros" perceived themselves as making a rather minor demand, and one that is in keeping with both secular law (anti-discrimination laws) and Jewish law (because the religious councils fill essentially secular functions). The Religious Establishment was split into two camps. One camp—the more liberal one—agreed to interpret the conflict as a secular one; that is, acknowledging that the religious council is not a halakhic forum, and so was able to concede.[6] The other camp interpreted the conflict as relating to authority and custom, and so did not concede. However, in light of the power of the Israeli judicial system and the economic benefits the "cons" stand to lose by boycotting the religious councils, even the most resolute "cons" do abide by the decision of the Court and cooperate with women on the councils. To put it differently, when forced to choose among changing their notions of appropriate gender roles (divinely decreed), their notions of halakhic authority (divinely decreed), or their notions of the function of the religious council (a modern political institution), they chose the latter, the only choice that allowed them to treat the case as a rebellion rather than a revolution and therefore to accept the outcome. It is crucial to bear in mind that in this case the "pros," with the help of the Supreme Court, made that choice an attractive one.

Women on the Electoral Bodies

Conflict surrounding women's right to serve on electoral bodies that select municipal and national chief rabbis has not received as much newspaper coverage as our other two cases. On the other hand, it has resurfaced several times, each time in a different city. The largest and most prolonged case was in Tel Aviv, where there was a two-year vacancy for chief rabbi because of orthodox opposition to the presence of women on the electoral body. The "cons" in this case were represented by Mayor Shlomo Lahat and the Tel Aviv Municipal Council, who were taken to Court because of their refusal to appoint women to the electoral body. Their refusal reflected the demands of orthodox political parties and influential rabbis. Only after the Supreme Court ruled that women must be allowed to serve did the chief rabbinate back down and allow the election of Tel Aviv's chief rabbi to proceed.

The electoral bodies that choose chief rabbis are composed of representatives from each of the political parties and of people appointed by the ministry of religion. Typically, each political party favors a particular rabbi, not because of the rabbi's religious or halakhic stance but because of his relationship with that party. Thus, women sitting on the electoral body would be unlikely to be perceived as having an influence regarding halakha, which as we saw in the previous case is the bottom-line definition of religious rather than secular activity.

Each time this issue has come up in a new municipality certain rabbis initially threaten to boycott the elections, but in the end they decide to participate despite the presence of women. Several years after the Tel Aviv case the same issue arose regarding the right of women to serve on the electoral body that chooses the national chief rabbis, and the newspaper headlines read like this: "For the First Time Women Will Participate in the Body That Chooses the [Chief] Rabbis: Unexpectedly, There Was No Opposition to Their Participation" (*HaAretz,* February 21, 1993). This newspaper headline indicates that the process of negotiation over women serving on electoral bodies has most likely been completed, that the "pros" and the "cons" have reached some sort of accommodation.

Opinions: "Pro" Women on the Electoral Bodies

The rhetoric here has been almost identical to that in the case of the religious councils: the electoral bodies are not halakhic forums. In the words of a liberal orthodox rabbi who has represented the Labor Party in the Knesset, "As far as I am concerned, the entire electoral body can be made up of women. The elections are not a religious matter" (*HaAretz,* November 25, 1993). Several of the candidates for chief rabbi said the same thing: "The election does not show anything about Torah stature or about Torah authority, rather about accepting [secular] legal authority" (*HaAretz,* November 18, 1992).

Note that the dating of these citations shows that they were uttered *after* that same line of rhetoric had already emerged as the most successful in the case of Leah Shakdiel.

Opinions: "Con" Women on the Electoral Bodies

The most commonly given reason for prohibiting women from serving on the electoral body is that men cannot sit with women for reasons of modesty. Yet, when the women elected to the Tel Aviv electoral body met with the chief rabbis and suggested that there be a room divider (*mehitza*) between men and women electors, the rabbis turned down this proposal (*HaAretz,* February 17, 1986), indicating that the issue at stake was not one of halakha but of custom and authority. This point was articulated by Chief Rabbi Lau who, after the Supreme Court ruling in favor of the women, "admitted that there did not seem to be any halachic bar to women being members of the electoral body, but said that the Rabbis felt there had been a deliberate attempt to erode the status of the religious authorities" (*Jerusalem Post,* December 12, 1987). Lau, in other words, chose to phrase the dispute in terms of rebellion: having women on the electoral bodies does not negate fundamental principles of Jewish law; it does, however, constitute a situation of subordinates turning against their leaders.

According to another ultra-orthodox rabbi, "I have no doubt that if the deciding voice is a woman's, then the election is no good. The stance of *halacha* is not totally clear, but it is an elementary principle that women do not choose rabbis" (*HaAretz,* November 18, 1992). Note the fuzzy rhetoric offered by even this hard-line "con" rabbi: "the stance of *halacha* is *not totally clear* [my emphasis]," a statement well designed to allow change to occur. And, in fact, the Religious Establishment now cooperates with the women on the electoral bodies: the women sit in the same room as the men, and the orthodox and (parts of the) ultra-orthodox communities acknowledge the legitimacy of rabbis chosen by a body on which women serve. (Some of the ultra-orthodox groups do not recognize the legitimacy of the Israeli chief rabbinate under any circumstances.) The post-facto rhetoric has been identical to that in the case of the religious councils: the electoral bodies are not really religious forums.

Women of the Wall

In comparison to the other two cases, the Women of the Wall seemed to hit some especially sensitive nerve in Israeli culture and elicited exorbitant public response (for an analysis of pilgrimage that stresses conflict rather than communitas, see Eade 1991). The Western Wall is the only standing remnant connected to the Jerusalem Temple that was destroyed almost two thousand years ago and is commonly believed by Jews to be the holiest place on earth. Before the destruction of the Temple, the priestly cult was centered there, and during the holiest segment of the Jewish ritual cycle, the High Priest would enter the "Holy of Holies" and engage in mystical communication with God. Religious Jews believe that the Shekhina (the immanent aspect of God) is more present at the Wall than at any other place. Written petitions to God are placed between the cracks of the stone wall, implying, perhaps, that God is in some way present to read the requests. In contemporary Israel the Wall is not only a religious symbol but also a national one: film footage of the recapture of the Wall during the Six-Day War is often shown on television; each year the paratroopers induct new soldiers into their ranks at a dramatic ceremony held at the Wall; secular Remembrance Day ceremonies take place there; and schoolchildren—religious and secular—visit the Wall as part of ministry of education programs to inspire patriotism.

Today the paved area in front of the Western Wall is divided by a barrier that separates the men's section from the women's section, as is customary in orthodox synagogues. On the men's side one commonly finds individual men praying and *minyanim* (prayer quorums comprised of ten adult men) engaged in vocal communal worship. On the women's side one finds only individual women praying. This is in keeping with traditional Jewish notions of men as constituting the public community and of women remaining private individuals.

The story of the Women of the Wall began on December 2, 1988, when a group of approximately one hundred women participants in the First International Jewish Feminist Conference in Jerusalem went to the Western Wall to hold a prayer service. American-born women for the most part, they were accustomed to the more egalitarian religious modes that characterize American Judaism. They went to the Wall holding a Sefer Torah (the Pentateuch written in a sacred manner on a decorated scroll that is traditionally read only by men), several of the women wore *tallitot* (the prayer shawls traditionally worn only by men), and many wore *kippot* (skullcaps, also traditionally worn only by men). The group entered the women's section and proceeded to conduct a communal prayer service. The response was violent: other women praying in the women's section, and men praying in the men's section, attacked the women both verbally and physically, telling them that it is forbidden for women to pray with a Sefer Torah and *tallit*.

The American women who attended the conference returned to the United States. The Israeli women, most of whom were American-born, pledged to return to the Wall on the first day of each month in order to carry out a prayer service. Following a series of incidents in which the women were assaulted, they sought a court order demanding, among other things, that the police offer them protection. The Court gave the government nine months in which to answer the women's charges and to find arrangements that would allow them to pray. On the last day of that nine-month period, in 1989, the ministry of religion issued a new ordinance prohibiting worship that is not in keeping with the "custom of the place" and with the "sensitivities of other worshipers" at holy sites—in other words, effectively excluding the Women from the Wall. The Women then filed a petition with the Supreme Court, asking that the Court enforce their right to pray at the Wall. In the meantime, the Court temporarily ruled that the status quo should be followed; the women could pray at the Wall but not as a group (i.e., without communal singing or prayer) and without a Sefer Torah or *tallit*. In January 1994 the Supreme Court verdict was handed down. Although each member of the three-judge panel expressed a separate opinion, the consensus was to return the case to the government to settle the matter.[7] At last account, in the spring of 1996, the government committee offered the Women of the Wall three alternative sites: an active archaeological dig, a spot outside the gates of Jerusalem's Old City (far from the Wall), and a legitimate holy place (called the "Little Wall") that has been used as a garbage dump for many years. Negotiations, as of this writing, continue.

The Women's Position

The Women's petition to the Supreme Court is based on several different arguments: religious freedom is a tenet of Israeli law; there is no uniform "custom of the place" at the Wall; their manner of praying is in keeping with Jewish law; and their prayer is genuinely spiritual and not a political stunt. Other sections of the petition address the jurisdiction of the Court, police, and government over holy places. They argue that the Wall is not the private fiefdom of the Religious Establishment or of the rabbi appointed by the government to serve at the Wall, and that the rabbi of the Wall has no right to say how people should pray at the Wall. They also contend that the 1989 ordinance of the ministry of religion is unjust and denies freedom of religion by implying that there is only one acceptable "custom of the place."

The Women of the Wall are an extraordinarily articulate group of individuals; they have written numerous pamphlets, fund-raising letters, letters to the editors of various newspapers, and magazine pieces. They have also been interviewed repeatedly by all of the major secular Israeli newspapers. The Women's rhetoric, for the most part, echoes the legal points raised in their Supreme Court petition.

The Women of the Wall consistently seek legitimacy not on the basis of sexual equality but on the basis of halakhic acceptability. They reiterate that they use a traditional orthodox prayerbook and that, in accordance with Jewish law, they do not recite certain prayers that can only be said by a *minyan* (quorum) of ten adult men. They are careful to refer to themselves as a "prayer group" and not as a "minyan," the distinction being that a minyan is a halakhically recognized group of ten or more men, whereas a prayer group has no official status. Their written statements are filled with opinions from orthodox halakhic experts who argue that what the Women are doing is permitted by Jewish law. In short, the arguments made by the Women are similar to the "pro" arguments in the cases of the religious council and the electoral bodies; that is, what they are demanding is a rather minor, nonrevolutionary change.

The Women repeatedly stress that they are not Reform Jews (Israeli mainstream Judaism is orthodox) but that they come from all affiliations and streams of Judaism and that their conduct is in strict accordance with halakha. The women reiterate these points almost every chance they get to represent their position freely. For example, the Jerusalem weekly newspaper *Kol HaIr* of March 24, 1989, published an article written by a reporter who is friend of one the Women's spokeswomen. He related an interview with her in which he clearly had offered her a chance to say whatever she wished. She chose to say that "most of the Women are orthodox and not Reform." Selecting this message to stand at the center of their rhetorical strategy serves to clarify that the Women are selling their struggle as a rebellion: they accept halakha and they are part of mainstream orthodox Judaism.

Publicly, the Women rarely make feminist comments. During an interview that I conducted with one of the Women's leaders, I asked if this is a feminist struggle. Her answer was evasive. The word "rights" appears in many of their statements, not in the context of women's rights but in the context of the "right" to pray.[8] They compare their own "rights" not to the "rights" of men but to the "rights" of other women who come to pray at the Wall. They claim that they are being discriminated against vis-à-vis other women (who are allowed to pray at the Wall as they wish) rather than vis-à-vis men (who are allowed to pray with a Torah and *tallit* at the Wall). Their legal documents focus on halakha and not on sex discrimination.

In an interview with another of the Women's spokeswomen, I was told that their decision not to use feminist rhetoric was tactical; they wanted to avoid the negative associations that the word "feminism" has in Israeli society (Izraeli and Tabory 1988). In short, the Women decided to package their stance in a way that they thought would "sell" in Israel.

The Religious Establishment's Position

In the following paragraphs I shall summarize the arguments and rhetoric used by the Religious Establishment.[9] Unlike the Women of the Wall who argued that their form of praying is permissible according to Jewish law, the Religious Establishment mostly avoided debate of Jewish law. They claimed that even if the women's style of praying is permitted by Jewish law, it is not the custom for women to pray in that manner, and the Women do not have the authority to change custom.

The state's legal brief, submitted to the Supreme Court in response to the Women's petition, drew on the opinions of Professor Eliav Shochetman, an expert in Jewish law: "Even if there are opinions in *halacha* that allow a woman to wear *tsitsit* [the ritual fringe attached to a *tallit*], the custom is not to let women wear *tsitsit* and there is no place to change this custom." Shuchtman and the state's attorney repeat the same argument regarding women carrying and reading from the Sefer Torah: even if it is possible to find opinions in Jewish legal sources that can be used to support women wearing a *tallit* or reading from the Torah, weight should not be given to these opinions because custom is the deciding factor in these cases. Shuchtman explains that in the framework of halakha the force of custom is equal to an absolute law, and there is no possibility of changing it.

Shuchtman quotes from a letter (responsum) of Rabbi Menashe Klein, one of the most important ultra-orthodox rabbis in the United States, who wrote concerning women's prayer groups (the kind of communal non-minyan in which the Women of the Wall participate): "And simply, we have never heard or seen of such a thing from the days of Moses until today, and maybe even the Reformers didn't think of such a thing . . . that these women are making a new thing whose source comes from that polluted place called women's lib, that comes in order to turn upside down the words of the living God and to turn the bowl on its lip (*hakeara al piha*) and [to turn topsy-turvy] the Table that is Set according to the Torah. And even if there were a clear permission [for this], just the fact that it wasn't customary in Israel . . . [means] that it is totally prohibited."

The point I would draw attention to in this statement is that the writer perceives the Women of the Wall to be engaged in revolution in the sense of seeking to change the basic order. The idea for women's prayer groups comes from outside the system ("that polluted place called women's lib") and the prayer groups are trying to turn the world upside down. Klein, like Shochetman, understands that the complex legal system known as halakha is made up of various opinions that can be manipulated in order to create change within the system. That is the reason that the concept of custom is repeatedly emphasized: custom, by tautological definition, is unchangeable.

The government-appointed rabbi in charge of the Wall, Rabbi Getz, has emerged as the Women's chief adversary. In the state's legal brief he is quoted as describing the Women as having "opened up in loud shouts [*bekolei kolot*]." In actuality, the Women of the Wall are a rather soft-spoken group and their praying style is quieter than that of many other groups and individuals at the Wall. I suggest that in describing the Women as shouting, Rabbi Getz was not purposely misleading the Court. Rather, he was describing his perception of the women as a group of screaming revolutionaries. Unlike the Women who downplay the issue of gender, Rabbi Getz adheres to a belief system in which gender is inescapable; there is no such thing as a non-gendered human being, and there are no such things as non-gendered "rights." Thus, women acting like men can never be insignificant, can never be unobtrusive.

A few months into the case Rabbi Getz wrote the Women a friendly letter begging them to stop "straying from the hallowed traditions of generations of Jews before you." He ended his letter by blessing the Women with the biblical blessing Eli the High Priest gave to the barren Hannah (the to-be mother of Samuel) when she prayed for a child: "The God of Israel should answer the request you have made of Him" (1 Sam. 1:17). At first look, this blessing seems incongruous. Why would a man who believes that his blessings carry a great deal of weight with God express a wish that God should grant his adversaries' request? I propose that from Rabbi Getz's point of view the Women have a great deal in common with Hannah: In the biblical passage Hannah appeared to be insane. But even more to the point, for Rabbi Getz women are so absolutely determined by their gender that he prays that the Women come to their senses and have children (like Hannah) and thus begin to act like "real" women.[10]

Some of the rabbi's other comments have been less moderate. The *New York Times* of February 12, 1988, quoted him as saying that a "woman carrying a *Torah* is like a pig at the Wailing Wall." This kind of comment is not lightly made. Pigs, in Jewish culture, are far more than a forbidden variety of meat. They symbolize all that is polluted and un-Jewish; one could claim that from a Jewish perspective pigs are the antithesis of Jews. Rabbi Getz's simile, then, suggests that the Women (whom he knows were born Jewish) are not Jewish when they insist on praying with a Torah at the Wall. In a variety of interviews and public statements, Rabbi Getz has endeavored to package the Women as not-really-Jewish.

The "cons" sometimes imply that not only are the Women not really Jewish but that they are actually Christian. In another newspaper article (*Jerusalem Post*, April 7, 1989) we read that according to Rabbi Getz, "They [the Women] need the Wall like I need a cross." The set of oppositions that he has built up is transparent: rabbis and the Wall versus Women and a cross. After the Women were prohibited by the Court from reading from the Torah at the Wall, they began to meet at the Wall for a quiet prayer service, and then to move to a nearby public archaeological garden to read from the Torah. The ultra-orthodox newspaper *HaModia* of April 7, 1989, describes this as follows: "The group . . . carried out their own cult [*pulhan mi-shelahen*] in the archeological garden in which were found relics of a Byzantine Church and signs of a Christian cultic site." Not only has the newspaper portrayed the move to the archaeological garden as if it were the Women's choice to pray there, but it has also introduced the Christian cultic character of the site, intimating, perhaps, that this is why the Women selected it.

Ultra-orthodox women at the Wall have grabbed the Women's prayerbooks, spit on them, bent them, and thrown them to the ground (normally, when a prayerbook accidentally falls to the ground, orthodox Jews pick it up and kiss it). In view of the fact that these were orthodox prayerbooks, which presumably most ultra-orthodox women could recognize as such, we understand that they were sufficiently upset to mutilate their own sacred symbols. I would venture to say that the ultra-orthodox women believed that the Women had in some way polluted the prayerbooks. That they felt it preferable to destroy the books than to allow the Women to pray from them expresses the extent to which the Religious Establishment perceived the Women's actions as revolutionary.

The Women of the Wall report that ultra-orthodox opponents have accused them of (mystically) causing all kinds of disasters. For example, they have been blamed for causing the Temple Mount Riots in 1997. These kinds of accusations are understandable in light of Gluckman's insight that "Even our modern societies embody contradictory principles and processes. These involve conflict. We allow room for divergence of opinion and interest within defined limits. If the limits are overstepped, the 'witchhunt' begins. It is a witchhunt as long as persons are blamed for misfortunes they are not responsible for" (1965, 107).

On a number of occasions ultra-orthodox women have torn off the Women's hair covering (by Jewish law married women cover their hair for reasons of modesty). This is a significant act: ripping off the hair covering is like "exposing" them for what they really are—impostors posing as religious Jews, outsiders who have tried to infiltrate the system in order to destroy it. Ripping off hair coverings is also reminiscent of the biblical bitter waters ceremony in which women suspected of adultery were uncovered and "tested" to see if they had indeed committed adultery (Num. 5:11–31). The insults shouted at the Women are telling: pigs, polluted (*tameh*), prostitute, gentiles (*goyim*). The Israeli newspaper *Yediot Ahronot* of March 21, 1989, reported that ultra-orthodox women screamed at the Women, "Nazis, go to monasteries and have Christian babies there!" The outsider status of the Women is epitomized by the single most frequent charge made against the Women—"Reformim." For Israelis, Reform Judaism is a foreign, American sect, and indeed, the American origin of many of the Women is frequently mentioned in the "con" press. (The "pro" rhetoric of course emphasizes the Israeli origins of certain members of the group, and the Israeli members often serve as the Women of the Wall's spokespeople.)

The ultra-orthodox newspapers have given the Women of the Wall a great deal of coverage. Much of that coverage serves to trivialize the Women. For example, *HaModia* of February 7, 1989, referred to them as the "Women of the Reform Sect." The word "sect" (*kat*) in Hebrew carries a connotation of a fringe group (such as Hari Krishna) or of a Christian group. The people who attack the Women are consistently referred to as "The permanent praying public at the Wall," implying that the Women are transient and not even part of "the public" but rather a peripheral phenomenon.

As we saw earlier, the Women insist that they come from all streams of Judaism, particularly orthodoxy, and that their praying is permissible by halakha. Their rhetoric aims to legitimize them, to "mainstream" their actions, and to prove that they are operating from within the system. The Religious Establishment, on the other hand, calls them "Reformiot," which carries a dual connotation of foreigners (Americans) and of lazy Jews who simply cannot be bothered to observe Jewish law. This rhetoric marginalizes the Women.

On July 5, 1989, the ultra-orthodox paper *HaModia* reported that the Women "made for themselves a custom" to go to the Wall on the first day of each month. *Yerushalayim*, the supplement of the secular paper *Yediot Ahronot*, published a biting critique of the "*Reformiot*" on August 31, 1989. The article began with: "The new gimmick of the Reform Movement women praying at the Wall with *tallit* and *Sefer Torah*." These and other similar remarks serve to paint the Women of the Wall as frivolous, as not rooted in any legitimate tradition.

Many articles in these papers accuse the Women of being a fund-raising stunt for one of the left-wing political parties (see *Yated Neeman*, April 5, 1989). A favorite term for the Women is "provocateurs," and what they do is frequently labeled "provokatsia," even by such supposedly "neutral" observers as the mayor of Jerusalem (*Jerusalem Post*, April 9, 1989). They are accused of coming to the Wall for profane rather than holy reasons. Unlike in the case of the religious council and the electoral bodies, the secular press is on the whole rather hostile toward the Women of the Wall.

At a meeting on July 12, 1989, Chief Rabbi Avraham Shapiro and Religious Affairs Minister Zevulun Hammer advised the Women of the Wall to pray individually, silently, and preferably at home—not at the Wall. If we take each of these suggestions seriously we see that they were given a recipe for male hegemony. Women should not act collectively, should not make noise, and should stay out of the public sphere. Disobeying these strictures is a revolution, it is a "provocation," it is "polluted," it is insane, and it is not Jewish.

Discussion

The Relative Weight of Symbols

In the case of the Women of the Wall the resource under dispute—the Wall—is understood to be a tremendous cultural resource. In the context of a study of conflict in Mennonite history, Fred Kniss has argued that cultural resources are different from other kinds of resources at least in part because they are indivisible and not commensurable by reference to some common metric. Whereas material and political resources can be exchanged and mobilized via units like dollars or votes, cultural resources lack such mediums of exchange and so are more likely to be "intense, all-or-nothing battles" (1996, 9).

In the Israeli context both the religious council and the electoral body can be understood as political or material resources. Both are made up of representatives from political parties; the religious council budgets funds for various services; and the chief rabbis chosen by the electoral body are employees of the state. Disputes over religious councils and electoral bodies can easily enter the currency of negotiation and compromise between orthodox and secular Israeli institutions. The councils and bodies can be divided, exchanged, and mobilized—they are made up of a number of categories of people. The Wall, on the other hand, is an ultimate example of a cultural or symbolic resource. It cannot be exchanged or traded for another piece of wall; it cannot be divided. By its very nature, it lends itself to all-out conflict. Kniss's approach helps explain the other religious-secular conflict in Israel that has repeatedly led to violent disputes: digging up graves at archaeological sites. Whereas disputes over funding for religious and secular education lends itself to exchange ("we'll give you one more secular school if you give us one more synagogue"), corpses—symbols of righteous ancestors—are not divisible. In disputes involving symbolic capital, resolution is much harder to come by because there is no logical unit of exchange. Thus, in the case of the Women of the Wall both sides fervently agreed on the uniquely high symbolic value of the Wall, and this understanding led to a zero-sum game in which for there to be a winner there has to be a loser.

My discussion until now has suggested that the assessment of a matter as symbolically valuable is a given, yet that is not entirely true. In the first two cases described in this chapter resolution was reached through a change of valuation—through redefining what the religious council and electoral body do (cf. Harrison 1995). Both sides agreed to shift the discourse from "who has rights over these religious bodies" to "what are these religious bodies worth." This shift led to resolution of the conflict through lowering the stakes and sharing the victory. In these cases women obtained seats on existing public assemblies, the assemblies stayed intact, and both sides found ways to justify and live with the outcome. The argument we heard repeatedly was that these bodies do not make halakhic rulings—they are secular bodies dealing with budgets and government bureaucracy. The implication, of course, is that within the halakhic system gender roles are part of the definition of the system and thus immutable; within the secular system gender roles are not part of the definition of the system, and so change is possible. By resolving the cases in these terms both sides gave up something: The "cons" have to sit with women as equals and the "pros" have to publicly proclaim that their victory is not really worth very much anyway (i.e., it is a secular and not a religious victory).

Whether it is possible to shift the valuation of a resource depends, as we have seen, on the nature of the resource itself. It also depends, as I shall now argue, on the structural locations of those contesting the resource.

Insiders and Outsiders

In the first two cases the women who demanded a larger share of the pie were nominated by large political parties. The women were, in a profound way, part of the system. Their arguments were drawn from the system: sexual discrimination is forbidden by Israeli secular law.

On the other hand, the Women of the Wall's outsider status was apparent to secular and religious Israelis alike. Whereas significant portions of the secular population had supported the other two changes discussed in this essay, the "American" Women of the Wall elicited hostility almost across the board. Their attempted appropriation of a state symbol, of a stone wall whose ancient façade bolsters the authenticity of national—not only religious—identity, alienated Israelis of almost all political persuasions.

Moreover, because feminism is understood by Israelis to be an American export, the Women of the Wall—despite their avoidance of the word—could not but be identified as feminists. Within a context of feminist discourse, rebellion (in Gluckman's terms) corresponds to liberal feminism; that is, the quest for equality within a legal system that is presumed to potentially encompass safeguards for human rights. Revolution corresponds to radical-separatist feminism that seeks to establish new systems, seeing prevailing legal, economic, and political systems as inherently patriarchal (Taylor and Rupp 1993). In Israel radical-separatist feminism is almost nonexistent, yet the word "feminism" is typically interpreted by the public to mean "man-hating" or "bra-burning" (which is repugnant to large parts of Israeli society) rather than "equal pay for equal work," which is supported by most Israelis (see Izraeli and Tabory 1988). The Women of the Wall believed themselves to be liberal feminists. However, because liberal feminism is an unrecognized political stance in Israeli society, the Women were invariably identified as revolutionaries—an unfortunate identity in terms of the likelihood of their being able to effect the kinds of changes they wished to produce. As revolutionaries stirring up trouble at the Western Wall, they were treated as jeopardizing the bedrock of both Judaism and Israeli nationalism.

In many of their interviews, the Women of the Wall opted for a line of rhetoric—"we come from all streams of Judaism"—that was meaningless to Israeli society because in Israel religious pluralism is not seen as a cultural value. In fact, they continue to be seen as "Reform," an American invention. The Women of the Wall's outsider status becomes apparent when we look at the kind of invectives used against them, invectives implying that they are not "really" Jewish. In the other two cases the "cons" imputed the "pros" with ulterior political motives but never called them pigs, Nazis, or gentiles.

"Woman" and "Women"

At the beginning of this chapter I argued that the outcome of gendered religious disputes may have a great deal to do with whether the dispute is understood as involving "Woman" or "women." "Woman," I argued, is a symbol whereas "women" are agents. In the first two cases presented, those involving the religious councils and the electoral bodies, the women were seen by both sides to the dispute as agents. The contested question was to what extent women should exercise agency—is women's agency equal to men's or less? Questions regarding, for example, women's right to lead or make decisions were raised by the "cons." In the case of the Women of the Wall the issue was understood to be one of "Woman." If we look again at the language used in the dispute we see that it is heavily symbolic: Nazi, pig, crucifix. The Women of the Wall were themselves seen as a symbol: symbolically desecrating Judaism's holiest symbolic site.

In the first two cases the gravity of gender was neutralized by—after some give and take—presenting the changes as secular and thus as fundamentally irrelevant to Judaism—as involving mere "women" rather than "Woman." The Women of the Wall, however, could not downplay religion (their struggle had to do with prayer) and thus chose to downplay gender (i.e., they rarely speak of women's rights). This strategy has not carried any weight with the Religious Establishment for whom gender is never a tangential category but a divinely created one. Because the Women of the Wall cannot make the claim that their case is a secular one, they are obliged to argue from within the halakhic system, and within the system of traditional Judaism, gender is immutable—gender roles are divinely ordained and upheld by custom, and changing them constitutes revolution.

The convergence of religious ideology and gender ideology elicits exceptionally strong affect because religions typically claim divine origin for gender roles: founding myths, creation myths, and etiological myths all proclaim that the way that "we" do gender is natural and sacred. Privileged communication with God is what, in the final analysis, justifies and sustains Jewish patriarchy. Because the Religious Establishment believes that sacred power is real, and more "real" than secular power, they perceive the case of Women of the Wall as having to do with power in its rawest sense: God is at the Wall, and whoever talks out loud to God at the Wall possesses tremendous power. In a system in which customary gender roles are championed by divine edict, women getting their hands on that kind of power threatens the system at its very core.

When we step back and look at Israeli society, we see that significant advances in the status of women have already taken place: education for girls, votes for women, women working outside the home, and women serving in the Knesset. Accordingly, in the case involving economic power (the religious councils) and in the case involving political power (the electoral bodies), women, backed up by the Supreme Court, negotiated mini-victories quite in keeping with Israeli secular norms. In the case involving sacred power, on the other hand, the Women lost. The Religious Establishment understood that the Women of the Wall are challenging the mythic charter of the Jewish people, because gender is part of that charter.

Packaging and Rhetoric

Because religious traditions typically protect themselves within a cloak of divine mandate, and because divinities often mandate "proper" gender roles, challenge to traditional gendered religious roles necessitates the use of creative rhetorical and ideological strategies, some of which prove more successful than others. The cases examined here suggest that the manner in which the change is interpreted and "packaged" can be the determining factor (Gamson and Modigliani 1987). In each situation, both sides used (and were used by) the mass media to present their arguments, frame events into "interpretive packages" (cf. Gamson and Stuart 1992), and negotiate the construction of social reality.

In the cases that we have seen here both sides to the conflict attempted to frame the proposed gender change in terms that constituted either rebellion or revolution—agency or symbolism, depending on whether they supported or opposed the change. In other words, these cases suggest that revolution and rebellion can be negotiable categories. How a demand for change is packaged and the readiness of the two sides to the conflict to search for mutually acceptable packaging can affect whether a particular conflict is treated as rebellion or revolution, which in turn is likely to determine the outcome of the conflict (cf. Capek 1993, 6). In general, opponents to change routinely argue that change is revolutionary (even if to outsiders the change seems quite trivial), often as a strategy to thwart change. Advocates of change, on the other hand, usually (not always) endeavor to present their demands as nonrevolutionary (even if to outsiders the change seems quite radical). The question is what kinds of rhetorical strategies are (un)successful in negotiating between these two antithetical stances.

Although religious conflicts are characterized by more or less the same kinds of political processes as other conflicts, proponents of religious change must seek especially creative rhetorical strategies in order to successfully neutralize claims of divine mandate, especially when the issue at stake is as emotionally charged as gender roles. As we have seen, a strategy that has worked more than once in Israel is to redefine the proposed change as nonreligious; this is a rhetorical strategy that offers opponents of change room to negotiate without explicitly backing down from their adherence to divine mandate. Redefining the issue as nonreligious is an obvious way of transforming a revolution into a rebellion.

The Women of the Wall, like the women in the other two cases, also proffered a rebellion rather than a revolution rhetorical strategy, arguing that what they are doing is in fact permitted by Jewish law. However, when the Religious Establishment made it clear that it was unwilling to enter into halakhic discourse with the Women, the Women did not modify their arguments in such a way as to offer any realistic rhetorical options to the "cons." To the contrary, the Women continue to flaunt symbols that fortify the Religious Establishment's perception of the Women as revolutionary. The Women, by appropriating male symbols—by acting like men—show themselves to be as topsy-turvy as a pig worshiping at the Western Wall or Rabbi Getz wearing a cross. The principal argument of the Religious Establishment is neither a political tactic nor a red herring; they say over and over that "this is not how it is done by us." Changing "how it is done by us" is an act of revolution, and the Women have not advanced (or, given their outsider status, cannot advance) an argument that can nullify the claims of custom.

In fact, contemporary customs at the Wall are not very ancient; they can be considered an "invented tradition" (Hobsbawm 1983). The point is that those in power are more likely to be able to package their version of tradition as "true." Given the outsider status of the Women of the Wall, they are in a poor position to be able to present their view of tradition in a persuasive way. Regarding the response of the press and the Israeli lay public, I would argue that non-specialists in general are unconcerned with researching the actual historicity of religious symbols. Rather, religious leaders, through the use of persuasive rituals and symbolic power, present their view of things as eternal (Geertz 1969). This would explain why the rabbis were unwilling to enter into halakhic arguments with the Women; halakhic argument leaves room for the possibility that there can be two legitimate opinions when the power of the religious establishment is contingent upon their holding a monopoly on "the truth."

Whereas the packaging in the first two cases allowed the "cons" room to negotiate, the Women of the Wall, adorned in symbols of male hegemony and advancing an argument drawn from outside Israeli culture, had packaged themselves as a revolution. Victor Turner, in the Ndembu case mentioned at the beginning of the chapter (1966), attributes the defeat of the upstarts to their lack of a compelling ideological stance: "This proved to be their undoing, since they thus committed themselves to accepting a system of values in which they occupied positions of lower status than the elders they sought to oust. In terms of the traditional standards of legitimacy, their rivalrous activities were weakly supported, and they could appeal to no new and authoritative criteria." Similarly, I would argue, the Women of the Wall have not offered a compelling ideological stance (in Israel feminism is viewed as marginal). Instead, they have made a point of allowing the traditionalists to determine the discursive frame—halakha. However, as the Women of the Wall are shown again and again, halakha and custom are a system of values in which women are by definition of lower status than men. By arguing from within the halakhic realm—a realm in which "Woman" rather than "women" is meaningful—the Women of the Wall seem doomed to failure.

Conclusion

The three cases presented here are specific to Israeli society, yet they offer certain broader insights into religious changes that have taken place around the world during the past half century, despite the adherence of most traditional religions to rigid gender ideologies. In the final section I turn to the question of which strategies and situations are likely to lead to successful efforts to effect gendered religious change.

First, change can be presented as not striking at the heart of the dominant gender ideology. A wonderful example of this process has been documented in Sri Lanka among *bhakti* fire walkers. According to Obeyesekere, "In the case of females, becoming a priest is a powerful source of 'liberation.' . . . But the cultural bias is still very strong against the idea that a pure divine being would reside in an impure vehicle [a female]. This resistance is overcome in two ways: the claim may be made that the spirit possessing the individual is not actually the deity but an attendant or servitor who conveys the commands of that deity; alternatively, a female may claim that she is possessed by a *female* deity like Pattini or Kali" (1978, 466). But—and here is a crucial social structural point—according to Obeyesekere this process is possible because of such socioeconomic variables as rapid urbanization (the loss of tight social control, which characterized village life), population growth, mass unemployment, and delayed marriage age for men and women. Put differently, cracks in the social structure leave room for "acceptable" change provided it is phrased in terms of the dominant gender ideology.

Second, whether the issue is understood to involve "Woman" or "women" can have an enormous affect on the outcome of conflicts. A good example here concerns ordination in Christian churches. In most Protestant churches the role of minister or pastor is understood to be one of agency—the minister or pastor leads and teaches. And, in most Protestant churches, after varying amounts of debate and dispute, women have been ordained as ministers. In the Catholic Church, on the other hand, where the role of priest is inherently symbolic, disputes over the ordination of women have not been resolved precisely because Christ's (and the priests') gender are seen as having symbolic value. Catholic priests, in other words, can be considered "Man" rather than merely "men."

Third, as I have shown in the examples of the Israeli religious councils and the electoral bodies, change can sometimes be presented as not striking at the heart or essence of the religious system. An intriguing variation on this theme involves situations in which male religious authorities commend women's increased religious activism, treating it as a laudatory return to ancient, authentic traditions that had been lost for a time but are now, rightly and properly, being reinstituted. This approach typically crops up in situations in which an outside authority has endeavored to suppress an indigenous religion but, for one reason or another, women more than men escape the constraints of the new hegemony. For example, Silverblatt writes that Andean women in the colonial period "were increasingly viewed by indigenous society as the defenders of ancient traditions and thus were encouraged to assume leading roles in the carrying out of native ritual" (1980, 177). Similarly, in modern Turkey the traditional ritual celebrating the birth of the Prophet Muhammad has changed significantly for men, while "the women seem to have become the repositories of [indigenous] spiritual values to which both women and men subscribe but which, paradoxically, only women can experience with performative immediacy because of their inferior status vis-à-vis past and present [Islamic] religious establishments" (Tapper and Tapper 1987, 87).

Alternatively, religious leaders can come to the conclusion that certain kinds of change are in their own interests and, therefore, choose to allow fictions or word games that permit them. This may be the reasoning behind the Catholic Church's new willingness to admit women pastors—shortages of male priests in many parts of the world have led to a situation in which women pastors are a necessary evil. These pastors may in fact function as community priests, but the fiction is preserved that they are not "really" priests. A parallel series of events occurred in Israel when ultra-orthodox rabbis decided to permit the women of their community to vote despite halakhic impediments: if their women were not to vote there would be fewer ultra-orthodox Knesset representatives and so a way was found for women's voting to not really be considered voting. It must be stressed, however, that these kinds of legal fictions can only be instituted by those who control the system (cf. Janeway 1981); the role of the advocates of change is to convince those in authority that it is to their benefit to go along with the fiction.

Finally, in some instances the religious establishment may see that changes are inevitable and seek to manipulate those changes to fit in with their own goals. Fundamentalist religious education for women in Jewish and Islamic societies is a good example of this process. Given that (secular) literacy for women has become unavoidable in the modern world, educating a generation of women to identify with the religious texts that teach female inferiority has proven a brilliant means of coping with modernity in societies as diverse as Israel (El-Or 1990) and Iran. A somewhat similar case has been described in regard to certain Buddhist leaders who, in response to the recent and rapid spread of Buddhism not only in Asia but in North America and Europe, have changed their views regarding women's religious vocations. According to Nancy Barnes, "Many very prominent monk-leaders have already become convinced [of the necessity to restore the traditional order of nuns] by the arguments of proponents of *bhiksuni samgha* [women's mendicant order] restoration, and by their own views of the possibilities for Buddhism [to expand] in the modern world" (1994, 145). In both of these situations, proponents of change tended to package even (what looks to outsiders like) revolutionary change in a way that looks to insiders like rebellion. Because the opponents of change either realize that change is inevitable or see some kind of benefit for themselves in the proposed change, this packaging is accepted and ample room is made available for fruitful negotiation.

In situations in which none of these strategies is tenable—when the proposed change strikes at the structural and ideological heart of the religious and gender system, when the change does not serve any even marginal interests of the religious establishment, and when the religious establishment has reason to believe that it can successfully avert change—the kind of violent conflict that characterized the case of the Women of the Wall is likely to erupt.

Afterword

In April 2003, the Israeli Supreme Court, in a 5–4 decision, voted against the right of the Women of the Wall to pray as a group at the Wall. In their decision, the judges said that allowing the women to pray at the Wall would be a danger to public safety. The nine-member panel also said that within twelve months the government should provide an alternative place for the women to pray at Robinson's Arch, an active archeological site located near the Wall. At first sight, this close decision does not seem to have added anything new to the discourse growing out of the Wall controversy. A recent book (Chesler and Haut 2003), provides additional perspectives of people deeply concerned with the subject.

Notes

I am grateful to the Israel Women's Network and to Jerusalem city councilwoman Anat Hoffman for allowing me to use their archives while doing research for this essay. I thank Ephraim Tabory, Leah Shakdiel, and Eyal Ben-Ari for reading and commenting on this chapter.

1. My argument here draws on Hawley and Proudfoot's (1994) analysis of patriarchy and religious fundamentalism, and on Wegner's (1988) analysis of women as agents and Other in the Mishnah (the second-century compendium of Jewish law). I concur with Moghadam that "When group identity becomes intensified, women are elevated to the status of symbol of the community and are compelled to assume the burden of the reproduction of the group" (1994, 18).
2. I discuss the case of the Women of the Wall in the context of a variety of other gendered corporeal conflicts in Israel (including conflicts around ultra-orthodox demands for women to dress "modestly," conflict surrounding Women in Black, and conflicts at the *mikveh* [ritual bath]) in *What Makes Women Sick: Maternity, Modesty, and Militarism in Israeli Society* (Sered 2000).
3. These cases are not the first ones involving issues of gender and religion that have made the front pages of Israeli newspapers. The right of women to vote and to be elected split religious Jews into two camps before the establishment of the State of Israel, and arguments concerning military exemptions for religious girls have reemerged periodically over the past fifty years.
4. The government committee, as of this writing, has not reached a decision. On July 6, 1995 (one year after the committee was appointed), the committee appealed to the Court for a six-month extension. The extension was granted (the Women of the Wall were not notified of the extension). The Women have now received a verbal promise from the Court that if by February 15, 1996, the committee has not come up with a reasonable recommendation, the Court will make a ruling.
5. The process by which members are chosen for religious councils reflects a complicated compromise between political parties. The minister of religion, the local town council, and the town's chief rabbi all nominate candidates, and they can veto each other's candidates.
6. Until the Supreme Court reached its verdict, *HaTsofeh,* the newspaper of the National Religious Party, was the most vociferous crusader against Shakdiel. After the Court decision, it began to support the idea of women serving on religious councils.
7. Israeli law gives the rabbi of the Wall authority over the Wall, so that on the face of it no court can declare his decisions illegal. Change regarding the Wall probably needs to be decided upon at the parliamentary and not the judicial level.
8. The only place gender equality is argued is in an additional petition to the Court filed by the Israel Women's Network, a secular women's rights organization. The Women's Network petition does not relate to the halakha. It merely says that even if the halakha discriminates against women, the secular state may not.
9. This includes the ministry of religion, the chief rabbis, the rabbi of the Wall, the orthodox and ultra-orthodox political parties, the orthodox and ultra-orthodox newspapers, and, by association, the state's attorney who filed the answer to the Women's Supreme Court petition. The answer to the Women's petition was filed on behalf of the rabbi of the Wall, ministry of religion, chief rabbis, police officer in charge of the police station in the Old City of Jerusalem, police officer in charge of the wall, and Israeli Police Department.
10. Leah Shakdiel has offered another interpretation of this letter. She suspects that Rabbi Getz may not have opposed the Women of the Wall in the beginning but gave in to ultra-orthodox pressure to force the Women to leave. Thus his reference to Eli, the shortsighted priest whose dynasty was removed from power, may have indicated that he understands that the religious establishment is sometimes wrong.

Bibliography

Abarbanel, J. 1974. *The Co-operative Farmer and the Welfare State: Economic Change in an Israeli Moshav.* Manchester: Manchester University Press.

Abbink, G. J. 1984. *The Falashas in Ethiopia and Israel: The Problem of Ethnic Assimilation.* Nijmegen: Institute for Cultural and Social Anthropology.

Abdel Fattah, A. 1987. "Ain Hod: The Story of a Man Struggling to Rebuild His Village." *Al-Fajr,* 28 June, p. 13.

———. 1995. "The Association of Forty Lifts the Veil of Silence and Sets a New Stage." *Sawt al-qura* 31 (6 February): 25–28.

Abou Zeid, A. 1996. *Al-mujtama'at al-sahrawiya wa-tahadiyat al-mustaqbal* [Desert Societies and the Challenges of the Future]. Cairo: National Center for Social and Criminal Studies.

Abrahams, R. 1969. "The Complex Relations of Simple Forms." *Genre* 2:104–28.

———. 1993. "Powerful Promises of Regeneration or Living Well with History." In *Conserving Culture: A New Discourse on Heritage,* ed. M. Hufford, 78–93. Urbana: University of Illinois Press.

Abrahams, R. D. 1993. "After New Perspectives: Folklore Study in the Late Twentieth Century." *Western Folklore* 52:379–400.

Abramovitch, H. 1986. "The Clash of Values in the Jerusalem Funeral: A Participant-Observer Study of a *Hevra Kadisha.*" Ninth World Congress of Jewish Studies, Jerusalem. World Union of Jewish Studies.

———. 1987. "Death." In *Contemporary Jewish Religious Thought,* ed. A. A. Cohen and P. Mendes-Flohr. New York: Scribner.

Abu El-Haj, N. 2001. *Facts on the Ground: Archaeological Practice and Territorial Self-Fashioning in Israeli Society.* Chicago: University of Chicago Press.

Abuhav, O. 2002. "Penei adam: 'Al terumatam shel ha'etnologim Erich Brauer we-Raphael Patai leheker ha'antropologia shel hayehudim" [The Face of Man: The Contribution of Ethnologists Erich Brauer and Raphael Patai to the Anthropological Study of Jews]. *Jerusalem Studies in Jewish Folklore* 20:155–73.

Abujaber, R. S. 1989. *Pioneers over Jordan: The Frontier of Settlement in Transjordan, 1850–1914.* London: Tauris.

Abu Kishk, B. 1981. "Arab Land and Israeli Policy." *Journal of Palestine Studies* 11(1):124–35.

Abu-Lughod, J. 1971. "The Demographic Transformations of Palestine." In *The Transformation of Palestine,* ed. I. Abu-Lughod, 139–64. Evanston: Northwestern University Press.

Abu-Lughod, L. 1989. "Zones of Theory in the Anthropology of the Arab World." *Annual Review of Anthropology* 18:267–306.

———. 1993. *Writing Women's Worlds: Bedouin Stories.* Berkeley: University of California Press.

Abu-Lughod, L., and C. Lutz. 1990. "Introduction: Emotion, Discourse, and the Politics of Everyday Life." In *Language and the Politics of Emotions,* ed. L. Abu-Lughod and C. Lutz. Cambridge: Cambridge University Press.

Abu Odeh, L. 1993. "Post-colonial Feminism and the Veil: Thinking the Difference." *Feminist Review* 43:27–37.

Abu-Rabia, A. 1994. *The Negev Bedouin and Livestock Rearing: Social, Economic and Political Aspects.* Oxford: Berg.

———. 1999. *Refu'a beduit masortit* [Traditional Bedouin Medicine]. Tel Aviv: Ministry of Defence Publishing.

———. 2000. "Employment and Unemployment among the Negev Bedouin." *Nomadic Peoples* 4(2):84–93.

———. 2001. *Bedouin Century: Education and Development among the Negev Tribes in the Twentieth Century.* New York: Berghahn.

———. 2005a. "Evil Eye and Cultural Beliefs among the Bedouin Tribes of the Negev." *Folklore* 116(3):241–54.

———. 2005b. "Indigenous Practices among Palestinians for Healing Eye Diseases and Inflammations." *Dynamis* 25:383–401.

———. 2007. "Breastfeeding Practices among Pastoral Tribes in the Middle East." *Anthropology of the Middle East* 2(2):38–54.

Achad Ha'am. 1916. "A Spiritual Center." In *Zionism: Problems and Views,* ed. P. Goodman and A. D. Lewis, 48–59. London: T. Fisher Unwin.

Achdut, L. 1990. *Seqira shenatit, 1989* [Annual Survey, 1989]. Jerusalem: National Insurance Institute.

Adam, A. 1950. *La population marocaine dans l'ancienne medina de Casablanca.* Rabat: Bulletin Economique et Social du Maroc.

Ades, D. 1978. *Dada and Surrealism Reviewed.* London: Westerham Press.

Adler, C. 1963. *Tenu'ot hano'ar bahevra hayisraelit* [The Youth Movement in Israeli Society]. Jerusalem: Szold Institute.

———. 1970. "The Israeli School as a Selective Institution." In *Integration and Development in Israel,* ed. S. N. Eisenstadt, 287–301. New York: Praeger.

Aescoli, A. Z. 1938. *Yisrael: Pirkei etnologia, yedi'at ha'am* [The Jewish People: Chapters in Ethnology]. Jerusalem: Yesodot.

———. 1956. *Tenu'ot meshihiot biysrael* [Messianic Movements in Israel]. Jerusalem: Mosad Bialik.

Aguirre, A., Jr. 1990. "Social Communication and Self Identification: Participatory Behavior on the Freeway." *Journal of Popular Culture* 24:91–101.

Agulhon, M. 1981. *Marianne into Battle: Republican Imagery and Symbolism in France, 1789–1880.* Cambridge: Cambridge University Press.

Al-Haj, M. 1979. "The Status of the Arab Hamula in Israel." M.A. thesis, Haifa University.

———. 1981. "Al-Hamulah al-'arabiyah fi Isra'il" [The Arab Hamulah in Israel]. *Afaq* 1–2:17–28.

———. 1987. *Social Change and Family Processes: Arab Communities in Shefar'am.* Boulder, CO: Westview.

———. 1991. *Education and Social Change among the Arabs in Israel.* Tel Aviv: International Center for Peace in the Middle East.

———. 1993. "Kinship and Local Politics among the Arabs in Israel." *Asian and African Studies* 27:47–60.

Al-Haj, M., and H. Rosenfeld. 1989. "The Emergence of an Indigenous Political Framework in Israel: The National Committee of Chairmen of Arab Local Authorities." *Asian and African Studies* 23(2–3):205–44.

———. 1990. *Arab Local Government in Israel.* Boulder, CO: Westview.

Allen, A. T. 1986. "Gardens of Children, Gardens of God: Kindergartens and Day-Care Centers in Nineteenth-Century Germany." *Journal of Social History* 19:433–50.

Almog, Oz. 1997. *Hatzabar-dyokan* [Portrait of a Native Israeli]. Tel Aviv: Am Oved.

Al-Qazzaz, A. 1977. *Women in the Middle East and North Africa.* Middle East Monograph no. 2. Austin, TX: Center for Middle Eastern Studies.

Altorki, S. 1977. "Family Organization and Women's Power in Urban Saudi Arabian Society." *Journal of Anthropological Research* 33:277–87.

Am'ad, Z., and M. Palgi. 1986. *Gormei nechonut lekabalat tafkidim tziburiim bakibbutz* [Causal Factors of Readiness for Managerial Roles in the Kibbutz.] Haifa: Kibbutz Research Institute.

American Jewish Year Book. 1950. *North Africa.* Ed. L. Shapiro. 51:426–32.

———. 1960. *North Africa.* Ed. J. Lazarus. 61:315–37.

———. 1970. *Jewish Communities.* Ed. V. Malka. 71:514–20.

———. 1980. *World Jewish Population.* Ed. L. Shapiro. 80:282–89.

———. 1990. *World Jewish Population.* Ed. V. O. Schmelz and S. Della Pergola. 90: 514–32.

———. 1994. *World Jewish Population.* Ed. V. O. Schmelz and S. Della Pergola. 94: 465–89.

American Joint Distribution Committee. 1990. *Africa and Asia Area Committee: Study Mission to Morocco and Tunisia.* Casablanca, Morocco: AJDC.

———. 1994. *Report by Albert Weizman.* Casablanca, Morocco: AJDC.

American Psychiatric Association. 1980. *Diagnostic and Statistical Manual of Mental Disorders.* Washington, DC: American Psychiatric Association.

Ammar, H. 1954. *Growing Up in an Egyptian Village.* London: Routledge and Kegan Paul.

Apfell-Marglin, F., and S. A. Marglin. 1990. *Dominating Knowledge: Development, Culture and Resistance.* Oxford: Clarendon.

Appadurai, A. 1986a. *The Social Life of Things.* Cambridge: Cambridge University Press.

———. 1986b. "Theory in Anthropology: Center and Periphery." *Comparative Studies in Society and History* 28:356–61.

———. 1990. "Disjuncture and Difference in the Global Cultural Economy." *Public Culture* 2(2):1–24.

———. 1991. "Global Ethnospaces: Notes and Queries for a Transnational Anthropology." In *Recapturing Anthropology: Working in the Present,* ed. R. G. Fox. Santa Fe, NM: School of American Research Press.

Applebaum, L., ed. 1974. *Lo 'al halehem levado: Hemshechiut utemurot bemoshav Nahalal* [Not by Bread Alone: Continuation and Recompense in Nahalal]. Rehovot: Center for Rural and Urban Settlement Research.

———. 1986. "Hagirot mishpahot 'iroiot lemoshavim biyisra'el." [Migration of Urban Families to Moshavim]. Ph.D. diss., Hebrew University of Jerusalem.

Applebaum, L., and H. Margolis. 1979. *Moshav ha'ovdim bemivhan hazeman: Defusei shinui ba'irgun* [Moshav Ha'ovdim in the Test of Time: Forms of Organizational Change]. Rehovot: Center for Rural and Urban Settlement Research.

———. 1983. *Hakefar halo haklai biysrael kemachshir lepituah: Reka, be'ayot, sikkium* [The Non-Agricultural Village in Israel as a Developmental Tool: Background, Problems, and Chances]. Rehovot: Center for Rural and Urban Settlement Research.

Aran, G. 1974. "Parachuting." *American Journal of Sociology* 80(1):124–52.

———. 1987. "From Religious Zionism to Zionist Religion: The Origins and Culture of Gush Emunim." Ph.D. diss., University of Jerusalem.

———. 1991. "Jewish Zionist Fundamentalism." In *Fundamentalisms Observed*, ed. M. E. Marty and R. S. Appelby. Chicago: University of Chicago Press.

Ardener, S., ed. 1975. *Perceiving Women.* New York: Wiley.

———. 1978. *Defining Females: The Nature of Women in Society.* London: Croom Helm.

———. 1981. "Ground Rules and Social Maps for Women: An Introduction." In *Women and Space: Ground Rules and Social Maps*, ed. S. Ardener. London: Croom Helm.

Arensberg, C. 1968 [1937]. *The Irish Countryman.* New York: Natural History Press.

Arian, A. 1970. "Consensus and Community in Israel." *Jewish Journal of Sociology* 12:39–53.

———. 1981. "Elections 1981: Competitiveness and Polarization." *Jerusalem Quarterly* 21:3–27.

Arieli, E. 1986. "A Barrier for Izrael Valley Kibbutzim." *Hashavua Bakibbutz Ha'artzi*, 14 November.

Aries, P. 1977. *L'homme devant la mort.* Paris: Editions du Seuil.

Arnon, Y. 1988. "Arb'im shana lameshek hayisra'eli" [Israel's Economy: Forty Years]. *Economic Quarterly* 138:251–58.

Aronoff, M. J. 1973. "Development Towns in Israel." In *Israel: Social Structure and Change*, ed. M. Curtis and M. S. Chernoff. New Brunswick, NJ: Transaction.

———. 1974. *Frontiertown: The Politics of Community Building in Israel.* Manchester: Manchester University Press.

———. 1980. "Centre-Periphery Relationships in the Israeli Labour Party." In *A Composite Portrait of Israel*, ed. E. Marx, 29–57. London: Academic Press.

Aronson, D. R. 1976. "Ethnicity as a Cultural System." In *Ethnicity in the Americas*, ed. F. Henry. The Hague: Mouton.

Aronson, E. 1988. *The Social Animal.* New York: Freeman.

Arzi, A. 1988. "A Cloud of Smoke." *Hedim* 22(132):9.

Asad, T., ed. 1973. *Anthropology and the Colonial Encounter.* New York: Humanities Press.

———. 1975. "Anthropological Texts and Ideological Problems: An Analysis of Cohen on Arab Villages in Israel." *Economy and Society* 4(3):251–81.

Asche, H. 1981. "Moderner Wandel und nomadische Bevölkerungsgruppen in der nordomanischen Küstenebene Al Batinah." In *Beduinen im Zeichen der Erdöls*, ed. F. Scholz, 101–59. Wiesbaden: Reichert.

Ashkenazi, M., and A. Weingrod. 1984. *Ethiopian Immigrants in Beersheva: An Anthropological Study of the Absorption Process.* Highland Park, IL: American Association for Ethiopian Jews.

———, eds. 1985. "Ethiopian Jews and Israel." *Israel Social Science Research* 3(1–2).

Association of Forty. 1993. *The Forgotten Ones.* Haifa: Association of Forty.

———. 1996. "The Association of Forty Calls on the New Prime Minister to Implement the Decisions of the Previous Government on the Subject of the Unrecognized Villages." *Sawt al-qura* (May–June):8.

Astington, J. 1991. "Narrative and the Child's Theory of Mind." In *Narrative Thought and Narrative Language,* ed. B. Britton and A. Pellegrini. Hillsdale, NJ: Erlbaum.

Atar, A. 1982. "Bamif'alim ha'eizoriim 'ein kol hadash" [Nothing Is New at the Regional Enterprises]. *Yahad,* 19 November.

Aviad, J. 1983. *Return to Judaism: Religious Renewal in Israel.* Chicago: University of Chicago Press.

Avishai, B. 1985. *The Tragedy of Zionism.* New York: Farrar, Strauss and Giroux.

Avrahami, E. 1993. "Tifkud hatakam: Dilemo turekiwunei shinui" [The Functioning of the UKM NFO: Dilemmas and Change Directions]. Ramat Efal: Yad Tabenkin.

Avruch, K. 1981. *American Immigrants in Israel: Social Identities and Change.* Chicago: University of Chicago Press.

Axelrod, R. 1984. *The Evolution of Cooperation.* New York: Basic Books.

Azarya, V. 1989. "Civil Education in the Israeli Armed Forces." In *Education in a Comparative Context,* ed. E. Krausz, 119–47. New Brunswick, NJ: Transaction.

Azmon, Y., and D. N. Izraeli, eds. 1993. *Women in Israel.* Studies of Israeli Society, vol. 6. New Brunswick, NJ: Transaction.

Babcock, B. 1978. "Too Few, Too Many: Ritual Modes of Signification." *Semiotica* 23:291–302.

Babylonian Talmud. 1959. Niddah 30b. Ed. I. Epstein. London: Soncino.

———. 1976. Baba Batra 12b. Ed. I. Epstein. London: Soncino.

Bachelard, G. 1964. *The Psychoanalysis of Fire.* Trans. Alan C. M. Ross. London: Routledge and Kegan Paul.

———. 1969. *The Poetics of Space.* Boston: Beacon Press.

Bachofen, J. J. 1967. *Myth, Religion, and Mother Right: Selected Writings of J. J. Bachofen.* Trans. R. Mannheim. Princeton: Princeton University Press.

Bacon, G. C. 1984. *The Jews in Poland and Russia: Bibliographical Essays.* Bloomington: Indiana University Press.

Bahloul, J. 1992. *La maison de mémoire: Ethnologie d'un demeure judéo-arabe en Algérie (1937–1961).* Paris: Anne-Marie Métailié.

———. 1996. *The Architecture of Memory: A Jewish-Muslim Household in Colonial Algeria, 1937–1961.* Trans. C. du Peloux Ménagé. Cambridge: Cambridge University Press.

Bakhtin, M. M. 1981. *The Dialogic Imagination.* Austin: University of Texas Press.

Balabkins, N. 1971. *West German Reparations to Israel.* New Brunswick, NJ: Rutgers University Press.

Baldwin, E. 1972. *Differentiation and Co-operation in an Israeli Veteran Moshav.* Manchester: Manchester University Press.

Banai, N. 1988. *Ethiopian Absorption—The Hidden Challenge.* Jerusalem: United Israel Appeal.

Banfield, E. D. 1958. *The Moral Basis of a Backward Society.* New York: Free Press.

Bank of Israel. 1960a. *Hahitpathut hakalkalit biysra'el* [Economic Development in Israel, 1959]. Jerusalem: Bank of Israel.

———. 1960b. *Seker* [Survey]. Jerusalem: Bank of Israel.

———. 1964. *Economic Development in Israel, 1963.* Jerusalem: Bank of Israel.

———. 1969. *Seker, No. 33* [Survey]. Jerusalem: Bank of Israel.
———. 1972. "Profit and Profitability in Industrial Firms in Israel, 1965–70." *Survey,* no. 40 (October 1972).
Bar-Asher, S. 1977. *Taqanot yehudei Maroko* [Regulations of Morocco Jewry]. Jerusalem: Zalman Shazar Center.
Barber, B. 1983. *The Logic and Limits of Trust.* New Brunswick, NJ: Rutgers University Press.
Bar-Gal, Y. 1980. "The Concept of Diffusion: Dimensions of Time and Space in Cooperative Agricultural Organization in Non-Jewish Villages in Israel." *Middle Eastern Studies* 16(3):236–45.
Bar-Ilan, M. 1975. "Achievements and Aspirations." In *Religious Zionism: An Anthology,* ed. Y. Tirosh. Jerusalem: World Zionist Organization.
Barnes, J. A. 1972. *Social Networks.* Reading, MA: Addison-Wesley.
———. 1973. "Genetrix: Genitor: Nature: Culture?" In *The Character of Kinship,* ed. J. Goody, 61–73. Cambridge: Cambridge University Press.
Barnes, N. J. 1994. "Women in Buddhism." In *Today's Woman in World Religions,* ed. A. Sharma, 137–70. Albany: State University of New York Press.
Barnett, H. G. 1953. *Innovation: The Basis of Cultural Change.* New York: McGraw-Hill.
Bar-On, D. 1988. "Re'ayon 'im psicholog" [Interview with a Psychologist]. *Hedim* 22(132):44–49.
———. 1993. "Peace Pre-Traumatic Disorder (PPTSD): The Israeli Experience." Paper presented at symposium of the Israeli Society for Family Therapy, 19 May, Tel Aviv University.
Bar-On, D., and M. Shelhav. 1984. *The Regional Enterprises.* Ramat Efal: Yad Tabenkin.
Bar-On, M. 1985. *Shalom 'achshav: Lediokha shel tenu'a* [Peace Now: Portrait of a Movement]. Tel Aviv: Hakibbutz Hameuhad.
Barrett, S. 1984. *The Rebirth of Anthropological Theory.* Toronto: Toronto University Press.
Bar-Tal, D., and S. Zoltak. 1989. "Hishtakefut demut ha'arviweyahasei yehudim-'aravim bemikra'ot" [The Reflection of the Character of the Arab and Jewish-Arab Relations in Readers]. *Megamot* 32(3):301–17.
Bartal, I. 1993. "Shimon ha-Kofer—A Chapter in Orthodox Historiography." In *Studies in Jewish Culture in Honor of Chone Shmeruk,* ed. I. Bartal, E. Mendelson, and C. Turnianski, 243–68. Jerusalem: Zalman Shazar Center.
———. 1994. "Knowledge and Wisdom: On Orthodox Historiography." *Studies in Contemporary Jewry* 10:178–92.
Barth, F. ed. 1969. *Ethnic Groups and Boundaries.* Boston: Little, Brown.
Bar-Yosef, R., and D. Padan. 1964. "Eidot hamizrah bagibush hama'amadi shel Yisra'el" [Oriental Jews in Israel's Class Structure]. *Molad* 12:504–16.
Basker, E., B. M. Beran, and M. Kleinhauz. 1982. "A Social Science Perspective on the Negotiations of a Psychiatric Diagnosis." *Social Psychiatry* 17:53–58.
Batchelor, D. 1993. "This Library and This Order: Art in France after the First World War." In *Realism, Surrealism: Art between the Wars,* ed. B. Fer, D. Batchelor, and P. Wood, 2–86. New Haven: Yale University Press.
Bateson, G. 1956. "The Message 'This Is a Play.'" In *Group Processes: Transactions of the Third Conference, October 7–10, Princeton, NJ,* ed. B. Scheffner. New York: Josiah Macy Foundation.
———. 1972a. *Steps to an Ecology of Mind.* New York: Ballantine.

———. 1972b. "A Theory of Play and Fantasy." In *Steps to an Ecology of Mind*. New York: Ballantine.

Bat Haim, H. 1954. "Ein Hod: Artists' Home." *Israel Speaks*, 22 January.

———. 1960. "Art among the Ruins." *Jerusalem Post*.

Baudrillard, J. 1983. *Simulations*. New York: Semiotext(e).

———. 1988. *The Ecstasy of Communication*. New York: Semiotext(e).

Bauman, R., ed. 1992. Introduction to *Folklore, Cultural Performances, and Popular Entertainments*. New York: Oxford University Press.

Bauman, Z. 1992. *Mortality, Immortality, and Other Life Strategies*. Cambridge: Polity Press.

Bebko, J. M., A. Perry, and S. Bryson. 1996. "Multiple Validation Study of Facilitated Communication: II. Individual Differences and Subgroup Results." *Journal of Autism and Developmental Disorders* 26(1):19–42.

Beck, L., and N. Keddie, eds. 1978. *Women in the Muslim World*. Cambridge, MA: Harvard University Press.

Beilin, Y. 1984. *Banim betzel avotam* [Sons Overshadowed by Fathers]. Ramat-Gan: Revivim.

Bein, A. 1952. *The Return to the Soil*. Jerusalem: Youth and Hehalutz Department of the Zionist Organization.

Beinin, J. 1988. "From Land Day to Equality Day." *MERIP Middle East Report* 150:24–27.

Beit-Hallahmi, B. 1992. "Back to the Fold: Return to Judaism." In *Tradition, Innovation, Conflict: Jewishness and Judaism in Contemporary Israel*, ed. Z. Sobel and B. Beit-Hallahmi, 49–72. New York: State University of New York Press.

———. 1993. *Original Sins: Reflections on the History of Zionism and Israel*. Brooklyn: Olive Branch Press.

Ben-Ami, I. 1984. *Ha'aratzat kedoshim bekerev yehudei maroko* [Folk Veneration of Saints among the Jews of Morocco]. Jerusalem: Magnes Press.

Ben-Amos, D. 1998. "The Name Is the Thing." *Journal of American Folklore* 111(441):257–80.

Ben-Amos, D., and J. R. Mintz, eds. and trans. 1970. *In Praise of the Baal Shem Tov (Shivhei Habesht)*. Bloomington: Indiana University Press.

Ben-Ari, E. 1987. "Disputing about Day-Care: Care-Taking Roles in a Japanese Day Nursery." In *Alternative Patterns of Family Life in Modern Societies*, ed. L. Shamgar-Handelman and R. Palomba, 119–31. Rome: IRP-National Institute of Population Research.

———. 1989. "Masks and Soldiering: The Israeli Army and the Palestinian Uprising." *Cultural Anthropology* 4:372–89.

———. 1992. *Conflict in the Military World View: An Ethnography of an Israeli Infantry Battalion*. Jerusalem: Truman Research Institute and Shain Centre.

Ben-Ari, E., and Y. Bilu. 1987. "Saints' Sanctuaries in Israeli Development Towns: On a Mechanism of Urban Transformation." *Urban Anthropology* 16(2):243–72.

———, eds. 1997. *Grasping Land: Space and Place in Contemporary Israeli Discourse and Experience*. Albany: State University of New York Press.

Ben-Arieh, Y. 1990. "Perceptions and Images of the Holy Land." In *The Land That Became Israel*, ed. R. Kark, 37–53. New Haven: Yale University Press.

Ben-Arieh, Y., and S. Sapir. 1979. "Reshita shel Beersheva be-shalhei ha-tekufa ha-'otomanit" [The Beginning of Beersheva toward the End of the Ottoman Period]. In *Beersheva*, ed. Y. Gradus and E. Stern, 55–68. Jerusalem: Keter.

Benas, B. 1969. "The Renascence of Jewish Aesthetics." In *Zionism: Problems and Views*, ed. P. Goodman and A. D. Lewis. London: T. Fisher Unwin.

Benayahu, M. 1983. "Mim hama'amadot vehamoshavot lameit ve'ad hahakafot veh'issur liytzi'at habanim aharei mitat avihem" [Concerning Death Processions, Circumambulations and the Ban on Children Following Their Father's Bier]. *Sinai* 92:58–65.

Ben-David (Gross), J. 1953. "Ethnic Differences or Social Change?" In *Between Past and Future: Essays and Studies on Aspects of Immigrant Absorption in Israel*, ed. C. Frankenstein, 33–52. Jerusalem: Henrietta Szold Foundation.

Ben-David, J. 2004. *Habeduim beyisrael: Hebeitim hevratiim vekarka'iim* [The Bedouin in Israel: Land and Social Issues]. Jerusalem: Jerusalem Institute for Israel Studies.

Bendix, R. 1998. "Of Names, Professional Identities, and Disciplinary Futures." *Journal of American Folklore* 111(441):235–46.

Ben-Dor, G. 1973. *The Military in the Politics of Integration and Innovation: The Case of the Druze Minority in Israel.* Jerusalem: Jerusalem Academic Press.

———. 1979. *The Druzes in Israel: A Political Study.* Jerusalem: Magnes Press.

———. 1980. "Electoral Politics and Ethnic Polarization: Israeli Arabs in the 1977 Elections." In *The Elections in Israel—1977*, ed. A. Arian, 171–85. Jerusalem: Jerusalem Academic Press.

Benech, J. 1940. *Essai d'explication d'un mellah (ghetto marocain): Un des aspects du judaïsme.* Paris: Larose.

Benedict, R. 1934. *Patterns of Culture.* Boston: Houghton Mifflin.

Ben-Ezer, G. 1983. *He'archut betzahal liklitat 'Beit-yisra'el' ('Hafalashim')* [The Israeli Army Prepares to Recruit Ethiopian Immigrants]. Tel Aviv: Matkal-Aka.

———. 1985. "Cross-Cultural Misunderstandings: The Case of Ethiopian Immigrant Jews in Israeli Society." *Israel Social Science Research* 3(1–2):63–73.

Ben-Gurion, D. 1963. "Vision and Redemption." In *The Mission of Israel*, ed. J. Baal-Teshuva. New York: Robert Speller.

———. 1971. *Israel: A Personal History.* Tel Aviv: American Israel Publishing.

Benita, E., and G. Noam. 1995. "The Absorption of Ethiopian Immigrants: Selected Findings from Local Surveys." *Israel Social Science Research* 10(2):81–96.

Benita, E., G. Noam, and R. Levy. 1993. "The Absorption of Ethiopian Immigrants: Findings from a Survey in Kiryat Gat." Discussion paper D-206-93. Jerusalem: JDC Brookdale Institute.

Benjamin, W. 1969. "The Work of Art in the Age of Mechanical Reproduction." In *Illuminations*, ed. H. Arendt, 212–52. New York: Schocken.

Ben-Menahem, Y. 1999. "'Al hativ'i we'al hahevrati" [On the Natural and the Social]. *'Iyun* 48:135–50.

Bennet, J., and J. Bowen, eds. 1988. *Production and Autonomy: Anthropological Studies and Critiques of Development.* Lanham, MD: University Press of America.

Bennett, J. W. 1975. *The New Ethnicity: Perspectives from Ethnology.* St. Paul, MN: West.

Bennis, W. G., and B. Nannus. 1986. *Leaders.* New York: Harper.

Ben-Porat, Z. 1985. "Bein-textualiut" [Intertextuality]. *Hasifrut* 34:170–78.

Ben-Porath, Y., and E. Marx. 1971. *Some Sociological and Economic Aspects of Refugee Camps on the West Bank.* Santa Monica, CA: Rand.

Ben-Rafael, E. 1982. *The Emergence of Ethnicity: Cultural Groups and Social Conflict in Israel.* Westport, CT: Greenwood.

———. 1988. *Status, Power and Conflict in the Kibbutz.* Aldershot: Avebury.

———. 1996. *Mahapeicha lo totalit* [A Non-Total Revolution]. Ramat Efal: Yad Tabenkin.

Bensimon-Donath, D. 1968. *L'evolution du judaïsme sous le protectorat français, 1912–1956.* Paris: Mouton.

Ben-Yehuda, N. 1985. *Deviance and Moral Boundaries: Witchcraft, the Occult, Science Fiction, Deviant Sciences and Scientists.* Chicago: University of Chicago Press.

———. 1990. *The Politics and Morality of Deviance: Moral Panics, Drug Abuse, Deviant Science and Reversed Stigmatization.* New York: State University of New York Press.

Ben-Ze'ev, E., and E. Ben-Ari. 1996. "Imposing Politics: Attempts at Creating a Museum of 'Co-Existence' in Jerusalem." *Anthropology Today* 12(6):7–13.

Ben-Zvi, I. 1966. *Nidahei yisrael* [Remote Jews]. Jerusalem: Yad Ben-Zvi.

Bercovitch, E. 1994. "The Agent in the Gift: Hidden Exchange in Inner New Guinea." *Cultural Anthropology* 9(4):498–536.

Berger, P. L., and T. Luckman. 1966. *The Social Construction of Reality.* Garden City, NY: Doubleday.

Berger-Sofer, R. 1979. "Pious Women: A Study of Women's Roles in a Hassidic and Pious Community, Mea Shearim." Ph.D. diss., Rutgers University.

Berglas, E. 1983. "Defense and the Economy: The Israeli Experience." Discussion Paper No. 83.01. Jerusalem: Falk Institute for Economic Research.

Bernstein, D. 1980. "Immigrants and Society: A Critical View of the Dominant School of Israeli Sociology." *British Journal of Sociology* 31(2):246–64.

———. 1981. "Immigrant Transit Camps: The Formation of Dependence Relations in Israeli Society." *Ethnic and Social Studies* 4:26–40.

Bertaux, D., and M. Kohli. 1984. "The Life History Approach: A Continental View." *Annual Review of Sociology* 10:215–37.

Bet-El, I., and A. Ben-Amos. 1995. "Rituals of Democracy: Ceremonies of Commemoration in Israeli Schools." Annual Meeting of the Israeli Anthropological Association. Ein Gedi, 4 January.

Bettelheim, B. 1967. *The Empty Fortress.* New York: Free Press.

Bien, Y. 1995. "Kibbutz in the Trap of the Consultancy Model." Paper presented at the 5th International Communal Studies Association Conference, Ramat Efal, Israel, 31 May.

Biklen, D. 1990. "Communication Unbound: Autism and Praxis." *Harvard Educational Review* 60:291–314.

Biklen, D., and A. Schubert. 1991. "New Words: The Communication of Students with Autism." *Remedial and Special Education* 12(6):46–57.

Bilu, Y. 1980. "The Moroccan Demon in Israel: The Case of 'Evil Spirit Diseases.'" *Ethos* 8(1):24–38.

———. 1982. "Pondering the 'Princes of the Oil': A New Light on an Old Phenomenon." *Journal of Anthropological Research* 37(3):269–78.

———. 1985. "The Taming of Deviants and Beyond: A Psychocultural Analysis of Dybbuk Possession and Exorcism in Judaism." *Psychoanalytic Study of Society* 11:1–32.

———. 1988. "Rabbi Yaacov Wazana: A Jewish Healer in the Atlas Mountains." *Culture, Medicine and Psychiatry* 12(1):113–35.

———. 1990. "Jewish Moroccan 'Saint Impresarios' in Israel: A Stage-Developmental Perspective." *Psychoanalytic Study of Society* 15:247–69.

———. 1993. *Lelo meitzarim: Hayav wemoto shel Ya'acov Wazana* [Without Bounds: The Life and Death of Rabbi Ya'acov Wazana]. Jerusalem: Magnes Press.

———. 1997. "Dybbuk and Maggid: Two Cultural Patterns of Altered States of Consciousness in Judaism." *AJS Reviews* 21(2):341–66.

———. 2000. *Without Bounds: The Life and Death of Rabbi Ya'acov Wazana.* Detroit: Wayne State University Press.

Bilu, Y., and H. Abramovitch. 1985. "In Search of the Saddiq: Visitational Dreams among Moroccan Jews in Israel." *Psychiatry* 48:83–92.

Bilu, Y., and E. Ben-Ari. 1990. "Netivoth's Western Wall." *Politika* (March):56–59.

———. 1992. "The Making of Modern Saints." *American Ethnologist* 4:672–88.

Bilu, Y., and A. Levy. 1996. "Nostalgia and Ambivalence: The Reconstruction of Jewish-Muslim Relations in Oulad-Mansour." In *Modern Sephardi and Middle-Eastern Jewries: History and Culture,* ed. H. Goldberg, 288–311. Bloomington: Indiana University Press.

Bilu, Y., and E. Witztum. 1993. "Working with Jewish Ultraorthodox Patients: Guidelines for a Culturally Sensitive Therapy." *Culture, Medicine and Psychiatry* 17:197–233.

Birenbaum-Carmeli, D. 2000. *Tzfonim: 'Al ma'amad beinoni yisraeli* [Tel Aviv North: The Making of a New Israeli Middle Class]. Jerusalem: Magnes Press.

Bishara, A. 1989. "Israel Faces the Uprising: A Preliminary Assessment." *MERIP Middle East Report* 157:6–14.

———. 1992. "Bayn makom le-merhav" [Between Place and Space]. *Studio* 37:6.

———. 1993. "On the Question of the Arab Minority in Israel." *Jusoor* 5–6:90.

———. 1995. "Representations of the 'Other' as Threat: Demonization and Anti-Semitism." Lecture at the conference "The 'Other' as a Threat: Demonization and Anti-Semitism." Hebrew University, Jerusalem, 12–15 June.

Bizman, A., and Y. Amir. 1982. "Mutual Conceptions of Arabs and Jews in Israel." *Journal of Cross-Cultural Psychology* 13:461–69.

Blalock, H. M., Jr. 1989. *Power and Conflict.* Newbury Park, CA: Sage.

Blau, P. M. 1964. *Exchange and Power in Social Life.* New York: Wiley.

———. 1968. "Social Change." In *International Encyclopedia of Social Science,* vol. 3. New York: Macmillan and Free Press.

———. 1974. *On the Nature of Organization.* New York: Wiley.

Blauner, R. 1964. *Alienation and Freedom: The Factory Worker and His Industry.* Chicago: University of Chicago Press.

Bledsoe, C. H. 1980. *Women and Marriage in Kpelle Society.* Stanford: Stanford University Press.

Bleuler, E. 1950. *Dementia Praecox: Or the Group of Schizophrenias.* New York: International Universities Press.

Blier, S. 1987. *The Anatomy of Architecture.* Cambridge: Cambridge University Press.

Bligh, S., and P. Kupperman. 1993. "Brief Report: Facilitated Communication Evaluation Procedure Accepted in a Court Case." *Journal of Autism and Developmental Disorders* 23(3):553–57.

Bloch, M. 1982. "Death, Women and Power." In *Death and the Regeneration of Life,* ed. M. Bloch and J. Parry. London: Cambridge University Press.

Bloch, M., and J. Parry, eds. 1982. *Death and the Regeneration of Life.* London: Cambridge University Press.

Blom, F. 1992. "Conception and Growth of Children." In *Medical Practices in Ancient America,* ed. M. G. Peredo. 3rd ed. Mexico: Ediciones Euroamericanas.

Bocock, R. J. 1974. *Ritual in Industrial Society: A Sociological Analysis of Ritualism in Modern England.* London: Allen and Unwin.

Boddy, J. 1989. *Wombs and Alien Spirits: Women, Men, and the Zar Cult in Northern Sudan.* Madison: University of Wisconsin Press.

———. 1994. "Spirit Possession Revisited: Beyond Instrumentality." *Annual Review of Anthropology* 3:407–34.

Boissevain, J. 1974. *Friends of Friends: Networks, Manipulators and Coalitions.* Oxford: Blackwell.

Boli-Bennett, J., and J. W. Meyer. 1978. "The Ideology of Childhood and the State: Rules Distinguishing Children in National Constitutions, 1870–1970." *American Sociological Review* 43:797–812.

Bomba, C., et al. 1996. "Evaluating the Impact of Facilitated Communication on the Communicative Competence of Fourteen Students with Autism." *Journal of Autism and Developmental Disorders* 26(1):43–58.

Bornstein, A. S. 2002. *Crossing the Green Line: Between the West Bank and Israel.* Philadelphia: University of Pennsylvania Press.

Borochov, E. 1989. "Hata'asia be'arei hapituah uve'ayoteiha" [Industry in the Development Towns and Its Problems]. *Economic Quarterly* (142):260–71.

Boserup, E. 1970. *Women's Role in Economic Development.* New York and London: Allen and Unwin.

Bossen, L. 1975. "Women in Modernizing Societies." *American Ethnologist* 2(6):587–601.

Bott, E. 1972 [1956]. *Family and Social Network.* New York: Free Press.

Bottomley, G. 1992. *From Another Place: Migration and the Politics of Culture.* Cambridge: Cambridge University Press.

Bourdieu, P. 1977. *Outline of a Theory of Practice.* Cambridge: Cambridge University Press.

———. 1984. *Distinction: A Social Critique of the Judgment of Taste.* Trans. R. Nice. Cambridge, MA: Harvard University Press.

———. 1986. "The Forms of Capital." In *Handbook of Theory and Research for the Sociology of Education,* ed. J. G. Richardson, 241–58. New York: Greenwood.

———. 1990a. *In Other Words.* Stanford: Stanford University Press.

———. 1990b. *The Logic of Practice.* Cambridge: Polity.

———. 1996. *The State Nobility.* Cambridge: Polity.

Bourdieu, P., and L.J.D. Wacquant. 1992. *An Invitation to Reflexive Sociology.* Cambridge: Polity.

Bourguignon, E. 1976. *Possession.* Corta Madera, CA: Chandler and Sharp.

———. 1979. *Psychological Anthropology.* New York: Holt, Rinehart and Winston.

Bourqia, R. 1987. "States and Tribes in Morocco: Continuity and Change." Ph.D. diss., Manchester University.

Bowen, J. R. 1993. *Muslims through Discourse.* Princeton: Princeton University Press.

Bowes, A. M. 1989. *Kibbutz Goshen: An Israeli Commune.* Prospect Heights, IL: Waveland.

Bowman, G. 1996. "Passion, Power and Politics in a Palestinian Tourist Market." In *The Tourist Image: Myth and Myth Making in Tourism,* ed. T. Selwyn, 83–103. Chichester: Wiley.

Boy Scouts of America. 1980. *The Official Patrol Leader Handbook.* Irving, TX: Boy Scouts of America.

———. 1984. *Fieldbook.* Irving, TX: Boy Scouts of America.

———. 1985a. *Firemanship.* Irving, TX: Boy Scouts of America.

———. 1985b. *The Official Scoutmaster Handbook.* Irving, TX: Boy Scouts of America.

Boyarin, D. 1990. *Intertextuality and the Reading of Midrash.* Bloomington: Indiana University Press.

Bradach, J. L., and R. G. Eccles. 1989. "Price, Authority, and Trust: From Ideal Types to Plural Forms." *Annual Review of Sociology* 15:97–118.

Braham, R. L. 1966. *Israel: A Modern Educational System.* Washington, DC: GPO.

Brand, L. 1988. *Palestinians in the Arab World.* New York: Columbia University Press.

Brandeis, L. D., ed. 1916. *Zionism: Problems and Views.* London: T. Fisher Unwin.

Brauer, E. 1934. *Ethnologie der jemenitischen Juden.* Heidelberg: Winter.

———. 1947. *Yehudei Kurdistan* [Jews of Kurdistan]. Ed. and trans. R. Patai. Jerusalem: Palestine Institute of Folklore and Ethnology.

———. 1993. *The Jews of Kurdistan.* Detroit: Wayne State University Press.

Brawer Ben-David, O. 1997. "*Tyul* (Hike) as an Act of Consecration of Space." In *Grasping Land: Space and Place in Contemporary Israeli Discourse and Experience,* ed. E. Ben-Ari and Y. Bilu, 129–45. Albany: State University of New York Press.

———. 2005. *Organ Donation and Transplantation: Body Organs as an Exchangeable Socio-Cultural Resource.* Westport, CT: Praeger.

Briggs, C., and A. Shuman. 1993. "Theorizing Folklore: Toward New Perspectives on the Politics of Culture." *Western Folklore* 52(2–4):109–34.

Briggs, L., and N. Guède. 1964. *No More Forever: A Saharian Jewish Town.* Cambridge, MA: Peabody Museum.

Brumann, C. 1996. "Materialistic Culture: The Uses of Money in Tokyo Gift Exchange." In *On Materialistic Culture and Consumption in Japan,* ed. M. Ashkenazi and J. Clammer. London: Kegan Paul International.

Bruner, J. 1987. "Life as Narrative." *Social Research* 54(1):12–32.

Bruno, M. 1989. "Hahitpathut hakalkalit: Sekira historit" [Economic Recovery in Historical Perspective]. *Economic Quarterly* 40(141):91–93.

Brunot, L., and E. Malka. 1939. *Textes judéo-arabes de Fès.* Rabat: École du livre.

Buber, M. 1952. *Israel and Palestine: The History of an Idea.* London: East and West Library.

———. 1971. *Meetings: Autobiographical Fragments.* La Salle, IL: Open Court.

Buijs, G., ed. 1993. *Migrant Women.* Oxford: Berg.

Burawoy, M., et al. 1991. *Ethnography Unbound.* Berkeley: University of California Press.

Burgansky, M. 1977. "The Kolel in Israeli Society: The Case of Merkaz Harav." Master's thesis, Bar-Ilan University.

Burgoyne, M., and A. Abul-Hajj. 1979. "Twenty-Four Medieval Arabic Inscriptions from Jerusalem." *Levant* 9:121–22.

Burnett, J. H. 1969. "Ceremony, Rites and Economy in the Student System of an American High School." *Human Organization* 28:1–10.

Burns, J. M. 1978. *Leadership.* New York: Harper.

Callaway, B., and L. Creevey. 1994. *The Heritage of Islam: Women, Religion, and Politics in West Africa.* Boulder, CO: Rienner.

Campbell, B., and H. Schuman. 1968. *Racial Attitudes in Fifteen American Cities.* New York: Praeger.

Canaan, T. 1927a. "The Child in Palestinian Arab Superstition." *Journal of the Palestine Oriental Society* 7(4):159–86.

———. 1927b. "Mohammedan Saints and Sanctuaries in Palestine." *Journal of the Palestine Oriental Society* 7(1–2):1–331.

———. 1933. *The Palestinian Arab House: Its Architecture and Folklore.* Jerusalem: Syrian Orphanage Press.

Canetti, E. 1966. *Crowds and Power.* New York: Viking.

Capek, S. 1993. "The 'Environmental Justice' Frame: A Conceptual Discussion and an Application." *Social Problems* 40:5–24.

Caplan, P. 1988. "Engendering Knowledge: The Politics of Ethnography" [2 parts]. *Anthropology Today* 4(5):8–12, 4(6):14–17.

Card, J. 1983. *Life after Vietnam.* Toronto: Lexington Books.

Carmi, S., and H. Rosenfeld. 1974. "The Origins of the Process of Proletarianization and Urbanization of Arab Peasants in Palestine." In *City and Peasant: A Study in Social-Cultural Dynamics,* ed. A. L. La Ruffa et al. *Annals of the New York Academy of Sciences* 220:470–85.

———. 1989. "The Emergence of Militaristic Nationalism in Israel." *International Journal of Politics, Culture and Society* 3(1):5–49.

———. 1991. "The Radical Change: From a Socialist Perspective to Militarism (Rejoinder to Ben-Eliezer and Shamir)." *International Journal of Politics, Culture and Society* 4:4.

Carmi, T. 1956. *Sheleg biyrushalayim: Shirim* [Snow in Jerusalem: Poems]. Merhavya: Hakibbuz Haartzi Hashomer Hatza'ir.

Carmon, N., and M. Hill. 1984. "Project Renewal: An Israeli Experiment in Neighborhood." *Habitat International* 8:117–32.

Carnoy, M., and H. M. Levin. 1985. *Schooling and Work in the Democratic State.* Stanford: Stanford University Press.

Carrithers, M. 1992. *Why Humans Have Cultures.* Oxford: Oxford University Press.

Case, C. E. 1992. "Bumper Stickers and Car Signs, Ideology and Identity." *Journal of Popular Culture* 26(3):107–18.

Cavendish, R., ed. 1970. *Man, Myth and Magic.* Vol. 7. New York: Marshall Cavendish.

Central Bureau of Statistics (Israel). Various years. *Statistical Abstract of Israel.* Jerusalem: Central Bureau of Statistics.

Chacour, E. 1984. *Blood Brothers.* Tarrytown, NY: Chosen Books.

Chaney, D. 1993. *Fictions of Collective Life: Public Drama in Late Modern Culture.* London: Routledge.

Chatty, D. 1996. *Mobile Pastoralists: Development Planning and Social Change in Oman.* New York: Columbia University Press.

Chesler, P., and R. Haut. 2003. *Women of the Wall: Claiming Sacred Ground at Judaism's Holy Site.* Woodstock, VT: Jewish Lights Publishing.

Chinas, B. L. 1973. *The Isthmus Zapotecs: Women's Role in Cultural Context.* New York: Holt, Rinehart and Winston.

Chodorow, N. 1974. "Family Structure and Feminine Personality." In *Women, Culture and Society,* ed. M. Rosaldo and L. Lamphere. Stanford: Stanford University Press.

Chow, Y. T. 1966. *Social Mobility in China.* New York: Atherton.

Chukwukere, I. 1981. "A Coffin for 'the Loved One.'" *Current Anthropology* 22(1):61–68.

Cirlot, J. E. 1962. *A Dictionary of Symbols.* London: Routledge and Kegan Paul.

Clifford, J. 1983. "On Ethnographic Authority." *Representations* 1(2):118–46.

———. 1986. "On Ethnographic Allegory." In *Writing Culture: The Poetics and Politics of Ethnography,* ed. J. Clifford and G. E. Marcus, 98–121. Berkeley: University of California Press.

———. 1994. "Diasporas." *Cultural Anthropology* 9(3):302–38.
———. 1997. *Routes: Travel and Translation in the Late Twentieth Century*. Cambridge, MA: Harvard University Press.
Clifford, J., and G. E. Marcus, eds. 1986. *Writing Culture: The Poetics and Politics of Ethnography.* Berkeley: University of California Press.
Cohen, A. 1965. *Arab Border-Villages in Israel: A Study of Continuity and Change in Social Organization.* Manchester: Manchester University Press.
———. 1969. *Custom and Politics in Urban Africa: A Study of Hausa Migrants in Yoruba Towns.* Berkeley: University of California Press.
Cohen, Adir. 1987. *The Image of the Arab in Israeli Children's Literature.* Haifa: University of Haifa Press.
Cohen, A. P. 1985. *The Symbolic Construction of Community.* London: Routledge.
Cohen, C. 1975. *Grandir au quartier kurde: Rapports de generations et modéles culturels d'adolescents israéliens d'ofrigine kurde.* Paris: Institut d'Ethnologie, Musée de l'Homme.
Cohen, D. 1964. *Le parler arabe des Juifs de Tunis: Textes et documents linguistiques et ethnographiques.* Paris: Mouton.
Cohen, E. 1967. "Matana" [Gift]. *Encyclopedia of Social Science.* Tel Aviv: Sifriyat Poalim.
———. 1970. "Development Towns: The Social Dynamics of 'Planted' Urban Communities in Israel." In *Integration and Development in Israel,* ed. S. N. Eisenstadt. New York: Praeger.
———. 1971. "Arab Boys and Tourist Girls in a Mixed Jewish-Arab Community." *International Journal of Comparative Sociology* 12:217–33.
———. 1972. "The Black Panthers and Israeli Society." *Jewish Journal of Sociology* 14:93–109.
———. 1977. "Expatriate Communities." *Current Sociology* 24(3):5–133.
———. 1979. "Phenomenology of Tourist Experiences." *Sociology* 13(2):179–201.
Cohen, E. G. 1982. "Expectation States and Interracial Interaction in School Settings." *Annual Review of Sociology* 6:479–500.
———. 1984. "The Desegregated School: Problems in Status, Power and Interethnic Climate." In *Groups in Contact,* ed. N. Miller and M. B. Brewer. London: Academic Press.
Cohen, M. 1912. *Le parler arabe des juifs d'Alger.* Paris: Honorè Champion.
Cohen, P. S. 1962. "Alignments and Allegiances in the Community of Shaarayim in Israel." *Jewish Journal of Sociology* 4:14–38.
Cohen, R. 1978. *The Singles Society.* Ramat Efal: Yad Tabenkin.
———. 1991. "The Problematic Absorption of Soviet Jews in Israel." *Innovation in Social Sciences Research* 4:439–61.
Cohen, S. 1985. *Visions of Social Control: Crime, Punishment and Classification.* New York: Polity Press.
———. 1988. "Criminology and the Uprising." *Tikkun* 3(5):60–62, 94–95.
Cohen, Y. 1991. *Women in Public Leadership.* Jerusalem: Hakibbutz Hadati.
Cohler, B. J. 1982. "Personal Narrative and Life Course." In *Life-Span Development and Behavior,* ed. P. B. Baltes and O. Brim, 206–41. New York: Academic Press.
Cole, D. P. 1975. *Nomads of the Nomads: The 'Al Murrah Bedouin of the Empty Quarter.* Arlington Heights: AHM Publishing Company.
Cook, M. C. 1995. "Four Villages Hit the Map." *Sawt al-qura* 32(6):26–27.
Cooper, J. C., ed. 1978. *An Illustrated Encyclopedia of Traditional Symbols.* London: Thames and Hudson.

Cooper, S. 1978. "Newgate: An Old-New Town in the Negev." Ph.D. diss. Washington, DC: Catholic University of America.

———. 1987. "The Laws of Mixture: An Anthropological Study in Halakhah." In *Judaism Viewed from Within and from Without: Anthropological Studies,* ed. H. E. Goldberg, 55–74. Albany: State University of New York Press.

Corradi, C. 1991. "Text, Context and Individual Meaning: Rethinking Life Stories in Hermeneutic Framework." *Discourse and Society* 2(1):105–18.

Corsaro, W. A. 1988. "Routines in the Peer Culture of American and Italian Nursery School Children." *Sociology of Education* 61:1–14.

Crapanzano, V. 1984. "Life History." *American Anthropologist* 86:953–59.

———. 1985. *Waiting: The Whites of South Africa.* New York: Random House.

Creyghton, M. L. 1992. "Breast-Feeding and *Baraka* in Northern Tunisia." In *The Anthropology of Breast-Feeding: Natural Law or Social Construct,* ed. V. Maher, 37–58. Oxford: Berg.

Crossley, Rosemary. 1992. "Getting the Words Out: Case Studies in Facilitated Communication Training." *Topics in Language Disorders* 12:29–41.

Csordas, T. J. 1985. "Medical and Sacred Reality: Between Comparative Religion and Transcultural Psychiatry." *Culture, Medicine and Psychiatry* 9:103–16.

———. 1994. *The Sacred Self: A Cultural Phenomenology of Religious Healing.* Berkeley: University of California Press.

Curtis, M., and M. S. Chertoff, eds. 1973. *Israel: Social Structure and Change.* New Brunswick, NJ: Transaction.

Czikszentmihalyi, M. 1975. *Beyond Boredom and Anxiety.* San Francisco: Jossey-Bass.

Dagan, S., and E. Yakir. 1996. *Shimon Avidan Giv'ati.* Givat Haviva: Yad Ya'ary.

Dahl, R. A. 1957. "A Concept of Power." *Behavioral Science* 2:201–18.

Dalton, M. 1959. *Men Who Manage.* New York: Wiley.

Danet, B. 1989. *Pulling Strings: Biculturalism in Israeli Society.* Albany: State University of New York Press.

Danforth, L. M. 1982. *The Death Rituals of Rural Greece.* Princeton: Princeton University Press.

Dangoor, E. 1994. "Shichvat mekabley hahahelatot bekibbutz Tzidon" [The Decision-Making Stratum of Kibbutz Tzidon]. Seminar paper, Sociology Department, Open University.

Daniel, E. V. 1984. *Fluid Signs: Being a Person the Tamil Way.* Berkeley: University of California Press.

Daniel, J., and G. Smitherman. 1976. "How I Got Over: Communication Dynamics in the Black Community." *Quarterly Journal of Speech* 62:26–39.

Danish, S. J., M. A. Smyer, and C. A. Nowak. 1980. "Developmental Intervention: Enhancing Life-Event Processes." In *Life-Span Development,* ed. P. B. Baltes and O. G. Brim, 3:339–66. New York: Academic Press.

Darrow, W. 1985. "Women's Place and the Place of Women in the Iranian Revolution." In *Women, Religion, and Social Change,* ed. Y. Y. Haddad and E. B. Findly, 307–20. Albany: State University of New York Press.

David, M. E. 1980. *The State, the Family, and Education.* London: Routledge and Kegan Paul.

Davidman, L. 1991. *Tradition in a Rootless World.* Berkeley: University of California Press.

Davis, N. Z. 2000. *The Gift in Sixteenth-Century France.* Madison: University of Wisconsin Press.

Dawes, R. M. 1992. "Social Dilemmas, Economic Self Interest, and Evolutionary Theory." In *Recent Research in Psychology: Frontiers of Mathematical Psychology,* ed. D. R. Brown and J. E. Keith Smith, 1–27. New York: Springer.

Degh, Linda. 1994. *American Folklore and the Mass Media.* Bloomington: Indiana University Press.

De Heusch, L. 1981. *Why Marry Her? Society and Symbolic Structures.* London: Cambridge University Press.

Deihl, C. 1985. "Wildlife and the Maasai." *Cultural Survival Quarterly* 9(1):37.

Denich, B. S. 1974. "Sex and Power in the Balkans." In *Women, Culture and Society,* ed. M. Rosaldo and L. Lamphere. Stanford: Stanford University Press.

Denzin, K. N. 1989. *Interpretive Biography.* London: Sage.

Deshen, S. 1966. "Conflict and Social Change: The Case of an Israeli Village." *Sociologia Ruralis* 6:31–55.

———. 1970a. *Immigrant Voters in Israel: Parties and Congregations in a Local Election Campaign.* Manchester: Manchester University Press.

———. 1970b. "Political Ethnicity and Cultural Ethnicity in Israel during the 1960s." In *Urban Ethnicity,* ASA Monograph 12, ed. A. Cohen, 281–309. London: Tavistock.

———. 1974. "The Memorial Celebrations of Tunisian Immigrants." In *The Predicament of Homecoming: Cultural and Social Life of North African Immigrants in Israel,* ed. S. Deshen and M. Shokeid, 95–121. Ithaca: Cornell University Press.

———. 1975. "On Religious Change: The Situational Analysis of Symbolic Action." *Comparative Studies in Society and History* 12:260–74.

———. 1976. "Ethnicity and Cultural Paradigms among Southern Tunisian Immigrants." *Ethos* 4:271–94.

———. 1981. *19th Century Responsa.* Ramat-Gan: Bar Ilan University.

———. 1989. *The Mellah Society: Jewish Community Life in Sherifian Morocco.* Chicago: University of Chicago Press.

———. 1993. "Doves, Hawks and Anthropology: The Israeli Debate on Middle Eastern Settlement Proposals." In *Beyond Boundaries,* ed. G. Palsson, 58–74. Boulder, CO: Sage.

Deshen, S., and D. Jaeger. 1971. "Culture and Politics in a Village of Immigrants from Djerba." In *Rural Settlements of New Immigrants in Israel,* ed. O. Shapira, 125–38. Rehovot: Settlement Study Centre.

Deshen, S., and M. Shokeid. 1974. *The Predicament of Homecoming: Cultural and Social Life of North African Immigrants in Israel.* Ithaca: Cornell University Press.

Despres, L. A. 1975. *Ethnicity and Resource Competition in Plural Societies.* The Hague: Mouton.

Deutsch, M. 1962. "Cooperation and Trust: Some Theoretical Notes." In *Nebraska Symposium on Motivation.* Lincoln: University of Nebraska Press.

de Vries, A. 1974. *Dictionary of Symbols and Imagery.* Amsterdam: North-Holland.

Diamond, S. 1957. "Kibbutz and Shtetl: The History of an Idea." *Social Problems* 5(2):71–79.

Dickenson, D. K. 1985. "Creating and Using Formal Occasions in the Classroom." *Anthropology and Education Quarterly* 16:47–62.

Dickson, H.R.P. 1949. *The Arab of the Desert.* London: Allen and Unwin.

Dillon, K. M., J. E. Fenlason, and D. J. Vogel. 1994. "Belief in and Use of a Questionable Technique: Facilitated Communication for Children with Autism." *Psychological Reports* 75:459–64.

Diqs, I. 1967. *A Bedouin Boyhood.* London: Allen and Unwin.

Dodgson, M. 1993. "Learning, Trust, and Technological Collaboration." *Human Relations* 46:77–95.

Doleve-Gandelman, T. 1987. "The Symbolic Inscription of Zionist Ideology in the Space of Eretz Yisrael: Why the Native Israeli Is Called Tsabar." In *Judaism from Within and from Without: Anthropological Studies,* ed. H. Goldberg. Albany: State University of New York Press.

Dolgin, J. L., D. S. Kemnitzer, and D. M. Schneider. 1977. "As People Express Their Lives, So They Are. . . ." In *Symbolic Anthropology,* ed. J. L. Dolgin, D. S. Kemnitzer, and D. M. Schneider, 3–44. New York: Columbia University Press.

Dominguez, V. R. 1989. *People as Subject, People as Object: Selfhood and Peoplehood in Contemporary Israel.* Madison: University of Wisconsin Press.

Don, Y. 1988. *Industrialization of a Rural Collective.* Aldershot: Avebury.

Donath, D. (Bensimon). 1962. *L'évolution de la femme Israëlite à Fès.* Aix-en-Provence: Faculté des Lettres.

Don-Yehiya, E. 1987. "Jewish Messianism, Religious Zionism and Israeli Politics: Gush Emunim." *Middle Eastern Studies* 23:214–34.

Dore, R. 1973. *British Factory—Japanese Factory.* Berkeley: University of California Press.

Dore, Y. 1988. *Industrialization of a Rural Collective.* Aldershot: Avebury.

Dorst, J. 1983. "Neck Riddle as a Dialogue of Genres." *Journal of American Folklore* 96:413–33.

———. 1990. "Tags and Burners, Cycles and Networks: Folklore in the Telectronic Age." *Journal of Folklore Research* 27(3):179–90.

Doughty, C. M. 1923. *Travels in Arabia Deserta.* 2 vols. London: Medici Society.

Douglas, M. 1966. *Purity and Danger: An Analysis of the Concepts of Pollution and Taboo.* London: Routledge and Kegan Paul.

Douglas, M., and M. Calvez. 1990. "The Self as Risk Taker: A Cultural Theory of Contagion in Relation to AIDS." *Sociological Review* 38(3):445–563.

Dow, J. R., ed. 1991. "Folklore, Politics and Nationalism." Special issue. *Asian Folklore Studies* 50.

Driver, H. E. 1973. "Cross-Cultural Studies." In *Handbook of Social and Cultural Anthropology,* ed. J. J. Honigmann. Chicago: Rand McNally.

Drori, I. 2000. *The Seam Line: Arab Workers and Jewish Managers in the Israeli Textile Industry.* Stanford: Stanford University Press.

Drori-Wilf, N. 1991. "Al mizbah omanut" [On the Altar of Art]. *Kolbo* (12 April):47, 62.

Duchan, J. F. 1993. "Issues Raised by Facilitated Communication for Theorizing and Research in Autism." *Journal of Hearing and Speech Research* 36:1108–19.

Duffy, M. A. 1985. "A Critique of Research: A Feminist Perspective." *Health Care for Women International* 6:341–52.

Dumont, L. 1977. *From Mandeville to Marx: The Genesis and Triumph of Economic Ideology.* Chicago: University of Chicago Press.

———. 1986. *Essays on Individualism: Modern Ideology in Anthropological Perspective.* Chicago: University of Chicago Press.

Dundes, A., and C. R. Pagter. 1978. *Work Hard and You Shall Be Rewarded: Urban Folklore from the Paperwork Empire.* Bloomington: Indiana University Press.

———. 1987. *When You're Up to Your Ass in Alligators: More Urban Folklore from the Paperwork Empire.* Detroit: Wayne State University Press.

———. 1991. *Never Try to Teach a Pig to Sing: Still More Urban Folklore from the Paperwork Empire.* Detroit: Wayne State University Press.

Durantez, C. 1985. "The Torch: The Great Olympic Symbol." *Olympic Review* 216:620–27.

Durkheim, E. 1933. *The Division of Labor in Society.* Trans. G. Simpson. New York: Free Press.

———. 1938. *The Rules of Sociological Method.* Trans. S. A. Solovay and J. H. Mueller. Chicago: University of Chicago Press.

———. 1969. *The Elementary Forms of the Religious Life.* New York: Free Press.

Durkheim, E., and M. Mauss. 1963. *Primitive Classification.* Chicago: University of Chicago Press.

Dwyer, D. H. 1978a. "Ideologies of Sexual Inequality and Strategies for Change in Male-Female Relations." *American Ethnologist* 5(2):227–40.

———. 1978b. *Images and Self-Images: Male and Female in Morocco.* New York: Columbia University Press.

Eade, J. 1991. "Order and Power at Lourdes: Lay Helpers and the Organization of a Pilgrimage Shrine." In *Contesting the Sacred,* ed. J. Eade and M. J. Sallnow, 51–76. London: Routledge.

Eaton, J. W., and M. Chen. 1970. *Influencing the Youth Culture: A Study of Youth Organizations in Israel.* Beverly Hills, CA: Sage.

Eberlin, M., S. Ibel, and J. W. Jacobson. 1994. "The Sources of Messages Produced during Facilitated Communication with a Boy with Autism and Severe Mental Retardation: A Case Study." *Journal of Pediatric Psychology* 19(6):657–71.

Eberlin, M., et al. 1993. "Facilitated Communication: A Failure to Replicate the Phenomenon." *Journal of Autism and Developmental Disorders* 23(3):507–30.

Edelman, M. 1988. *Constructing the Political Spectacle.* Chicago: University of Chicago Press.

Edgerton, R. B. 1979. *Alone Together: Social Order on an Urban Beach.* Berkeley: University of California Press.

Edwards, R. 1978. "The Social Relations of Production at the Point of Production." *Insurgent Sociologist* 8(2–3):109–25.

———. 1979. *Contested Terrain: The Transformation of the Workplace in the Twentieth Century.* New York: Basic Books.

Efron, J. 1994. *Defenders of the Race: Jewish Doctors and Race Science in Fin-de-Siècle Europe.* New Haven: Yale University Press.

Eickelman, C. 1993. "Fertility and Social Change in Oman: Women's Perspectives." *Middle East Journal* 47(4):652–66.

Eickelman, D. F. 1976. *Moroccan Islam: Tradition and Society in a Pilgrimage Center.* Austin: University of Texas Press.

Eilberg-Schwartz, H. 1990. *The Savage in Judaism.* Bloomington: Indiana University Press.

Eisenstadt, S. N. 1954. *The Absorption of Immigrants: A Comparative Study Based Mainly on the Jewish Community in Palestine and the State of Israel.* London: Routledge and Kegan Paul.

———. 1967. *Israeli Society.* London: Weidenfeld and Nicolson.

———. 1985. *The Transformation of Israeli Society: An Essay in Interpretation.* London: Weidenfeld and Nicolson.

Eisenstadt, S. N., R. Bar-Yosef, and C. Adler, eds. 1970. *Integration and Development in Israel.* New York: Praeger.

Ekeh, P. P. 1974. *Social Exchange Theory: The Two Traditions.* Cambridge, MA: Harvard University Press.

Elam, Y. 1980. *Hagruzinim beyisrael: Hebeitim antropologiim* [Georgian Jews in Israel: Anthropological Perspectives]. Jerusalem: Department of Sociology and Anthropology, Hebrew University.

El-Guindi, F. 1981. "Veiling Infitah with Muslim Ethic: Egypt's Contemporary Islamic Movement." *Social Problems* 28:465–85.

Eliade, M. 1954. *The Myth of Eternal Return.* Trans. W. R. Trask. New York: Pantheon.

———. 1956. *The Forge and the Crucible.* New York: Harper and Row.

Eliav-Feldon, M. 1982. *Realistic Utopias: The Ideal Imaginary Societies of the Renaissance, 1516–1630.* Oxford: Clarendon Press.

Elon, A. 1971. *The Israelis: Founders and Sons.* London: Weidenfeld and Nicolson.

Elon, E. 1991. "You Do Not Kill Mammy." *Nekuda* (November):44–45.

El-Or, T. 1990. "Educated and Ignorant: The Paradox of Knowledge among Ultra-Orthodox Women." Paper presented at the Israel-Canada Conference for the Social Scientific Study of Judaism, Toronto.

———. 1992. *Maskilot uburot: Mei'olaman shel nashim hareidiot* [Educated and Ignorant: Ultra-Orthodox Jewish Women and Their World]. Trans. H. Watzman. Tel Aviv: Am Oved.

———. 1993. "Are They Like Their Grandmothers: Literacy and Modernity among Ultraorthodox Women in the Hassidic Sect of Gur." *Anthropology and Education Quarterly* 24:63–82.

———. 1994. *Educated and Ignorant: Ultra-Orthodox Women and Their World.* Trans. H. Watzman. Boulder, CO: Rienner.

Endersby, J. W., and M. J. Towle. 1996. "Tailgate Partisanship: Political and Social Expression through Bumper Stickers." *Social Science Journal* 33(3):307–19.

Emerson, R. M. 1962. "Power-Dependence Relations." *American Sociological Review* 27:31–41.

Eppel, M. 1994. *The Palestine Conflict in the History of Modern Iraq: The Dynamics of Involvement, 1928–1948.* London: Frank Cass.

Epstein, E. H. 1978. "On the School as an Agent in Shaping National Identity." *Education and Urban Society* 10:107–12.

Eran, Y. 1989. *Vocational Absorption of Ethiopian Immigrants, 1984–1987.* Jerusalem: Amishav, Center for Aid and Employment Service.

Erikson, K. T. 1966. *Wayward Puritans.* New York: Wiley.

Escobar, A. 1991. "Anthropology and the Development Encounter: The Marketing of Development Anthropology." *American Ethnologist* 18(4):658–83.

Eshkoli, A. Z. 1956. *Hatenu'ot hameshihiot biysra'el* [The Messianic Movements in Israel]. Jerusalem: Mosad Bialik.

Etgar, T. 1977. *Honchim Vesomchot, Services for Assisting and Advancing Families.* Jerusalem: Ministry for Welfare and Labour.

Etzioni, A. 1988. *The Moral Dimension.* New York: Free Press.

Etzioni-Halevy, E. 1975. "Patterns of Conflict, Generations and Conflict Absorption: The Case of Israeli Labor and Ethnic Relations." *Journal of Conflict Resolution* 19:286–309.

Evens, T.M.S. 1995. *Two Kinds of Rationality: Kibbutz Democracy and Generational Conflict.* Minneapolis: University of Minnesota Press.

Even-Zohar, I. 1981. "The Emergence of a Native-Hebrew Culture in Palestine: 1882–1948." *Studies in Zionism* 4:167–84.

Evron, Y. 1980. *Defense Industry in Israel.* Tel Aviv: Ministry of Defense.

Ewen, S., and E. Ewen. 1982. *Channels of Desire: Mass Images and the Shaping of American Consciousness.* New York: McGraw-Hill.

Eyal, G. 1993. "Bein mizrah le-ma'arav: Ha-siah al ha-kefar ha-'Arvi be-Yisra'el [Between East and West: The Discourse on the Arab Village in Israel]." *Te'orya webikoret* 3:39–55.

Fadida, M. 1972. "The Dynamics of Career Patterns among Political Activists in a Kibbutz." Master's thesis, Department of Sociology and Anthropology, Tel Aviv University.

Faitlowitz, J. 1959 [1908]. *Masa 'el hafalashim* [A Journey to the Falashas]. Tel-Aviv: Dvir.

Falah, Ghazi. 1989. *Al-filastiniun al-munsiun: 'Arab al-naqb, 1906–1986* [The Forgotten Palestinians: The Negev Bedouin, 1906–1986]. Tayiba, Israel: Arab Heritage Center.

Farbridge, M. H. 1970. *Studies in Biblical and Semitic Symbolism.* New York: Ktav.

Farrell, R. A., and V. L. Swigert. 1982. *Deviance and Social Control.* Glenview, IL: Scott Foresman.

Fayence-Glick, S. 1957. *Kindergartens in Eretz Yisrael: The Book of the Fiftieth Anniversary of the Teachers' Union.* Tel Aviv: Israel Teachers Union.

Featherstone, M. 1991. *Consumer Culture and Postmodernism.* London: Sage.

Feige, M. n.d. *The Card Game and the Army: A Story a Reserve Unit Tells Itself.* Jerusalem: Hebrew University of Jerusalem.

Fein, L. 1967. *Politics in Israel.* Boston: Little Brown.

Feitelson, D. 1959. "Aspects of the Social Life of Kurdish Jews." *Jewish Journal of Sociology* 1:201–16.

Feld, M. F. 1977. *The Structure of Violence: Armed Forces as Social Systems.* Beverly Hills, CA: Sage.

Feldman, D. M. 1974. *Marital Relations, Birth Control and Abortion in Jewish Law.* New York: Schocken.

Feldman, J. 2001. "'Roots in Destruction': The Jewish Past as Portrayed in Israeli Youth Voyages to Poland." In *The Life of Judaism,* ed. H. E. Goldberg, 156–72. Berkeley: University of California Press.

Ferguson, K. E. 1984. *The Feminist Case against Bureaucracy.* Philadelphia: Temple University Press.

Fernea, E. W. 1969. *Guests of the Sheik: An Ethnography of an Iraqi Village.* Garden City, NY: Doubleday.

———. 1975. *A Street in Marrakech: A Personal Encounter with Moroccan Women.* Garden City, NY: Doubleday.

Fernea, E. W., and B. Q. Bezirgan, eds. 1977. *Middle Eastern Muslim Women Speak.* Austin: University of Texas Press.

Figley, C. R. 1978. "The Psychology Adjustment among Vietnam Veterans: An Overview of Research." In *Stress Disorders among Vietnam Veterans,* ed. C. R. Figley, 57–70. New York: Brunner/Mazel.

Figley, C. R., and S. Leventman, eds. 1980. *Strangers at Home.* New York: Praeger.

Fine, G. A. 1988. "Good Children and Dirty Play." *Play and Culture* 1:43–56.

Finkelstein, N. G. 1995. *Image and Reality of the Israel-Palestine Conflict.* London: Verso.

Fisch, H. 1978. *The Zionist Revolution.* London: Weidenfeld and Nicolson.

Flamand, P. 1960. *Diaspora en terre d'Islam: L'esprit populaire dans les juiveries du Sud marocain.* Casablanca: Presses des Imprimeries Réunies.

Flapan, S. 1987. *The Birth of Israel: Myths and Realities.* New York: Pantheon.

Foner, A. 1975. "Age in Society: Structure and Change." *American Behavioral Scientist* 19:144–65.

Fonrobert, C. E. 1999. "Yalta's Ruse: Resistance against Rabbinic Menstrual Authority in Talmudic Literature." In *Women and Water,* ed. R. Wasserfall, 60–81. Hanover, NH: Brandeis University Press.

Forte, T. 2002. "Shopping in Jenin: Women, Homes and Political Persons in the Galilee." *City and Society* 13(2):211–43.

Foucault, M. 1971. *The Order of Things: An Archaeology of the Human Sciences.* New York: Pantheon.

———. 1973. *Madness and Civilization.* Trans. R. Howard. New York: Vintage.

———. 1979. *Discipline and Punish: The Birth of the Prison.* New York: Vintage.

———. 1980. *Power/Knowledge: Selected Interviews and Other Writings, 1972–1977.* Ed. and trans. C. Gordon. Brighton: Harvester Press.

Fox, A. 1974. *Beyond Contract.* London: Faber.

Frank, G., and R. M. Vanderburgh. 1986. "Cross Cultural Use of Life History Methods in Gerontology." In *New Methods for Old Age Research,* ed. C. L. Fry and J. Keith, 185–212. New York: Bergin and Garvey.

Frankenberg, R. 1989. "Gramsci, Marxism, and Phenomenology: Essays for the Development of a Critical Medical Anthropology." *Medical Anthropology Quarterly* 2(4):324–37.

Frankenstein, C. 1953a. "The Problem of Ethnic Differences in the Absorption of Immigrants." In *Between Past and Future: Essays and Studies on Aspects of Immigrant Absorption in Israel,* ed. C. Frankenstein, 13–32. Jerusalem: Henrietta Szold Foundation.

———, ed. 1953b. *Between Past and Future: Essays and Studies on Aspects of Immigrant Absorption in Israel.* Jerusalem: Henrietta Szold Foundation.

Frazer, J. G. 1935. *The Golden Bough: A Study in Magic and Religion.* New York: Macmillan.

Freedman, M. 1958. *Lineage Organization in South-Eastern China.* London: Athlone Press.

———, ed. 1970. Introduction to *Family and Kinship in Chinese Society.* Stanford: Stanford University Press.

Frentz, T., and T. Farrell. 1976. "Language-Action: A Paradigm for Communication." *Quarterly Journal of Speech* 62:333–49.

Freud, S. 1964. "The Acquisition and Control of Fire." In *The Standard Edition.* London: Hogarth Press.

Friedl, E. 1967. "The Position of Women: Appearance and Reality." *Anthropological Quarterly* 40:97–108.

———. 1975. *Women and Men: An Anthropologist's View.* New York: Holt, Rinehart and Winston.

———. 1978. "Society and Sex Roles." *Human Nature* 1:68–75.

Friedlander, S. 1985. *Kitsch vamavet: 'Al hishtakfut hanazism* [Reflections of Nazism: An Essay on Kitsch and Death]. Jerusalem: Keter.

Friedman, M. 1987. "Life Tradition and Book Tradition in the Development of Ultraorthodox Judaism." In *Judaism Viewed from Within and Without,* ed. H. Goldberg. Albany: State University of New York Press.

———. 1991. *The Haredi (Ultraorthodox) Society: Sources, Trends and Processes.* Jerusalem: Jerusalem Institute for Israel Studies.

Friendly, A. 1981. *Israel's Oriental Immigrants and Druzes.* London: Minority Rights Group.

Fukuyama, F. 1995. *Trust.* New York: Free Press.

Fuks, A. 1976. *Politics and Society in Ancient Greece.* Jerusalem: Bialik Institute.

Furman, M. 1994. *Yaldut kemerkaha: Alimut vetzaytanut bagil harach* [Turbulent Childhood: Violence and Obedience in Early Childhood]. Tel Aviv: Hakibbutz Hameuhad.

Gaaton, A. L. 1969. "Economic Productivity in Israel." In *Seker Bank Israel.* Jerusalem: Government Printer.

Gabriel, A. 1992. "Grief and Rage: Collective Emotions in the Politics of Peace and the Politics of Gender in Israel." *Culture, Medicine and Psychiatry* 15:311–35.

Gabriel, R. A., and P. L. Savage. 1981. *Crisis in Command.* New Delhi: Himalayan.

Gaines, A. D. 1992. "From DSM I to III-R: Voices of Self, Mastery and the Other: A Cultural Construction of Psychiatric Classification." *Social Science and Medicine* 35(1):3–24.

Gal, R. 1986. *A Portrait of the Israeli Soldier.* New York: Greenwood.

Gambetta, D. 1988. "Mafia: The Price of Distrust." In *Trust,* ed. D. Gambetta. Cambridge: Cambridge University Press.

Gamliel, T. 2005. *Sof hasippur: Mashma'ut, zeihut, zikna* [End of Story: Meaning, Identity, Old Age]. Tel Aviv: Tel Aviv University Press.

Gamson, W., and A. Modigliani. 1987. "The Changing Culture of Affirmative Action." In *Research in Political Sociology,* ed. R. D. Braungart, 137–77. Greenwich, CT: JAL Press.

Gamson, W., and D. Stuart. 1992. "Media Discourse as a Symbolic Contest: The Bomb in Political Discourse." *Sociological Forum* 7:55–86.

Gamson, Z. 1977. "Is Kibbutz Culture in Conflict with Higher Education?" *Hakibbutz* 5:63–83.

Gans, H. 1979. "Symbolic Ethnicity: The Future of Ethnic Groups and Cultures in America." *Ethnic and Racial Studies* 2:1–20.

Gardner, A., and E. Marx. 2000. "Employment and Unemployment among Bedouin." *Nomadic Peoples* 4(2):21–27.

Garfinkel, H. 1963. "A Conception of and Experiments with 'Trust' as a Condition of Stable Concerted Actions." In *Motivation and Social Interaction: Cognitive Determinants,* ed. O. J. Harvey. New York: Roland.

———. 1967. *Studies in Ethnomethodology.* Englewood Cliffs, NJ: Prentice-Hall.

Gaskell, G. A. 1981. *Dictionary of All Scriptures and Myths.* New York: Avenel Books.

Gavron, D. 1986. "No Name Village." *Jerusalem Post,* 30 May, p. 12.

Gazit, D. 2000. *Tahalichei hityashevut behevel habesor biymei hasultan 'Abd el-Hamid hasheni* [Settlement in the Besor Region in Sultan Abd el-Hamid's Time]. In *Yerushalayim ve'eretz Yisrael: Sefer Arie Kindler,* ed. J. Schwartz, Z. Omer, and I. Ziffer, 183–86. Tel Aviv: Eretz-Israel Museum.

Gdor, U., R. Astman, and H. Salmon. 1985. *Klitat 'olei Etiopia, tochnit av* [Absorption of Ethiopian Immigrants, Master Plan]. Jerusalem: Ministry of Absorption.

Geertz, C. 1957. "Religion and Social Change: A Javanese Example." *American Anthropologist* 59:32–54.

———. 1963. *Agricultural Involution: The Process of Ecological Change in Indonesia.* Berkeley: University of California Press.

———. 1964. "Ideology as a Cultural System." In *Ideology and Discontent*, ed. D. Apter. New York: Free Press.

———. 1966. "Religion as a Cultural System." In *Anthropological Approaches to the Study of Religion*, ed. M. Banton, 1–46. London: Tavistock.

———. 1968. *Islam Observed: Religious Development in Morocco and Indonesia.* Chicago: University of Chicago Press.

———. 1973a. *The Interpretation of Cultures.* New York: Basic Books.

———. 1973b. "Theory of Culture." In *The Interpretation of Cultures.* New York: Basic Books.

———. 1977. "From the Native's Point of View: On the Nature of Anthropological Understanding." In *Symbolic Anthropology*, ed. J. Dolgin et al. New York: Columbia University Press.

———. 1989. "Toute Directions: Reading the Signs in an Urban Sprawl." *International Journal of Middle East Studies* 21(3):291–306.

Geertz, C., H. Geertz, and L. Rosen. 1979. *Meaning and Order in Moroccan Society.* Cambridge: Cambridge University Press.

Gefen, H. 1997. "Havnaya shel he'avar: Historia vezeihut hevratit" [Constructing the Past: Social History and Social Identity]. Ph.D. diss., Ben-Gurion University of the Negev.

Gelbard, R. 1993. *Kibbutz: Hasipur ha'amiti* [The Kibbutz: The True Story]. Dalia: Dalia Publishing.

Gellner, E. 1969. *Saints of the Atlas.* Chicago: University of Chicago Press.

Geneen, H. 1984. *Managing.* New York: Avon.

George, S. 1943. *Poems.* New York: Schocken.

Georges, R. A., ed. 1991. "Taking Stock: Current Problems and Future Prospects in American Folklore Studies." Special issue. *Western Folklore* 50:1–126.

Ghazanfar, Shahina. 1994. *Handbook of Arabian Medical Plants.* London: CRC Press.

Gilad, L. 1989. *Ginger and Salt: Yemeni Jewish Women in an Israeli Town.* Boulder, CO: Westview.

Gilligan, C. 1982. *In a Different Voice: Psychological Theory and Women's Development.* Cambridge: Cambridge University Press.

Ginat, A. 1979. "Hamaka hasheniya shel habotulizm" [The Second Stroke of Botulism]. *Hashavua Bakibbutz Ha'artzi*, 2 November.

———. 1981. "Ha'im richvei hape'ilim ya'amedu lireshut sadran harechev" [Will the Cars of Outside Workers Be at the Car Manager's Disposal?] *Hadaf Hayarok*, 7 December.

Ginat, J. 1987. *Blood Disputes among Bedouin and Rural Arabs in Israel.* Pittsburgh: University of Pittsburgh Press and Jerusalem Institute for Israel Studies.

Ginat, J., and E. J. Perkins, eds. 2001. *The Palestinian Refugees: Old Problems, New Solutions.* Norman: University of Oklahoma Press.

Glaser, D. 1969. *The Effectiveness of the Parole System.* Indianapolis: Bobbs-Merrill.

Glazer, N., and D. P. Moynihan. 1963. *Beyond the Melting Pot: The Negroes, Puerto Ricans, Jews, Italians and Irish of New York City.* Cambridge, MA: MIT Press.

Gluckman, M. 1965. *Custom and Conflict in Africa.* Oxford: Blackwell.

———. 1970. Foreword to *Immigrant Voters in Israel: Parties and Congregations in a Local Election Campaign*, by S. Deshen, xiii–xxi. Manchester: Manchester University Press.

Goffman, E. 1961. *Asylums: Essays on the Social Situation of Mental Patients and Other Inmates.* London: Penguin.

———. 1970. *Strategic Interaction.* Oxford: Blackwell.

———. 1971. *Relations in Public: Microstudies of the Public Order.* New York: Harper and Row.

Goitein, S. D. 1955. "Portrait of a Yemenite Weaver's Village." *Jewish Social Studies* 17:3–27.

———. 1983. *Hateimanim: Historia, sidrei hevra, hayei ruah* [The Yemenites: History, Communal Organization, Intellectual Activities]. Ed. M. Ben-Sasson. Jerusalem: Ben-Zvi Institute and Hebrew University of Jerusalem.

Golander, H. 1995. *Lihiot 'al kav haketz: 'Olamam shel keshishim bemahlaka sei'udit* [As the End Approaches: Social Life of the Disabled in a Geriatric Ward]. Jerusalem: Magnes Press.

Goldberg, H. E. 1967. "Patronymic Groups in a Tripolitanian Jewish Village: Reconstruction and Interpretation." *Jewish Journal of Sociology* 9:209–25.

———. 1968. "Elite Groups in Peasant Communities: A Comparison of Three Middle Eastern Villages." *American Anthropologist* 70:718–31.

———. 1969. "Egalitarianism in an Autocratic Village in Israel." *Ethnology* 8:54–75.

———. 1971. "Ecologic and Demographic Aspects of Rural Tripolitanian Jewry: 1853–1949." *International Journal of Middle Eastern Studies* 2:45–65.

———. 1972. *Cave Dwellers and Citrus Growers: A Jewish Community in Libya and Israel.* Cambridge: Cambridge University Press.

———. 1973. "Culture Change in an Israeli Immigrant Village: How the Twist Came to Even Yosef." *Middle Eastern Studies* 9:73–80.

———. 1978. "The Mimuna and the Minority Status of Moroccan Jews." *Ethnology* 17(1):75–87.

———. 1983. "The Mellahs of Southern Morocco: A Report of a Survey." *Maghreb Review* 8(3):61–69.

———. 1984. *Greentown's Youth: Disadvantaged Youth in an Israeli Development Town.* Assen, Netherlands: Van Gorcum.

———. 1985. "Anthropologie et études juives: Une perspective autobiographique." *Pardès* (Paris) 2:99–115.

———. 1987. "The Changing Meaning of Ethnic Affiliation." *Jerusalem Quarterly* 44:39–50.

———. 1990. *Jewish Life in Muslim Libya: Rivals and Relatives.* Chicago: University of Chicago Press.

———. 1992. "Potential Polities: Jewish Saints in the Moroccan Countryside and in Israel." In *Faith and Polity: Essays on Religion and Politics,* ed. M. Bax, P. Kloos, and A. Koster, 233–52. Amsterdam: Free University Press.

———. 1993. *The Book of Mordechai: A Study of the Jews of Libya.* London: Darf.

———. 1998. "The Breaking of a Glass at Weddings: An Anthropological Interpretation." In *Israel: Local Anthropology,* ed. O. Abuhav, E. Hertzog, H. E. Goldberg, and E. Marx, 595–608. Tel Aviv: Tcherikover.

———. 2003. *Jewish Passages: Cycles of Jewish Life.* Berkeley: University of California Press.

Goldberg, H. E., and O. Abuhav. 2000. "Physical Anthropology in Hebrew Zionist Writings." Paper presented at annual meeting of the American Anthropological Association, San Francisco.

Golden, D. 1996. "The Museum of the Jewish Diaspora Tells a Story." In *The Tourist Image: Myths and Myth Making in Tourism*, ed. T. Selwyn, 223–50. Chichester: Wiley.

Goldschlager, A. 1985. "On Ideological Discourse." *Semiotica* 54:165–76.

Gómara, F. L. de. 1992. "Children." In *Medical Practices in Ancient America*, ed. M. G. Peredo. Mexico: Ediciones Euroamericanas.

Gombrich, E. H. 1982. *The Image and the Eye*. Oxford: Phaidon.

Goodale, J. C. 1987. "Gambling Is Hard Work: Card Playing in Tiwi Society." *Oceania* 58(1):6–21.

Goode, W. J. 1969. "The Theoretical Limits of Professionalism." In *The Semi-Professions and Their Organization*, ed. A. Etzioni. New York: Free Press.

———. 1978. *The Celebration of Heroes*. Berkeley: University of California Press.

Goodman, H. 1986. "Police to Raze Three Houses in Ein Hud." *Jerusalem Post*, 3 August, p. 1.

Goodman, P., and A. D. Lewis. 1916. *Zionism: Problems and Views*. London: T. Fisher Unwin.

Goody, J. 1962. *Death, Property and the Ancestors*. Stanford: Stanford University Press.

———. 1968. "Restricted Literacy in Northern Ghana." In *Literacy in Traditional Societies*, ed. J. Goody, 198–264. Cambridge: Cambridge University Press.

———. 1976a. *Family and Inheritance*. Cambridge: Cambridge University Press.

———. 1976b. *Production and Reproduction: A Comparative Study of the Domestic Domain*. New York: Cambridge University Press.

Goshen-Gottstein, E. 1987. "Mental Health Implications of Living in an Ultraorthodox Jewish Subculture." *Israel Journal of Psychiatry* 24:145–66.

Gouldner, A. W. 1960. "The Norm of Reciprocity: A Preliminary Statement." *American Sociological Review* 25:161–78.

Gracey, H. L. 1972. "Learning the Student Role: Kindergarten as Academic Boot Camp." In *Readings in Introductory Sociology*, ed. D. Wrong and H. Gracey. New York: Macmillan.

Graeber, D. 1996. "Beads and Money: A Note toward the Theory of Wealth and Power." *American Ethnologist* 23(1):4–24.

Graham, J. W. 1991. "Servant-Leadership in Organizations: Inspirational and Moral." *Leadership Quarterly* 2:105–19.

Gramsci, A. 1971. *Selections from the Prison Notebooks of Antonio Gramsci*. Ed. Q. Hoare and G. N. Smith. New York: International Publications.

Granqvist, H. 1931–35. *Marriage Conditions in a Palestinian Village*. 2 vols. Helsingfors: Centraltryckeriet.

———. 1947. *Birth and Childhood among the Arabs*. Helsingfors: Söderström.

Green, A. 1977. "The Zaddiq as Axis Mundi in Later Judaism." *Journal of the American Academy of Religion* 45:327–47.

———. 1981. *Tormented Master: A Life of Rabbi Nachman of Bratslav*. New York: Schocken.

Greenberg, O. 1982. *Nashim bakele beyisrael* [Women in Jail in Israel]. Tel Aviv: Tcherikover.

———. 1989. *Hazmana le'ayeret pituah* [Invitation to a Development Town]. Tel Aviv: Hakibbutz Hameuhad and Jerusalem Institute for Israeli Studies.

———. 1999. *Nes 'amim: hayim bisetira* [Ness Amim: Life amid Contradictions]. Ramat Efal: Yad Tabenkin.

Grossman, D., ed. 1983. *Bein Yarkon we'ayalon* [Between Yarkon and Ayalon]. Ramat Gan: Bar-Ilan University Press.

Grossman, D. 1993. *Sleeping on a Wire: Conversations with Palestinians in Israel.* New York: Farrar, Straus and Giroux.

Guest, R. H. 1962. *Organizational Change.* London: Tavistock.

Gulick, J., and M. E. Gulick. 1974. *An Annotated Bibliography of Sources Concerned with Women in the Modern Middle East.* Princeton Near East Paper no. 17. Princeton: Princeton University Press.

Gumperz, J. 1982. *Discourse Strategies.* Cambridge: Cambridge University Press.

Gurevitz, Z., and G. Aran. 1991. "On the Spot: Israeli Anthropology." *Alpayim* 4:44–49.

Gvati, H. 1981. *100 shenot hityashevut: Toledot hahityashevut hayehudit be'eretz yisra'el* [Hundred Years of Settlement: The History of the Jewish Settlement in Eretz Yisrael]. Tel Aviv: Hakibbutz Hameuhad.

Hacohen, M. 1986. *Hayei adam: Kelulot* [Human Life: Weddings]. Jerusalem: Keter.

Ha-Cohen, Mordechai. *Higgid Mordecaï: Histoire de la Libye et de ses Juifs, lieux d'habitation et coutumes.* Ed. and annot. Harvey E. Goldberg. Jerusalem: Institut Ben-Zvi.

———. n.d. *Higid Mordechai* [Mordechai Narrated]. Ms. 8 1292. National and University Library, Jerusalem.

Hadawi, S. 1988. *Palestinian Rights and Losses in 1948: A Comprehensive Study.* London: Saqi.

Haddad, A. 1972. "Novellae." *Or Tora* 5:209–10.

Haidar, A. 1987. *The Palestinians in Israel: Social Science Writings.* Kingston: NECEF Publications.

———. 1990. *The Arab in the Israeli Economy.* Tel Aviv: International Center for Peace in the Middle East.

———. 1995. *On the Margins: The Arab Population in the Israeli Economy.* London: Hurst.

Haim, A. 1991. "Rachelim." *Nekuda* 154(November):12–14.

Hakohen, M. 1972. "Eulogy for R. Sassi Hakohen." *Or Tora* 5:134–35.

Halevi, N. 1983. "The Structure and Development of Israel's Balance of Payments." Discussion Paper No. 83.02. Jerusalem: Falk Institute.

Hallowell, I. A. 1955. *Culture and Experience.* Philadelphia: University of Pennsylvania Press.

Halper, J. 1978. *Ethnicity and Education: The Schooling of Afro-Asian Children in a Jerusalem Locality.* Ann Arbor, MI: University Microfilms.

———. 1993. "Between Practicing and Engaged Anthropology in Israel." *Practicing Anthropology* 15(2):27–30.

Halperin, A. 1987. "Military Buildup and Economic Growth in Israel." *Economic Quarterly* 37(131):990–1010.

Hamalian, A. 1974. "Shirkets: Visiting Patterns of Armenians in Lebanon." *Anthropological Quarterly* 47:71–92.

Hambrick, D. C., and G.D.S. Fukutomi. 1991. "The Seasons of a CEO's Tenure." *Academy of Management Review* 16:719–42.

Hamdan, O. 1974. *Horses in Palestinian Folklore.* Al-Bireh: Palestinian Folklore and Social Research Society.

Hammami, R. 1997. "Labor and Economy: Gender Segmentation in Palestine Economic Life." *Palestinian Women: A Status Report.* No. 4. Birzeit: Birzeit University, Women's Study Program.

Hammond, D., and A. Jablow. 1976. *Women in Cultures of the World.* Menlo Park, CA: Cummings Publishing House.

Hammoudi, A. 1993. *The Victim and Its Masks: An Essay on Sacrifice and Masquerade in the Maghreb.* Trans. P. Wissing. Chicago: University of Chicago Press.

Handelman, D. 1977a. *Work and Play among the Aged: Interaction, Replication and Emergence in a Jerusalem Setting.* Amsterdam: Van Gorcum.

———. 1977b. "Play and Ritual: Complementary Frames of Meta-Communication." In *It's a Funny Thing, Humor,* ed. A. Chapman and H. Foot, 185–92. Oxford: Pressman Press.

———. 1981. "The Idea of Bureaucratic Organization." *Social Analysis* 9:5–23.

———. 1990. *Models and Mirrors: Towards an Anthropology of Public Events.* Cambridge: Cambridge University Press.

———. 1991. "Symbolic Types, the Body, and Circus." *Semiotica* 85(3/4):205–25.

———. 1992. "Passage to Play: Paradox and Process." *Play and Culture* 5(1):1–19.

———. 2004. *Nationalism and the Israeli State: Bureaucratic Logic in Public Events.* Oxford: Berg.

Handelman, D., and E. Katz. 1991. "State Ceremonies in Israel: Remembrance Day and Independence Day." In *Models and Mirrors: Towards an Anthropology of Public Events,* by D. Handelman, 191–233. Cambridge: Cambridge University Press.

Handelman, D., and L. Shamgar-Handelman. 1997. "The Presence of Absence: The Memorialism of National Death in Israel." In *Grasping Land,* ed. E. Ben-Ari and Y. Bilu, 85–128. Albany: State University of New York Press.

Handels, S., and R. Bar-Zuri. 1994. *Hakelita hata'asukatit shel 'olei hever ha'amim biysra'el* [The Occupational Absorption of Russian Immigrants in Israel]. Tel Aviv: Histadrut.

Hannerz, Ulf. 1989. "Notes on the Global Ecumene." *Public Culture* 1(2):66–75.

Hanson, P. W. 1993. "Reconceiving the Shape of Culture: Folklore and Public Culture." *Western Folklore* 52:327–44.

Harding, S. 1986. *The Science Question in Feminism.* Milton Keynes: Open University Press.

Harlap, A. 1982. *New Israeli Architecture.* London: Associated Universities Presses.

Harrell, B. B. 1981. "Lactation and Menstruation in Cultural Perspective." *American Anthropologist* 83(4):796–823.

Harrington, C. 1973. "Pupils, Peers and Politics." Paper presented at "Learning and Culture": Annual Spring Meeting of the American Ethnological Society, Seattle.

Harris, M. 1968. "'Emics,' 'Etics,' and the 'New Ethnography.'" In *Readings in Anthropology,* ed. M. H. Fried. New York: Crowell.

Harrison, S. 1995. "Four Types of Symbolic Conflict." *Journal of the Royal Anthropological Institute,* n.s., 1:255–72.

Hart, K. 1988. "Kinship, Contract and Trust: The Economic Organization of Migrants in an African City Slum." In *Trust,* ed. D. Gambetta. Cambridge: Cambridge University Press.

Hart, M. 2000. *Social Science and the Politics of Jewish Identity.* Stanford: Stanford University Press.

Hartman, M., and H. Eilon. 1975. "Ethnicity and Class in Israel." *Megamot* 21:129–39.

Harvey, D. 1989. *The Condition of Postmodernity: An Enquiry into the Origins of Cultural Change.* Oxford: Blackwell.

Hasan-Rokem, G. 1996. *Rikmat Hayim-Hayetzira Ha'amamit Besafrut Hazal* [The Embroidery of Life: Folk Creativity in Rabbinical Literature]. Tel Aviv: Am Oved.

———. 1997. "Studying Folk Culture and Popular Culture." *Theoria webikoret* 10:5–13.

Hasdai, Y. 1982. "'Doers' and 'Thinkers' in the IDF." *Jerusalem Quarterly* 24:13–25.

Haskina, T. 1941. "Birthday Party in the Kindergarten." *Hed Hagan* 5:34–37.

Hastings, J., ed. 1951. *Encyclopedia of Religion and Ethics*. New York: Scribner.

Havakook, Ya'acov. 1986. *Mibeit hase'ar leveit-haeven: mishkenot habeduim betahalikhei shinui—mehkar etnografi* [From Goat Hair to Stone; Transition in Bedouin Dwellings]. Tel Aviv: Ministry of Defence Press.

Hawley, J. S., and W. Proudfoot. 1994. Introduction to *Fundamentalism and Gender*, ed. J. S. Hawley, 3–46. New York: Oxford University Press.

Hayden, R. M. 1996. "Imagined Communities and Real Victims: Self-Determination and Ethnic Cleansing in Yugoslavia." *American Ethnologist* 23(4):783–801.

Hazan, H. 1980. "Adjustment and Control in an Old Age Home." In *A Composite Portrait of Israel*, ed. E. Marx, 239–55. London: Academic Press.

———. 1990. *A Paradoxical Community: The Emergence of a Social World in an Urban Renewal Setting*. Greenwich, CT: JAI Press.

———. 1992. *Managing Change in Old Age*. Albany: State University of New York Press.

———. 1998. "The Time of Place: An Anthropological View of Rabin's Grave." In *Rav Tarbutiut behevra demokratit viyhudit* [Multiculturalism in a Jewish Democratic Society], ed. A. Sagi and R. Shamir, 731–53. Tel Aviv: Ramot.

———. 2001. *Simulated Dreams: Israeli Youth and Virtual Zionism*. New York: Berghahn.

Hehassid, J. 1957. *Sefer Hassidim*. Jerusalem: Mosad Harav Kook.

Heilman, S. C. 1983. *The People of the Book*. Chicago: Chicago University Press.

———. 1992. *Defenders of the Faith: Inside Ultraorthodox Jewry*. New York: Schocken.

Heilman, S. C., and M. Friedman. 1991. "Religious Fundamentalism and Religious Jews." In *Fundamentalisms Observed: The Fundamentalism Project*, ed. M. E. Marty and S. R. Appleby. Chicago: University of Chicago Press.

Heller, C. S. 1973. "The Emerging Consciousness of the Ethnic Problem among Jews in Israel." In *Israel: Social Structure and Change*, ed. M. Curtis and M. S. Chertoff. New Brunswick, NJ: Transaction.

Heller, J. 1949. *The Zionist Idea*. New York: Schocken.

Helman, A. 1987. "The Development of Professional Managers in the Kibbutz." *Economic Quarterly* 33:1021–38.

Helman, S. 1993. "Conscientious Objection to Military Service as an Attempt to Redefine the Contents of Citizenship." Ph.D. diss., Hebrew University of Jerusalem.

Helmreich, W. B. 1982. *The World of the Yeshiva: An Intimate Portrait of Orthodox Jewry*. New Haven: Yale University Press.

Hendry, J. 1986. "Kindergarten and the Transition from Home to School Education." *Comparative Education* 22:53–58.

Henry, J. 1957. "Attitude Organization in Elementary School Classrooms." *American Journal of Orthopsychiatry* 27:117–33.

———. 1965. *Culture against Man*. New York: Vintage.

Henslin, J. 1972. "What Makes for Trust?" In *Down to Earth Sociology*. New York: Free Press.

Herbert, Z. 1984. *Poems*. Tel Aviv: Hakibbutz Hameuhad.

Hernandez, F. 1992. "How Mexican Women Give Birth and the Double Bath for Children." In *Medical Practices in Ancient America*, ed. M. G. Peredo. Mexico: Ediciones Euroamericanas.

Herr, M. D. 1982. "Intermediate Days." *Encyclopedia Judaica* 4:1178–79.

Hertz, R. 1960. *Death and the Right Hand.* New York: Free Press.

Hertzberg, A. 1959. *The Zionist Idea.* New York: Atheneum Press.

Hertzog, E. 1996. "Mi marwiah mimedinat harewaha?" [Who Gains from the Welfare State?]. *Te'oria webikoret* 9:81–104.

———. 1998. *Habirokratia we'olei etiopia: Yahasei telut bemerkaz kelita* [Bureaucrats and Ethiopian Immigrants in an Absorption Center]. Tel Aviv: Tcherikover.

———. 1999. *Immigrants and Bureaucrats: Ethiopians in an Israeli Absorption Center.* New York: Berghahn.

Herzfeld, M. 1985. *The Poetics of Manhood: Contest and Identity in a Cretan Mountain Village.* Princeton: Princeton University Press.

———. 1997. *Cultural Intimacy: Social Poetics in the Nation-State.* London: Routledge.

Herzog, H., and R. Shamir. 1994. "Negotiated Society? Media Discourse on Israeli Jewish/Arab Relations." *Israel Social Science Research* 9(1–2):55–88.

Heschel, S. 1983. *On Being a Jewish Feminist.* New York: Schocken.

Hirschberg, H. Z. 1968. "The Jewish Quarter in Muslim Cities and Berber Arabs." *Judaism* 17(4):405–21.

Hirschman, A. O. 1970. *Exit, Voice and Loyalty.* Cambridge, MA: Harvard University Press.

———. 1982. *Shifting Involvement.* Oxford: Martin Robertson.

———. 1984. *Getting Ahead Collectively.* New York: Pergamon.

Hoben, A. 1982. "Anthropologists and Development." *Annual Review of Anthropology* 11:349–75.

Hobsbawm, E. 1983. "Introduction: Inventing Traditions." In *The Invention of Tradition,* ed. E. Hobsbawm and T. O. Ranger, 1–14. Cambridge: Cambridge University Press.

Hobsbawm, E., and T. O. Ranger. 1983. *The Invention of Tradition.* Cambridge: Cambridge University Press.

Hoch-Smith, J., and A. Spring, eds. 1978. *Women in Ritual and Symbolic Roles.* New York: Plenum Press.

Holland, J. L. 1973. *Making Vocational Choices: A Theory of Careers.* Englewood Cliffs, NJ: Prentice-Hall.

Holton, E. 1992. "The Cultic Roots of Culture." In *Theory of Culture,* ed. R. Munch and N. J. Smelser, 29–63. Berkeley: University of California Press.

Honigmann, J. J. 1977. "The Masked Face." *Ethos* 5:263–80.

Horodetsky, S. A. 1947. *Yahadut hasechel wiyahadut haregesh* [Judaism of the Intellect and Judaism of the Heart]. Tel Aviv: Tversky.

Horowitz, D. 1993. *Techelet weavak: Dor tashah-diokan 'atzmi* [The Heavens and the Earth: A Self-Portrait of the 1948 Generation]. Jerusalem: Keter.

Horowitz, D., and B. Kimmerling. 1974. "Some Social Implications of Military Service and the Reserve System in Israel." *European Journal of Sociology* 15:262–76.

Horowitz, D., and M. Lissak. 1978. *Origins of the Israeli Polity.* Chicago: University of Chicago Press.

———. 1989. *Trouble in Utopia: The Overburdened Polity of Israel.* Albany: State University of New York Press.

Hosmer, L. T. 1995. "Trust: The Connecting Link between Organizational Theory and Philosophical Ethics." *Academy of Management Review* 20:379–403.

Hughes, E. C. 1945. "Dilemmas and Contradictions of Status." *American Journal of Sociology* 50:353–59.

Hughes, J. 1989. "Thinking about Children." In *Children, Parents and Politics,* ed. G. Scarre. Cambridge: Cambridge University Press.

Huizinga, J. 1950. *Homo Ludens: A Study of the Play-Elements in Culture.* Boston: Beacon Press.

Humphries, S. C., and H. King, eds. 1981. *Mortality and Immortality: The Anthropology and Archaeology of Death.* London: Academic Press.

Hunt, R. C. 1973. "Power in the Domestic Sphere." *Science* 181:741–42.

Huntington, R., and P. Metcalf. 1979. *Celebrations of Death: The Anthropology of Mortuary Ritual.* Cambridge: Cambridge University Press.

Iadarola, A. 1985. "The American Catholic Bishops and Woman: From the Nineteenth Amendment to ERA." In *Women, Religion, and Social Change,* ed. Y. Y. Haddad, 457–76. Albany: State University of New York Press.

Idel, M. 1988. *Kabbalah: New Perspectives.* New Haven: Yale University Press.

———. 1995. *Hassidism: Between Ecstasy and Magic.* New York: State University of New York Press.

Ilan, S. 1995a. "Parliament Member Itzhak Levy Demands to Abolish Sessions with Autistic Children." *Ha'aretz,* 24 February.

———. 1995b. "The Talking Souls of the Autistic." *Ha'aretz,* 20 January.

Inhorn, M. 1994. "Kabsa and Threatened Fertility in Egypt." *Social Science and Medicine* 39(4):487–505.

International Committee on Project Renewal Evaluation. 1981. *Guidelines for Evaluating Research.* Jerusalem: Jewish Agency for Israel.

Isaacs-Elazari, J. 1999. "Ze lo 'oved" [It Does Not Work]. *'Al Hasharon* 429(22 October):58–62.

Ish-Shalom, M. 1948. *Kivrei 'avot* [Jewish Holy Tombs]. Jerusalem: Rabbi Kook Foundation and Palestine Institute of Folklore and Ethnology.

Israeli, E. 1961. *Peace, Peace, When There Is No Peace.* Jerusalem: Bohan.

Izraeli, D. N. 1991. "Culture, Policy and Women in Dual-Earner Families in Israel." In *Dual-Earner Families: International Perspective,* ed. S. Lewis, D. N. Izraeli, and H. M. Hootsmans. New York: Russell Sage.

Izraeli, D., and E. Tabory. 1988. "The Political Context of Feminist Attitudes in Israel." *Gender and Society* 2:463–81.

Jabbur, J. 1995. *The Bedouins and the Desert: Aspects of Nomadic Life in the Arab East.* Albany: State University of New York Press.

Jabrā, I. J. 1959. "Kharzat al-bi'r/kharzat al-bi'r" [Cistern's Circular Opening]. In *Tammuz fi al-madinah,* 68–69. Beirut: Dar Majallat Shi'r.

Jacques, E. 1990. *Creativity and Work.* Madison, WI: International Universities Press.

Jaggar, A. M., and S. R. Bordo. 1989. *Gender/Body/Knowledge: Feminist Reconstructions of Being and Knowing.* New Brunswick, NJ: Rutgers University Press.

Jakubowska, L. A. 1988. "The Bedouin Family in Rahat." In *Habeduim: Reshimot vema' amarim* [The Bedouin: Papers and Articles], ed. Y. Eini and E. Orion. Tel Aviv: Society for the Protection of Nature.

———. 1992. "Resisting 'Ethnicity': The Israeli State and Bedouin Identity." In *The Paths to Domination, Resistance and Terror,* ed. C. Nordstrom and J. A. Martin, 85–105. Berkeley: University of California Press.

Jamzadeh, L., and M. Mills. 1986. "Iranian Sofreh: From Collective to Female Ritual." In *Gender and Religion: On the Complexity of Symbols,* ed. C. Walker Bynum, S. Harrell, and P. Richman. Boston: Beacon Press.

Janeway, E. 1981. *Powers of the Weak.* New York: Morrow.

Jay, A. 1972. *Corporation Man.* London: Jonathan Cape.

Jehn, K. A. 1995. "A Multimethod Examination of the Benefits and Detriments of Intragroup Conflict." *Administrative Science Quarterly* 40:256–82.

Jewish Agency. 1984. "A Model for the Absorption of Ethiopian Immigrants in Transition Frameworks." Working paper for the Planning Team, Directors of Absorption Centers for Ethiopians. Jerusalem: Jewish Agency.

Johnstone, J. C. 1970. "Age-Grade Consciousness." *Sociology of Education* 43:56–68.

Jones, D. P. II, ed. 1994. "Autism, Facilitated Communication, and Allegations of Child Abuse and Neglect." *Child Abuse and Neglect* 18(6):491–537.

Jung, C. G. 1956. *Symbols of Transformation.* New York: Pantheon Books.

Kafih, J. 1962. "Women's Status in Yemen." *Mahanaim* 78:68–71.

Kafkafi, E. 1992. *Emet 'o emuna* [Truth or Faith]. Jerusalem: Yad Itzchak Ben-Zvi.

Kahana, Sh.Z. 1985. *Ha'otiot wesodoteihen* [The Letters and Their Secrets]. Jerusalem: Shem Publications.

Kahana, Y. 1977. *Ahim shehorim* [Our Black Brothers: Life among the Falashas]. Tel Aviv: Am Oved.

Kalish, R. A. 1985. *Death, Grief and Caring Relationships.* Monterey, CA: Brooks/Cole.

Kalkin-Fishman, D. 1981. "Tune and Control: The Acquisition of the Concept of Music in the Kindergarten." *Notebooks for Research and Criticism* 6:5–25.

Kanaana, S. 1975. *Survival Strategies of Arabs in Israel.* Bir Zeit: Bir Zeit University Publications.

———. 1992. "What Made the Palestinians Leave?" In *Still on Vacation! The Eviction of the Palestinians in 1948,* 1–32. Jerusalem: Jerusalem Center for Palestinian Studies.

Kanaana, S., and L. Abd al-Hadi. 1986. *Salamah.* Bir Zeit: Markaz al-Watha'iq wa-al-Abhath.

Kanaana, S., and B. al-Ka'bi. 1987. *'Ayn Hawd.* Bir Zeit: Markaz al-Watha'iq wa-al-Abhath.

Kanari, B. 1989. *Laset et 'amam: Hahageshama, hashelichut wehadimuy ha'atzmi shel Hakibbutz Hame'uhad* [Hakibbutz Hameuhad: Mission and Reality]. Ramat Efal: Yad Tabenkin.

Kandyoti, D. 1991. *Women, Islam and the State.* Philadelphia: Temple University Press.

Kanner, L. 1943. "Autistic Disturbance of Affective Contact." *Nervous Child* 2:217–50.

Kanter, R. M. 1972. "The Organization Child: Experience Management in a Nursery School." *Sociology of Education* 45:186–212.

Kapferer, B. 1988. *Legends of People, Myths of State.* Washington, DC: Smithsonian Institution Press.

Kaplan, A., and Y. Amit. 1979. *Tichnun labeduim* [Planning for the Bedouin]. Tel Aviv: Kaplan and Amit.

Karim, W. J. 1992. *Women and Culture: Between Malay Adat and Islam.* Boulder, CO: Westview.

Kashti, Y. 1979. *The Socializing Community: Disadvantaged Adolescents in Israeli Youth Villages.* Tel Aviv: School of Education, Tel Aviv University.

Kasl, E., V. J. Marsick, and K. Dechant. 1997. "Teams as Learners: A Research-Based Model of Team Learning." *Journal of Applied Behavioral Science* 33(2):227–46.

Katerbursky, Z. 1962. *Binetivot hagan* [The Garden Paths]. Tel Aviv: Otzar Hamore.

Katriel, T. 1982. "Mesibat kiturim ketekes leshoni basiah shel Yisraelim" [Griping as a Verbal Ritual in Israeli Discourse]. *Iyunim Bechinuch* 35:151–62.

———. 1986. *Talking Straight: "Dugri" Speech in Israeli Sabra Culture.* Cambridge: Cambridge University Press.

———. 1991a. *Communal Webs: Communication and Culture in Contemporary Israel.* Albany: State University of New York Press.

———. 1991b. "Picnics in a Military Zone: Rituals of Parenting and the Politics of Consensus." In *Communal Webs,* ed. T. Katriel, 71–91. New York: State University of New York Press.

———. 1997. *Performing the Past: A Study of Israeli Settlement Museums.* Mahwah, NJ: Erlbaum.

Katriel, T., and P. Nesher. 1986. "'Gibush': The Rhetoric of Cohesion in Israeli School Culture." *Comparative Education Review* 30(2):216–31.

Katz, D., and R. L. Kahn. 1978. *The Social Psychology of Organizations.* 2nd ed. New York: Wiley.

Katz, E., and S. N. Eisenstadt. 1960. "Some Sociological Observations on the Response of Israeli Organisations to New Immigrants." *Administrative Science Quarterly* 5:113–33.

Katz, E., et al. 1992. *Leisure Culture in Israel: Changes in Patterns of Cultural Activity.* Jerusalem: Louis Guttman Israel Institute of Applied Social Research.

Katz, J. 1961. *Tradition and Crisis: Jewish Society at the End of the Middle Ages.* New York: Free Press.

Katzenelson, B. 1946. *Collected Papers.* Vol. 3. Tel Aviv: Labor Party Publishing.

Katzir, Y. 1976. "The Effects of Resettlement on the Status and Roles of Yemenite Jewish Women: The Case of Moshav Ramat Oranim." Ph.D. diss., University of California, Berkeley.

———. 1983. "The Preservation of Jewish Ethnic Identity in Yemen: Segregation and Integration as Boundary Maintenance Mechanisms." *Comparative Studies in Society and History* 24:264–79.

Kaufman, D. 1991. *Rachel's Daughters: Newly Orthodox Jewish Women.* New Brunswick, NJ: Rutgers University Press.

Keesing, R. M. 1974. "Theories of Culture." *Annual Review of Anthropology* 3:73–97.

Kellett, A. 1982. *Combat Motivation: The Behavior of Soldiers in Battle.* Boston: Kluwer.

Kennedy, J. G. 1970. "Circumcision and Excision in Egyptian Nubia." *Man* 5(2):175–91.

———, ed. 1978. *Nubian Ceremonial Life: Studies in Islamic Syncretism and Cultural Change.* Berkeley: University of California Press and American University in Cairo Press.

Kets de Vries, M.F.R. 1993. *Leaders, Fools and Impostors.* San Francisco: Jossey-Bass.

Khalidi, R. 1988. *The Arab Economy in Israel.* London: Croom Helm.

Khalidi, W. 1959a. "What Made the Palestinians Leave?" *Middle East Forum* 35(7):21–24.

———. 1959b. "The Fall of Haifa." *Middle East Forum* 35(10):22–32.

Khalidi, W., et al. 1992. *All That Remains: The Palestinian Villages Occupied and Depopulated by Israel in 1948.* Washington, DC: Institute for Palestine Studies.

Khamaisi, R. 1990. *Planning and Housing Policy in the Arab Sector of Israel.* Tel Aviv: International Center for Peace in the Middle East.

Khan, M. M., ed. 1974. *Sahih al-Bukhari.* Vol. 7. Medina: Islamic University.

Khawalde, S. S. 1994. *Beduinen im gelobten Land: Die Stämme der Krad il-Het, Krad il-Ghannama und Krad il-Baggara.* Hamburg: Kovač.

Kibbutz Beth Alfa. 1968 [1922]. *Kehillatenu* [Our Community]. Emek Izrael: Kibbutz Beit Alpha.

Kimmerling, B. 1974. "Anomie and Integration in Israeli Society and the Salience of the Israeli-Arab Conflict." *Studies in Comparative International Development* 9(3):64–89.

———. 1985. *The Interrupted System: Israeli Civilians in War and Routine Times.* New Brunswick, NJ: Transaction.

———. 1992. "Sociology, Ideology, and Nation-Building: The Palestinians and Their Meaning in Israeli Sociology." *American Sociological Review* 57:446–60.

———. 1993. "Patterns of Militarism in Israel." *European Journal of Sociology* 2(1):1–28.

Kipnis, D. 1976. *The Powerholders.* Chicago: University of Chicago Press.

Kirmayer, L. 1992. "Taking Possession of Trance." *Transcultural Psychiatric Research Review* 30:51–57.

Kirschner, S. 1987. " 'Then What Have I To Do with Thee?' On Identity, Fieldwork, and Ethnographic Knowledge." *Cultural Anthropology* 2(2):211–34.

Kirshenblatt-Gimblett, B. 1988. "Mistaken Dichotomies." *Journal of American Folklore* 101:140–55.

———. 1992. Presidential Address Delivered at the Annual Meeting of the American Folklore Society in Jacksonville, Florida.

———. 1996. "Topic-Drift: Negotiating the Gap between the Field and Our Name." *Journal of Folklore Research* 33:245–54.

———. 1998. "Folklore's Crisis." *Journal of American Folklore* 111(441):319–21.

Kleinberger, A. F. 1969. *Society, Schools and Progress in Israel.* London: Pergamon.

Kleinman, A. 1980. *Patients and Healers in the Context of Culture: An Exploration of the Borderland between Anthropology, Medicine and Psychiatry.* Berkeley: University of California Press.

———. 1988. *Rethinking Psychiatry.* Berkeley: University of California Press.

Kleinman, A., and B. Good, eds. 1985. *Culture and Depression.* Berkeley: University of California Press.

Kniss, F. 1996. "Ideas and Symbols as Resources in Intrareligious Conflict: The Case of American Mennonites." *Sociology of Religion* 57:7–24.

Kohut, A. 1955. *Aruch Completum sive Lexicon Vocabula et Res, quae in Libris Targumicis Talmudicis et Midraschicis.* Vol. 7. New York: Pardes.

Koltun, E. 1976. *The Jewish Woman.* New York: Schocken.

Kook, Z.Y.H. 1975. "Zionism and Biblical Prophecy." In *Religious Zionism: An Anthology,* ed. Y. Tirosh. Jerusalem: World Zionist Organization.

Korazim, J. 1983. "Israeli Families in New York City: Utilization of Social Services, Unmet Needs and Policy Implications." Ph.D. diss., Columbia University, School of Social Work.

Kostiner, J. 1991. "Transforming Dualities: Tribe and State Formation in Saudi Arabia." In *Tribes and State Formation in the Middle East,* ed. P. S. Khoury and J. Kostiner, 226–51. London: Tauris.

Kouzes, J. M., and B. Z. Posner. 1993. *Credibility.* San Francisco: Jossey-Bass.

Krausz, E., ed. 1983. *The Sociology of the Kibbutz.* New Brunswick, NJ: Transaction.

Kressel, G. M. 1974. *"Mikol ehad lefi yecholto": Rivud mul shiwion bakibbutz* ["From Each According to His Ability": Stratification versus Equality in a Kibbutz]. Tel Aviv: Tcherikover.

———. 1975. *Pratiut le'umat shivtiut* [Individuality versus Tribality]. Tel Aviv: Hakibbutz Hameuhad.

———. 1982. *Rivei-dam bekerev beduim 'ironiim* [Blood Feuds among Urban Bedouins]. Jerusalem: Magnes Press.

———. 1983. *"Lekol ehad lefi tzerachav": Rivud mul shiwion bakibbutz* ("To Each According to His Needs": Stratification versus Equality in a Kibbutz]. Tel Aviv: Tcherikover.

———. 1984. "Changes in Employment and Social Accommodations of Bedouin Settling in an Israeli Town." In *The Changing Bedouin*, ed. E. Marx and A. Shmueli, 125–55. New Brunswick, NJ: Transaction.

———. 1991. "Managerial Blunders in the Kibbutz Enterprise: The Problem of Accountability." *Journal of Rural Cooperation* 19:91–107.

———. 1992a. *Descent through Males.* Wiesbaden: Otto Harrassowitz.

———. 1992b. "Reducing Collectivity in a Kibbutz." International Conference on Labor-Managed Firms, Ramat Gan, Israel, 28 May.

———. 2003. *Let Shepherding Endure: Applied Anthropology and the Preservation of a Cultural Tradition in Israel and the Middle East.* Albany: State University of New York Press.

Kretzmer, D. 1990. *The Legal Status of the Arabs in Israel.* Boulder, CO: Westview.

Krohn, A. 1978. *Hysteria: The Elusive Neurosis.* Psychological Issues, Monograph 45/46. New York: International Universities Press.

Krue, E. 1983. "The Vocational Side of a New Start in Life: A Career Model of Immigrants." *Journal of Vocational Behavior* 23:270–85.

Kruse, D., and C. Sowerwine. 1986. "Feminism and Pacifism: Women's Sphere in Peace and War." In *Australian Women: New Feminism Perspectives*, ed. N. Grieve and A. Burns. Melbourne: Oxford University Press.

Kuhn, T. S. 1962. *The Structure of Scientific Revolutions.* Chicago: University of Chicago Press.

Kunda, G. 1992a. "Criticism on Probation: Ethnography and Cultural Critique in Israel." *Theoria webikoret* 2:7–24.

———. 1992b. *Engineering Culture: Control and Commitment in a High-Tech Corporation.* Philadelphia: Temple University Press.

Kung, L. 1981. "Perceptions of Work among Factory Women." In *The Anthropology of Taiwanese Society*, ed. E. M. Ahern and H. Gates, 184–211. Stanford: Stanford University Press.

Kunz, P. R., and J. Summers. 1979–80. "A Time to Die: A Study of the Relationship of Birthday and Time of Death." *Omega* 10:281–89.

Kuper, A. 1983. *Anthropology and Anthropologists: The Modern British School.* Rev. ed. London: Routledge and Kegan Paul.

Kushner, G. 1973. *Immigrants from India in Israel: Planned Change in an Administered Community.* Tucson: University of Arizona Press.

Kynan, O. 1989. "In Our Own Image: Hashomer Hatzair and the Mass Immigration." Master's thesis, Department of History, Tel Aviv University.

Lakoff, G., and M. Johnson. 1980. *Metaphors We Live By.* Chicago: Chicago University Press.

Lambek, M. 1989. "From Disease to Discourse: Remarks on the Conceptualization of Trance and Spirit Possession." In *Altered States of Consciousness and Mental Health*, ed. A. C. Ward, 36–61. Newbury Park, CA: Sage.

Lamm, M. 1969. *The Jewish Way in Death and Mourning.* New York: Jonathan David.

Lancy, D. F. 1975. "The Social Organization of Learning: Initiation Rituals and Public Schools." *Human Organization* 34:371–80.

Landau, J. M. 1993. *The Arab Minority in Israel, 1967–1991: Political Aspects.* Oxford: Clarendon Press.

Lane, E. W. 1981. *Manners and Customs of the Modern Egyptians.* Cairo: Livres de France.

Lang, K. 1972. *Military Instructions and the Sociology of War.* Beverly Hills, CA: Sage.

Laqueur, W. 1962. *Young Germany: A History of the German Youth Movement.* London: Routledge and Kegan Paul.

———. 1972. *A History of Zionism.* London: Weidenfeld and Nicolson.

Lash, S., and J. Friedman, eds. 1991. *Modernity and Identity.* Oxford: Blackwell.

Laskier, M. M. 1983. *The Alliance Israélite Universelle and the Jewish Communities of Morocco, 1862–1962.* Albany: State University of New York Press.

———. 1990. "Developments in the Jewish Communities of Morocco: 1956–76." *Middle Eastern Studies* 26(4):465–505.

Laufer, R. S. 1988a. "The Aftermath of War: Adult Socialization and Political Development." In *Political Learning in Adulthood,* ed. R. S. Sigel, 415–57. Chicago: University of Chicago Press.

———. 1988b. "The Serial Self." In *Human Adaptation to Extreme Stress,* ed. J. P. Wilson, 33–53. New York: Plenum Press.

Lavie, S. 1990. *The Poetics of Military Occupation: Mzeina Allegories of Bedouin Identity under Israeli and Egyptian Rule.* Berkeley: University of California Press.

Lavie, S., and T. Swedenburg, eds. 1996. *Displacement, Diaspora and Geographies of Identity.* Durham: Duke University Press.

Lawson, E. D. 1963. "Development of Patriotism in Children: A Second Look." *Journal of Psychology* 55:279–86.

Leach, E. R. 1954. *Political Systems of Highland Burma.* Boston: Beacon Press.

Leacock, E. 1981. *Myths of Male Dominance.* New York and London: Monthly Review Press.

League of Arab Nations. 1965. *Ri'ayat al-badu wa-tahdirhum wa-tawtinhum* [The Protection, Sedentization, and Settlement of Bedouin]. 2 vols. Jerusalem: League of Arab Nations.

LeClair, D. 1996. "Teams: Economic Theory and Managerial Applications." *American Business Review* 14(1):60–66.

Lefebvre, H. 1991. *The Production of Space.* Oxford: Blackwell.

Lehman-Wilzig, S. 1993. "Copying the Master? Patterns of Israeli Arab Protest, 1950–1990." *Asian and African Studies* 27:129–47.

Lehn, W., with U. Davis. 1988. *The Jewish National Fund.* London: Kegan Paul International.

Lenski, G. 1966. *Power and Privilege.* New York: McGraw-Hill.

Leshem, E. 1969. "Defusey setiya betafkid rakaz hameshek bakibbutz" [Patterns of Deviation from the Economic Manager's Role in the Kibbutz]. M.A. thesis, Sociology Department, Hebrew University of Jerusalem.

Levenberg, S. 1945. *The Jews and Palestine: A Study in Labor Zionism.* London: Poalei Tzion-Jewish Socialist Party.

Lever, H., and C. Huhne. 1985. *Debt and Danger: The World Financial Crisis.* Harmondsworth, UK: Penguin.

Levi, Z. 1976. *Structuralizem bein metod utemunat 'olam* [Structuralism: Between Method and Worldview]. Tel Aviv: Sifriat Hapoalim.

Leviatan, U. 1992. *Involuntary Leadership.* Haifa: Kibbutz Research Institute.

———. 1995. "The Heavy Price of Working Outside." *Kibbutz Trends* 17:49–50.

———. 1997. "What Is Happening in the Kibbutz Industry?" *Hadaf Hayarok,* 6 May.

Levin, O. 1992. "From the Knesset." *Arabs in Israel* 2(3):10.

Levine, L. W. 1992. "The Folklore of Industrial Society: Popular Culture and Its Audience." *American Historical Review* 97:1369–99.

Levinger, E. 1993. *Andartot lanofelim biysra'el* [War Memorials in Israel]. Tel Aviv: Hakibbutz Hameuhad.

Levinson, A., and Y. Ze'evi. 1995. "Sticker Now." *Kol Ha'ir,* 8 December, part 2, pp. 10–13.

Lévi-Strauss. C. 1962. *La pensée sauvage.* Paris: Plon.

———. 1966. *The Savage Mind.* Chicago: University of Chicago Press.

———. 1987. *Introduction to the Work of Marcel Mauss.* London: Routledge and Kegan Paul.

Levy, A. 1994. "The Structured Ambiguity of Minorities towards Decolonisation: The Case of Moroccan Jews." *Maghreb Review* 19(1–2):133–46.

———. 1996. "Jews among Muslims: Perceptions and Reactions to the End of Casablancan Jewish History." Ph.D. diss., Department of Sociology and Anthropology, Hebrew University of Jerusalem.

———. 1997. "To Morocco and Back: Tourism and Pilgrimage among Moroccan-Born Israelis." In *Grasping Land,* ed. E. Ben-Ari and Y. Bilu, 25–46. Albany: State University of New York Press.

Levy, A., and A. Weingrod, eds. 2005. *Homelands and Diasporas: Holy Lands and Other Places.* Stanford: Stanford University Press.

Levy, Shlomit, and L. Guttman. 1976. "Zionism and the Jewishness of Israelis." *Forum* 1:39–50.

Lewis, A. 1979a. "Education Policy and Social Inequality in Israel." *Jerusalem Quarterly* 10:101–11.

———. 1979b. *Power, Poverty and Education: An Ethnography of Schooling in an Israeli Town.* Ramat Gan, Israel: Turtledove.

Lewis, H. S. 1989. *After the Eagles Landed: The Yemenites of Israel.* Boulder, CO: Westview.

Lewis, J. D., and A. J. Weigart. 1985. "Trust as Social Reality." *Social Forces* 63:967–85.

Lewy, A., and M. Chen. 1974. *Closing or Widening of the Achievement Gap: A Comparison over Time of Ethnic Group Achievement in the Israeli Elementary School.* Tel Aviv: School of Education, Tel Aviv University.

Lieblich, A. 1983. "Between Strength and Toughness." In *Stress in Israel,* ed. S. Breznitz, 39–64. New York: Van Nostrand.

———. 1987. *Aviv shenot* [Spring of Their Years]. Jerusalem: Schocken.

———. 1989. *Transition to Adulthood during Military Service: The Israeli Case.* Albany: State University of New York Press.

Lieblich, A., and M. Perlow. 1988. "Transition to Adulthood during Military Service." *Jerusalem Quarterly* 47:40–76.

Liebman, C., and E. Don-Yehiya. 1983. *Civil Religion in Israel: Traditional Judaism and Political Culture in the Jewish State.* Berkeley: University of California Press.

Lifshitz, O. 1983. "Uncontrolled Power." *Hadaf Hayarok,* 6 June, 18 July, and 15 August.

———. 1990. "Thin Is Nice." *Al Hamishmar,* 11 March.

Lifton, R. J. 1973. *Home from the War: Vietnam Veterans—Neither Victims Nor Executioners.* New York: Touchstone.

———. 1979. *The Broken Connection: On Death and the Continuity of Life.* New York: Simon and Schuster.

Lincoln, B. 1989. *Discourse and the Construction of Society: Comparative Studies of Myth, Ritual and Classification.* New York: Oxford University Press.

Lipset, S. M., M. Trow, and J. S. Coleman. 1956. *Union Democracy.* Glencoe, IL: Free Press.

Lissak, M. 1969. *Social Mobility in Israeli Society.* Jerusalem: Israel University Press.

———. 1971. "The Israel Defence Forces as an Agent of Socialization: A Research in Expansion in a Democratic Society." In *The Perceived Role of the Military,* ed. M. R. Van Glis, 327–39. Rotterdam: Rotterdam University Press.

Littlewood, R. 1990. "From Categories to Contexts: A Decade of the New 'Cross-Cultural Psychiatry.'" *British Journal of Psychiatry* 156:308–27.

Livav, A. 1980. *Abu-Hilmi rotse otonomyah* [Abu Hilmi Wants Autonomy]. *Ma'ariv,* 27 June, pp. 1–4.

Lomsky-Feder, E. 1994. "Patterns of Participation in War and the Constructions of War in the Life-Course." Ph.D. diss., Hebrew University of Jerusalem.

Lomsky-Feder, E., and E. Ben-Ari. 2000. *The Military and Militarism in Israeli Society.* Albany: State University of New York Press.

Looz, E. 1982. "Spiritual Leadership in the Kibbutz Community." In *Jewish Spiritual Leadership in Our Time,* ed. E. Belfer, 213–21. Jerusalem: Dvir.

Lorenz, E. 1988. "Neither Friends nor Strangers: Informal Networks of Subcontracting in French Industry." In *Trust,* ed. D. Gambetta. Cambridge: Cambridge University Press.

Lugo, A. 1997. "Reflections on Border Theory, Culture, and the Nation." In *Border Theory: The Limits of Cultural Politics,* ed. S. Michaelson and D. E. Johnson, 43–67. Minneapolis: University of Minnesota Press.

Luhmann, N. 1979. *Trust and Power.* Chichester: Wiley.

———. 1988. "Familiarity, Confidence, Trust." In *Trust,* ed. D. Gambetta. Cambridge: Cambridge University Press.

Lustick, I. 1980. *Arabs in the Jewish State: Israel's Control of a National Minority.* Austin: University of Texas Press.

Luthans, F. 1988. "Successful versus Effective Managers." *Academy of Management Executive* 2:127–32.

Lynd, Staughton, Sam Bahour, and Alice Lynd, eds. 1994. *Homeland: Oral Histories of Palestine and Palestinians.* New York: Olive Branch Press.

Maccoby, M. 1976. *The Gamesman.* New York: Simon and Schuster.

MacCormack, C., and M. Strathern, eds. 1980. *Nature, Culture and Gender.* Cambridge: Cambridge University Press.

Macleod, A. E. 1992. "Hegemonic Relations and Gender Resistance: The New Veiling as Accommodating Protest in Cairo." *Signs* 17(3):533–57.

Maher, V. 1974. *Women and Property in Morocco.* Cambridge: Cambridge University Press.

Mainwaring, S. 1990. "Presidentialism in Latin America." *Latin American Research Review* 25:157–79.

Majalli, N. 1990. "Yawm al-ard 1990." *Al-Itthihad,* 23 March, pp. 6–7.

Makhlouf, C. 1979. *Changing Veils: Women and Modernization in North Yemen.* Austin: University of Texas Press.

Malinowski, B. 1948. *Magic, Science and Religion.* New York: Free Press.

Malka, E. 1946. *Essai d'ethnographie traditionnelle des mellahs.* Rabat: Imprimerie Omnia.

Manna', 'A., and K. Haj-Yehia. 1995. *Mabruk: Tarbut hahatuna ha'arvit Beyisrael* [The Culture of the Arab Wedding in Israel]. Ra'anana: Institute for Israeli Arab Studies.

March, J. G., and J. P. Olsen. 1989. *Rediscovering Institutions.* New York: Free Press.

Maron, S. 1997. *The Kibbutz Population, 1990–1995.* Ramat Efal: Yad Tabenkin.

Mars, L. 1980a. "Leadership and Power among Ashdod Port Workers." In *A Composite Portrait of Israel,* ed. E. Marx, 81–112. London: Academic Press.

———. 1980b. *The Village and the State: Administration, Ethnicity and Politics in an Israeli Co-Operative Village.* Westmead, UK: Gower.

Martin, J. 1992. *Cultures and Organizations.* New York: Oxford University Press.

Marty, M. E., and S. R. Appleby, eds. 1993. *Fundamentalism Project.* 2 vols. Chicago: University of Chicago Press.

Marx, E. 1967. *Bedouin of the Negev.* Manchester: Manchester University Press.

———. 1976. *The Social Context of Violent Behaviour: A Social Anthropological Study in an Israeli Immigrant Town.* London: Routledge and Kegan Paul.

———. 1977. "Communal and Individual Pilgrimage: The Region of Saints' Tombs in South Sinai." In *Regional Cults,* ed. R. P. Werbner, 29–51. London: Academic Press.

———. 1979. Foreword to *Power, Poverty and Education: An Ethnography of Schooling in an Israeli Town,* by A. Lewis. Ramat Gan: Turtledove.

———, ed. 1980a. *A Composite Portrait of Israel.* London: Academic Press.

———. 1980b. *Halifin vehagigot brit mila etzel beduei hanegev* [Exchange and Circumcision Celebrations among Negev Bedouin]. In *Readings in Social Anthropology,* ed. M. Shokeid, E. Marx, and S. Deshen, 29–37. Jerusalem: Schocken.

———. 1980c. "On the Anthropological Study of Nations." In *A Composite Portrait of Israel,* ed. E. Marx, 15–28. London: Academic Press.

———. 1987a. "Labour Migrants with a Secure Base: Bedouin of South Sinai." In *Migrants, Workers, and the Social Order,* ed. J. Eades, 148–64. London: Tavistock.

———. 1987b. "Relations between Spouses among the Negev Bedouin." *Ethnos* 52(1–2):156–79.

———. 1990. "Advocacy in a Bedouin Resettlement Project in the Negev, Israel." In *Anthropology and Development in North Africa and the Middle East,* ed. M. Salem-Murdock and M. M. Horowitz, 228–44. Boulder, CO: Westview.

———. 2000. "Land and Work: Negev Bedouin Struggle with Israeli Bureaucracies." *Nomadic Peoples* 4(2):106–21.

Marx, E., and A. Shmueli, eds. 1984. *The Changing Bedouin.* New Brunswick, NJ: Transaction.

Matras, H., and Y. Mazor. 1999. "The Transformation of Zalman Schneur's Poem 'Yad 'anuga' into a Popular Song." *Jerusalem Studies in Folklore* 19–20:431–59.

Matras, J. 1965. *Social Change in Israel.* Chicago: Aldine.

Matras, J., and D. Weintraub. 1977. *Ethnic and Other Primordial Differentials in Intergenerational Mobility in Israel.* Jerusalem: Brookdale Institute.

Matthiasson, C. J. 1974. *Many Sisters: Women in Cross-Cultural Perspective.* Riverside, NJ: Free Press.

Mauss, M. 1954. *The Gift.* Glencoe, IL: Free Press.

Mayer, J. P. 1944. *Max Weber and German Politics: A Study in Political Sociology.* London: Faber and Faber.

Mazumdar, V., ed. 1977. *Role of Rural Women in Development: Report of an International Seminar Held at the Institute of Development Studies.* Bombay, Delhi, and Calcutta: Allied Publishers.

McCorkle, L. W. 1970. "Guard-Inmate Relationships." In *The Sociology of Punishment and Correction,* ed. N. Johnston et al. New York: Wiley.

McDonald, J. G. 1951. *My Mission in Israel.* New York: Simon and Schuster.

McGilvray, D. B. 1982. "Sexual Power and Fertility in Sri Lanka: Batticaloa Tamils and Moors." In *Ethnography of Fertility and Birth,* ed. C. P. MacCormack. London: Academic Press.

Mcintosh, M. 1978. "The State and the Oppression of Women." In *Feminism and Materialism: Women and Modes of Production,* ed. A. Kuhn and A. Wolpe. London: Routledge and Kegan Paul.

Mead, M. 1956. "Tamtzit hanekudot midin weheshbon 'al bikur beyisrael, yuli 1956" [Essence of the Points from the Report of My Visit to Israel, July 1956]. Unpublished Report.

Mechling, J. 1980. "The Magic of the Boy Scout Campfire." *Journal of American Folklore* 93:35–56.

———. 1993. "On Sharing Folklore and American Identity in a Multicultural Society." *Western Folklore* 52:271–89.

Meggitt, M. 1968. "Uses of Literacy in New Guinea and Melanesia." In *Literacy in Traditional Societies,* ed. J. Goody, 298–309. Cambridge: Cambridge University Press.

Meghdessian, S. R. 1980. *The Status of the Arab Woman: A Select Bibliography.* Westport, CT: Greenwood.

Meijers, D. 1986. *Hasidic Groups and Other Religious Collectives in Orthodox Judaism.* Amsterdam: Free University Press.

Meir, A. 1997. *As Nomadism Ends: The Israeli Bedouin of the Negev.* Boulder, CO: Westview.

Memmi, A. 1973. *Portrait du colonisé.* Paris: Payot.

———. 1975. *Jews and Arabs.* Chicago: J. Philip O'Hara.

Mernissi, F. 1975. *Beyond the Veil: Male-Female Dynamics in a Modern Muslim Society.* New York: Schenkman.

———. 1976. "The Moslem World: Women Excluded from Development." In *Women and World Development,* ed. I. Tinker and M. Bo. Washington, DC: Overseas Development Council.

———. 1977. "Women, Saints and Sanctuaries." *Signs* 3:101–12.

———. 1995. *Dreams of Trespass: Tales of a Harem Girlhood.* Reading, MA: Addison-Wesley.

Meron, D. 1992. *Mul ha'ah hashoteik* [Facing the Silent Brother]. Jerusalem: Keter.

Messing, S. D. 1982. *The Story of the Falashas.* New York: Balshon.

Meyer-Brodnitz, M. 1967. "Changes in the Physical Structure of the Arab Villages in Israel." Master's thesis, Technion-Israel Institute of Technology.

Michaelson, E. J., and W. Goldschmidt. 1971. "Female Roles and Male Dominance among Peasants." *Southwestern Journal of Anthropology* 27:330–52.

Michels, R. 1959 [1915]. *Political Parties.* New York: Dover.

Milgram, N. A. 1986. "An Attribution Analysis of War-Related Stress: Modes of Coping and Helping." In *Stress and Coping in Time,* ed. N. A. Milgram, 9–25. New York: Brunner/Mazel.

Miller, P. J., et al. 1990. "Narrative Practices and the Social Construction of Self in Childhood." *American Ethnologist* 17:292–311.

Miller, S. G. 1999. "Dhimma Reconsidered: Jews, Taxes, and Royal Authority in Nineteenth-Century Tangier." In *In the Shadow of the Sultan: Culture, Power and Politics in Morocco,* ed. R. Bourqia and S. G. Miller, 103–26. Cambridge, MA: Harvard University Press.

Mindel, N. 1973. *Rabbi Schneur Zalman of Liadi.* 2 vols. Brooklyn: Kehot Publication Society.

Minkovich, A. 1969. *The Disadvantaged Child.* Jerusalem: Hebrew University and the Ministry of Education.

Minns, A., and N. Hijab. 1990. *Citizens Apart: A Portrait of Palestinians in Israel.* London: Tauris.

Mintz, A. 1984. "The Military Industrial Complex: The Israeli Case." In *Israeli Society and Its Defence Establishment,* ed. M. Lissak, 103–27. London: Cass.

Minuchin-Izigsohn, S. D., R. Ben-Shaul, A. Weingrod, and D. Krasilowski. 1984. "The Effect of Cultural Perceptions on Therapy: A Comparative Study of Patients in Israeli Psychiatric Clinics." *Culture, Medicine and Psychiatry* 8:229–54.

Mitchell, D., and L. Plotnicov. 1975. "The Lubavitch Movement: A Study in Context." *Urban Anthropology* 4:303–15.

Mittleman, R. 1987. "The Meknes Mellah and Casablancan Ville Nouvelle: A Comparative Study of Two Jewish Communities in Transformation." Ph.D. diss., Department of Anthropology, Temple University.

Modell, J., and T. Haggerty. 1991. "The Social Impact of War." *Annual Review of Sociology* 17:205–24.

Moghadam, V. 1993a. *Gender and National Identity: Women and Politics in Muslim Societies.* London: Zed Books.

———. 1993b. *Modernizing Women: Gender and Social Change in the Middle East.* Boulder, CO: Rienner.

———. 1994. "Introduction: Women and Identity Politics in Theoretical and Comparative Perspective." In *Identity Politics and Women,* ed. V. M. Moghadam, 3–26. Boulder, CO: Westview.

Mohanty, C. 1988. "Under Western Eyes: Feminist Scholarship and Colonial Discourses." *Feminist Review* 30:61–88.

Moldavski, E. 1983. "Patterns of Exchange and Gifts on Conditions of Change and Continuity: Between Tradition and Progress among the Community of Georgian Jews in Their Country of Origin and after Immigration to Israel." Master's thesis, Haifa University.

Moldenke, H. N., and A. L. Moldenke. 1952. *Plants of the Bible.* New York: Ronald Press.

Montee, B. B., R. G. Miltenberger, and D. Wittrock. 1995. "An Experimental Analysis of Facilitated Communication." *Journal of Applied Behavior Analysis* 28(2):180–200.

Moore, H. 1988. *Feminism and Anthropology.* Minneapolis: University of Minnesota Press.

Moore, S., B. Donovan, and A. Hudson. 1993. "Brief Report: Facilitator-Suggested Conversational Evaluation of Facilitated Communication." *Journal of Autism and Development Disorders* 23(3):541–52.

Moore, S., B. Donovan, A. Hudson, J. Dixtra, and J. Lawrence. 1993. "Brief Report: Evaluation of Eight Case Studies of Facilitated Communication." *Journal of Autism and Development Disorders* 23(3): 531–39.

Morgan, G. 1986. *Images of Organization.* Beverly Hills, CA: Sage.

Morgenstern, J. 1966. *Rites of Birth, Marriage, Death and Kindred Occasions among the Semites.* Chicago: Quadrangle Books.

Morris, B. 1989. *The Birth of the Palestinian Refugee Problem, 1947–1949.* Cambridge: Cambridge University Press.

Morsy, S. 1978. "Sex Differences and Folk Illness in an Egyptian Village." In *Women in the Muslim World,* ed. L. Beck and N. Keddie, 599–616. Cambridge, MA: Harvard University Press.

———. 1982. "Childbirth in an Egyptian Village." In *Anthropology of Human Birth*, ed. M. A. Kay, 147–74. Philadelphia: F. A. Davis.

Moskos, C. C., Jr. 1975. "The American Combat Soldier in Vietnam." *Journal of Social Issues* 31(4):25–38.

Mosse, G. L. 1990. *Fallen Soldiers: Reshaping the Memory of World Wars*. Oxford: Oxford University Press.

Mundi, P., and D. Adreon. 1994. "Commentary-Facilitated Communication: Attitudes, Effects and Theory." *Journal of Pediatric Psychology* 19(6):677–80.

Murray, D. 1977. "Ritual Communication: Some Considerations Regarding Meaning in Navajo Ceremonials." In *Symbolic Anthropology: A Reader in the Study of Symbols and Meanings*, ed. J. L. Dolgin, D. S. Kemnitzer, and D. M. Schneider, 195–220. New York: Columbia University Press.

Murray, G. W. 1935. *Sons of Ishmael: A Study of the Egyptian Bedouin*. London: Routledge.

Musgrove, F., and R. Middleton. 1981. "Rites of Passage and the Meaning of Age in Three Contrasted Social Groups: Professional Footballers, Teachers, and Methodist Ministers." *British Journal of Sociology* 32:39–55.

Musil, A. 1928. *The Manners and Customs of the Rwala Bedouins*. New York: American Geographical Society.

Myerhoff, B. G. 1980. "Life History among the Elderly: Performance, Visibility and Remembering." In *Life Course: Integrative Theories and Exemplary Population*. AAAS Selected Syposium 41, ed. K. W. Back. Boulder, CO: Westview.

———. 1984. "A Death in Due Time: Construction of Self and Culture in Ritual Drama." In *Rite, Drama, Festival, Spectacle: Rehearsals Toward a Theory of Cultural Performance*, ed. J. J. MacAloon. Philadelphia: Institute for the Study of Human Issues.

Myerhoff, B. G., and J. Ruby. 1982. Introduction to *A Crack in the Mirror: Reflective Perspectives in Anthropology*, ed. J. Ruby, 1–35. Philadelphia: University of Pennsylvania Press.

Nakhleh, K. 1977. "Anthropological and Sociological Studies on the Arabs in Israel: A Critique." *Journal of Palestine Studies* 6:41–70.

Naor, Y., ed. 1949. *Ha'eish* [The Fire]. Merhavia: Hashomer Hatzair Education Department.

Naroll, R. 1964. "On Ethnic Unit Classification." *Current Anthropology* 5:283–312.

Nash, D. 1970. *A Community in Limbo: An Anthropological Study of an American Community*. Bloomington: Indiana University Press.

Natanson, M. 1962. *Literature, Philosophy and the Social Sciences*. The Hague: Martinus Nijhoff.

National Insurance Institute of Israel. 1996. *Israel National Report, 1995*. Jerusalem: Ministry of Labor and Social Affairs, National Insurance Institute.

Natur, S. 1980. "Wa-ma nasina Ayn Hawd" [And We Have Not Forgotten Ein Houd]. *Al-Jadid* 6:14–16.

Nazzal, Nafez Abdullah. 1974. "The Zionist Occupation of Western Galilee, 1948." *Journal of Palestine Studies* 3(3):58–76.

Near, H. 1992. *The Kibbutz Movement: A History*. Vol. 1. New York: Oxford University Press.

———. 1997. *The Kibbutz Movement: A History*. Vol. 2. London: Littman Library.

Neitz, M. 1987. *Charisma and Community: A Study of Religious Commitment within the Charismatic Renewal*. New Brunswick, NJ: Transaction.

Nelson, C. 1974. "Public and Private Politics: Women in the Middle Eastern World." *American Ethnologist* 1:551–63.

Neusner, J. 1974. "Death in Jerusalem." In *Jewish Perspectives on Death,* ed. J. Reler. New York: Schocken.

Nevo, O. 1987. "Irrational Expectations in Career Counseling and Their Confronting." *Career Development Quarterly* 35:239–50.

Nig'al, G. 1983. *Sipurei dibbuk besifrut yisra'el* [Dybbuk Tales in Jewish Literature]. Jerusalem: Rubin Mass.

Niv, A., and D. Bar-On. 1992. *The Dilemma of Size from a System Learning Perspective: The Case of the Kibbutz.* Greenwich, CT: JAI Press.

Nordau, M. 1916. Introduction to *Zionism: Problems and Views,* ed. P. Goodman and A. D. Lewis. London: T. Fisher Unwin.

Norman, K. 1991. *A Sound Family Makes a Sound State: Ideology and Upbringing in a German Village.* Stockholm: Department of Social Anthropology, University of Stockholm.

Nudelman, A. 1997. "Beri'ut weholi batefisa hatarbutit shel no'ar 'ole mi'etiopia" [Health and Illness in the Cultural Perception of Ethiopian Immigrant Youths]. In *Shoresh ehad we'anafim rabim,* ed. E. 'Amir, A. Zehavi, and R. Pragay, 99–121. Jerusalem: Magnes Press.

Nunn, M. K., ed. 1993. *Creative Resistance: Anecdotes of Nonviolent Action by Israeli-Based Groups.* Jerusalem: Alternative Information Center.

Nutini, H. 1965. "Some Considerations on the Nature of Social Structure and Model Building: A Critique of Claude Lévi-Strauss and Edmund Leach." *American Anthropologist* 67(3):707–31.

Obeyesekere, G. 1978. "The Fire-Walkers of Kataragama: The Rise of Bhakti Religiosity in Buddhist Sri Lanka." *Journal of Asian Studies* 37:457–76.

———. 1981. *Medusa's Hair.* Chicago: University of Chicago Press.

———. 1990. *The Work of Culture.* Chicago: University of Chicago Press.

Oded, Y. 1964. "Land Losses among Israel's Arab Villages." *New Outlook* 7(7):10–25.

Ofer, N. 1993. "Open House." *New Outlook* 36(1):48–49.

Ofrat, G. 1991. "The Fading of the Khaki." *Studio* 27:6–11.

Ogien, R. 1980. "A Slum Area in Tel Aviv." In *A Composite Portrait of Israel,* ed. E. Marx, 211–38. London: Academic Press.

Olin, U. 1980. *Rural Women's Participation in Development: Evaluation Study No. 3.* New York: United Nations Development Program.

Ong, W. 1982. *Orality and Literacy.* London: Methuen.

Oppenheimer, J. 1985. "The Druze in Israel as Arabs and Non-Arabs: Manipulation of Categories of Identity in a Non-Civil State." In *Studies in Israeli Ethnicity: After the Ingathering,* ed. A. Weingrod, 259–79. New York: Gordon and Breach.

Oring, E. 1981. *Israeli Humor: The Content and Structure of the Chizbat of the Palmah.* Albany: State University of New York Press.

Orlick, T. 1978. *Winning through Cooperation.* Washington, DC: Hawkins and Associates.

Ortar, G. 1953. "A Comparative Analysis of the Structure of Intelligence in Various Ethnic Groups." In *Between Past and Future: Essays and Studies of Aspects of Immigrant Absorption in Israel,* ed. C. Frankenstein, 267–90. Jerusalem: Szold Foundation.

Ortiz, S. 1979. "Labour and Value among Paez Farmers." In *Social Anthropology of Work,* ed. S. Wallman, 207–8. London: Academic Press.

Ortner, S. 1973. "On Key Symbols." *American Anthropologist* 75:1338–46.

———. 1974. "Is Female to Male as Nature Is to Culture?" In *Women, Culture and Society,* ed. M. Rosaldo and L. Lamphere. Stanford: Stanford University Press.

Ostor, A. 1984. "Chronology, Category, and Ritual." In *Age and Anthropological Theory,* ed. D. I. Kertzer and J. Keith. Ithaca: Cornell University Press.

Pagis, D. 1986. *'Al sod hatum* [On a Sealed Secret]. Jerusalem: Magnes Press.

Paige, K., and J. Paige. 1981. *Politics of Reproductive Ritual.* Berkeley: University of California Press.

Paine, R. 1983. "Israel and Totemic Time." *Royal Anthropological Institute Newsletter* 5:19–22.

———. 1992. "Anthropology beyond Routine: Cultural Alternatives for the Handling of the Unexpected." *Journal of Moral and Social Studies* 7(3):183–203.

Palgi, P. 1963. "Immigrants, Psychiatrists and Culture." *Israel Annals of Psychiatry and Related Disciplines* 1:43–58.

Palgi, P., and H. Abramovitch. 1984. "Death: A Cross-Cultural Perspective." *Annual Review of Anthropology* 13:385–417.

Palumbo, Michael. 1987. *The Palestinian Catastrophe: The 1948 Expulsion of a People from Their Homeland.* London: Quartet.

Pandolfo, S. 1989. "Detours of Life: Space and Bodies in a Moroccan Village." *American Ethnologist* 16:3–24.

Panoff, M. 1970. "Marcel Mauss's *The Gift Revisited.*" *Man* 5:60–70.

Papanek, H. 1973. "Purdah, Separate Worlds and Symbolic Shelter." *Comparative Studies in Society and History* 15:298–323.

Parizot, C. 1999. "Enjeux tribaux et élections nationales en Israël: Les élections du 29 mai 1996 chez les Bédouins du Néguev." *REMM* 85–86:237–58.

Parkinson, C. N. 1957. *Parkinson's Law and Other Studies in Administration.* Boston: Houghton Mifflin.

Parsons, T. 1939. "The Professional and the Social Structure." *Social Forces* 17:457–67.

———. 1959. "The School Class as a Social System." *Harvard Educational Review* 29:297–318.

———. 1969. *Political and Social Structure.* New York: Free Press.

Pascon, P., and D. Schroeter. 1982. "Le cimetière juif d'Iligh (1751–1955): Étude des épitaphes comme documents d'histoire sociale (Tazerwalt, Sud-Ouest Marocain)." *Revue de l'Occident Musulman et de la Méditerranée* 34(1):34–67.

Patai, R. 1947a. *On Culture Contact and Its Working in Modern Palestine.* Memoir No. 67. Menasha, WI: American Anthropological Association.

———. 1947b. *Mavo le'antropologia* [Introduction to Anthropology]. Tel Aviv: Yavne.

———. 1970. *Israel between East and West.* Westport, CT: Greenwood.

———. 1971. *Society, Culture, and Change in the Middle East.* Philadelphia: University of Pennsylvania Press.

———. 1983. *The Arab Mind.* New York: Scribner.

———. 1988. *Apprentice in Budapest: Memories of a World That Is No More.* Salt Lake City: University of Utah Press.

Pattie, S. P. 1997. *Faith in History: Armenians Rebuilding Community.* Washington, DC: Smithsonian Institution Press.

Pavin, A. 1994. *Haye'utz ha'irguni bakibbutz* [Organizational Consultants in the Kibbutz]. Ramat Efal: Yad Tabenkin.

Peacock, J. 1975. "Units of Consciousness: Symbols." In *Consciousness and Change.* New York: Wiley.

Peirce, C. S. 1955. *Philosophical Writings.* Ed. J. Buchler. New York: Dover.

Pels, P., and L. Nancel. 1991. "Introduction: Critique and the Deconstruction of Anthropological Authority." In *Constructing Knowledge,* ed. P. Pels and L. Nancel, 1–22. London: Sage.

Peres, Y. 1971a. "Ethnic Relations in Israel." *American Journal of Sociology* 76:1021–47.

———. 1971b. "Modernization and Nationalism in the Identity of the Israeli Arabs." *Middle East Journal* 24(4):479–92.

Peres, Y., and Z. Levy. 1969. "Jews and Arabs: Ethnic Group Stereotypes in Israel." *Race* 10(4):479–92.

Peretz, D. 1958. *Israel and the Palestine Arabs.* Washington, DC: Middle East Institute.

Peters, E. L. 1990. *The Bedouin of Cyrenaica.* Cambridge: Cambridge University Press.

Peters, T., and N. Austin. 1986. *A Passion for Excellence.* London: Fontana.

"Photo Exhibition in Haifa: 'The Forgotten.'" 1993. *Arabs in Israel* 3(2):8.

Piaget, J. 1969. *The Child's Conception of Time.* New York: Basic Books.

Pilssbury, B. 1982. "Doing the Month: Confinement and Convalescence of Chinese Women after Childbirth." *Social Science and Medicine* 12:11–22.

Pinkley, R. L. 1990. "Dimensions of Conflict Frame: Disputant Interpretations of Conflict." *Journal of Applied Psychology* 75:117–26.

Piore, M. J. 1979. *Birds of Passage: Migrant Labor and Industrial Societies.* Cambridge: Cambridge University Press.

Pisharoty, P. R. 1993. "Notes from Kerala." *Honey Bee* 4(4):12.

Pitt-Rivers, J. 1977. *The Fate of Shechem or the Politics of Sex.* Cambridge: Cambridge University Press.

Plascov, A. 1981. *The Palestinian Refugees in Jordan, 1948–57.* London: Frank Cass.

Plessner, H. 1970. *Laughing and Crying: A Study of the Limits of Human Behavior.* Evanston, IL: Northwestern University Press.

Plimpton, G. 1984. *Fireworks: A History and Celebration.* New York: Doubleday.

Polany, K. 1957. *The Great Transformation.* Boston: Beacon Press.

Preuss, J. 1978. *Biblical and Talmudic Medicine.* Trans. F. Rosner. New York: Hebrew Publishing Company.

Prior, M., and R. Cummins. 1992. "Questions about Facilitated Communication and Autism." *Journal of Autism and Development Disorder* 22(2):331–36.

Putnam, F. W. 1989. *The Diagnosis and Treatment of Multiple Personality.* New York: Guilford.

Qleibo, A. H. 1992. *Before the Mountains Disappear: An Ethnographic Chronicle of the Modern Palestinians.* Cairo: Ahram Press.

Quinn, N. 1977. "Anthropological Studies on Women's Status." *Annual Review of Anthropology* 6:181–225.

Rabinow, P. 1975. *Symbolic Domination: Cultural Form and Historical Change in Morocco.* Chicago: University of Chicago Press.

———. 1989. *French Modern: Norms and Forms of the Social Environment.* Chicago: University of Chicago Press.

Rabinowitz, D. 1992. "Trust and the Attribution of Rationality: Inverted Roles amongst Palestinian Arabs and Jews in Israel." *Man* 27(3):517–37.

———. 1997. *Overlooking Nazareth: The Ethnography of Exclusion in Galilee.* Cambridge: Cambridge University Press.

———. 1998. *Antropologia wehapalestinim* [Anthropology and the Palestinians]. Ra'anana: Institute for Israeli Arab Studies.

Rabinowitz, E., ed. 1958. *Hagim umo'adim behinuch* [Holidays and Times in Education]. Tel Aviv: Urim.

Radner, J., and S. Lasner. 1993. "Strategies of Coding in Women's Cultures." *In Feminist Messages: Coding in Women's Folk Culture,* ed. J. Radner, 1–30. Urbana: University of Illinois Press.

Rahat Municipality. 1997. *Seker Toshavim* [Survey of Inhabitants (of Rahat)], by R. Yisraeli. Tel Aviv: Al-Midan.

Ram, U. 1989. "Civic Discourse in Israeli Sociological Thought." *International Journal of Politics, Culture and Society* 3(2):255–73.

Raphael, D. 1975. *Being Female: Reproduction, Power and Change.* The Hague: Mouton.

Rapoport, L. 1983. *The Lost Jews: Last of the Ethiopian Falashas.* New-York: Balshon.

Rapoport, T., and E. Lomsky-Feder. 1994. "Israel." In *International Handbook of Adolescence,* ed. K. Hurrelman, 207–23. Westport, CT: Greenwood.

Rapp, R. 1979. "Anthropology." *Signs* 5:497–513.

Rappaport, R. 1979a. *Ecology, Meaning and Religion.* Richmond, CA: North Atlantic Books.

———. 1979b. "The Obvious Aspects of Ritual." In *Ecology, Meaning and Religion,* ed. R. Rappaport, 173–221. Richmond, CA: North Atlantic Books.

Ravicz, M. E. 1980. "Ephemeral Art: A Case for the Functions of Aesthetic Stimuli." *Semiotica* 30:115–34.

Ravid, M. 1999. *Tochnit mit'ar Rahat, 11* [Rahat Trace Plan, 11]. Ramat Gan: Ravid.

Ravid, S. 1992. *Ha'im 'over hakibbutz shinui 'erki* [The Kibbutz's Process of Change]. Ramat Efal: Yad Tabenkin.

Ravitzky, A. 1993. *Hakeitz hameguleh umedinat hayehudim* [Messianic Zionism and Jewish Religious Radicalism]. Tel Aviv: Am Oved.

Redfield, R. 1953. *The Primitive World and Its Transformations.* Ithaca: Cornell University Press.

Reese, H. W., and K. A. McCluskey. 1984. "Dimensions of Historical Constancy and Change." In *Life-Span Developmental Psychology,* ed. H. W. Reese and K. A. McCluskey, 17–45. New York: Academic Press.

Reichheld, F. F. 1996. *The Loyalty Effect: The Hidden Force behind Growth, Profits and Lasting Value.* Boston: Harvard Business School Press.

Rein, M. 1985. "Women, Employment and Social Welfare." In *The Future of Welfare,* ed. R. Klein and M. O'Higgins. Oxford: Blackwell.

Reinharz, S. 1992. *Feminist Methods in Social Research.* New York: Oxford University Press.

Reiss, A. J., Jr. 1971. *The Police and the Public.* New Haven: Yale University Press.

Reiss, N. 1991. *The Health Care of Arabs in Israel.* Boulder, CO: Westview.

Reiter, R. 1975. *Toward an Anthropology of Women.* New York: Monthly Review Press.

Rekhess, R. 1981. "Arviyei yisra'el" [Israeli Arabs]. In *Ehad mi-kol shishah yisre'elim* [Every Sixth Israeli], ed. A. Hareven. Jerusalem: Van Leer Institute, 1981.

Richardson, F. M. 1978. *Fighting Spirit: A Study of Psychological Factors in War.* London: Leo Cooper.

Riker, W. H. 1974. "The Nature of Trust." In *Perspectives in Social Power,* ed. J. T. Tedeschi. Chicago: Aldine.

Riley, M. W., and J. Waring. 1976. "Age and Aging." In *Contemporary Social Problems,* ed. R. K. Merton and R. Nisbet, 385–410. New York: Harcourt Brace Jovanovich.

Ring, P. S., and A. Van de Ven. 1992. "Structuring Cooperative Relationships between Organizations." *Strategic Management Journal* 13:483–98.

Ringel-Hofman, A. 1988. "28 Years of Singular Rule." *Yediot Acharonot,* 29 July.

Rizzi, B. 1985 [1939]. *The Bureaucratization of the World.* London: Tavistock.

Robin, E. 1972. "Attitudes, Stereotypes and Prejudices among Arabs and Jews in Israel." *New Outlook* 15(9):3–17.

Rodinson, M. 1973. *Israel: A Colonial-Settler State?* Trans. D. Thorstad. New York: Monad Press.

Rogers, S. C. 1975. "Female Forms of Power and the Myth of Male Dominance: Models of Female/Male Interaction in Peasant Society." *American Ethnologist* 2:721–56.

———. 1978. "Women's Place: A Critical Review of Anthropological Theory." *Comparative Studies in Society and History* 20(1):123–62.

Rohlen, T. P. 1974. *For Harmony and Strength.* Berkeley: University of California Press.

Roniger, L. 1990. *Hierarchy and Trust in Modern Mexico and Brazil.* New York: Praeger.

Roniger, L., and M. Feige. 1992. "From Pioneer to Freier: The Changing Models of Generalized Exchange in Israel." *Archives Européennes de Sociologie* 33(1):280–307.

———. 1995. "The Culture of the Freier and Israeli Identity." *Alpayim* 7:116–36.

Rosaldo, M. 1974. "Women, Culture and Society: A Theoretical Overview." In *Women, Culture and Society,* ed. M. Rosaldo and L. Lamphere. Stanford: Stanford University Press.

Rosaldo, M., and L. Lamphere, eds. 1974. *Women, Culture and Society.* Stanford: Stanford University Press.

Rosaldo, R. 1987. "Where Objectivity Lies: The Rhetoric of Anthropology." In *The Rhetoric of the Human Sciences,* ed. J. Nelson, 87–109. Madison: University of Wisconsin Press.

———. 1989. *Culture and Truth: The Remaking of Social Analysis.* London: Routledge.

Rosen, C. 1985. "Core Symbols of Ethiopian Identity and Their Role in Understanding the Beta Israel Today." *Israel Social Science Research* 3(1–2):55–62.

Rosen, L. 1968. "A Moroccan Jewish Community during a Middle-Eastern Crisis." *American Scholar* 37(3):435–51.

———. 1972. "Muslim-Jewish Relations in a Moroccan City." *International Journal of Middle East Studies* 3:435–49.

———. 1984. *Bargaining for Reality: The Construction of Social Relations in a Muslim Community.* Chicago: University of Chicago Press.

Rosen (Wasserfall), R. 1981. "Female Symbolism or the Women in the Judeo-Moroccan Representational System on a Moshav in Israel." Master's thesis, Hebrew University of Jerusalem.

Rosenblatt, P. C., R. P. Walsh, and D. A. Jackson. 1976. *Grief and Mourning in Cross-Cultural Perspective.* New Haven: Human Relations Area Files Press.

Rosenfeld, E. 1951. "Social Stratification in a 'Classless' Society." *American Sociological Review* 16:766–74.

Rosenfeld, H. 1958. "Processes of Structural Change within the Arab Village Family." *American Anthropologist* 60(6):1127–39.

———. 1960. "On the Determinants of the Status of Arab Village Women." *Man* 60:66–70.

———. 1964a. "From Peasantry to Wage Labor and Residual Peasantry: The Transformation of an Arab Village." In *Process and Pattern in Culture,* ed. R. A. Manners, 211–34. Chicago: Aldine.

———. 1964b. *Hem hayu fallahim* [They Were Peasants]. Tel Aviv: Hakibbutz Hameuhad.

———. 1968. "Change, Barriers to Change, and Contradictions in the Arab Village Family." *American Anthropologist* 70(4):732–52.

———. 1975. "Non-Hierarchical, Hierarchical and Masked Reciprocity in the Arab Village." In *Being Female,* ed. D. Raphael, 112–19. The Hague: Mouton.

———. 1978. "The Class Situation of the Arab National Minority in Israel." *Comparative Studies in Society and History* 20(3):374–407.

———. 1980. "Men and Women in Arab Peasant to Proletariat Transformation." In *Theory and Practice,* ed. S. Diamond, 195–219. The Hague: Mouton.

———. 1988. "Nazareth and Upper Nazareth in the Political Economy of Israel." In *Arab-Jewish Relations in Israel,* ed. J. Hofman, 45–66. Bristol, IN: Wyndham Hall.

Rosenfeld, H., and S. Carmi. 1976. "The Privatization of Public Means, the State-Made Middle-Class, and the Realization of Family Value in Israel." In *Kinship and Modernization in Mediterranean Society,* ed. J. G. Peristiany, 131–59. Rome: American Field Staff.

Rosenfeld, M. 2004. *Confronting the Occupation: Work, Education, and Political Activism of Palestinian Families in a Refugee Camp.* Stanford: Stanford University Press.

Rosner, M. 1992. *Kibbutz Work.* Tel Aviv: Open University Press.

———. 1993. "Organizations between Community and Market: The Case of the Kibbutz." *Economic and Industrial Democracy* 14:369–97.

Rosolio, D. 1993. *Hashinium bakibbutz weheker hakibbutz* [A Study of a Kibbutz in the Process of Change]. Ramat Efal: Yad Tabenkin.

———. 1999. *Hashita wehamashber* [The System and the Crisis]. Tel Aviv: Am Oved.

Rotem, Z. 1988. "The Military Production Function and Trends in the Israeli-Arab Military Balance Throughout 1950–1986." *Economic Quarterly* 38(138):289–304.

Rouhana, N. 1986. "Collective Identity and Arab Voting Patterns." In *Elections in Israel—1984,* ed. A. Arian and M. Shamir, 121–49. New Brunswick, NJ: Transaction.

Routh, D. K. 1994. "Commentary: Facilitated Communication as Unwitting Ventriloquism." *Journal of Pediatric Psychology* 19(6):673–75.

Rubenstein, A. 1984. *The Zionist Dream Revisited.* New York: Schocken.

Rubin, N. 1995. *Reishit hahayim: Tiksei leida, mila ufidion haben bimekorot hazal* [The Beginning of Life: Rites of Birth, Circumcision and Redemption of the First-Born in the Talmud and Midrash]. Tel Aviv: Hakibbutz Hameuhad.

Ruddick, S. 1989. *Maternal Thinking.* New York: Ballantine.

Rudey, J. 1971. "Dynamics of Land Alienation." In *The Transformation of Palestine,* ed. I. Abu-Lughod. Evanston, IL: Northwestern University Press.

Rudge, D. 1986. "Ein Hud: Village under Siege." *Jerusalem Post,* 17 August, p. 4.

Ruppin, A. 1934. *Hasoziologia shel hayehudim* [Sociology of the Jews]. 2nd ed. Tel Aviv: Shtibel.

Russell, R. 1991. "The Role of Support Organizations in the Development of Cooperatives in Israel." *Economic and Industrial Democracy* 12:385–404.

Ryff, C. D. 1984. "Personality Development from the Inside: The Subjective Experience of Change in Adulthood and Aging." In *Life-Span Development and Behavior,* ed. P. B. Baltes and O. Brim, 243–79. New York: Academic Press.

Sabella, E. Z. 1971. "The Leading Palestinian Hamayil (Families) and Socio-Economic and Political Organization in Palestine (1917–1948)." Master's thesis, University of Virginia.

Sachar, H. M. 1976. *A History of Israel: From the Rise of Zionism to Our Time.* New York: Knopf.

Sachau, E. 1883. *Reise in Syrien und Mesopotamien.* Leipzig: Brockhaus.

Sadan, E., and D. Weintraub. 1980. "Ethnicity, Nativity, and Economic Performance of Cooperative Small-Holding Farms in Israel." *Economic Development and Cultural Change* 28(3):487.

Safran, W. 1991. "Diasporas in Modern Societies: Myths of Homeland and Return." *Diaspora* 1(1):83–99.

Sahlins, M. D. 1969. *Tribesmen.* Englewood Cliffs, NJ: Prentice-Hall.

Said, E. 1980. *The Question of Palestine.* London: Routledge and Kegan Paul.

Salamon, H. 1994. "Making a Point with Knives: Wedding Gifts and Intergroup Relations." In *New Trends in Ethiopian Studies,* ed. H. Marcus, 966–74. Tel Aviv: Red Sea Press.

———. 1999. *The Hyena People: Ethiopian Jews in Christian Ethiopia.* Berkeley: University of California Press.

Sanady, P. R. 1973. "Toward a Theory of the Status of Women." *American Anthropologist* 75:1682–1700.

———. 1974. "Female Status in the Public Domain." In *Women, Culture and Society,* ed. M. Rosaldo and L. Lamphere. Stanford: Stanford University Press.

Sandberg, N. C. 1974. *Ethnic Identity and Assimilation: The Polish-American Community.* New York: Praeger.

Sanjek, R. 1990. *Fieldnotes: The Makings of Anthropology.* Ithaca: Cornell University Press.

Sarbin, T. R. 1986. "The Narrative as a Root Metaphor for Psychology." In *Narrative Psychology,* ed. T. R. Sarbin, 3–21. New York: Praeger.

Sarsour, I. 1993. "From Mosque to Mall." *Challenge* 16:25.

Sasson-Levy, O. 1993. "A Case Study of Religious Women's Political Representation in Israel." Paper presented at the Annual Meeting of the Association for Israel Studies, Atlanta.

Sayigh, Rosemary. 1979. *Palestinians: From Peasants to Revolutionaries: A People's History.* London: Zed Press.

Schachter, H. L. 1972. "Educational Institutions and Political Coalitions: The Case of Israel." *Comparative Education Review* 16:462–73.

Schatzker, C. 1969. "The Jewish Youth Movement in Germany between the Years 1900–33." Ph.D. diss., Hebrew University of Jerusalem.

Schely-Newman, E. 1995. "Sweeter than Honey: Discourse of Reproduction among North-African Israeli Women." *Text and Performance Quarterly* 15(3):175–88.

———. 2002. *Our Lives Are But Stories: Narratives of Tunisian-Israeli Women.* Detroit: Wayne State University Press.

Scheper-Hughes, N., and M. Lock. 1986. "Speaking 'Truth' for Illness: Metaphors, Reifications, and a Pedagogy for Patients." *Medical Anthropology Quarterly* 17:137–40.

Schlegel, A. 1975. "Three Styles of Domestic Authority: A Cross-Cultural Study." In *Being Female,* ed. D. Raphael. The Hague: Mouton.

———, ed. 1977. *Sexual Stratification: A Cross-Cultural View.* New York: Columbia University Press.

Schneider, D. M. 1979. "Kinship, Community and Locality in American Culture." In *Kin and Communities,* ed. A. J. Lichtman and J. R. Challmore. Washington, DC: Smithsonian Institution.

———. 1980. *American Kinship: A Cultural Account.* 2nd ed. Chicago: University of Chicago Press.

Schneider, H. 1988. "Principles of Development: A View from Anthropology." In *Production and Autonomy: Anthropological Studies and Critiques of Development,* ed. J. Bennet and J. Bowen. Lanham, MD: University Press of America.

Schneider, J. 1971. "Of Vigilance and Virgins: Honor, Shame, and Access to Resources in Mediterranean Societies." *Ethnology* 19:1–24.

Schoenberger, M. 1975. "The Falashas of Ethiopia, an Ethnographic Study." Ph.D. diss., University of Cambridge.

Scholem, G. 1946. *Major Trends in Jewish Mysticism.* London: Thames and Hudson.

———. 1965a. *On the Kabbalah and Its Symbolism.* New York: Schocken.

———. 1965b. "Tradition and New Creation in the Ritual of Kaballah." In *On the Kabbalah and Its Symbolism.* New York: Schocken.

———. 1971a. *The Messianic Idea in Judaism.* New York: Schocken.

———. 1971b. "Gilgul." *Encyclopedia Judaica* 7:573–77.

Schubert, A. 1991. *Facilitated Communication Resource Guide.* Brookline: Adriana Foundation.

Schumaker, L. 2004. "The Director as Significant Other: Max Gluckman and Team Fieldwork at the Rhodes-Livingstone Institute." In *Significant Others: Interpersonal and Professional Commitments in Anthropology,* ed. R. Handler, 91–130. Madison: University of Wisconsin Press.

Schuman, H. 1982. "Free Will and Determination in Public Belief about Race." In *Majority and Minority: The Dynamics of Race and Ethnicity in American Life,* ed. N. R. Yetman and C. H. Steele. Boston: Allyn and Bacon.

Schutz, A. 1944a. "The Stranger." *American Journal of Sociology* 49(6):499–507.

———. 1944b. "The Homecomer." *American Journal of Sociology* 50(5):369–75.

———. 1970. *On Phenomenology and Social Relations.* Chicago: University of Chicago Press.

Schutz, A., and T. Luckmann. 1974. *The Structure of the Life-World.* London: Heinemann.

Schütze, F. 1992. "Pressure and Guilt: War Experiences of a Young German Soldier and Their Biographical Implications." *International Sociology* 7(2):187–207, 7(3):347–67.

Schwartz, B. 1970. "The Social Psychology of the Gift." *American Journal of Sociology* 73(1):1–11.

Schwartz, M., and D. Giladi. 1993. "25% Agriculturalists? Reality and Conceptions during the Formative Decade of Israeli Agriculture: 1949–1959." *Economic Quarterly* 40(3):391–414.

Seeman, D. 1996. "The Silence of Rayna Batya: Torah, Suffering, and Rabbi Baruch Epstein's 'Wisdom of Women.'" *Torah u-Madda Journal* 5:91–128.

Sefer Yetsira [Book of Creation]. 1962. Jerusalem: M. Atia.

Seger, K., ed. 1981. *Portrait of a Palestinian Village: The Photographs of Hilma Granqvist.* London: Third World Centre for Research and Publishing.

Segev, T. 1991. *Hamilyon hashevi'i* [The Seventh Million]. Jerusalem: Keter.

Selwyn, T. 1995. "Landscapes of Liberation and Imprisonment: Towards an Anthropology of the Israeli Landscape." In *The Anthropology of Landscape: Perspectives on Place and Space,* ed. E. Hirsch and M. O'Hanlon, 114–34. Oxford: Clarendon Press.

———, ed. 1996. *The Tourist Image: Myths and Myth Making in Tourism.* Chichester, UK: Wiley.

Selzer, M. 1967. *The Aryanization of the Jewish State.* New York: Black Star Publishing.

Semionov, M., and N. Lewin-Epstein. 1987. *Hewers of Wood and Drawers of Water: Noncitizen Arabs in the Israeli Labor Market.* Ithaca: ILR Press, Cornell University Press.

Semler, R. 1993. *Maverick.* New York: Warner.

Sered, S. S. 1992. *Women as Ritual Experts: The Religious Lives of Elderly Jewish Women in Jerusalem.* New York: Oxford University Press.

———. 2000. *What Makes Women Sick? Maternity, Modesty and Militarism in Israeli Society.* Hanover, NH: Brandeis University Press.

Sexton, L. 1987. "The Social Construction of Card Playing among the Daulo." *Oceania* 58(1):38–46.

Shabtai, M. 1999. *"Hachi ahi": Masa' hazeihut shel hayalim 'olim mietiopia* ["Best Brother": The Identity Journey of Ethiopian Immigrant Soldiers]. Tel Aviv: Tcherikover.

———. 2001. *Bein reggae lerap: Etgar hahishtaychut shel no'ar yotze Etiopia beyisra'el* [Between Reggae and Rap: The Integration Challenge of Ethiopian Youth in Israel]. Tel Aviv: Tcherikover.

Shaffir, W. 1974. *Life in a Religious Community.* Toronto: Holt, Reinhart and Winston.

Shahar, R. 1988. "Choice of Marriage Partners among Israeli Youth." Ph.D. diss., Bar Ilan University.

Shaked, G. 1983. *'Ein makom aher: 'Al sifrut wehevra* [No Other Place: On Literature and Society]. Tel Aviv: Hakibbutz Hameuhad.

———. 1988. "Three Authors on the War." Paper presented at the seminar "Reading War in Literature, Film and the Media." Open University and Tel Aviv University.

Shalli, S. M. 1963. *Sefer karmi sheli* [My Vineyard]. Jerusalem: N.p.

Shamgar-Handelman, L. 1981. "Administering to War Widows in Israel: The Birth of a Social Category." *Social Analysis* 9:24–47.

———. 1990. *Childhood as a Social Phenomenon: National Report—Israel.* Eurosocial Report 36/5. Vienna: European Centre Childhood Programme.

———. 1995. "Sociology of the Family in a Small Academic Community: Investigation of the Israeli Family." *Megamot* 1–2:136–66.

Shamgar-Handelman, L., and D. Handelman. 1986. "Holiday Celebrations in Israeli Kindergartens: Relationships between Representations of Collectivity and Family in the Nation-State." In *Education in Comparative Context,* ed. E. Krausz, 71–103. New Brunswick, NJ: Transaction.

———. 1991. "Celebrations of Bureaucracy: Birthday Parties in Israeli Kindergartens." *Ethnology* 30(4):293–312.

Shammas, A. 1983. "Diary." In *Every Sixth Israeli: Relations between the Jewish Majority and the Arab Minority in Israel,* ed. A. Hareven, 29–44. Jerusalem: Van Leer Institute.

Shapira, R. 1978–79. "Autonomy of Technostructure: An Interkibbutz Regional Organizational Case Study." *The Kibbutz* 6–7:276–303.

———. 1979. *'Avodat haverot bemif'alei fa'asia kibbutziim* [Women's Employment in the Kibbutz Industry]. Tel Aviv: Kibbutz Industry Association.

———. 1980. *The Absorption of Academics in Kibbutz Plants.* Tel Aviv: Kibbutz Industry Association.

———. 1987. *Anatomia shel holi nihuli* [Anatomy of Mismanagement]. Tel Aviv: Am Oved.

———. 1990. "'Automatic' Rotation and Organizational Conservatism in a Kibbutz." *Megamot* 32:522–36.

———. 1993. "Split Elites, Conflicts and Renewal Failure in a Large Veteran Kibbutz." *Kibbutz Trends* 11:55–57.

———. 1995a. "'Fresh Blood' Innovation and the Dilemma of Personal Involvement." *Creativity and Innovation Management* 4:86–99.

———. 1995b. "The Voluntary Resignation of Outsider Managers: Interkibbutz Rotation and Michels' 'Iron Law.'" *Israel Social Science Research* 10:59–84.

———. 2008. *Transforming Kibbutz Research: Trust and Moral Leadership in the Rise and Decline of Democratic Cultures.* Cleveland: New World Publishing.

Shapira, R., and H. Herzog. 1984. "Understanding Youth Culture through Autograph Books: The Israeli Case." *Journal of American Folklore* 97(386):442–60.

Shapira, R., and R. Peleg. 1984. "From Blue Shirt to White Collar." *Youth and Society* 16:195–216.

Shapiro, S. P. 1987. "The Social Control of Impersonal Trust." *American Journal of Sociology* 93(3):623–58.

Shapiro, Y. 1976. *The Formative Years of the Israeli Labor Party.* London: Sage.

Sharma, U. M. 1978. "Women and Their Affines: The Veil as a Symbol of Separation." *Man* 13:218–33.

Sharni, S. 1974. *Characteristics of Moroccan and Yemenite Women.* Israel: Prime Minister's Office, Demographic Center.

Sharot, S. 1982. *Messianism, Mysticism and Magic.* Chapel Hill: University of North Carolina Press.

Shavit, M. 1985. "Maheshavot 'al hahanehaga hahistorit—ule'ahareiha" [Thoughts on the Topic of the Historical Leadership—and Afterward]. *Hedim* 122:54–61.

Sheaffer, Z., and A. Helman. 1994. *Brain-Drain: The Israeli Kibbutz Experience.* Haifa: Kibbutz Research Institute.

Shelhav, Y., and M. Friedman. 1985. *Hitpashetut toch histagerut: Hakehila hahareidit biyrushalayim* [Growth and Segregation: The Ultraorthodox Community in Jerusalem]. Jerusalem: Jerusalem Institute for Israel Studies.

Shenhav-Keller, S. 1993. "The Israeli Souvenir: Its Text and Context." *Annals of Tourism Research* 20(1):182–96.

Shepher, I. 1983. *The Kibbutz: An Anthropological Study.* Norwood, PA: Norwood Editions.

Shields, R. 1991. *Places on the Margin: Alternative Geographies of Modernity.* London: Routledge.

Shiman, L. L. 1986. "Changes Are Dangerous: Women and Temperance in Victorian England." In *Religion in the Lives of English Women, 1760–1930,* ed. G. Malmgreen, 193–215. Bloomington: Indiana University Press.

Shlaim, A. 1995. "The Debate about 1948." *International Journal of Middle East Studies* 27:287–304.

Shokeid, M. 1963. "Extended Families' Adjustment to the Moshav." *Megamot* 12:281–84.

———. 1967. "Old Conflicts in a New Environment: A Study of a Moroccan Atlas Mountains Community Transplanted to Israel." *Jewish Journal of Sociology* 9:191–208.

———. 1971a. *The Dual Heritage: Immigrants from the Atlas Mountains in an Israeli Village.* Manchester: Manchester University Press.

———. 1971b. "Social Networks and Innovation in the Division of Labor between Men and Women in the Family and in the Community: A Study of Moroccan Immigrants in Israel." *Canadian Review of Sociology and Anthropology* 8:1–12.

———. 1974. "An Anthropological Perspective on Ascetic Behavior and Religious Change." In *The Predicament of Homecoming: Cultural and Social Life of North African Immigrants in Israel*, ed. S. Deshen and M. Shokeid, 64–94. Ithaca: Cornell University Press.

———. 1979. "The Decline of Personal Endowment of Atlas Mountains Religious Leaders in Israel." *Anthropological Quarterly* 52:186–97.

———. 1982. "Jewish Existence in a Berber Environment." In *Jewish Societies in the Middle East*, ed. S. Deshen and W. P. Zenner. Washington, DC: University Press of America.

———. 1984. "Cultural Ethnicity in Israel: The Case of Middle Eastern Jews' Religiosity." *Association for Jewish Studies Review* 9:249–72.

———. 1988. *Children of Circumstances: Israeli Emigrants in New York*. Ithaca: Cornell University Press.

———. 1990. "Generations Divorced: The Mutation of Familism among Atlas Mountains Immigrants in Israel." *Anthropological Quarterly* 63(2):76–89.

———. 1992. "Commitment and Contextual Study in Anthropology." *Cultural Anthropology* 7:464–77.

Shokeid, M., and S. Deshen. 1974. *The Predicament of Homecoming: Cultural and Social Life of North African Immigrants in Israel*. Ithaca: Cornell University Press.

———. 1977. *Dor hatemura: Shinui wehemshechiut be'olamamshel yotz'ei tzefon-afrika* [The Generation of Transition: Continuity and Change among North African Immigrants in Israel]. Jerusalem: Yad Ben-Zvi.

Shoresh, D. 1988. *Farming Differentiation in the Workers Moshavim*. Rehovot: Center for Rural and Urban Settlement Studies.

Shryock, A. 1996. "Tribes and the Print Trade: Notes from the Margins of Literate Culture in Jordan." *American Anthropologist* 98(1):26–40.

Shumsky, A. 1955. *The Clash of Cultures in Israel: A Problem for Education*. New York: Prentice-Hall.

Shuqayr, N. 1916. *Ta'rikh Sina al-qadim wal-hadith wa-gighrafiatiha*. Cairo: Matba'at al-Ma'arif.

Shuval, J. T. 1963. *Immigrants on the Threshold*. New York: Prentice-Hall.

Shweder, R. 1991. "Cultural Psychiatry—What Is It?" In *Thinking through Cultures*, 73–110. Cambridge, MA: Harvard University Press.

Sibley, D. 1995. *Geographies of Exclusion: Society and Difference in the West*. London: Routledge.

Siegel, D. 1998. *The Great Immigration: Russian Jews in Israel*. Oxford: Berghahn.

Silverblatt, I. 1980. "Andean Women under Spanish Rule." In *Women and Colonization: Anthropological Perspectives*, ed. M. Etienne and E. Leacock, 149–85. New York: Bergin.

Silverstein, M. 1976. "Shifters, Linguistic Categories, and Cultural Description." In *Meaning in Anthropology*, ed. K. H. Basso and H. B. Selby, 11–55. Albuquerque: University of New Mexico Press.

Simon, L. 1916. "Modern Hebrew Literature." In *Zionism: Problems and Views*, ed. P. Goodman and A. D. Lewis. London: T. Fisher Unwin.

Singer, M. 1978. "Chassidic Recruitment and the Local Context." *Urban Anthropology* 7:373–83.

Sivan, E. 1991. *Dor tashah: Mitos, diokan wezikaron* [The 1948 Generation: Myth, Profile and Memory]. Tel Aviv: Ma'arachot.

Slouschz, N. 1927. *Travels in North Africa.* Philadelphia: Jewish Publication Society of America.

Slyomovics, S. 1998. *The Object of Memory: Arab and Jew Narrate the Palestinian Village.* Philadelphia: University of Pennsylvania Press.

———. 2007. "The Rape of Qula, a Destroyed Palestinian Village." In *Nakba: Palestine, 1948 and the Claims of Memory,* ed. Ahmad Sa'di and Lila Abu-Lughod, 27–51. New York: Columbia University Press.

Smart, A. 1993. "Gifts, Bribes and Guanxi: A Reconsideration of Bourdieu's Social Capital." *Cultural Anthropology* 8(3):388–408.

Smilansky, M., and S. Smilansky. 1967. "Intellectual Advancement of Culturally Disadvantaged Children: An Israeli Approach for Research and Action." *International Review of Education* 13:410–29.

Smith, E. M. 1976. "Networks and Migration in Resettlement: Cherchez la Femme." *Anthropological Quarterly* 49:20–27.

Smith, H. 1988. "Badges, Buttons, T-shirts and Bumperstickers: The Semiotics of Some Recursive Systems." *Journal of Popular Culture* 21(4):141–48.

Smooha, S. 1972. "Israel and Its Third World Jews: Black Panthers—The Ethnic Dilemma." *Society* 9:31–36.

———. 1978. *Israel: Pluralism and Conflict.* Berkeley: University of California Press.

———. 1984. *The Orientation and Politicization of the Arab Minority in Israel.* Haifa: Jewish-Arab Center.

———. 1988. "Jewish and Arab Ethnocentricism in Israel." In *Arab-Jewish Relations in Israel,* ed. J. Hofman. Bristol: Wyndham Hall.

———. 1989–92. *Arabs and Jews in Israel.* 2 vols. Boulder, CO: Westview.

Smooha, S., and Y. Peres. 1975. "The Dynamics of Ethnic Inequalities: The Case of Israel." *Social Dynamics* 1:63–79.

Sobel, Z., and B. Beit-Hallahmi, eds. 1991. *Tradition, Innovation, Conflict: Jewishness and Judaism in Contemporary Israel.* New York: State University of New York Press.

Soja, E. 1989. *Post-modern Geographies: The Reassertion of Space in Critical Social Theory.* London: Verso.

Soloveitchik, H. 1994. "Rupture and Reconstruction: The Transformation of Contemporary Jewry." *Tradition* 28(4):64–131.

Sontag, S. 1972. "Fascinating Fascism." In *Under the Sign of Saturn.* New York: Farrar, Strauss, Giroux.

Speer, A. 1976. *Spandau: The Secret Diaries.* New York: Macmillan.

Spencer-Brown, G. 1971. *Laws of Form.* London: Allen and Unwin.

Sperber, D. 1989. *Minhagei yisra'el* [Customs of Israel]. Jerusalem: Mossad Harav Kook.

Spiro, M. E. 1956. *Kibbutz: Venture in Utopia.* Cambridge, MA: Harvard University Press.

———. 1958. *Children of the Kibbutz.* Cambridge, MA: Harvard University Press.

———. 1987. "Collective Representation in Religious Symbol Systems." In *Culture and Human Nature,* ed. B. Kilborne and L. L. Langness, 161–84. Chicago: University of Chicago Press.

Spradley, J. 1979. *The Ethnographic Interview.* New York: Holt, Rinehart and Winston.

———. 1980. *Participant Observation.* New York: Holt, Rinehart and Winston.

Stacey, M. 1969. "The Myth of Community Studies." *British Journal of Sociology* 20:134–47.

Stachura, P. 1981. *The German Youth Movement, 1900–1945: An Interpretative and Documentary History.* New York: St. Martin's Press.

Stack, C. 1974. "Sex Roles and Survival Strategies in an Urban Black Community." In *Women, Culture and Society,* ed. M. Rosaldo and L. Lamphere, 113–28. Stanford: Stanford University Press.

Statistical Yearbook of the Negev Bedouin. 1999. Vol. 1. Beersheva: Center for Bedouin Studies and Development and Negev Center for Regional Development, Ben-Gurion University.

———. 2004. Vol. 2. Beersheva: Center for Bedouin Studies and Development and Negev Center for Regional Development, Ben-Gurion University.

Stein, L. 1967. *Die Sammar-Gerba: Beduinen im Übergang vom Nomadismus zur Sesshaftigkeit.* Berlin: Akademie-Verlag.

Stephans, M. 1986. "The Childbirth Industry: A Woman's View." In *Visibility and Power: Essays on Women in Society and Development,* ed. L. Dube, E. Leacock, and S. Ardener. Delhi: Oxford University Press.

Sternfeld, Z. 1988. "Intifada Diary." *Iton* 106–7:93–95.

Stewart, F. H. 1988–90. *Texts in Sinai Bedouin Law.* 2 vols. Wiesbaden: Harrassowitz.

Stewart, S. 1984. *On Longing: Narratives of the Miniature, the Gigantic, the Souvenir, the Collection.* Baltimore: Johns Hopkins University Press.

Stillman, N. A. 1973. "The Sefrou Remnant." *Jewish Social Studies* 35(3–4):225–69.

———. 1979. *The Jews of Arab Lands: A History and Source Book.* Philadelphia: Jewish Publication Society of America.

———. 1982. "Saddiq and Marabut in Morocco." In *The Sephardi and Oriental Jewish Heritage,* ed. I. Ben-Ami, 489–500. Jerusalem: Magnes Press.

———. 1988. *The Language and Culture of the Jews of Sefrou, Morocco: An Ethnolinguistic Study.* Manchester: Manchester University Press.

Strathern, M. 1988. *The Gender of the Gift.* Berkeley: University of California Press.

Strauss, A., et al. 1963. "The Hospital and Its Negotiated Order." In *The Hospital in Modern Society,* ed. E. Freidson. New York: Free Press.

Strizower, S. 1966. "The Bene Israel in Israel." *Middle Eastern Studies* 2(2):123–43.

Stromberg, P. G. 1993. *Language and Self-Transformation.* Cambridge: Cambridge University Press.

Stryjan, Y. 1989. *Impossible Organizations.* New York: Greenwood.

Suleiman, M. W. 1989. "Morocco in the Arab and Muslim World: Attitudes of Moroccan Youth." *Maghreb Review* 14(1–2):16–27.

Super, D. E. 1980. "Life-Span Approach to Career Development." *Journal of Vocational Behavior* 16:282–98.

Suransky, V. P. 1982. *The Erosion of Childhood.* Chicago: University of Chicago Press.

Sutton, S. B. 1977. "The Fine Art of Fire." *Harvard Magazine* 7–8:19–27.

Sutton-Smith, B., and D. Kelly-Byrne. 1984. "The Masks of Play." In *The Masks of Play,* ed. B. Sutton-Smith, and D. Kelly-Byrne, 184–99. New York: Leisure Press.

Swedenburg, T. 1995. *Memories of Revolt: The 1936–1939 Rebellion and the Palestinian National Past.* Minneapolis: University of Minnesota Press.

Sweet, L. E. 1967. "Appearance and Reality: The Status and Roles of Women in Mediterranean Societies." *Anthropological Quarterly* 40(3):551–63.

———. 1974. "Visiting Patterns and Social Dynamics in a Lebanese Druze Village." *Anthropological Quarterly* 47:112–19.

Swirski, B. 1984. *Benot Hawa benot Lilit: 'Al hayei nashim biysra'el* [Daughters of Eve, Daughters of Lilith: On Women in Israel]. Givataim: Second Sex Publishing Company.

Swirski, B., and M. F. Safir, eds. 1991. *Calling the Equality Bluff: Women in Israel.* New York: Pergamon.

Swirski, S. 1989. *Israel: The Oriental Majority.* London: Zed Books.

———. 1990. *Hahinuch beyisrael: Mehoz hamaslulim hanifradim* [Education in Israel, School for Inequality]. Tel Aviv: Breirot.

Sykes, G. M. 1958. *The Society of Captives.* Princeton: Princeton University Press.

Sykes, G. M., and D. Matza. 1957. "Techniques of Neutralization: A Theory of Delinquency." *American Sociological Review* 22:664–70.

Syna-Desivilya, H. 1991. *War Experiences in the Israeli Veterans' Lives: A Life Course Perspective.* Zichron Yaakov: The Israeli Institute for Military Studies.

Tal, U. 1963. *Fire Parades.* Hanoar Haoved Youth Movement.

Talmon, Y. 1972. *Family and Community in the Kibbutz.* Cambridge, MA: Harvard University Press.

Tamarin, G. R. 1971. *The Israeli Ethnic Landscape.* Vol. 3/4. Givatayim, Israel: Monographs of the Institute of Socio-Psychological Research.

Tapper, N., and R. Tapper. 1987. "The Birth of the Prophet: Ritual and Gender in Turkish Islam." *Man,* n.s., 22:69–92.

Taylor, V., and L. J. Rupp. 1993. "Women's Culture and Lesbian Feminist Activism: A Reconsideration of Cultural Feminism." *Signs* 19:32–61.

Tessler, M. A. 1978. "The Identity of Religious Minorities in Non-Secular States: Jews in Tunisia and Morocco and Arabs in Israel." *Comparative Studies in Society and History* 20(3):359–73.

———. 1981. "Ethnic Change and Non-Assimilating Minority Status: Jews in Tunisia and Morocco and Arabs in Israel." In *Ethnic Change,* ed. C. F. Keyes, 154–97. Seattle: University of Washington Press.

Tessler, M. A., and L. L. Hawkins. 1980. "The Political Culture of Jews in Tunisia and Morocco." *International Journal of Middle East Studies* 11:59–86.

Tessler, M. A., L. L. Hawkins, and J. Parsons. 1979. "Minorities in Retreat: The Jews of the Maghreb." In *The Political Role of Minority Groups in the Middle East,* ed. D. R. McLaurin, 188–220. New York: Praeger.

Teveth, Shabtai. 1990. "The Palestine Arab Refugee Problem and Its Origins." *Middle Eastern Studies* 26:214–49.

Thoden van Velzen, H.U.E. 1973. "Coalitions and Network Analysis." In *Network Analysis: Studies in Human Interaction,* ed. J. Boissevain and J. C. Mitchell, 219–50. The Hague: Mouton.

Thurley, K., and H. Wirdenius. 1973. *Supervision: A Reappraisal.* London: Heinemann.

Thurow, L. 1997. "The Rise and Fall of Brian Power." *Industry Week* 246(11):114–17.

Tibi, B. 1990. *Islam and the Cultural Accommodation of Social Change.* Trans. C. Krojzl. Boulder, CO: Westview.

Tiffany, S. W., ed. 1979. *Women and Society.* St. Albans, VT: Eden Press.

———. 1980. "Anthropology and the Study of Women." *American Anthropologist* 82:374–80.

Tiger, L., and J. Shepher. 1975. *Women in the Kibbutz.* New York: Harcourt Brace Jovanovich.

Tinker, I. 1976. *Women and World Development.* Washington, DC: Overseas Development Council.

Tirosh, Y. 1975. *Religious Zionism: An Anthology.* Jerusalem: World Zionist Organization.

Tishby, I. 1949. *Mishnat Ha-Zohar* [The Teachings of the Zohar]. Jerusalem: Mosad Bialik.

Tittmuss, R. M. 1970. *The Gift Relationship: From Human Blood to Social Policy.* London: Allen and Unwin.

Toledano, H. 1973. "Time to Stir the Melting Pot." In *Israel: Social Structure and Change,* ed. M. Curtis and M. Chertoff. New Brunswick, NJ: Transaction.

Topel, M. 1979. "'To Build and to Be Built': Power Elite in an Egalitarian Community." Master's thesis, Department of Sociology and Anthropology, Tel Aviv University.

Trachtenberg, J. 1974. *Jewish Magic and Superstition: A Study in Folk Religion.* New York: Atheneum.

Trevor-Roper, H. R. 1967. *The European Witch Craze of the Sixteenth and Seventeenth Centuries and Other Essays.* New York: Harper and Row.

Trope, Y. 1989. "Stereotypes and Dispositional Judgment." In *Stereotyping and Prejudice: Changing Conceptions,* ed. D. Bar-Tal et al. New York: Springer.

Tsur, M. ed. 1988 [1922]. *Kehyliyatenu* [Our Commune]. Jerusalem: Yad Yitshak Ben-Zvi.

Tuchinski, Y. 1948. *Gesher hahayim* [Bridge of Life]. Jerusalem: Jerusalem Burial Society.

Turner, V. W. 1966. "Ritual Aspects of Conflict Control in African Micropolitics." In *Political Anthropology,* ed. M. J. Swartz, V. W. Turner, and A. Tuden, 239–46. Chicago: Aldine.

———. 1967. "Betwixt and Between: The Liminal Period in Rites de Passage." In *The Forest of Symbols,* 93–111. Ithaca: Cornell University Press.

———. 1969. *The Ritual Process.* Ithaca: Cornell University Press.

———. 1974. "Religious Paradigms and Political Action: Thomas Beckett at the Council of Northampton." In *Dramas, Fields and Metaphors: Symbolic Action in Human Society.* Ithaca: Cornell University Press.

———. 1976. "Social Dramas and Ritual Metaphors." In *Ritual, Play and Performance,* ed. R. Schechner and N. Schuman. New York: Seabury Press.

———. 1977. "Symbols in African Ritual." In *Symbolic Anthropology,* ed. J. L. Dolgin, D. S. Kemnitzer, and D. M. Schneider, 183–94. New York: Columbia University Press.

———. 1982. *From Ritual to Theater: The Human Seriousness of Play.* New York: Performing Arts Journal Publications.

Turner, V. W., and E. Turner. 1978. *Image and Pilgrimage in Christian Culture.* New York: Columbia University Press.

Tyack, D. 1966. "Forming the National Character." *Harvard Educational Review* 36:29–41.

Tyler, S. A. 1987. *The Unspeakable: Discourse, Dialogue and Rhetoric in the Postmodern World.* Madison: University of Wisconsin Press.

Tzachor, Z. 1997. *Hazan—Tenu'at haim* [Hazan—A Life Movement]. Jerusalem: Yad Itzchak Ben-Zvi.

Tzalmona, Y. 1993. "Hummus with Whipped Cream?" *Mishkafayim* 19:9–14.

Tzur, Y. 1980. "The Car Is a Status Symbol." *Hadaf Hayarok,* 19 November.

Udovitch, A. L., and L. Valensi. 1984. *The Last Arab Jews: The Communities of Jerba, Tunisia.* London: Harwood Academic Publishers.

Vald, E. 1987. *Kilelat hakeilim hasheburim* [The Curse of the Broken Tools]. Jerusalem: Schocken.

Vancil, R. F. 1987. *Passing the Baton.* Boston: Harvard Business School Press.

Van den Berghe, P. L. 1973. "Pluralism." In *Handbook of Social and Cultural Anthropology,* ed. J. J. Honigmann. Chicago: Rand McNally.

Van Maanen, J. 1976. "Breaking In: Socialization to Work." In *Handbook of Work, Organization, and Society,* ed. R. Dubin. Chicago: Rand McNally.

Van Maanen, J., P. Adler, and R. Adler, eds. 1990. "Special Issue: The Presentation of Ethnographic Research." *Journal of Contemporary Ethnography* 19(1).

Van Velsen, J. 1967. "The Extended-Case Method and Situational Analysis." In *The Craft of Social Anthropology,* ed. A. L. Epstein, 129–49. London: Tavistock.

Vinitzky-Seroussi, V. 1998. "'Jerusalem Assassinated Rabin and Tel Aviv Commemorated Him': Memorials and the Discourse of National Identity in Israel." *City and Society* 10(1):183–203.

Vital, D. 1975. *The Origins of Zionism.* Oxford: Clarendon Press.

Wagner, R. 1986. *Symbols That Stand for Themselves.* Chicago: University of Chicago Press.

Walesgrove, R. 1984. "Press Coverage." *Space Rib,* 21 May.

Wallace, R. 1993. "The Social Construction of a New Leadership Role: Catholic Omen Pastors." *Sociology of Religion* 54:31–42.

Wallace, S. W. 1971. "On the Totality of Total Institutions." In *Total Institutions,* ed. S. W. Wallace. Chicago: Aldine.

Wallman, S., ed. 1979a. *Ethnicity at Work.* London: Macmillan.

———. 1979b. *Social Anthropology of Work.* ASA Monograph 19. London: Academic Press.

Walter, E. V. 1969. *Terror and Resistance: A Study of Political Violence.* New York: Oxford University Press.

Warnock, K. *Land before Honour: Palestinian Women in the Occupied Territories.* London: MacMillan, 1990.

Warren, R. 1973. *The Community in America.* Chicago: Rand McNally.

Wasserfall, R. 1987. "Gender Identification in an Israeli Moshav." Ph.D. diss., Hebrew University of Jerusalem.

———. 1990. "Bargaining for Gender Identity: Love, Sex and Money in an Israeli Moshav." *Ethnology* 29:327–40.

———, ed. 1999. *Women and Water: Menstruation in Jewish Life and Law.* Hanover, NH: Brandeis University Press.

Watson, L. C. 1976. "Understanding a Life History as a Subjective Document." *Ethos* 4(1):95–131.

Weber, M. 1964. *The Theory of Social and Economic Organization.* New York: Free Press.

Wegner, J. R. 1988. *Chattel or Person: The Status of Women in the Mishnah.* New York: Oxford University Press.

Weidman-Schneider, S. 1984. *Jewish and Female.* New York: Simon and Schuster.

Weil, S. 1977. "Verbal Interaction among the Bene Israel." *International Journal of the Sociology of Language* 13:71–85.

———. 1985. *The Occupational Perceptions of Ethiopian Jews.* Final report submitted to JDC Israel. Jerusalem: JDC.

———. 1986. "The Language and Ritual of Socialization: Birthday Parties in a Kindergarten Context." *Man* 21:329–41.

Weingrod, A. 1962. "Administered Communities: Some Characteristics of New Immigrant Villages in Israel." *Economic Development and Cultural Change* 9:69–84.

———. 1965. *Israel: Group Relations in a New Society.* New York: Praeger.

———. 1966. *Reluctant Pioneers: Village Development in Israel.* Ithaca: Cornell University Press.

———. 1979. "Recent Trends in Israeli Ethnicity." *Ethnic and Racial Studies* 2:55–65.

———. 1990. *The Saint of Beersheba.* Albany: State University of New York Press.

———. 1995. "Dry Bones: Nationalism and Symbolism in Contemporary Israel." *Anthropology Today* 11(6):7–12.

———. 1998. "Working at Home: Some Reflections on Reflexivity." Lecture at 50th Jubilee of Brandeis University.

Weingrod, A., and M. Gurevitch. 1977. "Who Are the Israeli Elites?" *Jewish Journal of Sociology* 19:66–77.

Weintraub, D. 1971. *Immigration and Social Change: Agricultural Settlements of New Immigrants in Israel.* Manchester: Manchester University Press.

Weintraub, D., M. Lissak, and Y. Azmon. 1969. *Moshava, Kibbutz, Moshav: Jewish Settlement and Colonization in Palestine.* Ithaca: Cornell University Press.

Weir, S. 1975. "Hilma Granqvist and Her Contribution to Palestine Studies." *British Society for Middle Eastern Studies Bulletin* 2(1):6–13.

Weiss, M. 1998. "Engendering Gulf War Memories: Israeli Nurses and the Discourse of Soldiering." *Journal of Contemporary Ethnography* 27(2):197–218.

Weissman, D. 1976. "Bais Yaakov: A Historical Model for Jewish Feminists." In *The Jewish Woman,* ed. E. Koltun. New York: Schocken.

Weitz, Y. 1965. *Yomanai we'igrotai labanim* [My Diaries and Letters to My Sons]. 6 vols. Tel Aviv: Masada.

Werblowsky, R. J. 1977. *Joseph Caro: Lawyer and Mystic.* Philadelphia: Jewish Publication Society of America.

Wesley, D. A. 2005. *State Practices and Zionist Images: Shaping Economic Development in Arab Towns in Israel.* New York: Berghahn.

Westermarck, E. A. 1968 [1926]. *Ritual and Belief in Morocco.* 2 vols. London: Macmillan.

Whyte, W. F., and K. K. Whyte. 1988. *Making Mondragon.* Ithaca: ILR Press and Cornell University Press.

Willensky, H. L. 1964. "The Professionalization of Everyone." *American Journal of Sociology* 70:135–58.

Williams, J. A. 1979. "A Return to the Veil in Egypt." *Middle East Review* 3:49–54.

Willis, P. 1981. *Learning to Labour: How Working-Class Kids Get Working-Class Jobs.* Aldershot, UK: Gower.

Willner, D. 1969. *Nation-Building and Community in Israel.* Princeton: Princeton University Press.

Wolf, E. R. 1966. "Kinship, Friendship, and Patron-Client Relations in Complex Societies." In *The Social Anthropology of Complex Societies,* ed. M. Banton, 1–22. London: Tavistock.

Wolf, M. 1972. *Women and the Family in Rural Taiwan.* Stanford: Stanford University Press.

Wolf, T. 1994. "Meanings Invested in the Homes of Arab Villagers: A Case Study of Spontaneous Settlements of Sedentarized Bedouins in Northen Israel." Master's thesis, Urban and Regional Planning, Technion-Israel Institute of Technology.

World Health Organization. 1992. *The ICD-10, Classification of Mental and Behavioral Disorders, Clinical Descriptions and Diagnostic Guidelines.* Geneva: World Health Organization.

Ya'ar, E., E. Ben-Rafael, and Z. Soker. 1994. *The Kibbutz and Israeli Society.* Tel Aviv: Open University Press.

Yadlin, A. 1989. "The Budget of the Movement for 1989." *Kibbutz,* 4 January.

Yanagisaco, S. J. 1979. "Family and Household: The Analysis of Domestic Groups." *Annual Review of Anthropology* 8:161–205.

Yancey, W. L., E. P. Erickson, and R. N. Juliani. 1976. "Emergent Ethnicity: A Review and a Reformulation." *American Sociological Review* 41:391–403.

Yaniv, G. 1990. *Unemployment: An Annual Survey 1989.* Jerusalem: National Insurance Institute.

Yankelovich, D. 1991. *Coming to Public Judgment.* Syracuse: Syracuse University Press.

Yekutiel, D. 1990. *Present Absent: Short Stories.* Tel Aviv: Yaron Golan.

Yisraeli, R. 1997. *Seker Toshavim* [Survey of Inhabitants (of Rahat)]. Tel Aviv: Al-Midan.

Yogev, A., and H. Ayalon. 1987. "Tuition-Free Secondary Schooling and Equality of Educational Opportunities: Social Aspects versus Economic Considerations." *Economic Quarterly* 37(131):873–83.

Zamir, D. 1979. *Ha'avoda hasechira bata'asia hakibbutzit* [Social and Structural Phenomena of Hired Labor in the Kibbutz Industry]. Tel Aviv: Kibbutz Industry Association.

———. 1996. *Economic Success and Coping with Crisis.* Haifa: Kibbutz Research Institute.

Zand, D. E. 1972. "Trust and Managerial Problem Solving." *Administrative Science Quarterly* 17:229–39.

Zarhi, S., and A. Achiezra. 1966. *The Economic Conditions of the Arab Minority in Israel.* Tel Aviv: Social Research Institute, Trade Union Federation.

Zaydan, M. 1993. "Paper Presented to the Cairo Conference on Human Rights Calls for the Right of Return." *Arabs in Israel* 3(2):2.

Zemach, M. 1980. *Attitudes of the Jewish Majority in Israel towards the Arab Minority.* Jerusalem: Van Leer Jerusalem Foundation.

Zenner, W. 1963. "Ambivalence and Self-Imaging among Oriental Jews in Israel." *Jewish Journal of Sociology* 5:214–23.

———. 1965. *Syrian Jewish Identification in Israel.* Ann Arbor: University Microfilms.

———. 2000. *A Global Community: Jews from Aleppo.* Detroit: Wayne State University Press.

Zerubavel, E. 1986. *Hidden Rhythms: Schedules and Calendars in Social Life.* Berkeley: University of California Press.

Zerubavel, Y. 1992. "New Beginning, Old Past: The Collective Memory of Pioneering in Israeli Culture." In *New Perspectives on Israeli History,* ed. L. Silberstein. New York: New York University Press.

———. 1995. *Recovered Roots: Collective Memory and the Making of Israeli National Tradition.* Chicago: University of Chicago Press.

Zilberg, N. 2001. "In-Group Humor of Immigrants from the Former Soviet Union." In *Language and Communication in Israel,* ed. H. Herzog and E. Ben-Rafael, 129–50. New Brunswick, NJ: Transaction.

Zilka, I. 1970. *Fire in Ritual, Ceremony and Parade.* Jerusalem: Youth Department, Ministry of Education and Culture.

Zionist Library. 1972. *The Voices of Jewish Emancipation.* Jerusalem: Zionist Library.

Zisling, A. 1988. *'Ein-harod viyrushalayim* [(Kibbutz) Ein-Harod and Jerusalem]. Tel Aviv: Yad Tabenkin.

The Zohar [The Book of Splendor]. 1956. Trans. H. Sperling and M. Simon. London: Soncino Press.

Zucker, D., et al. 1983. *Research on Human Rights in the Territories Held by the IDF.* Jerusalem: International Center for Peace in the Middle East.

Zucker, L. G. 1986. *Production of Trust: Institutional Sources of Economic Structure, 1840–1920.* Research in Organizational Behavior, vol. 8. Ed. B. M. Staw and L. L. Cummings. Greenwich, CT: JAI.

Zureik, E. 1979. *The Palestinians in Israel: A Study in Internal Colonialism.* London: Routledge and Kegan Paul.

Zussman, P. 1988. *Individual Behavior and Social Choice in a Cooperative Settlement: The Theory and Practice of the Israeli Moshav.* Jerusalem: Magnes Press.

Contributors

HENRY ABRAMOVITCH is a senior lecturer in the Department of Behavioral Science at the Medical School, Tel Aviv University. He studies medical anthropology, psychology, and the anthropology of dying.

ORIT ABUHAV is a lecturer in the Social Science Department, and in the anthropology program at Beit Berl College. She studies Libyan Jews and gift giving in Israel and the development of Israeli anthropology.

AREF ABU-RABIA is an associate professor in the Department of Middle East Studies, Ben-Gurion University. His research interests include Middle East and Islamic societies, ethno-medicine, medicinal plants, culture and health, violence, ethics and human organ transplants, and education.

GIDEON ARAN is a senior lecturer in the Department of Sociology and Anthropology at the Hebrew University. He studies Jewish orthodox settlers in the occupied Palestinian territories.

EYAL BEN-ARI is a professor in the Department of Sociology and Anthropology at the Hebrew University. His interests lie in Japanese white-collar communities, childhood education in Japan, and the Israeli military.

YORAM BILU is a professor in the Departments of Psychology and Sociology and Anthropology at the Hebrew University. He studies psychological and psychiatric anthropology and popular religion in Israel.

SHULAMIT CARMI is a sociologist who lives in Jerusalem and writes on the kibbutz and the social history of Palestine and Israel.

SHLOMO DESHEN is a professor emeritus in the Department of Sociology and Anthropology at Tel Aviv University. His research interests are Israeli Judaism, North African immigrants to Israel, and physically disabled persons.

ISRAEL DRORI is a professor at the Academic Studies College of Management, School of Business, and visiting professor at the Faculty of Management, Tel-Aviv University. His areas of specialization are organizational ethnography, work culture, entrepreneurship, and the evolution of organizations.

TAMAR EL-OR is an associate professor in the Department of Sociology and Anthropology at the Hebrew University. She studies women, religious groups, and literacy.

HARVEY E. GOLDBERG is a professor emeritus in the Department of Sociology and Anthropology at the Hebrew University. He studies North African and Middle Eastern Jewry, particularly Libyan Jews, and the anthropology of Judaism.

YEHUDA C. GOODMAN is a lecturer in the Department of Sociology and Anthropology at the Hebrew University. His interests lie in psychological and medical anthropology and the anthropology of religion.

OFRA GREENBERG is a senior lecturer at Western Galilee Academic College. She studies alternative medicine, new towns in Israel, total institutions, and communities.

DON HANDELMAN is a professor emeritus in the Department of Sociology and Anthropology at the Hebrew University. He studies ritual, play, bureaucracy, and mythology in South India and Israel.

HAIM HAZAN is a professor of social anthropology at Tel Aviv University and editor of *Israeli Sociology*. His main areas of research cover the life course, time, cultural and interactional aspects of old age, total institutions, community, nationalism, and collective memory.

ESTHER HERTZOG is a senior lecturer and head of the Anthropology Program at Beit Berl College. She studies bureaucracy, immigration, gender, and welfare policy.

TAMAR KATRIEL is a professor of anthropology in the Departments of Education and Media Studies at Haifa University. She studies communication, language, and museums.

YAEL KATZIR is a staff member of Levinsky Teacher's College, where she established the Department of Research and Development and served as its head for ten years.

GIDEON M. KRESSEL is a professor emeritus at the Blaustein Institute for Desert Research and the Behavioral Sciences Department of Ben-Gurion University.

He studies the kibbutz and other cooperative villages, Bedouin, and pastoralists in the Middle East and East Africa.

ANDRÉ LEVY is a senior lecturer in anthropology in the Department of Sociology and Anthropology at Ben-Gurion University. He is interested in topics such as diasporas, identity politics, and ethnicity in Israel.

ARNOLD LEWIS is an anthropologist who lives in New York. He was formerly a lecturer in the Department of Sociology and Anthropology at Tel Aviv University and studies education in Israel.

EDNA LOMSKY-FEDER is a senior lecturer at the School of Education at the Hebrew University. Her current areas of interest are immigration, culture, and identity. She has written on military service, war experience, and life stories.

EMANUEL MARX is a professor emeritus in the Department of Sociology and Anthropology at Tel Aviv University. He studies Bedouin in Israel and Egypt, labor migration, Palestinian refugee camps, and violent behavior.

DAN RABINOWITZ is associate professor in Social Anthropology at Tel-Aviv University and CEU. His research focuses on the Palestinian citizens of Israel, ethnicity, nationalism, and sociopolitical aspects of environmental issues.

HENRY ROSENFELD (1924–2007) was a professor emeritus in the Department of Sociology and Anthropology at Haifa University. He studied Arabs in Israel and the history of Zionism in Palestine.

HAGAR SALAMON is a senior lecturer in the Department of Jewish and Comparative Folklore and senior research fellow at the Harry S. Truman Research Institute for the Advancement of Peace, both at the Hebrew University. Her research interests include cultural expressions of interethnic relations and racial perceptions, with a focus on Ethiopian Jews and Israeli folklore.

SUSAN STARR SERED, formerly an associate professor at Bar Ilan University and research director at Harvard University, is an assistant professor at Suffolk University in Massachusetts. Her research has addressed gender and religion, women's health, and the anthropology of religion.

LEA SHAMGAR-HANDELMAN (1934–1995) was associate professor of sociology and education at the Hebrew University. She specialized in the sociology of the family and was studying the social construction of childhood at the time of her death.

REUVEN SHAPIRA is a senior lecturer of social anthropology at Western Galilee Academic College, Acre. He studies the kibbutz, especially industry and management.

MOSHE SHOKEID is a professor emeritus in the Department of Sociology and Anthropology at Tel Aviv University. His research themes are immigration, ethnicity, sexuality, and homosexuality.

DINA SIEGEL is a professor of criminology at the faculty of law, University of Utrecht. Her spheres of interest include post-Soviet immigration to Israel, organized crime, terrorism, drugs, and women trafficking and criminality in the diamond sector.

SUSAN SLYOMOVICS is professor of anthropology and Near Eastern languages and cultures at the University of California, Los Angeles. Her work includes the study of memory among Arabs and Jews in a Palestinian village and oral poetry in Egypt.

RAHEL WASSERFALL is a scholar in residence at the Women's Studies Research Center, Brandeis University. Her research interests are gender, religion, yoga methodology and identity, and Jewish education in the United States.

ALEX WEINGROD, professor emeritus of anthropology in the Department of Behavioral Sciences, Ben-Gurion University, studies North African Jewry and ethnicity.

Index

Permissions Acknowledgments

Some of the chapters that appear in this book have been previously published in the following books and journals:

CHAP 24 Abramovitch, Henry. 1991. "The Jerusalem Funeral as a Microcosm of the 'Mismeeting' between Religious and Secular Israelis." In *Tradition, Innovation, Conflict: Jewishness and Judaism in Contemporary Israel,* ed. Zvi Sobel and Benjamin Beit-Hallahmi, 71–99. New York: State University of New York Press. Reprinted by permission. © 1991 by the State University of New York. All rights reserved.

CHAP 17 Ben-Ari, Eyal. 1989. "Masks and Soldiering: The Israeli Army and the Palestinian Uprising." *Cultural Anthropology* 4(4):372–89. © 1989 by the American Anthropological Association. Reprinted with permission.

CHAP 25 Bilu, Yoram, and Yehuda Goodman. 1997. " 'What Does the Soul Say?': Metaphysical Uses of Facilitated Communication in the Jewish Ultra-Orthodox Community." *Ethos* 25(4):375–407. © 1997 by the American Anthropological Association. Reprinted with permission.

CHAP 19 Carmi, Shulamit, and Henry Rosenfeld. 1992. "Israel's Political Economy and the Widening Class Gap between Its Two National Groups." *Asian and African Studies* 26:15–61.

CHAP 1 Deshen, Shlomo. 1975. "Ritualization of Literacy: The Works of Tunisian Scholars in Israel." *American Ethnologist* 2:251–59. © 1975 by the American Anthropological Association. Reprinted from *American Ethnologist* by permission of the University of California Press.

CHAP 22 Drori, Israel. 2000. "The Supervisors: Go Betweens." In *The Seam Line: Arab Workers and Jewish Managers in the Israeli Textile Industry,* 133–65. Stanford: Stanford University Press. Reprinted with permission.

CHAP 16 El-Or, Tamar, and Gideon Aran. 1995. "Giving Birth to a Settlement: Maternal Thinking and Political Action of Jewish Women on the West Bank." *Gender and Society* 9(1):60–78. © 1995 by Sage Publications. Reprinted by permission of Sage Publications.

CHAP 2 Goldberg, Harvey. 1973. "Culture Change in an Israeli Immigrant Village: How the Twist Came to Even Yosef." *Middle Eastern Studies* 9:73–80. Available at http://www.tandf.co.uk/journals. Permission granted by Taylor and Francis.

CHAP 12 Katriel, Tamar. 1987. "Rhetoric in Flames: Fire Inscriptions in Israeli Youth Movement Ceremonials." *Quarterly Journal of Speech* 73:444–59. Available at http://www.tandf.co.uk. Permission granted by Taylor and Francis.

CHAP 3 Katzir, Yael. 1983. "Yemenite Jewish Women in Rural Development: Female Power versus Male Authority." *Economic Development and Cultural Change* 32(1):45–61. © 1983 by the University of Chicago.

CHAP 11 Kressel, Gideon M. 1995. "'He Who Stays in Agriculture Is Not a *Freier*': The Spirit of Competition among Members of the Moshav Is Eroded When Unskilled Arab Labor Enters the Scene." In *Rural Cooperatives in Socialist Utopia: Thirty Years of Moshav Development in Israel,* ed. M. Schwartz, S. Lees, and G. M. Kressel, 155–83. West Point: Praeger. Reproduced with permission of Greenwood Publishing Group, Westport, CT.

CHAP 4 Lewis, Arnold. 1985. "Phantom Ethnicity: 'Oriental Jews' in Israeli Society." In *Studies in Israeli Ethnicity: After the Ingathering,* ed. A. Weingrod, 133–53. New York: Gordon and Breach. Permission granted by Taylor and Francis.

CHAP 26 Levy, André. 2000. "Playing for Control of Distance: Card Games between Jews and Muslims on a Casablancan Beach." *American Ethnologist* 26(3):632–53. © 2000 by the American Anthropological Association. Reprinted with permission.

CHAP 15 Lomsky-Feder, Edna. 1995. "The Meaning of War through Veterans' Eyes: A Phenomenological Analysis of Life Stories." *International Sociology* 10(4):463–82. © 1995 by Sage Publications. Reprinted by permission of Sage Publications.

CHAP 18 Rabinowitz, Dan. 1997. "Risk, Rationality and Trust." In *Overlooking Nazareth: The Ethnography of Exclusion in Galilee,* 119–45. Cambridge: Cambridge University Press. Reprinted by permission of Cambridge University Press.

CHAP 14 Salamon, Hagar. 2001. "Political Bumper Stickers in Contemporary Israel: Folklore as an Emotional Battleground." *Journal of American Folklore* 114(453):1–32. Reprinted courtesy of the American Folklore Society, http://www.afsnet.org.

CHAP 7 Shamgar-Handelman, Lea, and Don Handelman. 1991. "Celebrations of Bureaucracy." *Ethnology* 30(4):293–312. Reprinted by permission of the Department of Anthropology, University of Pittsburgh.

CHAP 8 Shapira, Reuven. 2001. "The Vanishing of High-Moral, Servant Leaders and the Decay of Democratic, High-Trust Cultures in the Kibbutz Field." *Sociological Inquiry* 71(1):13–38. Reprinted by permission of Blackwell Publishing.

CHAP 27 Shokeid, Moshe. 1988. "The Hassidic Option." In *Children of Circumstances: Israeli Emigrants in New York,* 139–60. Ithaca: Cornell University Press. © 1988 by Cornell University. Reprinted by permission of Cornell University Press.

CHAP 20 Slyomovics, Susan. 1999. "Post-1948: The New *Ein Houd.*" In *The Object of Memory: Arab and Jew Narrate the Palestinian Village,* 99–136. Philadelphia: University of Pennsylvania Press. Reprinted by permission of the University of Pennsylvania Press.

CHAP 30 Sered, Susan. 1997. "Women and Religious Change in Israel: Rebellion or Revolution." *Sociology of Religion* 58 (1):1–24. © by the Association for the Sociology of Religion.

CHAP 29 Wasserfall, Rahel. 1991. "Menstruation and Identity: The Meaning of *Niddah* for Moroccan Women Immigrants." In *Mishpahot Be-Yisrael,* ed. R. Bar-Yosef and L. Shamgar-Handelman, 239–56. Jerusalem: Akademon.

CHAP 28 Weingrod, Alex. 1993. "Changing Israeli Landscapes: Building and Uses of the Past." *Cultural Anthropology* 8(3):370–87. © by the American Anthropological Association. Reprinted by permission of the University of California Press.

www.ingramcontent.com/pod-product-compliance
Lightning Source LLC
LaVergne TN
LVHW080403090826
844660LV00054B/1254

* 9 7 8 0 8 1 4 3 3 0 5 0 0 *